EDITOR'S NOTE.

My father at his death in 1893 left in manuscript a partially finished history of the Town of Canaan. It has been my intention since that time to print it. I remember of my mother saying that my father had said the history would all have to be rewritten before it was printed. I did not realize then, and not until within a few years, how true that was. Every year since 1893 I have spent more or less time in getting the material into shape, every year realizing how little I knew and how incompetant I was to perform the task. The mass of material, and the condition in which it was, seemed to me stupendous. Not in the slightest degree familiar with any of the past of the town, being absent from it from the time I was thirteen years old, with only periodical visits at home during vacation. During these times I took no interest in my father's work. For thirty years he had been accumulating the material. A good part of it was from personal observation but much of it was obtained from the reminiscences of old people, indefatigable search in old garrets for letters, books, deeds, diaries, scraps, anything that would lead to a clew on some forgotten incident.

My father says of himself: "I grew up to strong youth on the shores of the beautiful pond that fronts our street. It was a pleasant resort for thoughtful people. Old and young used to linger about there, and many confidences were imparted, some of which I shall never reveal. I was very near, and was conscious of much that was said and done in society, in politics, and in religion. Opinions were freely expressed before me, because, being merely a duplex tree, no one supposed my ears might ever give tongue to my voice. I made note of many things and treasured them up. Some of these events occurred so long ago that it is safe to write of them. They had an interest for those who took part in them as similar events have today, and formed epochs in men's lives."

In my youth I spent days riding over the hills with him in search of anything about Canaan, visiting the old graveyards. He rarely trusted to his memory, which is fortunate in some respects, for he had a very powerful remembrance of all events that occurred during his life, whether in Canaan or in other parts of the country. He was accustomed to jot down his notes on anything that was at hand, small scraps of paper, pieces that had already been used on one side, sometimes on both, cross writing and interlining with some other notes, but never scratching out or rewriting. When once written it expressed his thoughts unchangeably. This habit was acquired by reason of his profession,— printer, reporter and editor.

To arrange these small scraps and put them in their proper place has been at times like tracing out a labyrinth, for in my ignorance of men and things I knew not where they went. Neither did I know where they came from, and was tempted not to believe them, but in no instance have I found any item, however small, to be incorrect. I often heard my father disputing with others about some old occurrence. He always afterwards ascertained whether he was right or wrong.

When the old house burnt in 1898 many people asked me if my father's papers were destroyed. At that time I said they were not, and not until within a few years have I realized that some of them must have been burned, for there are gaps in some of the work that can not be accounted for in any other way. I take little credit to myself for this book. It is my father's work, with the exception of some chapters which I wrote and which the reader can readily tell. And these chapters contain some of his notes, but his death prevented him from carrying his search farther.

It will be observed that this book is a history of the early days, down to about 1860. It contains as just an account as could be gotten. From that date much is within the memory of those living. Some future historian can set himself that task. I have, however, where things of interest have happened since 1860, made some mention of them. The strenuous life of this town happened before that date. Since the Rebellion the life of the people has run smoothly. History is not made in that way.

After my father had been working some years upon this book there was an article in the warrant for town meeting to see if the town would financially assist in completing the history of

The History of Canaan, New Hampshire

William Allen Wallace

Editor: James Burns Wallace

Alpha Editions

This edition published in 2020

ISBN : 9789354010200

Design and Setting By
Alpha Editions
email - alphaedis@gmail.com

As per information held with us this book is in Public Domain.
This book is a reproduction of an important historical work. Alpha Editions uses the best technology to reproduce historical work in the same manner it was first published to preserve its original nature. Any marks or number seen are left intentionally to preserve its true form.

THE
HISTORY OF CANAAN
NEW HAMPSHIRE

BY
WILLIAM ALLEN WALLACE

EDITED BY
JAMES BURNS WALLACE

Concord, N. H.
THE RUMFORD PRESS
1910

the town. It was voted down. He then made up his mind that the book should be printed without their assistance. The amount of time and labor he spent in collecting this material can only be imagined. That there should not be patriotism enough in the town to care for its history is, of course, deplorable. This lack of patriotism has often been commented upon by many who think more of this town than any other place on earth. It is not only so in this town but in many others.

JAMES B. WALLACE.

CANAAN, N. H., January 1, 1910.

PREFACE.

All history should be the history of the people. It is what the people are doing in villages, communities and families, that lie at the foundation of national character, and sentiment, and consequently of national events. Those matters which possess a natural interest to a particular neighborhood, from association with the familiar names and places, are of interest to every one who seeks in the experience of the past for that wisdom that may be desired from a knowledge of what those who lived before us have done and suffered.

These records present to us pictures of human life, its virtues and failings, such as we can best understand. The village disputes, religious quarrels, and political discussions of past times, are analagous to those to which the present generation is exposed. They afford examples of character and conduct of which we can see the beginning and the end, and may draw therefrom most useful lessons. We are living over the same lines with some variations, but subject to the same general laws of action, inasmuch as we possess the same natures and are governed by the same passions and motives, which lead to similar results.

The historic genealogy of a village may be made as useful a guide through the devious paths of life as the chart of the mariner to him who sails among the breakers of the great deep, pointing out the track that others have pursued, and showing where and how they have advanced in safety, and also wherein they have become the victims of passion, folly and heedlessness.

By reference to various authorities it appears that so late as 1760 there were no settlements in New Hampshire north of Charlestown, which was then called "No. Four;" nor were there more than three towns settled south of Charlestown in the Connecticut valley within the present limits of New Hampshire. Hinsdale, or Fort Dummer, was settled in 1683. Westmoreland or "No. Two" in 1741, and Walpole in 1752. With the exception of Walpole, these towns were all settled by Massachusetts men, for until 1741, it was supposed the north line of Massachusetts would include these towns. At Hinsdale and Charlestown forts were built at an early period of their settlement and soldiers were stationed there for the double purpose of affording protection to the inhabitants and arresting the progress of the Indians from Canada, while meditating incursions upon the frontier towns. And so little interest did New Hampshire feel in the settlement and development of this country that in 1745, when Governor Wentworth recommended to the Assembly to take and sustain their newly acquired "Fort Dummer," which fell to them upon the establishment of the line between the two colonies, the lower house declined the acceptance of this place and also of "No. Four," alleging that the fort was fifty miles distant from any towns settled by New Hampshire; they did not own the territory, and that they were not equal to the expense of maintaining the places.

It was not until 1752 that the Governor of New Hampshire was permitted to adopt any measures to secure to that colony this valuable country. He then made several grants of townships on both sides of the Connecticut River, and a plan was formed for taking possession of it, the great richness of which they had heard from hunters and returned Indian captives. There was a term of years, from 1752 to 1760, during which the governors of New Hampshire and Massachusetts were too busily occupied in prosecuting the war with the French and Indians to allow them to give much attention to the extention of their settlement. But in the year 1760 the last act in the bloody struggle was accomplished in the capture of Montreal by the forces under General Amherst, and Canada was reduced to a British province.

It is said during the war the seasons were fruitful, and the colonies were able not only to supply their own troops with provisions, but also the British fleets and armies with food and refreshments of all kinds. But after the close of the war there followed two years, those of 1761–62, of great scarcity; so great as to make it absolutely necessary to seek supplies from abroad. During the drouth of 1761 disastrous fires raged in the forests in various parts of the state. And in the succeeding years the emigrants who passed northward in search of new homes traversed immense tracts of territory covered with the charred remains of forests, whose naked trunks and leafless branches were fast going to decay.

It was in the year 1761 that His Excellency Benning Wentworth turned his attention to this wilderness, and with the assistance of his secretary, Theodore Atkinson, resolved to change its forests into fruitful fields and cover them with cheerful homes. In this vicinity the towns of Canaan, Dorchester, Enfield, Grantham, Groton, Hanover, Lebanon, Lyme, Orford, Plainfield and Rumney were incorporated by separate charters.

TABLE OF CONTENTS.

			PAGES.
CHAPTER	I.	THE CHARTERS OF CANAAN	1–8
CHAPTER	II.	THE FIRST AND SECOND SETTLERS	9–21
CHAPTER	III.	PROPRIETORS' MEETINGS, 1768-1785	22–39
CHAPTER	IV.	PROPRIETORS' MEETINGS, 1786-1845	40–48
CHAPTER	V.	TOWN MEETINGS, 1770-1785	49–62
CHAPTER	VI.	TOWN MEETINGS, 1786-1797	63–78
CHAPTER	VII.	TOWN MEETINGS, 1798-1818	79–88
CHAPTER	VIII.	TOWN MEETINGS, 1819-1909	89–97
CHAPTER	IX.	THE PITCH BOOK AND PROPRIETORS' SURVEYS	98–125
CHAPTER	X.	PUBLIC RIGHTS	126–138
CHAPTER	XI.	THE COMMON, BROAD STREET, THE MEETING HOUSE	139–152
CHAPTER	XII.	DAME'S GORE AND STATE'S GORE	153–160
CHAPTER	XIII.	THE SURPLUS REVENUE AND LITERARY FUND	161–165
CHAPTER	XIV.	THE BAPTIST CHURCH	166–206
CHAPTER	XV.	THE CONGREGATIONAL CHURCH	207–230
CHAPTER	XVI.	THE METHODIST CHURCH	231–247
CHAPTER	XVII.	SCHOOLS	248–254
CHAPTER	XVIII.	NOYES ACADEMY	255–296
CHAPTER	XIX.	CANAAN UNION ACADEMY	297–311
CHAPTER	XX.	LAWYERS	312–342
CHAPTER	XXI.	SOLDIERS	343–383
CHAPTER	XXII.	DOCTORS, COLLEGE GRADUATES	422–429
CHAPTER	XXIII.	ROADS	384–421
CHAPTER	XXIV.	TEMPERANCE IN CANAAN	430–434
CHAPTER	XXV.	HOW SOME OF OUR HOUSES WERE BUILT	435–447
CHAPTER	XXVI.	WHEEL CARRIAGES, TANNERIES, POTS AND PEARL ASHES	448–455
CHAPTER	XXVII.	INCIDENTS	456–480
CHAPTER	XXVIII.	SECRET ORGANIZATIONS	481–492
CHAPTER	XXIX.	OLD FAMILIES	493–579
		GENEALOGY	581–654
		MARRIAGES	654–665
APPENDIX: VOTES FOR GOVERNOR; REPRESENTATIVES; SELECTMEN; MODERATORS; TOWN CLERKS; TOWN APPROPRIATIONS FOR CHARGES; CENSUS OF 1790; INVENTORY OF 1782; LIST OF VOTERS, 1825; ENROLLMENT LIST, 1864			669–694

HISTORY OF CANAAN.

CHAPTER I.

THE CHARTERS OF CANAAN.

The charters of Canaan are interesting documents, their tone and style are kingly, such as our Republican ears are unused to. The first and original charter signed and granted July 9, 1761, having lapsed by reason of the non-performance of its conditions by the grantees, they made application to Gov. John Wentworth, who renewed the old charter by a second charter dated February 23, 1769, and granted them a further term of four years to fulfil the conditions of the first charter.

The first charter commences with the royal declaration:

Province of New Hampshire,

George the Third, by the Grace of God of Great Britain, France and Ireland, King, Defender of the Faith &c.

To all persons to whom these presents shall come Greeting Know ye, that wee of our special Grace, Certain knowledge and Meer motion, for the Due incouragement of settling a new Plantation within our said Province, by and with the advice of our trusty and well beloved Benning Wentworth Esq, our Governor and Commander in chief of our said Province of New Hampshire. Have upon the conditions and Reservations hereinafter made, Given and Granted and by these presents for us our Heirs and Successors, do give and grant in equal Shares unto our Loving Subjects Inhabitants of our said Province of New Hampshire and our other Governments, and to their heirs and assigns forever whose names are entered on this Grant to be divided to and amongst them into sixty eight equal shares, all that tract or parcel of land, situate Lying & being within our sd Province of New Hampshire containing by Admeasurement Twenty three Thousand acres, which tract is to contain six miles square and no more out of which an allowance is to be made for highways and unimprovable lands by Rocks ponds mountains and Rivers one Thousand and Forty acres free according to a plan & survey thereof made by our said Governors order, and returned into the Secretary's office & hereto annexed, butted and bounded as follows; viz: Beginning at the South East Corner of Hanover from thence North fifty five Degrees East by Hanover Six miles to the Corner thereof, from thence South Sixty one degrees East six miles, from thence South forty one degrees West six miles from thence North fifty eight degrees West seven miles and one quarter of a mile to the bound first mentioned, and that the same be and hereby is Incorporated into a Township by the Name of Canaan, and the inhabitants that do or shall hereafter Inhabit the said Township are hereby declared to be enfranchised with and Intitled to all and every, the privileges and Immunities that other Towns within our Province by law exercise & enjoy and further that the said Town as soon as there shall be fifty families resident & Settled thereon shall have ye Liberty of hold Two fairs one of which shall be held on the . . . and the other on the . . . annually which fairs . . .

And as soon as the sd Town shall consist of fifty families, a market may be opened and kept one or more days in each week as may be thought most advantageous to the Inhabitants.

Also the first meeting for the choice of Town Officers, agreeable to the laws of our said Province shall be held on the third Tuesday in August next, which said meeting shall be notified by Thomas Gustin, who is also appointed the Moderator of the First Meeting, which he is to notify and Govern agreeable to the Laws and Customs of our said Province, and that the annual meeting forever hereafter, for the choice of such officers for the said Town shall be on the second Tuesday of March annually.

To have and to hold the above tract of land as above expressed together with all privileges and appurtenances to them and their respective heirs and assigns forever, upon the following conditions:

1st viz: That every Grantee his heirs and assigns shall plant and cultivate, five acres of Land within the term of five years for every fifty acres contained in his or their share or portion of land in said Township, and continue to Improve and settle the same by additional cultivations on penalty of the forfeiture of his Grant or share in said Township and of its Reverting to us our heirs and successors to be by us or them Regranted to such of our subjects as shall effectually settle & cultivate the same.

2nd. That all white and other Pine trees within the said Township fit for Masting our Royal Navy be carefully preserved for that use and none to be cut or felled without our special license for so doing first had and obtained upon the penalty of the forfeiture of the Right of such Grantee his heirs and assigns to us our heirs and successors as well as being subject to the penalty of any act or acts of parliament that now are or hereafter shall be enacted.

3rd. That before any division of the land be made to and among the Grantees a tract of land as near the centre of the said Township as the land will admit of shall be reserved and marked out for Town Lots, one of which shall be allotted to each Grantee of the contents of one acre.

4 yielding and paying therefor to us our heirs and successors for

the space of ten years to be computed from the date hereof the Rent of one Ear of Indian Corn only, on the Twenty fifty day of December annually, if lawfully demanded, the first payment to be made on the Twenty fifth day of December 1762

5 Each Proprietor settler or Inhabitant shall yield and pay unto us our heirs and successors yearly and every year forever, from and after the expiration of ten years from the above and twenty fifth day of December which shall be in the year of our Lord 1772, one shilling proclamation money for every Hundred acres he so owns settles or possesses and so in proportion for a greater or less tract of land, which money shall be paid by the respective persons above said their heirs or assigns in our Council Chamber in Portsmouth or to such officer or officers as shall be appointed to receive the same and this to be in lieu of all other Rents and services whatsoever.

In testimony whereof we have caused the seal of our said Province to be hereunto affixed.

Witness Benning Wentworth Esq our Governor and Commander in Chief of our said Province the Ninth day of July in the year of our Lord Christ one thousand seven hundred and sixty one and in the First year of our Reign

By his Excellency's Command with advice of Council Theodore Atkinson Secty.

BENNING WENTWORTH.

Province of New Hampshire July 9th, 1761

The names of the Grantees of Canaan

Thomas Gustin	George Harris
Gibson Harris	Caleb Whiting
Ebenezer Harris	Willm Fox Ju^r
Daniel Harris	Stephen Kellogg
Joseph Babcock	Thomas Gustin
Amos Walworth	Richard Wibird Esq
Joseph Eames	James Nevins Esq
Ebenezer Eames	Capt. John Wentworth Somers-
Ebenezer Peck	worth
Allen Wightman	Thomas Westbrook Walden
Jared Spencer	Daniel Fowle
Eph^m Wells Ju^r	Israel Kellogg
Thomas Wells	Aaron Cady
Thomas Gustin Ju^r	Aaron Cady Ju^r
Jedidiah Lathrop	Nathaniel Cady
Clement Daniels	Asa Daniels
John Chamberlain	John Tribble
Benj Chamberlain	Samuel Dodge
Abner Chamberlain	Samuel Meacham
David Chamberlain	Isaiah Rathbun
Richard Sparrow	William Chamberlain

Willm Chamberlain Jur	Rufus Randal
Thomas Gates	James Jones
George Lampheer	Jonathan Beebe 3rd
Thomas Minor	Jabez Jones
Phinehas Sabine	George King Mercht
Joshua Rathbun	Willm King do
Sylvester Randal	Capt Willm Wentworth
Saml Dodge 3rd	Thomas Parker
Eph^m Wells	Daniel Rogers
Josiah Gates Jur	John Newmarch Esq
Lewis Loveridge	

His Excellency Benning Wentworth Esq, a tract to Contain five Hundred acres as marked on the plan B. W. which is to be accounted Two of the within shares. One whole share for the Incorporated Society for ye propagation of the Gospel in foreign parts

One share for the first Settled Minister of the Gospel

One share for the benefit of the School in said Town & one share for a Glebe for the Church of England as by law established.

Province of New Hampshire July ye 9th 1761

Recorded in the book of Charters

THEODORE ATKINSON *Secretary*

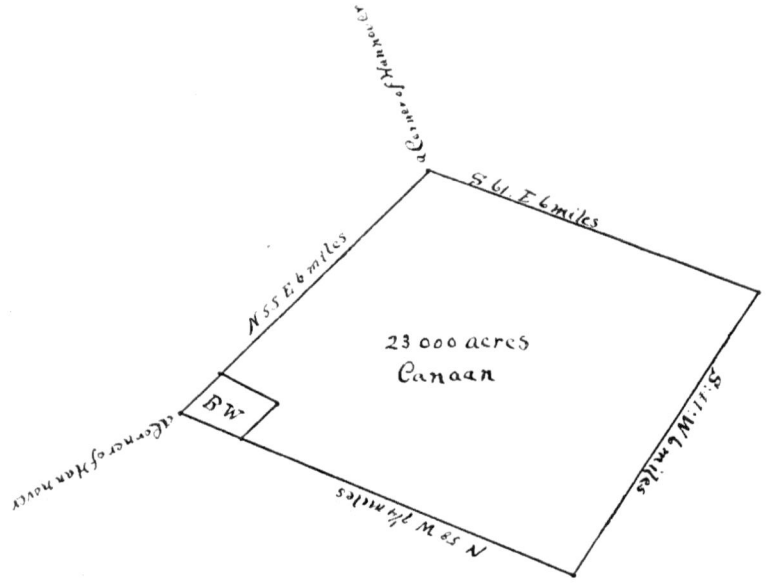

The Charters of Canaan.

The above is copied from the Proprietors' Records and was supposed to have been copied from the original charter which was in the possession of the Proprietors' clerk at one time, but where it is now is not known. The following is from the State Papers and is the renewal of the original charter:

Province of } George the Third by the Grace of God of Great Britain, New Hamp. } France Ireland King defender of the Faith &c.

Whereas we of our special Grace & mere Motion for the due encouragement of settling a new Plantation within Our Province of New Hampshire by our letters patent or Charter under the seal of our Said Province dated the 9th day of July 1761 in the first year of our reign a tract of land equal to six miles square bounded as therein expressed & since surveyed admeasured marked & ascertained by our order to Isaac Rindge Esq our surveyor general of lands for said Province Granted to a number of our loyal subjects whose names are entered on the same to hold to them their heirs & assigns on the conditions therein declared & to be a Town corporate by the name of Canaan as by reference to the said chapter may more fully appear And whereas the said grantees have represented unto us that by reason of the great Inconveniences which occur in the Settlement of the new Townships so remotely situated from any other Townships or Settlements that can afford any assistance hath rendered it impracticable for the whole number of grantees to perform that Part of the Conditions that relates to the cultivation of such a Proportion of the said Grant That there are families now settled on the premises which affords them hopes of a final Settlement without delay and humbly supplicating us not to take advantage of the breach of said Condition but to lengthen out & grant them some further Time for the performance thereof. Now Know ye that we being willing to promote the end proposed have of our further Grace & Favor suspended our claim of the forfeiture which the said Grantees may have incurred and by these presents do grant unto the said Grantees their Heirs & Assigns the further Term of Four years from this date for performing and fulfilling the conditions matters & things by them to be done as aforesaid, except the Quit Rents which are to remain due & payable as expressed & reserved in the original Grant or Charter.

J' Wentworth.

Feb. 23. 1769.

Attached to the charter are the names of sixty-two men as original grantees, and among them all it does not appear by any record that more than ten or twelve of them ever saw their "grants"—Amos Walworth, Ebenezer Eames, George Harris, Daniel Harris, Samuel Meacham, Thomas Gates, Thomas Miner,

James Jones, Samuel Dodge, Ephraim Wells, Jr., Josiah Gates, and possibly Thomas Gustin, whose name was discovered as a witness to a deed executed before William Ayer in Canaan. These men appear to have made explorations and to have performed various labors, and they left honorable names upon the records of the town. But there were other men than those named in the charter, to whom Canaan is indebted for opening up highways into the wilderness which developed all her hills and valleys. But few authentic documents exist relating to the early settlement of this town. No diaries detailing the events of that early life have ever been discovered, showing the hardships endured or the dangers avoided by those men and women whose resting place among us at this day is perhaps an obscure mound of earth without a stone to indicate whose bones have there decayed. Nor are there any letters to friends detailing the fate or prospects of those who came here. But little information is to be gained from the public records. These record the appointment of officers and of committees to perform certain duties, whose reports being "accepted," no more can be learned from them. They show that money was "raised" for building roads, laying out pitches, and for other purposes, but it does not appear how this money was expended, no one being held accountable for it.

Nor for sixteen years after the first settlement of the town, is there to be found in the town archives a list of the taxpayers. There is a partial list of the taxpayers for the year 1782 and a more complete list for the year 1786 in the handwriting of Ezekiel Wells, and which is a copy of the original record. The list for 1782 contains the names of forty-seven, three of whom were non-residents, that of 1786 contains seventy-eight names, three were non-residents. Not until 1793, more than twenty-six years after the settlement of the town, appears the first complete recorded list and it embraces 124 names. The old settlers are dead, their children are dead and their grandchildren, except here and there, one whose memory has become obscured by years, and whose recollections of the times of their fathers are little to be relied upon. With these difficulties in view at the starting point it will be seen that the task of the annalist becomes almost one of imagination. Of course it is of little consequence whether the history of Canaan be written or unwritten, like the man whose lineage ran back into obscurity, from whence little light is visable.

Years before the events described occurred, this country with all its ponds and streams, had been explored by trappers and hunters whose success always equalled their industry. It was related to me by Ensign Colby, that an ancestor of his from Haverhill, Mass., with a partner named Tribble, was one of the earliest explorers here, and that the reports these men made upon the natural products of the soil, influenced many persons in Haverhill, Amesbury, Plaisted, etc., to seek new homes here. On one occasion Colby and Tribble arrived on the shores of Hart Pond late in the afternoon, weary and discouraged by their toilsome journey through the forest. Dense woods lined all the banks, no trace of human life visible anywhere. They struck a fire and ate their scanty meal. Tribble weary and in ill humor, told Colby it was useless to trap in such a place. He didn't believe there was any game in this region. For himself, he was going to sleep, if Colby choose to set the traps, he was welcome to all the skins he could catch. The traps were set, and in the morning the trapper was rewarded by finding each one sprung, and holding fast a beaver, otter or a mink. Tribble apologized for his ill nature and unbelief of the night before, saying: "Hereafter the meaner the country looked the greater would be his expectations of game." It is fair to state, that Colby in the division of the furs, took no advantage of his partner's unbelief of the night before. They continued to trap some three weeks, with various success, about the pond and on Mascoma River, near the present village, always camping on the shores of the pond at night. One day, the sun about an hour high, they heard or supposed they heard, the report of a gun fired in the direction of their traps on the river, believing it to be a signal gun of the Indians and that they had discovered their traps. Without stopping to ascertain the truth, they took counsel of their fears, seized their skins and guns and hastily and fearfully took the trail that led to the settlements. They continued their flight through a wild forest for forty miles, to a place now called Boscawen. Here they sat down on the brow of a hill for rest and refreshment. Upon reflection they concluded they had fooled themselves out of their property, so they took the same trail back, to reclaim their traps, and were not surprised to find them all safe, many of them being sprung. Nor were there any indications of Indians to be seen.

The Indians, one hundred and more years ago were sufficiently numerous and hostile to cause the settlers to be extremely watchful. Evidence exists of two Indian camps in this town. One of these was situated upon the shores of Hart Pond, upon land now owned by Mr. George E. Cobb. Another has been located near the outlet of Goose Pond. Various rude implements, such as axes made of stone, jugs, etc., have been unearthed at these points, which confirms the belief in their former existence. The tribe is not known nor their language. They have disappeared like the trees, and few in our generation will care to inquire whence they came or whither they went. They probably belonged to the great family of Abnakis who inhabited this part of New Hampshire and northern Maine. But as our settlers had little to do with Indians, neither have we.

Wild game was in abundance, and the rivers were full of fish. Venison was plenty in the humble houses of the settlers. Bears and wolves were troublesome; besides serving to frighten crying children into silence, they often made sad havoc among the flocks. Moose, deer, rabbits, foxes, partridges, with beaver, otter, martin, mink, etc., abounded, and in their way each served to settle and open up this town to the institutions of civilization.

CHAPTER II.

THE FIRST AND SECOND SETTLERS.

The story of the first settlement of Canaan is legendary and has been brought down to us by generations. There are no documents to offer as proofs of its truth, and if any ever existed, they have been carefully gathered up and sold for paper rags. But the legend runs, that in the wintry December of 1766, the old man Scofield, who had been knocking about the country in search of a home while wandering in the neighborhood of Lebanon, from passing trappers and woodmen, heard of the rich intervals, the huge trees, and game in abundance, to be had in the wilderness, where as yet, no man had settled for a longer time than was needed to take up his traps. He started for the new region on snowshoes, hauling his effects on a handsled, followed by his wife and four children, two young sons and two daughters and settled here, the first white man, among the great pines and maples, the black bear and wolf his only neighbors. The old man must have possessed a stout heart and infinite faith in himself, for I take it, no man even in these devout days would go forth into the wilderness upon snowshoes and a handsled with simply a trust in God. Such a trust might do in the summer time, when the earth is generous in fruits and flowers, and a bed of grass or leaves is easy for the bones of the weary; but when the frost cloud descends and settles upon the earth, and feathers of young frosting give a nap to all things, a stern reliance upon self is a safer trust. Faith in God may do for a man in the agonies of inexorable death when he knows it is unsafe to postpone faith any longer, but it will never prevent his freezing with the mercury at zero and below. And so thought old John Scofield, for he brought his axe and shovel, removed the snow, felled trees, built him a great fire and a brush house and left a name in the local ananls that will live forever.

It is related that the next morning after his arrival, the old man left his family, and set out for Lebanon for such of his goods as he had been unable to bring the day previous, intending to return the same evening. But a heavy rain occurred which swelled the Mascoma so as to make it impassable. He arrived on the banks of the river after dark, but was unable to cross it, remaining there all night. And this was in the month of December, 1766. The experiences of that lonely traveler as he struggled to shelter his family from the inclemency of those December days, partake very little of romance, but they were common to the people of those days.

John Scofield was an Englishman, born in 1715. He had been a resident of Norwich, Conn. He was not a very social man, liked to have his neighbors so far away that when he visited them they would be glad to see him; would "welcome the coming, speed the parting guest." Early in the spring of 1766, finding himself embarrassed with near neighbors, he traveled up the river leisurely looking for a place to set up his family altar. After many hardships he reached Canaan in the manner before stated. Here he found land and space enough to satisfy his most lonely desires. He erected his first brush house in the valley, about twenty-five rods north from the schoolhouse in the old District No. 10, and afterwards built one of logs in the same place. The rocky remains of the old cellar are still to be seen there, overgrown with briars and bushes. There was also an oven built oval of stone, which was standing within forty years. It was taken down many years ago by Nathaniel Wilson and the stones laid into a wall in the vicinity. It was from this place he heard the report of Thomas Miner's gun on the eventful morning in the following spring, and which was a signal to him that he was no longer to live alone. Some time after this event, and before the lands were pitched upon by the slowly arriving grantees, he built a house nearer to the river, where he spent the remainder of his life. The field where his remains now lie was his own property, deeded to him by the proprietors. He cleaned it and dedicated a portion of it for a burial place. Several young persons were buried here before his own death. Mrs. Sarah Scofield, his widow, who died in 1794, is supposed to have been the last person buried there.

It does not appear that John Scofield's intention to set apart this spot as a burying place was ever completed. It was never enclosed, nor was there ever any record made of the fact. And when the farm was sold to Capt. Daniel Pattee in 1799, no reservation was made in the deed in reference to these graves, although it was well known that they were there. The practice of using it was doubtless abandoned from the inconvenience of getting to it. And the present graveyard on the sand knoll at West Canaan was substituted for it. The circumstances attending the laying out of the burying ground on the Street were similiar in their nature. The land was given to the people for a burying place by the then owner, Nathan Messer, but when afterwards he sold it to Mr. John Fales, he neglected to reserve the graveyard in the deed. Then Mr. Fales laid claim to the enclosure and threatened to plow it up, and plant potatoes upon the graves, if it were not paid for. The town paid him thirty-seven and one-half dollars, and in the deed a reservation was made of two rods square as a burial place for the Fales family. There was a stone wall around the original lot which was removed on the east side by Franklin P. Swett in the '60's and a picket fence built in its place. The town has bought four additions. A small strip was added by G. H. Goodhue and the tomb of William D. Currier was accepted by the town.

Mr. Scofield brought with him to Canaan a wife and four children: Delight, who afterwards married Gideon Rudd; Eleazer, aged twelve years; John, Jr., aged ten; and Miriam, aged eight years. The latter afterwards married Maj. Samuel Jones, who came in early from Connecticut. The old man was strong-minded and self-reliant; he had early nerved himself to make his own path in the world, and here we find him on that December night, the only man in Canaan, with his axe and rifle, making a brush house to shelter his little family and keep them from suffering. He was fifty-one years old at that time and had been accustomed to the comforts of social life, but he left all these to build himself a home in these wild woods. That his labors and virtues were appreciated, is evident from the fact that when the proprietors awarded sixty dollars to those pioneers who had contributed most to effect the settlement of the town, Mr. Scofield was the first of the four among whom it was divided, his proportion being rated at twenty-six dollars. The early settlers of Canaan were men of brave patience. Words fail in describing the reality to the occupants of comfortable homes at this day. They were rich only in stout hands and strong faith, and they conquered the wilderness of swamp and forest because they wanted a home. The earth which bore such trees would yield rich crops of grain and fruit. They set themselves down in the wild wood, it made little difference where, and attacked the trees. There was another man into whose life a good deal of romance was crowded, and as his appearance here was almost co-equal with Mr. Scofield, their relations to each other render it proper that we should refer to him now.

Thomas Miner, named a grantee in the charter, was the second man who came to this town. He resided at Norwich, Conn., and at the date of the charter was eighteen years of age. Notwithstanding his youthful years, his name appears as one of the grantees. He was a restless man, full of energy and activity all his life, a poor writer and not much of a scholar and not always mindful of the courtesies of life. This temperament led him at an early age to seek excitement in the varied career of a sailor. This life ever full of danger and hardship, at length it became dull and monotonous to him and he sought change in inland adventure. His ventures at sea had been fortunate, he had laid by a sum sufficiently large to secure him independence of labor. He married Eleanor Lamb in Norwich, 1765, at the age of 22, and his first child, named Allen, was born in September of the following year, 1766. He was at this time out of business, somewhat disgusted with the restraints of the Blue Laws that governed the civilization of Connecticut, and waiting for some exciting event to shape his course in the world. While in this frame of mind, it occurred to him that he was joint proprietor of a wild uninhabited tract of land in New Hampshire, which he had never seen. He was one of the sixty-one proprietors named in the charter. He could learn but few particulars concerning this land. Emigrants to the Upper Cohos had passed through it by the foot trail, but could give no description of it, except that it was covered with goodly trees, plenty of stone for fencing purposes; the waters abounded in fish, and the woods with game,— some of it dangerous. He resolved to explore that wild land, even if he had to go alone. This scheme just suited his present state of mind. He had explored the ocean whose waste of waters left no trace behind. Now he would explore the land and leave trace of himself that should make him famous in local story.

Many of the grantees were residents of Norwich, Colchester and the adjoining towns, the Harrises, George, Gibson, and Daniel; Dr. Ebenezer Eames, James Jones, Amos Walworth, Josiah Gates, Jedediah Lathrop, Samuel Meacham. Then there were Joshua and Ezekiel Wells, John and Samuel Jones, and others who were proposing to migrate. Mr. Miner made known to many of these men his intentions, but at first got little encouragement. Meeting Mr. Harris one day, he said to him: "Mr. Harris, I've got tired of this humdrum sort of life in a village, where everybody has to be so proper and religion is a pretense for a great deal of meanness. And I don't want to stay any longer in a place where I'm not allowed to kiss my wife on Sunday. I'm going to get out er this, and try the bears and wolves for neighbors, and live on fish and venison. Come along, and let's look after our six miles square."

To this Mr. Harris replied: "No hurry about it, Mr. Miner, it's a long way, and a hard way, on foot or horseback, it's slow traveling, but few places to stop at. You are young and active, with a young wife and child. You don't want to leave them behind. We'll get ready this fall and winter, and in the spring we can go in company; and others will go along too. In that way we shall be able to defend and support one another, and on that long road there will be need enough of it."

"Well," says Miner, "I did think of starting out alone, because you see, I've been used to doing that. I thought I'd leave my wife here and run up there and spend the winter looking round. Now I'm a poor writer and a worse scholar, and the bad of it is, that I should have to write to my folks. You're a scholar and understand all about these land voyages. Your advice is good. We'll spend the winter in getting ready and start out early in the spring, and build us a home up there where 'tain't unlawful for a man to say 'damn it,' if he's strongly tempted."

It was intended to start out a company of several families, and take along such conveniences as could be transported. But when spring came they were not ready. Some of them hesitated —that the journey was too long—they wanted to learn something more of the country, and they would wait longer. Mr. Miner's temperament was not of the waiting kind. When the spring came and he found the company still undecided, he took his wife and child and such implements and conveniences as he could pack upon a horse and with a compass in his pocket, to guide him when he became uncertain of his way, he started out for his territory driving a cow. His journey through Connecticut and Massachusetts was comparatively easy. There were many settlements and roads had been laid out. After getting into the Connecticut valley the woods seemed to close in upon them in long stretches, the clearings were few and very small and the roads dwindled down to a single trail, at times only discernible by the blazed trees which marked the way.

In all western New Hampshire but four towns had been incorporated. In each of these towns a block house or fort had been erected and they had attained prominence from the fact that being on the frontier they were often exposed to attack by the Indians from Canada. At these places he stopped for rest, and to hold intercourse with the people. His journey was a quiet one, unmarked by any disturbing incident. He and his young wife enjoyed the constantly varying scenery, which roused within him new impulses, and thoughts to which his life had heretofore been a stranger. In some of the reflective moods which fell upon him he would say: "Wife, I've loved the sea and was never afraid when the strong winds lashed it into fury, but it was a desert without a flower or tree and all that fell into it was swallowed up and disappeared forever. But this new road we are traveling is dotted all along with fragrant flowers, and the great trees, always stretching their long arms out before us, are calling us to a new destiny. We are started upon the long road. We are young, and life which a few months ago, seemed like an old wornout coat, now rises up all before us. Whatever may be our fate, we will have confidence in one another, and trust in God." And so they passed leisurely along on their way, past all the settlements, until they approached their land of promise and stopped to rest upon the rising land afterwards called "South Road," that gave them a bird's-eye view of much of the northern part of the town. Here they rested and decided to pitch their camp. Not a house in sight, not a smoke, not a clearing; no sign of civilization.

This young man of twenty-three years, who thought he had already enjoyed and exhausted the pleasures of the sea, and had found the charms of social life unsatisfactory, stood thereon that evening, the past all behind him, facing the new present, and looking through the great trees at a future crowned with fruitful fields and houses filled with comely faces. He stood there like a prophet and "viewed the landscape o'er." There was fearless resolution in his heart, and he turned to his wife who was near by caressing the boy, and said: "Wife, this is a goodly place. I think we'll build us a home here. This seems to be a great point in our lives. You know I'm not much of a hand a-praying, but we'll begin now, and thank God that we are here, and pray that he will give us strength and grace to accomplish the labors that are before us, and length of days that we may see the generations that are to subdue and utilize these forests and streams." And it was right here and on this occasion that all the romance departed out of his young life. The sun was setting in crimson and gold. His wife and boy were resting upon the ground, the horse and cow weary with their long journey, were turned loose to graze. The scene was not a rural one; it engendered a feeling of insecurity which called for immediate action. The past glimmered for an instant before his mind, with all its religious and social opportunities, but it was only a gleam that flitted rapidly away and left him standing there on the brow of that hill, filled at once with the resolves of ripe manhood. Henceforth there was to be only work, not a mere struggle for existence, but earnest active labor that the years to come would be proud of.

His reveries were disturbed by his wife, who said: "Well, Thomas, the sun is getting low. Where shall we make a bed? The little boy is tired; he must have his supper and go to rest." Thomas seized his axe, and in a short time had cleared away the brush and arranged the branches of the trees, so as to form a shelter from inclement weather. Then with flint and steel, he struck a fire and while his wife mixed the coarse bread and baked it before the fire, he milked the cow, and they sat down at their first frugal meal, not far from the spot where he afterwards erected his dwelling.

On awakening, the next morning, it is related that his horse was not to be found. After making hasty preparations, Mr. Miner seized his hat and coat and started out in pursuit, following the trail by which he came back as far as Charlestown, or No. 4, where he found his horse secured in the stable of a man who three days before spoke with the travelers as they passed along, and who, supposing the horse had strayed from his owner, secured him in his stable. Mr. Miner hastily retraced his steps to his camp, where he found his wife safe, but in much anxiety of mind lest he might be waylaid by evil-minded persons. After relating their mutual experiences while separated, she said to him: "Thomas, I think we are not alone here. While you were away I heard sounds resembling the chopping of an axe, followed by other sounds as if large trees had fallen and one time I thought I recognized the report of a gun, and these sounds all came from the direction of the valley yonder. Shan't we be glad to have a neighbor?"

"Indeed you surprise me, wife; I thought I was the first and last man here. But we'll rest tonight, and in the morning I'll beat about in the valley cautiously, and see what discoveries I can make; can't be that Mr. Harris, or any of the others down home have stolen a march on us! We'll soon see."

On waking the next morning his ears were greeted with sounds as of an axe in the valley below. The idea of an axe implied a white man, of course. So he discharged his rifle and waited the effect. This was soon answered by the report of another gun. He felt sure then that he had a neighbor, and in due time he found himself in the presence of our first settler and oldest inhabitant, John Scofield.

When he had made himself known the two men greeted each other with friendly salutations. Mr. Miner exclaimed: "It's good to see you here, my friend! Thought I was 'monarch of all I surveyed,' but I'm willing to divide with ye!" "How is it," said Mr. Scofield, "about those other men that are down in the charter, if they ever come in they'll about fill up the town; and if I'm going to be crowded here, I'll go off to Canada, where I've had my eye for a long time?"

"No need of that," replied Miner, "I've thought it all over as we came along, you just stay where you are and you'll get these lands about as cheap as you want them."

THE FIRST AND SECOND SETTLERS.   17

"I've been jammed in crowds all my life," says Scofield, "and I'm up here to get away from them, can't bear to be crowded, never could; came away from Connecticut because there was too many people and too much law."

"Just you hold and listen a minute," says Miner. "I've seen a good many of these proprietors down there in Norwich and Colchester and there's soft spots in more than half of them. They will never come up here because they are afraid of the journey, and if we can make them believe there's to be assessments on their rights, they'll be glad to sell out cheap and you and I can have the benefit of their indolent fears."

"It looks very probable, perhaps you're right. But how are ye for venison at your camp?"

"None at all, seen nothing to shoot at," says Miner.

"Well, you'd better come in and take some along with ye. We killed a bear that was snuffin' round the pig pen, two days since and the boys brought in a deer, so we are well supplied; and mind you bring the dame soon to see the old woman; its natural they should want to talk with one another."

"So I will," says Miner, "this venison is much like the land, it don't cost much after you get it."

It was not long before the women came together with very cheerful greetings. Mrs. Scofield was a middle-aged, motherly woman, who had followed her husband in all his wanderings for a home. They had a cabin which afforded them a shelter for themselves and their children. She was hopeful all her life; and, humble as it was, cheerfulness reigned in her home. Thus it was that at their first meeting, the old and the young couple being mutually pleased, formed a lasting friendship which continued during their lives and afterwards, in another generation became stronger by family ties.

Mr. Scofield, on learning that the proprietors of these lands were preparing to occupy them, naturally felt anxious as to his position here. He had after much wandering got his family in a position to secure a comfortable home. He had cleared a small patch of ground and was preparing to put in seed. Mr. Miner had assured him that there was land enough in Canaan for all the people who were coming, without any one of them being crowded, "and further," said he, "and to remove all your anxieties, I pledge my word to you that should any dispute arise, as to your occupancy here, I'll divide my share with you, for I am an equal owner and have a right to do what I will with my own. Then we will take advantage of circumstances and when we find a disgusted proprietor, we'll step in and buy him out before he has time to change his mind."

They resolved to be neighbors. Mr. Miner would plant his stakes at a convenient distance from Mr. Scofield, who should retain the land whereon he had made improvements and whatever lands they occupied, their rights should be recognized by the grantees. Having made this friendly covenant, they each set themselves diligently to work, and in due time they had green fields

> "Where the rain might rain upon them;
> Where the sun might shine upon them;
> Where the winds might sigh upon them;
> And where the snows might die upon them."

And now, having brought these two men together, who were so long apart, we will leave them while we go back and look after some other men, who, though willing, were not strong enough to come alone, but who, in the following years left records of honorable lives and actions.

Other Early Settlers.

Of the sixty-one grantees named in the charter, fifty-one were residents of Norwich, Colchester, and the surrounding towns in that vicinity in Connecticut. The other eleven were the friends of the Governor, and their names were written in the charter by court favoritism, a system that has always been understood in courts and cabinets, and by which men of genius get lands or profits without work.

After the departure of young Miner, in quest of his unknown lands, the subject of emigration often came to the surface in conversation between the proprietors, but several months passed away before they arrived at a conclusion. And then instead of coming as settlers, a few started out as explorers, who were to visit the lands and report upon its beauty and loveliness, its fertility and the uses to which industrious men might put it. The party consisted of George and Daniel Harris, brothers, Amos Walworth, Samuel Benedict, Samuel Jones, Lewis Joslyn, Asa Williams, Joseph Craw and Daniel Crossman, some of these gentlemen brought along their families. The expedition was delayed until summer and they reached Canaan by the same route as that traveled by Mr. Miner. It is supposed they were heartily welcomed by the two first families, who were anxiously awaiting for news from home. Mr. George Harris, who from his energy and superior intelligence, was recognized as a leader among them, soon after their arrival organized parties for exploration, and in a few days they had examined the southern, western and northern portions of the town. The following incident relating to one of their parties is handed down as a legend: George Harris and his party, in 1767, came upon a sheet of water near Hanover, whose surface seemed to be alive with wild geese and ducks. They killed a goose — an old one — and cooked it, all day, and then it was tough. It never got to be a tender goose, and to commemorate this circumstance they named that water "Goose Pond."

Another of these parties, in traversing the northern part of the town, came upon the camp of James Clark, who, with his family, had just come in from the Piscataqua settlements, and had pitched upon the hill, which he afterwards sold to Joseph Bartlett. This man Clark lived here until 1772, when Governor Wentworth built his road to Hanover. It was laid out north of Clark's house. The governor offered to take Clark into his service, which he accepted and followed on in the train to Hanover.

These exploring parties returned to Mr. Miner's camp at the time appointed, expressing themselves well pleased with the lands they had examined, particularly with the numerous ponds and streams which indicated abundance of water. In their travels, each one had selected a spot upon which to pitch his home. George Harris, Amos Walworth, Samuel Jones, Joseph Craw and Daniel Crossman selected lands upon what is now "South Road," so as to form a neighborhood. Crossman, Craw and Benedict, who had brought their families along, went into the business of brush housekeeping, like Miner and Scofield. While Samuel Jones, who was unmarried and had been a major of militia, for the time being, attached himself to the family of Mr. Scofield, from which he afterwards took a wife, and began improvements on his own pitch, which was not far away. Mr. Harris and Walworth returned to Colchester to convey the result of their observations to the waiting ones who came eagerly to hear the reports from New Hampshire.

But they were not ready to start, and did not come yet for more than a year, except Mr. Harris, who, with his wife and family, and accompanied by Samuel Dodge and Capt. Josiah Gates, returned to his new home the same season, and busied himself in assigning lands, laying out roads and other matters in the interests of the grantees. Before winter set in, each of these families had built log houses, and were prepared with their slender means to meet the rigors of the season. Joseph Craw's child died during the winter of 1768, the first death in the township. There was much to discourage these new settlers. No roads to pass from house to house. No corn mills nor saw-mills, no crops of grain to be gathered. The way of their coming was not favorable for the transportation of grain or food. Their slender stock slowly diminished, until the colonists began to feel alarm lest they might come to want and their families suffer. Here was a great trial approaching and it needed brave men to meet it. And under it some of those strong men grew faint and wished they had not come. Some, it is said, even turned back and sought their old homes in Connecticut. There was no mill nearer than Lebanon, nor roads leading to it, nor bridges upon which to cross the streams. Only a foot trail led through the forest, obstructed by swamps and fallen trees, and rafts of logs served for bridges.

For several years it occurred that a man must walk to Lebanon, where a mill had been built, work a day to earn a bushel of "bread corn" and have it ground, then pack it upon his back to his home in the forest, by that blind trail through the forest. We can imagine how carefully that bushel of bread corn was husbanded and dealt out to the laborers. The times afforded no room for tramps, nor vagabonds, nor idlers, or other non-workers to lounge about and eat up the hard-earned bread of honest industry.

> "Here eyes do regard them,
> In eternity's stillness,
> Here is all fullness,
> Ye brave, to reward you,
> Work and despair not."

It happened, a few years after the settlers came in, there was a failure of crops. There was but one man in town who had corn in his crib, our old friend, Maj. Samuel Jones, who was a man of wealth and influence, living on South Road, west of Beaver Brook. He was a kind man, considerate to his poor neighbors, to many of whom he gave employment. It is related that Col. Ezekiel Wells, also a man of wealth and influence, went to the major to purchase corn, confident that his social position was such as to bar a refusal, and thus he would save the trouble of going to Lebanon. But the major was inexorable. He replied: "Colonel, you have a good horse and plenty of money, and can get your corn with but little personal inconvenience. I want a good deal of work done, and these neighbors of mine have nothing else to pay for my corn. It wouldn't be right for me to sell you my corn and send these men all the way over to Lebanon on foot. No, Colonel, can't do it, we must help one another." Colonel Wells was an irascible and profane man, but the major was not moved thereby. Returning home, the colonel stopped a moment at a place where young Thomas Baldwin was hewing timber and made this remark: "By God, I wish I was a devil." Thomas stopped his work, and looking at the colonel quietly replied: "Put your foot upon this log and I'll make a devil of you at one blow of the axe."

CHAPTER III.

PROPRIETORS' MEETINGS, 1768–1785.

During the winter and spring of 1768, there was but little variation in the labors of the settlers. Some progress had been made in laying out roads, and several acres of trees had been felled and the land burned over preparatory to putting in seed.

Until this season, it does not appear that any organization of grantees had ever been made. It was necessary that some persons should be authorized to transact the business of the grantees, in order that the settlers might feel secure in their titles. Accordingly a meeting of the Proprietors was warned and was held, probably at the house of John Scofield, although the record does not say, on the nineteenth day of July, 1768. This is the first meeting of the people of Canaan. They met as proprietors of the Township of Canaan, owners of the land and not as citizens in a municipal capacity. The doings of the proprietors as recorded in the Proprietors' Book of Records, was concerned mostly with the laying out and dividing of the land, the appointment of officers for the purpose of allotting the land, called the "Lot Laying Committee," the appointment of assessors for the purpose of assessing the taxes to pay the expenses of the proprietary in surveying the lots, surveying and building roads and bridges, the appointment of a collector to collect the taxes, a treasurer to hold the money, and a proprietors' clerk to keep the records. Committees were appointed at different times for different purposes, mostly to see that the proprietors' money was laid out in a proper manner towards the object for which it was raised.

Not till two years later was a town meeting held, and during these two years the town affairs were conducted by the proprietors. The town officers were also officers of the proprietary, sometimes holding the same positions in each body. There were really more offices to be filled than men to fill them and some held two positions. Up to 1787, the proprietors assessed taxes on the lands for the purpose of building and mending roads and bridges, after that time the care of roads and bridges was assumed by the town and appropriations were made by the town alone. From 1770 to 1787, appropriations were made by both town and proprietors for that purpose.

The first meeting of the proprietors is as follows:

Province of New Hampshire: Canaan July 19th. 1768. A Meeting Legally warned of the Proprietors of the Township of Canaan in said Province, the following votes were passed (viz.):

1st. Chose Mr. George Harris Moderator.
2nd. Made choice of Mr. Joseph Craw Proprietors Clerk.
3rd. Made Choice of Mr. George Harris first Committee Man.
4th. Chose Captain Josiah Gates 2nd. Committee Man.
5th. Chose Samuel Benedict 3rd. Committee Man.
6th. Chose John Burdick 4th. Committee Man.
7th. Chose Mr. Joseph Craw 5th. Committee Man.
8th. Chose Mr. Samuel Benedict Asseser.
9th. Chose Mr. John Burdick 2nd. Asseser.
10. Chose Mr. Joseph Craw 3rd. Asseser.
11. Chose Mr. Samuel Dodge Collector.
12. Chose Mr. John Scofield Treasurer.
13. Voted to raise a tax of three dollars upon each Proprietors Right to defray the Charges of Making & Mending Rodes in the Township of Canaan.
14. Voted that the above mentioned tax of three dollars on each Prors Right for making and Mending Rodes be worked out under the care and direction of the Proprietors Committee and to be done by the middle of November next & ye sd Committee alow 4/ [shillings] pe day for sd labor.
15. Voted to raise one dollar upon each Proprietors Right which the Proprietors will give with one hundred acres of upland to be layed out in the undivided land with a stream where it shall be judged best & most convenient to build Mills on to any person who will appear and build a good Corn Mil & Saw Mill within twelve months from this time. So as to have said Mill well done and going for the benefit of the Town.
16. Voted that the Proprietors Committee are hereby directed to lay out to those Proprietors as are already settled in said Township of Canaan Ten acres of Meadow and allso one hundred acres of Upland where they have already made their Pitch, to be allowed towards their Right or share in Said Township, and also the said Committee are further directed to lay out ten acres of Meadow and one hundred acres of upland as above said as shall appear to make speedy settlement in said Town & furthermore the Proprietors Clerk is hereby directed to put the returns sd ten acres & hundred acres lots upon Record as they

shall be layed out and returned by the Committee to each proprietor as aforesaid.

17. Voted that the owners of more than one sixteenth Part of the Rights or Shares in the Township of Canaan shall make request to the Proprietors Clerk, setting forth the reasons for calling said meeting and also the articles to be acted upon and of the time and place of holding said meeting. That the Clerk warn a meeting by duly posting a notification Agreeable to said request (10) days at least before the time of holding at the house of Mr. John Scofield in said Canaan. Shall be a sufficient warning for the future.

18. Voted to raise six shillings on each Proprietors Right Labour or Provitions to be given to the first settlers in said Canaan as was proposed to be given them Encouragement, to be proportioned amongst them as (viz.):

to Mr. John Scofield of Vallew of 26 dollars
to Mr Asa Williams 18 dollars
to Mr Samuel Jones of Vallew of 8 dollars
to Mr. Daniel Crossman of Vallew of 8 dollars

Test GEORGE HARRIS *Moderator*,
JOSEPH CRAW *Pro C*

Soon after this meeting the proprietors realized that their charter had lapsed for non-performance of its conditions, and without its renewal in their favor they were liable to be deprived of the results of all their labors; that the township might be granted to others. Accordingly they prepared a memorial and presented it to the governor, followed on December 3, 1768, by a petition of George Harris in behalf of himself and the other grantees, praying for a new grant of the township:

A memorial of the Proprietors of the Township of Canaan in sd Province humbly represents that your Excellency memorialists having obtained A Royal Charter of the sd Township of Canaan Did A number of them soon begin A Town in the second range, & the Town between it & Conn River not having begun to settle [namely, Hanover] and indeed all the towns thereabouts being destitute of Roads and also of Provisions (to Spare) which rendered the settlement impractible at that time; Whereupon the adventurers withdrew until the Spring of the year 1766. At which time (the difficulties being in some measure removed and the proprietors having given New Encouragement to the first settlers) Canaan began to settle indeed and Encreases fast to this time & bids fair to Encrease still — that whether the Proprietors are engaged to settle the Town your Excellency may determine something by A copy of part of Canaan Proprietors records which we herewith transmit to your Excellency But your Excellencys memorialists being sensible that the time limited in their sd Charter for Duty to be done is

Expired, & the duty not done in full as required in the sd Charter, although they have made Good proficiency hereto — Therefor your Excellency memorialists humbly pray your Excellency would be Pleased to renew their Chareter, that so the further settlement of Canaan may be Encouraged and those who have advanced their interests thereon not Deprived thereof, and the Hopes of all your Excellencys Dutiful Memorialists Resolved into Gratitude, and furthermore your Excellencys memorialists (apprehending it to be requisite to have the lines of the Township of Canaan ran and the bounds Ascertained), Humbly beg Leave to recommend Mr Aaron Storrs to your Excellency as a fit person for s^d purpose (he being A Surveyor that is well approv^d of and pray your Excellencies favor (if it may also be your Pleasure) to appoint him to that service. Whom we also appoint to be our agent to Lay this our Memorial befor your Excellency & to Receive your Excellencys answer to this our Memorial & your Excellencys Memorialists as in Duty bound Shall Ever Pray.

At a Meeting of the Proprietors of the Township of Canaan held in Canaan Aug ye 12 day 1768 Chose Mr Aaron Storrs to Lay the above Memorial before his Excellency the Govr of New Hampshire.

Test JOSEPH CRAW. *Prop^r Clerk*

The meeting referred to on August 12, 1768, was never re-recorded in the Proprietors' Book of Records.

Petition of George Harris of Norwich in Colony of Conn husbandman in behalf of Himself and other Grantees of Township of Canaan, unto your Excellency & the Honble Council humbly shews:—

That y^r Petitioner & his associates have expended large sums in bringing forward the settlement of said Township, which (on acc^t of the many Obstruction & Difficultys they have met with for want of necessary Roads & Mills) they have not been able to effect, till his majestys grants to them was expired & as the settlement of new land is a heavy and weighty work, y^r Petitioners pray they may be indulged with a New Grant of said Township for such time longer as y^r Excellency may judge necessary & your Petitioner as in duty bound shall ever pray —

GEORGE HARRIS in
behalf of Himself & associates

Dec. 3, 1768.

Their application was successful and Gov. John Wentworth granted them a renewal signed February 23, 1769.

For two years subsequent to the first recorded meeting, there does not appear to be much increase in the population, but few of the grantees arrived and some who were here returned to Norwich. Among the new settlers we find Deacon Caleb Welch, who "pitched" upon the farm once owned by Harrison Fogg. He cleared the land of trees and dead brush, built a house, and planted an orchard of apple and pear trees, from which he lived to make thirty barrels of cider in one year, which he and his boys drank. He was very close with the fruit, jealous of his apples and pears. He came here with four boys, Caleb, Martin, William and Russell. William married and settled in Enfield, Martin married and died in Jerusalem. Deacon Caleb died with old Moses Low, who lived near him. He was buried in the Cobble, but no stone marks his grave. His wife went to live with her son in Enfield, where she died at the age of ninety years.

The Deacon's was the eighth family that settled in town. His son, Caleb, afterwards built the house where once Rufus Richardson lived and was its last occupant. Young Caleb sold it to Joshua Currier, who lived in it sixteen years, sold it to David Richardson and then bought the house where his son, Farrington, once lived, the first house east of the Gulf.

Dr. Ebenezer Eames, along with whom came Thomas Baldwin, a youth then sixteen years old. Joshua and Ezekiel Wells, two brothers; Samuel Chapman, who kept an inn on South Road, and was afterwards known as the old lame basket maker; Jedidiah Hibbard, Asa Kilburn and Samuel Meacham and his family, the three latter men being residents of Lebanon as early as 1764, followed Harris upon his return from Connecticut.

The power to call a legal meeting by the proprietors seems to have lapsed and application had to be made to Israel Morey in January, 1770, one of His Majesty's justices of the peace at Orford, who called a meeting to be held at the inn of Mr. John Man at Orford on May 10. At this meeting John Scofield was chosen moderator and the meeting adjourned to six o'clock the next morning at the house of John Scofield, in Canaan, to meet for the future and forever hereafter in Canaan.

It appears now that the settlers are much depressed and disaffection is apparent from the hardships they encountered and the scanty harvests. The want of a mill was every day increasing, and no relief seemed to be at hand. The bread corn had still to be carried to Lebanon as for four years past, by the same trail first blazed by Scofield and now not much improved.

It was voted that the proprietors of Canaan build the desired mills, and that they be completed in a workmanlike manner by the twenty-fifth day of December, 1770. A tax of twelve shillings was laid on each right, to be paid to the person who should build the mills. And as further encouragement to some such person, a grant of three hundred acres of land from the undivided uplands was voted, one hundred of these acres to be laid out so as to include all privileges convenient to said mills. But in vain did they hold out their twelve shillings tax, about $125, and three hundred acres; no millwright appeared yet for many months.

At this meeting Jedidiah Hibbard was chosen clerk, the duties of which he fulfilled until 1773. John Scofield was chosen treasurer and held the office until his death, in 1784. Jedidiah Hibbard was chosen collector and John Scofield, Joseph Craw and Asa Kilburn assessors. The clerk was authorized to warn meetings upon the request of ten of the proprietors and until there be twelve families settled herein by posting a copy of the warning in a public place, also sending a copy to Mr. Fowle, the printer at Portsmouth, and one to George Harris at Colchester, Conn., to be inserted in the public prints, if he see cause. And whenever twelve families are settled here the notification may be posted in said town alone.

From all the evidence we have gathered, it appears that at this time, 1770, nearly four years after the arrival of Mr. Scofield, there were not yet twelve families in the town, and these were chiefly settled upon or near the present "South Road." Their names were John Scofield, Thomas Miner, Joseph Craw, Daniel Crossman, Asa Williams, George Harris, Amos Walworth, Caleb Welch, Samuel Chapman, Ebenezer Eames and Samuel Benedict. Several other names appear, as Samuel Jones, John Burdick, Samuel Dodge, Jedidiah Hibbard, Asa Kilburn, Josiah Gates, Thomas Baldwin, but they were not reckoned as family men. A large majority of the proprietors living in Connecticut had not arrived and failed ever to come. They entered into the proprietary as many do in these days for the purpose of selling out at enhanced prices.

The meeting adjourned to meet again at the house of John Scofield. The proprietors' meetings were all held up to the time of the building of the meeting house at the homes of the settlers, then a few meetings were held in the meeting house, for the most part they were held at the different dwelling houses. Until 1774 the meetings were held at John Scofield's, until 1780 they met at Samuel Chapman's, and thereafter at different places as suited their convenience. At the meeting on June 12, 1770, each proprietor was authorized to make choice of one hundred acres of upland and ten acres of intervale. A tax of fifteen shillings was laid on each right to defray the expenses of laying out said lots. It was voted to ratify and confirm the several taxes which had been assessed upon the rights but not all collected, up to this time, and Mr. George Harris was appointed to collect each and every of the aforesaid taxes.

The first tax granted August ye 18 1761 being on each proprietors right	1.	3	0
The second granted November ye 16 1762 on each Right	0	8	7½
The Third tax granted Mar 31 1763 on each Proprietors Right	0	3	0
The Fourth tax granted Sept ye 23 1765 on each Right	0	6	0
The Fifth tax granted March 11 1766 on each Right	0	6	0
The Sixth tax granted Sept 3 1767 on each Right	0	6	0
The Seventh tax granted March the 21 1769 on each Right	1	7	9

The ratification of these taxes was followed by the sale of thirteen of the original rights for non-payment of taxes and charges.

The mill still troubled them and it was further voted "six shillings on each right, to be paid in labor, and the time for completing then be extended to August 15, 1771." Eight months longer we must pack our bread corn to Lebanon and back.

In the following October, through infinite exertions, the architects were discovered, and the mills for which we sighed were located. John Scofield, Joseph Craw and Asa Kilburn were appointed "to make and execute good deeds of three hundred acres of land unto Nathan Scofield and Ebenezer Eames, as encouragement for building Mills in Canaan as soon as they think fit," and extending the time for completing the cornmill to December 1, 1771, on account of the difficulty of procuring mill stones. How anxiously they watched the work in that mill.

From the foundation to the cap-board, they saw it rise and become more and more a mill, and when it was announced that on a certain day, the miller would hoist the gate, every man started early in the morning with a bushel of corn, hoping to be first on the spot, so that he might be able to boast that his was the first grist ground at the new mill. But perhaps we may imagine the disgust of these early risers, who on arriving at the mill, discerned one of those irrepressible, everlasting Yankees, who are never behind anybody, already there, quietly sitting upon his bag, waiting for the door to open. He had been there nearly all night.

The mill was built at the "Corner," near the old tannery of F. P. Swett, on the stream running from Hart Pond. It was built by Dr. Ebenezer Eames. The contract was for a corn and sawmill. The sawmill was not located at the Corner. From all we can learn it was located in the southerly part of the town, and another party got the benefit of the town appropriation for it. Doctor Eames was one of the grantees of the town and his share in the town land was set off to him, one hundred acres of which he occupied near his mill. The mill was a clumsy and uncouth affair, but it ground well the corn of the people. The stones were turned by an overshot wheel about twenty-five feet in diameter. We used to watch the slow revolutions of that great wheel and wonder how it would effect us to take a ride upon it. The deed given to Doctor Eames by the committee of the proprietors in 1771 was for one hundred acres of land, called the "1st. Hundred of the Mill Right," and in the Proprietors' Book of Records is described as follows:

Beginning at an old hemlock stump, at the end of the lower dam at the lower end of Hart's Pond. Then S 35° W about 12 rods across said Pond to a stake and stones, then S 26° E 31 rods to the N. E. Corner of a 50 acre lot in the 1st. Division of the Right of Samuel Dodge. Then S 78½° W 164 rods in said Dodge's line to a stake and stones, thence N 12° W 100 rods to a stake and stones then N 78½° E 164 rods to a stake and stones standing in the south line of the 1st. 100 of George Lamphere, then S 12° about 64 rods to the first bound.

JOHN CURRIER & EZEKIEL WELLS.
Committee of Proprietors.

It is not known what became of Doctor Eames and his wife. His last appearance as a taxpayer was in 1794. And the "1st.

100 of the Mill Right" in that year was given in for taxation by Henry French. Two years afterwards, in 1796, it is given in by Dudley Gilman. In 1797, it becomes separated, sixty acres is owned by Hezekiah Jones and forty acres by Joshua Clement. Then come Nathan Messer, in 1799, and Cyrus Carlton, who came here from Orange, where he had continued lawsuits with Nathan Waldo, which afforded both gentlemen great pleasure until the lawyers scooped in pretty much all their estate and then Mr. Carlton escaped to Canaan, bought the grist-mill and built a house, long owned and occupied by Hough Harris, and now by A. S. Green.

Excepting the laying out of roads and the survey of lands, the mill was the first solid improvement made in Canaan. Nearly all the houses so far were thrown up for temporary shelter, being built of logs and brush. There were no school houses, the schoolmaster had not yet arrived. No teams: hospitality was universal. The people were all workers and struggling for existence.

At the meeting of October 16, 1770, a tax of nine pence was laid on each right to defray the expense of sending John Scofield to Portsmouth and George Harris to Colchester, to collect money due the proprietors from the grantees. These moneys were the taxes before referred to which the absent proprietors neglected to pay, and which they did pay. Other taxes were only collected upon the sale of the rights, the owners of which were pleased with such a release from their obligations to the propriety.

In January, 1771, at an adjourned meeting, Jedidiah Hibbard, having procured a law book for the proprietors, it was voted to be received and paid for. John Scofield's bill of 16 pounds, 8 shillings, and Ezekiel Wells' bill for 1 pound, 2 shillings, for labor on the highway, was allowed.

Subsequently, in the same year, it was voted that each proprietor should clear one acre of intervale and cut and girdle two acres of upland before he should have title to his lands.

Five acres of land to each right, in the most convenient place, near the mills, were voted, for the convenience of timber, and from this day no proprietor might choose any land that might be thought necessary for such five-acre lots. Then followed several adjourned meetings, which record only the division of land among the proprietors, and the laying of taxes for the building of roads. And this building of roads seems to have been the great burden of the settlers and who can wonder at the burden. Not much else is done in those days. Many of these roads are traveled now, and the traces of those which have been changed are distinctly visible.

The only historical road built this year was the Wolfeborough or "Governor's Road," to pay for which each right was assessed two pounds L. M., for the purpose of making and clearing. This vote was passed in May, 1772. Joseph Craw, Samuel Benedict and Samuel Jones were appointed to lay out the one hundred and twenty-four pounds forthwith, and for each faithful day's labor they were to allow each man five shilling and six pence.

This road was surveyed from the Pemigewasset River to Dartmouth College, October 30, 1771. The direction of the road in Canaan, according to the survey, was: "W $15°$ N $13\frac{3}{4}$ miles to line of Canaan & Hanover." This road cut across the northwest corner of the town, crossing the bridge across Marshall Brook at the head of Goose Pond, and continuing on the line of the present road to Tunis, and from there to Dartmouth College. It is still known in Hanover as the Wolfeborough Road and the land lying along was laid out to its line. In the spring of 1772, Gov. John Wentworth started in his four-horse state coach from Wolfeborough, to visit his possessions towards Connecticut River. He was accompanied by an escort of sixty soldiers, and the road was cleared for him as he passed along through forest and swamps, over hills and through valleys, building bridges of logs over the streams and corduroy roads over the impassable mud. He passed over Moose Mountain to Hanover, where the new college had but recently been organized under the care of Dr. Eleazer Wheelock. In Canaan this road is a matter of legend for the most part; it is grown up to trees where the land has not been cleared. The line of it is visible from the distinctive color of the foliage, being the light green of white birch. A portion of this road is sometimes traveled, although it has been discontinued.

On the twenty-ninth of November, 1773, an adjourned meeting was held, when Capt. Caleb Welch was made moderator and a new committee was appointed, and the minister's lots and the school lots were voted to be laid out. And then the meeting was dissolved, after having been in session, by adjournments, more than three years and half. On June 1, 1773, a vote was passed, and is recorded in the handwriting of George Harris, confirming and ratifying all the transactions of the proprietors, relative to grants of land and calling public meetings, "notwithstanding any want of form, legal and proper terms or defects and defaults of process relative to the premises." And the dissolution of this meeting closes an epoch in our town history. For all these years the records are slim, affording scanty information of the lives of the people. There were town meetings and proprietors' meetings, to elect officers, to repair roads, to allow bills, to appoint committees to lay out "hundred acre lots." But as yet there appear no votes nor reports, upon loyalty, religion or education. Only once in a while is there a gleam of light upon the thoughts of this busy people.

Jedidiah Hibbard, having left town, in the latter part of November, 1773, Thomas Miner was appointed proprietors' clerk. From the records he has left it is very evident that Thomas spoke the truth, when he said to Mr. Harris, at his first setting out for the new lands, "that he had little or no education." The ink is well preserved, black, but the chirography, spelling and grammar are a little peculiar. There is no punctuation, rarely was a new sentence begun with a capital letter.

At a meeting in June, 1774, Capt. Caleb Clark, who lived near the old Fales place, was allowed to lay out a certain hundred acre lot "lying on the east side of the road that goeth from Eames mill and adjoining to Capt. Dame's Gore. Said Clark is to have said lot in room of his second hundred, in consideration that he pay the expense of laying it out and give the proprietors five pounds, one half to be done on the road and the other half on the bridge, to be built across the Mascomy river near John Scofield's at the lower Meadows."

Thomas Miner was to have the liberty of pitching one hundred acres, given him as "encouragement for building a Saw-mill." Capt. Caleb Clark, Capt. Charles Walworth and John Scofield were appointed agents to make Miner a deed.

This sawmill is stated to have been erected upon Moose Brook, south of the road, and some imagining persons affirm that many of the foundation stones are still visible, and that a flat stone with a square hole in the center was hung as a grindstone, but was not much used. It also lies there now, still washed by the ever-flowing waters of Moose Brook. But Mr. Miner received the deed and by the terms of it the people of Canaan were "well accomodated." The deed is very neatly written, in the fair hand of Thomas Baldwin and is dated "This 15th. day of September, annoque domini 1777," with Thomas Baldwin and Asa Kilburn as witnesses. A part of this deed is copied below as follows:

> Know all men &c, That we Caleb Clarke of Newmarket, in the province &c, Gent, Charles Walworth of Canaan &c, Gent, and John Scofield of Canaan aforesaid, husbandman, being chosen or delegated by the Propriety of Canaan, to be a Com'tee in the name & behalf of said prop'y to execute and deliver unto Thomas Miner of Canaan aforesaid, Gent, a Good Authentic Quit Claim Deed of One hundred acres of the undivided lands in said Canaan in such place as him the said Miner shall think fit to pitch one hundred acre lott not incroaching on the undivided in travail nor any other pitch made before it, which privilege of pitching said lott is Granted unto him the said Miner by the aforesaid propriety, for that he the said Miner hath erected a Sawmill in said Canaan, which well accommodates the inhabitants of said town. Wherefor we the named Caleb Clarke, Charles Walworth and John Scofield, by virtue of the authority delegated to us by said prop'y for the purpose aforesaid in the name and behalf of said prop'y. Do by these presents, in consideration of the aforesaid service Done by him the said Miner for said Prop'y to their full satisfaction Give Grant bargain Sell Release Alien Convey and confirm to him the said Miner his heirs, assigns &c.

Sixty acres of this hundred was pitched north of the Wells farm, east of Hart's Pond.

Several adjournments of this meeting took place, the matter of which was recorded in the uncouth hand of Mr. Miner, and then between the years 1774 and 1780 a hiatus occurs in the Proprietors' Records. This was during the Revolution and many of the proprietors were in the Continental Army. It is a pity to lose sight of this struggling settlement, during these years, and our loss is hardly compensated in freeing us from the almost unreadable cipher of Mr. Miner. In the year 1780, George Harris was appointed to settle with Lieut. Thomas Miner and make a request of him for the book of records he held. A request was also made upon Ebenezer Eames for a proprietors' book, containing a record of the pitches. Whether it was a different book from the one Thomas Miner had is not known, for there is but one Proprietors' Book of Records in existence. There may have been another book and if so it contained the record of those who owned the land, and in which right and division it was pitched.

This book was "once committed to the care of Asa Kilburn, late of this town." Mr. Kilburn, after residing in Canaan several years, laboring hard to improve his lands, had sold out and returned to Connecticut, not satisfied with life in our town. He left Canaan in 1777 with Jedidiah Hibbard and joined Col. Jona Chase's regiment at Ticonderoga.

At this date the land had become concentrated in few hands, that is, a large part of it. For while a few men had taken advantage of the necessities or fears of many of the grantees, a large number of small farms, hundred acre lots, had been planted and were being improved by the owners. The grantees had, for reasons heretofore pointed out, been glad to part with their rights, and now new men appear as proprietors, who had come in during the time there was no meeting, from 1774 to 1780. Many of the proprietors held their lands for speculation, driving close and snug bargains with the new settlers, while some of them were very liberal. It is said that Mr. Harris, who was anxious to have the town populated with industrious families, upon several occasions gave an hundred acres of land for a day's labor. He believed he would be richer for giving away a part of his land for actual settlement, than to keep it as wild land.

James Treadway, sometimes called Elder Treadway, with his wife, was an early settler resident here. He came from Dutchess County, New York, about 1770. He had purchased a large number of original rights and all the land Asa Kilburn owned in 1770, excepting what Kilburn lived on. He built a log house in the woods back of the barn on the old Dustin farm, where he lived for many years. He was a preacher, too, before there was a pulpit,— the first preacher to the settlers. The people gathered into barns and houses to hear him, but he was not liked, being a man of strong prejudice, very opinionated, and in all his disputes manifesting much selfishness. His name appears but once in the town records, and then in a manner to throw suspicion upon his integrity. Owning many of the original rights, some of which were not located, and having obtained possession of the "Pitch Book," he made many records for himself, of choice lands without regard to the rights adjoining, in many cases lapping over upon pitches already made, causing great annoyance. He located some lands from the shores of Hart's Pond westward, adjoining the lands of Capt. Robert Barber, and he claimed all the lands north of Captain Barber's line. Persons aggrieved by his arbitrary acts, remonstrated with him, but he paid no attention to their complaints. At last, they brought the matter before the proprietors, at a legal meeting held January 17, 1780, when the following votes were passed: "That those Pitches which were made by Mr. James Treadway while he held the Pitch Book in his possession contrary to the former vote of the proprietors shall be void and of none effect." "That those other Pitches that ware farely made by the other Proprietors that do not interfere on former Pitches shall stand good and remain valid." These votes had the effect, of course, to put a stop to Mr. Treadway's encroachments.

Mr. Jonathan Dustin bought of Mr. Treadway thirteen rights, embracing the lands of the old Dustin farm, which at that time extended from the shores of Hart Pond to Town Hill. Mr. Dustin first lived in a house of logs, built near the site of the house of Mrs. Levi George.

There were men in those days, who believed there was land enough and wild enough, and that where land was so plenty and people so few, they needed not to purchase anybody's right to settle upon it. Leonard Horr, Elijah Lathrop and William Record, believed this dogma firmly and became, in fact, squatters. But they were soon hunted out by the vigilant committee, and were solemnly warned, that in order to become owners, they must procure a good and authentic deed of one hundred acres of upland from or under one or any of the proprietors, and should make their pitch according to usage and shall improve it by building a house thereon and continue to occupy and cultivate it for six months. A failure to comply with any of these conditions will work to their discomfort.

The next year, in 1781, Leonard Horr was permitted to retain the lot he had already selected "northwesterly of the Saw Mill on Mascoma river, provided he makes speedy settlement."

On September 12, 1781, it was decided to lay out the three public rights: the Glebe right for the Church of England, the first settled minister's right and the school right, but it was several years afterwards that these rights were laid out.

A bed of clay had been opened near Hart Pond, a piece of six acres had been laid out on West Farms, near where Nathan C. Morgan lived, and two acres of land more was laid out adjoining the six acres as a common field.

This meeting of the proprietors, first called in 1780, was continued by adjournments, from time to time, until June, 1782, when it was supposed to have been dissolved. Nothing more of interest is to be gleaned here, only votes to lay out roads, for committees to divide the common lands, for taxes, and the dry details relating to the propriety, and then, for four years, there is no record. At this period in our history there seems to be a clew lost as in a mine, when the lead drops away. There are neither town nor proprietors' records.

And now, while waiting for some further events to come around, let us look in upon some of our old friends, and see how they lived, and first we will premise that in those days coal as a fuel had not been known; the same may be said of illuminating gas, made from it. No iron stoves were used and no contrivances for economizing heat were employed until Doctor Franklin invented the iron-framed fireplace, which still bears his name. All the cooking and warming was by means of fire kindled upon the hearth or in ovens. Tallow candles or pine knots furnished the light for the long winter evenings, and sanded floors supplied the place of rugs and carpets. The water used for household purposes was drawn from wells by the aid of sweeps. Pumps were not invented until after the beginning of the last century. Friction matches were not made until within seventy-five years. If the fire went out upon the hearth over night, and the tinder was damp, so that the spark would not catch, the alternative remained of wading to the nearest neighbor through the snow for a brand. It was seldom that more than one room was warmed in any house, except in case of illness of some member of the family, and the winter nights of over a hundred years ago were long and dreary. The men and women undressed and went to their beds in a temperature colder than that of our modern barns and sheds, and they did not complain, because they were used to it.

"Simple is that olden story,
   Of the years now pale and hoary,
  When the church, the farm, the schoolhouse,
    Made the round of country life,
  When amid these northern mountains,
  By these clear cool hillside fountains,
  Lonely households lived and labored
    Far from noise and city strife.

"Here the sturdy youthful farmers
  Early found their maiden charmers,
  Wooed them in the country fashion,
    Won them for a life of toil.
  Wed them in their simple dresses,
  In their own soft curling tresses,
  And new households thus were planted,
    On the rough and rocky soil.

"Was this life all toil and labor?
  When some neighbor met with neighbor,
  Was the talk alone of cattle,
    Flocks and herds and crops of corn?
  Had the scene no gentler pleasures?

Did it know no joyous measures?
Yea, for out of hills and valleys,
   Richest hopes and joys were born.

"Many a church was minus steeple,
And in winter time the people
Gathered from their scattered dwellings
   To a house without a fire.
But it had a charm for keeping
Men and little boys from sleeping,
As the sermon struggled onward,
   To the fifteenth head and higher.

"But the women, maid and mother,
Passed their stoves to one another,
Those convenient tin arrangements,
   Made to hold the slumbering coals.
While the male sex held from napping,
Spent their weary time in rapping,
Rapping their stiff boots together,
   Those were times that tried men's soles.

"Say ye not that life is barren,
Sweeter than the rose of Sharon,
Are the memories that gather
   Round a life in honor spent.
Bright with an immortal beauty,
Is a long life linked to duty,
Ever toiling and aspiring
   In a patient sweet content.

"But with all the buzz and hurry,
And with all this work and worry,
Matrons found more time to visit
   Long before the setting sun,
Than in these our days, so pressing,
When more time is spent in dressing,
And the day is just beginning
   When the olden day was done.

"How these olden memories muster,
  How around the heart they cluster,
  How the thoughts come thronging backward
    From those sturdy scenes of old.
  There are no days like the old days,
  There are no ways like the old ways,
  And in every generation
    The old story must be told."

CHAPTER IV.

PROPRIETORS' MEETINGS, 1786–1845.

During a period of more than four years, the proprietary makes no records for the clerk, George Harris, to record as would appear from the absence of the least scratch of a pen or the leaving of any space in the record book which might be filled up afterwards. On the contrary, the last four years which are blank on all town records, were full of happenings, perhaps so much occurred that the clerk of the proprietors as well as the town clerk, had not the courage to narrate events. Canaan was in the secession movement to join Vermont, so anxious were the other fifteen towns to belong to the sovereignty across the Connecticut River, that all the town, as well as proprietary officers, neglected their duty. The proprietors awoke at last to find themselves in debt, and George Harris, the owner of ten rights, Joshua Harris, the owner of one right, John Harris, the owner of one right, Ezekiel Wells, the owner of five rights, and William Richardson, the owner of one right, and owners of more than one-sixteenth part of the rights of land in town, requested the clerk to call a meeting at Maj. Samuel Jones' on the 27th day of June, 1786. They voted to raise one shilling and six pence on each hundred acres of upland to defray the cost of running the lines between Canaan and Enfield; John Scofield, the son of our first settler (the old settler is now dead two years), is appointed collector and to pay the money over to the selectmen of the town. This debt is the result of a meeting back in 1781, and five years after they are ready to pay the bill. Samuel Jones, Ezekiel Wells and Joshua Harris were appointed "Assessors." Another meeting is held in December to lay a tax on the "wild lands," for the purpose of "making & repairing the Rodes." Daniel Blaisdell is chosen collector to collect the tax of sixty pounds, as well as the balance of the previous tax of one shilling and six pence on each right, which John Scofield did not collect, "made in order to defray the charge of settling the lines in sd Town between Canaan & Enfield."

This is the first appearance on the proprietors records of the name of Daniel Blaisdell. The December meeting was adjourned until the next June, 1787, and again adjourned until July. The proprietors failed to meet then.

They were earnest, industrious men, working always with a purpose, and whose hours of leisure were all filled with labor, but they were not men fitted by education to make a record. When their day's work was over they sat down and thought of the next day, letting the past take care of itself, and the life of one day was only a repetition of the day preceding. The disinclination to think of what was past, shows itself in a niggardly manner throughout all their records. The town clerks were illiterate and bungling and often neglected to record most important events. Selectmen, assessors and committees were equally negligent. Thus it occurs that there are several hiatuses in our history which greatly mars its continuity, and leave many blank years. Thus the record for 1787 closes June 3d, with George Harris for clerk. In the meantime Mr. Harris died, "made his exit out of time in a sudden and unexpected manner," as the old record has it, and then for nearly ten years until January 10th, 1797, the clerk gives no sign. Not a line to show that those men kept records, and so long had the proprietors neglected their affairs that they had lost the right to control their property and were obliged to call in the assistance of the law to reinstate them in their rights. Joshua Wells, Robert Barber, Joshua Harris, William Richardson, William Ayer and Ezekiel Wells, made application to Jesse Johnson, a justice of the peace of Enfield, who issued a warrant, came over and restored life to the defunct "propriety" by organizing a meeting with legal officers. Meantime in all these years they had not been idle. Their committee had kept at work with a surveyor laying out hundred-acre lots and intersecting them with highways. In 1788 a road was laid out "commencing at Grafton line, at a corner bound between Nathaniel Whittier and Daniel Blaisdell's, to be four rods wide to the head of Broad Street, so called; thence eight rods wide. 288 rods to Mr. Elias Lathrop's." In 1793 the road leading from "Capt. Joshua Wells' to Dame's Gore," a distance of 1,240 rods, was surveyed. There were evidences all over town of work, in surveys and pitches, but no record of any deliberative meeting is recorded. At this meeting, warned for the second Tuesday of January, 1797, provision is made by empowering the clerk, so that the life of the corporation might hereafter be continued and in case of his death, the "Lot laing Committee," shall have the power to call a meeting "upon the petition of one-sixteenth part of the proprietors." Ezekiel Wells is appointed clerk, which office he holds until 1808. During this period nearly all the land in town is surveyed and recorded in his handwriting. Ezekiel Wells is given the privilege "of laying out a second hundred-acre lot, insted of a lot the Governors lot has took, which was No. 1 in the 2nd. Range."

After nearly nine years the books and papers of the propriety are scattered and Ezekiel Wells, Daniel Blaisdell and Capt. Robert Barber were chosen to look them up. Capt. Caleb Clark, one of the lot laying committee, has died in the meantime and Lieut. William Richardson is appointed in his place. And Nathaniel Bartlett takes the place of Samuel Jones, who has left town in 1795, although he appears as the owner of land until 1797. This meeting remains adjourned for more than a year. For more than four years there is no record, then the clerk is applied to to warn a meeting for August 27th, 1801.

The article respecting any further division of the undivided lands is passed. Thomas Miner, Daniel Blaisdell and Jehu Jones are appointed assessors and Ezekiel Wells collector to collect the one dollar tax on each right voted to defray the "charges of the proprietary." This meeting remains in session by adjournments for nearly two years, when the clerk is again requested to warn a meeting on the 17th of May, 1803. The proprietors voted that Ebenezer Clark, then the representative to the General Court, "present a memorial praying them to grant the disputed lands that Esq. Hoyt, in behalf of the Proprietors of Grafton petitioned for at the last session of said Court, adjoining the easterly line of Hanover." Clark had been urged by the town to remonstrate against Hoyt's petition. This land was State's Gore, called also Gates's Gore from the name of the person who purchased it of the state. Later in September, Daniel Blaisdell is allowed four pounds, two shillings, "which is in full, except on Clark's action." This was for legal services in the adjustment of the disputes over Dame's Gore line. William Richardson is allowed six pounds "in full," for like services.

At an adjourned meeting on March 29, 1804, Daniel Blaisdell, William Richardson and Joshua Harris were chosen a committee "to prosecute any person who have or shall hereafter trespass on any common lands of the proprietors." This meeting finally, after more than a year and seven adjournments, dies, and the Clerk in September, warns another meeting for the 8th of October. At that time all the articles are passed and this meeting is adjourned six times. Finally on the 12th day of February, 1805, the proprietors vote to have Daniel Blaisdell and William Richardson, their committee chosen in 1801, settle the action with the proprietors of Orange. That town had sought to evict Josiah Clark; the result was that Orange paid all the costs. Daniel Blaisdell received $17.10 for his services and John Currier $1.10 and William Richardson $4.50. In November, 1805, they raised $186 to establish the line between Canaan and Hanover. John Currier, Ezekiel Wells and William Richardson were chosen assessors to assess the tax on the rights. Daniel Blaisdell to collect it and pay it to John Currier, the treasurer, the old assessors are to pay any money they have to the treasurer. Nathaniel Barber had pitched seventy-seven acres of land on the 3d hundred of Richard Sparrow, and he was given the liberty to lay it out somewhere else on land not already taken.

In 1806 Richard Clark, Jr., son of old Richard, has "the liberty to pitch and lay out as much land as falls short on the third Hundred of Thomas Gustin Second Right on undivided land adjoining said Clark land." The time for laying out the first, second, third hundred-acre lots of upland and the first ten acres of intervale continues to be extended to the 13th day of November, 1809, with warnings from time to time against trespassers, that the committee will prosecute them if they settle on any lands which belong to the propriety. The proprietors are anxious to ascertain how much land had been taken up, and by so doing determined how much there is left and it takes many years with much prodding on their part to get the settlers to survey and record their pitches. During these years there are numerous adjourned meetings held, at which the time is continually extended. The meeting warned in 1806, keeps in session until

1808. Taxes are assessed on July 27, 1807, of $13 on each proprietor's right for the purpose of laying out the lots.

On October 8, 1807, the proprietors voted that the real owner "of the 3rd. Hundred of Lewis Loveredge have the privilege of pitching and laing out 50 acres of said lot on any lands wich is pitched or laid out to any other person notwithstanding the survey made to Jonathan Page." This land lay a little northerly and west of Bear Pond and for many years no owner had paid taxes on it nor for some years to come.

On February 22, 1808, John Currier was chosen the new clerk. The old clerk had become tired of writing adjournments. He continues in that office thirteen years until June, 1821.

On June 23, 1808, a committee, consisting of Capt. Joshua Harris, Daniel Blaisdell, Esq., and Capt. Ezekiel Wells, is chosen to ascertain the quantity of land in town not divided. At this meeting Micah Porter's intervale was voted to be surveyed. Thomas Baldwin sold it to Samuel Jones and Jones sold it to Porter, but the right to which it had been laid was forgotten, and the title was defective. In 1809 it was surveyed as sixteen acres adjoining Joshua Harris' land. Thomas Miner had deeded twenty acres of William Chamberlain's right, which was entitled to only ten acres of intervale, and the proprietors confirmed ten of the acres to the right of Clement Daniels. In 1809 the proprietors having brought suit against Robert Barber to eject him from a piece of intervale, agreed to settle and pay the costs, and leave Barber in possession.

From November, 1809, to July, 1812, there was no meeting of the proprietors. During this time they had evidently ascertained the amount of undivided land, for when they meet on July 9, 1812, they proceed to vote to lay the 4th Division of Upland of seven acres. The trespass committee are impowered to make settlement with all trespassers. This meeting by various adjournments continues until December. Then there is no meeting until March, 1814, when the clerk warns a meeting for the 10th. They then authorize the trespass committee to bring actions against those who have forfeited their pitches by failing to have them recorded and surveyed in the manner laid down, and for cutting timber on the forfeited pitches. A second Division of Intervale of one acre is voted to be laid out to each right. From

June, 1814, to June, 1816, there is no meeting. Ezekiel Wells, John Currier and Daniel Blaisdell are chosen the lot "laing committee in futer;" Daniel Blaisdell is chosen treasurer, Joshua Harris committee to prosecute trespassers with Moses Dole. A further division called the 5th, of seven acres is voted to be made of the land in the proprietary. Then for nearly five years the records are silent, until April 17, 1821, the clerk warns a meeting and an agent is chosen to "inquire into each survey bill and make a new and complete index of the same, to take notice of any apparent mistake has been made in any survey." They choose the best man in town for their agent, Daniel Blaisdell. And the records bear witness of his work. He found three rights that had two ten-acre lots of intervale laid out to them, and that there were three rights, Thomas Miner, Abner Chamberlain and Clement Daniels, "hath had no ten-acre lot laid out to them." It was apparent that some of the former owners had deeded the same right twice. In 1821, June 4, Elijah Blaisdell is chosen clerk, and continued in the office until 1845. No meeting is held until 1823, when at the request of Daniel Blaisdell, "owner of the shares of Rufus Randal, Ephraim Wells, Thomas Gustin, James Nevins, Esq., and forty other shares or rights, a meeting is held on the 22 day of March." John M. Barber prays the proprietors to set off a piece of land to him in consideration of his deeding the rights of Thomas Miner, Benjamin Chamberlain, Asa Daniels and Joseph Eames, to them. They voted to deed him a strip of land lying between Josiah Barber's and the river, to satisfy these rights of their full share of land. And on the 5th day of April, 1823, Barber deposited the deed with the clerk and it was recorded in the book of records and those rights cancelled.

On June 14, 1823, the proprietors voted that all the undivided lands between the following limits, "beginning at the Meeting house, thence on the road leading to Lebanon by William Campbell's farm, to the schoolhouse in his district, thence northerly on the road by Daniel Kimball's to Deacon Pillsbury's, thence southerly in the road to the meeting house begun at, be reserved to make out the fourth and fifth divisions of upland, on all the rights not as yet laid out or otherwise cancelled." There was in this a lot of land lying around Bear Pond, for the most part worthless and included the Pond, which at that date was many rods larger than now. Daniel Blaisdell prays the proprietors to set off to him land to satisfy twenty-two rights of which he is the owner, viz.: William Chamberlain, Joshua Rathburn, Josiah Gates, Jr., Capt. John Wentworth, Rufus Randall, James Jones, Thomas Gustin, second right; Amos Walworth, Stephen Kellogg, Joseph Babcock, William Fox. Jr., Thomas Gates, John Tribble, Jonathan Beebe, 3d, Ebenezer Peck; Ebenezer Harris, Daniel Harris, Ebenezer Eames, Samuel Meacham, Richard Sparrow, Sylvester Randall and Caleb Whiting, the first Division of Intervale of John Newmarch and Thomas Miner. Land within the following limits was set off to him: "to begin at the Grafton Turnpike road on Orange line, thence northerly on said Turnpike road to the corner by Joshua Wells farm, thence to follow the road leading from said Wells to Dames Gore thence to follow the line of said Gore to Orange line, thence by said Orange line to the place begun at" "Provided he reserves within said limits enough land to satisfy the second division of intervale of one acre to each of those rights which has not yet been laid out or cancelled." The quitclaim deed was executed within six days and the rights cancelled.

They also voted at this meeting to lay out a sixth Division of Upland of six acres. On March 18, 1824, Daniel Blaisdell, owner of the right of Ephraim Wells, receives "the strip of swamp land adjoining the intervale of Asa Paddleford and Deacon French, near Enfield line southerly and the lands of Reuben Gile easterly, the land of Joseph Follensbee westerly and adjoining northerly on the road that leads from said Follensbee's to said Giles, extending on said road from the line of Giles land southerly about forty-four rods, to a stake and stones being the corner of said Follensbee's land, near his orchard." "Also a small strip adjoining the westerly side of the Turnpike road, and Orange line and between Orange line and lands of said Blaisdell," and this right or share is cancelled. On June 30th, Daniel Blaisdell, owner of the School, Minister and Isaiah Rathburn rights, receives the "strip of swampy land lying westerly of Goose Pond Brook, adjoining land of Daniel Pattee and Levi George, and adjoining westerly on upland of Ahimez Wright, and easterly on upland of Jason Kidder and extends northerly as far as Wright's and Kidder's lands extends," and these rights are cancelled. Moses Lawrence, owner of the rights of Samuel Dodge, 3d, Lewis Loveridge, Stephen Kellogg, Thomas W. Waldron and John Newmarch, has set off to him to satisfy these rights the following land: "within the following limits, beginning at Dames Gore line on the road by Joseph Bartletts, thence on the road to the corner of the road between Bartletts and Josiah Barbers, then on the road by Lawrences, to the road by Nathan Cross, then on the road northerly to Dames Gore line, thence westerly on Gore line to place begun at." "Also all the undivided land not laid out southerly of and adjoining said Lawrence home farm and adjoining westerly on land belonging to Josiah Barber and David Richardson and easterly on lands owned or occupied by Lieut. Richard Clark and Elijah Blaisdell, and to extend southerly the whole width of the piece, to land of Uriah Welch, supposed to contain thirty-five acres." The proprietary seems now to have about finished its labors, but there are still some rights uncancelled. And these are the property of the estate of Daniel Blaisdell. After slumbering for nearly twenty-one years, Joseph Dustin and Elijah Blaisdell, son and son-in-law of Daniel Blaisdell, request Jonathan Kittredge, a justice of the peace, to call a meeting of the proprietors at Heath's Inn for the 21st day of July, 1845. They seek to choose a moderator and a new clerk. Elijah Blaisdell, the old clerk, had removed from town and became thus incompetent. They met and chose Jonathan Kittredge clerk. And he proceeds to call a meeting according to law that the proceedings which they are about to take may be legal, and afford them a good title to the undivided lands they propose to sell, for during those years Mr. Dustin has found numerous gores and pieces, not included in the old surveys and which have descended to the heirs of Daniel Blaisdell. On the 2d day of December, 1845, they meet and confirm a deed of land which Daniel Blaisdell gave James Eastman, dated November 24, 1832, of land on the west side of Goose Pond. Blaisdell was the owner at the time of his death of all the rights uncancelled except the rights of Richard Wibard, Daniel Rogers and William Wentworth, George and William King. The proprietors vote to cancel ten rights, in consideration of this conveyance, viz.: John Chamberlain, Abner Chamberlain, William Chamberlain, Jr., Aaron Cady, Aaron Cady, Jr., Nathaniel Cady, Daniel Fowle, Samuel Dodge, Thomas Gustin and Thomas Gustin, Jr.

They voted to reserve the common land lying on the westerly side of the Mascoma River, northerly of H. G. Lathrop's and adjoining Dame's Gore, for the right of Richard Wibard. Joseph Dustin and Elijah Blaisdell are appointed a committee to dispose of the remaining undivided land which is not enough to make any further division and account to the proprietors "for their equal share of the proceeds, excepting the land adjoining Bear Pond and the piece reserved for Richard Wibard's right." So ends the records; there was no accounting so far as recorded. It is, however, well known that Mr. Dustin under that vote sold several pieces of land. The land around Bear Pond he claimed as his own and was not sold out of the family until long after his death. It was never surveyed.

There still remain uncancelled the rights of George and Gibson Harris, Allen Whitman, Jared Spencer, Ephraim Wells, Jr., Thomas Wells, Jedediah Lathrop, Clement Daniels, David Chamberlain, Israel Kellogg, George Lamphere, Phineas Sabine, Jabez Jones, Richard Wibard, James Nevins, George King, William King, William Wentworth, Thomas Parker, and Daniel Rogers. The right for the propagation of the Gospel and the Glebe Rights were not cancelled, but the proprietors assumed ownership of them after the Revolution, and sold the land set off to these rights to different parties who occupied them.

CHAPTER V.

TOWN MEETINGS, 1770-1785.

The first town meeting of which there is any record was called by Benjamin Giles, justice of the peace, "upon the petition of more than ten freeholders, inhabitants of the Township of Canaan," on the 3d day of July, 1770. The charter provided that the first town meeting should be held on the third Tuesday in August, 1761; it certainly was not held in Canaan. Thomas Gustin was to be the first moderator and all annual meetings were to be held on the second Tuesday of March "forever hereafter." At the first meeting at John Scofield's house. John Scofield was chosen moderator; Samuel Benedict, clerk; John Scofield, Joseph Craw and Samuel Benedict, assessors; Asa Williams, tithingman; Ezekiel Wells, surveyor of roads. And all future meetings shall be warned in the manner following:

> The annual meeting on the second Tuesday in March to be annually warned by the Town Clerk, for the time being, by setting up a warning of Notification at least ten days before sd meeting, at some public Place in sd Canaan. And also the Clerk for the time being, shall at any time when applied to by seven Freeholders of sd Canaan, or the Assessors for the time being. Warn a meeting of the Freeholders of sd Town to be held at any proper place in sd Town, by setting up a Warning seven days at least before sd meeting at some public place in sd Town.

The same names appear on this occasion, with the addition of Ezekiel Wells, who with his brother, Joshua, arrived the previous year, that we are already familiar with in the Proprietors' Records. The Wells brothers were both unmarried, Joshua being a disappointed man of thirty-five and Ezekiel eleven years younger, who came because Joshua did. In 1771, at the second annual meeting, the same names appear as before, only a little changed about; Samuel Jones is constable; Asa Williams, fence-viewer; Ezekiel Wells, tithingman; Samuel Chapman, surveyor. In 1772 appears the same scant records of Samuel Benedict as clerk, not a profitable clerk for us, who are striving to learn philosophy by studying the history of persons who first cut down trees, and made roads in Canaan. The names of Ebenezer Eames and Caleb Welch are added to the previous list. This is the first year in which selectmen were chosen; they had been called assessors.

In 1773 the place of holding the annual meeting was changed from John Scofield's to the dwelling house of Thomas Miner, when Caleb Welch was chosen town clerk; Thomas Miner, moderator, and Samuel Chapman, the lame basket-maker, tithingman.

A census of the town was requested this year and it was made up in the following manner:

Unmarried from 16 to 60	12
Married from 16 to 60	11
Boys 16 years and under	16
Sixty years and upwards	—
Females, unmarried	11
Females, married	12
Widows	—
	62

The number of ratable polls was nineteen. In 1774 the annual meeting was "lagally warned" and held at the "dwelling house of Samuel Chapman." And here is an addition to the old list of names: Charles Walworth as selectman and Ezekiel Gardner, tithingman. And here also on this occasion, for the first time, appears the name of "Thomas Baldwin Surveyor of highways." Young Baldwin is, just before this time, twenty-one years old, and has now cast his first vote. He has already made himself useful to the people because of his superior intelligence.

Nearly all these people were of Connecticut, of the old Puritan stock, and brought their peculiar notions of the sanctity of the Sabbath to Canaan. They used to assemble in barns and houses, where the elders led in prayer and they all hummed a song of praise, and this young man was elected to read a printed sermon. On this occasion it was "voted that they would build a pound, between Mr. Samuel Chapmans and Moose Brook, to be built by the inhabitants on the first Monday in May next." And they built the pound on the west side of the brook, not far from Mr. Miner's mill. But the pound, like the mill, has long ago disappeared from sight. In 1775, January 16, the selectmen were directed to send a letter to the "Committee of Correspondence" at Exeter, "to answer their request." John Scofield was appointed to carry the letter. He assured the committee that the people were in sympathy with the movement for the redress of wrongs. The committee of correspondence was appointed by a convention of deputies, which met at Exeter January, 1775, to consult on the state of affairs, appoint delegates to the next general Congress to be holden at Philadelphia in May following. They issued an address to the people, warning them of their danger and exhorting them to union, peace and harmony; to frugality, industry, manufactures and learning the military art, that they might be able, if necessary, to defend the country against invasion.

A circular was sent out to the towns in New Hampshire in which they said:

You are requested to desire all males above twenty one years of age to sign the declaration on this paper, and when done to make return thereof, together with the name or names of all who shall refuse to sign the same, to the General Assembly or Committee of Safety of this Colony.

On the first day of July the list of subscribers to the "Association Test" was made out and forwarded. It was found that 8,199 male persons over twenty-one years of age, then living in New Hampshire, had solemnly promised to risk their lives and property in defense of their country and families against British aggression, while 773 for various reasons refused to sign. The greater part of the latter class were hostile to colonial independence. There were twenty-four Canaan signers, by which it will be seen that at that date, which was nearly ten years after the settlement of the town, there were but twenty-four males in it over twenty-one years.

This paper sent to Exeter is as follows:

We, the subscribers do hereby solemnly engage and promise, that we will to the utmost of our power, at the risque of our lives and fortunes, with arms oppose the hostile proceedings of the British Fleets and Armies against the United American Colonies.

CANAAN SIGNERS.

Ebenezer Eams
Richard Clark
James Treadway will
  on certain conditions
  (viz) (1)
Caleb Clark
Thomas Miner
Samuel Jones
Joseph Walter
Thomas Baldwin
Jehu Jones
          his
Thomas Baxter ×
          mark
Robert Burts

John Scofield
Samuel Lathrop
Ezekiel Gardner
John Scofield Jr
Gideon Rudd
Joshua Wells
Samuel Joslen
Richard Joslen
Charles Walworth
Ezekiel Wells
Eleazer Scofield
Caleb Welch
Job Scipio

Canaan July 1st. 1776

To the Honble Committee of Safety for the Colony of New Hampshire. These are to certify that every man in this town signed this agreement.

Attest
EBENr EAMES } Select-
SAMUEL JONES } men

(1) 1st On Condition that no man who is taken a Captive from the British forces be made an officer or let to be a Soldier in the Continental Army a2ly that every American found and taken in a arms against the United Colonies be Immediately put to Death and 3ly that all and every of the British Troops that are Captivated by the Continental forces by Sea or land or any other way taken shall be kept in Prison or Close Confinement and 4ly than every Commanding Officer or a Soldier or any Person or Persons imployed in any Business whatever in the Cintinental Forces who is found & proved to be a Traitor to the United Colonies in America be put to Death Immediately.

Upon these aforementioned Conditions do I sign this Declaration.

Witness my hand

JAMES TREADWAY

With the above was sent the following request from the Committee of Safety of Canaan and Enfield. Each town had its own committee appointed to look out for its defense.

To the Honble Committy of Safety For the Colony of New Hampshire,

A Request from The Comitty of Safety for the Towns of Canaan And Enfield alias Relhan in sd Colony;

Whereas we Being in Eminent Dange of being Ravaged and Destroyed by the Savages, and other of our Unnatural Enemies, And we Being Unable to Defend our Selves in the Lest: for the want of guns

Town Meetings. 1770–1785.

& aminition We therefore humbly Request that your Honors Would send us Sixteen guns, forty two pounds of Gunpowder and 168lbs of Lead 21 Dozen of flints B Lieutt Saml Jones of sd Canaan and Mr Elisha Bingham of Enfield Which men are chosen for the Said Purpose. Gentn your Compliaire with this Request will Greatly Oblige & Enable us to Defend our Selves in these frontier Towns.

Ebenr Eames
Saml Meacham   } Committee of Safety
Thos Baldwin

The Reasons Why this Paper was not Signed By two of the Committee is Because one is Absent and the other is the Bearer

S. Meacham

The Provincial Congress on July 5, 1776, "voted that Samuel Jones of Canaan and Elisha Bingham of Enfield have and receive out of the treasury 5 pounds for the purpose of purchasing Lead and flints for the use of the inhabitants of said towns. They giving good security for repayment of said sum when requested." The council on the same day voted to give them twenty-five pounds of powder and five pounds in money.

There are no more records for the year 1775, but a warning for the annual meeting. If Paul Revere's message was heard in Canaan we do not know. The fires of Bunker Hill and Lexington did not illuminate these forest homes; but these laborers did join the band of patriots, although they left no record of it. Their actions spoke louder than any words they could write.

The Committee of Safety of New Hampshire, in order to determine the strength of the colony, requested a census of the town, which was as follows:

The accompt of Inhabitants,
- Males under 16 yrs................................ 16
- Males over 16 yrs. to 50 not in army.............. 17
- Males above 50 yrs................................ 3
- Persons gone to the Army.......................... 3
- All females....................................... 28
- Negroes and slaves................................ —

Canaan Sept. 22. 1775   67

Upon diligent search we find that we have a Gun for every one capable of yousing them. As for Power & ball we have none with us.

Asa Kilburn   } Selectmen.
Ebenz Eames

In 1776 more new names appear: "Chose Thomas Baldwin Constable." Jonathan Bingham was surveyor and Jehu Jones tithingman; Asa Williams, pound-keeper. Capt. Samuel Jones, Thomas Miner and Caleb Welch were appointed to look out for a burying-place. They selected and laid out the grounds known as "The Cobble," near Jehu Jones' house on South Road. Under date of September 30, 1776, the towns of Canaan, Hanover and Cardigan were notified to meet to elect someone to represent them in the General Assembly and Council at Exeter the next December. They met at Hanover November 27 and refused to elect anyone, being dissatisfied with the methods of representation and that their advice was not taken in the government. They had been requested two years before, in 1774, and had declined. In 1774-'76 Lebanon, Hanover, Relhan, Canaan, Cardigan and Grafton were classed together and entitled to one representative, but they failed to send anyone. On September 18, 1776, Hanover, Canaan and Cardigan were classed together as being large enough to send one representative, but they did not send anyone in 1777. And here ends the record for that great year.

In 1777 the annual meeting was held at the house of Joshua Harris, son of George. The records of this meeting are unusually elaborate, which is due to the fact that they "Chose Insign Thomas Baldwin, Clerk." In this case Mr. Baldwin has recorded himself. The name of Richard Clark, 3d, is added to the list of freeholders. "Voted that the Committee of Safety be desired to administer the oath to the other officers." This committee was a patriotic committee, deriving its powers from the Council and Assembly, and had charge of military affairs when the Council and Assembly were not in session. John Scofield was a member and beyond this fact nothing is known. That some of our friends and neighbors did shoulder their muskets in the cause of popular liberty is evident from the following liberal bounty offered by the town:

Voted that every person that has ever been in the Continentals service, or may enlist the ensueing year, and may be gone through the usual season for business, shall not be liable to pay any taxes in this town for that year he is so gone.

Here appears the first vote of the town to defray town charges: "Voted to raise by a rate on the Poles and ratable Estate of the

Town Meetings, 1770-1785.

inhabitants of this town the sum of 3 pounds L. M. for the defraying town charges. What is paste and for the Insuing year."

All the back rates on the highways were to be worked out this year. The penalty for not paying the rate on polls and estates should be the same as for not working on the highway.

The only other business is contained in the following:

> Voted to appoint Capt. Joshua Wells, Caleb Welch and Eleazer Scofield fence-viewers, to examine fences, where any damage is done by hogs, and see if such fence is sufficient to stop hogs yoked according to law. If they adjudge the fence not sufficient then the owner of the fence shall not be liable to pay the damage, provided the swine are yoked and ringed according to law.

It might be interesting to those concerned to learn who, by the terms of this vote, is "holden to pay the damage." The owner of the fence is exempted. The swine, if yoked according to law, are not liable to pay, and the owner of the swine is not mentioned. Now who is to pay the damage when Joseph Craw's hogs pass through Samuel Jones' poor fence, with their yokes and rings on, and commit trespass to Samuel Benedict's garden?

By the record it appears that Thomas Baldwin was elected clerk for three years, 1777, 1778, 1779. Beyond the record of 1777 he confines himself to a copy of the warnings of the other two years; no record of the doings of the meetings, and thence onward for six years longer the record is a failure — years of great events to the town and nation — until 1786. All is blank; nothing appears save a few marriages, births and deaths among the people, and these are in an unknown handwriting. Thomas was unfaithful to his trust. He might have done much for our enlightenment, for he was a young man of ability. He gained a great reputation in the Baptist Church, but as a town clerk he was a fraud.

There was increase in population; new names appear, old names disappear. What were all these toilers doing in these long years? Who can tell us? Lands were surveyed and roads built, taxes were voted and many of the people joined the three regiments that were voted to support the War of Independence. Beyond these facts we shall never be able to look into the social condition of those times. Had they preachers or schoolmasters, and what were their names? During this time town meetings were held; petitions in the archives of the state department show that. The warning for the town meeting in 1779 contained an article "to take into consideration a tax bill from the Treasurer of New Hampshire." The town evidently voted to have William Ayer present a petition respecting it, as the following shows, but with what result is not known.

> To the Honorable Council & House of Representatives of said State. The petition of William Ayer of Canaan in the County of Grafton in said State in behalf of said town humbly sheweth that by means of the unsettled state of said County & the claim of Vermont they have never made their state tax but are now desirous to make the said taxes & to discharge the same; but the said town being much too high in the proportion of the State tax the petitioner prays the same may be examined & set right & said town will immediately proceed to make & discharge their taxes & as in duty bound shall ever pray.
> Exeter June 17. 1779.
> WM. AYER.

The petition was successful, for the Assembly voted to adjust the rate at twenty shillings on every 1,000 pounds of state and continental money for the years 1777, 1778, 1779, "said taxes now being all in arrears."

On the 20th of October, 1780, the Indians from Canada attacked and burned Royalton, Vt. An express was sent with the exciting intelligence for relief from the neighboring towns. A company of twenty men was instantly raised in Canaan to join those from Lebanon to go to the assistance of the unfortunate people of Royalton and to scout along the frontiers, lest the enemy should fall upon other settlements unawares. Joshua Wells was placed in command of this company. The names of those volunteers are known and their service also recorded by their captain, who sought payment for their services.

There seems to be no further inconvenience in regard to mills. The people were fully accommodated. Mr. Eames' grist-mill was running at the Corner. Mr. Miner's sawmill was running on Moose Brook. Jonathan Carlton of Amesbury had built a sawmill on the Mascoma at the outlet of the pond, and Capt. Robert Barber had come in from Newmarket and built the mill afterwards known as Welch's. He also built a second mill on the Mascoma, not far from the site of the old paper mill.

Town Meetings, 1770-1785.

The first settlers in Canaan, except James Clark, were all from Connecticut, and came here chiefly through the influence of George Harris, who, as one of the grantees, was much interested in the new settlement. Craw, Williams, Jones, Benedict, the Wellses, Welch, Joslyn, Walworth, Gates, Lathrop, Eames and others came with or followed after Mr. Harris. It was a long and weary way they traveled, on foot or on horseback. Roads were not marked out in many places. In others they were obstructed by stumps and logs. They left Colchester and Norwich in the opening spring and arrived early in the summer. These first-comers, most of them, located upon the ridge of land now called South Road, extending from John Scofield's, near Mascoma River, near West Canaan, to the farm once owned by S. D. Gorham, which was the homestead of Charles Walworth, a half brother of Amos Walworth, the grantee. These men and families endured much of hardship and suffering. They found here no shelter, no food, no ground fit for tillage, and but little seed to put in the earth when it should be prepared with axe and brand. These were soon followed by families from Haverhill, Amesbury, Plaistow, Hampstead, Newmarket and other eastern towns, inclined to settle here chiefly through the influence and representations of the friends of the governor, who had been made grantees and were anxious to realize something from their grants. Among these were the Dustins, father and sons, the Blaisdells, Clarks, Ayer, Bartlett, the Barbers, Sawyer, the six Richardsons. Some of these found their way to Sawyer Hill and to various other parts of the town, but chiefly upon the uplands, believing that they thus received the best lands for corn, vegetables and grass.

The inventory for the year 1783, seventeen years after the settlement of the town, shows some progress. Two hundred and seventy-nine acres of land had been subdued and made use of by the settlers.

A true Inventory of the Polls and rateable Estate in town of Canaan in said State in the year Anno Domini 1783—

No. Polls	50
No. Horses	28
No. Cows	62
No. Oxen	29

No. of 3 years old 14
No. of 2 years old 20
No. of yearlings..................................... 10
No. acres pasturing 118
No. acres mowing 127
No. acres tillage 34
No. acres wild land fit for improvement.............. 12,000

      WM. AYER } *Selectmen.*
      WM. RICHARDSON }

It was during the years of unwritten history that the secession of the sixteen towns took place. Canaan was one of these towns. The people severed their connection with New Hampshire and voted themselves a part of the new territory of Vermont. The history which records this peaceful uprising is substantially as below condensed:

The original grant of New Hampshire was made to John Mason, and extended sixty miles from the sea. The line passed from the town of Rindge through the west part of Concord, striking Winnipesaukee Lake. Later grants extended its western boundary to Lake Champlain. Under these later acts, grants of townships were made on both sides of the Connecticut River. In 1764 a decree of the king in council was passed limiting the boundary of New Hampshire on the west to the Connecticut.

The grants to New York were not more definitely bounded, and in consequence a fierce strife arose as to the right of New York to control the lake and the river. The inhabitants of the towns on both sides of the river were mainly from Massachusetts and Connnecticut, and their views of public policy coincided. They were not well satisfied with the line which separated them from each other, and after the Revolution, when New Hampshire adopted measures for framing a constitution, their dissatisfaction was expressed in acts as well as words. Vermont petitioned Congress to be received into the confederacy as an independent state, and a majority of the people in many towns on this side of the river desired to unite with them, by petition dated June 11, 1778, the result of conclusions they had reached in March. There were sixteen of these towns, as follows: Cornish, Lebanon, Dresden (now Hanover), Lyme, Orford, Piermont, Haverhill, Bath, Lyman, Apthorp (now Littleton),

Dalton, Enfield, Canaan, Orange, Landaff, New Concord (now Lisbon), and Franconia. They took the position that since the government of Great Britain was overthrown, they were left to their own natural sovereignty, that the original grant of New Hampshire extended but sixty miles from the sea, that these townships were independent grants, each in itself a sovereign political organization and that as the power which had created them was thus overthrown, they were at liberty to attach themselves to whatever state they pleased. On the other hand it was maintained that by their own acts in receiving grants and protection from New Hampshire, they had acknowledged the sovereignty of that state over them. There was much discussion in the towns bordering on the river. They refused to send delegates to the convention which formed the constitution of New Hampshire, but united in a petition to the Vermont assembly, which then met at Windsor, to be received as a part of that state. The question was submitted to the people of Vermont in their general assembly and the union with the sixteen towns was accepted June 11, 1778. They were accordingly admitted as a part of that state and gave notice to New Hampshire to that effect, and asked for an amicable settlement of the boundary line between the two states. The government of New Hampshire was by no means disposed to recognize the right of secession. The president of New Hampshire, Hon. Meschech Weare, wrote to Governor Chittenden of Vermont, August 22, 1778, reclaiming these towns, making a strong argument therefor. He said: "Were not these towns settled and cultivated under the grant of the governor of New Hampshire? Are they not within the lines thereof? Did not the most of these towns send delegates to the convention of this state in 1773? Have they not from the commencement of the war applied to the State of New Hampshire for assistance and protection? It is well known that they did, and that New Hampshire at her own expense supplied them with arms, ammunition &c, to a very great amount. I earnestly desire that this matter may be seriously attended to, as I am persuaded that the tendency thereto will be anarchy and confusion." He also made an appeal to Congress to interpose and prevent, if possible, the shedding of blood. Congress by a resolution on August 2, 1781, made it an "indespensible preliminary" to the admission of Vermont as a state and freeing them from the claim of sovereignty of New York, that Vermont give up all claim to the towns on the east side of the Connecticut River. The movement of these towns received no encouragement from Congress and Canaan was not in sympathy, as appears by the following petition:

Canaan January 22 1782

To the Honorable and Generable assemble of the State of New Hampshier greating we haveing for a Long time bin under a broken situation the pretended State of Vermont pretend to Exercise athority over us which causis a great confusion among us & there being more than one half of the inhabitants of this town that have bin and now are willing subjects to this state pray that we mite be put in sum regularasion that we may have a Justice of the peace & militare officers that we may be in a way to defend our selves against the Enemies of the united States for we think our Selves in great danger having no authority amongst us but the pretended athority of vermont which we are not willing to be under if we can have any other N. B. we the subscribers beg the privilege that the Honorable Cort wold commisonate William Ayer as Justice of the peace & that we mite be led to the choyce of miletery officers

Joseph Stickney	Thomas miner
Joseph flint	Daniell Carr
Daniel farnum	William Smith
Samuel Chatman	Leonard hor
Nathl Barlet	Benjaman Sawer
Joshua wels	Samuel Meacham
Samuel Josen	Robard Barber
Mathew Man	Jonathan Stickney
Josiah hall Bartlet	Ezkel wels
Benjamin Burt	David fogg
James woodbury	John Bartlet
henry springer	Samuel Hinkson
Jaspur barber	

At the first meeting of the assembly of Vermont, February 22, 1782, after the people had voted to receive these towns and the delegates from this side had taken their seats, the question arose whether these towns should be erected into a separate county. This was refused, whereupon the delegates again seceded and left the Vermont assembly in disgust. Their friends on this side of the mountains, bound more strongly to them than those on the other side, proposed to unite with them to form a new state on both sides of the river, to be called New Connecticut. Then followed a series of contentions between New York, Vermont and New Hampshire, which is not interesting here, all of which were finally settled by the admission of Vermont with her present boundaries into the confederacy of the United States, a settlement which was hastened by the shrewd policy of Ethan Allen, who conferred with the British authorities in Canada and elsewhere as if he desired a union with them.

In some of the towns concerned in this contest there was manifested a spirit of lawlessness and disorder. In others Committees of Safety were appointed with unlimited powers. A meeting of the Committee of Safety for Canaan, Hanover, Lebanon, Plainfield and Grantham was held at Lebanon and the following vote was passed: "That the laws of our country ought and shall be the rule of our procedure in judging of the qualities of offences and punishing the same only with such variations as the different channel of administration requires." It appears from the record that in 1786, after the question of sovereignty had been settled, that the people of the town, like honest men, voted that the uncollected taxes during the years of their secession should be paid. The amount is not known.

At the beginning of the year 1785 two petitions were presented to the president and council, which show the unsettled condition of affairs in town:

To his Excellency the Pres & Honble the Council

That as we are not represented in the house to our satisfaction we can not rest easy to have advice taken from that quarter in your Honorable Board respecting the appointment of Civil & Military officers.

We take liberty to inform you that Caleb Clark Esq will give best satisfaction for a Civil Magistrate of any man in town

Canaan Jan 26 1785

Asahel Wells*
Josep Stickney
Benj Harris*
Robart Barber
Joseph Flint
Jehu Jones*
Ezekiel Gardner*
Caleb Welch
George Harris*
Turner Peterson*
Samuel meacham*
benjamen burts*

Jonathan Stickney
Zebulon Gates
William Richardson*
James woodbury
Samuel Hinkson*
William Smith
William Douglass*
Elias Lothrop*
Thaddeus Lothrop
Humphrey Nichols
Abel Hadley*
Benja Sawyer*

Another petition of the same date requested the appointment of Capt. Robert Barber for a field officer: "that he would give much the best satisfaction. We understand a certain Mr. Jones has been mentioned, who will not answer the valuable purpose of peace in s^d Town." It was signed by seventeen men, twelve of those on the above petition marked * and Joshua Harris, Elisha Lathrop, Ezekiel Wells, Richard Clark, and Isaac Walker. Samuel Jones was a major in the Twenty-Fourth Regiment the previous year.

It was in 1785 that a petition was presented to the General Assembly by Col. Elisha Paine and others, to form a new town out of portions of territory of the towns of Lebanon, Hanover, Canaan and Enfield. The part of Canaan to be included was in the southwest corner. The petition was not successful.

CHAPTER VI.

Town Meetings, 1786–1797.

It is now nine years since our town clerk made any record. His name was Thomas Baldwin, and in that time he had become converted to the Baptist belief, had studied divinity, theology, been ordained as an evangelist, and placed in charge of the new Baptist Church, which was organized six years ago. In that capacity he served well and left a large mark for future theologians to look at, but his style of keeping town records is not commendable.

Our new clerk, Mr. David Fogg, who had recently married Ruth Dustin, daughter of old Jonathan, lived in a log house some fifty rods southerly from the house John M. Barber afterwards built. Some of the apple trees he planted are still standing. He wrote a firm, even hand, and his record is diffuse as to the appointment of officers. Mr. Fogg's name comes to sight several times in the few coming years, and then he disappears, and there is not even a grave-stone to perpetuate his exit.

When Demophile was near her end she said to me: "Do you ever go and read those names and bits of verses on the stones yonder? You and Aspasia used formerly. Some of them tell us to be sad and sorry for folks who died a hundred years ago; others to imitate men and women we never should have had a chance of seeing, had they been living yet. All we can learn from them is this — that our country never had any bad people in it, but has been filled with weeping and wailing from its foundation upward."

In 1786, twenty years after the first settlement of the town, the census of the inhabitants was 142 males and 111 females. This year appears the first vote in reference to schools. "Voted to raise fifteen pounds L. M. for the support of schooling," and Capt. Robert Barber, Eleazer Scofield and Richard Clark were appointed a committee to divide the town into school districts. The schools had not been a feature in the town, no system existed, any respectable person, who could strike a good square blow with a ferrule or rod, had merit sufficient to become school-master And sometimes persons were employed who had to spell words of a reading exercise before pronouncing them. Ignorance was rather winked at, other desirable things being equal. Two months in the winter, when there was nothing else to do, was all that could be afforded by these hard working settlers for schooling.

New names appear: Joseph Flint and John Hall Bartlett as tithingmen; among the six surveyors of highways is Abel Hadley; Richard Otis and William Douglass are hogreaves; Benjamin Sawyer and Esquire Ayer are fence-viewers. "Voted to raise 16 pounds L. M. to defray town charges." Compare with March 9, 1886, a hundred years later: "Voted to raise $3000 to defray town charges." The selectmen had grown to be as careless as the clerks. The finances and affairs of the town had fallen into confusion. It was voted to have a thorough investigation thereof for the years from 1781 to 1786, and Joseph Flint, Daniel Blaisdell and Richard Otis, were appointed for the purpose. They made a full report, which was "excepted," but they fail to inform us if they discovered any "rings" by which the town had been swindled. It is fair to infer that after James Treadway left, honesty was a prevailing virtue, although sometimes harrassed by incapacity and ignorance. Ten shillings on the pound was raised for the repair of roads, not to include the large bridges. A new pound was voted to be built near the "South end of the town." It was located on South Road at the northeast corner of John May's. Joseph Flint was appointed as constable to collect back taxes for the year 1781, "and an extent for the deficiency of soldiers for this town."

It was a sin unpardonable to be a pauper, or unfortunately poor. Our tramps were treated with more consideration, as the following will show:

State of New Hampshire. Grafton, ss.

To Mr. John Scofield Constable for the town of Canaan for the present year. You are hereby required in the name and government of the people of said state, to warn off said Canaan, sundry persons now dwelling in said town, viz., Abigail Cooley and Theodate Flanders with Coffey her child. Their neglect of departing within fourteen days will expose them to the penalty of the law. Therefore fail not and make return of your doings.

                WILLIAM RICHARDSON ⎫
                CALEB WELCH   ⎬ *Selectmen.*
                JEHU JONES   ⎭

Canaan Aug 9 AD 1786.

The constable states in his return that he read this precept within the hearing of these unfortunate women, who, looking in vain for some hospitable door to open to them, wearily passed over our bounds, and were heard of no more. In the following year similar warnings were given to Francis and Mehitable Kenniston and their seven children, to Hannah Stevens and to Sargent Blaisdell, a brother of Daniel and Parrott Blaisdell, a soldier who had failed to gain a residence anywhere. Also to Abigail Finch "to depart from this town that they may not become chargeable." "Those people that will make oath that they have paid their poll tax in any other town for the year 1781 shall be exempt from paying in this town for that year."

William Richardson, Major Jones and Benjamin Sawyer were appointed "to lay out a road from the old Wolfeborough road to Mr. Bradbury's land." That road has been made fourteen years, and now they call it "old." It is doubtful if it ever was traveled by any one after the governor's journey. William Bradbury had moved on to his farm which was then the northwest corner of the town, next to the old town line, in 1785, from Newburyport. He cleared it up by hand, and while doing it lived with William Richardson.

"Voted that we instruct our representative in order to incourage the making of paper money." Jesse Johnson of Enfield was the representative of the towns of Canaan, Enfield, Dorchester, Cardigan and Grafton, and he was instructed by the following notice:

    At a legal meeting holden in Canaan on Tuesday the 8'day of August 1786 the inhabitants of s^d Town unanimously voted to have paper money made.

                                DAVID FOGG, *Town Clerk.*

And Major Jones, Esquire Ayer and David Fogg were chosen a committee "to instruct our representative." The reason for this vote we learn from other sources. In January, 1777, one hundred pounds of silver or gold was equal to the same in Continental money. In February it took 104 pounds of Continental money to equal one hundred pounds of silver or gold. In January, 1778, Continental money had depreciated so that it took 325 pounds to equal one hundred pounds of gold. In 1779 it took 742 pounds; in January, 1780, 2,934 pounds, and in June, 1781, one hundred pounds of silver or gold would buy 12,000 pounds of Continental money. Neither debts nor taxes could be paid, and much distress existed in every community. The great struggle for independence had terminated in the emancipation of the people from foreign jurisdiction, but the people were suffering from the lack of any system by which values could be approximated. A large debt accumulated by the war remained to be discharged. Requisitions for this purpose were made by Congress and by the state governments. The course of trade was not in favor of the colonists, consequently the silver and gold gradually disappeared. So large was the balance of trade against the colonies that it seemed impossible that any system of imposts could be adopted by which the coin could have been retained. Recourse was had to the usual mode of taxation on polls and estates, by which means heavy burdens were laid upon the husbandman and the laborer. Private creditors, who had suffered long by forbearance, were importunate for their dues, and the courts were full of suits. Various remedies were suggested by the people, who felt themselves oppressed, but that which offered quickest relief was a new emission of paper bills founded on real estate and loaned on interest. The cry for paper money was incessant and universal. It was to be the panacea for all troubles. But to all the clamors of the people there could be but one response, that it was not in the power of any legislature to pass any law that would secure paper from depreciation. A law was passed, called the "tender act," by which it was provided that executions issued for private demands might be satisfied by cattle and other enumerated articles, at an appraisal of impartial men under oath. This act was limited to two years, before the expiration of which it was revived with alteration and continued for three years longer. The effect of this law, where attempts were made to execute it, was that the most valuable kinds of property were either concealed or made over to third parties, and whenever the sheriff appeared he could only levy upon articles of little value. Attempts were made by the legislature to encourage the importation of money from abroad by exempting goods from port duties. But all these efforts were in vain. No encouragement could be given for the circulation of money while the tender act was in force, because every man who had money felt it was safe only in his own pocket.

The cry for paper money was like a raging fever. In every town there was a party in favor of it, and against all laws which obliged men to pay their debts. This same party also clamored against courts and lawyers. The abolition of the courts was demanded, as being sinecures, whereby clerks, judges and lawyers enriched themselves at the expense of the people.

To still the alarm and collect the real sense of the people on the subject of paper money, the assembly formed the plan for the emission of fifty thousand pounds, to be let at four per cent., on landed security; to be a tender in payment of state taxes and for the fees and salaries of public officers. This plan was immediately printed and sent to the several towns, and the people were desired to give their opinion for and against it and make return at the next session of the assembly.

The excitement upon the subject was kept up by interested parties, who spread false reports in regard to the acts of the government. When the assembly again met at Exeter they were surrounded by a body of two hundred armed men, who in a threatening manner, demanded an issue of paper money, an equal distribution of property and a release from debts. Sentries were placed at the doors and the whole legislature was held prisoner, the mob threatening death to any person who should attempt to escape before their demands were granted. They continued their riotous demonstrations through the day, when they withdrew and spent the night upon a hill a mile away. The next morning they were attacked by the militia and dispersed, some forty being made prisoners, who were subsequently discharged upon making humiliating submissions. The dignity of the government being vindicated, its lenity became conspicuous. The plan adopted by the assembly for the issue of paper money was not sustained in the returns made by a majority of the towns and all the questions touching upon it were determined in the negative. And in Canaan it was "Voted that the handbill respecting paper be not adopted."

It was found by many patriots that the American Revolution would not produce that sum of political happiness, which its warmest advocates had formerly predicted. The efforts of the factions in several of the states had produced alarming results. But the powers of government being exerted with vigor, the spirit of anarchy was suppressed and the hopes of good men grew strong. Major Jones was appointed collector "to collect what remains due on a tax bill for the year 1779 in certificates agreeable to the scale of depreciation at the time it was due to the treasury."

In 1787, twenty pounds was raised to defray town charges, and ten shillings on the pound for highways. "Voted to sell the necessary wood for Mr. Walters' support at Vendue to the lowest bidder," and a committee was appointed to let out his place as long as they shall think proper. Joseph Walters was an invalid soldier and needed daily care. He was poor also, but owning land and being an old resident, he could not be warned off the town. Mr. Baldwin was voted thirty pounds in labor and produce this year and his estate was exempt from taxation, as it had been last year. The votes for a president on the thirteenth day of March, 1787: John Langdon, 23; John Sullivan, 9. Joshua Harris was appointed the first coroner in town, this year, by the president and council, and this office he held for ten years. Oliver Smith held the office one year, in 1798.

In 1788, Mr. Walters' care is bid off to Richard Otis for nine pounds. "Mr. Otis is to support the fire, that is wood convenient be found at the door cut suitable for the fire, and when necessary the fire be made, and also two cows shall be well pastured on the place in case there is feed enough grows, and that they be provided for in winter, or so long as it is necessary that this should be fed with hay, and fed therewith when it shall be needful, to be kept on the place while they give milk." The town was to pay the bill in wheat or other grain at the rate of five shillings per bushel. Mr. Otis was to have all the feed over

Town Meetings, 1786-1797.

and above what was needed to keep the cows. But Mr. Walters was to have the privilege of keeping two hogs, the town to inclose a small spot to pasture them. John Currier's name appears for the first time as surveyor of highways, Samuel Noyes as a selectman, and Thaddeus Lathrop as a fence-viewer. The votes for president this year were: John Sullivan, 1; John Langdon, 21; Josiah Bartlett, 7. And here appear the first votes for senator: Jonathan Freeman, 4; Colonel Payne, 18; and Bezaleel Woodward, 7.

At this meeting, March 11, it was "Voted to build a Meeting House." On May 9, a meeting was called to see about the building of the meeting house, and a committee was appointed to report on June 10, at which time the people got into a controversy as to the size of the house, the spot upon which to build it, its shape and other matters, got badly out of humor and went home. They said no more about a meeting house for several years. On December 15, "in obedience to an act of the State of New Hampshire," the legal voters met at Capt. Robert Barber's and voted for representatives to the first Congress and for the five electors for the first president of the United States. The votes for representative were: General Sullivan, 11; General Peabody, 10; General Bellows, 12; Judge Livermore, 18; Judge Calf, 5. For the electors: Jonathan Freeman, Esq., 19; Colonel Toppin, 19; Col. P. Long, 19; General Dow, 19; Maj. Daniel Tilton, 9; General Badger, 10. The "Selectmen are to provide things for the support of the Widow Birt and her family, that they are under necessity for." Her husband, "Ben Rob," had served in many campaigns, and had come home wounded and broken in health, and was now dead.

Maj. Samuel Jones was appointed treasurer without any other bonds than his own for the present year. The selectman are as loath to account as our tax collectors were before the passage of the law that compelled them to close their books every year. And "Mr. John Harris, Ensign Daniel Blaisdell and Capt. Joshua Harris were chosen to settle with the selectmen for the years 1787-1788. Also to settle with former Selectmen which have not already settled, and act discretionary in the matter."

Jesse Johnson of East Enfield was appointed delegate to the convention in 1788 to ratify the Federal Constitution. He represented the towns of Canaan, Enfield, Dorchester, Orange, Hanover and Grafton.

In 1789, Jehu Jones warns Eliphalet Norris and Lydia Norris and four children, also Francis Kenniston, who does not seem to have paid much attention to the first warning; Ichabod Honey, Betty Honey and Ebenezer Honey to "depart out of this town" for fear they might become town charges.

At the annual meeting there are twenty-eight votes cast for president of the assembly. "Voted not to raise any money for schooling this year." Times are bad, money scarce and hard to get, wages low. Other things must be had, so we will let the school-master wait awhile and study at home by the blazing back-log. But we will vote to pay the county tax of 1783 of thirteen pounds, which we repudiated, and twenty pounds to defray town charges.

Some of these good men worried lest the selectmen had been or might be led into temptation, and become thievish, so they voted "the selectmen for 1785 be put upon oath respecting the towns money from the year 1781 to 1786," but they neglected to tell us how hard they swore or what they swore about.

The poor they always had with them, and they needed care. Wood for the poor was vendued by the cord to the lowest bidder. Ezekiel Gardner bid off one cord to draw to the Widow Birt and cut it fit for the fire for six shillings. Capt. Robert Barber bid off one cord for six. Parrott Blaisdell bid off one cord for seven and six pence, the latter to be drawn to Lieut. Thomas Miner's for Mr. Walters. In 1790, Mr. Walter, whose serious illness had been a severe trial upon the sympathy and good nature of the people, was finally disposed of. An agreement was made with Thomas Miner, that he should receive a deed of all Mr. Walter's interests in Canaan, and take him and support him during his natural life, both in sickness and health. And the selectmen conveyed to Mr. Miner and took bonds for Mr. Walter's support. And David Dustin was to take "Widow Birts son Will that lives with her for ten pounds." "Uncle David," as he was called in after years, was a friendly man, kind-hearted, and the widow's son had a good home while in his house. So, also, it was voted "to let Jehu Jones have the order of the town upon the Treasurer for twenty pounds or upward and excuse him from collecting the hard money bill committed to him, he engaging to collect a bill in certificates in room of it, which bill shall be made out to him hereafter by the selectmen." And "that Jehu Jones pay back to those persons who have paid him their tax on the hard money bill that the Town excused him from collecting." Thirty pounds was raised for the support of Elder Baldwin, "excepting those who are conscience bound that they can not support ministers that way." Wheat at five shillings a bushel was made a legal tender for town taxes. And the selectmen were instructed "to provide a measure for a standard to try half bushels with."

Richard Otis warns William Hukins, Samuel Folsom, his wife Anne, and five children, Joshua Cushen, Deborah and Soloman Cushen, Sarah Walter and Sarah Fox, to leave town, because they are poor. The first jurors' meeting was held on March 30, 1790, and Thomas Miner was chosen the first grand juror from this town and Ezekiel Wells the first petit juror.

This year the town sold the Lock lot "for the purpose of discharging a debt the town owes in state notes and certificates. Which were hired for the town's use in the year 1789." The census of the town, taken in 1790, gives the number of inhabitants as 483, an increase in four years of 230.

In 1791, no money was raised for town charges, but the usual rate was voted for highways. Thirty-seven votes were cast for Josiah Bartlett for president. David Dustin was town clerk.

In 1792, nine pounds was raised for town charges and wheat could be taken in settlement. Deacon Welch is exempted from paying "pole tax for his son Dan that was taken away by death." Widow Worth was cleared of all taxes due Mr. Gilman, he being the constable and collector. "Voted if Grafton will agree to the same we will for the Futer meet at Mr. Clifford's for the choice of representative." On the 7th of May a special meeting was called to act upon the amendments to the constitution of the state. Sixty affirmative and thirteen negative votes were received. Deacon Welch "is permited to erect a number of small buildings on the highway opesit to his house and barn not to extend more than twenty feet from Jehu Jones line for the term of Twenty years." On August 27 was held the presidential election and the following electors received the following votes: Daniel Rindge, 25; Gen. Joshua Colby, 23; Jonathan Freeman, 34; Judge Thomas Cogswell, 36; Capt. Daniel Warner, 27; Gen. Benjamin Bellows, 32.

In the warning for October 10 there is this article: "3rd. To see if the Town will agree to have the enockalation of the small pox set up under propper Restrictions:" At the meeting they voted "not to have the Small Pox set up by enockelation."

About 1785, an institution for sanitary purposes was established under the shadow of Cardigan Mountain. It was called "The Pest House," a name suggestive of contagion, disease, death. It was a place of refuge for persons afflicted with smallpox, where they could receive the best treatment which the limited knowledge of the disease could suggest. It has been said that the house was once the residence of Col. Elisha Paine, a proprietor and one of the first settlers in Cardigan, and in his day a prominent and troublesome man, both socially and politically. This is a mistake. Colonel Paine built his house over an ancient cellar hole nearer the center of the town. Some time in the eighties smallpox appeared in this state. The people were terrified at its ravages and in many places fled at its approach, and left the hapless victims to care for themselves. Benevolent and thoughtful men began wearying themselves with projects for the treatment of the scourge, and how a cordon could be drawn about it, so as to confine it within narrow limits, and the residents in exposed localities feel safe to return to their usual labors. The idea of establishing a pest house was brought out at an assembly of gentlemen who had met to confer upon the demoralized condition of the people and if possible provide a remedy. The suggestion was adopted at once and a committee appointed to select the location for the house. Some of these gentlemen were familiar with the topography of Cardigan region. Its dense mountain loneliness had not yet attracted settlements. And a pest house filled with smallpox patients would be a signal to all who might wish to lay down their burdens here to seek some other asylum. A cellar was dug and wells were sunk and a house 36 x 30, two stories high, was erected, together with convenient out-buildings. And to this lonely asylum of wretchedness, the unfortunate victims of that terrible disease wended their sad way, from various parts of the state, in order that they might receive the needed care and kindly treatment which was denied them at home.

It is reported that at one time some thirty students at Dartmouth College were sent there and some of the professors also repaired thither. Among these exiles were some who afterwards were distinguished in their various callings. Thomas G. Fessenden was a well-known agricultural journalist; Parker Noyes became a distinguished lawyer; Philander Chase became a bishop, and was founder of several western colleges; Seth Currier, brother of John, of Canaan, a merchant. They were of the class of '96. These young men were detained at the pest house six weeks, long, dreary, heart-breaking weeks of sickening disgust to all of them, during which time they were not permitted intercourse with friends outside. Some of the patients died, and were quietly buried on the grounds, a short distance from the house, but no stones ever marked the resting place. Nathan Briggs, a farmer of the vicinity, was a patient for six weeks, and was constantly reminded of the sickening danger by the strong antiseptic remedies used to purify the air. The old man used to tell of the homesickness and feeling of loneliness which seized upon the young persons confined there, and seemed to be almost as bad as the disease they were forced to face day by day. It was in 1796 that Doctor Jenner made his first experiment of transferring the pus from the pustule of a milkmaid, who had caught the cow-pox from the cows, to a healthy child. The result was published and the practice spread throughout the civilized world. But it was not accepted everywhere. Two years after Doctor Jenner's experiment, the practice had not been adopted in the pest house under the shadow of old Cardigan.

In February, 1793, the matter came up again and it was again voted "not to have the Small Pox by enockalation set up in s^d town." So much excitement prevailed that a special meeting was called in March "to see if the town will have the Small Pox come into sd Town by way of enockalation under proper restrictions." And it was voted "not to have the Small pox come into sd Town by way of enockalation" under any proper or improper restrictions. Again, after two years, an effort was made to induce the town "to adopt the practice of inoculation for small pox," but the doubts in regard to the success or utility of the practice were so strong among the intelligent voters of that age that it was voted "to pass the article." It was about this time that the pest house was gradually cleared of its patients, either by death or successful treatment. And the buildings were left for the winds and storms to howl among their decaying timbers until they rotted away and became a part of the soil upon which they stood. And the only knowledge we possess of this institution is the unwritten legends that come down from those sad days.

The purveyor of the house was Daniel Blaisdell of Canaan, who lived on the farm once Prescott Clark's. He contracted to furnish vegetables and wholesome provisions to its inmates at reasonable prices. In order that he might approach the house without danger of contracting the disease, he arranged by building roads so that he could always approach the house to the windward. Then driving his cart and oxen as near to the house as prudent, he would stop and call loudly to announce his arrival. Then, unloading, he would depart as he came, having little intercourse with the inmates. It is further reported that he was a faithful purveyor, and that his provisions were fresh, wholesome and abundant.

The physician in charge was Doctor Tiffany from Connecticut, a skillful, self-reliant man. He had brought with him as an assistant, a young man named Storrs. One day, in the absence of the doctor, Mr. Storrs decided to vaccinate himself in his own way. He did so by injecting the virus between his eyes. On the doctor's return the young man reported to him what he had done. The doctor examined him with anxiety, for some moments, and then very quietly said: "If you, my young friend, have any communications to make to your friends, it will be wise for you to do so without delay. You have committed a fatal error, and I know of no remedy that can save you from death." The young man died.

On October 10, 1792, the town voted "that the selectmen settle with Mr. Joslin with Regard to Mr. Treadway's taxes discretionary." Mr. Treadway had left town and did not pay his taxes.

In 1793, the collectorship of the taxes was set up at public vendue for the first time "to the lowest bidder and him to be the collector providing he gits bonds to the Satisfaction of the town." "That the man that bids of the collectorship shall not be holden unless he hes the Constables both likewise." These two offices continued to be held by one person for many years afterwards. It was voted "that John Burdick procure a standard of weights and measures." And here is the first vote for governor: Josiah Bartlett, 35 votes; John Langdon, 7 votes.

Here is a curious vote. Some one had been "up against it"; somebody's feelings or otherwise had been hurt, and even to this day some people go to the legislature and enact laws out of spite against some one whose property has offended them. "Voted that if any mans Ram is found in his neighbors inclosures from the tenth day of September to the middle of November, the owner of such stray Ram shall pay One Dollar or forfeit his Ram which he pleases."

Jacob Hovey's wife and child are still paupers, their care to be paid for in "Grane."

There are two burying grounds at this time and it is voted to fence them "with Boards and Posts." Lieut. William Richardson, Mr. Jon. Carlton, Lieut. R. Whittier, committee for the "North Burying Yard"; John Burdick, Jehu Jones and Lieut. Thomas Miner for the "South Deestrict."

In 1794, the population of the town was, by the New Hampshire Register, 483. John Harris is paid by the town "for going after Jacob Hovey." Jacob may have deserted his wife and left her a town charge. He is brought back and his family no more appear as town charges. Hovey lived on the north side of the Wolfeborough Road, afterwards Luther Kinney's farm. The collectorship is bid off to Dudley Gilman for one half-pence on the pound.

On the thirteenth day of March the inhabitants of Canaan, Grafton and Orange met at Simeon Arvin's and elected John

Burdick representative to the General Court. This is the first Canaan man to serve in that capacity. On April 22, the town met at the meeting house for the first time. Nine pounds was raised to defray town charges.

On October 28, the town met at the meeting house for the second time, and continue to thereafter, although the building is still unfinished. The town voted "to make up this town's proportion of Minute Men forty shillings per month, togather with what the State and Continent gives them when they are called into actual service." John Worth is chosen "to officiate in the office of Justice of the Peace in the town of Canaan and for the County of Grafton." This is the first justice chosen in the town, although William Ayer had held a commission from the state for several years and continued to until he left town.

At the annual meeting in 1795 they met at the meeting house, but after transacting a little business they adjourned to Simeon Arvin's. The present selectmen are "to settle with Jehu Jones and other collectors as far back as they find anything due the town." Money was found due the town uncollected, but the collectors wanted further remuneration for making any further efforts, and the town voted "not to pay them anything," and "to prosecute all Town Collectors which are delinquent in settling with said town, as soon as may be convenient."

Thirty pounds was raised for town charges and eight shillings on the pound for highways. John Currier is collector at the rate of "three pence three farthings on the pound."

In 1796, twelve pounds was raised to defray town charges, six shillings rate for roads and four for bridges. Clark Currier is appointed collector of school money.

On October 16, the people met to cast their votes for six electors for president of the United States: Beza Woodard, Esq., 23 votes; John T. Gilman, Esq., 23 votes; Benjamin Bellows, Esq., 22 votes; Oliver Peabody, Esq., 22 votes; Ebenezer Thompson, Esq., 20 votes; Timothy Farrer, Esq., 25 votes.

On October 20, 1796, the people of Hanover appointed an agent, Jonathan Freeman, to prefer a petition to the General Court to have the land east of Moose Mountain annexed to Canaan or some other town, as may be convenient. Canaan took no action nor appeared. This land was a part of a gore which ran across the north line of the town from the Connecticut River to Canaan. No action was taken upon this petition other than the natural consequences, which would result from the situation of the land. It belonged to Hanover and there it is now.

The first book of records of the town closes with a meeting on the twenty-fifth of January, 1797, called in regard to preaching, and the town vote to "procure a book for records for the use of the town." The town meetings through this first volume relate to but few subjects, the election of town officers, roads, schools, and preaching, which will be dealt with elsewhere. (This book of the first records of the town has disappeared and no one seems to know where it has gone. My father, in his life time, made a copy of them for his more ready reference. It is the only copy known.)

The inventory for the year 1793 contains 127 names, the list is probably defective, one leaf may be missing. Quite a number of familiar names are absent. This is the first year the selectmen have made an inventory. The largest taxpayer was Samuel Jones, who had four acres of tillage, twenty acres of mowing, twenty acres of pasturing, twenty-two animals, and his tax was five pounds, six shillings and eleven pence. John Scofield paid a tax of four pounds, sixteen shillings, and six pence, on four acres of tillage, twelve acres of mowing, twenty-five acres of pasturing and fourteen animals. Thomas Miner had two acres of tillage, nine acres of mowing, twelve acres of pasturing, two animals and paid a tax of three pounds and ten shillings. These three men were large landowners of undeveloped land.

The inventory for 1794 contains 141 names, three of them non-residents. The total amount of tax raised was 161 pounds and two shillings. Under the head of "money on hand or at interest," "Samuel Noice" is taxed for fifteen pounds for 1793. No other person has "Money on hand." In 1794 this fifteen pounds is taxed to Allen Miner, which is a mistake, as it, no doubt, should have been taxed to Samuel Noyes, who was a man of means. It would appear that all the rest of the people traded on "Grane," calves, pigs, or whatever they could produce for "exchange."

Samuel Jones, John Scofield, Robert Barber, Ezekiel Wells, Caleb Welch and Thomas Miner are the largest taxpayers, in order, all large owners of undeveloped land.

There are 141 names on the inventory for 1795. The sum total of the tax is 182 pounds, 3 shillings and 8 pence. The largest taxpayers, in order, were John Scofield, Samuel Jones, their taxes being about $22 each; Caleb Welch, Joshua Harris, Ezekiel Wells and Richard Clark 3rd.

CHAPTER VII.

Town Meetings, 1797–1818.

At the annual meeting on the fourteenth of March, 1797, the vote for governor was forty-seven votes for John T. Gilman and sixty-four votes for Moses Dow. Daniel Blaisdell had forty-three votes for senator. On the next day the towns of Canaan, Enfield and Orange met at the "Meeting House and chose Daniel Blaisdell representative."

At the annual meeting, William Richardson was chosen justice of the peace by a majority of nineteen. Six shillings on the pound was raised for highways, and two shillings and six pence to defray town charges and "making and mending bridges."

The collection of taxes was struck off to Richard Clark, 3d, at two pence on the pound. Ezekiel Wells, Daniel Farnum and William Richardson were chosen hogreeves. The hogs were not much restrained of their liberty, for that reason the duties of these officers was not more than complimentary. This office was held in so little honor that the men appointed to it were chosen more as a joke, and in later years, to make it the more ridiculous, as many as twenty were appointed, of which the first was called the "General," and the others held subordinate positions on his staff, as "major," "captain," "corporal." Hogs found in trespass were placed in the pound. Some expense attended their release, and this fact made men observant of the ways of their hogs.

In 1798, the competition for the collection of taxes was spirited. Several bidders appeared and the excitement was high. Bidding began at three per cent. and went down until Richard Clark, 3d, determined not to be beaten, offered "a onepenny on the pound, for the privilege of collecting the money." The next year Richard paid only "a happenny on the pound for the privilege." William Richardson is justice of the peace this year.

In 1798, no money seems to have been raised to defray town

charges. In 1799, sixty dollars was voted to be raised, and six shillings on the pound to repair highways and bridges. The Widow Folsom and her children were "on the town." Mrs. Folsom was bid off to John Perley at "20 cents per week so long as he keeps her." She was the widow of Samuel Folsom, mentioned in 1790, and there were eight children. The selectmen wrote twice to her father, "Capt. Steaven Harriman of Hopkinton," to come to her relief and save the town any more expense. No doubt he did, for her name does not appear again.

In 1800, Timothy Johnson is chosen collector of taxes, and "he is to have one penny on the pound for collecting." One hundred dollars is raised for town charges, and eight shillings on the pound for highways. The selectmen are to "act discretionary, respecting taxing non-resident proprietors." At this time so much of the land was owned by non-resident proprietors, who never came to see their possessions and would not pay their tax that it led the town into as much expense to get the tax as the tax amounted to, the land being unimproved and unoccupied, if sold at tax sale there was not likely to be any one to buy it. Besides the greater portion of the land in town was still "common," had not been divided. The Widow Judkins is bid off to Prescott Clark at seventy-nine cents a week for one year.

Ruth Woodbury and her child were vendued to Samuel Welch for $32.50 for five months, and another child was sold to Daniel Farnum for twenty dollars "until he is twenty-one." The husband and father was James Woodbury, a Revolutionary soldier, who came to Canaan about 1780. He fell in love with Sally Springer, and wanted to marry her, but she preferred Daniel Blaisdell. The old man afterwards married and had a large family, some of whom were paupers and lived on the town. Daniel and Sally had a son James, who was a vain man, filled with conceit, very pompous and overbearing. He would always wear gloves when he could get them, and was usually on a swell when the older people were about. One day, having on a little larger swell than usual, old Esquire Richardson, who had been a justice of the peace since 1798, took him down as follows: "Um, you needn't feel so damn smart with your old gloves on, it's only an accident you didn't have ole Jim Woodbury for

Town Meetings, 1797–1818.

your father." The census of the town for 1800 was 835 inhabitants, an increase in ten years of 352.

At this date there were four sawmills in town, Trussell's at the "Village," Matthew Greeley's at Goose Pond, Robert Barber's, afterwards Welch's, and Scofield's at West Canaan. The mill at Goose Pond was built previous to 1790 by John Perley, who had come from Gilmanton, and had passed into the possession of Mills Olcott, Esq., of Hanover, and then into Mr. Greeley's hands. Clear pine lumber was worth $14 per thousand, common lumber $5, and there was no market beyond the immediate vicinity of the mills.

In 1801, Reuben Kimball took the Widow Miriam Judkins for $80 during the rest of her life, $20 a year until paid, he to give bonds. One hundred and thirty dollars is raised for town charges and thirty cents for highways.

At the annual meeting a prayer was addressed to the grantees of the town, asking them to fix a "Right or share in the town lands at 310 acres and to deed the remainder of the territory to the town." But the proprietors had not yet arrived at the unselfish conclusion that 310 acres was equal to 330, and the prayer was answered in the negative.

In 1802, they voted not to have a town treasurer, the selectmen were to perform that duty. The same appropriations were made for town charges and highways as last year.

In 1803, the same amount was voted for highways and $80 for town charges. They voted, with the consent of the proprietors of the meeting house, to build a "Pound" on the "Common," between the meeting house and the Pond. "Thirty-six feet square, of hewn timbers, eight feet high from top of sill to top of plate," to be finished in an acceptable manner by the first of September. The building of it was bid off to Prescott Clark for twenty-five dollars. The old pound was built among a lot of alder bushes. The timbers rotted away in a few years, and it was removed. It was also voted to fence the burying grounds "with good wall or posts and boards spiked on." There were five of these grounds at that time, namely: The "Street," "Wells," the "Cobble," West Canaan and West Farms. "Lt. Whittier, Wm. Richardson, Capt. John Currier, Capt. Ezekiel

Wells, and Lt. Thomas Miner" were the committee chosen to see the work completed. In 1804 the town voted fifty dollars for town charges and the same as before for highways. It also voted forty-five dollars to procure "weights and measures as the law requires."

On June 19, 1804, Canaan Social Library was incorporated into a proprietorship by the following men: John Hoyt, James Doten, Caleb Welch, James Johnson, Jr., Ebenezer Clark, Caleb Welch, Jr., Micah Porter, Hubbard Harris, Joshua Pillsbury, Levi George, Joshua Harris, Richard Otis, Elias Porter, John Currier, Ezekiel Wells, Jacob Trussell, Thaddeus Lathrop, Jr., Jacob Dow, Nathaniel Tucker, Nathaniel Bartlett, Moses Dole, Robert Wilson, Richard Clark, 3d, Caleb Pierce, Micaiah Moore and Nathaniel Barber. They could receive subscriptions to the amount of $1,000. Jacob Trussell was to warn the first meeting. Capt. Moses Dole was to purchase the books. Something like two hundred volumes were purchased, and Doctor Tilton covered them with sheepskin from Jacob Dow's tannery. Such books as Boswell's "Life of Johnson," Cooke's "Voyages," Davidson's "Translation of Virgil," Buchan's "Medicine," "Pilgrim's Progress," etc., were among them. The following is a copy of the subscription paper which led to the incorporation:

We, the subscribers, tacking in to considderation the Benefit of having a Libra in this town, as sune as we Can get phifty shairs sind for at two Dollars a shair. Tharefore we think it is Best to meat at the meeting house on Monday, the 27th day of June, at wone o'clock p. m. to set a time when the money shall be paid and what method the proprators will tacke to get the books. 1803, Canaan, June 15.

Thirty-five shares were all that was ever issued.

In 1832, there was an article in the warrant to see "if the town will vote $50 for new books for their Lyceum." It was not acted on. Assessments were made each year, some paid and others did not; their shares were sold and the new owners failed to pay assessments. The books became old and were finally divided up amongst the members. Some of them are to be found in the Town Library.

In 1805, $150 was raised for town charges, and the same as before for roads. Joshua Richardson, John Currier and John

Fales were chosen by the town to settle with Gordon Burley, "on the vendue deed he holds from the town of land of Joseph Randlett." Randlett's land had been sold for taxes, during the time he was having a dispute with Homer, the then owner of Dame's Gore. The town having no jurisdiction of the Gore land, had presumed to tax what they had no right to. In a subsequent meeting, the town voted to have the selectmen "settle with Burley as reasonable as possible." This land was the third one hundred acres of the right of Samuel Meacham, and was located north of the old Nathan Cross farm. John Currier was appointed to go to Wentworth "to find Ruth Woodbury a place to board."

In 1806, crows had become so troublesome that twenty cents a head was offered for dead ones by the town. Thirty dollars was raised for town charges, and the highway rate was raised to fifty cents. The question of taxing non-resident land came up again in the warrant, and the town dismissed the article. Ezekiel Wells was appointed pound-keeper of the new pound. He lived then in the old house of the Wallaces, burned in 1898.

In 1807, $200 was raised for town charges, and forty cents for roads. An "able bodied man shall receive six cent per hour for labor on the highways and the same for oxen." And probably the men performed as much labor in an hour at that price as they did later for seventeen cents per hour. They also voted to tax non-resident lands. The people objected to bearing the burdens of others.

In 1808, $150 was voted for town charges and forty cents for roads. In 1809, seventy-five dollars was raised for town charges and thirty cents for roads. Some men were employed to build a bridge over the river near Josiah Clark's mill. It required a gallon of Micaiah Moore's rum to complete it, the workmen drank it all, and then asked the town to pay for it, which was declined with thanks.

In 1810, $200 was raised for town charges, and the same as last year for roads. Joshua Harris was appointed the first postmaster of the town and held the office for three years. The census of the town in this year, 1,094, showing an increase in ten years of 259.

84   HISTORY OF CANAAN.

In 1811, $200 was raised for town charges and "fifty cents on a hundred dollars" for roads. William Campbell is to "find bed and board for Widow Pattee and abigail, keep their clothes good, until next March meeting for $1.89 per week. The town to pay their doctor's bill." Mr. Fisk gets $100 for Ruth Woodbury.

In 1812, $300 was raised for town charges and fifty cents for roads. Robert Williams, Jr., bid off the Widow Pattee and her daughter for seventy-five dollars for the year.

Canaan was a strong federal town and was, of course, opposed to the war with Great Britain. Party lines were closely drawn, and much bad language uttered. Some personal altercations occurred, which left bad feelings, and threats of chastisement were heard. In reference to the war of 1812, both parties held meetings and passed resolutions, but the Federalists only, being largely in the majority, were able to put themselves upon record.

On the 27th of July, 1812, a town meeting was held. Thomas H. Pettingill was moderator and John Currier clerk. A committee composed of Mr. Pettingill, Caleb Seabury, William Richardson and Jacob Trussell was appointed to make report of the opinions entertained by the people. The committee introduced their report with a lengthy "whereas," detailed the country's grievances, and followed by "Resolves" of a highly patriotic nature, as follows:

Whereas the constituted authorities of our country have declared this nation to be in a state of war with one of the great belligrant nations of Europe, and in pursuance of that declaration have caused a call to be made for a number of training bands to hold themselves in readiness to take part in the service of their country. Which call we acknowledge they have a constitutional right to make for the purpose of executing the laws of the union to suppress insurrection and quell invasion. And, whereas, it hath been the modern custom of Europe degraded by the iron yoke of its present military despot, to select by conscription such subjects as his sovereign pleasure dictates to fight it battles. And, whereas, the tyrannical and slavish custom hath of late been introduced into this land of liberty and equality, and there is danger of its becoming the permanent usage for raising troops. And, whereas, we trust there is yet in this town too much of the true spirit of seventy-six, to suffer such a degrading and unequal custom to prevail here while the citizens who compose the training band, (although respectable) are by no means the most wealthy and although the general government compensates with a lebral hand, with regret we perceive, that the compensation offered by law for the services of the non-commissioned officers, and soldiers is by no means an equivalent and while we conceive it to be equally our duty to obey every constitutional call of our government and frown with indignity on every uncinstant infringement of our rights, we deem it also our duty not to suffer the poorer class of our citizens to protect the lives and property of the wealthy without due compensation. Therefore, resolved, and voted that if the non-commissioned officers and privates, who are to be detached from the training band in this town, shall be called into actual service, for either of the above purposes, that the selectmen be hereby authorized and directed to assess a sum of money on the poles and ratable estate, liable by law to be taxed, sufficient to make up said troops the sum of ten dollars per month, including the pay they shall actually receive from the government, whether they volunteer their services or are drafted. And it is our duty to believe that they will not be called for any but the above purposes. And we earnestly recommend the former, as to occupy the ground of slaves is humiliating to free men.

Voted to pass the second resolve, which is in the following words:

Whereas, the publick concerns of our beloved country have of late assumed a dangerous and alarming aspect. And our government having in our opinion quit the highly honorable prudent and natural position taken by that man whose wisdom prudence and discernment united all classes in the best means to promote the great interest of the commonwealth.

And, whereas, the government of the United States, hath declared this nation to be in a state of war with Great Britain, who was at the time of that declaration the purchaser and consumer of about ⅞ of that vast amount of our domestic productions exported abroad for market, the income of which enriches our citizens and filled our national treasury. And while we acknowledge their right by constitution to declare war, and our duty to obey every constitutional injunction of our government, we claim with equal confidence the right guarranteed to us by the same constitution, and that of the State of New Hampshire, of freely expressing our opinions, of that as well as all others of a publick nature, without being put in fear by every engine of tyranny or even of mobs with the disgrace of the American name hath been set on foot and executed in the city of Baltimore and Savannah.

Therefore, being assembled to consult upon the common good. Resolved, in the opinion of this meeting, that in the present critical situation of the European world, it is the heighth of imprudence for this nation to enter into and prosecute a war with either of the great contending parties, in our opinion, a declaration of war against either Great Britain or France, is and to the least discerning mind must be considered as taking part with its enemy, and thereby subjecting this nation to the ruinous effect of that destructive war, which at present and for many years past, hath involved Europe in that wretchedness and distress, which shakes human nature even to name, the termination of which no mortal eye can see nor the most sagestive mind can conceive.

Resolved, that whereas, the present majority both in Congress and in our Cabinet, have in the opinion of this meeting, either turned a deaf ear to or have treated with neglect the remonstrations of the people against the late declaration of war and measures of restrictions on our own commerce. That at this critical period, it is not only the privilege, but the solemn duty of every citizen (while he religiously submits to the powers that be) to use all legal and constitutional measures to convince the unconvinced, that a change of public officers is absolutely necessary in order that the privileges liberty and prosperity, which our ancestors purchased with blood and immence treasures may be handed down to posterity unimpaired.

Resolved that every constitutional attempt to suppress the people or their representatives from freely expressing their opinion as well against as in favor of the measures of administration (which such opinions grounded 'in truth) is in the opinion of this meeting a gross infringement of the most valuable right of free men, and that every office holder or office seeker or any other person who either directly or indirectly shall threaten any citizen with a coat of tar and feathers, or any other art of mobbery, to deter him from freely expressing such opinion, merits and ought to receive the sovereign contempt of a free people, and we shall ever hold ourselves ready to aid government with our lives and fortunes in suppressing any mob, under whatever name it may assume or in whatever garb it may be clad.

A copy of these resolutions was forwarded to Hon. Nicholas Gilman, one of our senators in Congress, and through him the voice of Canaan was uttered in the halls of Congress, but the war still went on.

In November of this year, New Hampshire had the high honor of discovering Daniel Webster. His first election was announced. Canaan gave him 159 ballots. His opponent receiving forty-six. In 1813, the town voted $250 for town charges and fifty cents for roads. The selectmen of Orange asked Canaan to receive the jurisdiction of a part of that town. Canaan declined to accept. Much expense and more annoyance had already occurred from the litigous disposition of Nathan Waldo, Esq., whose influence was paramount in Orange, and it was through this trait in the man's character, that led a portion of the people of Orange to ask protection from Canaan. Upon the slightest pretext, and upon no pretext, he was ready to appeal to the courts, and when beaten upon one point would try another. But he was finally beaten himself, and having wasted all his property, was carried to Haverhill jail for debt, upon the limits of which he and his wife died and were buried by the county.

In 1814, $200 was raised for town charges and fifty cents for highways. Non-residents' lands were released from taxation excepting hundred acre lots. This was done at the instance of the proprietors. Robert Wilson takes the Widow Pattee and her daughter for $50, and the selectmen are requested to provide for James Woodbury and family and the Widow Buntin and her family. Mr. Buntin had owned, at one time, Barber's mill.

In 1815, Lawyer Pettingill is elected representative, town treasurer and moderator. He held these offices for four years in succession. For being treasurer he received the munificent sum of two dollars. Daniel Blaisdell, for being first selectman, the sum of $16.06; Daniel Pattee, second selectman, $9.01; Nathaniel Bartlett, third selectman, $3.52; Moses Dole, town clerk, $2.50.

The militia, having returned from Portsmouth, the town was asked to make up "any addition to their wages," to $12 per month. The town, in a long series of resolutions, in 1812 had patriotically voted to give them a just amount for guarding rich men's property, but they are not of the same opinion now, and refuse to make up anything. The poor are vendued as usual — James Woodbury is bid off by John Currier for nothing per week; Mrs. Woodbury goes to William G. Richardson for thirty-eight cents per week, and Widow Pattee and her daughter to Jacob Jewel, who lived near the Gore, for $67.95. Two hundred and sixty dollars was voted for town charges and the same rate for roads as last year.

In 1816, $150 is raised for town charges, and the same as last year for roads. The Widow Pattee is bid off to Daniel Pattee for seventy dollars, the Davis family are left for the selectmen to care for and Mrs. Wells, James Woodbury, Jr., and his father go to "Biley" Hardy.

In 1817, $300 is raised for town charges, roads the same as

before. The Widow Pattee is bid off to Jonathan Foster for $66.75. Mrs. Woodbury and James for $100 to Joseph Clark. The town is asked to provide a work house for their poor. The paupers have become so numerous that some cheaper way is sought to take care of them, but the town refuses to do otherwise than it has been doing for all the past years. Hiring their poor taken care of by the lowest bidder. The selectmen are requested to provide a pall for the use of the town.

In 1818, $400 is raised for town charges, roads the same as last year. Widow Pattee and her daughter go to David Gould for $66.50; James Woodbury to Mr. Gould for $68, and Mrs. Woodbury to Elisha Miner for $36.

And so closes the second book of town records. The men prominent in these years are: Daniel Blaisdell, Ezekiel Wells, John Currier, Caleb Seabury, Jacob Trussell, Daniel Pattee, Elias Porter, Thomas H. Pettingill, Hubbard Harris, Daniel B. Whittier, Nathaniel Currier, Jacob Dow, George Walworth, Nathaniel Bartlett, Daniel Hovey, John Worth, Jim Woodbury and young Jim.

In the year 1797 we find Clark Currier was licensed "to keep tavern the present year," also in 1812 and 1813. "Lt. Simeon Arvin has our approbation to keep tavern, and sell spirituous liquors by retail." "Capt. Joshua Harris to be a person well qualified to retail spirituous liquors." "Theophilus Currier to keep a public house." "Wm. Parkhurst, of Canaan, living on the Broad Street near the Meeting house, be a person well qualified to sell spiritous liquors." Also, in 1798 and 1799, Simon Smith is licensed to sell liquor on parade day, October 7, 1812, in the street, between Simeon Arvin's and Jacob Dow's. Moses Dole holds a license for a tavern and retailer of rum from 1800 to 1821. Joshua Harris from 1802 to 1809. Simeon Arvin holds a license from 1799 to 1814; Dudley Gilman in 1798–1800; Mary Gilman in 1801 and Dudley in 1802; John Perley in 1799; Oliver Smith, 1798; Hubbard Harris, 1799; John Wilson, 1802–'03; Micaiah Moore from 1803 to 1812; John H. Harris in 1805, 1815–1817; Joshua Harris in 1806; and the last two in 1817–'18; Nathaniel Barber in 1806; Daniel Blaisdell, Jr., on parade day, September 28, 1809, and 1810.

Cardigan Mountain and Canaan

CHAPTER VIII.

TOWN MEETINGS, 1819-1909.

The third book of town records begins with 1819. The Widow Pattee was sold to Warren Wilson for $65, James Woodbury also for $67; Mrs. Woodbury and Lewis Lambkin's children are left to the selectmen to dispose of. Amasa Jones got $14 for taking care of Mrs. Lambkin. The pay received by the selectmen the last year for their services was as follows: Elias Porter, $13.93; John H. Harris, $11.13; Daniel Blaisdell, $13.33; Thomas H. Pettingill received $2 for being treasurer and Daniel Hovey $4.50 as clerk. Four hundred and ninety-nine dollars was voted for town charges and to build and repair bridges. The rate for highways is fifty cents. In 1820, $350 was voted for town charges. Parrot Blaisdell of Orange took James Woodbury for $39, the other poor are left to the selectmen, as well as Prescott Clark's children. The census of the town this year shows 1,198 persons, a gain of 104 since the last.

In 1821, $750 was voted for town charges, roads at the same rate. The poor are left to the selectmen to dispose of: James Woodbury, Widow Pattee, Betsey Colby, — who is to be taken to her husband and relieve the town, — Mrs. Lambkin and her son, Abigail Flint, Prescott Clark and his four children. The selectmen are to procure guideboards.

In 1822, the time for calling the annual meeting passed and recourse was had to Daniel Blaisdell, as justice of the peace, to call it. The selectmen were voted sixty-seven cents a day for taking the inventory and fifty cents in other matters. They voted "to purchase of John Fales a convenient place for a burying ground." This is the first addition to the Street Cemetery. One hundred dollars was voted to fence it and the other grounds. Two hundred dollars was voted "for extra expenses."

The Canaan Musical Society was incorporated this year with a charter from the legislature, dated June 27, 1822. John Currier, Timothy Tilton and Moses Kelley were the incorporators. The society had the privilege of holding $1,000 worth of property. In 1823, $450 was voted for town charges. In 1824, $400 was voted and the same amount in 1825. In 1826, $500 was raised for town charges; in 1827, $600; in 1828, $800. In 1830, population was 1,428, a gain of 230.

In 1836, abolitionism was rampant over the country, both sides did not hesitate to express their opinions of each other and many of them, personal friends and neighbors, became enemies of the bitterest kind. Canaan was not without its sympathizers on both sides and feeling ran high. The opponents of the abolitionists were in power and they did not hesitate to "resolve" at the town meetings, against the other side expressing their contempt of the principles of the abolitionists.

At the annual meeting in 1836, the opponents expressed their spite against Hubbard Harris in the following manner: "Voted that if Hubbard' Harris refuses to present to the committee chosen for the purpose of examining the doings of said Harris while treasurer, the orders and papers in his hands for their inspection, the selectmen are authorized to commence suit." In October of the same year a town meeting was called and Dr. Thomas Flanders, Capt. Joseph Wheat, and James Pattee were appointed a committee to draft resolutions "suited to the condition and state of abolitionism" in the town, which they did in the following way:

Whereas, we the legal voters in the town of Canaan, understanding the abolitionists in the town are about to petition Congress to abolish slavery in the District of Columbia, would take this opportunity to express our opinion, on the subject in open town meeting, notified and warned for the purpose of choosing electors of President and Vice-President of the United States, and would respectfully remonstrate against Congress interfering with the institution of slavery in said District of Columbia, or any of the States of the United States. As we believe it to be unconstitutional and inexpedient, as has been ably and candidly shown by the Committee of the House of Representatives.

Resolved, that we view abolitionism in the present form to be the seed of Toryism, the spirit of the Hartford Convention, the scum of Anti-masonry, and the foe to Democracy, which requires the vigilence of the people to detect its secret plans.

Resolved, that these remarks, remonstrances and resolutions, be signed by the selectmen and town clerk and transmitted to some of our delegation in Congress and also a copy be sent to the N. H. Patriot and States Gazette.

Not satisfied with this they further reported:

That whereas abolitionism has of late attempted to hold incendiary meetings headed by infamous hirelings from abroad, calculated to disturb the Public Peace. Therefore, resolved, that a committee of Vigilence be appointed to consist of 23 persons, that in case any more of such meetings should be appointed, that they use such measures as they in their wisdom should think proper to put a stop to such meetings.

Resolved, that it be recommended to the several school districts not to employ any instructor or instructors to teach any of the schools in said districts (who may be tainted or suspected of taint of this cursed heresy).

The last was omitted from the record.

The following persons were appointed for the committee of vigilence:

March Baber	John Fales jr
Daniel Pattee	Peter Stevens
Daniel Campbell	Ezra Nichols
Nathaniel Shepherd	Wm. Campbell
James Pattee	Daniel Pattee jr
Nathaniel Eaton	Herod Richardson
John Shepherd	Benj. Porter
Elijah Colby	Americus Gates
Amos Miner	Daniel Currier
Henry C. George	Chamberlain Packard jr
Joseph Dustin	Wesley P. Burpee.
John Fales	

In 1837, there is an attempt to get the town to purchase a poor farm. The article is dismissed and it is not until 1839 that the farm is purchased.

In 1840, the town votes not to pay anything for ringing the bell. The census of the town this year was 1,576 persons, a gain of 148.

In 1842, Phineas C. Dunham, who lived in the old tavern, the Grand View House, was to receive "$6 for ringing the meeting house bell for meetings on the Sabbath and for all funerals, and that said sum be paid to said Dunham's wife in monthly installments provided he rings said bell suitably and regularly." He was a little inclined to be irresponsible at times from the effects of too much stimulants.

In 1843, the town voted to accept proposals from any one who would take the poor farm for the ensuing year. Bartlett Hoyt was allowed $6.75 for coffin, grave clothes and digging grave for his father-in-law, Robert Wilson.

In 1844, the disposition of the poor farm is left with the selectmen. The farm had become a burden. They let it to James Tyler and received $130.

In 1844, Hannah Page was a town charge. She had owned a part of the Jenniss farm. The town was asked to sell their interest and distribute the proceeds as they had done with the surplus revenue. This the town refused to do. Stephen Jenniss wanted the farm and the town offered it to him if he would take care of Hannah and take her off the town. He was to have the use of the farm as long as she lived by taking care of her. At her decease he was to have the farm. In 1845, the town was asked to quitclaim to Jenniss the part of this farm taken by the Northern Railroad and it refused. In 1854, the town deeded the farm to Jenniss.

There was some talk of a hearse this year, but the town refused to purchase one. The selectmen wanted more pay per day and asked for seventy-five cents. The town refused it. This year they voted that Sawyer Hill should be known as Prospect Hill. The name never stuck. There seems to be a fad among some people to change old names which mean so much to new ones which have no meaning at all. The new names last long enough to be confusing and then die out, never to be heard of more, like those who invented them. Before Benjamin Sawyer settled there, in the old surveys it was called the "Hill east of Goose Pond." Along about 1800 it was called Prospect Hill. It then became Sawyer Hill.

In 1844, the temperance spirit appeared again in the warrant, that the selectmen should not license any "person to sell spirituous liquors." Examination of the old account books of the traders and tavern-keepers, shows that the greatest number of items in almost any man's account was for rum and molasses. License to sell liquor was granted by the selectmen without any apparent qualifications, except the ability to keep a stock of it on hand. The fee charged was two dollars.

All the traders held licenses and the tavern-keepers. Licenses were also granted to many others for muster day, to sell in the street. The common, the field north of C. P. King's store, and A. W. Hutchinson's field, on the side of the Pinnacle, were used as muster fields. James Wallace was a trader whose store was located a few rods south of the present Wallace house. He sold rum in 1818 and for many years. The store was moved and a part of it is now the barn attached to Doctor Shrigley's house. Nathaniel Currier whose store was at the upper end of the "Street," sold rum. So did Capt. Joseph Wheat, Elder Wheat's son, James Arvin, Simeon Arvin's son, at the lower end of the street; Daniel Porter, John Clough, Seth Daniels, who lived on George W. Davis' farm; James Pratt, Benjamin Blake. On muster day, October 11, 1819, these men could have been seen selling liquor either on the street near "Widow Hannah Arvin's" or at their own stores.

Rum was sold on the street on election day — in fact, any day that any one wanted it. John Worth at East Canaan, Guilford Cobb on the street, Eleazer and Jesse Martin, James B. Wallace and Albert Martin, Currier & Wallace, Perley & Pattee, Charles Hutchinson, Jonathan Barnard, Calvin Pressey, Phineas Eastman, B. P. George, Eleazer Barney and James C. Pattee are those whose names appear from 1818 to 1855.

In 1846, there were eight candidates for representative in the field and after balloting all day they adjourned until the next morning. Jonathan Kittredge's friends stood by him and he was finally elected.

In 1847, the town voted to "prohibit Horses, Neat Cattle, Sheep and Swine from going at large in any Street highway or Common." This vote was reiterated in 1865 by imposing a fine of $2.

In September of this year the Northern Railroad had laid its rails as far as Grafton and in November the trains ran as far as Lebanon. Before that date the village at the station consisted of but a few houses and most of those were on the Turnpike. After this it began to assume the size of a village and for many years was known as East Canaan, and not until it had changed itself into a fire precinct did it leave off the word "East."

At the annual meeting in 1849 the town balloted for three days for town clerk and then voted to pass the article. This entry is found on the record: "After three days hard labor and twenty hard and hotly contested Ballottings, concluded to let the 'Old Coon' remain in his (the) hole, James Burns Wallace therefore remains town clerk until another clerk is chosen."

The town also voted six times for representative and then voted not to send one. James Burns Wallace was a candidate for that office, and they could neither defeat him nor elect him.

In the next year, 1850, "After three unsuccessful ballotings for town clerk, voted to pass the article, and Wallace remains, he thinks the people of Canaan are a spunky lot of fellows." There was no choice for representative this year, the independent vote, represented by Caleb Dustin, serving to defeat both Allen Hayes, the Whig candidate, and W. P. Weeks, the Democratic candidate.

Benjamin P. George was employed this year to take charge of the town house. Mr. George continued in this position as long as he lived. He lived in a house on the site of C. W. Dustin's. Before this he had lived in the Gore, in a house now no longer in existence, but the cellar hole still remains, next above the house J. W. Hoyt built, and on the other side of the road. The census of the town for 1850 shows 1,683 persons, a gain of 107.

In 1851, the town offered $100 reward to discover the person who burned Sam Avery's barns, and William W. George was appointed town agent to discover the person, but without avail. Samuel Avery had three barns burned by an incendiary some time previous to this date. Avery worked away from home most of the time. No one was seen to go there, as the farm was off the traveled road. One barn burned and he hired a man by the name of Dudley to hew out timbers and build a new one. This burned and Avery hired Dudley to build another. This burned; and Avery, becoming tired of rebuilding, traded with Levi Hamlet, in 1852, for the house now occupied by Mrs. Mary A. Robie, which Hamlet had built. Avery thought his wife set fire to the barns, as she did not want to live there. His son, Thomas D. Avery, ran away to sea, was gone several years, came back and bought the John Smith place, northeast of Hart's Pond, sold out and went to London.

In 1853, the old poor farm, having been sold in 1846, the town was asked to purchase another, the experience having been disastrous, and the town refused. John M. Barber and Bartlett Hoyt were appointed agents to purchase the first hearse, harnesses and house for the same, at an expense not to exceed $150.

In 1854, the town voted to accept and print 500 copies of the report of the superintending school committee. This report was the work of Mr. C. C. Webster, who was then teaching in the academy. Dr. Arnold Morgan and John M. Barber were the other members of the board, but they performed little service. This first report of any town officers ever printed is as true today as then — it is the best report ever printed.

In 1855, the town voted to print 400 copies of the auditors' report. This is the first town report printed. In 1856, the town voted to have the school committee's report printed with the selectmen's.

In 1857, the town voted to hire a farm for their poor and also made the same vote in 1860. In 1859, the town voted to choose the state, county and town officers on one ballot. Before this they had been voted for separately. The "Canaan Grenadiers" was formed this year, under state law, and the town accepted them as a volunteer company. The south side of the town house was shingled this year. The census for 1860 shows 1,762 inhabitants, a gain of 79.

In 1861, the Rebellion having begun, the town voted to borrow such sums of money as would be necessary to take care of the indigent families of volunteers. They paid out during the year $800.42. In 1865, the town voted to issue $10,000 in bonds, payable in from three to ten years at six per cent. interest, payable semi-annually.

In 1870, the town voted to apply the railroad tax on the town debt, which at that time was $61,173.39. They also voted to establish a cemetery in the northeast corner of the town near Hiram Jones'. This vote was never carried out, although many people had been buried there. But in 1909, the town procured a deed of the land. The census this year showed the largest population the town ever had, 1,877, a gain of 115 in ten years.

In 1876, the town voted not to establish the East Canaan fire precinct. Thirteen years later, on November 4, the selectmen were petitioned to lay out Canaan fire precinct, which was done on the seventh.

In 1878, the town voted to bond its indebtedness, which at that time amounted to $44,316.18. The interest was to be at four per cent., free from taxation. Ten thousand one hundred dollars' worth of bonds, payable in from one to seven years, at the option of the town, and ten thousand dollars' worth of bonds payable in from seven to fourteen years, were issued by the town. The last of these bonds was paid in 1890.

In 1879, the town voted to notify the Northern Railroad to protect the crossing at Welch's mill. In February, 1877, Enoch Call had been killed at that crossing. It was many years afterwards before there was adequate protection by discontinuing that part of the road which crossed the track and building a new one north of the grist-mill.

In 1880, the town pound was abolished by vote and ordered sold. The census this year showed 1,762 inhabitants, a loss of 105 in ten years. The town also adopted a seal for its weights and measures, which was the figure "2."

In 1884, the town adopted the act relating to blank inventories. The law was carried out for a few years until now the blanks are carried around and very rarely sworn to, and are practically useless for the purpose for which they were designed — to make a man give in all his taxable property to the assessors.

In 1887, the town received its first trust fund for the benefit of cemeteries. Hiram Richardson bequeathed $500, the income of which was to be expended in the care of Sawyer Hill Cemetery. In 1888, the increasing demand for better sidewalks led the town to instruct the selectmen to spend part of the highway money upon them. Chapter 79 of the Public Statutes relating to sidewalks and sewers was accepted, and on September 5 the selectmen laid out certain sidewalks at the depot. The census of the town in 1890 was 1,426 persons showing a loss of 336 in ten years, two less persons in town than sixty years before, in 1830. The library law was adopted in 1892 and the town received $100 worth of books from the state. This was the beginning of the town library. It was kept for some years in Miss Emma A. Bell's house, the librarian, until it became so large that

Town Meetings, 1819-1909.

more room being needed the upper floor of the academy building was fitted up. In 1907, Abram L. Williams bequeathed to the library $500, to be expended in the purchase of useful books, provided the town would raise a like amount for that purpose. The town raised $125 at first, and the next year raised the balance. There are now in the library about 3,000 volumes, besides many unbound books and pamphlets. In 1894, the town received the Jesse Martin fund of $500, the income of which was to be expended upon the care of the Martin and Blodgett lots in the Street Cemetery.

The police court was established by vote of the town in 1895, and Warren B. Richardson was appointed by the governor and council, police justice. He resigned in April, 1907, and James B. Wallace was appointed.

The Hiram M. Cobb bequest was received by the town in 1898 of $300, the income to be expended on the care of the Cobb lot in the Street Cemetery. The William D. Currier mausoleum was accepted as a part of the Street Cemetery in 1900. The population of the town had slightly increased this year to 1,444, from ten years ago. The Pattee fund of ten shares of Northern Railroad stock was received by the town in 1901, one half the income to be expended on West Canaan Cemetery and the other half to be used by the town. In 1902, the Lura G. Milton fund of $500 was received, and the income was to be expended upon the care of the Milton lot in the Street Cemetery. In 1905, the Wells' fund of $200 was received and the income was to be expended upon the care of the Peter S. Wells lot in West Canaan Cemetery. In 1907, the town received two bank books, one of $100, the other of $300, bequests of Abram L. Williams, the income of the first to be expended in cutting the bushes along the roadside about the West Farms Cemetery, the income of the $300 to be expended in the care of the Williams, Longfellow and Knowlton lots in the same cemetery. In 1908, the town accepted $200 from C. H. Hackett, the income to be expended in the care of his lot in the Street Cemetery.

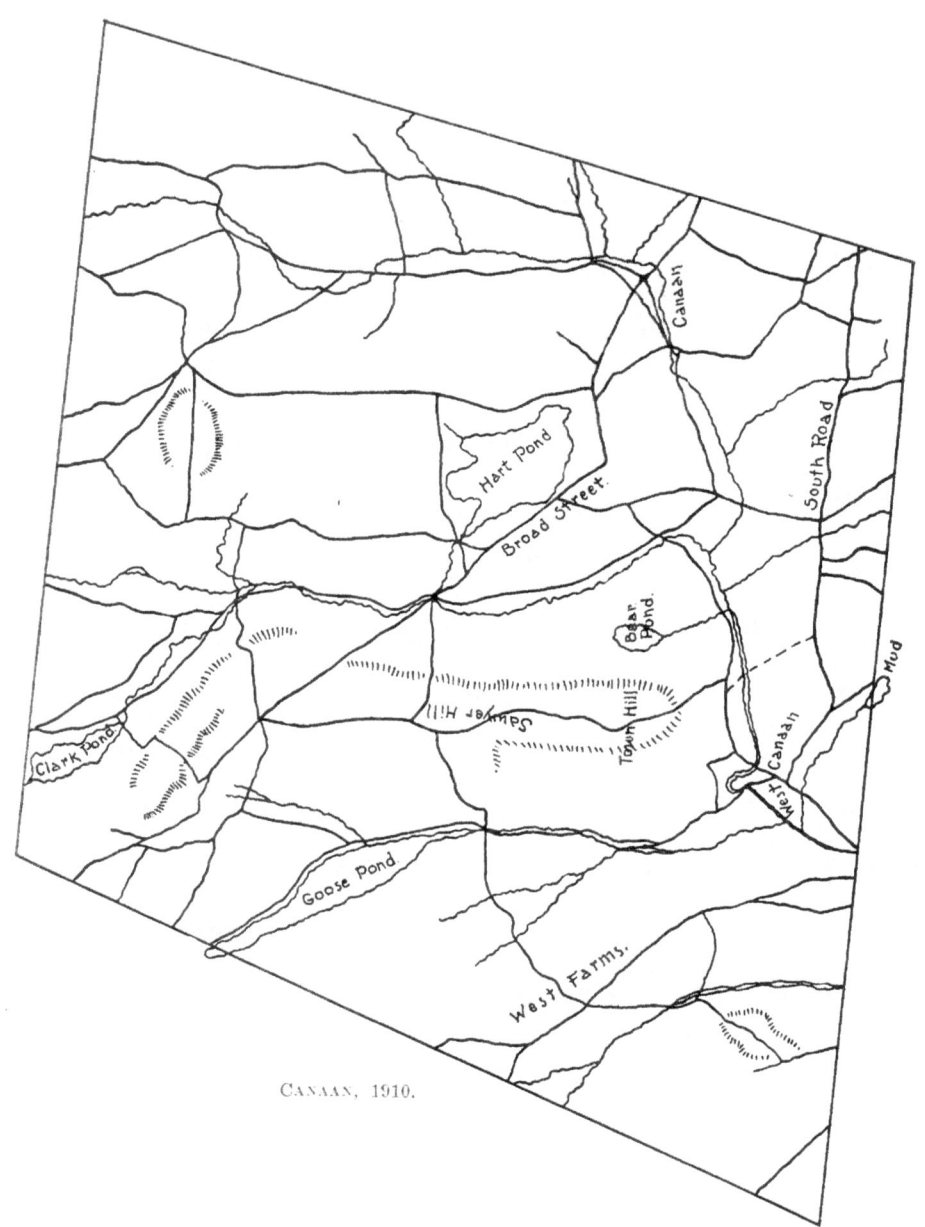

CANAAN, 1910.

CHAPTER IX.

THE PITCH BOOK AND PROPRIETORS' SURVEYS.

The Pitch Book was a book of records kept by the proprietors' clerk, in which were recorded the pitches or claim of any owner of a right to any parcel of land, setting forth to what right the land should be allotted, the quantity, where it was located and bounded generally, the date, and to whom the pitch was made, to be hereafter surveyed. For a number of years this book was the only evidence of ownership, except occupation, which the early settlers had. When the lots or pitches were surveyed by the committees appointed by the proprietors, these surveys were recorded in the Proprietors' Book of Records.

The "Lot laing Committee" attended to the laying of the lots and they were surveyed at the instance of the committee by a surveyor for the person who had first recorded his pitch or claim, or to other persons who were entitled to them by purchase of the rights upon which such lands were laid, or by purchase from those who had bought the rights, or by gift for certain purposes by the proprietors. The old Pitch Book was lost. It no doubt saw hard usage and went to pieces. One piece of it is still in existence, in the handwriting of Ezekiel Wells. The earliest pitch recorded in it bears date May 1, 1795. There is also in existence the Pitch Book of lands in the Fourth Division, in the handwriting of John Currier, proprietors' clerk, consisting of a few leaves of paper sewed together with a string. There are two pitches recorded in the Book of Proprietors' Surveys, one of which is as follows:

Oct 21. 1806. Then Nathaniel Whicher made return of a pitch of 50 acres of the 3rd. 100 of the Glebe lying east and west of the road that leads to Dorchester by Thomas Bedwell's joining west on a tract of land called the Green land.

EZEKIEL WELLS *Proprietors Clerk.*

The charter signed on the ninth day of July, 1761, by Benning Wentworth, divided the land in the town into sixty-eight shares and two plots or parcels. Sixty-two shares were granted to sixty-one men. Five shares were granted as follows: One share for the Incorporated Society for the Propagation of the Gospel in Foreign Parts; one share for the First Settled Minister of the Gospel; one share for the benefit of schools in said town; and one share for a Glebe for the Church of England, as by law established. One parcel of 500 acres, accounted as two shares, Benning Wentworth reserved for himself. One parcel was to be laid out as a town plot, before any other division of lands, as near the center of the town as the land would admit, for town lots, one lot to each grantee of the contents of one acre. One hundred acres was also given to Thomas Miner as encouragement for building a sawmill in 1774.

On July 19, 1768, the proprietors voted to raise one dollar on each right and to give one hundred acres of land with a stream where it shall be adjudged most convenient, to any person who shall appear and build a good corn and sawmill. In 1770, a further tax was raised and the amount of land was increased to three hundred acres, to induce someone to build a mill. The first hundred was to be laid out upon a stream and the remaining two hundred to be laid out in quality in proportion to the other lands in town. The first hundred was laid out at the outlet of Hart Pond and extended to within a few rods of the Mascoma River, in a westerly direction. The second hundred was laid out in two parcels to Joseph Bartlett, on the north side of the "old town line," above the land owned by Josiah Barber. The third hundred was laid out on the hill, on the east side of the road, where lately E. C. Bean lived, and included the farm now owned by J. A. Green. The one hundred acres given Thomas Miner was laid out in two pieces, one of sixty-two acres, adjoining on the north of Joshua Wells' old farm, and extended down the hill towards George W. Hazeltine's. The other parcel of forty-three acres was laid out south of Josiah Clark's old intervale farm and north of Mud Pond at East Canaan. The deed to Miner gave him the right to pitch his land wherever he saw fit. Both parcels were pitched by Nathaniel Barber, who must have purchased the right of Miner.

The proprietors' surveys do not show directly that the proprietors conformed to that article of the charter respecting the laying out of a town plot, as there is no survey of it recorded. But two surveys, one recorded October 8, 1801, on the right of Thomas Miner, began at the "South west corner of the Town Plot," and another on the right of Thomas Parker, which is now known as the "Currier Pasture" began at the "South-east corner." There is also a "draft of a Town Plot," in which the grantees are named and opposite is a number of the lot and range. But there is no key to it to indicate what its meaning may be.

The first meeting in which it was mentioned was in August, 1772, and it was voted "that the Town Plot be laid out in ye most Convenient Place In sd Town." In October, Joshua Wells was placed upon the committee, "In the room of Samuel Benedict," to complete the laying out. Other matters took up the attention of the proprietors, and the town plot did not come up again until 1781, when it was again voted to lay it out. It did not come up again until January, 1797, when Capt. Ezekiel Wells, Daniel Blaisdell, Esq., and Capt. Robert Barber were appointed a committee to look it up and see what situation it was in, report a plan and a location. In 1801 it was again voted to lay out the plot and a committee was appointed to look into "the state of the timber on the Town Plot." This is the first intimation that it had been located. At last, in 1802, the committee reported a plan and the plot, and it was voted "that it be annexed to the proprietors' records next after this meeting." If the plot was pitched as those two surveys would indicate, it was located northwest of Factory Village. Several old deeds refer to it as located in that section and forming a part of the farms of George W. Daniels and Fred Butman.

The draft of all the pitches of the town does not leave any place for it and although several votes were passed by the proprietors in their meetings and committees appointed for the laying out of the same, it was probably never laid out as planned. Many of the charters of other towns contained this provision, and it was inserted, no doubt, so that the settlers might build their houses and form a settlement near each other.

The five hundred acres of the governor's right was located in the southwest corner of the town adjoining the towns of Relhan, now Enfield, on the south, and Hanover on the west. Capt. John

Scofield purchased the five hundred acres of Martha Wentworth, the widow of Benning Wentworth, for two hundred dollars, on February 22, 1797. The proprietors surveyed two hundred acres of this right and laid it to Eleazer Scofield. The remaining three hundred was laid out in a parcel of four hundred acres to Mescheck Blake and was surveyed north of and adjoining the first parcel in 1799. The one hundred acres remaining of the four hundred parcel was laid out to the right of Rufus Randall, and lay north of the governor's land, extending along Hanover line. It was owned by John Scofield, the settler, and in the settlement of his estate it was set off to his son, John. This land was all at one time the property of the Scofields. Afterwards it was occupied by William and Israel Harris, Joseph Follensbee, Mescheck Blake, John May and Joseph Stevens.

Of the sixty-two names entered as grantees, the name of Thomas Gustin occurs twice. Whether this is a mistake, or it was intended to give him two shares, is not known. But the proprietors evidently inferred that he was to have two shares, for they laid out land on his "first" right and also on his "second." The Gustins were friends of the governor, so were Richard Wibard, a councilor and judge of probate; Thomas Westbrook Waldron of Dover, who was a representative at Exeter in 1768 and a councilor in 1773; James Nevins, who was collector of customs at Portsmouth; John Newmarch, Daniel Fowle, the printer, at Portsmouth; Thomas Parker, George and William King, merchants. George King was deputy secretary of state in 1772, and clerk of the supreme court of judicature in 1773 and in the Louisburg expedition of 1745 was an artificer; Daniel Rogers, who was a councilor in 1772 and a doctor by profession; Capt. William Wentworth and his son, Capt. John Wentworth, of Somersworth, a cousin of the governor. They were all from the vicinity of Portsmouth.

The charter granted 23,000 acres, which was "to contain six miles square and no more. Out of which an allowance is to be made for highways, unimprovable lands by Rocks, Ponds, Mountains and Rivers 1049 acres." It was bounded as follows: "Beginning at the S. E. corner of Hanover, thence North 55° East by Hanover six miles to the corner thereof. Then South 61°

East six miles, then South 41° West six miles, then North 58° West seven and one quarter miles."

The charter of Hanover gives the line as running North 45° West. The difference between the town directions would leave a gore of land which was not intended. In 1772, an addition was made to Hanover, 180 rods wide. Hanover at that time claimed this addition included a part of Dame's Gore and all of State's Gore. But the adjustment of the line between the two towns made the line run North 45° West.

The old maps made from surveys by both towns in 1805 run the line North 45° East. The Hanover surveys made the distance six miles to Dame's Gore and 165 rods on the Gore to the northeast corner of Hanover. John Currier, the Canaan surveyor, made the distance 1,897 rods to Dame's Gore. His minutes were: Hanover line, "Began at a stake & stones being the south east corner of Hanover run N 41 E 45 rods to the top of the mountain, then 1457 rods to Goose Pond Brook then 132 rods to Lyme road, then 263 rods to the Beach tree the corner of Canaan."

After the disputes over Dame's and State's Gores had been adjusted and State's Gore annexed to Canaan, the line was continued 182 rods to Lyme on Hanover.

The town, in 1805, raised $186 for the purpose of establishing the line between Canaan and Hanover, and according to the survey of the town, made by John Currier, in 1805, this line was run North 45° East 1,897 rods to Dame's Gore. The map made by Hanover at this time gives the line as running North 45° East six miles, then 165 rods on Dame's Gore.

The other lines have been disputed and do not now run straight. Almost from the first settlement of the town disputes and contentions prevailed with Enfield and Orange in relation to boundaries. By the charter, the boundaries began at the northeast corner of Lebanon and this same point is also the corner bound of Hanover and Enfield. The north line of Enfield was run out, their surveyors ran in upon Canaan nearly a mile, which was the cause of unhappiness to those people who had built themselves homes in the belief that they were living in Canaan. After many discussions and much hard feeling, in 1771, Capt. John Wentworth, George King and John Penhallow were appointed to settle the dispute, "and act everything that should be thought necessary Relative thereto." The matter dragged along for nine years, when in 1780 George Harris, Samuel Jones and John Scofield were appointed to examine all the papers in the case and to make a new survey of the lines, if thought necessary. This commission discovered what they thought to be a clerical error in the charter of Enfield, by writing sixty-eight degrees instead of fifty-eight, as it was in the charter of Canaan. By this error the lines of Enfield intercepted and confounded all the lines of the adjoining towns. It was found, also, that the line as claimed by Enfield left a gore of land, ten degrees wide, between Enfield and Grantham, and which was not claimed by the proprietors of Grantham. By correcting this apparent error, it was insisted that all these conflicting claims would be reconciled and the charters made uniform. A petition was presented to the General Court and in 1781, in a joint meeting of the town and the proprietors, George Harris was appointed their joint agent "to appear before the honorable General Court this March instant at Exeter, then and there to support a Petition, which he preferred at the last session, relative to establishing a proper line between Canaan and Enfield." The General Court appointed Jeremiah Page, Henry Gerrish and William Chamberlain of Boscawen, a committee to survey the disputed lines and boundaries and report thereon on the ninth of July following. They reported that "the Northeasterly corner of Enfield and the Southeasterly corner of Canaan were at the same point of beginning, thence running North 58° West seven miles and sixty rods to a birch stump which is the Northeasterly corner of Lebanon and the Southeasterly corner of Hanover." This report was received and filed away, but was not acted upon. Enfield thereon ceased to claim any of the Canaan lands, and extended its jurisdiction over the unclaimed gore on the north of Grantham, no one disputing her right thereto.

In 1802, twenty years afterwards, this report was called up and adopted by the legislature. This line was accepted by both parties and a year or two afterwards the proprietors asked the town to divide the expense of the surveys and litigation which had been incurred. This the town declined to accede to, on the ground that the proprietors, who were advertising their lands for sale, were bound to give a good title for the money they received. Having paid once for a title, the people did not feel called upon to pay again.

The map of the survey of John Currier, in 1805, made this line run North 58° West, 2,390 rods, but the minutes of his survey were as follows: Enfield line:

Began at the above bound, run S60E 34 rods to the top of the mountain, then 767 rods to Enfield road, then 8 rods to Mascum River then 7 rods across said river, then 180 rods to the road by Widow Sawyers, then 171 rods to Mud Pond, then across the pond 152 rods to an ash tree, then 280 rods to Otis road, then 791 rods to the south east corner of Canaan.

The map of Enfield survey, at this time, gives the same course and distance as the Canaan map, each town assisting the other in running the line. For eighty years no question of its correctness arose until in 1883, Henry H. Wilson, who had been a continuous selectman, after close examination, became convinced that the covered bridge over the Mascoma, called Blackwater or Scofield Bridge, was in Enfield and should be cared for by that town. The interest in that cause was kept up two seasons and several skillful surveyors were employed. At first the bridge was thrown into Enfield, which was a triumph for Wilson and Canaan. The defeated party then put on an additional surveyor and there was a victory for Enfield. Mr. Wilson then put on Prof. Charles H. Pettee, a civil engineer and surveyor, in whose skill and exactness he had the greatest confidence, and decided to abide the result of his labors. The bridge was in Canaan by a few feet. The method pursued was as follows:

By placing a signal on Moose Mountain at a point known to be only a few feet from the line, a trial line having been run with the compass from the western bound to this point. Then a point on Grafton hills beyond the eastern bound and on the prolongation of the town line was found and a signal was erected, this point giving a view of east bound in Grafton west line and Moose Mountain stations. Then the position of Moose Mountain station was corrected by sighting on Grafton station and running a line to west bound. Intermediate stations on Howe and Coggswell Hills were determined from which the position of the various roads was obtained and marked by temporary stakes. The bearing of this line from Grafton station, Coggswell Hill and various intermediate points was N 52¾° W, from Howe Hill it was N 53½° W, showing a slight variation.

And to establish the line so that there should be no further cause for dispute the selectmen of the towns traversed the seven-mile line and placed thirteen stone posts firmly in the ground, one at each highway leading from Canaan to Enfield. The expense of this campaign against the bridge to the towns was about $175. It appears, therefore, that there is a variation of the magnetic meridian of four and one-half to five and one-quarter degrees in about 107 years, in comparing the two surveys of the town line.

The east line of the town is the west line of Orange, and a part of the west line of Grafton. The town of Grafton, according to the record of perambulations, extends on the line of

Canaan 400 rods, the points of compass have varied from North 41° East to North 44° East. John Currier, in 1805, surveyed two lines. One claimed by Grafton and one claimed by Canaan. He ran the line as claimed by Canaan, South 41° West 387 rods from the southwest corner of Orange, which made a straight line with the old charter line between Canaan and Orange. But Grafton claimed a line west of the charter line, which took off a corner of Canaan amounting to about 240 acres. Grafton had a dispute with Enfield over a strip extending along its west side and, as Grafton lay to the east of Canaan, in order to maintain its western boundary as a straight line against Enfield, it was obliged to run into Canaan. John Currier surveyed this disputed line in Canaan to run from the southwest corner of Orange North 65° West 100 rods, thence South 43° West 385 rods, to the disputed corner of Enfield. The contention of Grafton was not recognized. In 1812 the record of perambulation is: "Met Henry Springer of Grafton and perambulated N 41 E about 400 rods to S. W. corner of Orange. According to act passed Feb. 8, 1791."

In 1826, the record was North 40½° East; in 1844, it was North 41° East; in 1868 North 43° East. The line on Orange begins at the northeast corner of Canaan and has been perambulated for years, South 61° West 226 rods to the southwest corner of Cushing's Gore, then South 44° West 1,740 rods to the Grafton line. John Currier's survey was of the "old line" and the "new line." They both ended at the northwest corner of Grafton and southwest corner of Orange.

The minutes of his survey are as follows: Orange line. "Begun at a large rock then run S35W 1600 rods to the south west corner of said Orange, then S39W 92 rods to the first road then 105 rods to the second road then 200 rods to Enfield Corner."

The course of the Orange "old line" was South 41° West 1,612 rods, and of the "new line," South 35° West, 1,595 rods, both starting from Dame's Gore, about 250 rods apart. At this time Orange claimed the westerly line as its west boundary. The Orange map of 1805 gave the line as running South 35° West 1,600 rods, and as part of Orange on the east end of the gore as South 39° West 160 rods from the northeast corner of the gore. The line on the south line of Dame's Gore was run North 65°

Deed of
Proprietors of Canaan }
to } Aug 12, 1807
Proprietors of Orange }

Whereas disputes have arisen and for a long time subsisted about the dividing line . . .

Beginning at a stake and stones near Daniel Blaisdell's field, N. W. Cor. of Grafton, Established by Gerrish etc, 1781, N 35 E 5 m. 20 r to a rock about 3 feet across in present supposed line of Canaan and Dames Gore to be N. E. Cor. Canaan released all lands to Orange East of new line. Daniel Blaisdell, Joseph Flint, Treadway land, Brown lot Morrill lot, Shepard lot, 402.63 whole amt. located.

Blaisdell N line 140 r. from Grafton Corner, from said Corner to new road is 220 r. to S. edge of Pond is 234 r., to S. line of Puffer 396, to Orange road 556

50 r. across Puffer land.

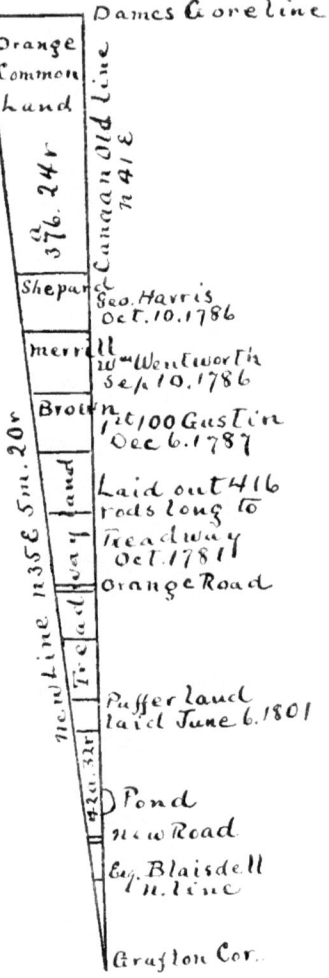

West 240 rods. There being so much dispute over the dividing line, the proprietors' committees of the two towns came together, had the line surveyed, and agreed upon a "new line," in distinction from the old or charter line. The new line agreed upon ran from Grafton corner North 35° East five miles and twenty rods, to the rock corner on Dame's Gore. It ran through all the lots which had been surveyed and bounded on Orange's "old line," leaving part of the land on Canaan side and part on Orange side. Accordingly the proprietors of Canaan, by deed dated August 12, 1807, released to the proprietors of Orange, who had appointed a committee "to pass deeds and settle the title with Canaan," all the land on the east side of this new line, amounting to 778 acres and eighty-seven square rods. The first mention in the records of the proprietors of Orange of this dispute occurs December 12, 1798. At this time the Shepard lot was the most northern lot located southeast of the old farm of Stephen Worth. All north of it was undivided.

One hundred and eight rods of the north line of that lot was released to Orange out of one hundred and sixty. This seemed to have settled the dispute. For over thirty years this "new line" was the accepted boundary. In 1840, the selectmen of Orange sought, by petition dated June 10, 1840, to the "Honorable Senate and House of Representatives," to have "that part of Canaan situated east of the line as Canaan was first surveyed by the proprietors annexed to Orange." Canaan instructed its representative to oppose it "with all his might." The hearing came up in 1841 and leave was given to withdraw the petition, which the selectmen of Orange did. Then the matter slumbered for nine years, until September, 1850, when John Flint of Lyme attempted to survey the disputed line for Canaan. He "began at Grafton Corner and ran thence N $37\frac{3}{4}°$ E nearly 1692 rods to the rock corner, then S 61° E 152 rods to the S. E. corner of Gore, then N 60° E 260 rods to Groton corner, a beech tree." This was the old compromise line. "The bearing and distance of the line Canaan claims as her east line will be N 43° E nearly and nearly 1700 rods to the S. E. corner of the Gore." Dame's Gore projected beyond the "new line" as claimed by Orange, 152 rods. Between the "new line" and the "old line" was a strip of land 152 rods wide at the north end and running to a point at Grafton corner. Orange had claimed this strip as far back as 1803 when the proprietors of Orange brought action of ejectment against Josiah Clark and lost their suit.

Application was made to the court of common pleas to settle and establish the line, which it did on November 13, 1850, having appointed D. C. Churchill, Isaac Ross and N. T. Berry commissioners. The line was established as follows:

Beginning at the northwest corner of Grafton, which is the southwest corner of Orange, thence running North 42¾° East, 1,700 rods to a stake and stones, which we set up and establish as the southeast corner of Dame's Gore, as it was when annexed to Canaan. Thence running North 60° East 254 rods to the southwest corner of Groton, being a beech tree standing on the west side of a brook. No trees were found marked on the east end of the Gore, but we marked them with spots on the sides and three marks acrost the tree with a marking iron.

The expense of this survey was $430.94 to the two towns. The strip disputed became Canaan land. The north line of the town extends on the line of the towns of Dorchester and Lyme. The perambulation of the line between Canaan and Lyme fails to show any distance. But the survey made when State's Gore was annexed to Canaan, began at the northeast corner of Hanover and ran thence South 64° East 277 rods to the "corner of Lime and Dorchester." This survey was made after Dame's Gore was annexed to Canaan. The map of Lyme from the survey of 1805 gives the same distance but the direction was South 64½° East.

The old town line of Canaan was bounded on the north by Dame's Gore, a strip of land which lay between Canaan and Dorchester. In the charter this line ran North 61° West six miles. The north line of all the old pitches have this bearing, but the proprietors pitched and surveyed many lots of land on the other side of the "old town line," which were in Dame's Gore, and the south line of these pitches do not follow that bearing. Some of them run North 64° West and North 65° West. John Currier's survey in 1805 runs on the gore line South 61° East 2,074 rods to Orange new line. Orange claimed its new line ran through the Gore and into Dorchester, a distance of sixty-two rods, taking off 220 rods on Dorchester's south line and Dame's Gore north line. Orange did not establish its claim.

The minutes of Currier's survey were as follows: Dame's Gore line:

Begin at a beach tree being the N. E. Corner of Hanover then run, S61E 310 rods to Clark's Pond then S29W 40 rods then 116 rods to the lower end of sd Pond, the Pond is 12 rods wide at the lower end, the general course of the Pond is N23W about 200 rods, then on the town line 368 rods to Mascum River, S34W is the general course of said river, then 274 rods to Dorchester road then 166 rods to Lary's pond on the west side and 30 rods wide, runs north 60 rods, South 140 rods, the general course is North and South, then 216, rods to Jones's road, then 266 rods to Indian River, then 228 rods to a large rock with stones thereon being on Orange line.

About the time of the annexation of Dame's Gore to Canaan, in 1846, application was made to the Court of General Sessions by the towns of Dorchester and Canaan to settle the line between them. Walter Blair, D. C. Churchill and N. S. Berry were appointed commissioners to settle the line and they established it, and it was confirmed by the court October 31, 1848, as follows:

Beginning at a beech tree marked standing on the southerly side of a small stream, running from a small pond, said tree being shown to as the southwest corner of Groton, running thence North 64 degrees West 250 rods to a small beech, spotted on the side and marked crosswise with a marking iron, thence North 65 degrees West 250 rods to a brown ash, standing between three small spruce trees about six rods west of Indian River, thence North 59 degrees West 950 rods to a stake and stones standing near the south end of a stone wall, thence 60 degrees West 309 rods to the South east corner of Lyme. It being a stake and stones. Monuments were marked with spots on the sides and three marks acrost the tree or stake with a marking iron.

The north line of the town, taking the survey confirmed by the court, extends 2,036 rods. The perambulations of this line have been for many years South 60° East, 1,536 rods to the northwest corner of George W. Hadley's, then South 64° East 524 rods to Groton and Orange corner. John Flint's survey in 1850 shows the old town line to be South 61° East and the gore line evidently from Hadley's South 64½° East 490 rods. In 1845 and 1864 the line was perambulated North 60° West 1,556 from Hadley's.

It will be seen that this town corners with Lebanon, Hanover and Enfield at its southwest corner; with Hanover on the Lyme line at its northwest corner; with Dorchester, Orange and Groton at its northeast corner, and with Enfield on Grafton line at its southeast corner.

The following letter written by Ezekiel Wells and sent to the state department, in explanation of the old map and survey of 1805, soon after the map was made, will serve to explain many things about our boundaries:

Sir, in answer to your letter accompanying the plan of the Town of Canaan which you seem to wish us to correct or explain, we can only make the following observations, (viz) as to the information which you first give us that by the plan of Hanover you find that they run in upon Canaan "about half a mile on one side & nearly a mile on the other" seems to be too indefinite to admit of an explanation; but you add that we have not given you any account of this contested line, and say that you want an actual accurate survey of the true & contested line with all the corses & distances marked on our plan, the line which we have laid down on our plan between Canaan & Hanover is the only line ever run between the two towns by any person, & is the line which has been mutually holden to & perambulated by them ever since the settlement of the Town, and their Charters bore date about forty years ago and the corse marked on our plan is the same corse given by Hanover Charter and the Compass of our surveyor followed the old line without variation to be perceived altho by sd compass in general there is a small variation, and the distances on the plan is agreeable to your Requirement, Horizontally if Hanover Selectmen have given you an account of any line easterly of the one on our plan we are authorized to say that they have done it without ever surveying any such line or even ever seeing the ground on which they say it is run as you may be further informed of by applying to Esq Blaisdel, and we further say that the beach tree marked on our plan as the south west corner of Canaan is the Established bound at which Lebanon Hanover, Enfield and Canaan corners . . . secondly you say that we have laid down on our plan what we call Orange old line but have not given the corse nor distance of it this neglect if it was one we have corrected, you say that we dont agree with Orange in the meeting of our road by more than a mile, & you expect us to be correct, which we have once said that we wore & now without hesitation say it again. You say that by laying down the plans of Canaan Grafton and Orange together you find that Grafton runs in upon Canaan about 100 rods and request us to make it certain whether the station at which you have marked A on our plan is actually the south west corner of Orange and the northwest corner of Grafton, to which we can only say that it ever has been considered as such by the selectmen of the two towns in their taxation; & their jurisdiction has, we believe always bin bounded there since a Committee from the Legislature abought 24 years since established that as Grafton corner altho the selectmen of Grafton say that their Charter & act of incorporation ran in upon Canaan & Enfield (as you have observed & as we have worked out on our plan) and this is all for they peosebly consent to be bounded in their taxation at that station . . . You perticularly wish us to let you know if the south east corner of Canaan & the northeast corner of Enfield are at the same station; to which we reply that they are & as laid down in our plan & as we suppose in the plan of Enfield whose selectmen helpt us to survey the line between us. The old line between Orange and Canaan was the Charter line but the new line is the one permenently agreed upon by the proprietors of both towns & acgnized in by sd Towns. The line between Canaan & Enfield and between Canaan & Dames Gore as also that between Canaan & Hanover are the points of compass mentioned in the several Charters and by compasses in general may vary from one to two degrees as the lines was run abought 40 years since . . .

With due respect permit us to subscribe ourselves your most obedient & very Humble servts.

The governor's plot having been taken out and the charter fixed the location of it the proprietors appointed committees to divide the land among the sixty-seven remaining rights, each grantee owning one share or right in the undivided lands. But few of the proprietors or grantees ever came to Canaan or paid any attention to their claims, and their rights were sold at auction to satisfy taxes and assessments made upon the rights for laying out roads, building bridges and dividing the lands. Taxes were not laid upon the land because it was as yet undivided and without owner.

On January 3, 1771, a meeting was held in Colchester, Conn., at the house of Thomas Wells. Aaron Cady's right was sold for eight pounds, fifteen shilling to Amos Wells; Gibson Harris' right was sold for two pounds to William Caldwell; Jared Spencer's right was sold for one pound, fifteen shillings to Samuel Joslyn. On May 15, 1771, in Lebanon, at the Inn of Cas. Hill, Nathaniel Cady's right was sold to Samuel Benedict for four pounds; William Fox, Jr.'s, right was sold to James Jones for four pounds; Thomas Gates' right was sold to Thomas Miner for four pounds, ten shillings; William Chamberlain's right was sold to Bartholomew Durkee for four pounds, five shillings; William Chamberlain, Jr.'s, right was sold to Benjamin Wheaton for four pounds, five shillings, as was also the right of Jedediah Lathrop, and was resold to Thomas Gates for five pounds.

The proprietors first voted to lay out hundred acre lots in 1768, known as a "First Division of Hundred acre Lots" of upland and a "First Division of Intervale" lots containing ten acres. Subsequently there were two further divisions of hundred-acre lots of upland, then a fourth division of upland into seven- or eight-acre lots, a fifth division into seven-acre lots and a sixth division into six-acre lots. There was also a second division of intervale lots into one acre. The pitches on these divisions were not always exact, sometimes more land was inclosed and sometimes less than was allotted to the division. Along South Road there was no allowance for the most part for roads. The lots being laid out to the "Road." South Road (often called the "Post Road"), in the early days, was laid out by the county court about 1774. It was intended to be nearly a straight road, extending across the south part of the town about two hundred rods from the town line. It was laid upon undivided lands of the grantees, and should the road ever be thrown up or its course changed the land would not become the property of the adjacent owners. A distinction must be drawn between ownership by the town and the grantees, also between the proprietors and the grantees, men who were named in the charter. Very few of the inhabitants of the town were proprietors and still less of them grantees. The town means the inhabitants of the town, the proprietors mean those who owned the original rights — they may not have been grantees, but they became proprietors for the most part by purchase.

The Proprietors' Book of Surveys is the source of title of all lands in Canaan, the beginning of an abstract. To it all titles lead for confirmation, as to points of compass and distances. It is a book of records in which the proprietors' committees confirmed the lands as laid out. Many of the lands had been settled upon before they were surveyed, some were resurveyed, the old survey having been lost, and the date of record is sometimes the date of resurvey. But this record shows that the proprietors confirmed them to those who had settled upon or purchased them. The register's office of this county does not contain any of these old surveys, or pitches, only so far as subsequent owners have followed the old descriptions, which are omitted often enough to make much confusion. No plot or map was ever made of these pitches or surveys by the proprietors, and it is not to be wondered at that they should make some mistakes; and there are some instances where they ran over on to land previously pitched, but it was discovered, sooner or later, and the lines adjusted or further allowances made of land somewhere else.

In beginning the search of a title at the present time, for the purpose of establishing the bounds, deeds are found as far back as 1864, in which the description is only by adjoining owners. In the '50's we begin to find points of compass and distances, only in part, and further search must be made to find all the bearings and distances. It finally leads back to the Proprietors' Book of Surveys, in which nearly every piece of land in town is recorded and described by points of compass and distances. Descriptions of property by adjoining owners is of very little value; points of compass, owing to the variation of the compass needle, which so far has constantly gone west, are not much to be depended upon; but distances do not vary, — they should be as they were a hundred years ago, allowing for the probability of human error.

Once an owner loses his bounds, he must get back to some record that will give him a definite course to follow. The old pitches began at the corner of some other lot, for the most part, and stakes and stones were used for the corner, sometimes trees, and the intervale lots were often bounded by the river. Stakes and stones have disappeared and trees, as well. Sometimes an old stump is left, or there is someone who remembers where the old stump was, — like the stump which was the beginning of the 1st Hundred of the Mill Lot by the dam at the "Corner." The river is still there, but its course is changed in many places. Still there may be instances where an old corner may be located. A survey made to Moses Dole, in 1809, mentions an island in the middle of the river. That island is there today, a little way below the site of the old paper mill. Lots, in the beginning, rarely gave any points of compass on the river, but they gave distances. The intervale lots, laid out in the meadows, sometimes included the river, the land extending on both sides. But, for the most part, the rivers, ponds, and brooks were taken as boundary lines.

The bearings of the lines of the old surveys having been determined many years ago, some of the surveys having been made more than one hundred and thirty years, and the compass needle having traveled westwardly, it becomes necessary to determine how far it has traveled from the bearing run by the old surveyors, before any new line can be run that will coincide with the old line. So far as known there is no way to determine the amount of variation. The line is where it always was, it has not changed; but the needle will not point at the same number of degrees it did when the old surveyor ran it. To say that the needle has traveled so far in any definite number of years is not correct. It cannot be averaged. By setting a compass on a number of old lines this will be apparent. The forty acres of the church right and lying on the north old town line, shows a variation of three and one-half to three-quarters degrees. The south line of the 1st Hundred of the Mill lot between A. M. Shackford and F. B. L. Porter shows a variation of five and one-half degrees. This lot was first surveyed in 1771 and resurveyed in 1806. The south line of A. B. Howe's and the north line of John Currier's, surveyed in 1805, shows a variation of seven degrees. The south line of J. B. Wallace's and the north line of A. M. Shackford's, on the east side of Hart Pond, probably surveyed in 1846, shows a variation of seven and one-half degrees. The latter is abnormal and extraordinary and cannot be accounted for, but taking that variation for the other lines the land surveys correctly. Broad Street, was first surveyed in 1788, North 11° West, and resurveyed by the Grafton Turnpike Company in 1804, and again in 1828 by the town which relaid the road over it, North 12° West, it now runs North 8½° West. The common, surveyed in 1793, shows a variation of three degree and one half. The only way is to determine the variation of the compass upon each piece of land sought to be surveyed. This can be found by running a line between two established and well-known corners, taking some old wall, known for a long time to have been on the line. The old bearing having been found by reference to old deeds, the present bearing having been found, the difference between the two bearings can be used as the variation to run the remaining lines. But if two bounds are not known, nor any walls or fences, reference must be had to the adjoining land and the survey becomes more complicated.

There are a few surveys of old pitches missing from the old book of surveys. The first one hundred acres of Israel Kellogg, located about the shore of Hart Pond, south of the road by R. H. Haffenreffer's, the third one hundred acres of the mill right, where Jonathan Carlton lived, and where E. C. Bean lately lived; the second one hundred acres of Clement Daniels' right, extending along the road by where F. P. Carter lives, and on the north side of the road from the Tontine settled by John Colcord, and upon which Daniel B. Whittier, the carpenter, lived in 1831; fifty acres of the third one hundred acres of the school right and fifty acres of the third one hundred acres of Josiah Gates, Jr., lying side by side on the north side of the old town line, being a part of the old Danforth and Tristram Sanborn farms.

The divisions of land were not laid out in one parcel, as the allotments would seem to indicate, as well as the votes of the proprietors, nor were they adjoining. The first hundred of Samuel Dodge, 3d, was laid out in five parcels of three, fifty, fourteen, thirty-three, and nine acres, and many others in like manner. Nor was land in each division laid to all the rights. Neither of the George and William King rights received any land in the fourth, fifth and sixth divisions of upland, or the second division of intervale. Some of the pitches refer to the lots being laid out in ranges, but there is nothing to indicate the lines of the ranges or how many or how they extended. The only references are to land in the "2nd. Range." No reference to any in the first. The implication drawn from the references is that the lands in the first range extended along South Road to the Enfield line, across the south line of the town. These lots are laid out systematically, about 200 rods by 80 rods on the road, and those on the north side of South Road are laid in like manner. But the land referred to as being in the second range lies north of these surveys and towards the west side of the town, above West Canaan and extending to Hanover line. The land supposed to be laid out in the second range are not all adjoining. In 1797, the proprietors voted "that Ezekiel Wells shall have the liberty of laying out a second hundred acre lot instead of a lot the Governors lot has took which was No. 1 in the 2nd. Range the lot belonged to sd Wells." This "No. 1" must have been towards the southwest corner of the town. Some of the lots bear numbers. "No. 1" was the "First Penhallow" lot, which, with the second and third "Penhallow" lots, after they were laid out on the three divisions of Richard Wibard's right, remained unoccupied or non-resident land for many years, being sold for taxes many times. These lots are what is known as the "Penhallow Pasture." "No. 2" laid on the right of Daniel Fowle. Ezekiel Wells lived here before he moved to the Street. "No. 3" is south of and adjoining "No. 2," all on Town Hill. "No. 8" was the first one hundred of Ephraim Wells, pitched to Samuel Converse and owned by James Treadway, who, when he had the Pitch Book, pitched six hundred other acres of land to himself, and which the proprietors afterwards nullified, to the extent of four hundred acres. This lot was the farm which Jonathan Dustin bought of James Treadway, but there is some conflict between the pitch as surveyed and the deed to Jonathan Dustin. The latter calls for fifty acres only of that right. There are numerous mentions of numbered stakes: "No. 2 in the 2nd. Range," "No. 4 in the 2nd. Range," located in the west side of the town. Nos. 16, 17, 18, 20, 21, 25, 27, 29, 33, are the starting points of lots extending northerly of Town Hill and northeasterly and east of Goose Pond. They are not regularly placed and seem to have no connection with any definite system of arrangement of lots. In attempting to make a plot of these old surveys, there are many discrepancies. Lines were run at different dates, the compass changed, old roads have been thrown up, and the names of the owners of lots have changed many times. The surveyor who ran the lines failed to find the bounds of an adjoining piece from whence he wanted to start. The towns of Dorchester and Hanover laid their land in lots, symmetrically arranged and numbered in order. Canaan laid its lots without order or arrangement, and of many different shapes. This arose from letting the settlers who were on the land have whatever they pleased, and in some cases instead of laying out the land to a certain right the right was laid out to the land. In 1768, the proprietors "voted that their committee lay out to those proprietors already settled, ten acres of meadow and one hundred acres of upland, where they have already made their pitch, to be allowed towards their right or share in the township." "And they shall lay the same amount to any who should appear and make speedy settlement." In 1770, agreeable to the encouragement from the proprietors, a number of settlers appeared and made sundry pitches, and as these were to contain ten acres of intervale to each right, some thinking themselves injured in not having their proper quantity, a committee was appointed to adjust the injury, by making up to each "that may be deficient, his proportion of intervale until his ten acres is completed, and to be adjoining what he now improves or as near as may be and not to interfere with other pitches." It was also voted that each settler "already on his hundred acres of upland should have the first choice of his lot before any other proprietor." The remainder of the intervale, if any, was to be divided among the whole of the rights equally. There are three instances where a pitch was made and the right to which it belonged was forgotten. Thomas Miner's intervale and Micah Porter's, situated on the Mascoma River. There was also a hundred-acre survey in the southeast part of the town, laid to Francis Whittier, upon a right the name of which does not appear. This is an extra hundred, as all the rights have their full share of hundred-acre lots.

In the first vote to divide the town land there was no condition attached. In 1770, the time for making pitches of upland and intervale was extended to the fifteenth of November, and to entitle any proprietors making such pitch to the property thereof as his estate, to be held by him or his heirs, he must cut and girdle one acre of trees on the hundred acres of upland and one acre on his intervale in good husbandlike manner, by the fifteenth of November. And in case any proprietor should make his pitch of one hundred acres of upland and ten acres of intervale at any time before the committee appointed shall lay out and lot the same, such proprietor shall be entitled to his pitch so made, and the committee are hereby empowered to confirm the same by ordering a record thereof to be made by the proprietors' clerk, also the fulfilling the conditions which entitles any proprietor to his pitch to be adjudged by the committee to lot said hundred acres and report to be made accordingly under their hands to the clerk to be recorded. The time was extended to November 1, 1771, but for the future each proprietor making his pitch must girdle two acres of his first hundred acres of upland, and at the next meeting the proprietors voted that two acres of intervale should be girdled. In June, 1773, the proprietors voted that each proprietor should have the right to make a pitch for his second hundred-acre lot of upland.

Asa Kilburn was appointed a committee to enter the pitches, on the day and time of day the pitch was made. The proprietor must attest that he has, after the time of pitching, cut bushes and girdled trees, and also set the first two letters of his name on a tree on said lot, and make his return to the clerk, and the first one doing this shall have the lot. The time for pitching second hundreds commenced in September and continued for nine months.

In 1781, it was voted that those who neglect to have their second hundred-acre lots properly laid out shall lose their chance of holding by pitching and have their lots flung into a "draught." The proprietors began to pitch their third hundred-acre lots on May 7, 1782, and "each proprietor shall pay the cost of laying out his own lot." But before making their pitches in the third division, each person must show to the committee his right for pitching by deed or power of attorney or letter from the proper owners.

More stringent conditions were imposed upon some of the proprietors in pitching. Thomas Miner must show a good and authentic deed from one of the original grantees and fell or cut twenty acres of land in ten months. This was really a rebuke to Mr. Miner, who had pitched upon a lot without asking permission of the proprietors. William Record, Leonard Horr and Elijah Lathrop must produce good deeds, build houses and proceed to cultivate the land. Silas Miller must clear and cultivate four acres of land; Isaiah Booth must clear, cultivate and build a house; Jacob Hovey must cultivate and manure his land The seven latter men were squatters. Capt. Charles Walworth can have a hundred acres if he will lay out another hundred-acre lot in square form, pay the proprietors seven pounds and leave a three-rod road through his land. Caleb Clark can have a hundred acres if he pay the proprietors five pounds. William and Caleb Douglass can have hundred-acre lots in the third division, provided they make speedy settlement and build a house.

The surveying and recording of the hundreds and intervales dragged along until August, 1805. The proprietors voted that as many persons who had made pitches had not complied with the former vote "in regard to getting their lands so pitched laid out and recorded," and it being "impossible to ascertain what quantity of undivided land there yet remain," "therefore voted that any lands, upland or intervale, which have been pitched and improved or pitched only, and have not been laid out by the proprietors Committee and recorded and shall continue in that situation until the first day of November next shall be liable to be pitched and laid out by any other person having lands to pitch, notwithstanding any former pitches or possessor which the law doth recognize as a good title." There was still undivided land and it was impossible to find it, for many claimed land over the hundreds they were entitled to and there was no way of telling how much unless all the land should be surveyed. The proprietors' committee proposed to do this. In 1808, another committee was appointed to ascertain the amount of undivided land.

The time for recording was again and again extended until Nov. 13, 1809, at six o'clock, "after which time no former pitches shall avail the holder." It was not until July, 1812, that the proprietors were able to make their fourth division of upland of seven acres. The pitching was to begin at six o'clock in the morning, "by cutting or girdling trees and by Marking the first two letters of the owners name on a tree, and the one making his return first to the Proprietors Clerk shall be intitled to said land until the first day of October by that time to be surveyed or to forfeit his pitch."

On the tenth of March, 1814, it was voted to lay out the second division of intervale of one acre. The manner of pitching was the same as before, but each person must have his land surveyed by a certain time. In June, 1816, the fifth division of upland was voted to be pitched of seven acres. In June, 1823, it was voted to lay out six acres of upland as a sixth division to each proprietors' right. This was the last division of lands.

An examination was made of the records and the surveys corrected and computed by Daniel Blaisdell, and many small strips and gores, marshy and swamp land, were found not yet divided. John M. Barber, in 1823, was the owner of four rights, and asked that a strip be set off to him to satisfy those rights. It was done. Barber deeded the rights to the proprietors and they were cancelled, as having received their full share of lands in Canaan. Daniel Blaisdell asked that land might be set off to him. This was done and twenty-two rights were cancelled, and afterwards four more rights were cancelled in the same manner.

In 1824, Moses Lawrence deeded five rights to the proprietors for thirty-five acres of land and these rights were cancelled.

At the time of his death, Daniel Blaisdell was the owner of all the rights uncancelled, excepting the rights of Richard Wibard, George and William King, Daniel Rogers and William Wentworth, which meant that he owned nearly all the undivided land in town. In 1845, Elijah Blaisdell and Joseph Dustin, son and son-in-law of Daniel Blaisdell, called a meeting of the proprietors and appointed themselves a committee to dispose of all the remaining land and to account to the proprietors for their equal share in the proceeds. This was the last meeting of the proprietors. Many deeds are found recorded from these two men, nearly all of them small parcels and of irregular shape.

There are still many farms in town that have remained in the possession of the descendants of the first owner, in the same form. The farm of John Currier, upon which his grandfather, John Currier, settled, is the first hundred acres of George Lamphere. The farm of Warren E. Wilson, and the farm now owned by Mrs. Colburn, were settled by her grandfather, William Harris.

What was known as the "Barber Farm," was the first hundred of Isaiah Rathburn and was laid to John M. Barber. It extended from the Mascoma River to the line of his father, Robert Barber's farm on the east. The latter's farm extended from the shores of Hart Pond to Indian River, beginning near the corner of L. B. Hutchinson's and O. H. Perry's land, extending down the shore of the Pond to the Wells line, then southerly, including the Pinnacle, to the river, where Barber's mill was located, then around on the Cochran farm, where Ezra Nichols settled, to the corner of the fifty acres of Allen Whitman's, then in a straight line to the pond, three hundred acres.

The fifty acres of the first hundred of Allen Whitman extended from the shore of the pond to the Dustin farm and from what is now the north line of O. H. Perry's, on the west side of Broad Street (the line on the east side was changed) to the north line of R. H. Haffenreffer. North of Whitman's was the first hundred of Phineas Sabine, extending to the south line of F. B. L. Porter's land. Then came fifty acres of Samuel Dodge, 3d, to the North Church, then the first hundred of the Mill Right.

Joshua Wells' farm lay on the east side of Hart Pond to Richard Whittier's land, extending towards the east, five hundred acres. The proprietors' surveys also give us the clew to where the old settlers lived, as the surveys are described by bounds on adjoining owners and occupants. A map of the old pitches has been made, so far as possible.

The difficulty to be overcome is to join the lots lying along the banks of the rivers. Both the Mascoma and Indian, because of their extremely irregular and winding courses, made it very difficult to measure their banks, and in many instances the distance must have been averaged, for lots on one side of the river do not have corresponding lengths on the other. The farm of Simon Blanchard, upon which John Scofield, Jr., lived, lying northerly of South Road, and at the westerly end, and extending around the vicinity of West Canaan, consisted of 340 acres, bounded by the river on the north and Mud Pond Brook on the south. It is not possible to close the plot by allowing the distances on brook and river. It may be interesting to know who owned the rights of the grantees during all those years, while the land was being divided, when some of the proprietors, failing to pay their taxes, their rights were sold at auction for non-payment. There was so much land it would seem that no one would be anxious to have more than he could use, but such was not the case. There was as much desire to be a large landowner as today. There was little change in the ownership of the rights from the original grantees, for the first few years. In 1780, Ezekiel Wells owned four rights, Eleazer Scofield two, Capt. Robert Barber one and one half, John Scofield, Jr., one, George Harris nine, Charles Walworth six, Samuel Jones one, John Scofield two, Caleb Clark nine, Jehu Jones one, Thomas Miner four and one half, besides several hundred-acre lots amounting to 2,500 acres; Joshua Wells two rights, James Treadway and Jonathan Dustin fifteen. In 1786, Joshua Harris owned one right, Ezekiel Wells five, John Harris one. In 1823, Daniel Blaisdell was the owner of forty-five rights, John M. Barber of four, William Richardson two, and Moses Lawrence five. In accordance with an act of the legislature, passed December 30, 1803, to cause the several towns to make surveys, in order to make a map of the state, the town at their next annual meeting dismissed the article approving of such survey, but at a meeting in March, 1805, they voted to put the making of the survey up at auction, and reconsidered their previous vote. John Currier made the survey, and this old map on file in the office of the secretary of state is a very interesting relic. The "plan is a present actual survey by careful admeasurement horizontally." The principal roads are given, not all of them. The road to Eames' mill is left out. This does not, of course, include the gores, subsequently annexed to the town.

The first recorded survey in the Proprietors' Book bears the date August, 1773, and the last July 6, 1837. After that date the deeds of the proprietors' committees were recorded in the county clerk's office. Most of the land in town was surveyed and allotted before 1806. Daniel Blaisdell, John Currier, Ezekiel Wells and Moses Dole made most of the surveys. The "Lot laying Committee" between those dates embraces the names of Ezekiel Wells, John Currier, Joshua Wells, Joshua Harris, Samuel Jones, John Scofield, John Scofield, Jr., David Blaisdell, Robert Barber, Charles Walworth, William Richardson, Nathaniel Bartlett, Caleb Clark. The leading men among the proprietors were Daniel Blaisdell, John Currier and Ezekiel Wells. The land surveyed and set off, so far as it is possible to determine, amounted to 22,254 acres. Of this 417 acres was made in allowances for roads. The allowance for roads to each hundred acres ranged from three to nearly thirteen acres. The largest allowance was to the first hundred of Isaiah Rathburn, the "Barber Farm." Surveyors, in settling boundary lines and partitioning land, have not taken these allowances into account.

The Proprietors' Book of Records is still in existence, badly dilapidated, every leaf separated from the binding and yellow with age and use. Its leaves had to be ironed to bring out the ink, which from much handling had become very dim. It was bound in sheepskin, with two leather straps, one at each end, to tie it together. The records of the proprietors are mixed in with the surveys; nor are the surveys in order. Spaces were left by different clerks and these spaces were filled up by subsequent ones. Deeds from the owners of the original grantee rights to the propriety are inserted at different places.

After all the divisions of upland and intervale had been laid out on the rights, for certain considerations, the owners of them conveyed them back to the propriety. In some instances, the conveyance was made to the selectmen. So that now, should there be found any undivided land left in town, the town might be the owner of a part of it by reason of being the owner of some of the rights.

CHAPTER X.

Public Rights.

The charter of the town provided that one share should be given to the "First Settled Minister in said Town." In 1773 the proprietors of the town voted to lay out the school and minister's lot. In 1781 they voted "a one hundred acre lot in the first division and a one hundred acre lot in the second division and one ten acre lot of Intervale" to three public rights, the Church of England right, the first settled minister's right and the school right. Samuel Jones, John Scofield, Caleb Clark and Ezekiel Wells were appointed a committee to "pitch and lay them out." In 1782 this committee were requested to lay out the third hundred-acre lots to the same "Publick Rights." In 1797 the "laying out" had not been completed, and it was voted "to compleat laying all the Publick Rites mentioned in the charter." The first settled minister's share was set off and assigned to Rev. Thomas Baldwin in 1783, the year he was ordained an evangelist and placed in charge of the newly organized Baptist Church. In 1790, when Mr. Baldwin dissolved his connection with the church and people of Canaan, a town meeting was called to make a final settlement with him and the following vote was passed:

Voted that we do hereby ratify and confirm a vote passed in the year 1783 (which vote is now lost) regarding the settlement of Elder Thomas Baldwin, in which vote the town voted to approve and confirm what the church had done in calling Eldr Baldwin to be ordained as an Evangelist, and to exercise pastoral care over the Church and Congregation so long as he should judge it duty to continue here, by which he was considered as the minister of said town, though not confined for any certain time.

At the same meeting Elder Baldwin, as testimony of his kindly regard for the people with whom he had lived and labored for twenty years and from whom he was about to separate, tendered to the town a deed of one half of his land, which was accepted in the language following:

Corner and North End of Street from Currier Hill

Voted to accept a deed of Eldr Baldwin of the right of land allowed or granted by Charter to the first Ordained Minister, excepting the first and half of the third hundred acres which is considered as one half of sd right.

Elder Baldwin had sold the hundred acres of the first division on November 1, 1783, to Samuel Noyes for 58 pounds, 10 shillings, soon after he became the owner of the right. According to the Proprietors' Records, this land was surveyed to Samuel Noyes November 5, 1805, and he lived on it. It was located in the southwest corner of the town, adjoining Grafton and Enfield. Half of the third hundred he had sold to Daniel Blaisdell and was included in a survey of 288 acres laid out October 26, 1805, and lay along the northwesterly corner of the first hundred and was a part of Blaisdell's old farm. This half interest was offered by the town to Rev. Aaron Cleveland to induce him to settle here in 1799, but he did not accept. Mr. Baldwin did not at this time give the town a deed because the town owed him for preaching. The excuse for not paying the claim was the hard lot of the people and the scarcity of money, cattle, calves, wheat and other grains, which formed the circulating medium. The claim ran along until 1800, when it was voted "to make a settlement with Elder Baldwin agreeable to his request." John Currier, Richard Whittier and Ezekiel Wells were appointed a committee to settle. Mr. Baldwin came up from Boston, met the committee and conveyed to the town by deed dated October 1, 1800, all his interest in the minister's right, excepting the first hundred and half of the third hundred acres, they agreeing to pay his claim and account, which had been unsettled for nearly eleven years. The remainder of the minister's right was then parceled out and sold.

Fifty acres of the second division was surveyed to John Worth, Jr., July 6, 1807, and is where the present village of East Canaan is. Forty-five acres of the same division were laid out to Ezekiel Wells October 8, 1807, and began at a "stake on the east side of the highway leading from Canaan to Grafton, about two rods south of the bridge over the Indian River, thence about 200 rods by the road to Orange line, then on the Orange line N 34 E 14 rods to a small pond, then by the waters of the pond and the brook that runs out of it 131 rods"; then in a very devious course "to the first bound." This is the land through which the railroad now runs on the west side of Mud Pond. Twelve and three-quarters acres in the third division was laid out to Nathaniel Barber on February 10, 1809. It extends from the Turnpike bridge, near C. O. Barney's, up the river, and is the meadow land north of his house. It was a part of Dea. Josiah Clark's farm. Five acres of the third division was laid out to Ezekiel Wells, "near where Captain Arvin lives," now owned by George W. Davis, adjoining the old Howard farm. Fifteen acres of the third division was laid out to Daniel Blaisdell November 13, 1808, on the east side of Goose Pond and adjoining on the easterly line of school lands. Seven acres of the third division were laid out to Simeon Arvin October 11, 1810, near Barber's sawmill. Seven acres of the fourth division were laid out to Israel Harris June 14, 1814, on West Farms, near Hanover line.

One acre of the second division of intervale was laid out to Charles Church of Lebanon May 27, 1814, and thirteen acres of the third division were laid out June 3d to the same. Seven acres of the fifth division were laid out to Moses Dole September 16, 1816, on the Mascoma River, below the paper mill site. Ten acres of intervale of the first division were laid out to Nathaniel Barber October 16, 1801. This was sold by Barber to Josiah Clark and is a part of Carey Smith's farm. Two and one-fourth acres of the third division were laid out to Nathaniel Barber May 15, 1817. This piece is between C. O. Barney's house and the river, extending down "Orange Pond Brook." One hundred and seventy-five acres of this land was the property of the town and was sold by them, there being 325 acres laid out to the right altogether. This right, as well as the school right, became the property of Daniel Blaisdell. Neither right received any land in the sixth division of upland because Blaisdell deeded them back to the proprietors and they were cancelled before the sixth division was laid out.

The charter granted "One Share for the Benefit of Schools in said town." And it will appear that our school never received the benefit of a dollar from the sale of the 325 acres laid to that right. The land was distributed as follows: The first hundred acres of upland was laid out November 28, 1782, "on a hill east of upper Goose pond, beginning at a stake, marked No. 33, thence

S 15 W 100 rods to a stake, thence S 75 E 163 rods to a beech tree marked, thence N 15 E 100 rods to a spruce tree marked, thence N 75 W 163 rods to the first bound with an allowance of three acres for roads." This lot remained unoccupied for several years. In 1796 the town voted "to sell the improvement of the School Lot (on Sawyer Hill) for three years to the highest bidder." "The Above said improvement struck off to Dudley Gilman for seventeen dollars for three years, said sum to be Paid in Clearing and Fencing on said Lot." Mr. Gilman did but little and at the expiration of his lease in 1799 it was voted "to sell the income of the School Lot for four years to the Highest bidder and rent to be laid out on sd lot in Clearing and Fencing yearly." "Struck off to Mathew Greeley for fourteen dollars and five cents yearly." Mr. Greeley made a good trade, cleared the great pines and spruces off to his mill, pastured the open field and with stones and brush built a fence.

Mr. Greeley's lease having expired in 1803, the lot was again put up and bid off to Jacob Tucker for $20 a year for three years, "to be paid in building a stone wall in front, acceptable to the selectmen." Mr. Tucker made good use of the land in a way profitable to himself. Before his lease expired Warren Wilson, whose lands adjoined, asked the selectmen to sell him a part of the lot. The town voted in 1805 "that the selectmen may sell a piece of land off the school lot to Warren Wilson." But he did not get the land at this time. In 1806 the town voted "to leave the school lots for the selectmen to dispose of." And now comes in another factor which caused great discussion and contention in the town for many years.

On June 21, 1804, the Grafton Turnpike Company was incorporated, with thirteen incorporators, residents of the towns of Lyme, Orford, Canaan, Grafton, Orange and Dorchester. Three of the incorporators were from Canaan: Daniel Blaisdell, Ezekiel Wells and Moses Dole. They were given the power to make bylaws, build a toll road with gates and establish the following rates of toll: For ten sheep or swine, one cent; for ten cattle or horses, one cent; for one horse and rider, one cent; for a sulky, chair, chaise with one horse and two wheels, two cents; for a chariot, coach, stage, wagon, phaeton, with two horses, four cents;

for the same with four horses, five cents; pleasure parties in proportion to their size; a cart or carriage of burden, one and a half cents; and when drawn by two beasts, two cents. Daniel Blaisdell was the treasurer; the other officers were from other towns. There were two toll gates in town. The first gate was erected at Worth's Tavern, which Dr. E. M. Tucker tore down and erected a more pretentious mansion. The facility for evading toll was more than the company could bear, so the gate was moved down near the house of Elijah Whittier, nearer the Orange line. The second gate was at Gates's Tavern, near Hanover line; George C. Bradbury's. The Turnpike approached Canaan across a corner of Orange and took possession of the old highway, "beginning at the center of two stakes, standing in the westerly line of Orange, near Orange Pond," surveyed in 1789 by Ezekiel Wells, and covered nearly the same ground as it traversed the town to the northeast corner of Hanover. The Turnpike was freely advertised as a bonanza, which, with its toll gates and bridges, was to fill the empty pockets of its proprietors. In 1806–'07 its books were still open and subscriptions solicited. Many people had great faith in its future profits and took shares of its stock. On the fourth day of July, 1807, a meeting was held at the inn of Moses Dole and action was taken as to how the Turnpike should be constructed. Contracts for construction were let to Thaddeus Lathrop, and John Currier agreed to build one hundred and thirty rods for two hundred dollars, the payment to be made upon his shares. The Pike was to be thirty feet, excepting causeways, which were to be twenty-four feet wide. It was first to be cleared two rods from the center each way of stones, trees and stumps. The road should be two feet higher in the center than the sides.

Dr. Caleb Pierce in the Pinnacle House subscribed for fifty shares, but it does not appear that he paid for them or was even a stockholder, but to please the doctor the company changed the route of the Pike from the north side of his house next the pond, laying a new road from near the Bickford road to the corner at A. W. Hutchinson's. Daniel Blaisdell subscribed for fifty shares, but took only six. Micaiah Moore owned eighteen shares, Moses Dole six, Nathaniel Barber four and one half, Robert Barber two, Jacob Dow three, Reynold Gates two, Simeon Arvin eight and one half, Clark Currier three, Joseph Bartlett two, John Bean three, Phineas Eastman one and one half, Joseph Wheat two, Richard Clark, Jr., eight, Josiah Clark two, Thaddeus Lathrop three, Jacob Trussell two and one half, Thaddeus Lathrop, Jr., two, John Currier two, Thomas H. Pettingill one half, Amasa Howard one half, John Fales two, John M. Barber, Caleb Seabury, Jonathan Carlton, Amasa Clark, Abel Hadley, Samuel Noyes, John Worth, Jr., Joseph Wheat, Jr., Wales Dole, John Currier, William G. Richardson, Mathew Greeley, Benjamin C. Sawyer, Moses Shepard, John Hoyt, Moses Lawrence, Ezekiel Wells, Daniel Carlton, Samuel T. Gates and William Richardson one share each. One hundred and seventeen shares were owned in Canaan of the three hundred issued. The stock was to be paid for in assessments, as the money was needed in the construction of the road. The par value was one hundred dollars, ten dollars of which was paid by the subscriber upon his agreeing to pay all future assessments and on receiving his stock. In 1807 the public confidence in the success of the Pike was undiminished, and the subject got into town meeting. The disposition of the school lots was again in the warrant and the people voted "to sell the School lots and lay out the money in a turnpike road." Later, at an adjourned meeting, Jacob Trussell moved to reconsider the late vote and proposed to sell all the public rights, school, minister's, glebe and propagation of the gospel, and invest the money in some safe fund, the income of which should be appropriated to the use of schools and the support of the gospel forever. But the "pike" had possession of the meeting and Mr. Trussell's proposition was voted down. They then voted "To sell all the public rights unsold." "To purchase shares in the Grafton Turnpike road to the amount of the sums for which the Public rights may be sold for." "That the selectmen be agents to take care of the sale of the Public Rights, and see to the laying out of the property arising from the same." "To sell all the remaining part of the Ministers and School Rights." "That the selectmen give notice of the sale of the Public Rights at publick vandue by giving six weeks notice, by an advertisement in the Dartmouth Gazette, and take notes for one half for one year, the other half in two years with interest." And "to purchase as many shares as the lands can be sold for

Hundreds of Dollars." "That the sale be the Monday preceding the sitting of the Supreme Court at Plymouth."

The "Public Vandue" was held on the 30th of June, 1807, by the selectmen, John Currier, Hubbard Harris and Amos Gould, who, for the consideration of $503, conveyed the first hundred acres of the school right to Nathaniel Barber. On the same day Barber quitclaimed the same to Warren Wilson "for a valuable consideration." Wilson lived on the present Loverin farm. Soon after he sold sixty-three acres to William Richardson. The land is now owned in part by Eugene A. Shepard and John D. Loverin. The second hundred acres was laid out December 12, 1784, and surveyed as follows:

Beginning at a stake standing in the south line of the town, thence S 58 E 84 rods to a stake marked No. 3, thence N 32 E 200 rod to a stake and stones, thence N 58 W 84 rods to a stake and stones standing by a brook, thence S 32 W 200 rods to the first bound. With an allowance of five acres for roads.

The brook referred to is Beaver Brook. This had remained wild and unoccupied up to the time of the "Vandue," when the selectmen conveyed it to Richard Otis for the sum of $290. This land lies about one hundred rods southwesterly from Henry H. Wilson's old farm.

The ten acres of the first division of intervale was surveyed to Nathaniel Barber October 16, 1801, and was included in an eighty-acre intervale farm, which he sold Josiah Clark. Barber had occupied this land for several years when a misunderstanding in regard to the title occurred and the same selectmen sold it by auction to Micaiah Moore, and also ten acres in the first division of intervale of the minister's right for $158. This title was quitclaimed to Barber August 21, 1807.

Fifty acres of the minister's right was sold to Jonathan Carlton for $145. The remainder of land due this right and subsequently laid is as follows: Twenty-eight and one-half acres was laid out December 6, 1808, and twenty-one and one-half acres was laid November 20, 1809, both to Jonathan Carlton, located on the west side of Goose Pond and between the two ponds. Both parcels were in the third division, as well as fifty acres, which was included in the farm of Ashel Jones, now owned by Alvah Dodge.

Seven acres of the fourth division were laid out to Simeon Arvin June 10, 1814, and is included in the old Howard farm. Seven acres of the fifth division were laid out to Moses Dole September 23, 1816, northwest of Factory Village. The second division of intervale, one acre, was laid out to Charles Church May 27, 1814, on the south side of the Mascoma River, where Goose Pond Brook runs into it. These several divisions of land were sold and deed given. The notes received by the town amounted to a little over $1,500, but the sale did not put money in the town treasury, the sale being on one and two years' time. The selectmen decided to take shares in the turnpike without further orders from the town. The following is a copy of the old certificate of the town:

Town of Canaan 15 shares.

Know all men by these presents that I E. Kingsbury Junr, Esq of Orford in the county of Grafton and State of New Hampshire, for the consideration of $150 paid to me before the delivery hereof by the town of Canaan, in the County of Grafton and State of New Hampshire, the receipt whereof I do hereby acknowledge, do hereby give, grant, sell and convey to the sd Town of Canaan, its assigns, the following shares in the corporation called the Grafton Turnpike Road, to wit the shares numbered from 234-248 both inclusive. To have and to hold the sd granted shares, with a right to give one vote for each share in all matters proper to be transacted by sd Corporation, and all other privileges and appurtenances to the same belonging to the sd Town of Canaan and to its assigns, and I the sd E. Kingsbury Junr, do covenant with the sd Town of Canaan that I have full power to convey the aforesaid shares in manner aforesaid.

In Witness whereof I have hereunto set my hand and seal this 4th. day of July 1807.

E. KINGSBURY JUNR.

This old certificate turned up in 1904 amongst some old papers that had been in the possession of David Bagley for many years. It no doubt came to him from John Fales and to Fales from Hough Harris, who was in later years a selectman. Persons interested in the pike became clamorous; they talked like demagogues of the present day, accusing the selectmen of trying to defeat the will of the people. Many of the good people did not take stock in the pike; they lacked confidence in its success. They told the people if they put their money in that pike they would never see it again. The pike was not finished. Indictments were already pending against it for damages; their money would soon be absorbed and assessments in money and labor would be called for to make the road passable. These arguments convinced nobody. The next year, 1808, the town voted "to direct the selectmen to sign the articles of agreement of Grafton Turnpike Corporation, certifying that they will carry on and pay their assessments on those shares taken by said town." It is supposed that the selectmen obeyed this vote, signing the agreement with the pike, and for more than a year the proprietors went on with their improvements, encouraging themselves and the stockholders by brave words. But no dividends had yet been announced, and the pike was still unfinished.

During the year 1809 no vote upon the subject is recorded, but the people were good enough to promise that they would exchange the road from "Dr. Maxwell's to Capt. Arvin's whenever the turnpike is opened and made passable." The road referred to was laid through the swamp near the pond. In March, 1810, an article appeared in the warrant to see if the town would open the road from S. Arvin's to the Wells farm "till such times as the turnpike shall be passable." It was dismissed. The road was still unfinished and in an almost impassable condition; but there seemed to be some urgency in the case and to give the people some chance to relieve their minds a meeting was called in May and it was voted "that the selectmen make the best distribution they can of those notes they hold against individuals to pay the assessments on those shares taken by the Town of Canaan." These assessments had been apportioned among the taxpayers and money being hard to get, many objected. At the annual meeting in March, 1811, the town voted "to raise a sum of money sufficient to pay the assessments on the 15 shares taken by the town in the Grafton Turnpike Co." Fourteen persons entered their "decent" against paying these taxes:

Levi George.	William Campbell.
Joshua Richardson.	John Porter.
Jacob Straw.	Stephen Williams.
William Longfellow, Jr.	Joshua Meachan.
Nathaniel Bartlett.	William Longfellow.
Reuben Gile.	Lewis Lambkin.
Daniel Pattee.	Robert Williams.

Not one of these men lived on the pike. There had as yet been no dividends and nothing but the assessments had been thrust at the stockholders. Nevertheless, in June following the town voted "not to sell their turnpike shares nor any part thereof." This vote was immediately reconsidered and Daniel Blaisdell, Thomas Miner and Micaiah Moore were appointed a committee to take the subject into consideration, "to see how they can dispose of the Turnpike shares belonging to the town and report September next." On November 11 they voted "To sell 15 shares of the Grafton Turnpike Corporation and all the privileges and immunities thereunto belonging to Daniel Blaisdell Esq, for $100, he paying all assessments now laid by the corporation and all future assessments, excepting $110 on each share, which is already paid by the town." And that "the selectmen execute a deed to said Blaisdell, on his giving bonds with sureties, to indemnify the town agreeably to the above vote."

"Voted to suspend the collection of the Turnpike tax for the space of ten days, and then if the said Blaisdell shall comply with the above votes, the selectmen are directed to stop the collection eventually."

On December 4 they voted "not to collect the Turnpike tax that was assessed in May last amounting to $372 on the principle."

In the adoption of this vote we infer that the town and Mr. Blaisdell had traded and that for $100 he received a deed of property which had cost the town nearly $1,700 and against which there were unpaid assessments of $372. Rather a bearish speculation! Looks as if the town, the school and the church would have been happier to have adopted Mr. Trussell's resolution. A proposition was made and earnestly advocated to collect and pay to the Turnpike Company the sum of $372 on condition that the directors give bonds to furnish and keep in repair a good, passable road, including bridges, from Hanover line through Canaan to Orange line, in place where the Turnpike is now laid, to be free of toll to all inhabitants of Canaan, to pass and repass for the term of twenty years. But they voted it down. They were not ready to enter into any further contract with the corporation. Their experience had not been agreeable.

The company had not provided a good road; it was defective in several places and unfinished, and the resolution was gently passed out of sight.

Several years after the above vote an article was inserted in the warrant to see if the town would allow the inhabitants living on the line of the pike to work out their highway taxes on said pike. But this article was coolly passed by unnoticed and the Grafton Turnpike Company was left to keep its roadway in repair from its own income, and thereafter the company, its feverish struggles with assessments insteads of dividends, its good or bad fortune, passes entirely out of our records. It worried along for several years, hoping for a surplus in its treasury, but the turnpike business was overdone and to escape from their difficulties they asked the Legislature in 1828 to receive back their charter and let them go into liquidation, and they went.

In 1823 the town voted that half the tax of those living near the turnpike be laid out on it, provided the inhabitants pass free of toll. In 1827 the town voted to accept the turnpike and lay a road over it, provided the corporation surrender their whole charter; and in 1828 the selectmen re-surveyed the road, "Beginning at the center of two stakes, standing in the Westerly line of Orange near Orange Pond," and thence passing over and including all the lands over which the Grafton Turnpike was laid through Canaan to Hanover line, and proclaimed it a highway over which all mankind were free to travel and enjoy themselves.

Seven assessments were made upon the stock. The first was made July 4, 1807, of $15 on each share and the town paid $225 on November 30. On January 25, 1808, two assessments were made, one for $15 and the other for $25, and the town paid $600. The fourth and fifth assessments were made January 30, 1809, of $35 and $10, and the town paid $675. The sixth assessment was made in January, 1810, of $14, and the seventh and last assessment was made in January, 1811, of $13.85. The town paid none on the last and only part of the sixth. It paid in all $1,692.

The first dividend of $1.25 per share was paid in 1813; the next in 1814 of fifty-five cents; another in the same year of fifty cents. In 1815 there was a dividend of one dollar. There were two dividends of one dollar each in 1816, one of sixty-six cents in

1817 and one of fifty cents in 1818, making a total payment of dividends of $6.46 on each share, or about $1,938 on all the shares. It cost the people of Canaan the sum of $15,688.19 for their experience with the "Pike," of which amount about $755.82 was returned in dividends. The total cost of the shares of the town was $2,067.75. Daniel Blaisdell paid part of the sixth assessment and the seventh. It cost Micaiah Moore $2,481.30, Simeon Arvis $1,102.28 and Richard Clark, Jr., the same. Each share cost the owner $137.85, less the small dividends he received.

The remaining two public rights, "for the Incorporated Society for the Propagation of the Gospel in Foreign Parts and for a Glebe for the Church of England, as by law established," were inserted in the charter to afford a source of income for those religious associations established in England. They were exclusively English concerns and had no place in this country; no more in olden times than now. No land was laid out to these rights before the Revolution and the result of that struggle was to forfeit all rights of property on American soil belonging to English people or corporations to the American people. The proprietors assumed ownership of these rights; they were not cancelled, but received their share of land in the several divisions, excepting the propagating right, which received none in the sixth division. In 1781 the proprietors voted to lay out the glebe right, but it was not done. Daniel Blaisdell became the owner of these two rights and much of the land was surveyed to him.

The first one hundred acres of the glebe or church right was laid out in 1804 to Daniel Blaisdell, and was the old farm Moses Lawrence lived on, and adjoined the east line of Josiah Barber's "long lot" on the "old town line."

Forty acres of the second division was laid to Clark Currier on Sawyer Hill in 1805, and another forty was laid out to Thomas and Mark Cilley in 1809, and is part of the "Hoyt Place" on the present Gore road.

Twenty-two and one-half acres of the same division were laid out to Nathan Cross in the "Gore," as was also eight and one-half acres of the third division in 1823. Fourteen acres of the third division were laid out to Moses Dole in 1809, where the old paper mill stood. Fourteen acres of the same division were laid out to "Samuel Whitcher" in 1806, on the west side of the Indian River, above the watering trough by the fair grounds. Eleven and one-quarter acres of the same division were laid out to Thomas Miner in 1806, on the south side of the river, opposite George W. Davis's, and fifty acres were laid out to Nathaniel "Whitcher" in 1806, near the Gore line. The first division of intervale of two acres was laid out in 1805, and extends from the Turnpike bridge at the depot down the river, embracing the railroad station and yards and part of the village. The fourth, fifth and sixth divisions were located in different parts of the town. No land was laid in the second division of intervale, and only one acre in the sixth division of upland. The whole number of acres laid out to this right was 325.

Daniel Blaisdell sold the first hundred of the propagating right to Stephen Worth and it was surveyed to him in 1807. It was the old Watts Davis farm near Tug Mountain, on Orange line. The second division was laid out in five different parcels, amounting to $105\frac{1}{2}$ acres. The third division was laid out in two parcels, amounting to ninety-one and one-half acres. The first division of intervale was laid out in two parcels, amounting to thirteen and one-half acres, and the second division was one acre. Seven acres were laid out to the fourth and fifth divisions. No land was laid out in the sixth division, and the whole right amounted to $325\frac{1}{2}$ acres. In 1811 the town voted "to examine the rights and title the town may have in the Church and Propagating rights." No report was made. They probably came to the conclusion that the town did not own them, although they were hard pushed to get money to pay their assessments on the turnpike.

The Protestant Episcopal Church is now the owner of these last two rights in this country. It became the owner by purchase from the two English societies. Some land in other towns in this state is still held by that church under these rights, leased by them and an income derived therefrom. Should any of the land pitched to these two rights be still unoccupied and in a wild condition it would be the property of that church. In this town all has been occupied that was set off to those rights, and it would be impossible to disturb the adverse title.

CHAPTER XI.

THE COMMON, BROAD STREET, THE MEETING HOUSE.

The proprietors' committee, in their efforts to determine the center of the town for the purpose of laying out the town plot mentioned in the charter, examined the land, struck out their lines and found the western shore of Hart's Pond to be near the center of the grant. But this land was already laid out to certain rights, nevertheless, the committee had an eye for the picturesque and they decided that this beautiful sheet of water should be one of the attractions of their new village. But how should they ever be able to make such a swamp passable and habitable! They traveled through it by the aid of rotten logs, fallen trees, ridges of moss, and then after much hard labor they laid out "Broad Street" in 1788, eight rods wide, and nearly one mile in length.

In the year 1800 the traveler across our Broad Street, which at that time was famous for its great two-porched meeting-house and for the great frames of unfinished buildings along its way, saw standing upon the fields on either side and upon the shores of Hart's Pond a continuous forest of huge pine trees, dead to the top, leafless and the earth strewn with fallen branches. These great trees had been girdled years before by the early settlers and left to die, that being the manner of death allotted to those monarchs of the forest. When dead and dry they were more easily burned standing than if cut down.

Part of the land along "The Street" was divided into acre lots; but those who settled there bought of the first owner.

"Broad Street" passed through Robert Barber's farm, through fifty acres of the first hundred of Allen Whitman, which William Douglass bought for twelve shillings and two pence at tax sale for the taxes assessed in 1782, through the first hundred of Phineas Sabine, and through Daniel Colby's fifty acres of the first division of Samuel Dodge, 3d. The first owners sold these lots running to "Broad Street." The road was not granted; it was and always has been the property of the adjoining owners.

There was but one clearing on the "Street" when it was laid out. It embraced about three acres and was owned by William Douglass, the shoemaker who lived in a log house built in the orchard back of the old Pierce Tavern or Grand View House, torn down in 1909. Mr. Douglass planted this orchard with seeds brought from Connecticut, the first orchard planted in the village.

To this day "Broad Street," now called "Canaan Street," is one of the most attractive and beautiful places in the state. It is 1,164 feet above tide water, 204 feet higher than the railroad station. At one end of it is the "Pinnacle," 263 feet above the "Street." Towards the east is Mt. Cardigan, 3,156 feet. To the north are Smarts and Moose Mountains, the latter 2,326 feet high. Towards the west one looks off into the long valley of the Mascoma River, and in the distance, through a break in the hills, can be seen the highest peak of the Green Mountains. Extending along the whole length of the "Street" is Hart's Pond, whose shores for the most part are surrounded by forests, which rise still higher upon the hills.

After the town had voted to build a meeting-house and their committee had reported upon the "spot" to place it, a long discussion arose upon the propriety and convenience in having an open "common." The proposition was acted upon favorably and a committee was appointed to wait upon William Douglass, the shoemaker, and negotiate for a deed. This deed reads as follows:

Know all men by these presents that I, William Douglass of Canaan, in the County of Grafton, State of New Hampshire, cordwainer.

For and in consideration of the sum of Eleven pounds five shillings lawful money to me in hand before the delivery thereof well and truly paid by Caleb Welch, John Burdick and William Richardson, in behalf of the proposed Meeting house in Canaan and in the county and State aforesaid.

The receipt whereof I do hereby acknowledge have Granted Bargained Sold and by these presents do give grant Bargain sell aliene enfeoff convey and confirm unto the said Caleb Welch, John Burdick and William Richardson in their capacity acting in behalf of the proprietors their Heirs and assigns forever a certain tract of Land being and lying in the Township of Canaan and situate as follows;

Beginning at the Northeasterly corner a few rods south of Mr. William Douglass Dwelling house adjoining easterly on Broad street so called thence running S 12°E 30 Roods to a stake and stones thence running N 78°W 12 Roods to a stake and stones thence N 12°W 30 Roods to a stake and stones from thence to the first bound. Likewise a piece of Land Lying Easterly from the above mentioned piece of Land between Broad street & Harts pond so called and Bounded as follows. Beginning at a stake and stones by the Pond thence running S 78°W 14 Roods to a stake and stones thence S 12°E 11 Roods to a stake and stones thence N 72°E 14 Roods to the pond from thence to the first mentioned Bounds to have and to hold the sd granted premises with all the privileges and apertainances to the same belonging to them the said Caleb Welch, John Burdick and William Richardson in their capacity as aforesaid to their Heirs to their only proper use and benefit forever and I the same William Douglass my Heirs Executors and administrators do hereby covenant grant and agree to and with Caleb Welch John Burdick and William Richardson in behalf of the proprietors of the proposed Meeting house in Canaan their Heirs and assigns that until the delivery hereof I am the Lawful owner of the sd premises seized and possessed thereof in my own Right in fee simple and have full power and Lawfull authority to grant and convey the same in manner aforesaid that the sd premises free and clear of all and every incumberance whatever and that I my Heirs executors and administrators shall & will warant the same to them the sd Caleb Welch, John Burdick and William Richardson as aforesd their Heirs and assigns against the Lawfull Claims and demands of any person or persons whomsoever in witness whereof I have hereunto set my hand and seal this 26 day of December 1792.

           WILLIAM DOUGLASS (LS)

Signed sealed and delivered
 in presents of
Wm Parkhurst
 Sally Parkhurst
   Grafton Ss Canaan Jany 14th 1794

Personally appeared William Douglass signer and sealer of the above instrument and acknowledged the same to Be his free act and Deed

Before Me WILLIAM AYER *Just. Peace*.

The price paid was about thirty-seven and one-half dollars.

A powerful argument used in favor of the second parcel was that in course of time many people would have to be baptized, because it was a divine ordination necessary to salvation; and eventually everybody would have to come to the meeting-house to hear the Word and witness God's ordinances, so they had better have a wide common opening down to the pond, that on occasions of baptism there might be room enough for all the people. This argument prevailed. The "Common," when William Douglass sold it to the "Proprietors of the proposed Meeting House," was a swamp crowded with stumps, trees, rotten logs and frogs. It was deeded unconditionally. For several years afterwards this swamp was drained off westwardly by ditches, until by cutting and clearing away obstructions it became settled land. In the fall of 1793 the use of the common was sold by auction to Simeon Arvin for two years, at two dollars per year, he agreeing to level the land and get out the stumps, but he failed to comply with his contract and nothing was done. For several years it remained in its natural condition, when Ensign Colby offered to clear and level the land if he could have the use of it for two years for his labor. The first year he did little else but cut and clear away. The second year the ground was ploughed and worked over, and he raised 123 bushels of shelled corn. As this crop did not sufficiently remunerate him the proprietors gave him the use of it another year, during which he raised 1,600 pounds of pussed flax, which his mother and sisters worked up into cloth, as was the custom in those days.

B. P. George enclosed a strip of it on the north side and fenced it in, but the fence is gone now. The academy grounds enclosed one rod of it on the south line and that fence is gone, too. Jesse Martin cleared his field of stones and left them on the west side, where they remained, occupying about twenty feet of space, until his son-in-law, Hon. Caleb Blodgett, paid for having them built into a wall in 1899. And the Canaan Street Improvement Society ploughed, leveled and seeded the piece on the west side the same year, having leveled the piece on the east side two years before. The "Street," laid out eight rods wide, has been encroached upon by adjoining owners every time a fence or wall has been built; even houses have been built into it, so that now but a small part of it is as wide as it was laid out.

It was many years after the settlement of the town before our ancestors decided to build a meeting-house. The subject came up at their religious gatherings, but it was only in the form of hopes and wishes. And even after the Baptist church was organized in 1780 their new house seemed just as far away. Thomas Baldwin, who for several years had had charge over the church and people, preaching in barns and other buildings at great inconvenience, had long urged the necessity for a meeting-house, which should really be a "stated place for worship and dedicated to God."

Dea. Caleb Welch and Dr. Ebenezer Eames also urged the need of a place of worship. For a long time a majority of the people were either indifferent or hostile to the project. They pleaded poverty and hard times and desired to wait a little longer. At length, at the annual meeting March 11, 1788, they voted unanimously "to build a meeting house, and the meeting adjourned to April 2d. Nothing was done at that meeting; but a special meeting was called May 9 for the purpose of arriving at some definite conclusion. Lieut. William Richardson, Daniel Blaisdell, Thaddeus Lathrop, Jehu Jones and John Harris were chosen a committee "to pick upon a spot to set a Meeting house and what method shall be taken for the building of the same." The committee reported at once and the place proposed was accepted, "which is about 60 rods from David Fogg's towards Mr. Dustin's." This would fix the place a little northeasterly of Israel Sharon's barn on the old Barber place. David Fogg's log house was in the south corner of the old Lebanon road, where there is now a clump of apple trees. Then Deacon Welch, Lieutenant Wells, John Scofield, Lieutenant Richardson and Daniel Blaisdell were appointed to prepare the spot ("prefix" is the word used), "and likewise propose some convenient method to build sd house." The meeting adjourned to Thursday, June 2.

The committee began to clear the ground and rocks, as directed, but dissensions arose among themselves, and several parties sprang up in town, each with its objections as to the details of the plan, locality, etc. An objection urged very earnestly by one party was that it would not accommodate the people, most of whom lived upon South Road, Town Hill and Sawyer Hill. The discussion became so energetic and irritating that the project was dropped to give time for "second thoughts." What transpired at the adjourned meeting on the "2nd thirsday" in June will never be known. No record was made. But it has traditionally come down through the old men, Elijah Miner, Ensign Colby, Nat Gilman and others, that there arose a serious and bitter contest regarding the location of the house, which resulted in the postponement of further action on the subject. Mr. Baldwin, who was the minister, and a few other good men continued to urge the necessity for a house, but he left town before the people became sufficiently united to start out seriously a second time. After four years of discussions, which oftentimes became harsh and bitter, developing much passion and ugliness, the people were summoned together on August 27, 1792, and voted to build a meeting-house, "provided the town can agree upon a spot to set it, and the method how to build it." John Scofield, William Richardson, John Currier, John Burdick, Dudley Gilman, Ezekiel Wells, John Worth, Abel Hadley and Richard Clark, 3d, were chosen a committee "to find a spot to set sd Meeting house, propose a method how to build it. Likewise to draw a plan of sd house and make report at some future meeting." At the adjourned meeting on October 10 the committee reported, the purport of which is left to conjecture from the results which followed: "Voted to build a Meeting house in town by Proprietorship." "Voted to accept the Report of the Committee respecting the spot to set the Meeting House."

"Voted to sell the Pue ground in order to bring the matter into Proprietorship." John Currier, John Burdick, Dudley Gilman, William Ayer and Samuel Jones were chosen to sell the "Pue ground." "Voted to accept the size of the Meeting House proposed by the Committee."

Dea. Caleb Welch was chosen treasurer, "to receive the obligations in behalf of the Committee."

Voted that each person that bids off a pue in sd Meeting House when he gives his obligation, may take a bond for a deed.

The meeting dissolved and the meeting-house disappears entirely from our town records, but not from the minds and determination of the people. The town stepped aside and left the details of the work in the hands of the proprietors.

The next step taken was to sell the pews upon the plan submitted and approved by the committee. "At a public Vandue holden at the house of Mr. Nath'l Barber in Canaan on Monday the 5th. day of November, A. D. 1792, for the purpose of selling the pew ground in the proposed meeting house, the following gentlemen bid off pews by number for the sum set against their names respectively:

The Common, Broad Street, the Meeting House.

		£	s
29	Jonathan Carlton	30	6
30	Joshua Wells	30	0
24	Capt. E. Wells	27	18
47	John Burdick	27	6
38	John Burdick jr	25	10
29	John Currier	24	6
22	Capt. Robert Barber	24	6
25	Lt. William Richardson	24	0
11	Thadeus Lathrop	23	14
10	Richard Clark	23	14
28	John M. Barber	23	14
2	Dea. Caleb Welch	24	0
46	Oliver Smith	23	17
12	Abel Hadley	24	0
31	Lt. Nath'l Bartlett	23	17
27	Warren Wilson	23	17
26	David Dustin	24	
14	Nath'l Barber	23	11
4	Lt. Richard Whittier	23	8
19	J. Wilson	22	8
7	Lt. Daniel Blaisdell	22	19
8	Reynold Gates	23	5
44	John Kesley	22	16
39	Ezekiel Gardner	19	4
41	John Worth	15	6
43	Simeon Arvin	22	13
42	Richard Clark jr	22	4
37	Hubbard Harris	21	9
40	Simeon Arvin	21	0
3	Clark Currier	21	0
35	David Dustin	20	10
33	Nath'l Gilman	19	10
6	Joseph Flint	19	13

PEWS IN THE GALLERY.

		£	s
20	John Burdick	14	14
1	Capt. E. Wells & O. Smith	15	15
3	Samuel Heath	13	16
19	Levi Straw	12	
9	Nath'l Whittier	12	6

PEWS BELOW.

		£	s
34	John Bean	16	16
36	Jehu Jones	16	16
5	Joseph Clark	20	2
18	John Scofield	15	12
20	Samuel Heath	15	12
18	Capt. E. Wells	17	13
13	Half to Henry Springer	5	8

The land as above described was purchased of William Douglass. The notice for the construction of the building follows:

1792 ADVERTISEMENT.

Public Notice is hereby given that the building and finishing of the new proposed meeting house in Canaan, will be sold at Public Vandue to the Lowest Bidder (or the person who will do it for the least sum) at the dwelling house of Capt. Robert Barber, on Wednesday Dec. 26 instant at 10 of the clock in the forenoon. Every person wishing for a good bargain is invited to attend.

DANIEL BLAISDELL, *Vandue Master.*

Canaan Dec. 3 A D 1792.

Dec. 26. 1792 Vandue opened according to Advertisement and Proceeded as follows. viz: the building and finishing of the above said Meeting House is struck off to Mr. William Parkhurst for £561.

OLIVER SMITH, *Proprietors Clerk.*

1. The building and finishing of said Meeting House is to be struck off to the lowest bidder, and he to be the builder and purchaser of said house, providing he give his obligation with sufficient bond to the satisfaction of the Proprietors.

2. The dimensions of said house are to be as follows: 42 feet in width and 52 feet in length, and the posts to be 26 feet long between joints, & the roof in proportion thereunto.

Also two porches, one at each end, each porch to be 12 feet square the posts to be 23 feet long.

3rd. The underpinning is to be raised one and a half foot, with rough stones and gravel on the lowest corner, and leveled off properly, and one foot three inches with hewn stones, and pointed with lime. The steps at each door to be of hewn stone, well proportioned & properly placed.

The painting of the outside is to be done in the same manner and exactly like the lower meeting house in Salisbury as to color. The house is not to be painted until the summer after it is covered. The windows are to have 40 lights of 7 x 9 glass. The Pews are to be made and placed exactly according to the plan by which they are sold, and the inside work to be done and completed in every respect equal to the upper meeting house in Salisbury.

The frame of the house is to be raised and outside by the first day of October next. And the Meeting house is to be built finished and completed in every respect in a neat and workmanlike manner, by the first day of September 1794.

The builder is to be compensated in the following manner: At the time of giving bonds he shall receive an obligation signed by the proprietors committee to deliver to him by the 10th. day of March next, good authentic notes of hand signed by the prptrs of pews on said house to the amount of the sum for which he is to build and finish it with sufficient power to collect the same; one quarter of said sum to be raised in money one quarter to be paid in lumber, and one half to be paid in neat stock; The lumber is to be paid to the acceptance of the prptrs, as to qualify and sorts, and at the following rate of prices, viz: 18 shillings per m for good merchantable white pine boards, delivered on the spot, and 33 shillings per m for good merchantable white pine split clapboards; and 7 shillings per m for good merchantable short shingles delivered on the spot, all other sorts of lumber to be estimated at the same rates.

These prices were afterwards modified: "Merchantable boards 16s, clear boards 27s per M. Clapboards 30s per M and shingles seven & six pence per M all to be delivered on the spot."

At a subsequent meeting the proprietors voted that half the lumber should be delivered by the middle of June, 1793, and the other half by the middle of September next. "One half of our money payment shall not be called for until the first day of August next, 1793. And the committee shall hold the obligations against the several prptrs until the 10th. day of March next (1793)."

At the time of the building of the house, Douglass clearing did not embrace much of the Common. On the east towards the pond, there was no clearing except a roadway that led to the water. A swampy jungle of bush alders and hemlocks obscured the view. South, to the lower end of the street where Robert Barber then lived, nearly all the clearing was the street along whose sides and even in the traveled way pine stumps obstructed the traveler. On the west, towards David Dustin's, it was only forest and jungle. It was not until September, 1793, that the great timbers for the frame of the house were ready to be put together. The sills were twenty inches square, the plates the same, and all the other timbers in the same proportion. During all this year the people and propriety had watched the work which they thought slow and halting. Robert and John M. Barber were sureties for Mr. Parkhurst and they were often appealed to to hurry the work, but without effect. It still lingered, one of the chief causes of the delay being found in the free use of Sampson Ballard's extract of molasses.

On the day early in September, appointed for the raising, the people for miles around were present. "Everybody was there."

A barrel of rum had been procured from Jesse Johnson at East Enfield to steady the nerves and increase the emulation of the workmen.

Mr. Parkhurst built and lived in the house for a long time the residence of S. P. Cobb, and kept a store in it. He married Sally Barber, daughter of Robert, who had provided well for his children. After the raising of the frame there was to be a grand banquet to the workmen at his house.

It is said that Mr. Parkhurst, who was a handsome young man, cool headed and of firm nerves, while working upon the ridge pole, was called to assist in arranging the heavy plate, and that he walked down the western rafter upright with his axe upon his shoulder, and several times during the raising exhibited feats of surprising coolness. At last, he proposed riding up astride one of the heavy timbers, but when near the top some of the rope tackling broke, and he was precipitated to the ground. He was seriously injured by the fall, and remained unconscious for a long time. His wife, assisted by the neighbors, was preparing dinner for the men engaged in raising the frame. The news of the accident soon reached her, and she left her work to go to him, supposing him to be dead. She came upon the ground weeping bitterly. After a while he opened his eye and, upon learning what had happened, said to her: "Sally, don't you see, if you spend your time crying and wringing your hands, that you won't have dinner ready, and all these men will be hungry? Now get home as soon as you can, and I'll come after you in a little while." He was carried home, but never recovered the use of his limbs, nor did any more work upon the building. He made money in after years by trading in patent rights. But he and his family disappeared from our midst, like many others who figured in our early annals, and left no trace behind.

But the work went on under the direction of the committee and the Barbers, and was completed the following day. The first meeting held in the new house was on the 19th of September, when it was not yet entirely covered. It was a business meeting, called at 12 m., when they "proceeded to sell several more pews," and "to allow Lt. Daniel Blaisdell's act of 5 shillings" and "Dr. John Harris' act of 9 shillings." During the winter and spring of 1794, no work was done on the house, but the workmen were always getting ready. Major Levi George of Salisbury, was hired to build the pulpit and do much of the panel work. The contractors were directed "not to build the pulpit and canopee like Salisbury, but that he build them exactly like the Pulpit and canopee of Chelmsford Meeting house." They also "voted that the sides and wall of the house be colored a stone couler, the roof a Spanish Brown, and the doors a sky blue." It was also "voted to receive neat stock instead of lumber from any proprietor to whom the change might be most convenient."

The house was still unfinished on the first of September, 1794, the day it was appointed to be delivered to the proprietors. It was not completed during the year 1795, and the work was still incomplete up to February 1796, when they voted that William Richardson, Lieut. Daniel Blaisdell and Capt. E. Wells be a committee to wait upon Captain Barber, respecting the completion of the house. In November of this year the proprietors finally got mad with Captain Barber and his son, John M., and deliberately threatened that "if the meeting house is not completed by the first day of May next," they will immediately prosecute the contractors on their bond. It was completed and offered for acceptance. The proprietors were not entirely satisfied with the work and after examination their committee made the following report:

We do not accept of the work upon the house at large.
The frame good
The underpinning Bad.
The outside Good
The wall pews in the gallery Good.
The seats not Good.
The plastering Good.
The seats not Good.
The breastwork good.
The insides of the porches bad.
The floors in the Galleries not good.
The Singing seats bad.
The Pulpit Good.
The pews on the walls below Good.
The body Pews on the West side Good.
The body Pews on the East side Bad.
The Glass badly set.
The bottom floors good.

Though not "excepted" in all its parts, it was received and occupied as a house of public worship, and for the transaction of town business. There is no record of the dedication of the house to God, either by sermon, prayer or anthem, neither the day nor the reverend men who took part in it; but their names are doubtless written along with Ben Adhems, nor the banquet which followed at Caleb Pierce's new tavern.

The house was built without steeple or bell, with three entrances, one on each end, under the porticoes, and one on the south. The pews were square boxes, those in the center placed in squares of four, and a row of pews round the walls, raised one step above the floor. The pulpit was reached by a flight of ten steps, and from this elevation the minister could look into the gallery. A picturesque and large-toned sounding board was suspended over the desk. The original clapboards were split from pine logs and then sawed — shingles the same. The timbers were cut, mostly, near the Common or near by, and the boards were sawed by Jonathan Carlton at his mill at the village. The nails were of wrought iron, cut out of nail iron of various thicknesses, by the aid of a machine made for that purpose, and set up in Mr. Carlton's mill.

In 1804, pew No. 48 was sold by auction to Jacob Trussel for $36, and the committee had to "call" upon him several times before he paid it. This pew was sold to pay the expense of repairing the house. At the same time "Chose Dr. Caleb Pierce to keep the kee and sweep and take care of the house for one year, and to give him one dollar therefor." A division was made for the "occupancy of the house, by the several denominations in their several proportions," and to "fix on the days when each should improve their opportunity." In 1812 the town voted "to paint and repair the outside of the meeting house at the expense of the town, whatever repairs are necessary. The town having the privilege as usual of holding public meetings in said house. It shall be painted with white lead and a Red Rough."

In 1814, it was "voted to repair the meeting house doors and windows but not to exceed the sum of twenty five dollars cost."

In 1820 there was a strong feeling that the town should own its building for public meetings and the warrant contained an article to see "if the town will build or hire a house for town meetings." They voted to spend $50 in repairing the old meeting house for the privilege of holding meetings for five years. And the proposal of the proprietors to repair the meeting house from time to time for the privilege of holding meetings was accepted. They also voted to take a lease of the house and repair it and voted $25 additional.

In 1825 they voted to shingle the meeting house. In 1829, "voted to raise $400 to repair the meeting house provided the proprietors of said House will lay out and expend $200 more. And also that the said proprietors convey to the said town, the use of the said house for the purpose of holding all their town meetings in." Jonas W. Smith and John Fales were appointed to lay out the money in behalf of the town.

The 12th of April, the same year, at a meeting of the proprietors of the meeting house, Daniel Blaisdell was appointed an agent to convey such title to the house as would be satisfactory to the town. Mr. Blaisdell made a deed according to his instructions, in which he conveyed to the town, the control of the house and "the right to use it for a town house forever," upon consideration that the town should make all necessary repairs upon the house. On June 9, 1829, by formal vote, the town accepted the deed. On this occasion the house was clapboarded and shingled, the western porch removed and placed upon the eastern one, forming the present tower, about fifty-three feet high. The sounding board was also removed, apprehensions being felt that it might fall and harm some one.

About the year 1841, a change was made in the interior of the house. Some persons procured the written consent of the proprietors to have the box pews removed and seats arranged as at present. The Baptists, also, had permission at this time to put a floor across the gallery and fit up the upper hall as a place of worship, but they failed to realize all their wishes. The floor was put in and the upper part left in dilapidation and confusion, relic hunters carrying off the old pew doors and wide panels until, more than fifty years after, in 1884, the Canaan Lyceum Hall Association was formed, and a hard wood floor was laid, for roller skating, about four feet above the floor the Baptists laid, and it was otherwise finished and decorated for the use of public and private gatherings. A stairway was also added to reach the hall from the outside. In 1849, $200 was appropriated by the town for repairs on account of damage done by some ruthless persons.

When the first bell was placed in the belfry is not known, but in 1853 Eleazer Martin was appointed an agent to sell the old bell and buy a new one of 1,200 pounds and hang the same. This bell has tolled for the dead and dying, for young and old to assemble, for the scholars in the academy, who always took delight in turning it over as many times as possible, and it was considered a great feat for any boy. It swung for many years, pulled by a long rope running down to the ground floor of the belfry. Its tongue has pealed the alarm for every fire in the vicinity, and on almost every night before the Fourth of July it has not been forgotten. Its tones are so clear that it can be heard in Tunis. In 1894, a clock was added to the tower, just beneath the bell, and the bell was fastened, that the clock might strike the time of day upon it, so that it no longer swings. In 1870, the town voted $400 to repair the house.

CHAPTER XII.

DAME'S GORE AND STATE'S GORE.

In the granting of townships in New Hampshire and the adjustment of their boundary lines, there were found to be numerous strips, or gores of land, not large enough for a whole township. These strips or gores Governor Wentworth granted to those who had done him some personal service and were his friends. One of these strips lay between Canaan and Dorchester. It was discovered in 1772, when the southern line of Dorchester was run and Gov. John Wentworth, in 1773, granted it to Capt. Theophilus Dame, then high sheriff of Strafford County, for his services in the late war, in the following terms:

Province of New Hampshire.

George the Third by the Grace of God of Great Britain France and Ireland King Defend of the Faith &ca—

To all to whom these Presents shall come Greeting—

Whereas we have tho't fit by our Proclamation at St. James the Seventh Day of October in the year of our Reign Anno Domini 1763— among other things to testify our Royal Sence and Approbation of the Conduct & Bravery of the officers & Soldiers of our armies and Signified our Desire to reward the same & have therein com'anded & Impowered Our Several Governors of Our Respective Provinces on the continent of America to grant without Fee or reward to Such Reduced officers as have Served in North America during the late War and to such Private Soldiers as have been or Shall be disbanded there and Shall Personally apply for the Same Such Quantities of Land respectively as in & by our aforesaid Proclamation are particularly Mentioned Subject Nevertheless to the Same Quit Rents & Conditions of Cultivation and Improvements as other our Lands are Subject to in the Province in which they are Granted; and whereas Theophilus Dame of Portsmouth in our County of Rockingham & Province Aforesaid Esq, had our appointment as Captain and Served during the late War and having personally applied & Solicited for such Grant agreeable to our aforesaid Proclamation KNOW YE that we of our Special Grace certain knowledge & mere motion do Signify our Approbation as aforesaid & for encouraging the Settlement & Cultivation of our lands within Said Province of New Hampshire in New England Have by & with the advice of our Trusty & well beloved JOHN WENTWORTH Esq Our Governor & Com'ander in Chieff of Our Said Province and of Our Council of the Same agreable to our aforesaid in part recited Proclamation, and upon the Conditions & Reservations hereafter mentioned given & granted & by these Presents for us our Heirs & Successors do give & Grant unto the Said Theophilus Dame and to his Heirs' & Assigns forever a Certain Tract or Parcel of Land Situate lying & being within our Said Province of New Hampshire and containing by Admeasurement Four thousand Two hundred & Seventy Two Acres including Ponds Roads & unimprovable Mountains according to a Plan or Survey thereof exhibited by our Surveyor General of Land for our Said Province by our Said Governor's order & returned into the Secretarys office of our Said Province a Copy whereof is hereunto annexed butted & bounded as follows (Viz) beginning at the North West Corner of Canaan from thence running South Sixty one degrees East Six miles to A spruce Tree which is the North East Corner of Said Canaan thence running North fifty three Degs East One Mile & Sixty Eight rods to the South East Corner of Dorchester thence North Sixty one degrees West Six Miles to the South West Corner of said Dorchester thence South fifty three degrees West one Mile & Sixty Eight rods to the Bounds first mentioned TO HAVE & TO HOLD the Said Tract of Land as above expressed with the Appurtenances to Him the Said Theophilus Dame & to His Heirs and assigns forever upon the following Terms (Viz)

First—That the said Grantee Shall cut Clear & make Passable for Carriages &ca a road of three rods Wide thro' the Said Tract as Shall at Any Time hereafter be directed or ordered by the Governor & Council aforesaid which road shall be compleated in one year from the Date of Such Order or Direction aforesaid on Penalty of forfeiture of this Grant & its reverting to us our Heirs & Successors—

Second—That the Said Grantee shall Settle or cause to be Settled Five Families in five years from the Date of this Grant in failure whereof the Premises to revert to us our Heirs & Successors to be by us or Them entered upon and regranted to such of our Subjects as Shall effectually Settle & Cultivate the Same—

Third—That all White & other Pine Trees fit for Masting our Royal Navy be carefully preserved for that Use & none to be Cutt or fell'd without our Special Licence for so doing first had & obtained on Penalty of the forfeiture of the right of the Grantee in the Premises his Heirs & Assigns to us our heirs & Successors as well as being Subject to the Penaltys prescribed by any Present or future Act or Acts of Parliament—

Fourthly—yielding & Paying therfor to us our Heirs & Successors on or before the Tenth day of May 1778 the rent of one Ear of Indian Corn only if lawfully demanded—

Fifthly—That the Said Grantee his Heirs & assigns shall yield & Pay unto us our Heirs & Successors Yearly & every Year forever from & after the Expiration of Ten Years from the Date of this Grant which will be in the Year of our Lord Christ Seventeen Hundred

DAME'S GORE AND STATE'S GORE.

Eighty Three, ONE SHILLING Proclamation Money for every Hundred Acres he so owns Settles or Possesses and So in Proportion for a greater or lesser Tract of the Land afore Said — which money shall be paid by the Proprietor Owner or Settler in our Council Chamber in Portsmouth or to such officer or officers as shall be appointed to receive the Same and these to be in Lieu of all Other Rents & Services whatsoever—

Sixthly — That this Grant Shall not interfere with Any of our Grants made as aforesaid & now in force nor Interrupt the Grantees in their Improvements making thereon agreable to the conditions thereof—

In Testimony whereof We have caused the Seal of Our Said Province of New Hampshire to be hereunto affixed.

Witness JOHN WENTWORTH Esq Our Afore Said Governor & Commander in Chieff the Seventh Day of May in the Thirteenth Year of our Reign Annoque Domini 1773.

J^r WENTWORTH

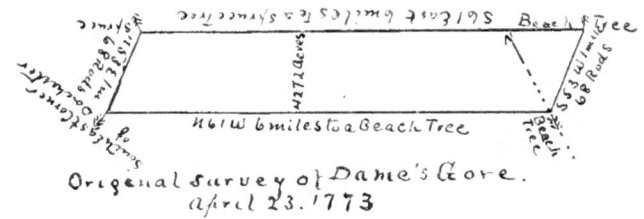

Original survey of Dame's Gore.
april 23. 1773

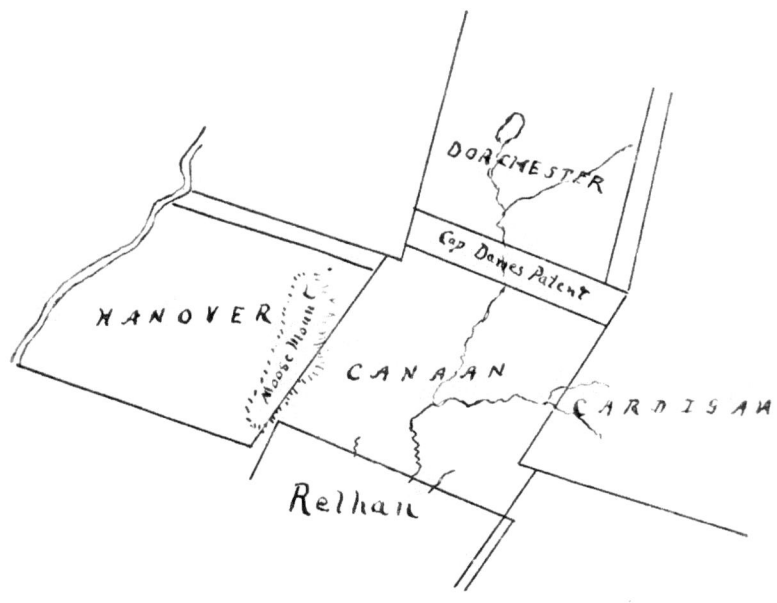

The proprietors of Canaan laid out land in the gore, thinking that it was a part of Canaan. Several rights were allotted land north of the "old town line." Joseph Randlett was one of these; also Josiah Clark. Daniel Lary settled there, buying his land of Dame. Caleb Clark bought five hundred acres of Dame, in 1774–'77. Captain Dame was not a thrifty man. It passed from him into the hands of Rev. Jonathan Homer, of Newton, Mass., for the consideration of 143 pounds and 12 shillings, on November 5, 1787. It was described in that deed as "Beginning at the north-east corner of the line lately run by the proprietors of Canaan through the Gore, thence running S 61 degrees E to the north-east corner of said line, then N 53 E to the south-east corner of Dorchester, then N 61 W to the south-west corner of Dorchester, then S 53 W to the first bound, Containing 4272 acres." It will be observed that the west line ran from the southwest corner of Dorchester to the northwest corner of Canaan. The direction of the line in the grant and deed are the same, but it was discovered by Homer that the bearing of that line was not correct, and he employed John Currier to survey it, and the line was run South 88° West, and the east line was also changed. Homer was called a hard man, perhaps because he wanted what he owned. There were several squatters, so considered by Homer, who had settled on his land, and would not atone to him. Joseph Randlett was one of them, and he began an action of trespass against him. Randlett called upon the town and proprietors to make good his title, as he had purchased the land of them. At the annual meeting in March, 1801, the town was asked to take into consideration the claim of Dame's heirs against Randlett, and Col. Henry Gerrish was appointed to settle the "disputed lines of the town." Later in October the town appointed Daniel Blaisdell and William Richardson "agents, empowered to defend in the two actions, viz: one brought by the proprietors of Dame's Gore against Joseph Randlett, and the other brought by the proprietors of Orange against Josiah Clark, in case the proprietors of Dame's Gore and Orange will not enter into a reference, for the settlement of the same, and to take every measure to maintain our lines according to our charter and the survey." These suits dragged along until 1804, when the town was able to make a satisfactory settlement with Homer. The action against Josiah Clark, was for ejectment from 100 acres and damages to the amount of $500. Clark won, and judgment was entered in his favor for the costs in February, 1804. Clark's land did not belong to Orange.

In 1803 a petition had been presented to the General Court, respecting a gore of land lying between Hanover and Canaan. Ebenezer Hoyt had been appointed commissioner to determine it. The town voted "to remonstrate with the General Court against the petition, of those praying for the land and to postpone the granting until the suit be determined between Col. Dame's heirs and the proprietors of Canaan, which involves in measure the same land." Homer had discovered that Dame's Gore did not include all the land on the north line of Canaan, that there was a small piece between Hanover, Lyme and the gore, which Dame's grant did not include, probably because at the time Captain Dame's patent was issued it was not known that Lyme extended beyond the line of Hanover. Homer wanted this piece, which afterwards became known as "State's or Gates' Gore." Homer did establish his right to Dame's grant, but it did not include the other piece.

The inhabitants of the gore being few, and under no government of their own, or able to protect themselves against the encroachments of adjoining towns, thought best to make application to the Legislature to be annexed to some town. Accordingly, in 1808, Daniel Lary petitioned the General Court to be annexed to Dorchester. Others of the inhabitants opposed this and wished to be annexed to Canaan. Homer opposed the petition, and asked the Legislature to postpone any action in the matter for three years until such a time as the people knew what they wanted. Some of the inhabitants asked Canaan to accept them, should the Legislature grant their request to be annexed to Canaan, and in November, 1808, the town voted, "that Dame's Gore may be annexed to Canaan, agreeable to the petition of the inhabitants of the Gore to the General Court in June last"; but the Legislature refused to act upon or grant their petition, and it was many years before they succeeded.

In 1833 the town voted to petition the General Court to annex

Dame's Gore. In 1837 the town was asked to vote for the annexation of "that part of Dame's Gore lying West of the Mascoma, and also that part of Dorchester lying west of the river and south of a line drawn from the North-east corner of Enoch Fifield's land westerly to Lyme line." The article was dismissed. In 1841 the town was asked to annex Dame's Gore, and again refused. In 1844 they refused again; but at the meeting on March 14, 1846, they voted to annex Dame's Gore, but dismissed that part of the article which referred to the annexation of State's Gore, and on July 2, 1846, the Legislature by enactment made Dame's Gore a part of Canaan.

By virtue of a resolve of June 20, 1815, William A. Kent, treasurer of the state, appointed Ebenezer Hoyt, to ascertain the quantity and appraise the value of a piece of land lying west of the line of Dame's Gore, adjoining Hanover and Canaan. This resolve authorized the treasurer to convey. And on December 27, 1815, he conveyed to Samuel Jones Gates and Adam Pollard for $220, the triangular-shaped piece described as follows "Beginning at the north-west corner of Canaan, thence running N 45 degrees E 182 rods to the north-east corner of Hanover, thence running S 64° E 277 rods to the corner of Lime, & Dorchester thence W 2° S 380 rods by Dame's Gore to the first bound containing 149 acres and 100 square rods." This is State's or Gates' Gore.

Of the early settlers on Dame's Gore Caleb Clark lived on the West end, then came Joseph Bartlett on the east side of the River. David Jones of Epping who married Hannah Dow, lived for a time at the Corner, but in 1794 moved to the gore and lived on what was afterwards the Lary farm. He was taxed in Canaan for the years 1793–'95. On the east end towards Orange was Josiah Clark, Daniel Lary and next Tristram Sanborn. Jonathan Homer purchased the gore in 1787 and on September 20, 1788, he made a personal visit to the gore to take formal possession of his new purchase. He made Josiah Clark his agent, to see that no trespass was committed, trees cut or any squatters allowed. At that time he showed his good will by giving Lary and Clark the privilege to make sugar from the maples on Sugar Hill. This hill Homer afterwards sold to Sanborn in 1817. Abner H. Cilley was an early settler. He was industrious and obstinate, and succeeded in the face of many annoyances from Mr. Homer in making himself a pleasant home. He was served with writs and summonses by the agents of Homer who were instructed to bring suits for larceny or trespass on every tree that was cut. Thomas H. Pettingill had good gleanings there, so also did Elijah Blaisdell. But Mr. Cilley lived and died at a good old age in his own house, the first built on that part of the gore, which is still standing in good condition, the property of R. H. Haffenreffer. Daniel Sherburne was an agent for Mr. Homer, and built the second house on that part of the gore owned by Mr. Haffenreffer. The third house was built by David Pollard, who was the father of eighteen children, fourteen of which lived to grow up; the fourth house was built by Amos Kinney, the fifth by Elwell Eastman, who lived there but a short time. Then B. P. George built on the west side of the road. Edwin May also built and lived there. The last man who was brave enough to finish a house on the gore was John W. Hoyt, whose family resided there while he was away in the army. Joseph Pollard, who married Abner H. Cilley's daughter, lived there and took care of old Abner, receiving the latter's property for so doing. After Pollard closed his house, all of the buildings were vacant for some time, until Mr. Haffenreffer purchased as much of the gore as he could and repaired all the buildings, that were not too much dilapidated. But for all the hard labor and money that have been put upon that land it still refuses to make anyone rich.

Mr. Homer died and Charles C. Curtis was appointed executor; he proceeded to sell the remainder of the land and accordingly held an auction in May, 1846, and closed out all of Homer's interests. Homer had sold land to Joseph Bartlett, Josiah P. Haynes, Caleb P. Wells, David Richardson, Mary Sanborn, Samuel J. Gates, Nathaniel Derby, Adam Pollard, Amos Kinney, Abner H. Cilley, Joseph Sherburne, Obadiah Eastman, Tristram Sanborn and Josiah Clark. Curtis sold to E. and J. Martin, Orrin and George Fales, Alexander Caldwell, John Rockwell, Asa Ham, Jonathan Kittredge and John Lougee, John L. Pressey, John B. Flanders, Joseph Hapgood, Wesley P. Burpee,

William P. Weeks, Moses Hadley and the balance remaining was bid off to Curtis' son. Joseph Worthen and others, not succeeding in getting Homer to build a road across his land petitioned the court in 1821 and compelled him not only to lay out the road, but to pay the costs of the action. He employed John Currier, who surveyed a road across the gore May 23, 1821.

CHAPTER XIII.

THE SURPLUS REVENUE AND LITERARY FUND.

In the year 1836 Congress voted to distribute thirty-six millions of dollars of surplus revenue, then lying in the treasury, among the several states. These millions had accumulated from the sale of public lands, and were still increasing. The national debt had been all paid. General Jackson told his party that this money was a source of danger to the liberties of the country. The Democratic party in those days was hostile to internal improvements, and opposed them everywhere. Railroads were built by individual energy; rivers were obstructed by snags, sawyers, rafts, and sand bars, and even the harbors of the lakes and the St. Clair flats were found pretty much in the condition nature left them. This money was to be distributed in four installments, three of which were paid when an angry cloud hovered over our northern borders, threatening war with England, and the fourth installment was retained to pay the expenses of transporting troops to Maine, to Niagara, and to the Indian Stream country in northern New Hampshire. The amount paid over to our state exceeded over $800,000. The Legislature voted to divide the money among the towns in proportion to population. At the annual meeting on March 14, 1837, the town voted to receive the money, and William P. Weeks was appointed financial agent in relation to it. The money, $3,003.75, was ordered to be loaned at six per cent. interest, paid in advance, in sums of not over three hundred dollars nor less than one hundred to any one individual, the interest to be appropriated to the schools, and to be divided among the several school districts in town according to the number of scholars; and an inventory of the scholars was to be taken the following April 1st of all scholars under 21 and over 3 years of age.

The agent received the money and loaned it to such persons as complied with the terms agreed upon; no discrimination being made in regard to the politics of the person applying for it. In

1837 the amount of interest was $180.22, and the next year it was the same, things moved on smoothly and the scholars got the benefit of the interest money. At this date there was a heap of malignant cussedness slumbering in the hearts of our people. It came in with the mob that destroyed the academy, and cropped out upon all occasions of excitement. In December, 1838, when George Drake destroyed the windows in the academy, the town appointed Caleb Blodgett, Thomas Flanders and James Pattee an "Investigating Committee," and it was their duty to try and fix the outrage upon the abolitionists, Jonathan Kittredge, Nathaniel Sumner, William W. George, and their associates. So positive were they that this injury had been done by the abolitionists that they proceeded at once to pronounce sentence upon them, by voting that "all the surplus revenue in the hands of the abolitionists be collected forthwith by the treasurer." And that there might be no doubt where Jonathan Kittredge stood they voted that he "be consigned over to the abolitionists." The committee reported that they had not been able to fix any charge upon anybody except the town, and the town paid their charges, $59.68. At the same meeting they voted to repair the Academy, the expense of which, amounting to $28.37, was paid out of the surplus revenue. At the March meeting in 1839 they voted "to collect a sum of the surplus revenue sufficient to buy a farm for the poor, and to stock it, and to furnish the house on said farm." James Pattee, Chamberlain Packard, Jr., and Joseph Dustin were appointed a committee to buy the farm.

The farm they proposed to buy was the old Deacon Welch farm, then owned by Moses Pattee, consisting of one hundred acres and also another piece of forty acres in the north part of the town above John Currier's. The Pattee homestead had cost the impecunious Moses about eleven hundred dollars; but his brothers, Daniel and James, held a mortgage against it. They were willing and anxious to receive their money back, and as Daniel was chairman of the board of selectmen, it was not difficult for him to pursuade the "Board," and as James was chairman of the buying committee it was not difficult for him to persuade the others that the farm was worth much more than the sum it cost Moses, and that it would be greatly to the interest of (the Pattee family) the town and the poor thereof to purchase it at the price asked. The town became the happy possessor of these valuable pieces of real estate on March 18, 1839, about a week after they voted. The poor had a farm, the Pattees got their money back, and a large hole was made in the sum total of the surplus revenue. But there were many voters who were not satisfied with this disposition of their money. They thought there was too much family interest at work in getting rid of that farm for so much money,— $1,450 for the land, and $550 to carry out the second part of the "vote." The town worked this farm with the usual results to such speculations — that mean losses every year — for a little over seven years, and then was glad to find a purchaser on August 8, 1846, at $1,200, in Moses French of Enfield. The furniture and stock were sold for what they would bring at auction. The loss to the town in this operation amounted to 10 per cent. per annum on its investment, without reckoning the diminished amounts paid to schools.

For two years, 1837 and 1838, the interest on the surplus revenue distributed to the schools was $180.22 each year. In 1839 the amount fell off to $60; in 1840 it was $60; and in 1841 it was $60; and the sum total of this revenue which accrued to the benefit of the schools during the five years it attracted the greed of the people was $540.44. After 1843 it ceased to appear in the records, because it had then been absorbed into the pockets of the taxpayers. One thousand dollars of the surplus revenue went into Canaan Union Academy, and with it $300 of the literary fund, and never came out. In 1843 the amount of the surplus revenue was $775.58, when the town voted to distribute it, as a result of the trouble which had arisen over the collection of the notes of the proprietors of the academy. In 1844, March 9, the amount of surplus revenue paid to Daniel Campbell was $814.32, and then it disappears from the records. When Dame's Gore was annexed, the town received $113.95 as the share of the gore. This also was absorbed and disappeared into the town treasury to pay the town debts.

In 1821, at the March meeting, the town voted "that the notes for the school fund be lodged with the town treasurer and kept and managed by him under the direction of the selectmen and the town." What this vote refers to is not known, unless it is a resurrection of the old funds received from the sale of the school lands in 1806, for the literary fund was not created by act of the Legislature until June 29, 1821. This law was designed to distribute the bank taxes collected by the state amongst the schools in the several towns according to their scholars. In 1822 the school fund comes up again and the town voted "that all persons indebted to the school fund by note, procure two sureties, and no notes to be renewed without two sureties." In 1829 the town was asked to make some disposition of the literary fund and the "old school fund," but they refused. In 1830 the town voted that "the first selectman take the direction of the school fund and put it to the best interest of the town." In 1832 the town voted to divide the interest and principal of the literary fund over $1,00 and distribute it into the several school districts, according to polls and estate, and to let out the school fund of $1,000 to best advantage with sureties. In 1833 the town voted to purchase a poor farm not to exceed $1,000, and immediately afterwards voted $300 to purchase the poor farm, and also to place the school fund in the treasurer's hands.

Elijah Blaisdell had the school fund and did not pass it over, so the town appointed Luther Kinne agent to prosecute Elijah to "final execution." Later, in July, the town voted to use the $300 appropriated for the poor farm towards the road around Clark Hill, and then tried to appropriate the school fund to buy the farm, but the town dismissed the latter article. In 1834 the town appropriated the interest on the school fund and $120 of principal of the literary fund "to be received from the state." They, then, that there might not be any doubt as to how the funds were to be disposed of in the future,

Resolved, That it is the duty of the treasurer to take charge of the school and literary fund, keep a regular account of the same in a book appropriated for that purpose, see that the notes are regularly renewed at least once in two years on the first day of February and made amply secure. Collect the interest and make a regular transfer of the money received from the state, and so much of the interest of the permanent school and literary fund as will make the sum of $120 annually, from the amount of the literary fund to the amount of the school money raised by the town, and to pay the same with the school money for the order of the selectmen for the support of schools and for no other purpose.

On January 19, 1837, the town

> Voted that the money in the hands of John H. Harris, George Harris and Nathaniel Currier, being a part of the school fund and belonging to the town, be collected and appropriated to the payment of the expenses and charges of the town the current year as far as it may be needed, and that the selectmen of the town give their notes in behalf of the town to the treasurer for the amount. And that the treasurer collect the same as soon as may be.

So vanishes the school fund, the literary fund continues to be received from the state and in 1839 amounts to $766.04, represented by notes of persons who had borrowed the money. And the town continues to divide the interest among the several school districts. In 1847, $233.96 of the town money is added to the literary fund and in 1851 $300 of the principal with the interest is appropriated for the use of schools "immediately." The town, however, receives each year from the state "interest on the literary fund" for the benefit of schools, which is raised from the tax on banks, railroads, telephone and telegraph companies. In 1865 the literary fund, which was loaned in several notes at six per cent. interest, the income to be used for the benefit of schools, amounted to about $1,000. The interest was not always promptly paid. The town decided to collect this money, and "adding enough to it to purchase a state bond or some other good paying security for $1,000, the same to be kept; and the interest to be used for schooling." In 1879 the state redeemed the bond and the town applied the money on the town debt. So disappears the literary fund. It is still put down in the selectmen's report of the financial condition of the town as a permanent debt, and the town pays interest on it for the benefit of the schools, being compelled to by the wording of its receipt to the state treasurer.

CHAPTER XIV.

THE BAPTIST CHURCH.

From the earliest settlement of this town its people have been strongly sectarian in religious matters. Personal recollections of the old people are, that they conceived it to be a vital importance to make a public confession of religion, and to be constant in their attendance upon its ordinances. Without reflecting that (in many cases) it was only an outside garment for Sunday use, the sentiment grows upon one that these solemn faced old gentlemen, whose constant appearance at the meeting-house, riding on horseback and bringing their wives upon a pillion behind them, were men of God to whom no evil could come nigh. My own increasing years and a more extended knowledge of human frailties and infirmities has considerably modified that sentiment. But that which used to excite my admiration greatly was the individuality that marked the rugged character of those men. There were none learned among them — nor were they much given to reading, except in the Bible and a few religious books they brought with them. Each man was his own expounder of the faith and doctrine he held to. They were all more or less given to expressing their views on Sundays, and having once announced their beliefs, they were not inclined to modify them, however they might differ from received opinions. There were strong voiced persons among them, who gradually monopolized the time, and at length crowded out the feeble. These men and women were never favorable to being taxed to pay for preaching, because they considered themselves qualified to preach for nothing. The records for many years give us only negative votes upon the subject. At length, when young Thomas Baldwin, one of their own boys, sprightly, eloquent and consistent, by hard study and steady application, had been set apart and ordained as an evangelist, and placed over this young church and people they yielded gracefully to him as their leader. The women loved and petted him, and the men honored and respected him for his manly, yet gentle

Paper Mill

Catholic Church

M. E. Church, Street

Congregational Church

character — and 35 pounds was readily voted for preaching for his support. But in the flush of their pleasure at having a leader, and while they were congratulating themselves upon their unanimity, there was heard one little piping voice and then another very feeble, sounding much as if ashamed of its own weakness, and then another — until five men came haltingly forward and "descented" to raising the tax. They did not believe it Scriptural to support a man for doing nothing but preach,— it would be encouraging laziness. They liked for the brethren to have a chance to tell of the Lord's doings, and not pay for a man's speech when his hands were idle. "No, they wan't a going to do no such thing." Everybody in that hard working community ought to have a chance to free his mind in his own way. It was put to vote, and those dissenting fellows were excused from paying any part of the tax. Each day while clearing away the forests, or working the lands, these strong minded men were rehearsing the thoughts they intended to speak at the next Sunday gathering. Among them were many fluent speakers — men, who with education, might have shone in the world of letters. With such men for fathers it is no wonder that many of the sons became preachers, and that several of them should attain eminence in the denomination to which they attached themselves.

The first preacher of whom we have any record was James Treadway, who came here as a settler in 1770. We know but little about his doctrine, and what is known of the man, is not any evidence of Christian principles, but rather a desire to better himself during the temporary lethargy of the proprietors, who, when they realized that all men are not honest, promptly rebuked him, and in a few years he disappears.

The first church established in Canaan was Baptist, the record of this event has been laid aside, but it was probably about 1780, that is, that denomination seemed to have the most followers, and in the early days the most control over who should preach. Before the meeting-house was built there was no stated place of worship, they met where it was convenient. Late in the summer of 1780 there came to town two Baptist evangelists, illiterate, but very zealous in their intercourse with the people. Their homely talk roused a large interest in religious matters. Their names have passed out of story and we cannot, if we would, give their address. They remained here several weeks. Some old professors were worked up and several young persons converted, among the others was Thomas Baldwin. He had already, since the death of his boy, Erastus, become a studious and serious young man. After these strangers had departed a suggestion was uttered that a church organization would be desirable, which led in a short time to the calling of a conference. Elder Elisha Ransom of Woodstock, Vt., was consulted. Other clergymen, including Rev. Samuel Ambrose, of Sutton, were invited to take part, and a church was organized in Caleb Welch's barn on South Road, that being the most convenient place for that purpose. It has come down in tradition that William Plummer, afterwards governor, preached his Tory sermon in the Deacon's barn, in 1780. It was also the place where many religious meetings were held in pleasant weather. Caleb Welch and John Worth were elected deacons. Deacon Worth invited himself to take charge of the singing, and it is said that he clung to that office with great tenacity. About thirty persons were admitted to membership. For a while the new church was ministered to by preachers from neighboring towns, and when these failed they relied upon the talent which circumstances had developed among them. No effort was made to settle a preacher for many months. Mr. Baldwin frequently conducted the exercises, and at length decided to prepare himself for the ministry.

In the spring of 1783 the church invited him to receive ordination and become their pastor. A council was called in June and he received ordination as an evangelist, and was put in charge of this church. Thomas Baldwin was a son of Thomas Baldwin; his mother was the second wife of Dr. Ebenezer Eames, who built the first mill in town. He was born in Bozrah, Conn., December 25, 1753, and came to Canaan with his mother and Doctor Eames in 1769. He worked as a carpenter for several years, and built a house near the old James Pattee place on South Road. Some of the old barns he framed, stood for many years, that of Joshua Wells, on the old Wells farm and the old Worth Tavern, which was torn down to make room for the new house built by Dr. E. M. Tucker, where Mrs. St. Armand lives. He built a house on the intervale, about a hundred rods from the house once occupied by B. M. Howard, now owned by George W. Davis. He planted his apple seeds; several trees were standing a few years back, in the vicinity of the old cellar, and hurried back to Colchester, Conn., where a young friend was waiting for him, Ruth Huntington. He was nearly twenty-two years old and she was several years younger. They were married on September 21, 1775, and soon afterwards set out on their return to Canaan. He had but one horse, which carried his little store of goods and his young wife, she occasionally resting herself by walking with him along the single trail that led through almost unending dense forests. Through Connecticut and Massachusetts there were occasional settlements, with roads passable for such vehicles as the people possessed. After passing into New Hampshire the places of refuge were seldom met. Several times during their journey they camped by the wayside. They arrived in Canaan about the last of October and were duly received by the people and installed in their new home. Here they lived several years; here their children were born. In the old record we read as follows: "May 19, 1777 Erastus Baldwin son to Thomas and Ruth Baldwin, was born." In the graveyard on the Street is an old slatestone slab that used to bear the following inscription.

ERASTUS
Son of Elder Thomas and Ruth Baldwin.
Died Nov. 2, 1777, in his 7th month.
This fading flower
Cut down and
Withered in an hour

It is the oldest stone in the yard, but the storms of nearly a hundred and thirty-three years have crumbled it to pieces so that the words are not decipherable. It is said Mr. Baldwin cut this stone with his own hands, and this is the only relic of the famous old elder which exists in Canaan. It was probably not erected until several years after the child's death, and exhibits a trace of vanity that is not objectionable. When the child died, in 1777, the father had not become an "Elder," but he had already experienced religion in Deacon Welch's barn, chiefly through the strong religious sentiment that pervaded the heart and character of his wife. In this house was born to them three other children, Sarah on June 8, 1780, Ruth on August 31, 1782, and Thomas, Jr., on August 29, 1784.

This house was bought by Oliver Smith, a very precise old man; when town clerk he used to place on record the day of the week and the hour of the birth of each one of the numerous Smith family. After Smith's departure it passed into the hands of Stephen Jenniss, whose advice to his son will long be remembered, "That in a dark night when it rains hard, the middle of the road is the safest place to walk." When the railroad was built, the old house was sold at auction to Mr. Weeks, who wanted it for the memories of Doctor Baldwin that clung around it. He took it down and built a house with its timbers at East Canaan. After this he took it down again, carried the timbers to the old Pinnacle House, then his residence on the Street, and built a carriage house and sheep barn of them, where it stood for many years until torn down a few years ago.

He was raised and educated in the doctrine of the Puritans, and became a convert to Baptism on reading a book entitled, "The Divine Right of Infant Baptism." The town records are silent during the first three years of young Baldwin's service, he was town clerk, but he, no doubt, considered his time more valuable for saving souls that telling what was done in town meeting. But a vote passed October 7, 1790, at a town meeting held at the house of Capt. Robert Barber, gives something of what was done as follows:

Voted that we do hereby ratify and confirm a vote passed in the year 1783 (which vote is now lost), respecting the settlement of Elder Thomas Baldwin, in which vote the town voted to approve and confirm what the church had done, in calling Elder Baldwin to be ordained as an evangelist, and to exercise pastoral care over the church and congregation, so long as he should judge it his duty to continue here, by which he was considered as the minister of said town, tho not confined for any certain time.

The first mention of his receiving any pay for his services, or rather not receiving any, was a vote passed in December, 1786, when it was "voted that a vote passed to give Mr. Baldwin 40 pounds be reconsidered." On March 22, 1787, the town voted "to give Mr. Baldwin 30 pounds in Labor and produce the present year," and that his estate be exempt from taxation.

In 1789 Mr. Baldwin received a call from the Baptist Church in Tunbridge, Mass., and about the same time one from Hampton, Conn. In February the town voted "that Elder Baldwin is not under obligation to this town any longer than it appears to him to be his duty to stay and preach in it." It was also voted "that Elder Baldwin would continue and preach in Town, so long as he can see it to be duty." He set out early in the summer and on the way received a call from the second Baptist Church in Boston. He preached at both Tunbridge and Hampton and received unanimous calls from both. He then went to Boston and on July 4, 1790, preached his first sermon there and then returned to Canaan. On March 9th, 1790, the town voted "to raise 30 pounds for the support of Elder Baldwin, excepting those who are conscience bound that they cannot support ministers that way" and "that any person who shall pay Elder Baldwin and take his receipt, it shall answer to the Constable for his proportion." On August 22, 1790, the church in Boston gave him a unanimous call. He continued to minister to this congregation until September 18, 1790, after being the first settled minister in town for seven years, when he accepted the call to Boston and was installed November 11, 1790. The church here increased in numbers under his preaching, and at his departure there were some seventy or eighty members. The general feeling in the church is represented to have been good, although as in all such bodies, there were some irrepressible persons who became impatient at having their talents ignored.

Coming into Canaan a poor boy he left it a wealthy man, as owner of the Minister's right, he realized from that, as well as from the purchase of other rights, and from the sale of land which he had purchased and mortgaged back. In 1794 he received the degree of A. M. from Brown University, and in 1803 the degree of D. D. from Union College. He edited the *Baptist Magazine* from 1803 to 1817. His election sermon, preached in 1802, went through three editions. His 250 page answer to Rev. Samuel Wonston, showed his best efforts. He was founder of Waterville College, Maine; on his annual visit to attend the commencement in 1824, he preached twice at Hallowell, Me. The next day, August 29, he spent in walking over the college grounds and upon going to bed, slept for a short time, groaned and died, aged 71 years, and was buried in Boston. He is described as a large man, well formed, and pleasing countenance. In appearance much like Webster; of military carriage and a splendid figure on horseback.

William Kimball, 85 years old, in 1881 remembered hearing him preach in the old meeting-house in 1817. "He drove up from Boston in a chaise, accompanied by his daughter, stayed at Joshua Harris' Inn; the people all thronged to see him and offered him hospitality, but he remained at the Inn. He preached once from the text 'Grieve not the Spirit.' The house was thronged with eager listeners. Pushee led the choir, with his violin, and the music was grand and full-toned. No more eloquent prayers have ever been spoken in Canaan from that day to this. They were complete, and so effective that everybody but Pettingill were in tears before they knew it. Everything that needed praying for was brought in, and got a short and eloquent blessing without any effort. The beauty of his prayer was it was short and comprehensive. I was a young man, but I have never heard another prayer that has or can displace that in my memory."

Ruth, his wife, died February 11, 1812. He married second Margaret Duncan of Haverhill, Mass., who survived him many years.

After the departure of Mr. Baldwin, there was no stated preaching. Various "trials" had been made, but no preacher had given such satisfaction as to induce the town to vote upon that subject. At length, about the 17th of June, 1793, there came along a young elder, whose gifts excited in them a gleam of hope, and on this day the inhabitants held a public meeting at the house of Capt. Robert Barber, to see, "1st. If the town would agree to hire Elder Elisha Ransom to preach for one year. 2nd. To see what sum of money the town will agree to raise for the support of said Ransom; and 3rd, to see if the town will provide any house for said Ransom to live in." The doings of the town are dispatched on this occasion in two brief lines. "Choose Lt. Thomas Miner Moderator. Voted to dissolve this meeting," and Elder Elisha Ransom disappears forever from our records. A committee on preaching had been previously appointed. They continued their search for a preacher, and on the 19th of November, of the same year, they reported another candidate, but the town declined to accept their report. However, the town voted 35 pounds lawful money "to support a preacher of the Gospel for one year," and Dea. Caleb Welch, Lieut. William Richardson and John Benedict were chosen a committee "to lay out the above sum of money in procuring Mr. Hooper if he can be obtained, if not some other man agreeable to the town." The time when Mr. Hooper was to begin was left discretionary with the committee. The "hireing" never began; Mr. Hooper disappears without coming to sight. During the year 1794, but little effort was made to procure preaching. The good people lamented the sad state into which they had fallen. They talked of one another as being obstinate and by their prejudices as being stumbling blocks to Christian progress. Each one asked the other to yield, but declined to give up his own preferences. It was a condition of society which has had its counterpart many times since. Up to the 10th of March, 1795, there was no success in procuring preaching. It was deemed impossible to unite the people upon any one person. But on this day, they made an effort and directed their committee to send to Mr. Uriah Smith to come and preach upon trial. All former votes were reconsidered and "30 pounds lawful money was raised to hire preaching the ensuing year." Smith was put "upon trial," and on the 29th of July, 1795, he was "hired to preach with us three months," at the rate of $10 per month. On November 2, Mr. Smith was hired to preach "till the Second Sunday of March next," at the same compensation.

At the annual meeting in 1796, forty pounds were voted for preaching. In consequence of this vote, five gentlemen entered their dissent and protested against "raising money this way," to support a preacher of the gospel. In order to quiet their opposition, it was voted that these five gentlemen, Thomas Miner, Dudley Gilman, John Richardson, Robert Williams, and Asa Paddleford might be excused from paying their rates, which they refused to accept. They made themselves so busy in creating public opinion, that on the 15th of March, seven days after the former vote, when the town "voted to hire Mr. Smith for six months at $10 per month, he to board himself" the dissenters showed a strong and growing opposition. This time they reconsidered the vote to raise forty pounds and voted thirty pounds, and the number who entered their dissent against paying the "thirty pounds" and also against hiring Mr. Smith had increased to twenty-five. The best men in town their names are below:

Thomas Miner	Shubal Burdick
Robert Williams	Hubbard Harris
Robert Wilson	E. Scofield
Moses Hadley	James Morse
Reuben Kimball	Asa Kimball
John Richardson	Joshua Richardson
Joseph Clark	John Wilson
Henry Springer	Daniel Kimball
Dudley Gilman	Simon Blanchard
Asa Paddleford	Caleb Wilder
Abel Hadley	John Worth
Josiah Barber	Joseph Flint
Levi Straw	

The town adhered to its vote and refused to release them from paying the tax. Mr. Smith continued to preach and to receive $10 per month until March, 1797, after which date he did not appear again in the pulpit. He lived several years in town, after he ceased to preach, and taught school in a schoolhouse that stood in the old orchard of Jacob Tucker, nearly opposite the house of Mr. Gideon Spencer on the old road to Dorchester. Afterwards he moved to Enfield, where he died.

There was still but one church in Canaan, but it was not strong enough to support itself and the great obstacle to securing "stated preaching" was found in the unwillingness of the members of this church to listen to preachers of any other belief. It was not strong enough to pay the expense of a Baptist preacher. There were Congregationalists, Universalists, and a few Methodists, and also a few impracticable men, who like some persons in these days, thought their own teachings good enough for the people, and were not inclined to yield their rights to any new comer. Each belief was jealous of the others, and refused to coöperate lest they might lose individuality. The result was they had no stated preaching for several years. Whenever a religious meeting was held, Dea. Richard Clark, Dea. John Worth, or Mrs. Miriam Harris would seize the opportunity to deliver their melancholy rhapsodies to an impatient audience, and this had got to be so severe a trial, that they at last resolved to form a society upon the "principles of equality," as they termed it. Elder Tyler said Dea. Richard Clark was a powerful exhorter, would sometimes lose himself in his zeal. Spittle would fly from both sides of his mouth, one corner at a time, and his nose was a river of snot, which he used to blow about him first from one nostril and then the other, stopping one with his thumb. He was long winded and very annoying to Thomas Baldwin.

To give the movement greater force a legal meeting was called, on the 28th of August, 1797. At this meeting the opponents of the society were so demonstrative, as nearly to break it up. After severe discussion, the house was divided, when it was found that the disorganizers were few in numbers but large in noise. Then Jehu Jones, Joseph Wadley and Richard Whittier were elected a committee to confer with a like committee appointed from the church, consisting of John Worth, William Richardson and Deacon Welch, who were to report a constitution for the society at an adjourned meeting. On the 4th of September, the committee made their report, which was accepted by the town. It was signed by a large number of men in columns according to their belief. I have thought it proper to print this report, together with the names attached to it, to show something of the form of thought which characterized the religious mind of those days. The manuscript is the original draft of the report, and the names were written by the individual owners. The paper is much worn, as if it had passed through many hands, before it slept the long sleep, before it came into my possession.

CONSTITUTION.

We, the subscribers, inhabitants of the town of Canaan, taking into consideration the importance of having the gospel preached among us, and the benefits and privileges that will accrue to us, our families, and the community at large, thereby do for the better promoting the same mutually and by our free consent enter into and join in a society to act agreeable to the following sentiments rules and regulations, namely

First, That we will support a minister by an equality, among ourselves according to what we are possessed of.

Second. That we will pay our several proportions of the sum or sums that the society shall raise from time to time for the support of the minister as they shall direct.

Third, That the minister be one that can bring credentials of his being a member of a regular gospel church, and in good standing with them, and can give evidence of his call to the work of preaching the gospel.

Fourth, That when the church have called a minister, and the society like him they will manifest their agreement with them in the matter.

Fifth, That it is the privilege of the minister and the church to lead in the worship, but if the society take the singing from the church, we will not contend so as to make a disturbance in the meeting, but will endeavor patiently to bear it as a trial.

Sixth, That it is not our intention to debar any of the proprietors or society from enjoying their privilege in the meeting house according to their interest.

Seventh, That all prudential matters shall be determined by the majority of the society, which shall consist of two thirds of the members present at the meeting.

Eighth, There shall be a standing committee, whose duty it shall be to warn meetings when applied to by seven members of the society.

Ninth, There shall be a clerk who shall make a fair record of the doings of the society.

Tenth, That there shall be a treasurer, assessors, and a collector or collectors for the society.

Eleventh, The above agreement made and entered into this 4th. day of Sept., A. D. 1797 to stand for the term of one year, as witness our hands.

Baptists.
John Worth
Caleb Welch
Ezekiel Wells
Caleb Pierce
John M. Barber
Joseph Wadley
Ezekiel Gardner
Nath. Whittier
Joshua Wells
Oliver Smith
Hubbard Harris
Israel Harris
William Harris
Jehu Jones
Timothy Johnson jr
Abel Hadley

Jacob Miller
Robbard Barber
Richard Whittier
Nathaniel Barber
John Currier
Stephen Worth
Caleb Welch jr
Thomas Miner
Joshua Clement
Nathan Beebe
Richard Clark
Simeon Arvin
Daniel Colby
Josiah Clark
Richard Clark jr
Ebenezer Clark
John Worth jr

THE BAPTIST CHURCH.

Caleb Seabury
Elam Meacham
Enoch Sweat
David Pearson
Samuel Chapman
Samuel Noyes
Nathaniel Gilman
Reynold Gates
Samuel Welch
Thomas Morse
Samuel Welch jr
Thaddeus Lathrop
Eliphlet Clark
Joshua Meacham
Thomas Cole
Judah Wells
James Morse
Jabez Smith
William Parkhurst
Bailey Cross
Elijah Whittier
Jonathan Dustin
David Jones

Universalists.
J. M. Colcord
Joshua Harris

Congregationalists.
William Richardson
Levi Bailey
Reuben Currier
Hezekiah Jones
Eliphlet Norris
Joshua Pillsbury
Moody Noyes
Dudley Noyes
Richard Otis
Clement Goddard
David Smith
John May
Moses Richardson
Richard Clark
Enoch Richardson
Joshua Richardson
Mathew Athaton
John Perley
Daniel Johnson
Warren Wilson
John Richardson
John Sweet
Jacob Richardson
John Wilson
Thomas Bedel
Timothy Johnson

At the meeting on the 4th of September, Oliver Smith was chosen clerk; John Worth, Jehu Jones and William Richardson, were appointed the "standing committee" to procure preaching. They also voted $100 to pay for preaching for one year. The committee were successful in finding a candidate who was willing to serve in the pulpit.

His name was Ezra Wilmarth. He stayed several weeks, preaching and visiting among the families, and won the good will of the town to such an extent, that on the 28th of November, 1797, they voted to hire him and pay him "fifty-two pounds as compensation for preaching with us one year." They also agreed to move his family to Canaan and provide a house for them to live in. It was "voted to give Lt. Richard Whittier $13.50 for bringing half a ton — either Mr. Wilmarth's family or his goods from Fairfax, Conn., to Canaan — if his family, the society is to pay their expense on the road. Lieut. Whittier is to have two-thirds of the money before he starts from home."

"Voted to give Lieut. Thomas Miner ten dollars for bringing half a ton from Fairfax to Canaan, meaning Mr. Wilmarth's family or goods." The committee was ordered to make "provision for Mr. Wilmarth respecting a house to live in and some necessaries of life, &c." Thirteen pounds were raised for "moving" Mr. Wilmarth and providing him a house to live in when he gets here. "Sunday the 14th day of January, 1798, the Rev. Mr. Wilmarth returned to Canaan with his family, and moved in with Mr. Josiah Clark. His time began on said day."

Mr. Wilmarth went about his labors serene and happy in the belief that he was appreciated for his faithfulness.

The people had concluded they had found the man they needed. A town meeting was called in August, when John Currier, Jehu Jones and Caleb Seabury were appointed "a committee on the part of the town to be joined by such of the hon. church as they may appoint to consult and propose a method for the settlement and support of Rev. E. Wilmarth." The committee made a detailed report of the method and then the town appointed William Richardson, John Worth and John Currier, a committee to present a call to Mr. Wilmarth, ask his acceptance and confer with him respecting his settlement over them in the gospel ministry.

Considerable diplomacy entered into the question right here between the church and town. Deacon Worth and Richard Clark, whose "gifts" in long prayers and longer exhortations, never came at a timely moment, would not cut off their privileges. Besides these brethren had pitched the tunes and sung the solemn singing in their own way, without harp or sackbut. Fiddles and fifes were an abomination to these pious souls. They made no objection to Mr. Wilmarth if all their rights were preserved. The town yielded all they claimed, and then a united call was given to the preacher, who was asked to accept it and name a day for his installation. Right here occurs a hiatus in the records, the result of old Oliver Smith's usual negligence. Several meetings were held of which he have no account and some of the terms agreed upon between the high parties are left to conjecture. But it is plain enough that somebody was getting jealous, and couldn't agree.

On the 17th of December the town voted to settle Mr. Wilmarth, agreeably to the conditions reported by the committee and which had been assented to by all parties. Previous to this date, several persons who disliked Deacon Worth's hum-drum music, astonished that worthy man by taking the wind out of his mouth without asking his consent. It was an insult he would not forgive. They might as well stop his praying and exhorting as his singing. So he rallied his forces, and called upon the church to rise up and vote a rebuke of this audacious outrage.

He got himself appointed the avenger of the church and issued the stately document which follows:

The church in Canaan hereby inform the town that in consequence of their assuming the authority of governing the singing in a way that they knew was disagreeable to the Church without any condescension or regard to them in the matter and of the Selectmen's making a tax or rate for the support of preaching without giving the Church notice of it that they might take off their proportion according to the proposal made by the Church which the town voted to comply with, therefore they have withdrawn their call of Elder Wilmarth till the town shall satisfy them on the above particulars.

JOHN WORTH,
By order of the Church.

Dec. 1st. 1798.

N. B. That although we agreed to bear a trial for one year we do not feel willing always to bear it.

Then followed a letter from Mr. Wilmarth declining to settle. It was addressed to Messrs. John Worth, John Currier and Richard Whittier, Committee, Canaan:

CANAAN, Dec. 3rd, 1798.

Gentlemen: As the worthy and respectable inhabitants of this town have been pleased to honor me with a call to settle among them as a minister of the gospel, and you were the committee thro' whom it was communicated to me, I esteem it my duty to make a reply via you to them.

I feel myself under a present necessity of answering you in the negative — and my reasons here follow:

1st. When the town voted the request it was with a promise that nine-tenths of the town were in favor of it, and were I to give my answer in the affirmative, it is possible, and even probable, that there would not be such a proportion in favor of my settlement, and consequently I might fall into the disagreeable predicament of being rejected after having consented.

2nd. The church in this town have seen fit to discontinue their call and vote me a letter of dismission and recommendation to any other church of the same faith and order — their reasons for withdrawing their call will be communicated to you via their committee.

These, gentlemen, are some of my reasons for not, at present, accepting your request. It is possible, however, that they may be removed.

Whether I ever settle among you or not, I assure you of my best wishes for your welfare, as a people, and should I leave you, it will be with painful anxiety for your future happiness. I am, gentlemen, yours and the public's devoted humble servant.

EZRA WILMARTH.

After this date, although the town yielded the points in dispute and renewed its call to the preacher, a coolness grew up between them which increased from day to day, until the year expired. On the 17th of April, 1799, it was voted not to permit "Mr. Wilmarth to make up the time he lost in preaching but there shall be deducted twenty shillings for every day he has lost."

Ezekiel Wells was appointed a committee "to ascertain what Mr. Wilmarth has received and what there is due him."

It took the committee until the 10th of May to make up a bill of particulars, when it reported that "according to the receipts exhibited by the collector.

Mr. Wilmarth has received......................	£24:5:1
That he was absent five days, went away one day before his time was out, and three days preached only a half day.................................	7:10:0
Deducted from...................................	52:0:0
Leaves due Mr. Wilmarth........................	21:4:11

And Mr. Ezra Wilmarth stepped out of Canaan without being settled which seems to have afforded mutual pleasure to all parties, particularly to the gifted ones, John, Richard and Miriam. On leaving Canaan he was settled over the church in Rumney in April, 1799, and was dismissed in May, 1811.

Notwithstanding their promptness in dismissing him it was two years and upwards before they paid him the balance due and part of this he took in due bills and personal promises.

Dea. John Worth, who lived across the Pond on the Landon place, was a poet, also, but the productions of his genius, like his dust, have long since mingled and become a part of the common things of this life. All that has survived of his wonderful poetic talents are the following lines, addressed to "Pride":

> Pride, don't come on!
> Thou hast undone,
> Many a son.
>
> Pride, don't come arter!
> Thou hast undone
> Many a darter!

Soon after Mr. Wilmarth's departure Rev. Aaron Cleveland, great-grandfather of Grover Cleveland, a clergyman from Norwich, Conn., visited friends in Canaan, and was invited to preach. He preached in the unfinished meeting house, and being a Congregationalist, like many of the settlers from Connecticut, they offered him inducements to remain here. A town meeting was called on the 12th of August, 1799, and "$100 was voted to be raised and to be appropriated for the purpose of hiring Mr. Aaron Cleveland if he can be obtained." Dea. Joshua Pillsbury, Micah Porter and Richard Otis were chosen a committee to confer with him, and report their success to the town. Everyone was confident that Mr. Cleveland would stay for the "$100." They expected no refusal, for why had he wandered so far from home, if he was not in search of employment. They took another vote, as if to confirm their resolution. "Voted that we will hire preaching." And another: "Voted that we hire Mr. Cleveland until March meeting, if he can be obtained." But against the two last votes, there were vigorous protests from the following gentlemen, "as the law directs," Jehu Jones, Reynold Gates, Joshua Wells, Josiah Clark and Daniel Colby, the first three from Colchester and the last from Newmarket and Haverhill. Mr. Cleveland seems to have been willing to remain in Canaan, but he pointed out to the committee that $100 was small compensation for the continued services of a minister of the gospel. They proposed to give him as a further inducement the half of the minister's right which had been deeded to the town by Elder Baldwin.

He remained here until September 1st, without accepting their invitation. Then pressing duties calling him to Connecticut, he sent the committee the following letter:

Messrs. Otis, Pillsbury and Porter, Committee:

Gentlemen—In answer to your request that I should stay a week longer than was proposed, let me observe:

That should the town wish to convene again to make me some further proposals, a meeting may be warned on Monday next and Mr. Otis will attend, who proposes a journey to Connecticut immediately after. By him, therefore, the proposals of this town can be forwarded to me, which I shall lay before our Association and be directed by them respecting my future steps. Mr. Otis can also be present at the Association and represent the essential matters respecting the town, and respecting myself.

And you may rest assured that the cause of Zion lies so near their hearts that they will point out the line of my duty in the case. Respecting the proposal of the town as it now stands, this I should lay before the Association. Should the town proceed no further, and should be determined in the case as sd Association should advise.

It appears as a matter of importance to me that I should commence my journey on the first week in September, as I have mentioned from the first day I came to this town, and Mr. Otis going to Connecticut will supply the difficulty of my longer stay at this time.

I am gentlemen, yours,
and Canaan's well wisher,
AARON CLEVELAND.

The church sent Deacon Otis to urge their request, but the town did not offer him any further compensation. The Association advised him to remain in Connecticut, and nothing further was heard from him except the bill for his services in the pulpit amounting to $50. And at the next annual meeting in 1800 the town voted "to raise money enough to discharge the committee from the demands Mr. Cleveland has made against them for preaching."

No money was voted for preaching in 1800, excepting that which was to pay Mr. Cleveland; they were without a pastor. In 1801 Elder Samuel Ambrose, Elder Crowell, Elder Jones and Rev. Mr. Webster occupied the pulpit. In 1801 they voted $60 for preaching from June to the next annual meeting and from this time on to May, 1808, the town refused to pay for preaching. Many persons were annoyed at the persistency of Deacon Clark and Deacon Worth and their followers, in demanding too much recognition for themselves. And when in 1802 the warrant contained an article about preaching, Samuel Joslen, before it was put to vote, entered his dissent. He said it was time enough to get money, when it was found out who was going to get it, and he did not intend to be involved in any more blind taxes.

Thus far it appears that the good people of Canaan had assembled together in the meeting-house, all denominations, with a church organization, consisting mostly of Baptists, and a society consisting of many others, not members of the church. No denomination had separated itself, or organized itself into a separate association. The denominational feeling had become so strong that on February 16, 1802, the Baptists constituted themselves into "The Baptist Church of Christ in Canaan." On this date "Brother Richard Clark was chosen moderator and brother John Worth, Deacon and Clerk."

On June 17th following, Josiah Clark was chosen Deacon. From the records it does not appear that the work of the church or the labors of the brethren were of sufficient importance to merit being written. There was stupor and indifference and petty rivalries among the members, that prevented them from seeing any good however little it might be in each other.

At the date above written desire was expressed on the part of some of the brethren to have the church separate itself from all other denominations, and constitute itself simply the Baptist church in Canaan.

In the effort to revive the church the brethren engaged in it appointed a committee to emasculate the list of members, so that none but the worthy might have a place therein, and this they did so thoroughly that if we take their record as truth, they left but few disciples of John Calvin in town, and these were Josiah Clark, Nathaniel Gilman, Richard Clark, Daniel Kimball, Job Tyler, Esther Clark, Sarah Gilman, Pernal Clark, Lydia Pearson and Abigail Cole who was excommunicated in 1836.

We know from other sources that the Baptists, in numbers, exceeded all the other sects in town, between sixty and seventy names being found on a former record. We should have liked it better had they retained all the original names, so that we might know who and how many among the brave settlers were written down "as those who love the Lord."

Up to August 19, 1804, the record is blank, but at this date they voted to join the Woodstock Association. The number of members at this date is stated as thirty-eight, but only these additional names are found: Moses Kelley, Nancy Kelley, Samuel Welch, Moses Hadley, and Molly Hadley. After this statement there is more blank in the record, but it is evident that it was blanker in the church. It was a little before this time that the Congregational Church had been established. And the Baptist denomination among themselves had lost control of the organization. There seemed to be no controlling intelligence, and few or no educated persons to manage affairs. They talked of doctrine, and purifying the church; it was all talk and no action. They talked when they had nothing to say, and when the listeners were all bored instead of edified. As in the former years when the same men pursued the same course, they soon fell into by and forbidden paths, and got lost in the great desert of the world. To extricate themselves from this unprogressive condition, the brethren prayed to be enlightened. It was made plain then as it has often been since that no religious sect in the town of Canaan was strong enough in men and money to give proper support to a respectable preacher.

The preaching by the resident orators was little attended to and the candidates for the favor of the church and people gave no satisfaction. They just appeared above the religious horizon and vanished like a summer cloud. The singing, then as now, was a fruitful theme of irritation. Benjamin Trussell, a musician of more than ordinary ability, a good singer, and performer upon the violoncello, had moved into town and was invited to contribute his part in the devotional exercises of the people. Like a true musician, Mr. Trussell believed that singing is only another form of praising God, and that the more sweet sounds he brought to his aid, the greater was God's pleasure. He took his violoncello into the seats, and tuned it before the congregation. Deacon Worth, who was counted as one of the guardians of all the proprieties in the church, and a leader of the singers, was more shocked than he had been on the occasion of the call of Mr. Wilmarth. That was simply a vocal interruption, but this was an invasion of the house of God, with the strains that the devil used to tempt young people to dance. A few other impulsive enthusiasts joined the deacon in denouncing the "devil music," and threatened to call a meeting of the church and expel the offender. They talked a good deal of nonsense, and some of the old singers, with Deacon Worth at their head threatened to leave the choir, and not sing any more, only that this was just what the other party wanted, and they would not afford them that gratification. The gentle spirit of Christian forbearance had nearly fled from the church, when good old Samuel Meacham, an early and devout Methodist, raised his hands in the midst of the half angry company and quietly remarked: "Brethren, let us pray," and then, "We pray thee, good God, turn the thoughts of these wrangling singers from themselves unto Thee! Fill their hearts with harmony and love, and if there be a single chord of music in Brother Trussell's bass-viol, that will tend to increase our devotions to Thee, let us have it in all its fullness, and, O Lord, forbid that we should ever cast away any good or pleasant thing that falls across our lives, and now give us thy blessing, and send us courage to clear out the angry thoughts that have invaded our hearts, and when we meet again, may it be in love and affection. Amen." And Caleb Seabury and Moses Dole responded "So mote it be." And the singing after the mutual jealousies had become self-exhausted settled itself.

Mr. Trussell's viol became a favorite, with everyone except the inharmonious Deacon, and he never ceased to talk about it. In 1807 there was no preacher, and no prospect of one unless the people would unite upon some person and stand by him. So they agreed to lay aside their dogmas and personalities and form a "Union Society," while like all union societies in religion proved to be no union at all. Daniel Blaisdell was appointed to write an agreement, such as all would sign. A part of the agreement is copied here, not particularly for any intrinsic merit it contains, but as showing the involved and long-winded theology these people cherished, and how thoroughly they were convinced of original sin, and depravity, and the difficulty of making its meaning plain.

We, the subscribers, taking into consideration not only the salutary effects that morality and religion rightly grounded upon evangelical principles, hath upon society in general, but especially upon the rising generation, and being fully convinced that to have the gospel statedly preached amongst us by a regular methodical preacher, who is not only a man of good moral character, but is reputed to have his communion from on high, will not only have a tendency to lay in the hearts of men in general the strongest obligation to due subjection; but we profess to view it as an institution of Heaven, whereby to convince sinners of Adam's fallen family of their deplorable condition, and bring them to embrace offered grace through a glorious Mediator, as the only means to escape the displeasure of an angry God. And having for a long time viewed with anxiety the deplorable situation of the town of Canaan in this respect, and fearing lest we should not be able to answer at the bar of injured Justice, for our neglect to our children and society, do agree and covenant with each other, &c."

No subscription was to be binding until two-thirds of the common inventory of the town assented to the union.

Rev. Mr. Young of Salisbury, had preached several Sabbaths and many of the people were pleased with him, and were desirous that he should come and settle with them. They sent Richard Whittier and Richard Otis down to invite him to come up and "preach two Sundays more," when they hoped to be able to determine whether he was a suitable man. Mr. Young came as desired and spent a week getting acquainted with the people, and was received with much effusion. The "Union" embraced the Congregationalists and Methodists who were well enough pleased with Mr. Young, but to make it agreeable every way, it was agreed that Mr. Young should exchange at the request of the Congregationalists, once in eight weeks with "some minister of that order," residing within a radius of thirty-five miles. But it is doubtful if he ever had an opportunity to exchange with any one. He did preach here a few weeks after this invitation, but there is no means of telling either of his success, or the time of his exit. We do not know that he was "settled."

In 1808 the town voted to raise $150 to hire preaching, and that each religious denomination lay out their money agreeably to their conviction. The selectmen were directed to post a notice for six weeks, at Captain Arvin's, Lieutenant Moore's and Moses Dole's Inn, calling upon all the people to come forward, and state to what denomination they wished to pay their minister's tax, otherwise they would be taxed as Baptists. The record shows that while this vote was being discussed, Reynold Gates, Richard Clark, Jr., Josiah Barber and Stephen Worth "has come forward and entered their decent against paying a tax to hire preaching."

Stephen Worth had disputed with some of the brethren the correctness of all Baptists beliefs. And was for his rashness stigmatized "an infidel." The others were Baptists by birth, education and conviction, and their "decent" probably arose from sympathy with the long winded Clark.

This arrangement continued satisfactorily for a few years. In 1811 the town voted $100, "and each denomination to lay out the money their own way," a committee of three, Josiah Clark, Baptist; Joshua Pillsbury, Congregationalist, and Caleb Seabury, Methodist, were appointed to lay out the money. Again in 1812 the town voted to raise $150 to hire preaching during the year, and Caleb Seabury, Methodist; Daniel Blaisdell, Baptist, and Amos Gould, Congregationalist, were a committee to "hire preachers of each denomination." And they added a cruel amendment to this vote "that no part of the $150 should be paid to Lt. Richard Clark." Lieutenant Clark was opposed upon principle to paying money to preachers. He was a talking man and the Lord had given him gifts sufficient unto the needs of the people. He had asked the town to give him the whole or part of the money, claiming that on all occasions when there was no stated preaching, he had conducted religious services freely and often at much inconvenience. Many people were not pleased with Mr. Clark's use of his gifts and took this occasion to express their opinion.

In 1813 they voted to raise $100 for preaching, and once only after this, in 1819, did the town vote money for preaching and that vote was vigorously protested. The "Union Society" went to pieces in 1812, and there was a relapse into the old order of things, each denomination raising their own money in their own way by assessment, and hiring their own preachers. In 1813 a successful effort was made to unite the church and people, and a committee was sent to Grafton, with an invitation to Elder Joseph Wheat, to come and settle here, which he accepted.

Elder Wheat was a Baptist and preached to that church and society for twenty-three years. From the time of his installation in March, 1814, until during the year 1827, he lived as the pastor and teacher of the people, going out and in before them as an example of an honored and revered man. Inquiries among his descendants have failed to discover his birthplace. It is supposed that he originated in Newmarket. In the war of the Revolution he served seven years, and was discharged when twenty-three years of age. His subsequent career down to his arrival in Canaan is unknown to us. In 1813 he was preaching in various places hoping to get a home, and on two or three occasions occupied this pulpit. For many years previous to this date there had been no "stated" preaching. The people who professed to be Christians, were divided into cliques, and there were several persons who aspired to do the preaching. They could talk long and loud, and because of this "gift" they successfully opposed the raising of money to pay "hireling" preachers from abroad.

The people endured these gifted talkers with long suffering patience, and there seemed to be no remedy except in quiet submission or in active opposition. The same persons who had disturbed and driven Elder Baldwin out of town, had exercised their gifts upon Elder Uriah Smith, upon Elder Ezra Wilmarth, upon Rev. Aaron Cleveland and other candidates for the pulpit down to 1813, when a united effort was made to break up the gifted monopoly and introduce an era of things that should be respectable, orderly and systematic. Elder Joseph Wheat was then preaching occasionally in Grafton, 53 years old, ripe and manly, with large experiences of human grief and suffering; would he come to Canaan, take charge of the souls in this church, and gather up and soften the flinty hearts that were laughing at the dissensions among the saints? They sent their committee, he came, and preached a sermon two hours long. He told them he was a Baptist, but he was a Christian. They liked him, organized a society, and gave him an invitation to join his fortunes with theirs. The following is the preamble to their agreement which was written by Hon. Daniel Blaisdell:

> To all to whom these presents shall come, know ye, that we, the subscribers, believing that the preaching of the gospel was intended by the all wise Governor of the Universe as a mean whereby to communicate his special grace to a ruined world, and believing also that a regularly preached gospel tends to promote good order, and strengthen

The Baptist Church.   189

the bonds of society, Do agree to form ourselves into a society by the name of the First Baptist society in Canaan, for the purpose of hiring Elder Joseph Wheat to preach amongst us; And to that end we do agree that if he can be obtained to remove to Canaan and preach to us so many Sabbaths as forty five in a year, and attend to such lecters and funerals and elsewhere as is common for a settled minister to do. That we and each of us, will pay our proportion according to our inventory, taken by the selectmen for the time being, of the sum of one hundred and twenty dollars, to be assessed and collected by a collector, and to be appropriated and paid over for the support of our said minister and his family yeraly, the whole to be paid in cash, if paid to the collector, but if any choose to carry to his house corn, wheat, rye, flour or wool, he is to receive one half the sum due to him, and give his receipt for the same. . . . provided nevertheless, that the agreement and every part thereof shall be null and void, unless such and so many persons shall join said society, so as that the assessments made as aforesaid shall not exceed the sum of thirty cents on the poll.

This agreement contains the signatures of ninety-three men, subscribing in sums from fifty cents to two dollars and fifty cents. These men have long since passed off the stage of life.

"Thomas H. Pettingill agrees to pay Elder Joseph Wheat $1.00 a year so long as he shall preach in Canaan." "Daniel Blaisdell one half of inventory added if necessary." John Currier, Nathaniel C. Pierce, Harry Leeds, Job Tyler, Josiah Clark, Abraham Pushee, Timothy Tilton, Joshua Currier, Amasa Jones, Adam Pollard, Oliver Smith and Nathan Willis, one dollar each. John M. Barber, Samuel Willis and Daniel Pattee will give two dollars each. Cyrus B. Hamilton will pay $2.50. Then there are Daniel Colby and John Worth, and Levi Bailey and Wales Dole and Amos Gould and William Campbell, at fifty cents each; then come Moses Shepherd, Nathaniel Wilson, Ephraim Wilson, Abner H. Cilley, six Richardson brothers, and many more all eager to join the society so as to settle the long vexed question of who was to do the preaching to this patiently waiting people.

A committee of invitation — Daniel Blaisdell, John Currier and Sewall Gleason — waited upon Elder Wheat and lost no time in making known the wishes of the people that he become their spiritual guide. The old man listened smilingly and approvingly to their solicitations, and his eyes rested benignly and lovingly upon the long list of names guaranteeing support to him and his family. He came and was duly installed in that pulpit which he abandoned only at the close of life.

Elder Wheat was a careful man in his intercourse with the people. He had cheerful words and friendly advice for every one. His labors in the pulpit were arduous; his prayers and sermons were almost of indefinite length, and he delighted in the loud music of his great choir, never omitting any of the stanzas in the longest hymns. He labored everywhere, and was called often to attend funerals. In those sad occasions he was a very effective speaker, being naturally sympathetic and weeping with the mourners. It was his custom whenever he heard unfriendly criticisms upon the life and character of a deceased person, to say, "we should tread lightly upon the ashes of the dead." The preaching of Eder Wheat and the high reputation which he enjoyed as a patriot soldier, were powerful influences in forming the habits and characters of many of our people. He was generally modest in relating his exploits. As a soldier he had endured great hardships. One incident in his camp life he used to relate with much feeling. He was captured by the Indians and taken through the woods to Canada. After a time he made his escape and started out alone through the then unbroken forest, two hundred miles. There were a few houses and small clearings along the upper waters of the Connecticut River, the smallpox prevailed in Canada, and the people along the clearings placed him in quarantine, not allowing him to come near their houses by day or night. He would come near a house and call to the people for food, then he would retire a considerable distance while they brought out victuals, and placing it upon a stump, eat and go on his way. He passed through Canaan on that journey on his way to his friends in the southern part of the state. On being asked if he ever killed any person during his seven years' service, he would pause, draw a long breath, and say with a sigh, "I s'pose I've been the death of six hearty men." He was not an educated man; in fact, he used to boast of his lack of education, but he had a retentive memory, and his mind was well stored with facts and fancies, which leaped out on all occasions, and gave interest to his most tedious sermons. He would sometimes say that, "Edication don't make a man any better Christian, unless it's in him. College larn't folks can't come nigh to God, with their high-sounding phrases. Bible larnin' was good enough for him. He had traveled nigh on to fifty years with it, and he thought he could get nigher to God with his humble ignorance than the man with his head swelled full of theology and divinity." His style was monotonous and singsong, with cadenzas uttered in a loud tone of voice, so that his words could be heard at long distances. He was very effective in prayer. He used to talk very familiarly with God; seize him by the hand and hold on till he got his blessing — a good old man with all his ignorance. In summer he always wore a loose wrapper, made of calico, that was always flying in the wind. His congregation was not always wakeful. His style and long-drawn utterances were favorable to drowsiness on the part of those hard-working men and women, and when he ceased speaking the sudden stillness would react with energy upon the sleepers.

He was much liked and sought after in all the region about wherever the Baptist Church prevailed. He was tender-hearted and easily put himself *en rapport* with his audience. Under his preaching many souls were converted and led safely through all the ordinances into the folds of the church. He was a great stickler for baptism; there was no salvation without going down deep into the water. It was his custom to wade far out until the water nearly reached his arm pits and when he had said the formula in that loud singing tone that echoed back from the woods on the opposite shore, he would plunge the candidate nearly to the bottom, bringing him up again with a jerk.

When he came to live here he bought a small farm and built a house a short distance below "Peggy's Tavern," on the turnpike. This farm he cultivated with his own hands, and by this means added something to his small salary, which was paid very tardily and oftentimes with ill grace, very much as ministers salaries are paid now. He possessed a powerful constitution, capable of sustaining great physical labor, but the infirmities of age crept in upon him, and he gave up preaching, and took refuge in the family of his daughter, Mrs. Samuel Gilman, who lived on the Carlton Clark farm, where, after months of suffering, he quietly went to sleep in 1836, at the age of 77 years. The legend upon his tombstone is, "Although dead, he yet speaketh."

Richard Clark, grandson of that Richard who used to spread his gifts freely before the people,— Richard the son, had also exercised his talents as a speaker,— and Richard, the grandson, had an ambition to preach like his fathers. He had but few opportunities for study, but he improved them all, and being a good-natured speaker, received ordination as a minister. He occasionally preached the Baptist doctrine for Elder Wheat. His mind was so absorbed by his ministerial duties that he lived and died a poor man in his own hired house. He was born about 1793, and died at Rumney at an advanced age.

On December 2, 1824, "Brother Ebenezer Clark was chosen clerk, upon the resignation of brother Richard Clark." Then, for several years up to July 30, 1830, Brother Ebenezer Clark, who was a clothier at Factory Village, entirely neglected the duties of his office, even if he had any to perform. During these years the record shows that forty-three names were added to the church. Several extensive revivals occurred among all classes of people, but the fruits thereof were divided among the Methodists and Congregationalists. The treasurer's book, 1827–1838, in the handwriting of Daniel Blaisdell, who was treasurer for many years, shows that several different preachers were hired and paid for. From the resignation of Elder Wheat to Elder John Peacock's call, preachers were hired by the Sunday. Elder Jesse Coburn preached several times in 1827, and also in 1828; Elder Mitchell preached in 1827, Elder Coombs in 1828, Elder Hall in 1829, and Elder Coburn again in 1830; the church numbered 89 members. These men received from three to five dollars a Sunday.

The Baptist Society from the time of the agreement with Elder Wheat, continued to pay its pastor by means of the assessments, and in the manner laid down in that agreement. The list of persons assessed for the year 1827, contains thirty-five names, some of whom were of other denominations than Baptist. It amounted to $42.47. For the year 1828 the tax amounted to $44.67; for 1829, the tax was $48.29; for 1830, $41.72; for 1831, $34.65; for 1832, $34.09; for 1833, $80.84; for 1834, $108.93; for 1836, $93.18, and for 1837, $66.05. In 1838 the number of members had dwindled to eleven, and although a tax of $62.58 was levied, there was $22.16 abated. The clerk has added,

"Josiah Clark, Nathaniel Gilman, Samuel Welch, John Fales, jr, are not as it appears members of the Society." In 1839 the tax raised was $34.55, with ten members; in 1841 the tax was $12.14. This was the last tax assessed, against the following, who were all that were left of the society: Joshua Currier, Ensign Colby, David Currier, Samuel Gilman, Daniel Kimball, Eben F. Currier, John Flanders, Benjamin Bradbury, Daniel W. Chase, and William Chase. In 1829 there was a desire to have a parsonage; some thought it would give the church a better standing to provide their minister with a place to live; that it would be more of an inducement for a good man to come and preach. Subscriptions were taken, ranging from fifty dollars by Daniel Blaisdell, to two dollars by March Barber and Phineas Eastman. The whole amount subscribed amounted to $477.50 by 44 different men, and the names of Congregationalists and Methodists are found on the list. They purchased the land now occupied by L. B. Hutchinson. The old parsonage house was for many years occupied by Albert Pressey; after his death it was sold and then torn down to give place to the present building. From January to June, 1830, Elder Nichol preached occasionally.

On July 15, 1830, the record continues, "voted unanimously, that we give brother John Peacock a call to labor with us so long as his labors may be thought profitable by himself and the church, for to take pastoral care of the church, and receive ordination as an evangelist."

The ordination was appointed to take place on the 25th of August, following. Elder Wheat at this time had become infirm both from age and the hardships of his earlier life. He occasionally preached, but the interests of the church seemed to require the presence of a more active man.

The exercises at the ordination of Mr. Peacock, August 25, 1830, were as follows: Prayer, by Rev. S. Coombs of New Chester; sermon, by Rev. George Evans of New Hampton, from II Tim. 6:5. "Do the work of an evangelist"; ordaining prayer, by Elder Joseph Wheat; charge, by Rev. Shub. Tripp of Campton; right hand of fellowship, by Rev. Noah Nichols of Rumney; concluding prayer, by Rev. Amos Foster of Canaan. The conference minutes of the Meredith association to which Canaan belonged, says this year: "The ancient church is no longer without one to take her by the hand."

Mr. Peacock was a man of earnest piety, of great activity and full to overflowing with magnetic persuasion. He started out so hopefully enthusiastic, that young and old flocked to listen to him. Religion became respectable and was much sought after in Canaan. And under his leadership the church realized her greatest prosperity. The congregation was increased by the attendance of persons in the habit of staying at home; the singing was greatly improved, a lively Sabbath-school sprang up, and members were added to the church, sixty-five, of whom forty-nine were by baptism. It was noted, too, as a good sign, that several chronic difficulties were cured, and it was believed forever settled.

Mr. Peacock remained here two short years, far too short for the prosperity of the church; and then he began his wanderings as an evangelist, which did not cease until he was called home, full of honor, at a ripe old age. His memory remained green among the old people long after his departure, who never ceased to recall his labors here but with expressions of love and reverence. He was a nervous, uneasy, good man, full of sympathetic magnetism and never could rest anywhere. His passion was to be always correcting somebody. Whatever else they did, everybody in his range must "come to Jesus and be baptized." A great many did not escape him. He seems to have stopped about everywhere in New England, preaching and praying and sincerely believing that to be his chief aim in life. He was an earnest, well-meaning man, and the world esteemed him good.

Below are a few extracts copied from the records of the church:

Sept. 15; 1832, Elder Peacock has preached with us two years and ten months, and now thinks it his duty to go to some other place. Voted to dismiss Elder Peacock and companion, and recommend them to the church in Danbury.

Then for a few months they were like sheep without a shepherd, and some went astray. The church numbered in 1832, 123 members.

March 1833. Gave Elder George Evans, a call to come and live with us and Mr. Peacock.

Sunday May 1, 1833. Elder George Evans was recognised as pastor of this church, and minister for the congregation, and received the Right hand of Fellowship from Elder Cheney. We hope that Elder Evans' labors with us may be blest of God to the awakening up of the church, and the conversion of many sinners.

This is the honest prayer of the pious clerk Jonathan Swan, To all which we say Amen, and may the conversion stick!

May 30, 1833, was the monthly meeting, Brethren and sisters related their experiences in the church. It is a low time although some are happy and rejoicing in the Lord.

There was a grievance with brother Moses Hadley, with whom we labored awhile, but getting no satisfaction his case was waived for the present. And then we took measures to increase the interest in the Sabbath school.

After waiting one month in prayerful consideration of our grievance with Brother Moses Hadley, on the 31st. of June. We voted to withdraw the Hand of Fellowship from him and from bro. Moses Hadley 3rd, also.

The business affairs of the church had been neglected, but this year they appear to receive special attention.

We taxed ourselves to support the table and other church expenses, and appointed Bro. B. Bradbury to collect and expend it.

We taxed ourselves $60 to repair the parsonage and appointed Jonathan Swan and Bailey Welch to expend it.

During the year several brethren were given letters to join other sister churches. John and Sarah Fales to Lyme. "Bro. Isaac Merrill was recommended to any other church of our faith and order." Joshua and Dorothy Merrill recommended to the church in Lowell. And "Sylvia Merrill having related her Christian experience before us, she was, on Sunday, November 10, baptised in the name of the Lord, in Hart Pond."

From this time on, until near the close of the next year, our friend, the clerk of this venerable church, was too busy with worldly affairs to write up his records. He simply tells us that Elkanah Phillips, and Jonson Welch and Elihu Derby were received by letter. And on "December 17, 1834, Sarepta Currier was received into our fellowship by baptism" and in the waters of Hart's Pond, cold as the baths of Apollo, she sealed her faith. At a church conference held this month, "but few were present."

The sisters held a prayer meeting while we retired to talk about arrears. It was then made known that several brethren were getting out into the highway of the world, and that we must send out guides to lead them in. Elder Geo. Evans was appointed to visit bro. J. L. Richardson, and some others who were using unfriendly and unchristian words in relation to the colored pupils of the newly opened Noyes Academy. It was also voted to admonish brothers, Amos and John Kinne, Eliphlet Gilman, Bartlett Bryant, Richard Clark, and sisters Rhoda and Sarah Blaisdell and sister Cole of Orange.

We also voted to give Joshua Currier jr, a letter of approbation as a preacher.

Joshua E. Currier, was son of Deacon Joshua and Mary Currier, born 1812; was converted and baptized by Elder Peacock, studied for the Baptist pulpit, preached many years successfully in the West, and during his later life, preached occasionally at East Canaan.

For a year,— a year of griefs to the brethren on account of the tumults and riots incited by wicked men, and joined in by many of our members, who seem to have forgotten God and all their covenant obligations, and with hearts filled with malice and wickedness, are striving to harm those who do not think with them. Perhaps God will soften their hearts and bring them humbly to see their errors, and with that hope, we will blot out the record of one full year, 1835. The church membership decreased from 138 in 1834, its highest record to 113.

January 1, 1836, It has been a very low time with the church, the year that is past. In Nov. the church held a protracted meeting and the Lord as we trust met with us and revived the hearts of some of his people. And some sinners appeared to be anxious to know that they would be saved.

At this time "Mr. Sewall Kinne, a young man of earnest convictions, was invited to improve his gifts in preaching. And brother Evans was appointed to convey this invitation to him."

Mr. Kinne was son of Luther and Esther Kinne, born in 1809, studied at New Hampton, was ordained at Jefferson, where he labored three years; then preached two years in Dorchester, two years in Danbury, then two and a half years in Weare. He then moved to Groton, where he preached twelve years. After that, for three years, he preached in the schoolhouse in the Gates district half the time. He died in Groton, August 19, 1872. A man of good abilities, much respected for his equable and harmless life.

The church voted "that it was the duty of the brethren who remove so far away that they cannot attend with us, to write letters and let us know their condition in spiritual things." On "April 28, 1836, Voted to give Elder George Evans and Mrs. Chloe Evans, a letter of dismission." Mr. Evans had labored here acceptably to the people, but to him it was a strain and trial, because during his years here, the thoughts of the people were far away from religion. Many things operated to discourage him. He asked dismission that he might go and labor in more congenial fields.

On June 30, Elder Harrison W. Strong and his wife, Serena, were received into the church. He occupied the pulpit about ten months, when he received a letter of dismission. It does not appear that Mr. Strong, by his preaching and example, left any deep impress upon the scene of his labors, and he left because many members of the church appeared to know more than he did. During this year the hand of fellowship was withdrawn from several brethren, others "were admonished for neglecting their covenant obligations, by absenting themselves from public worship and for refusing to bear any of the burdens of the church." Committees were appointed to visit various other derelict brethren and ascertain the state of their minds.

At a church meeting in November, Deacon Currier presented a grievance, which had been presented before, on account of certain members assisting in the moving and suppression of the Noyes Academy. "Talked the matter over a little, with some feeling. Got no satisfaction, brethren defiant, and unchristian. Adjourned the meeting two weeks." On the "8th of December We met and talked the matter over again, but the trials are not removed," and were not, until death closed over the graves of all the actors in that wild, sad scene. Eight months pass by and more grievances are presented. "Grief seems now to be the chief virtue in the church. If it will only purify our hearts, and make us humble! Kind and courteous!"

Sept. 7, 1837 at 9 o'clock in the morning, the meeting was opened with prayer, and then the brethren appointed to effect a settlement of a trial between four of the brethren, that after much persuasion and prayerful labor with the grieved brethren, the trial was taken out of the way. And the church expressed their satisfaction by unanimously rising to confirm the same, and when we had sung a hymn we adjourned.

It would have been more satisfactory had the names been written of those whose griefs "had been taken out of the way."

The next record is a wail for help. "Our lamps are burning dimly because the oil is not replenished."

August 1, 1838, The church has for a long time been wading through trials, many and severe. Elder Boswell, has preached a part of the time with us this year. But we are now destitute and the Lord only can tell what may become of us.

This looks as if faith was weak, and trust not strong. Cheer up brother; day will break, and we shall have a glorious resurrection morning!

On the 24th of September, 1838, a council met for the ordination of Brother Joshua Currier, Jr., as an evangelist, with intention of serving as a missionary in the West. The council was composed of delegates from the churches in Dorchester, Orange, Grafton, Hill, Rumney, Alexandria, and Hanover. The candidate having related his Christian experiences, his call to the ministry and his views of Bible doctrine, the council voted their satisfaction and proceeded to ordain him, assigning the parts as follows: Reading the Scriptures, Bro. V. E. Bunker; introductory prayer, Bro. D. W. Burrows; sermon, Bro. Henry Tonkin; consecrating prayer, Bro. J. Clement; charge, Bro. E. Crockett; concluding prayer, Bro. L. Conant (Congregationalist); benediction, by the candidate. Not a note of music is mentioned. Was none heard? Did those solemn brethren believe a man could be properly set apart for the service of God without a hymn or an anthem? It looks like it; and the town full of great harmonious voices! Where was Moses and Norman?

Jan 10 1839 the church related their experiences with some good feeling, Elder Palmer C. Himes and his wife Adelphi W. Himes were received into fellowship, and bro. Himes is recognised as Pastor of the church.

The membership has decreased to 97.

"Lydia Flint was received into fellowship by baptism," through a hole in the ice. In March, Hannah Welch, Hannah Cilley, and Mary Bradbury, were received into fellowship by baptism, through a hole in the ice.

In April "there is a growing interest among the members.

Our congregation has considerably increased since Bro. Himes has preached to us."

In November the church related their experiences and then "voted to withdraw the hand of fellowship from Hannah Cilley on account of immoral conduct." This is the Hannah who only last March, went down under the cold waters through the ice. Our good clerk should have added that "Hannah's immoral conduct" consisted in dancing all night to the music of a fiddle.

Mr. Himes continued to preach here until May 5, 1842. During his ministry a good degree of union was established. Some warnings were given to "derelict" brethren, but on the whole, he left an honored name behind him and departed with the prayers of all the brethren for his future happiness.

July 3 1842 the Methodists preached in the meeting house The Baptists met in the school house for a conference, and agreed to have a monthly meeting July 7th. This is the first time in many months the church have met. Brother Charles R. Nichols is with us now.

On the 7th "we met and were revived a little. We invited Brother Nichols to preach to us a few Sabbaths." Mr. Nichols remained and preached through the year, giving much pleasing instruction to the congregation. On the 18th of January, 1843, he was ordained as an evangelist. Almost every meeting of the church developed the fact that many of the brethren were more or less human. Was the standard of morals and piety of life placed too high, so that these everyday men and women, who were always in the way of the temptations of business and social pleasures, could not attain to it? We fear so. Their covenants, vows and church obligations, composed of platitudes and high sounding phrases, which few of them could comprehend, very soon ceased to have binding effect upon their minds. They seized upon this religion with the firm determination to hold on during life. Sober reflection afterwards failed to convince them that their hearts were much different from their old life, and so they fell away from their vows and became merely men and women as before.

On the 29th of January, 1843, it was just previous to the destruction of the world under the preaching of William Miller, when comets were blazing across the heavens, and the lights were dancing coldly in the North, three persons offered themselves for baptism. They went through the ice into the cold waters underneath, and came out baptized in the name of the Lord. Before this event, their lives had not been exemplary, not always kind neighbors, nor altogether honest, but fairish sort of people. It was hoped they might grow to be better. They attended church services faithfully for a season, bearing some burdens, but they proved after all they had endured to be merely human, and in seven months one was dropped and the other two ex-communicated from the church for a wilful neglect of all covenants, vows and obligations, and never afterwards was there any suspicions that these persons might have been Christian brethren. Who were these? Ah, they have gone with the great majority!

March 9, 1843, a committee reported upon their visit to Bro. Peter Wells and Bro. Nathan Gould. Then voted to withdraw the hand of fellowship from Brother Wells for total neglect of the church, and all its interests, "but we voted to bear with Brother Gould two weeks longer, hoping he may accomplish some of his promises." Brother Nichols prepared a temperance pledge for the church, but a large number of the brethren were not prepared to sign it. Finally, on the 10th of April, "having exhausted all argument out of self-respect, as well as from duty to God and this church, we withdraw the hand of fellowship from Bro. Nathan Gould for his continued neglect of all the ordinances of the church."

On the 20th of April, a few of the brethren met for prayer and conference, and the Lord was with us. The snow being deep in drifts hinders some from attending. Dea. Currier got his horse into a drift and had to leave the road in coming to meeting.

At a church meeting held June 29, 1843, "after some talk, mostly against it, we voted nearly unanimously to withdraw the hand of fellowship from slaveholders and from slaveholding churches, believing it a wicked violation of God's law, to hold a man in bondage."

In September "the religious temperature of the church is very low. Several are finding fault with Bro. Nichols, our young minister. And we are not agreed as we ought to be. Looks as though we might be destitute again."

On the 4th of October "Brother Peacock returned among us,

full of zeal for the Master's service, and as he proposed to remain with us a few days, we became hopeful for the good he might do us." He soon began a protracted meeting which was continued for twelve days.

> Many of the church members are quickened in their minds. Sinners were solemn and expressed desire for religion. Things are in a low state. The meetings at first were thinly attended, but increased in numbers and interest. Brother Peacock preached twenty-four sermons and attended twenty-four prayer meetings. Had evidence of the presence of God. Professors were revived, old hopes strengthened, evils corrected and good impressions made on the people. Some became anxious about their souls and one indulged hope. Had this meeting continued much good would have resulted. This church has been destitute of preaching for a long time and is very much discouraged.

Twenty-four sermons, and twenty-four prayer meetings; and only one to indulge a hope! Seems as if the labor was not proportioned to the harvest gathered in.

At the meeting in November, Bro. Benjamin Bradbury was chosen to the office of deacon, the honors of which office he wore with dignity and humble faith to the day of his death.

During the year 1844 church meetings were held irregularly. The attendance was small, but generally union and harmony prevailed. They had no preacher, but Brother Cutting of Lyme occasionally occupied the pulpit.

In 1845 the report is about the same, very friendly and united, "but we are like those who sleep. Brother Walker preached to us occasionally until July, when we were left without preaching."

The year 1846 is not distinguished for any lively signs of awakening. "Church meetings were held regularly during the year once in two weeks. There was union among those who met, but the number of these is quite small, and easy to count." The same may be repeated about the year 1847. Once a spasm of life seized the brethren. A special meeting was called at Sister Bartlett's,

> To consider the expediency of establishing regular meetings on the Sabbath. A proposition was received from the agent of the Baptist State Convention to assist the church in sustaining preaching, if the church thought there was sufficient encouragement to ask such aid. After a full and free discussion of the subject, it was voted to ask for the proffered assistance.

But we are left in ignorance of the further action of either party. There were, however, some very lively Baptists here at that time and it is fair to suppose that they had preaching. The conference minutes for this year report: "We are without a pastor; prospects discouraging; preaching only few Sabbaths; meetings held for prayer and conference, first Thursday of every month. They still pray, O Lord, revive thy work!"

During the next three years the records are not written, but it is certain that the church was held together by frequent meetings, and they had occasional preaching. They were too feeble to venture to promise a salary to any preacher. During the year 1851, the church met irregularly with small attendance, and not much enthusiasm. Elder J. Clements preached one fourth of the time. It was a weary year for the brethren, as was also the year following, when tired of trials, admonitions and warnings, the church nearly collapsed.

The year 1853 is marked by three distinct records, which are as follows:

> July 9. A few of the members met to renew their covenant obligations and to consult about sustaining preaching. Brother Eastman Preaches half the time for the present.
>
> Aug. 2. After conference voted to send a letter to the Association by Brother Eastman.
>
> Mrs. Hinkson brought trial against Mrs. Gates. Voted to admonish Mrs. Gates.
>
> Sept. 3. Church met and accepted the letter to the Association. Sisters Gates and Hinkson were brought forward, and talked upon it awhile. Then agreed to drop it, and forgive each other, and never meddle with it again, and shook the friendly hand at the close of the meeting.

Then for fourteen years the records of the Baptist Church are blank. The good clerk, wearied of writing the same phase over again and again, and so he wrote nothing at all.

In 1859 Elder J. Clements preached part of the time.

In 1867 the church was reorganized at East Canaan. After great trials, an elegant church edifice was built; a corner-stone was laid with solemn pomp in the southeast corner, and it was dedicated in June, 1872. Rev. Doctor Gardner preaching the sermon. It lingered along almost exhausted for many years, making no history worth recording. At the time of Rev. E. M.

Fuller's pastorate, new life was infused into it, and grew under his ministrations, but since its reorganization, it has not been strong enough, financially, to support a preacher for any length of time. There have been intervals when it has been without.

FREEWELL BAPTIST CHURCH.

David Cross was born in Wilmot, lived in Canaan many years on the Clifford farm; was an elder when he came here and was instrumental in organizing the Freewell Baptist Church of Canaan and Orange. On the 12th of January, 1828, "twelve precious souls met togather at his house and took the right hand of fellowship as a church by signing the creed." In connection with his name and because of his influence in organizing the church here, the following simple story is copied from the records of that lively church:

There were a few Freewell Baptist families from different churches that took up their abode in Canaan and Orange about the year 1825, and there being no church of their order there they felt to go alone until such times as would be convenient for them to have a church or branch of a church that they could unite with in full fellowship, so that they could enjoy all the privileges that belong to God's house in a free and open manner, believing that God owns such for his people.

Those brethren feeling as if the time of gathering a church was drawing nigh, appointed the 4th day of July 1827, to meet and see if they could have meetings set up for the purpose of declaring the dealings of God towards them, and that they might be help-meets to each other through life.

When met they agreed to spend the afternoon of each second Saturday, of each month as follows,— for each one to meet where they could be accommodated and declare the state of their minds views trials and determinations for the encouragement of each other,— believing God will own and bless them in such meetings, for as he says, "where two or three are gathered together," etc, and Paul says, "forsake not the assembling of yourselves together, as the manner of some is but exhort one another so much the more as ye see the day approaching."

At length the Lord began to pour out his spirit upon the hearts of his people, in such a manner that sinners began to cry for mercy, backsliders awoke, and saints rejoice in God the Rock of their salvation.

In short our numbers began to increase so that when met for monthly meeting in the house of brother David Cross on Jan. 12, 1828, there were twelve precious souls that took the right hand of fellowship as a

Church, to be called the First Freewell Baptist church of Canaan and Orange.

The church flourished; it gathered into its brotherhood more than one hundred members. It has never had a place for public worship, but its full-blooded activity has been felt by other churches. For many years it was the liveliest of them all and held more members than all the others. One reason for its success is doubtless its freedom from covenants, and the small cost of maintaining its organization. The elders take what is given them of the small collections made; they build no houses, but preach in schoolhouses, forests or other convenient places. It is a marvelous system of worship, and has great fascination for that large portion of the people who wish for cheap and lively religion. The schoolhouses have been crowded with attentive listeners, and scarcely a week would pass without conversions followed by baptisms, witnessed by large numbers of spectators. It works among the people who have little time to read and think for themselves and draws them all within its folds.

Of all its preachers and elders, no one deserves more credit than Elder Solomon Cole of Lebanon, who for years in summer and winter drove his horse from Lebanon to Factory Village to show sinners the path to God. Through a long life, devoted to that religion, his was always the hand held out to any who asked; a man of means, with a large business that required his constant care, some part of each week saw him exhorting his brethren in stentorian tones to praise the Lord. I do not believe he ever wrote a sermon; his words came naturally from a heart full to overflowing. Unmindful of interruptions, he never failed to carry the conviction that he was an earnest man. Collections were sometimes taken for him to buy him a new hat for instance, but that like all others, went to the poor and needy. He preached because he liked to, and no obstacle was too great, no storm too severe for Elder Cole. As sure as Kelley's Hall was to be packed to its doors, so sure was Elder Cole to be there. He preached in the schoolhouse,— anywhere the people asked him. All who knew him admired him. He was sincere, and the word of a sincere, honest man, whom the people believe to be such, goes farther than gold or riches. I remember distinctly of one incident, when I wanted to buy some clapboards of him. He said:

"I will guarantee those to be clear; as to those, I will guarantee there is not a good one in the bunch." He died April 3, 1902.

The following are some of the men who preached this faith: Joseph Flagg, born in Grafton about 1799; was an original member of this church; he was ordained in 1831, in company with Job C. Tyler, by the Weare Quarterly Conference; married Relief Springer, daughter of Henry; he is represented as a man of good talents, a very effective preacher, sincere and true in his friendships and attachments; he died in Vermont some years ago. John Sweat was born in Gilmanton in 1813; he was the son of Nathan, who for many years lived on the old Clifford farm; he and Otis Willis of Hanover, married daughters of Moses Lawrence, studied for the ministry, and were ordained together about the year 1840; Mr. Sweat labored acceptably many years in northern Vermont, and then went to live with his daughter in Hanover. Job Colman Tyler, son of Job and Ann (Pike) Tyler, born March 1, 1799, a man of slight education, but very confiding and intimate with God; he was very sympathetic and emotional, always earnest and interesting, and in his prayers and exhortations seemed to be standing in the immediate Presence; he had a strong desire to be counted an elder, because his perfect trust in God would give him more strength to help heavy-laden sinners lift the cross; he was ordained by the Weare Quarterly Conference in company with Joseph Flagg in 1831; his ill health was a bar to his being settled in the ministry, because he could not assume its cares and responsibilities; he was several times chosen pastor of the church in Canaan and Orange, and so far as he was able, performed its duties acceptably; he was often called to weddings, to the sick bed, to funerals, and though not great at preaching, his prayers were wonderful for elasticity and confidence; he lived to be an old man, and died in Canaan, September 1, 1879, at the age of 80 years and six months.

Nathan Jones was born in Wilmot, September 1, 1818; he came to Canaan in January, 1845, and was for a greater part of his life a resident of the town; was ordained an elder in May, 1847, at Weare; from that time on he preached in Wilmot, Canaan and Orange, until his death at Campton, January 13, 1894; he established a hammer shop on the stream that runs out of Hart's Pond and worked at that trade for many years; he was a close reasoner and a good debater, and was respected for his sincerity and perseverance; he married, first, Polly C. Bailey of Newbury, with whom he lived nine years; he then married Mary A. Gile of this town, and was the father of six children.

Elder George Davis, born in 1812, died in 1872; he attained to the name of "Shouting Davis"; he was an irrepressible Christian, and his heavy voice startled many a worshiper, who was quietly listening to the preacher.

CHAPTER XV.

THE CONGREGATIONAL CHURCH.

In 1795 four Congregationalists of this town joined the Rev. Eden Burroughs' church at East Hanover. In 1799 the town wished to settle Rev. Ezra Wilmarth as preacher, but the church refused to conform and the town voted to raise no money for preaching, which was a set-back for the long-winded deacons. Meantime Rev. Aaron Cleveland of Norwich, had arrived here to visit Connecticut friends. He preached in the unfinished meeting house. He was a Congregationalist, as were many of the settlers from Connecticut. They offered Mr. Cleveland $105 and 150 acres of land, half of the Minister's Right under the charter, to come and be their preacher. It was not much of a temptation to the old gentleman, and when he left town he had raised such desires in the hearts of the brethren of his faith that they sent a committee to Hanover to lay their hopes and desires before the church in that town. As a result of this day's work, Rev. Eden Burroughs and one of his deacons came over to Canaan, where they found thirteen persons willing to enter into covenant relations as Congregationalists, after which they were constituted a branch of the Hanover church, and this relation continued until the spring of 1803, then Doctor Burroughs and Rev. Mr. Dickenson of Meriden, came here and the "branch" was lopped off from Hanover and became the Congregational Church of Canaan. Joshua Pillsbury was the first deacon. This church was never self-sustaining, even in its best days. It was always a beneficiary of the New Hampshire Missionary Society. During several years the church enjoyed preaching by missionaries and neighbor preachers. Rev. Curtis Coe used to come up here from Newmarket and spend a few weeks, preaching in the meeting house, for each denomination had to use it; laboring lovingly without pay or the hope of reward in this world. After him, Rev. Broughton White come occasionally and preached pure Congregational truth to the people. The labors of these men were acceptable and fruitful. Additions were made to the church, which gave the brethren courage and confidence to go on with their work.

In 1814, Mr. Rolfe preached to them half of the time and a part of 1815. The church then consisted of thirty members. In 1819 there was a strong feeling to form a society, to which any and all persons could belong, of any denomination, like the Baptists had done, its object being to assist the church in the management of its affairs in a worldly way. Accordingly application was made to the legislature for a charter, which was approved on June 17, 1819, incorporating the "First Congregational Society of Canaan." The incorporators were Amos Gould, Elias Porter, Charles Walworth, Joshua Pillsbury, Joshua Pillsbury, Jr., "and their associates and those who may hereafter be associated with them." They were incorporated into a "religious society for the support of the gospel ministry, with all the powers and privileges usually enjoyed by corporations of a similar character and with the power of holding any estate, the annual income of which shall not exceed $1200." "Any person may join by signing the book of records and may leave the same by giving six months notice, and discharging all taxes legally assessed on him and his proportion of all debts contracted by the society during his membership." Money could only be raised at an annual meeting. The first meeting was held at Dole's Tavern, August 12, 1819. Amos Gould was moderator, Timothy Tilton clerk and Daniel Hovey treasurer. Jacob Trussell, Elias Porter and Amos Gould were the first assessors. The ten articles of the by-laws were read and adopted.

The next meeting was at the meeting house on March 6, 1820, when they adjourned to James Wallace's. Jacob Trussell was chosen collector and $60 was voted to be raised to "hire preaching." Elias Porter, Amos Gould and Samuel Noyes were chosen a committee on preaching. On September 4, 1820, the committee were empowered to engage Rev. Charles Calkins to preach one year.

The names of the members of the society for that year were as follows:

Amos Gould
Elias Porter
Samuel Noyes
Charles Walworth

Josiah Barber, 2d
Moses Dole
Joshua Pillsbury
Joshua Pillsbury, Jr.

THE CONGREGATIONAL CHURCH. 209

Timothy Tilton
Nathan How (Enfield)
Wm. Atherton
Daniel B. Whittier
David Gould
Jacob Dow
Joshua Blaisdell
Samuel Sanders
Joseph Bartlett
Alfred Porter
Bartlett Hoyt
Abraham Pushee
Nathaniel Currier
Shubel Towle
Mathew Greeley
James Wallace

Joshua Harris
Abraham Kimball
James Blaisdell
Robert Hoyt
Levi Bayley
Elijah Blaisdell
Jacob Trussell
Jacob Richardson
John Hoyt
Daniel Hovey
Abram Page
Richard Otis
Nathaniel Derby
Thomas Wood (Orange)
James Eastman

The amount of money assessed against these men was $61.05. And the collector was to "collect the same in case of refusal as the law directs."

On November 22, 1819, a tract society was formed with Dea. Amos Gould as moderator and Josiah Barber, 2d, clerk. It was called the "Canaan Moral and Religious Tract Society, Auxiliary to the N. E. Tract Society." Any one could become a member by paying twenty-five cents; the object was to distribute tracts. Nearly all the subscribers were Congregationalists. Amos Gould, Josiah Barber, 2d, Joseph Bartlett, Elias Porter, Richard Otis, Jacob Trussell, Benjamin Trussell, and their wives. James Blaisdell, Charles Walworth, John Hoyt, Robert Hoyt, Joshua Pillsbury, Jr., Polly Lathrop, Ephraim Noyes, George Richardson, David Richardson, Jacob Dow, Joshua Richardson, Jr., Thomas Wood, Timothy Tilton and his wife, Persis F. Austin, Anna Richardson.

Rev. Charles Calkins came in 1820, he had been preaching in Salisbury; Mrs. Hubbard Harris, his cousin, heard him there in 1819, on her wedding journey; he was a son of John P. Calkins, one of the early settlers on South Road. He was not a great man, and was too much afflicted with nerves to be successful as a teacher and evangelist. The old Baptists of Canaan were not men of refinement, nor were they apt to choose soft words in reference to rival ministers. As a class they saw no good in anything but baptism, all other isms were to be talked about and treated with contempt. They never missed an occasion to speak sharp words of Mr. Calkins and his church, thus engendering annoyance and ill-feeling. Mr. Calkins remained about four years, bearing as he thought a heavy burden all the time.

John Farmer, in the *New Hampshire Gazetteer* of 1823, says of Canaan: "There is a small Congregational Church, of which Rev. Charles Calkins is pastor."

In 1823 he decided that preaching was not his strong point, and his relations with the church were brought to a close without regret on either side. For several months after this event there was no Congregational preaching in Canaan. Mr. Calkins engaged Mr. Trussell to go with him to Waterbury, Vt., and build a sawmill, the pay being contingent upon the success of the mill. When it was completed and ready to operate there came a great rain, the swollen river crowded against the mill and carried it off. This catastrophe, Mr. Calkins received as a demonstration of God's anger for abandoning His peculiar service. He returned for a time to New Hampshire and preached in Boscawen, but he was unsuccessful there also. He had evidently mistaken his calling, and discouraged by his continued ill-success, started out upon what was then a perilous undertaking, a journey into the unsettled West. He reached western Pennsylvania and there we lose all trace of him.

In the New England Conference minutes, Canaan belonged to the Orange Association and in 1824 appears as a separate church, but no pastor. The number of church members is given as 34. Rev. Broughton White came occasionally to preach and when the brethren could do no better they waited upon the services of Elder Wheat. There was a young man in Hanover who had just completed his studies and was waiting for an opening to preach. Mr. White sent him over here in the spring of 1824. He was about here more than a year, gaining friends by his sincerity, his pleasant ways, his refined manners and the Christian graces which adorned his life everywhere. Even those rough natures that saw only pride and dandyism inside of a nice fitting suit of clothes, withheld their surly remarks when they became acquainted with the sentiments which governed the life of Amos Foster. On his first visit, Mr. Foster rode horseback from Hanover to Canaan, arriving here on Saturday afternoon. He stopped at the house of James Wallace, whose wife was an ardent Congregationalist. He found there also Mrs. Jacob Trussell, whose husband was the miller at the village. He accompanied Mrs. Trussell to her house. The next morning Elder Wheat came plodding along on his way to church. Mr. Trussell hailed him with the remark: "Elder, I've got a young man here from Hanover and he will preach for you a part of the day, if you like?" "Ha! wa'al," replies the elder, "le' me see," and turning shortly about, he went into the house without rapping, and without removing his hat or waiting for an introduction, addressed the young minister with: "Wa'al, what part of the day do you want to preach?" "Oh, the part that will suit you best," was the modest reply. The elder took a full survey of the young man, and without making any further remarks started on his way. But he lingered at the door of the church, talking with the people, until Mr. Foster arrived, when the elder went to him and said abruptly: "I guess you'd better preach all day, if you want to," and escorted him into the pulpit, where he sat all day listening, declining to take any part in the exercises. The old man was greatly pleased, and afterwards displayed all the friendliness he was capable of feeling during their lives. The old man was very opinionated, and never was known to own up that he was wrong in anything. As a general rule, he despised "edication." He "never had no larnin'; he was like the 'postles whom Christ selected for their ignorance, and thought he knew he could get closer up to God than college-larnt men, because his head and heart wan't full of dictionary words and high notions that only make men proud." "He'd preached the gospel nigh on to forty year and Bible larnin' was all he could make any use of."

The elder when once he commenced his services, was oblivious to all outside influences. He had a great sonorous voice that rebounded from the sounding-board above him and filled every corner of the house. Once in that spacious pulpit, and he had neither ears nor eyes, nor the perception of time, till his subject was exhausted. The galleries were well filled with singers, young people from all over town, who came to Elder Wheat's meeting to have a good time singing his long psalms, and whispering together during his long prayers and longer sermons. But on this occasion their levity and playfulness annoyed Mr. Foster, and nearly interrupted the services. He supposed they might be laughing at him, but when he learned they were only engaged in their usual pastime, he thought the matter over, and concluded to give these young persons some good advice. Not long afterwards the elder invited him to preach again, and this time he took for his text the famous paragraph: "Rejoice, O young man, in thy youth, and let thy heart cheer thee in the days of thy youth," etc. It is said to have been a very excellent sermon, and was addressed very pointedly to the gallery, so that for a time they were shamed into a decent observance of the proprieties of the place. But they pretended also to be very much annoyed at the rebuke administered to them. To show their resentment and to make the minister and the congregation feel it also,— they all stayed out of the seats in the afternoon and there was no singing, neither was there any disturbance. This event afforded a whole week's gossip for the town, and it was improved to such good advantage that before Sunday came around again, the principal singers went to Mr. Foster and apologized for their rudeness. And he ever afterwards had good singing and attentive listeners. The arguments and teachings of that sermon had a life-long influence upon the life and conduct of at least one man. Old people tell us of the early life of Joseph Dustin, how his days and years were a continued profane riot, and that on all occasions he led the crowd when any violence was contemplated. He had always scorned religion and laughed at the clumsy way Elder Wheat had of bringing souls to God. There was nothing cheerful or loving or refined in his religion, and his God was a good deal like himself,— without "edication or larnin'," and rendered blind and deaf by his own thunder. But here was a style of argument and refinement of expression, in speaking of God's love to man, that arrested Joseph Dustin's attention and struck such deep conviction into his mind that it was time for him to begin a new life. It was not long afterwards that he became a professed Christian and a praying man, and for more than fifty years he did not fail to proclaim his belief in the God who "took his feet from the horrible pit and miry clay and placed them on the rock of Jesus

Christ." But what created surprise was, that instead of uniting with Mr. Foster's church, to whom he had always been much attached, he should join the Methodists, after which he was always identified as one of the leading pillars. But this is readily accounted for when we consider that his temperament was always very demonstrative, and it is only among Methodists that religion is allowed to fill a man bursting full, so that it runs over and displays its happiness in shouts of Amen and hallelujah, and in songs and praise. Mr. Foster was always earnest and there was a gentle dignity in his manners that attracted all hearts to him, but it was not common for his congregation to interrupt him with shouts of approval.

On January 17, 1825, the committee of the church and society sent a letter to Mr. Foster, giving him a call to be pastor of the congregation, to which Mr. Foster on the 28th wrote this reply:

Dear Brethren and Friends:
With no ordinary feelings of interest have I viewed the mysterious and unexpected providences, which, at first, directed my steps to this place; and with no less interest have I viewed those happy occurrences, which have contributed to prolong my stay among you. At the commencement and during the prosecution of my preparatory and professional studies, it was my endeavor to place fully in view the solemn and awfully responsible undertaking in which it was my object to engage. And, when after having struggled with many and complicated embarrassments, which, through the interposition of a kind providence, I was enabled to surmount, it pleased God to introduce me into the Work of the Holy Ministry, I endeavored to give myself up to the leadings of divine providence; that He, who orders all things rightly and well, might make such a disposition of myself and my services as should most subserve the promotion of His own Glory and the interests of his kingdom. Nor do *I now* wish to call back the surrender I then made. If I do not greatly mistake my feelings, and the motives by which I am governed, it is my great wish to pursue the path of duty, without being governed by selfish or interested feelings — Wherever the voice of providence calls, *that* voice I wish to obey. In relation to the event in which my coming among you has resulted, I have only to remark, that it is one of which I had not the most distant thought. Of the wisdom of that providence however, which has directed to that event, we must not have the presumption to entertain a doubt. He, who orders all things after the counsel of his own will, knows what is best, — and if he gives direction to all events, if the minutest occurrences do not take place but by his premission, and if not a sparrow falls to the

ground, without his notice, then it is a fact that all those circumstances that have contributed to bring about this event, are under the immediate government and direction of an all wise and over-ruling hand. Shall the motions of this hand be disregarded? Shall those circumstances be attributed to the capricious operations of chance? Or shall man presume to say that he can advise to a safer and better course than here seems to be pointed out? If duty can be learned from the leadings of providence in any cases, perhaps, it may be discovered in this instance before us. I should not dare to oppose *my* judgment against what here seems to be the plain and obvious dictates of the divine hand. Another consideration has operated powerfully on my own mind in relation to the subject of your communication, which is, the high importance, that every town should enjoy the stated and regular means of grace, and the necessity of making strenuous exertions to supply destitute towns with these means. To the lovers of vital godliness it must be delightful to discover the increasing interest that is felt for the general prosperity of Religion. A deep sense of the condition of millions of our race, who are destitute of a knowledge of the Savior, seems to have been awakened; and altho' the means brought into operation for the general diffusion of Christian light thro the world, are very inadequate to the object to be accomplished, yet laudable efforts have been made; and, that these efforts may be continued, extended and increased, till the whole world shall be filled with the knowledge of the Lord, must be the spontaneous effusion of every pious heart. But while it is a matter of joy, that so much is done for the advancement of religion abroad, still it must be obvious that the claims of the destitute at home, should by no means be overlooked. Those even in Christian lands, without the means of grace, without repentance and faith, are in a condition equally as deplorable as those who inhabit the deepest shades of heathenish darkness. To cast an eye over the dreary wastes of our own domestic Zion, and view the moral desolations, which sin has produced, must excite an anxious sympathy for the inhabitants of those places. Many have been apprized of the importance of doing something to repair those wastes, to supply destitute flocks and congregations with the stated means of grace, that the wilderness and solitary places within our own borders may be glad and blossom as the rose.

The regular and systematic enjoyment of gospel means and ordinances, furnishes the most efficient safeguard of moral principle; and of course, is the best security of individual right. It induces sobriety temperance, industry; and hence promotes peace, health, prosperity and general happiness. That the gospel should therefore be supported in every parish and town is of vital importance as to the temporal interests of the people. But when we look back at its influence on their spiritual and eternal interests, none can possibly estimate its value. It hence becomes very desirable that every parish and town should be supplied with the stated administration of the word and ordinances of the gospel; — and hence also, it becomes the duty of every well wisher to human happiness to contribute his share in bringing about an event so desirable. And when divine providence opens the way by which one may be instrumental in accomplishing such an object, and renders his duty obvious, who shall shrink from going forward in the cheerful performance of this duty? With these views before me, My Brethren and Friends, I, after a sober, deliberate and prayerful consideration of the subject; and at the same time under a solemn sense of the obligations which I impose upon myself, and relying alone on the assistance of divine grace to make me to discharge these obligations I am induced to comply with the respectful invitation extended to me through your committee to settle over you as your minister, in thus yielding to your request, I can not but feel penetrated with a sense of my own insufficiency for the undertaking in which I consent to engage. Let me entreat you to remember, that he, whom you have invited to be your spiritual guide, is a frail, unworthy, sinful worm of the dust. He therefore entreats an interest in your sympathies and prayers, in this let him not be disappointed. His earnest supplications will ever be engaged in your behalf. Many things, during my residence here, have occurred, which have been the occasion of mutual rejoicing; and created ties, which, I trust, the long lapse of eternity will only serve to strengthen. Let it be our united prayers, that the connexion, which may hereafter be formed may be crowned with still happier results. Let us be duly impressed with a sense of the imperfection of human nature, and be prepared to bring into exercise a spirit of mutual forbearance and forgiveness. Let every step in relation to this important matter, be taken as in the near view of eternity; remembering, that we are amenable, for our conduct, and the motives by which we are actuated, at the tribunal of an omnipotent Jehovah. May we then find that the solemn engagement into which we are about to enter shall have met the divine approbation.

Wishing you grace, mercy and peace, I subscribe myself your Brother and servant in the Lord.

AMOS FOSTER.

On March 7, 1825, the society accepted of the doings of its committee, John H. Harris, Moses Dole and Elijah Blaisdell, and the contract they had made on February 28, 1825, with Mr. Foster. The committee appointed from the church on this occasion to contract with Mr. Foster were Jacob Trussell, Elias Porter and Samuel Drake. This contract provided to pay Mr. Foster annually $250, for the term of five years, the first payment to be made on the first day of January, 1826. Mr. Foster agreed to assign to the committee "for the benefit of said church and society the subscriptions which have been heretofore made to him, amounting to the sum of $200." Mr. Foster was to receive any further sums from the New Hampshire Missionary Society to an amount so as to make his salary $400. If the sums received from the Missionary Society were not enough to make his salary $400, he had the privilege to preach out of town, to an extent so as to make up the $400, and no more.

Mr. Foster had married on the 29th of June, 1825, Miss Harriet Amelia White, oldest daughter of Rev. Broughton White; they lived in the house now occupied by Mrs. Caleb Blodgett. The parsonage house was not fit for use, and was on the other side of the street. He had to pay rent all the time he was here. It was several times voted to pay his rent, but during all the time he was here the church and society were in debt to him and he left here with the society owing him. It is a wonder that Mr. Foster, all through his long life should have entertained such strong affection for the people of Canaan. They did not treat him well; in fact, they never really appreciated him. He came here from school, in debt for his education. He lived here and worked faithfully about nine years, and then his debt was not paid,— was scarcely reduced — and when he left, he had borrowed money from one of his brethren, who threatened to sue him if it was not paid,— and suing a man without money in those days, was to shut him up in jail. Up to that time our laws in relation to debt were barbarous, relics of ages when poor men had no rights and the grave was often more merciful than the creditor. Mr. Foster went from this town to Putney, Vt., and it was friends in Putney who came to his relief when threatened with such dangers.

No better description could be given of the condition of the people and Mr. Foster's pastorate than that written by himself and in his words, which is also a history of his life:

I was born in Salisbury, N. H., March 30, 1797, and was the son of Richard and Esther (Jewell) Foster. When I was one year old my parents removed to Hanover, N. H., where I spent most of the early years of my life. From my childhood I was in the habit of attending public worship, and this habit with the teachings of a pious mother deeply impressed upon my mind a sense of the reality and importance of religion. In the spring of 1815 there was a revival in Hanover under the ministry of Rev. Josiah Towne; in that revival, I trust, I embraced religion, and on the first Sabbath of January, 1816, I made a public

The Congregational Church.

confession. Then my thoughts turned to the question of becoming a minister of the gospel, but want of means stood in my way. Kimball Union Academy was opened about this time, with a considerable fund for the express purpose of assisting indigent students in the pursuit of an education for the ministry. In the spring of 1816 I entered that institution as one of its beneficiaries. In 1818 I entered Dartmouth College and graduated in 1822. During my college course I was assisted by the Ladies Benevolent Society of Acworth. I immediately after graduation commenced my theological studies under the instruction of Rev. President Tyler. In February, 1824, the Windsor Ministerial Association held a meeting at Norwich, Vt., at which time I was licensed to preach the gospel. Rev. Broughton White was present, he had just come from Canaan, having spent a short time in missionary labor in that place, and knowing the state of things there, he requested me to go and spend a Sabbath with the people. In accordance with the request I came to Canaan in March, 1824, and preached my first and as I supposed my last sermon to that people. In April following, I visited the town again by request, and preached a second time. I was now invited to return and spend several weeks more. Accordingly in June I returned. Soon after I received a commission from the N. H. Missionary Society to labor in Canaan and Orange ten weeks.

At the expiration of this service, efforts were made to retain me for a longer time. On the 17th of January, 1825, an invitation was given me to become the pastor. An affirmative answer being returned, an Ecclesiastical Council was called on March 2, 1825, and I was then ordained as the first pastor of the Congregational Church and Society in Canaan. The sermon was preached by Rev. President Tyler of Dartmouth College.

It is well to state some other interesting things which Mr. Foster does not mention at his ordination. Rev. Broughton White gave the charge; Rev. Baxter Perry of Lyme, offered the introductory prayer; Rev. Samuel Goddard of Norwich, Vt., made the consecrating prayer; Rev. Josiah Towne of Hanover, gave the right hand of fellowship; Rev. Abraham Burnham of Pembroke, addressed the people, and Rev. Charles White of Thetford, offered the concluding prayer. Elder Wheat was an invited guest. The several pastors and one delegate were present from each of the following churches: Washington, Pembroke, Hanover, Lyme, Norwich, Lebanon and Thetford. The singing was conducted by Ashiel Smith from Hanover, who was a famous conductor of singing schools and choirs. The seats were filled with singers, for in those days singing was taught freely every season. Benjamin Trussell played the bass-viol and Bracket Tilton worked on the violin. Betsey Pratt sang treble firmly and pleasantly. There were several counter-tenor singers, a part that would not be agreeable now, and was not particularly so then. Music was not yet arraigned for alto voices. The music was selected from the anthems of "Village Harmony" and the "Bridgewater Collection," and included "Strike the Cymbal." The solos were sung by Miss Pratt, Doctor Tilton and James Currier. It was great music and very effective giving us an idea of force and power of harmony in subjection. There was a feast served at James Wallace's after the services. It was customary on all convivial occasions to serve rum to the guests. Out of respect to the habits of Mr. Foster and Mr. White, it was dispensed with at this time, to the no small annoyance of a number of those present.

Mr. Foster continues:

During the whole of my ministry in Canaan embracing a period of nearly nine years, some sixty persons united with the church. At the time of my leaving, it consisted of seventy members. In the meantime several had been removed by death or otherwise. The building of the meeting house, dedicated Jan., 1829, promised much as to the prosperity of our society. The congregation on the Sabbath was considerably increased, more attention was paid to religion, the Sabbath school was attended by larger numbers, our prospects every way seemed encouraging. The state of morals was much improved while I was a resident of Canaan. At first a desecration of the Sabbath was very prevalent. Gunning, fishing, riding out for pleasure were common practices in that day. Often on the Sabbath did I hear the report of guns from one direction and another, and much disrespect for the sacred day was manifest by those improprieties in which the young indulge themselves in the house of God. Not only in regard to keeping the Sabbath, but also in regard to temperance a change for the better took place. The reformation of Jonathan Kittredge, Esq., always seemed to me a signal and happy event. It took place, I think, in the spring of 1826. Mr. Kittredge had one of his fits of intoxication about the time of the state fast. I frequently saw him pass my house, staggering as a drunken man does. His appearance suggested the thought of preparing a sermon on the subject of intemperance, which I did. When Mrs. Plastridge returned from the meeting, he was then becoming sober, he asked her, "What did Mr. Foster preach about today?" She said "About Intemperance." "Oh," said he, "I am the cause of it." Which was true. He came at once to see me. His agony of spirit was beyond anything of the kind I had scarcely ever witnessed. I saw him often afterwards and did all I could to encourage him in his reformation, which then commenced. In a week or two after this, at the close of my afternoon service on the Sabbath, Mr. Kittredge arose and gave the audience a most interesting and affecting account of himself, acknowledging his past intemperate habits and expressing his determination by the Divine help thenceforth to lead a sober, temperate and Christian life. He soon removed to Lyme and after several years returned to Canaan. In principle and practice he was ever afterwards, so far as I know, a consistent friend and supporter of the cause of temperance. Before I left Canaan there were influences set to work which I thought were useful. A Temperance Society was organized, and we had some able and interesting addresses on the subject, by such men as President Lord of Dartmouth College, Dr. Muzzey of Hanover, Rev. Charles White and Dr. Palmer of Thetford, Vt. With the people of the "early days" of Canaan, I had no knowledge. But at first it seemed to me that there was a strong sectarian prejudice existing among the different denominations. As an illustration of this let me state an incident. It occurred in the old Meeting house, on the day of my ordination, Dr. Tyler was preaching the sermon on the text in Hebrews 5: 4, "And no man taketh this honor unto himself, but he that is called of God, as was Aaron." In the midst of the sermon as Dr. Tyler was describing the qualifications of one called to the ministry, a man in the side gallery at the right hand of the preacher, spoke in a loud voice that could be distinctly heard; "It's all college call, it's all college call." It was designed as was supposed to express his contempt of an educated minister. Before I left Canaan it was evident this sectarian prejudice had diminished and I think the effect was owing in a degree at least, to the policy I adopted, which was this, finding several Christian denominations in town, I said to myself, "I will meet these Christian brethren more than half way and I will not lift a finger to pull down another denomination with a view to build up my own."

Adopting this principle practically, I have reason to hope, I gained the confidence and esteem of all classes of people. Elder Wheat always manifested fraternal kindness and good will, and my intercourse with him was agreeable. I remember distinctly a call I made at his house awhile after my settlement in Canaan. In the interview, he gave me a little sketch of his own life, spoke of his having been in the war of the Revolution, and of his religious experiences, among other things he remarked, "I haven't got no larnin', I was edicated in the school of the devil." His wife sitting by, raised her head and closed the interview by saying, "Well, you'll have t' die in your ignorance. It's hard to learn old dogs new tricks." If silence gives consent always, the old gentleman accepted the retort, for no more was said. The Elder was a good man, but I never knew of a revival of religion under his ministrations.

For Judge Daniel Blaisdell, I always entertained a very high esteem. He was a man of very correct principles, sound judgment, and exemplary conduct, and he made himself highly useful, both in his public and private life. There were other citizens whose names come to my remembrance, and whom I held in high esteem. Dr. Tilton, Capt. Dole, the Harrises, Joshua Pillsbury, Charles Walworth and Mr. Porter on

South Road. I often call to mind my first pastorate and the pleasant associations and friendships I there enjoyed and it would have been a pleasure to us both to have made that place our permanent home. But circumstances such as I need not name rendered it necessary to make a change.

Mr. Foster received a call to the pastorate in Putney, Vt., and was installed February 13, 1833. After remaining in Putney twenty years and seven months, on November 7, 1853, he became the pastor of the church in Ludlow, Vt. In 1857 he was installed in Acworth, N. H., where he labored as pastor nine years and feeling the infirmities of age, asked for his resignation, and was discharged June 13, 1866. He then returned to Putney, having come into possession of a home there, and finding the church without a pastor was asked to serve, which he did for seven years, closing his labors December, 1872. He did missionary work, however, for about a year in Cambridgeport, Vt. "Counting up my labors," said Mr. Foster, "from the time I was licensed the time amounts to half a century." Seven children were born to Mr. and Mrs. Foster. On the 29th of June, 1875, their friends and relatives united in celebrating their golden wedding at Putney, Vt. He died Sunday, September 21, 1884, in his eighty-eighth year.

It has been stated that the Congregational church in Canaan was never strong enough to sustain itself. It increased and flourished in those years and promised to do more for itself than it ever performed. Soon after Mr. Foster's arrival it became apparent that there was need of a house of worship apart from the other denominations. Although Elder Wheat and the Baptists claimed the old meeting house, because they had possession of it, they very kindly yielded the pulpit sometimes to Mr. Foster, still there was considerable inconvenience in it and some feeling. There was no question as to the title to the house. It was the property of "the proprietors" and they embraced all the beliefs in town. But the Baptists were most numerous and had maintained an organization in it ever since it was built. They disliked to yield it up and they did not. Several years previous to this time the Methodists had formed a church and though they were not in the habit of yielding any of their rights, yet that they might have the good will of the people while they were weak, they prudently went to work and in 1826 dedicated a church on South Road, and there they shouted and sung; and many of them got as near to God and talked as familiarly and lovingly to Him as if their names had been Elisha and Moses. Simple times those were; and simple Christianity, seemed a second time to have found a resting place upon earth. Brotherly love prevailed and charity and forbearance abounded so largely that they almost ceased to be virtues. My mother would sometimes allow me to go over there of a Sunday. It was sixty years ago (1888). The experiences of half a century, traveling side by side with my fellow-men, have not realized to me the truth of the impression then made upon my boyish mind.

It seemed to be necessary that there should be another house, wherein Mr. Foster could preach all the time. A religious society makes slow progress when it has to alternate with another in the occupation of a place of worship. They thought so here, and finally through the enthusiasm of George Kimball, Esq., and the energy of Jacob Trussell, the project assumed form. A deed of land from John Fales secured a location on the brow of a bleak hill, where the air currents are always strong. The deed was made to the First Congregational Society, dated May 10, 1828, and was for eighty-one square rods of land, described as follows: "Beginning at the northwest corner of Colby land on east side of Grafton Turnpike, then east six rods on Colby line, then north ten degrees west till it intersects with road to my house, then southwest on road till it intersects the Turnpike." The conditions were that a house should be erected within one year for public worship, and used as such. For conditions broken, the land would revert to Fales and his heirs.

The house was built in 1828 and dedicated in January, 1829. Bailey Welch was the builder. He fell from the steeple to the ground, but lived many years after. For this the town voted him $100 at its annual meeting in 1829. The church was paid for from the sale of the pews, as the Baptists had done. At the annual meeting in March, 1829, the society accepted of the house, "so far as to take care of it." Josiah Barber 2d, William Kelly and Otis Fields were to furnish the wood and build the fire. Mr. Foster's contract having run out, he continued to stay, and in March, 1832, they tried to contract with him for five years longer. But he severed his connection with the church

January 2, 1833. At the time he accepted the charge of the church, there were on the records fifteen male and thirty female members. At the time of his dismission the list contained the names of Elias Porter and his family of five, Nathan Howe and his wife, Richard Otis and Dea. Joshua Pillsbury, who died during his stay; Joshua Pillsbury, Jr., and his family of three; Amos Gould and his family of two; Charles Walworth and family of two; Ezra Chase, who was ex-communicated and family of two; Thomas Wood and family of two; Joseph Morse and wife; Edward Carlton, Mrs. Clark, Betsey Doten, Ruth H. Kimball, Caroline Waldo, John Hoyt and wife, Mrs. Jacob Richardson, John Sawyer and wife, James Pattee, Eliza Carlton, Harriet Hamilton, Mary Shephard, Samuel French, Samuel Drake, wife and daughter, Josiah Barber, wife and daughter, Otis Field, Caleb Gilman and his wife, Timothy Tilton and his wife, Hubbard and George Harris and their wives, Sally Smith, Mrs. Joseph Bartlett, Mrs. Lathrop, Sarah Clapp, Mrs. Daniel Pattee, Lucy Dole, and her daughter Mary D. Plastridge, Rebecca Currier, Mrs. Lazarus Page, John Nevins and wife, Bartholemew Heath and wife, Isaac Towle and his wife, Nathaniel Barber and his wife, Hannah Towle, and "old" Mrs. Towle, Charles W. Richardson, William B. Kelly, George Nelson, Alfred B. Dustin, Sarah Harris, Polly Wallace, Jane Chapman, Zilpha Clark, Mary F. Harris, Sarah Stetson, Sarah Fletcher and Anna Flanders.

Mr. Foster had charge of Orange during the first part of his ministry up to April, 1828, and some of the above were residents of Orange. They severed their connection and organized a separate church in Orange. Two cases of discipline are recorded during his pastorate. Mrs. Hannah Felch, who "had embraced sentiments and opinions, fundamentally erroneous and of very dangerous tendency." "And her deportment before the world had been such as to forfeit her claim to Christian character." For these she was excluded from communion. The other was Ezra Chase, who "had altogether neglected the duty of family worship." "Withdrawn himself from the Lord's table." "Used language and exhibited conduct wholly inconsistent with Christian character." For this he was ex-communicated.

In April, 1833, the society joined with the church to give the

Rev. Edward C. Fuller a call. An agreement was signed with Mr. Fuller April 27, 1833, for $400 annually "so long as he shall stay." Mr. Fuller was here through the stirring times attending the moving and destruction of the colored school, and was one of the friends of that school. The church passed through many trials and tribulations at that time because some of its prominent members were arraigned against each other on the question of the colored school. Mr. Fuller was not diplomatic and his short sightedness led him into difficulties which caused him to ask dismission, which was granted March 1, 1836.

Mr. Fuller found himself in the position of having recommended a church member to another church, who was under suspension at that time and who was afterwards ex-communicated. Jacob Trussell, for his part taken in the removal of Noyes Academy, was, as hereafter related, tried and on the 7th of March, 1836, ex-communicated. Mr. Trussell obtained from Mr. Fuller a letter of dismission to the church in Franklin. On the same date the church chose George Harris and Timothy Tilton to join with the three deacons of the church, Nathaniel Barber, Samuel Drake and Amos Gould, in sending a letter to the church in Franklin, "informing them of the accusations against Jacob Trussell for which he is ex-communicated." And thereupon the church resolved, "that we disapprove of the measures taken by our late pastor by giving Jacob Trussell a letter, as we think Mr. Trussell unworthy to be connected with any regular church after taking into consideration his past conduct." The sequel to this is written more than eighteen years afterwards, on October 29, 1854. The church was requested "to tarry" after meeting, and Esquire Kittredge read the following letter from Mr. Trussell:

To The Congregational Church in Canaan.

Difficulties having heretofore existed between your body and myself in relation to certain events in the removal of Noyes Academy in 1834 which led to a dissolution of my connection with the church, I take the liberty of saying to the church, that it would be a pleasure to me to have a reconciliation of all past differences take place. Those difficulties occurred in relation to a measure about which there was at that time great difference of opinion and at a time when the public mind was in a state of intense excitement. You are aware that a great majority of the people approved of the course taken in the removal of the Academy, including some who were members of churches beside myself. The church in Canaan with which I was connected disapproved of those measures and the part which I took therein was contrary to their wishes, and injurious to their feelings. Without entering into any discussion of the measure themselves, I feel free to say to the church, that I am sorry to have wounded the feelings of my brethren, and should be glad to have Christian fellowship restored between the church and myself.

It will be seen that Mr. Trussell was not sorry for anything he had done, and there is no intimation that his opinions had changed from the time he had led the mob. But the church accepted his excuse and restored him to fellowship and communion, and he thereafter became one of the pillars and supports of the church. During Mr. Fuller's pastorate only four united with the church. Then Rev. Liba Conant came as a candidate and on January 15, 1837, the church voted "to extend an invitation" to him, and that the sum of $315 be paid him. He was installed February 22, 1837. Fifty-three united with the church during his ministry, and there were two cases of discipline. Nancy Morgan, from whom the right hand of fellowship was withdrawn on account of her "misconduct," and Roswell Austin, who was ex-communicated. Mr. Conant remained until the spring of 1845. He became interested in politics and in 1844 represented the town in the legislature. His course was not approved of and his ministerial usefulness was spoiled. In 1838 the church reached its strongest position with eighty-six members. Then came Rev. Heman Rood, who stayed one year and taught in the academy also. He left the people with no interest and discouraged. From 1846 to 1851 the church was without a settled minister, and its doors were seldom opened to occasional preachers.

In 1851 Rev. Henry Wood, editor of the *Congregational Journal*, offered to preach one year for a small salary. He stayed two years. During his service the church was repaired, both outside and in and rededicated July 10, 1853. Rev. Moses Gerould was invited to preach four Sabbaths and entered on his labors July 24, 1853, at the end of that time, August 15, he was asked to remain on a salary of $500, which he accepted. Five days later a committee was appointed, consisting of George Harris, Jonathan Kittredge and Joshua Pillsbury, to revise the Confession of Faith, and on September 4th the revision was adopted. In the afternoon eight men and fifteen women were present and signed it. During the first five years of Mr. Gerould's ministry there were only four deaths among the church members; no cases of discipline; harmony prevailed. But the pastor began to feel discouraged. "To deplore a want of general spirituality and absence of the converting influences." None came forward to unite with the church. Alfred Nesmith intended to, but died. At the end of his sixth year, Mr. Gerould wrote: "Small indeed have been the fruits of these labors in the conversion of souls, and less in the increase of the church. Whether this want of spiritual success has been owing to the unfaithfulness of the acting pastor, or to local causes or to something else, eternity must decide. With the pastor, these years have not been years of indifference and inactivity, but he has striven to labor and pray as earnestly as in other years."

For the first three years, Mr. Gerould received from the New Hampshire Missionary Society $200 each year, it was then cut down to $150, and then to $100. In September, 1861, he again writes: "Another ecclesiastical year of this church and its ministerial service has gone, never to be recalled; and we may exclaim, 'my leanness! my leanness!' Not one has been added to the church! Oh, that God would arise and have mercy upon Zion, the time to favor her, the set time being come." "My heart is smitten and withered like grass," when I think of her low estate. "The word preached has seemed like water falling upon a rock."

Mr. Gerould tried to close his labors with the church, but he continued through the next two months, and in December commenced preaching through the winter "without stipulated salary." The people gave what they could, and the Missionary Society continued its contribution, which was to cease in August of the next year. He "reluctantly" commenced another year in the following April, with more courage. During the ten years of his ministry ten members died, twenty-one united with the church, five by confession. In May, 1863, Mr. Gerould writes, after having closed his labors over the church the month before: "How solemn the account the pastor must render of these years of unblest labor! Will the blood of these unconverted be found upon his skirts?" "Oh, my God, enter not into judgment with him who so many years has stood in that sacred desk for the purpose of showing the people their trangressions and the house of Jacob their sins, and yet has brought no more to that

'Fountain filled with blood,
Drawn from Immanuel's veins.'"

From April, 1863, to April, 1864, there was no congregational preaching. The Congregationalists united in worship and in sustaining the Methodist Church. For four years this situation continues, and the church became scattered. On the first of May, 1867, Rev. Robert Sloss, fresh from Princeton Theological Seminary, began to preach and continued through his vacation of four months until August. On the following 16th of December, they voted to give the Rev. Robert Sloss a call and pay him a salary of $800. But he never came back. From May 1 to August, 1868, Rev. James H. O'Brian from Princeton Theological Senimary, preached through his vacation. Then came another student, A. W. Hubbard, who preached four months from May 1, 1869. At that time there were twenty-one members, and then the house was closed, not to be opened again to this day for congregational service. On February 24, 1879, a committee came here to locate a Unitarian school; they looked at the Academy and Congregational Church and went away.

In 1885, the Catholics, under the leadership of Elder Joseph Hebert, the blacksmith at the "Village," held several services there and made an offer of $100 for the building. This was not accepted, much to the disgust of Elder Joseph. Repairs have been made from time to time by private subscription. In 1890 the house had become very badly dilapidated and Mathew H. Milton undertook to superintend the repairs and expend the money raised for that purpose. It was shingled and painted and the underpinning righted. In 1904, through the efforts of Mrs. Sarah A. Blodgett, daughter of Rev. Moses Gerould, assisted by Mr. G. H. Goodhue, a grandson of George Harris, for many years clerk of the society and church, the plastering, which had nearly all fallen from the ceiling, was cleared and the walls and ceiling covered with steel, the roof shingled and the floor timbers, which had become rotten, replaced by new ones. It is hoped to replace the inside of the church as it was originally built.

In 1853 the pulpit was cut down and a seat, which was in

front of the pulpit facing the congregation taken out. There were three steps leading to the pulpit also. It was built much like the other churches in those days with as strict adherence to the architecture of that period as possible, both inside and out. The pews have doors, which were always the delight of the children. In the northwest corner of the gallery is the "nigger pew." In 1828, when the church was built, there were two negroes in town, Nancy, a freed servant whom Mrs. George Kimball brought from Bremuda, and Dennison Wentworth, a black boy, living with Mrs. Plastridge at the old "Dole Tavern." So scrupulous were those people not to mix the races, that this pew was built for their special use. This did not look as if religion was an even thing all round, and some of the old people who had never seen before any difference in anybody in church, made amusing remarks about it. Mr. Kimball was not pleased with the arrangement and declined to let Nancy occupy the pew. They all sat together like one family. Dennison had associated with the boys and had been considered about as good as any of them. He also declined the honors intended for him and the pew fell entirely into disuse.

A letter from N. P. Rogers to George Kimball, dated August 5, 1829, in reference to Nancy and the trouble in changing servants, reads much as people talk now. The inference suggested by that pew, that the help was not as good as the rest of the family, would not tend to produce harmony. Mr. Rogers had been to visit Kimball in Canaan and had driven home to Plymouth.

We got home after a dismal ride. I was sick, wife tired, Daniel restless, spirits depressed, visit over, journey ended, road rocky, hilly — hilly as Satan; picked raspberries all along the wayside; unwell several days; money scarce; business dull. Wish we had as good a little Bermudese as Nancy, instead of the white bird of passage. They are as restless and troublesome as the French Jacobins. I can't keep one a week. Our Lydia is about retiring to her Peeling and then we have got the whole planet to circumnavigate for another. This notion of having a president only one term is making these jades as restless as king birds. They want to keep in perpetual rotation. When you next go to Bermuda you must bring Mary a neat little Bermudean she-Othello, as black as a blackberry and as clean as a penny. Blind her when you start or she will find her way back in six weeks on foot. You are better situated than anybody on earth. Your dwelling is an elegant retirement in a truly original neighborhood. Your faithful servant is cut off by her ebony hue, and by the waves that wallup towards our shores and the "vexed Bermoothes" from all propensity to quit your service and run home among white clowns and send you polling after another witch, to run away as soon as you have got her half learned. You have no better enemies except poor Elijah (Blaisdell), and his enmity is as good as a milch cow to you in Canaan. You are a scholar, with inexhaustible resources to amuse and entertain. You are an Episcopalian, and your piety is not of a sort to disquiet or alarm you; and your wife is a Christian, if you are not, and may sanctify her unbelieving husband.

The sons of several of the old church members became preachers. Ithamar Pillsbury, son of Joshua and Elizabeth Pillsbury, was born on South Road about 1798. In 1812, he ran away and enlisted in the army then marching for Canada; was followed by his father and brought back; was educated partly at Meriden; graduated at Yale college in 1822, and studied divinity at Yale, and became a Congregationalist preacher. He was appointed city missionary for Boston, which position he held several years; afterwards was appointed city missionary in New York. While here he married a wife eighteen years older than himself. She died and he married a young girl of eighteen, by whom he had several children. He was a man of great energy and very earnest in what he undertook. At a late period of his life he went to Illinois and located a tract of land which he intended to colonize. He named it Andover. He laid out his lands upon paper into streets and squares, ornamenting them with churches, schoolhouses, public buildings, printing presses, and all the resultants of a first-class community, and came East to sell his lots. His success did not answer his expectations. But in whatever he engaged he continued to preach. He died at Andover, Ill.

Caleb Clark, Baptist, was the son of Joseph and Abigail Clark, in the Porter neighborhood on the Turnpike; born July 4th, 1797. When a young man was not of much account in the family, but would often say smart things at the religious meetings. Was a timid boy and youth, often fearful of being eaten up by bears. Under Elder Wheat's dispensation, he received a "call" to preach by way of a dream. He was sent to school to New Hampton, and there trained to be a minister and then went forth as far as Rumney; here he settled down to preaching and farming, until his death, much respected for his piety and simplicity of life.

George Richardson, Episcopalian; born July 30, 1795, son of Joshua and Betsey Walworth Richardson; graduated from Dartmouth College in 1820. His brother, Charles Walworth Richardson, born June 11, 1801; after his brother George had been ordained, decided to devote his life to preaching the Congregational creed. It is supposed that he was ordained in Lancaster. He was in charge of the Congregational Church at Colebrook for several years and was much respected for his pulpit efforts. He was appointed chaplain of the twenty-fourth regiment of militia in 1845. Afterwards he was settled at Lancaster and Guildhall for several years. Then he had some connections with missionary efforts in Maine, and was active as agent and correspondent of some religious journals. In this town, he was for several years placed in charge of the public schools, going on foot through the twenty-one districts and accepting as compensation twenty-five dollars. His last years were not happy. Not being a thrifty man, his property slipped away and left him discouraged. His personal habits became an offence against neatness and good order. Indolent he was, and not possessed of that great virtue which comes after godliness. His personal appearance often indicated an aversion to the use of water. As he grew older, he used to imagine himself a desirable match for young ladies. His annoyances in that respect were laughable and sometimes so great as to call for the interference of neighbors. All the plans of his life seemed to have failed, and doubtless his disappointments, distress and poverty shattered his mind, so that he was hardly accountable for his acts. He was a man of good abilities, but lacked tact and skill to apply them to useful purposes. He died in 1872, a wayworn, weary old man, and was buried by the town.

William B. Kelly, Baptist, son of Moses and Nancy Kelly, born in 1806, was a hatter and clothier by trade; was converted under the preaching of Rev. Amos Foster and then turned his attention to divinity. He was ordained and installed over the Baptist Church in Peterborough, where he died in 1836, and lies buried in the Street Cemetery.

Thomas N. Jones, Congregationalist, son of Amasa, born about

1821, studied at Meriden and Gilmanton; was first settled in Loudon for several years; then called to Reading, Mass., where he labored until his death in 1869; an amiable, sincere man, who made many friends and retained them through his life.

So stands today this old house, one of the landmarks of the town. From whatever elevation or depression the street is viewed it is the most prominent but one. But not like the old meeting house, whose portals, although once dedicated to the service of God, now resound with that "devil music," which good old Deacon Worth so much abhorred. The old North Church is still ready to receive the children and grandchildren of those who struggled to upbuild it for the same service of God. More memories for this generation cluster round its doors than any other spot. With no feelings of curiosity, but of veneration, do we look upon it. We can well say with Daniel Webster, "There are those who love it"; love those memories, which grow stronger and stronger as we look across the way at the silent sentinels which mark the resting place of our fathers and mothers, who loved the old church before us and taught us to do the same.

Methodist and Baptist Churches at Canaan

CHAPTER XVI.

THE METHODIST CHURCH.

Methodism came into Canaan with the early settlers, but there was only a trace of it; it was many years before it developed itself. Samuel Meacham, who built the Gould house, long since torn down, and lived on Town Hill, came into town with George Harris, Samuel Benedict and Lewis Joslin in the spring of 1768 from Lebanon, N. H. He was a settler in that town as early as 1764 and came from Lebanon, Conn. He was an unsmiling, sedate man, who had the appearance of being very thoughtful, although the world is not much wiser for his thoughts because they were unuttered. He was a Wesleyan from the beginning He, with his family, brought his faith with him from Connecticut and kept it. He waited patiently for his brethren, who came afterwards, like the birds in summer, and made the whole atmosphere vocal with their songs and shouts of Glorias and Amens. He had six sons and five daughters: Jeremiah, Joshua, who lived on Town Hill beyond his father's house; Joseph, who married Sarah Basford; Andrew, who married Abigail Eastman; Elam, who married Polly Williams; and Thomas; Polly, who married William Bradbury and was the mother of Deacon Benjamin; Sarah, who married Amos Worthen; Phœbe, who married Ezekiel Wells; Miriam, who married Asa Kimball and was in want all her life; Betty, who married Moses Worthen.

Caleb Seabury was another good man who believed that way, and his wife with him. They lived here more than twenty years without reproach, honored in their lives, and departed peacefully to their great reward in some other land.

Capt. Ezekiel Wells was another: not a very religious man, not much given to prayer; somewhat profane, in fact, upon occasion. But his wife was a daughter of Samuel Meacham, and like that good old man, a sincere Methodist. Her influence seemed to bring her husband into the same fold, and he conformed as far as he was able to her discipline, and was accepted for whatever he was because he was an influential man. These three men conferring together formed the first class in Canaan.

Soon afterwards good old David Dustin joined them; then "Esq." Arvin applied and was admitted into that sacred circle. Arvin kept store at the north end of the Street then and sold rum, and he was often drunk upon his own liquor, which seriously scandalized the class and the brethren. It was common for them all to drink Arvin's rum, but he was drunk oftener and worse than the others.

There was a man named Warren Bannister who came here in 1810 as the Methodist minister. He had some duties to perform in regard to Arvin, disagreeable duties to him, because he was neither brave nor shrewd. Arvin's conduct annoyed them all, but being a prominent man, Bannister feared to apply the discipline. He prayed over his dilemma and then with desperate courage seized its horns and excommunicated the whole class together, serving the innocent and guilty alike. It occurred this was the quickest way to get the sinner out! Then he reorganized the class; Arvin and his friends were enraged, and much ill-feeling cropped out in the community. Bannister invited Mr. Dustin to rejoin the class. He replied, "No! he had been turned out once without cause, and he would stay out, lest he might be treated worse next time." Mr. Dustin lived and died a Methodist, but never again joined the class. There was Elder John Broadhead, for many years a presiding elder and resident here in the early part of the century. He lived in a house that once stood on the ground that was covered by the house resided in by Mr. Walker, afterwards burned, on South Road. He owned the land down as far as the corner, where afterwards the first Methodist church was built in 1826.

The elder was a Democrat of the sternest, most unyielding kind. Even at that time, it was doubtful whether religion or politics had the strongest hold on his conscience. It appears that most of the Methodist clergy of the early days were Democrats, a fact which at this day seems singular, since Jefferson, the father of the Democratic party was an avowed infidel and a great admirer of Voltaire. Democracy in those days was not the thing of shreds and patches which is today honored with that name. It meant then a system of government founded upon the direct will of the people and opposed the principle of Federalism as tending to consolidate the powers of the government in few hands. Elder Broadhead sometimes occupied the pulpit in the meeting house. In his prayers and exhortations he seldom failed to mingle religion with the politics to the infinite disgust of the Federalists who heard him. It is said that it afforded him great satisfaction to lash his opponents from the pulpit, because it gave them no opportunity for reply. Years afterwards (in 1829) he left the pulpit for the honors and emoluments incident to the life of a representative in Congress. A famous old man he was and held in honor in church and state. Canaan was a federal town, the home of Daniel Blaisdell, who never liked Methodists any better than he liked Democracy. He and the elder often encountered each other in debate and they seldom separated until both had become more or less enraged. On one of these occasions after an unusually stormy talk, the elder said to some of the neighbors that he had a great mind to "thresh Blaisdell." The next time they met was in passing through the woods between their houses — Blaisdell lived on the Prescott Clark farm — Blaisdell stepped out and said to the elder that "he was ready for a threshing if he thought he was able to do it." The elder replied "I think I can do it now and evermore, but I won't at this time." He said he was mad when he made the threat and thought the most Christian course was to own up.

At the beginning of the last century the country had been divided into circuits, the Hanover circuit to the west and the Bridgewater circuit to the east, and so far as they could be found, ministers assigned for their special care. Canaan, Dorchester Enfield, Springfield and a part of Grantham constituted the Hanover circuit, and the minister spent a week in each town. It was only once in four weeks they had services here.

In 1806 the N. E. Conference met in Canaan; it was arranged that there should be a grand camp-meeting on the shore of Hart Pond, in Robert Barber's woods, near the Wells place. Bishop Asbury presided. Ministers and brethren from far and near came to assist him, and there was a great multitude of people present, curious to see and hear that famous apostle of Methodism, who had been ordained a bishop by the sainted John Wesley himself and sent here to do his Master's work. Great success attended the labors here. Stevens says, "On Wednesday, May 11th, Asbury arrived in Canaan, where the conference began its session. The next day about forty four members were present besides probationers and visitors. On Sunday, May 15, 'I ordained,' says Asbury, 'eleven elders in the woods. At three o'clock I preached in the Meeting house. It was a season of power." The tenets of that faith were adopted into many families and continue to this day.

After this period we lose sight of the active element in the church. We only know that they never ceased to work and pray. There was a reaction; no gushing or striking scenes were heard of. The tide ebbed and flowed smoothly. The Conference Report for the year 1809 contains the first mention of a preacher for Canaan, Ebenezer Blake, and the membership is put down at 155. In 1810, under Warren Bannister and Joseph Lull, embracing the Canaan and Bridgewater circuit, the membership is 170. It is not known how many of these were residents of Canaan, although the report would indicate that all were. It is, however, improbable. Canaan is not mentioned again until 1817 when Eleazer Phelps is the preacher with a membership of 69. This would seem to be nearer the right number taking into consideration the number of families in town. In 1818 John Paine is the preacher and the membership is 71. The records from 1815 are very meagre, with an occasional omission, often consisting of only a statement that a meeting was held. In 1815 Jacob Marston was local preacher, Robert Williams, exhorter, with Thomas Cotton, Benjamin Norris, John Nevins, Moses Lawrence and Jonathan Snow were leaders. John R. Dustin and Thomas Cotton, stewards. In 1820 Joseph Killam reports 139 members. In 1822 and in 1823 the same. In 1825 Caleb Dustin and Giles Campbell preached to the Canaan and Lebanon circuit with a membership of 213, and in 1826 the number is increased to 235. The records for May 9, 1818, are "Voted to give Samuel Norris a recommend to the yearly Conference." He was admitted the following June, superannuated in 1840 and died in 1880.

Among the old band of Methodists we find the names of Solomon Sias, Jacob Sanborn and B. F. Hoyt as presiding elders. Then there was Moses Lawrence, John R. Dustin, Nathaniel and Samuel Norris, Jacob Marston, Joseph Killam and Samuel Gile as leaders, preachers and exhorters, and Robert Williams, who in his last years lived in constant fear of the sheriff. The old man got into debt and had nothing to pay it with. The fear of the sheriff was great upon him. He scarcely dared leave his house, fearing he might be carried off. When he went for his cows he would take his axe upon his shoulder. His neighbors all knew of his fears, and one of them, Maj. Levi George, thought to give him a scare. One evening while driving his cows home accompanied by his axe as usual, the Major came up behind him, and seizing him by the shoulder said, "Mr. Williams, you are my prisoner." The old man's face became white with fear. He turned suddenly upon the Major, who said to him quietly, "You see, neighbor Williams, I don't fear your axe, but you needn't be afraid, for I've got no papers agin you." Those were the days when poor men were shut up in jail for debt, as if that might help it. After that Major George himself fell into debt, by way of an indorsement for his son-in-law, but he took precautions before trouble came, to put his property into Lawyer Pettingill's hands for the benefit of his family. Joshua Blaisdell, the merciless, was sheriff and was ordered to arrest the Major. When arrived at the house the Major said, "You can take me to Haverhill as soon as you please, I have provided for my family and shall be glad to go with you, because I don't want to be bothered with thinking of you any more." The sheriff departed with a promise to return soon, but much to the annoyance of the Major he never troubled him afterwards. It was one of the peculiarities of that sheriff to annoy people who fell into his power. If letting them alone was most agreeable, he would arrest them, and if to arrest them gave great pleasure, he would stand off with his papers in his pocket, leaving his victim a prey to his own uncertain expectations.

At last there came over the church days of heaviness and indifference when neither preaching nor prayers availed anything. They were just drifting, drifting. In the year 1824 a long-wished for revival commenced, primarily it was the result of a sermon preached in the old church by Mr. Foster from Hanover, who was sent here to minister to the Congregational church. All religions had to use the same pulpit. The people had been listening weekly to the long monotonous sermons of Elder Wheat or Elder Hardy, for whom they never had much respect, and to Caleb Dustin and William McCoy, whose chief merit consisted in constantly offering "wine and milk without money and without price," but offered in so indifferent a tone and manner, that none would accept it, thinking it was for somebody else. McCoy preached in Enfield and South Road and once in four weeks on the Street. Most of the people, particularly the older ones went to sleep in the corners of the pews, and only waked up at the slamming of the seats by the boys and girls as they rose to the last prayer. The seats were narrow and the backs high and straight. They had followed those old saints for years through all their arguments, and had come to believe that there was no variation nor shadow of change in their discourses, and for this cause they regarded it as perfectly safe and proper for them to sleep away the weary hours that lingered about this old temple. Mr. Foster's manner was very impressive and earnest. His sermon was an eloquent plea, addressed to the young, urging them to live soberly and flee for their lives to the throne of grace and seek refuge there from impending danger. There was a charming refinement and fascination in the style of this new preacher, that interested the sleepers at the start and kept them awake. And the boys were not permitted to slam the seats when they rose for the benediction. After the sermon the men and women gathered in routs, and passed opinions upon the man and his doctrines. They "guessed" he was "all right," and his talk was right to the "pint." Mr. Haynes said it was time for all of them to wake up and remember that they had a Lord and Maker to whom they were all accountable, and not trust their entire salvation any longer to Elder Wheat and Elder Hardy or Caleb Dustin. Moses Lawrence said it was full time for them to do some praying on their own account, and let us begin now said other brethren. Those old fossils got waked up lively, and a great solemnity like a shroud fell upon them, and they bowed before it. They all began to flee to the mountains, as if it was their last chance to escape from remorse of conscience. There was great rejoicing for many were converted, some, who seemed to be more reprobates than the devil, became submissively Christians. After this great harvest of souls had become ripe, the churches went to work to gather them in.

 The Methodist church was most active, and was greatly increased and strengthened in the numbers that entered its portals. The old members renewed their vows, and promised to be forever afterwards more brightly shining lights in the Church and before men. There was old Robert Martin, and Benjamin Haynes and Orpha Currier and Levi George, Benjamin Davis and Thomas Miner and Amasa Jones and Jacob Dow and Moses Lawrence and John R. Dustin, with all their families who had been so long born again, as to have nearly forgotten it, and being in grace, didn't believe they could ever fall, whatever else might happen to them. With this firm belief in their own sure salvation, they had grown snowy cold and prayerless, except when their minister happened to be around, and then they were ever lamenting that the state of religion was so low — so lost sight of in the affairs of life! They had so long stood in the front ranks with their backs to the worldly crowd and their broad shoulders caught all the cheerful rays of heavenly light, and absorbed them like sponges, so that there seemed to be no visible access to the Rock of Ages. And long they had thus stood like the weatherbeaten stumps of the dead pine trees along the highway of the town.

There was a density and opaqueness about those solemn old saints and their notions about being "elected," that excited no interest among the young and gay, and there were large numbers of them in those days, who had festive seasons everywhere. And then old people talked in parables and proverbs, about their own security and then went about their business like other men who had never boasted of their grace. Sometimes it seems as if that generation of Christians did not die in their appointed time, but lapped over into another age, and have been lingering all the way down until now. They used to make the women wear bonnets plain, *sans* ribbons or flowers, and calico dresses made from scant patterns. They used to call these tricks, denying themselves, bearing the cross, and being in contempt of the world. But we used to think these plain and cheap clothes indicated more stinginess than grace. Suppose the ladies now should be seized with a freak to appear in church, like those plain primitive sisters, and they should fill the church full of cheap calicoes and hats plain without ribbons or feathers. It would be a sight! Perhaps they would boast of it as an act of humility! Well, those old men who always walked about like John Gilpin, as if they "carried weights," in the wilderness of their hearts heard the warning voices, and waked up as they had never been waked before. They withdrew their faces from the sunlight and fell upon their knees with their faces to the ground and let the flood flow over them. And when they rose if they were not washed clean of some of their nonsense, that, like barnacles to a ship, had been clinging to them, at least they said they were renewed, and declared with emphatic humility that they would never again stand in the light of divine truth. And to signalize their new earnestness and sincerity they proposed to build a new house.

The great harvest of members that had been gathered in, made it necessary that they should have a place of their own, where they could assemble and counsel each other often. By the arrangement with the other churches they were entitled to occupy the old meeting house but once in four weeks; that was not often enough to keep up a wholesome organization. So they drew their plan and after some lively discussions upon the spot, located it on South Road where the roads intersect. This spot being central and of easy access would best accommodate the brethren of Enfield and South Road, who were supposed to constitute a majority of the church. It did not cost much to build the house. The hearts of the people had been recently paralyzed by fears of hell-fires. It made them generous. Some gave labor, some gave lumber, others furnished provisions for the laborers, and all gave something. Their zeal was great and on the 1st day of January, 1826, the house was dedicated. Henry J. Wooley, a young Irishman preached the sermon. He was a dark haired man, an exhorter of wonderful power, and of strange skill in the application of language. His descriptions of hell and its torments were weird and unique, giving the impression of being personal experiences. Oftentimes in their prayer-meetings and love feasts he would psychologize the sensitive members of the meeting, and when they would awake from the trance into which they had fallen, they would present marvelous pictures of their experiences in foreign lands and spheres, some of them not very agreeable.

One of the most notable things that occurs to me at this long distance, was the choir and the music. Music has all my life long been to me a passion. It has absorbed a great many hours of my life. The rehearsal of it has given great pleasure, and I never tire of listening to it. "Thinking in the midst of music is one of the sweetest things in life, when the heart is at ease. When we feel the harmony, are harmonized by it, and yet lose not one thread of the golden woof we are weaving." I learned to sing in those old days, and I often feel the vibration of those old melodies, when my mind reverts to those old days. There were singers then everywhere, every house was vocal with singing. There were no fifes or fiddles allowed in that house in the first years; their tones were not harmonious to pious ears. But the seats were filled with young men and maidens, and in the center stood Reuben Welch, a tall man of large bulk, a most inveterate stutterer, but what seemed strange was that a man who was unable to articulate any sentence intelligibly, could sing all day without any impediment. And I have wondered since then, why, knowing he could sing any sentence, he did not carry on his ordinary conversation by the aid of minims and semi-breves, rather than stumble about his words like a person who wants to but cannot sneeze. He used to hold a singing book in one hand, the hymn book in the other, and mark the time by each alternately, and his heavy bass voice would roll out over them and control all the rest. The music they sung was solemn and plaintive, such as was best adapted to the serious condition of the Christian mind. They had no Bliss, no Sankey, no Gospel Hymns; these delicious melodies which give us so much pleasure were unheard by them. It was not known that anything pleasing or cheerful could enter into divine worship.

For many summers and winters these old brethren came up to worship God in the house they had built. They grew older and passed away one by one, let us hope to enjoy the heavenly felicities they believed in store for them. As the years passed by the congregation diminished, it grew more and more inconvenient to attend there. The members had gravitated away from that house. Some days the audience would resemble ours upon a rough day. Some days the doors would stand gaping widely for those who should but did not come. It seemed to have served the purpose for which it was built, and like an old garment was left by the wayside. Phineas Eastman bought it, took it down at the time the Northern Railroad decided to establish a station at East Canaan, removed to that place, and made a store out of its timbers, and from that day the voice of prayer has not been heard within its walls. Previous to this event, in 1841, Rev. George W. H. Clark, an earnest faithful man, was appointed to take charge of the church here. During the following year under his auspices a very extensive revival occurred, and very large numbers were added to the church, from the north and east part of the town.

In June, 1842, a camp-meeting was held in the woods near the Wells burying ground, where members were converted and united with the church. Many of the new Christians were disinclined to worship in the house on South Road, it being far to travel, and besides they wished to be where they could mingle with other Christians. This feeling increased rapidly and ere long it was decided to build a new house on the Street, which they could occupy and control together. A building committee was appointed, subscriptions solicited, land purchased and in due time the people saw a new spire rising towards heaven. Everything was completed, orderly and judiciously, and when the new house was dedicated it was already free from debt. This event occurred on the 2d day of October, 1844. The sermon was preached by Rev. Mr. McCurdy.

Mr. Clark, in 1892, wrote regarding his pastorate here:

I arrived in Canaan July 9, 1841, after dark, went directly to the old parsonage on South Road, called up the family opposite, as they had retired, to get the key. I found the church in a very low state. My preaching places for the Sabbath were three fourths of the time at the old chapel on South Road, and one fourth at the church at the Street. Held meetings in schoolhouses in different parts of my charge. A series of meetings were held on South Road where twelve to fifteen were converted in the fall. In March, 1842, when my Presiding Elder Rev. C. D. Cahoon, came to the Third Quarterly Conference, I asked him if he could not arrange for a camp meeting for his next visit. The presiding elder came, June 6th, and brought with him John Mars, a colored man. Camp meetings began with small attendance, but increased, some six were converted by Friday night. Saturday morning it began to snow and continued all day, but it was a great day of power. In our first preaching service the presiding elder preached; fourteen were converted; meeting held in the Enfield tent. Saturday morning Mars preached and 125 came to the altar. Monday morning closed the meeting. We went to the old church on the Street Monday evening, Mars

THE METHODIST CHURCH.

was with me. We held meetings nearly every afternoon and evening for four weeks. The whole country was moved religiously as never before. In the Autumn we held a union meeting with the Congregationalists, Baptists and Free-will Baptists. Three weeks in the Congregational church about 80 were converted. As a result of the work I baptized about 132. Early in the winter we began talking about building a church on the Street. That winter the timber was cut and carried to the mill. In the spring before I left the job was let for building. I returned in a few weeks and saw it raised.

Mr. Clark died in Fairfax, Vt., February 27, 1897. In Canaan his labors had been productive of harmony and good fellowship, and in 1843 he was sent to another field. Then the Rev. Erasmus B. Morgan fiery, fractious, irritable and opinionated, was placed in charge of this church. He was a very positive man, one of that rare class who believe they are called to improve upon God's own work, neither humble nor charitable; exacting; a wordy man of narrow intellect, embracing not much beyond his own intellect; very passionate withal, and apt to take offence at trifles. He began preaching on South Road, and sometimes occupied Heath's Hall on the Street. He had not been here long before there was a called meeting of the church, and about half of the brethren refused to attend further upon his ministrations. He was displaced by Elder Cahoon and a Mr. Eaton put in charge, but the cross fires were too sharp for Brother Eaton and he left. Mr. Morgan had a strong and earnest party here and he was reinstated. And he, with those who believed in him made war upon the other side. The feeling ran higher than at a presidential election, and the lies and slanders that followed were unbecoming professed Christians. The anti-Morgan lambs were without a pastor. They prayed and talked well, but they lacked a head. About February, 1844, a smart preacher named C. V. Caples, a colored man, received charge of the indignant half of the church, and then the wars of Morgan and Caples began, and are a part of the church history. Religion and society got badly mixed,— dynamite would have been dove-like compared to the explosions that shook and shocked the community. The joy and peace of believers was laid aside, and great bitterness and soreness resulted from the wicked words and deeds that were not restrained. It is related that one of the Morgan brothers in a prayer, asked the Lord "to seize on Sister ——

and shake her well over hell, but be careful and not let her drop in."

Morgan revoked Caples' license to preach but Elder Cahoon came in and vouched for him as a regular preacher. Mr. Conant, Congregationalist, vouched for him; Elder Clements, Baptist, however, called him an uncertain character. Mr. Caples made charges against Mr. Morgan and cited him to appear and answer at the next conference. The doors of the new church were closed against Morgan, and he preached in halls and schoolhouses. The moral atmosphere was heated and murky, too much so for the leading combatants. On the 8th of July, 1844, "Brother Morgan packed up his goods" and retired discomfited, and on the 16th, of the same month, "Brother Caples goes off to the State of Maine," and is no more seen in Canaan. The effect of that controversy was like a great blister on the church, it was years in healing but it purified many hearts and wrought out much Christian charity.

In 1844 the Circuit was divided on the line of Canaan and Enfield, leaving Canaan, Dorchester and a part of Hanover in the Canaan Circuit. Rev. Reuben Dearborn stepped into the breach left vacant by the retreating hostile forces. It was not a pleasant place to put a new man, but he was equal to the occasion. Carefully avoiding and ignoring the past troubles, he gradually brought the brethren together and a degree of harmony prevailed. The church increased in numbers and for many years was prosperous. They have had many preachers since that day with many of whom the brethren felt no regrets on parting after one year's intercourse, and there were others whose stay might have been lengthened until this day with profit. And they have always preferred to have the services of their preachers. But a change has come over the spirit of this country church. Once they were hardly content with two sermons and a prayer meeting on the Sabbath, now their hunger and thirst after righteousness is appeased by one sermon, and no prayer meeting on Sunday. They are content also to share their preacher's services with East Canaan. In 1883 the pastor was required to divide his time between the two churches. During the term of Rev. Joshua Holman the present parsonage on the

Street was purchased and repaired, and in 1869 the debt upon it was removed.

In June, 1843, Stephen Eastman was licensed as a local preacher. He was born February 10, 1818, and married Laura L. Loverin of Loudon. He was the sixth of eleven children born to James and Polly (French) Eastman. He attended two terms at Canaan Union Academy and several terms at the Newbury (Vt.) Seminary, joining the N. H. Conference in 1846 at Lebanon, Bishop Waugh presiding. He was stationed one year at Hopkinton, one year at North Charlestown, two at Walpole, then at Alexandria and Hebron where he closed his labors on earth March 14, 1854. On May 14, 1847, Larned L. Eastman was licensed as a local preacher. He was born March 12, 1813, the fourth son of James and Polly Eastman, married April 3, 1839, Lucy A., daughter of Henry Currier of Enfield. His life as an itinerant was one of great mental and physical activity. He relates his journeyings so modestly and concisely that it is best told in his own words.

My education what I have, was in the town school and during a four years' course of study while in charge of a church. Several years before joining the Conference I endeavored to improve to the best advantage in qualifying myself for the gospel ministry. I joined the Conference in 1848, at Manchester, Bishop Hedding presiding. Here I think Brother Stephen was ordained Deacon. I was appointed to Alexandria and Hebron, and reappointed in 1849. At the close of this second year I was ordained Deacon and Brother Stephen, Elder, by Bishop Norris at Newmarket. The two succeeding years I was appointed to Warner and Wentworth. At the close of this term was ordained Elder by Bishop Baker at Nashua. During these first four years I was favored with gracious revivals, many were converted each year. The two following years I was at Lancaster, where there was a great revival. The next two years at Littleton, and here we had a good time also. The next move was to Winchester, where we had two successful years. Then two years each at Plymouth and Amesbury, Mass., at Peterborough and Sunapee, and then three years at Methuen. Here my health began to fail, still I consented, being strongly urged to be appointed a second time to Warner. At the close of this year I asked for a supernumerary relation to the Conference without appointment, that we might rest and travel a little. We spent several months in Illinois and New Jersey, with our children; returned to Moultonborough and supplied for the year out, and was reappointed for the following year. Meanwhile I built me a house in Methuen, and moved into it, but retained my relation to the Conference, and preached at Kingston. The next year I rested until September. We then went to Londonderry and supplied the year out; rested again and then went to Groveton, and supplied the year out. Was then made effective and appointed to Groveton again. This was in 1875-6. And closed my effective service as a traveling minister. I am still an unworthy member of the N. H. Conference, broken down with labor and disease, having lost one eye by a cancer, and was near losing life from the same cause. I am now able to do something for this Children's Home, which is perhaps as trying a position as we ever occupied. God has been and is wonderfully good to us, and we intend to work for his cause while our day lasts. It seems but a little time since we were all children,— now we are stooping with age. But let us be glad we have lived and toiled for a time in the vineyard of the Lord.

The parents of Stephen and Larned Eastman moved into Canaan in 1795 from Hampstead, N. H. The father, James, was born April 28, 1780; the mother, Polly French, daughter of Jonathan French of Enfield, was born December 29, 1787.

Caleb Fales was a Methodist preacher, son of John and Sally Fales. He had a natural call to preach without being educated to it. A man of fair abilities, and being of good name and fame among his brethren. He was born about 1800, and when last heard from resided in Sharon, Vt.

Robert Williams, son of Robert, who emigrated from Barrington or Dunbarton, and settled in Enfield, it is not known where young Robert was born, he married Mercy Hardy of Lebanon, sister of the late Mrs. William Campbell, by whom he had several children. He was an industrious and thrifty farmer, owning at different periods several farms in this vicinity. From here he went to Illinois where he continued his farmer's life. He died several years ago, leaving a handsome property to be divided among his children. He was possessed of fine natural abilities, and was an earnest, effective speaker. When or where he was licensed to preach is not known but he was known as a Methodist preacher, and was much respected for his piety and eloquence. Early in the old temperance movement he espoused that cause and died a rigid abstainer from alcoholic drinks. He also enlisted early in the anti-slavery cause and did some good and earnest lecturing in behalf of oppressed humanity. On a Fourth of July more than sixty years ago, he was appointed to give an anti-slavery lecture in the Congregational church on the Street. At that time negroes and anti-slavery meetings were

THE METHODIST CHURCH. 245

interdicted in Canaan. The "Vigilance Committee" appointed by the town "legally" to disperse incendiary meetings, were notified of this proposed outrage upon the nice royalty of public opinion, and they hastened with drum and fife to disperse that little band of earnest thinkers whose prayers and hopes for the slave threatened to upheave the foundations of republican government. But that heroic committee for once came too late. They were so long getting upon the track that when they arrived at the church they learned that the speech had been spoken and the audience gone home.

Enoch Davis was another local preacher, of whom nothing can be learned except that he lived here some eighty years ago and let his light shine very freely.

AT EAST CANAAN.

Leonard Davis was the only person at East Canaan who was a member of the Methodist church in 1862. He was at that time a member of the church at the Street and afterwards transferred his membership. The church building now occupied by the Methodists was a union church, and was built by the citizens. There was religious worship in the house but no church organization.

Rev. C. U. Dunning in the spring of 1862 was closing his labors at Enfield, having preached and delighted the people at East Canaan, a request was sent to the annual conference asking for him to be sent for a year. He came and was the first pastor of the church. He remained until the spring of 1866, one year under missionary rule and three as preacher in charge of the church which was organized into an independent church by Bishop Osman C. Baker in 1863, it having been considered as a part of the church at the Street. Dunning reported at the close of his term, "Four years ago there were but fifteen persons who were considered to be members of the East Canaan class. By the blessing and good hand of our God upon us we are able to report 60 members and 29 probationers. Within three years three members and three probationers have deceased, all dying in the triumph of faith."

Under J. W. Adams eleven persons were baptized. But a very unfortunate division took place and the church, which had been strong and full of promise, divided into two weak ones. And from this disaster the church never recovered. During the pastorate of Mr. Farnham considerable interest prevailed and twenty persons were baptized, by Rev. J. Pike, presiding elder, and in spite of this interest there were two less on the roll than when he came. In 1873 the church was repaired at an expense of $400. In 1883 the church was united with the church at the Street. In 1892 $250 was spent in repairs and in 1900, $850 was spent in decorating the interior.

The following is a list of the preachers at the Street:

HANOVER CIRCUIT.

1801 Martin Ruter
    Thomas Branch
    Reuben Jones
    Joshua Crowell
1802 Oliver Beale
    Thomas Skeel
    Joel Winch
    Paul Dustin
1803 Joseph Broadhead

1803 Andrew Kernagen
    Joseph Fairbanks
    Thomas Skeel
    Dexter Bates
1804 Elijah Hedding
1805 Dyer Burge
1806 Joseph Barker
1807 Dan Young
1808 Dan Carr

CANAAN CIRCUIT.

1809 Ebenezer Blake

CANAAN AND BRIDGEWATER CIRCUIT.

1810 Warren Bannister
    Joseph Lull
1811 Abner Clark
    Leonard Bennett

1812 John W. Hardy
    Richard Emory
1813 John Lewis
    John Paine

CANAAN CIRCUIT.

1814 Jacob Sanborn
1815 Walter Sleeper
1816 Benjamin Burnham
1817 Eleazer Phelps
1818 John Paine
    Isaiah Emmerson
1819 Orrin Roberts
1820 Joseph Killam
1821 Ezra Kellogg
1822 Herschel Foster
    John Foster
1823 Joseph Killam
    Nathan Howe

1824 Joseph Killam
    William McCoy
1825 Caleb Dustin
    Giles Campbell
1826 Caleb Dustin
    Eleazer Steele
1827 Benjamin Paine
    Henry J. Wooley
1828 Benjamin Paine
    Joseph Sylvester
1829-30 Dan Fletcher
1831 H. Wheelock
    J. Sweat

THE METHODIST CHURCH.

1832 Caleb Dustin
    S. Hackett
1833 Caleb Dustin
    L. H. Gordon
1834 Supplied Mr. Robbins
1835 John H. Stevens
1836 B. Brewster
1837-8 Haines Johnson
1839 A. Heath
1840 Charles Cowing
1841-2 G. W. H. Clark
    Nathaniel B. Smith
1843 Erasmus B. Morgan
    Kimball Hadley
1844 Reuben Dearborn
1845 John Jones
1846 Silas Quimby
1847 Russell H. Spaulding
1848-9 H. H. Hartwell
1850-1 Nathaniel L. Chase
1852 Smith Aldrich
    or M. Newhall
1853 John Taggart
1854 T. J. Andrews
1855 H. A. Mattison
1856 John English
1857 Nelson Greene

1858 Nelson Martin
1859-60 Joshua Holman
1861 Joseph Hayes
1862 C. U. Dunning
1863-5 Reuben Dearborn
1866 J. W. Adams
1867 George N. Bryant
1868 A. S. Kendall
1869-71 A. C. Coult
1872-3 J. Mowery Bean
1874-6 S. J. Robinson
1877-9 J. H. Hillman
1880 A. F. Baxter
1881-2 J. A. Steel
1883-5 Irad Taggart
1886-7 S. G. Kellogg
1888-9 J. H. Trow
1890-2 C. E. Eaton
1893 H. G. Hoisington
1894-5 D. W. Downs
1896-9 C. A. Reed
1900-1 W. T. Carter
1902 A. M. Markey
1903-4 Herbert F. Quimby
1905-6 W. A. Mayo
1907-8 Cyrus L. Corliss
1909 C. W. Taylor

Preachers at East Canaan:

1863-5 C. U. Dunning
1866-8 J. W. Adams
1869-70 C. H. Chase
1871 Supplied
1872-3 S. C. Farnum
1874-5 G. N. Bryant

1876 Supplied by F. W. Johnson
1877 O. P. Wright
1878 Supplied
1879-80 A. C. Hardy
1881 Supplied by H. S. Parmlee
1882 None

From 1883 the church has had the same pastors as the Street.

CHAPTER XVII.

Schools.

Looking back over all the years my mind uncovers the events of early life like a ploughshare in the grass. There were school scenes for all of us. A little square-roofed school house stood upon the common; it was painted yellow. Many of us learned our letters in that house under the arbitrary rule of old Olive Cross, whose father built the Landon house, as well as the house where he lived and where Mr. Brais now lives. I say old Olive Cross, because I have no recollection of her as ever having been young. Her years seemed to have been perennial and eternal. A brother of John P. Calkins and uncle of Rev. Charles Calkins, who lived in a log house near H. G. Elliott's old farm, once besieged the affections of this prim Methodist teacher. Olive's castle was impregnable — she declined to yield to his proposals, as she did to every one else, and died an old maid. She was a stern old Puritan, and required pure submission to her rules, and her punishments were such as the Inquisition could hardly have improved upon. She was considered a very good woman, very religious and proper in her manners, and seemed to have earned the prescriptive right to teach the rudiments of education to all the children in town. She won the confidence of the parents by her zeal in watching for offences and in punishing offenders. I have often thought if she had children of her own she would have been gentler in her nature, and would have learned that love in a school room, or in a family, is a more powerful weapon than fear. But the parents of those days were great sticklers for force. Children needed flogging as much as horses, and they got it too. There were the Dows, the Wallaces, the Athertons, the Averys, the Barbers, the Wellses, the Tiltons. What would any of them ever have amounted to if they had not been flogged? And what would a school have been good for, unless it conformed to the parental discipline at home? I have often wondered if in the happy home to which, when her spirit ceased from troubling, good old Oliver Cross was triumphantly

Grist Mill

Fair Grounds

removed, she ever has visions of the little girls and boys in that old yellow school house, standing in the floor, their noses pinched with split sticks, holding heavy books out at arm's length until they fell to the floor through weariness; or with screws vibrating between the fingers until the blood flowed, and that great, wide ferule, that raised blisters wherever it fell. But these were facts which seemed all proper and right and served to develop the self-respect and intelligence of the pupil! She was the embodiment of despotic tyranny, and seemed to have absent spells while she invented new tortures for the little ones. I sometimes observe the comity which exists in families, that is, the reciprocal sentiments that pass between parents and children. I never saw a boy yet who discovered much affection for the "old man" who "licked" him upon occasion. He did it again, and he lied about it, too, if it would redeem the whip. In families where they keep a whip you do not see much caressing. The little boy when he comes home all tired out, does not drop into his father's arms and kiss him as he falls asleep. Little boys think: they observe the ways and the temperaments of men. A boy always looks in a man's face when he passes by. He is ever watching for little acts of courtesy, or a recognition from older persons. Speak to him pleasantly and notice what a joy pervades his face and shines out in his eyes. He sees that the little manhood that fills his jacket is recognized, and he goes on his way happy.

Many men and women forget they were ever boys or girls, and look down upon them so far off that they seem never to distinguish them from birds or cattle. Thank God! I always loved children; I always liked to be with them; I like to have them in my house, filling my yard and playing in the shade of my trees. They are like the birds among the branches thereof. Their voices are music to me, because they are the voices of innocence and happiness. And there is a far-off future for them in the coming years, when they like me, will be grey-headed, looking back over the events of half a century, and perhaps, unlike me, singing.

> "Oh! would I were a boy again,
> When life seemed formed of sunny years."

My recollection of the teachers in that old school house is that they were all alike. They never appealed to the manhood and self-respect of the pupils. Their laws like Draco's had penalties, and could only be appeased by corporal suffering. There was Edward Olcott, a rusticated student; and Elijah Blaisdell, who spared nobody — somebody was being punished all the time; and the Rev. Joseph L. Richardson, who afterwards became notorious as one of the leaders of the mob that destroyed the academy; he used to believe that children could endure cold and thirst as well as bodily tortures. He would tell us that these things, although they appeared to be severe judgments, were intended as blessings, and if we profited by them we should receive a crown of righteousness at some future time; but I never seemed to appreciate his prophetic promises in our behalf.

In 1793, a meeting of the Center district was held for the following purposes:

"CANAAN, December 9, 1793.

At a meeting of the inhabitants of the Center District holden at the house of Capt. R. Barber For the purpose of consulting a spot to set a schoolhouse and the time when and the method how to Build said School House. Proceeded as follows:

1st Chose Capt. Joshua Wells Chairman.

2nd Voted to build a school house and set said school house on the north side of the road leading from Capt. Barbers to Capt. J. Wells as near the corner of the old road leading to Capt. Barbers mill as the land will admit of.

3rd. voted to build the frame of the above said house 18 feet wide and 24 feet long and cover the same with boards.

4th voted to build the chimney with stone as far as the beams.

Meeting disolved.

OLIVER SMITH, *Clerk*.

This is the first mention of the building of a school house. There were three districts in town at this time.

The first vote to raise money for schooling was passed in 1786, when 16 pounds L. M. was voted. And Eleazer Scofield, Jehu Jones and Richard Clark were appointed a committee to divide the town into districts. There were no school houses, and the children had been taught by their parents at home. The people had begun to realize that more competent instruction was needed. But their efforts are feeble. They are not yet willing to give their children much of a chance. They thought that as their own

SCHOOLS. 251

education was obtained for the most part by hard knocks and experience, there was no reason why their sons and daughters cannot get it in the same way. Knowledge that could be learned from books was no qualification, in knowing how to cut trees and burn brush. So little did they value book learning, that no mention is made of raising any more money for schools until 1789, when they voted not to raise any.

At the annual meeting in 1795 we find that the town voted to abate Asa Paddleford's school tax. It would seem that the town had been supporting schools. The schools had not been well fostered, although the town had been divided into districts no school house adorned the forks of the roads. The schools were held where any convenient place could be obtained, and for the most part the teacher was paid by those who had subscribed to have a school. One of the subscription papers is as follows:

We the Subscribers, Do Agree to have a Woman's school, to begin as early Next Spring, as we shall think Proper & to last Five months the School is to be Kept where the School House Frame is Near Capt. Joshua Wells's in Canaan, and that we & Each of us Do Promise to bear our Equal Proportion in Getting, Boarding and Paying the Mistress for Teaching According to the Number of Scholars We Subscribe to send, as witness our hands.

CANAAN, February 6 A. D. 1795.

SCHOLARS.

Jonathan Farnum	1½	Levi Bailey	1½
Robert Barber	1	Joshua Wells	2
John M. Barber	1	Caleb Pierce	1
Peter Pattee	2	Enoch Sweat jr	2
Josiah Clark	3	Ebenezer Hanson	1
Richard Whittier	3	Oliver Smith	2

In this school Olive Cross commenced her long career as a teacher, at $4 a month, "boarding round" with the scholars. The frame spoken of, had been put up and covered in at the forks of the old road leading to Orange a little westerly from Joshua Well's. This frame was afterwards taken down and rebuilt into the schoolhouse that used to stand near John Worth's tavern.

In 1795 the town voted, "that the School rates collected by

Dr. Pierce Constable, shall be refunded back and paid the individual it was taken from." "That the northeast district where Abel Hadley lives, or those who have not schooled out their money, shall have the privilege of schooling it out in their own district, and that they all have an order on the constable if they have paid it." "That John Harris and Henry Springer have back their school money." "That those who live in the district where Lt. R. Whittier lives, who have sent their children to the north district to school the winter past, shall pay their money to that district."

In the warrant for the annual meeting in 1796 there was an article "to see if the town will vote to raise money to furnish the town with necessary school houses. No action was taken upon it. But this year for the first time the town chose school money collectors — John Currier, Ezekiel Wells, Jonathan Carlton, Clark Currier.

In 1798 John Bryant taught on West Farms and the other teachers were Job Wilson, Amasa Jones and Eliphalet Norris.

In 1799 Ezekiel Wells, Thomas Miner and Enoch Richardson were appointed a committee to divide the school districts "that are dissatisfied." Nine districts were made.

In 1800 Oliver Smith, Selding Pattee and Ebenezer Clark taught school in southeast district one month. In 1801 John Bryant taught on West Farms and at John R. Dustin's.

In 1803, a strong effort was made to provide the town with suitable accommodations for the schools, and a vote was passed "to raise a sum of $500 to build school houses in each district, allowing each the privilege of building its own, if they build within 7 months." The $500 was not assessed, through negligence of the selectmen. But the next year (1804) the town passed a similar vote, with this change, that the sum to be raised be $1,000, "allowing each district the privilege of building its own schoolhouse, if built within seven months." A committee of nine was appointed to ascertain the limits of each district. And nine collectors were chosen to collect the money, one in each district. Moses Dole, John Cogswell and Benjamin Haynes taught the schools. A committee appointed the previous year to redistrict the town reported that they had divided the town into ten districts, and that the money appropriated was not

SCHOOLS.   253

sufficient to build the needed schoolhouses. And in the following year (1805) the town voted an additional $500, "to finish the schoolhouses." The town also made twelve districts and appointed twelve collectors. The tenth district, called also the Center "Deestrick," as reported, was contained within the following boundaries: "Taking Jonathan Carlton (C. P. King) and thence northerly to Mascoma river around by Joseph Flints (G. W. Davis) and all Broad Street and Caleb Welch jr. by request." The schoolhouse in this district was located near Dudley Gilman's Tavern, not far from the site of the residence of the late H. C. George, now Mrs. G. H. Robinson's. It was built about the year 1800, and was the first schoolhouse built on the Street. It was a large one-story building with two stacks of chimneys. As the Street was to be the village it was called the "Academy."

After being occupied for a term of years as a school, it was burned one night by one of the pupils, named Zebulon Barber, who came from the Gore. At this late day the reason for Zebulon's incendiary act does not appear. This school was taught by "Master" Parker. The studies were not numerous, but embraced branches sufficient for what was then considered a fair education — spelling from "Webster's Spelling Book," and writing according to the method of those days. There were no arithmetics; even Pike's had not found its way into our schools. The pupils were instructed in "figures" and "cyphering" by means of sums written out by the master, whose importance increased in the same ratio as his figures. From a little book of about one hundred pages called "The Ladies Accedence," the rudiments of grammar were taught. The reading was confined to the few pages found in the spelling book, and to the New Testament, from which two long readings each day formed the opening and closing exercises. After the burning of "The Academy" the school was kept in a log house, situated in the field a little back of Miss Emma A. Bell's barn, and was taught a term by Lawyer Blaisdell, who often found scant gleanings after Hale Pettingill had picked over the ground. This was the first house built on the "Street" by William Douglass the shoemaker, for a dwelling. And it was still doubtful whether this would be the "Village," so deep and unfathomable were the mud obstructions.

In 1810, thirteen school districts existed, and the same number of collectors were appointed.

In 1811, the first school committee was chosen, "Esq" Pettingill, John H. Harris, and "Esq" Blaisdell. The next year Abel Brown takes the place of John H. Harris.

In 1812, the "Center Deestrick" is divided at Moses Dole's, he having his choice to which district he will belong "with his property."

In 1813, Pettingill, John H. Harris and John Currier are the school committee. In 1814 there are fourteen collectors of school money appointed. In 1816 there are fifteen school collectors representing so many districts. In 1826 a committee was appointed that divided the town into fifteen school districts. This was not satisfactory, so in 1828 the number was increased to seventeen. In 1854 there were twenty districts. In 1861 they had increased to twenty-one. This number continued until 1886. After the passage of the new school law the town in 1885 voted to redistrict the town. The superintending school committee was abolished as well as the prudential committee for each district and a school board was elected by vote of the school meeting.

The town, in 1886, was redistricted into eleven divisions; in 1887 there were ten. This continued down to the establishment of the High School district, which made two districts out of the town. The town school district has been divided into ten divisions, but most of the time there have been nine schools. There are twelve schoolhouses in the town district. The High School district comprises the southeast corner of the town.

CHAPTER XVIII.

Noyes Academy.

In the early part of 1834 several energetic citizens of Canaan, and prominent among them was the lawyer, George Kimball, procured subscriptions sufficient to build a house, and to buy half an acre of land, for grounds. It was located in the field next south of the Congregational Meeting House, with an ornamental fence in front. There were sixty contributors to the enterprise, and chief among them stood the venerable farmer, Samuel Noyes, for whom the contemplated school was named. The amount subscribed was $1,000, of which sum only $80 was subscribed by the opponents of the school, and only $20 of that was ever paid, the friends of the school offering at that time to assume the whole $80. Application was made to the legislature for a charter which was granted July 4, 1834, to Samuel Noyes, George Kimball, Nathaniel Currier, George Walworth and John H. Harris, as incorporators of Noyes Academy. The charter provided for the "education of youth." That the corporation could hold estate not to exceed $15,000, to be divided into one thousand shares of $15 each. Property by way of gift could be held to any amount. The stock was not assessable. On the 4th of July it occurred to some of the enthusiastic and philanthropic donors of the institution, to propose having it established, as they said, "upon the principles of the Declaration of Independence," whereby its privileges and blessings should be open to all pupils without distinction of color, coming with suitable moral and intellectual recommendations. A general meeting of the patrons of the school was warned to be held on August 15, 1834. Previous to this meeting the plan was proposed to many of them individually and met their prompt acceptance.

The nation at this time was at the height of the anti-slavery agitation. During this month anti-slavery riots had taken place in New York City, and had been continued into New Jersey. The people of Canaan sympathized with both sides and the line was as sharply drawn between the abolitionists of Canaan and their opponents as anywhere in the country. Several abolition orators came to Canaan and served to keep the people stirred on that question, which was not solved for more than twenty-five years after. The friends of the school realized there was going to be a struggle, excitement was in the air; both sides did not hesitate to show their whole strength, and every effort was made to bring it out and place every man either on one side or the other. This was a question that it took a man of great ability to straddle. An extract from a diary written at that time, shows that the friends of the school were intent upon carrying out their proposed plan: "Thursday, Aug. 14th, 1834. Rode around town, electioneering, exorted a promise from every man I called upon to appear on Canaan Street tomorrow at 2 o'ck."

Other trusty messengers were dispatched about town to notify all persons interested to appear. At the general meeting the plan was formally laid before it and discussed fully by friends and opponents.

The opposition was led, with much bitterness of spirit, by Hon. Elijah Blaisdell, a gentleman who was not a subscriber, having no pecuniary interest in the institution. Other prominent opponents were present — Dr. Thomas Flanders and Rev. Joseph L. Richardson, all of Canaan.

After a deliberate hearing, a ballot was taken when thirty-six of the fifty-one proprietors present voted in favor and fourteen against it. Two did not vote at all, and declined to express an opinion. Two of the fourteen negatives afterwards declared themselves in its favor. One who was not prepared to vote at this meeting afterwards gave in his assent. Two others hoped the school would go on upon the proposed plan and flourish, and six others who were not present afterwards sent in their decided assent, making a total of forty-nine subscribers who favored the proposed plan. The plan submitted was thus adopted, the proprietors proceeded to elect a board of trustees, and fix on a day for their meeting and organization.

An extract from the same diary brings us a little nearer to those times:

Friday, August 15. Attended the meeting of the proprietors of the Academy. N. Currier, Esq., was called to the chair, which he took without making a speech, as he never pretended to be an orator. I was much gratified with the proceedings of the meeting. 17 trustees were chosen. Mr. Kimball spoke with considerable warmth and energy on the wrongs of slavery. N. P. Rogers was present and spoke cheeringly of the future of this school. Mr. Blaisdell with his usual malignant disposition, bitterly opposed the object of the meeting, as subversive of the cause of good morals. Elijah does not win confidence in his assertions for his bitterness. Several resolutions were passed, among others it was resolved and approved that Dr. Cox of N. Y. City a notorious abolitionist, a friend, be among the trustees. Great events are on the gale.

Paine says "there is a mass of sense, lying dominant in man, which often descends with him to the grave for want of some stimulus to bring it forth to action. Nothing so well contributes to that important end as agitated or revolutionary times. This allusion seems to fit our present conditions."

But the enemies of the school — perhaps that phrase should not be used, it is not probable that any one was opposed to the Academy, as it was originated — but the plan to introduce negroes into this white community was revolting to the white sense of propriety. Negroes were not recognized as a part of the social system. This negative idea in regard to the negro was not new at this time. There are hardly any old enough to remember the first negro who came to Canaan. It was a boy, who came over from Hanover about ninety-five years ago, to live with Captain Dole. How curiously he was examined — the flat nose, thick lips, kinky hair, and more wonderful than all, the blackness that enveloped his skin. The boys gathered about him in a circle, and wondered to see him talk and laugh like themselves. But the novelty at length disappeared, and then Dennison Wentworth was only a "colored boy."

But the Christian men and women of those days were never ready to recognize his equality before God. And when the Congregational Church was built in 1828–29, that there might be no misunderstanding, as to the sentiment of the builders or projectors, a pew was built in the northwest corner of the gallery, and dedicated to the negro race as the "Negro Pen," and there it remains today, a witness to the prejudice that was to culminate in after years, in outrages and mobs all over the land, producing bitterness and wounds in society, that a whole generation has scarcely been able to heal. The negro could go into that pen, and listen to the prayers, the hymns and sermons of the preacher, but he must come no nearer the altar of God.

The opponents of the negro part of the plan were not idle. They gathered together in caucus, after the meeting of the proprietors, and decided that a "town meeting" should be called to procure if possible an unfriendly expression from the voting population of the town. The names of the men who were most prominent in this opposition were: Elijah Blaisdell, Joseph L. Richardson, Dr. Thomas Flanders, the Pattees — father and son — Jacob Trussell, William Campbell and many others. There was another reason aside from the social aspect of the affair, that led them to a public expression of disapproval of the negro question in the school. The Southern politicians were getting excited at the spread of Abolition sentiments, and it was a fondly cherished belief of our good men, that they could contribute something towards soothing their Southern brethren, by passing resolutions, denouncing the Abolitionists, having them published in the *New Hampshire Patriot*, signed by the selectmen and clerk and then sending carefully marked copies to their senators and representatives in Congress. It was only a murmuring ripple of popular opinion, not very loud as yet but harsh, a murmur that was to develop an untamed wild beast.

Indications of the mob spirit are foreshadowed in an extract from the diary before mentioned, under date of

August 26, 1834. There is certainly something pertaining to aristocracy in every village, Yea, in every community, of individuals. The man of wealth has his retainers as well as the religionist his proselytes. There are those who are ready to act in any capacity, even at the head of a mob whose intentions have been declared. Jefferson says "the mobs of great cities add just so much to the support of the pure government, as sores do to the strength of the human body."

August 29, 1834. It seems that the principles of abolition are as contagious as the cholera. All seems to be infected with the mania. Amalgamation would be frightful, but that would be the result if these principles were carried out.

A school is about to be opened here, where spirits of all colors are to receive instruction together.

The master spirit of the age is *benevolence*. The earth, the atmosphere, everything seems pregnant with the spirit of benevolence. What must be done, can be done. What ought to be done, will be done.

A town meeting was warned to be held September 3d, "To take the sense of the qualified voters relative to the contemplated Institution about to be established in this town, avowedly for the purpose of educating black and white children and youth promiscuously and without distinction and what measures to adopt in regard to said Institution." The meeting was held on the appointed day, and the following resolutions were passed:

Whereas divers of the inhabitants of the town of Canaan have erected a building and obtained an act of the legislature incorporating them into an association by the name of Noyes Academy for the avowed purpose of literary instruction, and whereas George Kimball, Nathaniel Currier and a few others, in contempt of the feelings and wishes of their associates, and contrary to the views of the good citizens of the town, (and as we believe of the adjoining towns) have determined by their vote to dedicate said building and act of incorporation, to the establishment of a school for the purpose of mingling promiscuouly, for the purpose of instruction the Black as well as the white children of our country, and have by their vote and declaration, declared that they will receive such blacks into said Academy for instruction and into their families as boarders on the same terms as the whites, and compel their own children and boarders, and all who may attend said Academy to associate with them, without regard to colour, thereby not only outraging the feelings of the inhabitants of said town, setting aside the very distinction the God of Nature has made in our species in colour, features, disposition, habits and interests, but inviting every black, who may obtain means by the aid of his own friends and by the aid of a Society heated by Religious and Political zeal, to a degree that would sever the Union for the purpose of emancipation. Therefore resolved That we view with abhorence every attempt to introduce among us a black population, and that we will use all lawful means to counteract such introduction.

Resolved that we most devoutly wish for the emancipation of every black slave in our country, and that whenever any method shall be devised to effect that object consistant with the rights, views and interests of our Southern brethren, who are immediately interested, we shall be ready to make any sacrifice to effect it, provided it is not to mix them with our own free white population.

Resolved that while we contemplate with sorrow, the hard fate of the African race, and lament that any of that race should be slaves, we are not prepared to sever the happy union of these states and inbue our hands in the blood of our brethren for the purpose, of having Black Presidents, Black Governors, Black Representatives, Black Judges, nor for the purpose of gratifying the religious zeal of any class of discontented citizens.

Resolved, that we view with abhorrence the attempt of the Abolitionists to establish a school in this town, for the instruction of the sable sons and daughters of Africanus, in common with our own sons and daughters and that we view with contempt every white man and woman who may have pledged themselves to receive black boarders or to compel their own children to associate with them.

Resolved, that we will not send our children to any Academy or High school, where black children are educated in common with white children, nor in any way knowingly encourage such schools.

Resolved, that we will not associate with nor in any way countenance any man or woman who shall hereafter persist in attempting to establish a school in this town for exclusive education of blacks, or for their education in conjunction with the whites.

Daniel Pattee, John Shephard and Elijah Blaisdell were chosen to procure the publication of the foregoing preamble and resolutions. And to nominate "seventeen" persons in different parts of the town with instructions "to use all lawful means to prevent the establishment of said school and if established to counteract its influence."

These men were:

James Eastman	Jacob Trussel
March Barber	Sylvanus Morgan
E. Blaisdell	Daniel Pattee, Jr.
Stephen Ward	D. B. Whittier
John Shephard	Samuel Paddleford
Elijah Miller	Timothy B. Dudley
George Walworth	William Campbell
Adam Pollard	Joseph L. Richardson

Under date of the same day the diary says:

The people of Canaan assembled this day at the Town House to consider the recent measures of the Abolitionists in reference to the School. After listening for some time to the mobocratic vituperation of Elijah, a long list of inflammatory resolutions pertinent to the occasion were read and passed. Ah, me! the old Jacobins are determined not to have the niggers here.

Great efforts were made to rally the disaffected and to create disaffection. Mr. Blaisdell took hold of the growing sentiment of opposition, petted it, rubbed it the wrong way of the fur, to irritate it, then presented the resolutions, all of which together with his speech, were duly reported in the *New Hampshire Patriot*.

No one raised an objection, no friends of the school took part in the meeting. The number voting for the unfriendly resolutions was 86, out of over 300 votes on the check list. The friends of the school were jubilant and considered themselves to be a strong and decided majority among the people. Poor, deluded mortals! Little did they realize the aggrieved spirit that animated those 86 votes. So firmly convinced that they were attending to their own affairs, and that no one ought to molest them, they took measures to open the Academy.

On the 11th of September, 1834, the trustees met for the first time in the Academy, when such business as came before them was transacted, and the following circular was passed to be printed, and put in circulation:

To The American Public.

The undersigned Trustees of the Noyes Academy, in conformity with the wishes of a large majority of the donors of said Academy, and with the unanimous vote of the corporators, named in the act of the Legislature, have come to the resolution to admit to the privileges of this Institution, colored youth of good character on equal terms with whites of like character. In adopting this principle the Trustees deem that they are reducing to practice the spirit and letter of the Declaration of our National Independence, of the Constitution and laws of New Hampshire, and the Bills of Rights of all the States of this United Republic, except those which have made literature a crime, and prohibited the reading of the Bible under heavy penalties.

In the State of New Hampshire *according to the law*, character and not complexion, is the basis of every distinction, either of honor or infamy, reward or punishment. But what greater punishment can there be, what greater degradation, than to deprive the soul of its proper sustenance, the knowledge of divine and human things? Much better were it to kill the body than to doom the mind to ignorance and vice.

It is unhappily true, that heretofore the colored portion of our fellow citizens, even in the free States, while their toil and blood have contributed to establish, and their taxes equally with those of the whites, to maintain our free system of Education, have practically been excluded from the benefits of it. This Institution, propose to restore, so far as it can, to this neglected and injured class the privileges of literary, moral and religious instruction. We propose to uncover a fountain of pure and healthful learning, holding towards all the language of the Book of Life: "Ho! EVERY ONE that thirsteth let him come and drink." We propose to afford colored youth a fair opportunity to show that they are capable, equally with the whites, of improving themselves in every scientific attainment, every social virtue, and every Christian ornament.

If however we are mistaken in supposing, that they possess such capacity; if, as some assert, they are naturally and irremediably stupid, and incorrigibly vicious, then the experiment we propose will prove this fact; and will in any event furnish valuable data, upon which the excited patriotism and piety of the land may predicate suitable measures in time to come, or may relapse into undisturbed repose, and forever forbear to form designs upon this agitating subject.

There are in the midst of this republic, of slaves and men nominally free, a number much greater than the population of the six New England States, and about nine times greater than the entire people of the State of New Hampshire. This mighty mass of human beings, of intelligent spirits and active passions must remain here, for weal or for wo, until the Creator of all shall come to judge the world. They must not only remain here but they must in spite of all human efforts, go on to increase in a ratio, which inspires apprehension in those who are conscious of doing them continual wrong.

If, therefore, there really exists between them and the whites, that natural and invincible antipathy, which many allege as an argument against our plan, how important and necessary is it for the welfare of this whole country that some of their own color should be humanized, christianized and qualified to gain that access to their minds and that control over their evil propensities which upon the above proposition it is impossible for any white ever to acquire.

It is a familiar remark, that it would be an incalculable injury to this country, if the restraint which the influence and instructions of the Catholic Clergy impose, were to be removed from the uneducated and depraved among the Irish emigrants. The total number of those emigrants does not exceed *one fifth* of the colored Americans! If, on the other hand, the alleged antipathy does not exist, then one of the most common and formidable objections to the free and equal participation of all our youth in the means and opportunities of improvement, vanishes at once and forever.

We propose to do nothing for the colored man — but to leave him at liberty to do something for himself. It is not our wish to raise him out of his place nor into it — but to remove the unnatural pressure which now paralizes his faculties and fixes him to the earth. We wish to afford him an impartial trial of his ability to ascend the steeps of science and to tread the narrow way, which leadeth unto life. We wish to see him start as fairly as others, unconfined by fetters, unincumbered with burdens and boyant with hope; and if he shall then fail, we shall at the worst have this consolation, that we have done our utmost to confer upon him those excellent endowments, which the wisdom of God and the solemn appeal of our fathers have taught us to regard as the appropriate distinction of immortal and infinitely improvable beings.

We profess to be republicans, not jacobins, nor agrarians; we think with a great and liberal Englishman, that political equality means "not a right to an *equal* part, but an *equal* right to a part," not a right to take from others, but an equal right with others to *make* for ourselves. We profess to be Christians and we look with humble reliance for the blessing of Him, with whom "there is neither Greek nor Jew, Barbarian nor Scythian *bond* nor free, but Christ is all in all."

This declaration is intended to be preliminary to a detailed plan for the instruction and government of the Academy, which with the terms of tuition, the qualifications for admission, the time of commencement, and the name of the instructor, will form the subject of a future and early communication to our fellow citizens.

     GEORGE KIMBALL, Canaan, N. H.
     NATHANIEL CURRIER, DO,
     TIMOTHY TILTON, DO.
     JOHN H. HARRIS, DO.
     DAVID L. CHILD, Boston, Mass.,
     SAMUEL E. SEWALL, DO.
     WILLIAM C. MUNROE, Portland, Me.,
     N. P. ROGERS, Plymouth, N. H.,
     GEORGE KENT, Concord, N. H.,
     SAMUEL H. COX, New York City,
            Trustees.

CANAAN, N. H., Sept. 11th, 1834.

The same day there was a public meeting at the Congregational Meeting House. Rev. Mr. Robbins, a Methodist minister, was invited to open the meeting with prayer. He almost declined, but finally consented. He prayed very cautiously, asking God to bless the enterprise if it was to be for His glory, but as he did not believe it was God's intention to mix blacks and whites, he prayed that all the efforts might be put to confusion. A careful man, this Robbins, but not honest as God and the law require men to be honest. The meeting was then addressed by Mr. David L. Child of Boston, followed by Samuel E. Sewall of Boston and N. P. Rogers of Plymouth.

This meeting was interesting to all the friends of the school. The principal points upon which Mr. Child dwelt were: (I.) The unlimited power and control of the master over the slave. (II.) The capacity of the black to receive needed knowledge, and (III.) the possibility of safe emancipation. He illustrated these points with facts, some of them revolting to human nature.

"Sept. 12, 1834," the diary goes on: "An address was delivered at the Academy by Mr. Abdy from England, a traveler, upon the subject of slavery as it existed in Europe, contrasted with it here. Mr. Child followed with some cheering words.

Then George Kimball, the lawyer, being filled with zeal, prophesied glowingly of the great benefits that were to result to the human race from the small beginnings here in Canaan." At length, "Sept. 14th. Tranquility is again restored to our village. The Abolitionists are gone, and Elijah and Jacob have retired from sight to their several occupations in life. Now let us wait for the next moment for both parties have become so hostile that aggressions must follow."

In those days there existed a class of men, whose minds were constantly seizing upon new and unheard of horrors, with which to influence and arouse the indignation of such as are always shocked at the recital of outrage and wrong. This class of persons like to pass from one state of indignation into another with abruptness, and always find the succeeding condition more intense than the preceding. This morbid feeling had been strained to a high tension, by the recital of the outrages and murder committed upon William Morgan, by the Masons of New York, and by the revelations of imaginary horrors, that were daily transpiring, within the guarded recesses of the lodge room. It was not difficult to transfer the sympathies of these awful imaginings to the actual horrors which were being daily recited, in relation to the black slaves. Their wrongs were visible, tangible realities, and seemed to cry to Heaven for redress. That cry was heard in every hamlet and village in New England, and awoke the sympathies of philanthropists into sudden and sometimes unhealthy activity.

It is possible, that the action of the trustees, inviting "colored youth," to partake of the benefits of the Academy, might have had its origin in a desire to secure to itself the benefits of the fund which several philanthropic gentlemen had set apart for the education of "colored youth," but certain it is, that some two years before the establishment of "Noyes Academy" efforts were commenced for the establishment of a Manual Labor School, somewhere in New England, to promote the improvement of the free people of color. Several thousand dollars, the sum was stated as high as $15,000, were subscribed and several places were recommended as suitable for such an undertaking. George Kimball, Esq., who was an enthusiast in everything he undertook, exerted himself with great assiduity, to influence the trustees and patrons of Noyes Academy to admit pupils without regard to color, to the advantages of the institution.

When this decision was announced, as it was by the trustees in their circular of the 11th of September, it was decided that the subscription with all its patronage, should be bestowed upon Noyes Academy, thus securing to it a permanent fund and placing its success beyond a doubt. But the hostile sentiments which met them at the threshold, and which soon developed into ungoverned rage, caused the withholding of these funds, and it has not been possible to trace them with certainty. But it is probable, when the difficulties in Oberlin College, Ohio, which were caused by the same sentiments, were settled by opening its doors to blacks and whites alike, that generous subscription went to swell the funds of that institution.

But to go back to the facts. After the meeting of the trustees on the 11th of September, a committee was dispatched to Andover Theological Seminary, for a "sound and accomplished teacher." Doctors Skinner and Woods, recommended Mr. William Scales, of the senior class, who accepted the position, and appointed the first of March as the date of opening the school.

Encouraged by the cheering call of the circular of the trustees, fourteen colored youth and children resorted to the school, advancing with trembling steps to the enjoyment of privileges, to them at least unexpectedly presented. Besides these there were twenty-eight white pupils, at the opening. And it looked as if the school was going on in peace and prosperity. Of the demeanor of the colored pupils, and it is upon good authority, that "they were modest and inoffensive in their deportment, in their manners polite and unassuming, their lives unblemished, in their application and improvement their capacities and intellectual attainments they compared favorably with the other pupils." The friends of the school believed they saw in all the signs a token of God's approbation of their endeavors, and they rested securely upon their labors.

In examining a lot of old manuscripts, I find several letters from friends, which give a little insight into the affairs of the school. Several short extracts follow: "Oct. 22, 1834. May Harris commenced the female department three or four weeks ago. Has about twenty scholars." "Canaan, Oct. 28, 1834.

Mr. Currier has returned from Boston. He brings intelligence that David L. Child, Esq., will come on in about six weeks and take charge of the school. The receipt of this interesting news affected each party in a different manner. There was a joyous rubbing of hands among our friends. Kimball had to holler long and loud. Old Dr. Tilton smiled all over. He has declared that the only epitaph he desires upon his tombstone is that he was 'The Slaves' Friend.' Col. Isaac Towle gave a grunt of satisfaction. You know, he is a very positive man. His 'I will' and 'I won't' settles all controversy with him. The hostiles were not pleased,—in fact they were mad — very mad! Trussell, Arvin, old Cobb, and Blaisdell, were hardly peaceable for some days. Their minds were much preoccupied. I am told that persons who approached them upon business matters received only such answers as 'Abolition scum,' 'villains,' 'perjured Masons,' 'unconstitutional acts,' &c. But for these men, who like Cassius 'have a lean and hungry look' there would be general cheerfulness among the people. Parson Fuller will teach the school until the arrival of Mr. C. He entered upon the task yesterday. Probably not more than twenty pupils attend. I do not go yet.''

"One thing further. I understand the circular is published, and the picture of this town is drawn with a master hand. I give you one sentence, which ought to melt and soften the hard hearts of those creatures who are base enough to oppose this wonderful scheme of Philanthropy.'' This sentence is the one which refers to their doing nothing for the colored man, but to leave him at liberty to do something for himself.

Miss Mary Harris was engaged to teach the female department. "Canaan, Dec. 23, 1834. The school building stands where it was placed, a monument of the rashness of the projectors.'' As time passed on the excitement increased, until the town was a scene of bitterness, suspicion and hatred mingled in society, and all kindliness seemed to be crowded out. The friends of the school were sanguine and fearless. The opponents were sullen and thoughtful. Old Mrs. Nichols said: "Mr. Kimball ought to 'a-been abed and asleep before he got us into such a tarnation scrape.'' Col. Daniel Pattee was greatly alarmed and threatened "extermination by fire and sword.''

Mr. Wesley P. Burpee, with pugnacious gravity, bobbed his head and declared, "This thing is unconstitutional. Sir! We must put it down, Sir!" Many secret caucuses of these men were held during the winter, and it was not until after long and mature deliberation, that a positive plan was resolved upon.

Another letter of January 22, 1835, says: "Thirteen colored persons are now attending school. Kimball has just returned from Providence with six. He intends building a large boarding house."

During the winter Mr. Kimball devoted himself to collecting funds for the school, and on his return in February, he announced that he had been more successful than he even hoped. The school was now assured of permanence. He sold his house, next north of the Currier store at that time, now the second, and moved into the Wilson house at the corner, opposite A. S. Green's, with the intention of boarding all the black pupils, some twenty of whom were announced as coming on the first of March, when it was anticipated the "Nigger school" was to begin. He also announced his intention of building a boarding house in the field near the Academy, for the accommodation of black and white pupils. An earnest effort was now made by the good people to raise money to purchase a bell for the Academy, but they were not successful. Mr. Scales came on Sunday, the first day of March. On March 31st a mulatto came from Boston to attend the school.

I now refer to the diary, date of April 10, 1835. "Oscar goes to school." "One colored man by the name of Thomas Paul, from Boston, has arrived. Did you suppose mother would board the *blacks*. No! She has enough else to do."

"May 21. Great exertions are making to rouse up a revival of religion. Another colored person, a lady from Boston, has arrived. Show 'em in! No aristocracy here."

A letter of June 10th says: "As yet only six 'colored youths' have arrived. Two of them black as night. Kimball boards them. This week is vacation. We cannot yet tell what the result of this school will be. Nothing but rare courage and devotion in the projectors to push their plans through good and evil reports will preserve it. The fact that the whole slave population of the South are coming here, shocks the sensibilities of the toothless, eyeless, senseless part of the community. The old, superannuated dotards sigh at the coming events, and wish they had never been born. Because, forsooth, a black man has come among us."

Rumors of the most absurd character were set afloat against the school and the people. The village was to be overrun with negroes from the South; the slaves were coming here to line the streets with their huts, and to inundate the industrious town with paupers and vagabonds. Other tales, too indecent to be reported, were circulated with wicked industry. As the Fourth of July approached violence began to be threatened, and it was announced that on that day an attack was to be made on the house. The day arrived and hundreds of men assembled, some as actors, others as spectators. The building was approached in a threatening manner by a body of about seventy men, many of whom were from adjacent towns, armed with clubs and other missiles and uttering fierce threats and imprecations. They drew up in front of the house. The leader of this brave band was Jacob Trussell, who announced to his followers that the object of their "virtuous wrath was before them." Several approached and attempted the door. There is in every man a sense of right and wrong which makes even the most hardened criminal hesitate to commit an unlawful act, even in the presence of his fellow conspirators. A sudden paralysis seemed to seize them. A window in the second story was suddenly thrown open and Dr. Timothy Tilton, a magistrate, appeared and after addressing a few words of warning, began to take down the names of the visitors in a loud voice. Thus he called the names of "Jacob Trussell, Daniel Pattee, Wesley P. Burpee, Daniel Pattee, Jr., Salmon P. Cobb, March Barber, Phineas Eastman," and so on. Then the band of rioters hesitated, fell back a little, and soon retreated, with undisguised speed, leaving behind them only their leader, who stood his ground valiantly for a while looking defiantly at the offensive building.

I will incorporate part of a letter dated July 15, 1835, relating to the movements of the allied forces of Canaan, Enfield, Dorchester and Hanover. The letter says:

On the 4th of July the "Jacobins," we call them "Jac's" from old Jacob, their leader, held a caucus in the hall of E. Martin, to concert measures for the ejectment of Kimball, Scales and the blacks from this town. In the meantime a large number of persons from this and adjoining towns had collected, and waited to hear the result of their deliberations. They thronged the street and fields of Canaan, clamorous and excited. At last the hall door was thrown open, and out came old Campbell, Daniel Pattee and sons, old Kinney, &c, &c, who proceeded immediately to the Meeting House, where Joseph L. Richardson, a man of fame and years, harrangued them from the deacon's seat. He told them of his love for the whole human race, of his indefatigable exertions in the Legislature, to cause the petitions of his constituents to be "read a third time and passed." But, alas! they were lost! He spoke of rights and equity, of public nuisance and mobs, he deprecated any coersive measures on the part of any people. In fine, the tender sympathies of the multitude were touched by the glowing imagery of this great and far-famed man. May he live to a good old age and always imagine himself quelling mobs. The fact is, the people had met on the Fourth, as notice had been previously given for the purpose of tearing down the Academy. But they did not do it.

A procession was formed at the hotel headed by Ben Porter and marched to the academy; an attempt was made to enter, when several gentlemen who were, unexpectedly by the mob, inside, hoisted a window, and proceeded to take the names of the leaders. The crowd dispersed as speedily as possible, muttering curses and menaces, and adjourned for one week. On Saturday, the 11th, they met at the old church in large numbers as before. William Campbell was moderator; they were noisy and excited, more so, if possible, than on the previous occasion. The only point I could gather in their proceedings was that the "*nigger*" was a nuisance, and must be removed from town. In the midst of their confusion, Doctor Flanders told them that the corporation had not in any respect proceeded according to law. There was a momentary lull in the assembly and a committee was appointed to inquire into the legality of the proceedings. This committee are to report at an adjourned meeting in two weeks.

When the people again assembled to hear the report of the committee, there was as before much excitement and they were united in one respect at least — hatred to the blacks. But they were divided in sentiment when the cry was raised to destroy the building. It was no doubt the intention of the leaders on each of these occasions to destroy the building and break up the school, but they could not rouse their followers up to that lawless act. So it was resolved that a legal town meeting should be called on the 31st of July to see what "measures the town will take to expel the blacks from the town of Canaan," and to act in relation to the black school.

Aside from the political aspect of the question, the results of which were of momentous importance to the country, there was a large portion of the community, who could not tolerate the negro in their society. To show the animus of the feeling that prejudiced this class of the community, I copy from the *New Hampshire Patriot* of June, 1835; the grammar belongs to the press:

Since the establishment of the school, it has been no uncommon spectacle to witness *colored gentlemen* walking arm in arm with what ought to be *respectable white females*. And that respectable people opposed to the school, as well as others, have been invited to parties where the colored portion of the school were also invited guests. It is said that one of the principal agitators of the slave question in this state, George Kimball, Esq., and his family, sit at table with a half dozen colored people, while a *white* girl attends upon them as servant. We do not wonder that the white people of Canaan should consider such an establishment a "nuisance," and that they should adopt all lawful measures for its removal. The people of this state have more than once been reproached as favoring the pernicious schemes of the Abolitionists, and as encouraging a practical amalgamation of colors, on account of this school. And while we would counsel our friends in that part of the State to persevere in their efforts until the "Nuisance" is abated, we would suggest to them the propriety of *mild and peaceable* measures, such as the public sentiment and laws of the State will justify.

From the other side we learn that Mrs. Hubbard Harris had a tea party, and invited the blacks — they attended. This was very shocking to several who attended. This party gave occasion to much very bad scandal. Mrs. Wallace had a tea party, — and did *not* invite the blacks. Kimball and wife, Mr. Seales and a score more were present. Mrs. Flanders was also invited. "What an insult!" exclaimed Mrs. Flanders, supposing the blacks had had an invitation. She declared "she was so mad she was insane for half an hour," the which no one doubted who knew her.

The 31st of July, 1835, is memorable in the annals of Canaan, memorable for the disorder it evolved as well as for the remarkable resolutions that were permitted to go upon its records, where they remain as a perpetual memento of the slow progress of public opinion. Joseph L. Richardson was moderator. The house was crowded with men filled with rage, rum and riotous intentions. They had worked themselves into the belief that a "legal" town meeting could do lawfully what it was unlawful for an individual to do. They were willing to shift the odium of the outrage of what they were about to do upon the "legal" town meeting. A committee was appointed to report a plan for the action of the town. After much labor, that committee presented a series of resolutions, embracing within their tortuous folds the plan that was to destroy the school, or rather as those who were seeking an excuse for their acts to "abate the public Nuisance." And now we come to the reports, the author of which sleeps in obscurity:

Whereas believing certain individuals, by the practice of fraud and deception have abused public opinion abroad in reference to the state of feeling in this town respecting the colored school here, and believing that designing demagogues and desperate Politicians abroad in connection with a few sordid spirits in this town who are influenced more by the love of gain than the love of God and man, are determined to continue their black operations in this town against the wishes of a large majority of its citizens. Although they have once and again expressed their disaprobation and have borne and forbourn until forbearance had ceased to be a "virtue." Therefore Resolved That from what our own eyes have seen and our ears have heard respecting the close intimacy that exists between some of the colored boys and white females, we believe if suffered to go on, it will not be long before we shall have living evidence of an amalgamation of blood. Resolved That we consider the Colored School in this town a Public Nuisance and that it is the duty of the town to take immediate measures to remove said nuisance.

Voted the town take immediate measures to remove the house in which the colored school is kept.

Voted that the Selectmen select the spot on which to set said building.

Voted that a committee be chosen to superintend the moving of said building at the expense of the town.

Voted that a committee of 15 or 20 persons be chosen for said committee and the following were chosen viz.:

Jacob Trussell (still at 90 broken and defiant)
Chamberlain Packard Jr (killed by God)
Wm Campbell (a foolish old infidel)
Herod Richardson ⎫
Elijah R. Colby ⎬ (dead and rotten and now forgotten)
Americus Gates ⎭
Daniel Pattee Jr (a blasphemous cripple)
Nathaniel Shepherd (Common drunkard)
Luther Kinne (Ossified legs)
Peter Stevens

Robert B. Clark (dead in his bed)
Salmon P. Cobb (an old witch too mean to live or die)
Daniel Campbell
James Pattee (a drunkard)
John Fales Jr (an idiot)
Wesley P. Burpee (an awful death from cancer)
Benj. W. Porter (drowned)
Bartlett Hoit (killed by God after having stolen money sent him)
   to keep his wife's father from starving or thrown on the town.)
March Barber (old foolish jealous and insane)

The words inclosed in the parentheses after each name are on the town records but were put there by someone afterwards.

Voted that the measures adopted by the town for removing said building, be commenced by the 10th day of August at 7 a. m. and be continued from day to day, without intermission, so as to satisfy the calls of nature, until the moving of said building be completed.

Voted unanimously that the following Preamble and Resolutions be sent to the editor of the Christian Register and Boston Observer, with a request that he would give them an insertion in his paper:

Whereas a report of the managers of the Mass. Antislavery Soc. has been published in the Christian Register and Boston Observer bearing date July 11th 1835, containing statements, that the inhabitants of Canaan, N. H., are generally in favor of the colored school in said town. Therefore resolved that the publication in that paper relating to said school is without foundation in truth and a libel upon the publick as more than four fifths of the inhabitants of this town in the estimation of this meeting are decidedly opposed to said school and are determined to take effectual measures to remove it.

Resolved that a copy of these proceedings be sent to the N. H. Patriot and State Gazette and be signed by the Selectmen and Town Clerk. With the request that all the papers in New England insert them once.

The meeting then dissolved and the noisy crowd left the village uttering threats and imprecations. But the chiefs in this "legal" conspiracy, it is said, held a private conference in the hall that lasted until morning. Wherein they discussed the responsibilities they were assuming, and some of the more cautions desired that they might receive counsel from some eminent lawyer. They accordingly consulted Josiah Quincy of Rumney, but his views conformed so greatly to their own, that they suspected there might be more sympathy than law in his opinion. They then consulted Ichabod Bartlett, who it was known was very outspoken against the Abolition excitement, but still was a careful and safe adviser. Mr. Bartlett's opinion did not arrive, however, until it was too late to save the building, but it is said to have been of such a nature that many of those who were engaged in the outrage of moving the building were rather anxious that that act in their lives should be forgotten. He told them, as I heard from the late Caleb Blodgett, Esq., who was high sheriff at the time, and had recently moved into town, that no vote of the town could "legalize" a mob; that the outrage they were about to commit was felony at common law; that each individual engaged in it was personally responsible for all the damage that might accrue, and that each and every man became lawless and criminal whenever he or they deprived others of their property or of the right to live peaceably in the community. But, after all, he thought there was little danger to be feared from prosecutions, because in the then exasperated state of public opinion upon the slavery question, there was no jury in the state who would find them guilty; but all high excitements are reactionary, beware of the "second thought." For this advice the town paid Mr. Bartlett $5. They had better have paid him thousands and sought his advice sooner.

The particulars which follow are taken chiefly from letters written at the time, by parties, as may readily be seen, who were not unfriendly to the school. As this is the only record of those eventful days I adopt it as authentic, believing it to be a veracious tale. The first letter is dated August 15, 1835, and commences thus:

The whole world will soon be awake to the transactions here. Since the 31st every cloud has been black with rumors. Upon the wings of every breeze was blown an account of coming events. From the tongue of every tattler escaped a direful foreboding. Emaciated groups of human forms, were to be seen in sheds and secret places, plotting and planning affairs for the 10th. Sometimes a silence not unlike that which precedes the earthquake prevailed. Scandal, "damnable innuendoes," hell-engendered lies, were eagerly received by the loquacious humor of this public. This is not a vision. It is a fact. But I pass now to the 10th. The day dawned, the sun never rose with more loveliness. Its meridian splendor is not an apt comparison in dog days. In the morn we greet him, at noon we flee from him. The cloud that had so long hung threateningly over us, now assumed a most fearful aspect. The people led by villains were mad, and in their madness had become destroyers. I was standing at my desk writing. Saw a man, Mr. B., pass with an iron bar. Soon I saw several more pass with bars and axes. Now a wagon loaded with chains hurries along. I looked out at the door. The street was full of people and cattle in all directions. A "string" of fifty yoke are just turning the corner by the old Church, all from Enfield. William Currier at their head. Thomas Merrill was also a leader. The destruction of that beautiful edifice has already begun. Trussell was the first man on the ground. He is Captain of the gang. His features show the smile of satisfied revenge. He thus addressed them: "Gentlemen, your work is before you. This town has decreed this school a nuisance, and it must be abated. If any man obstructs you in these labors, let him be abated also. Now fall to, and remove this fence."

The first blow was struck by Benjamin Porter, who seized an axe and attacked the fence. He was an active lieutenant of his master and was everywhere present encouraging the lookers-on to labor. Stephen Smith was at work for Sheriff Blodgett that day. Mr. Blodgett stayed at home. He would not by his presence, show sympathy with the brave band who were working for applause from the South, but was interested in the progress of the work. He sent Mr. Smith up to bring him reports. Mr. Smith said that he stood looking at the wreckers, thinking what a pity to see that beautiful edifice destroyed! The master came around that way and seeing a man idle he spoke out promptly: "Smith, here take that axe and help clear away that fence." Mr. Smith seized the axe and when the fence was cleared away, wondered why he had allowed that man to influence him to do that bad work. Many others have worked under the same subtle influence, and had no regrets until the will of the master was accomplished. The account continues:

When they first appeared and seized upon the front fence to pull it away, they were met by Doctor Tilton, who, as a magistrate, commanded them to disperse and begun to read the riot act.

There was a perceptable hesitation when Trussell stepped forward, seizing an axe and exclaimed: "Well, we have heard all that before, but it won't pass with us today. Boys, fall to here! If that man interrupts you any more remove him." Then striking the first blow, he encouraged his crowd to deeds unheard of before in this town. I need not say that there was sadness among our friends. We were sad at the unappeasable madness of the people, who blindly followed that revengeful man, but in the days to come there will be reaction. The reading of the riot act by Doctor Tilton was the only obstruction offered by the friends of the school. They chose to suffer affliction and the destruction of their property rather than shed the blood of these misguided men. They got the shoes under a little past 12 at noon. Trussell stands upon the front to give orders. The team is attached. Ninety-five yoke of cattle. It is straightened. The chains break. They try again and again the chains break! Almost in vain do they try. Thermometer ranges at 116 in the sun. At half past 7 they had succeeded in drawing it into the road, when they adjourned till next day. The cattle were in the meantime driven down to William Martin's meadow, where they were turned loose for the night. I need not tell you of the band of earnest philanthropists,— men and women,— who met together in secret that dark night and wept and prayed because of the destruction that had befallen their beautiful hopes. A man from Enfield, Joshua "Devil" Stevens, as he was called, set fire to the building that night, intending to destroy it, but the attempt failed.

The chains were weak, doubled they were still weak. A swift messenger was dispatched to the Shakers at Enfield and to Lyman's Bridge at Lyman for the cables used there. He returned before morning. Tuesday, the 11th, the progress of destruction was more rapid. The chains held firm when the order was given "to straighten the team." A little before noon they had reached our store where they halted in front, and at once demanded that a barrel of rum should be rolled out or they would demolish the doors. Mr. C. and myself thought it best to yield to their threats, but William said "No, he would sooner die than yield an inch to these fanatical villains." He backed himself against the door, determined to resist to the last. But he was removed after much struggling, and they had the rum. Do you believe we did not wish it might be hell fire to their bodies?

Another scene occurred here worth relating. Mrs. Wallace came out of the house, mounted the fence, and began to harangue that crowd as only an earnest woman can when the spirit moves her. She was telling them some very wholesome truths, when Mr. C. came up and seizing her from behind, carried her into the house exclaiming, "Get into the house and shut up your mouth. Don't you see, if you get 'em mad they'll pull my house down too."

Any person, man or woman, who, passing quietly along the street, then, did not hurrah with them, was insulted by those ruffians from Enfield, Hanover and Dorchester.

The cattle were allowed to rest in the heat of the day while the company ate the food prepared for them by the selectmen. Joseph Dustin was an abolitionist; he did not go to the hauling the first day. He fed the company to the amount of $16.44, which the town paid. The second day Mr. Blodgett requested him in behalf of the town, to prepare a dinner for the crowd. He killed a beef and cooked it all. It was eaten and paid for, by the selectmen out of the town treasury.

It is said that the selectmen were never averse to the advice of Mr. Weeks and Mr. Blodgett, who did not appear as open advocates of violence, but whenever any suggestion or motive particularly diabolical was offered, these men would give it strength and courage by clothing it in legal language.

Having rested and refreshed themselves the crowd were in no better humor than before. The rum had not made them peaceable. The team was hitched up and "straightened" with loud imprecations and curses and progressed slowly. When they were about opposite Parson Fuller's house, they rested for water. Mrs. F., a very plucky woman, when she saw the intent to use her water bucket, rushed out and cut the rope, thus dropping the bucket into the well, and declaring loudly that "her bucket should not be polluted by the touch of such foul lips." The men spoke to her with oaths and threats, she replied "She had been used to such acts for some time past she would be disappointed if they ever repented of their crimes or became gentlemen."

This day was hotter than the preceding, yet with redoubled ardor these men persisted in their crime, until they hauled the house on to the corner of the Common, in front and close by the old church. They arrived upon the spot just at dark, so completely fagged out, both oxen and men, that it was utterly impossible to do anything further. There it stands, shattered, mutilated, inwardly beyond reparation almost, a monument of the folly of and infuriated malice of a basely deceived populace.

Four weeks from last Thursday, they are to assemble again to draw it upon the spot chosen by the selectmen for its location. Many aggravating circumstances accompanying this transaction cannot be related here. The Institution is broken up. The aggressors declare boldly that they fear no retribution at the hands of the law. They rely upon public opinion and the authorities to sustain them in taking the accomplishment of their unlawful wishes into their own hands.

When the building had rested in front of the Church, the company was called to order by Jacob Trussell, when several sentiments appropriate to the occasion, were prepared and read on the ground by Phineas Eastman, and received with great applause.

1st. *The Constitution of the United States.* Based on a compromise between the North and the South, each pledging themselves to protect each others rights and privileges, it can only be maintained by a due regard to the rights of the respective parties.

The second . . .

3rd. *The Revolutionary Patriots of the North and South.* They fought togather for the privilege of making their own laws, their sons would be unworthy of their sires, if they should surrender their rights into the hands of the Abolitionists.

4th. *The Patriots of New Hampshire.* They will fight for the rights and privileges of the Southern brethren which are guaranteed them by the Constitution, so long as there is a man that can shoulder or handle a gun.

5th. *The Abolitionists.* They must be checked and restrained within Constitutional limits or American liberty will find a speedy grave.

6th. Let there be a union of all honest men, throughout all the United States, and an undivided and uncompromising opposition be presented to irredicate Abolition wherever found.

These resolutions with a description of the day's doing were sent to the *New Hampshire Patriot,* signed by Jacob Trussell, committee, and printed in that paper.

The second one was received with immense noise, it reads as follows:

The Abolitionists, a combination of disorganizers led on by an Englishman sent to this country to sow seeds of discord between the North and South. May he be removed from the continent as suddenly as the Noyes Academy has this day been removed from the control of the Abolitionists.

It was then voted that Scales, the teacher, and the blacks have one month in which to leave town. That if, on the reassembling of this company on the 10th of September, they were found within its limits, they would be removed by force.

On separating, Mr. March Barber, in behalf of the town and the committee, tendered his thanks to the people of Enfield, Hanover and Dorchester, for their efficient and energetic assistance. The chiefs from Dorchester were Benjamin Dow, Joshua Burley, and Jacob Blaisdell.

There were seven young colored boys from Rhode Island, and one young girl from Boston, a light mulatto, about 16 years old, of quiet ladylike demeanor. She boarded with Mrs. George Harris. She afterwards married a sailor named Castle, and lived in Boston. One other young girl about the same age was Miss Maria C., daughter of Edward Bracket of Concord, for many years a barber in that place. She was sprightly and lively in manner and voice. She had sandy hair, blue eyes and light complexion. She arrived at noon on the first day of the attack upon the house and went to board with Mrs. Harris. That night there was much riotous noise in the street. The mob had their grog, and many of them had doubled their rations, which made them forget to go home; and some of them forgot they ever were gentlemen.

They traversed the village shouting ribald expressions and coarsely threatened to attack the house that sheltered those two young girls. There were resolute men among the abolitionists but during that sad day of disorder they had advised themselves that it would be prudent to remain in the background.

Col. Thomas Hill lived in the house long the residence of Dr. Wheat, a stately man, tall and resolute. He called upon Col. Isaac Towle, a man of good presence, and equally resolute. These two went to a woodpile and hewed out two clubs sufficiently large as to need but one blow upon an assailant. They posted themselves about the house and remained until morning. Probably the darkness made cowards of these prowlers. Several times they came near but they neglected to make any attack. It was an anxious night in more than one house.

The account continues:

Mr. Kimball was absent during all this storm. He returned on the 12th, after an absence of five weeks. Three students came with him, 12 more were coming, all white.

There is a spirit of recklessness here, and it says the blacks must leave the town or die before the "last drawing." There are six little boys, one girl, so white you would not see the difference in a crowd, and four as large as myself. They know their rights, but perhaps dare not maintain them. Just now there are threats of attacking Kimball's house, where they board. Just so sure as the mob assails that house, there will be blood shed. The awful "beware" has been sounded. I believe they intend to repair the academy and open a white school.

Again the writer says:

It is not yet in evidence that the men of Canaan are brave or persistent in wrong doing. Knowing our own people as well as we do, all through their lives, these men of brag, our fears were not excited when they threatened. Richardson, Flanders, Burpee, Cobb, the Pattees or old Campbell, and all the rest of them with Trussell added, would never have caused us anything but regrets. Had the lawless and reckless people of Enfield, who volunteered to assist in this disagreeable affair stayed at home, we should not now see Trussell and his tail now triumphing over us. The high minded people of Enfield would hardly esteem it an honor to have participated in this outrage, could they see that they have simply been used by Trussell to avenge a *private pique* of several years standing. Had it not been for Trussell and the foreign element which rode over and insulted us for two days, we know that the Academy would never have been touched. Jacob Trussell is an intolerant bigot, opinionated, unforgiving, not a drop of warm blood in his veins except what is warmed by the passions that animate him. He never forgave an injury and he never had a friend. He never performed an act of pure charity, and he never forgot to be selfish. He is a member of the Congregational Church and of the Lodge of Masons here, and into each of these memberships he carries the obdurate obstinacy of his nature. His hatred of George Kimball, Nat Currier and Hubbard Harris, is an unquenchable fire in his breast. These men are all Anti-masons, the two last are seceding Masons. And here is the secret of the destruction of our Academy. He has been the moving spirit through it all.

He had twice before led the Canaan mob up to the door of the building with weapons in their hands, but the sight of our good natured Dr. Tilton, standing there as a magistrate, to take down their names, for future use, restrained them even in the presence of their leader, and caused them quietly to disperse. And when having invited the people from the neighboring towns to participate in the *move*, he knew his third attempt would be successful, for with his "legal town meeting" and these foreigners to back him, he was satisfied that Campbell, old Cobb, the Pattees, Burpee, and others would not fail to be there. He was not disappointed and our village is sad and gloomy with contending emotions. Jealousy and distrust pervades the minds. Can we ever forgive those insults, will this community ever be happy again? "When a generation has passed away then who are here will see." "How courageous one is on paper! Had you been here and taken a stand 'not on a widows jointure land,' but on the front of the Academy, and had old 'kernel' Pattee seen you, he would have winked you down for a 'tarnal abolitionist, Sir!'"

The days passed on without much interest to the friends of the school. The fruits of all their labors through individual malice "turned to Dead Sea ashes upon their lips." They were listless alike to threats or curses. There was an occasional ripple on the surface, the most considerable of which was the animosity shown to Rev. Mr. Fuller, for the part his wife took on the day of the "Great hauling," when not having the fear of the mob before her eyes, she audaciously removed the bucket from her well, and thus prevented these misguided souls from slaking their thirst. Mr. Fuller was repeatedly warned by ghostly looking messengers upon white horses at the dead of night, that unless he recanted his Anti-slavery principles ere the approaching 10th of October he would be severely dealt with There is no evidence to show at that time, at least, that Mr. Fuller heeded those solemn warnings.

A letter of August 26, 1835, says, "The Academy stands so near South Church as to render the travelled road impracticable. But for Trussell, the Academy would not have been touched." Another letter of September 9, 1835, "Tomorrow is the day for locating the Academy. Yesterday was preparatory drill. Muster takes place the 11th. Those who come to assist in moving the Academy will probably not go home."

On the 10th of September, according to the previous notice, the same men of Canaan, together with their friends, from Enfield, assembled with their cattle, on the Common and proceeded to the business before them, that is, to "locate" the Academy. The spot had been previously selected by the selectmen. These officers were, James Arvin, William Martin and Sylvanus B. Morgan, all now gone to their long home. The last two were men who honestly believed they were acting for the good of the human race, in opposing the introduction of negroes here. The first was an assistant worthy of his leader. A man of ability, whose later years could not redeem the vicious habits of his early manhood. His political friends sought to encourage him, by giving him town offices, but his life was embittered by early recollections and through them he lent a willing ear to the destructive schemes proposed to him by a "brother."

The men who considered themselves leaders were all there early. All of them ready with counsel, which under other circumstances, few of them cared to follow. There was first and foremost, Trussell, Campbell, March Barber, the Pattees, Burpee, Flanders, Arvin, Old Cobb, Richardson, Eastman, Kinne, Benjamin Porter, indeed, no name or face was missing. The thirty days they had given themselves for thoughtfulness, had not let in a single ray of softening light to their hardened understandings. There is no evidence that personal insults were offered on this occasion. They proceeded promptly as if the business they were about were a pleasure, and with loud cries to the work, all the forenoon, five hours, with all their cattle, they labored to haul the building across the road, and locate it in the corner of the Baptist Parsonage field. Then at twelve o'clock it was placed upon the spot. The cannon was then dragged through the street, and discharged at the house of every Abolitionist, breaking glass in abundance at every discharge. Then they adjourned for dinner, which had been prepared by Joseph Dustin, under the direction of the selectmen. The cattle were taken to the side of the Street near Gordon Burley's and fed. Speaking of this fact, Mr. Blodgett told me, that he and William Martin, pitched a ton of hay out of Burley's field on that occasion, quicker than any two men ever did the same work before. After dinner and refreshment the men were called to order, to receive the thanks and congratulations of the chiefs, who by their wisdom and virtue had thus saved Canaan from being the Asylum of the negro race. Several speeches were made and received with noisy demonstrations. Phin Eastman was garrulous and happy. Doctor Flanders was vindictive and triumphant. They were much alike in their tone. But one of them has been preserved. Mr. Trussell, it seems, could not trust himself to do justice to his subject in an extempore manner. Its great magnitude and importance required thought. So he put his thought upon paper and headed it "Farewell Address." The manuscript was for years hidden away in the archives of the author. But death often discloses lost gems. This eloquent piece of thankfulness was thus restored to light that it might be preserved as part of this veracious history.

Farewell Address of Jacob Trussell:

Gentlemen, the work is done! The object is attained! The contest has been severe, but the victory glorious! No sable son of Africa remains to darken our hemisphere! The Abolition Monster, that ascended out of the bottomless pit, is sent headlong to perdition, and the mourners go about the streets. To you, Gentlemen, who have assisted in attaining this glorious victory, I present you hearty and sincere thanks, for your prompt attention and your unexampled exertions in repelling an enemy, far more to be dreaded, than the pestilence that walks in darkness, or the destruction that awaits at noonday. May the sun of liberty continue to shine on you with increasing splendor, and never be obstructed by the sable clouds of Africa. And should it be your misfortune to be invaded by a similar foe, we pledge ourselves to unite our exertions with yours in putting down by all lawful exertions, every plot that threatens the subversion of our liberties, or disturbs the public tranquility. May that being who presides over the destinies of nations, reward you a hundred fold in this life and in the world to come, life everlasting.

After the tumultuous applause which followed the delivery of the "Farewell Address," had subsided, they again assembled for labor, and the building was placed in order for underpinning. About sunset the work was accomplished, when the procession was again formed, with cannon in front and was paraded through the Street, accompanied by the stirring peal of fifes and drums. As before the cannon was discharged at the house of every Abolitionist. At each discharge the broken glass jingled in unison with the yell of triumph that went up from the crowd, the firing and shouting was kept up until late at night. Just before night one chivalrous fellow ascended the cupola of the Academy, painted the black ball thereon white and nailed a *white* flag to the spire. And the spirited people of Canaan and Enfield caused this history!

On the 19th of September a town meeting was called to hear the report of their committee on removal. To see if the town would repair the house and set up a school and appropriate the School and Literary Fund for that purpose. And adopt some measures to suppress the dangerous doctrine of the Abolotionists.

The report of the committee chosen by the town to superintend the removal of the building in which the colored school was kept was accepted, and Jacob Trussell, Daniel Pattee and Daniel Campbell were appointed to collect subscriptions to repair the building. The other articles were dismissed.

On the 10th of October another town meeting was held, and William P. Weeks, Caleb Blodgett and Thomas Flanders were chosen to get an instructor to superintend a school in Noyes Academy, for tuition fees to begin as soon as the house is in shape. The following resolutions were also passed:

Resolved that the Chairman of the Superintending committee, chosen by the town for the purpose of removing Noyes Academy, togather with persons associated with him, merit and receive the thanks of the town, for the prompt and energetic and praiseworthy manner in which he and they discharged their respective duties.

That the selectmen send to the Post-master of Natchitochez and at

NOYES ACADEMY.

New Orleans, each an Anti-slavery Almanac and direct their attention to the name of Hubbard Harris Esq.

So far the work was complete. The school was destroyed, the children who had gathered into it, fled from the scourge that pursued them. The chief actor in the scene had still one more duty to perform. It was to bring in his bill of items of expenses. It is inserted here, *in extenso*, as below:

The Committee chosen by the town to superintend the removal of the building in which the colored school was kept, have in discharging the duty assigned them, incurred the following expenses on the credit of the town:

Aug. 10, 1835 Joseph Dustin, furnished beef and lamb to the amount of	$ 16.44
Aug. 10, 1835 E. & J. Martin, furnished refreshment consisting of Biscuit cheese &c to the amount of	13.64
Aug. 10 & 11 Amaziah Carter's bill of expense	14.48
Aug. 10, 1835 Daniel Balch's bill	3.03
Aug. 10, 1835 Nathaniel Ingram's bill for mending chains	2.00
Sept. 10, 1835 E. & J. Martin's bill	7.43
Sept. 10, 1835 Joseph Dustin's bill for victualling	29.37
Sept. 10, 1835 Gordon Burley's bill for hay	15.00
Sept. 10, 1835 Rufus Richardson expenses in procuring chains at Shakers	6.
And returning them &c supposed to be	5.00
Sept. 10, 1835 S. S. Smith & J. Norris bill	1.00
Sept. 10, 1835 Ichabod Bartlett's bill	5.
Sept. 10, 1835 Mr. Barber's bill (of Grafton)	1.00
	$118.39

The addition is as the committee presented it. The following additional bills were afterwards audited and paid by the town treasurer:

Guilford Cobb for chains lost	7.50
Daniel Currier (Enfield) for chains lost	3.00
James Pattee repairing chains	5.25
Amaziah Carter procuring chains	.75
D. Currier Chains	.50
	$17.00

And now, having "abated the nuisance," and located it upon a spot selected by themselves, the bills audited and paid, the resolutions of thanks passed, "Farewell Address" spoken, the cannon fired and the windows broken, and all these duties performed by virtue of a "legal town meeting" these patriotic men and boys retired to the solitude of their beds and slept upon roses, the sleep of the righteous! Perhaps! But at this late day we do not propose to trouble their dreams.

There did, however, question arise, in days afterwards, which somewhat puzzled them. They had taken the house from the proprietors, and now what should they do with it? There was talk of liabilities for personal damages, actions of trespass, etc., but the politicians, the men in office, the clergymen generally and the public mind, now all known to be so unfriendly to the proprietors, and especially to the *color* of their cause, that it was not deemed prudent to invoke the law, and there the case rests to this day. In after years, it is said, that many of these men regretted the part they took in that outrage. Joseph L. Richardson, a man of education, elected to all the offices in town, when upon a bed of sickness, and the vision of his past life returned to him, regretted that part of his life, and wished it had never occurred. The Faleses, father and sons, afterwards became earnest Abolitionists. It is said that Capt. James Pattee when the excitement had passed, and reason regained its control over him, was very demonstrative in regretting the part he took in that great folly, but it is said that his regrets were caused more by the fears of prosecution for trespass, etc., than from a change of sentiment.

On the other hand, it is said, that some were hardly satisfied with moving the building. Their vindictiveness would only be satisfied by making all the Abolitionists endure some personal affliction. Old Cobb was one of this class. He was deputy sheriff under Blodgett, and was always ready to serve any process against those obnoxious persons. It is well known that on all such occasions he more than performed his threats. Many families were reduced to distress and suffering through his inhumanity and the only rebuke he ever received, was that he "should keep within the law." He never repented the part he took in producing the chaos of those days. It is said, that for a long time after those events, he was in the habit of hissing and spitting at clergymen whom he knew to be Abolitionists, as he passed them on the highway. Rev. Robert Woodbury was one of those thus annoyed. Rev. Jonathan Hamilton another.

Dr. Thomas Flanders, was noted for his violent sentiments and his frequent threats, but he could not face the public opinion that came afterwards. He disappeared forever from the face of this people.

James Doten was at that time an earnest Abolitionist. He looked upon the excited crowd as they destroyed the building and raising his hands he said "he wished God would strike them all dead for their crimes."

James Tylor joined the Abolition Society, but a few days afterwards was persuaded to withdraw his name, through the influence of Mr. Weeks and Mr. Blodgett.

Jacob Trussell, like old Cobb, never repented the part he took on that occasion. He was expelled from the Congregational Church, and left town threatening that he would return upon occasion, and lead the "people" upon any similar occasion. In this connection it is proper, as a part of the history of the times to present a digest of the proceedings of the Congregational Church in relation to some of its members. One month after the last "hauling" on the 10th of October, 1835, Col. Isaac Towle presented the following paper, which was also read to Mr. Trussell, thus:

Brother Trussell, you have grieved not only me but other members of our church in the course you have taken in regard to the removal of Noyes Academy.

Charge 1st. In introducing resolutions to that effect at a meeting of the people, contrary to the known wishes of many of your Brethren in the Church.

2nd. By still persisting in moving the building as a leader of the party, when one of your brethren, a Magistrate, commanded you and others to desist.

3rd. By being instrumental in distributing ardent spirits to the people when highly excited and at a time when many of the citizens and Brethren of the Church, considered themselves in danger, in consequence of threats against their persons and property.

Colonel Towle lived on the old Randlett farm, had fourteen children; he calculated to have them come along every March; was a very positive man, a strong abolitionist and saw no good except in the Congregational Church.

The foregoing articles of grievance were read before the church by Brother Isaac Towle against Jacob Trussell. On the 31st of October the last charge was withdrawn. Jacob Trussell refused to answer the charges, as he said "the previous steps" had not been taken. The church considered this a mere pretext to evade the question, but to show their clemency towards him, voted to adjourn two weeks, that Brother Towle might again take "the previous steps" so as to remove any excuse on Trussell's part.

The church met again on November 9th and a long and fruitless discussion ensued. Various propositions were offered for the settlement of the difficulties. To none of which would Mr. Trussell consent. It was then voted that the church will proceed to settle the dispute in their own way. Meantime as a preliminary step, Brother Trussell was suspended from Church Communion.

On November 27th an adjourned meeting of the church was held in the church and open to the public. There was "a large attendance." A long and desultory discussion ensued upon the subject with Brother Trussell, and he not denying the charges alleged against him, nor giving the brethren aggrieved any satisfaction, but persisting in his own justification, together with his trifling with the feelings of the brethren, and his abusive language, it was

Voted, that Mr. Trussell withdraw while the Church consult for a few moments. Whereupon the members of the Church after deliberation voted to suspend Brother Trussell from the Church indefinitely.

And now there was discord between the church and the pastor, Rev. Edward C. Fuller, growing out of this business. It seemed that he had given a letter of Christian fellowship to Mr. Trussell to transfer his relations to the church in Franklin, and this is done while he is under discipline of suspension in the church. The following is a copy of the original letter:

Canaan Jany 11. 1836

This may certify to whom it may concern that Mr. Jacob Trussell is a member of the Church of Christ in this place of which the undersigned is pastor. He is in regular standing with the exception of censure for assisting in the removal of the Noyes Academy, and in all other respects is recommended to the care and fellowship of any other church, where God in his providence may locate him. And when admitted into the fellowship and care of another Church his relation to this Church will cease.

E. C. FULLER,
Pastor of the first Congregational Church in Canaan N. H.

On the first day of March, 1836, Bro. Bart Heath was arraigned upon the same charges and passed through the same ordeal as Mr. Trussell, but with less resolution. It was "voted to excuse Brother Bart Heath for the part he acted in the removal of the Academy, in consequence of his confessions and explanations." A letter of "recommendation" was also granted him. Brother Heath also expressed a strong desire to be forgiven for any and all his expressions derrogating to a Christian, or against his brethren, expressing his sorrow and asking forgiveness of the church, which was freely granted. Afterwards on the 7th of March, "Voted that Brother Jacob Trussell be excommunicated from this Church."

A committee of five was chosen to send a letter to the Congregational Church in Franklin, informing them of the accusation against Jacob Trussell for "which he is excommunicated from this Church." Then finally it was resolved, "that we (members of the Congregational Church) disapprove of the measures taken by our late Pastor in giving Jacob Trussell a letter, as we think Mr. Trussell unworthy to be connected with any regular Church after taking into consideration his past conduct." The members of the church most conspicuous in these proceedings were Timothy Tilton, Nathaniel Barber, George Harris, Hubbard Harris, Jr., Joshua Pillsbury, Isaac Towle, Samuel Drake, Jesse E. Emerson, Caleb Gilman, Amos Gould.

Here we take leave of the church records and return to the affairs of the world. So far as Noyes Academy is concerned, our history is about finished. It only remains to record two or three striking events. The town by vote, repaired the building, appropriating the money from the Surplus Revenue Fund, and the spirit that "hauled" it from its first foundation was evoked to make good the pledges it made itself. A teacher was hired and a few pupils attended for a few weeks, six or eight, and the money or the disposition failing, the school was discontinued. Several attempts were made to open it, but they ended in failure.

An attempt was made by the "town" or those who had abducted the building, to compromise with the proprietors, but these stood aloof, believing and hoping a day of redress would come, but it never came. These unlawful acts which it was claimed public opinion demanded, have been atoned for, but not in human courts of justice. On the morning of December 31, 1838, it was found that seven windows had been removed the night before. Search was made for them; a pile of fragments of sash and broken glass, pounded almost to powder, were found on the shore of the pond.

A town meeting was called on the 17th, to see what "the town will do towards repairing the injury done to the Academy by a *Midnight Mob*. Got up by a party who professes all the Religion Mortality and Humility and who preaches so much against the Mob, Mobites and the Mobs Committee." And Caleb Blodgett, Thomas Flanders and James Pattee were chosen to "search out and bring the perpetrators to justice." It was also voted to repair the injury. This outrage was believed to have been committed by George Drake, who took this method to receipt a blacksmithing bill, which he had against the present owners of the Academy. The failure by the town to establish a school in the Academy after they had taken possession of it, and the proprietors had looked on at their failure, with probably no feelings of sorrow, aroused the old feeling against the Abolitionists. The diary again says:

The Abolition question at this time (1839) was one continued theme of excitement. The heart grows sick and disgusted at the repetition of the slang and abuse of the self-constituted club of Jacobins, at the lower end of the Street. Weeks, Blodgett and Flanders, sly and wicked beyond redemption, because of the unholy influence of their secret councils, the soft Martins (E. & J.), the ferocious Pattees, the tiger acting Campbells, that coterie of a D——n, the devil, for diabolism can be compared to none other now in existence.

The building had been standing several years a silent monument of all the bad feelings of the human heart. Its doors were seldom opened to the student. Many persons had expressed a wish that it might burn down, and its ashes scattered to the four winds, and that the recollection of it might cease from the recollection of man. On the night of March 7, 1839, a great light illuminated the heavens. All the people leaped from their beds, and saw the building, the cause of so much sorrow and sin, enveloped in flames. No efforts were made to extinguish it. And the ashes were indeed scattered to the four winds.

James Richardson of the class of 1841 of Dartmouth College, was engaged to teach in the Academy in the spring of 1839, after it was burned his school was transferred to Burley's Hall. Five days after the burning the annual town meeting occurred. The question of personal damages had recently been revived and had caused some uneasiness among that "Committee of Removal." Several of them, including Jacob Trussell, who at this time was residing in Franklin, had asked the town to protect them, and on this occasion, a resolution was adopted of which the following is a copy:

Resolved, that we, as a town, will defend Jacob Trussell, or any others, engaged with him, in the removal of Noyes Academy, against any suit or suits, that may be brought against said Trussell or others on account of said removal.

In announcing this vote, James Arvin said: "Of all the Isms that ever were introduced into Canaan, Abolitionism has done the most mischief. It has arrayed brother against brother in the same church, neighbor against neighbor, and engendered more strife and contention than anything else combined. I am gratified to know that we have put it down so that it will be perfectly harmless for one year."

Before closing this history, which I have detailed tediously perhaps, though with scarcely a shadow of the transcendant brutality that attended it, I ought to say that as far as possible, I have been impartial. Except two men, whose names are herein present, there was not infatuation enough in the town of Canaan to have perpetrated this outrage. It was charged to the people of Canaan, but it was the deed of the whole community. It was tauntingly called the "Canaan Mob," by men ashamed of the imprudences of their allies, but it was *one of the mobs of New Hampshire*. It was a legitimate outbreak of a very *general "public sentiment,"* and the honor or odium of it should be shared accordingly.

People from Canaan indisposed to molest the school, were taunted wherever they went for living in "nigger town." Guide boards were nailed to trees by the wayside, indicating so many miles to "nigger town." Rev. J. L. Richardson, representative for that year, appealed to the legislature for an act of some sort to remove the "nuisance," as "public sentiment" was pleased to call the school. The legislature unaccountedly refused to interfere. Individual members, however, advised their reverend brother, that as the constitution and law was against him, he must take the matter into his own hands. "Public sentiment" was found to be all right, and at the appointed time, it foamed and boiled over on the ill-fated school.

A letter written at this time to Mr. Trussell by James Arvin, will show the situation of the friends of the school, who were in the minority, as well as informing Mr. Trussell of what he most desired to hear that the town would stand back of him.

Canaan, Mar. 12th., 1839. Dear Sir. Yours of the 3rd inst. was duly received and I thot proper to defer answering it until I should be able to give you the result of our elections. We have given our Political opponents the soundest drubbing they ever received since our party got in the ascendency; we chose our representative by 94 majority; our state and county officers by an average 80 majority, as also our representative to Congress by the same. I believe there is not a Whig abolitionist that holds office in town excepting Nathl Currier, a weigher of hay, and it was with some difficulty that the voters would consent he should hold the office. Thus you see we have carried all before us today. The trustees of Noyes Academy, allies of the Negro school, have waited in vain until after our March elections for a more favorable prospect to push on their unhallowed designs upon us. You may rely I think upon those men that co-operated with you and stood by you through the fiery ordeal you were doomed to pass while here in consequence of the active part you took and the efficient services you rendered in the removal of that building which is now reduced to ashes by some of the abolitionists or their tools. You were appointed at the head of a committee to superintend the removal of that house, which was considered a nuisance, and you were appointed by the town and your duty assigned by the town, and they are legally and morally bound in my opinion to see you harmless, and, sir, we have passed a resolution today, in solemn town meeting, which reads as follows. [It is given above.] . . . Thus you see Canaan is yet awake and still on right ground as it respects the removal of that house and still duly appreciates the important services you rendered us on that trying occasion.

I was pleased to hear from you and am happy in having it in my power to give a copy of the resolution which amounts to what you desired, I believe.

It is in evidence that Canaan would not furnish the requisite team, so that cattle were invited from the neighboring towns, some volunteering, others being impressed. It is safe to say that had this same "public sentiment," *out of Canaan*, stayed at home, and refrained from intermeddling, the school might have been in successful operation to this day.

Among the colored people were four youths, whose names deserve record in the story of the school, and some of them have made names that will be illustrious in all future time, when the names and lives of those weak mortals who opposed them, shall only be recorded upon obscure tombstones. These youths were Henry Highland Garnet, Thomas Paul, Thomas S. Sidney and Alexander Crummell.

Garnet was 19, coal black, and until ten years of age was a slave. His father, by hard toil, had ransomed himself, his wife and children from American slavery. A year before he came to Canaan young Garnet became a Christian and united himself with the Presbyterian Church. He was afflicted with a knee disease which threatened his life. This had been much aggravated on his way through New England by exposure in bad weather on the outside of the stage, the place allotted "all niggers" by "public sentiment." He reached Canaan exhausted and enfeebled by his hard journey, and with his crutch under his arm, hobbled up to the school, tidings of which had reached his ears; with all his discouragements he flew to the fountain of knowledge opened to him at "Noyes Academy," where he was distinguished for his modest, exemplary conduct, and won the respect of everybody that knew him. But the human wild beasts set themselves upon his track. He escaped like a startled deer, and lived eminent for his learning, revered and beloved for his sincerity and Christian benevolence, and when he spoke his eloquence filled his audience like a current of electricity. He became a doctor of divinity, and was appointed United States Minister to Liberia, where he spent many years of his life in the discharge of duties for which he was well fitted among his people. He died and was buried in Liberia.

Two years after these events, Garnet returned to Canaan and lectured in the Congregational Church. There was no disturbance. The vigilance committee failed to appear. He was listened to by an earnest, thoughtful audience, and received much attention from the citizens. He was the guest of Mr. George Harris and he had a reception the same evening. Among the callers was Ben. Porter, who had been active in driving him from town. He took Garnet by the hand and told him he had heard his speech, and that he had come there to express to him his sorrow and regret he had felt on account of his bad work on the other occasion. He had only lacked a little moral courage to make him go up at the close of the speech and make public confession to the whole audience. Porter retired to private life, taking no more interest in politics. A few years later he, with his wife and family, emigrated to Michigan. He was drowned by the wrecking of a steamer on Lake Erie.

Thomas Paul was the son of a late clergyman of Boston, of graceful manners, of amiable and courteous disposition, of respectable talent and attainment, twenty years of age and lighter in his complexion than many of those who denied him the right to study.

Sidney was seventeen, quite white, a scholar of graceful person and demeanor and an accomplished writer and speaker.

Crummell was sixteen, of full African descent, his father was stolen from Africa, but he was released from slavery. He was born in the city of New York; his mother and her ancestors for several generations, were never subjected to servitude. But his father early in life, although he came of a royal family, was made a slave. His father was a native of Timanee, West Africa, a country adjoining Sierra Leone, and lived there until he was thirteen years old. Alexander Crummell's grandfather was King of Timanee, and the incidents of his early life appear to have impressed themselves very strongly upon his son's memory. He was fond of describing the travels that he took with his father's caravans in the interior of Africa and of the royal receptions given to them by the various kings. Young Crummell in his early life was sent to the Mulberry Street school in New York City, which was provided by the Quakers, afterwards receiving further and better instruction from white tutors provided by his father. After leaving Canaan he studied for three years at Oneida Institute, working at farming to pay his way. In 1839 he became a candidate for Holy Orders and at the same time applied for admission as a student in the General Theological Seminary of the Episcopal Church. He was admitted to Priests Orders in Philadelphia. He pursued his studies in the University of Cambridge in England. After this he sought a home in Liberia, where he remained for many years, taking the double duty of the Rectorship of a Parish and a Professorship in the College. While a citizen of this new Republic, he was frequently called upon to officiate as orator of the day; and his addresses were marked by great breadth of vision and foresight, profound historical research and decided rhetorical power. It is said of him that if he had not been called to the work of the Christian Ministry, he might have become eminent as a statesman. After spending the bloom of his days in Liberia, he returned to the United States, to take up his work among his race at the capital of the Nation, where he was Rector of St. Luke's Church, until the time of his death. He wrote two books, the "Future of Africa" and "The Greatness of Christ," besides many contributions to various periodicals.

Many remember the visit which this man paid Canaan in 1895, with his friend, Mr. Downing. He had not been in Canaan since the night Oscar Wallace had driven him and Paul down the Lebanon road, out of town to escape the dangers which threatened their lives, and they were real, for he related how one man had discharged a pistol through the door of the Cross house at the Corner where they roomed and boarded with the family of George Kimball. Upon his arrival on the street he went to the hotel with Mr. Downing and was refused admission on account of his color. Hon. Caleb Blodgett received and entertained them and when his arrival became known, there was not one but what was glad to shake his hand and listen to his words from the pulpit of the Methodist Church. It was a pathetic spectacle to see this old man, tall and spare, gray, almost blind, with a dignity befitting the position which he had held among his fellow-men, delivering a sermon to the descendants of those who sixty years before had driven him out of town. The contrast between the two receptions received, the first when a boy and the second as an old man, serve to prove that the principles of truth and justice will always prevail. Although shadowed in enmity and spite for a time they will in the end rise and bury all bad feelings underneath.

These young men fled from the "wrath that pursued them," to Oneida Institute, New York, where they were received and pursued their studies. A letter written on the 4th of July, 1835, by N. P. Rogers, one of the trustees of the school, to the *Liberator* in Boston, gives an interesting account of a celebration held at Plymouth, where these young men were present.

The speakers on this occasion failed to respond and they were about to give up that part of their exercises, when George Kimball, Esq., a zealous Abolitionist of Canaan, send word that "if our Anti-slavery was of the standard to deserve the honor," he would visit us with some fine young men of Noyes Academy, whom he had prevailed upon to come and offer their support on the occasion. "Hospitality," he said, "must open its doors in the true spirit of emancipation or we could not expect them." We promptly accepted the offer and on the third had the honor of welcoming Brother Kimball and his wife and four young gentlemen of the school to our homes. I will give you some account of their history, names and what is quite important now, their color.

Paul, son of a Baptist minister, a scholar and a gentleman, quite in advance of the standard of our educated young men, of mitigated color, complexion quite endurable.

Garnet, of full unmitigated, unalleviated, unpardonable blackness, quite "incompatable with freedom," crippled, with severe lameness, nine years ago a slave in Maryland, an enlightened and refined scholar, a writer and speaker of touching beauty.

Sidney, an orphan literally, as well as by caste, more fortunate in complexion than our friend Paul, even an accomplished scholar, graceful and eloquent orator. It might raise the envy and the emulation of our young patricians at the higher Seminary, coveting the glories of eloquence, to see and hear him speak.

Crummell, a mere boy in years, but in talent, learning and character anything but a boy; black, sable as Toussant of the undeteriorated aspect of that land whence his father was stolen. I talked with him on the subject of insurrection. He denounced it because of its midnight slaughter of women and children. To open war for liberty, he had less objection, but it was too like murder to fall upon unarmed men, a scrupulosity more like knight-errantry than is common in these *shrewd* times. I asked him before a *Colonizationist* what the colored people would do with the colony at Liberia, if it were left to them. "Send and bring them home," said he with animation, "every man of them." "Every man you find alive," said young Garnet.

Mr. Garnet was introduced to the audience with a response, prefaced with some beautiful remarks on the contrast of his own feelings with those proper to the joyous day, and supported them in an address of some thirty minutes with great simplicity and pathos. His response was in substance, that it was the duty of every patriot and Christian to adopt the principles of the abolitionists, for the sure and speedy overthrow of slavery, that every man who walked the American soil might tread it unmolested and free. There were many passages of touching eloquence in his address, and when he told of the objects that met his earliest vision and shed natural tears, at the remembrance of his own and his parents bondage, I found many moistened eyes in the audience besides my own. Young Crummell followed Garnet in a spirited and manly speech, which was listened to with much attention.

Mr. Sidney was called to the platform under a strong expression of favor, which he amply repaid by a very eloquent address. The young gentlemen tarried with us until Monday, the 6th, and offered us an opportunity to disperse some of the prejudice and uneasiness we are wont to feel at the fine appearance of our colored brethren. We had the satisfaction of attending our young friends to the house of God on the Sabbath, and their presence proved no interruption to the services. They amalgamated with the congregation. The pew doors of our yeomanry, too respectable to be sneered down by the dandyism of the land, were opened to them, and they had the satisfaction of associating with their brethren and countrymen and fellow sinners, on proper and Christian footing. This I call *practical Anti-slavery*.

New England at that time was degenerated into guilty and dastardly servility to the South. She was enslaved by her prejudices until she trampled her own laws and peace under foot. The descendants of the founders of Puritan Seminaries broke up the *free school. And such a school!* Had it been undisturbed it would have taken the lead of all others in the country, and enjoyed patronage unknown to any other. Abolitionists everywhere would have sent their sons and daughters, animated by the high toned principle and lofty purpose that distinguished them from their abusers. The flower of the colored youth would have found their way to it from every part of the country. God would have blessed it with his abundant favor. Its breaking up and dispersion left the quiet and beautiful village to the bats and owls. The stillness of the desert succeeded.

Rev. Mr. Fuller found his usefulness gone and he went, and the meeting house was soon closed up and forsaken. Has not the curse of that "legal mob followed this village to its latest days?" Alas for Canaan! her prominent men have never been her friends.

The following is from a letter written by the Rev. Amos Foster, the first pastor of the Congregational Church, before Mr. Fuller:

The most I can say is to express my astonishment that a class of men should be found so reckless, so regardless of law and human rights, and so devoid of moral principles, as to engage in such an undertaking. As the account shall hereafter be read on the page of history, it will fix a most unfavorable impression on the mind respecting the character of those most prominent in the undertaking. One of the principal men engaged in the matter was a member of the church. He was excommunicated. On his return to Canaan he was, I learnt, restored to his standing in the church, after making some partial retractions and confession. But my impression is that he really maintained his former opinions and did not in fact regret the course he had taken. I was absent from Canaan while these unpleasant scenes were transpiring, and of course could not be advised of the facts on both sides of the question, as if I had been in the place. But from some things I heard, I judge that some friends of the school were rather indiscreet and pursued a course which provoked the indignation of those on the other side. I refer to the partiality showed to the colored students and the positions given them at the social gatherings. Certainly they should have been treated kindly, but whether it was wise to invite them or any of the Academy students to their social parties is, at least, doubtful. But I do not say that by way of apology for those engaged in the crime of removing the Academy. That terrible act yet dwells in the memory of many now living, and the records of it will be read by hundreds who will have a being in future years, and who, we may ask, will there be to justify so outrageous an act? The moral sentiments of the people will be so changed, I may say, so corrected, and the colored race will be brought to sustain such a position among their fellow beings, that the matter of wonder will be that there could once have been a class of people in the world, as should commit such a crime as breaking up an institution for the education of youth, both black and white. Since the outrage in Canaan, we can see the wonderful change that has taken place in the moral and political condition of the colored race.

CHAPTER XIX.

CANAAN UNION ACADEMY.

A few weeks after the excitement attending the burning of the old academy building had subsided (it was never known who the incendiary was) a number of men assembled in Mr. Weeks' office and proposed to erect a new academy upon the site of the one burned. It was estimated that thirteen hundred dollars would defray all charges. An attempt was made on April 15th to get the town to appropriate money from the surplus revenue to build a new town house and academy, but the article was dismissed and a vote was taken "not to build." Subsequently, these men decided to make thirteen notes of one hundred dollars each, each note to be signed by five men, and each man to be a member of the new corporation on payment of one fifth of his note. Thus there were to be sixty-five shares in the new building at twenty dollars each.

The names of the signers of only twelve of the thirteen notes have been obtained. They are the following:

On the first note were Eleazer Martin, March Barber, James Arvin, Bartlett Hoyt and Jesse Martin.

On the second, William Gordon, Ensign Colby, Thomas Flanders, John Fales and William Kimball.

On the third, William Martin, William P. Weeks, Guilford Cobb, Henry Martin and Horace Chase.

On the fourth, Caleb Blodgett, William Doten, Tilton Nichols, Joseph D. Smith and Salmon P. Cobb.

On the fifth, Joseph L. Richardson, Benjamin Bradbury, Joshua S. Lathrop, Alvah Richardson and Benjamin Kidder.

On the sixth, Daniel G. Patten, Abram Page, Jr., Josiah Richardson, Joshua W. Richardson, James B. Wallace and Amos B. Clark.

On the seventh, Joseph Dustin, John Shepherd, Josiah P. Haynes, James Tyler and Nathan M. Currier.

On the eighth, Simeon Hadley, William Campbell, Peter S. Wells, Daniel Campbell and Nathaniel Shepherd.

On the ninth, Amos Miner, Daniel Pattee, Jr., James Pattee, Chamberlain Packard, Jr. and Sylvanus B. Morgan.

On the tenth, Francis Welch, Moses W. Jones, James Doten, Jr., Nathan Willis and Elijah R. Colby.

On the eleventh, Nathaniel Barber, Nathaniel Currier, William W. George, Moses G. Kelley and John Jewell.

On the twelfth, Carey Leeds, Eliphalet C. Gilman, Jesse Clark, Josiah Clark, Jr., Francis Robbins and C. S. Hubbard.

It was decided to take these notes to the town agent and ask the loan of thirteen hundred dollars of the surplus revenue remaining on hand. The money was loaned from time to time during the construction of the building. One thousand dollars of the amount was loaned from the surplus revenue and three hundred from the literary fund. Afterwards a charter was procured from the legislature and approved June 27, 1839, in which Eleazer Martin, Jesse Martin, Caleb Blodgett, James Arvin, Guilford Cobb, Ensign Colby, William P. Weeks, Daniel Pattee, Jr., James Pattee, Joseph Dustin and William Doten were named as incorporators, to establish an institution for the "education of youth," under the name of "Canaan Union Academy." With this money they built the academy, believing it would prove a successful and profitable investment; but this belief was a delusion, if not a snare. No steps were taken by the dominant party to conciliate the large number of citizens who were aggrieved; no kind words were spoken, nor did anyone propose any method to harmonize the antagonisms; and there the two nearly equal hostile factions stood, making faces at each other, the one pointing to that building as a monument of acts of aggression unatoned for and the other flinging back contemptuous epithets *ad libitum*.

A piece of land was purchased from Jonathan Kittredge, but was not conveyed until February 13, 1840, for $50. It was one-half an acre, taken off the north side of the Baptist parsonage land, a part of the same land that was deeded to Jonathan Swan by the Baptist Society, and by it to Kittredge. The land was described "to run from the east side of Broad street to Hart Pond, with width equal at both ends." Dr. Thomas Flanders contracted to erect the new building, and deliver it complete into the hands of the trustees on the first of September, 1839.

He engaged a number of efficient workmen and the work proceeded rapidly until the outside of the house was finished. And here came in a little episode that created some amusement at the time. The doctor boarded all his workmen. His wife was pleased with the progress of the work, and spoke cheerfully to all the men as long as the outside was unfinished. The finishing of the inside was slower work, which she could not appreciate. She said the men were getting lazy, and she would have them all discharged. On the 30th of May, 1839, she called upon Mr. Weeks, who held the contract, and asked to be permitted to read it. He placed it in her hands and turned away to attend to other affairs. She sat down, read it through very deliberately, then quietly tore it into small pieces, and placing them in a heap on the table, passed out of the office saying: "I guess I've taken the life out of that thing anyhow!" She went home and when the men came in to dinner, they found nothing to eat. She told them she had got done boarding lazy men, and they must go elsewhere to board. When the doctor learned of the affair, he went to Mr. Weeks and renewed the contract, and the building was ready for occupancy at the time appointed.

The school was organized on the first of September, 1839, with a formidable board of officers. William P. Weeks was president of the corporation; Hon. Caleb Blodgett, vice-president; Eleazer Martin, secretary; Rev. Joseph L. Richardson, treasurer. The executive committee consisted of Guilford Cobb, March Barber, James Arvin, Sylvanus B. Morgan, James Pattee and James B. Wallace. The board of visitors were Edwin D. Sanborn of Dartmouth College, Leonard Wilcox of Orford, William H. Duncan of Hanover, Hon. David C. Churchill of Lyme, Arthur Latham of Lyme, Rev. Liba Conant of Canaan, Rev. Palmer C. Himes of Canaan, Rev. Abel Heath of Canaan, Rev. Ephraim Crockett of Danbury, Caleb Plastridge of Lebanon, John Jones and Hon. Converse Goodhue of Enfield. Mr. J. Everett Sargent, an undergraduate of Dartmouth College, who had taught the last term in the old building, was engaged as principal. The trustees feeling very confident of success, engaged to pay him $40 per month and board for three months. Miss Mary A. Blaisdell was engaged as assistant. Great efforts were made by the proprietors of the school to fill all the seats and it opened with one hundred and twenty pupils. A catalogue of the institution was issued. The following is a list of the scholars, all are from Canaan except where otherwise indicated:

Gentlemen:

Albert G. Arvin
Edwin W. Atherton
Franklin W. Barber
Hiram Barber
Horace H. Barber
James P. Barber
John M. Barber, Jr.
Caleb Blodgett, Jr.
George W. Bryant
Roswell S. Chapman, Enfield
Joseph D. Clark
Hiram M. Cobb
Frank Currier
George Currier
Guilford Doten
Caleb Dow
Isaac W. Dow
Joseph Dow
John B. Dustin
Albert Eastman
Stephen Eastman
George S. Eastman
Ransom Farnham, Topsham, Vt.
Abraham H. Flanders
David Fogg, Enfield
Harrison Fogg, Enfield
John S. Gilman
Stephen S. Gilman

Simeon Hadley
Henry S. Hamlet
Levi W. Hoit
James Huse, Enfield
John Ingram
James H. Kelley
Charles W. Kidder
Alfred H. Kittredge
Edw. C. D. Kittredge
John H. Lathrop
Albert Martin
Nathan C. Morgan
J. Monroe Pattee, Enfield
Wyman Pattee
Daniel F. Sanford, Mansfield, Mass.
Alpha B. Stevens
Moses Stevens, Jr., Enfield
John A. Swett
Augustus W. Taylor, Danbury
Charles A. Welch
Horace B. Welch
Charles H. Wells
Horace B. Williams
Samuel Williams, 2d
Henry Wilson
John Worth, Jr.

Ladies:

Martha M. Atherton
Caroline E. Atherton
Martha J. Barber
Rhoda Blaisdell, Orange
Emily R. Blodgett
Clarissa J. Chapman, West Rumney
Mahala Choate, Enfield
Chastina Clark
Dorothy B. Clark
Abby P. Cobb
Adelia F. Cobb

Elizabeth F. Cobb
Lucretia B. Cobb
Phebe P. Cobb
Susan Frances Cobb
Elizabeth J. Conant
Sarah Ann Conant
Eliza Ann Currier
Marion M. Davenport
Mary Dow
Emeline Dustin
Harriet B. Dustin
Rebecca Dustin

CANAAN UNION ACADEMY.

Caroline P. Eastman
Miriam Eastman
Abigail Fales
Sarah Fales
Sarah Ann L. Flanders
Offranda A. Follensbee, Grafton
Harriet S. George
Isabel M. George
Julia Ann Gile, Grafton
Lucy Gile, Grafton
Lydia H. Gile, Enfield
Arabella Harris
Frances S. Harris
Celinda Hazen, Hartford, Vt.
Olivia W. Heath
Emily E. Jones, Enfield
Maria C. Jones, Enfield
Malinda Jones, Enfield
Nancy L. Kimball
Julia L. Kittredge
Susan B. Lathrop
Celina Martin
Hannah C. S. Martin
Roxilana B. Martin
Lucy Ann Miner
Hannah S. Morse
Almeda Nichols, Enfield
Eleanor Nichols, Enfield
Julia Ann Nichols, Enfield
Mary E. Page
Rachel R. Page
Sarah Ann C. Pillsbury
Lucy Ann Richardson
Mary R. Richardson
Elsa A. Smith
Harriet A. Smith
Hannah L. Stevens, Enfield
Mabel E. Stevens, Lebanon
Tryphena Stark
Catherine R. Swan
Harriet O. Wallace
Sophia J. Wallace
Hannah S. Willis

Sixty-nine ladies and fifty-four gentlemen; and the spring term was to begin on the first Monday of March. The prospectus was as follows:

This institution in its location combines every advantage of a salubrious climate and pleasant scenery. No pains will be spared by its officers or instructors to render it a favorable resort for young persons who wish to pursue a thorough course of study. There are two rooms for recitation, and the Scholars are classed according to the branches pursued, but all are under the care and direction of the Principal.

COURSE OF STUDY.

Instruction is given in the various studies required for admission to College, in the French Language, and in all the English branches taught in similar institutions.

EXPENSES.

The Tuition is $3.00 per term. After the present term an additional charge of $1.00 will be made to those attending to the languages. Board can be had in good families for from $1.00 to $1.50 per week. Students who wish to board themselves can obtain convenient rooms near the Academy, at a moderate rate.

TERMS AND VACATIONS.

There will be three terms in the year, the fall term to commence the first Monday in September, the Spring term the first Monday in March, and the Summer term the first Monday in June, each to continue 12 weeks.

BOOKS.

English, Porter's Rhetorical Reader, Smith's and Sanborn's Grammar; Olney's and Huntington's Geography; Goodrich's History of the United States; Adam's New and Davies' Arithmetic; Day's and Davies' Algebra; Playfair's Euclid, Flint's Surveying, Comstock's Philosophy and Chemistry, Burrett's Geography of the Heavens; Political class book, Watts on the Mind, Abercrombie's Intellectual Philosophy, Upham's Mental Philosophy, Paley's Natural Theology. Ancient Languages: Andrew's and Stoddard's Latin Grammar, Andrew's Latin Reader, Latin Tutor, Cooper's Virgil, Anthon's Sallust, Cicero's Select Orations, Fiske's Greek Grammar and Exercises, Jacob's Greek Reader, Greek Testament, Leverett's Latin Dictionary, Donnegan's Greek Lexicon, Lampriere's Classical Dictionary. French: Bolmar's Levizac's Grammar, Bolmar's Phrase Book, LeBrun's Telemaque, Voltaire's Charles XII, Meadow's and Boyer's Dictionary.

REQUIREMENTS.

All students are required to attend at all the regular exercises, and observe all the regulations of the Institutions, and at all times to maintain a correct moral deportment. In case of non-compliance, neglect of study or immoral conduct, the delinquent will be reported to his parents, and if he does not reform, will be immediately removed that others may not suffer thereby. During each term there are weekly exercises in compositions and declamations.

EXAMINATIONS.

There will be a public examination at the close of the fall and spring term, in the various branches attended to, which the board of Visitors will be expected to attend.

The other party also organized a school in Currier's Hall and employed Mr. I. N. Hobart, a classmate of Mr. Sargent, to teach it. He drew in about sixty pupils; but these efforts were strained. Many of the pupils who trod those unclassic floors were there by reason of the social and political antagonisms, which had not been allayed or softened as the years went by. There always was a trace of stinginess in the people of Canaan in matters pertaining to schools, and it is not surprising that the interest in this school should fall off, when it became a matter of paying out money for board and tuition.

Mr. David H. Mason of the class 1841, who afterwards became United States district attorney in Massachusetts, taught the spring term of 1840, to a diminished number of pupils, so much so that the speculation looked likely to prove a failure and on the 30th of May, 1840, the proprietors offered the building and its privileges "to any suitable person who would take the school upon his own risk." Mr. Mason accepted the school upon those conditions and conducted it two terms. Thus suddenly the hopes of these sixty-five men faded out, and they found themselves indebted to the town in the sum of thirteen hundred dollars and accruing interest.

In the spring of 1841 the corporation opened the academy with the following officers: William P. Weeks, president; Caleb Blodgett, vice-president; Eleazer Martin, secretary, and Jesse Martin, treasurer. The executive committee were March Barber, James Arvin, Sylvanus B. Morgan, James Pattee, Nathaniel Shepard, Peter Wells, Daniel Campbell, Nathaniel Currier, William W. George and Dea. Nathaniel Barber. The preceptor was T. L. Wakefield, who graduated from Dartmouth College in 1843. Twenty-eight gentlemen and seventeen ladies attended. The fall term of that year was taught by Edward E. Sargent, a classmate of Mr. Wakefield's, with forty-five gentlemen and twenty-two ladies attending.

Socially, things were not much changed: there still existed a good deal of sullenness, but there was a decrease of personal vituperation. The proprietors were, however, not pleased with their investment. The terms of the loan required the interest on their notes to be paid in advance, and the town was now asking for the principal also. The most interesting query with many of them was how to avoid payment and free themselves from their obligations. The suggestion that was acted upon and accepted was made by S. P. Cobb and J. L. Richardson, namely, to sell the land and buildings to the town.

At the beginning of the annual meeting on March 8, 1842, the interest on the surplus revenue and school fund was voted to be divided as before among the schools. At the last part of the day, after many had gone home and after all the articles in the warrant had been disposed of, and nothing remained to do but sort and count the ballots for state and county officers, the motion was made to reconsider the vote regarding the disposition of the surplus revenue and school fund and voted: "That the Treasurer of the Town of Canaan remit to the proprietors of Canaan Union Academy the interest on the notes given by them to the Treasurer of the town of Canaan or to the agent of said town." They also voted: "That said notes be given up to said proprietors when they make and deliver to said town of Canaan a deed of academy land and buildings thereon, owned by said proprietors." This led to an outburst of wrath and indignation, seldom equalled and never excelled, against the men who had borrowed the public money and had attempted by a trick to vote away that money to pay their private debts. There was a very radiant atmosphere in Canaan for the next two weeks, as the following "whereas" and "resolved" witness.

At the close of the annual meeting the proprietors of the academy appointed Joseph Wheat their agent to convey the property to the town, and he hurried the matter so rapidly that the deed was made and delivered to the town on the 23d of March, the day before a town meeting was held, which put a stop to their plans. At this meeting William Eastman was moderator. Jonathan Kittredge, bravely seconded and assisted by James Eastman, took the lead in the services and offered the following preamble and resolutions, which seems to be weighted down with indignant distinctness:

WHEREAS, at the close of the annual meeting on the 8th. instant a vote was passed purporting to be a vote of the town of Canaan to the effect, as recorded, that the Treasurer remit to the proprietors of Canaan Union Academy the interest on the notes given by them to the treasurer of the town of Canaan or to the agent of said town, and also that said notes be given up to said proprietors when they make and deliver to the town a good and valid deed of the academy land, and buildings thereon; and whereas the design in passing said vote was carefully concealed from the legal voters of said town in the article in the warrant for said town-meeting under which said vote was pretended to be passed, giving no sufficient notice thereof; and whereas, the absence of a majority of said legal voters was designedly and fraudulently taken advantage of by said proprietors to secure the passage of said vote; and whereas, said vote was carried by the votes of said proprietors contrary to the wishes of a large majority of the legal voters of said town; and whereas, the said vote is for the above reasons illegal and void, therefore

Resolved by said town, in legal town meeting assembled, that the said pretended vote be, and the same is hereby rescinded. That the town will not accept of any deed of the academy, and the selectmen have no right or authority to accept the same, or to perform any other act in relation thereto, obligatory upon the town. That the records of said pretended vote be expunged and that the town clerk now in the presence of the town draw black lines around the same and write across the same the following words, "Expunged by order of the town this 24th. day of March A. D. 1842."

Resolved that the said agent be authorized to collect said notes and right of authority to give up to the said proprietors the said notes and that he be directed not to give the same.

Resolved that Jonathan Kittredge be and is hereby appointed an agent of the town to demand and receive of Wm. P. Weeks all the notes in his hands, given to the town or to him as Treasurer or agent of the town or for the towns money, and that his receipt for the same to said Weeks shall be his discharge from the town therefor on his procuring bonds to the acceptance of the town.

Resolved that the Treasurer of the town has not, nor had he any to take any other steps to secure the interest of the town in its public money or in the said notes that he may think proper.

They also voted that the agent collect the notes or that the signers procure sureties acceptable to the agent. George Harris, Dexter Harris, James Eastman, Daniel Sherburne and William E. Eastman were Kittredge's bondsmen. And then to further show the state of their feelings and rake up the old trouble, Jonathan Kittredge, Joshua Richardson and James Morse were chosen a committee "to look up and report the facts in relation to the account of the Investigating Committee of 1839, appointed to ascertain by what means the Academy was burned."

They voted to "divide the Surplus Revenue and School Fund equally among the schools." A motion was then made to reconsider all the votes and resolutions, and it was voted "not to reconsider any of them."

The other party was much disturbed at the passage of these votes. They met and talked earnestly together, but feeling quite confident that they could maintain their position, they requested "William P. Weeks, Esq., to consult some learned counsellor-at-law, and procure his opinion as to the binding force of the vote passed at the annual meeting," concerning the remission of interest and deed of the academy. On the 11th of April, Kittredge demanded the notes of Mr. Weeks, who refused to give them up.

A special town meeting, called April 23d for various purposes, gave rise to some lively talk. Mr. Kittredge was severely criticised and unceremoniously dismissed as agent of the town, 127 voting for his dismissal and none against, upon a poll of the house; but Kittredge did not stay dismissed. He had already on March 29th, applied for a temporary injunction restraining Mr. Weeks from doing anything, and had on the 11th of April, after Mr. Weeks' refusal, filed a bill in equity against Mr. Weeks to compel him to turn over the notes to himself as agent of the town. Kittredge was also determined to bring suits against the makers of the notes, and to push them to judgment, either as agent of the town or as an interested citizen, and the party was late in discovering that they had passed one more illegal vote, as the subject was not named in the warrant for the town meeting.

The "learned counsellor-at-law" (Mr. Josiah Quincy of Rumney), whose opinion they procured, in view of the suits which had been commenced against the makers of the notes, advised them to compromise with the town's agent upon the best terms they could obtain, as Mr. Kittredge was in a frame of mind to push them to the utmost extent of the law, and his costs might soon exceed the principal of the notes. The "learned counsellor" held the same opinion of the action of the town and of the proprietors of the academy as did Mr. Kittredge — that it was unlawful for a part of the taxpayers of the town to vote away the public money to pay the private debts of the proprietors of the academy, without first giving notice, in the warrant to that effect.

In August the proprietors held a meeting and offered to pay into the town treasury the principal due on their notes to the town, and to take back their deed, "provided, at their next meeting, the town would vote to give the said proprietors the interest due on their notes."

They made one desperate effort to check the strong measures adopted by the town agent, by calling a town meeting on the 22d of August, 1842, to reconsider the work of March 24th, but they failed. William E. Eastman was chosen moderator, much to their chagrin, and then it was voted "to dissolve the meeting"; and thus the frost of public condemnation once more struck a chill to their hopes and expectations. From August until the next February no public steps were taken, but the proprietors rallied and got their partisans well in hand, so that on the first of February, 1843, feeling confident of their case, they called a town meeting, at which it was voted

To give the proprietors of Canaan Union Academy the interest on their notes given to the town, for the surplus revenue and literary fund, on condition that they take back their deed of the academy land and buildings to the town, and pay into the treasury the principal due on their notes, and they shall give satisfactory bonds for the payment of their notes to the town.

Passed by, yeas 149, nays 139. The bill in chancery and all suits brought by Mr. Kittredge against the individual proprietors, were ordered to be dismissed and stopped and "Jonathan Kittredge is dismissed and discharged as agent of the town in regard to said notes and all other matters in which he is authorized to act as agent for the town."

This vote caused much dissatisfaction with a large number of voters, who were not present at the meeting, inasmuch as it gave to a few men the accumulated interest on the money of the whole people. They said "it was not a fair division, and if the public business was to be done in that partial manner, they would all turn out next time and make it musical for some of them." It soon became evident that something must be done to soothe and placate these stay-at-home fellows; but they became troublesome. Various schemes were considered and abandoned, but at the annual meeting in March, one month afterward, the following extraordinary vote, which seemed to meet the worst features of the case, as it gave everybody a grab at the bag, was passed:

To give all the inhabitants of the town, including widows and maiden ladies, paying taxes, a sum of money out of the Surplus revenue equal to the sum voted to the proprietors of Canaan Union Academy, Feb. 1, last;

And then

That the remainder of the money be equally divided among all the inhabitants, including said widows and maiden ladies, as also said proprietors, who are in town on the 1st. day of April, and who are liable to the assessment of public taxes, not including persons seventy years of age.

The amount of surplus revenue in the treasury at this date was $814.32, and the division *pro rata*, among the taxpayers was

$2.34. At the same meeting, the following respectful language was adopted in regard to Messrs. Weeks and Kittredge, the gentlemen employed as counsel in the suits brought against the proprietors of the academy, that they be requested to dismiss all suits now pending against any and all of said proprietors, and that request was subsequently complied with.

On the 12th of March, 1844, the people declared that the proprietors of the academy had got more than their share of the surplus revenue and ordered them to pay into the town treasury an amount equal to the excess they had received above the rest of the inhabitants, but it does not appear that any one of those proprietors ever complied with the request of the people. They took all that ever came into their hands and kept it. At one of the proprietors' meetings, the venerable and respected Joseph Dustin, introduced the old fire-brand in these words:

That the school be opened for the benefit of the colored as well as the white children, and that all his Methodist brethren vote on the motion and not attempt to dodge it.

This provided a discussion characteristic of the times and people. It was promptly voted down and from that day onward, no colored person has been seen in any of our schools.

On May 10, 1845, the proprietors of the academy voted to appoint J. E. Sargent "as agent of said proprietors to execute and deliver to S. P. Cobb a good and valid deed of said academy, buildings and land for the sum of $400." It does not appear that this deed was ever executed, for what reason is not known, but it seems queer that a company of men should embark in such an enterprise and after spending so much money, and feeling, not to say passion, in five years be so anxious to get it off their hands.

But little remains of interest concerning the academy. The institution was re-established in 1852, its fortunes having varied with the years up to 1854, when, under the care of Charles C. Webster, it reached its greatest fame, with a total of 206 scholars, 114 males and 92 females; with a classical department designed to prepare for college, a higher English and common English department, and four terms a year. Eleazer Martin was president of the corporation; Jonathan Kittredge, vice-president; Jesse Martin, secretary, and Horace Chase, treasurer. William P. Weeks, S. P. Cobb, Jonathan Kittredge, Arnold Morgan and Caleb Blodgett were the executive committee of the corporation. There were seven instructors and the scholars came from all over the country, although for the most part from Canaan and the surrounding towns. Mr. Webster gave up the school in 1856, having been here three years, and removed to Minnesota. Burrill Porter, Jr., continued it for another year, with a corps of six teachers and 171 pupils. Since that it ceased to be a corporation and became simply a private school, with wide intervals of time when the building was closed. Occasionally some one came along who would open a school and continue it for one or two terms, contributing nothing towards the support or care of the building, and little towards their own.

Through the energy of J. D. Weeks and William A. Wallace as trustees of the academy, the school was revived in 1870, and continued with different teachers until 1878. Some of them were Herbert Norris, J. Clement Story in 1876; William Sharp and B. E. Goodrich in 1877. For fourteen years its doors were closed and then in 1891 it was opened by Prof. Luther Purmot. Hugh Moore was the last person to open a school.

In 1854 the town was asked to paint the academy, fix up the yard and put a fence around it; they refused to do it and the fence was built by private subscription. Parts of it are still in existence on the line between the academy land and the adjoining owner on the south. Repairs have been made to the building by private subscription from time to time. In 1904 the town library having attained such proportions, it was deemed advisable to move it into the academy building, where it occupies the upper floor. The town having appropriated part of the money to fit it up for that purpose and the balance being raised by voluntary contributions.

The question has arisen, who owns the academy? In reading this detailed statement of the facts, relating to the doings of the proprietors of the academy, it is evident that so long as the corporation existed it considered itself the owner of the building. The town having refused a deed from the proprietors, exercised no control over their doings. The money which built the academy was borrowed, and the town was only a creditor of those sixty-five individuals who signed the notes. What was done with the money was immaterial to the town. The town at first sought to replace this money in the funds from which it had been taken, but a change of feeling led it to distribute the balance of the surplus revenue among the other inhabitants. Realizing that the proprietors had had more than their share, they sought to make them pay the difference back to the town; this they never did. The town is in the position of having paid for something which they would not accept, and not enforcing their demand for their money to be returned, but silently allowing it to remain. Some might say that by their silence, they had accepted the disposition which had been made of their money, and are really in the position of being owners of the property, since their money paid for it.

At this day some are jealous of the apparent exercise of ownership of some people over the building, but no one claims it. If one person or another does anything to protect and preserve this old landmark of the Street, it is done with a feeling of respect for the memories which must cluster around its portals. Unique in its position, it stands as a monument to the expression of the most trying times in the history of the town. Deserted and alone, it attracts the attention of every newcomer, who wonders that it should be so neglected. Like a bone that has been quarreled over by two dogs, it has been dropped, never to be taken up again. The generation in whom the worst parts of man's nature was aroused has passed away. More than sixty years have elapsed since it was a disturbing factor; not one of the signers of the thirteen notes is alive today; not one of the men who opposed their plans. The questions disputed at that time and at the bottom of all their hard feeling has long since been settled, and their children and grandchildren have grown up with no remembrance of the spite and abuse thrown broadcast by their parents and grandparents. The issue is dead and forgotten; the slave question has ceased to be; abolition, too; and we of this day can little realize the depth to which men's feelings were stirred. Such is the history of the attempts to establish a school of learning in Canaan, and when we look back upon its stormy course at no time having the good will and sympathy of all the people of the community, bitterly opposed and as bitterly favored, living along from year to year on the persistence some men have to accomplish their ends, and using the object in dispute only as a means, blind to the good there might be in it itself, if spite and revenge be eliminated, the good in it became secondary to the success of their plans for revenge, resorting to trickery, force and unlawful means to bolster up or oppose. Is it any wonder that such a cause should fail, when dependent upon such influences, that people who had not become involved should hesitate to take any part?

CHAPTER XX

LAWYERS.

There were no lawyers among the early settlers of Canaan, and from the appearance of all the written documents that have come into my possession not any very learned men. There was very little use for law or lawyers so long as these men were contending simply with forests and wild beasts. Disputes relative to land titles were easily adjusted by the proprietors' committees and the surveyor with his compass. It was many years after the first arrivals before the people had need of courts of justice or of lawyers. Every man felt himself constrained to be neighborly, friendly and forbearing, because each one was dependent upon every other one for some of the comforts in their rough life. In like communities, where the labor of the day was followed by the rest of the night, there was no place for the idle and dissolute either to rest or amuse themselves.

George Harris, who followed close upon the footsteps of Thomas Miner in 1767, was an intelligent business man with a good education. Having the interests of the new colonists greatly at heart, he exerted a wise influence over them, so that while he lived, the uneven tempers were held in subjection, and for many years there were more precautions taken against wild beasts than dishonest men. In those first years, when it was necessary to observe forms of law, in order to give binding effect to the wishes of some grantee, recourse was had to Bezaleel Woodward of Hanover, or Benjamin Wheaton of Lebanon, both of whom held commissions as justices of the peace under the king.

About the year 1779 William Ayer, holding a commission as justice of the peace from the governor of Massachusetts, came with his wife to make his home in Canaan. Nathan Follensbee, a young friend, accompanied him; they came from Amesbury, Mass., and on their arrival were very hopeful of their future in the new settlement. They secured lands on South

West Canaan

Road, near enough to be neighbors, and built log houses for their first shelter, as did all the early settlers, because of the scarcity of sawed timber. Mr. Nathan's father and a hired man came with them also and located upon the farm once owned by Farrington Currier, and Mr. Ayer upon the next adjoining, afterwards owned by Daniel Farnum. After building his log house, Mr. Follensbee, with his father's assistance, felled five acres of trees, burned over land and raked in the seed, but the early frosts killed the crop; then he returned to Haverhill and brought back a wife, Anne Sawyer. They lived here several years and had three sons born to them. It is related that after the fire which had burned the brush and timber which her husband had felled, that the ground was black with ashes and coal, there was nothing green left growing near his cabin. Mrs. Follensbee visited her neighbor, Mrs. Ayer, and told her how dismally black everything was about her home, and begged of her a handful of green turf, which she carried home in her handkerchief and transplanted. The seasons from 1785 to '90 were severe; untimely frosts cut off the crops of the farmers and even their seed was lost. Discouraged by the unpropitious seasons, Mr. Follansbee sold his lands and moved to Hampstead, where his eldest daughter, Martha, was born, July 30, 1793. She married Hubbard Harris, Jr., who was a trader on the Street and built the house long the residence of Dr. Arnold Morgan, now owned by Mrs. Henry Martin. One other sister, Betsey, was born in Hampstead in 1795. Afterwards, not pleased with his manner of life he was persuaded by his friend Paddleford and Capt. James Huse, to return to this region and buy lands on Shaker Hill in 1796. In 1797 his daughter Sarah was born. She married George Harris, a brother of Hubbard. Mr. Follensbee died in Enfield after a long and eventful life.

Mr. Ayer had received a good education and was somewhat familiar with legal lore. He was not too modest to let his townsmen know that he could make his services as valuable to them as those of Wheaton and Woodward and at less trouble. The legal business of the colonists consisted chiefly in the making and acknowledging of deeds. The days had not yet come when they could afford to spend their time and substance in litigation. Mr. Ayer served the people as justice, conveyancer and adviser, and also in many town offices. He was an honored resident of Canaan about twenty years, when the failing health of his wife induced him to sell out his farm to Daniel Farnum and return to Massachusetts. But there were other men in town competent to perform all the legal services which the people required in their business intercourse. Thomas Baldwin was one of these men. Being a ready writer, he was often called upon to make deeds and wills, some of which are quaint and picturesque in their phraseology. I have several of them in my possession written in a fair, round hand.

Daniel Blaisdell, also, the first of the name, was a growing man and became so familiar with legal forms and requirements that he was generally selected to present questions to the courts, duties which he performed satisfactorily and for small compensation. He was not a learned man, but possessed a good judgment and a retentive memory. Then there was "Esq." John Currier, who was almost uninterruptedly engaged in business of a public kind all his life. These were the lawyers in those early days who were sufficient unto the wants of the people. Lawyers as such found little encouragement to stop here for several seasons, but chiefly because there was neither time nor money to squander on such luxuries. In nearly all bargains or trades it was agreed that payments should be made in farm products, labor, etc.

At or about the time of the building of the meeting house, there came into town a lawyer, who with strong assurance told the people that they needed him, or at any rate he needed them, for they appeared to be thrifty and ought to have a good many nice questions in law to talk over, and he proposed to stay and get his living among them. His name was Nathanial Farrer, but the people did not take kindly to him. He secured board with Capt. Moses Dole. He remained here a year or more, and in that time occurred the first lawsuit in Canaan. Capt. Robert Barber had bought a nice horse, at a low price, from a stranger who was passing through town, and was much pleased with his bargan. The captain was a short, pussy man, wore breeches and a long waistcoat, like old Uncle John Barber, and was a good sort of a man, but always busy, too much so to pay much attention to children; in fact, children got very little away from home. About the only salutation they got from him was "take care boy, don't meddle with things." A short time afterwards a man from one of the Vermont river towns appeared in our street, inquiring for a horse which he said had been stolen from him. He described the horse and the thief, saying he had traced them as far as this village. Being directed to Captain Barber, he saw and claimed the horse as his property, but Captain Barber declined to part with it without consideration, whereupon the claimant set Lawyer Farrer upon him, brought him into court and replevined the horse. The captain paid the costs with an ill grace. He said it was "all along of harboring a lawyer in town, whose only means of living was by the misfortunes of honest people." The captain's chargin at being cheated by a horse thief was very great, and he continued to pour out the vials of his wrath upon lawyers as the natural allies of thieves, until the sympathies of the people were awakened in his favor and Mr. Farrer was regarded as a man who might make mischief among them. Be that as it may, our hardworking ancestors were not yet ready to engage in suits at law. They knew it to be expensive, and so they continued to rely upon their friends, whose previous faithful services were a guaranty for the future. Mr. Farrer, finding his cases did not multiply, and that his clothes were getting seedy, left town, and there is no further trace of him to be found in our annals. In part payment for his board bill due Elias Lathrop, he pledged two blank books, unruled and bound in sheep, with his name upon the fly-leaf. These books are now in my possession, containing valuable memoranda concerning the meeting house, and the reorganization of the Baptist church in 1802.

For several years little variation was noticeable in the lives of our people. They labored diligently upon their lands and prayed for the prosperity of the church, which was without a pastor, but was feebly, yet vainly, struggling to find a man to take charge of their spiritual affairs, one whose teachings they could follow with faith and trust; but it was many years yet before those prayers were answered. For amusement they had for a long time an adjourned town meeting, which they regularly attended, and scolded about the dilatorious conduct of the contractors in building and finishing the meeting house.

In 1808 Thomas Hale Pettingill, a graduate of Dartmouth College in 1804, and just then admitted to the bar, visited relatives in Canaan, and concluded it would be a good field for him to work in. He was the son of Benjamin and Polly Pettingill of Salisbury, born November 20, 1780. He read law with John Harris of Hopkinton. He built the house, later the residence of Jesse Martin, and opened an office in one of the rooms in the spring of 1808. At first he met with indifferent success. The old prejudice against lawyers was active and demonstrative; but he persevered, and when told they had no use for his kind of man, he would shrug his shoulders and wait. He had not long to wait, not more than a year, before he had the whole town by the ears. His labors necessitated the appointment of a sheriff, and this officer planned how he could gain a living by this office. The next thing of importance was a court; and from that day onward until now Canaan has never been without a lawyer, with his attendant sheriff and court, and the evidence is conclusive that all of them escaped the fate of Farrer. No one of them has ever since been starved out, with the exception of George Kimball and John H. Slack. Mr. Pettingill's diligence and success surprised his friends. His legal machinery ground slow but sure. Many of the best and most quiet citizens were taken in his toils, and paid him homage. One record shows that from the 2d day of July, 1808, to February 23, 1811, a period of two years and eight months, Mr. Pettingill brought 193 suits before John Currier, Esq., the court's fee in each case being charged at sixty-seven cents. The first case this young lawyer brought was Nathaniel Tucker v. J. Smith. The case was a trivial one, a misunderstanding in the settlement of a small account, but it served for a beginning as well as if it were of national importance. Mr. Pettingill was aggressive in his temperament, was not famous for courtesy or neighborly kindness; he was persistent in the pursuit of an object, and no mere personal consideration turned him aside from the attainment of his fixed purpose to get rich. He liked directness and hated all shams, but he was never a great favorite with the people, although they appreciated his ability, and for three years he held three town offices at one time. He was representative in 1814, 15 and 16, moderator from 1813–20, town treasurer from 1813–20, and member of the school committee from 1811–20. In his earlier years he was a Federalist. In 1817 he published a burlesque upon Jefferson and his friends, called "The Yankee Traveller; or, the Adventures of Hector Wigler"; later he changed his opinions, became ashamed of the literary venture and tried to recall it from circulation. When he left town he had made no impress upon its institutions nor upon the hearts of the people that would lead them to cherish his memory. Many incidents are remembered of him which illustrate his sharp wit and self-reliance. His imperious disposition manifested itself in all the walks of his life. He was the first candidate for the rights and benefits of Masonry in the then new Mt. Moriah Lodge, which was organized in 1814. The records show that he carried his temper into the lodge room. Another lawyer, Elijah Blaisdell, of whom we shall hear more further on, had located in Canaan; he also was a member of that lodge. Being of the same profession and of similar traits and habits, they had frequent altercations. Then there were complaints; one day it was the complaint of Brother Pettingill against Brother Blaisdell, and a committee appointed to consider the same. At the next communication was a report that the belligerants had settled their difficulty, and there was nothing further to report. Next time it would be a complaint Blaisdell v Pettingill, and the committee would go over the same routine; then there would be difficulties with Nathaniel Pierce, and again with Doctor Tilton, and all ending in the same way, and each showing arbitrary temper on the part of the members of the bar.

A demand against Amasa Jones was left with him for collection. He sent Amasa a letter which brought him quickly to his office. Amasa objected to paying fifty cents for the letter and began to plead his hard times. Pettingill took up his pen and wrote figures. Amasa asked him why he wrote. Pettingill replied, "I'm charging you ten cents a minute for the time you keep me waiting, I can't afford to do all this talking for nothing," and then Amasa made haste to pay the bill without further objections to the price of the letter.

In 1813 he subscribed one dollar towards the support of Elder Wheat; three years afterwards, when Mrs. Stephen Worth died, and the elder at the funeral charged Stephen with being an infidel, greatly offending the whole congregation, Pettingill, Colonel Wells, John M. Barber and William Richardson, withdrew their promises of support, and declared they would never hear him preach again. Mr. Pettingill resided in Canaan until 1822, and his going was much like his coming. His father, grown old, desired him to come home and live with him. He declined; his chances for wealth were too good to be abandoned here. As a further inducement the old man told him to sum up all his gains during his residence in Canaan and if he would come to him he would double the sum. The lawyer counted up his gains, until they amounted to over ten thousand dollars, which surprised the old man into the remark that he feared Tom had not been very considerate; but he made good his promise and in 1822, with reluctance, Lawyer Pettingill turned his back upon the field of his legal triumphs, leaving it in possession of his antagonist, Blaisdell, and settled down in his native town of Salisbury, where he continued to reside, with the exception of two years spent in Franklin, until his death, August 8, 1856, at the age of 75 years. He married Aphia Morse at Cornish in February, 1810. They had one son and two daughters.

Old Jim Woodbury was a Revolutionary soldier, whom Pettingill often met, and to his salutation, the old man's uniform answer was "I'm a leetle better than I was yesterday, Mr. Pettingill." Pettingill's reply to this refrain was, "Well, Uncle Jim, you've been a leetle better every day since I knew you, and you are about as miserable now as a man can be and live; you must have been an almighty mean man before anyone else knew you."

There was Henry French of Grafton, who applied to him for a certificate to teach a district school. After a short examination, Pettingill gave French a certificate reading that "he was fully competent to teach school in any district where there were no scholars."

Elijah Blaisdell, born in Canaan October 29, 1782, was the son of Hon. Daniel Blaisdell. November 14, 1802, he married Mary

Fogg of Hampton, daughter of John Fogg, and settled down in Pittsfield as a shoemaker. At the age of twenty-seven, with a wife and three children dependent upon him, he concluded that shoemaking was not his strong point! he might get rich, but he never would become famous; so laying aside his last and apron, he entered an office in Montpelier, Vt., and for three years applied himself to the study of law, and was admitted to the bar. For a few years he loitered about in search of a location. He tried Grafton and Danbury, but the people were not sufficiently litigious. About 1812 he located on Canaan Street, in the house afterwards occupied by Albert Pressey. About the same time he was appointed "side" judge of the court of common pleas for the county of Grafton. He resigned in 1834 and was appointed county solicitor and reappointed five years after. He was also the colonel of a regiment of militia. His second wife was Mrs. Mary Kingsbury of Plainfield. Here Pettingill already had a court with all its machinery in full blast. Here he lived and labored until 1833, when he sold out and removed to Lebanon. He died in Lebanon October 10, 1856. In politics he began a Federalist, and was elected to various town offices, also to the Legislature in 1827–28. Upon the election of General Jackson in 1828, he visited Washington to see the inauguration ceremonies, and he was received with so much affability by the old general that he became his warm supporter and forever afterward voted and talked as a Democrat. In 1835, when for a season Abolitionists had no legal rights and public opinion was as merciless as an octopus, he returned to Canaan, and harrangued the assembled people upon the importance of "driving the niggers out of our beautiful town," even if it became necessary to destroy the academy building to accomplish that purpose. He was made a Mason in Mount Moriah Lodge in 1814, and he soon became upon all occasions the rival and antagonist of his brother Pettingill. In their temperaments, these two men were much alike, arbitrary and overbearing, impatient of restraint, not scrupulous of the rights and feelings of others, and in the innumerable suits which they promoted, were always pitted against each other. Their language to each other was far from polite, and a stranger would suppose them to be bitterly hostile, but when the time arrived for making up bills of costs, they would come readily together to divide the spoils in great seeming friendliness.

Mr. Blaisdell held the office of judge of probate for several years, during the supremacy of the Democratic party. He was sent to the Legislature in 1826; was selectman in 1822-24-25-28-31 and 32. But with all his long years and his opportunities for usefulness, he left no memorial of services by which a succeeding generation will recall his name as a benefactor.

George Kimball was born in Harvard, Mass., in 1787, son of Benjamin and Nancy (Wilder) Kimball; he graduated at Dartmouth College in 1809; read law with Stephen Moody at Gilmanton, and was admitted to the bar and settled in practice at Union, Me., in March, 1813; from thence he went to Warren, Me., in 1814. For many years he was a successful teacher in the public schools in Concord and in Richmond, Va., and also in the island of Bermuda in 1815, where he married a lady who was the owner of many slaves. On his return he brought one of them, named Nancy, as a servant for his wife, and through all the vicissitudes of their lives, Nancy remained faithful and true to her mistress. In 1824, he turned his attention to journalism, and became editor of *The Concord Register*. He was a gentleman of refinement and intelligence, companionable and of amiable disposition, a good storyteller and a writer of fair ability, but he was indolent, exceedingly fond of snuff and good whiskey, too much so to meet with success in a calling that requires active industry, tact and a quick perception. Of the duties of editorial life, he was a dreamer and oftentimes when his mind should have been active in his business, he would sit for hours nibbling his pen or gazing into vacancy, and when at last roused by the call of the boy for "copy," he would start up with "Yes, yes, boys, in a few minutes"; and instead of sitting down to his work himself, would start off and beg his friend, George Kent, to "help him out just once more."

In the fall of 1826, he had become weary of journalism; it interfered with his fixed habits of indolence. His friends advised him to return to the law, and that Canaan would be a good place to locate. There were sheriffs here, and justices and all the machinery for making a first-class reputation. Pettingill was gone and Elijah Blaisdell alone remained as an antagonist. He came here and opened an office and in a few months after received the appointment of postmaster. He was a scholar and an agreeable speaker, but his manner of life had not made him familiar with legal practice. Business flowed in upon him, but in the details of legal forms he made mistakes and was often obliged to ask leave to amend his declarations. Blaisdell harassed and annoyed him and he as usual had recourse to his old Concord friends for relief. Moody Kent was his mentor and N. P. Rogers of Plymouth, his *fidus Achates*. They partially directed his cases and carried him triumphantly through many difficulties.

Mr. Rogers was a man of rare talents. His mind was severely disciplined by study, reading and observation. His brain was active, and scattered gems of thought through the columns of the papers of that day. Whoever was fortunate enough to secure his friendship, found in him a great soul, true as the magnet, full of noble and unselfish sentiments. As a letter writer, he was without an equal in his time. He stood watch over Kimball as if he was his own child, and his advice will be worthy of attention ages hence. The following is dated May 3, 1829:

I must request you to act as to Nell in *loco guardiani* (if this is grammar), as to her school ("Nell" was Ellen Farrand, Mrs. Rogers' sister, who was teaching in Canaan) and assist her in her studies *ad interim* (pater again). Converse well in her hearing, for you can advise and instruct as well as Burns could, whether you "peek the sede" any better than that adviser, I don't judge. One thing I want to say you, don't run in debt at the store; estimate your stores of little articles, and muster money and pay down for all you buy and buy at cash prices; otherwise you will always be thinking about it or you will forget that you owe and will spend what will pay the debts. Pay your sheriff often, and make your magistrate work cheap, pay him but part entry fee. Make out all your ex'ons yourself, and let him sign them, and pay him nothing for signing blanks. Debt is the worst evil on earth, next to dishonesty. Of all things a classical gentlemanly spirit should keep free of dependence on the vulgar traders that we sometimes find in the world. Of all tyrants in the world, the most tyrannical is the brute that gets power by vending rum and tobacco. Don't suppose that I have in my eye any of your neighbors, I have not. But I give you and suggest this caution — that's all.

Here is another that is so well salted and spiced that I cannot withstand the temptation to copy it entire:

Plymouth, Aug. 5, 1829. Dear K———. Court, like a pay day or a day to be hung on, draws nigh apace, and I find among other perils that await you and me, is the case of *Gilman v. Dutton*. Sit down and write me the facts in the case as they occurred, and as we can prove them. You must see the witnesses and hear their stories, and take fire at them. We must prepare that case well. Ascertain whether the witnesses will testify *viva voce* better than on paper, i. e., whether their lies will appear most plausible in a deposition or from the tongue.

I want you to be as industrious as a pis-mire. There is no reason why you and I, having common sense, should be less diligent than those who have not got it. What a miracle it would be if we should devote four hours each day to the study of the law, and now in our "sere and yellow" time of life rise like a couple of Darien eagles to the very mid-heaven of eminence! Would it not be worth while, eh! No more of this, which prudence (if you had it) would lead you to burn. All that your worldly friends think you lack is hawk-eyed cunning, sharpness at money-getting, ambition and industry to cut and thrust in the law, and to heap up gain, as some of them are doing. I tell them your happiness and excellence and safety consist in your freedom from that infernal disposition to clutch at everything you see, like most of them,—though I want you to study law a little harder (I mean I am doing it) and be as economical as Franklin and prudent in your bargains, not sharp; to be sharp is imprudent. I am at the end of my sheet and entirely your friend. N. P. R.

In the money matters, Mr. Kimball was not a prudent man. He had all the business he could attend to, but it only tended to poverty. He had a bad habit of paying his sheriff and court fees, and charging them to his client, and then instead of collecting his costs, would borrow money, and buy everything on credit. He was an enthusiast and, like his Plymouth friend, a natural reformer. He was largely instrumental in building the Congregational Church in 1828. In connection with Rev. Mr. Foster and Jonathan Kittredge, he joined the new and untried temperance movement, which has been moving ever since. The anti-Masonic wave, which started from Buffalo in 1826, reached through New Hampshire in 1829. With his friend, Rogers, he plunged enthusiastically into its seething vortex and though not a Mason, he successfully talked about the "wicked deeds of that horrible institution, that was afraid of the light," and through his influence, Nathaniel Currier, John Shepherd and

Hubbard Harris, were induced to make public renunciation of their Masonic obligations. This greatly enraged the Masons, and Jacob Trussell and Elijah Blaisdell said "they might just as well have renounced everything else, for although members of the lodge, neither of them could explain what they had renounced."

Mr. Kimball was naturally sympathetic. When Garrison appeared as the champion of the enslaved race, Kimball with Rogers, joined him and were ever after identified with the movement. They were greatly instrumental in building "Noyes Academy" and in changing its original features so as to admit colored pupils. They had a right to do this; but the public opinion of those days was as much enslaved as the negroes, and was fierce and brutal in its instincts as the hyena. The beautiful fabric which those unselfish men had erected and whose dedication to freedom of thought ought to have made it sacred, was rudely thrown down, and the grand object for which it was so carefully nursed into being, disappeared forever in one day. The mob, which on the 10th of August, 1835, defied law, violated private rights and destroyed the germs of what would have become one of the most flourishing institutions of learning in the country, was simply the creature of public opinion, remorseless and cruel, which pervaded the land through all its widespread territory. It was not a Canaan mob, for with all their evil passions then fired up, there was a lack of courage in the men of Canaan to perform such deeds. They gave Ichabod Bartlett five dollars to tell them if they had any legal rights to destroy the "nigger school." He did tell them that every man standing by and consenting thereto made himself liable to the penalties of the law — provided public opinion should ever allow a jury to find them guilty. This contingency was so remote that it placed no restraint upon the mob. This digression is made because Mr. Kimball was acting as the agent of such men as Samuel E. Sewall, Samuel H. Cox, Arthur Tappan, David L. Child, Benjamin Lundy, and the great body of Abolitionists of the country, who cherished the hope that this free academy might be instrumental in developing the capacities of the negro, and in some degree mitigating the social rigors that environed his race. The ferocity of the mob spirit amazed and for a time paralyzed the friends of that school. The people were seized with the idea that Abolitionists were to be exterminated with or without law. At public meetings, finding themselves in a minority and treated as public enemies, they for a time refrained from attending them and waited for the reaction of the public mind, which was sure to come.

Mr. Kimball found it to his interest to leave town. In 1836 he went to Alton, Ill., and in company with Hubbard Harris engaged in mercantile business; Nathaniel Currier furnished $6,000 as part of their capital. When the mob of Alton attacked Lovejoy's office, killed Lovejoy and threw his press and type into the Mississippi, Kimball was present, but not as one of the defenders. He was not successful in trade, and he returned to the East. He remained East a short time, for fortune did not favor him, being almost constantly embarrassed. At his wife's solicitation, they returned to Bermuda about 1840, where for twenty years he was a teacher and lawyer in the town of Hamilton. In 1858 he died, a weary old man.

John Hancock Slack, A. M., son of John and Betsey (Ide) Slack, was born at New London in June, 1789, and died at Loudon County, Va., August 2, 1857, aged 68. He was graduated from Dartmouth College in 1811, and taught school at Hopkinton. He read law with Hon. Moses P. Payson of Bath, and Hon. John Harris and Baruch Chase of Hopkinton, and was admitted to the bar in 1817; practised at Andover, Pembroke, Goffstown and New Castle (Hill); was a resident of Canaan in 1829 and 1830, where he taught a select school in the hall of Gordon Burley's store; and occasionally, when other lawyers were out of sight, had some practice. Leaving Canaan about 1830, he went to Canada and then drifted southerly to Georgetown, D. C.; thence to Fairfax County, Va., and afterwards to Loudon County, where he died. He married Lydia, daughter of Levi Hastings of Wilton, about 1825. When he resided here in the old Baptist parsonage, which Albert Pressey last occupied, he was a poor man; he had never been successful, either as a teacher or lawyer; he often appeared like a hunted man, and many reports to his disadvantage were circulated and he seemed generally to be under a cloud. He often said he was confident he would live down all the evil that was said of him. At Georgetown he established a college and referred to many of the leading men of Washington as trustees and visitors. He started out well, but had not the faculty of holding on, therefore, he often fell by the wayside. He belonged to a class of men who make good servants, but cannot serve themselves; they need a directing mind. Perhaps some part of the ill success which attended his life was due to his partner. His home life was neither cheerful nor tidy, and he seemed to think that apologies for personal blemishes were due as a matter of course to visitors. To his boy scholars, he was always kind and friendly; for myself I always had a warm place for him in my heart.

Jonathan Kittredge, LL. D., was the son of Dr. Jonathan and Apphia (Woodman) Kittredge, born in Canterbury, July 17, 1793; graduated at Dartmouth College in 1813. He read law with Bleecker & Sedgwick at Albany, N. Y., and Roswell William Lewis of New York City, and began practice at the last place in 1817. It is not known how long he remained in that city, but soon after the departure of Mr. Pettingill in 1822, he opened an office in Canaan and resided here until 1827, when he removed to Lyme, where he married Julia Balch on February 8, 1829; he resided there until 1836. Before he came to Canaan he had contracted an appetite for strong drink, his case seemed almost hopeless; no man could have been worse; he had thrown off self-respect, lost caste in society, his brethren of the bar shunned him, and clients seldom sought his counsel. In those days when rum was almost as common a drink as cider, and many drunkards traversed the highways crookedly, the trail of Mr. Kittredge was the crookedest. Some efforts were made to reclaim and save him by a few friendly brethren of the bar, and particularly by that great-souled gentleman, N. P. Rogers, whose hand and heart always went out to the weary and heavy laden; and there were some too, who for reasons of their own, urged him on, apparently pleased with his self-abasement. The appetite for drink clung to him like the shirt to Nessus, and dragged him down until he could get no lower and no word of reproach or kindness could rouse him to contend with the demons that had seized him, but to the Rev. Amos Foster, is due his reformation in 1825, as elsewhere related. While at Lyme he wrote and delivered an address upon temperance, January 8, 1827, which when published, gave him almost a national reputation. The address was reprinted in England, France and Germany, and exerted a powerful influence for good upon the thoughtful world. The State Temperance Society appointed him its agent in 1832 and he edited its newspaper in 1834.

There was not much need of lawyers in Lyme, either before or since that period, but Mr. Kittredge continued to reside in that town among friends who tenderly watched over him, until he should gain courage and strength to meet his old enemy and all his bad forces in the wide world's arena. In 1836 he returned to Canaan, a period when society was almost resolved into its original elements; that is, the professed Christian men of the town had gone back to original sin. Hatred, vituperation and slander filled all hearts and mouths. It was here during the next eight years he won an honorable reputation as an able, skilful and well-read lawyer, for fair dealing and humanity as a man, for sincerity as a Christian and proved himself resolute and fearless in the pursuit of an object. Bad men avoided him, and when charged with slandering him, slunk away and denied it.

In politics he was a Whig, and disclaimed any sympathy with Abolitionists or Free-soilers, but in the excitements of those days, he never forgot that strength and numbers, even when upheld by public opinion, were not always guarantees of justice; and thus he soon found himself in full accord with the opposition to the wild elements that disturbed society and called itself patriotism. He was rough and uncouth in many ways, even with his friends, and those who disliked him sometimes called him "hog," or some equivalent phrase without defining whether they intended it as a compliment to him or it. He was considered a safe counselor, always true to his clients. Only on one occasion did we ever hear his integrity impugned, and that was in the settlement of an estate, when upon rendering his final accounts, the judge after looking over the items and seeing an enormous fee charged by the executor, exclaimed: "Mr. Kittredge, Mr. Kittredge, that is a most outrageous fee!" After some rough scolding, the fee was allowed, minus two hundred dollars. He was a politician, of course, and sought his own advancement; he was the leader of his party and could control all its elements. He succeeded very skilfully in throwing out a Democratic postmaster here and secured the place to himself, which he held several years in a very lax manner. Five times he was elected to represent the town in the Legislature in 1846-48 and 1851 and 1855. He held various town offices, especially such as were agreeable to him; was selectman in 1851 and moderator eight years; he went as delegate to the Philadelphia Convention in 1848, that nominated General Taylor, and was an active worker for his election.

In 1856 he was appointed chief judge of the court of common pleas, and held the office until the court was reformed out of existence in 1858. He was respected as a lawyer and judge, but he was not popular with either lawyers or clients. His brusque manner with other peculiarities among other members of the court, begat a hostility on the part of the bar that resulted in reforming the whole court, and several of its members, including Mr. Kittredge, were left out in the cold. In 1858 Dartmouth College conferred upon him the degree of LL. D. In the spring of 1859 he moved to Concord, where he continued to reside until his death, April 8, 1864, aged 71 years. His manner of leaving the court was not agreeable to him; he felt as if he had been struck by his political friends and it soured him towards many with whom he had always worked. The act was said to have been engineered through the Legislature by Cragin of Lebanon, who had been treated coarsely by Mr. Kittredge and took that method to be revenged. Both parties seemed to enjoy great pleasure in "reforming" that court.

Jonathan Kittredge's greatest victory was achieved over himself in his earlier years. He was held in honor and esteem by the good people here; he was a man of large ability. I do not feel myself competent to give an anaylsis of his capacity as a lawyer, but I can speak of him at home and in his neighborhood life and of his influence in affairs, some of his disappointments and his old age. His famous temperance address was given in the Congregational Church in 1829; I heard him speak it. There was a time here once when the waves of popular madness ran so high and wild that the law and the right of individuals were trampled upon and justice and truth were fallen in the streets. Jonathan Kittredge was the one courageous man to buffet the howling mob and rescue truth and justice from the evil passions that threatened them. His children, Ellen Maria, born December 7, 1838, died August 11, 1839; Edward C. Delevan, referred to elsewhere, and Jonathan Perry, born in Canaan December 13, 1840, married Ellen S. Bond of Worcester, Mass., December 26, 1872; enlisted in Company B, third New Hampshire Volunteers, August 23, 1861, was appointed hospital steward, September 9, 1862; mustered out August 23, 1864; was in the drug business in Concord under the name of Underhill & Kittredge.

William P. Weeks was the son of Brackett and Sarah (Pickering) Weeks, born at Greenland, February 22, 1803; graduated from Dartmouth College in 1826. He read law with Hon. William A. Hayes and Charles N. Coggswell of South Berwick, Me. Admitted to the bar in 1829 in Maine; November of that year he located here at the instance of his brother-in-law, Gordon Burley, whose large business affairs had become entangled and Mr. Weeks was set to work to straighten them out. Three other lawyers were already in practice on the Street, Blaisdell, Kimball and Slack. He soon afterwards entered the office of Mr. Blaisdell as a partner, and continued there for a short time, two or three years. There seemed to be small room for him, but he stayed on, believing that some or all of the others would soon have occasion to emigrate, and he would have an open field. Mr. Slack did leave within two years. Mr. Blaisdell in 1833, concluded to make his future home in Lebanon, and two years later Mr. Kimball formed a mercantile partnership in Alton, Ill., and quitted the field of his victories and defeats. When Mr. Weeks came to Canaan there existed here two parties with strong antagonisms, which arose chiefly from business complications, but politics was also a large factor. It was a vicious sentiment that delighted in tearing reputations, and showed itself in nearly all the walks of life. As events developed, it was impossible for any intelligent man to remain an indifferent spectator. He was a Democrat by natural inheritance, and when his party called the roll, he answered, and even until the day of his death, he was a strong leader here. The only time he was ever ashamed of his party was when the Legislature of 1854 passed resolutions hypocritically reciting that the extension of slavery into the territories was good cause for the dissolution of the Union. It was to catch the Abolition vote and failed of its object, because it was plain that neither the men nor the party were sincere in enacting those words. It placed the party in a false position, and it lost prestige for consistency. He might have added, had he lived, that in thirty successive years, it never regained its lost character. During the sad years when the Abolition trouble disturbed the social harmony he was a strong partisan. He took no active part in the early disputes, but his counsel and advice as well as sympathy were always at the service of the destructors. Threats of violence were freely made against the prominent men and women, and particularly against the colored boys.

It was through his timely counsel that the ruffians laid aside their clubs and stones. That party was made up of strong-minded, wilful, determined men, with none too much intelligence or education, but with brains enough to carry out their plans in their own way, which was not always gentle. Mr. Weeks always held these fierce spirits in restraint by quietly quoting the penalties of the law to them. His practice was extensive and lucrative, but it was chiefly in the branches of law relating to debt and credit, and the validity of titles. In these matters he made himself an authority.

He was never counted a great lawyer, but he was a correct business man and carefully attended to all affairs placed in his hands.

When the town voted to receive the surplus revenue, Mr. Weeks was appointed agent to receive and loan it to responsible parties. When the Academy was rebuilt, with money borrowed from the agent by the proprietors, they, finding the property a poor investment, influenced the town to take a deed of the building and give up the notes. There was strong feeling on the delivery of these notes. On being questioned, Mr. Weeks said: "Gentlemen, you need not be alarmed for those notes. They are safe in my possession, and when you make a proper call for them they will be forthcoming."

On July 28, 1833, to him a most important occasion, he married Mary Elizabeth Doe, daughter of Joseph Doe of Derry, and as the years went by three sons and two daughters were born to them.

In 1839, 1840, 1852, 1853 and 1854 he represented the town in the Legislature; he was also in the State Senate in 1848-49, being its president the last year; was also in the Constitutional Convention in 1850, a famous body of politicians, who went up to Concord, drank brandy and smoked cigars at Gass' Hotel for several months, and ripped and tore away at the old Constitution so fiercely that scarcely a fragment was left, and when at last they sent it out to the world the people saw nothing in their labors to approve, and sat down hard upon it and squeezed the life all out of it. The cost of that mutilating convention was about $60,000, the payment of which was the only new fact the people realized concerning it. The honors attending the doing of that body of men never matured — verdict of the voters — killed by too much wet nursing.

Mr. Weeks, in the earlier years of his practice, was not always scrupulous of the means he used against his adversaries, and was unmerciful to debtors. Like many other young lawyers, his first rule of practice, was fees, costs and charges, and his second rule was to collect them. He had for a deputy for many years S. P. Cobb, whose levies were like the marches of the legions of Attila, the grass disappeared behind him. During the early days, and before the Northern Railroad was built, it was customary for the merchants in town to go to Boston to buy their goods. Before making this yearly trip it was necessary for them to have money to pay for what they wished to buy. All the merchants with the exception of Jesse Martin never had money enough ahead to pay for their goods, so that just before starting they would take their ledgers to Mr. Weeks and ask the loan of money upon their accounts. Mr. Weeks always loaned them, never charging more than $10 on a hundred dollars. The next day he would set his partner or clerk to writing letters to those whose names appeared as debtors on those books, asking them to call the next day and settle. These letters were not mailed, but were placed in the post-office in plain sight behind a string which held them up to the sight of every one. Very few failed to appear the next day if they received the letter, but as sometimes happened the debtor did not go to the office or hear of his having a letter, for some days, but when he did and hastened to Mr. Weeks' office he was told, "I waited twenty-four hours, and a writ has been made out, but I did not have it served, so I saved you that much. It will cost you about three dollars for the writ." Mr. Weeks was known to have had as many as 100 writs returnable at a single term of court, and not one of them contested, upon all of which he collected costs.

In the course of his forty years' practice he accumulated a large property, all of which descended to his children. His habits were all close. His sympathies were with the Methodist Church, but he seldom attended the service after their clergy began to pray for the slaves. He always read the *New Hampshire Patriot* and conformed to all the legends of the Democratic party. He never expressed sympathy for the Union cause during the war, but always maintained with Mr. Buchanan that the government had no right to coerce a state. In business his writs and summonses were always profitable; here he had no weaknesses. His liberality was not profuse. With all his success in business, his gains multiplying year by year for the long period he resided here, his name does not appear as a patron either of religion, learning or arts, and the only monument erected to record his virtues is that which stands above his grave.

In his later years he became in reality a banker, and his loans were great accommodations to persons in need of money, and it is only just to say that in his transactions as a banker he was lenient and honorable with his clients. He was a great lover of sheep and cattle and spent much time caressing his nice flocks. There were times during his practice here when he formed copartnerships. The first has already been referred to, the other two were with young gentlemen who had been students in his office, both of whom have risen to eminence in their profession, first at the bar, and then upon the bench of the state courts. These young men were J. Everett Sargent and Isaac N. Blodgett.

Mr. Weeks died suddenly, on January 8, 1870, by hanging himself from a beam in his barn, aged 66 years. He was a social and genial man and good story-teller.

Old Uncle Sam Whitcher carried the mail on horseback from Lebanon to Plymouth and return weekly for many years. After the postoffice department at Washington was burned, about 1838, the old man came into Mr. Weeks' office with a bundle of papers and asked him to look them over and collect what was due upon them. Upon examination they were found to be quarterly bills for carrying the mail for the entire period the old man had been in service. "Have you never received any pay for your services in carrying the mail, Mr. Whitcher?" asked the lawyer. "No — them's the bills," stuttered the old man. Mr. Weeks took off his spectacles and looking the old man straight in the eye, said very deliberately, "Mr. Whitcher, the vouchers in the postoffice department at Washington were not burned, as was at first reported; they are found to be all safe. Shall I collect these bills?" The old man listened awhile for something more to be said, then slowly gathered up his papers and as he opened the door to depart, turned and said, "I — I guess you needn't do nothing about these papers till I come again." But he never came.

Jonathan Everett Sargent, son of Ebenezer and Prudence (Chase) Sargent, the youngest of ten children, was born in New London August 23, 1816. The father was a poor farmer and the children had early in life to strike out for themselves. He worked upon his father's farm until he was seventeen. This was in 1833. His desire for knowledge grew upon him, and he arranged with his father that the remaining four years of his minority should be his own, to board by teaching school and any other labor that would pay, and clothe himself and call for nothing more from his father.

Mr. Sargent first came to Canaan as a teacher in Noyes Academy in 1838. He was the last teacher in the old building and the first in the new Canaan Union Academy. He was then an undergraduate at Dartmouth College of the class of 1840. At the opening term of this school there were 123 pupils. The following is in Mr. Sargent's own language:

I first went to Canaan in September, 1838, and taught that fall in the old academy building. Mr. Hobart, a classmate of mine, teaching in a hall at the north end of the Street the same term. I also taught in the old Academy the next winter. Three months after my return to Hanover, the latter part of February, 1839, the old academy building burned. A Mr. James Richardson, another classmate of mine, taught school during the spring term of 1839 in Martin's Hall, over the store of E. & J. Martin, at the south end of the Street, and during that spring and summer the new academy building was erected and was in readiness the first of September. I was employed to teach the first term at $40 per month for three months. I returned to Hanover that winter and remained till Commencement, 1840.

Mr. Sargent then entered the law office of Mr. Weeks and remained there until 1841, when he went South and taught there until the summer of 1842; then he returned to Canaan and formed a partnership with Mr. Weeks. He had been admitted to the bar in Washington, D. C., in April, 1842. In July, 1843, he was admitted to the bar of Sullivan County. During the season of 1843 he built the house now occupied by George E. Cobb, married Miss Mary C. Jones, daughter of John Jones of Enfield, and moved into the new house on Thanksgiving Day of that year. Here he lived until the summer of 1847, in partnership with Mr. Weeks. In a letter to me he says: "I recollect very well the first case I ever tried. It was in Mr. Weeks' office, before Eleazer Martin as justice. It was a complaint for assault and battery by a Mr. Sanborn against a Mr. Whittier. They lived at what is now East Canaan, not far from where the depot stands. It was before the railroad was built. I appeared for Sanborn, the plaintiff, and Mr. Kittredge appeared for the defendant. I succeeded in getting the defendant fined $3 and costs, which was a great success for my first effort. In the summer of 1847 I moved to Wentworth, where I lived and practiced law twenty-two years; since that time my residence has been in Concord."

During his residence in Wentworth he achieved all the judicial honors which the state could confer. During his residence in this town he was not unlike other young lawyers who have started out in their life career with ambitions first to gain money then to win honors. Lawyers are not much different from other classes of money-getters, except in the value they put upon their services. With them the making of the fee bill is reduced to an exact science, and the facility with which his work is itemized proves that in the study of the law this department of jurisprudence is seldom overlooked. He had a proficient teacher, and he was too apt a pupil not to take advantage of all his opportunities. He taught school here; he studied law here; he built a house and married here; he was an active politician and as such became postmaster, and he took a deep personal interest in the success of his party, which being the only party which could point a moral in its platform, was always to be successful. It seems here that wealth and its comforts began to pile up around him, but the blushing honors which he sought did not envelop him until after his departure, and then he had his fill,—a pleasant neighbor and intelligent gentleman.

In 1844 he was appointed solicitor of Grafton County. He was sent as representative from Wentworth in 1851, 1852 and 1853, and the last year was speaker of the House. He was translated to the Senate and became its president in 1854. In 1855 the Know-nothings swept the state like a cyclone, and every Democrat was swept overboard in the whirl. The same year Governor Metcalf generously offered him a seat on the bench of the court of common pleas. He held this office four years, when his court was abolished and he was translated to the bench of the Supreme Court, and became chief justice in 1873. In 1874 the Democrats elected the Legislature and that court was immediately abolished for the benefit of the party. Mr. Sargent then became simply an attorney, in partnership with William M. Chase of Concord. He held various other offices and trusts, and among them he worked up through all the secret mysteries of Masonry and was elected grand master of Masons in New Hampshire, a position as honorable, as exalted and desirable as any other he ever held. Then he retired from active business, and sat serenely back to enjoy the comforts and honors which long years of economy and study had showered upon him, a beneficent, courteous old gentleman, the most distinguished of all the great names which Canaan has furnished to adorn the bar of the state.

George W. Murray, son of John and Ruhannah (Wells) Murray, was born in Hill, July 31, 1830. He was educated at Andover Academy, taught school in Bristol and Wilmot; read law in the office of Nesmith and Pike at Franklin, and was admitted to the bar at the April term at Concord in 1855. In the same year he opened an office at East Canaan, being led to Canaan because of the appointment of Mr. Kittredge to the court of common pleas, thereby removing the most prominent lawyer in town at that time. That village grew up around him and during his thirty-five years' practice he won an enviable reputation as a sound lawyer. In 1857 he married Jeanette F. Barnes of East Lebanon, and six children were born to them. His advice and assistance was sought by all who could afford his charges, because it was believed his opinions were founded upon an absolute knowledge of the law. Like William P. Weeks, he became a sort of banker in the town, loaning much money to those who had security.

He was a Democrat until Fremont's campaign in 1856 and ever afterwards was a Republican. He served two terms in the Legislature, but although many men were his debtors whom he had helped out in tight places, he was not popular among the voters. He rarely sought office, knowing that the prejudice against a man with a little money was not favorable to political advancement unless some of that money was used. Mr. Murray was a Methodist and the most generous contributor to the support of that church at East Canaan. He was liberal in many ways where he saw that it was for the benefit of the town, but more particularly for his own village; his love for that led him at times to oppose everything that seemed to be for the benefit of any other part of the town. It is said of him that he has been the only lawyer in the state of New Hampshire who acquired as large a fortune by the practice of the law solely. His business transactions, however, always netted him a profit. Very careful, he never loaned money unless he knew where he was to get it back; this also made him enemies, for there are plenty of people who remain one's friends until they borrow money of you, then upon the first demand to pay they become more bitter enemies than they were friends. As has been said, "if you loan your friend money you will lose your money as well as your friend."

He died January 5, 1900.

Joseph D. Weeks, son of William P. Weeks, was born October 27, 1837, graduated from Dartmouth College in 1861, studied law with Daniel M. Christie of Dover with whom he practised for a short time; was admitted to the bar in 1864. At the request of his father he returned home, and was a resident in Canaan all the rest of his life. It was hinted at the time that the real reason for his being called home, was that his intercourse with the loyal men of Dover begat a desire to enlist in the Union army, but his father used such arguments as induced him to abandon his design, and he was discharged. He was a victim of the draft of '63 but paid John Moriarty $300 to go as his substitute. In the years of his practice here he ever manifested a disposition to bestow favors upon friends and other needy persons. He entered with enthusiasm into all schemes for the success of the Democracy, to which he bore unswerving allegiance. His legal attainments, although not profound, were equal to all his needs. And he devoted more time to cattle, horses and farming than to books. He was generous and friendly and was never charged with oppressing any poor wretch who happened to fall into the fangs of the law. This trait gave him great power in politics and he seldom met with defeat. Three times he was sent as representative from this town, in 1869, 1870 and 1880, and twice to the Senate, in 1875 and 1878. It was in the latter rôle that he distinguished himself under the Weston régime, by planting old John Proctor in Natt Head's seat, thereby making that body Democratic to the great disgust of the Republicans, who called it a fraud, and perhaps it was, but his party liked him all the better for it.

He was quite regular in attendance on Methodist preaching and often held a handkerchief to his eyes — to protect them from strong rays of light. He claimed that his attendance upon Sunday service was to set a good example; it was not often that he could repeat the text, or the substance of the preacher's remarks unless he involved himself in natural history. He was a liberal contributor to the church and paid it in such a free manner as to make one think it was doing him a favor in accepting it. Either as a lawyer or as a man, he was large of heart, sympathetic and friendly. He was very genial and entered heartily into all schemes to "drive dull care away."

He contributed willingly to everything that in any way affected the Street, not only in money, but with his influence. Every one called him "Joe." A good story-teller, and the story lost nothing in the telling if it could be made better by any additions. He never married, but was often suspected of having tender sentiments. It is not too much to assert that no man in Canaan ever won a stronger grip upon the respect and esteem of our people than he. With education and wealth, both of which give men high standing, the uses he made of these gifts won the hearts of men. Seldom a man applied to him in vain for help financially or otherwise. He lived among the people on the Street fifty-three years and died of apoplexy December 1, 1890.

William B. Weeks, a brother of Joseph D. Weeks, was born in 1839; educated in Canaan Union Academy, and graduated from Dartmouth College in 1861, read law with his father, and was admitted to the bar; practised in Canaan a short time and then emigrated to West Virginia, with the intention of making a home there, but the war was raging everywhere and northern men were not welcome. The people were not at all friendly and in a few months he wandered back to his native hills, and became an attorney in Lebanon, where he continued to reside. He married Miss Henrietta Bridgeman of Hanover in 1866.

Isaac Newton Blodgett was the son of Caleb and Charlotte (Piper) Blodgett. Caleb Blodget was born in Hudson in 1793, and moved from Dorchester to Canaan in 1833, and for a time lived in the old house torn down by O. H. Perry across the street from H. P. Burleigh's, where Isaac was born March 6, 1838. Caleb Blodgett was sheriff of Grafton County for many years, a clear-headed man whose advice was worth attention. He represented Canaan in the Legislature of 1841 and 1842, was a selectman from 1838 to 1841 and in 1849. He died October 5, 1872. Isaac N. was educated in Canaan Union Academy and was tutored for a time by his brother Caleb, at Leominster, Mass.; read law in the office of William P. Weeks and Anson S. Marshall, and was admitted to the bar in April, 1861. On May 24, 1861, he married Sarah A., daughter of Rev. Moses and Cynthia (Locke) Gerould of Canaan. For six months after the date of his admission to the bar he was a partner with Mr. Weeks, when he bought out the business and continued to practice in the same office until 1867. The building stood until the winter of 1906 just south of Miss Emma Bell's and was moved by H. P. Burleigh to be used by him for a carpenter's shop. In 1867, receiving an offer of partnership from Hon. Austin F. Pike of Franklin, he moved there, and under the firm name of Pike & Blodgett continued the practice of the law until 1878, when on November 19th he was appointed associate justice of the Supreme Court. On August 18, 1898, he became chief justice and held that position until his resignation in 1901. He was always a politician and a Democrat. He represented Franklin in the Legislature in 1871, '73, '74 and '78; was a member of the state Senate in 1879 and 1880; and of the Constitutional Convention of 1876, 1889 and 1903. He was chairman of the Democratic committee in the disastrous campaign of 1875, when the Senate "fraud" in favor of old John Proctor of 1874 reacted upon his labors and all the bright dreams of his party vanished into thin air. He was several years town treasurer of Franklin and proved himself a successful financier. He was successful as a lawyer and the conduct of his cases won for him respect and esteem from all parties. After retiring from the bench it was his wish to pass the remainder of his life in the quiet enjoyment of his last days. He did not wish to die in the harness, like his brother Caleb. But his fellow citizens would not leave him alone. He served two terms as mayor of Franklin without opposition, and he was called in consultation and as counsel by the brother members of his profession. He died at his home in Franklin, November 27, 1905.

Frank Dunklee Currier, son of Horace S. and Emma (Plastridge) Currier, was born in Canaan October 30, 1853; read law with Mr. Pike of Franklin and was admitted to the bar at Concord in April, 1874; spent one year with Mr. Murray at East Canaan, and then opened an office for himself in the same place. At the start he was fortunate in having a friend in Mr. Murray, who being ill was advised to take a two years' vacation from business. He turned many of his clients over to his young friend. Before entering seriously upon the labors of his profession, he took a look at the marvels and natural wonders of the country to the Pacific, including the mountain region. He was studious and energetic and managed his cases with a skill that gave him good standing as a lawyer, and his conduct was such as to give his friends confidence in his future success; but his ambitions lay in politics; its fascinations were more attractive than the abstruse themes of law. There was a Greenback craze and he was seized with it and was only rescued from being swallowed up in its vortex by a promise from his friends that he should be sent to Concord. He went to Concord one term, in 1879, and like other young men became conspicuous for much speaking. His ambition was to be conversant with all subjects, wise or otherwise. He asked for another trip to Concord, but the favor of the people was always uncertain; a breath of air, or a five-dollar bill has made and unmade many a reputation; he was defeated, but not discouraged. He still believed in political advancement, but had lost some confidence in popular favor; the same man is not always the favorite. Heroes of today are often laid upon the shelf tomorrow. He was secretary of the Republican State Committee from 1882 to 1890.

His quick memory, wit and knowledge of men and localities was of great service in closing out the campaign. He was clerk of the New Hampshire Senate from 1883 to 1887, exhibiting an active intelligence and knowledge of legislative matters that greatly facilitated business and gave him favor among the senators; was delegate to the Republican National Convention in 1884. He was elected senator in 1886 and was the president of that body; was naval officer at the port of Boston from 1890 to 1894. He was elected again in 1898 to the House of Representatives and was chosen speaker of that body. In 1901 Dartmouth College gave him the honorary degree of A. M. He was elected congressman from the Second District to the Fifty-Seventh, Firty-Eighth, Fifty-Ninth, Sixtieth, and Sixty-First Congresses. As a presiding officer his ability is recognized by the speaker of the House, who calls him oftener to the chair than any other congressman.

Irving C. George, son of Henry C. and Eleanor H. George, was born in Canaan in 1855; was educated at Canaan, Tilton and Meriden; read law with Mr. Mugridge of Concord; was admitted to the bar at Plymouth in November, 1877, and located at Newmarket. He married at Newmarket, in 1878, Miss Nellie A. Palmer, and had six children. At the request of his father he returned to Canaan and opened an office here; upon the death of his father he returned to Newmarket, where he now is.

Joseph Clement Story, son of Otis J. and Harriet (Clement) Story, was born August 20, 1855. His education was obtained from the schools of this town, Kimball Union Academy and Phillips Andover Academy in Massachusetts. He taught school at Canaan in the old academy on the Street, in 1876; his rule was strict, his ruler was stricter and many of us can remember being obliged to stand on the tops of the desks when we did not have our grammar lesson, or helping one another to hold a slab or a book at arm's length in the middle of the floor, when some of us did not return at recess or when the bell rang. He studied law in the office of George W. Murray, Pike & Blodgett at Franklin and E. B. S. Sanborn of Franklin; he attended Boston University Law School in 1879, and was admitted to the bar of this state in 1880; commenced the practice of law at Wentworth in 1880, where he remained for three years, when he went to Plymouth, where he continued the practice of his profession.

He married in March, 1881, Helen Smith. He died January 27, 1895, in Burlington, Vt.

William A. Flanders, son of Sylvester and Lois Flanders, born in Canaan, February 26, 1835; educated at Canaan Union Academy; read law in the office of G. W. Murray, and at that time was a much better scholar than his teacher; admitted to the bar in 1861 and opened an office in Wentworth, where he was not successful. He was a famous mathematician, good memory, well stored with knowledge, but his wisdom was all vanity,— one of those unfortunates who for lack of good advice fall by the wayside and are lost in the rubbish that falls over them. In 1866 he married Miss Angelina M., daughter of Prescott Clark of Canaan. He died in Wentworth in July, 1909.

Caleb Blodgett, elder brother of Isaac N. Blodgett, was born in Dorchester on June 3, 1832. He came to Canaan in 1833 with his parents; he was educated at Canaan Union Academy, and was graduated from Dartmouth College in 1856.

After graduation he taught in Leominster, Mass., with the intention of making this his life work, but after a few years he became tired of it and returned to Canaan, where he began the study of law. He completed his studies in the office of Barton & Bacon in Worcester, Mass., where he opened an office. He also practised in Stoughton, Mass., and in 1860 opened an office in Boston, Mass., where he practised successfully twenty years. In 1882 Governor Long appointed him to the bench of the Superior Court. Governor Russell offered him a place on the bench of the Supreme Court, which he refused, believing that his health and ability were better fitted for the trial and decision of jury cases, in which he held a unique position. Not a jury lawyer during his practice, when elevated to the bench where those cases were the principal ones tried, he became and was recognized as the ablest trier of civil cases with a jury on the bench. He married Miss Roxalina B. Martin, daughter of Jesse Martin of Canaan in 1866. Owing to failing health, he resigned from the bench September 1, 1900, and died on December 11, 1901, at his residence on Canaan Street, where he had spent his summers for many years. His love for his native village was great; no suggestions were ever made to him for its benefit but he was always ready to contribute, not only with money, but with his personal presence. His generosity towards the Street is proverbial; he was ready at all times to make up any deficiency. "If you want any more, come to me," I have heard him say many times. He took great pleasure in books in his library, which he had built just before his death on the north end of his barn.

Frank B. Clark, son of Henry W. and Emily E. (Rowe) Clark, was born in Enfield September 30, 1873. His education was obtained from the Enfield High School and a three years' course at the New Hampshire State College, after which he taught school, and in September, 1896, began the study of law in the office of Charles A. Dole at Lebanon; was admitted to the bar in July, 1899; he came to Canaan September 15, 1899, and has continued the practice of the law here since that time. He was married September 15, 1897, to Bernice E. Trescott, daughter of James A. and Abbie E. (Lamphiere) Trescott; she was born in Lyme, May 3, 1870. They have four children, Hugh T., born in Hanover, August 1, 1899; Earl L., born in Canaan April 26, 1901; Frank K., born May 1, 1905; Bernice P. A., born July 29, 1909. Mr. Clark has been a member of the school board of the High School District for five years, and tax collector for 1909 and 1910.

James Burns Wallace, son of William Allen and Mary (Currier) Wallace, was born in Canaan August 14, 1866; was educated in the district schools of the town, Canaan Union Academy, Hanover High School, New Hampshire Agricultural College; from 1881–82, St. Johnsbury Academy, graduating in the class of 1883; then entered Dartmouth College and graduated from the academic department in the class of 1887; taught one term of school on the Street in the winter of 1885; went to New York City in the fall of 1887, and for thirteen years was an instructor in mathematics in Cooper Union; was employed in the Seventh National Bank, and in the Bank of the State of New York until August, 1888, when at the instance of his cousin, William J. Wallace, presiding judge of the United States Court of Appeals, entered Columbia Law School in the fall of 1888. He studied there two years, and the last year was in the law office of Tracy, McFarland, Ivins & Platt; was admitted to the bar in New York County in November, 1890, and continued in the practice of the law in that city until 1905, when he removed permanently to Canaan. In 1900 was admitted to practice in the courts of New Hampshire, and although never having hung up any shingle, does not refuse to practice his profession. He married December 22, 1889, Alice Hutchinson, daughter of Lucius B. and Alice M. (Rollins) Hutchinson of New York City. He has been trustee of the town library since 1907; was a member of the town school board in 1907 and 1908; representative to the General Court in 1909, and was chairman of the committee on liquor laws and a member of the committee on revision of statutes; was appointed justice of the police court June 19, 1907. Mr. Wallace is a thirty-second degree Mason, with membership in Summit Lodge of Canaan; St. Andrew's Chapter, and Washington Council at Lebanon; Sullivan Commandery at Claremont, and the New Hampshire Consistory at Nashua; he is also a member of Kimball Chapter, Order of the Eastern Star, at Lebanon, and a noble of Bektash Temple of the Mystic Shrine at Concord.

CHAPTER XXI.

SOLDIERS.

Canaan ought to be a loyal and patriotic town. It has been largely fertilized with the remains of patriotic men. In all her graveyards repose the dust of those who in the gloom of the uncertain result of the Revolution, enlisted in the three New Hampshire regiments and went forth from pleasant homes to fight and win liberty and independence for themselves and the unborn millions with whom their most prophetic visions would never have dared to people this great country. They went forth cheerfully, supplying their own necessities. It is a list to be proud of and each one of them is deserving of more honor than we are able to bestow. Their example and habits of thought doubtless did much towards forming the character of our people. As citizens, they are known to have been law-abiding, and to have exercised a powerful influence for good morals. They were not educated men, but they were reverently religious and were constant attendants upon the service of God. The remains of forty-three of these soldiers lie buried in Canaan; some of the graves are marked by stones and many of them rest in unmarked graves and their ashes mingle with the common soil of the town.

Thomas Baldwin, died in Waterville, Me., and was buried in Boston, Mass. Joseph Wheat, Joshua Richardson, John May, Reynolds Gates, Robert Martin, Salmon Cobb, Eliphalet Richardson, Enoch Richardson and Ezra Nichols, were buried in the Street Cemetery; the last two have no headstones, but Enoch Richardson is undoubtedly buried beside his wife. Daniel Blaisdell, John Worth, Daniel Colby, Henry Springer, Ezekiel Wells, Jonathan Dustin, David Dustin, Josiah Clark, Joshua Wells, Jonathan B. Cross, Richard Whittier and Robert Barber, lie buried in the Wells Cemetery; the grave of the last is not marked by any stone, and the headstone of Ezekiel Wells is not over his grave. Warren Wilson, Samuel Meacham and Richard Otis lie in the Cemetery at West Canaan. William, John and

Moses Richardson, brothers, Nathaniel Bartlett, Moses Sawyer, Daniel Kimball, Mathew Greeley and James Woodbury, lie in the cemetery on Sawyer Hill. William Longfellow and Abraham Knowlton (Mrs. Knowlton died in Pembroke) lie buried on West Farms. Thomas Miner lies in the Cobble Cemetery.

From the recollections of men who were contempory with many of these veterans, valuable information was obtained: from Charles W. Richardson, son of Joshua; George Harris and Mrs. Harris, a daughter of one of them; from Joseph Dustin —of the War of 1812, son of one and grandson of another; from Jacob Richardson, son of William, an officer; and from Jacob Trussell, whose memory was very retentive up to the day of his death, at the great age of ninety-one years and eleven months.

The names of these soldiers are given below:

Elisha Bingham	Asa Kilburn
Daniel Blaisdell	Richard Clark
John Richardson	Parrott Blaisdell
William Richardson	Joshua Wells
Joshua Richardson	Abraham Knowlton
Eliphalet Richardson	Joshua Springer
Enoch Richardson	Samuel Meacham
Ezra Nichols	Josiah Clark
William Longfellow	Joshua Harris
Moses Sawyer	Mathew Greeley
Warren Wilson	Jonathan Dustin
Caleb Welch	John May
Richard Otis	Robert Barber
John Worth	Ezekiel Gardner
Benoni Tucker	Samuel Lathrop
William Ayer	Nathan Follensbee
John Beedle	John Hoyt
Daniel Colby	Samuel Hinkson
Robert Martin	Joseph Walters
Robert Hoyt	John Bartlett
Henry Springer	Jehu Jones
John Follensbee	Caleb Welch, Jr.
Samuel Jones	Samuel Gates
Daniel Kimball	Francis Smith
Gideon Rudd	Thomas Gates
Thomas Miner	Thomas Baxter
John Scofield, Jr.	Asa Williams
Jeremiah Meacham	James Jones
Benjamin Robert Birts	Jedidiah Hibbard

Soldiers.

Thomas Baldwin
Mesheck Blake
Nathan Springer
Reynold Gates
James Woodbury
Joseph Wheat
Salmon Cobb
David Dustin
Ezekiel Wells
Nathaniel Bartlett

Jacob Clifford
Nathan Durkee
Daniel Hovey
Richard Whittier
Jonathan B. Cross
Jonathan Lock
Theophilus Currier
Daniel Parker
Moses Richardson

Parrott Blaisdell and Joshua Springer were mustered out in Vermont; Nathan Follensbee lies in Enfield, while his brother John (who a hundred years ago lived on the Howard farm), Mesheck Blake, Robert Hoyt, and John Beedle, have passed beyond recognition and their names only are known.

In 1780 twenty men of Canaan marched to Rutland and Royalton, Vt., under the command of Capt. Joshua Wells, and then marched back again. The enemy did not wait for them, but they came back greatly exasperated against their captain, whom they charged with being ignorant of his duties and very overbearing, giving many vexatious orders for the purpose of exercising his authority. The following is a pay roll made for part of Capt. Joshua Wells' Company in Col. Chase's Regiment of Militia, who were called forth in an alarm October 20, A. D. 1780:

A Pay Roll Made for Part of Capt Joshua Wellse's Company in Col Chases Regiment of Militia who were Called forth in an Alarm Oct 20 A D 1780

	Days out.	Milds travel.		Days out.	Milds travel
Capt Joshua Wells	9	90	Nathaniel Bartlett	9	74
Lt Saml Jones	9	90	Caleb Welch Jr	9	74
Ensgn Thomas Baldwin	9	90	Jonathan Sprague	9	90
Sergt Caleb Welch	9	90	Daniel Blaisdell	9	90
Samuel Hinkson Private	9	90	Thos Miner	9	90
John Scofield Junr	4	30	Saml Gates	9	90
Jehu Jones	9	90	Ezek Gardner	9	90
Samuel Meacham	9	90	Benj Robert Birts	4	30
Robert Barber	9	90	Joshua Harris	9	90
John Bartlett	9	74	Francis Smith	9	90

N. B. Thirty Mild allowed out of said Travail on account of Drawing Provisions on the way for a distance of Thirty Milds.

A true Return Errors Excepted. Signed in behalf of the Company CANAAN Decr 15 A D 1783

JOSHUA WELLS *Capn*

Thomas Baldwin came home an ensign, Samuel Jones a lieutenant, Caleb Welch a sergeant, and Thomas Miner was afterwards called "leftenant." Thomas Miner was in Captain Russell's Rangers in 1776; sergeant in Colonel Chase's Regiment at Saratoga in 1777, and one of the scouts mentioned in the following:

To the Hon the General Court of the State of New Hampshire—
The Petition of the Town of Canaan Humbly Sheweth that we the inhabitants of Said Town the Summer past Conceived our Selves in Danger From the Canadain and other Savages (our Frontier being in great measure Neglected) and therefor by a vote of the Town Did agree to Raise and pay Three men for Six months to Scout and Guard &c to which men we have paid and are obligated to pay ten pounds Each — the men were raised by no order nor by the authority of No State but only by the vote of the Town — Altho they went into a Regiment Raised by The authority of Vermont but Should your honors think they Rendered any Service to This or the United States your Petitioners pray that their Money Paid sd Soldiers may be Reimbursted them or abated on thier Taxes. All which is Humbly Submitted and your Petitioners as in Duty bound Shall Ever Pray &c

                          THOMAS BALDWIN } *Come in behalf*
                          WM AYER   } *of Said Town*
CANAAN STATE OF NEW HAMPSHIRE June 8th 1782.
(Recd and ordered to lay)

Abraham Knowlton was in Captain Lunt's Company, Colonel Little's Regiment, in Massachusetts and was at Bunker Hill. Early in 1776 he enlisted in the naval service and made one cruise under Captain Williams. In the latter part of the year he enlisted under Captain Skinner and made two cruises on the schooner *Lee*. On the last cruise he was captured, carried to Halifax, imprisoned a year, then impressed on the British ship of war *Culloden*, and sailed for Wales, where he was taken sick, was taken ashore and detained as a prisoner until the close of the war.

The following anecdotes are told of Enoch Richardson by the Rev. Charles W. Richardson: "He was, perhaps as daring and persevering a patriot and soldier as has been found in any war. When quite young, at the battle of Bunker Hill, he was one of the bravest. He said many soldiers would say they did not know that they ever killed one of the enemy, but said he: 'I know that I killed one at Bunker Hill. I was one of the last who left the breast works when our ammunition failed. I had put my last charge in my gun, and attempted to fire it, but my gun, an old-fashioned flint-lock, missed fire; snapping two or three times. I dropped on my knees behind the breast works, catching out my jack-knife and picking the flint with it, by which time the soldiers near me had all retreated. At that instant a red-coat soldier, who had run forward of the British advancing column, came up to the breast work and thrust his gun and bayonet over at me, exclaiming: "D——n you! now I've got you!" I struck his gun aside, springing on my feet and fired my gun, the muzzle touching his body, making a hole through him, I should judge, as large as my arm. As my last charge was gone and my gun old, I jumped over and seized the dead man's gun and cartridge box, sprang back and loaded and fired his few remaining cartridges, sending his British bullets among the British as they advanced, and then I turned and retreated.' This same Enoch Richardson was one of the soldiers who went in that daring expedition up the Kennebec River, and through the awful, woeful forest to Quebec. He was one who entered the city, but as it became necessary to escape immediately, he jumped down about eighteen feet, where his fall was broken by about three feet of snow and made his escape, and after a long time made his way back to his home after great hardship and suffering. When he was a soldier at Ticonderoga, the time of his enlistment, and of two of his brothers and some of their old neighbors expired a very short time before the taking of Burgoyne's Army. They came home across Vermont by hilly and rough roads without shoes, and begged what food they had by the way, as their money was worthless. They arrived home weary and destitute. Three days after their arrival a recruiting officer came for volunteers to hasten to Ticonderoga, as there was a prospect of capturing Burgoyne's whole army. This Enoch Richardson put down his name, turned around and walked directly back over those hard and hilly roads and was there at the surrender of Burgoyne's Army. Few soldiers ever had such courage and perseverance as Enoch Richardson, whose remains are in Canaan Broad Street Cemetery. I have often, when a child, listened with, as it were, a breathless attention to anecdotes of that war by my father Joshua, who was one of the army who were successful in driving the British out of Boston. He said that just previous to the cessation of hostilities, and the agreement to evacuate Boston, our army threw shells into the town for three nights in succession, and that from the hill they occupied, Copp's Hill, he could hear the rip and tear of the roofs of the buildings as those shells entered. The last evening of the time the British were allowed in which to get on board their fleet and depart was a busy, noisy night in Boston. He said that he and many of the soldiers remained up and listened all night to the rattle of wheels on the pavements, to the voices of men and women, to the barking of dogs, etc., two miles distant, as the air was favorable to make the sounds distinct. It was a kind of music under the circumstances which pleased our soldiers well.

"He used often to tell of toils and hardships and sufferings at or near Ticonderoga. He was with our army in its retreat some time previous to the surrender of Burgoyne. The British were successful in fortifying a high eminence, where they could play upon a portion of our army without any danger of being reached in return. Our troops were under the necessity of leaving in great haste, and were pursued some distance and annoyed by the enemy. Men were frequently killed and wounded by cannon shots. While on the march one soldier, marching at his side, was shot through the body by a cannon ball and pitched against him as he fell, pushing him out of the ranks. They were under the necessity of passing through a considerable forest to reach a place where they could obtain food and rest. This forest was infested by Indians, in what numbers they did not know, and this part of the army was under the necessity of scattering and getting through the woods as best they could. He was in the rear and after they got into the woods and night was approaching, he and a few with him, found a soldier who had just been killed and scalped by an Indian. It soon became dark; they lost their small path and not agreeing in their opinions, which way the path was, they became separated and my father found himself alone hunting for the path in perfect darkness. He got down and crept on his hands and knees, feeling for the foot-path and immediately caught hold of a man's leg. He and the other were both frightened, thinking of the Indians in the woods but he soon learned that the man he had found was his brother, John Richardson. He told him to stay where he was till he crept on and found the path which he believed was near. He soon found it and called softly to his brother and they felt their way along together, until the path led them out into a small low meadow. At length the path seemed to be gone, and he being forward, suddenly stepped off into a creek of deep mud with a little water, falling on the breech end of his gun and driving it down, muzzle foremost the whole length into the mud. He clambered out with the assistance of his brother, being careful to save his gun and they traveled up the creek until they felt out a place where they could get across. They soon saw a light up on higher ground and carefully picked their way till they arrived at the place where there was a house and barn filled with soldiers who had arrived there and were packed close in almost every place where a man could lie down for rest under shelter; and none of them had any food that day unless it was some small and hasty lunch in the morning as they were starting. But he said there was an officer and assistant there with a light beside of a cask of good wine, which they had obtained and they told him and his brother that it was the rule for each one as he arrived to drink a pint of wine, which they did, and find the best place they could and lie down. The house was full and the barn also. In the house his brother crowded down between two soldiers. He could find no place for a time, but at length he discovered some low shelves, far enough apart so that a man could crowd in between them, but not long enough for him to straighten himself in. He crowded himself in between two of these shelves with his feet drawn up considerably and lay until his limbs began to ache from contraction and then he crept out and got his feet down on the floor between some of the men and stood a short time, and then crawled in between the shelves again. He passed the night without any sleep. By morning some provisions had been obtained, though they were then poorly supplied, and soon after they reached Fort Edward."

Enoch and his brother were stationed at Newcastle for three months, in November, 1776. Enoch was a corporal there and at Saratoga. He was sergeant in the Rhode Island campaign from March, 1778, to January, 1779. John was stationed at Great

Island in November, 1775, and was also at Saratoga and Rhode Island. On the evening of May 2, 1777, dispatches were received by the Committee of Safety of this state, informing them that the garrison at Ticonderoga was threatened with capture by the enemy, and urging immediate reinforcements to that important post. The matter was considered by the committee and on the following day the chairman, Hon. Josiah Bartlett, dispatched messengers to Colonels Ashley of Winchester, Benjamin Bellows of Walpole, and Jonathan Chase of Cornish, entreating them "by all that is sacred to raise as many of your militia as possible and march them to Ticonderoga." In accordance with that request, Colonel Ashley marched with 109 men, Colonel Bellows with 112, Colonel Chase with 159, and Capt. Josiah Brown with fifty-four men from Col. Enoch Hale's regiment.

In the pay roll of Colonel Chase's regiment are the names of Ezekiel Wells and Daniel Kimball, sergeants; James Jones, corporal; William Richardson, Asa Williams and Josiah Clark, privates. These men were in the company commanded by Joshua Hendee of Hanover. They marched to Ticonderoga May 7, 1777, 112 miles, and finding the alarm premature, were discharged after service of forty days. For this service they received eight pounds, six shillings.

The second alarm from Ticonderoga was more serious than the first. Maj. Francis Smith of Plainfield took command of Colonel Chase's regiment and marched to Ticonderoga on the 27th of June and with him were the following men: Thomas Baldwin, who was discharged an ensign after seven days' service, and Corp. Thomas Gates. The latter was one of the grantees in the charter. Jeremiah Meacham and Asa Kilburn, who served eight days each; Jedidiah Hibbard, William Richardson, John Scofield, Samuel Lathrop and Daniel Hovey. The ferriage of 209 horses over the Connecticut River is put down at two cents each, amounting to three pounds, nine shillings and eight pence.

Ticonderoga was garrisoned by 3,000 men under General St. Clair. General Burgoyne was approaching with an army of 8,000, and on the 4th of July planted a battery on Mt. Defiance, 750 feet above the American works. St. Clair, seeing that resistance would be hopeless, abandoned the fort on the night of

SOLDIERS.

July 5th and escaped with the garrison into Vermont. The British pressed upon the fugitives and overtook them at Hubbardton, seventeen miles from the fort. Here a sharp engagement ensued in which the Americans fought so obstinately as to check the pursuit. We learn from Rev. Charles W. Richardson's tale that the brothers Enoch and John Richardson were there.

In September, 1777, there was a call for help from the army of General Gates at Saratoga. Colonel Chase's regiment responded with enthusiasm; Joshua Wells was captain; Jedidiah Hibbard, sergeant-major; John Scofield, Josiah Clark, Richard Clark and Enoch Richardson were privates. These men are believed to have joined in the battles of Bennington and Saratoga. On July 23, 1777, Capt. Joshua Hendee of Hanover, of Colonel Hobart's regiment, with two-months men, marched to join General Stark's brigade. In this company were Sergeant Ezekiel Wells and Privates Nathaniel Bartlett, Josiah Clark and Elisha Bingham. Ezekiel Wells also served in the defense of Portsmouth two months from September 27, 1777. In Captain Webster's company were John Hoyt, sergeant, and Robert Barber. Thomas Baxter, Ben Rob Birts, and Gideon Rudd were in Captain House's company, Colonel Chase's regiment of Stark's brigade, in September, 1777, from Canaan.

Among the absentees from Colonel Cilley's regiment at Valley Forge, January, 1778, was Thomas Baxter, who was then thirty years old, left sick at Albany in hospital. He enlisted in 1777 for three years under Colonel Chase. Birts was crippled in his campaigns. He enlisted in 1777 for three years when twenty-six years old. He returned to Canaan, where he had a wife and child, and became a charge upon the town. Gideon Rudd married Delight, eldest daughter of John Scofield, the old settler, who "for divers good causes me thereunto moving, but more so especially for the love and good will I bear unto my well-beloved daughter Delight, wife of Gideon Rudd," conveyed to her one hundred acres of land. Mr. Rudd lived in Hanover afterwards, and his name is commemorated in the "Rudsboro Road." John Richardson served in Rhode Island in August, 1778, under Captain Page of Colonel Gates' regiment. In 1779 volunteers were slow in coming forward. An earnest call was made for reinforcements. It was not advisable to enforce a draft; Congress voted $200 and the state $300,—$500 for recruits. William Ayer of Plaistow, afterwards of Canaan, served in General Whipple's brigade in the expedition to relieve Rhode Island in 1778. He was at Winter Hill in Colonel Burnham's regiment as second lieutenant in December, 1775. Nathaniel Bartlett was at Saratoga, was a sergeant in Captain Runnell's company on the western frontier, and served from Bunker Hill to 1780.

John Beedle was in Captain Osgood's company of rangers and joined the Northern army in July, 1775; afterwards he was in Captain Russell's company of rangers for service in New Hampshire, then in Captain Richardson's company for the defence of the frontier adjacent to the Connecticut River.

William Richardson was in the Revolution before he came to Canaan. He was in Capt. Ezekiel Gile's company of Col. Stephen Peabody's regiment, as second lieutenant; enlisted January 1, 1778, for service in Rhode Island, and was discharged January 6, 1779. He enlisted from Hampstead in Hezekiah Hutchins' company of volunteers, as a corporal, and marched from Hampstead to Saratoga in September, 1777. He was appointed second lieutenant in the Rhode Island campaign when he was thirty-two years old. He was at Bunker Hill and Ticonderoga at every alarm. He died February 25, 1829, nearly 83 years old.

Daniel Blaisdell enlisted from Hopkinton in Captain Clement's company and served at Newcastle and was at Ticonderoga. His brother, Parrott, was in Captain Marston's company and marched to Rhode Island in June, 1778. He re-enlisted in Captain Downe's company and served up to January 1, 1779.

Elisha Bingham was in Captain Hendee's company for two months and was at Stillwater as a corporal. Jonathan B. Cross enlisted from Methuen, Mass. He resided in Enfield and was town clerk of that town in 1784, but the pay rolls give him as serving from Canaan.

Josiah Clark served at Fort Washington and Kittery Point from November, 1775, to February, 1776, in Captain Salter's company. He was at Ticonderoga, Bennington, Stillwater and Saratoga. William Longfellow, said Abram L. Williams, was a minuteman in 1775 at Bunker Hill, served under Moses Little, was a sergeant on his second enlistment; was in New York and New Jersey in 1776, Trenton in 1777; the same year went privateering with Paul Jones and was captured in August and confined in England; was exchanged from Mill Prison. Another account told by one who heard him tell it, is, that he was captured and imprisoned. A plan of escape was made to dig underground. The dirt was to be carried out in the seats of their pants and the man who could carry most was to get out first. Longfellow was a very large man and weighed about three hundred pounds. There was only one other man larger than he. He was a very harsh and rough man and at the time of his death, when sitting in a chair gasping for breath, with his wife at his side feeding him medicine with a spoon, he said, "Faster, faster, you old devil." He died half an hour afterwards. He had an old straight sword four feet long which was sold after his death.

Richard Clark was at Saratoga in Colonel Chase's regiment in September, 1777. Daniel Colby served at Great Island in Captain Downe's company in 1775.

Nathan Follensbee enlisted from Plaistow when seventeen years old in 1779, and under Major Scott in 1781, was in Captain Webster's company.

Mathew Greeley enlisted from Salisbury in 1777 for three years in Captain Morrill's Company, Colonel Scammell's regiment. He served up to November, 1781. He fought with Washington, Gates and Greene; was one of those who conveyed Major Andre to Tappan and was at Stony Point under Clinton, when they passed up the Hudson and marched weary and foot-sore over the narrow defiles and ragged rocks under the guidance of the negro Pompey. He would tell of the boy and his curious antics.

Joshua Harris was at Ticonderoga in June, 1777.

Jedidiah Hibbard was at Ticonderoga and at Saratoga; was a sergeant-major.

James Jones enlisted from Lebanon; was at Bunker Hill and Ticonderoga twice.

Samuel Jones was at Fort Washington in November, 1775; joined the Northern Continental Army in 1776 and was an applicant for prize money at Portsmouth of the ship *Prince George*. He signed a petition for more pay in 1777, on the ground that "forty shillings was better when war began than six pounds now." He was a second lieutenant at Ticonderoga in October, 1776, and in July, 1780, was enlisted in the first New Hampshire Regiment, and is described as being forty-eight years old, five feet four inches tall and of dark complexion.

Daniel Kimball was a sergeant at Ticonderoga in 1776; was at West Point in July, 1780, an ensign in Capt. Abel Stevens' Company and adjutant and ensign on Colonel Nichol's staff.

Robert Martin from June 26, 1777, to January 7, 1778, was a drummer with the troops at Rhode Island. He was at Mount Independence at the surrender of Burgoyne, and for a time was at Newcastle in Captain Calfe's Company in 1776, and from 1785 to January 14, 1787.

Jeremiah Meacham joined the Northern Continental Army in Captain Hayward's Company in 1776; was at Ticonderoga from October 28 to November 18, 1776, and in June, 1777.

Richard Otis was a corporal in Captain Canfield's Company at Ticonderoga in June, 1777, and in July.

Eliphalet Richardson was at Saratoga in September, 1777, and served also in the Rhode Island campaign in 1778.

Joshua Richardson served in the Rhode Island campaign.

Gideon Rudd was engaged in the New York service in 1779.

Moses Sawyer was at West Point in 1780 in Captain Butler's Company with John Hoyt. The latter was a sergeant at Bennington and Stillwater and was at Saratoga.

John Scofield, Jr., was in Colonel Chase's Regiment at Ticonderoga in June, 1777, with Daniel Hovey, Ezekiel Gardner, Jacob Clifford, Nathan Durkee and Samuel Lathrop. They were also at Saratoga the September following.

Henry Springer was enlisted in Captain Stone's Company from Haverhill, Mass., for three years in 1777, and in 1780 he enlisted to 1781, in Captain Dennett's Company.

Benoni Tucker enlisted for the campaign in Canada in July, 1776.

Joseph Wheat was on the pay roll of Captain Everett's Company in 1776; he marched to reinforce the army in New York in December and in April, 1777, was in Captain Walker's Company. At the alarm in June, 1777, from Ticonderoga, he was in Captain Emmerson's Company. He was also in the same company in Rhode Island in August, 1778. In June, 1779, he enlisted for one year in Captain Hawkins' Company, which was the Ninth Company of the Third New Hampshire Regiment. He was corporal in Captain McGreggor's Company in April, 1780.

Asa Williams was at Ticonderoga in Colonel Chase's Regiment in 1776 and again in June, 1777. He took up his residence in Enfield in 1779.

Warren Wilson was in Captain Sinclair's company at West Point in 1780.

John Worth served in the Rhode Island campaign.

Joshua Wells was in Captain Dearborn's company August 1, 1775, and as captain with ten other Canaan men. Jedidiah Hibbard, Thomas Miner, John Scofield, Jacob Clifford, Josiah Clark, Richard Clark, Nathan Durkee, Samuel Lathrop, Ezekiel Gardner and William Richardson marched to Saratoga in September, 1777, and joined General Gates. His brother, Ezekiel, was at Ticonderoga in May, 1777, and a sergeant in Captain Hendee's company at Stillwater and in Captain Lovejoy's company in September, 1779. Richard Whittier was at Saratoga in 1777 as corporal, and was a sergeant in Captain Robinson's company in the army in New York.

Robert Barber and Sergt. John Hoyt were in Capt. Ebenezer Webster's company. Robert Barber was appointed an ensign in the fourth company of the fourth regiment by Gov. John Wentworth in 1770. On September 6, 1777, the following letter was addressed to Capt. Robert Barber:

Sir, Agreeable to a request of Congress, and pursuant to order of the Committee of Safety of this state. You are hereby required forthwith to Draught or otherwise engage the one sixth part of your companies, not already in the war, including the Alarm list that are fit to bear arms, and able to march and perform their duty; to march from their homes at the farthest by the 15th. of this month, September, and proceed to Bennington and put themselves under the command of General Stark or the commanding officer there, or thereabouts, to serve until the last day of November next unless sooner Discharged. They are to be under the officers of this Regiment. The officers to have the same wages as the Continental Army and the soldiers $15.00 per month, and 3d per mile for travel to Bennington one months pay to be advanced, every man to equip himself with a good Firearm and also a Bayonet and Cartridge box if possible. Given under my hand at Newmarket the day and year above written.

JAMES HILLS *Leut. Col.*

The United States Pension Bureau has published a roll of the Revolutionary War pensioners for 1834 and for 1840:

LIST OF THE PENSIONERS ON THE RECORDS IN 1834.

Daniel Lary, private, Massachusetts Continental line, died May 13, 1827, aged sixty-eight years.

William Longfellow, private, Massachusetts Continental line, died in 1834; was eighty-three years old.

Richard Otis, private, Connecticut Continental line, died in 1834; was eighty-nine years old; transferred from Windham Co., Vt.

Eliphalet Richardson, private, Massachusetts Continental line, died October 3, 1831, aged eighty years.

Enoch Richardson, private, New Hampshire Continental line, suspended act 1820, aged sixty-six; died, 1820.

Joseph Wheat, private, New Hampshire Continental line, suspended act 1820, aged sixty.

James Woodbury, private, Massachusetts Continental line, suspended, seventy-eight years old.

LIST OF REVOLUTIONARY PENSIONERS AND WITH WHOM THEY RESIDED JUNE 1, 1840.

Bridget Wheat, age eighty-three; resided with Joseph Wheat.
Warren Wilson, age seventy-seven; resided with Joseph Wheat.
Elizabeth Currier, age seventy-four; resided with Theophilus Currier.
Josiah Clark, age eighty-two.
Nathaniel Bartlett, age eighty-three; resided with John Pressey.
Daniel Parker, age eighty-three.
Joshua Richardson, age eighty-two; resided with Joshua W. Richardson.
Daniel Colby, age eighty-seven; resided with Andrew Elliott.
Sarah Poland, age seventy-nine; resided with Elijah Gove.
Sarah Longfellow, age eighty-eight; resided with Stephen Williams.
Lydia Whitney, age eighty-eight; resided with Isaac Whitney.
Daniel Kimball, age seventy-seven; resided with David Townsend.
Nathan Follensbee, seventy-eight, and Mathew Greeley, aged eighty, are put down from Enfield.

Jonathan Locke was a recruit, as the following order shows:

CANAAN Mar 13, 1790

To William Gardner Esq Treas, Pleas pay to Jehu Jones or bearer the sum of twenty pounds with the interest due thereon being a Town bounty paid by the Town of Canaan to one Jon^a Lock a Recruit in 1782.

SAMUEL JONES WM RICHARDSON *Selectmen*

To be allowed on Mr Jones tax for 1784.

The Militia After the Revolution.

The militia law passed in 1792 divided the militia of the state into brigades, regiments and divisions. Each regiment was divided into two battalions. The towns of Lebanon, Enfield, Canaan and Grafton formed the first battalion of the Twenty-Third Regiment; and the towns of Hanover, Lyme, Dorchester and Orange the second battalion. In 1796 the office of major of the first battalion is shown to be vacant by the adjutant-general's report. In 1808 it is the same. There is no evidence that any militia assembled for training in Canaan before 1808, but it is probable they did, as a petition was presented to the president and council in January, 1786, requesting the appointment of Capt. Robert Barber for field officer, and intimating that Samuel Jones, who wished for the position, was not desirable. Before 1792 this town was included in the Twenty-Fourth Regiment. John Currier was commissioned lieutenant in the fourth company of the Twenty-Fourth Regiment on September 20, 1794. He was appointed captain in the same company, from which he resigned in 1800.

In 1784 Samuel Jones was second major.

In the latter part of the year 1808 the Legislature passed a new law, which led to a new arrangement of the militia of the state. Free, able-bodied, male citizens, from sixteen to forty years of age, were to be enrolled without exceptions; there should be at least a company of light infantry or grenadiers to each battalion; one cannon, with carriage, harness and apparatus, should be furnished each company of artillery, also music, money and a color. There should be no more than one company of cavalry to each regiment; that these companies should be furnished music, money and colors; that each company should turn out for inspection of arms and military exercise on the last Wednesday of June, annually; also annually in August or September, and as often as the commanding officer should think proper, not exceeding four times a year. Each regiment should be called out annually during the months of September or October; that suitable meats and drinks, or thirty-four cents in lieu thereof, should be furnished each non-commissioned officer and private within the several towns and places on regimental or battalion musters; that the captain-general appoint as many aids as he thought proper, with the rank of lieutenant-colonel; that gun houses should be provided for the cannon at the expense of the state; that each town should be kept provided with certain amounts of powder, balls, flints and camp-kettles.

The Adjutant-General's report for 1808 mentions the existence of thirty-six regiments, and it would seem that there were no companies training in Canaan recognized by the state. That there were muster days is evident by the vote of the town in August, 1808, which is the first vote on the records to refer to the militia. The warrant contained an article, "to see if the town will find non-commissioned officers refreshments on Muster Day." The article was dismissed. It was customary on muster days to drink as much rum as possible, and booths were set up along Broad Street where the thirsty might obtain strong drink. The selectmen issued licenses to persons desiring to sell, and the first one mentioned was to Daniel Blaisdell, Jr., in 1809 at the training on the 28th of September. William Parkhurst also received a license. Licenses were issued to these two men again in 1810.

Between 1808 and 1812 one new regiment was formed, the thirty-seventh, composed of men from Canaan, Dame's Gore, Orange, Enfield and Grafton. The officers at that time were: Caleb Seabury, lieutenant-colonel commandant; Levi George, major, first battalion; and Benjamin Choate of Enfield, major, second battalion. At the annual meeting in March, 1812, the town voted, "That each company have their choice whether they have 34c. or suitable meats and drinks on Muster Day, and each captain take the minds of his company at June training." This refers specifically to the law of 1808, which the town has first taken notice of.

The Thirty-Seventh Regiment held its musters in Canaan, and Canaan men were its officers. It was probably organized and recognized by the state in 1809. The adjutant-general's report for 1868 says, that in 1810 there were thirty-seven regiments of militia in the state. John H. Harris was appointed captain of the First Company of Infantry of the Thirty-Seventh Regiment on October 1, 1810, and resigned in 1812. In 1820 the officers were Otis Barney of Grafton, colonel; Daniel Pattee of Canaan, lieutenant-colonel; and William Livingston, major. Joseph

Dustin resigned as a lieutenant in the Sixth Brigade Second Division of the Thirty-Seventh Regiment in 1824. Under the law of 1830, Joshua Blaisdell was division inspector of the Second Division, Second and Sixth Brigades. Josiah P. Barber was colonel of the Thirty-Seventh Regiment, Elijah Blaisdell lieutenant-colonel, both of Canaan, and Fauntleroy Caswell, major. Under the revised statutes of 1840, the officers for 1843 were Eliphalet C. Gilman, colonel; O. A. J. Vaughan, adjutant, and Horace S. Currier, quartermaster, all of Canaan. Vaughan had been appointed adjutant in 1841, and in 1844 was appointed lieutenant-colonel. He read law in the office of Jonathan Kittredge, and in 1857 moved to Laconia.

On August 29, 1838, John M. Barber was appointed ensign of the Fourth Company of the Thirty-Seventh Regiment. He was appointed captain of the First Company, April 5, 1841, and resigned March 29, 1842. There were forty-three men in this company. He was appointed fourth sergeant in the Granite Phalanx, of which J. Everett Sargent was captain, June 26, 1843. John B. Dustin was sergeant, and in the absence of his captain twice delivered an address to his company. It serves to explain the object which was sought to be accomplished by the militia, and is as follows:

Gentlemen, Officers and fellow soldiers. You are called together on this occasion by the laws of the State and country, for the performance of a duty, and the accomplishment of an object of no small moment to the interests of our common country and to the peace and safety of us all. I presume none of us are prepared to question the propriety and utility of the law which requires us thus to meet once in each year to revive, quicken and renew our martial spirit and to acquire that knowledge of military discipline which shall the better prepare us to defend our rights as men and as freemen and the better to secure to us those blood-bought privileges which our fathers bequeathed to us as the richest blessings of our inheritance.

If the law then requiring us thus to meet is right and proper surely this duty on our part should be esteemed a privilege and an honor, rather than as an irksome and laborious task. And thus it is considered by all those who truly know and feel the real spirit and value of martial exercise. To be sure the manner in which our military performances are sometimes and I may say frequently passed over, or absolutely shunned by many of our fellow citizens, both of those in military rank and honors and those of less distinction down to the common soldiers, is not at all creditable to our military system. But you know there are those always and in all professions who are far more ready to receive the honors of office than they are to perform the duties which their offices demand at their hands.

But this is no objection to the real merits of our militia system. By training the great body of our citizens to act the part of soldiers we at once avoid the dangers arising to free institutions from a standing army, and render ourselves invincible by any foreign force that may arise against us. For tyranny would stand but a poor chance to success in conducting her battles with soldiers who fight for hire, and care not whether the victory or defeat attends them provided the pay be good — against citizen soldiers who know the value of their country and their homes, and know also and feel that death is much better to them than defeat. We would hope, gentlemen, that you feel in some good degree the importance of the true martial spirit. And from your appearance this day we are led to feel a strong confidence that there will be a still greater increase of this spirit in your future performances. When a company or regiment are both ready and willing to learn their duty and then do it, when they go through their military performances with spirit and pride and just ambition, there is a majesty in it, which enkindles a flame of patriotism in the heart of every true lover of his country. Gentlemen, the inspecting officer informs me that there are but few and very slight deficiencies in your arms or equipments today. The general appearance of the regiment will certainly suffer nothing by a comparison with its appearance on former occasions, or in comparison with those of other neighboring regiments. We hope to see still greater improvement in your appearance hereafter. Let more of your companies be uniformed, more of them drilled in a truly soldier-like manner, and let us see every man in the old Thirty-Seventh proud to show himself a soldier. My present limits will not permit of going into any topics in any degree foreign from my subject. I will merely remark that though we may and should as citizens take an interest in all the great questions which agitate our country and though we may have our individual preferences as to the candidates for governor or president, who may from time to time be held up as the candidates for those offices, yet as soldiers we are to love our country, and whether Polk or Clay or Captain Tyler, or the Mormon prophet, is president, we are to love our country with a soldier's love and defend her with a soldier's devotion. Gentlemen, in conclusion, may you have a safe return after this day's exercises are closed to your homes and families, and may you feel more than ever resolved to maintain and preserve our free institutions which render those homes so happy and those friends so prosperous.

Gentlemen, had I a general's commission to found a speech upon I could, of course, give you a much longer, if not a better address, but as I have not I will no further weary your patience, except by wishing you and yours a happy life in a happy home and in a free country.

An artillery company was organized in 1820. The militia system of New Hampshire was then doing its level best to make citizen soldiers of every man. It was complete in all arms but one. They lacked a six-pounder gun — brass one. They wanted it badly. At the date above named a meeting was called of all interested, to assemble in the hall of Capt. Joshua Harris' Tavern on the Street, to organize an artillery company and to appoint a commission to ask the state to loan them a gun. John Jones of East Enfield was elected the first captain. Nathaniel Currier of Canaan, lieutenant; and John Barney of Grafton, second lieutenant. After the election of officers they all drank freely of Captain Harris' rum, at the expense of Capt. John Jones and went home.

The application to Governor Bell was successful. Orders were sent to purchase land and build a house upon it, in which to store the gun. Captain Harris gave the deed of the land, and the house was built upon contract by Shubel Greeley of Goose Pond. Thus those citizens obtained their gun and were proud of it. They used upon occasion to exhibit their delighted patriotism by dragging it up and down the Street, and make a thundering noise firing off blank cartridges wadded with green grass. They kept this up for eighteen years, and about the last use they made of it was in the grievous days when liberty of speech was believed to be a crime, and that the ladies ought not to be allowed to meet together even in secret, to pray against slavery and oppression.

They would harness themselves to it and drag it through the Street, and fire if off at the closed doors of the offending abolitionists, yelling like wild Indians as the glass rattled from the sash, and that was about the last triumph under the old militia system. Soon afterwards the artillery company was disbanded, and the state conveyed its title to the town. Capt. Robert B. Clark was commander of the cavalry, or "troop," they called it. The troop was organized some years previous to 1820, and practiced horsemanship about twice a year. They were placed upon the retired list about the time the artillery fired its last wad.

In 1851 the Legislature passed a law, that the militia of the state should not be subject to active duty, except in case of war, invasion, riot, or inability of the civil officers to execute the laws. This led to the militia becoming mere names on paper, and it soon ceased to have much vitality. At this date Caleb A. Sleeper was colonel; Daniel Follensbee, lieutenant-colonel; A. A. Currier, major, and William B. Follensbee, quartermaster. In 1857 the system of 1851 was abolished, and a new one instituted by the Legislature. This seems to be the end of the Thirty-Seventh Regiment, it did not reorganize under the new law. In 1859 an independent company was formed called the "Canaan Grenadiers," and was accepted by the town. Jacob Peters was captain, Gilman W. Clark, lieutenant, and Augustus F. Blake, ensign. It numbered thirty-seven men. This company existed until the outbreak of the Rebellion.

War of 1812.

In the war of 1812 fears were entertained of an attack upon Portsmouth by the British fleet. In April, 1812, the President of the United States, ordered the Secretary of War to request Gov. William Plumer to order into the service of the United States such part of the quota of the militia as he should deem necessary for the defence of the sea coast of the state. Volunteers for the defence of that port did not offer with sufficient alacrity, and a draft was ordered. The quota for Canaan was fifteen men, for two months' service. Five men at once volunteered, namely: James Dustin, born in 1791, son of David and Rebecca (Cross) Dustin, leaving the trade of a tanner with Jacob Dow. After his discharge, he in company with Abner H., Joseph, Aaron C., Reuben and Daniel Colby, sons of Daniel, emigrated to Ohio, which was then the West. Jehiel Clark, born December 3, 1790, son of Richard, 2d., cousin of Colonel Josiah, enlisted as fifth sergeant. He married and lived on the farm afterwards owned by Col. Isaac Towle. Never was a prosperous man. Washington Wilson, son of John and Sary, born October 11, 1792. Joseph Dustin, brother of James, our "Brother Joe," born October 25, 1795. Frederic Noyes, son of Dudley, who in 1795 lived on the Howard Farm, and at this time on the Farrington Currier farm.

Nine men were drafted, of these only the following names have been preserved. Elijah Flanders, eldest son of Joshua, usually called "Corker," born in 1794 on the farm next north of Joseph Bartlett's, brother of Sylvester. He procured a substitute a day or two after reaching Portsmouth and came home. James Blaisdell, son of Daniel and Sally, born January 17, 1784, who went as a substitute for Nathaniel Derby. Nat. Barber, known as "Devil Nat," for his wild tricks, brother of Zebulon of Dorchester. He had been a soldier before, and went as a substitute for Timothy Sanborn. Amos Richardson, son of William. Joseph Blake, who was appointed an ensign. David Lary and Rufus Wilson, son of Warren. These men all enlisted in Colonel Sias' regiment, and Capt. John D. Harty's company, some on the 27th and 28th, and others on the 29th of September, 1814, for sixty days. They were stationed at what is known as "Portsmouth Plains," about a mile southeast of the court house. Four others are reported to have enlisted but their names are not on the rolls. Samuel Williams, a brother of Robert, who married Pernal B. Worth. Samuel Sawyer, and a man named Gile. Paul Cook, who was afterwards a partner with his brother-in-law, Abraham Pushee, harness maker at the "Corner." Cook afterwards died in Lyme. These men marched to Concord where they were mustered into service. David Dustin went along to carry their baggage. They were marched to Portsmouth and in two or three days were discharged and ordered home, the threatened attack having been a false alarm. Nathaniel Currier, many years a trader on the Street, was on duty as a soldier near Oswego, N. Y., one season during the war. Dan Welch, brother of Simeon, son of "Bomination" Welch, born on the Rufus Richardson farm, was in this war. He married Huldah Gould and died in Lowell, Mass., a poor man, without a pension. She applied for a pension, but died waiting for it. The Old Ladies' Home in Lowell pursued that pension, caught and captured it. Joseph Dustin and Dan Welch, both gifted men, left Portsmouth destitute of money. They proposed to each other that they become traveling evangelists, and in that way work their passage home. They began praying and exhorting, by the wayside or in houses, whenever they could find two or three gathered together. They were successful and returned home, neither tired nor hungry. Josiah Clark wanted to enlist and go to Portsmouth but had a lame foot and could not march.

MEXICAN WAR.

In Company H, Capt. Daniel Batchelder, of the Ninth United States Infantry are the names of four Canaan men, who enlisted May 1, 1847, for the war, James Andrews, Benjamin Bean, Sanford Gardner, and Bernard McCluskey. They sailed from Newport on the *North Bend*, May 21, 1847, landed on the 21st of June at Vigara, on the 14th of July began their march and were the first regiment to enter the fortress of Chepultepec, on the 12th of September. Asel Burnham was in either Captain Bodfish's or Captain Rowe's company of the Ninth Regiment.

WAR OF THE REBELLION.

May, 1861.*

The most exciting subject now is the war. There are occasionally flag raisings. Union badges and flags are everywhere seen. The old flagstaffs of the political parties serve the common sentiment. The young ladies wear rosettes of red, white and blue, and the boys wear medals decorated with the immortal colors. Every individual act of patriotism is greeted with three loud huzzas. All the old patriotic songs are being learned by the young patriots. There are no more any Republicans or Democrats. The Preceptor of our Academy has closed out and opened a recruiting office; he belonged to the inevitable Smith family, and enlisted for the war. There is a wildness about this enthusiasm that astonishes everybody, and it is very contagious; old and young throw up their hats and hurrah for the union. Clergymen have abandoned the everlasting negro question, and now preach upon the war. They pray for the confusion of traitors. Even here, where money was supposed to be as scarce as honesty and patriotism at as large a discount as veracity, the people will not tolerate traitors. They do not allow men to talk treason now. A few days ago a man who had no sense came into an adjacent village with a load of potatoes and attempted to exercise the freedom of opinion by abusing Government. But the men and dogs took after him so finally that he was obliged to leave his potatoes and flee to safety. Similar scenes are occurring every day.

My old mother, whose patriotism increases with her years, often wishes she were a man. She would go and fight the rebels. She has just prepared 300 bandages for the use of the wounded and is going about town inviting other ladies to do likewise. She is talking now of getting up a lot of white linen caps for the soldiers in the hot sun. Every day she is impatient to hear the news, and she prays that President Lincoln may hurry up matters and give the rebels a great

*Written in a letter of that date, by W. A. W.

battle, a crushing battle that shall smite them to the earth. Our Postoffice exhibits a scene of excitement every day. Men who never took a paper now take a daily, and they are always present when the mail arrives. And those who are not able to take a daily are there also, and are impatient until some one reads the telegraph reports of the night before. A hundred questions are asked of the probable result of the war, and today there has been great rejoicing because the telegraph reports the President to have said that the war shall not cease till the Flag of the union waves over every fort, arsenal, custom house, and other public building within the national domain. Every one concurs in such sentiments. It is wonderful what universal burst of enthusiasm has escaped from northern hearts. There seems to be but one breast and its great throb reaches East, west, north and south, from the Atlantic to the Pacific, from the Canadas downward. It is thrilling to see a nation rushing to the service of its government, in such compact, glittering, intelligent, relentless masses. The world never before saw so sublime a spectacle, because the world never before saw so great a treason, so great a necessity for prompt, impulsive action. I would be glad to go, but my weak back would falter by the wayside under the weight of arms and blankets. In after years, when the events of this great treason are rehearsed by the winter firesides, these soldiers will enjoy a glorious and enviable pride in saying, "I was there — I helped put out the fires of treason." And what epitaphs the heroic acts of those soldiers are to furnish for the eye of future generations! Whole lives of uselessness are now to be illustrated by one act of patriotic devotion, that shall fill fame's trumpet so full, as it sends its swelling candenzas with prolonged reverbrations down to the remotest posterity. These are the times of great thieves and greater heroes, and each will win immortality in their degree.

Sixteen men volunteered in 1861, Charles Robie, Joseph Sylvester, Elijah W. Johnson, Job B. Jenness, Andrew J. Darush, Placid Adams, Thomas McNabb, William Tolbert, George B. County, Stephen Shephard, Frank T. Dustin, Peter Pieron, Henry Hoffman, James Kimball, Anthony Welch and William E. Allard.

On August 9, 1862, the town were requested to meet to see what should be done in regard to furnishing the town's quota of soldiers. They voted to pay each volunteer a bounty of $100. Whereupon David Barnard offered to give the first man who should volunteer $5. Twenty men came forward and gave in their names as volunteers for three years, and the individuals named opposite gave each man $5:

John N. Ford,	paid $5 by	David Barnard
Almond R. Decato,	" " "	Dexter Harris
Thomas S. Marshall,	" " "	William A. Wallace
William R. Call,	" " "	Warren W. Wilson
Nathaniel W. Bean,	" " "	William A. Wallace
Philip G. Prescott,	" " "	Levi George
George M. Richardson,	" "	Horace S. Currier
John J. Burns,	" " "	Dexter Richardson
Abel Hadley,	" " "	Frank Currier
John W. Philbrick,	" " "	Darius Barnard
Sidney L. Colby,	" " "	George Hinkson
Thomas E. Jones,	" " "	Charles Day
Charles T. Langley,	" " "	Thos. D. Avery
Frank Morey,	" " "	Lewis C. Pattee
Orville Goss,	" " "	J. S. Davis
Moses H. Marshall,	" " "	Isaac Davis
Leedus Hebert,	" " "	A. H. Cilley
John B. Lovering,	" " "	Stephen Morse
Chas. D. Washburn,	" " "	Eleazer Barney
Orson Makepeace,	" " "	Joseph Dustin

Caleb Jones attended this town meeting fired with patriotism, and when the call was made for volunteers, he gave a pledge that if his boy Tom would not go he would, for he was bound to have the family represented, and he put down his name as proxy for Tom who took his place in the ranks and came home to die from the effects of exposure in camp life.

William W. George proposed to give each volunteer a dinner at Sanborn's Hotel the day they left for camp. Fourteen of these men received the bounty of $100. Orson Makepeace, Charles T. Langley and William R. Call never enlisted. John N. Ford and Sidney L. Colby went afterwards. Thomas S. Marshall went but did not receive the bounty. Oliver B. Childs, William Digby, Aaron Sargent, Allen H. George and Ephraim Adams received the bounty besides the above fourteen, enlisting about the same time. The town voted to give volunteers for nine months' service $100 and $50 more if called out of the state. The selectmen with L. C. Pattee, William L. Harris, William P. Weeks and William W. George were appointed a committee to get recruits to make up the town's quota, and they were to receive one dollar for each recruit, but if the recruit went to the selectmen he was to receive the dollar. Every man who brought a

SOLDIERS.

volunteer was to receive five dollars, and the families of the nine months' men were to be taken care of the same as the three year men. The following men enlisted for nine months receiving $155, all in the Fifteenth Regiment:

Everett W. Dow	Gilbert J. Robie
Levi Martin	Rufus S. Goss
Hiram Jones	William W. Dustin
Austin Dunham	Don C. Washburn
David Legro	Albert Bradbury
Alvah Gilman	Edgar D. Aldrich
Dexter E. Bradbury	William A. Gordon
Abiel Sharp	Edwin D. Aldrich
James Furlong	Fred B. Wells
William Adams	

In 1863 the town voted to pay each drafted man $300, agreeably to the law of the state passed June, 1863. The following received $300:

Joseph D. Weeks	H. R. Norris
George T. Wells	L. K. Currier
Wm. A. Flanders	Albert F. Davis
E. H. Pressey	Edwin Shephard
Byron Edwards	George W. Davis
S. B. Morgan	Charles N. Morse
David H. Butman	Burns Edwards
George D. Harris	George Tilton
H. A. Nichols	Jas. M. Eaton
Samuel A. Colby	Denis County
J. S. Jones	

For these drafted men the following substitutes were furnished:

John Moriarity	for	J. D. Weeks
Loftus Reed Mager	"	Tilton Nichols
Henry Wallace	"	George W. Davis
James Simpson	"	Wm. A. Flanders
Alfred Marland	"	George D. Harris
Adelbert O. Williams	"	Edwin Shephard
Enos Gloggett	"	Geo. T. Wells
James Harris	"	Mathew H. Clark
John Lamontaine	"	Sam L. A. Colby
Daniel Doherty	"	H. R. Norris
John Mulholland	"	George Tilton
Alfred Jones	"	S. B. Morgan

George Thomas	for L. K. Currier
Thomas Ayers	" Albert H. Davis
Albert H. Currier	" David H. Butman
Robert Smith	" J. M. Eaton
James Smith	" Byron Edwards
Edwin Gerush	" Burns Edwards
Theodore Shoemaker	" E. H. Pressey
John Marshall	" John S. Jones

On December 7, 1863, the town voted to borrow $14,000 to fill out the quota of the town in response to the call of the President for 300,000 men on October 17, 1863, and the selectmen were requested to contract with William W. George and Albert M. Shaw to fill the quota, at $500 per man unless they could be found for less. Elijah W. Johnson and John W. Hoyt volunteered and received $555. Robert M. O'Connell, a veteran, received $600, and George F. Taplin received $250. The town paid Hollis B. Whitney $500 for one volunteer and W. W. George $10,633.50 for nineteen volunteers.

In 1864 the town voted to pay reënlisted men who had gone to fill out the quota $100, and who were now in service, and to pay C. N. Homan $300, who had been drafted. The following were the reënlisted men:

Timothy A. Dunham	Peter Perron
Alonzo Mitchell	Frank W. Carroll
Joseph Graville	Charles Prew
Albert York	Tyler Heath
Placid Adams	

The town voted that the "selectmen put in volunteers (to fill out quota) provided that any persons in town that are enlisted shall pay to the selectmen $200 for exemption papers for three years to the number of 24, and the first 24 men who make application to the selectmen, shall be the ones that are entitled to the benefit and balance to be paid from the town treasury, and to pay future drafts $300 or their substitutes. Bounties repaid to be divided equally with town and ones receiving benefit of foregoing vote." Twelve thousand dollars was voted to be raised to accomplish the foregoing. The following men received $76, who paid $200 for substitutes:

Soldiers.

James P. Barber	George E. Cobb
Elijah Smith	D. G. S. Davis
Geo. L. Whittier	Aaron Aldrich
William Hall	Daniel Hazeltine
Benj. P. Nichols	Chas. H. Leeds
Daniel H. Campbell	Wm. G. Somers
Jeremiah Whittier	Geo. W. Murray
Geo. W. Randlett	Elijah Whittier
Augustus Shephard	Warren F. Wilson
Albert E. Barney	Moses E. Currier
H. H. Wilson	Newton B. Gates
Chas. Davis	Geo. C. Bradbury

On August 29, 1864, a town meeting was called "to see what the town would do to fill out the quota required by the call of the President for 500,000 men." The town resolved to pay the largest bounty provided by the act of August 19, 1864. They resolved to pay $400 bounty to all persons having residence in the town three months prior "who volunteer," and to hire $4,000 to accomplish it. Five hundred dollars bounty was paid the following volunteers:

Daniel Stickney	Sidney L. Colby
John Holt	Jas. W. Atherton
Geo. P. Clark	Edson J. Fifield
James Wilson	Everett W. Dow

William W. George furnished five volunteers and three substitutes, also fifteen volunteers, and substitutes for 24 enrolled men.

On November 30, 1864 the town voted that the "Selectmen should put men into the military and naval service in anticipation of a call," and to hire $20,000.

At the annual meeting in 1865 William W. George was appointed "Military Agent of the town with exclusive control."

The men arranged by regiments is as follows, some of the names occur twice because of reënlistment:

SECOND REGIMENT.

George B. County, Company B; enlisted May 27, 1861; mustered in June 7, 1861, for three years; transferred to Fifty-Seventh Company, Second Battalion, Infantry Company, September 9, 1863; discharged May 26, 1864.

Charles A. Pratt, Company C; enlisted May 20, 1861; mustered in June 1, 1861, for three years; deserted, Concord, May 24, 1863.

Benjamin W. Adams, Company I; enlisted May 20, 1861; mustered in June 7, 1861, for three years; deserted, Concord, April 8, 1863; apprehended February 28, 1864; discharged April 14, 1865.

Dennis County, Company I; enlisted May 18, 1861; mustered in June 7, 1861, for three years; discharged, disabled, January 1, 1863. (See First New Hampshire Light Battery.)

Michael C. Miner, Company I; enlisted May 19, 1861; mustered in June 7, 1861, for three years; mustered out June 21, 1864.

Lyndon B. Woods, Company I; enlisted May 25, 1861; mustered in June 7, 1861, for three years; mustered out June 21, 1864.

Jonathan Merrill, Company I; enlisted May 20, 1861; mustered in June 7, 1861, for three years; wounded severely, Gettysburg, July 26, 1863; discharged, disabled, May 2, 1864; mustered out June 21, 1864.

RECRUITS.

William Thompson, Company K; enlisted December 3, 1863, for three years; promoted corporal May 1, 1865; mustered out January 19, 1865.

Joseph Saunders, Company K; enlisted December 3, 1863, for three years; wounded, Cold Harbor, June 3, 1864; mustered out June 26, 1865.

Carlos Smitz, Company K; enlisted December 3, 1863, for three years; transferred to navy April 29, 1864; served on *Mt. Vernon* and *Connecticut;* discharged August 11, 1865.

John McCullom, Company F; enlisted December 3, 1863, for three years; promoted corporal January 1, 1865; to sergeant September 1, 1865; mustered out December 19, 1865.

Robert McConnell, Company H; enlisted December 11, 1863, for three years; discharged, disabled, May 22, 1865.

Patrick Ledlow, Company —; enlisted December 6, 1864, for three years; deserted December 10, 1864.

John W. Hoyt, Company E; enlisted December 29, 1863, for three years; wounded, Cold Harbor, June 3, 1864; transferred Company C, Twelfth Regiment, June 21, 1865; absent detached service December 19, 1865; discharge to date December 19, 1865.

John (alias William) Dorsey, Company F; enlisted November 30, 1863, for three years; deserted April 11, 1864; apprehended; promoted corporal January 1, 1865; promoted sergeant June 25, 1865; discharged December 19, 1865.

Francis Bearo, Company F; enlisted November 30, 1863, for three years; discharged December 19, 1865.

James Green, Company F; enlisted November 30, 1863, for three years; deserted, Point Lookout, Md., January 3, 1864.

Thomas Presly, Company F; enlisted December 3, 1863, for three years; transferred to navy April 30, 1864; served on *Mt. Vernon* and *Tacony;* discharged July 25, 1865.

Thomas Kerby, Company F; enlisted December 3, 1863, for three years; transferred to navy April 30, 1864; served on *Quaker City;* discharged July 25, 1865.

SOLDIERS.

John Kelley, Company F; enlisted December 3, 1863, for three years; wounded June 3, 1864; deserted on furlough November 10, 1864.

Henry Preston, Company F; enlisted November 30, 1863, for three years; deserted, Bermuda Hundred, Va., June 1, 1864.

RE-ENLISTED VETERANS.

George Young, Company K; enlisted December 4, 1863, for three years; transferred to Company B April 28, 1864; discharged May 25, 1865.

William Whitmer, Company F; enlisted November 30, 1863, for three years; deserted, Point Lookout, Md., January 18, 1864.

The Second Regiment was at the battles of First Bull Run, Siege of Yorktown, Williamsburg, Fair Oaks, Savage Station, Peach Orchard, Glendale, First Malvern Hill, Second Malvern Hill, Bristow Station, Second Bull Run, Chantilly, Fredericksburg, Manassas Gap, Gettysburg, Wapping Heights, Swift's Creek, Drury's Bluff, First and Second Cold Harbor, Petersburg, Proctor's Creek, Chesterfield, Darbytown, Spring Hill and the occupation of Richmond.

THIRD REGIMENT.

Horace L. Davis, Company E; enlisted July 22, 1861; mustered in August 23, 1861, for three years; detached; musician Second Brigade Band, Tenth Army Corps; mustered out August 23, 1864.

James Simpson, Company A; enlisted October 12, 1863; killed, Drury's Bluff, May 13, 1864.

Stephen Hadley, Company E; enlisted July 26, 1861; mustered in August 23, 1861, for three years; wounded slightly, Drury's Bluff, May 13, 1864; again, Deep Bottom, August 16; mustered out September 9, 1864.

Tyler Heath, Company E; enlisted August 14, 1861; mustered in August 23, 1861, for three years; re-enlisted January 1, 1864; killed, Drury's Bluff, May 15, 1864.

Abel Hadley, Company E; enlisted September 1, 1862, and mustered for three years; died of disease, Morris Island, S. C., September 16, 1863.

RECRUITS.

Orville Goss, Company E; enlisted August 16, 1862; mustered in September 5, 1862, for three years; appointed corporal November 19, 1863; wounded severely, Drury's Bluff, May 13, 1864; discharged, disabled, May 10, 1865.

John N. Ford, Company H; enlisted August 9, 1862; mustered in September 6, 1862, for three years; killed, Charles City Roads, Va., October 27, 1864.

Edwin Gunsch, Company G; enlisted October 8, 1863; mustered in September 6, 1862, for three years; discharged, Philadelphia, Pa., October 28, 1864.

Zephraim Forties, Company K; enlisted February 1, 1865; mustered in September 5, 1862, for three years; mustered out July 20, 1865.

John Mulholland, Company D; enlisted October 14, 1863; mustered in in September 5, 1862, for three years; mustered out July 20, 1865.

John W. Philbrick, Company E; enlisted August 11, 1862; mustered in September 5, 1862, for three years; wounded, May 15, 1864, Drury's Bluff, and February 11, 1865, Sugar Loaf Battle; discharged June 26, 1865, Goldsboro, N. C.

RE-ENLISTED VETERANS.

Charles Prew, Company E; enlisted January 1, 1864, for three years; mustered out July 20, 1865.

Albert York, Company E; enlisted January 1, 1864, for three years; appointed sergeant; appointed first sergeant January 10, 1865; wounded, Fort Fisher, N. C., January 15, 1865; mustered out July 20, 1865.

This regiment was at Secessionville, S. C., Port Royal, James Island, Morris Island, Fort Wagner, and its siege, Drury's Bluff, Half-way House, Bermuda Hundred, Deep Bottom, Petersburg, Laurel Hill before Richmond, Fort Fisher.

THIRD REGIMENT.

Henry S. Hamlet, Company D; enlisted March 1, 1862; mustered in March 18, 1862, for three years; musician; appointed corporal; captured May 16, 1864; died, Millen, Ga., November 12, 1864.

Beletson Hoffman, Company K; enlisted October 16, 1863; wounded, Cold Harbor, June 4, 1864; died disease, Point of Rocks, Va., August 7, 1864.

John Lamoutaine, Company C; enlisted October 20, 1863, for three years; mustered out August 23, 1865.

Albert H. Currier, Company C; enlisted October 20, 1863, for three years; missing, Deep Bottom, Va., August 14, 1864; returned; mustered out August 23, 1865.

Warren W. Hamlett, Company F; enlisted March 15, 1862; mustered in November 3, 1862, for three years; wounded, August 16, 1864, Deep Bottom; mustered out March 23, 1865.

Orra H. Hardy, Company F; enlisted March 26, 1862, for three years; musician; died disease, Beaufort, S. C., November 20, 1863.

Alfred Marland, Company K; enlisted October 15, 1863, for three years; promoted first lieutenant, Company H, February 17, 1865; mustered out August 23, 1865.

Oscar F. Washburn, Company K; enlisted March 18, 1863, for three years; promoted corporal; died disease, Fort Munroe, August 13, 1864.

Samuel Sleeper, Company K; enlisted March 26, 1862, for three years; discharged April 16, 1865.

SOLDIERS.

Thomas Ayers, Company B; enlisted October 21, 1863, for three years; transferred to navy April 27, 1864.

George Thomas, Company H; enlisted October 16, 1863, for three years; deserted July 6, 1864; sent to regiment May 29, 1864, from hospital Beaufort, S. C., N. F. R.

Theodore Shoemaker, Company I; enlisted October 17, 1863, for three years; deserted, White House, Va., June 1, 1864.

RE-ENLISTED VETERANS.

Peter Perron, Company I; enlisted September 18, 1861; re-enlisted February 14, 1864, for three years; wounded July 26, 1864; discharged July 20, 1865.

Timothy A. Dunham, Company I; enlisted September 18, 1861; re-enlisted February 18, 1864, for three years; mustered out August 23, 1865; wagoner.

This regiment was at Port Royal, Pocotaligo, Fort Wagner, Fort Sumter, Drury's Bluff, Bermuda Hundred, Cold Harbor, Deep Bottom, Fort Andrews, Fernandina, Morris Island, Petersburg, Fort Fisher.

FIFTH REGIMENT.

Elijah W. Johnson, Company I; enlisted August 23, 1861, for three years; discharged January 28, 1862; was a recruiting officer of this regiment in 1861; received sixty-three recruits and was appointed first lieutenant October 12, 1861.

Richard K. Martin, Company I; enlisted August 27, 1861, for three years; corporal; killed, Antietam, September 17, 1862.

Ezra Cutler, Company I; enlisted September 23, 1861, for three years; deserted October 19, 1862.

George E. Cilley, Company I; enlisted October 11, 1861, for three years; discharged, disabled, February 28, 1862.

Placid Adams, Company I; enlisted September 12, 1861, for three years; re-enlisted January 1, 1864; discharged December 6, 1864.

Henry Evans, Company I; enlisted September 27, 1861, for three years; discharged, disabled, August 16, 1862.

Job B. Jenniss, Company I; enlisted September 9, 1861, for three years; wounded, December 13, 1862, Fredericksburg; May, 1863, Chancellorsville; July, 1863, Gettysburg; deserted, Point Lookout, February 12, 1864.

Ephraim Adams, Company I; enlisted August 14, 1861, for three years; wounded, June 3, 1864, Cold Harbor; transferred Second Battalion, V. R. Company, October 25, 1864; discharged June 22, 1865.

George W. Kimball, Company I; enlisted September 16, 1861, for three years; wounded, Chancellorsville, May, 1863; killed, Gettysburg, July 2, 1863.

Alonzo Mitchell, Company I; enlisted September 2, 1861, for three years; re-enlisted January 1, 1864; killed, Deep Bottom, Va., July 27, 1864.

Thomas McNabb, Company I; enlisted September 12, 1861, for three years; wounded, Fredericksburg, December 13, 1862; Cold Harbor, June 3, 1864; discharged, disabled, November 3, 1864.

Willie Martin, Company I; enlisted September 25, 1861, for three years; wounded, Fair Oaks, June 1, 1862; discharged, disabled, August 18, 1862.

Charles Robie, Company I; enlisted September 19, 1861, for three years; discharged, disabled, October 29, 1862.

Henry H. Sherburne, Company I; enlisted July 27, 1861, for three years; died, disease, May 6, 1862.

Daniel C. Smith, Company I; enlisted September 16, 1861, for three years; deserted June, 1862.

Joseph Sylvester, Company I; enlisted August 23, 1861, for three years; deserted, December 4, 1862, Falmouth, Va.

Andrew J. Darush, Company I; enlisted August 21, 1861, for three years; discharged, disabled, October 9, 1862.

Stephen Shephard, Company I; enlisted September 12, 1861, for three years; killed, June 1, 1862, Fair Oaks.

RECRUITS.

Henry Wallace, Company K; enlisted October 12, 1863, for three years; deserted, Point Lookout, Md., April 15, 1864.

Patrick Shea (alias Welch), Company H; enlisted October 3, 1863, for three years; transferred to navy April 23, 1864; discharged, disabled, October 15, 1864.

Frederick Flury, Company I; enlisted September 10, 1861, for three years; deserted August 30, 1862.

Francis Augustus, Company G; enlisted August 16, 1864, for three years; deserted, Petersburg, October 12, 1864.

Owen F. Bacon, Company H; enlisted August 11, 1864, for three years; promoted corporal; wounded slightly April 7, 1865; mustered out June 28, 1865.

Darby Carrigan, Company H; enlisted August 8, 1864, for three years; mustered out June 28, 1865.

Daniel Doherty, Company I; enlisted October 6, 1863, for three years; transferred to navy April 20, 1864; discharged July 12, 1865.

Alfred G. Jones, Company H; enlisted October 1, 1863, for three years; mustered out June 21, 1865.

Loftus R. Mager, Company H; enlisted October 1, 1863, for three years; discharged, disabled, April 20, 1865.

John Moriarity, Company H; enlisted October 1, 1863, for three years; promoted corporal; mustered out June 28, 1865.

Orrin Wade, Company I; enlisted August 9, 1864, for three years; discharged, imbecility, December 23, 1864.

John Marshall, Company H; enlisted October 6, 1863, for three years; wounded June 16, 1864; dishonorably discharged September 30, 1864.

SOLDIERS.

James McGee, Company I; enlisted August 8, 1863, for three years; sent to regiment August 27, 1864; N. F. R.

Lindor Maruize, Company K; enlisted August 16, 1864, for three years; deserted to enemy October 28, 1864; apprehended; sentenced to be hanged; commuted to dishonorable discharge and five years' imprisonment.

Robert Smith, Company I; enlisted October 6, 1863, for three years; died, DeCamp Hospital, July 17, 1864.

James Smith, Company I; enlisted October 6, 1863, for three years; mustered out July 15, 1865.

James Harris, Company G; enlisted October 3, 1863, for three years; deserted, November 14, 1863, Point Lookout.

RE-ENLISTED VETERANS.

Joseph Gravelle, Company I; enlisted September 25, 1861, for three years; re-enlisted January 1, 1864; deserted, Point Lookout, March 31, 1864.

The Fifth Regiment took part in the battles of Rappahannock River, Yorktown, Fair Oaks, Peach Orchard, White Oak Swamp, Charles City, Malvern Hill, Antietam, Fredericksburg, Chancellorsville, Gettysburg, Cold Harbor, Petersburg, Deep Bottom.

SIXTH REGIMENT.

Thomas J. Carlton, Company B; enlisted for Enfield October 7, 1861, for three years; re-enlisted for Canaan December 28, 1863; promoted second lieutenant, Company H, January 9, 1864; wounded June 3, 1864; September 30, 1864, at Poplar Springs Church; appointed first lieutenant, Company B, August 1, 1864; appointed captain January 10, 1865; resigned June 17, 1865.

William E. Allard, Company B; enlisted November 27, 1861, for three years; deserted August 13, 1862, on march from Fredericksburg; went to Canada.

Lucian N. Gordon, Company B; enlisted November 9, 1861, for three years; wounded December 13, 1862; appointed sergeant; re-enlisted from Enfield December 23, 1863.

James Kimball, Company B; enlisted November 6, 1861, for three years; deserted August 16, 1862.

Edwin E. Shattuck, Company B; enlisted November 27, 1861, for three years; discharged, disabled, December 1, 1862.

Anthony Welch, Company B; enlisted December 7, 1861, for three years; killed, Bull Run, August 29, 1862.

John W. Towle, Company B; enlisted December 9, 1861, for three years; wounded, August 29, 1862, Bull Run; discharged December, 1862.

RECRUIT.

John Carter, Company H; enlisted June 29, 1864, for three years; transferred from Eleventh New Hampshire June 1, 1865; promoted corporal July 1, 1865; mustered out July 17, 1865.

The Sixth Regiment took part in the battles about Camden, Second Bull Run, Chantilly, South Mountain, Antietam, White Sulphur Springs, Fredericksburg, Vicksburg, Jackson, Wilderness, Spottsylvania, Cold Harbor, Petersburg.

SEVENTH REGIMENT.

Frank T. Dustin, Company C; enlisted October 22, 1861, for three years; transferred Second Battalion, V. R. C., May 7, 1864; discharged November 8, 1864.

Henry J. Gile, Company C; enlisted October 7, 1861, for three years; killed, Fort Wagner, S. C., July 18, 1863.

Daniel F. Hinkson, Company C; enlisted October 7, 1861, for three years; killed Fort Wagner, S. C.; promoted corporal July 18, 1862.

This regiment up to June, 1863, saw little field service. After that it was in the battles of Morris Island, Fort Wagner, Olustee, Drury's Bluff, Chester Hill, Bermuda Hundred, Deep Bottom, New Market Heights, Petersburg, Laurel Hill, Darbytown Road, Richmond.

NINTH REGIMENT.

George W. Richardson, Company B; enlisted July 5, 1862, for three years; absent in confinement, Fort Nelson, June 6, 1865; no discharge furnished; corporal.

Jerome Gay, Company B; enlisted June 30, 1862, for three years; deserted, September 24, 1862, Antietam.

James S. Holt, Company F; enlisted June 12, 1862, for three years; died, disease, February 16, 1863.

RECRUITS.

Jacob Christensen, Company F; enlisted July 5, 1864, for three years; transferred to Sixth New Hampshire June 1, 1865; mustered out July 17, 1865.

Daniel Conway, Company I; enlisted July 5, 1864, for three years; deserted en route to regiment, City Point, Va., February 10, 1865.

James Green, Company A; enlisted December 24, 1863, for three years; deserted en route to regiment January 26, 1864.

James Murphy, Company —; enlisted December 8, 1863, for three years; deserted en route to regiment December 31, 1863.

George Lester, Company —; enlisted December 24, 1863, for three years; deserted en route to regiment, N. F. R.

Martin Smith, Company A; enlisted December 24, 1863, for three years; deserted, Camp Dick Robinson, **Ky.**, January 26, 1864.

Ferdinandt Meyer, Company F; enlisted July 5, 1864, for three years; transferred to Sixth New Hampshire June 1, 1865; mustered out July 17, 1865.

SOLDIERS.

Henry Rider, Company C; enlisted December 23, 1863, for three years; transferred to Sixth New Hampshire June 1, 1865; died, disease, September 19, 1865; mustered out July 17, 1865.

William Kehoe, Company A; enlisted December 24, 1863, for three years; deserted January 26, 1864.

Oliver Yarden, Company D; enlisted December 23, 1863, for three years; deserted, Camp Dick Robinson, Ky., January 27, 1864.

Frank Jackson, Company D; enlisted December 23, 1863, for three years; deserted, Loudon, Ky., March 6, 1864.

James H. Walker, Company F; enlisted June 19, 1862, for three years; wounded July 30, 1864; killed, September 30, 1864, Poplar Springs Church.

This regiment was at the battles of South Mountain, Antietam, White Sulphur Springs, Fredericksburg, Vicksburg, Jackson, Wilderness, Spottsylvania, Cold Harbor, Petersburg.

ELEVENTH REGIMENT.

Allen H. George, Company H; enlisted August 17, 1862, for three years; honorably discharged, disabled, May 23, 1864; appointed second lieutenant September 4, 1862.

George H. Richardson, Company H; enlisted August 9, 1862, for three years; corporal; transferred to Company F, V. R. C., August 3, 1864; discharged June 30, 1865.

Frank Morey, Company H; enlisted August 9, 1862, for three years; corporal; promoted sergeant May 1, 1864; wounded slightly June 16, 1864; mustered out June 4, 1865.

John O. Barnes, Company H; enlisted August 17, 1862, for three years; died, wounds, May 15, recevied at Fredericksburg May 12, 1864.

Nathaniel W. Bean, Company H; enlisted August 11, 1862, for three years; died, disease, Alexandria, Va., June 29, 1864.

Oliver B. Childs, Company H; enlisted August 11, 1862, for three years; wounded felling trees February 17, 1864; mustered out June 4, 1865.

William Digby, Company H; enlisted August 9, 1862, for three years; transferred to Second United States Artillery October 14, 1862; died August 23, 1863.

Ledus Hebert, Company H; enlisted August 7, 1862, for three years; wounded slightly May 6, 1864; promoted corporal May 1, 1865; mustered out June 4, 1865.

Thomas E. Jones, Company H; enlisted August 11, 1862, for three years; wounded severely May 6, 1864, Wilderness; discharged, disabled, July 6, 1865; died July 27, 1865.

John B. Lovring, Company H; enlisted August 6, 1862, for three years; mustered out June 4, 1865.

Moses H. Marshall, Company H; enlisted August 8, 1862, for three years; transferred to Eleventh Company, Second Battalion, I. C., March 5, 1864; discharged August 15, 1865.

Thomas S. Marshall, Company H; enlisted August 6, 1862, for three years; discharged, disabled, May 6, 1864.

Philip G. Prescott, Company H; enlisted August 9, 1862; discharged, disabled, July 15, 1863, Washington, D. C.

Aaron Sargent, Company H; enlisted August 9, 1862, for three years; killed near Petersburg, June 16, 1864.

Almond K. Decato, Company H; enlisted August 9, 1862, for three years; mustered out June 4, 1865.

Charles D. Washburn, Company H; enlisted August 6, 1862, for three years; discharged, disabled, February 25, 1864.

RECRUITS.

John Carter, Company E; enlisted June 29, 1864, for three years; transferred to Sixth New Hampshire Volunteers June 1, 1865; appointed corporal July 1, 1865; mustered out July 17, 1865.

Elijah W. Johnson, Company H; enlisted December 29, 1863, for three years; transferred to Company E, Twenty-First V. R. C., January 24, 1865; discharged August 8, 1865.

Joseph Sherry, Company E; enlisted July 1, 1864, for three years; transferred Sixth New Hampshire Volunteers June 1, 1865; promoted corporal; mustered out July 17, 1865.

John Taylor, Company D; enlisted June 30, 1864, for three years; transferred to Sixth New Hampshire Volunteers June 1, 1865; mustered out July 17, 1865.

George F. Brooks, Company —; enlisted July 20, 1864, for three years; deserted *en route* to regiment.

Joseph D. Bliss, Company —; enlisted July 20, 1864, for three years; deserted *en route* to regiment November, 1864.

August Champagne, Company —; enlisted June 30, 1864, for three years; deserted *en route* to regiment.

Thomas H. Desmond, Company —; enlisted June 30, 1864, for three years; deserted *en route* to regiment.

Samuel Evans, Company —; enlisted July 29, 1864, for three years; deserted *en route* to regiment.

John McCauley, Company —; enlisted July 2, 1864, for three years; deserted *en route* to regiment.

John Piero, Company —; enlisted June 24, 1864, for three years; deserted *en route* to regiment.

James Richards, Company —; enlisted July 2, 1864, for three years; deserted *en route* to regiment.

Charles H. Allerton, Company —; enlisted June 30, 1864, for three years; deserted *en route* to regiment.

Horace A. Johnson lived in Canaan and was credited to Hebron.

The Eleventh Regiment was in the battles of Fredericksburg, Vicksburg, Jackson, Wilderness, Spottsylvania, North Anna,

SOLDIERS. 379

Polotopomy, Bethesda Church, Hatcher's Run, Petersburg, Weldon Railroad, Poplar Springs Church, Cold Harbor.

TWELFTH REGIMENT.

George F. Taplin, Company F; enlisted August 18, 1862, for three years; discharged, disabled, December 5, 1862; re-enlisted November 3, 1863; wounded June 3, 1864; discharged, disabled, April 18, 1865.

John W. Hoyt, Company C; enlisted December 29, 1863, for three years; wounded June 3, 1864; transferred to Company E, Second New Hampshire Volunteers, June 21, 1865; discharged December 19, 1865.

This Regiment was in the battles of Swift's Creek, Drury's Bluff, Fredericksburg, Chancellorsville, Gettysburg, Wapping Heights, Cold Harbor, Petersburg, Bermuda Hundred, Richmond.

FOURTEENTH REGIMENT.

Enos Glogelt, recruit Company K; enlisted September 29, 1863, for three years; wounded October 19, 1864; discharged November 20, 1865.

This Regiment was at Deep Bottom, Antietam, Winchester, Fisher's Hill, Cedar Creek.

FIFTEENTH REGIMENT.

Company F; nine months' men mustered out August 13, 1863.

William Gordon, captain; enlisted October 2, 1862; mustered in November 11.

Fred B. Wells, first sergeant; enlisted September 8, 1862; mustered in October 10; re-enlisted, Company B, headquarters troop, Department of the Gulf, July 5, 1863; discharged July 24, 1864.

Alvah Gilman, corporal; enlisted September 8, 1862; mustered in October 15; died, Baton Rouge, June 3, 1863.

Everett W. Dow enlisted September 2, 1862; mustered in October 10.

Abiel Sharp enlisted September 15, 1862; mustered in October 10; wounded June 14, 1863.

Don C. Washburn enlisted September 5, 1862; mustered in October 10; wounded May 27, 1863; discharged August 13, 1863.

Levi Martin enlisted September 5, 1862; mustered in October 10.

James Furlong enlisted September 5, 1862; mustered in October 10.

Edwin D. Aldrich enlisted September 5, 1862; mustered in October 10; killed, Port Hudson, La., May 27, 1863.

Albert Bradbury enlisted September 15, 1862; mustered in October 10.

Hiram Jones enlisted September 15, 1862; mustered in October 10.

William Adams enlisted September 15, 1862; mustered in October 10.

William W. Dustin enlisted September 2, 1862; mustered in October

10; died, July 21, 1863, New Orleans, of wounds received at Port Hudson, La., June 11, 1863.

Edgar D. Aldrich enlisted September 8, 1862; mustered in October 10.

Dexter F. Bradbury enlisted September 8, 1862; mustered in October 10; died, disease, St. James Hospital, New Orleans, July 9, 1863.

Austin Dunham enlisted August 30, 1862; mustered in October 10; wounded May 27, 1863.

Gilbert J. Robie enlisted September 8, 1862; mustered in October 10; died, disease, Memphis, Tenn., August 3, 1863.

David Legro enlisted September 1, 1862; mustered in October 10; wounded May 27, 1863.

Rufus S. Goss enlisted September 1, 1862; mustered in October 10.

This Regiment was on duty about Carrollton and Port Hudson, La.

EIGHTEENTH REGIMENT.

Andrew J. Darush, Company G; enlisted December 3, 1864; discharged by order December 28, 1864.

John Moores, Company G; enlisted December 10, 1864; mustered out August 11, 1865.

Henry Thomas, Company G; enlisted December 10, 1864; deserted January 14, 1865.

Cornelius Creed, Company H; enlisted February 25, 1865; mustered out July 29, 1865.

John M. Lee, Company H; enlisted February 25, 1865; deserted March 15, 1865.

John S. Webster, United States Navy; enlisted June 8, 1863, for one years, as landsman; served on *Ohio, Princeton, Saratoga, Powhattan;* discharged July 7, 1864.

NEW HAMPSHIRE BATTALION, FIRST NEW ENGLAND CAVALRY, TROOP K.

Asa A. Hall, enlisted October 9, 1861; wounded August 9, 1862; captured June, 1863; re-enlisted for Strafford January 2, 1864.

TROOP M.

James H. French enlisted December 3, 1861; transferred to Company K January 1, 1862; appointed bugler; re-enlisted January 2, 1864, for Manchester; discharged August 31, 1866.

They were at Cedar Mountain, Second Bull Run, Chantilly, Fredericksburg, Culpeper, Bristow Station.

FIRST REGIMENT, NEW HAMPSHIRE CAVALRY, RECRUITS.

James Bond enlisted February 27, 1865; deserted *en route* to regiment.

George Langdon enlisted February 15, 1865; deserted May 13, 1865.

Charles Bradley enlisted February 15, 1865; mustered out July 15, 1865.

They were at Cold Harbor, White Oak Swamp, Weldon Railroad, Winchester, Cedar Creek.

FIRST LIGHT BATTERY, NEW HAMPSHIRE VOLUNTEERS, RECRUIT.

Dennis County enlisted November 7, 1863; transferred to Twelfth Company, Heavy Artillery; mustered out June 9, 1865.

This Battery served with the Reserve Artillery until November 5, 1864, when it consolidated with the Heavy Artillery. After November 1863, it was at Brandy Station, Wilderness, Spottsylvania, North Anna River, Sheldon's Cross Roads, Cold Harbor, Petersburg, Deep Bottom.

FIRST REGIMENT, HEAVY ARTILLERY.

James W. Atherton, Company H; enlisted September 3, 1864, for one year; mustered out June 15, 1865; sergeant; enlisted June 8, 1863; one year United States Navy as landsman on United States ships *Ohio*, *Princeton*, *Saratoga*, *Powhattan*, *Neptune*; discharged July 7, 1864.

George P. Clark, corporal, Company H; enlisted August 31, 1864, for one year; mustered out June 15, 1865.

Everett W. Dow, corporal, Company H; enlisted September 1, 1864, for one year; mustered out June 15, 1865.

Sidney L. Colby, Company H; enlisted September 1, 1864, for one year; mustered out June 15, 1865.

Edson J. Fifield, Company H; enlisted September 1, 1864, for one year; mustered out June 15, 1865; promoted corporal February 26, 1865.

John Hoyt, Company H; enlisted September 1, 1864, for one year; mustered out June 15, 1865; promoted corporal January 19, 1865.

Daniel Stickney, Company H; enlisted August 31, 1864, for one year; mustered out June 15, 1865.

James Wilson, Company H; enlisted August 31, 1864, for one year; mustered out June 15, 1865.

Dennis County, Company M; enlisted November 7, 1863, for three years; mustered out June 9, 1865.

Frank W. Carroll, Company H; enlisted September 16, 1863, for three years; discharged, disabled, June 5, 1865.

RECRUITS.

Andrew Blair, Company M; enlisted November 11, 1864; mustered out June 9, 1865.

James Lahey, Company —; enlisted December 23, 1864; deserted *en route* to regiment.

John Miller, Company —; enlisted December 3, 1864; deserted en route to regiment.

John Gilman, Company M; enlisted December 2, 1864; deserted, New York City, April 29, 1865.

This regiment was assigned for duty in the defences about Washington.

Adelbert O. Williams served in Company H, Thirtieth Massachusetts Infantry; enlisted December 3, 1861; discharged for disability March 30, 1862.

Sylvanus J. Dow served Company I, Twelfth Massachusetts Infantry; enlisted June 26, 1861, for three years; mustered in same day as corporal; appointed sergeant January 1, 1864; first sergeant-major March 1, 1864; wounded; discharged July 8, 1864; term expired.

The names of the volunteers furnished by brokers, is as follows:

James Green	Asa A. Hall
John Kelly	John M. Lee
Patrick Welch	Jerome Gay
Henry Preston	Jas. H. French
Thomas Presley	Andrew J. Darush
Frank Jackson	Jas. H. Walker
Thomas Kirby	Francis Augustus
George Young	John Miller
Charles H. Allerton	Jas. S. Holt

The substitutes furnished by brokers to make out the quota of the town were:

Francis Bearo	James McGee
John McCullom	George Young
Wm. Thompson	Oliver Yarden
Orrin F. Bacon	William Dorsey
Orrin Wade	Joseph Saunders
Henry Rider	Wm. Whitmer
Thos. Kirby	Darby Carrigan
Wm. Kehoe	Jacob Christensen
Martin Smith	Joseph Sherry
John Carter	Danl. Conway
Saml. Evans	James Murphy
Thos. Prew	Geo. F. Brooks
John Moores	August Champagne
James Bond	John Mahr
Chas. Bradley	John Perron
James Lahey	Henry Kelley

John Gilman	George Lester
Zephriam Forties	Joseph D. Bliss
Robert McConnell	Thos. H. Desmond
Orra C. Hardy	John McCauley
Patrick Ledlow	Jas. Richards
Chas Smith	Cornelius Creed
Saml. Sleeper	George Langdon
Linder Maruize	Andrew Blair
Ferdinant Meyer	Warren W. Hamlett
John Taylor	Thos. Presley
James Green	Oscar F. Washburn

In the adjutant-general's report the Canaan enrollment on April 30, 1865 was 139 men, the total quota under calls since July, 1863, up to that time was 93 men. The total credit by enrollment and draft was 108 men, there being a surplus of 15 men. The number of male citizens in town between 18 and 45 years liable to military duty was 139, the estimated number who entered the army and navy from April 15, 1861, to April, 1865, was 49 as reported, but the latter number must be a mistake. The number of men the town was required to furnish during the war can not be told nor the number it did furnish. But so far as the records go every name has been taken that has been credited to Canaan, some whose residence was unknown are known to have enlisted from this town. This record includes only the names of those who enlisted from this town and went to fill out the quota required. Some of them were residents, others were hired by the brokers employed by the town to obtain men in place of those drafted or volunteered. Some men reënlisted after their term of service had expired. Many of the hired substitutes deserted.

The foregoing lists contain the names of 183 men.

CHAPTER XXIII.

ROADS.

The settlers traveled from house to house by means of paths, which by constant treading and use became harder and harder and more distinctly roads. There were no wheeled carriages and the people went on foot or horseback. They traveled straight, with no reference to inequalities of hill or valley. The first paths were worn along South Road, between the houses of the settlers, and to Lebanon, where they had to go for grain. As other settlers came and built their log huts in other parts of the town, paths were trod to their houses. When the corn mill was built a path was made to Eames' mill from the south part of the town, subsequently a road was laid over this part, "as now trod to Eames Mill." This road ran through the north field of the old Barber farm, nearly on the east line of M. E. Cross', across his road to the town house, through his field and so on towards the northeast to the mills at the outlet of Hart's Pond. Traces of this road are still visible just inside the west line of wall on J. B. Wallace's land.

Another road to the mill led along the north side of Hart's Pond, and was called the "old Cardigan Road," over much the same course as the road now used, until it reached the corner, then turning and running south by Joshua Wells', turning again southwesterly over the hill towards the Bickford place and so on towards Orange over the bridge by the fair grounds. Another path led to the mill from Dorchester, and came out near the Putney house on the previous road.

The road across Sawyer Hill dates back to an old path trod between Nathaniel Bartlett's and South Road, by the houses of Ezekiel Wells, Samuel Meacham, Warren Wilson, William Richardson, Clark Currier and Amasa Clark.

These paths, which gradually became roads capable of travel with ox teams and horses, were built for the accommodation of the settlers only; there was no traveling for pleasure, and with the exception of Governor Wentworth when he passed over his

Factory Village

Street and Hart Pond

road to Hanover, no one passed through the town expecting to find any direct route to any other town. Hills were not avoided, the early settler knew where his neighbor lived in a straight line and he went that way, not round about, with no regard for any other traveler but himself. These paths and roads wore out early, and it was not like the western prairie, where there is no sign of tree or rock, and when the ruts get too deep, another track is made along side of the old one with no labor.

The settlers would have had to cut trees and remove stones, and even when they did begin to build new roads for team travel, they did not avoid hills, but kept as near the old path as possible. The first road turnpiked and rounded up was from South Road to the Street. The old settlers were nearly all proprietors, owned one or more rights of the grantees, and as the charter provided an allowance for roads to be made in the surveys and pitches of land, they considered it their duty to lay them out and make repairs. For nearly two years after the settlement of the town there does not seem to have been much money spent upon roads, nor any laid out, whatever repairs had been made were done by the settlers without expense. Up to 1776 the town had voted no money for roads. In that year it voted 15 pounds, the proprietors had raised all the money and built all the roads. From 1776 to 1787 both town and propriety voted money for roads and bridges. After that date the propriety seems to have left that public duty to the town, and from that time on, for forty years, the records of the town are mostly the record of the acceptance, survey and discontinuance of roads.

At the first meeting of the proprietors in 1768, three dollars tax on each proprietor's right was raised for roads. This amount was to be worked out at the rate of four shillings per day. The proprietors' committee were to see that it was worked out. At the first town meeting in 1770, Ezekiel Wells was appointed surveyor of roads, the duties of his office were to survey the roads to be laid out, and not to superintend their construction, as is done today by that officer. In 1774 the town appointed two surveyors and their duties began to tend towards the laying out and constructing.

In 1770 the proprietors raised six shillings on each right for roads, and later in the year a further tax of 18 shillings was laid. In 1771 John Scofield was paid 16 pounds, 8 shillings for labor on the highway, Samuel Jones 2 pounds, 10 shillings and 2 pence, Samuel Benedict 12 shillings and 8 pence, Joseph Craw 8 shillings. They were the road committee. In 1772 James Jones received 8 shillings for labor. This was all for the repairs on the old paths. The Governor's Road from the Pemigewasset River to Dartmouth College was voted to be built at a proprietors' meeting May 19, 1772, and they "Voted a Tax of Two pounds lawfull money be & hereby is laid on each Proprietors Right & Share of land in sd Canaan to defray the Charges & Cost of Clearing & making the Governors Rode thro sd Town." (a)* Joseph Craw, Samuel Benedict and Samuel Jones were appointed a committee to lay out the "sd one hundred and twenty four pounds in making sd Rode forthwith," and a day's work was to be worth 5 shillings and 6 pence. In July they voted to lay a road from the "Lower Meadow across Town Hill to ye road that goes to the Mills." There is no survey of this road recorded nor of the road voted to be laid the following October. "from the Mills southerly to the town Line."

In 1773 a road was wanted through a corner of Relhan (Enfield) and application was made to the Court of General Sessions. There is no evidence in the court records that this road was obtained. In June, 1773, they voted "to lay out a road from the road that leads (from ye Lower Great Meadows across Town Hill to ye Mills) on ye North Bank of Masquamy thro Mr John Scofields Entervale lot to Ezekiel Wells Enterval lots shall lay out a road for sd Wells."

In 1774 Caleb Clark was to pay five pounds in labor for a lot, "one half to be done on the road and the other half to be done on the bridge to be built acrost the river by John Scofields at the Loer Interval." In October they voted "That the Rode that goeth from Thomas Miners Intervale to Mr John Scofields should be laid out in a more straight form and a bridge built under the care of the comite across the river." "That there should be a Rode laid out from Capt.Waleworths (Walworths) to the rode that goeth from Samuel Chapmans to Mr. Eames mill." No one of these was ever recorded nor are they in existence now. The

* Refers to layout of roads.

"Lower Meadow," "Lower Great Meadows," and "Loer Interval," are the same and were in the vicinity of West Canaan, so was John Scofield's intervale. Thomas Miner's intervale was near G. W. Davis's. Captain Walworth lived at the east end of South Road, and Samuel Chapman and Ezekiel Wells on Town Hill.

In 1777 the town chose three surveyors of highways, "Richard Clark in the Northeast District, Charles Walworth in the South district, Samuel Jones in West District." The care of the roads had given one man too much work and we will see that as the roads increase the number of surveyors also increases. This is also the first indication of dividing the town into districts, it was a division made by custom and not by any vote of the town.

In 1780 the proprietors voted to "lay out a Rode from Samuel Jones to Barbers Mil where they think it most Convenient for the South part of the Town." This led by the old graveyard down past the old Haynes house, and is now thrown up. In 1786 the proprietors raised 60 pounds for roads and bridges, "Forty pounds of this amount was to be laid out on the road appointed to be laid out by the court through the town." No road was recorded on that date on the court records. Fifteen pounds was to be laid out on the road "from Lime to Grafton." Five pounds was to be laid out on the bridge, "from Town Hill so called over the river."

Four shillings a day was to be allowed for labor in summer and three shillings in winter, three shillings for ox work. This is the last vote made by the proprietors about roads. That question had become too large for them, there are too many roads and the proprietors are few, and it is left to the town hereafter. The town this year raises its road money for the first time by the rate, ten shillings on the pound.

It was also voted to lay out a road to "John Curriers land," (he lived then on West Farms), also from "Mr. Calkins house," who lived at West Canaan, "to Town Hill." In April a committee was chosen to survey all the roads in town. Whether they ever reported or not or performed this work is not known. In August, 10 shillings on the pound were raised "to make good the Post Road through the town," and six days' notice was to be given of the time to work. In November the committee "to compleat the Post Road in this town, call on the inhabitants to make good the Bridge over the Mascoma river on said day by way of a land tax." The "Post Road" called the County Road and "South Road" also, and even to this day, was laid out by the County Court about 1774. The old deeds of that date refer to it, but it was probably laid out by the General Sessions Court October 26, 1785, as a Post Road. In 1791 the post route over it was called No. 2. That court was the Court of General Sessions and had jurisdiction of highways. Upon petition signed by inhabitants living near the proposed road, the court appointed commissioners, who held a hearing and if impressed with the necessity or desirability of such road proceeded to appoint a day to meet upon the proposed route and lay out the road. The County was not organized until 1773.

There is a small record book of His Majesty's Court of General Sessions for several terms, from April, 1774, to April, 1775, at Haverhill. The next term appears to have been held at Plymouth in November, 1782. John Wentworth, the provincial governor, left in May, 1775, and no court was held during the Revolution. There is no record of South Road ever having been laid out by this court. That it was laid out before the proprietors made the survey of land along the Enfield line is evident, for the old surveys run to the road, and the range line followed the road for a distance of 800 rods. It became the traveled highway from the lower towns to the north. From the height of land in Grafton it plunged down into the "Gulf" up over the long hill by the Joneses, down again over Moose Brook, and so on up and down, over Town and Sawyer Hills, till it passed beyond our boundaries. This road has remained unchanged, only it is not so much the traveled road to Lyme now. Congress in 1793 established post routes through the state, one of these routes started from Concord and went through Boscawen, Salisbury, Andover, Newchester, Plymouth, Haverhill, Piermont, Orford, Lyme, Hanover, Lebanon, Enfield, Canaan, Grafton, Alexandria and Salisbury to Concord. Each post rider was required to perform his route weekly. The riders received twelve pounds each. Postage on single letters was fixed at six pence for forty miles and four pence for less than forty. Once a week citizens in Canaan could send a letter to other sections in the state, by the rider. If directed to a town on one of the other routes, six to twelve days would be required for its delivery.

In 1786 a road was laid out from the "old Wolfeborough road" to Mr. Bradbury's land, and a bridge was built over the Indian River. Six highway surveyors were appointed this year and the next year, 1787, eight. The old roads are beginning to be inconvenient, easier travel is required, and a committee is appointed to see "where the road should be turned by Daniel Blaisdells land." "To alter the road from Mr. Joslens house to Enfield line, and a road was laid out from the 'Brick Yard' on West Farms, 'to John Harris land,' also from David Foggs to the Post road on Quaker Hill." Daniel Blaisdell lived on the turnpike below the depot. Mr. Joslen lived at the west end of the South Road near West Canaan, John Harris' land was north of the brick yard. David Fogg lived at the corner of the Lebanon and switch roads from the Street.

In 1788 is found the first appropriation for making the roads passable in winter "Voted to raise 5 shillings on the pound for the purpose of breaking rodes and clearing out fallen trees the ensueing winter, if sd money is not laid out in sd time to be laid out on the Roads next Spring." They also voted to petition the selectmen of Grafton to lay out a road "from the Main Road that leads thro sd Grafton, to meet the road that leads to Capt. Barber's Mill" (1). A survey of a road from "Thomas Baldwin's dwelling house to Enfield line was accepted, and to give Mr. Baldwin the allowance of land left for a road by the proprietors of sd town in exchange for the above said road." They voted to lay out a road from "Thadeus Lathrops to strike the public road." Thaddeus Lathrop lived on the east side of the road from the village opposite the house of J. W. Colburn (3). A committee was appointed to complete the bridge over the Mascoma, "by Lieut. E. Wells," and another committee was appointed to complete the bridge "on the Post road over Maskum river."

In 1789 no new roads were laid out or voted. In 1790 nine highway surveyors were appointed but no new roads laid. In 1791 the selectmen were requested to lay out a road to "Mr Thadeus Lathrops" and a committee was requested to alter a road from "where Mr. Calkins formerly lived to Major Jones Saw mill, if they think best."

In 1792 nine highway surveyors were appointed, as follows:

    John P. Calkins for Sugar Hill.
    John Scofield for the south district.
    Asa Paddleford for West Farms.
    Samuel Meacham for Town Hill.
    Ensign Joshua Richardson for N. W.
    Richard Clark for north district.
    Jonathan Dustin for Dogester district.
    William Douglass for Centre district.
    Oliver Smith for middle district.
    Elijah Wicher for Eastern District.

"Voted to build a bridge over the Mascoma river, near where the old one stands." "To send a petition to the town of Hanover requesting them to make a Good Passible Road Through the Corner of Their Town which Lies betwixt Canaan and Lyme as the Road Goes." "Voted not to open the road through the Intervale from Mr. Flints to the bridge." The inhabitants north of the Wolfeborough road were incorporated into a separate highway district.

Lieut. William Richardson, Maj. Samuel Jones and Capt. Ezekiel Wells were appointed a committee to survey "necessary Roads." The building of the bridge over the Mascoma was to be sold to the lowest bidder.

In 1793 "Voted that the former committee chosen to survey the road from Grafton line to Sawyer hill (viz) William Richardson, R. Barber and J. Harris, make a proper return of their poceedings to the town clerk and him to record the same." It was never recorded. The town voted to allow for labor done on the highway three shillings, six pence per day for the months from May to August, and two shillings per day for oxen. "Voted to build a bridge over Mud Pond Brook upon cost of the Town." "To sell the same to the lowest bidder for wheat at 5 shillings per bushel." This bridge was struck off to John Currier for $47. Thomas Miner, Joshua Wells and Robert Barber were to "lay out a road from West Farms to the center of the Town." "Voted that the road from John M. Barbers to J. Flints be opened and recorded." This was not recorded until 1795 and extended from the south end of the Street to the Switch (8). A committee was appointed to inspect the bridge built by Thomas Miner over the Indian River. In 1794 there were ten highway surveyors and districts. "Voted not to accept the road from Mr. Flints to Shubal Burdicks." "Voted to present a petition to the Sessions respecting the road from Prospect Hill to Lyme." This matter was brought up at the town meeting in Hanover and it was postponed. There is no mention of this among the court records. The town voted "to accept the survey of a road from Ebenezer Eames to Dames Gore" (5). "Voted to accept survey of road from Enfield line near Asa Paddlefords by the Brick Yard to North Branch Bridge" and from "Steven Eastmans to Daniel Morses." To lay out a road from "the Meeting house to the Widow Steven's or near by in the most convenient place." Nothing is known of this road nor of the one accepted later from "Widow Stevens to Joshua Stevens."

Almost everyone wanted a road at this time to go anywhere, and any one could call out the committee and ask the town to accept of the road, all at the expense of the town. The town began to realize that much unnecessary work was done which had to be paid for so they voted to put a stop to it in the following: "that if any man calls out the committee, and lays out a road, and the town does not accept of said Road, that the man which calls out said committee, pay them himself for their services."

In 1795 they voted "to petition the County Court to have the road made passable from Prospect Hill to Lyme through Hanover." This petition was dated August 22, 1796. Lyme appointed Jonathan Freeman its agent to go before the Court of Common Pleas. The road from "Mr. Flints to Mr. Peaslee's South bound" was accepted. In 1796 the highway surveyors were increased to twelve, and no new roads were laid out or asked for.

In 1797 Ezekiel Wells was made agent of the town at the next term of the "Inferior Court Respecting the Lyme Road," on a petition for a road from Lyme to Canaan meeting house. This petition was dismissed February 26, 1798 (2).

The road to Lyme through the northeast corner of Hanover had been a source of much annoyance to the people of Lyme and Canaan. Hanover persistently refused to lay out the little piece of road in that town to join on to the ends of the road from

Canaan and Lyme. A petition dated July 6, 1796, was sent to the selectmen of Hanover by the selectmen of Canaan, informing them, "that the cryes of the injured Travellers are continually ringing in our ears, on account of the intolarableness and almost impractacableness of Travelling the Road." No attention was paid and Canaan applied to the court. The court required notice to be given Hanover. After the dismissal of the petition for what cause is not known, the inhabitants of Lyme and Canaan at once petitioned Hanover to lay out the road, and on August 31, 1798, the selectmen of Hanover, appointed a place to meet the selectmen of the other two towns in Lyme on the 20th of September "and see where a suitable place for sd road can be found."

The town "Voted to lay a rode from Moody Noyes on his line to Joseph Flint's land, and from thence in the most convenient place to sd Flints." This is the same road not accepted in 1794 when Shubel Burdick lived on Moody Noyes' farm. "To lay a road from Mr. Flints to the Meeting house in the most convenient place and that the road be established when the committee lays it" (9). It was laid in 1798 and Moody Noyes conveyed a strip of land four rods wide and two hundred long to the selectmen of Canaan for it. A road was laid out "from the road that goes by Mr. Carlton's in the most convenient and best place by Nathaniel Whichers to the road that goes to Dorchester by Nathaniel Gilmans." This was recorded in 1800 (12). In 1798 no roads were voted nor in 1800. In 1801 the town voted not to "change the road from Ezra Nichols to the Meeting house." This requested change was afterwards granted. "Voted to reconsider Ezra Nichols road to Nath Barbers." "To establish a road from John M. Barbers to Nichols." Ezra Nichols lived on the Cochran place, and Nath Barber at A. W. Hutchinson's.

The town voted "to lay out a road from West Farms to the Meeting house," to exchange road from Joshua Harris' northerly down the hill (8) from where it "is now trod, into the Range way between Harris and James Doten to the North end of Dotens land" (9). "Voted to give Moses Richardson $12, on condition that he give a deed to the town of a road four rods wide from near his house to Francis Kinneson," and "Daniel Farnum $10 for a four rod road through his land and Francis Kinneson's land." "where the road was run to Moses Richardsons land." This road went from South road to the road to Grafton (17). The highway from West Farms to Prospect Hill was accepted (16), and one from Clark Currier's by Richard Clark, 3d's, to Reynold Gates's, and from said Clark's by Levi Cilley's to Ambrose Chase's (14), also from Clark Currier's to Josiah Barber's (15). Directions were given to open a road from Deacon Harris' barn to Thaddeus Lathrop's. In 1802, "Voted to move road to the north line of Jonathan Carlton's lot" (20). The road was first laid in 1800. The bridge over Goose Pond Brook on the West Farms road was bid off to Jonathan Carlton for $36, to be 16 feet wide of $2\frac{1}{2}$ inch plank. The road from Captain Wells' orchard to Moses Chase's house through J. and Elam Meacham's land to the old road was discontinued, and a road to Moses Chase's another way was voted to be laid out (20a). This is the first vote of the discontinuance of any road by the town, many roads hereafter were voted discontinued and passed out of use, many others by not being used have been closed and fenced in by adjoining owners.

The laying out of roads in the early days was sometimes done by committees and sometimes by selectmen, contrary to the law. Nor were roads discontinued legally. Some roads were laid out by the courts, and some became roads from constant travel by the public. Efforts made in the interests of private individuals to close roads have, when opposed, met with disaster, and the roads have continued open. It is oftentimes a question for the courts to decide and is the only safe method to pursue in closing a highway for a long time traveled over by the public.

In 1803 John Currier, William Richardson and Daniel Farnum were appointed a committee to lay out necessary roads. There were fourteen highway surveyors, and thirty cents was raised by the rate for roads. The town "Voted to open road from the head of Broad Street to Thadeus Lathrops on as reasonable terms as they can with the owners of the land." "To raise $75 for a new road from Joshua Wells to Orange line towards Grafton" (21). "To Discontinue road from Nathaniel Gilmans to Joseph Randletts as soon as new road is passable." New road was recorded 1802 (19).

In 1804 fifteen surveyors were appointed, but no new roads were voted, and the town refused to build a bridge from Levi George's to Town Hill. Mr. George lived opposite George Ginn's. In 1805 there are 17 surveyors, the town offers fifty cents per day from June to August and thirty-four cents after that time for work on the road. The town "voted to build a bridge over the Mascoma at or near William Campbell's saw mill, and the committee to call upon the inhabitants to build the same." This is the bridge refused in 1804. In 1806 they voted again "to build a bridge at William Campbell's new mill over the river"— the bridge near the old tray factory. The town voted "That Capt. George keep two gates free on the road from his house to Wm. Campbell's for two years." "To exchange old road for land to Wm. Campbell's new mill to the place where new bridge is to be built" (25). "To examine road that leads from near Jehu Jones and comes out to the road below Lt. Follensbees mill" (22), and that the survey, "of Jehu Jones road to Welches Mill be opened by surveyor."

The September Term of the General Sessions, laid out a road from South Road to Enfield line. This is the first road recorded in the court record as laid out in Canaan (26), and the next is in 1822.

In 1807 six cents per hour was paid on the highway for men and oxen. There are seventeen surveyors. The survey of Blake's road was accepted (23), in the southwest corner of the town and also a survey of South Road (24).

In 1808 Daniel Pattee, Joshua Harris and John Currier were chosen to fix a place to build a bridge "over the North Branch of Mascoma and make survey of road from where it crosses said river to where it intersects old road." "The old road from near Codfish Hill to river where old bridge was," was discontinued (28) and also the road from near Joshua Harris to Town Hill Bridge, which was the last seven or eight courses (8). This road led from South Road north to the river, on the line between Joshua Harris', afterward Sylvester Jones' and James Doten's. After the road was discontinued Joshua Harris pitched upon it in the right of Daniel Harris and it became a part of his farm. The road through "George Waleworths land so far as it goes 'was thrown up', he giving liberty to travel to the burying ground and keeping gates or bars convenient to pass" (22). This is the road by the Cobble Graveyard to South Road.

In 1809 they voted to exchange the road beside the pond from Wells' to Broad Street as soon as the turnpike is passable. And also "to explore ground for a road from Broad Street on direction to Lebanon City to Canaan line." This refers to what is now called the "Lebanon Road." As a continuous road it was never laid out so far as known. There was a road or path from Eames' mill by John M. Barber's (Israel Sharon) down the hill to the bridge and across the flat to William Campbell's, known in early times as the road across Town Hill from east to west. From there on it passed through interval lots of Wells and Eleazer Scofield to Enfield line. There were numerous changes in these roads until it is probable the present road was the final development.

In 1810 the committee "are to measure Mr. Walesworths lot of land and if there is any allowance for a road they are to lay out and open the road from Jehu Jones to Welchs Mill which was discontinued." The road from the north end of Broad Street near the burying ground, southerly as far as David Dustin's house was discontinued, a part of the old path to Eames' mill, and a road from "Dustin's to the Street near Capt. Moore's" was opened but not laid until 1821 (48). The road "from the brook near David Lawrence's house northerly, as far as the old schoolhouse on the northwest corner of Samuel Welch, Jr.'s land," was changed to a place further west and also the "road from the brook as far northeasterly as Welch's house," was changed to near Eliphalet Richardson's orchard (39). John Currier was allowed fifty cents a rod for building extra fence on account of these changes.

In 1811 it was voted, "to make a road passable on the best ground from some place on Broad street by the Brick yard to Enfield line, near Asa Paddleford's." "To settle with Job Tyler for a road through his land" (32). "To discontinue road from William Chase's barn northerly as far as Levi Cilley's house, also from Luther Kinney's northerly by Richard Clark, Jr.'s, to Turnpike at Hovey pasture" (14). And the "road from Richard Clark, Jr.'s, north by Josiah Clark's to turnpike near

Saml. Gates" (14) was discontinued. They voted "to lay a road from near Caleb Seabury's to the road that leads from Clark Currier's to Amasa Clark's." "To exchange road from Wells barn easterly as far as Abel Hadley's orchard, for a road on the west side of said Hadley's orchard to the turnpike." One hundred and eighty dollars was to be laid out on the road to Enfield by John H. Harris, "that was fined by the court." Roads, like persons, in those days were indicted and fined for being bad. Abel Brown's request "to remove a road by building a bridge over a run of water in Dist. No. 8, and to straighten road from the bottom of the hill, near Lawrence mill to the turnpike on the south line of land lately sold to Saml. Church," was granted.

The old Scofield bridge and the log bridge, a little east of it, were rebuilt. It was voted that the "selectmen lay out a road from Ezekiel Wells, Jr.'s, to old Post guide on County road that leads to John Willises" (35); "from the Meeting house to back road near John M. Barber's (31); and discontinue road to burying ground near Daniel Colby's"; "to alter road on hill, south of John M. Barber's." "To assist the Town Hill district so much as to make their part of the new road from Center district to old road in Town Hill district." "To lay out a road on the east route, according to plan exhibited by selectmen acrost Clark Currier's land."

In 1812 the road from "Dea. Josiah Clark's bridge to turnpike, near John Worth, Jr.'s barn," was accepted (34), and the road from "Saml. Whittier's to Dea. Clark's bridge," was exchanged for it.

The road from Clark Currier's to the burying ground was exchanged for the road from the burying ground to Amasa Clark's. Esquire Pettingill was asked to procure a continuance for those roads which were indicted. If the road could be fixed before the return of the indictment and trial, there would be no fine. The road from the old brick yard easterly, "crossing the Intervale to the County road at the Post guide, and the road from near Stephen Clifford's, easterly to northwest corner of E. Wells, 3d's, orchard," were discontinued. In place of the latter was (35).

In 1813 the road from the north end of "Broad street to Gore line, near Asel Jones's," was straightened. One hundred and sixty dollars was raised this year for making roads and bridges. The road from "Thadeus Lathrop, Jr.'s, to the bridge between the two sawmills," was discontinued. The committee were ordered to explore the ground for a new road from Greeley's mills to the West Farms' road. The report on straightening the road from Gore Road to Broad Street was not accepted. The selectmen were requested to lay out a road from Seth Daniels' to Welch's Mills (37), to straighten the road from the meeting house to Judah Wells', and a survey of a road from Mescheck Blake's to Hanover was accepted (36). The road from Esquire Currier's to Wood's mills was straightened and Currier allowed $30.

In 1814 Stephen Goodhue petitioned Canaan for a road from Canaan's meeting house to Plymouth and the town voted to oppose it. In 1815 the road from Joseph Clark's to the turnpike was laid, and the road from Ensign Colby's to Daniel B. Whittier's was discontinued (20). John Fales was given the "old road against his land southerly, which is discontinued, lying between the two brooks, for the present contemplated road crossing his land." Eliphalet Richardson is given "one rod off, westerly side of old road from southerly side of the Mill brook, four rods northerly as far as where the new road leaves the old one to sd Richardson's orchard." The two last votes refer to the road at the Corner, voted to be changed in 1810 (39).

In 1816 the town quiets John Currier in the possesion of the old road, between his land and Bailey Welch. And D. B. Whittier, Nathaniel and Ephraim Wilson are quieted in the possession of another old road (20).

In 1818 it is voted to lay out a road "from Adam Pollard's by Caleb C. Bartlett's to highway near Nathl. Bartlett's" (43). The survey of a road by Stephen Worth's is accepted (42).

In 1820 the road from March Barber's to the meeting house was straightened (44). March Barber lived on the old Benjamin Norris farm and the old road came up over the hill southwest of Israel Sharon's in a straight line to meet the road from the Switch and continued to the south end of Broad street over the latter road. The old road was given to J. M. Barber from the north side of James Wallace's land, down the hill to the Nichols or Cochran land. The road as straightened, is now the traveled road from the town house to the Norris bridge.

The road from Deacon Clark's bridge to the fair grounds was continued by Job Jenniss's to Orange line (45).

The road to Sewall Gleason's had been indicted on the north end of Sawyer Hill and a postponement was asked to repair it. The bridge across the river at Caleb Welch's mill was rebuilt. It was voted to lay out a road across Capt. Joshua Harris' land to David Dustin's land (48).

This was laid out in 1821 and is the present road from the town house to M. E. Cross'. In 1821 it was voted to ascertain the boundaries of the old Mill road, and in 1822 it was deeded to Joshua Harris for the land which the new road took. In 1821 it was voted to make a survey of a road from Job Jenniss' by Deacon Clark's field and east side of his house to corner of Robert B. Clark's field. William Campbell had agreed to repair the Scofield bridge and desired to be relieved from his obligation, the town agreed to relieve him if he would give the town "1500 feet of good merchantable pine plank 2½ inches thick and 16 feet long, and no plank to be received unless as thick as above specified." The road from Abel Aldrich's to Enfield line was accepted and Aldrich had the privilege of straightening the road if he would give the land (47). In 1823 the old road was discontinued.

In 1822 the Lebanon road was indicted and the town voted $150 to repair it. The County Commissioners laid out a road from Hanover line by William Harris's into Enfield to the Lebanon road (49). The town voted to lay out a road for Amos Richardson, but would not accept of his survey and the road was not laid until the next year (50). This road led off the Lyme road in the northwest part of the town. In 1823 the road near Lewis Simmons' was straightened.

In 1824 the road from Amasa Clark's to Hanover line was straightened; this road led off from the turnpike at the north end of Sawyer Hill.

In 1825 Ezekiel Wells was given the old road through his land, for the land the old road took. In 1826 the survey of the road from Reuben Giles' to John May's, was accepted, but was not laid out until 1827 (54). In 1825 the selectmen were requested to make minutes of the survey of a road from Deacon Clark's bridge to Ezra Gales'.

In 1826 Jacob Richardson's petition for a road to Amos Gould's was granted, in 1827 the road from Nathan Cross' to and along the Gore line to Josiah P. Haynes', was accepted (57). This began at the old road from Nathaniel Gilman's. The road from Lieutenant Miner's on South road to the bridge, was left with the selectmen to open in their discretion.

Daniel Blaisdell's petition for a road was granted. In 1828 $400 was raised to build bridges injured by the freshet. In 1827 the town voted to accept the Grafton Turnpike and the selectmen were ordered to lay out a road over the same (58).

In 1831 the Clark Hill road was voted to be laid out, but it was not until 1833 that it was accepted and recorded (65). It began at the turnpike, taking a westerly course and ended at the turnpike near the Gore line. It is now the traveled road and took the place of the turnpike which continued by Fred Avery's house. In 1830 a road was laid out from the south end of Wells' bridge to South road (59), and in 1831 the old road from the same point was discontinued over the saddle to the county road. The road from the foot of Gilman hill across the meadow to near Moses Flanders', was discontinued and a new road laid to take its place (62).

In 1832 $50 was laid out on the new Gore road and the road from the Congregational meeting house to John H. Harris's at the corner, was opened four rods wide. At a meeting in September, there was an article in the warrant to discontinue the road from Daniel Blaisdell's to Job C. Tyler's, the town refused to discontinue it, but in 1836 the town agreed to throw up the old road when Tyler should build sixty-seven rods of new road. There was a dispute between Ephraim Wilson and John Fales over the ownership of an old road at the Corner which had been thrown up. Wilson began proceedings against Fales for trespass. The town voted to relinquish all claim to the land to Wilson by his paying the town $5; Fales was to move his barn off Wilson's land; the town was to give Fales $40, and he was to give up his claim. Wilson lived in the Fred Cross house at the Corner. In 1834 the old road from the top of the hill west of Indian river, at the begining of the new road to intersection of new with old, near the line of Joshua Martin's, was discontinued and a new one laid (66). This was in the northeasterly part of the town from the Plymouth road.

In 1836 the survey of the road from Deacon Clark's bridge to Deacon Sleeper's, was accepted (68), but the road was not laid and recorded until 1839. This is the road from the depot, known as the river road to Dorchester. Joshua S. Lathrop petitioned for a road and it was laid out in 1840, and is now the road from a little below E. M. Adams' to Dorchester (71).

It was voted to lay out a new road on the petition of John Hoyt and others, and another on the petition of Benjamin Wells. In 1841 the selectmen were requested to lay out the Lathrop road on the east side of the Mascoma to the turnpike near Joseph Wheat's shop or Trussell's bridge.

In 1842 the town was asked to lay out a road from Deacon Sleeper's house to the new road from Canaan to Dorchester, and also a road from Harrison Pillsbury's to the Lebanon road, near March Barber's. In 1847 the town was asked again and again refused. But the latter road was laid out by the court in 1848 (77).

In 1844 the road from Campbell Hill to the Lebanon road was discontinued. Luther Kinney petitioned for a road and Joseph Wheat also and the town voted to lay out both roads.

In 1845 the town voted to make alterations in the turnpike from Harrison Porter's to Gates' Gore. This discontinued the turnpike from beyond Fred Avery's house to where the Clark Hill road intersects the turnpike. The town voted not to lay out a road from Simeon Arvin's to the Dorchester road, near Andrew Dewey's, but afterwards reconsidered and the road was laid in 1846 (75). The town refused to lay out a road from Daniel Campbell's to the Lebanon road. Jeremiah Whittier's petition for a road was dismissed, but it was afterwards laid out. In 1847 the town was asked to lay out a road from Eaton's mills to the Lebanon road at West Canaan; it was refused, but it was laid out by the court in 1848 (76). Levi Wilson's petition was dismissed and this road was laid out by the court in 1848. The road from the east line of Currier and Wallace's land, near Stephen Wells' to the Dorchester line was discontinued, also that portion of the old road superseded by the new road (75) from Pillsbury's to Jenniss'.

In 1848 the road from the depot to the turnpike was voted to be laid out.

In 1849 the "Potato Road" was laid out by the court (79). The road from James Arvin's to March Barber's, was voted not to be discontinued, but in 1861 it was discontinued and the selectmen were requested to lay out forty-two rods of it, subject to gates and bars from the end of Broad street (94). The old road from Chamberlain Packard's to Harrison Pillsbury's was discontinued.

In 1852 Daniel B. Cole's petition for a road was dismissed, but the road was laid in 1855 (88). Joshua L. Lathrop's petition for a road was granted and the road laid in 1853 (84). Watts Davis' petition was also granted and the road laid in November (83).

In 1854 Otis Jones petitioned for a road and it was granted.

In 1857 the court laid out a road from near A. C. Lovejoy's, down the valley of Committee Meadow brook to the Shaker Hill road in Enfield, a few rods east of the schoolhouse in district No. 9 (89).

In 1857 the railroad having built a bridge over the river above Scofield or Blackwater bridge, so changed the current of the stream that it undermined the foundations of Scofield bridge, and William W. George was appointed agent of the town to settle with the railroad. It was adjusted by the railroad putting in stone abutments on the north side of Scofield bridge, to prevent the wearing of the water against the roadway.

In 1859 the road from Moses Knights' to Hanover line was discontinued.

In 1865 the road laid by the county commissioners on the east side of Goose Pond, on John Shepard's land near the brick knoll, where the new road intersects the old road, was discontinued north 100 rods to near the intersection of the Gates road.

In 1866 John L. Perley petitioned for a road and for the discontinuance of an old road; both were granted.

In 1867 the road about fifty rods from Wells' hill, near where the French shanties formerly stood, to the intersection of the road by John Stevens' to Enfield, was discontinued, and also a part of the road east of Wells' hill to S. B. Morgan's.

In 1868 the road near Kelly & George's store, northeast about eight rods, was discontinued to the intersection of the new road.

In 1869 the road from F. H. Wells' sawmill, following the brook to Enfield line, was discontinued.

In 1870 the road from near Warren Wilson's to tray factory, Town Hill road, was discontinued.

In 1884 the road from "near the watering trough below N. C. Morgan's over the hill to Enfield line," was discontinued. Also the road from Lary Pond to Hiram Jones'.

In 1886 the road from the "Jerusalem road to Orange, near David Cole's house," and the road "beginning at the intersection of Levi Hamlet road, thence northerly to road leading by G. W. Murray place," were discontinued. The latter road had been discontinued by vote of the town many years before.

In 1888 the town voted to discontinue "road on west side of road leading across Sawyer hill, near J. E. Cilley's; thence west to the Gould farm."

In 1892 the road on the "east side of the brook, near Lovejoy's mill; thence west to the road from Enfield by the mill to West Farms," was discontinued by vote.

In 1894 the "road over the crossing at Welch's Mill," was discontinued, and in 1896 the town voted not to discontinue it.

In 1896 the town voted to discontinue the road from "G. W. Davis's to the intersection of the Lebanon road." Mr. Davis, under advice of counsel, had purchased the land on both sides of this road; his counsel advising him that by so doing, he could close the road by vote of the town. The matter was carried into court and the case was decided against Mr. Davis. Judge Chase writing the opinion. The court held that highways should be laid out either by the selectmen or by the court; this power was not conferred upon towns to be exercised by direct vote or by a committee chosen by the town. This was a highway solely because it had been used as such for twenty years, and could not be discontinued without the consent of the court. Upon the facts shown the court would not consent to close the road.

In 1897 the town voted to discontinue the road through Wells' Cemetery. An addition had been made to the cemetery on the other side of the road, which made it advisable to build a new road around the west side of the cemetery, so that there might not be any traveled highway through it.

In 1902 the town discontinued a "piece of road north of Henry Sorrell's house; thence east past the old sawmill site of Lovejoy's mill, to west end of road formerly discontinued."

In 1906 the "road from Campbell's to Stephen Peaslee's old mill" on the road from Factory Village to Dorchester, was discontinued, as well as a short piece leading westerly from the turnpike opposite the post office at Factory Village.

LAYOUTS OF ROADS.

(a) Road from Pemigewasset River to Dartmouth College October 30, 1771: W 10 N 260 to line between Cokermouth (Wentworth) and Dorchester W 260. W 23 S one mile. W 4 miles. W 15 N 1¾ miles to line of Canaan and Hanover. That part of Governor's or Wolfeboro road in Canaan.

(b) Report of road commissioners in 1785 for a road from Boscawen to Dartmouth College: . . . thence by spotted line 15 rods from Nathaniel Hovey's sugar camp, thence nearly straight course to bridge over Mud Pond Brook, thence as road is now trod 10 rods (South Road), thence on straight course by Eleazer Scofield's house, thence to stump 3 rods to the south side of Joseph Bean's barn.

1788.

(1) Road from Grafton to Barber's Mill. Isinglass Hill road to grist mill at East Canaan: Beginning on Grafton line between Danl Blaisdell's and Whittier's, then N 41 W 208 r., N 28 W 26 r., N 18 W 72 r., N 48 W 28 r., N 28 W 18 r., N 9 W 46 r., N 45 W 30 r., N 32 W 180 r., to Robert Barber's mill.

(2) Road from grist mill by Wells Cemetery: Beginning opposite Joshua Well's house S 97 r., S 19 E 44 r., S 14 W 20 r., S 19 E 48 r., S 14 W 20 r., S 9 E 48 r., S 11 W to Barber's mill. First course discontinued.

(3) Broad Street: "N 11 W 288 to the road near Mr. Elias Lathrop's farm." See Turnpike.

1793.

(4) Road from Wells' east side of Hart's Pond to Nathaniel Gilman's: Beginning near Joshua Wells' house. Data not complete on first course; probably N 14 E 20 r., N 80 r., N 22 E 40 r., N 40 E 204 r., N 24 E 112 r., N 22 E 192 r. It then met (19).

(5) Road to Dorchester by John Currier's: Beginning near Eames' mill at corner, then N 30 E 75, then N 27 E 326. From this on the data is lost, but the old surveys would indicate that it followed the range lines N 24 E 20, then crossing Abner Colby's land northeasterly to the southwest corner of Prescott Clark's land, then on his land and Josiah

Barber's N 29 E about 300 r. to the gore line, then in the gore N 6 E 50 r. to Joseph Bartlett's house N 65 E 73 r. The first course was discontinued and (39) took its place. The last course is not used. It was a part of the Governor's road. This road existed as early as 1784 as a traveled way.

(6) This road led from John Currier's in a nearly straight course across his land to Caleb Clark's, then to meet the road from Wells' to Dorchester, following the range lines, S 75 E 44 r., S 68 E 100, S 61 E 73, S 72 E 100 r., then in the same course to the Wells road. From Caleb Clark's or the Putney place to Currier's it was discontinued.

1795.

(7) From north end of Broad Street to Corner, N 33 E 60 r.

(8) From south end of Broad Street to Post Road, N 85 W 104, S 71 W 61, S 52 W 40, S 27 W 17, S 6 W 13, S 11 E 25, S 18 W 36, S 10 W 13, S 4 W 28, S 2 W 9, S 21 W 10, S 4 W 10, S 43 W 8, N 89 W 19, S 54 W 37, S 21 W 30, S 36 W 16, S 52 W 4, S 71 W 52, S 55 W 22, S 20 W 38, S 31 W 58 to Post Road, near Captain Harris' store (Jones' place). The first course was discontinued in 1861, but the selectmen laid out N 85 W 42, subject to gates and bars (see 94).

MARCH 13, 1798.

(9) Road from County Road near Moody Noyes' (S. W. Currier's) to Dea. Josiah Clark's (A. W. Hutchinson's): Beginning County Road at a bound on the line between Thomas Miner's and Moody Noyes', 2 rods on the east and 2 rods on the west, N 30 E 200 to northeast corner Noyes', N 38 E on west side of line between Joseph Flint's (G. W. Davis') and Simeon Arvin's, 41 r., N 64 E 40, S 80 E 12, N 44 E 46, N 20 E 30, N 34, N 4 E 36, N 46 E 119, to Clark's Corner at the south end of Broad Street.

Moody Noyes deeded this land to the town December 17, 1799: Beginning 4 rods west of the corner of Thomas Miner's on South Road, N 30 E 200, E 4 r. to Miner's, then southerly by Miner's 200 to South Road, then W 4 r.

JUNE 8, 1799.

(10) Near John Kimball's down Eastman Hill: Beginning at the Lyme Road, near Lieutenant Bartlett's house, N 12 E between Bartlett's house and barn 130, N 29 E 23, N 41 E 38, N 20 E 24, N 27 E 24, N 25 E 50, N 6 E 21, N 35 W 164 to Hanover line; 4 rods wide. Bartlett lived about 60 rods south of H. B. Gates'. Part of this road has been thrown up.

FEBRUARY 22, 1800.

(11) From David Bucklin's to Charles Whittier's: From Simeon Hadley's to highway leading from Grafton to Canaan meeting house, beginning northeast corner of Hadley's land, N 35 W 36, N 86 W 10, N 62 W 42; 3 rods wide.

ROADS.

MAY 29, 1800.

(12) From Dorchester road by Nathaniel Whittier's (Randlett place) to Jonathan Carlton's (C. P. King): Beginning northeast corner Jonathan Dustin's land, N 61 W 99 on the north side of Dustin's to northwest corner S 54 W 120, S 85 W 42, N 67 W 108, N 81 W 26, N 85 W 50 to highway near Carlton's. All discontinued.

AUGUST 1, 1800.

(13) Part of Jerusalem Spring Road: Beginning old road to Orange, southeast corner Peter Pattee's land N 41 E 1½ miles and 20 rods to northeast corner Harry Leeds', running range line between Pattee and Rich lots, between Dow lot and Levi and Job Wilson and David Brown; 4 rods wide (see 27).

NOVEMBER 10, 1800.

(14) Beginning Lyme road, near Clark Currier's (Edgar Ricard's), N 59 E 38 between Currier's house and shed, N 9 E 60, N 24 W 44, N 14 E 30, N 4 E 58, N 26 W 24, N 43 E 43, N 13 W 82, N 33 E 36, to a beech stump about 5 rods northwest of Richard Clark's house; N 33 W 64, S 63 W 42, N 73 W 60, to highway from Lyme road by Runeld Gates' to Hanover line.

Also from beech stump, S 35 E 76, S 29 E 158, S 35 E 25, S 18 E 44, S 15 E 55, S 6 W 32, S 25 E 23, S 14 E 104, to stake near Ambrose Chase's barns.

MAY 29, 1801.

(15) Road from Ricard's to Charles Lashway's: Beginning 25 rods northeast of Clark Currier's house in road from Currier's to Richard Clark's 3 rods, S 61 E 44 to line of land between John Currier's and Clark Currier's, S 75 E 130 on said line; S 42 E 26, S 49 E 20, N 82 E 44, S 64 E 30 to stump near Ambrose Chase's house (near Collins'), S 6 E 36 to land of William Richardson, E 96, S 54 E 20, S 79 E 16, S 54 E 46, S 22 E 14, N 21 E 22, S 71 E 16, S 85 E 22, to line between Josiah Barber's and Moses Colby's; S 61 E on said line 72 to highway from Barber's to meeting house; 4 rods wide.

JUNE 16, 1801.

(16) From West Farms to Prospect Hill: Beginning on road from old brick yard to Daniel Morse's on line between John Currier's and William Longfellow's, N 40 E 46, N 61 E 39, S 74 E 16, N 51 E 80, E 203, N 35 E 34, S 74 E 62, S 44 E 30, N 80 E 24, S 58 E 18, to Goose Pond Brook; N 57 E 92, S 33 E 24, S 63 E 20, S 84 E 28, N 74 E 48, S 67 E 36, to road near John Wilson's. Wilson to give land south of road so not to be narrowed by John Perley's house (Goose Pond).

NOVEMBER 4, 1801.

(17) Daniel Farnum, James Kinneson, Moses Richardson to selectmen of Canaan, deed for road 4 rods wide: Beginning north side Post Road,

near Farnum's (Charles Whittier's), N 48 E 60, N 45 E 66, to road from Joshua Wells' to Mr. Clifford's in Grafton.

NOVEMBER 7, 1801.

(18) Road from South Road to near William Hall's: Beginning northwest corner 3rd 100 Nathaniel Cady, owned by Josiah Barber, a little north of Barber's house on Dorchester road, S 61 E 180 to Ebenezer Davis' north end, across Barber's and Moses Lawrence's (Decato's). This road leads from the Dorchester road above the old poor farm to meet (38). It ran on the old town line.

NOVEMBER 20, 1802.

(19) Beginning southwest corner of Nathaniel Gilman's land, thence northwest in line of Gilman's and Thomas Beedle's to northwest corner of Charles Greenfield's, being 184 rods, thence same course 16 rods, N 11 E 74, N 64 E 98, N 42 E 42, S 58 E 64, S 61 E 40, to road near Joseph Rundlett's house. This road begins where (4) ends; leads down Gilman Hill to Birch Corner. Gilman and Thomas Beedle were adjoining owners, Beedle on the west side of the road. Beedle's line in the old surveys runs N 20 E, while Gilman's ran N 25 E.

(20) Beginning old road on line between Nathaniel Whittier's and Nathaniel Whittier, Jr.'s, near said junior's barn, N 61 W 30, N 86 W 50, S 84 W 67, to Jonathan Carlton's (C. P. King's) line, N 69 W on Carlton's line 126 rods to old road leading from Dorchester (by John Currier's). This road has been thrown up.

(20a) Beginning old road on line Moses Chase's land, S 90, near Samuel Chapman's, northwest corner south on Chapman land, 78 to southwest corner, S 10 E 76, S 4 W 64, to old road from east to west across said hill; from Reuben Puffer's to Campbell Hill, by Defosses'.

DECEMBER 15, 1802.

(21) Beginning at old road at bridge in first hollow, a little east of Joshua Wells' house, S 31 E 114, S 53 E 64, S 11 E 15, S 36 E 38, S 57 E 40, S 53 E 9, S 10 E 41, S 37 E 40, S 11 E 20, to bridge over Indian; S 38 E 23, S 21 E 28, S 38 E 48, S 18 E 25, S 30 E 41, S 46 E 20, S 27 E 14, S 53 E 14, to Orange line. Superceded by Grafton Turnpike.

It may possibly be the old road to the Bickford place. However, it plots out over nearly the same ground the turnpike covers, from Wells'.

DECEMBER 9, 1802, TOWN HILL.

Minutes of roads surveyed by John Currier for the making of a map required by the state in 1804: "Road from Grafton to Hanover, N 51 W 214 rods to Farnum road, N 23 W 80, N 35 W 54, N 10 W 50, N 37 W 38, N 35 E 68 rods to Cobble Road, N 20 E 26, N 48 E 32, N 5 E 24, N 52 E 34 rods to Follensbee's mill, N 6 E 50, N 12 W 44, N 8 E 27, N 20 W 39, due N 109 to Wells' corner, due W 54, N 55 W 44, N 70 W 85, N 79 W 47 to Arvin's corner, N 14 W 122 to meeting house, same course

192 rods, N 33 E 64 to Carlton's corner, N 64 W 12, N 81 W 44, N 46 W 32, N 35 W 42, N 42 W 44 to Mascum River, same course 120 rods, N 22 W 23, N 49 W 58, N 70 W 28, N 55 W 30, N 22 W 78 to Wilson's corner, N 21 E 178, N 30 W 60, due N 30 to Currier's corner, same course 33 rods, N 29 W 82, N 55 W 44, N 36 W 36, N 77 W 60, to Bartlett's corner, same course 49 rods, N 49 W 33, N 35 W 30, N 5 E 52, N 10 W 56, N 39 W 32, N 30 W 22, N 7 W 30, to Hanover line.

"Road from Cyrus Carlton's to Dorchester, beginning at the post guide at the corner: N 47 E 36 to Currier's corner, N 20 E 240, N 23 E 74, N 74 E 34, N 50 E 34, N 33 E 30, N 11 E 90, N 21 E 34, N 41 E 42, N 30 E 30, N 14 E 84, N 6 E 76, N 80 E 92, due E 14 rods, N 78 E 25, N 80 E 34, to the gore line.

"Road from Wells' corner to Orange line: Due E 10 rods, S 53 E 76, S 66 E 78, S 69 E 84, S 47 E 35, S 29 E 30, S 72 E 28, N 66 E 33 to Indian River; S 69 E 38, S 82 E 162, S 62 E 17, S 50 E 9, N 77 E 15, S 66 E 18, to a maple stub near Orange line."

May 16, 1804.

(22) Beginning at South Road, near Jehu Jones' house, N 28 E 60 on Jones' line, N 85 E 12, N 10 E 32, N 26 E 68, N 86 E 14, S 72 E 26, N 61 E 20, N 84 E 28, S 80 E 8, S 45 E 22, N 81 E 51, to road that leads from Canaan meeting house to Grafton. This road led by Cobble graveyard to near Alvin Davis' and is now discontinued.

June 15, 1805.

(23) Beginning Enfield line by path from Elijah Paddleford's to Meshech Blake's, N 12 E 40, near John May's house, N 8 E 157, N 34, to Blake line; 4 rods wide. This road leads by H. L. Webster's to Enfield line.

June 17, 1805.

(24) Beginning Enfield line, near bridge over Mascoma, near Asa Paddleford's, E 36, N 72 E 52, S 86 E 50, N 73 E 54, to Judah Wells' corner[1] N 56 E 40, N 15 E 40[2], N 73 E 44, S 57 E 44, S 30 E 60, S 40 E 42, S 17 E 43, S 38 E 69, S 85 E 144, S 59 E 177, to corner near Micah Porter's, then same course 113 rods[3], S 54 E 58, S 60 E 183, S 56 E 76, S 70 E 26, S 2 E 30, N 64 E 26, S 59 E 130, to Daniel Farnum's road (17), S 45 E 31, S 73 E 44, S 58 E 152, to Grafton line.

South Road, as resurveyed. "Excepted Apr 7, 1807" by town.

June 30, 1806.

(25) Survey of road exchanged by town from the first corner, about 12 rods east of William Campbell's old saw mill, by his new mill: Beginning at said corner S 16 E in line between Ezekiel Wells' and Chadwick's and Campbell's on east side of said line 46 rods to bridge near new mill, S 33 W 17, N 60 W 22, S 52 W 9, to said old road; 4 rods wide. Said

---
[1] Currier's Survey, N 74 E.
[2] Currier's survey, N 15 E 12, to Mud Pond Brook, same course 28 rods.
[3] Currier's survey, same course, 133 rods, to J. Porter's corner.

line is the center thereof from bridge to old road on south side of River Road to old Tray factory from Campbell's old mill to meet old road from South Road to river now discontinued.

1806. SEPTEMBER TERM OF GENERAL SESSIONS.

(26) Beginning at south side of South Road of Canaan, nearly opposite house of Joshua Harris, standing in line between Micah Porter's and Hough Harris' land, S 30 W 116, S 43 W 84, to road laid out by selectmen of Enfield on Canaan line. Road laid 2½ rods east of said line. Lockehaven Road.

DECEMBER 24, 1807.

(27) Beginning northeast corner of Harry Leeds' land, N 40 E 54, N 50 E 44, N 42 E 28, to where Stephen Worth is beginning to build a house. Continuation of (13) to Tug Mt. House.

Also from a road from said road to Orange line, east side of said road 34 rods north of Leeds' corner, S 6 E 41, S 23 E 48, to Orange line; 4 rods wide. This road is south of above and easterly.

MAY 1, 1808.

(28) Beginning north side of road from meeting house to Prospect Hill in first hollow, a few rods north of Codfish Hill, S 63 E 8, S 49 E 34, S 69 E 73, to west side of Grafton Turnpike, near John Llado's mills. From near Fred Butman's to Factory Village.

MARCH 14, 1809.

(29) Beginning northwest corner Samuel Sanborn's house in old road that leads from Timothy Clough's to Joshua Meacham's, N 45 E 20, N 24 E 4, N 15 E 48, to old road. Sanborn lived on Placid Adams' farm.

SEPTEMBER 5, 1810.

(30) Beginning gore line about 100 rods east of Clark Pond, where road is now traveled from this town to Dorchester, S 2 E 36, S 28 W 12, S 4 E 35, S 38 W 12, to brook that runs out of pond; S 67 W 13, S 74 W 29, to old road near house of Luther Kinney, S 26 E 40, to Levi Cilley's land, S 53 W 98, S 55 W 20, to turnpike at south side of schoolhouse, from near R. H. Haffenreffer's in gore to Clark Pond, by Stephen Morse's old place to turnpike by Daniel Goss'; 4 rods wide.

JUNE 28, 1811.

(31) Beginning west side of highway, 20 rods southerly from bridge over small brook, southerly from John M. Barber's about 80 rods, S 63 W 16 to west side of Mascoma, S 53 W 38, S 79 W 26, S 67 W 32, S 80 W 59, to said old road leading from river to William Campbell's; 4 rods wide. Part of it is Lebanon road, by Norris place.

JULY 10, 1811.

(32) From Job Tyler's to the turnpike: Beginning at highway near Tyler's house on south line of his land, N 41 E 6, N 19 E 11, N 36 E 9, E 42, N 74 E 10, N 53 E 9, N 44 E 12, N 64 E 35, N 50 E 26, N 43 E 16, N 39 E 38, N 63 E 6, N 34 E 10, to small brook, N 62 E 52 to turnpike; 3 rods wide. From David Bucklin's to H. A. Gilman's, below depot.

SEPTEMBER 5, 1811.

(33) Beginning southeast corner Richard Clark, Jr.'s house, S 60 W 94, to turnpike; road from Mrs. Lydia Shattuck's by Clarence Kinney's.

NOVEMBER 2, 1811.

(34) Beginning at old road on north bank of Indian River, south of house lately owned by John Follensbee, N 63 E 22, S 85 E 66, S 87 E 87, N 34 E 14, to west side of Grafton Turnpike, crossing turnpike 4 rods, thence same course 36 rods, N 26 E 12, N 70 E 18, N (99) 20 (probably due east), N 82 E 36, N 46 E 30, to west side of river, 4 rods south of bridge over river on old road to Orange, from thence easterly, crossing river in a direction to intersect the old road on the east bank of said river, with privilege of crossing old bridge so long as same is passable; 4 rods wide; from grist mill through to East Canaan by F. D. Currier's, over the hill to bridge by fair grounds.

1812.

(35) Beginning northwest corner of Ezekiel Wells 3rd's orchard, S 54 W 60, to near bank of Mascoma, S 71 W 9, to high bank on north bank of Mascoma, S 20 W 8, to high bank on south bank of Mascoma, W 36, S 71 W 18, S 41 W 68, to old road, a pine stub, 20 rods north of bridge over Mud Pond Brook. There is no road now that satisfies this.

MAY 18, 1813.

(36) Beginning north end of old road, near Elisha Blake's house, N 23 W 42, to near east end of Meshech Blake's house, N 94, to west line of land owned by Daniel Dow, to northwest corner, N 15 E 68, N 10 W 92, to Hanover line; 3 rods wide; southwest corner of town.

AUGUST 19, 1813.

(37) Beginning center of road against southeast corner of Seth Daniel's house (G. W. Davis'), S 76 E 90, to Simeon Arvin's land, S 88 E 12, to east side of saddle, N 80 E 45, S 70 E 16, S 53 E 35, S 86 E 24, to Stephen Jenness' land by the fore side of his house, N 80 E 31, N 76 E 65, S 70 E across the river 16 rods, S 84 E 15, S 52 E 42, N 88 E 80, to road by Caleb Welch, Jr.'s, house; whole distance, 1 m., 81 rods; 4 rods wide; from G. W. Davis' to grist mill.

July 1, 1815.

(38) Beginning northeast corner of Moses Lawrence's, S 61 E 164, to northeast corner of Ebenezer Davis', S 60 E 22, to road leading to Dorchester, near Nathan Cross' house; 4 rods wide. This road leads from (18) to (19).

(39) Beginning on the west side of the brook, between John Fales' shop and house where Pushee lives, N 36 E 28, to line of Eliphalet Richardson's, thence same point across Richardson's land 21 rods, thence same point to top of hill 16 rods, then N 52 E 28, to old road near Esquire Currier's house; 3 rods wide; up hill from corner to John Currier's.

Also, beginning 1½ rods below a large rock near old road in Eliphalet Richardsons's pasture, before the house that Bailey Welch lately purchased of David Richardson, S 49 W 21, S 88 W 13, S 86 W 46, to old road 4 rods above bridge over brook running to John Fales' shop, thence to the water course in the bridge, then across said bridge, then to a heap of stones in westerly edge of brook on road that leads to Esquire Currier's. Road from Putney place to Corner.

(40) Road from Corner to turnpike down the hill; N 62 W 15, S 85 W 22, N 67 W 22, N 51 W 23.

July 1, 1816.

(41) Between Daniel and Asa Kimball's, S 49 W 58, to southwest corner of Asa's land, then same course 80 rods to door yard of Amos Gould, 1½ rods north of northeast corner of his dwelling house; 2 rods wide.

October 23, 1817.

(42) Beginning at old road (27), 29 rods north of Harry Leeds' northeast bound, N 8 E 22, N 11 E 5, N 12 E 22, N 32 E 11, N 43 E 6, N 50 E 47, to house the late residence of John Worth, deceased, N 24 E 44, N 33 E 21, N 20 E 28, N 46 E 53, to east line Stephen Worth's land, then in his east line 29 rods to northeast corner, N 20 E 114, N 29 E 60, N 32 E 160, to south line Dame's Gore; 623 rods long. Road from Jerusalem north to schoolhouse.

June 10, 1818.

(43) Beginning north side of road against Sewal Gleason's barn, east end, N 26 W 4, N 5 W 8, N 2 E 6, N 14, N 10 E 12, N 35 W, to southeast corner of Nathaniel Bartlett's house 41 rods, N 53 W 50, N 58 W 80, N 36 W 36, to stump by old road near Adam Pollard's house; 4 rods wide. From old Hinkson place across H. B. Gates' field.

June 5, 1820.

(44) To straighten road from bridge, near March Barber's, to meeting house; Beginning south side road 18 rods east of bridge, N 48 E 60, to north line of Ezra Nichols' (Cochran's), N 80 E, on said line 12 rods to road by Nichols (9).

Second piece: Beginning at the fence on north side of road from James Arvin's (A. W. Hutchinson's) to John M. Barber's (Sharon's), opposite east side of road coming from Ezra Nichols', N 13 W 22, to Barber's field, N 41 E 89, to parade near schoolhouse.

OCTOBER 30, 1820.

(45) On line of old road near Josiah Clark's (Carey Smith's) house, S 10 E 10, S 32½ E 42, S 4 E 10, S 49 E 100, to Orange line; 3 rods wide.

MAY 23, 1821.

(46) Road across Dame's or Homer's Gore: Beginning at Canaan line at end of road, from Luther Kinney's to Dorchester, N 10 E 23, N 33 E 14, N 19 E 44, N 36 E 17, N 22 E 18, N 45 E 9, N 25 E 16, N 15 E 8, N 10 E 22, N 2 E 31½, to Dorchester line to south end of Dorchester road, 222½ rods; 4 rods wide. John Currier, surveyor. Laid out for Homer James Worthen, H. G. Lathrop, chairmen.

NOVEMBER 20, 1821.

(47) Beginning end Jonathan Sawyer's wall, on line between Canaan and Enfield, at end of Enfield road, N 18 E 70, N 4 W 60, to County Road.

NOVEMBER 21, 1821.

(48) Beginning 4 rods east of David Dustin's house, S 85 E 48, N 76 E 39, to meetinghouse common. Road is laid 2 rods south of above line.

MAY 4, 1822.

(49) February term of Court of General Sessions. Beginning on Hanover east line, where road in Hanover intersects Canaan, S 29 E 72, through James Ralston's to Israel Harris' heirs' land, S 29 E 19, S 14 E 26, to William Harris', S 14 E 24, S 15 W 28, to Sylvanus Payne's land, S 46 to Enfield line; S S E 54 on Asa and Benj. Choate's, then same point 78 rods on Daniel Huse's, to corner Choate's, then S 29 W on line between Choate's and David Huse's, 137 rods to county road leading from Follensbee's to Lebanon; 3 rods wide.

APRIL 23, 1823.

(50) Road to Amos Richardson's, between house and barn of Sewal Gleason, on south line of old road, S 24 W 71, to south line of Gleason land, same course 104 rods to south line of Amos Richardson's; 3 rods wide. From old Hinkson place south.

MAY 24, 1826.

(51) Beginning southeast corner of Daniel Sherburne's dwelling house, S 26 W 22, to highway that leads from Widow Abigail Clark's to turnpike; 3 rods wide.

September 9, 1826.

(52) Benefit and request of Elijah Gove: Center gate 16 rods north of William Harris' house, N 26 E 19, N 53 E 22, N 21 E 22, to center of Blake Brook; 2 rods wide. Discontinued April 17, 1827.

December 9, 1826.

(53) Benefit of George Flint: Beginning at Flint's barn, on piece of land he purchased of Judge Blaisdell, and on line of John R. Dustin's land, that he purchased of Blaisdell, S 30 W 36, S 15 W 44, S 27 W 16, N 77 W 8, N 47 W 16, to corner of Bartholomew Heath's, N 80 W 8, S 73 W 30, N 37 W 38, S 64 W 80; then by south line of land on which Nathaniel Barber lives to causeway near bank of Barber's land 80 rods, then through lane by Barber's house to road near Daniel B. Whittier's; 3 rods wide.

May 4, 1827.

(54) Beginning at the center of the road at the northwest corner of Giles' house, S 83 W 14, S 59 W 16, S 82 W 9, N 64 W 25, N 39 W 6, N 59 W 28, N 72 W 10, N 56 W 31, N 62 W 9, N 31 W 14, N 56 W 28, N 32 W 23, N 15 W 27, N 80 W 12, S 45 W 28, S 78 W 25, S 45 W 18, S 56 W 19, S 76 W 10, S 53 W 20, S 35 W 51, S 82 W 28, S 59 W 11, S 70 W 10, S 50 W 25, N 83 W 40; intersecting road between Paddleford house and schoolhouse.

May 9, 1827.

(55) Beginning west line of road from John Shephard's to Daniel Kimball's, one rod north of north line of Kimball's house, W 58, to Silas Dustin's.

June 2, 1827.

(56) Beginning in line between David Currier, Jr.'s, and Aaron Nichols', in Currier's door yard, N 68 W, in Currier's and Nichols' line, 143 rods, N 80 W 13, S 40 W 11, S 68 W 14, W 10, N 84 W 11, N 77 W 106, N 70 W 38 to intervale, N 80 W 14 to river, S 82 W 18, S 71 W 12, S 81 W 19½ to John R. Dustin's land, S 30 W 14, S 78 W 13, to George Flint's private road (53), S 10 W 14 on private road, S 31 W 12, S 88 W 14, N 75 W 10 N 44 W 12, N 78 W 8, S 69 W 20, N 50 W 6, N 32 W 28, N 69 W 7, S 76 W 21, S 78 W 14, W 14, N 66 W 52, S 88 W 27, N 50 W 14, N 73 W 12, to road by Daniel Whittier's at end of Nathaniel Barber's land to his house.

June 21, 1827.

(57) Beginning east side of road from Nathaniel Gilman's house to Dame's Gore, as you descend hill towards Nathan Cross' meadow, about 4 rods southerly of corner of Cross pasture, S 55 E 34, S 85 E 20, S 83 E 12 to east side of Cross meadow, S 48 E 42, S 84 E 12, N 70 E 22, S 68 E 108 to Flanders' dooryard, S 74 E 39 to line of Ashel Jones', then same point 28 rods, S 86 E 22, S 85 E 14, N 81 E 76, S 85 E 11 to east line Jones' land, N 8 E 16, N 58 E 31, N 76 E 14, N 88 E 26, S 69 E 8 to La-

throp path, S 60 E 17, S 32 E 6, N 75 E 12, N 85 E 7, S 82 E 15, S 50 E 18 to river, N 82 E 36, N 52 E 12, N 19 E 36, N 35 E 19, N 58 E 10 to south line of gore, near corner Josiah Haynes' and Caleb Wells', where they now live in gore; 4 rods wide. Began at Birch Corner and went to Henry Tormey's.

November 7, 1828.

(58) Beginning at the center of two stakes standing on the westerly line of Orange, near Orange Pond, N 47 W 41, N 30 W 166, N 20 W 100, N 40 W 152, N 33 W 80, N 61 W 96, N 81 W 26, N 52 W 28, N 58 W 40, N 65 W 100, 4 rods wide, then N 12 W 240, 8 rods wide, then N 12 W 80, N 26 W 124, N 2 W 80, N 20 W 50, N 7 E 20, N 66, N 7 W 120, N 14 W 116, N 10 W 120, N 16 W 100, N 22 W 68, N 14 W 54, N 24 W 154, N 12 W 108, N 3 W 32, N 14 W 118, to Dame's Gore line, near southwest corner thereof; meaning to be on same ground that Grafton Turnpike was laid out. The turnpike was first surveyed in 1804, and was 4th Grafton Turnpike from Andover to Orford bridge.

August 27, 1830.

(59) Beginning near south end of the Wells bridge, S 60 W 32, S 50 W 16, S 33 W 16, S 74 W 6, to the South Road; 3 rods wide.

September, 1830.

(60) Beginning north corner Samuel Whittier's apple house, S 77 E 13, S 70 E 28, on Samuel Whittier's, S 57 E 14, on Moses Whittier's, 2 rods east of Samuel Whittier's house, 2½ rods; laid out south of line. Samuel Whittier lived on Bickford place.

October 16, 1830.

(61) From Moses Sawyer's to Hanover line, 2 rods from northeast corner of Sawyer's house on west side of highway, N 30 W 4, N 75 W 12, N 55 W 12, N 34 W 30, to Hanover line; 2 rods wide.

December 9, 1830.

(62) Beginning near bridge east of Nathan Cross' house, S 31 E 18, S 15 E 30, S 12, to a road, then on said road S 58 E 66, S 61 E 21, to maple tree on road; 4 rods wide (57).

June 10, 1833.

(63) Beginning 87 rods east from Indian River, near small bridge on new road from Canaan to Plymouth, S 40 W 8, S 50 W 11, S 62 W 8, S 66 W 9, S 68 W 8, S 84 W 10, S 83 W 8, S 45 W 10, S 46 W 8, S 53 W 7, to river, then beginning on west bank of river, N 38 W 7, N 57 W 4, N 30 W 8, to highway; 4 rods wide.

September 2, 1833.

(64) Beginning southeast corner of James Follensbee's, S 68 E 32, through Jeremiah Whittier's land, S 59 E to road from Canaan to Dorchester, through Rufus Hoyt's; 4 rods wide.

September 3, 1833.

(65) Clark Hill Road: Beginning on turnpike near Joseph L. Richardson's (Daniel Goss') barn, N 59 W 30, N 61 W 8, N 28 W 14, N 48 W 8, N 51 W 6, N 34 W 10, N 36 W 7, N 51 W 9, N 66 W 10, N 44 W 11, N 37 W 7, N 8 W 8, N 6 W 7, N 3 E 6, N 7 E 11, N 1 E 6, N 11, N 10 W 18, N 41, N 2 W 42, to turnpike near corner of Nathaniel Derby's field; 4 rods wide; took place of turnpike from Daniel Goss'.

September 1, 1835.

(66) Beginning on New Plymouth road, foot of the hill, north side of Joshua Martin's, S 18 E 13, S 13 E 13, through Martin's, S 6 E 10, S 10 W 64, to pair of bars and through Aaron Whittlesey's; 4 rods wide.

October 1, 1836.

(67) Beginning on east side of turnpike, where road to Widow Abigail Clark's intersects, near John Flanders' house, S 75½ W, across turnpike and Flanders', 12 rods and 20 links, to Flanders' fence, east of new road round Clark Hill; 3 rods wide.

April 16, 1839.

(68) Beginning west end Deacon Clark's bridge, N 29 E 9, N 12, N 5 W 22, N 4 W 15, N 19 E 14, N 32 E 22, N 52 E 14, N 35 E 13, N 37 E 8, N 38 E 16, N 26 E 10, N 20 E 10, N 6 E 12, N 13 E 17, N 18 E 8, N 5 W 14, N 8 E 14, N 25 E 10, N 30 E 14, N 5 E 14, N 7 W 8, N 22 E 9, N 43 E 14, N 58 E 21, N 35 E 12, N 26 E 30, N 7 E 58, N 25 E 42 and 34, N 35 E 13, N 26 E 10, N 26 E 37, N 30 E 54, to Stephen Sleeper's house; road from bridge, near fair grounds, up river.

July 13, 1839.

(69) Beginning on east side of turnpike, about 8 rods below watering trough, N 65 E 10, N 73 E 72, N 27 E 17, N 28 E 36, N 35 E 18, N 34 E 18, N 50 E 20, N 38 E 12, N 20 E 34, N 33 E 23, N 43 E 22, N 46 E 25, N 10 E 14, N 5 E 26, N 3 E 24, N 30 E 30, to road leading from turnpike to Dorchester.

December 11, 1839.

(70) Beginning west side Sawyer Hill Road, at corner Daniel Kimball's mowing field, W 75, to Joseph Kimball's house; 3 rods wide.

1841.

(72) Beginning 15 rods south of the Frenchman's house, S 52 W 76, S 20 W 12, S 30, S 8 E 34, S 3 E 26, S 40 W 10, S 66 W 7, to turnpike by Eliphalet Gilman's; 3 rods wide.

June 10, 1845.

(73) Beginning on north bank of road from John Worth's to Orange, opposite Benjamin Y. Hilliard's barnyard, N 44 E 4, N 5 E 3, N 33 W 8, N 5 E 10, N 39 W 11, N 14 W 4, N 30½ W 16, N 26 W 17, N 60 W 36, near Moses Whittier's bars; 2 rods wide.

March 3, 1846.

(75) Beginning east side Simeon Arvin's house, N 42 E 33, N 31½ E 8, N 40 E 9, N 57 E 5, N 63 E 10, N 80 E 11, N 85 E 9, N 63 E 12, N 31½ E 5½, — 80 E 5, — 78 E 10½, N 60 E 12, — 47½ E 11, N 46 E 15, N 41 E 12, N 36½ E 9½, N 41½ E 29½, N 44 E 17, N 37 E 6½, N 30 E 17, N 66½ E 11½, N 70 E 13, N 52 E 40, to Dewey's road at junction of Dorchester road; whole district, 318 rods; 4 rods wide.

September 23, 1840.

(71) Beginning by side of fence near road southwest from Joshua S. and Thad S. Lathrop's barns, N 19½ E 63, to birch, N 29 E 26, to spruce, N 31 E 10, N 40 E 26, N 38 E 6, N 49 E 7, N 60 E 6, N 63 E 8, N 40½ E 9, N 31 E 5, N 17 E 27, N 21 E 24, to Dame's Gore line, N 21 E 9, N 4 E 18, N 10 E 8, N 6 E 10, N 25 E 8, N 24 E 4, N 45 E 6, N 57½ E 10, N 46½ E 12, N 37½ E 8, N 44 E 12, N 43½ E 10, N 48 E 7, N 23 E 8, N 16½ E 5½, N 10 E 7, N 3 E 7, N 23 E 35, N 31 E 8, to gore line, N 23½ E 23, N 2½ E 16, N 1 W 15, N 12 W 14, N 23 W 9, N 8 W 10½, N 14 W 12, N 46 E 24, N 30 E 7, N 31 E 12, N 26 E 10, N 25 E 32, N 36 E 29, to side of road by Jesse Jones'; Dorchester road by T. W. Young's.

October 9, 1846.

(74) Beginning north side of road opposite bars on hill east of Harrison Pillsbury's, S 82 E 12, S 87½ E 9½, S 77½ E 19, S 86½ E 17½, N 89½ E 15, S 78¼ E 31¾, S 74 E 12, E 16½ S 86½, E 17¾, S 82 E 18¾, S 79½ E 15, S 81¼ E 6, S 89¼ E 50, to north side of road near bridge below Simeon Welch's shops; 4 rods wide. See (37).

August 31, 1848.

(76) Court of General Sessions: Beginning on north side of Lebanon road, 52 rods southwest of south end of Wells' bridge in Canaan, N 23 E 7½, N 6 E 22, N 1¼ E 17, N 2½ E 12, N 2¾ W 16, N 22½ E 2 to south side of Mascoma, on north line of Warren Wilson's, N 43 E 5, across river, N 30 E 1½, N 24 W 22, N 20 W 22, N 15½ W 25, N 9 W 16½, N 8 W 14, N 24½ E 9½, N 40½ E 11, N 17 E

8½, N ½ E 8½, N 5 W 12½, N 9 W 16, N 16 W 11, N 26¼ W 14, N 28 W 10½, N 1¾ W 23, on north line H. C. George's, N 1¾ W 3, N 2½ E 12, N 17½ E 17, N 26¼ E 13½, N 25 E 13, N 20¼ E 10½, N 16½ E 21, N 17¼ E 16, N 23¾ E 16, N 25¼ E 15, N 44½ E 6¼, on north line Ezekiel and Peter Wells', N 49 E 11½, N 49¾ E 28½, N 49½ E 20, N 52 E 14½, N 12 W 2, to north line Huse, Conant & Co.'s, N 12 W 11, on north line David and James Pattee's, N 12 W 3, N 2½ W 13½, N 11 E 6¾, N 41 E 30, N 25 E 12½, N 12 E 13, N 27 E 7½, N 43½ E 13, N 42 E 12, N 44 E 11½, N 35¾ E 10¼, N 6½ E 20¼, N 24 ½ E 11½, N 11 E 8½, — 9¾ E 10, N 8½ E 5, N 30 E 17, on north line John Barker's, N 35 E 13, N 47½ E 14, to south side of road, 7 rods west of bridge across brook at outlet of Goose Pond, below Eaton's mills; then beginning north side of road, 3 rods east of east end of bridge, near a new building, N 40 E 10½, N 68½ E 26, N 18 E 20, N 5¾ E 12, N 1½ E 14, N 5¼ E 15, N 20 E 22, N 25 E 43, to north line Nathaniel Eaton's, N 16½ E 38, N 20½ E 24, N 8 E 8, to north line of John Shepherd's, N 8 E 9, N 15½ E 11, N 34 E 5, N 40 E 5½, N 36 E 10½, N 5 E 16, N 14½ E 10, N 19½ E 39½, N 5 E 16, to north line of D. Towle's, N 5 W 9, N 6½ W 11, N 11 E 8, N 18 E 8, N 9¾ W 11, to north line W. H. Duncan's, N 17 W 8, N 6½ W 12, N 1½ W 15, N 14½ W 10, N 18½ W 9, N 16 W 9, N 23½ W 11, N 33 W 8, to north line Amos Gould's, N 14 W 8, N 25½ W 12, N 32 W 12, N 43½ W 13, N 45 W 35, N 23¼ W 27, N 10 E 8, N 7½ E 8, N 10 W 11, N 7 W 8, N 18 E 10, N 6 W 9, N 4¼ W 16, N 7¾ W 22, N 16½ W 18, N 1½ W 17, N 10 W 16, N 6½ W 20½, to north line of Caleb Bartlett's, N ¼ E 54, N 2 W 22, on land of James Eastman to Hanover line, N 12 E 8, N 28½ E 4, N 59 E 7, N 28 E 61, N 26½ E 19½, N 11¾ E 8, on Eastman's land, N 22 E 18, on Eastman's to south side of old County Road, 11 rods north of James Eastman's house, occupied by Ira Eastman; $505.50 damages; Goose Pond Road from West Canaan.

OCTOBER 1, 1848.

(77) Court of General Sessions. Beginning at a stake standing in the road, S 10¼ W, from the northeast corner of Martin & Currier's store and three rods therefrom, thence S 67 W 10 r., to stake on Miner and Fairfield's land, S 60 1-3 W 12 r., 10 l., to southerly line of Fairfield's land, S 60 1-3 W 2 r., on Currier and Martin's land, S 47½ W 12 r. on the south line of Currier and Martin; S 47½ W 1 r., to land of Joseph Wheat, S 32 W 18 r. to the west line of Wheat's, S 32 W 9 r. to Martin and Currier's land, S 17 1-3 W 21 r. to the south line of Currier land, S 17 W 8 r. to George Harris' land, S 17 W 8 r. on Harris' land, S 6½ W 5 r. to south line of Harris', S 6½ W 1 r. to Joseph Wheat's land, S 9 W 7 r. to the south line of Wheat's, S 9 W 2 r. to the south line of J. H. Harris', S 11.25 W 6 r. to the south line of John Fales', S 11.25 W 4 r. to the line of George Harris', S 6 1-3 W 8 r., 7 l., to south line of Harris', S 6 1-3 W 2 r., on Wil-

ROADS. 417

liam Kimball's, S 10¾ W 8 r., 7 l., S 25.25 W 39 r., S 10 W 15 r., S 4.40 E 19 r., S 7½ W 7 r., to south line of Kimball's, S 19.20 W 20 r., to Caleb Blodgett's south line, S 21 1-3 W 75 r. to Joseph Dustin's, S 4 W 24 r., S ½ W 46 r., S 7¾ W 14 r., S 17 2-3 W 13 r., 9 l., to south line of Dustin's, S 1 1-3 W 16 r., on March Barber's land, S 2¼ E 11 r., S 9¾ E 9 r., 15 l., S 4½ E 11, to near the southeast corner of J. H. Harris' land, S 4½ E 12 r. on A. Cochran's land, S 11 2-3 E 12 r., S 20 E 11 r., 10 l., S 15 E 10 r., 8 l., S 3 E 12 r., S 5½ W 16 r., 12 l., S 3 W 9 r., 14 l., S 4 W 19 r., S 4 W 2 r., S 8½ E 10 r., 17 l., S 5 E 11 r., 16 l., on Cochran's, S 18 W 13 r., 13 l., over highway (4 rods out) to stake on Cochran's, S 21½ W 21 r., 17 l., S 23 E 43 r., 11 l., S 13 E 19 r., 5 l., to Harrison Pillsbury's land, S 31 E 7 r., 16 l., S 33 2-3 E 9 r., 14 l., S 7 E 9 r., 8 l., S 11 1-3 W 8 r., S 15½ W 10 r., S 14 W 7 r., S 6¾ W 7 r., S 25 1-3 E 46 r., to stake and stones standing on north side of the road leading by Harrison Pillsbury's to South Road, and N 63½ E 14 r., 5 l., from the railroad track at crossing southwesterly from Pillsbury's house; the above line to be the center of the road; road to be 3 rods wide; from Factory Village to Switch.

OCTOBER 1, 1848.

(78) Court of General Sessions. Beginning north side of road by John Jones', S 75 2-3 E 1½ rods from southeast corner of Daniel McKinney's blacksmith shop, N 15 E 11 r., 3 l., N 10¾ E 8 r., 24 l., and 9 r., 17 l., N 1 1-6 W 4, 18 l., and 10 r., 9 l., N 17 E 32, N 42 E 9 r., 12 l., N 33 E 9, N 9 E 11 r., 9 l., N 19 1-3 E 13, N 16 E 10 r., 21 l., N 14 E 11 r., 4 l., N 41 E 13 r., 10 l., N 39 E 15, N 40¾ E 41, N 24° 25' E 10, N 18 E 48, N 20 E 20, N 3½ W 45, N 8 2-3 W 25 r., 5 l., N 15¾ W 16, N 6 W 10, N 13 1-3 W 10, N 16¼ W 41, and 18 and 8, N 12½ W 8, N 10 W 8, N 10½ W 24 and 3 and 9, N 14½ W 49, N 6 2-3 W 76 and 17 to north line of Warren and Henry Wilson's land on south side of South Road.

OCTOBER 1, 1849.

(79) Court of General Sessions. Beginning at Canaan on bank of South Road, at intersection of road leading by William Doten's, to railroad, S 6 E 110, on Theophilus Currier's, S 6 W 66, on Currier's, S 4 W 11, on Currier's, S 13 E 10, on Currier's, S 15 E 6, on Currier's, to south line, and north line Daniel Gile's, S 17 E 8, S 19 E 9, S 18 E 10, S 15½ E 16, S ½ E 15, all on Gile's, to south line of Canaan, S 11 W 64, in Enfield on Gile's east line and west line Mathew Bryant's, S 4½ — 22 on Bryant's, S 5 W 21½, to north side of road by Daniel Gile's, S 1½ W 2, across road, S ½ W 20, S 4½ W 15, S 11 W 13; Potatoe Road.

FEBRUARY 18, 1851.

(80) Beginning on road from Canaan to Dorchester, on land of Dustin and Somers, N 2½ E 31, N 6½ W 9, N 8¼ W 13, in north line

27

of Dustin's and Somers', N 5 W 59, across Benjamin P. Wells', N 109, across Rufus Atwell's, N 80 across Uriah F. Lary's, to road by Asahel Jones' and Lary's, to Dorchester, near where old Sanborn house stood; 3 rods wide; Lary Road.

August 21, 1852.

(81) Beginning north of Hiram Philbrick's house, east side of road from Factory Village, by Thad. Lathrop's, to Dorchester, N 88½ E 40, N 80½ E 10, N 56½ E 20, N 56 E 13, N 58½ E 10, N 75 E 12½, near mill of Stephen Peaslee; 3 rods wide.

September 1, 1852.

(82) Gates Road: Beginning east side Goose Pond Road (76), on John Shepherd's, N 64¾ E 8, on Shepherd's, N 44½ E 18, N 51 E 29, to south line of Olcott lot, N 33¾ E 26 on Olcott's, N 30 E 13, to south line Nathaniel Eaton's, N 30 E 6 on Eaton's to south line Amos Gould's, N 26 E 16, N 27 E 22, N 26 E 28½, N 27½ E 19, to side of Gould Road; 3 rods wide.

November 30, 1852.

(83) Beginning east bank of road from Levi Wilson's to Dorchester, near house said to have been built by Stephen Worth, S 55 E 6½, S 88 E 7, S 56½ E 11½, N 60 E 7, across Lorenzo Jameson's, S 60 E 2, N 79½ E 7½, E 22, N 73 E 9, N 87½ E 12, N 54 E 6, across Edward Currier's to Watts Davis'. See (42) (27) (13).

October 26, 1853.

(84) Beginning on southeast side of road by George Davis' house to Dorchester, near William Gordon's, on land of Jones & Co., S 44½ E 11, S 48½ E 8, S 35 E 9, S 6½ E 20, S 15½ E 15, S 9 E 8, S 10 W 23, S 23½ W 8, S 20½ W 7, S 1 E 15, S 3½ E 10, S 17½ E 10, S 38 E 10, S 3½ E 8, S 5¼ E 7, to south line Stephen Morse's and north line of Charles Day's, S 18 E 12, on Day's, S 29 E 6, S 27 E 12, S 18 E 10, S 27 E 16, S 16½ E 14, S 19 E 16, S 6½ E 12, S 2¼ W 15, on Samuel Dow's, S 34 E 7, S 51 E 10, to north line of T. S. Lathrop's, S 47½ E 12, on T. S. Lathrop's, to Joshua L. Lathrop's north line, S 47½ E 1, on J. L. Lathrop's, S 31 E 9, S 44½ E 7, S 37 E 13, S 22 E 18, S 56 E 7, S 31 E 17, S 26 E 8, to east line of J. L. Lathrop's and west line Reuben Goss', S, on Goss', 24½ E 13, to west side of road from Factory Village by Goss' to Dorchester; 3 rods wide; Clark Pond Road.

November 5, 1853.

(85) Beginning near watercourse on line Richard Hutchinson's and Jonathan Barnard's, N 85½ W 23 r., 15 l., on Barnard's, N 85½ W. on Jonathan Sanborn's, to east side of depot road, north of Sanborn's wheelshop; 3 rods wide.

ROADS.   419

DECEMBER 23, 1853.

(86) Across Pattee & Perley's, Goose Pond: Beginning east side of road from Pattee & Perley's to Tavern House, occupied by G. Westgate, N 17 W 8, N 4 W 6, to road leading from tavern to Canaan Street and East Canaan; 2 rods wide.

AUGUST 19, 1854.

(87) Beginning south side of road from West Farms to Lebanon, on James Brocklebank's, S 8 E 8, on Brocklebank's, S 6½ W 9, S 31½ W 14, S 16 W 6, S 9 W 11, S 1 E 20, S 2 E 9, to north line of Shakers', S 2 E 9, on Shakers', S 7 W 16, S 1 W 10, S 6 E 9, S 3 W 10, S 5½ W 26, S 15½ W 13, S 29½ W 20, S 37½ W 31, S 5½ W 5, S 17 E 5, S 27 E 3, to Enfield line; 3 rods wide.

SEPTEMBER 13, 1855.

(88) Daniel B. Cole's road: Beginning on the northwest side of road from Cole's to Orange meeting house, N 31 W 11½, to west line Lorenzo Jameson's, N 35 W 11, N 68 W 14, N 53½ W 27, N 54 W 15, N 62 W 17½, N 31 W 14, to east side of road from Leander Jameson's to Dorchester; 3 rods wide.

1857.

(89) April Term County Court. Beginning at a stake standing opposite and near the house of A. C. Lovejoy in Canaan, S 18 W 41½ on Lovejoy's, S 6 E 83 on C. M. Dyer's, S 6 E 32 on Henry and William M. Currier's, S 11 W 86 on Lovejoy's, S 11 W 30 on William Currier and William C. Smith's, S 11 W 48 on William Currier's, S 11 W 31½ on Seth P. Follensbee's, to Canaan and Enfield line, S 11 W 38, S 11 W 64, to north end of Shaker Hill Road in Enfield. Down valley of Committee Meadow Brook.

JUNE 13, 1857.

(90) Beginning near Charles Hutchinson's house on road from Alpheus Preston's to Goulding's mills to Canaan depot, N 7 E 34 r. to turnpike; from Barney Brothers' store north.

JUNE 10, 1858.

(91) Beginning on William Digby's, south of his house, N 71 W 10, N 42 W 8, N 61 W 14, across Bailey Welch's, N 61 W 75, to road from Page's mill to Dorchester, across Horace Chase's; 3 rods wide.

JUNE 14, 1859.

(92) Beginning near John B. Cunningham's, N 77 W 20, to near meeting house, N 58 W 40, to near John Milton's; 3 rods wide.

October 19, 1859.

(93) Beginning at Jonathan Barnard's, opposite his stable and on north side of road from Depot Street to turnpike, N 60½ E 6, to turnpike, then across turnpike to westerly line of Richard Hutchinson's, N 61½ E 76, on Hutchinson's, N 65½ E 24, and 4, on Alfred Davis', N 74 E 10, N 38½ E 7, N 8 E 14, N 10 E 20, to bank of road leading from Orange to depot, opposite watering trough; 3 rods wide; road from Barnard's by Edwin Flint's to watering trough.

1861.

(94) Beginning 9 rods below southeast corner of Arnold Morgan's, on line of Morgan's and Mary Clark's, S 85 E 42, to old turnpike, near Edwin B. Miner's (A. W. Hutchinson's), it being course of old road lately discontinued; subject to gates and bars; 2 rods wide. See (8).

November 5, 1861.

(95) Beginning southeast corner of F. M. Wells' barn, west side of road from Wells', N 5 E 10, on Wells', then on land of Shakers, N 10 E 22, N 28 E 10, N 10 E 11 and 10, N 8 W 6, N 3 E 20, N 23 E 5, N 46 E 9, N 27 E 6, N 4 E 10, N 25 E 15, N 28 E 15, N 8 E 2½, to Harry Follensbee's, N 8 E 3½, to Leonard Hadley's, N 33 E, on Hadley's. The line between Hadley's and Follensbee's 162 rods to road leading over West Farms.

June 1, 1866.

(96) Beginning at road on east line Stephen Swett's, one and one half rods from Swett's southeast corner, S 9½ E 8, through land of John T. Milton, to west side of road from depot to street.

February 18, 1868.

(97) Beginning stake 6 feet north of old pine stump, east side of road from Canaan to Lyme, 6 r., 6 l., south of south bank of Mascoma, near bridge, E 14½ N 3 r., 3 l., E 19½ N 2 r., 4 l., E 44½ N 2 r., 17 l., E 53½ N 10 r., 13 l., to watercourse in road from Factory Village to Dorchester; 3 rods wide.

September 2, 1891.

Road laid in place of a part of Gore Road: Beginning at a stake and stones on the east side of Gore Road, and near a ledge in said road, thence N 25 E 13 r., 11 l., N 4 E 5, N 10 W 11, to stake and stones on east side of Gore Road. The selectmen laid this piece without mentioning any width.

May 30, 1893.

Road to N. J. Hill's: Beginning at stake and stones on east side of turnpike, one rod from southwest corner of E. C. Aldrich's land, thence

N 38 E 11½, N 43 E 15 r., and 23 l., to stake on a line with E line of N. J. Hill's land and one rod south of southeast corner of Hill's land; 2 rods wide.

SEPTEMBER 6, 1894.

Road that took place of road over railroad track to Welch's mill: Beginning 51 feet northeast of Fernald's mill, being an iron pin in side of road, and 10 feet north of said pin at a hemlock stake, it being center stake of roadbed, thence west by a stake marked 9 feet that stands in bank 26 feet northwest of said mill shed, then west in straight line to west line of Fernald's land, then west by a stake marked 12 feet and land of A. G. Arvin's, and by a stake marked 3276 on top of hill to Indian River, and across said river to an iron pin in side of road east of W. H. Welch's house and about 4 feet northwest of two spotted elm trees; width to be 3½ rods on north side of Fernald's mill shed and across his land, 5 rods wide across Arvin's land to the river, rest of road 3½ rods.

NOVEMBER 4, 1897.

Wells Cemetery Road: Beginning stake and stones in west side of road from Fernald's mill to Wells Cemetery, 142 feet north of southwest corner of wall around land of William Welch, thence N 45 W 11 r., and 13 l., N 30 W 8 r. and 20 l., N 39½ W 3 r., and 6 l., N 9 W 4 r. and 15 l., N 24 E 7 r. and 16 l., N 11 E 6 r. and 17 l., N 5 r. and 19 l., N 21 W 4 r., and 21 l., N 40 W 4, N 29 W 4 r. and 16 l., N 11½ W 22 r. and 19 l., to south side of turnpike; 40 feet wide.

AUGUST 11, 1909.

Beginning at a gate on the south side of South Road on land of Charles Whittier, thence S 19 W 6 r. S ¾ W 12 r., S 13½ E 6 r., S 12 W 6 r., S 27¾ W 8 r., S 17 W 8 r., 12½ feet and on Whittier's to Frank Lashua's land, thence S 19 W 11 r., S 3¼ W 14 r., S 41¼ E 20 r., 4½ feet on Lashua's to Whittier's, thence S 27½ E 26 r., 4 feet, on Whittier's, to a point 17½ feet west of Charles Abbott's barn.

CHAPTER XXII.

Doctors and College Graduates.

The first man to come into town with doctor in front of his name was Ebenezer Eames. He was a grantee and having built the first mill in town received the offer of the proprietors of three hundred acres of land called the Mill Right. Whether he ever practiced as a physician or not is not known, but it is to be presumed that if he knew anything of medicine the settlers made use of his knowledge as occasion required. He was a miller and a blacksmith, the latter title is given him in an old deed. He was the miller up to 1787, when he sold the First Hundred of the Mill Right with all the buildings and privileges to Henry Finch, taking back a life lease. Finch was his son-in-law. The mill continued to be run by them until January 3, 1795, when they sold out to Dudley Gilman and left town.

Dr. John Harris came from Colchester, Conn., about the same time. He resided many years in a small house on the corner opposite the Congregational Meeting House, near a clump of lilac bushes, which were placed there by himself. But the health of the people was against his success. It is not known into what part of the surrounding country he drifted.

Dr. Caleb Pierce came from Enfield, bought out William Douglass, built the old hotel on the Street, but he was not successful as a landlord, was a very talkative and vain man, like his son Nat, was not popular and the young people held their dances at Dudley Gilman's Tavern. He died, in 1813, of spotted fever in the Pinnacle House which he had bought of Robert Barber.

Dr. Amasa Howard came here in 1807 and in 1810 built the house O. H. Perry remodeled and now lives in. He left town in 1815, moved to Springfield and sold his house to Jacob Dow. He is reported to have been a very skilful physician. He was also a surveyor, but his obdurate habits of drinking were a bar to his success. It is reported further that he kept on drinking and moving and died in delirium.

Dr. Timothy Tilton for over twenty years traveled up and down on the back of a black pacer, drank wine, went to jail, laughed at or with his creditors, and never troubled his debtors, and in all the sad and weary phases of his life preserved the good nature and wit which well became him. He came here in 1813 while Doctor Pierce lay dead with spotted fever, and remained here until his death December 28, 1836, aged 60 years. He was an active Abolitionist, and took a prominent part in resisting the attacks on Noyes Academy. On his headstone was at his request engraved "The Slave's Friend." He brought his family from Alexandria. His oldest child, Harriet Brown, was born in Newchester, April 27, 1807, married Dexter Harris in 1825 and died October 16, 1878; William Brackett, born in Bridgewater, February 20, 1810; Joseph Chase, born in Bridgewater December 25, 1812, married Mary Jane Chapman July 4, 1837, and built the house now occupied by F. L. Sawtelle, in 1832. She died in Concord, September 7, 1851, aged 38 years; Dr. James Aaron, the last child was born in Canaan, December 18, 1815, graduated from Dartmouth Medical College in 1842, and practiced medicine in Newburyport, Mass., where he died in 1881.

Dr. George Nelson, who graduated from Dartmouth College in 1822, in the class with Rev. Amos Foster, graduated from the Dartmouth Medical College in 1828 and came here soon after; was received into the Congregational Church here June 24, 1829. He left here in February, 1835, and in 1836 was in Louisiana. He died in 1875, aged 78 years. His career here was rather a stormy one, and he was not successful. A letter written in 1833 says: "Dr. Nelson is ruined. He will sue Burley and Cobb, Tilton, Trussell and D. B. Whittier for Slander."

Dr. Cyrus B. Hamilton and Dr. Daniel Hovey practiced here about a year. Dr. Daniel Stark came here too poor to pay his matriculation fees. Doctor Jones, who married Sophia Martin, daughter of Eleazer, remained a few years and sold out to Dr. Arnold Morgan. Doctor Morgan was born in Northfield, Vt., December 10, 1816; his father was a Free Will Baptist preacher; he lived in Cavendish until 1840, then moved to Windsor. He attended the Norwich Military Academy one term, was fitted for college but never went. He studied with Doctor McEwen, and graduated from Dartmouth Medical College in 1840. "There are but few young men who are so well fitted for the profession," said one of his professors. He began practice in Quechee, Vt., was there five years and went into the mercantile business in Pennsylvania. He came to Canaan in January, 1849. He practiced here for twenty-nine years and died in Savannah, Ga., April 14, 1878, where he had gone in search of health. His widow and son, Ben, went West leaving his mother, who died here; one daughter, Lizzie M., married Henry H. Pattee; another, Frances A., married, September 4, 1869, Frank E. Barnard, son of Darius. He had sold out his practice to Dr. George E. Leet who remained on the Street several years and then moved to East Canaan, where he lived for a few years and moved to Concord.

Dr. Ara Wheat was born in Grafton in 1816 and was the son of Capt. Joseph, and grandson of Elder Joseph Wheat. The family very soon after his birth moved to Canaan. Some time in the thirties he went to Ohio and returned to begin the study of medicine with Dr. Jones. He graduated from Dartmouth Medical College in 1860 and began the practice of his profession here. He married Isabel M. George, daughter of William W. George. They had two sons, William G. and Allen A. He gave up active practice in 1892 and removed to Springfield, Mass., where he died September 18, 1896. His wife died August 25, 1872, aged 42 years and 17 days.

Dr. Edward M. Tucker was born in Springvale, Me., April 22, 1839. He was educated at Dover, N. H., and in Boston, Mass. He studied medicine in 1864, under Dr. Levi G. Hill in Dover, and continued his studies under Dr. J. F. Fisher and Dr. Edward Cowles, while hospital steward in the army. He enlisted in the Third Massachusetts Battery and was wounded at Shepardstown, Va., September 20, 1862. He was taken to the hospital in Philadelphia, and was discharged from service on account of disability after a partial recovery. He passed the examination as a surgeon and reënlisted September 8, 1864, in Company I, Forty-Fourth Regiment Veteran Reserve Corps. He was transferred to an independent company of the Veteran Reserve Corps and was discharged December 18, 1865, to reënlist as hospital steward in the regular army. He held that position until December, 1871, attending three courses of lectures at Georgetown Medical College. He attended the Medical Department of Bowdoin College from which he graduated in 1872. He began practice in Canaan, July 28, 1873, and remained here until October, 1907, when he removed to Derry, N. H., where he died December 8, 1908. He married, February, 1879, Mary Albina Kimball of Grafton, N. H.; she died in Canaan, September 5, 1902, aged 50 years, 2 months, 29 days. They had one child, Luie A., living in Derry.

Dr. Frank A. Bogardus was born in Carroll, N. Y., April 4, 1869. He has been married twice; by his first wife he had one child that died young; his second wife, Blanche M. Coburn, daughter of John B. and Hattie F. (Doten) Coburn, he married August 31, 1905. She was born in Canaan, August 3, 1876. They have had two children, Charles B., who died young and Stanley, born February 1, 1908. Doctor Bogardus was educated in the High School at Catskill, N. Y., after which he taught four years, some of the time studying medicine with Dr. Charles L. Dodge. He then entered Baltimore Medical College, graduating in 1894. He first settled in practice at Hill, N. H., remaining there less than five months; on August 14, 1894 he came to Canaan and has since been in practice here.

Dr. Persons W. Wing was born in Glens Falls, N. Y., April 11, 1877, son of Walton S. Wing, and grandson of Halsey R. Wing, the first surrogate of Warren County, N. Y. He attended the Glens Falls Academy, and Peekskill Military Academy, graduating in 1897. He studied one year at Cornell University, and entered Long Island College Hospital in 1898, graduating in 1902. He married, June 25, 1902, Elizabeth H. Clarke of Sandy Hill, N. Y. He practiced medicine in Grafton, N. H., before coming to Canaan, in May, 1908.

GRADUATES FROM DARTMOUTH COLLEGE.

The following list embraces all the Canaan graduates from Dartmouth College, so far as known. It is not a long one, but it is respectable and honorable, both as to numbers and standing of those named.

The first graduate was George Richardson, of the class of 1820, son of Joshua and Betsey Richardson, born July 30, 1795; died at Charlestown, March 17, 1829. After graduating he taught one year in Moor's Charity School, Hanover; was principal of New Hampton Academy from 1821 to 1825, having been recommended by the faculty of the college to the trustees of that institution to become its first principal. It is not known with whom he studied divinity, but it must have been during his residence at New Hampton, as he was ordained a deacon in the First Episcopal Church, and preached his first sermon at Charlestown, July 5, 1825. He preached at North Charlestown and at Drewsville on alternate Sundays. He was ordained a Presbyter at Charlestown, July 26, 1828, by Bishop Alexander Viets Griswold, of Rhode Island, surviving his full induction to the ministry less than eight months. A man of letters, respected for his sincerity and earnestness. He was the first clergyman who read the Episcopal service in this town. It was at the house of Lawyer Kimball in 1828, at the solicitation of Mrs. Kimball, who was an English lady from Bermuda, and a communicant in that church; he married Elizabeth, daughter of Capt. Joseph Dennison, of Leyden, Mass.

Daniel Blaisdell, class of 1827, son of Elijah and Mary (Fogg) Blaisdell, read law with Joseph Bell of Haverhill, and became a resident of Hanover. From 1835-75, treasurer of Dartmouth College; state senator from 1863-65, representative several terms and held various town offices. Died in 1875, aged 69 years.

James Joshua Blaisdell, Rev., born February 8, 1827, class of 1846, brother of the above, graduated from Andover Theological Seminary in 1852. Served as chaplain of the Fortieth Wisconsin Volunteers during the Rebellion. Made a D. D. in 1873, by Knox College. Professor of Rhetoric and English Literature, at Beloit College, Wis., from 1859-64, professor of Intellectual and Moral Philosophy, from 1864 until his death at Kenosha, Wis., October 10, 1896, by suicide.

George Warren Gardner, class of 1852, was born in Pomfret, Vt., October 8, 1828, and as he said "born again in Canaan,

1842. Elder Peacock sponsor." Prepared for college at Canaan Union Academy and at Thetford. Was the first principal of the New London Institution from 1853-61. Ordained a minister of the gospel at New London in 1858. Settled as pastor of the First Baptist Church in Charlestown, Mass., September, 1861, and remained there until 1872. Was chosen corresponding secretary of the American Baptist Missionary Union, and served until 1876. Was called to the pastorate of the First Baptist Church in Cleveland, Ohio, in 1876. Received the honorary degree of D. D., in 1867 at Dartmouth. Traveled extensively in 1870. In 1880 was preaching in Marblehead, Mass. Doctor Gardner was present at the dedication of the Baptist Church at East Canaan in 1872, and preached the sermon on that occasion. His father was a shoemaker, and resided many years at the "Corner."

Caleb Blodgett, son of Caleb and Charlotte, class of 1856. (See lawyers.)

Amos Noyes Currier, A. M., class of 1856, born October 13, 1832, son of Eben F., professor of Latin and Greek languages in Iowa Central University, 1857-61 and 1865-67, was a volunteer in the war of the Rebellion, 1861-65. In 1867-70 professor of ancient languages in Iowa State University. In 1870 professor of Latin language and literature in the same university and acting president in 1898.

Edward Cornelius Delavan Kittredge, born December 29, 1834, in Lyme, class of 1857, son of Jonathan and Julia (Balch) Kittredge. Read law and practiced in New York. Died June 20, 1879, at Demarest, N. J., aged 44.

Marcus Manilus Pillsbury, class of 1858, son of Harrison Pillsbury. Remained upon his farm in Canaan several years after graduation. Then engaged in selling books, and kindred merchandise in New York. He was last engaged in the manufacture of edge tools at Napanock, N. Y., with an office in New York City. He died in 1908, leaving a widow and two daughters, both married.

Samuel L. Gerould, born July 11, 1834, class of 1858, son of Rev. Moses and Cynthia (Locke) Gerould. Studied for the Congregational ministry; was sergeant of the Fourteenth New Hampshire Volunteers from 1862-63. Was pastor of the church in Goffstown many years, and then settled over the church in Hollis where he remained until his death.

Joseph Doe Weeks, class of 1861, son of William P. and Mary (Doe) Weeks. (See lawyers.)

William B. Weeks, brother of above and in same class. (See lawyers.)

James Burns Wallace, class of 1887. (See lawyers.)

Nathaniel S. Currier entered Dartmouth in the class of 1841, and remained two years, but did not graduate. Died in Homer, La., in 1852, aged 30 years.

Ithamar Pillsbury graduated from Yale in the class of 1822.

William B. Arvin, son of Simeon and Hannah Arvin, born in 1812 in the house now owned by A. W. Hutchinson; graduated from West Point in 1836. He was appointed a lieutenant of infantry and ordered to Florida, to fight the Seminoles. After one campaign he resigned his commission and located at Newark, Ohio, as a lawyer.

Dr. Thomas Flanders graduated from Dartmouth Medical College in 1832.

Dr. Ara Wheat graduated from the Dartmouth Medical College in 1860, and Dr. Lewis W. Morey in 1876.

Dr. A. H. Flanders, son of Dr. Thomas Flanders, studied at Harvard Medical College and graduated from Union College. He was born in the Pinnacle House. Practised in New York City. Built a house on Fort Nonsense, Morristown, N. J., where he died. He married and had one daughter, Grace, married and living in Morristown, N. J.

George Dexter Harris, born in Canaan, December 16, 1840; was the son of Dexter and Harriet B. Harris; was appointed assistant acting surgeon November 12, 1863, and served on the United States Steamship *Magnolia*, resigned May 1, 1865. Graduated from Dartmouth Medical College in 1864; commenced studying with Dr. Thomas H. Currie and Dr. Alfred R. Bullard in 1860. After his resignation he returned to Canaan and afterwards went into the drug business in Boston where he died October 8, 1890, unmarried.

William Martin Chase, son of Horace and Abigail (Martin) Chase, was born in Canaan, December 28, 1837; was educated at

Canaan Union Academy, and graduated from the Chandler Scientific Department of Dartmouth College in the class of 1858. For about two years he was assistant preceptor of Henniker Academy. He then entered the law office of Anson S. Marshall of Concord, where he studied until his admission to the bar in August, 1862. He soon afterwards formed a partnership with Mr. Marshall which continued until the death of the latter. He was also for a time a partner of Hon. J. Everett Sargent, who became chief justice of the Supreme Court. Later he was a partner with Frank S. Streeter of Concord, until 1891, when he was appointed to the bench of the Supreme Court. He received the degree of A. M. from Dartmouth College in 1879, and the degree of LL. D., in 1898, and was appointed trustee of that institution in 1890. On December 28, 1907, having reached the age limit, he resigned from the Supreme Court. He was in the Senate from the tenth district in 1909. He married and has one son, Arthur H., who is the state librarian at Concord, who is married and has two children, Marjory and Robert.

Wilfred Hiram Smart, son of Frank B. and Mary B. (Jones) Smart, was born in Dorchester, April 22, 1883. His education was obtained at the Canaan High School, New Hampton Literary Institution from which he graduated in 1903, entering Dartmouth College in the fall of that year; he graduated in the class of 1907. He entered the Harvard Law School the next fall and will graduate in 1910. He was married June 30, 1906, to Rachel G. Smith of Meredith. Has been the agent of the Mutual Life Insurance Company of New York for some years.

Earl C. Gordon, son of George H., and Emma F. (Noyes) Gordon, was born December 12, 1887. His education was obtained from the Canaan High School, New Hampton Literary Institution, from which he entered Bates College, where he spent one year, and then entered the class of 1911 of Dartmouth College. Was assistant clerk of the senate for the session of 1909.

CHAPTER XXIV.

Temperance in Canaan.

The old orchards of Canaan were famous in their early maturity. The seeds were brought from Connecticut and Massachusetts. After building a house and clearing a spot of land, the next duty of the settler was to plant an orchard. The farms laid out by the newcomers, almost without exception, were not considered complete until the apple trees were started. The soil was moist and rich, and well adapted to the growth of fruit trees. They grew rapidly in the new soil, enriched by the ashes from the burned forests, and they bore fruit so abundantly that cider mills were erected at convenient places all over town. As the yield of apples increased, so the appetite for cider, and something stronger increased, and with this increasing appetite some of the bad traits of human nature were developed. The gatherings of the people were usually held at places where they could gratify their appetites, and there as the day progressed, the looker-on would observe the various phases which the use of cider and other drinks produced. Some men became hoggish and wallowed in their filth; some men became devilish and needed only hoofs and horns to be such in fact; some became idiotic and foolish and drooled in their silliness; others were a prey to ugliness, very few went home sober, or even knew when it was time to go home; some who had left strong-minded and muscular wives at home, preferred enjoying the evening air until the fumes of inebriety were evaporated. These things were not confined to the low or vicious, but it was a great social evil; it was a part of the hospitality of the house to offer cider, wine or rum to strangers as a beverage. There were drunkards among all classes of people. Many a man died of strong drink upon whose headstone may be read some cheering verse from the Bible.

There were a number of strong men who fell by the wayside in their encounter with apple-juice; there was Dea. C. W. and his sons, Esquire A. and all his sons; E. and J. W.; Doctor T., J. D., and L. W., and others, over whose remains might well have been inscribed, "Woe to him that tarrieth long at the wine cup." There came a time when the men who planted these great orchards, knew not what to do with the fruit. Some years, when their bins had been filled with apples for family use and their casks were all filled with cider, the quantity left ungathered was almost fabulous. Cattle, hogs and horses were turned loose to grow fat upon them. The year 1822 by those who remember it, has always been called the great apple year. Many hundred barrels of cider were made and many hundred bushels of apples rotted on the ground. Joshua Wells, before his death, used to recall that year and gave the cider product something as follows: Joseph Bartlett, 150 barrels; Dea. Caleb Welch, 30 barrels; John M. Barber, 100 barrels; Joshua Wells, 200; Capt. Moses Dole, 30; William Campbell, 50; Col. Daniel Pattee, 60; Josiah Barber, 60; Reynold Gates, 75; Abel Hadley, 25. Cider was everywhere. The difficulty being to find casks to hold it, it was free to all. Men drank it and became ugly, both in body and mind — red noses, bleared eyes, and bloated bellies were the sights that marked the devotees to these frequent libations, and there was no man brave enough to rise up and cry out: "Taste not, touch not."

Years went by and the same unhealthy signs traversed our streets, sometimes upright, sometimes on hands and knees, and this tippling was not all confined to one sex. It was well known that wives, mothers and maidens had appetites and often indulged them. Many good men and women regretted the slavery which, like fiery serpents, was winding itself about souls and bodies; but the remedy for it was not apparent.

In the town lived a young lawyer named Kittredge. He had long scorned to follow anybody's example. He preferred to be a leader, and if anybody in the country excelled him in his methods of getting drunk, he didn't know it; and if anybody ever showed more contempt for the usages of society, the people were ignorant of it. Oftentimes he was a weary, heavy-laden man. Why should he not rest when and where he pleased! on the grass! in the ditch! by the roadside! And if he happened to reach his own home before he sank down to rest, why should he take off his muddy boots, his jammed hat, or bedraggled clothes, as he crawled into bed and lost consciousness! He fell low down — very low! He lost practice, caste, character, and was looked upon as a pariah. But he was not entirely lost. By a supreme effort of his will, he crushed out the snakes and cast out the demons that possessed him, and became a man again. From his own severe experience, he believed he could benefit the world by speaking against the evils of drunkenness.

It was in the year 1829 that an attempt was made to organize an association to oppose the excessive use of alcohol. The meeting was held in Mr. Foster's church. Mr. Kittredge delivered a thrilling address upon the evils of drunkenness, which was subsequently printed, and then there was a general discussion upon the merits of the question; whether it was right and proper for this community, where rum was as much a drink as cider or water, and about as cheap, to abstain from its use, when nine out of ten knew they could not do it. A pledge was laid before the meeting, but it was so worded that sickness and depression of spirits were to be an excuse for indulgence.

Good old Elder Wheat could not sign it, because through all his long life he had used rum and it had given him courage and strength to work. Mr. Trussell would not sign it, although he was not a hard drinker, because it restrained a man in his liberty to do as he pleased — freedom in all things was his motto. Bart Heath drank rum because he loved it; he knew it was good for him. His wife drank it also; and it was good for her, too. Now he wasn't going to throw away any good thing in this world, because it would be parting with his rights. Doctor Tilton would sign, with a mental reservation, that the pledges should be no bar to his present habits. Deacon Drake wouldn't sign it, because he didn't wish to submit himself to so powerful a temptation as an invitation to drink would subject him. George Kimball, the lawyer, was not a drinking man. He favored the pledge and his argument ran somewhat as follows: "Spirit is expensive and useless and, moreover, hurtful. Its cost we all know. Its uselessness is provable by the fact that it contains no nourishment, nothing that can give vigor or strength. It is good when a man is melted, in that condition, there might be propriety in drinking spirit; but until the natural state becomes a state of fusion, I should object to the use of ardent spirits. Instead of giving strength, it only deceives men into a false estimate of their powers, like madness and poor human nature has to pay for it afterwards. It produces poverty, engenders sickness, is dangerous to the reputation, to the contentment and happiness in families, and is destructive to usefulness; to friendship, and is an enemy to the body and soul. I denounce all kinds of excitable spirits, except when a man is ready to perish. We may give wine to one of heavy heart, if it be pure. I denounce cider except in small lots and pure. I denounce the filthy orchards that encumber the best part of farmers' lands where he ought to raise corn and grain." Mr. Kimball was not applauded for his murderous allusion to the orchards, nor did he get credit for the peculiar "exceptions" he allowed.

When a man is melted, as he called it, a man in those days would hardly take alcohol to cool his blood.

There was a strong objection to the pledge simply as such. Personal "rights" and "liberty" to do as they pleased, were powerful words, and kept their hands off that paper. My recollection is that it received no signatures at that meeting. The men went home to talk it over and the women also. They looked about them and saw three stores and two taverns on the Street where rum was sold over the counter by the glass. Several other taverns about town offered facilities for indulgence. Not a day passed but some one or more men staggered home from these resorts, either too drunk to be civil, or too stupid to reflect whether their appetites might be more dangerous to their liberties than the pledge which had been offered them. There was a man who had sold rum all his life and he used to boast that he had never tasted any of his own liquors and knew no difference between them; "rum, gin or brandy, were all the same to him." He sold it! But he was not honest. He would tempt men on to drink, and then charge them with bills of goods which they never purchased, but which he would compel them to pay for, because having drank his rum, they had become oblivious to business obligations as well as to the decencies of life. These sad sights and scenes presented themselves daily to the world, and one by one a generation of drunkards went down to the grave, some of them lingering along life's road, like decaying pine stumps, rotten and ragged, waiting for the slow tread of time to crush out their strong vitality. But the words spoken at that first temperance meeting were like good seed scattered broadcast over the earth; and through all the years have yielded an annually increasing harvest down to this day. Wisdom, folly, philanthropy and fanaticism, since that day have taken a hand in the crusade against rum. Something has been gained, but the worm of the still is undying, crushed out today; tomorrow it shows its leprous features in another place. The combined and concentrated wisdom of all our law-makers, and of all the political philanthropists for the suppression of the sale of liquors from that day to this, has resulted in the conviction that men will have it.

In the year 1855 it was thought better to deal it out through an "agent," so that the profits therefrom might be a part of the public income. John M. Barber was the first town agent, and the rules controlling the distribution and sale were as follows: "You shall purchase and sell only such liquors as are pure and unadulterated. All liquors costing less than one dollar a gallon, your profit shall be 25 per cent., all over that amount 15 per cent. Purchase as you need and not have an unnecessary quantity on hand." The year 1880 was also a famous cider and apple year. There were eight cider mills in town. Harris J. Goss' mill made 413 barrels; E. C. Flanders made 42 barrels at his mill; Lary's mill made 346 barrels and Mr. Lary gathered 715 bushels of apples from his own orchard. Charles H. Wells' mill made 339; John Currier made 42 barrels at this mill, and Enoch Fifield and Charles Day divided 48 barrels between them. At Gates' mill 361 barrels were made; Daniel Hinkson made 41 at this mill. William Hall's mill turned out 410 barrels. George L. Whittier made 65 barrels there. Henry H. Wilson's mill turned out 419 barrels, Philip Prescott's 351, and William Huggett's 329 barrels. That year the barrels were worth twice as much as the cider. The cider sold at $1.25 per thirty-two gallons. Probably the apple crop that year was not far from 41,000 bushels.

CHAPTER XXV.

How Some of Our Houses Were Built.

Jonathan Carlton moved from Amesbury, Mass., to Canaan about 1780 and "pitched" upon the top of the hill, where he died. He put up a log house and therein some of his children were born, while the only door to the house was a strip of hemlock bark, set against the opening. He "cleared that farm." Being a millwright, he accepted the proprietors' offer of "100 acres of timbered land," which was the third hundred of the mill right, and built the first sawmill on Mascoma River, near the present factory village. These lands were then covered with a heavy growth of white pine of great size. The first timber he sawed was for his own house, the great house on the hill, now owned by C. P. King. He also sawed the lumber and boards for the meeting house; also for Captain Wells, who was then building the Wallace house, and for Dr. Caleb Pierce, who was then preparing to build the old hotel (Grand View).

About the same time Capt. Robert Barber built the Welch mill, as it was afterwards called, and sawed the boards for his new house, afterwards the Pinnacle House. Captain Barber was more fortunate than some others; upon his land he found a number of hard pine trees, which he sawed into flooring for his house and which remain to this day. Captain Barber also built a sawmill below Mr. Carlton's on Mascoma River, the ruins of which may be seen not far from the ruins of the old paper mill. The nails used in these buildings were cut from wrought-iron hoops, manufactured for the purpose, with a cutting machine set up in Mr. Carlton's mill. The rum used to raise the buildings came from Jesse Johnson's at East Enfield, who for many years kept the only store in all the region round about.

Simeon Arvin was of Irish parentage and came here in 1790. A few years afterwards he kept a store in a red building near where now stands the house of the late George Harris, now his grandson's, G. H. Goodhue. He married Hannah, daughter of

Jonathan Dustin, and raised a family of boys and girls. In 1804 he bought the farm of Nathaniel Barber at the south end of the Street, where A. W. Hutchinson now lives. A Mr. Clark owned a blacksmith shop just north of Arvin's store, which he afterwards sold to Nathaniel Currier, who finished it up into a store, where he traded for many years. This shop was near the site of the stone house. Arvin sold his store to Micaiah Moore, brother-in-law to Blacksmith Clark, but it did not prosper after Arvin left it. Both Moore and Clark sold out and went West to "the Ohio," disappearing forever from among us. Arvin also owned the Welch mill.

Josiah Clark married Pernal Barber and built the house where A. W. Hutchinson lives; he bartered farms with Nathaniel Barber, his wife's brother, and moved down on the intervale, near the fair grounds.

Daniel Colby lived in a log house near the cemetery on the Street, where he raised a family of fifteen children and died at the great age of ninety-nine years. As full of crochets and eccentricities as any man could be.

Reynold Gates, son of Josiah, was a good worker. He came to Canaan about 1768, when a boy, from Colchester and without friends. Major Jones took care of him and when he married Lydia Clark, the major gave him one hundred acres of wild land. He took up land in the northwest part of the town and before his marriage, had his bread made at William Richardson's on Sawyer hill. Several times on his way home in the evening, he was chased by wolves and, to save himself, would drop a loaf; sometimes he found himself breadless on arriving at his log cabin. He lived north of where H. B. Gates now lives. His nearest neighbor was Nathaniel Bartlett, who came shortly after and settled the adjoining farm and married Susanna, a sister of Gates' wife, both daughters of Caleb Clark. These two men carried on their lands together. Bartlett came from Amesbury, and before his marriage, lived with William Richardson. One day he had set his dinner pail down, a bear came along, got into it and slipped the bail over his head, and away went bear and pail. He was heard of several times afterwards. The cellar hole alone remains of Bartlett's house, about sixty rods south of where H. B. Gates now lives, in the field.

Allen Whitman of Colchester, Conn., one of the original grantees of Canaan, never came here to look after the lands that were surveyed and assigned to him, and which were taxed for the making of roads and other expenses. The first division of one hundred acres was surveyed in two lots of fifty acres each, one on the easterly shore of Hart's Pond, the other on Town Hill. The first half has a history sufficiently interesting to induce its being traced out, as upon it are situated some of the old landmarks of the town.

In 1782 it was taxed at 12s., 2p., and on the 3d of January, 1786, it was sold by John Hall Bartlett for non-payment of the tax, to William Dougless, a shoemaker, who received a deed acknowledged "before me, William Ayer, J. P." and

> Beginning at a stake and stones standing by the side of Hart Pond,—thence S 80°W 113 rods to a stake and stones, then S 10°E 22 rods to a stake, then S 80°W 15 rods to a stake, then S 10°E 46 rods to a stake and stones, then N 80°E 118 to a heap of stones by the pond, then by the pond to the first bound.

The boundary lines of this land are still preserved to a certain extent. It is the land between the north line of O. H. Perry's on the west side of the Street, and the north line of R. H. Haffenreffer's, and from the pond to the old Dustin and Barber farms, now occupied on the west by M. E. Cross and Mary E. D. Weeks.

On October 23, 1790, "William Douglass, cordwainer," in consideration of £100, L. M. conveyed to "Samuel Dustin, yeoman," of Canaan, a brother of David, and son of Jonathan, the same lot of fifty acres, with the following additional description: "Lying southerly of Mr. Jonathan Dustin's land, that he now lives on, and joins on Capt. Robert Barber's land, and westerly on the road or path now trod from Mr. Eames' Mill, to the south side of the town."

January 20, 1791, "Samuel Dustin, yeoman, in consideration of £100 paid by William Douglass, cordwainer," conveys a house and fifty acres of land, situated on the west side of Hart Pond, and lying southerly of Mr. Jonathan Dustin's land, that he now lives on, and joins on Capt. Robert Barber's land, and westerly on the road or path now trod from Eames' mill to the south side of the town; said land being part of the first one hundred acres of the right of Allen Whitman.

The first break in the body of the fifty-acre lot, occurs November 26, 1792, when William Douglass, "in consideration of the sum of eleven pounds, four shillings, lawful money," conveyed to the committee of the proprietors of the "proposed Meetinghouse," the land now known as the "Common."

On July 14, 1793, "William Douglass, cord. sold to William Parkhurst, trader, for £74–10s., L. M., a certain fifty-acre lot or farm, bounded easterly on Hart Pond, so-called, northerly on Jonathan Dustin's land, westerly on the road from Eames' mill to the south side of the town, and southerly on land of Robert Barber, it being part of the first hundred acres, laid out in the original right of Allen Whitman, excepting three acres and one-quarter, which I have already deeded to the proprietors of the Meeting house, and on which said Meeting house now stands."

On August 5, 1793, William and Sally Parkhurst conveyed to Caleb Pierce of Canaan, physician, for £150 lawful money, the same fifty acres of land, and bounded as in the deed from Douglass to Parkhurst, with the following addition: "With the buildings thereon, excepting three and one-quarter acres, which belongs to the proprietors of the Meeting house, deeded to them by William Douglass, and being the same land on which the said house now stands."

Doctor Pierce built the old tavern and opened it in 1794; it was first known as Pierce's tavern, then Moore's store, Clark's tavern, J. Harris' inn, Cobb's tavern, and so on down to Crystal Lake House and Grand View Hotel. The lumber to build it was sawed at Jonathan Carlton's mill at the village.

The second division of this land occurred in 1793. Caleb Pierce sold five acres adjoining on Robert Barber's line, on the west side of the Street and the corresponding land on the east side to the pond, to Col. Ezekiel Wells, who up to that time, had resided on Town Hill. While building his house, he moved in with Doctor Pierce, who was from Enfield, and at that time occupied the only house on the Street. Colonel Wells erected the frames of two large houses, one on each side of the Street, and was ambitious to own the largest house in town, but he was not able to finish the houses he proposed to erect. The frame on the east side remained uncovered for several years, and was sold to a Mr. Tucker, who took the frame down and moved it elsewhere. The house on the west side, he covered in and two rooms were finished in panel. He lived in this house; some of his children and one grandchild were born in it. Then it passed into the hands of Gideon Morse and Josiah Clark in 1809. The last sold it to Col. Asa Robinson of Pembroke, in 1815, and he, desiring to return to Pembroke, traded it with James Wallace in 1817, then in business in Pembroke, for property valued at $1,000. The house was burned November 4, 1898. In 1815 Josiah Clark sold to William Atherton "one acre exact measure," "Beginning at the northeast corner of Robert Barber's land on the Broad Street," in consideration of $100. On August 10, 1805, Caleb Pierce conveyed to Micaiah Moore, "trader of Lime," for $1,600, a tract of land bounded as follows:

Commencing at a stake on Hart Pond, running westerly by the Dow land to Broad Street, crossing said street to the northeast corner of Jacob Trussell's old joiner shop, northerly 10 rods one foot to a stake and stones, then S 80°W 80 rods to a stake and stones by a strip of land formerly owned by Thomas Dow, then S 10°E 10 rods one foot to a stake and stones, then S 22 rods to a marked stake, then S 80°W 15 rods to a stake by the road leading from David Dustin's to John M. Barber's, then S 10°E 46 rods by said road, to a stake and stones by said Barber's land, then by said Barber's land easterly, to the southeast corner of a five acre lot that Ezekiel Wells now lives on, then N 12°W 12 rods, then N 82 E 46 rods to a stake and stones, then N 12 W 9½ rods to a stake and stones, being the southwest corner of the Meeting House land, then easterly by lands I sold Capt. Ezekiel Wells to Hart Pond, then by said Pond to the first bound, reserving three and one quarter acres of Meeting House grounds, the road that leads through it, and the land under Jacob Trussell's old joiner's shop, so long as it will stand without repairing.

On February 7, 1809, Micaiah Moore mortgaged for $500 to John Currier, the same land, reserving the meeting house land and "one-half acre and buildings I live in, being all the land I bought of Caleb Pierce." Moore afterwards redeemed this. In 1811 Moore sold to Eliphalet Clark of Boston, for the sum of

$1,750, fifteen acres of land, which sale included the old tavern, orchard and lands adjoining on both sides of the Street. The property was next conveyed to Joshua Harris, who occupied it as a store and tavern until 1822, when he transferred it to Salmon P. Cobb, and since that day it would require much labor to trace the title through the many changes of ownership.

James Doten owned it from 1838 to 1842, then George Powers; after him came David Heath, Harvey Angell, Guilford Cobb. Ann Dunham lived there in 1852. When Joseph Dustin and William W. George bought it for Amos Kidder in 1855, it was standing empty. Kidder never paid for it. Then came Charles Jones, who had a tinshop there in the old hall. Charles Day owned it when Willard Dunham, Peter Godet and Frank and Mercy Fox lived there. In 1878 William Gordon bought it of Charles Day. He christened it Crystal Lake House. After him came Mrs. Derby, Mr. Dale, Mr. Landon, Albert R. Wilkinson, who called it the Grand View Hotel; after making many repairs to it, he sold it at auction to R. H. Haffrenreffer, who tore it down in the winter of 1908-09, and used the timbers and boards to build a summer cottage. Thus ended one of the oldest hostelries on the Grafton Turnpike, where the coaches from Boston used to stop for change of horses.

In 1790 William Parkhurst built the house now occupied by Col. A. A. Haggett. He had married Robert Barber's daughter Sally and the old man gave him the land. He kept store in this house. After him it was occupied by Daniel Blaisdell for a time. On March 15, 1800, Parkhurst conveyed to Robert Barber for $350, "all the buildings that I built on said Barber's land in said Canaan, on the easterly side of Broad Street, so-called, with all the fences and appurtenances thereto belonging."

On January 17, 1809, Robert Barber conveyed to Dr. Caleb Pierce "the Home Farm, embracing 180 acres, in consideration of $3,000, bounded northerly on Hart Pond, westerly by land of Simeon Arvin, easterly by land of Joshua Wells, and the highway leading to Grafton, southerly by the road leading by Jonathan Follensbee's (formerly Oliver Smith's) and land of said Smith and John Tenney to Arvin's corner." This is the "Pinnacle" property. The remainder of his farm Barber had sold to Simeon Arvin. Doctor Pierce occupied the house until 1813, when he died of spotted fever. His family continued to live there until 1824, when it passed into the hands of Dr. Thomas Flanders. The house once occupied by H. P. Burleigh, was moved by him from the site where it was built, just north of O. H. Perry's barn. Jacob Dow built it in 1802 and 1803. He married Phœbe Wells, daughter of Ezekiel, in September, 1802, and his first child, Phebe, born June 21, 1803, who May 9, 1824, married David March, was born in her grandfather's house, while her father was building his new house, clearing the pine swamp and jungle of bushes which extended to the pond, and while Jacob cleared and drained the land and worked it into beautiful and fruitful fields, she became the mother of fourteen children. This house burned two years ago.

Henry Morse began the house where F. B. L. Porter now lives in 1844 and finished it in 1845; after living there a year, he sold it to William Kimball.

John M. Barber, son of Robert, pitched on 113 acres, 153 rods of land in December, 1794, extending to the west of his father's farm. It was in the right of Isaiah Rathburn, and like many of the old settlers, his first house was of logs. He married Sally Sanborn and moved into a small house near the site of the large house, wherein had lived David Fogg and his wife, Ruth Dustin. They had disappeared and given place to John M. and Sally, who like all the strong workers of those days, believed in the propagation of the species. Children came along at regular intervals until the little house was full: March, Deliverance, Polly, Sally, John, Jesse, Catherine, Irena and Miriam. He built the ell part of the new house about 1800, and moved into it. He was one of the most hardy of the early settlers, seldom wearing an overcoat or mittens in cold weather. He was heard to say that he raised potatoes on the ground where stood the tallest, most beautiful grove of pine trees in town at the time it was cut. In 1807 he hired Moses Richardson to bring down from Sawyer Hill the dressed underpinning for the addition he was contemplating. For this new house, he had selected a location unsurpassed for its scenic beauty. In the background was the old forest, lively with varieties of large and small game. It was in those woods that old Uncle David Dustin killed a bear and the wad of his rifle set fire to the underbrush that could not be quenched until a hundred acres of old growth timber had been burned and become valueless. Mr. Barber was as usual quite indignant at the "accident," but as every man in those days had all the timbered land he wanted, and there was no sale for lumber, he, like a good neighbor, soon recognized the fact that "accidents will happen," and was easily placated. It was in those woods that a bush called wickoby used to abound, the wood corklike, the bark as Major Trussell used to say, "tough as horn," and was sought for by Caleb Welch, the miller, to tie up his meal bags. These woods were in early days a grand place to shoot small game, but Uncle John Barber would not allow hunting in them with guns unless we would agree not to use tow for wadding. These woods renewed themselves and in 1888 were cut down and sawed into lumber. John M. Barber built his house of the best pine lumber, sawed at his father's mill. His work went on slowly, for the "Embargo" of Jefferson in 1807, and the "Non-Intercourse" of Madison in 1809, increased the price of nails, iron and other necessary materials, so as to discourage its completion. In 1810 money was scarce and Mr. Barber concluded, like many others, to wait for better times. But the better times never came for him. The house remained unfinished. He never drove another nail into its timbers. Afterwards when Hiram Barber came into its possesion, comfortable improvements were made. Three generations of Barbers occupied that house, and then it passed into the hands of Charles Day. After his death, the timber was cut off and the land then passed to Israel Sharon. The house burned on the night of the 29th of December, 1891.

Josiah Barber built the big house on the old "Poor Farm" and lived there. It was his boast that he would build a bigger stack of chimneys than any of his neighbors, the big chimneys exhausted his means to such an extent that he never entirely completed the big house. His son, Josiah P. Barber, was called "Black Siah Barber." "Smiling Siah Barber" was the latter's cousin. His father lived in Epping. "Smiling Siah" used to visit his uncle and assist him in his work. The old man gave him a piece of land as an inducement to settle here. The young man built the church house next below his uncle's, on the right; got married and lived there many years, when he sold out and moved to Nashua, where he lived to be over eighty years old. Beyond, still stands the old house of Joseph Bartlett, who came here about four years after Josiah Barber and bought out Caleb Clark's heirs. Clark was the first settler in that region. This old house is almost a ruin. It was afterwards occupied by Orrin and George Fales, the former married Bartlett's daughter, Polly.

The old farm where Charles Deeato lived was settled by Moses Lawrence and the old house was built by him. Bartlett and Lawrence were Barber's neighbors and each strove to outdo the other in building their houses. Not one of them ever finished the inside of his house. Barber owned a sawmill on the Mascoma River above the bridge on the road from Charles Lashua's. This mill afterwards passed into the hands of Moses Lawrence, who came to Canaan about 1800, lived here about thirty-eight years and died in Ohio. He was an ardent Methodist, believing all other doctrines sinful. He had six daughters and three sons. Two of the sons were John and Richard; Otis Willis, Fardey Norris and his cousin, Joseph Norris of Dorchester, married three of the daughters. One went away unmarried; also the boys. He built the small house near the Swett house for one of his sons. The style of these old houses was much alike. There are many of them standing now. With two stories, square-shaped and large square rooms, with a large hallway in the center, and four rooms on a floor, and two large chimneys, one on either side. Some were built with four-sided roofs, none of them had blinds on the outside, but had shutters inside disappearing into the partitions on either side of the windows, and when shut, the room was as dark as night. Their style of architecture verged on the colonial, more so as the means of the owner permitted. A little later, the style although still trying to preserve the colonial resulted in smaller houses, two stories high, but oblong and only one room deep and two rooms wide, with a hall in the center, but these two rooms were large ones, like the old Barber homestead. Then came a still further narrowing in width, like John Currier's, the Haggett and Dow houses. To all of these was added an ell, of an altogether different style, in fact no style at all, and which for the most part, was the kitchen and living room of the family. Later and along in the thirties, came the story and a half house, some of them built with four rooms on the first floor, and finished rooms on the second floor. The attics of the two-story houses were not finished, nor were all of the rooms on the second floor.

The "Stone house," the only one of its kind in town, was built about 1842 by Edmund Hazen. The stone came from the pasture back of the paper mill. It was built for a blacksmith shop and later Simon Dodge finished it into a house.

Gordon Burley built and kept the store which stood just north of Charles Seavey's house. He sold it in the latter part of December, 1834, to Eleazer and Jesse Martin who came from Grafton. Eleazer came with his family in the early part of January, 1835, and moved in with Mrs. Wallace. He afterwards moved into the house now owned by F. B. L. Porter. Jesse Martin bought the house Thomas H. Pettingill built and which had been occupied by Mr. Foster. It was then a one-story house and Mr. Martin built it over.

It may be interesting to know where the farms of the old settlers were, begining from the settlement of the town to 1813. The roads upon which some of them lived have been long since thrown up. Here and there as one traverses the fields and woods, an old cellar hole appears; upon close observation an old road can be found. Beginning at the southeast corner of the town and following the Enfield line along South Road, we first find Samuel Noyes, then Daniel Farnum, afterwards owned by Dudley Noyes and Daniel Hinkson, now Frank Lashua's. Then comes Amos Stevens in 1787, afterwards owned by Timothy Johnson and then by Daniel Davis, Elijah Miner and Reuben Welch. Next came Capt. Charles Walworth and on the opposite side of the road was his son George's farm, where the Cobble graveyard is. Then came the farm of Dea. Caleb Welch; on the north side of the road was Jehu Jones. Next was the farm of Theophilus Currier, through which the Potato Road runs. On the north side of the road was the farm of two hundred acres of Thomas Miner. East of Theophilus Currier was William

Ayer. On the west side of the Potato Road was James Morse, on the opposite side was Shubael Burdick, who sold to Moody Noyes. Next came Thomas Baldwin, who sold to Samuel Jones and he sold to Micah Porter. Opposite was Richard Otis, who sold to James Doten. Next came Samuel Jones, afterwards the Daniel Pattee farm; next was the farm of John Scofield, extending to Mud Pond Brook, afterward Samuel Jones', then Daniel Pattee, his son James, and beyond him Joshua Pillsbury, who swapped with Warren Wilson. On the opposite side of the road was George Harris and his son Joshua; next was John Scofield, Jr., who sold to Col. Levi George. Next was the farm of Eleazer Scofield, afterwards Simon Blanchard, who sold to Lois Evans. Robert Williams lived on the Blanchard farm also. The Scofield land included the vicinity of West Canaan. On the other side of Mud Pond Brook was the farm of Richard Aldrich, then came Samuel Joslyn, afterwards owned by Judah Wells, also known as the Richard Aldrich farm. Then came Asa Paddleford's farm as far as the governor's right of five hundred acres then from the Mascoma River, north of Asa, came James Paddleford. John Scofield owned the governor's right and his heirs sold to John May, William and Israel Harris, Daniel Dow, Elam Meacham, Joseph and Benjamin Blake to the Hanover line.

Extending along the north line of the town, east of Mascoma River, was Joseph Bartlett, then came Moses Lawrence, Ebenezer Davis, Nathan Cross, Joseph Randlet, Daniel Lary, Josiah Clark, Amasa Jones, Tristram Sanborn. Then coming down the River Road on the east side of the town was Stephen Worth in Jerusalem. Then Harry Leeds, Ezra Chase. On the Jerusalem Road, was David Brown, Levi Wilson, John Worth, Jr., Eliphalet Norris, William Wood, Jabez, Job and Jeremiah Wilson to the Nathaniel Barber farm, afterwards Josiah Clark's. West of David Brown was Peter Pattee.

Beginning on the Turnpike at Grafton line, was Elijah Whittier, Daniel Blaisdell and Parrott, his brother, to the bridge over the river at the depot, then following the Turnpike was John Worth, Jr.'s, tavern, and not a house from there to the top of Doten Hill; then on the Bickford Road was Ezekiel Gardner, John Sweet, afterwards Samuel Whittier's, on the Turnpike came Joshua Wells, then Robert Barber in the Pinnacle House; next Josiah Clark, William Parkhurst, Dr. Amasa Howard, Jacob Dow, William Atherton, Ezekiel Wells after he moved from Town Hill; above the town house was William Douglass; towards the west was Jonathan Dustin, extending to the Mascoma River, then on the Street Moses Dole, Nathaniel Currier in 1816, Daniel Colby and Dr. John Harris opposite the cemetery. Thaddeus Lathrop lived opposite J. W. Colburn's. At the corner northerly towards Dorchester, was Ebenezer Eames; afterwards Cyrus Carlton built A. S. Green's house and ran the mill; then John Currier, David Pearson, Wales Dole, Jonathan Carlton. Ensign Colby on the Robitoille place, Jonathan Carlton, Jr., lived on the Green place, then came "Smiling Siah Barber," then Josiah who built the poor farm to Joseph Bartlett's. On the road easterly from the corner was Eliphalet Richardson on the Haffenreffer place, Samuel Welch on the Putney place; then John Worth and John Colcord at the corner of the roads. On the west side of the pond between Wells and Colcord lived Richard Whittier. North of Colcord was Bailey Cross, Joshua Richardson, Jonathan Dustin, Jr., George Flint on the Elijah George place. To the west was Nathaniel Whittier on the Randlett place, Eliphalet Clark on the Levi Hamlet place, and off the present road on Gilman Hill, was Nathaniel Gilman, Benoni Tucker and Thomas Beedle, with Charles Greenfield. Then came Nathan Cross on the Murray place.

Extending along the Hanover line and on West Farms, north of the governor's right, was Shaker land, then Reuben Gile, who sold to his son Stephen and moved away in 1828. Stephen moved to Morristown, Vt., with Jacob Straw in 1826. Stephen had married Lydia Straw. Afterwards S. B. Morgan owned some of the Gile farm, John Day that upon which Henry H. Wilson lived; north of him was Timothy Clark, afterwards his brother Theodore's. Clement Stoddard lived there first. Next came John Currier, who sold to Jacob Tucker, then Abraham Knowlton. Next was Henry Springer, Elijah Paddleford, and after him William Longfellow. Then came Jacob Straw, afterwards Abram Longfellow. Then came Robert Williams; next William Straw, a brother of Jacob, of Hopkinton. Next came Daniel

Morse, afterwards Robert Williams, who sold to Stephen Eastman as well as William Straw, and extended to Hanover line adjoining the Eastman farm in Hanover. Then came common land to the north side of Goose Pond. Then came John Willis; then William Bradbury to the line of Gate's Gore settled by Samuel J. Gates. East of Bradbury was Reynold Gates; east of him for two hundred acres was Caleb Clark; south of Clark and Gates was fifty acres of Adam Pollard and 376 acres of Nathaniel Bartlett. South of him was Matthew Greeley, afterwards Sewell Gleason, at the Hinkson place. South of him was Clark Currier on Sawyer Hill. Then came William Richardson, his brothers, Enoch, John and Eliphalet, then Robert and Warren Wilson, afterwards Joshua Pillsbury and Moses Shepard. Next south came Jacob Richardson, John Wilson at Edwin Shepard's, then Lewis Lambkin, Richard and David Kimball, Samuel Clough, Moses Chase, afterwards Reuben Puffer and Samuel Chapman, where Lewis Defosse lived, then Samuel Meacham and Ezekiel Wells. East of Ezekiel Wells was William Campbell and east of him was waste land, east of which was the Barber farm to the Street.

Daniel Porter settled the farm now in the possession of Sigismond Wolfson. There was an old road which led easterly from Clark Currier's, now Ricard's. On this road east was Amasa Clark, then Ambrose Chase, afterwards John Hoit, and John Fales. Nathaniel Richardson settled the Err Collins place. Richard Clark, 3d, settled on the Delancy King place, Joseph Clark at F. F. Avery's. Levi Cilley on Fred Sharkey's old farm and Luther Kinne on C. H. Sweet's, at the corner of the road from Josiah Barber's. From the switch where Joseph Flint's farm was easterly, afterwards Seth Daniels, was Oliver Smith, Stephen Jenniss, Robert Barber's mill; John Follensbee at the present grist mill. On the road south from the grist mill lived Job Tyler, Moses Hadley, William Ayer, Thomas Cole, Moses Kelley, Jacob Miller, John Bean, Joshua Springer, Joshua Currier, David Currier. Amos Gould lived on the left below the old Hinkson place; Joshua Meacham lived on the Nathaniel Shepard place; Edwin May lived on the Caleb Jones place; having previously lived in the Gore.

CHAPTER XXVI.

WHEEL CARRIAGES, TANNERIES, POTS AND PEARL ASHES.

Caleb Welch brought a two-wheeled gig wagon into town when he came about 1769. The first four-wheeled vehicle seen here, was owned by Simeon Hadley. The body was roughly constructed and placed upon the axles without springs. On the rough roads of those days, it was not a great comfort to ride in it. Capt. Joshua Harris owned the first chaise. It was of a deep shining green color. He brought it from Connecticut in the first years of this century. He owned a very staid old horse, whose habits had worn into accord with the old man. It was his custom to leave that horse and chaise unhitched where he could eat grass, whenever he called upon his neighbors. The old man was famously absent-minded. On returning from those calls, he would uniformly forget his team, and would walk home with his head bent down talking to himself. Sometimes he would find his horse standing at his door; at other times he would go back and find him still feeding beside the roadside. The old man kept a diary in which he recorded things concerning town affairs as well as of individuals, doubtless much that would be interesting now. In the endeavors to find it, it only served to show that it had been lost forever, gone to rags. It was traced to the family of his son and to his granddaughter, and then it disappeared.

Captain Dole, who bought out Dudley Gilman and kept an "Inn" at the north end of the Street, where is now the Hotel Lucerne, owned a chaise which attracted much attention. It had a nearly closed top and was a grand affair.

TANNERIES.

The first tannery was established by Lieut. Richard Whittier on the north side of Succor Brook. It was discontinued a hundred years ago. The remains of it are still to be seen on the site where the steam mill was located that cut off the timber in 1904.

Mr. Whittier left his wife and five children in Methuen, Mass., and came to Canaan in 1788, where several of his neighbors had already settled, and purchased a hundred-acre lot of land on the east side of Hart's Pond, called the first one hundred of the right of William Fox, Jr. He remained long enough to cut over five acres of timberland, that being required by the proprietors, and returned to Methuen to close up his affairs and get ready to bring his family into his new home. Various and untoward events delayed his setting out, and it was more than a year before he was able to return to Canaan.

Capt. Joshua Wells, who lived near the old orchard back on the hill from the present Lovejoy house, was to be his nearest neighbor. On the north side of his land lived John Colcord and Bailey Cross. And still farther on towards Dorchester, Nathan Cross had made a clearing, on the farm since known as the Murray farm. It was in September or October of the year 1789, that he returned alone, for he was not yet prepared to give his family a home. The following letter, which is unique in its construction and rather unusual in its orthography, is one of the fragments of those days, which indicates the writer's purpose to make a home in Canaan.

> Cap. Wells: Sir, I haveing a opportunity to write a fue lines I would imbrace it. Sir: I should be glad you would git some person or parsons to loope the high limes upon my feel trees and seet them on fire the first opportunity, they be drye, and I will satisfy you and them when I come up. Sir, I expect to set out the first day of September. this from your friend
>
> RICHARD WHITTIER.
>
> methuen, August the 15 Day 1789
> Sir, I should be glad to board at your house.

He came and put up a log house, and later in the season his family joined him. He burned over the land he had cleared, and having put in crops of grain, he journeyed back to Methuen with his family, to settle up his affairs for a final move to his new home. But those were slow days, and small events often caused long delays. There is another letter very personal and peculiar which exhibits some of the customs and habits of thought in those days.

Methuen August the 2nd, 1790.

Sir: having a opportunity to send a fue lines, I now imbrace it to let you now of my affairs. that day I left your house it was very warm, but I had the headake very much, so I did not ride in the middle of the day, but I rode in the evening wich made me very late home, and it grew cold and I took cold and have been very sick, so that I have cepte house till a day or two agoe, and now grow some better. my family is all well, and I hope these lines will find you and your family in good health. mrs. Whittier sends hur regards to you and mrs. Wells, hoping to be better acquainted; my sons gives their Regards to your sons; my daughter gives hur cind regards to your daughters. Sir, I have nothing new to write. it is very weet and worm. we have great shours and heavi thunder. it is somewhat sickly but not many deaths. Sir, I have sent Letter to Daniel peaslee to bring my oxen down and he will bring them to your house the night before he set out with them, and if you will keep them I will Repay you. Sir, I am alike to be disipinted of sum of my stock and lode by Reason of my being sick and sceasness of munney, that I am afraid I shall not get up to Canaan till the eight or teenth of September, and if my grain should warnt Reaping before I come, Sir, if you will git mr. Runnels, or mr. Welch, or mr. Nathaniel Worth, or mr. Gardner or mr. Stickney. or sum of them, or all of them, to Reap it and secure it I will satisfy them, and if they fail anny boddy Els that will do it. but I am in hopes I shall be there before it will want Reaping. This from your affectionate friend,

RICHARD WHITTIER.

plese to give my regards to mr. miller. tell him I should be glad to have him look at that fence that he made if he pleese.

Mr. Miller was Jacob Miller, who came from Methuen with Mr. Whittier and helped him clear the farm. His daughter married Nathaniel Barber, who lived on the same farm at one time. Mr. Miller built a house on the farm Barak Smith lived on.

He did not arrive until late in the fall, when he found that Mr. Wells had reaped and stored his grain and Mr. Miller had "looked at that fence," and repaired it. It was too late in the season to build a comfortable house, but the neighbors were kind and afforded shelter to his family. There were three sons born in that first log house, Asa, who twenty-five years ago was living in Erie, Pa., and built the old house on the site of Hotel Rand, Abiah and Moses. The labor of clearing the land, the cares of the family, and his duties as a citizen, prevented his building a new house for a time, but in the course of four or five years, with the aid of his boys, he got out the timber, sawed his boards at Capt. Robert Barber's new sawmill and put up the frame of the new house and covered it in so as to make him a comfortable home. Two more children were born to him: Leonard in 1797 and Rufus in 1800. He was by trade a tanner, and soon after his family was made comfortable, he built his tannery about a hundred rods north of his house. He carried it on for several years, but it was not remunerative and he gave it up. Mr. Whittier lived in that house until he died about the year 1812 and was buried in the Wells cemetery, where a broken stone records: "In memory of Richard Whittier," no date, no age.

Several years afterwards it passed into the hands of Lazarus Page, who sold it and moved to Lowell, Mass., in 1827. Since that time it was owned and occupied by a great number of people and not for long by any one. It had a cheery aspect for summer, but it was a dreary place in winter. When it burned, August 24, 1879, it was occupied by H. E. Elliott. It was a sad sight to see; it was like assassinating an old friend. For more than two generations we had looked at that house and barn across the pond. The land upon which it stood is now owned by Mary H. Wendelstadt, who has built a cottage nearer the water. The well on the sight of the old house is one of the deepest, being twenty-eight feet, and its water is of the purest and coldest. So perfectly and symmetrically were its sides stoned that in attempting to place a pipe in it, no hole could be found large enough to insert a half-inch pipe below the surface and a crowbar had to be used to dislodge one of the stones, more than a hundred and fifteen years after it was built.

Theophilus Sanborn of Dorchester married Fanny Cross and built a tannery on the right bank of Cross Brook and carried on the business six or eight years and then abandoned it for lack of stock. This was about 1805.

About the year 1802 Jacob Dow of Concord married Phebe Wells and built a tannery on the Street, where he carried on the business until his death in 1831.

Daniel Porter came from Danvers, Mass., in 1825 and bought Peggy's Tavern, situated on the old Turnpike. He built a tannery in the field opposite his house, but he abandoned the business many years before his death.

Franklin P. Swett of Gilmanton built the last tannery in Canaan at the Corner below the present mill. The business was discontinued in 1861. The buildings fell down and were removed.

Pots and Pearl Ashes.

The manufacture of pots and pearl ashes was once an important business here. It was mostly confined to the vicinity of the Street, where nearly all the business of the town was transacted. The earliest building erected for this purpose was owned by Simeon Arvin, in the southeast corner of the field once owned by Bela B. Whitney and now owned by O. H. Perry at the south end of the Street. Then Joshua Harris put up a factory in the field back of the store of the late Jesse Martin, which stood north of and on land where Charles Seavey now lives, the factory was near the pond.

Nathaniel Currier built a factory in the field back of his store, now occupied by C. P. King, and towards the pond, about 1817. He also carried on the business at the village. Nathaniel Currier came to Canaan in the latter part of 1815, and bought land on the Street January 2, 1816, where he was a successful trader for many years. He was an active Abolitionist during the strenuous years of the town and died in 1863, aged 73 years. His son, Horace S. Currier, father of Hon. Frank D. Currier, was a trader at the village in company with Albert Martin. They sold out to James H. Kelly and William W. George. Martin went to California in 1858. Horace S. Currier was employed in his father's store and afterwards formed a partnership with James B. Wallace, also a clerk in his father's store. They carried on a successful business until the death of Mr. Wallace in 1853. Horace S. Currier died in 1866.

The last factory was erected by James Wallace, in the field opposite the house once owned by Stephen S. Smith, and now by O. H. Perry, about 1822. In 1829 it was pulled down and turned into a cooper's shop, where huge wagonloads of barrels for packing pork were regularly sent to market, by Aaron Quimby's four-horse team. On the death of Mr. Wallace in 1831, the cooperage passed into the hands of Stephen S. Smith. In those days ashes were a commodity, like any other article, and were paid for at the rate of twelve and one-half cents per bushel for hard and ten cents for soft wood ashes. Money was not easy to get and the demand for ashes became greater than the demand for firewood. The ashes were very abundant from the great fireplaces built to receive three and four-foot logs. Stoves had not come into common use and the value of ashes as a manure was unknown. Mr. Wallace was also a trader. His store stood just south of the old house. After his death the old store was sold to Whittier & Balch, traders, at the upper end of the Street, where they moved it and is now the shed of the present Shrigley house. The back store was sold to J. C. Tilton and another man who occupied it as a wheelwright shop.

In 1828 John Fales and Elijah Blaisdell, who owned the mill privilege at the outlet of Hart's Pond, contracted with Moses Richardson to build the frame of the "Tontine" at the Corner. It was to be one hundred feet long, divided into five equal sections, for $100. The timber was of clear pine, sawed at Greeley's mill at Goose Pond and hauled thence and put up according to contract. It was christened the "Tontine." Daniel B. Whittier who lived on the Frank Carter farm called it the "Spontoon." William and Moses Kelley put in a hat factory, Eliphalet Page a harness shop, John Fales a blacksmith shop, a grist mill, and Nathaniel Barber, cabinet-maker, a carpenter shop, filled the remaining space. Horace B. Welch and Lyman S., his brother, in 1851 began to make felloes; the former went to California and for many years, up to 1883, it was used by Lyman S. Welch for the manufacture of felloes. When it burned May 28, 1883, the fire also destroyed the house occupied by Leroy Colby across the road, between the Robert R. Morey place and the brook. Mr. Welch transferred his business to Lebanon. In 1885 Ira Fifield, with capital furnished, built the present building for a shop, where all kinds of jobs could be done, the latter abandoned it and the building and water privilege passed back into the hands of Mr. Welch, who had given up his business in Lebanon. Mr. Welch used the mill for making shingles and plaining boards, and dealt in finished lumber in a small way up to the time of his death. Since that time the business has been owned by R. H. Haffenreffer. The paper mill was first used as a casimere or woolen mill where the people could have their rolls carded and the woven cloth finished. At the time of the moving of Noyes Academy it was owned and operated by Nathaniel Currier. There was a bell in its belfry and it was to be rung when the signal was given that the academy was under way. The signal to be given was the firing of guns. But the one who was to ring the bell did not do so, and Betsey Ham, who in 1842 married Joseph H. Tilton of Meredith, rang the bell. Mrs. Tilton's father was Joseph Ham, who at that time was employed in Nathaniel Currier's potash works at the village. This old building was running as early as 1828, so Mrs. Tilton says, when she went to Factory Village into the family of Jacob Trussell, it was called the "Factory," and from it the village around began to be called Factory Village. Back in the 30's the village was called "Slab City." In June, 1857, it passed into the hands of Capt. William Gordon, whose family came the next August. He got it to running as a paper mill in the summer of 1858, being obliged to install new machinery and remove the old carding and woolen machinery. Captain Gordon ran it until 1862 when he leased it to William W. George and Horace S. Currier, and went to the war. He came back August 13, 1863, and ran the mill until 1870, when he sold it to William W. George. It passed into the hands of Stephen Peaslee, who refitted it with new machinery and enlarged its capacity. It never paid after Mr. Peaslee sold it and several owners subsequently kept up the manufacture of straw board. On December 3, 1890, it was destroyed by fire.

Hammer Shops.

Phineas Eastman, Dan Balch and Jonathan Kittredge started the manufacture of steel hammers on the stream that flows out of Hart's Pond. William Butterfield, who built and lived in the house once owned by Sarah Richardson, succeeded to the business. He was succeeded in 1855 by Nathan Jones, who built the lower shop and sold the upper one to J. S. Lincoln. For twenty-five years, until 1880, Elder Jones made nail, shoe, blacksmith and farrier's hammers by hand with the aid of such simple machinery as he had until more advanced methods of manufacture made it impossible for him to any longer continue the business with a profit, then the shop was closed and now only the ruins of its foundation remain.

Lincoln's Awl Shop.

Josiah S. Lincoln married Hannah Hoit; he came to Canaan and bought the old Jonathan Carlton farm of Elias Wolcott in 1861, he tried to farm for one year, and then turned his brains to making awls. He hired the upper hammer shop of Nathan Jones, who was using the lower hammer shop that was built by William Butterfield. Lincoln fitted up the upper shop and bought small rods of steel, set his forges and went to work. He would hammer the end down, cut them off the length he wanted, grind them on an emery wheel, put them in a small barrel with steel dust, which had a drum and belt to keep it turning, until they were polished and then box them for market. In 1863 he bought the upper shop of Jones. In 1867 he sold his farm to Alden E. Alford and bought the house built by Allen Hayes opposite Sarah Richardson's, which burned when William Kimball lived in it. When Frederick Simonds came back from the war in 1863 or 1864, he went into the shop to help Lincoln. The business was continued a few years and the shop and water privileges were sold to Lyman S. Welch.

CHAPTER XXVII.

INCIDENTS.

On the occasion of the burning of Noyes Academy on March 7, 1835, Doctor Flanders with many others came up very much excited, inquiring here and there, "Who did it?" "Can't some one tell us who was the villain?" "Ho, it must have been the d—d Abolitionists!!!" etc. Jonathan Kittredge came upon the ground while these queries were being put, remarking as he appeared, "Well, that's a better light than I ever expected to see from that institution." The doctor rushed up to him in great rage, and spoke thus, "You are a d—d Abolitionist, Sir!" "It was you who burned that building!" Kittredge was of course not pleased with that charge, and he sued Flanders for defamation and slander, before a justice from Lyme, taking him on behalf of the state, himself appearing as prosecutor. This court held Flanders to answer the charge at Plymouth. Meantime on the 12th at the annual town meeting, a motion was made and carried, as follows, "Voted that we hereby consign Jonathan Kittredge over to the Abolitionists."

This was but one of the long series of provocations that were heaped upon Mr. Kittredge by the *patriots*. He had some peculiarities of manner, in walking, spitting and coughing. In these he was followed, mimiced and mocked by several persons, and particularly by young John B. Dustin, who possessed a peculiar faculty for mimicry. Mr. Kittredge had borne patiently all these insults, hoping they would cease of themselves, but when the charge of arson was laid to him, he thought it time to protect his reputation. Hence, the prosecution of Flanders who, finding himself outside the pale of "public opinion," in a spot where the old cry of "Abolitionist" would not relieve him, one day, in the absence of Mr. Kittredge, summoned thirty or forty witnesses, taking their depositions before Mr. Weeks, in order to prove justification for his slanderous words, but it was of no avail. All this testimony was of a negative character. He thereupon, on the return of Mr. Kittredge, waited upon him and proposed a settlement. Mr. Kittredge consented to stop the suit on one condition, that if Flanders would sign such a retraction of his slanders as Kittredge might dictate. Flanders had no choice but to submit to any terms that Kittredge might impose. Mr. Kittredge drew up the paper in which, commencing with a "Whereas," he recited the defamatory and slanderous words that had been leveled at him, and closed it somewhat as follows: "In uttering these slanders, for the purpose of injuring the good name and fame of Mr. Kittredge, I have lied like a dog, I confess it with humility and shame, and I sign this confession and publish it to the world, in order that the suit now pending against me may be settled and discontinued. THOMAS FLANDERS."

This document Mr. Kittredge published in the Concord papers. It was indeed a source of humiliation to the "patriots." On the 27th of May Mr. Kittredge surprised his enemies by summoning young John B. Dustin to answer the charge of libel before Justices Turner and Flint of Lyme. John was sixteen years old, tall and reckless, and had made himself very offensive by his abuse of Mr. Kittredge. The trial caused great excitement.

Weeks was counsel for respondent. Kittredge for himself and the state. The trial commenced at ten in the morning and continued through the night until four o'clock in the morning, when the testimony being all in the court adjourned till one p. m. for deliberation. At one the decision was announced, that John B. Dustin recognize in the sum of $600 for his appearance at the November court to be holden at Plymouth. His father and Weeks came forward and bailed him.

The trial was held in Willis' Hall, which was crowded until the close. Kittredge had received several anonymous letters, containing threats against his person and property, accompanied with oaths most horrid. The last one was received after he had issued the warrant. The evidence tended to fix the authorship on John. But the case never went any farther. It was shown that the young man was acting by advice of older villains, who were jealous of Kittredge's success, and for a consideration the case was compromised and dropped. After this Kittredge and young Dustin became fast friends. John had ability beyond his years, and quickly learned the ways of the world. Kittredge often employed him to serve his writs, which service he performed in a satisfactory manner.

Our laws in regard to debt were at one time very severe. The poor man had no rights which a grasping creditor could not reach, when execution for a debt was to be imprisonment if not paid. There was a young tanner named David March. Just about that time he married Phebe Dow; he was industrious and steady but he owed a sum of money in Croydon. His creditor sent the sheriff here, who took March away from his young wife and from his labor and carried him to jail at Haverhill. The day he started I was the small boy looking on, and just beginning to think. Someone expressed sympathy, hoping he might soon return. March replied, "If I were dishonest I should feel disgraced to be in the hands of the sheriff, going to jail, but the laws are not friendly to the poor man." No, indeed, they were not; and it was not until years afterwards that an enlightened public sentiment demanded the abolition of that wolfish law that put poor debtors in jail. I remember another case that occurred about 1831, and which to me seemed to be a very hard one. Old Doctor Tilton, who used to ride a black pacing horse, and was welcomed into every house in town, was in debt. In fact, he never was out of debt. He was a learned man, a good lawyer as well as physician; but all his learning could not save him from the sheriff's hands, and he was sent to Haverhill. His indebtedness was an endorsement for a friend. He used to say he hoped "the time for sending men to jail for debt would soon come to an end. It was no benefit to the creditor nor to the community to take an able-bodied man from his business and shut him up because he was unable to pay his debts." The doctor remained in Haverhill several months.

David Greeley, son of Matthew, was the clothier, at the village. Col. Daniel Pattee, Maj. Levi George, Jo Morrell whose occupation was laying up stone wall, drinking rum and bragging about his accomplishments, and Bill Wood, would go down to David's shop, make a night of it, and go home sober in the morning. One night when the colonel was bragging heavily of his capacity, they made a paste of flour and rum and rubbed it into his hair, and each one struck him with a codfish and christened him "Grand Bashaw," which he afterwards retained. Next morning one of the neighbors called in and found his wife cleaning the paste from his head.

Nat C. Pierce in 1818 built the pound on the Pinnacle for $30, giving the land therefor. In placing the capstone over the gate it slipped and crushed his hand badly. A few months before the pound was built Nat had been raised in Mt. Moriah Lodge, No. 22. He swore very profanely at the stone, and so loudly that some of his Masonic brethren had him cited before the lodge, to declare why he should not be expelled for useless profanity, the stone was deaf, dumb, lifeless and senseless, therefore his swearing was wanton and unnecessary, and they expelled him, but afterwards restored him on his pledge to refrain from drinking rum and thus mistaking a stone for the heels of a colt.

He was a great beau among the girls, and he would drink rum and boast of his success among them. "He'd stayed with the Pattee girls, the Harris's, the George's, the Wells', and meant to stay with every decent girl in town, before he got married and then take his choice." He finally chose Dolly Pattee, and David Greeley married her sister. They emigrated to Princeton, Bernard County, Ill., where they took up lands, lived, labored, prospered and died. Old Squire Arvin used to furnish the rum.

There was one office in the early days, the duties of which could hardly have been agreeable. But then, as now, there were men whose capacities and temperaments adapted them to all the legal offices. The tithing-man was the terror of all the little boys and the Sabbath breakers. It was their special duty to see that all the members of each family attended public worship and to mark all violations of the Sunday laws. Some of these officers delighted in the legal espionage with which their appointment clothed them and never lost an opportunity to use their power to annoy their fellow-citizens. The office and the officer at length became so obnoxious that the duties were narrowed down to simply keeping order among the boys and girls during divine worship; and at length the office was abolished, and the vexatious annoyances of the man with the long white wand, with a ball at one end and a fox-tail at the other, have passed away forever. When the sermon became tiresome and men nodded in unconsciousness, they would find themselves rudely awakened by a rap from the ball in the hands of the soft-footed man, whose feet were muffled that his aproach might be like that of the thief in the night. To the ladies he was a little more considerate. Their awakening was secured by the brush of the fox-tail drawn gently under their noses. Many relics of tyranny and paganism were reproduced in our New England habits and customs by the men who had scorned to submit to them in another land. Several generations passed away before all these offensive offices and rules were abolished and the pure freedom of thought and action which we enjoy today was established.

But there was a humorous side to this annoyance which would sometimes crop out in the characteristics of the man who filled the office. Capt. Joseph Wheat was tithing-man during the earlier portion of his father's ministry. The old elder, when once he settled into his two hours' labor, was oblivious to all outside occurrences. On one occasion Captain Jo., seizing his wand, started out to quell a riotous disposition among several children, whose guardians had ceased from their labors and gone to sleep. As he cast his eyes about the house, he was astonished to perceive the whole congregation nodding, wholly unconscious and careless of the thunders that resounded from the pulpit. He was quick-witted and eccentric, particularly when seized with a profane sentiment. On this occasion he never said a word, but jumped up and jerked both his solid feet down square upon the floor. The concussion brought the whole astonished congregation to their feet. The old man stopped preaching, also, — lost his balance, in fact — but rallied in a moment and sternly demanded, "Jo, why do you disturb this meeting? Is that the way you keep order?" "Sir," says Captain Jo., "it lies between you and me to entertain and instruct this congregation. You've been telling them awful truths for more than an hour and they all went to sleep. I gave one solid jump, and they roused up as if Satan were already shaking his spread wings to carry them off. Your arguments are very persuasive, but you see mine are powerful."

John Sullivan got mad at one of his neighbors, mad enough to go to a lawyer and swear that he must have some law. He didn't care what it cost. The other fellow would have the bills to pay and the more there was, the better he would be satisfied. "But, you have no case," said the lawyer, "and you'll get beat if you begin on him." "Don't care a fig for that, — its law I want on the feller; give him as much as you can, blast him." A summons was served upon the "feller" to appear and answer. He did answer satisfactorily, and John was adjudged to pay the several items of costs; "How much is it?" he asked and laying down a V, told his legal friend to take it out of that. "The costs amount to $19.20," said his exact and muletive friend. "Howly Moses!" exclaimed John, "There's two dollars more, that's seven dollars, call it square and let me go." "Nineteen dollars and twenty cents, and not a cent of discount," was the slow response. John reluctantly drew his wallet, took out several bills, pinching them as he laid them down. "There's the money; now I'm done wid ye, and if all the dirty haythen in this wicked world insult me, I'll never go to law any more; I've got enough of it."

There was years ago a bank started in this town. It was called the Goose Pond Bank and its place of business was not far from the Rainey house. Jacob Trussell was the president. They proceeded to issue money, but the government got after them. Joseph Smith, Simon Blanchard and John Pearley were caught stamping money in Blanchard's barn. Selden Pattee, a brother of Robert Wilson's wife, and Rice Howard fled. Jacob Drew, who was a good deal at Trussell's courting one of the girls, disappeared when the arrests were made. Daniel Follensbee of Grafton was also under suspicion of being one of the gang. John Pearley served eight years in state prison for passing counterfeit money.

Some years ago Mr. and Mrs. Dimond of Orange sued the town for damages upon the highway, between the houses of Richard Hutchinson and George Hinkson. The town pleaded in defense that they were wrongfully parties to the suit, inasmuch as the Northern Railroad had graded the highway over the track, and had not properly finished their work. Having been repeatedly warned they had always neglected to comply with the law. The suit was continued in court for several terms, the railroad promising all the time to settle with the parties and make the highway safe for travel. It remained unchanged until Onslow Stearns desired the nomination for governor. He was naturally anxious to be elected, and he started out upon a tour of inquiry as to the friendly views of the voters. When he reached Canaan he met William W. George and asked him what his chances were. The reply was: "Very small! Very small indeed!" "That's not very encouraging!" "No," continued Mr. George, "not for you. The fact is we have no confidence in you. For years you have promised to repair that road and relieve us from the burden of these suits and we don't believe you mean to do either. The people of Canaan have very foolish notions about truthful men. They've tried you and don't believe in you." "Is that all there is against me?" "Well, ain't that enough?" "Well, suppose I go and settle those suits and fix the road, will you forget all about it and be kind to me?" "Well, we will see the road fixed first, then perhaps there won't be anything to remember." That same season the road was repaired and the costs of the suits were assumed by the railroad, and Mr. Stearns was elected governor.

Benjamin Spencer came with a small family from Colebrook, in search of employment to Canaan in 1825. He was a blacksmith by trade. He explained his wishes and his skill as a worker in iron to several persons, hoping to win their attention. James Wallace thought favorably of his capacity and built a shop for him on the north side of the road between Arvin's corner and the Pinnacle House, then the residence of Dr. Thomas Flanders. He worked faithfully at his trade for months and then suddenly disappeared without leaving his address. It was not long after this that an officer appeared with an order of arrest, charging Spencer with uttering a note for a considerable sum, and presenting the same to the Grafton Bank of Haverhill and receiving the money thereon; but he disappeared before it was discovered that the name of Ephraim H. Mahurin, a well-known citizen, the high sheriff of Coös County, attached to the note as endorser, was a forgery. Spencer received the money and left, but it was believed that he must have had an accomplice, because he was illiterate, with no skill in the use of the pen. It was believed impossible for him to have written Mr. Mahurin's name so as to deceive the cashier of the bank. Suspicions attached to Doctor Flanders, from some remarks made by his enemies, and dwelt upon until they ripened into a belief that the doctor was really the guilty person. There was a comparison of his handwriting by experts — they were not called by that name then — some of them even swore to their belief in the doctor's guilt. Doctor Flanders, like many others, felt a strong interest in securing the arrest of Spencer, who had fled so rapidly, but not in a manner to cover up his tracks. Joshua Wells was deputized to follow him and bring him back.

Mr. Wells started in pursuit in his high-backed sleigh, driving a nice, well-kept roan horse — roan horses were always his weakness — tracking and following his victim like one of his own hounds, all the way into western Pennsylvania, where he came up with Spencer, resting unsuspicious of danger, arrested him and started on his long return journey, delivering his prisoner safely into the custody of the jailor at Haverhill. Spencer was tried for the crime of forgery and convicted, but utterly refused to name any person as his accomplice. He owned that he lacked skill as a penman and that was all. He was sentenced to state prison for two years. He entered that prison and after his two years' service, came out and said nothing. He came back to Canaan, spent a few days in the family of Mr. Wallace and then disappeared. He acknowledged his action in the crime — that he got some money by it, but lost everything else, honor, character, business and all hopes of ever being able to hold up his head. He had been duped — had yielded to temptation, but he was not vindictive, and the law must be satisfied with one victim. Mr. Wallace and Mr. Wells, both very friendly to him, urged him to speak, but it was of no avail — he never named the man who instigated him. He did write a statement, however, vindicating Doctor Flanders, declaring his innocence of any knowledge of the forgery. This statement was left in the hands of Mr. Wells, to be used at his discretion. He laid it away and forgot it, and its existence was for a long time unknown. It was found by his son, Charles H. Wells, among some old notes, receipts and other papers. It is in Spencer's own handwriting, and is printed to relieve the memory of Doctor Flanders of the odium which unjustly attached to him during all his after life. The doctor was not popular. His impulsive temper often broke out without reference to propriety, and often gave offence. But he was regarded as a man of integrity, and incapable of committing an act of dishonor. These suspicions greatly annoyed him. To get away from them, some years afterwards he left town and died an old man in the town of New Durham. This is the statement:

Town Plot, Oct. 3d, 1827.

To the President, Directors, and Company of the Grafton Bank:

No doubt you feel yourselfs injured by me and want to seek all the recompense you can. Very good; that is your privilege. But let me tell you not to seek of an innocent man. Because I have done wrong I will assure you my feelings have been wounded as bad as my character, and was it in my power to make all restitution for all the injury done anybody by me I should be willing. Let me be called what I will yet I am not voyd of the natural feelings of mankind, and when I heard of Dr. Flanders being stripped of his property and his character my heart almost bleeds within me. My bosom is moved with pity and compassion, and can I pity, and not relieve I must try. I will tell you the truth as it is in Christ and lie not. Dr. Thomas Flanders is as innocent from signing Ephraim H. Mahurin's name to that note you allege against him or even seeing or knowing anything about it as the angels in heaven. I know it and God knows it; and I fear his enemies are intriving wrong evidences against him, and that is as bad as I have done. Mr. James Williams, if I am informed right has sworn to an absolute falsehood, and others have done no better. I am your well-wisher and never meant you no harm.

BENJ. SPENCER.

(The "Town Plot" referred to is Canaan Street.)

ELDER WHEAT'S REBUKE OF INFIDELITY AT THE FUNERAL OF MRS. STEPHEN WORTH.

The following was an incident in the history of the old meeting house, related by a person who was an eye witness of the scene. Stephen Worth, about the year 1797, married Molly, the widow of his brother, and settled down upon the farm where Watts Davis worked out his hard and disagreeable life, in what is known as Jerusalem. Stephen loved and cherished his wife all her days, and was a sincere mourner when she died in 1816. The funeral was held in the meeting house one Sunday, which was thronged with sympathizing friends. Elder Wheat preached a long sermon on death and the darkness of the grave, taking for his text a whole chapter, and placing special emphasis upon the phrase, "Where the worm dieth not and the fire is not quenched."

For the first hymn the elder requested the choir to sing that screed by Doctor Watts, which is supposed to have been written when the doctor was oppressed by nightmare or indigestion. The verse reads:

> "My thoughts on awful subjects roll,
> Damnation and the dead!
> What horrors seize the guilty soul
> Upon a dying bed."

Abraham Pushee was a young saddler here, a good singer and very skilful upon the violin, which instrument, greatly to the chagrin of Deacon Worth and Richard Clark, he had insisted upon bringing into the choir. When the elder read the hymn, Pushee refused to sing it. The sentiment it expressed was too horrid to be adapted to any music in his books. Turning to the singers, he requested them to sing the next hymn, commencing: "Why do we mourn departing friends," to the grand old tune of "China." When the choir struck at the first line of the hymn, the elder jumped to his feet and exclaimed: "That is not the hymn I wish you to sing!" but the choir kept on singing, paying no attention to the elder's exclamation.

After his sermon he made a general address to the mourners. Then he became personal, and the ludicrous incidents which followed are related by an eye-witness.

He said he "had always been told that Brother Worth was a courteous man, kind and considerate to everybody, lovin' and honorin' his wife as a true husband; but I learn with sorrow," he continued, raising his voice, "that he is a convert to the hell-damnin', heaven-darin', God-provokin' doctrines of Tom Paine, the infidel author of the 'Age of Reason' Now, my duty to my God and my people, required me, even here in the presence of the remains of his lamented partner, who this day is restin' peacefully in the arms of Jesus, to rebuke the devil and all." And there is no telling what the good elder might not have said, had he been permitted to finish his rebuke, but at this point an interruption occurred. Hon. Daniel Blaisdell rose in his pew with great energy and stood leaning forward with one hand extended, and mouth open to speak, with his wife, hanging to his coat tails. But Stephen Worth, the chief mourner, got the start of him, exclaiming, as he rose up that, "the time and place for such unfeeling remarks, even if they were well deserved, were ill chosen." He had never before heard of that awful book; both the "Age of Reason," and Tom Paine were strangers to him. He hoped they were good men and more considerate and charitable to others than the elder was towards him. He had done his duty as a husband and Christian in the fear of the Lord; and this attack upon him looked as if the evil one had entered into the ———."

Another interruption occurred right here. His brother John was so overcome that he was seized with a sudden illness and had to be taken out in a dead faint. Confusion was very great all over the house. Everybody was standing up in astonishment, and talking indignant nonsense. When quiet was restored, Mr. Worth concluded his remarks by saying he would "get those books and read them; for it couldn't be any worse for him to read them than for the elder, and then he could judge for himself if they were bad books."

Captain Wells and John M. Barber were greatly offended at the elder's remarks, and refused ever after to hear him preach. Many others were also very angry, but expended their ill-feeling in talk. The elder, like the rest of them, was in confusion and when the uproar subsided a little, he quite grimly declared that he had spoken from report. He was glad to learn that Brother Worth was not an infidel, and even if he were, perhaps it would not become him to judge him. Then the long services which had occupied nearly all day, were brought to a conclusion and the body laid away in the ground.

Afterwards, when Judge Blaisdell met the elder, he asked him "what evil spirit beset him to attack Stephen Worth at that funeral. It was an unheard of outrage, such as only a crazy or drunken man would commit. Had he — ?" "Well, he had — for his stomach's sake. It was good for him, and gave him courage and confidence." "Yes," retorted the judge, "and your courage, as you call it, caused you grievously to afflict a good man, whose heart is heavy with grief at the loss of a wife he loved. You, old man of God! to make a public scandal on such an occasion! Go, now; commit no more such folly!"

Elder Wheat preached in Canaan for seventeen years after that event, but never made a similar speech at a funeral. He was a good man, faithful to all the light that shone for him. The good he did will send its influence away down through the ages, and his memory will be green when others are forgotten. To show how important a character he was, the young men and maidens sought his counsel and assistance. The record of the marriages performed during his ministry was 308 in number.

Suit for Slander.

In this suit for slander, it will be noticed that the plaintiff received more abuse than cash from the defendant's lawyer. Benjamin and Keziah were married in 1820 and toiled happily on life's journey for several years. Then getting a little unsettled, they moved over to South Road, and lived in the same house with James, whose wife was named Rhoda. This was eighty years ago or more. It was pleasant and neighborly between the families for a season, but for all that, the house was never large enough for them. One day a neighbor came in and asked Mrs. Keziah if she had heard of the stories her friend in the other part of the house had been circulating? To be sure, it was none of her business, but it would trouble her to keep it, so she "out with it." It was how Mrs. Keziah had been to Mrs. Rhoda's cream pot, to her soap barrel, to her meal chest, and to her hen's nests and had declared that "she was no better than any other thief."

There were very grievous times under that roof after that neighbor's visit, and then Benjamin, to vindicate the good name of his wife, was persuaded to cite Mrs. Rhoda before a justice, either to prove her stories or acknowledge herself a slanderer. This she persistently declined to do; but in due time obeyed a summons and appeared before Hon. Daniel Blaisdell, who held his court in the hall of Cobb's Tavern. Mrs. Rhoda was there represented by Elijah Blaisdell, Esq., who, from a shoemaker, had by hard study and labor, risen to be a lawyer in the village. Mrs. Keziah was represented by C. B. Haydock of Hanover. Mrs. Rhoda had no witnesses to prove her assertions, but she testified very positively as to her losses; and "I know that I have told the truth, for nobody else has had a chance to steal my soap and eggs and things; and if Mrs. Keziah ain't guilty, she wouldn't be so awful touchy about it, there now!"

Mrs. Keziah just as positively denied all the allegations, and declared Rhoda to be a common gossip and slanderer, who wouldn't tell the truth even to keep friendly with the neighbors; and to prove these charges, she introduced several of the neighbors, who swore that Mrs. Rhoda was a common gossip, tattler and liar, and had always made mischief among her acquaintances, and this was no worse than some of her other stories, only she hadn't been brought into court before.

Blaisdell's defence of his client was not an argument, but simply a torrent of abuse and vituperation poured upon Keziah; and he claimed judgment for his client because she had only spoken the truth. Mrs. Keziah said afterwards she always hated the sight of Blaisdell after that speech. Up to that time she had never believed that for five dollars a man, who pretended to be decent, could be so mean a liar. The hall was crowded with men and women, all anxious to hear the outcome of this famous dispute. I was there also, a little boy, standing upon one of the side benches. Suddenly there was a crash, loud shrieks and a rush for the doors and windows. Everybody wanted to get out at once — not everybody either, only the timid and scary ones. The timbers of the flooring had given way, and the middle of the floor had sunk down about two feet, and was only held together by a few nails.

There sat Judge Blaisdell, cool as the north wind, and deliberate as Stephen Smith, when he begun to tell a story. His legs were crossed and he had slipped down so that his big belly rested against the table. "Men," he said, "don't crowd the door. There is no danger; follow each other out carefully and quickly and in five minutes you will feel better than you do now. And you women, struggling together there — just step back upon the bench near that boy, and then watch me! You'll be all right in a minute."

The hall was soon cleared of the excited crowd and then the judge very deliberately climbed up out of the wreck; and with no unnecessary delay, reorganized his court in another room, where, after the lawyers had each claimed the innocence and virtues of their clients, he proceeded to give judgment, which was that this matter, little in itself, had grown big by being talked about, and it had made several persons unhappy. It was not right for Mrs. Rhoda to charge her neighbor with stealing unless she had proof of it, because by so doing, she had placed herself in jeopardy. "She is brought before this court on a charge of wilful and malicious slander. Her answer is, that she stated the truth, — it is not slander, — but she offers no proof in support of this charge; while her neighbors come in here and swear her to a common gossip, liar, and slanderer. Mrs. Rhoda, your case is a bad one. There is a slow-moving finger pointing at you from all around and behind each finger is hissed one poisonous word — 'Slander!' It grieves me to announce my judgment in this case, as between two women who ought to live together in unity; but the evidence of your neighbors is conclusive that you are a slanderer, that you carry a viperous tongue, which you do not try to rule. You are fined ten dollars and the costs of this court; and when you go home, take this advice along with you, and act upon it: When you find your tongue inclined to utter another slander, sieze upon it and bite it before another word is spoken. And so may you continue to live in peace and in the love and respect of your household. This court is adjourned without date."

THE CRIME OF ISAAC DOLE.

In 1831 Mrs. Mary Wallace was left a widow with seven children. Her life had been all devoted to her family, and she was unpracticed in the ways of business. James Wallace, her husband, had died suddenly, without advising her of the condition of his affairs. She was named executrix of the estate, which she was desirous of settling by paying all demands as soon as possible. Isaac Dole, the chief character in this story, had been for several years a deputy sheriff. He lived on the mountain in Lebanon, and was in the practice of loaning money to needy persons. He had accumulated a fortune, all of which, except the farm he occupied, was in cash, which he loaned like a banker. This incident occurred soon after the death of Mr. Wallace, and related to the payment of a note which proved to have been forged, with a long story of the frauds practiced upon lone women by bad men. James Wallace had on more than one occasion borrowed money of Dole. These loans, the executrix had reason to believe, were all paid and the notes cancelled. The last one for $200 had been paid a short time before Mr. Wallace's last illness, which was sudden and fatal, and the cancelled note was filed among his papers. The spring following his death she received notice from Dole, that he held a note against the estate for $200, and desired to know when it would suit her convenience to pay it. She was a good deal surprised and annoyed, but having no suspicion of the dishonesty on the part of Dole, she invited Mrs. Martha Harris to ride to Lebanon with her in order to pay the note. They started out and had ridden as far as William Campbell's on Town Hill, when they met Dole on his way to visit her. They all stopped at Mr. Campbell's; the note was produced, the money paid, and they returned home. No suspicion of forgery was aroused that day, and had Mr. Dole on receiving the money, asked that he might retain the cancelled paper, she would have given it to him, and this story would never have been written.

After the return of the ladies, the peculiarity of the shape of the paper upon which the note was written was a subject of conversation. The signature, "James Wallace," was genuine. The body of the note was in the handwriting of Dole. But the writing was crowded into a space much too small to correspond with the boldness of the signature, below which there were two inches of blank paper. While talking upon the subject next day, the Rev. Mr. Foster came in and asked that he might examine the note. It was handed to him, and almost immediately he looked up and exclaimed, "Mrs. Wallace, this paper is a forgery!" and he tapped the paper with considerable energy with his forefinger. "It was cut off from the bottom of a bill of goods which your husband had receipted and here," continued he, "are the lower parts of the long letters in the words, 'received payment,' which could not be cut off without leaving the paper too small to write the note upon." Upon close examination, they were all satisfied that Mr. Foster was correct; and George Kimball, lawyer, was called in to advise upon the case. The result was, that that same day Jonas Smith of Canaan arrested Dole in his own house upon the charge of forgery, and at the same time attached the real estate of Dole, upon a civil suit for the recovery of the money paid.

There was a young lawyer in Canaan, who never refused a fee and who made a rule of his practice to look well after the interest of his clients — a man who, through long years of successful practice, was always true to his clients. Dole came to him and stated the trouble that had come upon him, and that if he could not make some arrangement with the widow he would be ruined. "Now," said he, "put your wits to work and the fee shall be ample." The lawyer listened patiently to the story and then waited a moment before speaking. "Mr. Dole, as your counsel, I must ask you to be very candid with me, and tell me in one word, if the charge of forgery be true? If I know the exact truth, it will enable me to change the ground of defence with more confidence." Dole told him to go to work as if the charge was true. "Indeed," said the lawyer, "I suspected as much! and you have got the widow's money in your pocket now! and the question is," continued the lawyer, "how to keep it there!" "Exactly," said Dole, "I see you are good on a trail." "Now," continued the lawyer, "Mrs. Wallace has got that fatal paper. If we could get it into our possession, we would doubtless make terms with her; suppose we go down and call upon her, perhaps we can persuade her to let us examine it."

They started out down the street, and called upon the widow, whom they found alone. Meantime she had seen them approaching, and had sent her little boy, anticipating a visit, to invite Lawyer Kimball to the interview. She greeted her visitors politely, but with a strong feeling of antagonism. The lawyer stated the object of their call, and with great suavity, asked her to allow him to look at the paper which she alleged to be a forgery. She replied to him very quickly: "Do you think, sir, that it would be safe or prudent for me to place that paper in the hands of two such disinterested and honorable men as you and Mr. Dole? Even if I were disposed to gratify you, which I am not, you ought to know that when the complaint was made on that piece of paper, it passed out of my possession." They then changed their plans. Mr. Dole suggested he could make it an object for her to stop the suit, as there was some uncertainty in the result of it. He would refund the money with interest and give her a hundred dollars as a bonus. She still declined their offers with some asperity of tone. Then Mr. Dole seeing that smiles and offers of bonus had failed, changed his batteries and made a demand for her dead husband's books and papers, intimating if she did not give them up some unpleasant things might happen. She was a resolute, brave woman, and she was alone, but she began to feel apprehension lest these two strong men, the fate of one of whom lay in her hands, might not possess themselves of those papers, which were in the desk in that same room, and among them the original note, cancelled, which was to be put in evidence whenever the case came to trial.

She had been looking very anxiously up the street for the appearance of her counsel, and was greatly relieved when Mr. Kimball at last appeared, accompanied by Mr. Foster, and both swinging hastily down the street. Then, turning to the two men, who stood waiting and hoping their threat might produce a favorable effect, she said, almost trembling with anxiety: "Gentlemen, as this is a matter of great importance, I do not feel brave enough to decide it alone, but as I see some of my friends approaching, I'll consult them, and with their approbation, will comply with your manly request." They had not noticed the disappearance of the boy and they supposed they had that lone widow entirely in their power, and were only waiting for her to yield quietly to their threats. The possession of those papers was of the utmost importance to Mr. Dole. His future life hung upon them, and he came prepared to use all means, even force, if necessary, to get them into his hands. They supposed Mrs. Wallace was upon the point of yielding; and when she called their attention to the approach of her two friends, they were struck into dismay and astonishment. The lawyer glanced out of the window, and turning to his client, said earnestly: "True enough, Dole! it's Kimball and Foster! They'll be here in five minutes! Whatever we do must be done quickly." But there remained nothing for them to do but retreat; their opportunity had passed and did not return. They both turned towards the door, but before they disappeared, stopped, with a sudden courtesy, that contrasted sharply with their previous threat, said: "Mrs. Wallace, the urgency of our case has compelled us to be ungentlemanly. You will excuse us, for life and reputation seems at stake; but if you can decide to accept of our proposal, we shall be glad to hear from you at your earliest convenience." They then left the house, taking a course that did not bring them into contact with the approaching party.

Mr. Foster and Mr. Kimball did not arrive any too soon, the strain upon the mental faculties of Mrs. Wallace had been so severe that a reaction had begun. They found her suffering from nervous prostration, and it was some minutes before she could describe to them her interview with Mr. Dole and his lawyer. They complimented her upon her prudence and bravery, and were duly grateful to the gentlemen for delaying the use of force until it was too late. After a full consultation, the gentlemen decided that it was not safe to leave those books and papers, upon which so much depended, in a house only guarded by a woman and young children, so they conveyed them to a place of safety and all the plans of the criminal who had come to Canaan, very hopeful of compelling or buying immunity for his bad acts, were frustrated.

Nothing now remained to him but to take his chances of escaping conviction in the courts by due course of law. Mr. Dole was advised to make an aggressive defence in the preliminary examination, which must now inevitably take place, and with that idea to retain several eminent lawyers, whose high standing might serve to overawe the justice. A swift messenger was sent to Haverhill to secure the services of Joseph Bell, who was eminent both as a lawyer and for his large presence. William T. Heydock, Esq., brother-in-law of Mr. Bell, and a lawyer, was also retained. Indeed, he had secured a very imposing array of counsel, and his last hope was by the mere weight of numbers, with their well-known intelligence and matchless impudence, to crush the prosecution, which was supported by George Kimball, assisted by N. P. Rogers of Plymouth, both of whom entered into the case as if success was vital to their reputations.

The examination took place at Lebanon, before Justice J. Hinds of Hanover. It drew together a large audience, many of whom were friends of Sheriff Dole, and were very demonstrative in the arraignment of a man like Dole, who had long been an active citizen in the community.

Mr. Dole was arraigned before the justice for the crime of forgery; and Mr. Kimball moved that, upon the allegations and proofs offered, the prisoner be held to await the action of the grand jury. This motion was vehemently opposed by Mr. Bell, who at the start assumed that no forgery had been committed, for even the prosecution admitted the signature to be genuine, and called the attention of the court especially to the improbability of a man with wealth, respected and honored like the respondent, committing such a crime. Two hundred dollars was a paltry sum for such a man to risk his reputation and life upon! Then he went into a bitter invective against the plaintiff. Among others, he said this was a scheme of hers to extort money; that she had offered to compromise the suit on refunding the face of the note and one hundred dollars, and that upon the refusal of his client to comply with her demands, she had threatened him with the vengeance of the law. This prosecution was the result of that threat. It was a great outrage upon the rights and liberty of a worthy citizen, and he closed a long speech with the very confident expectation of the discharge of the prisoner. The impudence of that speech, uttered in Mr. Bell's most sonorous tones and crushing style, gave the prosecution some anxiety, and they carefully watched its effect upon the justice; but they were greatly reassured when, after a moment's pause, he very quietly asked Mr. Bell if he desired to put in testimony in proof of his assertions. Of course he expected to be called upon to prove something; else, why did he so bravely enter court. But he pretended to be astonished and annoyed at the quiet remark of the judge, as if his word were not of sufficient weight to control the action of the court! But over-bearing impudence was the ground of his defence, and when this system of defence failed to influence the court, he knew that his case was hopeless. Mr. Bell did not attempt to prove by the lawyer that the plaintiff proposed a compromise for money, but he induced two of Dole's children, a son and daughter, to appear and swear that they were witnesses of the transaction between James Wallace and Isaac Dole, their father; that the note was genuine, and the money paid upon it was honestly due their father.

They were sharply cross-examined by Mr. Rogers, who at the moment held in his hands the genuine and the forged notes, cancelled, both of even dates and amounts. His skilful queries produced confusion in their minds, so that they were uncertain whether the money was paid or borrowed by Dole, or received or paid by the executrix. Then followed two speeches by the lawyers, which were variously opposed by the audience, but which produced no visible effect upon the court. Mr. Bell's speech exhibited a slight modification in tone, and was devoted chiefly to shameless slander of the widow, whose money had been stolen, and to panegyrics upon the character of Dole as a citizen and officer, and upon these grounds urged that he be discharged from arrest.

Mr. Kimball spoke last. He reviewed the character of Dole, and noted the hesitation of his witnesses, and closed his argument by eloquently urging upon the court to make an example of a bad man, and save the community from his further depredations by holding him to await the action of the grand jury. The trial occupied all day and was for a long time a theme for discussion in the community. Dole was ordered to recognize in $1,000 for his appearance in Haverhill. He gave the required bond upon the spot and then set himself to work to extricate himself from the certain fate that seemed to await him.

I insert the following letter, written the day after the trial. It is dated from Plymouth:

Dear Kimball: We got safely home at 11 o'clock. More I think of our trial at Lebanon, the mightier the concern seems to me to be, and your part in it seems a higher and more striking character. The whole seems a magnificent dream. But it is a terrible reality, and poor Dole stands convicted of forgery and subornation of perjury committed on the offspring of his own body. He has sacrificed his children to save himself from the consequences of his own crime. We ought to have said something more on the enormity of this crime. We ought to have warned all around us of the frightful consequences of imbibing the horrid principles of poor Dole. But we had much to do, and could not but omit many things.

Make out the costs of prosecution and send on to Justice Hinds, and direct him to make his record and how to make it, and to copy the whole and send it to you recognizances and all. Then you will have the record safe and I will have the proof safe and the county will have the $1,000 safe, and the community be safe and secure of being relieved of Dole by his absconding. You must have copies as soon as you can, or the complaint, record, etc., will be plundered.

Among Dole's subaltern counsel — some one among that throng, unknown to fame, who surrounded him and expected to swell the train of his triumphant discharge, but who in fact were only of his crew when he went down — some one of them will be shrewd enough to conjecture that if the record of the recognizance were stolen, Mr. Dole might retire (having paid his counsel) without forfeiture. You will see to this.

The more I think of your speech the grander it seems to me; which I mention merely to remind you that you have to answer for rejecting offers of mercy, made under great lights, and with extraordinary means of knowing duty.

Sat verbum sapienti.

N. P. ROGERS.

During the interval until the sitting of the court, Dole expressed great confidence in a favorable result in his case. He sold his real estate and got his resources well in hand. An incident showing his state of mind was related to me at the time. A man in Dorchester owed him money on a note. Dole notified him to pay it, saying he would call upon him. The debtor and creditor started from home the same day, and met on the road not far from Mr. Ben Choate's in Enfield. They went into Mr. Choate's house where the money was paid and the note cancelled; but as they were about to separate, Dole turned to the Dorchester man and asked that he might be allowed to retain the cancelled note. He said in explaining: "Since I was arrested for forgery, everybody who owes me, expresses the suspicion that I am practicing the crime again. It annoys me, and I want to retain this paper which is of no value to you as an evidence of your trust in me with Mr. Choate as a witness." He told the truth and he felt it too. More than one person, upon being called upon to pay, expressed suspicion that he was paying his note a second time, but could not prove it because he did not have his cancelled papers.

At the appointed time Mr. Dole rode to Haverhill, and put up his horse at Towle's Hotel. The same day he was seen in earnest consultation with some friends from Lebanon, and he had a long interview with his counsel in Mr. Bell's office. The grand jury met in the upper room in the old court house. On the afternoon that Dole's case was considered he ordered his horse harnessed, saying he would take a turn about town. He drove about the village common several times, each time riding slowly past the court house, watching it with apparent carelessness. The last time he approached the house, about four o'clock in the afternoon, he paused a moment and looked up at a south window. There was a movement in the jury room. A window was raised, and a red handkerchief waved for a moment outside and then disappeared. Dole carelessly turned his horse's head, and rode slowly through the street until he reached the bank building, where he received a nod of recognition from his council, Mr. Bell. Then urging his horse, he drove rapidly down the road that led across the river at Bradford, and beyond the jurisdiction of the court at Haverhill. He was never seen again in public in New Hampshire. He fled westwardly and his family followed him. It was afterwards known that he kept a hotel in Lockport, N. Y., under another name. His wife died soon after; his daughter became insane; and his son, after a time, studied and practiced as a lawyer.

When the case was called in court and no answer returned, his recognizance was forfeited. His bondsmen came promptly forward, and were discharged on payment of the $1,000. Judgment was also rendered in the civil suit for the recovery of the $200, which had been secured by attachment of real estate, and thenceforth the name of Isaac Dole became linked with the crimes of forgery and perjury, the memory of which not even Lethe's waters can wash out.

And now in regard to the waving of the red handkerchief: I give the story as I saw and heard it at the time, for I, a boy, saw Dole as he rode about the common at Haverhill, and disappeared on the road towards Bradford. Dole was a Mason. One of the grand jurors from Lebanon was also a Mason and a friend of Dole, and was the person with whom he had had a long consultation on his arrival at Haverhill. While his case was under consultation, he was to be prepared for the worst. He was to ride about in the neighborhood of the court house and watch for a signal, which was to be a red flag if the jury found a true bill against him. He watched, took due notice, and governed himself accordingly. He fled; preferring liberty even with a blighted name, to the degradation of a term of service in the penitentiary.

Dea. Jonathan Swan, after 1820, lived in the small house on the Street, afterward owned by Mrs. Durrell, and in which Albert Pressey lived until it was sold to Mrs. Rouillion and torn down. Deacon Swan was a worthy man, industrious and a Baptist. He emigrated to Iowa about 1850, with his family, and died in 1873, aged 87 years.

Lemuel Wilson, son of Jeremiah Wilson, was the second son of Robert. Lemuel had a brother Samuel; their mother's name was Betsey Carlton and they moved to Michigan in the early part of the last century. The father, Jeremiah, died when the boys were quite young. The mother, in her deep grief, conceived the idea that in order to secure the favor of God, she must return to Canaan and she and her children be baptized in the waters of Hart Pond, near the place of her birth. Accordingly, in the year 1827, she took her boys, then grown to manhood, and wended her slow way to Canaan, and they were all baptized by Elder Wheat in Hart Pond, in the presence of a great congregation of witnesses. They returned to their home in Michigan. Many years afterward Lemuel, who had drifted to California, was persuaded to abjure his early Baptist predilections and profess himself a Roman Catholic. His recollection of the baptism was so dim that the priest deemed it necessary to inquire if it was a fact, and the query seemed to turn upon the point whether Elder Wheat's baptism was sufficient to save him in his double character of Baptist and Catholic.

Maj. Samuel Jones lived in a large square house on South Road, which afterwards passed into the possession of James Pattee. It was burned at midday in December, 1828, through the carelessness of two boys, who were grinding apples for Elias Porter. There was a large cider mill and numerous barns and sheds so near that nothing could be saved. It was a grand sight; no wind. The flames went straight up and left only a pile of ashes. In one of the chambers were sixty bushels of wheat, two hundred bushels of corn in the crib, tons of hay and unthreshed oats. Only part of the furniture was saved.

The orthography of Hart or Heart Pond may be interesting. John Farmer in his *Gazetteer*, printed in 1824, spells it Heart Pond all the way through. Mr. Farmer was an enthusiastic antiquarian, and was regarded as good authority, and so that name is still used by some, out of deference to its supposed heart shape, which is more in the eye than in the pond. All the old grants bordering on this pond spell it "Hart." Daniel Colby, when a young man, 150 or 160 years ago, used to come up here from Massachusetts with his father and two others, named Tribble and Hart, and trap beaver and otter upon the shores of this pond. Ensign Colby, an old man who died forty years ago, said the word was spelled H-a-r-t by the early visitors, and was probably named for one of the old trapper's partners.

A letter dated May 30, 1838, says: "We have made one grand improvement on our Street this spring. We have caused to be set out two rows of beautiful rock maple trees, on each side of the street, its whole length. They will give it beauty and serve as a point of admiration with all lovers of artificial scenery." While many of these trees have grown to be stately and proud, a great number were mutilated and destroyed by vicious persons not resident here, but who deemed any annoying act they might commit, proper and right as against the abolitionists of the street. It was this bad temper that first broke the unity of the two rows of maple trees. It was so bad as even to affect the temper of horses. It was seriously related that on one occasion, Maj. Levi George, who lived on South Road, started with his wife to do some trading at Martin's store. When he reached the schoolhouse on the edge of the common, his horse gave a snort, turned suddenly round and trotted back home, so offensive was the scent of abolition to his nostrils. It is not known what became of that horse, but he was printed in the *New Hampshire Patriot* as being instinctively intelligent.

In 1857 James H. Kelley, F. P. Swett, Franklin Barber, James C. Furber and others, fenced a three-cornered park where the three roads meet at the "Corner," set out trees, set up a martin house, and made an arrangement for a fountain and flower beds, but it was never completed.

Milton Hall, Canaan

CHAPTER XXVIII.

SECRET ORGANIZATIONS.

Freemasonry.

Mount Moriah Lodge flourished for many years, and drew into its mysterious folds all the prominent men. Its influence was felt in society, religion, politics. It grew unwieldly from the number of men of small minds who secured its honors, and then bickerings and jealousies crept in, its benign influences were smothered and it passed away like a dream when one awaketh.

It was in the back parlor of Seth Bullock's hotel in Grafton, that eight earnest brethren met to confer upon their wants. A petition was written and signed on October 27, 1813, by Richard Currier, 3d, Seth Bullock, John Kimball and thirteen others and forwarded to the Grand Lodge for a charter for a lodge to be called Mount Moriah. Bro. Joseph Merrill was chosen an agent to attend the General Assembly of the Grand Lodge at Portsmouth and present the petition. Brother Merrill faithfully performed his duty and returned with the desired authority. On the second day of February, 1814, the brethren assembled at Moses Dole's hall in Canaan, to listen to and act upon the report of Brother Merrill. He said he had stated the wants of the brethren here, how they were few in number and scattered over a wild wide country,—and that they needed the bonds of an organization to bring them together for social and mental improvement, whereby much good would be effected and their solemn obligations to each other and to the world would be better appreciated.

The brethren of the Grand Lodge had kindly listened to his story and had then graciously authorized their grand master to grant us a letter of dispensation, which he would now read. It was in the words following:

{ Seal of Grand Lodge } By authority vested in me as Grand Master of Masons in and throughout the State of New Hampshire:—

Be it known, That I, Edward J. Long, on application and proper recommendation of Richard Currier 3rd., Seth Bullock, John Kimball and others, all Master Masons, for a new Lodge to be constituted and holden at Canaan, in this State

Do hereby empower said Currier and others to assemble at said Canaan as a Lodge of Masons; to perfect themselves in the several duties of Masonry; to make choice of officers; to make regulations and by-laws, and to admit candidates into the first degree of Masonry; all according to the ancient customs of Masons.

This warrant of dispensation to continue in full force and authority for three months from the date hereof.

Given under my hand and the seal of the Grand Lodge, this 27th day of January A. L. 5814.

EDWARD J. LONG, G. Master.

Attest CHARLES TAPPAN, *Grand Secretary.*

An informal meeting was held, Bro. Caleb Seabury being chairman, when after appointing Bros. Timothy Tilton, Moses Dole and Caleb Seabury, a committee to report a code of by-laws and to procure furniture for the lodge, "we adjourned to meet on Wednesday preceding the full moon in March, it being the second day, A. D. 1814, at Masons hall, in Canaan."

The brethren are now much interested in the business in which they are engaged, — and they travel many miles on horse back, and on foot, over rough roads and by blazed paths to be present at the first selection of officers, because the success of the undertaking demands that their first officers shall be intelligent, active, and interested in the work, — we assemble, fourteen of us, good men and true, — and the dingy old manuscript blurred with age and dust, uncovers to us the following names:

Caleb Seabury.	Dr. Timothy Tilton.
James Slocum.	Moses Dole.
Jesse Johnson.	Joseph Merrill.
Richard Currier.	Jonathan Jones.
Daniel Currier.	Seth Bullock.
Henry Currier.	James C. Drake.
John G. Colt.	John Jones.

The lodge was opened in due form on the first step in Masonry, — and then the following officers were chosen, namely:

Bro. Timothy Tilton, master; Bro. Richard Currier, senior warden; Bro. James C. Drake, junior warden; Bro. Joseph Merrill, secretary; Bro. Moses Dole, treasurer; Bro. Samuel Phillips, senior deacon; Bro. John Jones, junior deacon; Bro. Daniel

Currier and Jonathan Jones, stewards; Bro. Jesse Johnson, Seth Bullock and Caleb Seabury, standing committee.

And now the organization is complete and we are ready for work, and here it is. The first candidate presented, asking for the rights and benefits of our ancient institutions, is the lawyer on Broad Street, Thomas Hale Pettingill, whose writs and summonses were almost as numerous as autumn leaves or the pine stumps on the broad street and much more expensive. We made him an entered apprentice in due form and then our work being done, we adjourned, congratulating each other that we — vain men — had firmly established an institution that should abide the lapse of ages. *Sic transit* — the actors in these scenes have all gone to that bourne from whence no traveler returns. Meetings were held under the dispensation and candidates were initiated into the first degree of Masonry during this year. On February 14, 1815, the Grand Lodge appointed Henry Hutchinson a special deputy to install the officers and constitute Mount Moriah Lodge, No. 22, on Wednesday, February 22, 1815. On that date the lodge received its charter. It was not until the following October that any work was done in the second and third degrees. Its meetings were held on Broad Street in the hall over the store of Nathaniel Currier, a part of the time, and for many years in the old Wallace house. Up to December, 1815, they initiated nineteen candidates, for which they did not settle with the Grand Lodge, and on June 11, 1817, were reported delinquent since 1814. They had not sent any representative nor had any of their officers attended the assembly of the Grand Lodge. After this reprimand they were not negligent in their duties for many years.

In 1821 the district deputy visited the lodge and found they had appointed two fellowcrafts as stewards the previous election. In 1823 application was made to the Legislature for a charter, which was granted on July 2, in the following terms:

An act to incorporate certain persons by the name of the Mount Moriah Lodge No. 22 in the Town of Canaan.

SECTION 1. Be it enacted by the Senate and House of Representatives in General Court that Abraham Pushee, Ebenezer Chase, Stephen Folsom, Timothy Tilton and Samuel Morgan and all persons who may hereafter become members of said Lodge be and they are hereby incorporated and made a body corporate and politic forever by the name of Mount Moriah Lodge No. 22 in the town of Canaan and the said body corporate is hereby impowered to hold and possess real and personal estate not exceeding in value the sum of two thousand dollars and is vested with all powers, rights and privileges incident to corporations of a similar nature.

SECT. 2. And be it further enacted that Abraham Pushee may call the first meeting of said Lodge by giving fourteen days notice in the New Hampshire and State *Gazette* of the time and place of such meeting. At such meeting or any subsequent meeting the members of said Lodge may choose a secretary and elect such other officers and establish such by Laws, rules and regulations as may be deemed necessary for the government of said Lodge and for carrying into effect the object of the same provided said by Laws, rules and regulations be not repugnant to the Constitution and Laws of this State.

In 1825 Alpheus Baker of Lebanon, district deputy grand master, reported as follows: "On the first of February I attended Mount Moriah Lodge at Canaan. I found the brethren assembled at an early hour. I found their records well kept, and they seemed desirous of all necessary information for transacting the business on the different degrees. I heard them lecture on the first degree and found them generally correct; but on the fellowcrafts,' they were deficient; I then gave them a dispensation for raising the Rev. Amos Foster of that town, and found they were deficient in the work and lectures of that degree. Their master was not present, although he had summoned his lodge, on some very important business. The brethren told me they had not the lectures on the second or third degree." On this date Dr. Timothy Tilton was master, Jacob Trussell and Daniel Hovey wardens, James Wallace secretary, and Daniel B. Whittier treasurer. In 1826 Alpheus Baker reported the lodge well attended and in a flourishing condition. In 1828 the records of the lodge were reported well kept, and the brethren very correct in the lectures. The lodge continued to make reports until 1835. Then for five years it lay dormant through the trying times attending the destruction of Noyes Academy and the division of the people into two factions on the slavery question. These contentions were carried into the lodge and harmony ceased to prevail, neighbors and friends and brothers became bitter enemies and the tenets of the faith were not sufficient to keep them together. The formation of Social Lodge at Enfield in 1827, took from Mount Moriah all the Enfield members, and some of the most prominent ones: Richard Currier, 3d, Nathan Currier, Dexter Currier, Ebenezer Chase and others. Many moved away, many of those who had kept the lodge together so long died. The last entry upon the old treasurer's book was made in 1828. Neither the records of the secretary nor the charter of the lodge can be found.

There is in existence the report of a committee appointed to settle with the treasurer, dated in 1832, which showed $335.45 in his hands. The lodge was always in a prosperous condition, so far as its treasurer's records show, but the funds were often represented by more due bills than cash. Candidates were often initiated upon the giving of their notes for the fees, which afterward some of them failed to meet. The old by-laws dated July 23, 1817, are in the handwriting of Dr. Timothy Tilton. Their meetings were held at two o'clock in the afternoon, and "the lodge shall be closed by eight in the evening." When a negative was given against a candidate, the standing committee were to receive the reasons for said negative. Every member was furnished with a white ball and a black one, and as the ballot box was passed the members voted which they saw fit. If one negative was received the one so voting was to inform the standing committee of his reasons and if they judged the reasons sufficient the negative was to be effectual. And if the one giving the negative vote did not give his reasons, the negative was of no avail. All apprentices must work five months as such before they could be admitted to the next degree, and then they must work three months before receiving the third degree. The fees were twelve, three and five dollars. Every brother present on a regular lodge night was to pay twelve and one-half cents as a fee for the evening. The expenses of a special meeting were to be paid by the brother desiring it. No more than three ceremonies could be gone through with at one meeting. In 1823, upon the incorporation of the lodge, a new set of by-laws was made and printed, and at the end of the lodge copy was the names of the members; as associated under the act of incorporation of June, 1823:

Abraham Pushee.
Ebenezer Chase.
Stephen Folsom.
Samuel Morgan.
Timothy Tilton.
Daniel B. Whittier.
Richard Currier, 3d.
Jacob Trussell.
Jacob Blaisdell.
Elias Porter.
Samuel Withington.
William Atherton.
Daniel Hovey.
Ebenezer Clark.
Salmon Cobb.
Nathaniel Currier.
Elijah Miner.
James Wallace.
Moses Dole.
Bela Johnson.
Nathan Currier.
Grover Burnham, Jr.
Benjamin K. Gilman.
Benjamin Shattuck.
Willard Sayles.
James Doten.
Elijah Blaisdell.
David Barnard.
Francis Dustin.
Hubbard Harris.
John Blaisdell.
Robert Barber.
William Martin.
Frederick Hill.
Timothy Blaisdell.
Guilford Cobb.
Dudley Austin.
Jesse D. Arvin.
Dexter Currier.
Rufus Whittier.
John Shepard.
Asa Whittier.
Samuel Hoyt.
Ichabod S. Johnson.
James Saunders.
James Doten, Jr.
Micajah M. Smith.
Caleb Cushing.

The treasurer's book contains these names: David C. Peck, Thomas H. Pettingill, Samuel Noyes, Jacob Barney, Samuel S. Stevens, Amos Morse, Clark Aldrich, Ralph Roby, Nat Pierce, Daniel Currier, Amos Foster, Elihu Granger, James Pattee, Caleb Dustin, Theodore Tyler, William B. Kelley, Moses Kelley, Cyrus Adams, Aaron Wise, Thomas Page, Thomas Lathrop, Nathan Hobart, Samuel Saunders, Rowel Colby, Jr., Hilsey R. Stevens, Joseph S. Pratt, Ezra Kelley, Edward Evans, John Cooke.

The last surviving member was John Blaisdell, who died in 1892 or 1893. On June 9, 1840, the Grand Lodge declared the charter forfeited. This closed the first chapter of Mount Moriah.

For twenty-six years the old members were unaffiliated; some of them died, others moved away, and no new ones came until in 1866, after the return of Jacob Trussell, who had always been a prominent Mason, he, with William Martin, Charles U. Dunning, David Barnard, William A. Wallace, Stephen R. Swett, Isaac N. Blodgett and Allen H. George, petitioned the Grand

Lodge for a charter of a new lodge to be established at Canaan. The Grand Lodge refused to grant a new charter for a lodge at Canaan, but suggested that the charter of old Mount Moriah might be revived and then they would consent if the lodge be moved to Grafton. This was agreed to and Mount Moriah was again established and this time at Grafton Center in June, 1866. Some of the Canaan Masons attended Mount Moriah and some of them continued to go to Social Lodge at Enfield; there was but little difference in the distance. Isaac N. Blodgett, who was an officer, used to walk from the Street to Grafton Center to attend the meeting and back again, reaching home after midnight. At first there was much energy and hard work displayed in making the lodge successful. But private animosities and desires to hold offices soon began to crop out and the attendance to decrease. On February 22, 1870, Stephen Fellows was impeached for unmasonic conduct and privately reprimanded. In May the district deputy notified the lodge of his intention to visit the lodge, and upon his arrival he found only the master and secretary present. The reason for the absence of the other officers and members was a shooting match in the near vicinity. The master at that time said the condition of the lodge was due to the total absence of Masonic spirit of one member, and advised giving up the charter. Cromwell Kimball had made the remark: "If I can't be master of the lodge I will ruin it." Charges were preferred against him and the Grand Lodge, after a hearing, expelled him. This was the last of Mount Moriah. No meetings were held after 1870. I have been unable to determine what became of the charter, as it is not in the office of the grand secretary and the Grand Lodge records do not show that it was ever forfeited.

The records of the revided lodge are at Concord. Before the revival of Mount Moriah, many of its possible candidates had gravitated to Social Lodge and as the trouble increased, still more found favor where more harmony and Masonic spirit prevailed. For more than thirty years Social Lodge had jurisdiction over Canaan, several efforts were made to gain the consent of Social Lodge of Enfield, to establish a lodge here unsuccessfully until in 1901, the consent of King Solomon's, Kearsarge, and Social Lodge was obtained, and a petition was sent to the

Grand Lodge for a dispensation and the establishing of a new lodge. The dispensation was granted December 30, 1901. On January 15, 1902, Summit Lodge was opened under the dispensation by the district deputy grand master for work. At the meeting of the Grand Lodge in May, a charter was granted and on October 8, 1902, Summit Lodge, No. 98, was constituted by the officers of the Grand Lodge.

The charter members were: E. M. Tucker, A. M. Shackford, C. F. Everett, E. M. Adams, G. W. Chase, E. S. Hadley, H. B. Wooster, C. A. Kimball, R. A. Burgess, G. H. Gordon, C. P. King, S. R. Swett, W. B. Martin, Carey Smith, G. E. Muzzey, O. B. Sargent, J. A. Greene, O. L. Rand, F. D. Currier, T. M. Hoyt, A. H. George, G. O. Hadlock.

Its meetings have been held in the Knights of Pythias Hall. The first master was Charles F. Everett. The subsequent masters have been George H. Gordon, Charles P. King, Edwin S. Hadley, Will A. Dean and James F. King. The roster of the lodge contains the name of sixty-eight who have been members, but death has claimed seven of them.

Patrons of Husbandry.

Mascoma Grange, No. 68.

This Grange was organized in Enfield, October 26, 1875, and was afterward transferred to West Canaan, where its meetings are now held. Levi F. Webster was the prime mover in its organization, and was its master for ten years. There were forty-three charter members: Levi F. and Ann C. Webster, Mr. and Mrs. Leonard B. Warren, Harvey B. Jones, Ruth K. Jones, John C. Currier, Rufus Webster, Nathan C. and Carrie L. Morgan, Mr. and Mrs. Nathan S. Holt, Henry H. and Betsey L. Wilson, Mr. and Mrs. E. L. Hadley, Charles Dwinells, Webster and Ann Currier, Moses E. and Julianna Withington, Eben R. & Emily J. Dustin, Mr. and Mrs. David N. Ladd, Mr. and Mrs. Samuel Carlton, Mr. and Mrs. Harry Huse, Mr. and Mrs. Andrew J. Hadley, Ira G. and Emma Webster, Horace M. and Julia Jones, Mr. and Mrs. L. W. Rogers, Mr. and Mrs. John J. Walbridge,

Hannah Currier, John Hosmer, David Noyes, Moses A. Brocklebank.

There have been initiated in all 272; and the present membership is 133.

Indian River Grange.

The first meeting was held at the house of Alvin Davis, December 10, 1875, when the thirty-five charter members were instructed by Deputy D. E. Boyden. These members were: Mr. and Mrs. J. H. French, Mr. and Mrs. Alvin Davis, Mr. and Mrs. Reuben Bachelder, Mr. and Mrs. F. G. Dimond, Mr. and Mrs. Enoch Eastman, Mr. and Mrs. Frank Cogswell, Mr. and Mrs. G. W. Davis, Mrs. William Aldrich, Hubbard Aldrich, J. H. Blake, Fred B. Clark, John Pressy, Mr. and Mrs. N. G. Cilley, Mr. and Mrs. John Fernald, Mr. and Mrs. C. H. Ford, Mr. and Mrs. H. J. Goss, Mr. and Mrs. William Hall, Mr. and Mrs. Nathaniel Whittier, Mr. and Mrs. Samuel Hoit, Alton Nourse, James Morrill.

The inducements held out to join were that by banding themselves together in a body, they would be able to buy necessaries at a price much lower than was asked of a single individual. The high prices following the Civil War being particularly hard upon the farmers. The meetings during the first year were held at the houses of Alvin Davis, J. H. French, William Aldrich and John Fernald. These were rather social gatherings than anything else. The need of a hall where the members could assemble was apparent, and in the summer of 1876, a committee was appointed to construct a hall and in the early part of 1877 Grange Hall was completed and occupied.

In 1875 two members were initiated, in 1876 seven, in 1877 four, in 1878 three. In 1879 one, and six members were suspended for non-payment of dues. The next four years was a period of depression. Meetings were held infrequently and very little interest was manifested. To such a low ebb had their affairs reached that during the years 1884, 1885 and 1886, less and less and finally no meetings were held, the charter was finally surrendered and Indian River Grange ceased to exist.

In the early part of 1887, at the solicitation of the state master and secretary, the revival of Indian River Grange was suggested and effected. At an informal meeting, March 25, 1887, these two officers being present, a petition was signed by thirteen old members and sixteen new ones.

The grange was still in a very low condition during the year 1887, only six meetings were held and only one member initiated. In 1888 fourteen meetings were held and ten new members joined. The next two years was a period of inactivity, with no additions to membership. In 1891 six new members were received by petition. In 1892 and 1893, more members were suspended for non-payment of dues and the grange could hardly keep its head up. But the period of depression was nearly ended and in the early part of 1895 prosperity began to show itself. During this year all the regular meetings were held as well as several special for the conferring of degrees. In 1896 twenty-eight new members joined and the total membership was sixty-one, twenty-seven males and thirty-four females. The membership has constantly increased every year. In June, 1899, it reached the century mark. The membership has steadily increased. In 1901 eleven new members were initiated. During the last ten years 183 members have been initiated; death and withdrawals have left the number of members at the present time at 184. The town has never had any "Old Home Week" celebration. Several times articles have been in the warrant and each time passed. The grange in 1904, held an entertainment as an observance of that event. William Hall, Hubbard Ford, Alvin Davis, and Mr. and Mrs. George W. Davis are the only remaining charter members.

Knights of Pythias.

A petition to establish a lodge of this order was started in the summer of 1893, with twenty-eight names, who were to be the charter members. Few of these knew anything about the principles of the order and those who did not, were induced to sign by the representations of those who did, that it was an order that would be of benefit to them. The names of the twenty-eight signers were as follows: A. L. Young, G. H. Kinne, F. W. Barney, J. F. Wentworth, E. M. Allen, G. H. Gordon, B. E. Goss, H.

A. Gilman, Cary Smith, H. H. Woodward, W. C. Story, James Dubia, A. J. Barney, M. T. Furber, C. O. Ingalls, A. H. Barney, E. Fitzgerald, M. M. Wiggin, A. P. Follensbee, C. O. Barney, H. J. Goss, R. E. Allen, F. A. Trumbull, G. E. Cobb, C. P. King, F. E. Howe, J. E. Martin, B. F. Davis.

On the evening of the 11th of August, 1893, a lodge of emergency was opened in Grange Hall, at which the officers of the Grand Lodge were present, with the result that Mt. Cardigan Lodge, No. 31, was duly instituted. Meetings were regularly held in Grange Hall for a time, when it became apparent that it was not a satisfactory meeting place and a committee was appointed to make arrangements for Barnard Hall. Accordingly a five-year lease was secured and extensive changes made. The first meeting held in the new hall was on December 30, 1893. The lodge continued to hold its meetings there for seven years. During these years the lodge prospered beyond expectation. In December, 1894, when the lodge was sixteen months old it had a membership of forty-eight knights, one esquire and two pages. The debt incurred in fitting up Barnard hall had been paid off in October. In 1895 the membership increased to fifty-eight. At the close of 1897 the membership was seventy-four, and at the last meeting in 1898, the membership was ninety. In December, 1899, the membership was 101, and the lodge had nearly $1,000 in its treasury. The increase in membership and funds led to talk of a new hall, and an offer was made in March, 1900, for the Grange building. This offer was accepted and a committee, consisting of H. A. Gilman, G. H. Gordon and E. M. Allen, was appointed to make the necessary repairs and changes. Another story was added to the building, which is occupied as the lodge room and ante-rooms. Mrs. Lura G. Milton, whose son, Frank E. Milton, had been a member and who had died in 1894, donated $500 towards the improvement of the building in memory of her son, and the hall has since been called Milton Hall. The first meeting held in the new hall was on September 7, 1900. The membership at the end of this year was 109. Since that time forty-nine members have been initiated, making a total of 168 members admitted by initiation and four by card. Suspension, death and withdrawals have decreased the number, so that now the total membership is 123.

Pythian Sisterhood.

In February, 1900, Mrs. Adelaide H. Currier and Mrs. Mary A. K. Tucker circulated a petition for the formation of a Sisterhood. There was a Lodge of Knights, and why not have the auxiliary branch for the ladies? Twenty-seven ladies signed the petition and on the institution of the assembly, became the charter members. Their names were: Adelaide H. Currier, Mary A. K. Tucker, Lillian A. Barney, Mrs. I. B. Stevens, L. Idella Smith, Dell J. Goss, Blanche M. Coburn, Mrs. F. A. Doten, Emma F. Gordon, Ella M. Richardson, Romie E. Jones, Emma L. Sherburne, Roxie L. Allen, Bertha D. Hadley, Frances R. Kimball, Mrs. A. E. Smith, Georgie A. Sanborn, Minnie M. Folsom, Lucy R. Clarkson, Elvira Woodward, Kate R. Davis, Addie M. Follansbee, Mary E. Howe, Emma J. Dubia, Lora M. King, Helen M. Merrill, Blanche E. Bogardus.

An informal meeting was held on March 7, 1900, which was adjourned until the following March 13, when the officers of the Grand Lodge were present and Mascoma Valley Assembly, No. 22, was instituted. At the next meeting the name of the lodge was changed to Prosperity Assembly. They first held their meetings in the Grange building where the Knights were, and afterwards moved with them into Barnard Hall and then back again into Milton Hall. At the end of the first year they had thirty-six members, the next year eighteen more joined, in 1902 three, 1903, three, in 1904 two and in 1905 two, making a total membership of sixty-four. The next year there were none initiated because of the agitation at that time as to whether they were to be recognized by the Grand Lodge of Knights as the auxiliary body. The Grand Lodge refused to recognize them and it became necessary to reorganize, which was done February 14, 1907. Under the old system the Knights could not become members of the Assembly; under the new they could. Since the beginning, 107 have become members, death and withdrawals at the present time have left sixty-three ladies and twenty-four knights.

CHAPTER XXIX.

OLD FAMILIES.

The Scofields.

John Scofield was in his lifetime a prominent man in the affairs of this town. A well-poised, sincere man, and the people had great trust in his integrity and good common sense and conferred upon him all the offices and honors in their power to bestow. These offices he held almost continuously during the eighteen years he remained here and he had the pleasure of seeing his sons, Eleazer and John, Jr., as they grew up to be men, honored for the same sterling qualities that distinguished himself. Mr. Scofield lived to see the patriots successful in all their plans and the country freed from the rule of George the Third, of whom Thackeray says: " 'George, be a king,' were the words which the king's mother was forever croaking in the ears of her son. And a king the simple, stubborn, affectionate, bigoted man tried to be." Mr. Scofield wore knee buckles and breeches. Tall and of most enduring constitution. No respect for the weather; all kinds were alike to him; summer's heat and winter's cold. He was an Englishman and a Baptist. Mr. Scofield was not a soldier in the Revolution. "On the nineteenth of April in seventy-five," he was sixty years old, and beyond the age limit for service in the field. He was buried on the spot chosen by himself for that purpose, upon his own lands and a headstone of clay slate, which he wrought out with his own hands, excepting the date of his death, was placed over his grave, where it remained, exposed to the storms of more than ninety years, quietly marking the resting place of the brave dust that was gathered beneath, and might have continued to remain for ninety years longer a silent sentinel there, but for the foolish vanity of a man who thought to win renown for antiquarian research by lugging that stone off, and placing it in the dusty and damp cellar of the New Hampshire Historical Society at Concord, where the dust accumulated upon it so as to obscure the inscription. And that man signalized his ignoble feat by attaching to the stone a sketch of Mr. Scofield, which was only remarkable for its blunders and mistakes in dates. *Disce omnes cui bono.* This stone remained in the box it was received in in the cellar of the society until 1905, when the town at its annual meeting, saw fit to recognize the services and trials of this man by requesting that it be returned to Canaan.

The town also voted to place a fence around the spot where Mr. Scofield's dust lay, the better to preserve his grave and those buried beside him. The stone was placed in the Town Library on account of its condition, it not being deemed advisable to place it at the head of his grave. On the stone is carved this inscription:

IN MEMORY OF
JOHN SCOFIELD
Who died July 5th, 1784
In his 69th. year
Blessed are ye dead who die in the Lord.

On the footstone, now standing at the foot of his grave, was carved "Mr. John Scofield." The grave is located in the south part of the pasture of the old James Pattee farm on South Road, which Daniel Pattee bought in 1799. This farm was cleared by Samuel Jones, Mr. Scofield's son-in-law.

At some unknown date a burial place was laid out in that lone pasture. Years ago there were eleven mounds, arranged due east and west. At only one of them, Mr. Scofield's, was there a gravestone. Field stones are placed at the head and foot of some of the others. Five of them were short, indicating children. Mrs. Scofield was buried beside her husband and a Mrs. Floyd is said to have been buried in another. And this is all that is known of those buried there.

Mrs. Scofield, whose maiden name was Sarah Crocker, she who so bravely walked with her children, while her husband hauled his handsled from Lebanon, in that dreary December day in '66, survived her husband in her old homestead for twelve years. She died September 4, 1796, and her grave was never marked. The reason for this apparent neglect to mark the old graves was cogent with the people. There were no skilful workers in stone among them, and they could hardly afford the expense of sending abroad for monuments of marble or granite. Nearly all the old stones set up in our cemeteries are the handiwork of some member of the family of the deceased, wrought from stones which still have their counterparts in this town. The last will and testament of Mrs. Scofield, witnessed several years before her death, is copied below. It is written in the handwriting of Thomas Baldwin and is witnessed by him. The spelling and capitalization of the original are retained.

In The Name of God, Amen. The Last Will & Testament of Sarah Scofield of Canaan in the County of Grafton and State of New Hampshire.

Im primis, my Soul I Commend to God that Gave it. Trusting and Beleiving thro the Merits of His Dear Son to be accepted of Him in Peace. My body I resign to the Earth, to be Decently Interred Trusting and Believing I Shall receive it again in the Morning of the Resurrection Refined for Immortality.

My funeral charges together with all my Just Debts to be Paid out of my Estate. Item, I Give and Bequeath all my wearing apparel to my Children and Grandchildren, to be Equally Divided into Four Parts (viz) To my Beloved Daughter Merriam Jones one Quarter (and She to have the first choice). To Temperance Scofield my Beloved Daughter in law one Quarter, to my Beloved Daughter in law Lydia Scofield one Quarter, and to my Beloved Grand-daughters, Sarah Crocker and Esther Jones, one quarter to be equally Divided between them.

Item I give and bequeath to my beloved daughter Meriam Jones my bed underbed two coverlids one pair of Sheets one pair of Pillow cases.

Item I give and Bequeath al the remaining part of my Estate of Whatsoever Nature or kind to my beloved Sons Eleazer and John Scofield to be Equally Divided between them. With this Proviso that they pay To my two Grandaughters above named two pounds Ten Shillings Each to be paid out of my Household stuff or other ways to their Satisfaction Immediately after my Discease.——all and every of the Bequested Premises I Will and injoin that they be Divided and injoyed as above expressed.

In Testimony Whereof I have hereunto Set my hand and Seal this 23rd day of Jany A D 1786, Signed Sealed And Confirmed in Presents of

	her
THOMAS BALDWIN	SARAH + SCOFIELD.
EZEKIEL LUNT	mark

Ezekiel Lunt was a resident of Enfield. This will was never probated. Its terms were carried out without legal formality. The sons of Mr. Scofield were Eleazer, born in 1754, and John, born June 12, 1756. There were two daughters, Delight, who died in 1777, the wife of Gideon Rudd of Hanover, and Miriam, two years younger than John, all born in Connecticut. Before the death of their father, these young men exhibited traits of character which won the respect and confidence of their townsmen. Their opportunities for education were very limited, there being no public schools. But few of the people became distinguished for their learning, because the necessities of life compelled them to labor. They learned to read and write painfully, and if not disturbed could slowly reckon figures. The new settlements did not afford even so good advantages as the older settlements in Connecticut from whence they came and the young people had to depend chiefly upon their own efforts and the instruction of parents at home and the parents of these young people were but indifferent scholars. Mr. Scofield passed through a routine business education, while his wife was ignorant, both of letters and penmanship. But what the boys lacked in mental training was made up to them in good advice, which they stored up and followed all the days of their lives.

Eleazer married Temperance Calkins, whose father, John P., lived in a log house on the South Road, about ninety rods west of his father-in-law, Mr. George Harris. They had a family of three sons, Eleazer, Nathan, Benjamin, and two daughters, all born in Canaan. He built and lived in the house John Moore now owns. John married Lydia Clark, a sister of Dea. Josiah Clark. They had four sons and five daughters, all born in Canaan. John Scofield, Jr., was an earnest patriot of the Revolution. He was made captain of a militia company and marched on foot from Canaan to Saratoga, and had the gratification of being present at the surrender of Burgoyne. He always afterward was known as Captain Scofield, and as he grew in years, he got to be "old Captain Scofield."

The sister Miriam, married Maj. Samuel Jones. After living together several years, two children being born to them, they separated by mutual consent, a lack of harmony being the chief reason, and the major carried her back to her mother's house. It is reported that it gave him greater pleasure to restore her to her mother's house than he manifested when he took her away. She was a confirmed invalid and continued with her own kindred until her death, and was always known as "Aunt Miriam." Major Jones sold out; emigrated to New York and married again. One son, many years afterward, revisited the scenes of his father's early labors. Soon after the old settler's death, Mr. Eleazer and Captain John, who had assisted in cutting the first trees for actual settlement in Canaan, began to talk to each other of emigrating, selling out their lands and making a home in Canada. Strong as were their attachments, they seemed willing to yield them all and push on and begin as settlers anew farther off.

The industry and perseverance of the people had made this a flourishing community. Every season was adding to its numbers and respectability. Schools were organized in the new districts and a common education was possible under difficulties. Religion had many sincere votaries and the Baptist Church increased in numbers, although many of the good men were not within its fold.

The lands were being sub-divided, and distributed freely at low prices to induce settlements. It would not be long before every man would be reduced to a hundred acres or even less.

They felt crowded, and sterling men as they were and honored and respected as such, were sired of the same disease which attacked "the old man" thirty-five years before when he exiled himself from the pleasant town in Connecticut and by devious wanderings at length found a home upon the banks of the Mascoma at Canaan. They had heard that the soil of Canada was rich and easily worked, but few stones, and extended in long level stretches of forest. It was not until after the death of their mother, some years, that their desires began to assume definite shape. About the year 1800 Captain John and his son John Bunyan, traveled up to Canada for exploration, and decided upon the spot that should be their future home. They found it a great unbroken forest, with natural features far superior to these. They returned well pleased, and two or three years afterward, packed up their household goods, their lares and penates, their wives and children, cattle, sheep and hogs, a bag of apple seeds, for it was a rule with all our ancestors, to plant an orchard as soon as the first acres were felled and started out for their new home about a mile within the Canada line in the town of Dunspatten, now St. Armands.

They took up a large tract of land and in one year cleared thirty acres with their own hands. They built houses and barns, planted orchards and crops of all kinds, and increased and multiplied, as perservering industry always does. The entire race disappeared from among us, and their names never again appear in our records. Eleazer, his wife, three sons and two daughters, Captain John, his wife, four sons and five daughters, and Aunt Miriam, all departed together, leaving us only the graves of our first settler and his wife.

Captain John's children were: Sarah, born January 21, 1779, she married David Tallman and had eight children; Miriam, born May 4, 1780, married Robert Barber and had two children; John Bunyan, born March 31, 1781, died September 24, 1814, married Wealthy Basford and had seven children; Lucinda, born June 28, 1784, died December 2, 1857, married Benedict Tyler and had seven children; James, born August 10, 1786, died March 8, 1849, married Olive Basford and had eleven children; Jesse, born March 31, 1789, died October 23, 1828, married Eliza Martin and had one son; Lydia, born November 23, 1791, died July 2, 1860, she married Salmon Baker and had eight children and afterwards married David F. Carpenter; Lewis, born September 13, 1794, married Eliza Bowen and had one son; Betsey, born October 4, 1797, married John Ingalls and had four children.

Capt. John Scofield owned and lived upon the farm which he sold to Levi George of Salisbury in 1803, on the north side of South Road, opposite where George Ginn now lives. He owned the land on both sides of the old road leading to the mill. He deeded the land on both sides "to the road." That road was thrown up by the town, consequently the land reverts to the heirs of Captain Scofield. Every subsequent deed has followed the same description and no owner has recognized or assumed to give a description to a subsequent purchaser that included the road.

There were others who emigrated and went to make up the Canaan colony in Canada, either with the Scofields or soon after. Robert Barber, Jr., who had married Miriam Scofield; Allen Miner and his wife, Sally Flint, daughter of Joseph Flint, and three children; David Clark, son of Captain Caleb, married to Sarah Basford; Prescott Clark, his brother, married to Mary Basford. Two other Basford girls had married into the Scofield family; they were the daughters of Joseph Basford, a Revolutionary soldier, who had settled in Orange. He was not long a resident of Orange. Like many other settlers in that town, he left to get rid of the exactions of Nathan Waldo, and settled at East Lebanon, where he was employed by Elisha Paine in his mill at the outlet of Mascoma Lake. William Gates, son of Reynold, a young man about eighteen years old, joined the colonists, and after the death of David Clark in 1810, married the widow. Prescott Clark had eight children.

The Dustin Family.

The Dustin family were originally from Haverhill, Mass. Jonathan Dustin was a millwright and carpenter. He and his son David served in the Revolution and after their discharge in 1780, emigrated to Canaan and became purchasers of rights in the proprietary. In the old surveys, he is described as Lieut. Jonathan Dustin. The family always resided upon the farm known by that name, which Jonathan purchased of James Treadway in 1780 for "400 pounds L. M.," and David, the son, deeded to Joseph the grandson in 1840. It is now owned by M. E. Cross. Jonathan was the owner of the right of Phineas Sabine and when he came to Canaan, built his log house in the field northeasterly of where the present house of Mr. Cross is. William Douglass had the only house there before him in this section. Mr. Dustin's land was on the west and north of Douglass', and extended on the east to the shores of Hart Pond.

Jonathan Dustin died July 4, 1812; he lived to be over ninety-three years old. His children were David, Hannah, who married Simeon Arvin, Ruth, named after her mother, who married David Fogg November 23, 1788, Susanna, Daniel, Samuel, Jonathan, Jr. David Dustin died September 10, 1840, aged seventy-nine years, he married Rebecca Cross, daughter of Jonathan Cross of Methuen, Mass., and then of Canaan. She died November 24, 1849, aged eighty-two years. "Uncle David," he was always called, a kind friendly man, whom the young people always liked. He had several sons. James, born in 1791, who served an apprenticeship with Jacob Dow, the tanner, and was a volunteer of the War of 1812. He emigrated to Ohio. Caleb, born August 24, 1799, lived and died in Canaan January, 1891, at a ripe old age of over ninety-one years. He married first Nancy Miller, daughter of Jacob, January 27, 1824; she died December 3, 1857, aged fifty-five years. They had three children: Emily, who died February 28, 1841; Caroline E., who died March 8, 1841, and Loraine H., who married William G. Somers, March 12, 1849. He died April 13, 1880, aged fifty-seven. They had one son, William B., who died February 29, 1868, aged three months. Caleb Dustin was engaged in the lumber business with his son-in-law. He married second, Mary G. (Kelley) Gilman, daughter of Moses Kelley and widow of Col. Eliphalet C. Gilman. Franklin Dustin, another son of David, went to St. Augustine in the '30's and never returned. Dudley B., the youngest, was to take care of the old folks and have the farm, but Dudley and Betsey Pierce had a quarrel and she went with another man. Dudley grew restless and uneasy, and believing there were better chances in the world than the farm offered, sometime in 1825, gave up his place to his brother Joseph, and followed the western trail, until he reached the banks of the Williamette in Oregon, where he long resided and died, February 2, 1878, aged seventy-five years. He first went to Ohio; then to Iowa, where he lived until 1849. In Oregon he received 320 acres of land and became a man well filled with worldly riches, which descended to his four sons. There were two Betseys, daughters of Jonathan and Ruth, one of them died young and the other married Rev. Jonathan Hazeltine of Hebron, November 30, 1820, a Methodist preacher, who, when public opinion protected mobs and outlawed abolitionists, braved the whole of that bad element by denouncing the sin of slavery everywhere.

Joseph Dustin, another son of David, was born October 25, 1795, and died at one o'clock April 3, 1877. He was an old man with a young heart, and all the days of a long life manifested a hearty interest in all questions that occupied the public mind. Politics, religion, schools, town affairs, — upon all subjects he had decided opinions and up to the day of his death, was engaged in active business. He possessed a very tenacious memory of men and events, and possessed a large fund of information upon the occurrences of his last seventy years. No man has ever had so precise knowledge of all matters relating to the titles to real estate in Canaan. In connection with Hon. Daniel Blaisdell, he became the owner of all the undivided land in town. These lands consisted of corner lots, gores, and small patches, that fill in between hundred-acre surveys, and the looking up these surveys made him an authority upon boundary lines and titles. He was cheery and affable, and as his years increased, he delighted more and more in the society of children and youth. He had large charity for young men who were sowing their wild oats. For he had been young himself once and had sown an abundant crop. While still a young man, he became interested in religion. He had been Godless, oftentimes recklessly wild, exhibiting great contempt for the teachings of Elder Wheat's ponderous sermons, and the long prayers of his solemn deacons. But his hour of repentance came and he was a changed man ever after. He became an enthusiastic Methodist and was a liberal and cheerful supporter of the institutions of that church, sometimes making up from his own purse any deficiency there might be in the year's appropriations. He married on Thanksgiving day, November 27, 1818, Sally, daughter of Judge Daniel Blaisdell. Fifty-nine years they traveled the long road upon which they set out, and as "Brother Joe" and "Sister Joe," they ended their long lives. Brother Joe carried the mail for many years and no boy ever failed to get a ride. He held many town offices and was a selectman in 1844 and 1847.

Mrs. Dustin survived her husband and died March 18, 1885. She was born June 17, 1799. They had two sons and three daughters: James, who died September 20, 1826, aged six years; John B., born September 13, 1821, died single, April 18, 1851; Emeline, born December 12, 1822, died April 20, 1891, married Simeon Hadley, they moved to Lowell, Mass., where he died in 1853; they had two children, Lizzie and Emma, who married a Sleeper, and had two children, Ethel and Grace, who married a Stevens and had one child, Hazel; Rebecca A., who lived and died at home unmarried April 4, 1889, aged fifty-nine, and Harriet B., who married Mark Purmont, and after his death in 1878, came back to the old farm. She kept a millinery store before her marriage at East Canaan, and was burned out when Barney Bros. store was destroyed in December, 1872. She afterward, with the assistance of her father, built the building now occupied by the post office and carried on the same business.

Daniel Dustin, son of Jonathan, married Deborah Barber February 8, 1789, and had one daughter, Susanna, born April 8, 1791. Samuel Dustin married Eunice Martin, February 19, 1791, and had two children, Nathan, born November 14, 1791, and Sophronia, born March 24, 1795.

The Blaisdells.

Part of the following about the Blaisdell family is taken from a manuscript prepared more than half a century ago by Joshua Blaisdell, who died more than forty years ago. Mr. Joshua Blaisdell was the son of Daniel, the early settler of this town. It is a dingy and much worn account and so far as it relates to the origin of the family the credit of it is due to him, as well as the authenticity. Mr. Blaisdell says:

The family originated in Denmark and came to England after the Danes were subdued by Alfred the Great, and his successors, many of whom settled in the northeast part of Wales. From this quarter our family came to this country. They had been forgemen since they settled in Wales. Ralph Blaisdell married into the royal family (but how far "into" the record does not state). "Sir Ralph Blaisdell of Wales" Lord Eldon states, "was a noble generous knight." Several of the name were members of Parliament. The name should be "Blaisdale," with a Scripture name before it. We gloried also in a coat of arms, which I cannot describe, only as it had the name "Blaisdel" inscribed on it, and this was the way my father spelled it up to 1808, when he was elected to Congress, and his name was so spelled in his certificate of election, after which he spelled it "Blaisdell."

Three brothers came from the northeast part of Wales and landed in Newbury, Mass., previous to 1675. Their mother accompanied them, the father died before the family left England. His name was Enoch. Some time after their arrival she married a second husband named Satterlee. About the year 1811 my brother Elijah (of Canaan) visited Newburyport and had an interview with the daughter of a son by this

Sally (Springer) Blaisdell

Hon. Daniel Blaisdell

Hon. Elijah Blaisdell

OLD FAMILIES.

marriage. The daughter was over one hundred years old, and was called Granny Satterlee.

Enoch first, was a forgeman. The names of his three sons were Enoch, Abner and Elijah. Enoch settled in Maine, and for most part was ancestor of the Blaisdells in that state and in Strafford and Rockingham Counties in this state. Abner went to New York. Elijah settled at Amesbury, Mass. It is not known how many sons he had, but there were several of the name in Amesbury, and it is not easy to assign them any other origin. There certainly was one named Elijah, and nearly equally as certain there was a Jonathan. Jonathan went to Kingston to a place called Fishing Falls. He had two sons called Jonathan and William. Jonathan, Jr., had two sons, William and Ralph, who settled in Salisbury in 1740. Jonathan, Sr., was a blacksmith and went to Kingston on account of the superior facilities for iron working. His son Jonathan, born July 13, 1723, was also a blacksmith.

Elijah (third of the race) married a widowed woman and remained in possession of the old place in Amesbury. They had born to them four sons and one daughter, Elijah, Jonathan, Enoch, Jacob and Abigail. Jonathan once visited my father (Daniel) in Canaan on his way to search for a western home. Enoch also followed him to Ohio. Jacob was a forgeman as usual. He went to Burton and afterwards to Indiana. The reason for his leaving for the west was that the boundary lines between Burton and Eaton were changed somewhat, and he lost some property thereby. He declared he would stay no longer in a state where property was not protected. Abigail died when young. Elijah the father was a brave soldier, he lost an arm in battle and lived and died in his own home.

Elijah (fourth of the race) married Mrs. Mary Keazer Sargent, widowed daughter of Capt. Timothy Keaser, a sailor out of Newburyport. He lived and died at Amesbury, a schoolmaster. They had three sons born to them, perhaps more, Parrot, Daniel and Sargent. When Daniel was seven years old his father died leaving his family destitute. Some years after the father's death the widow moved her family to Henniker, N. H., and thence to Hopkinton, where she married Nathaniel Whittier. Daniel was twelve years old when his mother left Amesbury. He lived in Henniker two years and three years in Hopkinton, during which time he served a campaign as a soldier of the Revolution at forty shillings per month and twelve shillings blanket money. He left the army at seventeen years of age and went to Canaan.

Parrot Blaisdell, spelled "Parrit," was born in Amesbury, Mass., November 11, 1759, married on Thursday, May 5, 1785, Mrs. Ruth (Folsom) Ball, daughter of Josiah and Abigail Folsom, born in Haverhill, Mass., March 22, 1759. He lived in Canaan, Orange, Hanover and Montpelier, Vt., and died at Fort Covington, N. Y., August 3, 1836. He no doubt came to Canaan about the time of his brother Daniel, for his name appears on the inventory of 1782, which would show he was here in 1781. They had three sons and seven daughters:

1. George H., born the first day of March, 1784.

2. Abigail, born on Wednesday, February 8, 1786, on the old Cochran farm; she died at Stoneham, Mass., at the home of her granddaughter. She married Russell Putnam.

3. Ruth, born December 23, 1787; died December 4, 1836, "at quarter past four." She married Henry Howe.

4. Polly, born January 7, 1790; died November 20, 1790.

5. Polly, born May 22, 1791; died at Potsdam, N. Y., November 22, 1865; married her cousin, Joshua, son of Daniel Blaisdell.

6. Sally, born on Thursday, January 29, 1793; married Otis Standish.

7. Azurbah, born December 15, 1794, married Pierce B. Smith.

8. Parrit, Jr., born May 4, 1796; died August 3, 1839, at Fort Covington, N. Y., "of collery also his son Edwin of collery August 4, 1839." He had one son and one daughter. He was a sailor.

9. Clarissa, born October 4, 1798; married John C. Wolf.

10. Elijah, born May 5, 1801. He was editor and publisher of the *Vergennes Vermonter* in 1848. His cousin Joshua says of him: "He is hale fellow well met, drinks a glass with a friend and pays the bill, is a tattling bragging man, has one son of good promise and two others and one daughter."

Another account of the Blaisdells is here given, furnished me by Alfred O. Blaisdell from investigations made by Dr. W. O. Blaisdell:

The family were from Lancashire, where in Preston, there were at one time fifteen families of that name. Ralph Blaisdell and his wife came to this country in 1635, having embarked at Milford Haven, Wales, on the ship *Angel Gabriel*. The ship seems to have belied her name, for, arriving on the coast of Maine in a severe storm, she became a total wreck. All on board were saved. Ralph and his wife settled in York, Maine. In 1642 he sold his property as shown by the county records and moved to Salisbury, Mass., that part which was afterwards Amesbury, where for several years he kept an inn. He had but one son, Henry, who married Mary Haddon, and also a second wife, Elizabeth. By the two wives he had nine children, six boys and three girls. He combined the trades of farmer and tailor. One of his sons Jonathan, born October 11, 1676, was a blacksmith and at the age of twenty-two married Hannah Jameson of whom the seventh was Enoch, born July 9, 1714. Enoch married Mary Satterlee, had eight children of whom the third was Elijah, born December 31, 1740. Elijah married Mary Sargent March 14, 1759, and lived in the west parish of Amesbury until a year or two after his marriage when he moved to Warner, N. H. He was the father of Daniel, Parrot and Sargent.

In the town records for 1787, appears a "greeting to Samuel Joslyn, Constable of the town of Canaan." "You are required forthwith to notify and warn to depart from said Town of Canaan, the following-named persons now residing in sd Canaan that they not become chargeable in sd town, viz.: Sargent Blaisdell and his wife Susanna and you are to make due return of this warrant and of your doings unto the selectmen of Canaan." Samuel read the warrant in the hearing of the persons named, but it does not appear that he caused any of them to "depart from" Canaan. The name of Sargent Blaisdell's wife does not agree with Joshua Blaisdell's tale, but there is no doubt that he was Daniel's brother. Mr. Joshua says: "Sargent Blaisdell married Mary Blue, a woman with a lively tongue. They lived in Canaan, Enfield and Grafton. It was in the latter town he left his wife with three children, Sargent, Peter and Mary, and the last heard of him he was at Cherry Valley under the assumed name of Sargent Johnson. Sargent, Jr., found his father there, and resided there. Peter died in Canaan, was not considered a bright boy. Mary married and lived in New York state. The facts in regard to his elopement were these, which occurred probably about the years 1789-90. Daniel lived near to Samuel Noyes in the southeast corner of the town. Mr. Noyes had lost a horse by a thief. Sargent was at work for Noyes and was sent upon another horse to search for it. He also sent Daniel upon his own horse and charged them not to come back without the thief. Sargent in taking leave of his wife, repeated the order. She told him 'Go along and never show your face in this house again, without that thief.' Daniel went towards Hopkinton and caught the fellow. Sargent took a different route and, finding no trace of the thief, pushed on and was never seen here afterward. He left a good farm, implements and tools and took nothing but his horse, like a true knight."

The mother of these three boys, Mary Keazer, married in Hopkinton a third husband, Nathaniel Whittier, and died in Canaan May 15, 1806, aged seventy-nine years. She had four children by Mr. Whittier: Elijah, Samuel, Nathaniel and Abigail, who became the wife of Thomas Cole. Elijah married Nancy Kenniston, who was afflicted with a trace of insanity, which was transmitted to some of her descendants. Samuel married Mehitable Bedel October 23, 1796, who, in her old age, wandered from the Bickford place and was found drowned in Hart Pond. Nathaniel married Polly Sleeper. All had large families in Canaan.

Among the early settlers in Canaan, no one was more distinguished for good sense, for integrity and for uprightness in his relations to society than Daniel Blaisdell. He, with his brother Parrot, had done service in the War of the Revolution, and being honorably discharged about the year 1780, in company with other soldiers, emigrated from Amesbury, Mass., to this town, and here made his home during all the years of his long and honorable life. He was eighteen years old at the time of his arrival, with but little knowledge of books, but possessing a constitution inured to toil and hardship. He came here like many others, because it was reported to be a goodly land, where a man might make himself a home by the labor of his own hands. The soil was rich and fruitful and only needed persevering labor to be made to bring forth abundantly. After looking about among the scattered settlers for a few days, he engaged to work for Joseph Flint for six months at six dollars per month. Mr. Flint had been a merchant in Newburyport. About a year previous to this time he had come here from Hopkinton and began to clear up the farm where George W. Davis now lives. The work was very laborious and the master was hard and exacting upon all who fell under his control. Early and late they toiled, — daylight calling them to breakfast and candle light to supper. He used to tell young Blaisdell if he would remain in his service he would make a man of him and having a large family of girls, he supposed their company to be sufficiently magnetic to make the young man forget the hard labor to which he was subjected. He served his time faithfully and well and then hired himself to Capt. Charles Walworth, who lived on South Road. The captain was strongly religious, having imported his Puritan sentiments with him from Connecticut. He was a man of great natural kindness and often gave his young friend good advice. While employed with Captain Walworth, some of the ungodly young people got up a ball, to which they invited Blaisdell. The captain objected to his going, using all the arguments then in common use, against the sinfulness of dancing,—all of which failed to convince the young man. Then the captain told him if he would stay from that wicked gathering of scoffers, he would the next day, show him something that would be of great advantage to him. Daniel stayed away from the ball, but his heart was there all the evening, because little Sally Springer was to be there, and he had begun to believe that the angels had not all left the earth. The next day the captain took him down into a densely timbered region (the farm where Prescott Clark once lived), and advised him to buy it, build a log house, get married, and make himself a home; in two years he could pay for it with the crops. He bought one hundred acres, agreeing to pay Mr. Walworth $300 therefor, and went to work clearing it up and it is said, the first crop of wheat paid for the land. He built himself a log house, and then wooed and married the little girl (who was an angel to him), January 28, 1782, being scarcely twenty years old, and in due time they had sons and daughters born unto them — a house full. He worked hard and was rewarded with increase in various ways. He became a teacher; he studied politics and was elected to various town offices; he stored his mind with much practical knowledge, which he imparted freely to all his neighbors. He often acted as a justice and his decisions were regarded as just and right. In twenty-one years eleven children were born to him. More than a hundred years ago a tax was levied by the Legislature which was very burdensome to some of the new towns. Caleb Seabury was said to have been the occasion of it. He was sent to Exeter as a representative. He thought he would signalize his term of office by assuring the Legislature of the great wealth of Canaan. Its soil yielded spontaneously and enriched its people. The effect of this speech or talk was the passage of the law which burdened the people with taxes. The next year Mr. Blaisdell was sent to Exeter to ask for the modification of the law. He told them that it was true that the lands of Canaan were exceedingly rich and fruitful. It was like all other new soil upon which the timber forests had been reduced to ashes. If they would make wheat, rye and corn, legal tender for taxes, it would relieve the people greatly, but there was no money and no market for their commodities. Lands, cattle, hogs, ashes, grain, etc., were the circulating medium. Nearly all purchases were made by way of exchange. In this way he pleaded with them, until they consented to modify the law, which greatly pleased the people and made him more popular than ever. Before Mr. Baldwin left town, Mr. Blaisdell had passed through the mysterious process which men call "a change of heart, had joined the new Baptist Church and was ever afterward a consistent Baptist, and advocate for the stated preaching of the gospel." His manner of stating his opinions was somewhat diffuse and like a small piece of butter on a large slice of bread, was a good deal spread out. He sometimes stated it thus: "We believe that the preaching of the gospel was instituted by the all-wise Governor of the universe as a means whereby to communicate his special grace to a ruined world; and we believe, also, that a regular, peaceful gospel, tends to promote good order and strengthen the bonds of society." He was prominent in all the services of the church, and also in all the connections of his party. As a Christian, the Baptist Church was his strong tower; a belief in its tenets could alone save lost souls. His political faith was as fixed and unalterable as his religion. The Federal party had the immortal Washington for its head, and through that organization alone, could our free institutions be perpetuated. It was the sacred privilege of Federalists to hate Thomas Jefferson, as it was the duty of Baptists to avoid the devil, and flee from the wrath to come. These two principles governed all his actions in religion and politics. His first appearance in public life was as a legislator at Exeter in 1793. He was sent again in 1795 and remained there until 1799, representing the towns of Canaan, Grafton and Orange. He represented Canaan in 1812 and 1813, and in 1824 and 1825, and was a judge in the Court of Common Pleas for Grafton County. His sturdy sense and fearless expression of opinions attracted attention and won the applause of his party. He enjoyed the honors he was winning and had vivid dreams of future greatness. Several years he was elected senator and five times he was elected councilor and one term he served in Congress from 1809-11. While in Congress he was an active partisan and opposed all measures involving the peace of the country. He was an aggressive politician and many times came in conflict with the leaders of the war party. Being a rough de-

OLD FAMILIES.

bator with few courtesies of speech, he received from John Randolph the sobriquet of "Northern Bear," a title which clung to him all the days of his life.

Two letters are inserted here which have lain perdue for two generations. The spelling is a little unusual, also the use of capitals, showing defects in his early education. These have been corrected. The first letter might, with propriety, be made to refer to scenes and events of more recent date and both exhibit in strong light the unyielding nature of the man.

WASHINGTON CITY, Jan. 18, 1810.

Dear Sir:

I received yours only last evening, which I read with pleasure. You complain of Democratic orators dealing out falsehood; I thought you knew them better than this, for if I should find them dealing in any other commodity, I should think them insane, or that they had deserted their cause. This I apply to their leaders, and not to all who call themselves Republicans, for there are many among them who are well disposed men, and need only to be here one week, and hear the threats in Congress, to convince them they have been misled. A leader among them, three days since, in Congress, made a war speech, and in reply to a gentleman who had spoken against war, said: "Some gentlemen seem to regret the loss of blood and treasure more than submission to Great Britain. I, also," said he, "regret the loss of the blood of some of our citizens, but if we go to war with England, Canada must be taken, and we very well know what men must be engaged in taking that country." And many more such expressions, which would make the blood of our New England Republicans boil. I immediately went to him and required an explanation. He looked beat and paddled off as well as he could.

Let nothing deter you from duty at, and before the second Tuesday of March. For the darkest time is just before day.

I am sir, &c.,

DANIEL BLAISDELL.

To John Currier, Esq.

The next letter is interesting as showing the hostility of the Federal party to all measures for the defense of the nation at a time when England, supposing us to be weak, had become, day by day, more arrogant in her demands.

WASHINGTON CITY, Feb. 27, 1810.

Dear Sir:

I send you Mr. Epps' war speech, which seems to have originated in a fit of madness, that the Senate had seen fit to cut Mr. Mason's American navigation act of that part which they intended, instead of the Embargo or non-intercourse. It was sent back from the Senate to our House on Thursday, with only three out of thirteen sections left. The two first to interdict the armed ships of England and France from our harbors. And the other to repeal the non-intercourse act. To be sure, sir, it was a curiosity to see the embargo hands, with distorted features, rise in turn, and declare that it was treason against the party that had brought forward and supported commercial restrictions, to thus dispose of it without a substitute. Some of them said they would much rather the hall would fall in and crush them to death, than abandon the system in that way. And after a Sunday evening caucus at the president's, they (as it would seem) are prepared to plunge the nation into immediate war, for Epps did not deny, but owned it must have that effect. Seventy-four supported the measure and forty-nine opposed it. If so many of their war measures, resolutions and proclamations had not evaporated, all must see that we must have a war with England soon, for France is only mentioned to deceive the people. The president on Saturday, before the caucus, said openly, our affairs with France were in a fair way to be settled. Tell your demos if there is any dependence to be placed upon their leaders they may fix their knapsacks to go to Canada.

From your friend,
DANIEL BLAISDELL.

To John Currier, Esq.

At the expiration of his term in 1811, Mr. Blaisdell returned home, firmly believing it to be a Christian virtue to oppose the coming war. Public meetings were called for the purpose of concentrating public opinion. A series of resolutions, longer than one of John Worth's prayers, and more tiresome, setting forth the iniquities of the Democratic leaders and calling upon good men to defeat them, were passed. The excitement ran fearfully high and continued for years. Many worthy neighbors became estranged and the lives of many of them were too short to outlive the ill-feeling engendered.

For more than twenty years he went in and out among his neighbors and friends, exercising great influence in their affairs, honored and respected by all, even by the Democrats, whom, as a party, he never ceased to denounce as the enemies of his country. The struggles of his early life had given him habits of industry, temperance and economy. He lived first "one hundred and two rods down the road toward Grafton" from the bridge at East Canaan by Mud Pond. He then built a modest house on the farm afterward owned by James Doten and since burned, at the top of Doten Hill and readapted himself to the career of a farmer, and about 1818, lived in the Haggett house. His knowledge of law made him a safe counselor. He was sometimes called upon to carry business for his neighbors up to the courts. At one time he was solicited to carry a case to the court at Exeter. He started on horseback, as was the custom then, and on the road was overtaken by Gen. Benjamin Pierce, who was traveling the same way. Personally they were friendly, but very hostile in politics. Blaisdell was a man of even temperament, not easily excited and whom mere words could not offend; but he never yielded a point once settled in his mind. Pierce, in temperament, was the reverse of Blaisdell, but he was equally tenacious of his opinions. Blaisdell believed only Federalism and Baptism. Pierce believed only Democracy. They traveled together, discoursing pleasantly as they rode until they approached the subject of politics. Pierce quite earnestly denounced the Federalists as the enemies of the country and as desiring to destroy the liberties of the people by consolidating all power in the hands of a few families. Blaisdell, very coolly replied by accusing the Democracy of demagogism, of debauching the virtue of the youth of the country and, like Satan, of desiring to lead all things down to himself. This reply infuriated Pierce. He declared that he "would not ride with such a traitor any further" and, jumping off his horse, dared Blaisdell to take his chance of a "thrashing on the spot." Blaisdell declined to take the chances offered, not only because they were not favorable to him, but because he saw nothing to fight about. He said some soothing words to the governor, who finally remounted his horse and the two jogged on to Exeter as though nothing had occurred; but they talked no more politics on that ride.

There was never much poetry in his life. His habits of thought had always been so earnest, so convincing to his reason, that any position he ever assumed, whether in morals, politics or religion, became to him matters of fact. He never yielded a point to an opponent, because he never allowed himself to be in the wrong. It pleased him to see labor rewarded and mean, tricky people punished. But young folks never loved him, because he never seemed to see them. He would speak of "the rising generation," with a look so far away, as if he never expected to give place to them, or as if they were to drop from some distant sphere and slowly approach to greet him as he disappeared. We used to look upon him as the embodiment of dignity and wisdom,—a man with whom we could take no liberties. He was a wilful man, who liked to have his way. Like most men in his day, he ignored the presence of children. I do not remember of any boy who felt proud of his caresses or approving words. He never uttered them and he very seldom saw any boys. His own life from boyhood until long after he thought himself a man, was of hard toil, without school or books and all the way up hill. Did he never yearn for a word of encouragement? I often wonder when the manner of these men's lives occurs to me, how they could always pass by the children,—the boys who are coming right along to crowd them out of the way? In his day the old judge was a great power in politics, and he had the faculty of keeping his party in office nearly all his life. He never thrust himself forward for office, nor would he allow more than one of his boys to be in office at the same time. This policy made him strong. He did not use his political influence to keep his family in office. In this respect he understood human nature better than some of the leaders in later years. The people respected his advice because they knew him to be unselfish.

It was more than eighty years ago,— just before March election. There had been a sly caucus at Cobb's tavern in which Wesley Burpee, Daniel Pattee, William Campbell, with a few others figured, and Elijah Blaisdell had been nominated for representative. It was intended for a surprise and only such as were friendly to Elijah were present. Old Bill Wood and Levi Wilson had been there after their daily rum; going home about sunset, the judge hailed them for "the news up to the street." "O, nothin' much," replies Uncle Bill, "only we had a caukis, and sot up 'Lijah for representative." "What!" thundered the old judge, "Lige Blaisdell for rep! impossible! But who's done it? He 'aint fit for it, more'n my old hoss, and

I tell you he shan't have it." And he didn't get it. The judge mounted his old horse and rode up to Wallace's store, where a crowd had begun to gather. He dismounted, and after saluting them, inquired if anything of importance had transpired. They confirmed his first intelligence with more particulars. Then he smoothed his brow and replied: "Men, this will never do; because I was fit to hold office, it don't follow that all the Blaisdells are fit for it, and I ought to be pretty well acquainted with them all. And then the way this nomination was made is unfair. A man that plays tricks even in politics, is unworthy of your votes. We must get together, Saturday night at this store and talk it all over, and depend upon it we'll have a good man nominated." The other Blaisdells stayed at home that year. That Saturday night was memorable in the annals of Canaan Street. There was a large gathering and they drank rum freely; everybody did, except this matter-of-fact old judge. Asahel Jones, who belonged to the other party, appeared among them. He was accused of being a spy and he was ordered to prepare for instant death. They secured him, placed a rope about his neck and shoulders and drew him up to a beam in the store, several times letting him down hard. Asahel was badly hurt and worse frightened, and begged hard for a reprieve. Finally he was permitted to start for home. He went over the hill, 'round the pond, crying "Murder! help!" On the road the cold air began to freeze the rum out of his skin and he was sorely chilled. He grew mad as he thought how he had been assaulted and battered by those fellows on the Street, no better than he. Next morning he presented himself before his friend, Elijah Blaisdell, and complained of his assailants, three of whom were arrested and made to pay $20 for the wicked sport they had enjoyed. After the election of General Jackson in 1828, Elijah became a Democrat. The old judge was much annoyed at his son's apostasy from his own faith, but he pretended to be greatly pleased, "because," said he, "now we shall know where to find him all the time."

His children married and settled in town, and the third generation numbered sixty-nine persons. Of his eleven sons and daughters, Elijah, the lawyer, had twelve children; James, the sheriff, six; Daniel, the musician, seventeen; William, the painter, seven; Joshua, the sheriff, six; Parrott, the farmer, twelve; Jacob, the doctor, none; Jonathan, the trader, three; Sally, wife of Joseph Dustin, five; Rhoda, third wife of Eben Clark, deacon, who used to manufacture woolen cloth at the village, one; Timothy, the broker, seven. These families for years all resided in one neighborhood, and it was a common remark that the old folks could visit all their numerous offspring in one day. The name was once nearly as common as blackberries (Barney at East Canaan), but it has disappeared entirely from among us now, and is found only on old tombs and graveyards.

Blaisdell, Daniel, b. Amesbury, Mass., January 25, 1762; d. January 10, 1833; m. by Thomas Baldwin January 29, 1782, Sally Springer, dau. of Joshua, the ferryman, of Haverhill, Mass., b. October 15, 1761; d. June 10, 1838. Eleven ch.

1. Elijah, b. Canaan, October 28, 1782; d. October 10, 1850; m. November 14, 1802, at Pittsfield, Mary Fogg, dau. Dea. John, b. Hampton, September 6, 1781; d. Twelve ch. He m. 2d, Mrs. Mary Kingsbury of Plainfield.

 1. John, b. Pittsfield, May 13, 1803; d. Vineland, N. J., over 90 years old.

 2. Daniel, 3d, b. Pittsfield, August 25, 1806; d. 1875; m. Charlotte Osgood of Haverhill. Grad. Dartmouth College, 1827. Lawyer in Hanover from 1834–'75. Treasurer of Dartmouth College. Ch.: Alfred, now living in Brooklyn, N. Y., and Charlotte, who m. Professor Ruggles of Dartmouth College.

 3. Hannah, b. Grafton, December 13, 1808; d. June 27, 1811; buried near Ebenezer Hoyt Place in Grafton.

 4. Elijah, b. Danbury, March 11, 1811.

 5. Hannah, b. Canaan, August 5, 1813.

 6. Elizabeth, b. Canaan, May 15, 1815; m. a Morey and in 1892 lived in San Francisco.

 7. Mary Ann, b. Canaan, August 9, 1817; d. September 14, 1817.

8. Mary Ann, b. February 24, 1819; d. Beloit, 1905; m. Joseph Tyler of Boston. Ch.: Joseph, sugar manufacturer in Philippines, and Columbus, m. and d. at Seattle.
9. Rhoda, b. March 27, 1821; single; was teacher in Beloit, Wis.
10. Sarah, b. January 26, 1823; single; died 1906. Teacher in Beloit, Wis.
11. James Joshua, b. February 8, 1827; d. October 10, 1896; m. Susan Allen of Lebanon. Lived in Beloit, Wis. Two ch.: James and Philip.

2. James, b. September 20, 1784; m. February 17, 1805; Abigail Tyler, dau. Job. Six ch.: Abigail, Sarah, George, James, Sargent, ——.
3. Daniel, Jr., b. December 28, 1786; d. September 17, 1871; m. October 24, 1805, Sally Clark, dau. Josiah and Pernal, b. July 1, 1789; d. March 7, 1866. Seventeen ch.
   1. Elijah, b. March 30, 1806; was a doctor.
   2. Clark, b. January 8, 1809; m., had three ch.: one named Clark.
   3. Daniel, b. June 4, 1811.
   4. Josiah, b. June 4, 1811; d. June 22, 1811.
   5. Sally, b. June 5, 1813; d. single.
   6. Jonathan Homer, b. February 13, 1816; d. San José, Cal.; single.
   7. Suel Swett, b. August 28, 1818; single, lived Fairlee, Vt.
   8. Mary, single.
   9. Justin.
   10. Justus, d. San José; m. 1st, Clara Tyler; one dau.; m. 2d, a Bruce.
   11. Judge.
   12. Abigail.
   13. Harriet N., d. February 4, 1832, aged 3.
   14. Malvina.
   15. Harriet N., d. June 6, 1856; aged 9.
   16. Nancy, and one d. unnamed.
4. William, b. March 11, 1789; m. Hannah Follensbee of Grafton and had seven ch.: Alvah, who m. Margaret Dunbar at Nashua; m. 2d and had three ch. William A., son

of William, Horace, Harrison, Alzoa, and two nameless. At the funeral of one of them Elder Wheat preached the sermon, and stated his belief that "this infant was unregenerate, and is now writhin' in burnin' flames of hell." William was angry. Left the Baptist Church and joined the Congregationalists, and ever afterwards refused to listen to Elder Wheat's preaching. He was a painter.

5. Joshua, b. April 20, 1791; m. December 19, 1813, his cousin Polly, daughter of Parrot, b. May 22, 1791; d. at Potsdam, N. Y., November 22, 1865. M. 2d, his cousin, Mrs. Mehitable Springer Frost, and d. Thetford, Vt., September 29, 1872. Was deputy sheriff from 1818 to 1833. Lived in Haverhill, N. H., Fort Covington, N. Y., 1842. Potsdam, N. Y., 1844-66 as a merchant. Ch.: four sons and two dau. His second wife was a daughter of Joshua Springer of Canaan, b. in 1792 in old district No. 8. She was married three times, living all the time in Thetford, Vt., first to Judge Buckingham, second to Deacon Frost, she survived them all and lived nearly helpless for some years, but retained all her faculties. She d. in Thetford, Vt., October 12, 1883.

6. Parrot, b. August 4, 1793; m. June 1, 1814. Rhoda French Currier of Enfield. They had 12 children, two Marys, Theophilus, two Rhodas, Timothy, Emily, James, two nameless and Guilford.

7. Jacob, b. October 20, 1795; m. March 7, 1825. Eliza Harris of Canaan, dau. of Hubbard; b. July 17, 1800. No children. Both died at Keysport, N. Y. Being a seventh son he was advised that it was necessary that he should become a doctor.

8. Jonathan, b. February 19, 1798; m. 1st. Persis Ames; 2d, Hannah, dau. of Dr. Ezra Bartlett of Haverhill. Three children.

9. Sally, b. June 17, 1799; m. November 27, 1818. Joseph Dustin of Canaan; d. March 25, 1885. Five children.

10. Rhoda, b. September 1, 1801; d. January 10, 1891. Was a teacher about town until 1832 when she married Dea.

Ebenezer Clark April 19, 1832. One daughter. They separated and afterwards were divorced, because of differences of opinion respecting spiritualism.
11. Timothy Keazer, b. May 9, 1804; d. September 24, 1853; m. 1st, September 23, 1824, Phœbe Cobb; d. March 23, 1832; aged 36; m. 2d, Harriet Merrill of Haverhill, b. November, 1813; d. December 20, 1848. Had one child buried in the grave with his first wife, and three sons and two dau. by his second wife. He was a strong Abolitionist and member of the Congregational Church. He was a storekeeper in Haverhill after the second marriage where he failed in the panic of 1837. He afterwards lived in Boston, was agent of the Connecticut Mutual Life Insurance Company until his death. Ch.: Sarah, m. a lumberman; Harriet, b. Haverhill, November 11, 1834, m. April 30, 1856, Charles H. Cram of Chicago; b. Hanover, March 22, 1832. Nine ch.: Clara, b. January 19, 1857; d. March 18, 1900. Nathan Dow, b. August 2, 1859; m. Mary Queen, manager for Silver, Burdett & Co. in New York. Charles H., b. November 12, 1863; m. Ysabel Del Valle, a merchant and ranchman. Harriet Blaisdell, b. August 26, 1864; m. 1st, Dr. T. W. Miller; m. 2d, Dr. W. W. Quinlan; lives Chicago. Bessie, b. April 28, 1868; m. W. C. Reynolds, in the paint business. Timothy, b. April 26, 1870; m. Georgie Shores, railroad supplies in Chicago. Rupert, b. February 10, 1872; m. Cora Neidig, merchant and ranchman. Walter, b. January 10, 1874; m. Nina Del Valle, merchant and ranchman in California. Mildred, b. August 11, 1876; m. J. V. Paulson; d. March 5, 1900; lives with mother in Haverhill. Timothy, son of Timothy, was in the Rebellion, contracted consumption and d. single. Edward and Frank.

The Clarks.

Richard Clark came from Newmarket in 1773, bringing with him three sons, Richard, Eliphalet and Josiah. The old man settled on the farm afterwards owned by John Currier, then sold out to Nat Tucker and pitched upon the hundred acres embraced in the Hayward farm, then known as the first hundred of Israel Kellogg, which extended from the outlet of Hart Pond to the road running from Wells' and south of the old road from the Corner. He lived and died there and lies buried in the Wells cemetery. His sons, Richard and Eliphalet, built houses upon the farms lately owned by Jacob Randlett and Levi Hamlett. Richard died there; but Eliphalet went to Boston. The two Richards were strongly religious, never failing to give earnest testimony of their faith upon all occasions. Josiah at the age of thirteen, went to work on the Gore with his Uncle Caleb. He was set to cutting alder bushes, where black flies and mosquitoes were numerous. He endured their stings until he became disgusted with settler life and then resolved that he would run away back to Newmarket. But he did not, because Capt. Robert Barber, an old neighbor from Newmarket, arrived with his family, including his daughter Pernal, in whom Josiah was much interested. Then came the call for three regiments to fight for independence. Old Richard had become an invalid and could not go, but Josiah, young and strong, nerved up with the patriotism of a boy of sixteen, shouldered his gun and marched until he was discharged, and like a great number of his comrades, with his pockets filled with worthless continental script, was obliged to beg food to bring himself to his father's door. Arrived at home he rested a few days, when a message was sent over the country calling for recruits to join the army under Gates near Saratoga, to arrest the progress of Burgoyne' towards Boston. He started back with Enoch Richardson on foot. They fought with Stark at Bennington and were present at the battle of Saratoga and saw the surrender of Burgoyne. Then he came home and went to work. Once more he seized his gun in 1780, when the cry for help came from burning Rutland, and marched with Thomas Baldwin, Daniel Blaisdell, Thomas Miner, Samuel Meacham and others, twenty-two of them under the command of Capt. Joshua Wells, whom none of them liked, and arrived at Rutland in time to see the village in ashes and the Indians retreating, taking along one prisoner, a citizen, to Canada. This company traveled ninety miles and were out nine days. In 1782 Josiah married Pernal Barber and settled on the Gore near the Lary farm, and had for neighbors Tristram Sanborn and Daniel Lary. Here he settled down to a tranquil domestic life. Five children were born to him: Judith, who died in 1797, and was the first person buried in the Wells cemetery. Captain Wells gave an acre of land for that purpose and buried his own dead there; Betsey, who married John Worth; Robert B., who lived on the farm since occupied by David Kimball; Sally, who married Daniel Blaisdell, Jr., and Josiah. But the earth and trees on the Gore were too stingy for his necessities. After thirteen years' patient labor, he came back to Canaan and lived with his wife's father until he built him a house. He bargained for land with Mr. Barber and built the house where A. W. Hutchinson now lives. While here he with his wife, united with the Baptist Church, and was appointed a deacon. Nathaniel Barber, brother to his wife, lived on the intervale at East Canaan. The brothers often worked together. Several seasons Nat lost his crops from frosts, and he became discouraged. One day, while working together, Nat bantered Josiah to trade farms. They made the exchange and Deacon Josiah's home was on the intervale until his death, June 7, 1851, at the great age of ninety-three years. Pernal, his wife, through all that long sixty-nine years, survived him four years and was then placed to rest beside him at the great age of ninety-one years. Deacon Josiah's son Josiah, was born in 1795. He was a hard-working man all his long life of more than ninety years. His opportunities for education were few and at long distances, both in time and on the road. But few of the young men of his day were more favored than he. He went a few months or weeks in the winter to some pedagogue, who could scarcely read without spelling, and whose chiefest virtue as a teacher was the habitual use of the "ruler," thumb screw, or some other instrument of torture. Very few of the old people taught in the schools of Canaan ever laid claim to more knowledge than sufficient for their daily labors. As a boy and scholar, he lived in the "Centre Deestrick"—(so spelt in the handwriting of "Oliver Smith, T. C."). This district embraced all the territory within a radius of about two miles from the meeting house. The schoolhouse stood near Dudley Gilman's tavern. Most of the children got a whipping every day, either at home or at school, sometimes at both, and these whippings were oftener bestowed in school for not comprehending the large words in the lessons, than for any offensive conduct. Those old masters were muscular and knew more about "larrupin'" the boys and girls than they did of the contents of books.

Mr. Clark obtained his title from being appointed colonel of the Thirty-Seventh Regiment, New Hampshire Militia, which for many years mustered in Arvin's field on the side of the Pinnacle, or on the ridge back of Nat Currier's store. Those were joyous gatherings, at which every one treated himself to rum and sheets of gingerbread; and headaches were not the consequence of this sort of indulgence. In 1830 there was much rivalry inside the parties. The men who managed the politics would not work together. As in many of the years since, there were men who knew that their talents and abilities were deserving of recognition and because of being passed by from year to year, like balky horses, they hung back and refused to pull. In this year Colonel Clark's name was brought up and he was sent to Concord as a representative and also in the year following. But he was too industrious in his habits to sit idly by listening to motions and debates in that hall, when he might be engaged in some useful labor. He sought a shop where he might have the use of tools, and then got permission to absent himself from time to time during those tiresome talks. He did not neglect his duties, but when he came home he brought a wagonload of ox-bows as the fruit of his industry, and he thought and so did his neighbors that his ox-bows were more useful than his laws. For many years he lived a quiet life on the intervale farm. In 1814, at the age of 19, he married Betsey, daughter of Levi Bailey. They had five children, Sally, Dorothy, Jesse, Judith and Joseph. She, dying afterward, in 1827, he married Sally, daughter of Nathaniel Gilman, and two sons, Gilman and Horace, were born to them. And yet again, upon the death of Mrs. Sally, he married Mrs. Sally Hazeltine, who died some years ago.

Caleb Clark came to Canaan with his brother Richard, in 1773. He settled first on the Gore, where he owned five hundred acres of land having purchased the same of Theophilus

Dame on the west side of Clark Pond; he also owned land in the part of Dorchester, known as Martha's Vineyard, and adjoining his Gore land. He also owned land "on the hill northerly of Eames Mill," where he died in October, 1793. His two sons, David and Prescott Clark, resided in the same neighborhood. Prescott lived on the road near Charles Lashua. These two brothers married sisters. Prescott's wife was Mary Basford, and David's, Sarah Basford. Prescott had eight children, and with his wife and family moved to Canada in the spring of 1806. The two brothers resided in Dunham, P. Q., where they died of spotted fever in 1810. On their gravestones is the following: "Prescott Clark, died January 11, 1810, aged 42; David Clark, died January 19, 1810, aged 44."

Clark, Joseph d. November 2, 1853, aged 81; (d); m. November 30, 1794; Abigail Welch, b. 1770; d. November, 1846; (d). Eight ch.: Caleb, b. July 4, 1796; Chase, b. April 11, 1798; Polly, b. February 6, 1800; Sally, b. August 8, 1801; Hannah, b. February 6, 1804; Tilton, b. October 1, 1805; Samuel, b. November 2, 1807; d. October 29, 1872; (d). Esther, b. June 24, 1811.

Clark, Prescott, m. Lydia Bailey had four ch.: Amos, b. October 12, 1812; d. July 27, 1883; (b); m. Frances D. March, b. November 3, 1813; d. August 14, 1854; m. 2d. Sophronia C. Morey, b. November 29, 1811; d. January 3, 1898; (b). Three children: Sarah E., b. September 10, 1844; d. October 8, 1860. John H., b. June 11, 1846; d. July 18, 1887, Company F, Eighteenth New Hampshire Regiment. Jennie S., b. 1857; m. 1889, Russell A. Miller; d. February, 1909. Richard, son of Prescott, b. March 12, 1814; d. 1903. Prescott, Jr., third son of Prescott, b. April 13, 1816; d. September 4, 1893 (b); m. October 11, 1840, Susan Sanborn of Holderness. Ch.: Arthur B., d. June 18, 1850, aged 5 mo. 7d. and Frank P., d. December 13, 1901, aged 53 y., 5 mo., 7d. (b) m. January 23, 1872, Nellie P. Gray. Ch.: Charles R., b. May 2, 1877. Chestina, dau. of Prescott, b. August 21, 1818, m. Colonel Safford of Vermont. Angie L., m. August 31, 1843, William A. Flanders, son of Sylvester. Fred, b. 1857, b. November 27, 1881, Mary F. Jones.

Clark, Richard, m. a Marston. He was born in Greenland, N. H., in 1693. He had four sons, Caleb, David, John and Richard. John never came to Canaan, but the other three did. Caleb bought 300 acres of land of Theophilus Dame October 9, 1773, extending across the Gore and in 1777 he bought 100 acres more adjoining it. Captain Caleb d. in 1793; his wife's name was Mary. His children were David, Prescott, Susanna, who married Nathaniel Bartlett; Lydia, who m. Reynold Gates; Elizabeth, who married Jehu Jones; Mary, who married Josiah Bartlett; Caleb, Joshua, Jacob, Joseph, Anne. Prescott Clark's children were: Polly, b. May 29, 1794; m. William Chambers in Canada. Charlotte, b. May 31, 1796; m. Levi Clement in Canada. David 3d, b. April 15, 1798. John Basford, b. February 10, 1805; d. March 2, 1888. Betsey, b. January 15, 1802. Horatio Nelson, b. March 3, 1804. Leah, b. March, 1806; m. Jeremiah Potter in Canada. Henry Harris, b. April 2, 1809.

Richard, son of Richard, b. 1725; d. 1815; (d); m. Elizabeth Burley and had six children: Lydia, who m. John Scofield, Jr., Anna, Josiah, Richard, Jr., Eliphalet, who m. December 4, 1818, Charlotte Gates, Ebenezer. Colonel Josiah said his "grandsir was buried by the military," and there was a great gathering of people from all around to attend it, and there was a great drunk after it on Canaan Street.

Josiah, son of Richard, b. 1758; d. June 7, 1851; m. 1782, Pernal Barber, this is the way she spelled her name in deeds but it is spelled Purnel in other places, dau. of Robert; d. September 29, 1855, aged 91. They had five ch.: Judith, d. June, 1797, aged 13, the first person buried in Wells cemetery; Betsey, who m. John Worth (see Worth); Robert B.; Sally, who m. Daniel Blaisdell, Jr. (see him), and Josiah.

Robert Barber, b. August 17, 1787; d. January 29, 1857; (b); m. 1st, 1810, Betsey Currier, dau. of Theophilus; d. May 10, 1826, aged 35, they had ten ch. He m. 2d, February 27, 1827, Mrs. Eliza (Hewes) Currier of Lyme; b. December 6, 1794; d. September 28, 1849; had two ch. He

m. 3d, 1852, Mrs. Mary (Flint) Wallace; no ch. By his first wife he had Sophronia, b. November 29, 1811; d. January 3, 1898; Eliza, b. October 10, 1813; d. June 19, 1836, m. October 1, 1834, Leonard Davis, and had a dau. Arvilla (see him); Mary J., b. December 11, 1815; Robert Barber, b. February 26, 1818; d. in Dover, March 2, 1890, m. Elvira G. Stevens, b. in Wentworth, July 4, 1818; d. April 25, 1869. His children were Jemima L., who m. Fred Bane; Wyman R., who m. Mary Buckner; Frank B., b. May 27, 1851; m. November 20, 1877, Lillea M. Davis, b. December 8, 1858; one ch., Alice Benson, b. July 24, 1881. Richard O. and Austin E., Frank B., lives in Dover. Josiah 3d, fifth ch. of Robert B., b. February 26, 1818; d. November 14, 1850; m. Harriet Braley of Grafton. No ch. Eleanor Webster, b. February 12, 1820; d. July 24, 1907; m. August 18, 1847, David Kimball, b. March 14, 1817; d. February 1, 1909, one ch., Ella A., m. October 14, 1875, Daniel G. S. Davis, had one son, Orel K., b. July 3, 1879; m. Mary Martin and lives with his mother on the old Robert Clark farm.

Richard C., son of Robert B., b. May 30, 1822; d. August 9, 1844. Emily Swett, b. March 30, 1824; d. January 15, 1880; m. Hibbard P. Ross, lived in Groton, Mass.; two ch. d. young, Willie and Artemus. Betsey Currier, dau. of Robert, b. May 5, 1826; d. Cambridge, Mass.; m. April 3, 1854, Willard W. Balcom. Theoda Hewes, b. December 11, 1827; m. July 19, 1855, John Sanford Shepard (see him). Pernell Elisa, b. April 29, 1834; m. February 22, 1871; Freeman Wight of Boston, b. October 3, 1834; d. January 13, 1909, was in the fur business for many years in Boston. Two ch.: Freeman Clark, b. June 28, 1872; m. December, 1900, Mattie Eva Spafford; no ch. Robert Franklin, b. September 2, 1881; m. April 13, 1903, Blanche L. McIntire; had one ch. d. young.

Josiah, son of Josiah, b. January 9, 1795; d. July 3, 1892; (b); m. 1st, December 28, 1814, Betsey Bailey, dau. of Levi, b. November 8, 1793; d. April 16, 1825; three children. He m. 2d, September 19, 1827, Sally Gilman, dau. of

Nathaniel; d. March 16, 1843, aged 47; had two children. He m. 3d, Mrs. Sally Hazeltine, widow of William of Groton, d. December 31, 1838, aged 44. His ch.: Sally, d. March 3, 1824, aged 3. Dorothy, m. Roswell Elliott; 2 ch.: Belle and Carrie who m. Wallace G. Goss; Jesse, d. July 6, 1887, aged 71 y., 4 mo.; he m. Sarah M. Elliott, dau. of Asa and Betsey Elliott; d. June 20, 1852, aged 24 y., 9 mo.; Judith, m. a Woodard and Joseph, d. single; Gilman and Horace were the other sons by Sally Gilman.

Richard, Jr., son of Richard, b. October 28, 1761; m. September 16, 1788, Esther Jones, dau. of James and Sarah (Paddleford) Jones, b. December 9, 1768. They had four ch.: Jehiel, b. November 3, 1790; Lucy, b. July 23, 1792; Ebenezer, b. April 7, 1795; m. April 19, 1832, Rhoda Blaisdell, dau. of Daniel. His first wife, Nancy A., d. December 8, 1822, aged 22; (a); by whom he had one ch., Andrew J., d. February 23, 1823, aged 6 m; (a). His second wife, Ruth, d. September 21, 1831; (a); by whom he had two ch. Lucius G., d. September 11, 1827, aged 10 y. and Richard, d. November 21, 1830, aged 4 m.; (a); Richard, fourth ch. of Richard, Jr., b. December 9, 1798.

Clark, Anna, d. January 31, 1832, aged 12; (d); must have been of the last family, also Mary Ann, dau. of Richard and Abigail Clark, who m. April 2, 1838, John Rockwell and d. October 21, 1851, aged 41. (d).

The Genealogy of John Currier.

I. Richard Currier was born in England in 1617 and was one of the original settlers of Salisbury, Mass. He had two children, perhaps more, Hannah and Thomas. Richard died in 1687.

II. Deacon Thomas, b. Amesbury, March 8, 1646, m. December 3, 1668, Mary, dau. of William Osgood; he died 1687; she died 1712. Their children, born in Amesbury, were:

1. Hannah
2. Thomas
3. Richard
4. Samuel
5. William
6. John

Old Families.

7. Joseph
8. Benjamin
9. Ebenezer
10. Daniel
11. Mary
12. Ann

III. Joseph, b. 1674, m. December 9, 1708, Sarah Brown. Their children, born in Amesbury, were:

1. Nathan
2. Joseph
3. Ephraim
4. Abner
5. Sarah
6. Hannah
7. Ann
8. Mary
9. Miriam.

IV. Nathan, b. November 6, 1710; m. April 14, 1736, Mehitable Silver. Children born in Amesbury.
1. John, b. December 12, 1733; d. July 17, 1736.
2. Seth, b. March 10, 1735.
3. John (of Hopkinton), b. May 1, 1737.
4. Sarah, b. December 9, 1738.
5. Anna, b. January 8, 1740; d. 1781, in Hampstead; m. Peter Morse of Warner, father of James Morse, b. 1739; d. 1787, (see him).
6. Daniel, b. December 13, 1748.
7. Hannah, b. August 5, 1750; m. Zebulon Davis.
8. Nathan, b. July 27, 1756.

V. Deacon John, moved to Hopkinton, N. H., 1766; m. in Amesbury, Sarah Clark; he died December 23, 1804. Ten children:
1. John (of Canaan), b. January 6, 1762; d. May 10, 1826.
2. Clark (of Canaan), b. June 2, 1763; d. July 6, 1813.
3. Seth, b. December 8, 1764; d. Canaan, Me., January 1, 1842; Dartmouth College, 1796.
4. Anna, b. August 24, 1766; d. February 12, 1816.
5. Amos, b. August 25, 1768; d. November 29, 1846, grandfather of John F. Jones of Hopkinton.
6. Sarah, b. August 16, 1770; d. July 26, 1834.
7. Hannah, b. July 8, 1772; d. January 20, 1793.
8. Stephen, b. January 11, 1774. d. ———.
9. Persilla, b. Aug. 16, 1776; d. December 7, 1854.
10. James, b. January 20, 1778; d. April 19, 1813.

VI. "September 21, 1783. Then John Currier and Lois Morse were married in Hopkinton." Lois Morse was a cousin to John, dau. of Peter and Anna (Currier) Morse. She was brought up in the family of Deacon John of Hopkinton. She died October 17, 1816, aged 55 yrs. 10 mos. He m. 2d, March 5, 1822, Mrs. Abi Plummer Richardson, widow of Eliphalet Richardson, who survived him until January 3, 1851, aged 83 yrs.

Dea. John Currier of Hopkinton was a large owner of Canaan lands purchased at low prices from the original grantees, who had ceased to have a taste for forest speculations. It does not appear that he ever visited Canaan to examine his real estate. About the year 1781 he sent his two boys, John and Clark, to look after his interests, with instructions if they found the place agreeable, to "pitch" upon some of the lands and improve them as settlers. The young men were well pleased with their prospects. John built a log house on West Farms on the 100 acres his father had bought of John P. Calkins, cleared up an acre or two, and returned to Hopkinton for his cousin as a wife, and it seems he did not go any too soon. They had six daughters and one son born to them.

1. Anna, b. June 30, 1784.
2. Sarah, b. December 26, 1785.
3. Hannah, b. August 27, 1789.
4. James, b. November 2, 1791.
5. Lois, b. May 30, 1795.
6. Permelia, b. January 8, 1798.
7. Clarissa, b. October 10, 1799.

All his children were born on West Farms, for it was not until August 25, 1804, that he bargained farms with Jacob Tucker and went to live on the hill on the farm still in the possession of his descendants. Jacob Tucker afterwards sold his farm to Abraham Longfellow. Esquire John was one of the most prominent men in Canaan during the forty-five years of his life here. He was very influential, not only in the Proprietary, in the division and lotting of land, but in the affairs of the town, was a lieutenant and captain in 1793 and 1794 in the Fourth Com-

John Currier Homestead

OLD FAMILIES. 527

pany of the Twenty-Fourth Regiment. He was clerk of the proprietors from 1808 to 1821, one of the "Lot laying Committee" from 1805 to his death, and many of the lots were surveyed by him. He made a survey of the town in 1805 traversing all the boundary lines. He was sent to the General Court in 1810, 1811 and 1817. He was selectman in 1800 to 1803, 1805, 1807, to 1812, 1816 to 1817, 1819 and in 1823, fifteen years.

1. Anna, m. John Stanley of Hopkinton, March 3, 1802, and had eight children; she d. March 9, 1858.
   1. Julia, b. December 10, 1804.
   2. Lois, b. December 21, 1806.
   3. John Currier, b. Lyman, N. H., December 13, 1809.
   4. Henry, b. June 26, 1813.
   5. Lyman, b. September 13, 1814.
   6. James, b. April 14, 1819.
   7. Nancy, b. April 4, 1823.
   8. Lavina, b. November 13, 1826.
   Julia Stanley, m. John Smith, January 16, 1834, and d. June 18, 1835, leaving no children.
   Lois, m. April, 1832, George Hazeltine, and d. March 7, 1861; a daughter of Julia, d. September 27, 1850, aged 17 yrs. There were two other daughters, Ellen S. and P. Jennie and a son, George Henry.
   John Currier, m. June 21, 1843, Jane Beattie of Ryegate, Vt. Their children were:
      1. William J. B., b. April 13, 1844.
      2. Margaret Ann, b. September 3, 1845.
      3. Catherine Jane, b. September 23, 1846.
      4. Robert James, b. March 28, 1848.
      5. Harriet E., b. June 9, 1849.
      6. Hannah G., b. May 11, 1853; d. November 24, 1875.
   Henry Stanley, m. Feb. 5, 1846; Chloe Bartlett of Waterford, Vt. Three children:
      1. Ellen Francis, b. January 25, 1848.
      2. Martha Marian, b. April 22, 1851.
      3. Carrie Louise, b. November 28, 1856.
   Lyman Stanley, m. November 26, 1842, Laura A. Way of Barnet, Vt. Their children were:

1. L. Edgar, b. January 26, 1848.
2. P. Jennie, b. March 25, 1850.
3. Charles A., b. April 13, 1853.
4. Alfred, b. January 2, 1857.
5. Herbert A., b. March 9, 1862.

James Stanley, m. October 28, 1857, Julia F. Byron of Maidstone, Vt. Their children were:
1. Frederic James, b. August 29, 1858; d. August 1867.
2. Julia Emma, b. September 14, 1860; d. in August 1867.
3. Stella J., b. June 16, 1869.
4. Susie L., b. December 6, 1873.

Nancy Stanley, m. 1st, December 11, 1845, W. S. Hinman, no children; m. 2d, March 26, 1854, Lester S. Richards. She d. West Concord, Vt., May 13, 1872. Children were:
1. Oliver S., b. January 31, 1855.
2. William John, b. January 7, 1860; d. January 26, 1864.
3. George Sherman, b. July 31, 1866; d. April 20, 1868.

Lavina Stanley, m. 1st, January 27, 1848, William G. Paddleford; no children; m. 2d, October 28, 1857, Spofford A. Way. Her children were:
1. William J., b. December 1851.
2. Frank A., b. December 27, 1858.
3. Allen, b. July 21, 1860.
4. Anna, b. January 13, 1864.

2. Sarah, dau. of John (of Canaan), m. 1809, George Flint of Canaan; she d. at Cleveland, O., February 15, 1841; he d. Cleveland, O., October 20, 1869. Two children:

1. John Currier, b. November 10, 1810; m. 1833, Emma Storrs of Lebanon; b. April 14, 1814. He was killed by a falling tree while chopping alone in the forest, June 22, 1838 (a). Three children.
　1. Edwin, b. May 15, 1834; m. October 10, 1862, Sarah Buck of Cleveland, O., b. June 6, 1838; now living in Canaan. No children, but adopted a son, George, now dead.
　2. Horace C., b. December 29, 1836; m. March 13, 1861,

OLD FAMILIES.   529

Agnes Nichols; one child, Emma, living in Avon, Loraine Co., O.
 3. Oscar Wade, b. September 14, 1838; d. September 1862, single. Was adopted by a brother of Senator Ben. Wade of Ohio, and died while studying law in his office.
 2. Louisa, b. August 15, 1815; d. in Old Ladies' Home, Manchester, September 13, 1903; single.
3. Hannah C., m. November 3, 1810, Daniel Hoyt, b. July 7, 1787. She d. August 4, 1863. He was drowned in Goose Pond in 1813, July 29, while poling logs. Their ch.:
 1. Lois Maria, b. January 14, 1812; d. December 23, 1879; m. September 5, 1837, Levi French of Enfield, b. November 13, 1812; d. February 27, 1871. Their children were:
  1. George Hoyt, b. January 15, 1839; m. November 14, 1866, Luella Clement of Underhill, Vt. Their children:
   1. Guy Clement, b. June 10, 1869.
   2. Helen May, b. May 23, 1871.
  2. Darwin Gallatin, b. May 14, 1845; m. 1st, June 5, 1866, Hattie P. Wright; she d. May 27, 1868; one child, Hattie W., b. March 20, 1868. He m. 2d, Emma L. Mead November 2, 1869; one child, Emma Lillian, b. May 20, 1875.
  3. Lois Maria, b. September 6, 1851; d. December 23, 1869.
 2. George F., b. March 13, 1813; d. August 22, 1815 (a).
 Hannah C., m. 2d, David Goodhue of Underhill, Vt., one ch.
VII. 4. James, m. January 4, 1837, Louisa Wier, dau. of William and Nancy (Morse) Wier of Grafton, Vt.; b. January 4, 1802; d. July 25, 1884. He d. Canaan May 22, 1846. Three children. She m. 2d, May, 1847, Isaac W. Perkins of Lyme. He d. September 22, 1855; no. ch.
 1. A son died in infancy, b. December 12, 1837.
 2. Mary Duncan, b. November 20, 1838; m. January 8, 1865, William Allen Wallace, son of James and Mary (Flint) Wallace of Canaan, b. September 28, 1815. He d. Feb-

ruary 15, 1893. She d. December 25, 1898. One son.
James Burns, b. August 14, 1866, m. December 21, 1889,
Alice Hutchinson, dau. of Lucius B. and Alice Maria
(Rollins) Hutchinson; b. June 22, 1867. No children.
3. John, b. January 8, 1841; d. October 5, 1909; m. January
27, 1896, Mrs. Mary Puffer. No children.

John Currier passed all his days upon the farm which his father and grandfather had tilled before him and where they had lived and died. Three generations followed in each other's footsteps. Born in the old house his grandfather built, he was but five years old when his father died, leaving a large farm, for his mother and sister, then eight years old, to carry on. The burden was almost too much for his mother, who married the next year. Her second husband died when John was fourteen years old and from that time on, he had to assume the duties of the head of the household. His mother was strong willed and very set in her purposes and this characteristic was early instilled into and imbibed by him. His mother would never have any assistance in her household, and up to the last year of her life, insisted upon doing her own work. Her son was obliged to do the same, so far as he was able in his earlier years and as he grew older, the old lady was persistent in her efforts to hire as little help as possible. His early years were a ceaseless round of hard toil, with few pleasures. His mother's tastes were simple, and she insisted upon there being no extravagance. Everything was saved, it might be useful sometime. This trait followed him through his whole life. While she lived he was constant in his duty to her and her slightest wish was always granted. He was educated in the district schools of the town and Canaan Union Academy, attending at times when the farm work was not important. His sister would often go away to visit relatives, but he never went. He never would go away from home to stay over night without protest, and then to return as soon as possible. He first became interested in town affairs in 1877, when he was chosen selectman, again in 1878 and 1879. The politics of the town changed and he was not again in office until 1881, when he was chosen overseer of the poor and held the office the following year. He was on the board of select-

men in 1886, also in 1892, and in 1894 he began the longest term of continuous service of any one in the history of the town, being chairman of the board all the time, a period of fifteen years, making in all twenty years as selectman. He was the most prominent man in town affairs for the last ten years and his knowledge of them was not surpassed by any one. He was familiar with the ownership and location of every piece of land in town. His memory of events and persons was phenomenal and often served him to good purpose in town affairs. Great confidence was placed in his judgment. He made many wills and in consequence was called upon to administer many estates. He was trustee and treasurer of the Methodist Church on the Street for many years. The Currier family were Congregationalists, and his sympathies were with the old church at the upper end of the Street. Although not a church member, he was almost a constant attendent upon the Methodist service. Until within the last two years of his life, he was a man of great endurance, strong and powerful. He never smoked but once, and that made him so sick he never tried it again. His was an active life and he rarely stopped to think of himself. The last two years he contended with a disease which at times was very painful, but the end was peaceful. He was not of a nervous disposition and was never known to lose his temper, never seemed to be irritated in his dealings with men, and however much they might be angered, there was always a smile upon his lips. I, his nephew, can pay no better tribute to him, than to say he was my "Uncle," in all ways, "Uncle John," and such he gradually became to every one.

   5. Lois, m. January 26, 1818, Uriah Welch of Canaan, son of Samuel Welch, b. July 5, 1793; she d. January 24, 1821 (1831 on tombstone); he died August, 1839. He m. 2d. January, 1821, Sarah French. Removed to Concord, August 13, 1839, and while at work on the Free bridge over the Merrimac River fell in and was drowned. Their children were:

     1. George Porter, b. December 29, 1820; was a printer in Boston.

2. John Currier, b. October 18, 1826; d. January 18, 1827.
3. Unnamed infant.
6. Permelia, m. December 4, 1823, Samuel C. Sawyer of Enfield; she d. February 23, 1856, in the Insane Asylum at Taunton, Mass. They had six children: Anne, Olivia, Augusta, Mary, Burns, John.
7. Clarissa, m. November 13, 1828, Ezra Gilman of Canaan, both d. in Manchester; he, April 26, 1855; she July 21, 1869. Their children were:
   1. James Currier, b. January 31, 1831; d. 1909; m. Nancy Smiley of Bedford in 1868; d. 1908 in Manchester; no children.
   2. Daniel Hoyt, b. December 8, 1836; m. 1860, Mary Bennett of Indian Orchard, Mass.; one son, Elmer A. Daniel was killed by falling bricks in the Hazeltine house, Manchester.

VI. 2. Clark, younger brother of Esquire John, came to Canaan from Hopkinton, 1872. He settled on the hundred acres his father purchased of George Harris and now occupied by Edgar Ricard. He m. in Canaan, 1787, Margaret Norris whose father, Eliphalet, was a clothier at the Corner. They had four children. Mrs. Currier died about the year 1825. She was insane for many years previous, shut up in a pen and treated harshly by her family.

1. John, b. February 25, 1789, m. about 1812, Eliza Hewes of Lyme, by whom he had one daughter, Sarepta, m. to E. J. Morrill of Franklin. John lived with his wife some years and then disappeared from this part of the world. Several years afterwards he was recognized by a neighbor in Troy, N. Y. He denied his name and refused to give reasons for his strange conduct.
2. Margaret, b. August 22, 1791; m. August 25, 1816, David Norris of Cornith, Vt. Several children; she d. 1869. One, Clark C., d. November 2, 1817, aged 17d, is buried on Sawyer Hill.
3. Sally, b. April 18, 1796; m. December 25, 1816, Nathan Cass of Canaan, moved to Concord, Mass., had several children and d. February 23, 1880.

4. Infant dau. d. August 1800, aged 5d.; first person buried in Sawyer Hill Cemetery.
5. Hannah, b. 1807; m. 1828, —— Smith of Corinth, Vt. Several children.

VI. 4. Anna, sister of John and Clark, m. Moses Flanders of Hopkinton, lived and died on a great farm in Enfield. She d. February 12, 1816. Their children were:
1. Sally, m. Samuel Day.
2. Hannah, m. David Day.
3. Moses, d. unm.
4. Timothy, d. while attending Dartmouth College.
5. Mary, m. Daniel Smith, left two daughters:
   1. Anne, m. Levi F. Webster of Canaan, one son; Herbert L., b. May 31, 1866; m. December 31, 1891, Ida Belle Sargent, b. 1866.
   2. Mary F., b. June, 1841.

The Doles.

In the cemetery on the Street is a group of graves of the Dole family. It is many years since any additions were made to that group. The head of the family was Capt. Moses Dole, who came to Canaan in 1801, from Cheshire County, having recently married, March 1, 1801, Miss Lucy Poor of Charlestown. He bought the tavern and farm of Dudley Gilman and hung out a sign on which was painted, "Mr. Dole's Inn, 1802." That old tavern occupied the site of the present Hotel Lucerne. The sign swung there more than a quarter of a century, inviting travelers to partake of his hospitality. He was a courteous gentleman, and Mrs. Dole was distinguished for her refinement and intelligence. Socially and politically, they exercised a large influence. The captain was held in high esteem and was elected to various offices of trust, the duties of which he discharged with fidelity. He was chosen representative to the general court in 1808, 1809, 1818, 1819, 1820; selectman in 1804; town clerk from 1801 to 1806 inclusive, and from 1808 to 1817 inclusive, sixteen years longer than any other, with the exception of George H. Gordon. He was a member of Mt. Moriah Lodge; was born September 17, 1777, and on the 2d of June, 1828, was buried with Masonic honors. Mrs. Dole, born January 16, 1774, had died October 6, 1826, with an epidemic which raged fatally among young and old during that season. They had two children, Joseph and Mary. Joseph, born October 31, 1801, died May 16, 1817; Mary was born October 28, 1803, married first, August 15, 1823, Dr. Charles Plastridge, brother of Doctor Caleb of East Lebanon; he died October 16, 1826, aged 29. She remained here until 1829, and is the Mrs. Plastridge referred to by Mr. Foster. She married second in 1828, Hon. Joseph Sawyer, and became a resident of Piermont. Five daughters and one son were born to them.

Mr. Sawyer died in 1858, and being left nearly destitute, she took up her abode with her daughter in Cambridge, Mass. At the time of her death, February 1, 1885, she was on a visit to her daughter, Mrs. Kimball in Pontiac, Mich. She was strongly religious, having inherited her convictions, and was a member of the Congregational Church from the year 1816.

The Martins, Robert.

Robert Martin came to Canaan in 1819 from Pembroke. He was a distinguished soldier of the Revolution, serving faithfully in the campaigns in Rhode Island; in the disastrous attack upon Mount Independence, was present at the surrender of Burgoyne, and for a time was stationed at Newcastle. His son William and grandson Henry, came with him, the latter a boy of ten. They bought the great intervale farm, which had been cleared by Joseph Flint, who sold it to Seth Daniels. Mr. Flint came here from Hopkinton. He had previously been a merchant in Newburyport, Mass. He died in 1809 and was buried in the Street cemetery and was the father of nineteen children, all of whom grew up. The last one to die was Mrs. William Atherton, January 23, 1873, aged 79 years. Mr. Daniels gladly availed himself of the offer of the Martins, to purchase the farm and in 1819, being seized with the western fever by having received glowing accounts of the fertility of the soil in western New York, he started out with his family to seek a new home. Robert Martin died in 1839 and was buried on Canaan Street. William Martin was a farmer and blacksmith. In 1845 he sold

Old Wallace House, Town House and Hotel on Broad Street, 1880

his farm to Harrison Pillsbury and bought the house built by Gordon Burley, in which he died, aged 83 years. He was a good man, greatly respected for the sincerity of his convictions, a lifelong Democrat, faithfully supporting all the decrees of his party. A Methodist without stain, undeviating until his preachers began to pray for the abolition of slavery. He looked upon this as a crime against his southern brethren and it greatly grieved him. But he was a sincere and worthy man; friendly and generous according to his means. He became a member of Mt. Moriah Lodge in 1824, and was buried by Social Lodge of Enfield. He was a selectman of the town in 1826, 1827, 1831 and 1835. Henry Martin, the grandson, was a life-long Democrat like his father, and only once was ever known to fail to respond during the Greeley campaign, when he stayed at home. He was a blacksmith and his shop, since taken down, stood north of Mrs. Levi George's. He married first Persis Marston, granddaughter of that Richard Whittier who first cleared the farm on the east side of Hart Pond. He married second Lucy Burleigh. He was a schoolmate of the writer, in the old yellow schoolhouse on the common, under the severe, but chaste discipline of that lovely old maiden, Olive Cross. We traveled through long lives by different routes, but these all finally meet and end at the same place.

Martin, William, son of Robert d. July 20, 1866, aged 82 y. 9 mo.; (a); his wife, Mary Stannell, d. January 19, 1869, aged 82 y. 10 m.; (a); his son, Henry, d. December 24, 1894, aged 81 y. 1 mo. 10 d.; first wife, Persis W. Marston, b. 1808; d. 1865; m. 2d, February 15, 1866, Lucy J. Burley, dau. of Benjamin of Dorchester; by her he had Helen A., b. July 1, 1867; m. June 28, 1893, William A. King; one son, Ronald; Mary m. Ernest A. Barney, son of Albert E., and George H. m. Clara Jewel, one ch.; Jane, Abigail, dau. of William, b. January 26, 1818; d. March 27, 1901; m. 1st Horace Chase (see him); m. 2d, Hiram Barber.

The Wallace Family.

The family of Wallaces in Canaan were descended from the Scotch-Irish Wallaces who emigrated from Argyleshire, Scotland, about 1650, to Coleraine in the north of Ireland, where Joseph Wallace lived until he emigrated to America in 1726, with his wife Margaret whom he had married about 1718, and one son William, then about six years old. With Joseph came a sister Jean, and a brother John. Joseph lived in Londonderry, N. H., until his death in 1755; his wife died the next year; his son William moved to Milford, N. H., in 1756 with his wife, Mary Burns, and oldest son, Joseph; there were other children besides William, two or three daughters, but he was the only son.

William was born in Coleraine, Ireland, in 1720 and died in Milford May 24, 1793. His wife, Mary, was the daughter of John Burns who had emigrated from the north of Ireland in 1736 and was of Scotch-Irish descent. They were married in 1752. She was born in 1730 and died in Milford, May 24, 1815. They had five children:

Joseph, b. September 9, 1753; d. December 29, 1838; m. November, 1779, Letitia Burns, and had eight children.

John, b. March 20, 1756; d. July 23, 1835; m. September 12, 1780, Mary Bradford, and had ten children.

Mary, b. August 17, 1759; d. May 14, 1786; m. Israel Burnham, and had one child. William, b. April 5, 1764; d. October 10, 1790, single.

James, b. in Milford, October 17, 1766; d. in Milford July 23, 1828; m. 1st, September 19, 1786, Betsey Holton Kimball of Amherst, daughter of Maj. Eben Kimball, b. December 5, 1766; d. in Milford, October 13, 1807; m. 2d, February 22, 1817, Sophia Tuttle of Littleton, Mass. He was a merchant in Milford and also a manufacturer of pots and pearl ashes. He had nine children by his first wife, the oldest, James, was b. in Milford August 24, 1787, d. in Canaan August 7, 1831, through the fatal carelessness of the physician; m. June 21, 1811, Mary Flint of Middletown, Mass., daughter of Lieutenant John and Betsey (Fuller) Flint; she was b. January 5, 1791, and died in Canaan October 1, 1866. She m. 2d, 1852, Robert Barber Clark, b. August 16, 1787; died January 29, 1857.

James Wallace attended Phillips Andover Academy from November 2, 1802, to December, 1803; moved to Salem, N. H., after his marriage and lived there two years; he then moved to Pembroke, where he lived four years, engaged in business as a merchant. In October, 1817, he moved to Canaan with his wife and three children, having traded with Gen. Asa Robinson of Pembroke for the old house Ezekiel Wells built. He represented Canaan in the Legislature in 1827 and 1828, was a selectman in 1824, 1825, 1826, 1829, 1830, and postmaster from 1822 to 1827. In Canaan he manufactured pots and pearl ashes and was also a merchant. His store was located south of the old house. He had eight children.

John Flint, b. in Greenfield April 7, 1812; d. at sea of yellow fever in August, 1853, and was probably buried at sea, as nothing was ever heard of him after he left San Francisco for New Orleans.

He left home at the age of nineteen to go to sea, and was gone four years; was forty-three months on the water crossing the Pacific four times; visited Canton, Boston, to the Azores, Cape de Verd, St. Helena, Ascension, along the coast of South America to Queen Charlotte Inlet, Sandwich, Society and New Zealand Islands. He remained at home but a short time and never returned here. He then shipped upon a whaler from New Bedford and did not return to the United States, except to start again, until 1841. Nothing was heard of him again until March 16, 1852. His brother's diary of that date, written in a mining camp in California says: "John arrived at the Bar. Stayed until Sunday. Twenty-one years he has been a wanderer by land and sea. Present address Sandwich Islands." On the 4th of the next month my father went to Barnes & Ray's ranch near Stockton, Cal., and stayed over night with him. He was then employed there by the month. He stayed again with him on the 21st, and saw him again on the 20th of May, when he had decided to go to San José. On the 8th of July he went to see him again and found he had gone to the Sandwich Islands. There was no trace of him after this for a year, when my father learned of his being in Los Angeles. He tried to find him only to learn that he had gone to San Francisco; he followed there to learn he had shipped for New Orleans and was sick; he followed to New Orleans to await the arrival of the vessel. Upon its arrival the captain upon being questioned, would not give any information. The inference was that he had died and it being known that he had quite a considerable sum of money and valuables with him, they were stolen and his death concealed. He never married.

James Burns, b. in Salem, October 25, 1813; d. in Canaan, October 4, 1853; m. January 10, 1851, Susan Owen Chandler of West Randolph, Vt., b. October 15, 1822; d. in Thomasville, Ga., in 1904. She m. June 20, 1860, Dr. Thomas R. Reid of Thomasville, Ga. He was a persistent letter-writer and correspondent; nearly all his life he kept a diary.

His early years cannot better be described than in his own words, at the time he was twenty-one. "Oct. 25, 1834. I am no longer a minor. I have attained the age of 21, and no bones broken. Was it fashionable now as formerly, or rather was this cold water reform, anything like 'Jackson and Reform' or Past office reform. I should not hesitate to crack a bottle of old cognac. But I prefer to be a reformist, an abolitionist, a pure Radical. During the long period of my minority, there are but few incidents within my recollection of any importance before 1826. I was like all other boys full of mischief, and perhaps that disposition is still a trait in my character. I was sent to an Academy in Thetford, Vt., in the spring of 1826. The time passed away as it usually does at such places, cheerfully. At the expiration of the term, I of course went home, from thence I was sent to Plainfield Academy, where I spent another three months. In the Fall of 1826, my uncle, who then resided in Milford, N. H., requested of my father that I should live with him. I forthwith 'packed up.' For three long years, I remained with him acting in the complicated capacity of foot-boy, *valet de chambre*, ostler, informer, cow-boy. In fact I was both Squire and Knight, visiting home but once during my sojourn with my uncle. In 1829, in the Fall, I think in the month of September, my uncle deceased, consequently my official capacity was at an end. And bidding farewell to a land that had become endeared to me by many recollections, I again set sail for the land of Canaan.

1, 2, 3. Mary (Currier) Wallace. 4. Louisa (Wier) Currier 5. Mary (Flint) Wallace.
6. James Burns Wallace.

1830 again found me rambling over the fields of Canaan. During this year I was alternately in my father's store, and at school. Three years absence had made many alterations in the town. Some of the old inhabitants had moved away and others had appeared to fill their places. So I was obliged to regret their loss and form new acquaintances. 1831, Aug. I buried my father, from that period to the present a new era has been opened to my views. My younger brother had previously engaged as a printer in the office of the *Post* at Haverhill, N. H. Immediately after my father's decease I went to Concord, and engaged as a clerk in a store of Asaph Evans, in which capacity I acted for the space of three months. It was in Hills building I was situated. I paid a visit to the printing office. The employment I thought would suit me. I had previously heard the rumbling of the presses and conversed with several of the printers. I became afflicted with the printing mania, and thenceforth resolved to be a printer, made application to Mr. Hill, who without much '*talk*' agreed to employ me, *provided*. Accordingly in November, 1831, I entered the office of Hill & Barton, the publishers of the N. H. P. & S. G., as a — not a devil, but a printer, which employment perfectly coincided with my disposition and feelings. From my youth I had been very fond of reading. In my situation I could gratify that propensity. And it was not the least of my enjoyment, after the round of labor had passed off, to sit me down, one, two, three, sometimes a dozen hours, to spend in perusing such books as I could obtain from the extensive collection of Mr. Hill. Adapting the manner of David Hume, 'that as a man can not write long of himself without egotism,' I will hasten this sketch to a close. I was never destined to the command of a regiment of Hussars, or to pick type forever. In the Fall of 1832, whether it proceeded from my sedentary ambition, or from my sedentary habits, or from some other cause more immediate, or remote, I am unable to determine, I sickened of fever and fled the office, attributing meanwhile my sickness to the confined life I led. From the kind attention of my physician, and the kinder attention of my mother, I in a short time recovered, returned to the office, and after bidding farewell to the knights of the stick and type, took a retrograde movement again to the land of Canaan. Immediately after my return I contracted a bargain with Gordon Burley, to enter as clerk in his store, a man who has subsequently rendered himself so infamous in the annals of Canaan. Three months I tarried with him and left him in perfect disgust. This was in the winter of 1832 & 3. April 1, 1833, entered the store of Nathl Currier, where I remained eleven months. During this year 1833, the attention of the north was roused to the investigation of the system of slavery as carried on within the limits of U. S. A. Not since my recollection has a national subject received the attention which this has. In March, 1834, I left Canaan for Middlebury, Vt. I entered a store in that place acting as clerk. From some cause which is not immediately connected with my tale, after remaining there two months I departed for the land of Canaan. One would think from the many times that I had landed at C., I was so intensely attached to it, as to leave all else to a general wreck before I would abandon it. But it is far otherwise. On the other hand, I find it to be a convenient starting point. It is as of as much importance in my terrestrial voyages as the Pole star."

In the winter of 1834 to 35 he taught school in Canaan "in old Hadley's Sleepy Hollow," and attended dancing school. Abraham Pushee, who was a renowned dancing master and fiddler, opened a dancing school with an attendance of eighty. On January 27, 1835, he went to work as a clerk for Whittier & Balch in their store. On the 27th of March, Whittier sold out to Balch and he remained with the "Jr Partner." He remained with Balch until October. Nathaniel Currier had proposed to him to go to Louisiana with Hubbard Harris on a trading trip, with ready-made clothing, socks, etc. He was to carry $8,000 to $10,000 worth of goods. He left Boston on October 30 and reached New Orleans on November 19. He was sick thirteen days on the voyage. On the 6th of December he reached Natchitoches by boat up the Mississippi. He made a trip of fourteen days to Washington, Ark., on horseback, and after his return went to David Pratt's store in the Parish of Claiborne, traveling sixty-five miles through the wilderness to find only two buildings,—Pratt's store and a house of entertainment kept by one Drew, a superannuated planter. The first man whom he met was Doctor Nelson, who had left Canaan the March before. David Pratt was Mrs. Nathaniel Currier's oldest brother. His daughter, Elizabeth Pratt, was with him. From Pratt's store he set out for Spring Hill, Ark., and traveled three days to find three buildings in the pine woods. "We crossed creeks and bayous, plunged through cane brakes and mud so deep that we could not travel faster than a walk. The inhabitants are scattered here and there, so remote from each other and society, that their mode of life is little calculated to please a Yankee. The food is principally corn bread (chicken dough) and fried pork fried in soap grease. I was fourteen days on the road, traveled about 400 miles. Five merchants shipped their goods back north. There was an influx of merchandise. Harris is with me." This was Hubbard Harris, brother of George. He returned to New Orleans and on January 9 started by boat up the Mississippi to Columbus, Ohio; from there he staged across to Philadelphia, arriving on the 31st of January, 1836. "Feb. 2. I made arrangements today to leave for New York on the Camden & Amboy R. R., but owing to the extreme cold the cars did not arrive from N. Y. I am obliged to go in an open sleigh, 4 P. M. and will arrive in N. Y. tomorrow morn." On February 12 he reached Canaan. In March he went back into Balch's store. This store stood just above Mrs. Caleb Blodgett's house and is the shed of Mr. Shrigley's building. It was built by James Wallace and during his lifetime was used by him as a store at the lower end of the Street. After his death it was sold to Whittier & Balch. In the latter part of March Balch sold to Hiram Smart. In July, 1837, Smart sold out to him and he began business for himself, but it was not profitable and being unable to obtain a lease of the building, he traded back to Smart in October and the store was closed. On January 1, 1838, he formed a partnership with Nathaniel Currier, under the name of Currier & Wallace. Later he formed a partnership with Horace S. Currier at the Street and at the time of his death, they were in business at the depot.

He represented the town in 1852 and was town clerk from 1846–51. No children.

3. William Allen, b. in Pembroke, September 28, 1815; d. in Canaan February 15, 1893; m. January 8, 1865, by Rev. Reuben Dearborn in Canaan, Mary Duncan Currier, dau. of James and Louisa (Wier) Currier, of Canaan; b. November 20, 1838; d. in Canaan December 25, 1898; one child:

James Burns, b. in Canaan August 14, 1866; m. December 21, 1889, Alice Hutchinson, dau. of Lucius B. and Alice M. (Rollins) Hutchinson; b. June 22, 1867; no. ch.

4. Oscar Flint, b. in Canaan March 14, 1818; d. there May 27, 1842; single.

5. Amelia Melvina, b. in Canaan December 14, 1820; d. in San Francisco, Cal., March 20, 1868; m. Daniel G. Cummings; b. March 5, 1812. She was his second wife; one ch. He went to California in the latter part of 1854, and she followed in April, 1855, with her daughter.

Clara Amelia, b. May 14, 1846; d. Yokohama, Japan, November 19, 1900; m. April, 1868, in San Francisco, Cal., George E. Rice, who died in Nagasaki, Japan, December 17, 1901. She was employed in the English School of the Japanese government until it was abolished. He was eleven years in the employ of the United States government at Yokohama, Japan; three years as marshal and eight years as vice-consul general. They resided in Yokohama, Japan. Three children:

Mabel Amelia, b. at Hakadate, Japan, December 23, 1868; m. Henry W. Fraser; d. July 27, 1909, in New York City. Was with the Hong Kong, Shanghai Bank in Hong Kong and in New York City. No. ch.

Lillian Amelia, b. Hakadate, Japan, December 23, 1868; m. December 12, 1888, Frank Gillett of Walthamstow, England; b. January 14, 1854; d. December 9, 1900. During his life they resided in Yokohama, and upon his death she went to his home in England and has resided there since; one ch.

Evelyn Frances, b. October 12, 1889.

Clara Edwina, b. September 21, 1871; m. November 30, 1892, William Wallace Campbell of Quebec; b. in Quebec, August 22, 1860; reside in Kobe, Japan; he is agent

James B Wallace

of the Pacific Mail Steamship Company, White Star and Oriental Steamship Companies. Two ch.:

Dorothy, b. May 18, 1895.

Archibald Kenneth, b. October 2, 1896.

6. Sophia Jane, b. May 13, 1823; d. in Canaan, July 5, 1842; single.
7. Rodney Holton, b. February 22, 1826; d. April 6, 1826.
8. Harriet Olivia, b. January 22, 1830; d. in Canaan June 4, 1904; bur. in Oakland, Cal.; m. 1st, February 18, 1850, Albert Martin, son of Eleazer, of Canaan; b. in Grafton February 2, 1821; d. in San Francisco, Cal., November 28, 1883. They resided in San Francisco for many years until his death. He was in the banking house of Tallant & Co. After his death she came back to Canaan and married May 20, 1889, Matthew H. Milton, b. October 28, 1819; d. in Canaan in 1905. She was his second wife. She went to California with her daughter and brother in 1859; her husband had preceded her the year before; one ch. by her first husband.

Lillie Wallace, b. in Canaan, May 9, 1851; d. in East Oakland in 1905; m. August 27, 1868, Charles H. Daly; b. in Australia December 13, 1841; two ch.:

Gertrude Elizabeth, b. August 8, 1869; d. August 13, 1872.

Mabel Harriet, b. October 18, 1873; d. June 12, 1902.

William Allen Wallace.

William Allen Wallace was the son of James and Mary (Flint) Wallace. He was a descendant on his father's side of the Scotch covenanters who came from Scotland to the north of Ireland, and with the other emigrants from Londonderry, came to America and settled Londonderry, N. H. His mother came from Middleton, Mass.; her father was Lieut. John Flint a Revolutionary soldier and her grandfather, John Flint, was in the same army. Her grandmother was Huldah Putnam, a sister of Gen. Israel Putnam.

My father came to Canaan from Pembroke in 1817, with his father and mother and two older brothers, when he was two years old. His father was a stern man whom he feared rather than loved, who was too much engaged in his business to pay much attention to his children. This left their care to the mother, who was a sincere Christian woman whose first duty was to her children, then to her church. His education up to the time he was fifteen years old, was obtained at the schools in town, and he was prepared to enter Dartmouth College. Mr. J. L. Bunce of the *New Hampshire Post*, a paper printed at Haverhill, N. H., adverstised for a boy. He begged his parents to let him learn to set type and in May, 1831, his mother carried him to Haverhill and he was duly installed in that office as the youngest apprentice. He was the first of the family to leave home and the last to return. In August of that year, his father died and his mother being occupied in caring for the estate, closing up the store and cooperage business, his college life was overlooked. He remained at Haverhill two years, when the office was sold out and hauled off to Concord. He says, "about all I learned in the *Post* office was to set type, to work the rollers, and to sweep the office. This last operation I reduced to a science, and have often since been complimented for the skill with which I manipulated a broom over a dusty floor without raising a cloud." He went to Concord as a part of the office and remained about a year, not liking the owner, he left. He fell into the hands of a man who cared nothing for him, and when at the end of his service the only advice he received was to "Go and be hanged." He went; but was not hanged. In April, 1834, he engaged to work with Alfred Beard of the *Nashua Telegraph*, a genial, pleasant gentleman, whom everybody loved, but none more so than those who labored for him. He remained there two years and then took to wandering. He says: "I was often disgusted with myself for the instability of my resolutions. I was possessed with the idea that I was not appreciated at my full value; but with empty pockets, I got over that. There is nothing like a flat purse to take the conceit out of a boy."

In 1836 he had grown uneasy and wanted to be doing something else. His oldest brother had gone to sea and he thought to do the same. His brother Burns wrote him: "The idea of being a sailor is not ennobling, means can be furnished you to go to school six months, be contented until your time has expired."

In May he went to Plymouth to school where he remained until December. He was obliged to rise at 5 o'clock in the morning, study an hour before breakfast, and whenever he wished to smoke to go out of town. The first of December found him in the office of the *Bunker Hill Aurora*, Charlestown, Mass.; the last of December he was back again in Nashua, and on the first of January, 1837, in Charlestown again, when he was almost induced to enlist in the United States navy, and but for his brother Burns, would have been a sailor. However, he went back into the printing office and remained in Charlestown for about a year. He then went to East Bridgewater, Mass., and remained about six months in the employ of George H. Brown. He returned home through the summer and in October went to Boston, where he remained the rest of the year. In December he wrote: "A printer cannot, like almost any other mechanic, take his tools and set himself down by the roadside wherever he pleases and establish himself. He must wait, long years of anxious toil, frequently thrown out of work, and when at length grown grey in the service, his best life's blood exhausted and his eye growing dim, he thinks of passing his days in quiet, he examines his funds and finds, not full coffers, but as when he first set out, nothing but emptiness. I am a printer. I have been a journeyman over two years, and if not where I first began, I am so near it that you can scarcely perceive the difference, except that I have grown somewhat older. I have come to the conclusion I will stay in Boston as long as I can get work." One day in January, 1839, he found himself in Worcester, Mass., with $2.11 in his pocket. He went into the old *Spy* office and became its foreman. On the publication of the *Daily Spy* in 1846, he became one of the editors. In 1848 he went with the great host up to Buffalo and joined in the nomination of Martin Van Buren for the purpose of defeating Lewis Cass for president. He says: "I was always proud of that pilgrimage, for it broke up the seemingly interminable Democratic succession in office, and was one of the moving events which led to the abolition of slavery." In July, 1848, he became associated with Mr. Earle in the management of the *Spy*.

Mr. Earle was not an easy man to get along with. The *Spy*

was not a mint and the financial system was a source of irritation to my father. In December, 1848, he wrote: "I often think I could bring my mind down to estimate the value of money, because my friends tell me some day I shall see the necessity of it. But it is no use, my head is too full of wild thoughts, vagaries, dreams. It is only when I get out into the world, and then I have only learned its value when sometimes, at a moment's notice I have found myself in the cars, and half way to Springfield, Boston or Norwich, without a cent, and have had to borrow of the conductor to pay my passage." His money went as fast as he got it and his friends took advantage of his little regard for it by borrowing of him. Mr. Earle was one of those; and this eventually led to their estrangement. In the early part of '49 a cousin wrote him: "If I were a young man I would go to California." In answering it, he said: "The idea has taken strong hold of me. My mind is haunted with the visions of that golden land. I say to myself, why should I stay here, where only toil and labor are mine, and a mere pittance (which to be sure is more than I carry with me into another world), all I get for my toil. There are many associations and kind friends which it will be hard to part from, but partings and change are the order of nature. I can lose my life by going and I may by staying. I shall feel no more peace of mind here than I would there. It has long been my desire to leave New England, to go beyond the reach of influences that have made my heart, I was going to say, desolate, but it is not so. There is no feeling of desolation in my heart and cannot be as long as there is a good God above, and the woods and fields and glorious beauty all round me. In my younger days my chiefest delight was in rambling alone in the woods and fields and my recollections of thankfulness to the glorious Giver of all that is beautiful in the world, still have their influences upon me. My home is among the mountains and my youth was spent there. I studied the works of God, those old mountains seemed like altars and the trees and flowers pointing straight to Heaven, seemed like worshipers before the Majesty above. But I left them in their silent beauty and grandeur, to wander among men and engage in the strifes of the world. There is a vacuum, a longing after the past, and an intangible dream of love, an attachment stronger than time, back there in my young years, the memory of it and its sad termination, have made my life an active one, but a lonely one. My heart has not been hardened, though I have often feared it had, nor have any of its fine cords been blunted, but I often feel lonely and all my thoughts are tinged with sadness. I do not expect ever to get rid of it. But I do wish to change my residence. I want to run away from my fate. And for that reason, I am impelled to go and dig gold.''

In March, 1849, he wrote again: ''I am inwardly impelled strongly and constantly to go west. I am going to do something besides dabble in politics. Mr. Earle says I am sanguine, nervous and impulsive, and it is useless to try to make me otherwise.'' In July, 1850, he wrote: ''I am about to leave this city, probably forever, after eight years and a half of service in the old *Spy* office. I shall leave it with regret and yet with the consciousness that I have already been here too long. I would like to change my business. And will buy me a farm where I can enjoy the sweat of my labor, unannoyed by the political struggles that haunt an editor's life. On the 22d of this month I shall leave.''

After leaving Worcester, he went home to Canaan, visited relatives in Warrensburg, N. Y., and Burlington, preparing to go. In September, 1850, he started for the West on a tour of discovery for something to do, reaching Chicago by way of the Great Lakes. He returned to Canaan with his mind fully made up to go to California. On November 7, 1850, he wrote: ''This may be the last day I spend in the house of my childhood. My thoughts are not all sad for I feel an assurance that some day I may return. I know I am not formed to buffet the world. Quiet labor I enjoy. I shall go forth trusting in Providence that my future may be useful to some of the loiterers by the wayside. Privation and hardship and severe toil, I anticipate, but the hope that animates, will I trust, give me strength to bear and overcome the difficulties and dangers.'' He left home the next day, proceeded to New York to take passage on a vessel bound for the Isthmus. On the 17th they passed under the guns of Morro Castle, ran up the bay and visited Havana. On the 24th they arrived at Chagus, where ten of them hired a boat for $150 to go up the river. On the 1st of December they reached Panama, where they took passage in the *Constitution*, a vessel badly out of repair. There was much sickness on board, the accommodations and food being of the poorest kind. On the 14th they entered the Bay of Acapulco, where they landed and bought eggs for a dime apiece. My father bought eleven hens to take to California. They left Acapulco on the 16th, with 190 passengers. On the 29th of December he landed in San Francisco. He remained there three days and with five others in company with him, started up Napa Creek to lay claim to some unoccupied land to begin farming. They pushed on three miles beyond Napa, then a small village of fifty houses, hired a farm of a Mr. Brown and on the 15th of January, 1851, began spading up the soil with three spades. One of their number made a rake. The next day they set out onions, planted ruta-bagas and turnips. They succeeded in spading about a quarter of an acre, and made up their minds it was too slow. They went eight miles and bought two mules for $100 each, determined, if they could buy a plow, to plow all they could fence. He writes: "Why am I here in a region so little known, engaged in farming? Most people think there is nothing else to do in California but to dig gold, and the mines are the destination of almost everyone. I could have gone there with my New Hampshire friends and perhaps I should not have regretted it. But as we have tools and seeds fresh from home and did not wish to lose them after learning the price of vegetables in the various markets, we resolved to find land for cultivation. But farming is expensive and we must wait some months before we can get our crops to market. In the meantime we must live, and provisions are not cheap. Knowing this and believing that the woods and rivers might afford a small income, we sought for a country abounding in fish and game. This we have found, and as soon as our seed is in the ground we shall take advantage of what is before us. In the mountains twelve miles distant are grizzlys, whose flesh sells for fifty cents per pound, and whose hide is very valuable; elk, deer and hare abound. We have a boat and take our stores to San Francisco in one day. We did propose at first to go to the mines and carry on gardening and mining. We thought we should find plenty of land without an owner and we might squat anywhere. There is not a foot of land and never will be. We are about sixty miles from San Francisco and have large quantities of turnips and onions in the ground. Turnips bring about twelve and one-half cents each.''

In the four months he had been in Napa valley he had gained nineteen pounds, sleeping on the ground and climbing mountains, hunting and farming, chasing coyotes, wolves and bears from their hens, ducks and mules. The latter ran away and they spent ten days hunting them. "You know I always sang a heavy bass; and could never sing anything else. Since I came here I can run a scale from double D in the bass, to B flat in alto without changing a muscle. I do not know what it is attributable to, unless it be the healthy development of my system, that gives my nerves and muscles, free and equal action." He remained here until the last of June, when with two of his companions, they started for the mines up the Sacramento River. They reached Dry Creek on the 8th of July, and on the morrow began rocking at Winslow's Bar on the Yuba River. After their first week's labor they were able to pay for their tools and provisions and divide four dollars each. The severe cold at night and extreme heat in the middle of the day, caused my father to take a severe cold and on the 29th they returned to Napa to divide up the profits of farming. The chickens which they had paid $5.10 for in Acapulco, they sold for $75. About the only profit made. They had worked eight months and did not pay expenses. On the 8th of October he determined to leave Napa and seek his fortune in some other field. He paid $6 for a ride in a cart to Benicia and $100 by steamer to San Francisco, where he remained until the 13th and then started for Big Bar, a placer mining district on the Moquelumne River, where he began to work a race. But mining did not pay and on the 28th of December he wrote: "I sometimes think I will leave this country and return to the Atlantic. More money is to be made here than elsewhere, but money is not all I would live for. I have talent and education which ought to serve me better than they do here. I have aspirations which are stifled by physical pain and labor and my pride is often sorely hurt by some double-jointed ignoramus who laughs at my futile attempts to unearth some huge rock. Were it a question of politics, law or divinity even, I would have no fear of my abilities to meet it. I have but one passion, it is not for gold; it is not for honors or fame; it is for music. I love the forest, for the wind sighs mournfully through its branches. The pattering rain lulls me to sleep."

On the 25th of February, 1852, he wrote: "Now, how can I say anything to stay a man from coming to this place? There is plenty to eat, to drink, to wear, to be had for money. But these are not what men come here for, golden fortunes are the inducements to all; they start with a feeling that they will endure all necessary hardships in their strife for gold, and feel confident of success. They arrive at San Francisco, at Stockton, or Sacramento. Here commences the real strife; from either of these points they begin to feel that the elephant is not far off. At either place they are not forty miles from gold. They hire their goods packed to their diggings, themselves walking through the sandy plains, and over the tiresome hills. They are in the mines where they have so often sighed to be. Here they are to commence a new life in earnest. Now look at them. Here is a hill a mile and a half long, which they must descend. On their backs (for now they must be their own jackasses) are slung tent, clothes, camp kettles, picks, shovels, pans and their personals. Slowly and wearily they arrive at the foot of the hill, and lay down their packs to rest. They look anxiously around. The earth lies in heaps and furrows, in every direction. 'What shall we do next?' Says one. 'I am hungry and tired; let us stop here.' They sit down upon the ground, satisfy their hunger with bread and pork, and perhaps sleep. They wake in the morning refreshed and eager to begin the search; for gold has glimmered through all their night visions. With pick, pan and shovel they start out to prospect — to find a place where they may dig and wash dirt. They traverse the bars and river's bank up and down, washing out a pan of dirt here, another there; all day long they walk up and down, and return at night weary to their pork and bread. With their weariness comes a feeling of discouragement; for they have scarcely seen

the color of gold all day. In the morning they start again.
This day perhaps they will strike something — and perhaps
they will not. And this last is perhaps much more intelligible to
men now than in other days. Well, this day brings no better
success. They see the tracks of the elephant all around — the
beast cannot be far off. They eat their supper in silence and
with forebodings. They are not only sick at heart, but sore
afraid. The great tears roll down their cheeks as they sit with
their elbows on their knees, regretting the dollar a day, the
cheerful homes and sympathizing friends they have left so far
away. There is no joy for them in anything around. The anticipations of great riches with which they started have become
so modified, that had they sufficient to get back, they would
leave instantly. But they must work; for there are no poorhouses in this country. They conclude there is nothing for
them here. They make inquiries and are told that some eight,
ten or fifteen miles away, the miners are getting one or two
ounces a day. That is the place for them. They pack up their
chattels, and looking wistfully up the long hill on either hand,
start on their weary way — one hill only leads them to another,
worse than the first. They inquire of every one they meet, how
far they are from their destination, and each one names a distance longer than the first. They at last reach the two-ounce
diggings. The earth lies in heaps and furrows, as at the first
place and they know not what to do here. They find that here,
as at other places, a few holes and claims are paying well, but
that most of the miners are not averaging over four dollars. To
them California has become a great humbug, — the largest field
for repentance, and the most unavailing — the worst place to
find a friend, and the hardest to get out of. Now what is to be
done? They hear of great strikes in different directions; but
always at a distance. If they are foolish, they pack on after
the rainbow's dip, otherwise they settle down, and cleave the
earth and rocks like other men. As I said before, perhaps they
will be fortunate; but this is the most unintelligible word, perhaps, in all this great country. I dare say that at this time,
three men out of every five are getting little more than a living,
simply because they are men wholly unfitted for the task they

have undertaken. Did they understand this, they would think twice before they rushed off here, they would make experiments to ascertain whether they were able to pick, dig or shovel, in water, mud, or dry dirt, week in and out, as they have to do here. You reason, others get gold, why should not I? You can, if you will do what I propose, namely: take a common railroad pick and a shovel, go out into your field and select the stoniest spot you can find; mark out ten feet square and go at it. Sink a hole down to the ledge or bed rock. It may be five, ten or fifteen feet. Start early in the morning and work till sunset, until you finish the job. If you do not like this job, I will propose another, the easiest I have experienced. Take your pick and shovel, together with two buckets (common water pails), go down near the river, say fifty, or one or two hundred yards distant, fill your buckets with dirt, and carry them to the river; you ought to carry two hundred buckets in a day. When you get through the first day judge whether you will be able to do it a whole season. These are the two ways of getting out the gold. Remember that hard labor is not the only thing a man must encounter. Your intercourse is with men, with dirt and with Nature in her wildest forms. Yet they are not companions with whom man may commune a lifetime. Their sublime grandeur excites one, but does not satisfy the longings of the human heart. You must do your own cooking, washing and mending, for here are neither wives, mothers, nor sisters. You must roll yourselves in blankets, and when traveling, sleep in your clothes. Fleas swarm all over the country, and sometimes before he has thought of it, one gets lousy. When I speak of receiving so much as my share of a week's labor, I simply mean because I work in partnership with others. You ask me when I will get sufficient gold to induce me to return. Really I can not tell. The thought often comes to me that my talents and education ought to be of more service than digging here. Notwithstanding I am getting gold faster than ever before, a feeling of uselessness comes over me, and I long to be back."

He remained at Big Bar until April, 1852; the rains and floods carried away everything in March and they could dig only in the cañons. He returned to Stockton and on the 8th of April, with two Worcester men, started for Big Creek Flat on the Touwalumne River, eight miles from Jacksonville. Here he took out $45, became discouraged, returned to Oak Springs intending to return to the states, "Tired to death of the under life." On the 21st he returned to Stockton, stopped two days with his brother John and started for San Francisco. On the 26th he started for the mines again with a firm determination "of not leaving there without something." On the 7th of May he arrived at the old cabin again, found one of the party, worked a week and divided $8.50. He then started for Moccason Creek to see if he could do any better. The first week he took out $25 the next $26.80. On May 30th he wrote: "How many of these weary hot days must I dig to be able to return to my friends. I have not been fortunate here. The nature of the labor makes it impossible for a constitution like mine to succeed." He made during this month $89. In July he left Woods Creek, Dutch Bar, taking a mule train for Stockton and San Francisco on his way to Panama and home. He put off at Yuba Benna to find his brother, and then returned to San Francisco, where he remained three months. On the 27th of September, 1852, he went to Los Angeles. The next day he wrote: "This is my anniversary. 'I wish I was a boy again when life seemed formed of sunny years.'"

On the 12th of October he went into the office of the *Los Angeles Star*. In 1853 he became the editor and proprietor. He wrote: "The paper was a folio, five columns to the page, about half the size of the *Daily Union*, printed with bourgeois and nonpareil, and one-half the sheet was dedicated to the natives in the Spanish language. The price was $6 per year; advertising $2 per inch. There was money in it and danger also. Human life was held at a cheap rate in those years. Thieves and murderers were turned loose from Mexican prisons on condition that they left the country. In the autumn of 1852 these cholos became so daring that we appointed a tribunal which we named Vigillantes. Quite a number of the scamps were hung on the hill in front of Fremont's old fort in view of the whole city. On one occasion five were hung upon one gallows. On being told by Doctor Osborne that if they desired to leave any message for their friends they had better take that opportunity, as they would soon start for a country where the post office connections were uncertain, one of the victims with a noose around his neck, addressed several of his comrades standing in the crowd by name thus: "We made a mistake in coming to this country, *amigos*. They are too active for us. Go back, every one of you, to Sonora, and obey the laws, or you will soon be traveling this same road. And now," he added, turning to the doctor, who was to float them off, "sons of dogs, do your worst." But there was another element in that country equally as dangerous as those cholos, — the slave-holding intolerance of free speech. A large proportion of the new people were from Arkansas, Missouri and Texas, and they brought all their southern prejudice with them. California, in that day was as surely a slave state as Texas. To be sure she adopted and was admitted with a free constitution; but the influence of the slave power was so potent that for four years afterwards annually the Legislature enacted a law giving the owners of slaves, brought there for mining purposes, one year longer in which to secure profits from the labor of their slaves.

The courts were all friendly to this legislation, and if an appeal were made to them to interfere, the judges "reserved an opinion." Pistols and knives were the chief ornaments of men, and the ladies had not yet arrived. It was a time for constant active watchfulness, and it was years before confidence was firmly established among the motley crowd that had gathered there to form a social community. In August, 1854, after an absence of four years, he started for home by way of the Isthmus. On August 25 he arrived in New York, and on the 30th reached Canaan, where he spent thirteen days with his mother and sisters. His brother Burns had died in the meantime. During September he visited relatives in Warrensburg and Syracuse, N. Y., and in October went to Worcester. In Providence on the 12th of October, he wrote: "I have now no ambition, but to return to California. I want the free mountain air, my horse, rifle, woods and flowers." He made two visits to Professor Gray of Harvard College with flowers he had collected in California, and so pleased was the old man that he cried. The variety and beauty of the California flowers had never been shown him before, and he directed him how to collect and preserve further specimens which were to be sent him. On the 28th he went to Milford, N. H., to visit relatives, then to Warrensburg, N. Y., then to Providence, and to Danvers, Mass. On November 24, he wrote: "I, alone, am a wanderer up and down the earth, stopping like a rail car here and there for refreshments." On the 5th of December he left New York for Panama and San Francisco, where he arrived on the 31st. January 10, 1855, found him again in Los Angeles.

On the 25th of January he received the appointment as schoolmaster and taught until the 17th of June, "when he began to prepare for another journey home, wearied with teaching dullards from the frontiers." While teaching, he with some of his friends became interested in Spiritualism, and attended seances, but was never able to get much satisfaction out of that belief. It was new to that wild country and appealed to many men so far away from their kindred. The medium took advantage of those who had distant friends; his belief in mediums was never strong, and gradually died out. On the 4th of July he went to San Francisco, stopped with his sister Melvina and on the 16th set sail for the Isthmus; on August 1st he crossed the Isthmus and on the 11th landed in New York. On the 18th "started for the home of my childhood. Found old Atherton encroaching upon my lines, that we have occupied for forty years. Nearly all the trees were planted since my father's death. It is twenty-five years since I left my schoolmates here. Mother has filled the house with boarders for the school, of young people whose fathers and mothers were my playmates. I return from wandering over the face of the earth and find myself classed as old by those with whom it seems natural for me to associate. Though my hair is silvered, they knew of me from their parents, and they received me with the respect due to age and to travel, not with the familiarity of companionship. Surely I am getting old. I am the last of my family. My mother has married again, my sisters have married and their names no longer belong to me. My brothers and my father lie in yonder churchyard. There is a row of mounds there and all my kin are resting there. But I do not grieve; for what are these bodies, more than old garments we cast off? These beautiful scenes of my childhood, I become more enamoured of each time I approach them. The further I wander the more do I turn towards it." He remained at home but a short time and on the 6th of September visited relatives in Danvers and Salem. From there he went to Providence, New York, Philadelphia, Pittsburg, Cleveland, Syracuse, and on October 2, returned to Canaan to leave again on the 8th. On the 13th he reached New York and on the 20th set sail again for California. "I cannot wait, I must travel this world alone." On the 15th of November he landed in San Francisco, and on the 23d was back again to take up his old quarters in Los Angeles. On the 25th he began school at San Gabriel at $90 per month. He continued to teach more or less during the time he lived in Los Angeles while he was not editing a newspaper. In 1856 he was appointed school commissioner. In April he purchased the *Los Angeles Star* and edited it for a short time as proprietor. A month afterwards he sold it. "I could not advocate Buchanan for president, and the politicians wanted a Democratic press. I then edited a Spanish campaign paper called *El Clamor Publico*, and through its instrumentality carried the county for Fremont. The starting of the paper was a dangerous move. Grant Owry (who has since been a delegate in Congress from Arizona), came into town one day from Tuscon with a lot of his fellows, and said he had come to "clean out the black abolitionists," and had "brought along the ropes." He was met at the plaza and advised to take his band and ropes back into the desert, and told that no outrage upon any person whomsoever would be permitted; that the men of Los Angeles were capable of taking care of themselves, and, if occasion required, of him and his band also. He found us all "loaded," even the most peaceable of us, and took himself back silently to the left bank of the Gila River." "I was the first man who dared announce himself a Republican in southern California in 1856, spending much time and money upon this Spanish paper, but never happened to be on the winning side in that country; worse men than I got all the offices." When a member of the school board, the city council authorized them to build a schoolhouse of brick, two stories high, and to open and establish the first public school in that city. He was elected an honorary member of the California Academy of Sciences, for labor in the field as a botanist. "I was present at a ball in Don Abel Stearns' casa, when the managers expelled General Fremont and a woman he conducted there, and who was not his wife. At one time I was in the Mormon county of San Bernandino with Judge Hayes and was appointed by him special United States district attorney, in the absence of the proper officer, who was then in Rebellion against the government."

As a gatherer of news, he first made known the horrible details of the Mountain Meadow massacre. In January, 1857, he began writing as correspondent for the *Alta California*, a newspaper published in San Francisco. During this year he was engaged in teaching school, making many trips into the mountains in search of flowers. On one of them he met two bears in the trail, one a short distance behind the other, both of which turned out. Further along he met a panther whom he and his mule turned out for. In June, 1858, the proprietor of the *Alta California* sent for him to come to San Francisco. On the 28th he left the latter city for the Fraser River and the scenes of the latest gold excitement. It was the desire of McCrellish, proprietor of the *Alta* to stop the flood of emigration from California to those mines, and no better way was known than to send some one who could describe the hardships to be endured with so little chance of success. His own description of his journey was written and forwarded to the *Alta*, some parts of which may be interesting:

"The summer of 1858 will long be remembered in the annals of many a sad fellow upon the Pacific coast, who with bright hopes and excited imagination, threw away what fine chances remained to him in California and Oregon, and wishing to be the first man there rushed off, expecting to gather wealth from the golden sands of the Fraser River. Hustling themselves into crowded ships to get to Victoria, and here buying or building canoes, they paddled across the stormy Gulf of Georgia, 75 miles to the mouth of Fraser River, where with muscles firmly braced, they stemmed the fierce torrent that rushed down through the Cascade Mountains. Many of those adventurers lost their lives in those whirling waters. Many lost the earnings of years. A few gathered gold and came away to enjoy it. I was upon the editorial staff of the *Alta California* at San Francisco. In the interests of humanity it was desirable to check the increasing rush to the mines, which could be productive only of misery and poverty in thousands of cases. With this object in view, I was directed by the manager of the paper to proceed to Victoria, and thence to the scenes of excitement along the Fraser River, as high up as Fort George, in L. 60° N.

"I took passage with two companies of soldiers bound up the Columbia River 120 miles to Fort Vancouver. Here was one of the sublimest spectacles the lover of nature ever beheld. The snow-crowned monarchs towering far above the clouds, their cold white summits glittering in the sunlight rose before us. Mt. Adams, Mt. Rainier and Mt. St. Helens, were there in all their grandeur, their massive vastness seemed to fill the horizon. They were sixty to one hundred miles apart, and their great tops seemed to kiss each other, and the breeze which swept from them seemed laden with chilly particles. I have looked upon the tall peaks of the Sierra Nevadas, but these stand alone in all their magnificence and fill the heart with awe, a sense of fullness comes upon you as you gaze upon them towering up to the gates of Heaven."

On the 6th of July he reached Victoria: "2,000 men have gone up, 200 went home on the *Panama*" the steamer he went on. On the 13th he reached Fort Hope where he remained a week, and then proceeded by steamer to Fort Yale, where the sun rose at 2.30 in the morning. After remaining there a week he returned to Fort Hope, and on the 10th of August was back at Victoria. On the 25th he was at Napa, the place where he first started farming in California. He wrote of Napa "revisited," "this was once my dreamland, here on the banks of this little river my first dreams of wealth in California took form and grew and were on the point of being realized, but 'the next day came a killing frost.' It was from here I first wrote letters to my friends, assuring them that two seasons at least would close my exile. Those days were very happy, because there was so much to hope for; and the memories of them as we came up thronged upon me like pleasant shadows." From there he went to White Sulphur Springs, where McCrellish had sent him to recruit. He returned to San Francisco and was requested to make preparations for a trip overland to Salt Lake City across the plains. "There is excitement in the anticipated dangers and strange scenes I shall encounter. I love it, and shall start out with much pleasure." He left San Francisco on the 2d of September, 1858, by boat and reached Sacramento the next day. On the 4th he started by coach with nine others; the next morning they had made but twenty miles and stopped for breakfast. "The host was an Irishman, and he will never be nearer death than he then was until he meets it. Davis took offense at his impudence and would have shot him." The road wound along the south fork of the American river. "There was novelty and grandeur in those massive, round, naked, white rocks." At Placerville they watched for the mail, to learn that it had been attacked by Indians at Goose Creek mountains, the animals were run off and the clothing of the party taken. They climbed to the summit of the Sierras and down again through Eagle Valley, across the Twenty-Six Mile Desert to the sink of the Humboldt River, Alkali Lake. On the 11th they came upon a party of 300 Pah-ute Indians standing along the road, begging for tobacco, further along they came upon some Shoshones and on the night of the 12th an attempted attack was made upon them by Indians, but as they were prepared the Indians left. On the 23d they reached Salt Lake City. He remained there two weeks meeting and conversing with the Mormons in the streets and in their homes, and sending back letters for the *Alta*, of what he observed. On the morning of October 2d, he proceeded overland to St. Louis, having received word from McCrellish to go there. The route taken was the one General Johnston took the summer before when he had been sent by the government to subdue the Mormons, and the country showed the traces of their fortifications. They were continually stopped by soldiers and were obliged to give an account of themselves. They passed through Echo Cañon, across Bear River, by Fort Bridger, to Green

River, along the banks of the Sweetwater, with the Rattlesnake Mountains on one side, through the valley of the Platte to Laramie, Fort Kearney. On the 23d of October he reached St. Joseph, Mo., and on the 31st St. Louis, by boat from St. Joseph. To a friend he wrote: "My journey from Salt Lake was long and fatiguing, we ran through a hundred Indian villages, crossed the Rocky Mountains, and all the other mountains on the continent, ate buffalo meat, and chased buffalo bulls, saw the prairie all on fire, and tried to catch prairie dogs; chased mountain goats and ran away from prairie wolves." He left St. Louis the next day for Cincinnati, thence to Columbus, Cleveland and to Syracuse which he reached November 10, where he visited his uncle five days, and then to Albany and New York, from there he went to Worcester and on the 22d of November reached Canaan. "After ten years absence a snowstorm greets me in my old home. While breathing the warmer breezes of the South, I have come to look with dread upon the snow king."

He spent Thanksgiving in the old house, the first for twenty years. He stayed at home until December 11, and then went to Worcester, then to Boston and Cambridge visiting friends, and on the 16th was back in Worcester, to meet W. P. Weeks and to exact a settlement with Eaton, to whom he had sold his interest in the *Spy*, and who had not paid him. He remained there until December 24, and then went to New York where he spent the holidays. On January 6, 1859, he was in Philadelphia and on the 12th set sail for Norfolk and Petersburg, in the interests of the *Alta*. He visited Richmond and Fredericksburg. On February 10 he was in Washington, where he remained until February 19, when he went to New York to see Albert Martin, his brother-in-law and a son of Eleazer Martin, off for California. On March 2 he was in Worcester and on the 5th called on Doctor Gray at Cambridge and gave him all the plants he had collected. He returned to Canaan and on the 14th bade good-by to his mother, intending to return to California. He got as far as the depot and came back. He had made up his mind to join the Masons and called upon Jacob Trussell, who gave him a letter to the lodge in Enfield. During the following months he took the several degrees in Social Lodge. On May Day he wrote, "I am still lingering like the snowdrifts in this northern latitude. There are some little arrangements which it becomes me to make, to render more easy the path of the old lady who has long lived here rather than to take her away. To remove her it would be necessary to take the old house, the trees and the land along with her, whose heart strings 'round them cling. The fence posts are rotted off, the stone wall has fallen down, the orchard is dying, moss and lichens have overgrown the roofs, rocks and trees; the woodpeckers and the wrens, who always know where the wood is decaying, flit around, always keeping a large branch between themselves and danger. The old lady insists that she is still smart, and is able to take care of all these things; but she sometimes complains of weariness; her step is often feeble and she is becoming tremulous. She says it is not so, but I, who see her at intervals of long years, observe that like the fences and stone walls she needs to be cared for. Therefore, I am waiting here. Besides these evidences of decay and age, several little annoyances have arisen, which seemed to make it imperative to remove. One of these and perhaps the worst, was occasioned by the obstinate pertinacity of an old fellow who thinks the principle of squatter sovereignty applicable to the condition of things in this law-abiding state. He not only seized upon my land, but built his house upon it, and kept so mean a fence that his chickens and stray animals were always in the old lady's garden. I had to have a quarrel, of course; for how could I tolerate a squatter in my very garden? I threatened several things, and did get quite angry. I would chop his house down, or dig a deep ditch, or build a high wall, or sue the beggar and — pay all the costs myself. I made several rash resolves, but at length grew considerate; put up a close stout fence of huge rocks, with which all our lands abound and am now convalescent.

"I don't know that I am losing any time by stopping here. I think, in fact, I am making a little daily progress homeward, because I am in a country where it is profitable to watch the various pulsations of the human heart,—in labor, trade and religion,— the three elements that make up human nature in three parts. These are very distinct employments but they have a negative connection. Religion may sanctify and purify the miserable and friendless wretch for a first-class passage to the Spirit Land, but it is only successful trade and labor well rewarded that secures content and peace of mind. Faith in Divine Providence is at a discount unless unattended with strong and saving effort. 'God's love and care' are very pretty sentiments to talk about, but these people know very well that if they do not pile up the stones and burn the stumps in their fields, all the protection they get comes by way of the poorhouse. In this country everybody but old Daniel Campbell and Nat Currier go to meeting; but they put faith only in bone and muscle. There is no excitement, no wildness, no enthusiasm on any subject. The men hoe corn and potatoes, make hay, and plod to church to get the news of the week. The women make butter and cheese, get up 'circles' where some sewing is done and much sympathy is expressed for the poor in Africa and Hindustan, believe in the minister, pray for their friends, and go to church to hear the gospel, of course. Each day is the same, except that the wind is sometimes south and northwest. To sleep, to eat, to labor, to pray, to gossip, is the occupation of the people. No one gets angry but me, no one fights, but many talk! Indeed, if we were to lose the power of speech, our little jealousies and envyings would have no utterance. It is marvelous what a relief it is to be able to express one's sentiments distinctly, particularly where there is no danger of personal injury. Do you care to hear of this quiet country? It makes no noise in the world, because there is no class here to disturb the peace. The people live by will. They dine each day at 12 o'clock, and the hour is announced by the village bell. They toil hard upon the stingiest and stoniest land, and pay their debts, not so much perhaps from a principle of honesty as from a desire to avoid exposure. They seldom make presents, and they do not give away their subsistance. The winter was long and the spring backward, and the frost nipped all the fruit buds, so that we have no apples. Then the drouth came on and for two months there was no rain to ripen the corn and potatoes and fill up the grass bottoms and many fears have been expressed that there was to be a general caving in of nature. The grumblers have been active in their vocation, but I think the harvest will not disappoint the husbandmen. Indeed, the most inveterate grumbler among them, old Nat C. 'who never knew so bad a season since 1816, when the corn and potatoes were killed in July by the frosts,' now very contentedly says he has a better crop than he had last year.

"Sometimes I think I am staying here too long or that I am going away too soon. I don't know how my happiness depends upon it, yet I would not go alone, if I had the courage and confidence of a young man. There is poetry and sentiment and many imaginary pleasures in waiting; but like the redoubtable Miles Standish, I am terrified at the ghost of a 'thundering No!' from the lips of a pretty woman. The sensation is truly dismal, and can only be appreciated by similar unfortunates."

The "thundering No" had so many terrors for him that after making two attempts to leave without tempting his fate, he came back each time, in the same state in which he had departed. He continued to linger here until the 14th of October, when he wrote, "I shall leave the old country and go back to the old scenes that have so long had charms for me." My mother had refused him and he started for California. He went to Philadelphia, and returned to New York, where he met his sister Harriet and her daughter, Lilly, who took passage with him to join her husband in San Francisco. On the 28th of October, 1859, at Aspinwall he wrote:

"I had rather be at home building stone fences, digging rocks and picking up dry leaves and occasionally walking up the hill. Perhaps I might have won happiness. I shall have to travel this once more and that is the end." On the 12th of November they landed at the wharf at San Francisco, where he stayed a week and then took steamer for Los Angeles. December 16 he went to San Pedro and on the 20th he wrote, 'I know I am not to remain here." On January 23, 1860, he started for San Francisco again to go to Sacramento, where the Legislature was in session, at the request of the *Alta California*. The *Alta* in February asked him to go to the Geysers and Cinnabar mines. He took steamer and on February 23 was at Petaluma, from there he took stage up the valley of the Russian River to Healdsburg. From there he proceeded alone on horseback to the geyser country, sometimes finding it more agreeable to walk down the declivities than to lean back and hold on to the hair of his horse's tail. Everywhere was indication of prospectors; hardly a rock but what had been struck by a hammer. Claims had been staked out. The discovery of quicksilver was more startling than that of the precious metals. He remained there writing articles for the *Alta* until March 13 when he returned to Petaluma and on the 16th was back in San Francisco.

On that day he wrote his mother: "I have but just returned from the mountains where I expected to be gone only six days. I was absent four weeks on compulsion. I went down into one of the worst mountain cañons in the state and it came on to rain, hail and snow so that I was fastened up. The snow covered the tops of all the bushes, so that it was impossible to find the road, and during ten days I remained in the house, looking out in vain for the sun to peer down in upon us. At last he came, melted the snow, and raised the rivers, so that for several days we could not ford them. Do you wish to know what I was doing there? Nothing. I went partly for my own pleasure, partly to look after some rich quicksilver mines, supposed to be buried in the rocks of that country. I found the cinnabar in great quantities and some day it will be very valuable. But probably I shall not live to see it. It was a wild region, and I was well repayed, although I endured more hardship, and grew old faster than upon any other expedition I have ever undertaken. It was among the geysers, the boiling and steaming springs of sulphur, alum, ammonia, and various other chemicals are constantly issuing from the earth. The earth is all on fire there, and as we walk over it carefully, it has the resonance of a hollow chamber beneath. I trod very carefully over those burning cones, for it reminded me of what you used to teach me of 'the smoke of their torments ascending forever' and of the fire and brimstone lake. Here was almost positive proof of its existence. In the midst of all this fire the most beautiful flowers were blooming, and beautiful trees growing. Two days since I came down out of this summer and winter region. I don't think there is another place like it in the world,— so difficult to get at or to get away from, nor so fearfully interesting when you are there."

On the 23d of March he dined with his sister Harriet in San Francisco. He remained there until the 11th of April when he was sent to Sacramento on political business, to oppose what was called the Bulkhead bill. In the meantime the *Alta* had been thinking of sending him overland to St. Louis, and on the 17th he began his preparations, but was unable to get stage for a month. On the 21st he was in Sacramento again to carry congratulations to Governor Downey for vetoing the Bulkhead bill. On the 6th of May he returned to Los Angeles. On the 18th he wrote, "Have been waiting for two weeks for overland stage to take me to St. Louis, am impatient to get home. I have been a wanderer so long, homeless and unsatisfied." On the 20th he went to San Pedro to receive the governor, and on the 24th of May started from Los Angeles overland by the Butterfield route. On the 26th they were crossing the Colorado desert, on the 28th at the Colorado River ferry he stayed a week. On the 4th of June he was at Gila City. On the 11th the stage was full, so he could not get away. While waiting here he wrote his mother, "I did not intend to write you till I had crossed the country; till I was realizing the dreams of my life in my old home with the dim and intangible shadows of the past glancing around me; till I could see the old graveyard and the slabs that indicate my destiny; the old church where I sang psalms and never listened to the sermons of the sanctified saint 'who washed his garments from the blood of sinners who ceased not to harden their hearts'; the old mother whom I love the stronger as I go down myself into the vale of years, and whose pathway it is left for me to smooth and make pleasant. I, who have never known her, the first to leave her in early boyhood, and, after her children one by one, have left her shattered frame drifting upon the rocks of old age, the last to return and give her confidence as she travels down to the foot of the hill of life and till I have greeted another and a younger in whom I feel a strong interest, and whom I wish to be near. I have been dreaming today, oh, so delightful of the old home and the rest I shall take there, the solace from care, from fatigue, from the world, with my books, my music, my friends, and my thoughts, that I feel exalted, and I have waked suddenly and find myself still bound upon the desert banks of this Colorado River, the least interesting river in the world, which swells by us a flood of muddy waters, brought down from uninhabitable regions."

On the 15th he had taken stage and reached Tucson, then to Messilla, N. M., Fort Chadbourne, Texas, Belknap, Sherman and Fort Smith, Ark. From here he wrote home, June 29, 1860: "I am coming along slowly and shall reach you after awhile. I have had a very hard journey, and have sometimes thought I should never get through. I arrived here two days ago and intend to rest, for I am weak and nearly sick. I can scarcely walk and my throat troubles me badly, but I shall not remain here long. I am anxious to get to a stopping place. I have taken some pretty hard journeys in my life but this is the hardest and most dangerous. I never wish to go over that ground again. I have been on the way over sixty days and have not heard from anybody in that time."

On the 6th of July he reached St. Louis after having traveled a distance of 3,096 miles from San Francisco. He went to Columbus, Ohio, and from there to Philadelphia, which he reached July 9 and then home. He remained home until December 4, when he started for New York, Philadelphia and Washington. On February 12 he was in Philadelphia again and on April 13 was in Washington; from there he went into Virginia, to Fairfax Station, Manassas, Centerville and Bristow. This trip seems to have been made more for his own amusement, writing not so much for the *Alta* as for other papers. He came back home and remained through the summer and winter until January. On August 2, 1861, he printed the first copy of *The Reporter*, setting up his own type and from his own press printing the copies for free distribution. The second copy was printed on August 6, the third on August 21, of which he said "it has made a great sensation. One would think half the town were hit by the talk." The last copy was printed September 14, in which he says: "*The Reporter* is under no obligations to reveal its intentions. He prints for his own amusement, upon his own account, and at such times as he sees proper. So please don't ask him any questions. If his own efforts recoil and make him sick, he is not going to own it. If any other person takes a disgust at what he says, perhaps it will be wise for that person to make a great fuss about it; call *The Reporter* hard names and bad names; threaten not to speak to him; nor to sing with him; at any rate be furiously indignant, and when the indignation has effervesced, it will be quite proper for such persons to be ashamed of themselves." In October he received a proposition from McCrellish, editor of the *Alta California*, to spend the winter in Washington as correspondent, which he accepted. On December 7 he went to Washington, had difficulty in finding a place to live. "The country is full of soldiers; camps and regiments are met and passed everywhere, particularly after leaving Philadelphia. The crowd here is as ignorant of what is going on as they are in Milton's store after reading the *Journal*. Everybody is wondering what will happen next. A hundred dollars a month would be no temptation for me to stay here."

He wrote his first letter to the *Alta* on December 9, and the editor at the top of it made this comment: "The following is the first letter from our Washington correspondent, W. A. Wallace, who will remain at the Capital during the present session of Congress. The letters of this gentleman written for the *Alta* several years back, won for him a high reputation. The readers of the *Alta* in 1858 will particularly recollect his vivid letters from Fraser River written during the summer and fall of the great exodus to that locality. We have called him again from his peaceful home, away up among the valleys at the foot of the Green Mountains, where he had retired to a quiet life, and was attending the declining steps of a dear old mother, whose sands of life were ebbing away. At the summons, 'telegraph,' he has left his quiet home, and repaired to the din, bustle and hurry of Washington life, to give the readers of the *Alta* a lifelike history of the momentous events which roll day by day over the national Capital. We shall close this introduction of an old favorite writer for the *Alta*, and let him tell in his own language how he was employed at the time the summons reached him to repair to the busy scenes of active life." A part of this letter was as follows: "You directed me to pack my valise and abandon the cheerful old home, around which a thousand pleasures have circled during the short time I was permitted to enjoy it. Everything about that home is old and cheerful. The old lady who worries herself about labors which she ought to resign, but which her habits will never allow her to forego; the old books, whose well-read pages are familiar to all of us; the old apple trees, from which until this year, we have always made cider; the old neighbors, who all feel an interest in each other's business; the old graveyards where our fathers and brothers lie; and the old church, whose gospel is now preached out, and closed up. But doubtless our Christian people will not permit so great a means of salvation to fall by the wayside, and after I am gone their hearts will become softened, and the old fires will be again rekindled — oh, there are a thousand associations clinging like ivy around the old home, that fill me with regrets to leave. But this is a world of eternal changes; we are always having to say good-by to some friend. I had flattered myself that my travels were over, that weariness and fatigue were for somebody else and I should henceforth enjoy a euthanasia of happy reflections under the shade of my own trees, clearing the rocks from my fields, and watching the growths of my pigs and garden. The old longings to be in wild and strange places would occasionally come over me powerfully but they would soon be checked by my pleasant surroundings."

On the 10th he wrote: "The crowd in this town depends upon the New York papers almost exclusively for their news. I believe we are farther from the news than you are at home. We see the soldiers here all the time, but we hear no guns, and no battle is near us. The squads of soldiers that file in the streets hurry through without stopping, and we know no more of them. I have heard it intimated in high circles that Mr. Lincoln is not equal to his position, that he allows himself to listen to the cautious counsels of covert traitors, and his constitutional scruples are an attribute to these counsels. It is said that he puts much confidence in James Guthrie and James R. Speed of Kentucky, who pretend to be Union men but who are, in fact, traitors, and are using their influence upon the President to delay the advance of the Federal armies." He returned home the last of December to go back again to Washington on January 3, 1862. On January 17, he wrote: "I get disgusted with the administration, at the millions of money that have been wasted upon its favorites, and I have written to the *Alta* such letters as will, if they are published, show that one man, at least is not afraid to write against corruption. I can't express all my sentiments in language of sufficient force. But probably it will be just as well as if I did, for I presume any who might care for what I would say under other circumstances would now count me a sort of fanatic, an enemy of the government or something else or worse."

On January 22 he wrote: "I have just received a dispatch from the *Alta*, telling me I must not leave here for sickness or smallpox. The work is hard and tiresome. I have to travel in all weathers and since I came here have, on but few occasions, retired before 12 o'clock at night. There is an end to all things and I suppose there will be an end to my staying in Washington, and when the end comes I will go cheerfully to work on the old farm." On February 19 he came back from Washington but returned. On March 29 he was offered the position of collector of revenue for southern California, and refused it. In April he returned home and the *Alta* wished him to live in Washington and be their correspondent, but in June he returned to Canaan and did not again take up the pen as war correspondent of the *Alta*. On January 8, 1865, he married Mary Duncan Currier and settled down to peace and quiet on the old place, writing for various papers and magazines, picking stone and building wall. In 1870 he began to collect historical matter for the town history which he kept up all his life. Nothing can better illustrate his life from this time than his own writing. In 1880 he wrote: "The record says it is sixty-five years since I came hereabout. It hardly seems so long, and yet the events I recall took place in another generation, so many years since I was a boy, and used to think our horizon bounded the work, and were it not for the graves of the old people, whose lives I recognize, all the life would appear a dream. I had a father, mother, brothers, sisters, a houseful of us. One by one they are gone, scarcely a footprint upon the sands remain; only Harriet, and she so far away and so silent that she seems to have gone with the rest out of sight. I loved them all, but it did not keep them here. Do they ever, any of them, or any person, come about me? I almost doubt it, although I have wanted for many years to believe it. There is but one event which makes it certain to me, when I go to that Unseen Country, I shall realize all the life there may be in it. I shall know if friends recognize each other, or if it be only spirit intercourse, or if it be the silence of the grave from whose solemn darkness no soul ever returned."

In December, 1880, before starting for the golden wedding anniversary of Mr. Foster in Putney, Vt., he wrote: "I told him we should certainly meet him, and many other old and dear friends, after we get through here. His own ideas and beliefs in the future state might make him doubt our assertion, but we expected some time in years to come to give him a joyful greeting, and that he, before that day comes, would see the inconsistency of a great and good Creator, resolving in cold blood to send nine tenths of all his children into endless torment, because two of them, many thousand years ago discovered that there were pleasures in the world hidden from them, and a sight of their own nakedness brought them to light. I think Mr. Foster is too good a man to treat his own children under the laws he lays down for the use of his God, and I don't believe his God is any worse than he is. He has been preaching endless torment sixty years and he is the father of a family. I think he has more faith in God's love and affection than in his wrath and justice, which were the attributes of the God of Elder Wheat and Richard Clark."

"September 29, 1883. I am alone tonight in this great house, and the rooms seem peopled with silent memories of all the busy lives that have thronged it in the long years since we entered its walls. My father was a stern man, unapproachable to young persons. I feared him more than I loved him. My mother was a patient worker and a sincere Christian all her life. She had positive opinions, and expressed them fearlessly; she loved her children and made many sacrifices for them. She ought to wear a crown of glory in the bright home she now owns. And my brothers and sisters — they flit around me like shadows and disappear, leaving only my Mary and my boy, as the living active representatives of all who have gone before. And I have got to that point in life when I can almost see the end, when they will be looking back upon me as I look upon the already departed.

I only wish that my life may be such that they will remember me with affectionate respect, and feel some pride in recalling the associations that linked us together in life.

"January 8, 1884. Our nineteenth marriage anniversary; but unlike the first a strong southeast wind prevails, driving a wet snowstorm before it. That night John drove us down, and after staying round with mother and Mrs. Tilton awhile by the kitchen fire he went off timidly and shyly to bed. Tonight we sit here with nineteen years of varied experiences behind us, and while looking forward for a few days and looking back over all these years, and the long road we have traveled, with the rough hills and deep valleys, that sometimes obstructed the way, and the gently undulating plains, that stretched far on and far on, it seems now that it had all the way been plains, green with pleasant memories, that stretch way on in the future farther than the keenest vision extends. God bless us as He has done, and keep us from doing foolish things, and make our mutual faith and confidence strong and lasting. Amen!

"January 13, 1884. Minister preached a sermon on the devil. I wanted to ask him if he had ever seen that devil, and if he resisted him, so that he fled. The strongest proof of a devil is that he is so often mentioned in the Bible, devil, satan, adversary, enemy, all these names pointed to a person. I fear if I believed in him that I should become a dreadful coward, and should always be looking under the bed nights before getting into it.

"February 4, 1884. It seems to me life is not long enough to spend even a year of it in sulking at the envious and jealous remarks of neighbors whose numbers are not so great, that we can well spare even one from our social circle. If the past could only bury itself, and be forgotten, what a happy time we would all have in the near future. It seems as if to hate and slander were the normal conditions of human nature, and as long as men are happy in it, there will not be much change in our lives.

"September 28, 1884. My anniversary comes around again, oh, so quickly. I don't think I am any better than I was a year ago, perhaps not so perfect. I am not a Methodist so I don't go on to perfection, neither do I 'fall from grace,' but I rather promised myself a year ago, that if I was here another year,

I would congratulate myself on being a good reformer, but I rather failed in my own estimation. Twice I've been madder than a disturbed hornet. First when F— G— played dignity on poor Etta, second when the Silver Lake livery broke into my garden and destroyed the fruit of my toil and of my season's labor. Then I raged, but I shed no tears. I said 'for the future you will board your own horses, or I shall arrest them,' and they have not frequented our house since. I will make no pledges for the year to come, only I hope these horses will not compel me to tie them up in my yard.

"January, 1885. Twenty years we have been going on together! I remember many years ago before that quiet event, of reading with avidity, 'The Autocrat of the Breakfast Table,' the best of Holmes' books; the young man was called John, and the schoolmistress took a walk, and the conversation becoming personal, after a severe struggle he asked the young woman, would she like a longer walk over the long road. It recurred to me one day when walking with my Mary and I asked her the question more than once before she consented, and we fixed the day for the first of January, 1865, when we would start out on that road. But for some untoward event we did not come to time, but during the week the cake was made, Mr. Dearborn was invited and a few minutes after seven in the evening, he closed the service and excused himself saying we had no further use for his services, and he had another engagement, and then we started out on that road. And for twenty years, which today seems but a short time, we have traveled on, with no turning. Sometimes it has been rough and shadows have flitted about, but sunshine and the consciousness of honest purposes have prevailed. Twenty years we have had close communion together, in health, sickness, pain and distress, and we are here today to thank God, for the pleasures and happinesses that has been our lot. Is life all joy? is it only one great hope! O, no; no life is like that, sorrows come and misfortunes, and pains and deaths. We have laid old friends away in the ground to await resurrection in some brighter form, hours and days have seen us anxiously watching, almost hopeless, the doctor's fees have been paid and life flows smoothly on again. The long road grows longer, but it is fragrant with sweet confidences and pleasant hopes, and still the years go by and the burden of age is growing heavier day by day.

"January 18, 1885. We have been packing up for a little trip to Concord tomorrow, to the printers' banquet, and so long it is since we went anywhere, it seems a great effort to start. Once I could go round the world with a satchel and not be half so worried as this makes me. It is because the years are rolling on.

"September 28, 1885. Seventy times the years have rolled round in my life, and looked me in the face. A man at seventy ought to be a good man. He ought to have completed his character and won the respect, reverent esteem or otherwise of the people with whom he mingles. Pretty much all his life is behind him. He has not much to look forward to except the end, which may be nearer than he thinks. And I thank God that my good habits have enabled me so far to take care of myself, to be no burden nor care nor anxiety to any one. I hope I may have the courage to see and face the end, as fearlessly as for years I have been looking towards it.

"November, 1885. And here I am now just entering upon that eventful period of life called old age, and the boys and girls still call me Allen. Isn't that rather calling me back to 'youth and that time when first I heard the tuneful chime?' It seems as if, counting years, my life was all behind me, merely that I have not much now to live for, except to get ready to live forever. And who knows for what port we are bound when we put on immortality. I cannot lift the veil that hides the beyond, nor do I believe any one else alive can do it, but I want so to employ my days, that when the change comes, and I pass out of human sight, if there be any spirit relation in another sphere, I may find myself in the company of good men and women, whom love of God and man has made blest. I have no desire to go where they sing hallelujahs forever; not I. But I should like pleasant music and quiet converse. I have no time to speculate upon hereafter, let us live so that its coming to us shall cause no anxiety. But I am glad to be here now; that the Indians did not kill me in the mountains nor the rebels in Virginia. We will live hopefully for the future and pray that all changes may bring us nearer to one another. Selah.

"September 28, 1888. My anniversary: shall I ever see another? Who can tell? Will my work ever be done? Very doubtful. I can see and feel the changes which friends either do not see or they are considerate not to mention. I am glad to have lived so many years, and to have left a mark that will do honor to the name. Life may be long, but we will make it serene.

"September 28, 1815, 10 o'clock p. m.—September 28, 1890, 10 p. m. All other hours between these two dates I have been here. When a person has reached the age of 75 years, what is there in the future for him to look forward to? Only to see that his affairs are in order, and live in peace and charity with all mankind. The next journey may be to the graveyard. I have seen so many changes in this world that nothing surprises me. My boy is, I hope, so far settled in life that he will only need my good wishes in the future. My dear Mary whom I have loved and honored for thirty years, and to look back they seem so short! She is here always by my side; she looks at me anxiously at times. Perhaps she sees my failing strength, certainly I am losing the strong grip I once held on my muscles. Memory is still clear, eyes poor, dimness comes over them, hearing strong, voice grows tremulous at times, and singing sometimes tires me. I walk upright and neighbors speak of my activity as boyishly wonderful, but they don't see the weariness that comes over me after even slight exertion. There is small desire to go into company, home seems to be the happy place. Many things do not interest me today as of yore, politics are stale, with no honesty. Religion seems a great sham, its votaries are inconsistent, uncharitable, hypocritical, given to slanders and defamation. The Christianity of the world seems to be all outdoors. I fully realize there can be but little more work here for me. I realize, also, that I shall never, perhaps, be able to finish what I have begun, and I realize more than ever that I have not and never had the power of continuity of thought that would have led me on to success. Like Hyatt Smith I just fall short of achieving the desired end. But who knows whether in the great accounting a man's capacity will be considered. 'I am nearer my journey's end that I have been before.' I am thankful for all the pleasures vouchsafed me.

"September 19, 1891. The high wind last night blew over my mother's acacia, the only one in town. She brought it from Piermont (Jo Sawyer's) in May, 1831, when she carried me to Haverhill to enter a printing office, an event which changed the whole face of my life. Studies which it had been decided I should pursue were laid aside and never again taken up. My reading became of a desultory character such as all printers' boys fall into, and I became a man of general information and with no habit for study in any particular direction, my mind is superficial. But that old tree! I could have cried if it would have done any good. She cherished it and I grew old in the love of all things which she cherished. Trees are like people, they grow old and fall down.

"September 28, 1891. The idea of helplessness oppresses me, I want to grow old gracefully and quietly."

That was the last he wrote about himself, though he still continued to record events which interested him up to within a week of his death. He had kept a diary nearly all his life. His habit was to write it up at the end of the week. In later years it did not record events so much as his own thoughts upon them, the event serving as a text. My father did grow old gracefully and quietly as he wished. I think he minded it more than my mother or I. As a boy I can remember his activity as almost phenomenal. He was up at daylight, three a. m., every morning in summer and worked until breakfast in the garden, then all day long, only stopping to eat; no rest, rarely going to bed until ten o'clock at night, and then to read himself to sleep. As he grew older he realized that he got tired quicker and would take a nap after dinner. His habits of life were very regular, if he found anything did not agree with him he did not continue its use. He smoked, chewed and took snuff, for thirty years, stopped, and not in my lifetime did I ever see him use tobacco, but he always liked the smell of it and would give me cigars, much to my mother's disgust. Our house was always a Mecca for tramps. His early experiences led him to help anyone, greatly against my mother's wish sometimes, for she had been brought up as a farmer's daughter, where everyone was expected to work. He was very fond of dumb animals being particularly sensitive when seeing them beaten by someone else. I have seen him threaten to chastise a man beating his horse, in language which the horse-beater resented so much that his anger was quickly changed from beast to man. Nevertheless, his temper was quickly aroused by both man and beast, and at times by his own animals. When old Josie would kick him and the pail full of milk against the side of the barn (the kick never came until she knew he was about done milking), or when old Mattie, who lived to be thirty-three years old, bit the back out of a workman's coat, "Darn you," he said, "you bit me last week," and proceeded to belabor her. What made him realize his growing old more than anything else, was the weakness of his voice when singing. Up to the time he was seventy, his was one of the strongest voices I can remember of hearing. There was not a singer in his day in town that understood music so well; his voice was a clear tenor and full. There was hardly an entertainment or funeral in town at which he was not called upon to sing. He was always interested in politics, was always a Republican, his life led him to keep in it, but he cared very little for office, his profession led him rather to criticise those in office, and many a one has felt the force of his pen. Nothing gave him more delight than to bring forth a reply from the person he attacked. My father's life after his marriage became almost entirely a home one. When business compelled his absence he nearly always returned before he was expected, so great was his love of home. My grandmother tried to bring up my father as a minister; she was a strong-minded Congregationalist and Abolitionist. My father imbibed Abolitionism, but never became even a church member. Church creeds he had little respect for. He thought the use of common sense would obtain entrance into the Kingdom of Heaven as well as anything. Sermons preached about hell-fire and damnation were to him spectacular and without reason. He always liked to attend church, and was the leader of the choir for many years. Charles F. Livingston of Manchester, with whom he worked and roomed for nearly two years, when they were boys on the *New Hampshire Telegraph* at Nashua, and with whom his friendship grew stronger as they grew older, said of him: "In the line of his profession, he was good as a compositor, excellent as a foreman and manager, and superior as a reporter and editor. As a writer, he was clear, clean and concise." He was town clerk in 1864, '65, and '66, and superintending school committee twice. He died of angina pectoris, suddenly, as he had wished, not after a long illness, February 15, 1893, at the age of 77 years, 4 months and 17 days. He was the oldest member of Social Lodge of Free and Accepted Masons of Enfield, N. H., at the time of his death, and was buried with Masonic honors in the cemetery on the Street.

My mother survived him nearly six years, but always felt his absence. In November, 1898, when the old house was destroyed, which had sheltered the Wallaces for over eighty-one years, she was burned in securing a trunk containing valuable papers, from which she did not recover. She died, December 25, 1898.

The Wilsons.

There were four brothers, Robert, Warren, John and Levi, sons of Nathaniel Wilson, who came from Gilmanton about the year 1783, and settled in Canaan. They were told, as many of the early settlers were, that lands were cheap and of exceeding richness. John and Warren settled on Sawyer Hill, on the farms now owned by John D. Lovring and the old Chandler farm. Warren afterwards exchanged farms with Dea. Joshua Pillsbury, who owned the present George Ginn farm; he m. March 25, 1783, Anna Berry; he d. October 10, 1851, aged 89; she d. October 31, 1819, aged 63. They had nine ch.: Betsey, b. January 5, 1784; d. August 23, 1865; m. David Richardson (see him). Nathaniel, b. July 23, 1786; d. December 19, 1789; Ephraim, b. July 21, 1788; d. December 12, 1789. Nathaniel, b. April 14, 1790; d. May 7, 1873; m. March 9, 1818, Betsey Burley of Dorchester; d. September 28, 1862, aged 65. They had seven ch.: Gordon, Henry H., Warren F., one d. young, Helen, Rufus and George. Nathaniel lived on the George Ginn farm, and his first house was in the field towards Enfield line; afterwards he built the house now occupied by Mr. Ginn. His son, Warren F., succeeded to the farm, worked it for many years and then moved to Enfield. Warren F. was b. November

1, 1838; d. March 18, 1906; m. Kate E. Strate, b. August 19, 1839, and had ch.: Leon W., b. January 22, 1873; d. June 23, 1894; Hattie S., b. July 2, 1863; Ida B., b. 1871; m. October 11, 1894, Will A. Hoit; Fred B., b. 1865; m. September 21, 1886, Ella F. Childs, dau. of Oliver B. and Mary S. Childs.

Henry H., son of Nathaniel, bought the farm, which he afterwards sold to Lineius Dennis on West Farms. He was for years a prominent man in town affairs. His first term as selectman was in 1862, and was continued in office in 1863. He was always a Democrat, and the next year saw the Republicans in office. He was elected again in 1869 and served continuously to 1874. He served again in 1884 to '86, and in 1892, a period of twelve years; and the town showed prosperity under his guidance. He m. 1st., Betsey Day, and had two ch.: Frank P., d. February 6, 1862; aged 10 yrs. 4 mos., and Harriet F., d. April 23, 1862, aged 3 yrs. 7 mos. He married a second time, and during the last years of his life lived in Enfield, where he died. Ephraim, son of Warren, b. March 7, 1792; m. 1830, Lucy Harris. Levina, b. March 20, 1798. Rufus, b. April 21, 1796. Warren, b. April 20, 1798. Lavinia, b. April 8, 1800.

John Wilson, brother of Warren, m. Sarah Barber, dau. of Zebulon of Dame's Gore, July 16, 1792; and had six ch.: Washington, b. October 11, 1792; d. January 28, 1854; m. May 6, 1837, Mehitable Tucker; ch.: James, d. June 9, 1889, aged 49; m. April 19, 1889, Cynthia Atwell. George H., d. November 21, 1906, aged 59 yrs., 5 mos., 21 d. Jacob, son of John, b. October 29, 1795. Charlotte, b. January 26, 1798; Elizabeth, b. April 13, 1800. Presele, b. February 6, 1802; John B., b. May 27, 1806; d. April 24, 1877; m. Sophronia Averill, b. November 4, 1811; d. October 18, 1897; ch.: Albert H., b. September 17, 1842; d. August 1, 1885; m. Ola Smith, dau. of R. R. Smith; ch. John. Warren E., son of John B., Loraine, dau. of John B.; b. April 27, 1848; d. May 14, 1898; m. Andrew E. Bean, b. September 28, 1845. Effie A., b. December 3, 1856; d. November 1, 1895; m. Charles O. Ball, b. February 14, 1860; Angie, d. February 23, 1857; aged 21; m. Hiram E. Putnam, son

Old Families.

of Caleb S., d. May 2, 1857, aged 21; Orissa C., m. Jonathan A. Sanborn (see him). Abbie Bell, m. a Pond.

Robert Wilson, brother of Warren; m. 1787, Ednah Richardson, dau. of William, d. April 18, 1800 (a), and had five ch.: Prudence, b. April 26, 1792; d. July 18, 1796; Levi, b. June 15, 1794; Jeremiah, b. May 14, 1796; m. July 2, 1815, Betsey Carlton, and had two ch.: Lemuel and Samuel. Prudence, dau. of Robert, b. April 6, 1798, m. Bartlett Hoyt, had one son Levi. They moved to Genesee, N. Y. Robert, son of Robert, b. March 31, 1800; d. August 28, 1800. Robert, m. 2d, March 29, 1801, Sally Dole, sister of Moses Dole, and had one son Joel, b. August 2, 1802. She was an invalid for a long time and he hired Phœbe Pattee, a daughter of Peter, to do the work. Several children were born to Robert and Phœbe, while she lived in his house, and he claimed them as his own. When Sally got well she refused to live in that "crowd" and came back to live with her brother, who cared for her and when she died buried her. But before she died old Robert married Phœbe, June 14, 1810, and kept on having children. Phœbe is said to have died of hysteries brought on by holding in her temper too long while she was spinning, December 3, 1851, aged 75. Old Robert fell into bad hands after his property was gone and was buried by the town. He died April 26, 1843, aged 77 (a). One dau., Edna, d. March 10, 1894, aged 78 yrs., 6mos., 22 d.; m. December 3, 1835, Nathan Willis (both a), and had thirteen ch.: Holmes, m. in the South and was in the Southern Army; Otis F., went West and m. there twice; Lizzie m. John Follansbee and had no children; John Chase, m. Emma Davis of Plainfield; William Henry, m. out West; Clarabelle never m.; Perry m. out West; Ara m. out West; George Harvey, m. a Webster; Ardella, m. a Heath; James, m. a Cummings; Leona, d. single (a). Ursula, dau. of Robert and Phœbe; m. Harvey Tucker; Phœbe m. a Holmes, Matilda m. a Brown, and Jane m. a Brown of Bristol.

GENEALOGY.

GENEALOGY.

The following are not intended as complete records of any family. The labor necessary to complete them would take more time than is at the disposal of the compiler. They will, however, serve as a starting point for some future genealogist. They have been collected from the town records, some of which are not now in existence; from tombstones, family Bibles and recollections of old people. The records of the older settlers have been made as complete as possible. The letter (a) represents that the person is buried in the Street Cemetery, (b) Wells, (c) West Canaan, (d) Sawyer Hill, (e) West Farms, (g) Cobble, (h) Birch Corner, (i) Porter, (j) Jones, (k) Dorchester, beyond the Jones Cemetery.

Abbott, Jane, d. June 9, 1864, ag. 21 (c).

Adams, John S., d. June 15, 1876, ag. 68 (b); his wife, Mary J., also the wife of C. D. Washburn, d. Nov. 21, 1885, ag. 56y., 2m. (b).

Adams, Angeetta, dau. of John R. and Mary A., d. Oct. 24, 1860, ag. 2m., 6d.; Matta J., dau., d. April 4, 1862, ag. 3m., 17d.; Addie E., dau., d. March 25, 1863, ag. 4y., 23d. (c)

Akerman, Ernest S., d. Oct. 3, 1906, ag. 24 (b).

Aldrich, Richard, d. March 16, 1829, ag. 69 (c); his wife, Orpha, d. May 15, 1855, ag. 87.

Aldrich, Abel, d. Nov. 9, 1848, ag. 60; his wife, Rebecca, d. Sept. 23, 1859, ag. 72 (c). Children: Gilford, d. July 8, 1849, ag. 17 (c); Asahel B., m., March 7, 1837, Persis Ferguson of Sharon, Vt. Children: Persis Phinette, d. Jan. 21, 1853, ag. 15y., 7d. (c); Edwin D., d. May 27, 1863, ag. 17y., 8m., 4d. (c).

Aldrich, Welcome, brother of Leonard, William and Aaron, d. Dec. 29, 1879, ag. 65; m. Hannah C. Burnham, dau. of Grover and Hannah (Currier) Burnham; d. April 15, 1890, ag. 69y., 4m., 17d. Children: Sidney, d. Aug. 20, 1868, ag. 18y., 4 m.; Edwin C., d. Sept. 11, 1906, ag. 54y., 3m., 17d.; all (b); m., Aug. 19, 1877, Abbie E. Knowles, b. 1854; Mary E., m. David Bucklin.

Aldrich, Leonard, d. Aug. 17, 1872, ag. 56; m. Mary E. Hadley, dau. of Jacob and Caroline (Newton) Hadley; she m. (second) a Preston; d. May 4, 1888, ag. 72y., 6m. Children: Leonora S., d. March 28, 1856, ag. 5y.; Etta C., d. Jan. 6, 1865, ag. 5y., 3m.; Elbyne, m. Francis Welch (see him); Ora L., d. May 12, 1907, ag. 49y., 6m., 20d. (b), by his wife, Etta S., he had: Eva May, b. Aug. 6, 1881; d. Dec. 17, 1886.

Aldrich, William, b. Feb. 15, 1819; d. May 23, 1897; m. Louisa M. Davis, dau. of Samuel, b. March 6, 1831. Children: Hubbard W., b. 1854; m., Jan. 29, 1879, Flora M. George.

Aldrich, Aaron, d. July 10, 1887, ag. 66; m. Lucretia D. Evans; d. Aug. 15, 1899, ag. 75y., 6m. (b). Children: Anna D., d. Aug. 8, 1872, ag. 20; Mina M., d. Sept. 19, 1866, ag. 12y., 6m.

Aldrich, Harry, d. Aug. 26, 1845, ag. 21y., 8m., 16d. (a).

Aldrich, Milton, of Lebanon, b. Dec. 5, 1797; m. Eunice Buell of Groton, b. Feb. 28, 1806. Children: Harvey, b. Dec. 9, 1823; d. Aug. 26, 1845; Almon, b. Canaan, April 6, 1826; Lyman, b. July 30, 1828; Marcia Ann, b. Jan. 7, 1831; Emily, b. Feb. 22, 1833; Adelaide, b., Enfield, Dec. 11, 1835; Emergene, b., Enfield, July 10, 1838; Julia, b., Enfield, Dec. 27, 1841.

Allen, T. Wilfred, b. 1833; d. 1906; his wife, Emma A., b. 1839; d. 1905 (b). Children: Edwin M., m. Roxie L. Davis. Child, Lena F. Robert E., son of T. Wilfred, b. Keene, Dec. 7, 1872; m., Oct. 23, 1897, Estella M. Davis, b. March 25, 1876; dau. of B. F. Davis of Grafton. Child, Franklin M., b. July 31, 1899.

Arvin, Simeon, d. May 19, 1816, ag. 49; m. Hannah Dustin, dau. of Jonathan; d. June 13, 1852, ag. 79 (b). Children: William B., b. March 26, 1791; d. March 6, 1813 (b); Simeon, b. 1793; m. and had three ch., two of them Elizabeth and George; Ruth, b. March 27, 1795; m. John Jones of Enfield. Children: Mary C., m. Hon. J. Everett Sargent and had one ch., John, d. young; Emily, m. ——— Foster; Hannah, b. 1797; m. John Burnham of Lebanon; had one son, John; Susannah, b. May 8, 1809; d. Aug. 12, 1867; m. Guilford Cobb, son of Salmon (see him) (a); William Brickett, b. 1812; d. ———; James, d. July 9, 1852, ag. 59y.; m., April 25, 1825, Sarah B. Follensbee of Grafton; d. August 15, 1864, ag. 76 (b). Child: Albert Gallatin, b. November 17, 1826; d. ———; m. Malana Shepard, dau. of Nathaniel; had two daughters and lived in Hanover.

Atherton, William, d. Jan. 31, 1863, ag. 74y., 1m., 24d.; m. Lavinia Flint, dau. of Joseph, b. April 27, 1794. Children: Mary E., d. August 21, 1890, ag. 69y., 4d; George William; Harriet Augusta, d. Sept. 11, 1827, ag. 3m., 23d. (all a.); James Wilbur; Edwin; Martha, m. in California; Caroline, m. in California.

Austin, George W., son of Arthur A. and Mary A., d. April 16, 1896, ag. 24y., 7m., 9d. (c); Gertrude A., dau. of same, and wife of Truman J. Clark, b. 1873; d. 1908 (c).

Avery, Samuel, d. Nov. 24, 1871, ag. 70y., 6m., 12d.; his wife, Elizabeth F., d. Jan. 15, 1872, ag. 75y., 4m., 1d. (a).

Bachelder, Nancy, dau. of Bailey and Sarah A.; d. March 6, 1862, ag. 4y., 24d. (c).

Bagley, Charlotte, wife of Moses, d. May 16, 1892, ag. 72.

Bailey, Levi, d. April 22, ag. 77; his wife, Anna, d. Jan. 23, 1831, ag. 61 (b). Children: Lydia, b. Sept. 13, 1789; Salley, b. Feb. 25, 1792, d. Aug., 1821 (b); Betsey, b. Nov. 8, 1793; d. April 16, 1825; m. Dec. 28, 1814, Josiah Clark, Jr.; all (b); Levi, Jr., b. Aug. 10, 1799; m. Feb. 19, 1823, Betsey Stevens of Grafton, d. Jan. 4, 1844, ag. 40y., 11m. (b). Children: Rial, m. Mary Ann Rogers; Adelaide, m. Joseph Peters.

Baker, James, d. March 18, 1890, ag. 66y., 8m., 21d. (d); m. April 14, 1851, Mary J. Flanders, d. March 23, 1902, ag. 79y., 17d. Children: Climena L., d. Sept. 5, 1852, ag. 3m., 25d.; James M., d. June 10, 1892, ag. 40y., 3m. (d).

Baker, Ellen E. (Parmenter), wife of Enoch, d. July 6, 1854, ag. 22y., 2m., 28d. Child: George P., d. April 4, 1856, ag. 4 (b).

Barber, Capt. Robert, b. between 1740-'50; d. about 1809; his wife, Sarah March, survived him about one year. She was appointed administrator of his estate, and before it was settled John M. was appointed on both estates. His estate was appraised at $1,301.74. Came to Canaan in 1777 with a yoke of oxen and a sled. Their children were: John M., Nathaniel, Robert Purnell, Sarah and Catherine, who married Artemus Lawrence and went to Ohio. The latter had one son, William, who died about 1832.

Barber, John M., b. Feb., 1767; d. March 24, 1855 (b); m., June 20, 1791, Sally Sanborn, d. June 12, 1838, ag. 68. He was born before his father came to Canaan; lived and died on the old Barber farm, from whom it got its name, now owned by Mary E. D. Weeks; he was a farmer. Had nine children: March; Deliverance, b. April 14, 1796; d. Jan. 29, 1799, fell in the fire; Mary, b. June 9, 1798; d. July 4, 1858; m. Benjamin Kidder. Child: Emily C., d. Nov. 15, 1857, ag. 21 (b); Sally, b. Sept. 8, 1800, d. Sept. 6, 1865, was lame; John, b. Sept. 9, 1802, d. March —, 1805, scalded by boiling sap; Jesse, b. Dec. 31, 1804, d. Aug. 24, 1858, lame, went in wheel chair; Catherine; Irena; Miriam, b. Feb. 14, 1814, d. Sept. 13, 1833 (b).

Barber, Purnell, dau. of Robert, m. Josiah Clark. (See Clark.)

Barber, Robert, son of Robert, m. Miriam Scofield, b. May 14, 1780, and had two children. They went to Canada with the other Scofields.

Barber, Sarah, dau. of Robert, m., March 5, 1792, William Parkhurst, and had one child: Catherine, born here Aug. 24, 1792.

Barber, Nathaniel, son of Robert, d. June 3, 1857, ag. 85y., 10m. His wife Nelly, d. June 2, 1819, ag. 49; m. (2) Feb. 27, 1820, Sally Patten. Two children: Dea. Nathaniel, d. Aug. 23, 1862, ag. 66y., 10m; m. Dec. 23, 1817, Elizabeth B. Miller, dau. Jacob, b. 1800; d. June 18, 1886. Children: Frank, m. Eunice Fales, and Horace H., m. Marie Garfield, one son, Winthrop G., d. young; Nelly, d. Dec. 27, 1809, ag. 6y., 8m.

Barber, March, son of John M., b. June 21, 1794; d. Oct. 14, 1868; m. Nov. 14, 1816, Mehitable Fifield, dau. of Winthrop and Mehitable Fifield, b. July 18, 1793, d. Oct. 25, 1875; he lived first on the farm where Benjamin Norris afterwards lived; then he succeeded to his father's farm, where he died; he had five children: Capt. John M. Franklin, b. Oct. 7, 1819, d. May 4, 1882, married and had one child, Frank; Hiram; Martha Jane; James P.

Barber, Catherine, dau. of John M., m. William Doten. (See Doten.)

Barber, Irena, dau. of John M., b. Aug. 14, 1810; d. May 3, 1852; m. Stephen S. Smith, b. April 18, 1804; d. July 5, 1887; lived in the house now owned by O. H. Perry, just off the Street; was a cooper and mason by trade; had six children: Elsa A., d. Feb. 21, 1841, ag. 5y., 6m.; Charles M., d. March 26, 1831, ag. 7; Harriet A., b. Feb. 10, 1832, m., Oct. 10, 1878, Charles E. Cogswell, b. Jan. 29, 1824; Mariam E., d. Oct. 19, 1903, ag. 64y., 7m., 2d. (a), m. Sept. 7, 1864, Horace B. Tenney, b. Feb. 21, 1837. Child, Irene A., b. 1868, m. April 13, 1886. Arthur W. Hutchinson. Sophia, dau. Stephen, b. Dec. 7, 1840, d. ———; m. Nov. 3, 1880, Hendrick Hall, b. Nov. 19, 1837; William P., m. Mattie Conger, lives in Marysville, Cal. Children: M. Irene, b. Jan. 10, 1878; Inez C., b. April 3, 1881.

Barber, John M., son of March, b. April 29, 1818; d. Aug. 15, 1885; m. (1), Jan. 13, 1842, Sarah S. Chapman, dau. of Noah and Abigail (Currier) Chapman, b. July 2, 1819; d. July 16, 1848; they had one child: William P. C., b. Sept. 3, 1845; d. Dec. 16, 1847. He m. (2), July 4, 1849, Mary M. Fales, dau. of Orrin, d. Nov. 29, 1907, ag. 84 (a). One child: William M., b. May 25, 1852; d. Aug. 26, 1909 (a); m. (1), Dec. 25, 1872, Anna Belle Shattuck, d. ———; no children; m. (2) Julia A. Sullivan and had two children. John M. lived in the house now occupied by David H. Whittier and was a gunsmith and wheelwright; his son was in the flour commission business.

Barber, Hiram, son of March, b. Aug. 23, 1823; d. Feb. 18, 1892 (a); m. (1), Oct. 8, 1850, Lucy A. Fales, dau. Orrin, b. Jan. 24, 1830; d. April 22, 1881. Three children: Henry H., who m. ———; has one dau. m., and is in the dry goods business in Milford; George E., who m. Elizabeth Weaver, has one dau., Helen, and is in the dry goods business in Derby, Conn.; Alice, single. Hiram m. (2), May 2, 1883, Mrs. Abigail (Martin) Chase, dau. William Martin, b. June 26, 1818; d. March 29, 1901; no children. He succeeded to his father's farm and took care of his parents for it, paying $1,000 besides. He sold to Charles Day and moved on the Street, where Bela B. Whitney afterwards lived, after his second marriage he moved into the Chase house, next above.

Barber, Martha Jane, dau. of March, b. June 14, 1829; m. Alfred M. Shackford (see him).

Barber, James P., b. Sept. 20, 1830; d. Dec. 21, 1904; m. (1) Mary S. Wier, dau. of Thomas; d. Oct. 13, 1861, ag. 21 (a); m. (2) Pauline R. Colburn, d. Jan. 14, 1868, ag. 33; m. (3), Sept. 21, 1876, Abigail A. Hoyt, d. July 27, 1890, ag. 68 (a). Children: Byron J., d. Aug. 15, 1861, ag. 5m., 5d.; Jennie M., d. April 12, 1868, ag. 11m.; Nellie J., b. Oct. 6, 1864; m. Fred B. Currier and had one child, Bernard B. Marion Belle, dau. of James P., b. Dec. 10, 1865; m. (1), Sept. 1, 1886, Dexter H. Nichols, b. April 21, 1852; d. Aug. 8, 1888; no children; m. (2), Bert Blood.

Barber, Josiah, d. about 1830; m. (1) Anna, by whom he had five children: Josiah Perous, b. April 16, 1792; Sally Perous, b. Dec. 4, 1793, m., March 12, 1815, John Hoit, Jr. (see him); Nancy Clark, b. April 10, 1796; Betsey, b. April 10, 1802; Polly, b. Oct. 19, 1803, d. May 15, 1851, m., Sept. 23, 1839, Nathaniel Derby, d. Feb. 24, 1875, ag. 88y., 8m. His first wife was Irena Clark, whom he m. Oct. 10, 1821; she d. May 15,

1839, ag. 47. Josiah, by his second wife, Salome, had five children: Clarissa Ann, b. Feb. 15, 1814; Salome, b. March 28, 1816; Moses, b. April 24, 1818; Louisa, b. June 18, 1824; Daniel, b. Sept. 8, 1826.

Barnard, Jonathan, b. Aug. 28, 1819; d. May 8, 1888; his wife, Mary Ann, d. Feb. 15, 1870, ag. 43. Children: Francis H., d. Nov. 27, 1849, ag. 1y., 10m.; Ellen L., d. Feb. 19, 1859, ag. 5y., 2m.; Hattie F., d. Aug. 24, 1859, ag. 1y., 11m.; Cora Bell, d. ———; Clara, m. a Chase; Georgianna, m. Clara's husband.

Barnard, David, son of Thomas and Ruth (Eastman), b. April 27, 1819; d. Jan. 11, 1888; m. (2) Susana Leavitt Youngman, b. March 29, 1825. Children: Burns M., m. Nellie Stevens, dau. Wyman. Children by his first wife: Eugene A., m., Nov. 11, 1885, Alice A. Grimes; Emma J., m., June 17, 1885, Fred F. Avery.

Barnes, Fred O., d. Dec. 21, 1878, ag. 19y., 1m. (d).

Barney, Aaron, son of Jacob and Lois (Walker), of Grafton, b. June 2, 1810; d March 24, ——— (b); m., Dec. 29, 1836, Sarah Ann Chase, dau. Ezra, b June 11, 1816; d. Jan. 8, 1891. Children: S. Addie, b. Oct. 4, 1849; d. Jan. 10, 1876; Charles O., b. July 21, 1844; m., July 21, 1873, Mary E. Wilmarth, b. Sept. 23, 1851; d. Feb. 4, 1887. Children: Lester, O, b. July 24, 1874; d. March 12, 1890; Alice M., b. July 8, 1879; d. March 21, 1899; Addie; Edward A., b. July 22, 1881; m., Nov. 30, 1909, Bessie Hutchinson; Ralph T. Elsina H., dau. Aaron, b. 1854; m., Oct. 4, 1874, Walter B. Martin.

Barney, Polly M., wife of Melvin A., d. April 10, 1883, ag. 37.

Barney, Otis, d. Dec. 8, 1849, ag. 76; his wife, Alathea, d. Jan. 7, 1868, ag. 75 (b).

Barney, Eleazer, son of John of Grafton, b. March 29, 1814; d. Sept. 7, 1884; m. Emeline A. Durrell, dau. of Daniel and Augusta (Tilton) Durrell, d. Feb. 14, 1906, ag. 82y., 10m., 8d. Children: Helen, who died young; Albert E., who m. (1), July 2, 1862, Rosina E. Hutchinson, dau. of Richard, d. Sept. 11, 1863, ag. 19y., 3m.; m. (2), Jan. 22, 1867, Abby Hutchinson, sister of his first wife. Had two children: Ernest A., b. July 11, 1869, who m. Mary Martin, dau. of Henry and Lucy J. (Burley) Martin; John E., b. March 15, 1876, m. Lydia J. Kirkpatrick, b. Aug. 23, 1880, had two children: Marjory, d. Feb. 5, 1906, ag. 1y., 8m., 20d. (b), and Pauline, b. May 22, 1907.

Barney, Arthur J., son of Eleazer, m. (1) M. Josette Hosley, d. Jan. 2, 1878, ag. 27y., 3m., 9d.; m. (2), April 10, 1881, Lillian A. Smith. He had two children by his first wife: Harry A., m. Feb. 6, 1907, Mary A. Hornbrooke, and has one child: Maurice H., b. Dec. 20, 1907. Clarence E., m., June 19, 1906, Grace A. Safford.

Barney, Bertha E., dau. Eleazer, b. 1856; m. (1), Dec. 22, 1875, Hervey S. Dow, son of Samuel H. and Emily R. Dow, b. 1849; d. Oct. 8, 1890; m. (2) Albert L. Hadley. Children by first marriage: Edith Meriam, b. Jan. 27, 1878, m., Jan. 25, 1898, Perley J. Columbia, four children. Archie, son of Hervey S. and Bertha E., d. Dec. 3, 1886, ag. 3d.; Pearl E., b. 1880, m., June 11, 1901. Reginald C. Stevenson, b. 1880; one child.

HISTORY OF CANAAN.

Barney, Charles, d. Aug. 3, 1887, ag. 69; m. (1), Feb. 20, 1853, Elizabeth J. Wells, d. Nov. 18, 1854, ag. 22; m. (2), Nov. 5, 1856, Harriet Wells, d. June 3, 1909, ag. 77y., 7m., 3d. Children: Lizzie I., m. Carey Smith; Allen W., b. May 14, 1862; d. Sept. 28, 1903.

Barry, Jane, wife of William, d. Nov. 23, 1861, ag. 52; also a dau. Nella, d. Sept. 8, 1850, ag. 2y.

Bartlett, Joseph, d. July 19, 1837, ag. 72y., 10m. (a); his wife, Matty or Molly, d. Jan. 20, 1818, ag. 49 (a); he m. a second wife, Ruth. He purchased 100 acres of the old farm of Caleb Clark, April 2, 1793, and in the deed he is recorded as from Newtown, N. H. His children were: Lois and Polly. Lois was b. Nov. 3, 1792; d. Nov. 18, 1819 (a); m., March 10, 1810, Joseph Burley of Dorchester, b. April 28, 1784; d. March 21, 1866. They had five children: Joseph Bartlett, b. Feb. 11, 1811; m., April 21, 1840, Louisa York, and had five children: Annie McKim, Louisa, Joseph Bartlett, George Mathias, who d. young, and Fannie, who d. young. The second child of Lois was Lois, b. May 2, 1818, and d. young. Third child of Lois: Mathias, b. Nov. 22, 1814; d. April 27, 1816; John, b. Sept. 2, 1816; d. Aug. 19, 1861; he married. Fifth child of Lois was Louisa Maria, b. Jan. 15, 1819; d. April 8, 1874; m., Dec. 7, 1843, John Foster of Rumney.

Bartlett, Polly, dau. of Joseph and Molly, b. Jan. 25, 1795; d. Feb. 24, 1885; m., Nov. 30, 1820, Orrin Fales, son of John, d. Jan. 28, 1858, ag. 58. Children: Orrin Gilbert, b. Nov. 19, 1826; d. May 3, 1841 (a); Mary M., m. John M. Barber (see him); Lucy A., m. Hiram Barber (see him); Clara J., b. Feb. 23, 1841; d. Dec. 1, 1890; m., April 5, 1864, Charles S. Wilson. Child: Luella. Hannah E., dau. Orrin, m. J. Blood; Lois, m. James H. Thrasher; George, d. in Pepperell, Mass., by his second wife, Maria, he had Charles H., b. Feb. 1, 1862. Joseph B., d. Feb. 9, 1863, ag. 23, who resided in Nashua at the time of his enlistment, Sept. 19, 1861, in the Eighth Regiment; he died at Fort Independence, Boston Harbor (a).

Bartlett, Nathaniel, d. March 18, 1841, ag. 84 (d); he m. Susannah Clark, dau. of Caleb; her oldest son was of that name and she signed a deed of her interest as an heir in Caleb Clark's farm; she d. Aug. 13, 1825, ag. 69y., 8m., 24d.; her age is given as 76 on her tombstone. Their children: Caleb Clark, m. Sarah Huse, dau. Nathan, d. Jan. 12, 1865, ag. 73y., 7m. Their children were: Eliza H., b. Oct. 14, 1826; d. Jan. 3, 1903; m., Oct. 24, 1866, John W. Kimball, b. Aug. 8, 1824; d. April 14, 1901; Belinda L., d. Feb. 22, 1875, ag. 38; m., Sept. 6, 1866, Ephraim F. Withington, b. Jan. 21, 1830; d. Sept. 18, 1880 (d), and had one child, Sidney B., m. Mary A. (Jepson) Story, d. ―― (a); Cordelia H., m., Sept. 22, 1852, Samuel Carlton. Children: Mary J., d. Aug. 14, 1855, ag. 1y., 10m., and Charles H., d. June 9, 1859, ag. 1y., 1m. (d); Caleb Sidney, son of Caleb C., d. May 19, 1866, ag. 44. Eliza H. succeeded to the old farm of her father, Caleb, which was a part of Nathaniel's old farm. The last house on the old Lyme road in Canaan. Polly H., dau. of Nathaniel, d. Nov. 9, 1870, ag. 86; m. Luther Kinne (see Kinne).

Betsey, d. June 8, 1862, ag. 73y., 2m; m., March 29, 1815, John Flanders, d. Feb. 22, 1864, ag. 74. Nancy H., m., Jan. 23, 1821, Amos Gould of Piermont.

Bartlett, Molly, consort of John H. Bartlett, d. Jan. 16, 1789, ag. 37 (a).

Bartlett, Nathaniel E., d. Aug. 26, 1873, ag. 63y., 1m.; m. Susan Slade, b. June, 1801; d. Oct. 13, 1886; he came from Vermont. Children: Frank T., and Myra H., b. Nov. 30, 1854; m., March 7, 1877, Wyman P. Clark, b. May 6, 1855; no ch.

Bartlett, Sally, has a broken stone, no dates (d).

Bean, Lucia P., wife of Daniel F., d. Aug. 13, 1849, ag 28 (a).

Bean, John, and Polly, his wife, had: Folsom, b. March 2, 1789; John, Jr., b. March 28, 1791; Moses, b. Jan. 11, 1793; Susannah, b. March 13, 1795. His name appears on the inventories of 1793-'95, and in 1798 he owned land in the southeast corner of the town.

Benson, Grace E., dau. Eugene E. and Belle K., b. 1899; d. 1900 (a).

Berry, Charles D., d. Sept. 21, 1876, ag. 56; his wife, Sarah, d. Oct. 21, 1871, ag. 55 (a). He was the father of John W. Berry. Lived in house now burned, across the Pond, on Richard Whittier's old farm.

Bert, Dorcas, wife of Alanson, d. March 8, 1843, ag. 40 (a).

Bickford, Jonathan, d. May 24, 1873, ag. 61 (b); his wife, Sabrina C., d. March 15, 1901, ag. 87. Children: Joseph S., d. June 14, 1864, ag. 22 (b); Sarah M., b. Nov. 21, 1837; d. Oct. 21, 1898; m. Freeman S. Parker and had three children: Laura, Cora Bell, d. Dec. 17, 1880, ag. 15y., 6m. (b); George W. Ida M., dau. of Jonathan, d. Nov. 1, 1870, ag. 18y., 10m.; Jane, m. Charles Wells (see him); Amelia A., b. 1840; m., Nov. 28, 1871, Ozias Millet; Mary E., b. 1838; m., Dec. 3, 1867, William H. Bell; Carrie.

Blaisdell, Martha E., wife of Hiram G., d. March 8, 1869, ag. 22; their dau., Linnie N., d. Dec. 11, 1867, ag. 8m., 22d. (a). He m. (2), April 26, 1870, Caroline A. Westcott, b. 1854, and had two children: Fannie Ellen, m., June 27, 1906, Frank W. Chase, and Lora A., d. Dec. 27, 1905, ag. 24y., 8m., 11d.; she m., Nov. 6, 1897, Moses B. Wheeler and had three children (a).

Blaisdell, Sanborn, d. July 16, 1862, ag. 68; his wife, Mehitable, d. Sept. 11, 1867, ag. 62 (j).

Blake, Polly F., wife of Joseph, d. Aug. 17, 1863, ag. 69 (d).

Blanchard, Israel, b. Nov. 14, 1825; d. Jan. 20, 1902 (c).

Blodgett, Caleb, b. Dec. 13, 1793; d. Oct. 5, 1872; m., Sept. 17, 1824, Charlotte Piper, b. Feb. 12, 1804; d. Feb. 1, 1873 (a). Children: Caleb, b. June 3, 1832; d. Dec. 11, 1903 (a); m., Dec. 14, 1865, Roxalana B. Martin, dau. of Jesse, and had one son, Charles H., who married and has one son, Caleb; lives in Melrose, Mass. Isaac N., son of Caleb and Charlotte, b. March 6, 1838; d., Franklin, Nov. 27, 1905; m., May 25, 1861, Sarah Gerould, dau. of Moses, and had one child, Anna. Emily R., dau. of Caleb, d. Aug. 23, 1851, ag. 23 (a); m. Miles Jackson who d. Oct. 29, 1853, ag. 53 (a); their son, George, d. Sept. 28, 1848, ag. 4m.,

2sd. (a). He m. (2), April 12, 1852, Elsie T. Miner, dau. of Amos Miner.

Bogardus, Wilmer S., son of Dr. F. A. and Blanche E. (Sargent), d. Dec. 30, 1899, ag. 11m., 16d.

Booth, Isaiah, m., Feb. 18, 1784, Anne; one child: Joseph C., b. July 1, 1784.

Boyington, Huldah M., d. Sept. 8, 1884, ag. 60.

Bradbury, William, b. Haverhill, Mass., April 2, 1759; d. Dec. 27, 1834 (d); m. Polly Meacham, dau. of Samuel, b. Feb. 9, 1768; d. June 26, 1836. Nine children: Judith, m. William Gordon; Betsey, m. a Randlett; Sarah, d. April 11, 1875, ag. 77y., 4m.; m., Dec. 14, 1815, Abner H. Cilley, d. Feb. 4, 1872, ag. 78 (d). Children: Horatio G., d. April 25, 1864, ag. 29 (d); George J., b. 1840; m., Nov. 27, 1864, Clara J. Jewell, d. Jan. 7, 1866, ag. 19y., 10m. (a); m. (2), Dec. 24, 1868, Mrs. Ada E. Lowell, Dianey, and another daughter that m. a Wardsworth. David, son of William and Polly, m. a Richardson; Mary, single. Samuel, m. a Gould; Roswell, m. an Emerson; William, d. Oct. 15, 1853, ag. 54 (d); m., Dec. 11, 1817, Rebekah Gould, b. 1793. Twelve children: Joshua and Rebekah, d. young; Albert A., b. Oct. 9, 1838; d. 1901; m., May 29, 1869, Adeline E. Morse, dau. of Jesse, b. 1844; d. 1900 (e). Children: William J. and Addie R., m. Frank S. Fifield, son of Edson J.; Amos Porter, b. 1842, son of William, m. Adelia Elmer, b. 1846; Harriet Ann, m. (1), Dec. 22, 1842, Elbridge G. Stone; m. (2) Plummer Smith. Children: Lucy A., b. 1845; m., Aug. 9, 1864, William A. Libbey, b. 1843, of Piermont. Hannah, dau. William, m., Oct. 28, 1852, Alexander Jefferson; Aaron, b. May 5, 1828; d. July 4, 1861; m. Annette Richardson, dau. of Jacob and Elsie (see her); Mary, m. William K. Hadley, son of Silas; Celia, m., Aug. 21, 1849, Caleb B. Atwood; Fannie W., b. 1834; m., Sept. 25, 1862, Charles H. Kelley. William, son of William, m., March 15, 1855, Velina S. Spear; Dexter F., m., Nov. 12, 1857, Betsey A. Clark. Benjamin, son of Dea. William, d. Nov. 25, 1893, ag. 89y., 10m., 21d. (d); m. (1) Lydia Pollard, dau. David, d. March 17, 1875, ag. 68y., 2sd. Children: Amanda E. J., d. Nov. 2, 1838, ag. 8w.; Louis N., d. March 24, 1900, ag. 67y., 8m.; George C., m. (1), Sept. 11, 1853, Elzina Wheat, d. Oct. 11, 1864, ag. 33y., 2sd. (a); m. (2), Jan. 2, 1869, Mattie P. Story, dau. of Otis J., b. 1845. Benjamin, m. (2), July 16, 1876, Hannah S. Boston.

Bradbury, Samuel, m., Nov. 5, 1815, Phoebe Porter. Children: Phoebe, b. Sept. 4, 1816; d. March 3, 1879; m. George Davis, d. July 26, 1872, ag. 60y., 6m., 26d. (a). Children: Phoebe, d. June 28, 1856, and Leroy S., b. 1842; d. 1894 (a); m. Emma M. Merrill and had three children: Kitty, m. (1) John Harrigan, and had one child; m. (2) Albert Richardson; Etta Bell, d. Feb. 3, 1866, ag. 21d, and an infant, d. April 11, 1868. Samuel, son of Samuel, b. Dec. 16, 1817; Polly, b. Feb. 12, 1819; Enos Wells, b. Dec. 24, 1820.

Briggs, Howard C., son of C. B. and A. E., b. March 13, 1884; d. May 12, 1903 (b).

Brocklebank, Moses A., d. Sept. 8, 1898, ag. 79y., 5m., 10d. (c); m., Oct. 13, 1879, Sophronia Stevens of Enfield, d. Oct. 19, 1878, ag. 54; their dau., Laura R., d. May 17, 1862, ag. 11y., 5m., 20d.; Nellie A., d. Feb. 12, 1894, ag. 36y., 4m.; m. (1) Oscar Harris; m. (2) Henry Choate.

Brown, Susan F., dau. of B. and S. P., d. Sept. 15, 1873, ag. 21 (b).

Brown, Abel, b. Feb. 28, 1780; m., Jan. 3, 1811, Sally Folsom, b. Oct. 19, 1785. Child: Adaline Colby, b. Feb. 23, 1812.

Brown, John G., son of Charles and Mary, d. July 22, 1880, ag. 19 (b).

Bucklin, Mary E., dau. of Welcome Aldrich, wife of David, d. Aug. 14, 1871, ag. 29y., 9m. (b); Allie S., son, d. May 1, 1871, ag. 4m., 14d.; Arthur M., b. 1864; m., July 4, 1883, R. Clara Akerman, b. 1863.

Burke, Michael, d. Nov. 16, 1902, ag. 82y., 7m. (c); his wife, Honora, d. April 13, 1872, ag. 49; son, John W., d. Aug. 22, 1881, ag. 32 (c).

Burnham, James, d. March 16, 1849, ag. 74y., 7m. (e); by his wife, Elizabeth, he had Elzina, d. May 16, 1827, ag. 10; Dea. Silas d. May 4, 1887, ag. 81y., 6m. (c); m. (1), June 15, 1837, Ruth P. Colby, d. March 9, 1849, ag. 36y., 2m. (e); m. (2), Jan. 15, 1849, Lydia Sanborn, d. March 29, 1871, ag. 52 (c). Adelia A., wife of William H. Clough, d. March 24, 1891, ag. 42y., 4m., 7d. (e). James, probably the son of James, d. July 10, 1827, ag. 27; and Joseph d. Nov. 9, 1838, ag. 41, his wife, Lucy, d. March 6, 1836, ag. 37.

Burnham, Mason, b. Oct. 18, 1823; d. Sept. 1, 1891; his wife, Ruth L., b. July 27, 1824; d. Feb. 11, 1894.

Burnham, Nellie W., dau. of George W. and Mary L., d. Oct. 2, 1862, ag. 5y., 2m., 21d; another, Liona E., d. Sept. 25, 1862, ag. 2y., 10m., 1d. (c).

Butman, Mary, wife of Paul, d. April 23, 1850, ag. 45 (a). Children: Laura, m. (1) a Sanborn; m. (2), Aug. 18, 1861, David T. Ford; Frank, b. Dec. 27, 1824; d. Aug. 14, 1896 (d); m., Feb. 6, 1849, Susan T. Colby, dau. of Adonijah and Susanna Colby, b. Feb. 2, 1824; d. Oct. 21, 1893. Children: Frank H., d. Sept. 30, 1881, ag. 28y., 4m. (d); m., Jan. 1, 1874, Eva Gorham; George E., b. 1863; d. 1890 (d); Alma A. Clough, wife of another son, Charles H., b. Sept. 3, 1861; d. Feb. 4, 1895 (d). Another son of Frank: Fred E., is married and has three children: Blanche, Oscar and Grace.

Butterfield, son of William and Harriet Jones, d. Sept. 11, 1849, ag. 4w; another son, George, d. Aug. 11, 1849, ag. 2y., 4m. (a).

Call, Enoch, d. Feb. 23, 1877, ag. 76y., 4m., 18d. (d); by his wife, Ruth, he had: Sarah J., b. 1845; m., Nov. 29, 1865, John Wheeler of Dorchester; William R., b. 1838; m., Sept. 21, 1869, Abbie F. Harris.

Campbell, William, d. Aug. 7, 1863, ag. 88 (c); his wife, Hannah Hardy, d. July 7, 1862, ag. 83y., 6m. Children: Capt. Daniel, d. Dec. 11, 1850, ag. 52y., 10m. (c); m., July 11, 1821, Polly Wells, dau. of Ezekiel and Polly, d. Sept. 4, 1882, ag. 81y., 4m.; their children were: Daniel H., d. May 19, 1885, ag. 57y., 8m., 26d. (c); m. Angelina F. Webster, d. Jan. 26, 1886, ag. 55; their children were: Daniel W., b. 1855; m., April 30, 1882, Mary J. Clough, dau. of B. W. Clough, b. 1860; Sarah F., b. 1859;

m., June 15, 1887. Elmer E. Brown; Ella, m. a Carr; Mary, m. Frank Howe. Charles A., b. 1867; d. 1895; m., Dec. 7, 1887, Hannah A. Goss of Hanover; had four children. Alba A., son of Capt. Daniel, d. Oct. 10, 1853, ag. 19. Polly, dau. of William, b. March 31, 1807; d. Jan. 8, 1821. William, Jr., d. May 28, 1839, ag. 31. Betsey, d. Sept. 12, 1862, ag. 62; m., Nov. 22, 1821, Nathaniel Shepard, d. Oct. 27, 1881, ag. 82y., 11m. Hannah, m., Jan. 31, 1822, Timothy Sanborn.

Carlton, Jonathan, m. Molly; she d. Nov. 5, 1821, ag. 61. Children: Daniel, b. April 21, 1783; child, Moses. Jonathan, d. Dec. 3, 1878, ag. 78y., 2m.; m. Eliza Shattuck, d. March 26, 1852, ag. 53y., 4m. (a); Francis C. and Mary had a son, Miles, d. Sept. 26, 1821, ag. 9m. (a).

Carlton, Thomas L., and Edna, had a son, Albert, b. Nov. 3, 1839. Nancy, wife of Thomas J., d. April 2, 1860, ag. 24 (c).

Carter, William, d. April 12, 1871, ag. 84y., 10m.; he m. Abigail and had a son, George, d. Dec. 25, 1856, ag. 21.

Caverley, Harriet D., b. 1819; d. 1909 (c).

Chamberlain, William A., b. March 6, 1855; d. June 14, 1906 (c).

Chase, Ambrose, d. about 1803 (d), and Hannah, had Hannah, b. March 13, 1801, and William, who m. Abigail and had Elisa, b. June 11, 1811, Hannah Hawthorne, b. May 26, 1813, and John R., b. March 31, 1815.

Chase, Joseph, d. Sept. 6, 1820, ag. 46; Nancy E., his wife, d. Jan. 20, 1857, ag. 82. Children: Sarah, m. Uriah F. Lary (see him); Horace W., b. March 18, 1809; d. Jan. 3, 1877 (a); m. Abigail Martin, dau. of Robert, Dec. 24, 1835; b. June 26, 1818; d. March 29, 1901. Children: William M. (see lawyers); Henry M., b. Aug. 27, 1857; d. May 22, 1902 (a); m., June 1, 1878, Addie B. Smith, and had a daughter.

Chase, William, d. Oct. 14, 1857, ag. 61y., 3m.

Chase, Ezra, d. Jan. 14, 1864, ag. 84 (b); his wife, Sarah E. Morrill, d. March 17, 1848, ag. 63y., 9m. Children: Betsey M., d. Nov. 21, 1888, ag. 79; m., Aug. 1837, Gideon Lowell, d. Sept. 2, 1863, ag. 62. Children: Frank B. and Belle. Samuel B., son of Ezra, b. March 6, 1819; d. Nov. 15, 1893; m. dau. of Otis Barney. Sarah Ann, dau., d. Jan. 8, 1891, ag. 74y., 6m.; m. Aaron Barney (see him); Charles C., Francis M., son of Ezra, d. March 29, 1875, ag. 63 (b); m. Eliza J. and had Clarence J. A., d. Dec. 24, 1857, ag. 7w., 7d., and Viola J., d. Dec. 14, 1860, ag. 8y., 2m., 1d.

Chesley, Eleazer, d. Sept. 29, 1876, ag. 80y., 5m. (c); Ann, his wife, d. Aug. 15, 1869, ag. 67. Their son, Eleazer B., d. April 2, 1868, ag. 31.

Childs, Oliver B., m. Mary Stone, b. Feb. 5, 1844; d. Jan. 21, 1903. Almira T., b. Dec. 9, 1844; d. Nov. 7, 1879; m. George Barker. Mary Ella F., dau. of Oliver B., d. Aug. 8, 1898, ag. 36y., 9m., 18d.; m. Fred B. Wilson.

Clark, Amasa, son of Moses, b. in Warner, Aug. 10, 1777; d. Feb. 17, 1854 (d); m. Sally Ladd in Hopkinton, from the family of Daniel Flanders, came to Canaan in 1804. She d. Nov. 30, 1858, ag. 75. They had six children:

GENEALOGY.

1. Laura, b., Hopkinton, Feb. 14, 1803; m., Jan. 26, 1825, Noah Sawyer of Canaan; three children: one of them, Seraph, d. Jan. 11, 1835, ag. 8; Stephen, b. 1835; m., Jan. 7, 1871, Mary E. Cilley, dau of Mark, b. 1835.

2. Zilpha, b. Oct. 2, 1804; m., Feb., 1837, John Hobbs, Jr., of Andover; one child, Catherine, who married and died, leaving three children.

3. Samuel Stillman, b. April 15, 1807; d. April 25, 1876; m., 1833, Clarissa Porter of Canaan, b. Jan. 2, 1804; d. March 4, 1863, leaving three children. He died April 25, 1876; was blind many years. Children: 1. George Porter, m. (1) ———— Pettingill; she was divorced; m. (2) Ellen Bradish of Haverhill; several children. 2. Sarah, b. 1841; m., 1868, Benjamin Clay of Danbury; resides California. 3. Eliza P., b. 1841; m., June 13, 1870, Sigismond Wolfson of Germany; four children: Mabel M., d. Nov. 8, 1897, ag. 22y., 10m.; Clara F., d. April 15, 1874, ag. 29; Maurice S., d. Sept. 22, 1873 (d), ag. 1y., 1m., 21d.; Carl, who m. Lillian Jewel and lives with his father and mother in Canaan on old Porter farm.

4. Carlton Currier, b. Oct. 3, 1814; m., June, 1841, Lucinda Bowen of Grafton; no children; m. (2), Oct. 19, 1871, Mrs. Mary Sargent, who soon died, Sept. 14, 1874, ag. 47y., 5m., leaving an infant that died a few months after. He died Dec. 17, 1875 (d). Child: Alma C., d. March 14, 1876, ag. 1y., 11m., 16d.

5. Sarah, b. June 19, 1818; d., unm., Feb. 24, 1841 (d).

6. Mary, b. Oct. 20, 1820; m., Feb. 3, 1859, Joel Osborne of Chelsea, Vt.; she died Oct. 28, 1863; no children.

Clark, Theodore, d. June 13, 1858, ag. 85y., 6m., Sd.; bought his farm of his father, Timothy, who came from Pelham; his second wife, Betsey, d. Sept. 26, 1884, ag. 87y., 7m., Sd. Children: Daniel, d. April 17, 1892, ag. 78y., 5m., Sd.; m. (1) Dorcas Hadley, dau. of Stephen 1st, d. March 18, 1876, ag. 61 (e); m. (2), Nov. 19, 1876, Elizabeth Hale. Children: Emeline, d. Feb. 5, 1904, ag. 63; m. John W. Philbrick, son of Hiram; Irena, b. 1846; m., Aug. 6, 1865, Alexander Evans, b. 1836; Benjamin O. T., b. 1849; d. Oct. 7, 1867 (e); m., July 4, 1861, Carrie E. Philbrick, dau. of Francis and Abigail Welch, she was known afterwards as "Inda E."; Betsey, b. 1834; m. (1), Oct. 12, 1857, Anthony Welch; m. (2) Hiram Philbrick; m. (3) Willard Colburn, d. July 13, 1893, ag. 60y., 2m., 24d.; Rachel G., b. 1850; m., Oct. 11, 1865, Elijah W. Edwards, m. (2) John Ford; Leonard A., b. 1851; m., Oct. 8, 1874, Malvina Shattuck; Henry W., b. 1859; m., Sept. 1, 1879, Hattie J. Shattuck, b. March 7, 1864. Children: Dorcas, b. March 20, 1883; m. Ira A. Tarbell, and Josie m. Albert Goss; Mahala D., d. July 1, 1879, ag. 22y., 10m.; m. John Ford (e). Betsey, dau. of Theodore, d. March 1, 1824, ag. 2; Reuben, d. Oct. 29, 1884, ag. 66y., 2m., 24d. (e). Children: Jennie D., d. March 6, 1884, ag. 24y., 1m., 23d.; m. a Dunham.

Clark, Dorinda, first wife of Reuben, d. July 27, 1842, ag. 23 (e). His second wife, Miriam J., d. Sept. 13, 1898, ag. 68y., 8m., 6d. (e).

Clark, Helen A., wife of Frank E., d. May 15, 1903, ag. 31 (e).

Clark, Jacob S., b. 1799; d. 1881; his wife, Hannah S., b. 1811; d. Feb. 11, 1898 (a).

Clark, Mary E., dau. of O. A. and G. A., b. Nov. 3, 1904; d. Feb. 18, 1905.

Clark, Warren W., son of John B. and Susan B. (Waterman), d. Jan. 15, 1857, ag. 6y., 7m., 2d., and Warren T., d. Oct. 2, 1862, ag. 1y., 8m. (c); John S., son of John B., b. 1843; m. (1) Mary A. Morey; m. (2). Aug. 30, 1891, Mary A. Woodbury, b. 1853; Truman J., b. 1856; m., Oct. 27, 1906, Gertrude A. Austin, b. 1873; d. Dec. 27, 1908, ag. 35y., 1m., 8d. Child: Lizzie M., b. 1907; d. 1908 (c). Horace A., son of John B., b. 1848; m., Jan. 10, 1874, Mary E. Stark, dau. of Jonathan of Hanover.

Clement, O. F., Co. B, Fourth Vermont Volunteers. (c).

Clement, Annie B., wife of Frank A., b. 1874; d. 1895 (c).

Cleveland, William A., b. Nov. 22, 1816; d. Sept. 4, 1887; his wife, Deidamia, b. Dec. 7, 1824; d. Oct. 18, 1903. Children: Clara A., b. July 11, 1865; d. June 22, 1898; m. a Wright.

Clough, Samuel, d. Nov. 23, 1862, ag. 82 (d); his wife, Jerusha Clark, d. Sept. 22, 1853, ag. 74. Children: Miriam, d. July 20, 1827, ag. 19; Mary A., d. Sept. 14, 1884, ag. 61y., 11m., 21d.; m. ——— Williams; Clark, b. 1818; d. 1892 (c); m. Elsie (Miller) Richardson, b. 1817; d. May 30, 1897. Children: Sarah J., wife of John P. Daines, b. 1852; d. 1905; one son, Byron. Emma A., dau. of Clark, b. 1858; m., June 19, 1877, Albert Packard, son of John, b. 1858. Children: Ethel, Burton. John F., son of Samuel, b. 1820; m., March 13, 1844, Hannah E. Packard, dau. of Chamberlain, b. Feb. 1, 1827; d. Oct. 6, 1894 (d). Children: Allen J., d. Feb. 5, 1907, ag. 62y., 8m.; he m., April 19, 1864, Sarah Ann Whittier, dau. Elijah and Matilda, and had a son, Bert. Mary A., dau. of John F., b. 1854; m., April 9, 1879, Daniel Goss, Jr., son of Daniel and Loraine, b. 1852; one son, Albert, m. Josie Clark, dau. of Henry; one dau., Beatrice.

Clough, Clark, d. April 1, 1853, ag. 26 (d).

Cobb, Salmon, b., Mansfield, Mass., Oct. 22, 1760; d. Nov. 4, 1851; m. (1), Oct., 1785, Abigail Pratt, b. Oct. 1765; d. May 1, 1804; m. (2), May 1, 1811, Bathsheba Briggs, b. April 29, 1770; d. May 26, 1863. He was a Revolutionary soldier before he came to Canaan (a). Children: Seven by first and one by second wife: Polly, b. March 15, 1788; Abigail, b. June 2, 1790; Fanny, b. Aug. 19, 1792; d. Sept. 12, 1879, single; Salmon P., b. Dec. 19, 1793; d. Sept. 3, 1878 (b); m. Betsey Fisher, b. Dec. 31, 1801; d. Dec. 20, 1869. Children: Hiram, d. Feb. 21, 1824, ag. 5m., 3d.; Elizabeth F., b. 1828; d. 1884, single; Abbie P., d. May 6, 1849, ag. 21; Adelia F., m. James H. Davis (see him); Caroline, and Phoebe, d. Jan. 29, 1901, ag. 66y., 9m., 14d.; Lucretia B., d. Oct. 22, 1906, ag. 69y., 4m., 7d.; m., April 24, 1860, Albert A. Haggett; two children, one dau. died, and one dau., Minnie L., living with her father, single. Phoebe, dau. of Salmon, b. Oct. 25, 1795; d. March 23, 1832 (b); m., Sept. 23, 1824, Timothy K. Blaisdell, son of Daniel (see him). Guilford, b. July 17, 1799; d. April 23, 1853 (a); m., 1832, Susan Arvin, dau.

Genealogy.

of Simeon, b. May 8, 1809; d. Aug. 12, 1867. Children: Hiram M., b. July 21, 1828; d. April 12, 1897; m. Malvina Snell, b. Jan. 24, 1839; d. Jan. 14, 1907; Susan Frances, b. Dec. 4, 1833; d. Aug. 21, 1903, single. Hiram, son of Salmon, b. March 6, 1801. Edwin, b. March 8, 1812; d. Nov. 16, 1870 (a); m., March 19, 1837, Emma E. Brooks, b. July 27, 1815; d. June 28, 1885. Children: Emma E., b. May 27, 1840; m., Jan. 1, 1862, Wyman Stevens. Children: Ellen E., b. Aug. 11, 1862; m. Burns M. Barnard. Henry P., b. May 6, 1864; d., single. George E., son of Edwin, b. Feb. 20, 1844; m., Nov. 8, 1879, Lucia A. Folsom, b. May 21, 1860. Children: Fannie L., b. July 5, 1880; m., June 19, 1904, Ernest D. Fleetham, b. Sept. 14, 1869. Children: Constance, b. Sept. 12, 1906; Ernest D. Jr., b. Feb. 2, 1909.

Colburn, Leonard, d. Oct. 16, 1828, ag. 85 (d); his wife, Elizabeth, d. April 6, 1815, ag. 73 (e).

Colburn, Willard, d. July 13, 1893, ag. 60y., 3m.; his first wife, Mandana B., d. May 21, 1881, ag. 47y., 6m.; m. (2) Betsey Clark, dau. of Daniel.

Colby, Daniel, d. July 23, 1853, ag. 99y., 7m.; his wife, Mary Folsom, of Haverhill, Mass., d. March, 1850, ag. 92. He had fifteen children, one of them, Lucy, b. Feb. 25, 1799; d. Feb. 19, 1876; m., Jan. 19, 1815, Joshua Wells (see him). Ensign, d. Aug. 17, 1866, ag. 87 (a); m., March 16, 1806, Silvia Fales, d. March 12, 1850, ag. 62. Children: Mary, b. Oct. 22, 1806; d. May 18, 1881; m. Thomas J. Hardy, d. Sept. 20, 1883, ag. 78 (a). Alvin, b. April 2, 1808. John H., b. March 20, 1818; m., Sept. 2, 1838, Emeline D. Hadley. Children: Sidney L., b. 1846; m., Dec. 24, ———, Sophia L. Morse, b. 1850. Joseph, d. Feb. 22, 1825. Abner Chase, son of Daniel, m., Nov. 12, 1795, by William Ayer, Betsey Laff Flagg. Aaron H., m., March 23, 1814, Sally Haynes.

Colby, Adonijah, b. Gilmanton; d. Jan. 14, 1849, ag. 71 (a); m. (1) Susan Taylor, d. Dec. 5, 1818, ag. 39; m. (2), Dec. 2, 1819, Susanna Richardson, dau. of John, b. July 16, 1790; d. Oct. 23, 1855. Children: John, d. Sept. 30, 1887, ag. 60y., 5m.; Susan T., d. Oct. 21, 1893, ag. 69y., 7m., 21d.; m. Frank Butman, son of Paul and Mary Butman (see him). Capt. Elijah R., son of Adonijah, d. Feb. 20, 1864, ag. 53y., 10m., 6d. (a); m. Lucinda A. Lathrop, b. Oct. 2, 1809; d. May 7, 1899; she m. (2) Thomas Sanborn. Nancy R., dau. of Adonijah, b. Sept. 10, 1816; d. July 1, 1887; m., Dec. 17, 1846, Henry E. Joslyn.

Colby, Moses, old stone defaced (a); d. about 1804.

Colby, Enoch, had a dau., Sarah, b. Aug. 7, 1808; may have been wife of Harry Leeds.

Colby, Willaby, d. Sept. 28, 1858, ag. 79 (d); Elizabeth Tewksbury, his wife, d. April 29, 1849, ag. 66. Children: Sarah, wife of Israel Porter, d. Dec. 1, 1896, ag. 86; Willaba, d. May 31, 1848, ag. 26; Mary C., m., Nov. 28, 1845, Darious W. Copp of Sanbornton, and d. Sept. 22, 1884, ag. 61y., 4m., 9d.; he d. June 8, 1891, ag. 64 (d). John S., d. Sept. 30, 1887, ag. 60y., 11m.; single. Elizabeth, d. Jan. 28, 1881, ag. 69; m. a Jones.

596   HISTORY OF CANAAN.

Colby, Martha A. (Houston), wife of Moses T., d. April 25, 1903, ag. 68y., 2m., 24d. (c). Children: Ella J., d. Aug. 23, 1883, ag. 20; Charles M., d. June 25, 1860, ag. 2; Edna R., d. Dec. 6, 1874, ag. 4; Lizzie M., d. April 4, 1877, ag. 10. The last three buried in Hanover.

Cole, Joseph H., b. May 11, 1815; d. June 24, 1849; m., 1843, Melissa J. Lowell, b. May 1, 1820; d. July 26, 1867. Children: Daniel W., b. Oct. 16, 1847; d. March 4, 1868 (a); m., April 27, 1867, Ellen Dean; Amon H., b. Dec. 11, 1843; d. Nov. 4, 1867 (a); Etta M., b. Jan. 24, 1850; d. Oct. 21, 1874 (a); Alvin B., b. Oct. 12, 1845; m., Feb. 6, 1875, Lizzie M. Boyce. Melissa J. Lowell m. (2), 1852, William Digby, b. Nov. 4, 1825; d. Aug. 23, 1863. Children: Florence H., b. Aug. 30, 1854; d. Aug. 13, 1856 (a); Rosilla E., b. Sept. 28, 1857; d. Feb. 14, 1862; Joseph W., b. Nov. 7, 1859; d. July 23, 1867 (a).

Cole, Norman W., d. Sept. 29, 1891, ag. 29y., 11m., 22d.; Viola M., d. March 7, 1883, ag. 18y., 6m., 14d. Children of Justus and Caroline (Digby) Cole.

Collins, Nellie M., dau. of J. O. and C. F., d. Aug. 29, 1883, ag. 3y., 9m. (a).

Collins, John, b. April 3, 1788; m., April 5, 1819, Sally Stevens, b. Sept. 1, 1797; d. Jan. 16, 1824. Children: James Stevens, b. March 16, 1820, Olive Stevens, b. Nov. 27, 1822.

Columbia, Charles, d. Aug. 21, 1900, ag. 40 (b); Anthony, d. Nov. 30, 1893, ag. 80y., 10m., 2d.; his wife, Lasett, d. May 19, 1883, ag. 93y., 6m.

Conant, Henry F., son of Rev. Liba and Deborah, d. Nov. 28, 1836, ag. 7 (a).

Copp, Henrietta, d. Feb. 9, 1879, ag. 14y., 9m.; Elsworth W., d. Dec. 19, 1878, ag. 8y., 1m.; children of Lemuel M. and Lucy E.

Corliss, Joseph Folsom, son of Daniel and Rachel, d. Nov. 21, 1816, ag. 20 (b).

Crosby, Benjamin J., son of Stephen and Rhoda, d. Jan. 25, 1850, ag. 21 (b).

Cross, Bailey, son of Jonathan and Molly (Bailey) Cross of Methuen, d. March 12, 1812, ag. 41 (b), on tombstone; town records say d. Feb. 28, 1813; m., March 14, 1802, Susannah Bagley; she m. (2) Stephen Worth. Children: Leonard, b. Feb. 14, 1803; lived in Georgia; m; Luther, b. Sept. 16, 1804; a doctor, lived St. Catherine, Ont.; m., no children; Lemira H., b. Aug. 31, 1806; m. Henry J. Deaver; Calvin, b. Aug. 16, 1808; d. 1902; m. and had a dau. who m. Dr. Goodnow of St. Catherine, Ont. Amey, b. June 12, 1811; d. March 1, 1813; Susanah, b. May 12, 1813; m. Anthony Groves. The other children of Jonathan and Molly were: Nathan, d. Sept. 21, 1857, ag. 73 (b); Jonathan B.; Rebecca, m. David Dustin; Elizabeth, m. Caleb Welch; Olive, the school teacher, d. single; Fanny, m., Sept. 7, 1815, Theophilus Sanborn of Bridgewater.

Cummings, Martha, wife of William, d. Oct. 9, 1852, ag. 101 y., 7m., 11d. (b).

Currier, Nathaniel, son of William and Nancy, b. Oct. 6, 1791; d. Sept.

12, 1863 (a); m. Rebecca V. Pratt, d. July 24, 1872, ag. 78 (a). His mother, Elizabeth P., d. March 21, 1832, ag. 79 (a). Nathaniel's children were: William P., d. June 6, 1838, ag. 21; Horace S., b. April 25, 1818; d. June 17, 1866 (a); m. Emma C. Plastridge, d. April 6, 1888, ag. 65; their children were: William Darwin (a); m. Kate M. Woolfe Jennie W., who m. M. P. Pratt, and had two children, Louise and another dau. Frank D., b. 1854; m., May 31, 1890, Addie H. Sargent, dau. of Horace Rollins of Grafton; Charles Warren, b. Feb. 23, 1863; d. Dec. 6, 1891 (a), and Maud Mabel, b. March 16, 1860. Oliver C., third son of Nathaniel, d. Sept. 13, 1826, ag. 5. Frank, d. Jan. 13, 1889, ag. 65 (a); m., March 16, 1874, Ella R. Milton, and had two children: Helen R., b. March 13, 1875, single; and John Pratt, b. 1880; m., July 25, 1903, Ruby I. Goss, b. 1885, and has two children: Dorothy E., b. May 4, 1904, and Helen, b. Nov. 19, 1905. Oliver P., d. Dec. 25, 1826, ag. 4w. George K., d. Jan. 22, 1907, ag. 78y., 8m., 5d. (a); m. Mary Louise George, b. 1847. Henry K. W., d. Aug. 10, 1831, ag. 16m. Nathaniel S., d. Homer, La., Oct. 19, 1852, ag. 30 (a). Henry K., d. Dec. 28, 1883, ag. 46 (a); m. Mary ———; one son, Nathaniel, b. June 9, 1863, who is married, and one dau., Lizzie, d. Feb. 28, 1862, ag. 2y., 6m. Elizabeth P., dau. of Nathaniel, m., Dec. 5, 1856, John C. Dunklee; one dau., Helen, m. and had two children.

Currier, Reuben, m., Aug. 8, 1792, Abigail Clough, and had Reuben, Jr., b. Aug. 10, 1793; d. March 1, 1797 (b); Henry, b. Nov. 8, 1794, Theophilus S., b. April 11, 1797.

Currier, Dea. Joshua, b. Southampton, Mass., d. June 18, 1871, ag. 92y., 1m. (b); tombstone says d. June 16, 1871, ag. 93; his wife, Mary Farrington, d. April 2, 1864, ag. 85. Children: Betsey, b. 1808; d. Aug. 10, 1829; Farrington, d. Aug. 11, 1891, ag. 86y., 3m.; his wife d. June 16, 1873 (c); child, Amos; Eben F., m. Sophia Noyes, d. June 14, 1873, ag. 72. Children: Moses E., b. Feb. 5, 1836; d. April 8, 1887; m., Oct. 19, 1865, Arabel Hadley. Dorothy Jane, b. 1813; d. April 28, 1821. Sophronia D., b. 1815; d. Oct. 5, 1829; Ann, d. Jan. 3, 1818, ag. 7m.; William Ayer, d. Feb. 10, 1818, ag. 17m.

Currier, Theophilus, d. Sept. 28, 1837 (g), ag. 85; m. Elizabeth Follensbee; his dau., Betsey, m. Josiah Clark (see him). Theophilus, Jr., d. Oct. 9, 1865, ag. 72y., 10m., 17d. (g); m., Dec. 24, 1817, Sarah P. Tyler, dau. Job Tyler, d. April 20, 1866, ag. 73. Richard, son of Theophilus, d. Jan. 18, 1822, ag. 36 (g). John Wesley, son of Theophilus, Jr., b. Dec. 22, 1828; m. Catherine B. Doten (see her). Elizabeth, dau. Theophilus, Jr., m., April 4, 1841, Moses French. Fanny, m. John Cunningham; Alonzo, m. his cousin.

Currier, David, d. July 19, 1839, ag. 70y., 3m., 2d. (b); m., Feb. 2, 1797, Ruth Stevens of Enfield, d. Nov. 1, 1846, ag. 71y., 9m., 15d. Children: Edward, d. Jan. 13, 1892, ag. 86y., 7m., 1d.; Aaron, d. June 10, 1880, ag. 66; Hannah, m., Dec. 2, 1819, Grover Burnham. David, d. July 2, 1862, ag. 59y., 5m. (b); m. Rhoda Tyler, d. March 31, 1894, ag. 86y., 8m., 26d. Children: Rhoda M., d. Sept. 16, 1842, ag. 2y.,

1d.; Ruth, b. 1830; m., Oct. 22, 1879, Carey Leeds. Dorothy, dau. David and Ruth, d. Sept. 26, 1885, ag. 86y., 8m. (b). Abigail H., d. Jan. 28, 1892, ag. 88y., 14d. (d).

Currier, Simeon, son of Samuel and Mahala (Blaisdell), b. Feb. 23, 1839; d. Oct. 14, 1900; Co. H., Seventh Vermont Volunteers (c). Child: Samuel W., m. Etta Hadley. Children: Eva and Hammond.

Daines, Peabody M., b. 1814; d. 1887 (c); m. Hannah Peters. Children: Marcia M., b. 1851; d. Nov. 6, 1889; Sadie R., b. 1864; d. 1885; Louisa, d. Oct. 2, 1860, ag. 16y., 8m., 6d. (c), and John P., who m., Dec. 14, 1889, Sarah J. Brocklebank, b. 1852; d. 1905; had Bryon; m. a second time. Dalpha, Lida, dau. of D. J. and M. A., d. Sept. 20, 1886, ag. 4m. (a).

Davis, James H., d. Sept. 14, 1864, ag. 34y., 6m., 22d. (b); m., Feb. 23, 1854, Adelia F. Cobb, dau. Salmon P., d. Dec. 12, 1867, ag. 33y., 6m., 5d. Children: Frank A., d. Nov. 5, 1860, ag. 5y., 2d.; Charles H., d. April 9, 1862, ag. 2y., 5m., 4d.

Davis, Samuel, of New Grantham, d. Feb. 7, 1867, ag. 90 (b); m., March 11, 1817, Miriah Hadley, dau. Simeon and Lucy, d. June 5, 1872, ag. 76. Children: Isaac, d. May 9, 1894, ag. 74y. 1m.; m., Oct. 14, 1841, Eliza Ann Tyler, dau. of Job C. Tyler, d. Aug. 12, 1882, ag. 58; m. (2), June 26, 1884, Mrs. Lydia (Rogers) Wright; she m. (3), Feb. 8, 1898, James Morrill. Children of Isaac and Eliza: Herbert C., b. Oct. 20, 1845; m., 1864, Nettie Merriam. Three children: Herbert Eugene, b. Oct. 29, 1865; Everett Tyler, b. March 2, 1867; Fanny Elsie, b. Sept., 1880. Julia A., dau. of Isaac, b. April 8, 1854; m. (1) Charles Swett; m. (2), Dec. 4, 1893, Ben A. Goss. Charles, son of Samuel, b. Dec. 5, 1823; m. (1), Feb. 28, 1850, Caroline T. Miner, dau. of Elisha, b. March 2, 1826; d. Aug. 1, 1896; m. (2), Jan. 3, 1906, Mary J. Martin, b. 1851. Children: Wesley, Milan E., b. 1853; m., Dec. 26, 1876, Jennie P. Worthen; Roxie L., m., Nov. 29, 1888, Edwin M. Allen. Children: Lena F., b. Aug. 9, 1890. Martin, son of Samuel, d. Oct. 4, 1866, ag. 40; killed at Ruggles Mica Mine, Grafton; m., March 8, 1849, Lydia Aldrich of Hill. Alfred, son of Samuel, b. 1829; m., March 8, 1849, Abigail Aldrich of Hill, b. 1829. George W., b. 1834; m. Emeline L. Kilton, b. 1844. Children: Arthur L., b. 1863; d. 1905; m. (1), Dec. 24, 1887, Katherine R. Murray, dau. of George W., b. 1864. Children: Verne L., b. July 5, 1890; Lilla L., dau. Geo. W., b. 1868; m., Jan. 21, 1891, Irving B. Andrews, b. 1859; Lizzie Jane, b. 1871; m., June 15, 1904, Fred D. Taylor, b. 1870; Nettie E., m. Frank H. Webster; two children. Alvin, son of Samuel, b. 1840; m. Sarah C. Richardson, dau. of Willard, d. Nov. 30, 1897, ag. 56y., 8m., 4d.; m. (2), July 8, 1903, Abbie B. Boutwell. Children: Fred U., b. 1866; m. (1), Oct. 14, 1889, Hattie E. Worthen, b. 1871; m. (2), Feb. 4, 1897, Martha J. Bullock, b. 1873. Willie M., b. 1868; m., May 16, 1891, Belle M. Dresser, dau. of John of Enfield, b. 1872. Harry A., d. April 7, 1903, ag. 30y., 10m., 9d. Leon A., b. 1881; m., March 28, 1904, Eva M. Sanborn, b. 1882. Laura E., b. 1879; m., July 16, 1902, Ralph W. Gordon, b. 1882. Child: Lawrence D., b. Oct. 12, 1902.

Davis, Watts, d. Feb. 22, 1869, ag. 76; his wife, Mary, d. June 24, 1877, ag. 84.

Davis, Leonard, d. April 14, 1891, ag. 81; m. (1), Oct. 1, 1834, Eliza Clark, dau. of Robert B.; had one ch., Arvilla F. M.; d. March 30, 1861, ag. 25y., 6m. (b); m. (2) Nancy Stevens, dau. of Peter; d. Aug. 19, 1883, ag. 70. Children: Peter Lyman, d. Jan. 24, 1851, ag. 1y., 4m. (b); Wesley P., b. 1852; m., Feb. 21, 1883, Ida M. Coburn; Daniel G. S., d. July 17, 1887, ag. 46y., 11m., 21d.; m. (1), May 14, 1870, Susan Augusta Fowler; d. June 25, 1872, ag. 36; and an infant son d. June 25, 1872; m. (2) Ella Kimball, dau. of David; one son, Orel K., b. July 3, 1879; m. Mary Martin.

Davis, son of G. E. and M. J., d. Jan. 4, 1907, ag. 15d. (b).

Dean, Velous, d. Aug. 5, 1858, ag. 23 (b).

Decato, Etta, d. Feb. 23, 1892, ag. 14; Luella d. Oct. 13, 1884, ag. 1y., 8m., 20d.; children of Thomas and Mary B.

Derby, Elihu, d. April 25, 1800, ag. 73y., 5m., 7d. (d).

Derby, Foster May, son of Alvin H. and Catherine E., d. July 9, 1852, ag. 2y., 6m.; Lucy Cassandra, dau., d. June 30, 1852, ag. 4y. 6m. (d).

Dickson, Macauley, b. March 16, 1847; d. April 18, 1902.

Dodge, Ella S., dau. of Alvah and Mary C., d. July 30, 1877, ag. 20y., 11m., 14d. (j). Elmore J., son of Alvah, d. June 20, 1904, ag. 46y., 28d. (b); his wife, Hattie R. E., b. 1853; d. 1892. Children: Harry, b. 1881; d. 1890.

Dole, Wales, d. May 7, 1861, ag. 76 (a); m., Dec. 30, 1813, Sarah Burley, dau. of Gordon of Dorchester; d. May 21, 1844, ag. 52 (a); m. (2), July 5, 1846, Lois Blodgett. Elizabeth S., wife of Stephen Dole, d. Jan. 1, 1834, ag. 80; probably parents of Wales (a).

Doten, James, son of James and Elizabeth (Kempton) Doten, b. Plymouth, Mass., Sept. 28, 1766; d. March 26, 1859; m., in Plymouth, Oct. 25, 1789, Martha Torrey of Plymouth, b. 1767; d. July 29, 1810 m. (2) Mary ————; d. Feb. 27, 1832, ag. 60; all (g). He came to Canaan in 1797; had nine children: Martha Torrey, b. Dec. 20, 1791; d. Nov. 26, 1792; Mary Torrey, b. Feb. 23, 1795; d. Feb. 6, 1873; m., in Canaan, Nov. 19, 1822, Grover Burnham. They resided in Enfield; had six children. Martha, dau. of James, b. April 21, 1796; d. Oct. 27, 1841 (g); m., March 12, 1818, Thomas Burley of Dorchester; had two children; Maria, b. July 14, 1798; d. Nov. 9, 1890; m., Jan. 29, 1822, Heman Killiam; m. (2) James Crofoot; had four ch. by each husband; Betsey, b. June 14, 1801; d. Oct. 21, 1851 (g); single; James, b. Oct. 30, 1803; d. May 17, 1877; m., Nov. 12, 1829, Rebecca Jones of Enfield, b. Sept. 12, 1808; d. March 29, 1885. Their seven children were: Guilford, b. Oct. 14, 1830; d. 1905; m., Feb. 17, 1864, Mrs. Betsey Lowell Flagg, dau. of Daniel and Abby Lowell; b. Feb. 17, 1840; d. June 25, 1862. Three children: Nelly May, b. Jan. 16, 1865; m., Sept. 15, 1885, Alfred A. Stevens, b. 1849; Frank Albin, b. Oct. 29, 1866; m., Aug. 13, 1894, Ethel E. Dubia, dau. of James and Emma J. Dubia; ch., L. Linwood and ————. Hattie Maude, dau. of Guilford, b. June 28,

1874; m., Oct. 3, 1893, Frank A. Trumbull, b. 1867. George Williams, son of James and Rebecca, b. May 6, 1833; d. Nov. 27, 1833. Ambrose Cushin, b. Dec. 31, 1836; d. June 7, 1873; m., Jan. 11, 1868, Augusta Leeds, dau. of Carey; one ch., Mabel Pattee, b. Nov., 1870. Matilda Jane, dau. of James and Rebecca, b. May 18, 1840; d. March 9, 1841. Lizzie Maynard, b. Feb. 12, 1842; d. Feb. 13, 1871; m., March 2, 1869, Harrison C. Bryant. Ellen Frances, b. Aug. 6, 1846; d. Jan. 6, 1850. Hattie Frances, b. Oct. 7, 1851; m. (1), Feb. 17, 1876, John B. Coburn; he died Sept. 20, 1885; she m. (2), March 13, 1890, Henry P. Pitcher. Three children by first husband: Blanche M., b. Aug. 3, 1876; m., Aug. 31, 1905, Dr. Frank A. Bogardus. Two children: Charles B., b. Sept. 19, 1906; d. Oct. 22, 1907; Stanley, b. Feb. 11, 1908. Harry R., b. April 19, 1882, and Elizabeth are the other two children of Hattie F. William, son of James, b. Nov. 14, 1805; d. ——; m. (1), Nov. 27, 1827, Catherine Barber, dau. of John M., b. Oct. 23, 1807; d. Oct. 17, 1833; m. (2), Feb. 16, 1834, Mrs. Sarah Morse; d. April 24, 1879, ag. 85y., 10m., 22d., in Hanover. Two children: Helen Maria, b. Nov. 12, 1829; m., Feb. 4, 1854, Martin Van Buren Morse, b. Hanover April 3, 1829; four ch. Catherine Barber, b. Oct. 17, 1833; m., Sept. 9, 1855, John Wesley Currier, son of Theophilus, Jr., b. Dec. 22, 1828; d. May, 1884. Their four children are: Willie Doten, b. June 4, 1859; Nellie Bertha, b. Dec. 18, 1860; Grace May, b. May 1, 1865; Fred Roscoe, b. Manchester Oct. 1, 1873. Eleanor, dau. of James, b. Jan. 30, 1808; m., Nov. 29, 1827, Henry Morse, son of Gideon and Hannah Johnson Morse, b. July 8, 1799; d. ——; six ch. Loiza, b. April 27, 1810; d. Aug. 1, 1810; was the last ch. of James.

Dow, Charles S., b. Jan. 29, 1865; d. July 28, 1905; by his wife, L. A., he had Robert W., d. Oct. 30, 1892, ag. 5m. (b).

Dow, Jacob, d. Aug. 4, 1831, ag. 56 (b); m., Sept., 1802, Phebe Wells, dau. of Ezekiel; d. Feb. 19, 1867, ag. 84y., 10m. Children: Phebe, b. June 21, 1803; d. ——; m., May 9, 1824, David March of Croydon; Isophena, b. Oct. 9, 1804; d. Jan. 6, 1892 (b); single; Rozetta, b. April 21, 1806; d. Sept. 4, 1807; Jacob Trussell, b. Dec. 31, 1807; d. in the field July 24, 1880 (c); m. Nancy Ann Blaisdell of Dorchester; d. June 22, 1894, ag. 77y., 5 m., 22d. Their children were: Edwin B., d. March 14, 1841, ag. 4y., 9m.; Emma S., d. June 23, 1863, ag. 23y., 4m.; Everett, b. 1842; d. 1900; Sylvanus J., m. a Whaley. Elvira, dau. of Jacob, b. Nov. 23, 1809; m. Sylvester P. Gould. Armena, b. July 12, 1811; d. Aug. 13, 1831; Sarah, b. April 10, 1813; Mary, b. March 10, 1815; d. July 7, 1817; William Walles, b. Jan. 27, 1816; Mary, b. 1818; d. Dec. 8, 1852; Rozetta, b. Aug., 1825; d. June 3, 1828; Isaac, Joseph, Caleb.

Drew, Sally, wife of Joseph H., d. Jan. 10, 1839, ag. 22; dau., Roseanna, d. Jan. 1, 1838, ag. 5 (b).

Drew, Almary K., wife of Hiram T., b. 1854; d. 1895; son, Calvin S., d. April 28, 1891, ag. 18.

Drugg, Thomas, Company E, Twenty-First United States Infantry (c).

GENEALOGY.

Dunham, Almon, son of Phineas C. and Anna, d. Oct. 1, 1831; Francis R., son, d. Sept. 16, 1826; Hiram Uline, son, d. Oct. 6, 1850 (a).

Dunham, Phineas O., d. April 1, 1889, ag. 76 (c); his wife, Louisa, d. June 4, 1883, ag. 68; son, Eugene, b. Nov. 25, 1864; d. Aug. 26, 1883.

Duplesse, Ira I., son of Israel and D. M., b. Sept. 13, 1901; d. April 3, 1906 (c).

Durrell, Daniel, d. July 7, 1838, ag. 53 (b); Eunice, his first wife, d. June 20, 1827, ag. 35; Nancy C. Jones, dau. of John, his second wife, d. Nov. 25, 1862, ag. 63y., 4m. Children: Eunice S., m., Jan., 1840, David Goodhue of Essex, Vt.; Augusta E., m., Feb. 15, 1841, Ebenezer Barney of Danbury; and Emeline A., m. Eleazer Barney (see him); Elizabeth J., d. Oct. 7, 1864, ag. 31; m., Dec. 19, 1860, Hiram S. Worth, son of Edmond and Sally; Daniel I., b. 1848; d. Oct. 25, 1890; m., Feb. 16, 1862, Helen A. Leeds, dau. of Richard E. and Mary P.

Dustin, John R., d. Feb. 16, 1859 (a), ag. 75; m., June 14, 1805, Phebe Gilman, d. Oct. 26, 1868, ag. 85. Their children were: Sylvester, d. ———; Hannah, b. Feb. 3, 1808; Alfred Bartlett, b. Dec. 3, 1812; d. Aug. 26, 1895 (a), single; John Wesley, b. Sept. 27, 1810; d. July 25, 1882 (a); m. Mary Jane Parker; no children, but brought up Charles W. Dustin, d. Dec. 5, 1905, ag. 52y., 6m., 12d. (a); m. Sarah A. Fifield, dau. of Ezekiel, and had three children: Gertrude, b. March 14, 1880; m. R. R. Prescott; Minnie, m. James Mansur, and Blanche, b. March 6, 1887, m. John T. Knuckey. William Wallace, fifth child of John R., b. April 29, 1819; d. ———; m., Oct. 19, 1844, Jerusha Clifford of Dorchester; Melvina Jane, b. April 29, 1821; d. Dec. 4, 1893 (a), single; Franklin Tilton, b. Sept. 15, 1825; d. Feb. 15, 1899 (a), single.

Dwinels, James, b. Dec. 17, 1859, ag. 59y., 5m., 20d. (c); his wife, Louisa, d. Oct. 18, 1857, ag. 51y., 6m., 24d.; their children were: George, d. Feb. 25, 1841, ag. 5y., 2m.; Sarah C., wife of Stephen Hadley, 3d, d. June 28, 1868, ag. 31y., 3m. (c); Catherine, d. Feb. 23, 1841, ag. 1y., 7m., 26d.; Catherine M., d. Aug. 18, 1843, ag. 8d.; Julianna G., wife of Moses E. Withington, b. Feb. 23, 1833; Moses, b. Jan. 31, 1828; d. June 14, 1900 (c). Charles W., b. 1835; m. (1), May 16, 1861, Albina L. Richardson, dau. of Jacob and Elsie, d. Nov. 25, 1874, ag. 30y., 2m.; had two children: Cora B., d. April 25, 1875, ag. 8y., 5m.; and Daisy. m. (2), April 3, 1876, Mrs. Julia A. (Merrill) Richardson, b. Oct. 1, 1837; d. April 5, 1902 (c); no children.

Dyke, Lyman, d., ag. 83; Company I, First New Hampshire Heavy Artillery.

Eastman, Phineas, m. Susannah Cogswell; d. Aug. 27, 1842, ag. 68 (a). Children: Elwell, b. Dec. 31, 1795; Phineas, Jr., b. Oct. 30, 1798; d., Manchester, May 24, 1858; ch.; Cogswell, m. ——— Dow of Haverhill; Peggy, b. Dec. 18, 1800; d. Sept. 9, 1802 (a); John, b. Feb. 28, 1802; Simeon, b. Oct. 1, 1804; Moses, b. March 14, 1803; Rachel, b. May 4, 1814; Mary Ann, m., Sept. 1, 1845, Clark C. Walworth (see him); Persis T., m., Jan. 6, 1857, C. W. Webster of Wells River, Vt.; Josephine, m. Albert Hoyt; Caroline, d. single.

Eastman, Stephen, d. April 8, 1797, ag. 49; his wife, Miriam, d. Dec. 28, 1817, ag. 66y., 3m. (e). James, d. Dec. 17, 1851, ag. 71y., 8m.; his wife, Polly French, d. July 13, 1874, ag. 86y., 6m. (e); had eleven children; he came here in 1795 and settled on the west side of the town, and was the father of James, who m. Susan L. Williams (see her). Children: Larned, m., April 3, 1839, Lucy Ann Currier of Enfield; Stephen; Sophronia, m. ——— Smith; Mary, Miriam; Rhoda, m. ——— Piper; Bartlett; Moses F., son of James and Polly, d. June 1, 1843, ag. 13y., 5m.; J. French, d. April 22, 1871, ag. 47 (e).

Eastman, Allie S., son of J. B. and M. C.; d. June 28, 1868, ag. 4m., 15d. Margaret, wife of Zebulon Barber, m. March 12, 1815; d. Nov. 1854, ag. 34 (j).

Eaton, Ebenezer, d. Dec. 27, 1851, ag. 78; his wife, Susannah, d. Dec. 28, 1853, ag. 78. Nathaniel, d. July 6, 1861, ag. 56; his wife, Lucinda M., d. Dec. 18, 1843, ag. 39; his son, James M., m., Nov. 15, 1862, Mary E. Richardson, dau. of Alfred, d. Nov. 25, 1865, ag. 23y., 10m., and their dau. Mary Frances, d. Feb. 22, 1866, ag. 2y., 1m., 16d. Mary H., dau. of Nathaniel and Lucinda, d. April 9, 1848, ag. 19. Nathaniel, m. (2), Susannah, and had a son George M., d. June 3, 1854, ag. 9y., 5m. (all d).

Edwards, Nancy M. (Hadley), wife of Elijah W., d. Nov. 17, 1864, ag. 58y., 11m., 13d. (e); he m. (2), Oct. 11, 1865, Rachel G. Clark, dau. of Daniel; their dau. Lucinda, d. Sept. 26, 1848, ag. 1y., 6m., 11d. Benton, son by Rachel, d. Aug. 30, 1877, ag. 10m., 2d. Two other sons, Byron and Burns W., went West. Elijah W. and Nancy M. were m. Dec. 25, 1839; he d. 1878, ag. 57y., 6m. Perry, d. Jan. 2, 1891, ag. 21y., 6m., son of Elijah and Rachel Clark (e).

Elliott, Joel, d. Feb. 22, 1873, ag. 82 (b); his wife, Betsey, d. Oct. 8, 1861, ag. 61. Freeman E., their son, d. Oct. 18, 1861, ag. 21; he m. (2), May 4, 1862, Mrs. Dorothy (Springer) Chase, dau. of Henry and Hannah Springer. Child: Emeline, m. William Welch.

Elliott Roswell, d. Feb. 28, 1864, ag. 58y., 5m.; his wife, Dorothy B. Clark, dau. of Col. Josiah, d. Dec. 2, 1878, ag. 59y., 3m. (b).

Elliott, Henry E., d. 1909; his wife, Martha A. Peaslee, d. April 22, 1901, ag. 74y., 5m., 22d. Children: Henry E.; Hattie, m. Friend Pressey, b. Oct. 6, 1856, d. Sept. 19, 1902.

Emerson, Caleb, D., d. Jan. 9, 1851, ag. 53 (a).

Emerson, Charles E., son of Charles H. and F. M., b. Jan. 26, 1873; d. Aug. 11, 1891 (e).

Evon, Irene S., wife of Alexander, d. Sept. 25, 1886, ag. 38y., 3m (e).

Fales, John, b. Feb. 13, 1768; d. Oct. 10, 1858; m. Sally Carlton, b. March 16, 1768; d. Aug. 15, 1841. Eleven children: Silvia, b. Oct. 19, 1788; d. Aug. 15, 1841; m. Ensign Colby (see him); John, Jr., b. April 28, 1790; d. June 22, 1861 (a); m. ———. Children: Dorothy H., b. Feb. 25, 1813; m., Feb. 25, 1841, Joshua S. Lathrop (see him); Mary C., b. March 17, 1815; d. July 4, 1869; m. Joseph Sherburne (see him); Willard A., b. March 3, 1817; Eliza, b. April 9, 1818; d. Feb. 22, 1892;

GENEALOGY.

m. Horace W. Miller, son of Jacob; no children; Sarah, b. March 29, 1820; m. in the West; Abigail, b. Aug. 19, 1822; Eunice C., b. Feb. 27, 1828; m. Frank Barber, son of Dea. Nathaniel Barber. Arnold, son of John, b. April 25, 1792; d. Oct. 19, 1868; m., Oct. 29, 1815, Sarah Greeley. Children: Henry, b. March 11, 1827, and a dau. Polly, dau. of John, b. April 29, 1794; d. Aug. 17, 1863 (a); m. Joseph Blake; Laura, b. Dec. 13, 1795; d. Aug. 8, 1886; m., Sept. 3, 1865, George W. Leavitt, d. Oct. 4, 1875, ag. 71; no children. Horace, b. Aug. 12, 1797; d. June 12, 1881; m., March 30, 1841, Caroline Eldredge, d. May 8, 1885; Orrin, b. Aug. 18, 1799; d. Jan. 28, 1858; m., Nov. 30, 1820, Polly Bartlett (see her); David, b. Sept. 30, 1801; d. Nov. 9, 1875; m., April 13, 1824, Sophia Hadley; Caleb, b. Nov. 6, 1804; d. June 25, 1882; Jabez H., b. Nov. 4, 1806; d. Feb. 3, 1882, in Baltimore, Md.; m., July 8, 1829, Ruth Miller, dau. of Jacob, d. Sept. 7, 1881, ag. 75. Children: Loraine H., b. Jan. 31, 1831; m., Oct. 20, 1859, John B. Dickey; Martha Jane, b. May 2, 1835; Joseph H., d. June 24, 1842, ag. 5y., 1m.; Susan C., b. April 8, 1839; m., March 9, 1880, Frank C. Morse, b. 1852; Sarah, b. Aug. 16, 1808; d. April 12, 1856; m., Sept. 8, 1853, Cyrus Perkins.

The following were taken from the Fales' Bible: Mariah Fales, b. Dec. 2, 1818; Caroline Fales, b. March 27, 1819; Inda Fales, b. Aug. 2, 1820; Louisa Fales, b. 1822 (?); Caroline Fales, b. March 10, 1825; Julia Fales, b. July 6, 1826; Angeline S. Folsom, b. March 17, 1821; Horace Folsom, b. Feb. 21, 1819; Joseph H. Fales, b. May 14, 1844; Emily D. Fales, b. May 17, 1856; Augusta Ann Fales, b. Sept. 6, 1842; Caroline Fales, b. June 4, 1834; John D. Fales, b. June 26, 1831.

Farnum, Jonathan and Phebe, had children: Sally S., b. Feb. 8, 1828; m., June 10, 1847, Sargent Randall of Enfield; Hannah C., b. Dec. 12, 1829; Lucy S., b. May 1, 1831; John, b. April 26, 1833; George W., b. Jan. 24, 1839; Luther C., b. March 2, 1843.

Farnum, Daniel, d. Aug. 29, 1810, ag. 62 (g).

Fellows, Mercy Townsend, wife of Dea. Peter, d. Aug. 31, 1863, ag. 61y., 6m. (a).

Fifield, Georgiana M., dau. of Benjamin and Adaline, d. Oct. 12, 1848; ag. 9y., 15m.; also Alice, d. June 14, 1855, ag. 1sm. (a).

Fifield, Daranzel, son of Ezekiel, b. Feb. 12, 1848; d. Nov. 6, 1897 (a); his wife, Delia S. Columbia, dau. of William, b. May 2, 1852; d. May 29, 1895 (a).

Finch, Henry, m., Dec. 24, 1786, Mary Baldwin. Child: Ebenezer, b. April 4, 1788. He was the miller that succeeded Ebenezer Eames at the "Corner." His wife may have been the mother of Thomas Baldwin, who came with Eames.

Fish, Theoda, wife of Otis, d. Dec. 23, 1853, ag. 62 (b).

Flagg, Lois, d. Jan. 14, 1841, ag. 37; Albion W., d. June 25, 1862, ag. 25 (b).

Flagg, Hannah W., wife of George Eiffert, b. Nov. 30, 1840; d. June 30, 1906.

Flanders, Margaret, wife of Joshua, and dau. of Adam Pollard; d.

March 7, 1848, ag. 75 (a). Children: Sylvester, d. July 11, 1890, ag. 82y., 27d.; m.. March 5, 1834, Sarah S. Morse, dau. of James, b. June 7, 1802; d. April 3, 1880. Children: William A., b. Feb. 26, 1835; d. 1909; m., Aug. 31, 1863, Angeline L. Clark, dau. of Prescott and Susan, b. April 13, 1843. Children: William Arthur, b. April 24, 1865; d. Nov. 20, 1866; Frederick, b. Jan. 10, 1867; Susan, b. Nov. 9, 1868; William A., b. May 30, 1870; George M., b. March 16, 1872; Gracia, b. Sept. 5, 1873. George M., son of Sylvester, b. April 7, 1837; m., Nov. 20, 1859, Mary C. Aldrich, b. June 3, 1841; their children: Bertha Maria, b. Oct. 8, 1863; Sarah Elsie, b. June 12, 1868; Georgia, b. July 4, 1871. Julia Y., dau. of Sylvester, b. Nov. 2, 1839; m., Nov. 29, 1860, William Hall. Elijah Clark, son of Joshua, b. 1820; d. 1901 (a); m. Louisa H. Pollard, dau. of Adam Pollard. Children: Augustus Benton, d. July 28, 1863, ag. 12y., 8m., 19d.; Julia A.; Alice M., b. 1854; m., Feb. 25, 1880, Wallace G. Fogg, son of George W.; has one son, George W. Lydia B., dau. of Joshua, d. July 22, 1877, ag. 71; m., May 7, 1838, Abram Davis (a); Sarah J., b. 1817; d. 1890; m., April 29, 1851, William Burnham, d. June 17, 1886, ag. 72y., 3m. (a).

Flanders, John, son of Elijah and Sarah, of Weare, d. Feb. 22, 1864, ag. 74y., 8m. (d); m., March 29, 1815, Betsey Bartlett, dau. of Nathaniel, d. June 8, 1862, ag. 73y., 2m. Children: Betsey A., m. Horace Kinne (see him); Irad, d. March 3, 1826, ag. 10m., 13d.; Mary Jane, d. March 23, 1902, ag. 79y., 17d.; m., April 14, 1851, James Baker (see him); John C.

Flint, Joseph, of Hopkinton, d. April 13, 1807, ag. 61; his wife, Molly Harriman, d. Jan. 2, 1812, ag. 61. Children: Lucy, b. Aug. 29, 1780; d. Aug. 26, 1865; m. Daniel B. Whittier, son of Richard (see him); Polly, m. Ezra Nichols (see him); Sally, b. June 19, 1768; m., Oct. 10, 1790, Allen Miner; Edward, m., Oct. 20, 1791, Betsey Clark.

Fogg, Samuel, d. Oct. 23, 1874, ag. 77 (c); his wife, Lucy, d. Aug. 10, 1875, ag. 73; Harrison, b. June 30, 1823; d. Sept. 5, 1896 (c); m., Sept. 7, 1886, Jeanette E. Preston, dau. of Alpheus, b. Sept. 19, 1851; d. June 14, 1906.

Follensbee, Col. Lucian A., d. April 16, 1892, ag. 76y., 6m.; his wife, Sarah C. Sargent, d. Aug. 18, 1875, ag. 60y., 10m., 12d. (h).

Follensbee, Perley R., son of Parker and Sally (Blanchard), b. March 2, 1835; d. Feb. 27, 1905; his wife, Mary A., b. Sept. 18, 1836; d. March 7, 1908. Children: Clara D., b. Dec. 6, 1865; d. May 30, 1882: Nettie M., b. July 28, 1872; d. April 25, 1896; m. Will C. Tenney; Herbert E., b. Feb. 27, 1871; d. July 28, 1901; m. Maggie Ricard, one son.

Follensbee, Seth P., d. June 10, 1872, ag. 71 (c); his wife, Frances G., d. Sept. 6, 1863, ag. 52. Children: Arabella, b. Feb. 25, 1852, ag. 20; Abi, d. Feb. 10, 1856, ag. 22; Henry H., d. Sept. 15, 1868, ag. 28; Ida, d. Jan. 29, 1862, ag. 13.

Follensbee, Orrin M., son of Parker, b. Dec. 5, 1849.

Folsom, Joseph and Mary. Children: John C., b. March 29, 1819; Rufus H., b. Jan. 25, 1827; Cyrus, b. Feb. 11, 1829; Mary J., b. April 4,

1821; Elizabeth S., b. March 20, 1823; Harry H., b. Feb. 21, 1825; Hiram, b. Feb. 9, 1831; Naveissa, b. Orange, April 7, 1833.

Foster, Rev. Amos, b. March 30, 1797; d. ———; m., June 29, 1825, Harriet Amelia White, b. March 26, 1802; d. Oct. 18, 1882. Children: Harriet Eliza, b. May 27, 1826; Broughton White, b. Sept. 7, 1828; Ellen Maria, b. Oct. 18, 1830; Frances Jane, b. May 3, 1833.

Fox, Harvey, b. Aug. 30, 1844; d. Dec. 16, 1900; Company H, Eleventh New Hampshire Volunteers; Fannie O., wife of Harvey H., b. May 22, 1871; d. Sept. 10, 1904 (c).

Fox, Elizabeth, d. Aug. 10, 1901, ag. 66y., 5m. (a).

Fulsom, Samuel and Anna. Children: Samuel, Jr., b. March 2, 1784; Betsey, b. May 20, 1782; Sally, b. Oct. 5, 1785; Josiah, b. Dec. 27, 1787; Steaven, b. Feb. 17, 1789; Jeames, b. Feb. 27, 1791; Sheleb, b. June 20, 1792; George, b. May 20, 1794.

Garland, Hermie T., son of H. J. and S. M., d. Aug. 25, 1880, ag. 3y., 8m.; Louise J., wife of Joseph H., d. July 27, 1882, ag. 58y., 5m. (b).

Gates, Reynold, d. Dec. 26, 1836, ag. 75 (a); m. by Thomas Baldwin, Nov. 10, 1785, Lydia Clark, dau. of Caleb; d. Nov. 16, 1795 (a); he m. (2), April 9, 1800, Charlotte Basford of Essex, Vt. He came here in 1768 with Samuel Jones. Children: Capt. Samuel Jones, b. July 26, 1786; d. ———, (d); m. Eunice. Children: Horatio, d. Oct. 28, 1887, ag. 77y., 10m., 18d. (d); m., March 29, 1835, Sybel Hews, d. Dec. 3, 1898, ag. 91. Children: Newton B., d. Nov. 18, 1886, ag. 50y., 21d. (a); m. Sarah A. Bean. Children: Horatio B., b. 1872; m., Feb. 20, 1907, Nettie M. Morrison, b. 1885; Leora A., d. July 20, 1883, ag. 19y., 1m., 1d.; Maud S., d. July 27, 1888, ag. 20y., 11m., 13d. (a); m. Eugene A. Shepard; Pertie J., b. 1874; m., June 10, 1895, Eugene A. Shepard; Grace L., b. 1878; m., June 17, 1899, Charles E. Kenyon, b. 1876, William H., son of Newton B., d. Jan. 28, 1863, ag. 22y., 10m., 7d. and Eunice F., d. Jan. 21, 1874, ag. 27y., 8m; Lydia, dau. of Samuel J., d. Aug. 29, 1825, ag. 10; Hannah B., d. May 19, 1839, ag. 24; m., Oct. 15, 1835, Benjamin W. Porter, son of Daniel; William, d. June 22, 1839, ag. 22; Reynold, d. Sept. 16, 1825, ag. 6; Charlotte, d. Sept. 2, 1825, ag. 4; Amanda M., d. Oct. 6, 1825, ag. 2; Reynold, d. Dec. 20, 1832, ag. 2y., 2m., 11d.; Billa, son of Reynold, b. Dec. 1, 1787; Marvin, b. March 16, 1791; Joshua Clark, b. March 7, 1795; m., June 27, 1816, Rhoda Clark; Charlotte, m., Dec. 4, 1818, Eliphalet Clark.

George, Col. Levi, b. March, 1767; d. Feb. 4, 1848 (c); m. (1), 1790, Polly Pettingill, dau. of Capt. Benjamin of Salisbury, b. 1770; d. Jan. 30, 1809; m. (2), July 2, 1809, Betsey Sanborn, d. July 17, 1851, ag. 71. Nine children: Mary, d. June 5, 1818, ag. 27; m., April, 1818, David Ross; Betsey, b. 1793; d. Jan., 1869; m., March 3, 1816, Jacob Young, went to Pennsylvania; Hannah, d. Dec. 6, 1806, ag. 12; Benjamin Pimelton, b. June 15, 1797; d. July 28, 1878; m., Nov., 1821, Keziah Blake, dau. of David, b. Feb. 6, 1801; d. May 22, 1879. Children: Levi, d. Aug. 27, 1871, ag. 49; m., Sept. 9, 1849, Harriet May, dau. of Edwin. Children: Estelle Augusta, b. Jan. 14, 1851; m. Augustus Hayward.

Clarissa, b. 1799; m. and went West; Lucinda, b. 1801; d. Nov. 1855, single; Charlotte T., b. Aug. 15, 1803; d. March 26, 1882; m., March 20, 1823, William Whittier (see him); Isaac Kimball, b. March 6, 1806; d. Dec. 1891; m., 1835, Sirena Aldrich; Henry Clinton, b. May 8, 1808; d. Nov. 28, 1887; m. (1), 1835, Eunice P. Walworth, d. Nov. 23, 1841, ag. 29; m. (2) Mary Calef of Salisbury. Children: Henry Clinton, b. 1844; d. in the army, 1863; Eleventh New Hampshire Regiment from Salisbury; m. (3), 1852, Eleanor L. Hinkson, dau. of Daniel and Cynthia, d. April 27, 1894, ag. 72y., 11m., 27d. Children by first wife: Mary Ann, b. Oct. 13, 1837; single, lives in Los Angeles, Cal.; Carlos C., b. May 22, 1839; d. Sept. 24, 1863, in the army; Eunice W., b. Sept. 16, 1841; m., Feb. 14, 1867, Frank W. Stickney, b. April 8, 1840. Children: Clinton G., b. May 24, 1868; m., Jan. 1, 1896, Frances W. Sawyer; Carl, b. May 17, 1876; m., Jan. 1, 1902, Grace E. Murray; child: Clinton Murray, b. 1904. Irving T., son of Henry C. and Eleanor L., b. June 27, 1854; m., 1880, Nellie Palmer; lives in Newmarket, N. H. Children: Grace I., b. 1881; Henry C., b. March 1, 1882; Thomas Miner, b. April, 1883; d. ———; Bertha, b. April, 1885; Wallace Bruce, b. March, 1886; Eleanor Hinkson, b. Oct. 3, 1887.

George, William W., was born in Sunapee in 1807; when a boy he went to Croyden as an apprentice to the trade of manufacturing woolen cloth. He came to this town in 1832, having married Lucy B. Whipple in Croyden. With Nathaniel Currier he established the manufacture of woolens at the Village and also carried on a lumber business. He was fifteen years deputy sheriff, was once a candidate for state senator. He was representative in 1847 and 1866; was selectman in 1844-'46, 1855, 1856, 1858, 1865 and 1866. He d. Aug. 8, 1871, ag. 63y., 7m.; she died April 21, 1895, ag. 77. Isabelle M., d. Aug. 25, 1872, ag. 42y., 17d.; m., Oct. 28, 1856, Dr. Ara Wheat; Harriet S., d. Sept. 4, 1901, ag. 69; m., Dec. 15, 1850, James H. Kelley; Frances K., b. 1834; d. 1896; m. Jan. 15, 1852, Charles Day, b. Sept. 16, 1822; d. March 22, 1885; had two children: Flora B., b. March 18, 1853, and Mamie. Col. Allen H., b. Aug. 18, 1836; d. Feb. 20, 1904; m., Jan. 18, 1866, Jane E. Wheat, dau. of Solomon. Children: William W., Agnes L., b. April 18, 1876; d. July 3, 1881 (all a).

George, Col. Elijah, b. Sunapee; d. June 6, 1895, ag. 86y., 9m., 2d. (a); m., 1826, Caroline M. Eastman, b. March 3, 1802; d. Oct. 4, 1883. Children: Louisa, b. Sunapee, 1837; m. John Gile of Enfield; Moses Eastman, b. 1838; Artemesia, b. 1843; Charles, b. 1844; Celinda A., d. March 15, 1856, ag. 16y., 23d; Frank A., d. Oct. 9, 1865, ag. 14y., 5m., 28d.; Eudora E., d. April 17, 1858, ag. 1y., 5m., 13d.; Mary Jane, b. and d. 1857 (a); Mercyline, b. 1841; m., Jan. 21, 1860, H. J. Morrill; Carrie M., b. 1845; m., Dec. 6, 1871, Alphonso Eastman.

Gile, Amos, d. May 7, 1869, ag. 74; his wife, Mehitable, d. Aug. 20, 1847, ag. 56; m. (2), June 20, 1860, Mrs. Betsey Davis; a dau. Lucy, d. Aug. 27, 1857, ag. 26; and a son, Henry J., d. July 18, 1863, ag. 26; Mary A. m. Nathan Jones.

Genealogy.

Gile, Lovicy, wife of Jesse, d. Feb. 28, 1870, ag. 53. Warren N., son of Ira S. and Maria F., dau. Amos, d. Aug. 13, 1884, ag. 20y., 1m., 1d. (a); she m. (2) John Worthen.

Gillis, Albert S., b. Poultney, Vt., Jan. 6, 1826; d. June 20, 1882 (a); his wife, Lizzie, b. Poultney, Vt., Nov. 5, 1840; d. April 22, 1885.

Gilman, Nathaniel, d. Dec. 27, 1851, ag. 84y., 9m. (b); his wife, Sally, d. Oct. 1, 1841, ag. 70. Children: Lieut. Samuel, b. May 1, 1794; d. March 20, 1866 (a); m., Nov. 14, 1816, Lydia Wheat, dau. of Elder Joseph, d. Sept. 5, 1832, ag. 37. Children: Minerva W., d. Jan. 23, ag. 23; Hannah W., d. Oct. 21, 1832, ag. 2y., 5m.; Laura Phelps, b. Feb. 14, 1821; John T.; Lucia. Col. Ezra, son of Nathaniel, b. Dec. 29, 1795; d. Manchester, April 26, 1855 (a); m., Nov. 13, 1828, Clarissa Currier, dau. of John, b. Oct. 10, 1799; d. July 21, 1869 (a). Three children: James Currier, b. Jan. 31, 1831; d. Bedford, 1909; m., 1868, Nancy Smiley of Bedford; Louisa, b. March 3, 1835; d. Oct. 17, 1849 (a); Daniel Hoyt, b. Dec. 8, 1836; d. ———; m., 1860, Mary Bennett; one child, Elmer A., who m. and has one dau.; Sally, dau. of Nathaniel, d. March 16, 1843, ag. 47; m. Josiah Clark (see him); Jesse; Col. Eliphalet C., d. April 19, 1861, ag. 51 (a); m. Mary G. Kelley, d. Feb. 10, 1888, ag. 79y., 7m., 12d.; dau. of Moses and Annie (Tyler) Kelley; Alvah, d. June 3, 1863, ag. 46y., 6m.; m., June 29, 1842, Dorothy C. F. Gile, d. Sept. 6, 1875, ag. 53. Three children: Sidney A., d. Feb. 24, 1866, ag. 20y., 7m.; Horatio A., b. 1847; m., Dec. 18, 1869, Maria M. Stevens, b. 1846. Children: Fred B., d. Dec. 8, 1897, ag. 25; Charles H., b. 1875; m., Jan. 4, 1897, Ellen S. Underhill; Sidney B., and Josie; Arvilla, dau. of Nathaniel, m. ———; Caleb, m., Feb. 17, 1820, Sally Smith of Gilmanton; Betsey, wife of Winthrop Gilman, d. Sept. 19, 1833, ag. 88 (g).

Gilman, Dudley, and Mary, had Moses, b. May 28, 1790; Steven, b. Aug. 28, 1792; Uriah Smith; Edward Harriman, b. July 25, 1797.

Ginn, Mildred P., dau. of John and Mabel L., d. Nov. 26, 1904, ag. 4m., 26d.; Harold R., b. Dec. 20, 1905; d. March 8, 1907 (c).

Gleason, Winsor, d. July 10, 1878, ag. 82; his wife, Elmira Silsbury, b. Jan. 2, 1803; d. April 27, 1885. Emily S., their dau., wife of George H. Lathrop, b. Feb. 20, 1830; d. Nov. 25, 1899 (a).

Gobar, Charles O., b. July 1, 1869; d. Jan. 30, 1899; m. Martha Flanders, dau. of Sanford. Child: Lola A., b. Nov. 21, 1894; d. Feb. 16, 1896 (b).

Gordon, Capt. William, b. April 11, 1821; d. Aug. 16, 1904; m., Oct. 5, 1843, Augusta J. Sleeper, b. Oct. 17, 1823; d. March 21, 1897. Child: Charles S., b. Nov. 8, 1844; d. Nov., 1909; m., Nov. 9, 1866, Matilda A. Bucklin, two children. Frank L., b. Jan. 13, 1846; d. Aug. 9, 1846; Clemmie A., b. Oct. 5, 1847; m. (1), Dec. 11, 1873, John B. Cheney; m. (2), Oct. 22, 1887, Jacob F. Richardson. Frank L., b. May 10, 1849; m., Sept., 1885, Ella M. Rogers; Ella A., b. May 2, 1851; d. Aug. 28, 1852; Willie, b. March 10, 1853; m., May 14, 1876, Lizzie F. Eastman; Mary Ella, b. Oct. 27, 1855; d. April 8, 1876; m., Dec. 14, 1873, Wilfred

D. Fellows; George H., b. Sept. 27, 1859; m., Sept. 24, 1881, Emma F. Noyes, b. Aug. 14, 1861. Child: Ralph William, b. Feb. 25, 1882; m., July 16, 1902, Laura E. Davis, dau. of Alvin; Leila Mildred, b. Dec. 15, 1883; d. May 15, 1894; Earl Clifton, b. Dec. 12, 1887; Harold George, b. Dec. 21, 1889; Vaughn Lawrence, b. May 7, 1892; m., Nov. 9, 1909, Katherine A. Campbell; Mamie Gladys, b. Oct. 7, 1893; Ethelyn Augusta, b. July 1, 1899; Ruth Cheney, b. Jan. 10, 1902.

Goss, Joshua, d. April 8, 1854, ag. 64 (e); m. Hannah Gile, d. Dec. 29, 1868, ag. 75. Child: Jonathan, d. ————; Company G, Eighteenth New Hampshire Volunteers; m. Mrs. (Ross) Lillis. Reuben, d. Sept. 24, 1882, ag. 67 (a); m. 1) Susan (Lathrop) Beal, dau. of Harris G. and Susan (Stevens) Lathrop, d. Sept. 3, 1865, ag. 47y., 4m., 4d.; m. (2) Caroline E. Sherburne, dau. of Joseph, d. March 12, 1904, ag. 65 (a); one son, Charley, d. young; the other child, Harris J., b. 1845; m., Jan. 8, 1870, Lizzie B. Norris, dau. of Benjamin, b. 1847. Two children: Ben A., m. Dell J. Swett, dau. of Isaac Davis; and Ruby L., m. John P. Currier; two children. Bernice E., dau. of Reuben, b., June 27, 1887, Sarah A. Bullock, dau. of James B. of Grafton, two children. Lena, Calista S., dau. of Reuben, d. Aug. 14, 1897, ag. 46y., 5m., 9d.; m. (1), July 19, 1863, Alonzo Bucklin; m. (2) Milo Bucklin; m. (3) William S. Durgin; Elizabeth B., b. 1843; m., Feb. 19, 1865, Elijah Smith (see him); Wallace R., b. 1854; m., Feb. 20, 1875, Carrie E. Elliott, dau. Roswell. Daniel son of Joshua, d. April 12, 1890, ag. 69y., 8m., 10d.; m. Loraine P. Williams, b. July 8, 1828; d. Dec. 10, 1896. Children: Daniel, b. 1850; m., April 9, 1879, Mary A. Clough, dau. John, b. 1854. Children: Albert, b. Sept. 25, 1880; m. Josie Clark. Child: Beatrice. Abby F., dau. of Daniel and Loraine, d. March 8, 1864, ag. 10y., 4m., 8d., drowned in Scales Brook; Lizzie L., d. March 12, 1884, ag. 19y., 6m., 25d.; Emma, d. young; Nellie S., m. Delevan K. Williams (see him); Richard married and died in Enfield; Levi, d. June 20, 1866, ag. 35; m., June 23, 1855, Dorothy A. Philbrick, dau. of Hiram, d. March 30, 1856, ag. 24y., 3m. (a); Orville, d. ————; m., Aug. 21, 1856, Hannah Philbrick. Children: Dora, m. David Towle (see him); Anna D., m., Sept. 17, 1873, Burns W. Sanborn; Sarah, m. Bailey Batchelder; Abbie, m. Royal Abbott; Roxanna, m. March 30, 1856, Sylvester Withington.

Goss, Jethro, d. Nov. 10, 1857; Susannah, his wife, d. June 8, 1862, ag. 86 (e). Children: Russell, d. April 3, 1885, ag. 74y., 4m., 23d (e); m., Feb. 27, 1833, Rachel S. Clark, d. Dec. 20, 1865, ag. 54; Levi M., son of Jethro, d. June 25, 1897, ag. 84 (e); his wife, Elmira C., d. Aug. 29, 1884, ag. 69. Children: Walter, d. Feb. 14, 1858, ag. 2y., 5m., 6d.; Susie May, d. Sept. 23, 1889, ag. 3 (e).

Gould, Nathan, d. Jan. 18, 1854, ag. 72y., 3m. (e); his first wife, Abigail, d. April 19, 1830, ag. 40y., 6m., 23d. Children: Nathan, b. Jan. 20, 1815; d. April 4, 1837; Hannah, m. John Packard (see him); Nathan, m. (2) Sarah C., d. Feb. 12, 1853, ag. 51y., 6m., 4d. Child: Joseph T., d. Aug. 30, 1857, ag. 17y., 11m.

GENEALOGY. 609

Gould, David, m., Sept. 19, 1817, Susan Beal. Children: Alanson, d. Aug. 28, 1821, ag. 2; Diadema, d. April 19, 1824, ag. 1m.

Gordon, Judith, wife of John Gould, d. June 16, 1862, ag. 73.

Graham, George, b. 1850; d. 1895; George W., son by Margaret, b. 1879; d. 1880 (a).

Greeley, Mathew, son of Shubal and Hannah (Pettingill), b. Salisbury, Sept. 3, 1759; d. June 24, 1842 (d); m., Jan. 1, 1782, Abigail Emmons, b. Dec. 17, 1761; d. July 10, 1847. Children: Shubael, b. May 18, 1782; d. Rumney, March 24, 1867; m. (1), Jan. 1, 1804, Anna Hoit, dau. John and Hannah, b. April, 1779; d. Oct. 1, 1805 (d); m. (2), Aug. 25, 1808, Lydia Whitney, dau. Isaac and Lydia (Taylor), b. Oct. 27, 1782; d. Rumney, March 29, 1867. Children: Nancy, b. June 13, 1812; Ira, b. Dec. 28, 1813; Susan B., b. March 15, 1815; and six more: David, m., June 22, 1809, Judith Pattee, dau. Daniel; Ephraim, b. July 5, 1786; d. May 28, 1846; m. (1) Sally Clark, dau. of Timothy; Mathew, b. Nov. 1, 1788; d. July 9, 1847; m., Oct. 16, 1816, Orra C. Byington; Abigail, b. July 2, 1794; d. March, 1796; Abigail, b. Feb. 7, 1796; m. Isaac Whitney; Achsah, b. March 23, 1798; d. Jan. 2, 1838; m., Oct. 19, 1828, Silas Dutton, b. July 16, 1802; d. May 30, 1850; John D., b. Aug. 23, 1802; m., Sept. 1, 1832, Semia Sanborn; Lydia, b. Oct. 9, 1804; d. Jan. 10, 1851; m. Daniel Huse; Ira, b. July 27, 1806; d. March 27, 1807; Hannah, m. Shubael Towle; Sally, b. May 28, 1790; d. Oct. 19, 1868; m., Oct. 29, 1815, Arnold Fales, son of John and Sally, b. May 25, 1792; d. March 14, 1868.

Greenough, Robert, d. June 21, 1858, ag. 34y., 5m. (a).

Hadley, Abel and Lydia, had Simeon, b. Hopkinton, May 3, 1783; Jacob, b. Canaan, Oct. 23, 1785; Lydia, b. Nov. 2, 1887.

Hadley, Simeon, m., March 5, 1788, Lucy Martin. Children: Moses, b. Jan. 10, 1792; Miriah, d. Jan. 5, 1872, ag. 76; m., March 11, 1817, Samuel Davis (see him).

Hadley, Moses, b. May 1, 1769; d. June 20, 1858; m., May, 1793, Mary Martin, b. April 10, 1772. Children: Joshua, b. Aug. 29, 1795; m., Jan. 18, 1815, Ruth Davis, of Grafton; Relief, b. Oct. 15, 1797; m., March 15, 1815, Dr. Samuel S. Stephens; Sophia, b. Oct. 13, 1799; m., April 13, 1824, David Fales; Amos, b. July 9, 1802; m., July 3, 1823, Mehitable Briggs of Orange; Moses, b. March 22, 1806; d. Dec. 3, 1872 (h); m. Almira Procter; d. Dec. 16, 1885, ag. 80 (h). Children: Angie E., b. 1857; m., Sept. 18, 1875, Daniel L. Straw of Grafton; George, d. May 29, 1893, ag. 62y., 10m., 26d.; m. Mary A. Leavitt. Children: Albert L., d. April 14, 1906, ag. 48y., 15d.; m. (1), Feb. 6, 1884, Lillian M. Lovejoy; three children; m. (2) Bertha (Barney) Dow, dau. of Eleazer Barney; Edwin A. Norman, son of Moses 1st, b. March 22, 1813; d. May 29, 1890 (b); m., Feb. 3, 1836, Lucy D. Davis, dau. of Samuel, b. March 9, 1818. Children: Lucian, b. ——— 13, 1844; Arabel, b. Nov. 21, 1842; m., Oct. 19, 1865, Moses E. Currier, son of Eben F. and Sophia N.; Mariann, b. Jan. 12, 1837; d. April 8, 1887; Marcia, d. June 30, 1874, ag. 35; m., Oct. 25, 1864, Augustus Shepard (see him); Malvina,

b. Feb. 10, 1847; d. Nov. 10, 1864; Eva M., b. 1852; m., Feb. 25, 1875, Walter A. Swett, son of Horace; Etta M., m., April 4, 1878, Samuel W. Currier, son of Simeon; children: Eva, Hammond. Hamlin E., b. April 15, 1860; m. (1), Sept. 29, 1883, Minnie S. Whaley, d. April 3, 1889, ag. 27; m. (2), April 28, 1900, Clisty Whaley; two children, Howard and Marcia, by first wife; Lyman, son of Moses 1st, b. 1815; d. April 4, 1881; m., May 30, 1836, Lois Eaton of Grantham, d. Nov., 1889.

Hadley, Stephen, m. (1) Abigail Coburn, d. March 7, 1825, ag. 43 (e); m. (2) Sarah Williams, dau. of Robert, d. June 30, 1834, ag. 36y (e). Children: Stephen, Jr., d. Nov. 25, 1876, ag. 67; m., June 20, 1860, Harriet N. Towle, dau. of Shubel; she m. (1) Reuben Clark; Susan M., m. David Towle; Nancy M., m., Dec. 25, 1839, Elijah W. Edwards, his first wife (see him); Dorcas, m. Daniel Clark (see him); Leonard, d. Jan. 24, 1892, ag. 85y., 4d.; m. (1) Sally Marshall; m. (2) Mary G. Williams, dau. of. Stephen, b. Jan. 29, 1826; d. Sept. 22, 1886. Children: John M., d. Dec. 1, 1847, ag. 19y., 11m (e); Eben, d. Jan. 4, 1873, ag. 42y., 2m.; m., Feb. 28, 1855, Jane Philbrick, d. Jan. 6, 1875, ag. 37y. 7m. Children: Jennie, b. 1856; m., June 23, 1874, John Hopkins; Linnie C., d. Feb. 14, 1887, ag. 18y., 3m., 4d. (e); Abel, son of Leonard, died in army; Stephen, m. (1) Sarah Dwinnels; m. (2) Myra Biathrow, d. July 13, 1891, ag. 38 (e). Children: Warren B., d. May 23, 1888, ag. 16 (e); Dennis, son of Leonard, d. June 3, 1847, ag. 10. Moses M., son of Stephen and Sarah Williams, b. Hanover, April 28, 1828; m., March 20, 1855, Mahala D. Fisher; one child, Charles; Aaron, b. Hanover, June, 1829; m. Belinda Sanborn of Canaan; had one son; Gilman, son of Stephen and Mary, b. 1830; d. Oct. 20, 1834; Calvin, d. March, 1836 (e); Andrew J., b. Hanover, Aug. 11, 1832; d. 1909; m. Carrie Blaisdell, Aug. 7, 1870; one dau., Florence; Sarah, b. Hanover, June 22, 1834; m., May 11, 1859, Sherburn L. Corning of Manchester; both mutes; two children: Amos G. and Minnie L.

Hadely, Simeon, d. Oct. 5, 1859, ag. 39; his wife, Emeline Dustin, b. 1822; d. 1891. Child: Isabel R., d. Sept. 29, 1857, ag. 1.

Hadley, Obadiah, son of Nathaniel; m. Achsah G. Kimball, dau. of Abram, b. 1823; d. Sept. 25, 1890; his first wife, Caroline Stephers, d. June 26, 1851, ag. 27y., 10m. (d). Children of Achsah: Ida A., b. 1859; m., March 30, 1887, Edwin A. Muzzey; Orra, d. Jan. 14, 1881, ag. 16y., 9m.

Handerson, Anna M., wife of Charles H., d. Oct. 20, 1893, ag. 45y., 6m. 20d.

Hanson, Ebenezer and Lucy. Children: Hannah, b. Sept. 1, 1791; Jeremy S., b. Feb. 7, 1793; William G., b. April 18, 1795; John, b. March 9, 1797; Mariann, b. Aug. 4, 1799; Lucy, b. Oct. 13, 1802; Ben, b. March 4, 1805.

Hardy, Gilman, d. June 19, 1868, ag. 76 (c); his wife, Rachel C., d. Aug. 14, 1844, ag. 57; his second wife, Mary Colby, dau. Daniel, d. Dec. 30, 1858, ag. 50. Children: Mary E., d. Jan. 8, 1848, ag. 3 (d);

Thomas J., d. Sept. 20, 1883, ag. 78; his wife, Mary Colby, d. May 18, 1887, ag. 74 (a). Gilman m. (4), Sept. 5, 1860, Matilda Jones.

Hardy, Almira, dau. Daniel and Betsey, d. Feb. 18, 1904, ag. 6w. (c).

Harris, George, b. Feb. 1723; d. Nov. 13, 1790 (g); "Made his exit out of time," so the old record says, aged 67 years. "The memory of the just is blessed," says his tombstone. M. (1) Sally; m. (2) Mrs. Anna, d. Jan. 16, 1812, ag. 63; "Let not her virtues die" is on her tombstone. Children: Capt. Joshua, b. Norwich, Conn., May 10, 1754; d. Aug. 10, 1835 (a); m., June 1, 1781, Hannah Hough, d. April 2, 1783, ag. 22 (g); m. (2), April 1, 1784, Miriam Johnson, d. Feb. 29, 1840, ag. 79 (a). Nine children: John Hough, b. Feb. 18, 1782; d. Aug. 2, 1858; m., June 4, 1804, Lucy May, dau. of John and Mary, d. Nov. 2, 1864, ag. 80y. 5m. He kept a store at one time in a little house that now forms the ell of Wallace G. Fogg's house. It was sold to Daniel Pattee, who built on the two story addition, afterwards he lived where A. S. Greene now lives. Children: Mary Freeman, b. June 12, 1806; d. July 4, 1840, single; Lucy May, b. May 4, 1808; d. ———; m. ——— Wilson. Children: Harriet, m. ——— Bush; George, m. ———; Hannah Hough, b. Feb. 24, 1811; m. James A. Furber. Children: Sarah; Loraine; George C. and Ida. Sarah Sheldon, dau. of John H., b. March 10, 1813; m. (1) Rev. William B. Kelley and had one child, Williamine Loraine, b. Aug. 28, 1836, m. (1) Roger D. Smalley; m. (2), Oct. 13, 1869, Andrew Oliver; Sarah S., m. (2), Aug. 24, 1839, Calvin P. Fairfield of Lyme. Children: Payson E., b. July 22, 1841; m., Nov. 6, 1875, Caroline P. Churchill, resides in Lyme. Children: Arthur Perry, b. April 23, 1877; m., Dec. 23, 1902, Amelia B. Griffith. Children: Marion, b. April 22, 1908. Helen Francis, dau. of Payson E., b. July 26, 1879; m., June 25, 1908, Melbourne B. Tewksbury. Children: Edwin, b. Feb. 25, 1909; d. March 25, 1909; Marion Harris, dau. of Payson E., b. March 1, 1881; m., Sept. 5, 1907, Fred W. Lovejoy; Anna Churchill, b. April 24, 1884; m., June 12, 1907, P. Leon Claflin. Children: Dorothy, b. March 14, 1908; Alice Eva, b. Nov. 29, 1909. Sarah Loraine, dau. of Calvin P. and Sarah S., b. May 19, 1843; d. Feb. 12, 1849; Ella Harris, b. March 24, 1847; m., Oct. 25, 1876, John P. Southworth. Children: Calvin Porter, b. Sept. 1877; d. Nov. 1877; Sarah Loraine, b. Feb. 6, 1879; Adelia Maria, dau. of Calvin P. and Sarah S., b. June 5, 1852; d. Oct. 31, 1904. Marcia Maria, dau. of John H. and Lucy, b. July 7, 1815; m. (1) ——— Johnson; m. (2) John Stiles of Kankakee, Ill; one child by first: Alta. Eliza Ann, dau. of John H., b. Feb. 8, 1818; m., Dec. 1837, David J. Powers of Palmyra, Wis. Children: Loraine, William, Frank. Lemira Loraine, dau. of John H., b. Aug. 6, 1820; d. Oct. 9, 1885; m., July 4, 1838, Allen Hayes of Windsor, Vt., afterwards of Canaan. Children: John Henry, lives in Enfield; Idella May, m. a Burleigh. George May, son of John H., b. Jan. 31, 1823; m. ———. Children: Frederick M. and Kittie. John Adams, son of John H., b. April 9, 1826; m., Jan. 22, 1852, Mary Ann Swett, dau. of Elisha, of Canaan; no children. Polly, dau. of Joshua, b.

Jan. 12, 1785; Jesse, b. March 11, 1786; James Shepard, b. Jan. 27, 1788; Sally, b. Jan. 30, 1790; Hannah Hough, b. Feb. 13, 1795; m. Daniel Hovey (see him); George, b. July 2, 1796; d. July 16, 1806 (g); Betsey, b. March 19, 1800; Lenora Wheaton, b. July 28, 1802; Mary, dau. George, b. Jan. 23, 1767; m., Nov. 9, 1785, Oliver Smith (see him); Hubbard, b. Dec. 31, 1769; d. Oct. 19, 1845 (a); m., Jan. 14, 1794, Kitty Dexter, b. Dec. 16, 1771; four children; m. (2) Mehitable, d. March 2, 1846, ag. 74 (a). Children: Hubbard, b. Nov. 27, 1794; m., 1819, Martha Follensbee, dau. Nathan; George L., b. May 15, 1796; d. March 29, 1871 (a); m., 1822, Sarah Follensbee, dau. Nathan of Enfield, d. July 25, 1892, ag. 94y., 10m. (a). He came back to Canaan in 1825 and in 1831 built the house now occupied by his grandson, G. H. Goodhue. He also built the Hotel Lucerne the same year. Children: Arabella, d. July 7, 1848, ag. 23; m., Sept. 13, 1846, Albert Martin, son of Eleazer; he afterwards m. (2) Harriet O. Wallace; Sarah Frances, d. Nov. 22, 1890, ag. 58; m., Sept. 13, 1854, J. Merrill Goodhue, d. Oct. 12, 1881, ag. 54. Children: George H., b. 1856; d. 1910; m., June 27, 1894, Grace I. Wiswell, b. 1873. Children: Merrill and Elsie. Eliza, dau. of Hubbard, b. July 17, 1800; m., March 7, 1825, Jacob Blaisdell (see him); Dexter, b. May 16, 1805; d. June 17, 1865 (a); m. Harriet B. Tilton, dau. of Dr. Timothy, d. Oct. 16, 1885, ag. 78. Children: Eliza B., b. April 29, 1828; d. Dec. 18, 1906; m. Benjamin P. Nichols (see him); George Dexter, b. Dec. 16, 1840; d. Oct. 8, 1890, in Boston (referred to elsewhere); Oscar W., b. 1845; m., May 16, 1873, Nellie A. Brocklebank; had several children, one son Dexter. Lois, dau. of George, b. Nov. 28, 1770; d. Jan. 19, 1820; m., Nov. 22, 1793, James Morse (see him); Lucy, dau. George, m. (1), May 30, 1771, Capt. Charles Walworth (see him); m. (2), 1786, Henry Hall of Canaan. Four children: Sally, b. May 8, 1787; Polly, b. April 16, 1788; Henry, b. June 5, 1791; Joshua, b. Oct. 23, 1792.

Harris, Israel, b. Bozrah, Conn., June 22, 1775; m., Feb. 23, 1797, Miriam Eastman, b. May 6, 1778.

Harris, Benjamin and Sally, had children: Elizabeth, b. May 24, 1799; Lydia, b. Sept. 30, 1800.

Harris, William, b. 1772; d. 1852; m., Aug. 11, 1813, Olive Babbitt, b. 1788; d. 1859. Children: William Lathrop, b. Nov. 15, 1814; d. 1901; m. Sarah Pierce, b. 1819; d. 1895. Children: Georgianna, b. 1844; m., Oct. 4, 1868, James H. Little of Lowell; Octavia, b. 1840; d. 1842; Octavia, b. 1843; d. 1851; William, b. 1852; d. 1852; Willie, b. 1854; d. 1856; Emma J., b. 1851; d. 1866; Sarah J., b. 1847; m., May 13, 1869, Moses S. Perley; Isaac Babbitt, son of William, b. July 17, 1820; Jason Eaton, b. Dec. 7, 1822.

Harris, Anna, m., Aug. 24, 1800, John May, Jr., son of John.

Haynes, Benjamin, d. Oct. 26, 1836, ag. 67; by his wife, Ruthy, he had Sumner, b. June 2, 1800; Josiah Porter, b. Oct. 1, 1802; Francis Asbury, b. Nov. 21, 1805; John, b. Sept. 19, 1810; George, b. May 16, 1813; Martha Jane.

Genealogy.

Hayward, Wilmer H., d. June 8, 1879, ag. 21y., 2m. 4d. (h).

Hazeltine, William, d. Sept. 20, 1853, ag. 31y., 8m.; Sally his wife, d. Dec. 31, 1838, ag. 44 (b); George W., b. 1834; m. Melissa A. Whitney, b. 1844; d. 1905. Children: Minnie E., b. 1866; d. 1880; Alberto C.; Grace E., b. 1876; m., June 8, 1897, J. Frank King, b. 1871.

Heath, Sally, wife of Nathaniel, d. Dec. 24, 1840, ag. 47 (a).

Heath, Susan, wife of Eben, d. Dec. 17, 1863, ag. 64 (a).

Heath, John R., d. Aug. 15, 1883, ag. 56 (c); m., May 1, 1850, Miranda Eastman, d. March 29, 1889, ag. 59; a son, Lyman E., d. Feb. 5, 1852, ag. 4m., and an infant, d. March 29, 1862, ag. 15d.

Hebert, Esther, wife of Joseph, d. Jan. 31, 1871, ag. 49 (a); Joseph, m., (2), Dec. 26, 1872, Lovina Kemp.

Henderson, Isabelle E., wife of James, b. April 23, 1844; d. May 22, 1905 (c).

Hill, Moses, d. Aug. 15, 1852, ag. 26 (d); Frank, b. Oct. 31, 1823; d. Sept. 15, 1901; m. Odil Durocher, b. Dec. 23, 1828; d. March 31, 1902. Children of Frank, Jr., and E. Hill: Villa A. T., d. June 20, 1892, ag. 10y., 3m.; Freddie A., d. June 10, 1892, ag. 8y., 11m., 4d.; Willie G., d. May 19, 1892, ag. 16y., 15d.; Harry O., d. June 5, 1892, ag. 12y., 3m.; Charles, son of Frank, Sr., b. Feb. 2, 1866; d. March 13, 1893.

Hinkson, Daniel, d. March 26, 1846, ag. 67 (g); his wife, Cynthia, d. Dec. 26, 1848, ag. 67 (g). Children: Daniel, d. Oct. 30, 1881, ag. 75y., 10m. (c); m. Rachel C. Packard, Nov. 27, 1834; she d. Aug. 9, 1905, ag. 93y., 4m., 3d. Children: Delia L., b. May 14, 1837; d. 1909; m. Edwin Shepard, b. April 10, 1829; d. Oct. 23, 1905; Betsey M., d. Dec. 29, 1839, ag. 6w.; Daniel F., d. July 18, 1863, ag. 20y., 4m., 18d. (c); Chamberlain P., b. Nov. 25, 1845; d. Dec. 10, 1900 (c); m. and had a family; lived in Hanover. Leander, son of Daniel 1st, d. Dec. 11, 1855, ag. 44 (g).

Hoit, John, d. Oct. 17, 1832, ag. 80 (d); m. Hannah Rogers, d. March 15, 1813, ag. 59y., 8m., by whom he had Daniel, d. July 29, 1813, ag. 26 (d); John, Jr., d. Sept. 20, 1864, ag. 79y., 1m., 20d.; m. (1), March 15, 1811, Eliza Clark, d. Aug. 25, 1814; by her he had: Abigail, b. April 17, 1812; Daniel, b. Dec. 25, 1813; m., Oct. 7, 1837, Susan Bartlett; John, Jr., m. (2), March 12, 1815, Sally Barber, and had Nancy, b. Jan. 4, 1816; she m. Harrison Rogers; and John Gilman, b. March 6, 1817; d. Sept. 10, 1825; George, d. Sept. 17, 1825, ag. 3; Joel, d. Sept. 18, 1825, ag. 1y., 3m.; Hannah P., d. Sept. 14, 1825, ag. 6y., 3m.; Stephen B., d. Sept. 20, 1825, ag. 4y., 8m.; John, Sr., m. (2), May 25, 1815, Abigail Clark of Orford; a dau. of John, Sr., m. Josiah G. Lincoln.

Hoit, Nathan W., d. June 18, 1834, ag. 11m (a).

Hoyt, David, d. May 30, 1877, ag. 75y., 3m., 1d.; his wife, Judith, d. Aug. 11, 1855, ag. 55.

Hoyt, John W., d. Dec. 20, 1897, ag. 66; his wife, A. E., had Frank A., d. Oct. 19, 1883, ag. 7y., 4m. (a).

Hoyt, Persis Cross, dau. of Jonathan and Molly (Bailey) **Cross**, wife of Robert, d. April 3, 1858, ag. 83.

Hoyt, Rufus S., d. March 12, 1852, ag. 50; his wife, Eliza, d. Sept. 21, 1847, ag. 40. Children: Rufus A., d. Feb. 4, 1852, ag. 19; Benjamin Henry, d. July 30, 1854, ag. 20; Josephine A., d. Nov. 7, 1857, ag. 22; Eliza Jane, d. March 28, 1847, ag. 10; Warren E., m. Lydia Goodrich, b. Aug. 9, 1847; d. Jan. 29, 1899. Children: Ned Leon, b. June, 1878; d. Sept. 5, 1879 (c); Will A. m. Ida B. Wilson (see her).

Holt, Ann R., wife of Henry, Jr., d. Dec. 2, 1853, ag. 28 (a); William, b. 1832; d. 1905; George F., b. 1857; d. 1906; Sadie A., dau. of Charles and Jane, d. April 21, 1879, ag. 1y., 5m.

Hopey, Fath R., dau. of A. M. and M. E., b. March 24, 1902; d. Sept. 9, 1904 (j).

Hovey, Daniel, m., Jan. 12, 1817, Hannah Hough Harris, dau. of Joshua, and had George Harris, b. Sept. 24, 1817, and Edward Olcott, b. June 23, 1824; d. July 6, 1824 (a).

Howard, Edward and Hannah, had Salley Knight, b. June 5, 1804.

Howard, Elvira H., dau. of Caleb S. and Sarah P., d. March 31, 1881, ag. 44 (c).

Howe, Nathaniel, d. Nov. 6, 1856, ag. 85; his wife, Elizabeth, d. April 2, 1858, ag. 86 (c).

Huggett, William, b. 1841; d. 1908 (c); m., Nov. 19, 1873, Hattie Dana; son, Elmer E., m. Edna E., b. June 29, 1868; d. June 29, 1886; m. (2) ———.

Hunt, Phylendy R., d. July 17, 1856, ag. 51.

Hutchinson, Levi, son of Jonathan and Mary (Wardwell), was a hatter from Pembroke and Chichester; b. Aug. 12, 1781; d. May 4, 1873 (b); m., April 10, 1805, Sarah Page, b. Oct. 15, 1783; d. June 26, 1840. He came to Canaan in 1834, with his family. Three children: Charlotte P., b. Oct. 6, 1809; d. May 1, 1851; m., Aug. 18, 1833, Sylvester P. Gould. Children: Martha H., b. Dec. 18, 1833; m. William Paine; no children; and Mary, b. June 13, 1836; d. 1851. Richard Wood, son of Levi, b. Sept. 10, 1811; d. Feb. 27, 1889; m., Dec. 12, 1841, Mary Sanborn, dau. of Jonathan, b. April 30, 1820; d. May 30, 1899. Children: Rosina, b. June 13, 1844; d. Sept. 11, 1863; m. July 1, 1863, Albert E. Barney (see him); Abby Ann, b. Oct. 29, 1846; m., Jan. 22, 1867, Albert E. Barney; Mary Emma, b. March 19, 1849; m., Jan. 11, 1869, Joseph F. Stockbridge, no children; Charlotte L., b. Feb. 15, 1851; Charles B., b. March 31, 1853; d. Sept. 19, 1864; Arthur W., b. Jan. 27, 1858; m. (1), Dec. 30, 1882, Lizzie M. King, d. Feb. 6, 1884, ag. 19y., 5m., 22d.; m. (2), April 13, 1886, Irene A. Tenney, b. Sept. 7, 1868. Three children: Bessie, b. Dec. 22, 1886; m., Nov. 30, 1909, Edward A. Barney; Mariam, b. Jan. 14, 1890; Fred Richard, b. May 25, 1893; Charles, son of Levi, b. July 24, 1813; d. June 26, 1890; m., March 22, 1838, Mary Wells, dau. of Joshua, b. April 30, 1817; d. Dec. 21, 1897. Children: Lucy Jane, b. June 27, 1839; m. John Flanders. Children: Minnie, m. Edward Prentiss; three children: Laura, d. young; Edward and Laura; Gratia, dau. of Lucy J., b. Feb. 12, 1864, lives in Salt Lake City.

Jackson, Solon P., son of Heber and Sybil H.; d. Nov. 1, 1862, ag. 2;

GENEALOGY. 615

Lilla A., dau., d. Nov. 7, 1862, ag. 7; Carroll, a son, d. Nov. 13, 1862, ag. 9 (d).

Jameson, Leander, b. Sept. 22, 1818; d. March 24, 1897; his wife, Diana Kimball, dau. of Joel, b. June 26, 1820; d. March 4, 1894 (b). Children: Fred; Ada; Jerome, b. 1848; m., Jan. 1, 1872, Evelyn J. Stonning. Children: Wilbur, Edith.

Jenness, Dorothy, wife of Richard, son of Stephen, d. May 17, 1849, ag. 25; Roseanna, dau., d. Nov. 5, 1849, ag. 2y., 10m.; Sally, wife of Joseph H. Drew, d. Jan. 10, 1839, ag. 22 (b).

Jenness, Job B., son of Stephen, d. Oct. 16, 1905, ag. 79; m., March 28, 1847, Sarah Chellis, d. Oct. 25, 1868, ag. 40. Children: Oscar P., d. July 28, 1863, ag. 16; Lucy Jane, d. Oct. 18, 1867, ag. 17; Allen, d. Sept. 8, 1879, ag. 9; Oscar, d. Aug. 18, 1865, ag. 1; Malvina, b. 1850; m., Sept. 3, 1869, George W. Peabody; George B., b. 1855; m., March 12, 1876, Hattie E. Flanders.

Jepson, Francis, d. Nov. 24, 1901, ag. 75y., 3m.; his wife, Caroline M. Smith, d. Nov. 20, 1890, ag. 59y., 2m. (a); one dau., Mary A., d. March 10, 1906, ag. 51 (a); m. (1) Charles O. B. Story and (2), Nov. 14, 1892, S. B. Withington.

Johnson, James, son of Timothy and Anna, d. Jan. 13, 1801, ag. 10y., 9m., 11d. (g); Ellen R., wife of L. F., b. May 21, 1858; d. March 1, 1892 (c); Lura C., wife of Wilson D., d. Nov. 2, 1885, ag. 19y., 2m., 12d. (e).

Johnson, Lieut. E. W., b. May 9, 1824; d. ———; Mary, his wife, b. Feb. 29, 1822; d. April 2, 1888; dau. of Stephen Jenness. Child: Henry.

Jones, Jehu, b. Colchester, Conn., Dec. 17, 1749; d. 1813; m., Dec. 10, 1776, Betsey Clark, dau. of Caleb, b. March 13, 1755; d. ———. Children: Betty, b. Dec. 4, 1777; Amasa, b. Oct. 11, 1779; m., June 26, 1808, Sally Crocker. Children: Albert Amasa, b. March 5, 1809; Louisa Maria, b. Sept. 4, 1811; Harriet Stoddard, b. Dec. 3, 1813. Asahel, son of Jehu, b. Aug. 21, 1781; d. June 23, 1851 (a); m., Oct. 15, 1809, Bernice Crocker, b. Dec. 10, 1785; d. July 25, 1880. Children: William Pearl, b. July 23, 1810; Hiram, b. Feb. 16, 1818; d. Feb. 6, 1899 (j); m., March 1, 1843, Sarah Hoague, b. June 29, 1815. Children: Mary B., b. March 26, 1853; m. March 19, 1875, Frank B. Smart, son of Daniel, b. Dec. 10, 1852. Children: Leroy E., b. April 14, 1876; printer in Boston; Winnifred S., b. April 22, 1883; m., June, 1908, Adolph Langton; Wilfred H., b. April 22, 1883; m., June 30, 1906, Rachel G. Smith of Meredith. Lydia Ann, dau. of Hiram, b. Dec. 21, 1846; d. Aug. 13, 1868; Lucina A., b. May 29, 1849; m., May 1, 1882, Hiram Herbert Stevens, b. April 17, 1849; d. Sept. 2, 1909. Children: Julia C., b. Sept. 4, 1883; m., May 19, 1906, Herbert F. Withington. Child: William H. Charles R., son of H. H. and Lucina A., b. April 17, 1890. John A., son of Asahel, b. Nov. 13, 1812; d. June 9, 1886; Company E, Fifteenth New Hampshire Volunteers; Julia Caroline Amelia, b. June 10, 1821; d. Dec. 7, 1906; m. Abial Smart, d. April 26, 1895, ag. 81. Julianna, dau. of B. and A., b. Oct. 27, 1814; d. Sept. 6, 1818. Thomas W., b. April 28, 1823; d. May 1902. Mary, dau. of Jehu, b. Sept. 6, 1783; d. Dec. 4, 1848; m., Oct.

24, 1808, Tristram Sanborn, son of Tristram. Sarah, b. Sept. 1, 1786; Jabez, b. Sept. 28, 1788; Philura, b. Aug. 25, 1790; m. George Walworth (see him); James, b. Sept. 16, 1793; Jesse, b. May 15, 1796; m., April 17, 1826, Sarah Davis; Nancy Clark, b. July 13, 1798; d. Nov. 25, 1862; m. Daniel Durrell (see him).

Jones, Polly, wife of Nathaniel, d. Dec. 1, 1870, ag. 91; their son, Caleb, d. Jan. 21, 1881, ag. 71y., 6m. (d); his wife, Elizabeth Colby, dau. of Willaby (d); d. Jan. 29, 1881, ag. 68y., 7m. Children: John S., d. Jan. 22, 1894 (d), ag. 56; Thomas E., d. July 27, 1866, ag. 25 (d); m., Aug. 11, 1862, Sophia E. Hoffman. Children: Charles T., b. April 1, 1865; Melissa A., dau. Caleb, d. Oct. 19, 1884, ag. 50y., 7m., 26d.; m. Edwin A. Morse, son of Jesse; Irena, d. Aug. 28, 1878, ag. 34; m. Edwin A. Morse (d).

Jones, Sylvester, son of Isaac, b. March 5, 1811; d. Jan. 26, 1885; his wife, Nancy M. Currier of Enfield, dau. of Henry, d. June 10, 1879, ag. 54. Children: Emelie Currier, d. Sept. 16, 1863, ag. 18 (c); Florence M., b. 1853; m., Jan. 10, 1872, Charles H. Emerson.

Jones, Charles S., son of Ira, d. Jan. 3, 1886, ag. 58y., 11m., 3d. (a); m., June 20, 1850, Maria L. Pressey, dau. of John L. and Sarah; Frank B., b. April 14, 1856; d. March 15, 1904 (a); his wife, Ida M., was b. Jan. 21, 1855; Lena, dau. of Bert and W. R., d. Sept. 28, 1893 (d).

Jones, Mary S., d. April 30, 1873, ag. 80 (a), mother of Elder Nathan, d ———; by his first wife, Polly C., who d. May 13, 1849, ag. 32, he had Satira, d. Feb. 25, 1867, ag. 24; Alvin S., d. Sept. 13, 1849, ag. 1y., 4m.; Almeda, d. June 24, 1865, ag. 24y., 8m., 19d.; m. Charles N. Morse, son of Stephen (see him). Ednah, b. 1845, d. 1904; m., Oct. 25, 1862; Edson J. Fifield, d. Feb., 1888, ag. 47y., 9m.; son of Joseph and Sarah (Pollard) Fifield. Children: Elmer, Darwin, Frank and William, Adin G., b. 1872; d. 1873; Nathan m. (2) Mary A. Gile, dau. Amos, and had Arden, b. 1851; m., Dec. 26, 1870, Sarah M. Bagley, adopted dau. of David and Murilla. Lizzie A., dau., d. Oct. 13, 1873, ag. 12y., 10m.

Keenan, Christopher, d. Feb. 10, 1853, ag. 24.

Kelley, Moses, settled here in 1801; d. Oct. 2, 1850, ag. 73 (a); his wife, Nancy Tyler, dau. Job, d. Aug. 20, 1863, ag. 82. Children: Moses G., d. Sept. 27, 1875, ag. 71 y., 2m. (a). His first wife, Lydia W, d. Nov. 8, 1861, ag. 44y., 5m. Children: George W., d. Sept. 8, 1843, ag. 1y., 6m.; Marion Isa, b. 1846; m., April 30, 1864, Caleb N. Homan. Rev. William B., son of Moses, d. June 9, 1836, ag. 30; m. Sarah Sheldon Harris, dau. of John H. Children: Williamine Loraine; m. (1) Roger D. Smalley; m. (2) Andrew Oliver. Sarah S. m. (2) Calvin P. Fairfield (see her). Joseph T., son of Moses, d. June 12, 1862, ag. 51y., 8m. Moses G., m. (2), April 23, 1865, Mary Ann Marcy of Windsor, Vt., James Hamilton, d. April 10, 1882, ag. 61 (a); m., Dec. 15, 1850, Harriet S. George, dau. of William W., d. Sept. 4, 1901, ag. 69. Children: Jennie E., b. 1851; m., Oct. 16, 1876, J. Edward Lincoln, b. 1853; Hattie L., b. 1856; m., Jan. 15, 1878, Austin V. Dow, b. 1846; a son d. Nov. 2, 1863, ag. 10w.; George H., b. Oct. 16, 1864; m., June 19, 1889, Helen G.

GENEALOGY.

Cheney; another son of James H. d. Sept. 11, 1866, ag. 8m., 12d. (a);
Mary G., dau. of Moses and Nancy, d. Feb. 10, 1888, ag. 79 y., 7m., 12d.;
m. (1) Col. Eliphalet C. Gilman; m. (2) Caleb Dustin, son of David.
Ann P., dau. of Moses, m. Cyrus Perkins. Children: Elizabeth D., m.
Benjamin Morey; Cyrus E.; Isaac N.; Charles, m. Julianna Niles; and
Henry I. Flavilla, dau. of Moses, m. John Worth, Jr.

Kelton, Lorenzo F., d. Jan. 9, 1872, ag. 14. Almer F., d. Jan. 10, 1872, ag. 12. Edwin A., d. Jan. 3, 1872, ag. 2y., 5m., 20d. Children of Amos and Hannah M. (a).

Kent, Daniel, d. Jan. 6, 1852, ag. 84; his wife, Elizabeth, d. Jan. 14, 1864, ag. 90y., 1m., 12d. (a).

Ketcham, Sukey, wife of Samuel, and an infant d. March 28, 1813, ag. 30. (d).

Kimball, Daniel, d. Jan. 29, 1843, ag. 80 (d); m. Mary Stevens, d. Nov. 7, 1838, ag. 70. Children: Asa, b. July 3, 1787; m., Oct. 7, 1810, Miriam Meacham, dau. of Samuel; Daniel, Jr., b. Oct. 16, 1789; d. Feb. 4, 1872; his wife, Louisa, d. Aug. 19, 1859, ag. 68y., 7m. Joseph, son of Daniel, 1st, and his wife, Miriam, had a dau. Anner, d. July 9, 1839, ag. 13m. (d); Mary, d. Aug. 12, 1867, ag. 70; Pamelia S. ("Aunt Milly"), d. Feb. 18, 1868, ag. 72; m., Oct., 1837, David Townsend, d. Aug. 25, 1857, ag. 73 (d); she m. (2), Sept. 23, 1860, Samuel Stephens of Enfield; Moses d. County Farm, Dec. 23, 1860, ag. 80; m. Arvilla Stark of Hanover, d. April 5, 1860, ag. 48; one child: Elizabeth Ann, d. March 23, 1856, ag. 14 (a). Caleb P., son of Daniel, 1st, killed by lightning while ploughing in the field, May 15, 1843, ag. 35 (d); m. Susanna Richardson. Children: Nancy L. R., d. Aug. 28, 1852, ag. 25 (d); another dau. m. a Richardson, d. Jan. 7, 1850, ag. 50. Parkhurst K., d. Sept. 28, 1888, ag. 78y., 4m. (d); m. Lucy K. Miller, d. March 21, 1873, ag. 62. Children: Charles T., d. March 22, 1860, ag. 12y., 8m.; Horace W., b. Jan., 1845; d. Aug. 30, 1907; m., Aug. 30, 1863, Mary A. Call, dau. of Enoch, d. Aug. 12, 1867, ag. 20 (d).

Kimball, Abraham, d. July 2, 1855, ag. 70 (a); came from Weare, where he had married Eunice Watson, d. Jan. 7, 1876, ag. 81 (c); he was a lame shoemaker at Goose Pond and lived east of the Levi Davis house; was a member of Mr. Foster's church (Congregational) and a frequent attendant on Sundays. Children: Adeline, b. April 12, 1816; d. Dec. 12, 1891; m. Jesse Morse, b. Feb. 21, 1813; d. April 9, 1878; son of Jesse and Dorothy (see him); Arvilla, b. March, 1819; m. Peter S. Wells; Abigail Ann, b. 1824; d. Oct. 23, 1873 (c); m., Nov. 18, 1859, William E. Allard; Achsah G., b. 1823; m. Obediah Hadley (see him); Abram Fred, d. May 5, 1907, ag. 86y., 9m.; m., Jan. 19, 1850, Hannah L. Emory of Lyme, d. Aug. 29, 1882, ag. 48y., 1m., 9d. Children: Carrie E., b. 1862; m., March 24, 1877, Chellis E. Collins, son of Err and Mary Collins; Fred B., b. 1858; m., Jan. 4, 1881, Dora M. Columbia, dau. of William and Elizabeth (Hall); b. July 17, 1858, d. Sept. 2, 1903 (a). Children: Freddie B., b. Nov. 20, 1891; d. Sept. 2, 1894 (a); Eugene E. and Burnis J. John W., son of Abraham, b. Aug.

8, 1824; d. April 14, 1901 (d); m., Oct. 24, 1866, Eliza H. Bartlett, dau. of Caleb C., b. Oct. 14, 1826; d. Jan. 3, 1903; Alfred H., b. 1833; d. Nov. 2, 1861.

Kimball, Asa, and Betsey, had William, b. Nov. 6, 1787; d. Feb. 19, 1882 (a); m., Feb. 18, 1824, Sarah Richardson, d. June 5, 1844, ag. 40. Children: William Henry, d. March 18, 1847 (a), ag. 6w., 18d. Nathaniel, son of Asa, b. March 14, 1790; Hannah, b. May 24, 1792; Relief, b. April 17, 1794.

Kimball, Daniel, d. Jan. 6, 1852, ag. 84; his wife, Elizabeth, d. Jan. 14, 1864, ag. 90y., 1m., 12d.

Kimball, Burns C., son of D. H. and N. L., d. April 16, 1847, ag. 4y., 6m. (d); Oscar M., d. Jan. 31, 1880, ag. 32 (d).

Kineston, Samuel, and Abigail had William, b. Nov. 24, 1782 (b).

King, James M., b. March 30, 1830; d. March 30, 1903; m. Mary E. Hutchinson, b. Sept. 7, 1834. Child: Edwin R., b. April 8, 1858; d. Oct. 14, 1901. Charles P. m. Lora M. Milton; two children, Marion and James F. Lizzie M. m. Arthur W. Hutchinson (see him). James F. m. Grace E. Hazeltine. Vinia E. m. Elmore H. Plummer.

King, Georgie T., son of T. and P., d. Nov. 12, 1890, ag. 1y., 3m. (c).

Kinne, Luther, son of Amos, b. Dec. 15, 1779; d. Dec. 7, 1849 (d); m., May 2, 1802, Pasha Miller, b. Oct. 7, 1783; d. Jan. 14, 1830; m. (2) Polly Bartlett, d. Nov. 9, 1870, ag. 86. Children: Esther, b. Jan. 15, 1803; d. Sept. 20, 1806; Eunice, b. Nov. 13, 1804; d. Sept. 7, 1806; Amos, b. June 2, 1807; d. July 20, 1885 (a); m., Jan. 11, 1831, Sally A. Rogers, dau. of William, b. Sept. 8, 1811; d. March 29, 1900. Children: Eunice, b. Sept. 6, 1833; d. Feb. 13, 1834 (d); Martin Van Buren, b. June 18, 1836; m. (1), Sept. 17, 1856, Celina A. Kinne, dau. of John, b. Sept. 15, 1836; d. April 19, 1892; m. (2) Nelly Moore; m. (3) Addie Colburn. Child: Nellie, b. Jan. 10, 1861. Mary Ann, dau. of Amos, b. Aug. 2, 1838; d. Nov. 13, 1908; m., Oct. 22, 1856, Stephen D. Smith, b. May 29, 1833; d. ———. Children: Perley B., Lucilla A., Edna J. Rosina Jane, dau. of Amos, b. April 4, 1841; m., April 14, 1859, Charles A. Colby, b. April 13, 1839. Child: George M., b. Sept. 4, 1865. Ada Isabel, dau. of Amos, b. March 26, 1850; d. April 20, 1906; m. (1), March 14, 1872, Parker H. Stocker, b. Oct. 1, 1845; d. Nov. 23, 1884; ch.: Lilla M., b. Oct. 14, 1876; m. (2), June 11, 1890, William H. Huggins. Sewell G., son of Luther, b. Nov. 2, 1809; d. Aug. 19, 1872; m. Henrietta R. Stevens, b. June 30, 1820. Children: John N., b. June 7, 1842; Baron Stowe, b. March 20, 1853. Luther, Jr., son of Luther, b. May 30, 1812; d. May 10, 1884; John M., b. April 15, 1814; d. Feb. 16, 1886; m. Achsah Blake, b. Dec. 13, 1815; d. March 29, 1853; m. (2) Leafy Blanchard, b. Aug. 24, 1828; Louisa, b. Aug. 11, 1816; d. July 30, 1824; Esther, b. Jan. 3, 1820; d. Jan. 10, 1881; m. Stephen Morse (see him). Horace, b. March 24, 1823; d. Jan. 3, 1884 (d); m. Betsey Ann Flanders, b. June 20, 1817, dau. of John. Children: Climena, d. Aug. 11, 1854, ag. 5y., 7m.; Clarence L., b. 1856; m. (1), Jan. 11, 1882, Gertrude A. Eastman, d.

GENEALOGY. 619

Dec. 22, 1886, ag. 25y., 2m. (d); m. (2), May 4, 1892, Welthea W. Goodell.

Knowlton, Abraham, d. July 15, 1819, ag. 64 (e). His wife, Esther Billings, d. Feb. 25, 1812, ag. 54.

Lambkin, Lewis, m., Nov. 26, 1801, Nancy Miller. Children: Lewis, d. June 9, 1832, ag. 17y., 2m., 24d.

Lamott, Adolphus, d. Feb. 10, 1890, ag. 76; m. Nancy A. Plant; d. April 9, 1888, ag. 76y. Children: James, b. 1838; m., Dec. 17, 1863, Kate McBean, b. 1839. Children: Irving W., d. July 4, 1879, ag. 9y., 9m., 14d. Mary Ann, dau. of Adolphus, b. 1846; d. March 2, 1902, ag. 56 (a); m., April 13, 1863, Benjamin W. Adams, son of Placid; m. (2) a Currier; m. (3), April 28, 1885, Horace S. Groves. William m. Jennie ———; d. March 5, 1894, ag. 30.

Langley, Sarah J., wife of Charles T., d. April 15, 1864, ag. 24y., 10m., 14d.; dau., Iona, d. Aug. 27, 1867, ag. 8y., 3m., 25d. (a).

Lary, Daniel, d. May 13, 1827, ag. 71. His wife, Elizabeth, d. June 13, 1812, ag. 58. His second wife, Esther, d. May 16, 1834, ag. 57y., 8m. He was one of the early settlers in the Gore and is buried just across the line in Dorchester.

Lary, Uriah F., d. Aug. 7, 1869, ag. 72; m., Nov. 23, 1826, Sarah Chase, dau. of Joseph; d. July 17, 1891, ag. 87y., 10m., 11d. Children: Benjamin P., d. July 27, 1899, ag. 69y., 9m., 3d.; Walter P., b. Nov. 30, 1843; d. July 25, 1895; m., Sept. 23, 1893, Jennie M. Hubbard; Dema, b. 1846; m., Aug. 13, 1870, Cassius M. Dustin; Daniel W., d. Jan. 24, 1860, ag. 8y., 5m., 21d.; Alonzo L., son of Uriah, b. 1831; m., Oct. 7, 1855, Emily M. Clark, b. 1840; d. 1907 (b); has a son, Austin L.; m., Dec. 26, 1894, Margaret McKewen. Joseph C., son of Uriah, b. 1828; m., Jan. 2, 1872, Frances M. Learned, b. 1847. Children: Freddie L., d. Sept. 15, 1879, ag. 6y. 9m. (all j); Harley, Asa and a dau.

Lathrop, Thaddeus, b. Feb. 3, 1742; m., Oct. 28, 1761, Anna, b. Oct. 15, 1744; d. Dec. 18, 1815 (a). Children: Mary, b. July 4, 1762; Elisha, b. Sept. 16, 1764; Anna, b. Aug. 13, 1766; m., July 27, 1800, Dr. Samuel Hilliard of Cornish. Caroline, b. June 1, 1770; Pamela, b. Sept. 15, 1775; Thaddeus, Jr., b. Feb. 12, 1778; m., Nov. 1, 1804, Betsey Lathrop. Children: Nancy Greeley, b. Nov. 1, 1805; d. Oct. 21, 1812; Susan, b. July 13, 1807. Harris Gordon, son of Thaddeus, 1st, b. April 30, 1784; d. March 31, 1864 (a); m. Susanna Stevens; d. Jan. 22, 1869, ag. 69. Children: Daniel S., d. March 30, 1819, ag. 8; Harris, d. May 28, 1825, ag. 15 (a); Thaddeus S., b. April 23, 1823; d. Jan. 13, 1888 (a); m. Sarah C. Chase, b. Nov. 10, 1814; d. Oct. 20, 1868; her first husband was Nehemiah Muzzey. Children: Henry S., d. Dec. 28, 1906, ag. 58y., 11m., 20d.; m., Nov. 26, 1884, Luvia I. Blood. Children: Lulu Mabel, b. 1885; m., April 25, 1906, Ben A. Noyes, b. 1885; and Don. George H., son of Harris, b. April 13, 1826; d. Dec. 8, 1903 (a); m. Emily S. Gleason, dau. of Winsor and Sophia (Clark) Gleason, b. Feb. 20, 1830; d. Nov. 25, 1899 (a). Chilldren: Clara, m. William H. Sharp; d. ———; had a son, Earl C. Belle, b. 1857; m., Aug. 26, 1878,

Charles W. Neal, b. 1847. Emma L., b. May 10, 1860; m., Jan. 15, 1878, Lyman J. Sherburne, son of Joseph (see him). George Elwin, b. July 22, 1864; m. and has two children. John H., son of Harris, d. Nov. 7, 1878, ag. 57 (a); m. Urvilla M. Ross; d. Feb. 16, 1901, ag. 75y., 6m., 8d. (a). Children: Frank R., d. Sept. 10, 1871, ag. 18; Ellen Eliza, d. July 19, 1852, ag. 1y., 9m.; Hattie Alma, d. Nov. 19, 1867, ag. 7y., 3m.; Della C., b. 1857; m., Jan. 31, 1880, George Sloane, b. 1847. One son, d. Sept. 3, 1881 (a); Charles L., m. (1), Dec. 31, 1885, Anna B. Morse, dau. of Orrin; d. March 22, 1889, ag. 20 (a); m. (2), March 7, 1892, Angie Edwards. Two children: Earl, b. March 15, 1889, and Daisy. Lucinda A., dau. of Harris, b. Oct. 2, 1809; d. May 7, 1899; m. (1) Elijah R. Colby; d. Feb. 20, 1863, ag. 53; m. (2) Thomas Sanborn. Susan, dau. of Harris, d. Sept. 3, 1865, ag. 47y., 4m., 4d.; m. (1) a Beal; m. (2) Reuben Goss (see him). Thomas, son of Thaddeus, 1st, b. June 2, 1787, and Mary, his wife, had James Burr, b. Cohassett, Mass., Feb. 22, 1812; Benjamin Gorton, b. Canaan July 6, 1815. Margaret, dau. of Thaddeus, m. Caleb Clark.

Lathrop, Elisha, d. May 10, 1867, ag. 60; m. Nancy M. Richardson; d. May 22, 1902, ag. 85. Children: George E., b. March 10, 1853; d. Pioche, Nev., Sept. 1, 1907; Malvina C., b. Jan. 27, 1839.

Lathrop, Joshua S., b. April 23, 1812; m., Feb. 25, 1841, Dorothy Fales, b. Feb. 25, 1813. He went West Oct. 27, 1855, with his family. Annie, b. July 28, 1843; Horace W., b. May 16, 1848; d. Oct. 23, 1888; and Lucinda A., b. July 30, 1851.

Lawn, Robert, d. Jan. 20, 1892, ag. 92 (c); his first wife, Rebecca, d. Oct. 31, 1865, ag. 40; second wife, Mary, d. Jan. 27, 1892, ag. 75; dau., Margaret, d. Aug. 1, 1862, ag. 11y., 4m., 11d.

Laxson, Flora, dau. C. H. and M., b. 1890; d. 1891 (a).

Leeds, Harry, b. Feb. 25, 1779; d. April 18, 1831 (b); m., Oct. 28, 1802, Rhoda Follensbee, b. June 13, 1782; d. Sept. 16, 1863. Children: Rhoda, d. July 1, 1803, ag. 17d.; Jerusha, b. April 14, 1804; d. Sept. 7, 1806; Sarah Ann, b. Feb. 2, 1806; Betsey, b. Nov. 22, 1807; m., Dec. 9, 1829, James Follensbee of Enfield. Children: Clara P., b. 1835; m., Oct. 12, 1864, George H. Wood of Windsor, Vt. Harry, son of Harry, b. May 24, 1809; d. Nov. 24, 1886; m., May 3, 1838, Sarah Colby, dau. Enoch of New Boston; d. Dec. 13, 1893, ag. 85; son, Charles H., b. Feb. 4, 1844; d. Nov. 29, 1867. Orinda, b. Jan. 23, 1811; Carey, b. April 28, 1813; m., Feb. 6, 1834, Almeda E. Clark; m. (2), Oct. 22, 1879, Ruth Currier, dau. David and Rhoda (Tyler) Currier, b. 1830. Children: Augusta, m. Ambrose Doten (see him). Tryphoena m. Burns W. Pattee; Mary, d. single; Richard Clark, b. May 3, 1815; by his wife, Mary P. Rice, had Helen A., b. 1840; m., Feb. 16, 1862, Daniel I. Durrell, son of Daniel; Lizzie; Horace, who m. Lizzie Jones and had one son, and Hubbard. Elmina, dau. of Harry, b. Dec. 13, 1816; d. Nov. 6, 1892; m. Ruel Hayward; d. Aug. 26, 1877, ag. 66y., 6m., 21d. (b). Two children: Orinda L., b. 1841; m., Jan. 12, 1868, Frederick S. Simonds; d. Aug. 14, 1899, ag. 71y., 3 m., 23d.; one son, Charles F.,

b. 1870; Frederick S. m. (1) Mary E., d. May 1, 1867, ag. 31y., 6m.; Augustus R., b. 1850; m., April 13, 1875, Estelle A. George, b. 1851. Mary, dau. of Harry, b. Feb. 24, 1821.

Longfellow, William, b. Newbury, Mass.; d. Sept. 5, 1834, ag. 79 (e) (ag. 83, pension rolls). His wife, Sarah, d. Feb. 1, 1842, ag. 90 (e). His first wife, Hepzibah of Byfield, Mass., m., 1781; d. April 17, 1805, ag. 90. Children: Abraham, d. Nov. 25, 1850, ag. 56; William, drowned at sea near Boston in 1826, ag. 38; Susan, d. April 27, 1848, ag. 58; Elisabeth, d. March 12, 1843, ag. 58. Came from Boscawen and bought his farm in 1799 of Elijah Paddleford, the Harry Follensbee farm.

Lovejoy, Augustus and Sally; had a son, b. April 22, 1850.

Lovrien, Joseph H., d. Aug. 26, 1870, ag. 87 (e). His wife, Hannah, d. Jan. 27, 1864, ag. 79. Children: Lydia, m. Daniel Whitmore; d. Sept 8, 1872, ag. 47y., 5m. (e). Their children: Fannie E., d. Feb. 13, 1876, ag. 19y., 7m.; Lillie E., d. Nov. 17, 1870, ag. 5m. Susan, wife of Moses Sanborn, b. Aug. 4, 1812; d. Sept. 18, 1883.

Loving, John D., b. March 27, 1845; m. Clara F. Clement, b. Dec. 31, 1852. Children: Ernest D., b. Dec. 11, 1878; m. Grace F. Cunningham, b. Sept. 19, 1881; d. July 30, 1900; and Wilbur F. Nora E., d. Jan. 11, 1876, ag. 1y., 11m. (e).

Low, Mary (Jenness), wife of Moses, d. 1864, ag. 86; dau., Mary Ann, d. May 1, 1888, ag. 82 (a).

Lowell, Elisabeth, wife of Daniel G., d. Nov. 26, 1862, ag. 25 (a).

McCormick, George P., d. March 21, 1888, ag. 58y., 5m.

McConnell, Jane, wife of Robert, b. Nov. 29, 1824; d. Feb. 8, 1907; Charles H., son, d. April 29, 1880, ag. 26y., 8m., 4d. (e).

McLaughlin, John, d. March 3, 1858, ag. 76y., 9m. (d).

Marrs, Eliza A. (Tupper), wife of Daniel M., b. 1840; d. 1908 (e).

Marshall, Jane M., wife of Moses, d. Nov. 8, 1879, ag. 59y., 3m., 12d. (d).

Marshall, Thomas S., d. Nov. 25, 1881, ag. 69. Dorothy A., his wife, d. Feb. 10, 1890, ag. 71. Children: George, d. March 4, 1852, ag. 11m.; Frank, d. Sept. 1, 1863, ag. 8 (a).

Martin, Levi, d. Feb. 26, 1898, ag. 74. His wife, Chestina, d. June 1, 1876, ag. 56 (e).

Martin, Hannah (Kittredge), wife of Dea. Nathaniel Martin of Dorchester; b. Aug. 4, 1780; d. July 12, 1857 (a).

Martin, Jesse, son of Sylvester and Mary of Grafton, b. July 2, 1805; d. June 28, 1869 (a); m. Emily A. Green, b. Oct. 21, 1808; d. Nov. 6, 1870. Children: Roxalani B., m. Caleb Blodgett (see him); Susan A., b. Jan. 26, 1842; d. Oct. 9, 1883 (a).

Martin, Eleazer, d. March 27, 1865, ag. 75y., 6m. (a); son of Sylvester; his wife, Polly, d. Sept. 13, 1848, ag. 53. Children: Albert m. (1) Arabella Harris; m. (2) Harriet O. Wallace; Arthur.

Massuere, Charles H., son of Charles B. and Selinda, d. May 31, 1854, ag. 1y., 8m.; Francis H., son, d. May 15, 1850, ag. 2m.

May, John, came from Plymouth, Mass.; d. Feb. 19, 1836, ag. 79y., 8m.; m. Mercy Foster; d. April 27, 1830, ag. 72 (a). Children: John, Jr., m., Aug. 24, 1800, Anna Harris. Children: Lucy, m. John H. Harris (see him). Edwin, son of John, b. Dec. 11, 1793; d. Oct. 31, 1844; m., Dec. 31, 1821, Rhoda French, b. Nov. 26, 1801; d. May 4, 1879. Children: Harriet, b. Jan. 7, 1823; m., Sept. 9, 1849, Levi George (see him); Albert, b. Nov. 8, 1824; d. June 8, 1864; m. Susanna Morse; Emily, b. Dec. 23, 1829; d. June 18, 1858; m., July 28, 1856, John A. Cook of Lyme; no ch. Caroline Augusta, b. Dec. 18, 1834; d. Feb. 7, 1855; Edwin Harvey, b. Aug. 6, 1839; d. April 25, 1840; Marcia Ann, b. Jan. 20, 1842; d. Nov. 11, 1883; m., Sept. 16, 1871, Caleb Cheney, b. 1827. Children: Albert, b. Aug. 23, 1872; m. Lilla Day; Ethel, b. Nov. 4, 1876; m., 1894, William H. Searles. Children: Blanche, Alice. Mabel, dau. of Marcia A., b. June 27, 1880. William, son of John, went West. Charles; George, d. young; Thomas, d. Plymouth, Mass.; Foster, m. Sarah Elkins. Children: Helen M., d. May 27, 1841, ag. 11; Sarah A., d. May 20, 1841; Eddie F., d. Feb. 10, 1852 (a); Lucy and Sally, ch. of John.

Meacham, Samuel, d. Jan. 22, 1811, ag. 72 (c). Children: Jeremiah, m. Nov. 27, 1794, Abigail Davis; Joseph, m. Sept. 6, 1801, Sarah Basford; Joshua, m. Pamela Chapman; Andrew, m., June 18, 1801, Abigail Eastman and had two ch.: Olive, b. Feb. 9, 1802, and Andrew Main, b. April 18, 1805. Elam, son of Samuel, m. Mary Williams (see her); Thomas; Polly, m. William Bradbury (see him); Sarah, m., March 12, 1800, Amos Worthen and had a ch., Sally, b. March 9, 1801; Phœbe, m. Ezekiel Wells (see him); Miriam, b. June 14, 1794; m., Oct. 7, 1810, Asa Kimball; Bettish, m. Oct. 12, 1797, Moses Worthen.

Meewen, Lydia Ann, dau. of John and Lydia, b. Sept. 2, 1812.

Meloon, Abigail, wife of Jeremiah, d. Oct. 10, 1849, ag. 79y., 7m. (c).

Merrill, Betsey, wife of Benjamin, d. Dec. 29, 1853, ag. 79; dau., Elvira, d. Jan. 19, 1845, ag. 38 (a).

Merrill, Samuel, d. March 9, 1885, ag. 79y. 4m. (a).

Miller, Jacob, d. April 6, 1843, ag. 72 (b); m., Oct. 6, 1799, Elizabeth Davidson Ball of Orange; d. May 29, 1838, ag. 59; son, Horace W., d. Aug. 1, 1894, ag. 75y., 6m., 15d.; m. (1) Julia A. Nichols, dau. Aaron; d. Oct. 17, 1845, ag. 22y., 9m.; m. (2) Eliza Fales, dau. John (see her); Nancy, m. Caleb Dustin; Ruth, m. Jabez H. Fales; Elizabeth, m. Dea. Nathaniel Barber.

Milton, Joseph, b. July 22, 1789; d. Sept. 22, 1864. Priscilla Trussell, his wife, b. Aug. 3, 1781; d. Sept. 29, 1846 (a). Children: Mathew H., b. Oct. 28, 1819; d. March 19, 1905; m. (1) Antoinette Fellows, b. April 22, 1825; d. May 10, 1888. Children: Loraine H., d. March 23, 1862, ag. 16y., 7m.; Adda, d. Sept. 18, 1851, ag. 9y., 27m., 5d.; Ella, m. Frank Currier (see him); Fred, b. July 30, 1859; d. May 31, 1897 (a); Lora, b. 1863; m., May 8, 1889, Charles P. King, b. 1863. Children: Marion, b. Nov. 12, 1889; James, b. Nov. 14, 1895. John T., son of Joseph, d. Jan. 4, 1886; m., Dec. 9, 1850, Lura Gage; d. Feb. 26, 1902, ag. 76y., 2m.

Children: Frank E., d. May 27, 1894, ag. 42; and Bella A., d. May 25, 1883, ag. 29 (a). Jacob, son of Joseph, d. Medusa, N. Y.; had two ch.

Miner, Thomas, of Canaan was descended from Thomas, son of Clement, son of Thomas. The latter came from Chew Magna, Somersetshire, England, born in 1617. He married, April 23, 1634, Grace, daughter of Walter Palmer, born in 1608, who had come with her father to Charlestown. Thomas and Grace resided in Charlestown until 1636, when they removed to Hingham, where Clement was born, March 4, 1638. In 1645 they joined the first planters of New London, Conn. Thomas Miner of Canaan was born about 1743 and died July 12, 1827. He married in 1765 Elinor Lamb, who died Jan. 7, 1814. Eight children were born to them. He built the house now occupied by C. F. Everett and sold it to Caleb Gilman. He afterwards bought George and Joshua Harris' tavern of Joshua Harris, a large square-roofed house, where he lived until his death and was buried in the "Cobble," with no headstone. His son, Amos, took down the old tavern, replacing it with the house afterwards occupied by Sylvester Jones.

The children of Thomas and Elinor were:

Allen, b. Norwich, Conn., Sept. 13, 1766; d. May 29, 1843; m. by William Ayer, Oct. 10, 1790, Sally Flint, dau. of Joseph Flint, b. June 19, 1768; they joined the Canadian colonists and he became a doctor of medicine. Child: Lucy, b. Oct. 10, 1791.

Lovica, b. Feb. 20, 1771; d. July 26, 1806; m. Ezra Nichols (see him).

Thomas, b. Feb. 13, 1773; d. March 26, 1849.

Elijah, b. Oct. 29, 1777; d. Sept. 9, 1869; m., Jan. 1, 1804, Temperance Clifford, dau. of Samuel of Grafton, b. June 19, 1782. Six children were born to them in Canaan before he moved to Dorchester in 1818. He was a member of Mount Moriah Lodge. Their children were: Allen, b. Oct. 3, 1804; Lewis, b. Sept. 13, 1806; Marvin, b. Feb. 7, 1809; Lyman, b. Oct. 6, 1811; Avery Ann, b. May 28, 1814; and James Munroe, b. Nov. 18, 1817.

Cynthia, b. April 25, 1781; d. Dec. 26, 1849; Elisha, b. March 18, 1784; d. Aug. 8, 1844 (g); his wife, Elizabeth Tyler, d. April 8, 1860, ag. 70 (g). Children: Thomas T., d. April 10, 1823, ag. 11y., 4m. (g); Caroline Tyler, d. Aug. 1, 1896, ag. 70y., 4m., 30d.; m., Feb. 28, 1850, Charles Davis, son of Samuel. Sophia, dau. of Thomas, b. July 27, 1786; d. ———; Amos, b. Dec. 28, 1792; d. Aug. 24, 1866; his wife, Fanny Tyler, dau. of Job, d. May 2, 1863, ag. 70y., 11m. (a). Children: George, d. July 21, 1879, ag. 63y., 8m., 17d. (a); m., April 4, 1841, Nancy French of Enfield, d. July 16, 1869, ag. 53y., 10m. Children: George Byron, d. March 6, 1877, ag. 34 y., 10m., 6d. (a); m. A. E. ———. Children: Burtone, d. Dec. 13, 1891, ag. 19y., 10m., 1d. Henry H., son of George, d. Aug. 25, 1845, ag. 11d. Elsie T., dau. of Amos, b. Sept. 18, 1828; d. May 19, 1896; m. (1) Miles Jackson; m. (2) a Wiswell and had Grace, who m. G. H. Goodhue; m. (3) Nathan W. Morse, son of Jesse and Dorothy (Hibbard) Morse. Ellen, m. Samuel Smith; Clinton; John, m. and lived in Hanover; Leonard, m. (1) Helen Choate; m. (2) Helen Morse, dau. of Nathan W., d. Nov. 21, 1892; she m. (2) Merrill Owen.

Edwin B., son of Amos, d. Oct. 15, 1869, ag. 53y., 11m.; m., March 3, 1840, Lucy Wells, dau. Joshua, d. July 25, 1868, ag. 48y., 7m. Children: Allen E., d. Jan. 30, 1866, ag. 24y., 3m.; Charles W., d. June 27, 1848, ag. 1y., 14d., and Lucy Jane, dau. of Amos, m. Daniel Johnson. Child: George M., d. Feb. 10, 1854, ag. 2y., 10m. (a).

Mooney, Katie S., wife of Levi J., b. June 17, 1836; d. Jan. 14, 1904 (e); dau. Maud A., d. April 19, 1880, ag. 3y., 8m., 17d. (d).

Morey, Stephen, b. Dec. 14, 1804; d. April 20, 1849; m. Sophronia ———. Children: Robert C., b. Aug. 9, 1848; d. Dec. 16, 1849.

Morey, Robert R., son of Harley and Lucy (Tenney) Morey, d. Feb. 16, 1909, ag. 79; m. (1) Emeline C. Maynard, d. Jan. 15, 1863, ag. 23y., 11m.; m. (2), Feb. 12, 1867, Louise R. Maynard, b. 1840; d. 1905; m. (3), April 7, 1906, Clara L. Putney, d. Sept. 28, 1907, ag. 46y., 1m.; m. (4), Dec. 2, 1908, Mrs. Mary J. Dow, b. 1850; d. April 6, 1910. Children: Persis L., b. 1858; d. 1863; Mary A., b. 1861; d. 1881; Nellie L., b. 1876; d. 1883.

Morgan, Olive B., wife of James, d. March 4, 1886, ag. 85y., 5m. (a).

Morgan, Sylvanus B., b. March 24, 1793; d. Oct. 26, 1873; m. Nancy Currier, dau. Nathan of Enfield, b. Jan. 30, 1801; d. ———. Children: Nathan C., b. Dec. 6, 1821; d. May 14, 1888; m., Sept. 28, 1858, Carrie L. Carpenter of Plymouth, Vt., b. March 10, 1833. Two children: Ada C., m. Walter C. Story (see him), and Alva. Converse Goodhue, son of Sylvanus, b. Jan. 7, 1827; d. Nov. 3, 1880; m. Helen Bridgman. Children: Alice, m. George Huntoon, lives in Jacksonville, Ill. Thomas Benton, son of Sylvanus B., b. Dec. 9, 1834; d. April 19, 1891; m. Louise L. Carpenter, sister of his brother's wife. Two children: Edna, m. E. C. Stiles; and Clarence, d. young.

Morrill, Samuel A., son of Clara J., d. March 22, 1868, ag. 2m., 18d.(b).

Morse, Daniel, son of Daniel, uncle of Jesse, d. Jan. 1, 1831, ag. 67 (e); his wife, Mary, d. April 23, 1822, ag. 52, and his second wife, Mary, d. Nov. 8, 1842, ag. 58. Children: Silas M., b. Sept. 5, 1787; d. April 7, 1788; Silas M., b. March 25, 1790; Lucinda, b. May 7, 1792; Rachel, b. Jan. 13, 1795; Irene, b. Sept. 17, 1796; d. Jan. 6, 1804. Daniel lived at the end of the Pond from which Committee Meadow Brook flows.

Morse, Jesse, son of Jesse and Dorothy (Hibbard), b. Feb. 21, 1813; d. April 9, 1878 (e); m. Adeline Kimball, b. April 12, 1816; d. Dec. 12, 1891; dau. of Abram. Children: Edwin A., b. 1837; m. (1), July 4, 1864, Irena Jones, dau. Caleb; m. (2) Melissa A. Jones, dau. of Caleb, d. Oct. 19, 1884; m. (3), Oct. 8, 1885, Mrs. Eva S. (Gorham) Butman, b. 1855. Emily C., dau. of Jesse, d. Sept. 20, 1883, ag. 56 (e); m. Horace S. Groves, d. Aug. 10, 1901, ag. 66y., 5m.; he m. (2) Mary A. Lamotte, d. March 2, 1902, ag. 56 (a). Addie E., b. 1844; d. 1900 (c); m. Albert Bradbury. Orrin H., b. May 19, 1839; d. March 8, 1888 (a); m. Annabelle Sherburne (see her). Franklin Pierce, m. Helen French.

Morse, Stephen, of Haverhill, b. Jan. 1, 1815; d. Sept. 24, 1904 (a); m. (1), Dec. 4, 1837, Esther Kinne, b. Jan. 3, 1820, dau of Luther, d. Jan. 10, 1881 (a); m. (2), May 16, 1882, Augusta A. Weare, b. April 17,

GENEALOGY. 625

1832. Children: Charles N., b. Oct. 11, 1839; m., Oct. 20, 1861, Almeda Jones, dau. of Nathan and Polly, b. Oct. 1, 1840; d. June 24, 1865 (a). Children: Flora; Minnie; George; Carl E., d. July 29, 1864, ag. 6m., 21d. (a); m. (2), Nov. 29, 1866, Ellen Augusta Greeley, b. Dec. 26, 1843; d. Nov. 2, 1892; m. (3), Oct. 18, 1898, Mrs. Elizabeth C. Mahan, b. March 12, 1847. Persis P., dau. of Stephen and Esther (Kinne), d. June 10, 1866, ag. 24 (a); m., Sept. 26, 1863, Samuel N. Homan. He m. (2) Ruth A., dau. of Stephen, d. July 22, 1870, ag. 21. Her child, Mabel R., d. Aug. 8, 1870, ag. 28d. (a). Ellen, dau. of Stephen, b. Dec. 26, 1843. George, b. May 21, 1850.

Morse, James, son of Peter and Anna (Currier) Morse, b. Sept. 26, 1769; d. Nov. 12, 1818 (g); m., Nov. 22, 1793, Lois Harris, d. Jan. 19, 1820, ag. 45 (g). Children: James, Jr., b. Jan. 15, 1795; d. Dec. 1, 1861; m., April 5, 1821, Lucy Tyler, dau. of Job, b. July 29, 1796; d. May 25, 1869. Children: James, b. Jan. 21, 1822; m., Nov. 25, 1849, Arvilla Smith, b. Dec. 5, 1823. Two children: Georgianna, b. July 19, 1851, and James Byron, b. July 26, 1852; d. Sept. 9, 1852; Lucy, dau. of James and Lucy, b. Sept. 5, 1823; d. Oct. 11, 1857. Byron, b. Jan. 27, 1825; d. Aug. 5, 1840 (g). Emeline, b. Feb. 15, 1827; d. Aug., 1830. Caroline, b. June 15, 1830; d. March 25, 1840. Emeline W., b. Nov. 21, 1833; m. ———— Holcomb, and had four children: Elisa Jane, b. Nov., 1857; Lucy Evelyn, b. 1859; Mary Cordelia, b. 1862; James Norton, b. June 8, 1864. Mary R., dau. of James and Lucy, b. June 15, 1836; m., 1862, Abner R. Brush; one child: Caroline, b. Aug. 6, 1863. Elsie T., b. Sept. 25, 1838; m. Joseph J. Jerrole, b. 1833; had seven children: Frank Herbert, b. March 5, 1859; d. Sept. 8, 1861; Alonzo Edmund, b. Aug. 9, 1859; Mary Anna, b. July 16, 1861; Lucy Emeline, b. Dec. 3, 1864; Franklyn Michael, b. March 7, 1867; Elsie Mabel, b. April 27, 1871; Hattie, b. March 21, 1876. Julia, dau. of James, Sr., b. March 15, 1798; d. July 13, 1863; m., Aug. 5, 1822, Rev. Job C. Tyler, son of Job, b. March 1, 1799; d. Sept. 1, 1879; one child: Elsie A., b. Feb. 27, 1825; d. Aug. 12, 1882; m., Oct. 14, 1851, Isaac Davis, son of Samuel (see him). Lois, dau. of James, Sr., b. March 9, 1800; d. Oct. 1, 1853; m., March 20, 1825, Calvin Pressey, b. April 13, 1797; d. March 15, 1866 (see him). Sally, dau. of James, Sr., b. June 7, 1802; d. April 3, 1880; m., March 5, 1834, Sylvester Flanders, b. June, 1808; d. July 11, 1890 (see him) (b). Nancy, dau. James, Sr., b. Feb. 22, 1805; d. in Wentworth, May 30, 1874; m., Nov. 13, 1834, Benjamin Martin, b. Dec. 1, 1809; d. Oct. 10, 1864; two children: Roseanna, b. July, 1836; Benjamin F., b. Aug. 23, 1840; m., Feb. 11, 1872, Mary Jane Colburn, b. Aug. 16, 1850; two children: Charles, b. Jan. 31, 1873; Amanda Louisa, b. Aug. 13, 1874. Betsey, dau. of James, Sr., b. Oct. 11, 1807; d. April 21, 1854; m., April 3, 1839, John B. Smith, b. April 8, 1809; d. May 1, 1854; one child: Alvira, b. Aug. 1, 1840; d. Jan. 18, 1842. Lucy, dau. of James, Sr., b. Nov. 11, 1809; d. June 24, 1886 (b). George, b. March 19, 1812; d. 1832 or '33. John, b. June 4, 1816; m., Aug. 31, 1840, Ann Philbrick, b. April 10, 1822; d. May 21, 1867; m. (2), Feb. 7, 1869, Melissa Wilcox, b. 1839. Three children by first wife, and one by second; Mary F., b. Aug. 16, 1841; d. Sept. 3, 1854; George H., b. June 23, 1846; m., 1870; Julia T., b. June 5, 1850, m., July, 1873, Joseph Stermon. Children: Cora Belle, b. Aug. 6, 1874; Elizabeth May, b. Aug. 26, 1872. Mary, dau. James, Sr., b. Nov. 12, 1818; d. Nov. 19, 1820.

Morse, Sarah, d. Aug. 30, 1865, ag. 79. Martha E., dau. Valentine, d. Oct. 6, 1886 (d), ag. 33. William C. b. Feb. 23, 1861; d. June 25, 1903 (a).

Monroe, Agnes (Ryan), wife of Caleb P., b. Oct. 10, 1836; d. Nov. 16, 1899 (a).

Murray, John, b. Jan. 10, 1797; d. March 26, 1871; m. Rheuanah Wells, b. May 3, 1795; d. April 15, 1860. Children: Sarah W., b. June 10, 1825; d. Nov. 8, 1865; George W., b. July 31, 1830; d. Jan. 5, 1900; m. Jeanette F. Barnes, b. March 30, 1833. Children: Julia W., m., May 25, 1880, Oren P. Wright; one son d. young; Ellen F., b. 1863; m., Jan. 1, 1890, William A. Plummer, b. 1866; Charles Edward, b. Dec. 5, 1866; d. at Holderness School, Feb. 13, 1891; Katherine R., b. 1864; m. Arthur L. Davis; one son, Verne; Claude M., b. 1872; m., Oct. 27, 1898, Mabel A. Plummer, b. 1871. Carl B., b. 1872; m., Aug. 21, 1901, Flossie J. Stevens, b. 1876.

Nesmith, Erastus, b. 1803; d. 1870; his wife, Lucy R., b. 1809; d. 1898; son, Alfred J., d. Feb. 1, 1858, ag. 24 (a).

Nichols, Ezra, by his first wife, Betsey, had Ezra, b. Oct. 16, 1790 (a); by his second wife, Lovica Miner, dau. of Thomas, b. Feb. 20, 1771, d. July 26, 1806, he had Betsey, b. Sept. 18, 1795, and Nancy, b. May 18, 1800; by his third wife, Polly Flint, dau. of Joseph, he had Lovica Flint, b. March 13, 1813; d. June 9, 1883 (a); m., March 8, 1842, Albert Cochran, d. Aug. 25, 1875, ag. 64 (a). Children: Abby; Clarendon A., b. 1845; d. ———; m., Jan. 1, 1869, Mary A. French, b. 1850; Lizzie L.

Nichols, Enoch, d. March 11, 1871, ag. 82y., 9m.; m. Charlotte Powell, d. Sept. 15, 1875, ag. 86y., 5m., 26d. Children: Benjamin P., b. Jan. 3, 1827; d. Oct. 8, 1880 (e); m. Eliza B. Harris, b. April 29, 1828; d. Dec. 18, 1906. Children: Dexter H., b. April 21, 1852; d. Aug. 8, 1888 (e); m., Sept. 1, 1886, Marion B. Barber, dau. James P.; Kate; Ralph, b. April 27, 1867; Almanda P., d. May 30, 1904, ag. 84y., 11m., 27d.; m. a Fogg.

Nichols, Aaron, d. April 24, 1859, ag. 58; child, Tilton, d. May 27, 1873, ag. 58; his wife, Lydia, d. July 15, 1874, ag. 61y., 5m. Child: Mandana L., d. Dec. 5, 1863, ag. 24y., 6m. Julia A., dau. of Aaron and N———, d. Oct. 17, 1845, ag. 22y., 9m.; m. Horace W. Miller.

Nichols, Mary Ann, dau. of Benjamin and Lydia, d. Jan. 6, 1837, ag. 9m.

Nichols, Sarah M., wife of John N., d. June 18, 1882, ag. 66. Child: Josephine S., d. Sept. 23, 1883, ag. 33y., 7m.; m. John Burrill (a).

Norris, Benjamin, b. April 1, 1811; d. Dec. 3, 1897; m. Zaphira Ross, b. Jan. 10, 1813; d. Jan. 3, 1890. Child: Horace R., b. 1840; m., Nov. 26, 1868, Jennie M. Smith, b. 1847. Child: George, d. ———. Lizzie B. m. Harris J. Goss (see him).

GENEALOGY.

Noyes, Samuel, d. June 9, 1845, ag. 90y., 10m. (b); by his wife, Lydia, d. Jan. 23, 1833, ag. 75, he had Relief, b. Feb. 8, 1791.

Noyes, Moody, had Moody, Jr., b. June 26, 1793; Betsey, b. June 12, 1795; Theodore, b. Oct. 29, 1796.

Noyes, Amos L., d. Feb. 4, 1884, ag. 66y., 1m., 11d.; his wife, Hannah Peaslee, d. Oct. 21, 1889, ag. 64y., 6m., 15d. Children: Mattie H., d. Sept. 29, 1886, ag. 29; m. George Bailey; son, Alfred; Chas. E., b. 1854; m., Feb. 29, 1872, Eldorah V. Whittier.

Noyes, Amos, b. in Groton, Vt., April 9, 1822. Abigail, b. July 15, 1827. James, b. Jan. 27, 1829. Sophia Ann, b. Jan. 2, 1831. Joseph, b. Oct. 2, 1833; children of Stephen.

Otis, Richard, and his wife, Sarah, had children: Ethelinda, b. in Norwich, Conn., Aug. 18, 1766; m. by William Ayer, Dec. 29, 1791, Judah Wells (see him); Esther, b. Feb. 14, 1768; m. by Thomas Baldwin, Nov. 26, 1785, Clement Stoddard. Children: Ruth, b. Feb. 4, 1787; Polly, b. Jan. 3, 1792; Lucy, b. July 13, 1794. Israel Sabin, son of Richard, b. Jan. 27, 1770; Elisha, b. April 5, 1772; m. and had a child. Roxanna, b. Dec. 10, 1794. Richard, Jr., b. July 4, 1774; m., Feb. 7, 1799, Sally Chandler, and had Sally, b. March 1, 1800. Lucy, b. Aug. 6, 1776. Ezra, b. July 7, 1778. Annis, b. Aug. 11, 1780. Erastus, b. Oct. 24, 1784.

Paddleford, James, d. Sept. 3, 1826, ag. 29 (c).

Page, Abraham, m. Dec. 13, 1806, Hannah Richardson; he lived in the old school house at the Corner, which Arden Jones afterwards lived in. Children: Eliphalet R., b. Lebanon, April 26, 1807; d. ———; by his wife, Sarah F., he had children: Elizabeth, b. Aug. 3, 1833; George, b. Dec. 21, 1834; d. Aug. 22, 1836 (a); Caroline, b. Sept. 8, 1836; George Washington, b. Feb. 23, 1839; Sarah Jane, b. Feb. 16, 1841; m. ——— Edmondston; two sons lived in California; Clarabel Hammond, b. Oct. 6, 1842. Sarah Ann, dau. of Abraham, b. in Meredith, March 29, 1808; d. Nov. 1, 1855; m., Sept. 13, 1838, Josiah Richardson; Almira, b. June 29, 1809; d. single; Hannah, b. Sept. 14, 1812; d. April 11, 1828 (a); Abraham, Jr., twin of Hannah, had a son, Charles, who owned a saloon in Lowell. Leonard, d. Sept. 11, 1826, ag. 12y., 9m. (a). Samuel, b. in New Hampton, May 1, 1815, was an Advent preacher. Charles, b. in Canaan, May 24, 1817, was an Advent preacher.

Page, John, only son of Lazarus and Hannah, d. Sept. 21, 1826, ag. 7y., 21d. (a).

Packard, Chamberlain, d. March 23, 1861, ag. 76y., 10m. (c); m. Hannah Corser, d. March 30, 1861, ag. 76y., 7m. Children: Octavia, d. Dec. 15, 1844, ag. 40; m., July 11, 1822, Ezekiel Wells, Jr. (see him); Chamberlain, Jr., d. Dec. 31, 1867, ag. 62 (c); killed by a railroad train; his wife, Louisa W. Hinkson, d. May 2, 1880, ag. 75; a dau., Hannah E., d. Oct. 6, 1894, ag. 67y., 8m., 5d.; m., March 13, 1844, John F. Clough (see him). Rachel, d. Aug. 9, 1905, ag. 93y., 4m., 3d.; m., Nov. 27, 1834, Daniel Hinkson (see him). John, d. May 2, 1870, ag. 57; m., June, 1843, Hannah S. Gould, b. Feb. 1, 1821; d. June 3, 1880. Children: Albert, b. 1858; m., June 19, 1877, Emma A. Clough, dau. of Clark, b. 1858. Children: Burton C.; Ethel; Maud E., b. June 18, 1882. Samuel, son of Chamberlain, d. April 11, 1817, ag. 1y., 10m. Betsey, d. March 29, 1831, ag. 8y., 5m., 24d. Louisa, d. April 9, 1831, ag. 1y., 1m., 28d. Erastus, son of Chamberlain, m., April 27, 1835, Hannah Washburn.

Pattee, Capt. Asa, came from Warner with his son, Colonel Daniel, and settled on the old farm John Scofield cleared, and which Samuel Jones afterwards owned. Capt. Asa d. May 24, 1825, ag. 91 (e). Colonel Daniel brought with him his wife and family. He had six sons and seven daughters by his first wife, Judith, who d. Oct. 23, 1820, ag. 54, and one son by his second wife, Dorcas, who d. June 18, 1868, ag. 83. He died March 2, 1850, ag. 86 (e); he was a selectman in 1829 and in 1830. His children were:

(1) Miriam, who d. Aug. 28, 1813, ag. 21.

(2) Judith, m. David Greeley, the son of Mathew, June 22, 1809.

(3) Dorothy, m. Nathaniel C. Pierce, son of Dr. Caleb. She had Caleb, b. Feb. 24, 1813; m. Martha Paddleford; and Louisa Maria, b. May 5, 1816. The last two families went to Illinois.

(4) Sylvanus Barnard, b. April 18, 1797; d. July 22, 1886 (e); m. March 3, 1819, Betsey Howe, dau. of Nathaniel and Elizabeth Howe, of Enfield; she was b. 1801; d. Oct. 3, 1848. He m. (2) Maria P. Leslie, d. Aug. 28, 1874, ag. 62; he had three sons and one daughter. Lived in Enfield. Capt. Hiram, d. Nov. 25, 1855, ag. 29y., 9m., 11d. (e); the daughter m. a Howe. James C., d. June 14, 1882, ag. 54y., 11m; by his wife, Ann M., he had Hiram, who m. Alice Mosher. Calvin M., d. Feb. 16, 1892, ag. 35; m., June 23, 1876, Lou C. Garland. Hattie, and Sadie, d. Dec. 27, 1889, ag. 24; m. W. A. Mitchell.

(5) Daniel, Jr., b. in Canaan in 1799, d. in Canaan, May 12, 1875 (e); m., Dec. 28, 1820, Judith G. Burley, dau. of Gordon Burley, of Dorchester. She d. May 26, 1883, ag. 83y., 4m. They had six sons and three daughters. When 28 years old he was commissioned captain of a company of artillery in the Thirty-Seventh Regiment. Was selectman in 1841, 1842, 1843, 1849. Lived at West Canaan. Lewis C. m. Rebecca Perley, in 1858; carried on an extensive lumber business at Goose Pond and West Canaan for many years, and was one of the organizers of the Pattee Plow Company of Monmouth, Ill., with his brothers James H. and Henry H., b. 1840. He represented Canaan in the Legislature in 1863. Fred L., son of Lewis C., is in the lumber business at West Canaan; is married and resides in Winchester, Mass. Gordon B. was engaged in the lumber business in Ottawa, Canada, under the name of Perley & Pattee. James H. went to Monmouth, Ill., and resided there as well as his brother, Henry H., whose first wife was Lizzie B. Morgan, dau. of Dr. Arnold Morgan of Canaan; he m. June 18, 1867; she d. March 12, 1879, ag. 33. Allen W. d. April 11, 1855, aged 12y., 6m. John B. d. Sept. 23, 1824, ag. 3y. (d). Louise M. m. Ithamar P. Pillsbury, who was one of the Pattee Plow Company, and resided in Monmouth, Ill. Eliza D. m. John Q. Perley of Enfield. Elizabeth D. d. Aug. 18, 1830, ag. 4y., 4m. (d).

GENEALOGY.

(6) Moses D., d. April 11, 1851, ag. 47 (c); m. Hannah Huse, of Enfield, in 1832; was a farmer and had four children. Judith, d. Feb. 19, 1831, ag. 1y., 3m., 19d.

(7) James, b. June 25, 1802; d. Sept. 28, 1872 (c). His first wife was Rebecca Currier of Enfield, whom he m. Dec. 28, 1825; she d. March 12, 1841, ag. 36. His second wife was Rosamond Jones. He had five sons and one daughter by his first wife and one daughter by his second. He was a selectman in 1850 and 1854. Wyman, his son, was b. in Canaan Aug. 26, 1826; d. in Enfield in 1902; m., 1857, Mary Jane Burley, b. Dorchester Dec. 10, 1827; had two children: James W., b. July 27, 1864, who is m. and lives in Enfield, and John. Wyman was in the lumber business in Canaan from 1848 to 1859, and represented this town in the Legislature in 1855 and 1856. In 1859 he moved to Enfield. From 1860 to 1864 he was sheriff of Grafton County, representative from Enfield in 1875 and 1876, town treasurer for thirteen years, auditor of the Northern Railroad fifteen years, director of the Peterboro and Hillsboro Railroad and Mascoma Insurance Company and of the National Bank at White River Junction, Vt. James F., son of James, m. Marion F. Blake and d. in 1871. Ann R., b. 1835; m., April 23, 1860, James M. Currier of Enfield and resided in Springfield. Burns W., d. Oct. 28, 1888, ag. 51; m. Tryphœna Leeds of Canaan; he d. in Enfield, where he lived. Children: Jennie L., d. May 16, 1861, ag. 11; Fred D., d. Nov. 12, 1862, ag. 10m. George W., d. May 23, 1840, ag. 11y., 5m. Another son of James, George W., d. March 2, 1851, aged 11d., and a daughter, Angeline C., d. May 20, 1840, ag. 8m.; by his second wife he had Ella, who lives in Enfield.

(8) John, d. April 25, 1807, ag. 1y., 16d.

(9) Hannah D., d. Jan. 27, 1836, ag. 27y., 11m.; m. Capt. Albert Currier (c).

(10) Louisa M., d. Jan. 20, 1816, ag. 1y., 10m.

(11) Jesse, d. March 14, 1823, ag. 1m. (c).

(12) Betsey, who m. a Currier.

(13) Rhoda J., who m. a Stevens.

Pattee, Daniel F., d. July 22, 1854, ag. 22 (c). Peter, d. Nov. 16, 1800, ag. 52 (b).

Pearley, Nat, had a wife, Dorothy, and a wife, Lydia, by whom he had Stephen, b. March 18, 1806.

Peaslee, Jonathan, d. March 6, 1876, ag. 88; his wife, Miriam, d. Jan. 17, 1880, ag. 83; their son, Stephen, d. June 6, 1893, ag. 66; m. Susan Homan, dau. of Joseph and Sarah (Noyes); their child, Fred W., b. 1860; d. 1885, m. ———. George E., d. Feb. 9, 1859, ag. 6m., 28d. Charles H., d. Sept. 28, 1872, ag. 6y., 9m., 6d. Harry O., b. 1874; d. Feb. 19, 1889 (all a). Sanford, son of Jonathan (a), children: Allie and Frankie (a).

Peters, William, d. Dec. 18, 1881, ag. 87y., 3m.; his wife, Fanny, d. March 5, 1865, ag. 65y., 10m. Hannah, wife of John Peters, son of William, d. June 30, 1856, ag. 28; a dau., Druzilar, d. Feb. 27, 1858, ag. 6.

Eliza L., wife of Jacob Peters, d. July 25, 1857, ag. 30. Children: Mary, d. April 10, 1850, ag. 3; Joseph B., d. Oct. 7, 1854, ag. 1y., 9m.; Charles F., d. Feb. 11, 1857, ag. 1y., 21d. Anna Frances, dau. of J. C. and L. S Peters, d. Nov. 1, 1859, ag. 17y., 9m. (all c). Willie F., son of John, b. 1857; m., March 3, 1879, Emily F. Brown.

Philbrick, Hiram, d. April 20, 1876, ag. 76y., 8m. (e); his first wife, Mary, d. Dec. 5, 1863, ag. 56 (a); one son, Charles A., d. July 29, 1858, ag. 28y., 8m. (a). John W., b. 1844, m. Emeline Clark, dau. Daniel and Dorcas, b. 1841; d. 1904; Hiram m. (2), March 3, 1864, Mrs. Betsey (Clark) Welch, dau. Daniel and Dorcas Clark; a son, Daniel H., d. Jan. 10, 1866, ag. 10m., 27d. (e).

Pierce, Caleb, m. in Enfield, Feb. 19, 1788, Betsey Clough. Children: Lucy, b. Nov. 20, 1789; Nathaniel Currier, b. Aug. 27, 1791; m. Dorothy Pattee; went to Illinois. Their children: Caleb, b. Feb. 24, 1813; m., April 30, 1840, Martha Paddleford; Louisa Maria, b. May 5, 1816; Betsey, dau. of Caleb, b. July 14, 1806; m. a Blake.

Pillsbury, Deacon Joshua, d. Feb. 21, 1825, ag. 82 (e); his wife, Elizabeth, d. March 17, 1816, ag. 60y., 6m. Children: Deborah, d. July 8, 1826, ag. 40, Joshua, Jr., b. March 31, 1789; d. Oct. 19, 1858; m. Sarah Fletcher, b. Jan. 26, 1793; d. Oct. 30, 1874. Children: Joseph D., b. Nov. 4, 1817 (a); d. Andover, Ill., Oct. 25, 1847. Mary B., b. Nov. 4, 1817; d. June 20, 1867 (a), single. Sarah, dau. Deacon Joshua, m. Simon Dodge. Children: Ella S., b. 1842; m., June 14, 1866, Otis G. Turner; Arthur, Clarence, Lena and another girl and boy.

Pillsbury, J. Daniel Webster, son of Joseph D., b. June 30, 1847. Miriam, m., June 1, 1800, Charles Walworth. Betsey, m. Dec. 22, 1814, Thomas Evans.

Plummer, William, b. April 29, 1818; d. March 21, 1904; his wife, Lucy E. Smith, b. Dec. 21, 1823; d. July 24, 1903. Child: Elmore H., b. 1857; m., June 6, 1880, Vinia E. King.

Plummer, Reuben S., b. 1849; m. Millie E. Whittier, b. 1856.

Pollard, Adam, d. May 11, 1847, ag. 63y., 11m., 13d.; his wife, Mary, d. Sept. 27, 1880, ag. 88y., 9m., 7d. (d). Children: Louisa, b. Feb. 20, 1821; m. Elijah C. Flanders (see him); Sybil, m., Aug. 29, 1852, Heber Jackson of Hanover; and Solon K.

Pollard, David, was b. in New Boston, and his wife, Sarah Gale, was b. in old Haverhill, Mass. They had eighteen children; four of them, Perley, Hannah, and two others, d. in infancy; Lydia, d. March 17, 1875, ag. 68; m. Benjamin Bradbury; Benjamin, m. Sarah Jewett; Sarah, d. Oct. 25, 1884, ag. 79y., 1m., 15d.; m. (1) John Calef; two children: a son d. young, and Ann; m. (2) Joseph Fifield. Children: Edson J., m. Ednah Jones, dau. of Nathan (see her), and William H. Caroline, m. Alvah Richardson. Sylvenia, m. Joseph Welch. David went West, m. and d. there. Isaac, d. April 8, 1862, ag. 62; m. Maria Emerson. Children: Charles W., b. 1847; m., July 3, 1875, Nellie J. Harper; m. (2) Susan Blanchard. Rodney went West and d. there. Horace went West. Martha, m. Jeremiah Clough. Walker went West and d. there. Wil-

GENEALOGY. 631

liam went West and d. Oct. 4, 1909. Hannah, d. single. Fred R., b. 1833, lives in Lebanon.

Pollard, Joseph J., son of Benjamin; d. ———; m., April 7, 1861, Sarah E. Bridgman, dau. of Benjamin; d. Feb. 8, 1873, ag. 36. Children: Royal S., d. May 24, 1887, ag. 21y., sm.; Elnora, b. 1859; m., Oct. 20, 1887, Melvin A. Aldrich, d. March 5, 1892, ag. 26y., 10m., 5d. Eva, b. 1864; m., April 1, 1882, Henry W. Columbia.

Pollard, Isaac, d. Oct. 13, 1870, ag. 60 (c).

Porter, Micah, d. July 7, 1811, ag. 68; his wife, Mrs. Ruth Bates, d. Nov. 16, 1819, ag. 84 (g); he had several children: John, William, Reuben, Hannah, who m. William Laud, and Betsey, who m. a Straw; Noah, Josiah, David, Elias, who had a dau. Eliza by his wife, Sarah, d. April 10, 1805, ag. 5m. (g). Micah lived where S. W. Currier now lives, and his sons lived around him.

Porter, Daniel, b. Danvers, Mass., d. Oct. 19, 1852, ag. 81; his wife, Ruth M., b., Beverly, Mass., 1774; d. in Canaan, 1857. Children: Clarissa, b. in Beverly, Mass., Jan. 2, 1804; d. March 4, 1863; m. Col. S. S. Clark, son of Amasa (see him); Eliza R., b. in Beverly, Mass., April 28, 1799; d. May 31, 1881. Daniel R., d. May 11, 1837, ag. 28. Benjamin W., m. (1), Oct. 15, 1835, Hannah B., dau. of Capt. S. J. Gates, d. May 19, 1839, ag. 24, and he went West. William H., d. Dec. 3, 1845, ag. 31y., 27d. (all b).

Porter, Thomas J., son of Daniel and Clarese, d. March 14, 1876, ag. 70.

Porter, Osman, d. Feb. 27, 1878, ag. 62 (a); m., March 18, 1841, Lucy S. Bailey, b. Nov. 11, 1820. Child: Fred B. L., b. April 11, 1859.

Powell, Hannah D., b. May 5, 1836; d. March 31, 1894. Adna J., b. Nov. 6, 1870; d. Sept. 13, 1888 (b).

Pressey, Calvin, son of Moses and Hannah (Tucker), d. March 14, 1866, ag. 67y., 10m., 14d. (b); m. (1) Mary Tucker, d. Feb. 18, 1824, ag. 31. Children: Albert, d. Jan. 10, 1887, ag. 64y., 6m., 26d; by his wife, Elvira, he had Horace and Eva. John, son of Calvin, by his wife, Mary (a), had Celia C., d. April 8, 1879, ag. 27; m. Dixi C. Cross; Friend, m. Hattie Elliott; and Samuel. Calvin m. (2), March 20, 1825, Lois Morse, dau. of James, b. March 9, 1800; d. Oct. 1, 1853. Children: Julia M., b. Nov. 21, 1825; m., July 18, 1853, Alvin Tucker of Enfield. James, b. Feb. 28, 1827. Mary, b. Oct. 29, 1828. George, b. March 12, 1833; m. (1) Elizabeth A. Sanborn, dau. of Jonathan and Mary, d. Oct. 5, 1861, ag. 28y., 10m.; m. (2) Addie A. Pillsbury, d. Aug. 11, 1864, ag. 24y., 11m., and had a dau., Addie L., d. Sept. 14, 1864, ag. 1m., 9d.; m. (3), Sept. 19, 1865, Eunice C. Cummings. William D., son of Calvin and Lois, b. May 6, 1837; d. Nov. 2, 1854. Luca V., b. April 15, 1842. John L., son of Moses and Hannah, d. Aug. 25, 1874, ag. 70y., 2m.; his wife, Sarah, d. April 23, 1885, ag. 75y., 1m., 6d. (a). Children: Sarah B., b. 1839; m., Sept. 4, 1860, George W. Randlett, son of Jacob and Effie; Maria L. m. Charles S. Jones (see him). Moses, son of Moses, b. 1806; d. 1885; m. Laura E. Hibbard, b. 1807; d. 1881 (b). Children: George

P., b. 1831; Miranda R., b. 1837; Henry A., b. 1839; d. June 15, 1864; Elwin H., b. 1843; Albert L., b. 1846; d. 1848 (b).

Preston, Alpheus, d. Aug. 28, 1867, ag. 58; m. Almira Tucker, d. July 11, 1861, ag. 52 (b). Children: John Earl, b. Dec. 27, 1828; d. April 18, 1883; his wife, Margaret Elizabeth, b. May 19, 1839; d. March 28, 1903; Nelson, m., July 4, 1857, Paulina Lowell and had Florence J., d. April 7, 1858; George N., d. Feb. 19, 1888, ag. 25y., 8m.; Willie, d. March 23, 1878, ag. 5m., 11d. (a). Munroe, son of Alpheus, m. Sarah Robinson, and had a son Frank. Elizabeth, d. May 17, 1909, ag. 69y., 10m., 6d.; m. George E. Muzzey. Children: Nella A., d. April 20, 1862, ag. 2y., 1m.; Charley M., d. Oct. 15, 1864, ag. 1y., 3m. (a). Martin, d. in the army. Marcellus; Lydia; Jenette E., m., Sept. 7, 1886, Harrison Fogg (see him).

Prockter, Lucia Ann, dau. of Jonathan and Ruth, d. April 2, 1818, ag. 1y., 10m. (a).

Puffer, Minnie B., b. 1878; d. 1904 (a).

Putnam, Caleb S., d. Jan. 16, 1873, ag. 70; m. Elvira W. Wheelock, d. Feb. 13, 1888, ag. 81y., 3m., 8d. Children: Elvira, m. Charles H. Wells (see him); Sidney; Persis, m. John Follensbee of Enfield; Hiram E., d. May 2, 1857, ag. 21; m., Nov. 23, 1856, Angie M. Wilson, d. Feb. 23, 1857, ag. 21; Martha, m. William Huntoon; Florina W., b. Feb. 5, 1845; d. May 28, 1903; m. (1) Theodore Tyler, son of James; m. (2), Dec. 27, 1861, James C. Felch; had two dau., Cora and Ella (b); she m. (3) Sumner R. Truell, b. Sept. 20, 1842; d. Dec. 29, 1899 (b); Hattie S., m., May 8, 1869, Joseph C. Abbott.

Rainey, Albert I., son of Peter, d. Dec. 16, 1902, ag. 39; m. Eva A. Fisher, d. ———. Children: Loney E., Mary A., Albert R.

Rand, Oscar Shirley, son of Oscar F. and Frances C. (Dow), d. Feb. 25, 1902, ag. 28y., 2m., 22d. Herman S., son, d. April 1, 1881, ag. 1y., 5m., 15d. (b).

Randlett, John W., son of George J. and Sarah E., d. Feb. 2, 1864, ag. 2y., 10m. (a).

Ricard, Ada M. (Laughlin), wife of Edgar, b. Oct. 1, 1854; d. Sept. 10, 1904 (d).

Rice, Charles, d. Oct. 3, 1857, ag. 69.

Richardson, William and Elizabeth, both d. 1791 or '92, ag. about 84 on monument (a); not buried (a); their children:

Richardson, William, b. Newbury, Mass., March 8, 1746; d. Feb. 25, 1829 (d); m. (1) Prudence Morse, d. April 3, 1779; m. (2) Esther Sawyer, d. May 11, 1840, ag. 85; came to Canaan, 1784, with his five brothers, John, Joshua, Moses, Eliphalet, Enoch. Children: Jacob, b. Feb. 15, 1772; d. June 30, 1864 (d); m. Mary R. Morse, d. May 1, 1850, ag. 75. His children were Susan, Sarah, d. June 5, 1844, ag. 40 (a); m., Feb. 18, 1824, William Kimball (see him) (a); Nancy A. B., b. April 12, 1809; d. April 23, 1885; m. Ozias Daniels, b. Oct. 5, 1807; d. April 24, 1878 (d); one son, George Washington, m. Eugenia E. Hall; two children: Ida Louise, d. July 29, 1893, ag. 18y., 6m. (a), and Grace, who

Genealogy.

m. Edwin P. Stone. William, son of Jacob, d. Oct. 30, 1860, ag. 59 (d); m., Sept. 7, 1826, Dhoda Colby, d. May 6, 1879, ag. 78; his children: Dexter, d. May 9, 1900, ag. 69 (d); m. (1), March 13, 1854, Mrs. Lucy Ann (Hill) Kimball, d. Jan. 7, 1881, ag. 50; m. (2), April 13, 1882, Sarah E. Callemore; one son, William M., b. 1860; d. ———; m., Oct. 25, 1874, Ida M. Smith; m. (2) Martha M. J. Wright, Feb. 17, 1888. Mary Ann, dau. of William and Rhoda, b. 1846; m., May 25, 1865, George O. Hall. Children: Bertha, m. (1) a Barnes; Alfred, d. April 18, 1881, ag. 68 (d); m., Jan. 1, 1839, Eliza B. Welch, b. Dec. 10, 1812; d. April 6, 1904. Children: Mary E., d. Nov. 5, 1865; m., April 16, 1862, James M. Eaton, a son of Nathaniel. Sarah M., b. May 14, 1845; Jacob, Jr., son of Jacob, d. Sept. 25, 1852, ag. 37; by his wife, Elsie Miller, he had Annette, b. 1840; m. (1) Aaron Bradbury, and had a son. Melvin A., m., Nov. 1, 1888. Martha A. Daniels; and a dau., Rosie E., d. April 30, 1874, ag. 16; William C., b. 1860; m., Feb. 22, 1883, Lucy M. Daniels, b. 1862; she m. (2), March 11, 1864, Philip G. Prescott, b. Sept. 28, 1835; d. Oct. 13, 1903 (d). Children: Allie S., d. July 6, 1875, ag. 2y., 9m., and Alice F., d. Sept. 12, 1876, ag. 8w. Mamie B., b. 1881; m., May 10, 1898, Elmer W. Preston, b. 1873. Willard, son of Jacob, d. Feb. 15, 1887, ag. 69y., 4m. (b); m., March 24, 1839, Almira Towle, dau. of John. Children: James Burns, d. May 2, 1909, ag. 69y., 6m., 24d.; Ella, b. 1849; m., Feb. 7, 1870, Charles H. Hunter. Sarah C., d. Nov. 30, 1897, ag. 56y., 8m., 4d.; m. Alvin Davis. Edna, dau. of William, b. July 29, 1773; d. April 16, 1800; m. Robert Wilson; d. April 26, 1843, ag. 77 (see him). Ruhannah, dau. of William, b. in Hampstead, June 10, 1775. Nathaniel, b. in Hampstead, June 3, 1779; d. Nov. 15, 1849 (d); m. Hannah Tucker, d. April 4, 1856, ag. 72. Children: Caleb, b. Jan. 7, 1805; Esther, b. Sept. 25, 1808; Alvah, b. Aug. 22, 1810; m. Caroline Pollard. Joshua, Jr., son of William, b. Feb. 25, 1785; d. May 22, 1869 (d); m., Feb. 12, 1812, Lois Hoyt, b. Jan. 4, 1790; d. April 7, 1853; m. (2), June 7, 1859, Mary M. Jackson. Children: Herod, b. Dec. 13, 1812; Hannah Hoyt, b. Sept. 26, 1815; d. March 14, 1864 (a); m., June 3, 1848, James Hackett, d. Sept. 8, 1840. Children: Corcellus H., b. in Tunbridge, Vt., April 20, 1839; m., and has a family, lives in New York; she m. (2) Jacob P. Tenney, d. Nov. 17, 1893, ag. 80. Children: Mary M., d. Sept. 1, 1862, ag. 11; Grace L., d. Nov. 14, 1867, ag. 9y., 2m. (a). Persis Austin, dau. of Joshua, Jr., d. April 17, 1821, ag. 2y., 6m. Persis Austin, d. Dec. 10, 1854, ag. 29; m. James Carroll, d. Dec. 28, 1850, ag. 31 (d). George H., d. Sept. 7, 1872, ag. 37 (d); m., Jan. 28, 1857, Julia A. Merrill of Hanover, b. Oct. 4, 1837; d. April 5, 1902; she m. (2) Charles W. Dwinels; a son, Fred G., b. 1861; m., June 1, 1899, May Idella Fox, b. 1879; two children. Maria, dau. of Joshua, Jr., m. a Yeaton; a dau. Lois Maria is buried on Sawyer Hill. Hiram, d. Sept. 25, 1826, ag. 5. Amos, son of William, b. Dec. 21, 1796; m., Feb. 24, 1820, Elsa Eldredge and had Isaac Gleason, b. March 9, 1821; Mary Ann, b. April 18, 1824. William had a daughter, who d. young.

Richardson, John, brother of William, d. 1811 (d); his first wife,

Elizabeth, d. Aug. 17, 1821, ag. 64; he had: Elizabeth, b. April 9, 1780; m., March 18, 1798, Joseph Sawyer; Mary, b. May 13, 1782; d. Feb. 11, 1862; Sarah, b. June 30, 1784; Abigail, b. May 8, 1786; Susanna, b. July 16, 1790; d. Oct. 23, 1855; m., Dec. 2, 1819; Adonijah Colby (see him). John, by his second wife, Nancy, had: Ira, b. March 10, 1811; Eunice, b. Sept. 6, 1812.

Richardson, Joshua, brother of William, d. March 2, 1841, ag. 83 (a); m., March 25, 1792, Betsey Walworth, dau. of Amos and Elizabeth (Harris) Walworth of Norwich, Conn., a dau. of Gibson Harris, b. June 5, 1763; d. July 26, 1850. Children: Charlotte, b. April 30, 1793; d. Dec. 13, 1850 (ag. 67 on tombstone) (a), single; Prof. Rev. George, b. July 30, 1795; d. March 17, 1829 (a); m. Elizabeth Dennison, dau. of Capt. Joseph of Lyndon, Mass; Emily Betsey, b. Jan. 5, 1798; d. Jan. 14, 1824 (a); Rev. Charles Walworth, b. June 11, 1801; d. Nov. 18, 1871 (a), single; Joshua Washington, b. Jan. 20, 1804; d. Sept. 7, 1857 (ag. 58 on tombstone) (a); had a son Henry.

Richardson, Moses, brother of William, d. Jan. 21, 1822, ag. 59; m. Nancy Pollard, d. Dec. 25, 1804.

Richardson, Eliphalet, brother of William (d), d. Oct. 3, 1831, ag. 80; his wife, Abi, d. Jan. 3, 1851, ag. 83 (d).

Richardson, Enoch, brother of William, d. 1820, ag. 66; his first wife, Elizabeth, d. Aug. 16, 1809, ag. 46 (a); had a second wife, Phebe. Children: Moses, William G., lived in Lyme; John, m., Oct. 26, 1817, Susan Norris, lived in Leroy, N. Y.; Betsey, m., Feb. 8, 1810, John F. Huse, of Lyme. Enoch, lived in Leroy, N. Y.; and Sarah. David, m., Dec. 26, 1803, Mrs. Betsey Wilson, d. Aug. 23, 1865, ag. 81y., 7m., 18d., dau. of Warren. Children: Plummer and Abi Plummer, both b. Aug. 30, 1804; Joseph, b. Feb. 22, 1810; Benjamin, b. Jan. 8, 1812; Rufus King, b. Nov. 30, 1814; d. July 15, 1887 (b); m. Sarah Marston, d. Feb. 12, 1856, ag. 39. Children: Abby R., d. Feb. 21, 1855, ag. 2y., 6m.; Elizabeth, d. Feb. 17, 1855, ag. 9m., 6d.; Louisa P., d. April 11, 1858, ag. 18; Hudson M., d. July 10, 1864, ag. 26y., 1m.; Carrie M., d. April 12, 1890, ag. 46y., 10m.; m. Charles Seavey, had two children: Eugene and Henry, b. Oct. 1866; Belle, dau. of Rufus, single.

Richardson, John W., d. Oct. 19, 1892, ag. 63y., 5m.; his wife, Adeline R., d. Sept. 13, 1883, ag. 53. Child: Warren B., m., Sept. 25, 1878, Ella M. Davis.

Richardson, Theodore, d. July 4, 1845, ag. 72 (a); by his wife, Nabby, he had, Mary, d. March 27, 1854, ag. 52 (a); Hannah N., b. Aug 4, 1815; d. July 5, 1876; m., June 8, 1845, Charles D. Washburn, b. Sept. 1, 1819; d. June 13, 1903. Children: Delia S., b. Aug. 8, 1852; m. Eben D. Sanborn, b. Jan. 11, 1855; d. March 16, 1883; Georgia, b. Dec. 19, 1854; m., Nov. 21, 1874, Lewis T. Sanborn, b. June 14, 1847; d. Aug. 30, 1877; Charles and Horace.

Richardson, Rev. Caleb H., son of Samuel and Lydia, d. April 25, 1868, ag. 84 (d); his wife, Loanna, d. Dec. 1, 1873, ag. 92; a dau., Lydia P., d. Dec. 14, 1871; m. a Waldron.

GENEALOGY.

Richardson, Joseph L., d. March 16, 1842, ag. 40y., 8m. (d); his first wife, Hannah G., d. April 9, 1838, ag. 34y., 1m.; m. (2), Aug. 12, 1838, Sophronia Eastman; she m. (2), June 2, 1843, Daniel L. Smith.

Richardson, Samuel D., d. Oct. 29, 1884, ag. 78; his wife, Sophia, d. Aug. 20, 1874, ag. 68 (d).

Richardson, Adeline R., dau. of Moses and Anna (Lawrence) Boynton, d. Sept. 13, 1883, ag. 53y., 8m., 4d.

Ring, Harry F., son of Abner R. and Mary, d. April 5, 1816, ag. 13; Lucy P., dau., d. Oct. 24, 1817, ag. 5m. (e).

Roberts, Smith, d. Dec. 24, 1865, ag. 42 (e); his wife, Mary Ann, d. May 10, 1871, ag. 49; son George S., d. April 11, 1863, ag. 11.

Robie, Gilbert J., b. 1834; d. 1863; m. Mary Ann Loveren, b. 1834; one son, Horace G., b. 1861.

Robinson, Laurenza, dau. of Jacob and Mary, d. Aug. 25, 1848, ag. 1y., 8m. (a).

Rogers, William, b. 1867; d. 1905. Charles H., d. Sept. 27, 1861, ag. 64y., 11m. (a); his wife, Abigail S., d. May 27, 1852, ag. 50y., 7m. (a).

Rogers, John L., d. March 27, 1895, ag. 91y., 7m., 1d., son of Samuel and Rebecca (Haines) (b).

Ross, Willie J., son of James W. and Sarah J., d. Nov. 26, 1864, ag. 3y., 10m.; dau., Martha A., d. Aug. 2, 1865, ag. 7m., 2d. (b).

Sanborn, Tristram, d. Jan. 28, 1835, ag. 75; his wife, Comfort, d. Nov. 23, 1842, ag. 82. Children: Tristram, d. March 11, 1857, ag. 67; m., Oct. 24, 1808, Mary Jones, dau. of Asahel, d. Dec. 4, 1848, ag. 66. Children: Ann J., d. June 7, 1859, ag. 45y., 7m., 3d.; m. Rufus Atwell, b. June 16, 1816; d. Sept. 2, 1880. Children: Guy E., d. Nov. 1, 1846, ag. 9d.; George P., b. Feb. 11, 1850; d. Jan. 12, 1884; Sarah M., d. Aug. 16, 1864. Abigail, dau. of Tristram and Mary, d. Nov. 17, 1818, ag. 1y., 10m. Joshua, son of Tristram and Comfort, b. 1802; d. 1877; his wife, Mary P. Sawyer, b. 1806; d. 1867. Children: Maria, b. Feb. 11, 1833; d. Nov. 25, 1858; m. Palmer Woodard; Jane, b. 1843; d. 1863; Emmer, b. 1847; d. 1868; another child d. July 17, 1863, ag. 20y., 4m. Sue E., dau. of Tristram and Comfort, d. Aug. 15, 1840, ag. 48y., 5m. J. Clark, son of Tristram, b. 1810; d. 1900; his wife, Sarah, b. Jan. 19, 1896, ag. 79y., 10m., 12d. Herbert A., d. May 31, 1872, ag. 5. Georgie M. d. March 2, 1873, ag. 4. Charles H., d. Feb. 25, 1893, ag. 24y., 8m., 22d. Betsey, dau. Tristram and Comfort, m., Dec. 25, 1820, Isaac Sanborn of Sandwich. They are all descendants of Tristram and Comfort (j).

Sanborn, Jonathan, d. Nov. 25, 1870, ag. 76 (b); m. Mary A. Chellis, d. May 3, 1850, ag. 55; his second wife, Achsah, d. Nov. 28, 1872, ag. 79. Children: Jonathan A., d. Sept. 7, 1872, ag. 43 (b). Orissa C. Wilson, dau. John B., his wife, d. June 19, 1864, ag. 25, child: Lizzie J. Almer L., son of Jonathan, d. March 20, 1875, ag. 30y., 8m. Elizabeth A., d. Oct. 8, 1861, ag. 28y., 10m.; m. George Pressey. Mary, m. Richard Hutchinson (see him). Thomas, b. Feb. 7, 1817; d. July 29, 1892 (b); m. (1), Nov. 26, 1840, Arrosina Rollins of Grafton, d. Oct. 30, 1864, ag. 48y., 6m., 3d.; he m. (2) Lucinda A. (Lathrop) Colby. Children:

Addie Adella, d. Oct. 1, 1862, ag. 5y., 2m., 19d.; Morrison J., b. 1841; m., July 7, 1866, Rodosca K. Hinkson, dau. of George, d. March 1, 1883, ag. 41. Children: Lula Adella, d. Feb. 11, 1874, ag. 4y., 3m. Alma L., son of Jonathan, d. Feb. 20, 1875, ag. 30; m., Oct. 6, 1872, Mary E. Robinson. Gariophelia, dau. of Thomas, m. Herbert Garland. Abigail A., dau. of Jonathan, b. May 2, 1835; d. Jan. 16, 1892; m., Oct. 16, 1853, Benjamin F. Andrews of Orange, b. March 19, 1827; d. July 16, 1900 (b). Child: Dexter O., b. 1854; m., Oct. 24, 1872, Ida A. Whittier, dau. Elias. Hezekiah H., son of Jonathan, b. Dec. 29, 1835; d. Sept. 16, 1856.

Sanborn, Emeline F., dau. of Daniel and Mary B., d. Sept. 1, 1834 ag. 9 (a).

Sargent, Betsey, first wife of William, d. July 30, 1853, ag. 66 (a); his second wife, Frances M., d. June 17, 1887, ag. 77y., 4d. He d. Jan. 1, 1893, ag. 75.

Sawyer, Jonathan, d. April 16, 1860, ag. 76 (c); his wife, Sarah H., d. Aug. 18, 1857, ag. 73. John R., d. Aug. 6, 1862, ag. 45; his wife, Mary C., d. Nov. 12, 1866; Matilda, adopted dau., d. Nov. 7, 1858, ag. 17y., 10m. (c).

Sawyer, Azubah, d. April 5, 1893, ag. 87y., 8m. (b).

Scales, Stephen, d. Aug. 28, 1855; his wife, Ruth, d. May 31, 1850, ag. 71. Children: Abigail, d. Nov. 10, 1835, ag. 18; son, Isaac H., d. April 3, 1831, ag. 21 (c).

Shackford, Edrick, b. July 16, 1814; d. Jan. 10, 1885 (b); m. Caroline Huntoon, b. April 20, 1814; d. Jan. 4, 1904; Warren O., son, b. Sept. 1, 1842; d. Oct. 23, 1865; Ann A., dau., b. April 10, 1846; d. Sept. 12, 1865; Byron W., son, b. July 15, 1844; d. Sept. 19, 1865; m., Feb. 23, 1865, Emma F. Cogswell. Alfred M., b. Jan. 23, 1839; m., May 1, 1859, Martha Jane Barber, dau. of March. Children: Addie M., b. Aug. 11, 1860; m., Sept. 9, 1884, Arthur P. Follansbee; no children. Susan A., b. Oct. 30, 1862; m., Oct. 27, 1880, Will A. Tucker. Children: Howard H. Edrick S., Joseph M., m. Edith Neily, one child; Lawrence C.; Alfred B.

Shaw, Elias P., son of E. H. and M. A., d. March 23, 1867, ag. 15y., 23d.; Mary E., dau., d. Nov. 25, 1863, ag. 7y., 4m., 3d. (b).

Shepard, Moses, d. Dec. 8, 1826, ag. 54 (d); his wife, Abigail, d. March 26, 1838, ag. 66. Children: John, d. May 9, 1868, ag. 71y., 6m. (d); m. Roxanna Blodgett, d. June 3, 1871, ag. 73. Children: John Sanford, d. Nov. 3, 1867, ag. 43 (d); m., July 19, 1855, Theoda H. Clark, dau. of Robert B., b. Dec. 27, 1827. Children: Roxie Bell, b. Oct. 17, 1856; Herman Alphonse, b. July 18, 1858; John Sanford, Jr., b. Dec. 28, 1860; m. and lives in Franklin; Eliza Theresa, b. March 16, 1863; Seth Blodgett, b. Jan. 5, 1865; m. and lives in Franklin; Arthur Delbat, b. Feb. 20, 1866; d. July 5, 1867. Ann B., dau. of John, d. Dec. 6, 1873, ag. 47; m., June 4, 1860, William P. Stone; one son. Edwin P., b. 1870; m., Sept. 18, 1899, Grace M. Daniels, dau. of George W. Moses, son of John, d. Sept. 3, 1829, ag. 18m., 22d.; Edwin, b. April 19, 1829; d. Oct. 23, 1905 (d); m., Jan. 1, 1860, Delia L. Hinkson, b. May 14, 1837;

GENEALOGY.

d. 1909. Henry, b. June 16, 1831; d. March 14, 1899 (d). Augustus, b. 1834; m. (1), Oct. 25, 1866, Marcia Ann Hadley, dau. Norman, d. June 30, 1874, ag. 35; a son, Eugene A., b. Aug. 2, 1867; m. (1) Maud S. Gates, d. July 27, 1888, ag. 20y., 11m., 13d. (a); m. (2) Pertie J. Gates, b. 1874; two children: Alice Maud, b. July 19, 1900; Sarah, b. 1902. Augustus, m. (2), Jan. 7, 1875, Phoebe Ann Smith. Polly, dau. of Moses, d. May 2, 1883, ag. 82 (d); m. Benjamin Blake. Eliphalet, d. Nov. 27, 1814, ag. 12. Abigail, d. Dec. 26, 1877, ag. 66 (d); m. John F. Blake. Nathaniel, d. Oct. 27, 1881, ag. 82y., 11m. (e); m. Nov. 22, 1821, Betsey Campbell, d. Sept. 12, 1862, ag. 62.

Sherburne, Daniel, son of Joseph and Olivia, b. in Epsom, April 13, 1782; d. Aug. 31, 1860; his wife, Abigail, b. in Gilmanton, Feb. 9, 1787; d. March 22, 1863; moved from Epsom here in 1822. Children: Annah, b. Dec. 5, 1808; d. Dec. 25, 1831 (d); m. Daniel W. Clark, d. March 1, 1845, ag. 37. Joseph, b. June 13, 1811; d. June 29, 1864 (a); m. Mary C. Fales, b. March 17, 1815; d. July 4, 1860. Children: Caroline E., d. March 12, 1904, ag. 65y., 1m., 17d.; m. (1), Oct. 19, 1862, Elijah Bullock; m. (2), Aug. 7, 1870, Reuben Goss, d. Sept. 24, 1888, ag. 67 (a); Henry H., b. Jan. 10, 1841; d. May 6, 1862. Annabelle A., b. 1843; m., Nov. 20, 1864, Orrin H. Morse, son of Jesse, b. May 19, 1839; d. March 8, 1888. Children: Anna, d. March 22, 1889, ag. 20; m. Charles L. Lathrop; Freddie A., d. Sept. 10, 1878, ag. 13y., 8d. (a); Clarence H., b. July 30, 1887; Mary E., b. 1845; m., July 7, 1864, Rollin E. Davis of Vermont; Ella, and Lyman J., b. 1856; m., Jan. 15, 1878, Emma L. Lathrop, dau. of George H. and Emily. Children: Edith, b. July 3, 1880; m. R. L. Harris; Mary E. b. April 10, 1891, and Alice. Olivia Anna, dau. of Joseph, b. July 7, 1849; d. Aug. 2, 1861. Mary, dau. of Daniel, b. June 13, 1811; d. Sept. 15, 1843 (d); m., April 18, 1837, Joshua M. Hadley. Ivory Little, b. May 29, 1817; Caroline, b. Jan. 13, 1821; d. Dec. 8, 1824 (d).

Silloway, Andrew, d. April 13, 1853, ag. 56; Elizabeth Ann, dau. of Andrew and Almira, d. Oct. 9, 1849, ag. 3y., 8m., 16d. (a).

Smith, William, and Anna of Connecticut, d. Jan. 22, 1801, ag. 73, had Eliphalet, b. Sept. 18, 1748; William, Jr., b. Jan. 7, 1758; Joshua, b. April 20, 1760; d. Brentwood, Feb. 19, 1795; Francis, b. April 7, 1762; Anna B., b. Aug. 12, 1764; Oliver, b. Oct. 21, 1766; m., Nov. 9, 1785, by Thomas Baldwin, to Mary Harris, dau. of George, b. Jan. 23, 1767. Children: Hannah, b. Jan. 12, 1786; Polly, b. Feb. 9, 1788; Sally, b. Feb. 16, 1791; Ursula, b. Jan. 12, 1793; Oliver, b. Dec. 17, 1794; d. Feb. 24, 1795; Oliver, b. March 8, 1796; d. Sept. 5, 1798; Eliza, b. Sept. 25, 1798; d. Sept. 21, 1800; Oliver, b. Sept. 24, 1800.

Smith, Uriah, of Woodstock, m., Dec. 31, 1795, Caty Vale of Pomfret, by Aaron Hutchinson, V. D. M.; a son, Steven, b. Dec. 20, 1796.

Smith, Harriet N., b. Sept. 15, 1823; d. March 16, 1893 (b).

Smith, Moses, d. Feb. 7, 1855, ag. 89 (b). His wife, Mary, d. March 6, 1844, ag. 78. Children: Mary, b. July 1, 1800; d. Dec. 3, 1815; Sarah, b. July 7, 1802; d. March 3, 1872; Stephen S., b. April 18,

1804; d. July 5, 1887; m. Irena Barber (see her). Elsa, b. May 8, 1808; d. Oct. 23, 1833; Zenith, m. a Hood.

Smith, Moses, son of Nathaniel and Polly of Sanbornton, d. Oct. 23, 1878, ag. 81. His wife, Betsey, d. May 3, 1872, ag. 67y., 1m. (a); dau., Marilla C., b. 1833; m. David Bagley 3d, b. 1827; d. 1903 (a); adopted son, Henry, b. 1852; m., Nov. 13, 1871, Mary J. Whittier; Sarah m. Arden Jones, son of Nathan.

Smith, Francis H., d. Oct. 7, 1850, ag. 83 (b). His wife, Mehitable, d. June 13, 1838, ag. 63. Children: Sarah W., d. Feb. 19, 1824, ag. 23; Elizabeth, b. June 24, 1807; Leonard, b. May 10, 1810; Ruth Emery, b. March 15, 1812; John, b. May 30, 1805; d. March 23, 1861; William Jarvis, b. April 29, 1803.

Smith, Joseph Belnap, son of John and Sarah, b. Sept. 26, 1835; d. 1861; also George and another son, William J., d. May 21, 1843, ag. 5 (a). Betsey, wife of John, d. Sept. 9, 1826 (a). Frank W., son of Franklin and Louisa A., d. Aug. 18, 1849, ag. 5m., 25d.

Smith, Elijah, son of Micajah M. and Abigail (Cole) of Orange, d. Aug. 11, 1908, ag. 76y., 6m. (b); m. (1), April 11, 1857, Mary Eliza Davis, dau. of Leonard and Nancy; d. Oct. 29, 1863, ag. 25. Children: Alden E., m. March 22, 1878, Rosie E. Bullock; Carey, b. 1861; m., Sept. 13, 1891, Lizzie Idella Barney, dau. of Charles, b. 1859. Child: Ned, b. Feb. 16, 1893. Elijah m. (2), Feb. 9, 1865, Isabelle M. Goss, dau. of Reuben, and had Cora B., b. 1871; m., Nov. 20, 1892, Sidney R. Smith, son of Richard R., b. 1870. Children: Herman S., b. July 23, 1896; Ray, b. June 23, 1898. Harry R., son of Elijah, d. Jan. 24, 1908, ag. 27y., 9m., 21d.; m., March 10, 1901, Fannie E. Cross, b. 1884. Child: Harriet A., b. Sept. 2, 1908.

Southard, George H., b. 1869; d. 1904.

Springer, Henry, d. Feb. 10, 1833; m., Dec. 12, 1780, Hannah Straw; d. Dec. 3, 1821, ag. 59. Children: John, b. March 3, 1781; Susannah, b. March 7, 1783; Levi, b. Oct. 18, 1785; Betsey, b. Aug. 1, 1787; Lois, b. April 9, 1789; Hannah, b. Jan. 31, 1796; Dorothy, b. Nov. 21, 1797; m. (1) a Chase; m. (2), May 4, 1862, Joel Elliott. Relief Noyes, b. Dec. 26, 1799; another same name, b. May 27, 1802. Mary Elizabeth, dau. of Ezra and Sally (Miller), dau. Jacob, d. March 6, 1841, ag. 4.

Stanley, John E., d. Jan. 2, 1889, ag. 57y., 2m., 18d. (b).

Stebbins, Sarah Jones, dau. of Enos and Candar, b. Dec. 13, 1811.

Stevens, Samuel H., son of Jotham and Ruth (Barnes), b. Aug. 23, 1821; d. June 1, 1903. His wife, Belinda W., b. June 27, 1827; d. Dec. 14, 1863. Children: Charles C., d. Dec. 5, 1863, ag. 10y., 1m., 4d.; Georgia Anna, d. June 20, 1857, ag. 8m., 10d. Neldora A., d. Dec. 17, 1863, ag. 5y., 6m., 5d.; Benjamin H., d. Jan. 14, 1864, ag. 16y., 8m., 27d.; Franklin H., d. June 20, 1864, ag. 14y., 1m., 18d. Samuel H. m. (3), March 26, 1873, Sarah I. Allbee; m. (4), June 3, 1890, Nancy M. Batchelder. Ira B., son of Samuel H. and Belinda, b. 1860; m. Capitolia B. Colburn, dau. of Willard and Mandana, b. 1860. Children: Frank H., m. Fanny Bryant; Leon and Alice.

GENEALOGY.

Stevens, Peter, d. June 5, 1860, ag. 80 (b). His wife, Jemima, d. Jan. 15, 1859, ag. 79.

Stevens, Rhoda J., wife of John, d. March 23, 1854, ag. 53y.

Stickney, Daniel, b. 1827; d. 1893. His wife, Caroline, b. 1837; d. 1902 (b).

Stiles, Nathaniel, d. Dec. 2, 1851, ag. 43 (b).

Storey, David, son of Nathan and Elizabeth, d. July 29, 1810, ag. 3y., 7m. (e).

Story, Otis J., son of David and M. (Currier), b. Aug. 7, 1818; d. Sept. 21, 1891; m., April 4, ——, Harriet Clement, dau. of William and Harriet, b. March 29, 1816; d. Oct. 11, 1894. Children: Abbie, m. Sidney R. Hannaford; Mehitable P., m. George C. Bradbury (see him); Clara A., m., March 12, 1870, George A. Huntoon; Harriet P., m., Nov. 22, 1876, George W. Story; Charles O. B., b. 1851; m. (1), Feb. 26, 1873, Mary S. Jepson, dau. Francis. Children: Frank H., d. Nov. 14, 1877, ag. 7w. (b). J. Clement, b. Aug. 20, 1855; d. Jan. 27, 1895; m., March, 1881, Helen Smith; Walter C., b. Oct. 16, 1858; m., March 27, 1880, Ada C. Morgan, dau. of Nathan, b. March 26, 1860. Children: Carroll M., b. April 18, 1881; d. Oct. 17, 1904; m., July 22, 1902, Elsie Chase. Children: Leslie and Robin. Carl W., son of Walter C., b. Nov. 18, 1882; Ethel C., b. Aug. 22, 1884; Leslie, b. July 15, 1886; d. Sept. 14, 1886; Leon, b. July 15, 1886; d. Sept. 5, 1886; Mary A., b. Feb. 3, 1892; Bertha M., b. Nov. 8, 1899; d. June 13, 1904.

Straw, Mrs. Molly, d. March 26, 1813, ag. 55 (d).

Sturgeon, Rose Anna, wife of Eli, d. Feb. 15, 1890, ag. 39. Child: Willie D., d. April 9, 1883, ag. 13.

Swan, Charlotte A., dau. of Jonathan and Charlotte, d. Jan. 6, 1841, ag. 16 (a).

Swett, John, m., July 3, 1787, Mary Hawks and had Experience, b. Jan. 15, 1788; Lui, b. April 21, 1790; Lore, b. June 17, 1793. Charles F., son of Franklin P. and Sarah E., d. Jan. 19, 1851, ag. 3y., 3m. (a).

Sykes, Emily S., d. June 20, 1882, ag. 44 (a).

Talbert, Emily D. (Kimball), m., Nov. 29, 1856, William H. and d. Jan. 3, 1905, ag. 69. Georgie B. Daniels, dau. Henry, m., Dec. 1, 1883, William P., son of William H.; d. Sept. 13, 1885, ag. 21y., 1m.; dau., Isabelle N. Pope, m., May 11, 1879, William P.; d. Jan. 20, 1880, ag. 19y., 6m. (all c).

Tanner, Thomas, son of Jonathan and Susannah, b. Dec. 4, 1794.

Taplin, Dr. N. P., d. June 13, 1891, ag. 71 (b). His first wife, Eliza M. Rogers, dau. Dr. John, d. June 17, 1867; Eddie F., son, d. May 29, 1873, ag 13; George F., d. Dec. 23, 1870, ag. 24; member of Company E, Twelfth New Hampshire Volunteers. He m. (2), Oct. 7, 1868, Ella M. Washburn; Charles C., b. 1854; m., July 4, 1871, Hattie Drown; son, John.

Temple, Charles, d. Nov. 27, 1886, ag. 72 (b). His wife, Roxanna, d. Dec. 8, 1870, ag. 55. Child: Miria A., m. George W. Chase. Children:

History of Canaan.

Charles T., b. Dec. 8, 1875; d. May 10, 1897 (a). Mary Ann, d. Feb. 4, 1862; ag. 52; sister of Charles.

Thompson, Valentine, b. March 7, 1833; d. Nov. 15, 1896. Alice S., dau. of Valentine and Elsie F., d. Aug. 14, 1865, ag. 3y., 10d.; Ernest H., son, d. Dec. 24, 1866, ag. 4y., 4m., 20d.

Tibbitts, Jesse and Abigail, had Joseph, b. Feb. 10, 1807.

Towle, Shubel, son of Abraham, d. July 30, 1865, ag. 77 (d); m. Hannah Greeley, dau. Mathew. Children: Harriet N.; m. (1) Reuben Clark; m. (2) Stephen Hadley, Jr. John R., m. Mary M. Child; Mary A. C., d. Oct. 25, 1839, ag. 10w. (d).

Towle, John, d. Feb. 24, 1858, ag. 74; m. Miriam Watson; d. May 6, 1864, ag. 81y., 3m. Children: David, d. April 6, 1887, ag. 80y., 9m., 28d.; m., May 24, 1838, Susan M. Hadley, dau. of Stephen and Abigail. Children: Angeline L., b. 1838; m., Nov. 11, 1859, Ephraim F. Withington; Lucinda E., d. Sept. 16, 1848, ag. 1y., 11m., 16d. (e); Cynthia, d. 1861, ag. 14y., 6m.; Martha E., d. 1861, ag. 3y., 5m.; Stephen H., b. 1839; m., April 14, 1863, Ann M. Morey; David, d. Nov. 3, 1903, ag. 49; m., Sept. 4, 1875, Dora Goss, dau. Orvill and Hannah; d. July 27, 1881, ag. 22y., 9m., 18d.; Ephraim; John W., d. 1908 (a). His first wife, Mary S., d. Jan. 6, 1884, ag. 36. Children: Mary E., d. Dec. 26, 1863, ag. 6m.; Allie J., d. Aug. 17, 1881, ag. 4y., 1m. (a); m. (2). Elsina A., dau. of John, m. Hollis Whitney (see him). Sarah W., m. Albert W. Whitney (see him). Martha Jane, d. April 21, 1889; m., Aug. 1837. Nathan W. Morse, b. 1817; d. ———. Children: Frank W., d. Dec. 24, 1849; Nathan D., d. Feb. 4, 1867; Martha Ellen, m. (1) Leonard Miner; m. (2) Merrill Owen. Almira, dau. John, m. Willard Richardson (see him).

Towle, Col. Isaac and Rebecca, had Charles, d. Sept. 6, 1831, ag. 3; Mary Ann, d. Nov. 10, 1835, ag. 3m.; George, d. Nov. 19, 1836, ag. 6 (a).

Townsend, Ziba, d. Dec. 7, 1856, ag. 90. Nancy, his wife, d. July 4, 1856, ag. 80 (a).

Trowbridge, Cynthia C., wife of James, d. Aug. 31, 1863, ag. 56 (a).

Trussell, Jacob, b. Aug. 2, 1779; d. July 3, 1871 (a). His first wife, Persis E., d. March 26, 1863, ag. 82; m. (2) Mrs. Mary (Eaton) Smith of Manchester, June 18, 1864.

Trussell, Benjamin and Sally, had Charles, b. Jan. 20, 1798; Cyrus, b. March 15, 1799; Sally, b. Aug. 15, 1801; Farnum, b. Oct. 8, 1802; Lorenzo, b. Oct. 2, 1804; John Langdon, b. Aug. 30, 1806; Ira Man, b. May 26, 1808; Albert, b. Feb. 4, 1810; Horatio, b. Sept. 12, 1811; Elizabeth, b. Feb. 7, 1813; William, b. Oct. 9, 1814; Mary Ann, b. Oct. 21, 1816; Rozina, b. Jan. 10, 1819; Rozelta, b. Jan. 10, 1819.

Tucker, Moses, d. Sept. 1, 1849, ag. 78. Moses, son of Moses and Deborah, d. Oct. 11, 1878, ag. 75y., 6m. Sarah, his wife, d. Sept. 3, 1881, ag. 86y., 6m., 10d. Children: Jonathan K., b. 1834; m., June 4, 1865, Abigail W. Varnum of Dorchester, b. 1843; Eunice, d. Feb. 27, 1869, ag. 75; Marilla D., wife of Moses C., d. Aug. 25, 1874, ag. 39y., 4m.; a dau., Sarah E., d. March 3, 1865, ag. 3y., 3m.

GENEALOGY.

Tucker, Luzefor, son of David, d. Sept. 2, 1881, ag. 35 (a); m., March 16, 1869, Mary E. Bill; d. Feb. 7, 1905, ag. 51y., 11m., 28d. (a).

Tyler, Rev. Job Coleman, son of Job and Ann (Pike), b. Haverhill, Mass., March 1, 1799; d. Sept. 1, 1879; m., Aug. 5, 1822, Julia Morse; d. July 13, 1863, ag. 65y., 3m., 28d. Children: Eliza Ann, m. Isaac Davis (see him). James, son of Job and Ann, d. Sept. 26, 1879, ag. 78. His first wife, Polly, d. July 27, 1844, ag. 38; second wife, Clara, d. Aug. 12, 1872, ag. 53. Fannie S., dau., b. 1853; m., Nov. 30, 1871, Isaiah E. Emerson. Rhoda, dau. of Job and wife of David Currier, d. March 31, 1894, ag. 86y., 8m., 26d. Sarah P., dau. of Job and wife of Theophilus Currier, Jr., d. April 20, 1866, ag. 73. Theodore, son of James, d. Aug. 28, 1858, ag. 23; m. Louisa Putnam. Lucy, dau. Job, m. James Morse, Jr. Nabby, dau. Job, m. James Blaisdell (see him). Nancy m. Moses Kelley (see him). Fanny m. Amos Miner.

Underhill, John, d. Feb. 21, 1883, ag. 82 (b); m. (1), Jan. 12, 1823, Hannah Hadley; d. Oct. 2, 1839, ag. 37; second wife d. Aug. 7, 1875, ag. 85; Frank T. m. Susan A., b. 1847; d. 1898 (e); their dau., Addie B., b. 1867; d. 1898; and Anna, a dau., b. 1872; d. 1883.

Underhill, Edgar S., son of Robert, d. July 25, 1909, ag. 58; m. Carrie L. Burnham, dau. of Dea. Silas; d. Oct. 5, 1877, ag. 20; Robert d. Aug. 11, 1892, ag. 82y., 5m., 17d.

Vermont, Thomas, d. April 25, 1902, ag. 55 (c).

Wadley, Washington, son of Joseph, b. Dec. 13, 1797.

Walworth, Amos, was a grantee of the town; was here once. His half brother, Capt. Charles of Colchester, came here in 1768. Betsey Walworth, who m. Joshua Richardson, was a dau. of Amos. Charles came here to look after his brother's lands. His father, William Walworth, Jr., lived at Fort Hill, Groton, Conn.

Capt. Charles d. July 12, 1782, ag. 37 (g); m., May 30, 1771, Lucy Harris, dau. of George. Children: Lucy, b. March 13, 1772; m., 1832, a Chase; Emma, b. July 25, 1773; Sally, b. Oct. 30, 1774; Charles, Jr., b. June 1, 1777; m., June 1, 1800, Miriam Pillsbury; lived on South Road, opposite his brother, George. George, b. April 4, 1779, m. Philura Jones, dau. of Jehu. They went West and settled at Anamosa, Iowa, in 1839, with all their family of nine children with the exception of their eldest son, who went to Boston. Their children: James J., m. Elizabeth Nason and had one son, Arthur C.; George d. single in Texas; Clark C., m. Sept. 1, 1845, Mary Ann Eastman, dau. of Phineas, Jr. Children: Ella, Lula, Alice and a son d. young. Eunice m. H. C. George (see him). Mary Ann m. Edmund C. Booth, both deaf and dumb; Emily Jane m. Libius Fifield, a minister; Dennison married twice; William H. H. m. and had two children: Caroline Augusta, m. (1) Rev. Mr. Drummond; m. (2) Rev. Daniel Fiske. Simeon, son of Capt. Charles, b. Jan. 26, 1781; Susannah, b. May 1, 1782; d., ag. 96; lived unm. Her last years, many of them, were spent with Joshua Hall of Rumney, her half brother, her mother having married Henry Hall of Canaan in 1786, by whom she had four children.

Washburn, Nahum, d. July 23, 1862, ag. 75 (c). His wife, Polly, d. Jan. 30, 1841, ag. 51. Luther B. d. Sept. 17, 1853, ag. 40 (c). His wife, Laurella, d. April 27, 1863, ag. 52. Don Carlos d. Aug. 22, 1863, ag. 24y., 9m., 17d. (c); Charles D., b. Sept. 1, 1819; d. June 13, 1903 (a); m. (1) Harriet N. Richardson, b. Aug. 4, 1815; d. July 5, 1876 (a); m. (2), Feb. 6, 1879, Mary J. Adams. Children (first wife): Georgie A., b. 1855; m., Nov. 21, 1874, Lewis T. Sanborn.

Waterman, Elisha, d. March 19, 1871, ag. 88. His wife, Lucy, d. Feb. 13, 1878, ag. 92 (c).

Watson, J. S., d. Nov. 22, 1893, ag. 52. His wife, Allie V., d. Nov. 17, 1893, ag. 42 (a).

Webster, Alpheus S., d. Oct. 1, 1853, ag. 48. His wife, Betsey Sawyer, d. Jan. 18, 1849, ag. 35 (c); m., Sept. 12, 1849, Mary F. Jones of Enfield. Child: John S., d. Jan. 12, 1908, ag. 62y., 11m., 10d.; m. Ethel M. Parmenter.

Webster, Harry, d. Dec. 16, 1855, ag. 50y., 11m., 11d.; m. Eliza Little; d. Oct. 21, 1888, ag. 77y., 4m., 24d. Children: Emily F., d. March 24, 1841, ag. 2; Hiram L., d. Dec. 19, 1846, ag. 4y., 6m., 6d.

Weeks, Capt. Brackett, b. Oct. 18, 1775; d. Oct. 26, 1832 (a); m. Sarah Pickering and had: William Pickering, b. Feb. 22, 1803; d. Jan. 8, 1870 (b); his wife, Mary E. Doe, b. Aug. 30, 1812; d. Jan. 14, 1889. Children: Joseph Doe, b. Oct. 27, 1837; d. Dec. 1, 1890; Susan H., b. March 18, 1853; d. April 30, 1881; Mary E. D. Marshal and William B. Elizabeth Pickering, dau. of Capt. Brackett, b. Greenland Sept. 29, 1801; d. Ticonderoga, Vt., March 14, 1872; m., in Canaan by Rev. Amos Foster, about 1830, Gordon Burley, b. Aug. 25, 1795; d. Middleton, Oct. 1, 1864. He was the son of Joseph of Dorchester. He kept store on the Street for a time. Their children: Lucretia Morse, b. Hebron, Sept. 19, 1828; d. Glen Falls, Aug. 24, 1848; m. W. F. Jones; no ch.; Henry Gordon, b. Canaan June 2, 1832; m., Oct. 27, 1870, Jane Richards. Two children: Henry Gordon and Charles Richards. Brackett Weeks, b. Aug. 18, 1834; m., June 20, 1861, Minerva Smith, and had five children. Charles William, b. Concord, March 27, 1836; d. Nov. 16, 1837; Mary Elizabeth, b. Feb. 20, 1841; m., July 10, 1877, John C. Hollenback, a lawyer in Ticonderoga, Vt.

Welch, Dea. Caleb, d. about 1815. By his wife, Elizabeth Cross, dau. of Jonathan and Molly (Bailey) Cross of Methuen, Mass., he had: Daniel, b. Dec. 12, 1795; m. a Gould; had a dau., Sophronia; d. in Lowell. The records refer to another, Dan, who d. earlier. Caleb, Jr.; Simeon, d. July 29, 1876, ag. 72 (b); m. Deborah Richardson, dau. of Ephraim and Sarah; d. April 14, 1884, ag. 79y., 2m. Children: Francis, d. May 2, 1900, ag. 74y., 10m., 12d.; m. (1), Sept. 22, 1862, Elbyne Aldrich, dau. Leonard; m. (2), March 2, 1878, Mrs. Caroline (Digby) Cole; a dau., Emily D., b. 1846, m. (1) Charles H. Isham and had a son, Ferdinand; d. April 19, 1864, ag. 1y., 1m. 10d. She m. (2), June 7, 1866, Carroll M. Couch, b. 1843. William, son of Simeon, d. June 23, 1907, ag. 80y., 7m., 5d.; m., July 16, 1854, Emeline Elliott, dau. Joel. Children: William H.,

GENEALOGY.   643

b. 1855; m. (1), Nov. 18, 1876, Almira A. Preston; dau., Ethel. b. Sept. 1, 1880; m. (2), Feb. 5, 1901, Alice M. Rice, b. 1873. Charles, son of William, single. Eliza, dau. of Caleb and Elizabeth, b. Dec. 12, 1812; d. April 6, 1904; m. Alfred Richardson (see him). Reuben, son of Caleb and Elizabeth, by his first wife, Zephy, had Mary Ann, b. June 14, 1810; d. Oct. 20, 1826; Lydia Ann, b. Jan. 19, 1813; d. ———; m., June 19, 1834, Benjamin F. Nichols of Enfield; John Noyes, b. Oct. 22, 1815; d. Sept. 22, 1818. Reuben's second wife, Relief, d. July 4, 1818, ag. 28. Caleb had another dau., Sophia, who m. April 17, 1851, Samuel Dow, d. July 28, 1864, ag. 67. Joseph, Luther and Mary.

Welch, Jennie E. wife of James M., b. Aug. 14, 1868; d. Jan. 2, 1905 (b).

Welch, Francis, d. March 6, 1888, ag. 74y., 11m., 18d. (d); by his wife, Abigail Colby, d. June 30, 1874, ag. 56y., 9m., he had Lydia J., b. Aug. 30, 1848, d. Sept. 10, 1890; Carrie E., called Indie, d. May 7, 1905; ag. 64y., 6m., 15d.; m. (1) Charles A. Philbrick, d. July 29, 1858, ag. 28y., 8m., son of Hiram; m. (2), July 4, 1861, Benjamin O. T. Clark, son of Daniel and Dorcas (see him); m. (3) John A. Jewell.

Welch, Samuel, son of Joseph of Ipswich, b. June 26, 1742; d. Sept. 20, 1817 (a); m. (1) ——— Cheney, d. 1776; had five children: Lydia, b. 1768; m. David Pearson of Canaan; Abigail, b. 1770; d. Nov. 1846; m., Nov. 30, 1794, Joseph Clark (see him); Polly, b. 1772; m., 1800, Nathan Tucker of Salisbury, Mass.; Samuel, b. Aug. 27, 1774; d. 1848; m., 1804, Lydia Gill; Richard, b. 1776; d. Sept., 1817; m. and settled in Hartland, Vt.; Samuel m. (2), 1777, widow Anna (Chase) Cheney, d. May 22, 1795; six children: Daniel, b. 1778; m. Hannah Montgomery of Hampstead; Betsey, b. April 19, 1780; m. ——— Smith; Anna Chase, b. 1785; m. Jonathan Choate and d. soon after, leaving an infant dau.; Bailey, b. April 18, 1788; d. Aug. 20, 1863 (a); m., July 2, 1810, Priscilla B. Barbour, b. March 26, 1782; d. Oct. 9, 1871 (a). Children: Arnold, b. Nov. 27, 1811; d. Feb. 1, 1848; m. (1) Rebecca S. Sargent, dau. of Edward Sargent of Windsor, Vt.; d. Aug. 29, 1836, ag. 25; m. (2) Hannah A. Pierce, b. April 2, 1812; d. Sept. 10, 1847. Children: Henry Clay, b. July 8, 1839; m. (1), April 8, 1863, Sarah Cushing Lewis, dau. of Rev. James D. and Eunice R. (Jenkins) Lewis of Falmouth, Mass., b. Schenectady, N. Y., Jan. 1, 1840; d., Cleveland, O., Nov. 4, 1884. Children: Lewis Chamberlin, b. Falmouth, Mass., June 30, 1864; d. Hancock, Mich., Oct. 15, 1884; Eunice Jenkins, b. Cleveland, O., Aug. 14, 1866; d. April 23, 1889; Caroline Briggs, b. Cleveland, O., Dec. 2, 1868; George Arnold, b. Cleveland, O., May 29, 1879. Henry C. m. (2), Nov. 23, 1886, Amelia B. Roberts, dau. of James H. and Sarah F. (Reed) Roberts. George Pierce, son of Arnold, b. Oct. 12, 1841; m., June 25, 1873, Marian Howard Oliphant, dau. of James W. and Maria (McAllaster) Oliphant. Children: George Oliphant, b. March 25, 1875; d. Aug. 21, 1875; Henry James, b. Dec. 15, 1881; m., Sept. 11, 1907; Alice Andrews, dau. of Upson A. and Harriet B. (Warmington) Andrews, b. Dec. 1, 1886. Child: Henry James, Jr., b. Feb. 5, 1909. Arnold, Jr., son of Arnold, d. July 8, 1846, ag. 14m., 10d. Charles Arnold, b. Sept. 1, 1847; d. April 10, 1848. Willard Choate, son of Bailey, b. Feb. 26, 1814; d. May 12, 1895; m. (1), Oct. 9, 1836, Maria L. Smith, d. March 4, 1847, ag. 37; m. (2), June 9, 1850, Sarah F. Jennings, dau. of Lewis and Abigail Jennings. Children: William H. H., b. May 19, 1841; d. Aug. 30, 1866; Louisa Maria, m., Dec. 12, 1876, J. Alonzo Ford; Emma Rebecca, b. Feb. 9, 1846; m., May 17, 1867, Samuel M. Tucker, son of Samuel and Eliza H. Tucker. Child: Ross Francis, b. March 1, 1868. Arnold S., son of Willard, m., Oct. 21, 1874, Helen Scotchburn. Willard C., Jr., b. May 11, 1854. Alvin Colby, son of Bailey, b. April 28, 1817; d. Oct. 21, 1888, at Williston, Vt.; m., April 27, 1845, Abbie B. Chittenden, b. March 27, 1820; d. Feb. 12, 1877. Children: Jane Maria, b. in Underhill, Vt., Nov. 13, 1847; d. March 11, 1906; m., Sept. 22, 1879, Dr. A. L. Bingham; no children. Mary Abbie, b. May 26, 1851; m., May 11, 1870, Charles A. Murray of Burlington, Vt. Children: Elizabeth E., b. March 28, 1871; m., April 20, 1897, Frank C. Weeks; one child, Charles M., b. in St. Albans, Vt., Aug. 24, 1898. Katherine C., dau. of Charles A. and Mary Abbie, b. Jan. 29, 1874; m., Nov. 20, 1895, Daniel G. Emery; their children: Mary C., b. Chelsea, Mass., Dec. 12, 1897; Gwendolin M., b. Dec. 25, 1898. James Franklin, son of Bailey, b. April 18, 1821; d. Nov. 22, 1850; by his wife, Mary S. Merrill, b. Newbury, N. H., Aug. 6, 1822; d. Nov. 30, 1909, he had May B., d. July 16, 1867, ag. 19; Frank C., b. July 28, 1850; m. (1), April, 1868, Josephine Gilpatrick, d. Jan., 1869; m. (2), May 15, 1871. Mary S. Knapp, d. Nov. 7, 1877; m. (3), May 9, 1879, Martha S. W. Hall. Mary S. m. (2), 1852, Zenas D. Holden, and d. Nov. 30, 1909, ag. 87y., 3m. Charles Austin, son of Bailey, b. Dec. 6, 1824, d. Aug. 20, 1880; m. (1), Sept. 2, 1845, Sarah E. Davis, b. March 24, 1823; d. March 15, 1861; m. (2), Nov. 4, 1862, Elvira A. Boynton, b. Feb. 11, 1825; d. Dec. 24, 1877. Children: Lovena Agnes, b. June 7, 1846; m., Nov. 29, 1866, John K. Reed, son of William C. and Sarah E. Reed. Child: Minnie B., b. 1871. Charles Edward, son of Charles Austin, b. July 14, 1850; d. Aug. 4, 1850. Edward Austin, b. Aug. 9, 1852; m. ———. Lincoln R., son of Charles Austin and Elvira A., b. Lowell, Mass., April 19, 1865; m., May 14, 1891, Sarah L. Joyce, dau. of James H. and Alletha (Gibbs) Joyce, b. June 20, 1867. Child: Austin Horace, b. Dec. 2, 1896. Horace Barbour, son of Bailey, b. July 23, 1831; d., Sacramento, Cal., Sept. 17, 1882; m. ———; Lyman Stanley, b. April 2, 1827; d. Dec. 9, 1903 (a). James, son of Samuel, b. March 12, 1791; d. March, 1841; settled in Hartland, Vt.; his first wife d. 1841. Uriah, b. July 5, 1793; d. Aug., 1839; m., Jan. 26, 1818, Lois Currier (a), dau. of John (see her). Samuel m. (3), Dec. 19, 1797, Susanna Cheney.

Wells, Thomas, was of Essex, a shire town in England, and resting on the North Sea. Tradition says he fled to America, concealing himself in an empty cask, stowed among the water casks of an outgoing vessel. He landed in Massachusetts, but passed immediately to Rhode Island. Hugh, his son, was born in Essex, married there and ultimately came to New England. Thomas, his son, born about 1620, in England, settled at Hadley, Mass., where he died in 1676, aged 56. His wife afterwards married Samuel Belding. The children of Thomas and Mary were: Lieut. Thomas, b. June 10, 1652; m. Hepzibah Buell and d. in 1691. She suffered from an Indian raid, June 6, 1693. Mary, m. (1) Stephen Belding, and (2) Joseph Field. Sarah, b. May 5, 1655, m. David Hoite. Jonathan. John, who was drowned Jan. 20, 1680; and Ephraim, b. about 1674, m., Jan. 23, 1696, Abigail, dau. of John Allis. He lived in Colchester, Conn., where his wife died. He d. Sept. 13, 1748. His son, Ephraim, m., Feb. 2, 1726, or 1727, Lydia Chapman. He was a farmer and kept an inn at Colchester, Conn., where he died in Sept., 1786. He was a grantee of Canaan. Their children, so far as known, were: Ephraim, Jr., also a grantee; Thomas, a sailor, was seized by a press gang, forced on board a British ship, and held there three years. He was in Calais at the date of the great earthquake which destroyed Lisbon in 1755, and was nearly wrecked by the tidal wave that followed it. A letter written by him at that time to his brother, Joshua, is still in existence. During the Revolution he was in command of a privateer sailing from Norwich. He was a grantee of Canaan. Joshua, born in 1735, married Mrs. Jerusha Scoville Leeds and died in Canaan Sept. 1, 1804. Ezekiel, b. July 22, 1745; m. Phoebe Meacham, dau. of Samuel Meacham of Canaan, and died here Dec. 7, 1818; she d. Sept. 12, 1856, ag. 92y., 9m. Ephraim, Jr., Joshua and Ezekiel were residents and proprietors in Canaan. Ephraim, Jr., came here but only to dispose of his interests, and then depart. His land was located at the north end of Sawyer Hill. William Richardson, Joshua Richardson and Clark Currier purchased it. Joshua and Ezekiel came to Canaan previous to 1769, evidently to look out for their father's and brothers' interests. They took prominent parts in dividing and surveying the lands. Joshua was good at waiting; the girl of his choice had married Capt. Carey Leeds, a sailor. Capt. Leeds having died, Joshua on March 13, 1786, lost no time in hurrying to Colchester, where he arrived April 20, married the widow the same day and hastened back with a family of five children. He was kind and tender to her all her days, and he perpetuated her virtues upon the crumbling stone that marked her grave: "Sacred to the memory of Mrs. Jerusha Wells, late consort of Capt. Joshua Wells, who died Nov. 28, 1797, aged 60 years.

"She exemplified in life those virtues which adorn the female character. As a companion she was social, loving and sincere. As a parent, tender, affectionate and kind. As a friend, constant and faithful. She was beloved and respected in life and much lamented in death.

> "An angel's hand can't snatch her from the grave,
> Millions of angels can't confine her there.
> Cease then to weep, dry up your tears,
> She shall arise when Christ appears."

A daughter by her first husband, Sarah Ann Leeds, d. Aug. 18, 1794 (b).

Three children were born to them: Lydia, b. Nov. 6, 1788; d. Oct. 11, 1848; Joshua, b. Aug. 24, 1792; d. Aug. 23, 1873 (b); m., Jan. 19, 1815, Lucy Colby, b. Feb. 25, 1799; d. Feb. 19, 1876. Children: Lucy, b. Dec. 16, 1819; d. July 25, 1868; m. Edwin B. Miner, March 3, 1840 (see him); Charles H., m. (1), Jan. 3, 1849, Elvira W. Putnam, d. Oct. 13, 1858, ag. 30; m. (2) Lucy Jane Bickford, d. Oct. 8, 1889, ag. 54. Children: Frank C., b. 1852; m., Sept. 30, 1872, Etta Braley; Allen C., b. 1857; m., Jan. 19, 1878, Melissa L. Westcott, b. 1861; Julia, b. 1862; m., May 10, 1885, Fred W. Lovejoy, b. 1860; three children: Marion, Helen, Wendell. Freddie, son of Charles H., d. Sept. 25, 1858, ag. 3; Mary, dau. of Joshua, b. April 30, 1817; d. Dec. 21, 1897; m., March, 1838, Charles Hutchinson, son of Levi, d. June 26, 1890, ag. 77 (see him).

Hannah, b. April 17, 1794, died Jan. 3, 1795, dau. of Capt. Joshua. Capt. Joshua settled about half a mile above the present Wells house, and planted five hundred apple trees, many of which are standing today. Ezekiel settled near the house where Sylvanus Dow now lives. He was deputy sheriff from 1787 to 1798; proprietors' clerk from 1797 to 1808; selectman in 1787, 1796 to 1798; moderator from 1795 to 1801, 1803 to 1805; treasurer of the town, surveyor of both town and proprietary, tithingman, poundkeeper, and was a prominent man in the town. On Nov. 25, 1779, he m. Phoebe Meacham, at that time fifteen and a half years old. He fully obeyed the command to "increase and multiply," for in ten years they had nine children, and in 1809, Mrs. Wells had borne eighteen. They were as follows: Ezekiel, b. Nov. 16, 1779; d. May 25, 1863 (c); m. (1), Nov. 27, 1800, Polly Colby; b. Aug. 7, 1779; d. Nov. 9, 1874; m. (2), July 11, 1822, Octavia Packard, d. Dec. 15, 1844, ag. 40; built and lived in the house S. J. Dow now owns. Children: Ezekiel, 3d, d. Nov. 7, 1882, ag. 79; his wife, Nancy, d. Sept. 26, 1867, ag. 69. Polly, d. Sept. 4, 1882, ag. 81y., 3m., 29d.; m., July 11, 1821, Daniel Campbell (see him). Peter S., b. Sept. 8, 1807; d. Dec. 14, 1887 (c); m., March, 1819, Arvilla Kimball, b. March 23, 1819; d. March 15, 1893. Caleb, son of Ezekiel and Octavia, d. March 31, 1836, ag. 13y., 4m.; Ezekiel, d. Feb. 28, 1852, ag. 24; Alvin J., d. Feb. 5, 1853, ag. 22; Octavia M., d. March 15, 1854, ag. 19; Alanson, d. Aug. 3, 1840, ag. 1y., 10m.; Polly, d. Oct. 30, 1844, ag. 3. George F., b. 1833; d. 1907 (c); his wife, Mary A., d. Jan 4, 1891, ag. 52y., 11m., 22d.; dau., Ada E., b. 1863; m., May 22, 1887, Arthur E. Mooney, b. 1866. Phoebe, dau. Ezekiel, b. April 15, 1782; m., Sept. 15, 1802, Jacob Dow; she d. Feb. 19, 1867. Ephraim, b. June 29, 1784; m. Nancy Graves, d. July 27, 1846. A second daughter, b. Sept. 25, 1785, d. Oct. 14, 1785. A third son, b. June 12, 1786, and died. A fourth son, b. March 8, 1787, and died. Twins, b. March 8, 1788, one stillborn, the other died a few days after. A seventh son, b. June 1, 1789, and died. Enos, b. Feb. 14, 1791, d. Oct., 1862. Betsey, b. Dec. 26, 1793; d. Jan. 20, 1795. Sally, b. Dec. 6, 1794; d. June 13, 1883; m., Oct. 14, 1810, William Rogers,

b. Feb. 20, 1788; d. April 11, 1863. They are both buried in a small graveyard at the head of Goose Pond. They lived a short distance above in Hanover, on the road to Lyme. They lived in Canaan where F. B. L. Porter now lives. They had ten children: Sally A., m. Amos Kinne (see him); William M., b. Aug. 30, 1813; d. Jan. 29, 1892; m. Sarah Gibbs, b. Aug. 31, 1821; Nancy G., b. Aug. 24, 1815; d. Oct. 7, 1864; m. Hiram Pressey, b. March 26, 1812; d. ———; Mary D., b. May 8, 1818; d. May 15, 1884; m. Richard Fitts, b. Oct. 10, 1813; d. ———; Hannah W., b. Aug. 23, 1820; m., Oct. 26, 1848, John T. Hurlbutt, b. Aug. 8, 1819; Jane, b. June 24, 1823; d. May 7, 1867; m. Benjamin Piper, b. Oct. 10, 1816; d. Sept. 25, 1878; Wallis L., b. Sept. 23, 1826; d. Oct., 1908; m. Mary J. Mitchell, b. Oct. 4, 1822; Louise M., b. April 25, 1830; d. July 21, 1831; Lafayette W., b. April 18, 1832; d. Feb. 24, 1907; m. Abbie A. Saunders, b. March 6, 1842; George W., b. Jan. 31, 1836; m. (1) Mary E. Dickerson, b. Dec. 4, 1833; d. March 8, 1868; m. (2) Ann Pollock, b. June 14, 1834. Hannah, dau. of Ezekiel, b. Jan. 7, 1796, m. a Goodwin and d. June 23, 1831. Polly, b. March 20, 1798; m. John Flanders of Benton. Caleb Pierce, b. April 15, 1800, died. Betsey Pierce, b. March 4, 1802; d. Sept. 30, 1816. Delia Fayette, b. June 20, 1806; d. July, 1831. Mahala, b. May 1, 1809; m. an Eaton and died.

Wells, Judah, who is often mentioned in the early records of Canaan, was of Colchetser, Conn., where he m. (1), in 1755, Eunice Olcott; m. (2), in 1760, Ann, dau. of Isaac Bigelow; m. (3), Dec. 29, 1791, Ethelinda Otis, dau. of Richard Otis of Canaan, by William Ayer, justice of the peace. He was a relative of Joshua and Ezekiel Wells. He came to Canaan before 1793, and bought the farm known as the Aldrich farm, west of the Mascoma River on the Enfield line, the farm which Samuel Joslin first settled and sold to him. Ethelinda was b. in Norwich, Conn., Aug. 18, 1766. They had two children: Otis, b. Dec. 7, 1792, and Juda b. Jan. 27, 1795.

Westcott, James A., d. Feb. 24, 1883, ag. 64 (a); m. Permelia Chase of Danbury; a dau., Phebe A., m., April 2, 1876, William E. Allard.

Wheat, Elder Joseph, d. Oct. 28, 1836, ag. 77 (a); his wife, Bridget, d. Nov. 9, 1845, ag. 99. Children: Capt. Joseph, d. Sept. 9, 1855, ag. 69y., 10m.; his wife, Lydia Bullock, d. Oct. 18, 1868. Children: Lafayette; Dr. Ara, d. Sept. 18, 1896, ag. 80y., 6m.; m., Oct. 28, 1846, Isabelle M. George, dau. of William W., d. Aug. 25, 1872, ag. 42y., 17d. Children: William G.; m. and has Harold and Isabelle. Allen, son of Ara, b. June 14, 1863. Elzina, dau. Capt. Joseph, d. Oct. 15, 1864, ag. 33; m. George C. Bradbury (see him). Solomon, d. Oct. 4, 1848, ag. 29; m., Nov. 9, 1845, Emily Mackey of Thetford, Vt. Children: Elizabeth A., d. May 9, 1848, ag. 10m.; Jane E., b. 1846; m., Jan. 18, 1866, Allen H. George (see him). Lydia, dau. of Elder Joseph, d. Sept. 5, 1832, ag. 37; m., Nov. 14, 1816, Samuel Gilman (see him). Elvira H., d. Nov. 27, 1836, ag. 25; m., Dec. 20, 1835, Smith Rowe of Grafton. Capt. Alvah, d. Sept. 29, 1852, ag. 39; m., Feb. 10, 1841, Sarah King of Orange. Lois, who m. a Caswell; Sally who m. a Smith; Benjamin; Nathaniel.

Whitmore, Norman, d. May 31, 1863, ag. 70y., 1m.

Whitney, Silas, d. April 21, 1866, ag. 75; m. Sally Butler, d. March 31, 1871, ag. 83. Children: Moses S., d. May 8, 1863, ag. 37; Bela B, b. Oct. 21, 1819; d. May 24, 1897; his first wife, Louisa Jameson, d. Sept. 2, 1856, ag. 34. Children: Emma, m. ——— Heath, had a dau., Lora, who m. and had a son. His second wife, Sarah H. Burley, dau. of Benjamin, d. Aug. 11, 1879, ag. 57y., 2m.; had Flora M., d. Aug. 3, 1862, ag. 9m.; Albert, d. Sept. 15, 1863, ag. 7m.; Flora M., b. Nov. 6, 1866; d. ———; m. and had a dau. Fred, m. and has a son Philip and dau. Harriet. Bela B., m. (3), May 2, 1880, Mrs. Melinda (Colby) Darling, dau. of Sargent and Ruth, d ———; and m. (4), Feb. 20, 1889, Emeline B. (Colby) Bell.

Whitney, Isaac, and his wife, Lydia Taylor, who d. March 24, 1843, ag. 91 (e), had Esther, b. June 12, 1775; d. Nov. 2, 1847 (e); Isaac, b. March 17, 1784; d. March 15, 1866; m., Feb. 8, 1819, Abigail Greeley, dau. of Mathew, b. Feb. 7, 1796; d. May 30, 1891. Four children: Albert W., b. Jan. 11, 1822; d. March 31, 1897 (e); m., Oct. 17, 1842, Sarah W. Towle, dau. of John and Mary, b. Aug. 13, 1822; d. Oct. 1, 1907. Children: Charles A. C., b. June 16, 1849; d. July 18, 1857; Clara A., b. April 16, 1852; d. 1909; m., Aug. 11, 1870, Joseph Tucker. Children: Albert W., d. Aug. 5, 1878, ag. 5y., 10m. (a); Arthur, Leon, Carrie, Mina W., dau. Albert W., b. Nov. 12, 1858; m. Henry C. Melendy. Alice M., b. Nov. 21, 1860; m. Alden Hardy. Hollis B., son of Isaac, b. May 22, 1824; m., Dec. 17, 1843, Elsina A. Towle, dau. of John, d. June 8, 1896, ag. 70 y., 8m., 4d. (d). Children: Henry O., b. Nov. 12, 1845; m. Susie E. Ames. Children: James H., b. 1885; m., Oct. 20, 1908, Lettie M. Austin; James M., b. Oct. 8, 1849; d. Aug. 24, 1874; m. Ellen M. Butman. Louisa A., dau. of Isaac, b. Sept. 12, 1828; m., Nov. 25, 1847, Franklin S. Smith. Lucy J., b. May 24, 1835; m., June 6, 1852, Edwin E. Shattuck, b. July 8, 1830. Children: Frank E., b. Feb. 17, 1853; d. June 21, 1857. Malvena L., b. Nov. 6, 1854; m. Leonard Clark. Children: Mary B., Carrie C., George L. Burlingame, Emma. Isaac W., son of Edwin, b. May 11, 1856; m. ———; Frank E., b. Nov. 2, 1858; m. Jennie Robinson. Child: Frank E. Edwin H., b. May 11, 1856; d. 1909; m. Fannie Dowling. Hattie J., b. March 7, 1864; m. Henry W. Clark (see him). Lodena A., b. Oct. 19, 1870; m. John E. Smith; child: Perley E.

Whittier, Richard, (b), and Betsey, had Daniel Bodwell, b. in Haverhill, Mass., Nov. 6, 1778; d. May 20, 1834 (a); m., Jan. 7, 1802, Lucy Flint, dau. of Joseph, b. Aug. 29, 1780; d. Aug. 21, 1865. Their children: Almira, b. April 27, 1804; d. May 9, 1831 (a); m., May 27, 1827, Dr. Charles Heaton of Dorchester; Ruth C., b. Aug. 12, 1807; m., Nov. 22, 1831, Daniel G. Patten of Boscawen; Albion, b. Oct. 12, 1814; d. Oct. 8, 1861 (a); his wife, Emeline, d. May 25, 1851, ag. 31 (a); Augusta, b. March 19, 1821; went to California and m. Simeon, son of Richard, b. Oct. 20, 1780; Dorothy, b. Oct. 30, 1782; Richard, Jr., b. Oct. 25, 1784; Moses, b. Feb. 18, 1788; d. Aug. 22, 1791; Asa, b. May 5, 1791; Abiah, b.

GENEALOGY.   649

April 6, 1793; Moses, b. April 16, 1795; Leonard, b. July 10, 1797; Rufus, b. May 23, 1800; d. Sept. 28, 1828; his wife, Abi D. P., d. Oct. 30, 1828, ag. 24 (a). Children: Horatio N., d. Sept. 4, 1826, ag. 7w.; Augustus L., d. May 23, 1829, ag. 23m.

Whittier, Nathaniel, d. Feb. 21, 1814 (b); m. Mrs. Mary (Keazer) Blaisdell, mother of Daniel, d. May 15, 1806, ag. 73; had four children: Elijah, d. June 22, 1848, ag. 79 (b); m. Nancy Keniston; had eight children: Polly, b. March 3, 1789; m. Stephen Jenness; Salley, b. March 11, 1791; Elijah, Jr., b. Dec. 17, 1792; Abigail, b. Dec. 25, 1795; m., May 12, 1814, Levi Wood; Mehitable, b. Jan. 28, 1797; m. Wilks Edwards; Nathaniel, b. March 10, 1799, d. young; William, b. June 20, 1804; d. Feb. 4, 1890; m. Charlotte T. George, dau. of Col. Levi, d. March 26, 1882, ag. 78. Children: Louisa, b. March 1, 1824; Lucinda G., b. Jan. 20, 1826; d. Oct. 20, 1852; m., June 12, 1849, Andrew J. Powell; had a dau. Ida A., d. June 2, 1867, ag. 17y., 3m. Elijah, b. Feb. 9, 1828; d. Feb. 18, 1839; George L., b. Feb. 4, 1830; d. Feb. 22, 1890; m. Louisa C. Rowell, d. March 5, 1906, ag. 75y., 1m., 13d.; had a son Charles, b. 1858; m., Feb. 3, 1884, Mary E. Wallace, b. 1862; d. 1908; two children: Hattie L., d. April 12, 1889, ag. 1y., 9m., 14d.; Maude M., b. 1885; m., Aug. 8, 1906, Harvey A. Blanchard. Ira A., son of William, b. Aug. 27, 1832; d. April 27, 1834; Martha J., d. Oct. 30, 1836, ag. 2; David H., d. April 2, 1840, ag. 4; Mary A., d. April 23, 1840, ag. 6; Hermon D., d. Jan. 17, 1850, ag. 7y., 8m.; Isabelle, d. Jan. 22, 1850, ag. 1y., 5m. Samuel, son of Nathaniel and Mary, m., Oct. 23, 1796, Mehitable Beedle, d. July 14, 1854, ag. 84; Nathaniel, m. Polly Sleeper; Abigail, m., March 4, 1798, Thomas Cole; had a dau. Abigail, d. Nov. 26, 1880, ag. 80y., 8m.; m. Micajah M. Smith. Elijah, (b), m. (2) Lucretia Aldrich, d. June 25, 1869, ag. 76. Three children: Nathaniel, b. June 21, 1825; m., Nov. 7, 1862, Nancy J. Andrews, both of Orange; Belinda, m. Joseph Briggs; Webster, m. Lucinda Chapman. Abijah A., d. Feb. 1, 1850, ag. 16.

Whittier, Elijah, d. June 24, 1890; m. Ruth B. Eastman, b. 1826; son of Elijah and Melinda.

Whittier, Elijah, m. Melinda Roberts, d. July 7, 1826, ag. 31. Children: Elisha R., d. Jan. 27, 1903, ag. 75y., 11m., 6d.; m., April 26, 1849, Melissa Ladd. Children: David H., b. 1849; m., Aug. 28, 1870, Emma P. Cross, one son, Clinton. Sarah Ann, dau. of Elijah, b. 1840; m., April 19, 1864, Allen J. Clough; had a son Bert; she m. (2) Stephen R. Swett, Dexter.

Whittier, Enoch, d. Nov. 29, 1878, ag. 69; m., March 5, 1835, Sally Merrill of Thornton, d. Feb. 17, 1901, ag. 86 (h).

Whittier, Jeremiah, d. March 26, 1858, ag. 75; his wife, Nancy A., d. March 6, 1868, ag. 84; a dau., Harriet J., d. June 30, 1866, ag. 20 (h).

Whittier, Samuel W., d. June 15, 1885, ag. 66 (h). Miriam B., wife of Simeon, d. March 11, 1842, ag. 24 (h). Nathaniel, d. Jan. 23, 1892, ag. 71. Nathaniel Whicher, 3d, d. Oct. 28, 1816, ag. 11. An old stone in Wells Cemetery.

Whittier, Zenas, d. Nov. 26, 1874, ag. 76 (b); m., Sept. 3, 1820, Mehitable E. Merrill, d. Feb. 15, 1856, ag. 56. Children: Henry C., d. Dec. 7, 1832, ag. 4m.; Isabel, d. June 16, 1836, ag. 21d.; Jane, d. July 13, 1826, ag. 2d.; E. M., d. June 18, 1829, ag. 4m.

Whittier, Carrie J., wife of Aaron, b. 1858; d. 1896 (a).; dau. of Willard Colburn; his first wife, Mary Ann, d. March 14, 1871, ag. 21; buried in Orange.

Whittlesey, Polly, wife of Aaron, d. May 9, 1846, ag. 64 (h).

Wier, Thomas, b. 1814; d. 1899; Makala E., his wife, d. Aug. 2, 1889, ag. 77y., 10m., 25d. Children: Emma L., d. Oct. 17, 1861, ag. 14 (a); Ellen F., m., Dec. 7, 1880, Frank H. Lowell; Sarah; Martha, m. Joseph J. Follansbee.

Williams, Robert, b. 1749; d. May 14, 1823, at Shakers in Enfield; buried there; m., Jan. 13, 1777, Sarah Pinkham, d. about 1819; buried on West Farms. Came from Barrington to Enfield; lived with Shakers before he came to Canaan in 1797; left Shakers, because he had to give up his property. Bought farm of John Harris on West Farms and gave the land for the West Farms Cemetery. Several of the older children were born in Barrington. Children: Mary, b. 1778; d. 1816; m., March 1, 1798, Elam Meacham, son of Samuel. After his wife died he moved to Pennsylvania with his children and married again, having two children. In Canaan he lived opposite the Knight house and his wife was buried on the Ezra Day farm. His children were Elam, who was a preacher among the Mormons in 1847; Polly, m. a Gallaway, who was killed; she joined the Mormons, angry at her brother, David, who opposed her course. John was an ironworker in Erie, Penn.; Nancy, m. a Couch and lived in Richland City, Wis.; a child, William. Sarah, m. Elam Hanchett, and d. in the 40's in Illinois; three children: Nathaniel, Samantha, Diantha, Sylvester, d. LaSalle County, Ill., 1848; m., Delila Burch. Children: Roseanna, m. Ferdinand Renne, lived in Oregon; Marinda, m. Aaron Woodbury, lived in Citronella, Ala.; Frances, m. John Kelly, lived in Chicago. David, son of Mary and Elam, m. Sarah Joslyn. Six children: Darius; William, m. Eleanor Craddock and had five children; James, m. Amanda Burnham and had three children; Roseanna, m. Porter Hubbard, one child; Sylvester, killed at Chickamauga. Thomas, son of Robert, b. 1782; m. Deborah Pinkham, his cousin, d. Nashua, April 2, 1837, lived several years in Canada, where their children were born; came to Lowell in the 30's. Robert, son of Robert, b. Feb. 6, 1784; d. Riley, Ill., Feb. 8, 1872; m., June 29, 1808, Mercy Hardy, b. Hopkinton, Oct. 30, 1787; d. Hampshire, Ill., Dec. 13, 1852; they resided on Town Hill while in Canaan. Sold to his son Sylvester in 1841 a farm in Hanover on which was a new brick house. Children: Sylvester, b. April 16, 1809; d. 1874, at Marengo, Ill.; m. (1) a Partridge. Children: Orion H.; Gratie; and by a later wife, Mary. Was a member of the New Hampshire, Vermont and Troy Conferences and finally owner of his father's farm in Illinois. Valorous C., b. Canaan, March 8, 1811; d. Marengo, Ill., May 11, 1887;

m., March 1, 1834, Luana D. Rundlet. Cared for his father's Grafton farm a few years and went to Illinois about the time his father did. Owned a farm at Riley, Ill. His wife lived several years after his death. Five children: Sylvester D., Valorous T., Robert M., J. Frank, Albert J. Horace P., b. Canaan, April 16, 1813; d. Aug. 4, 1881, at Kinsley, Ill. Four children: Flora, Owen, Eva, Etta. Sias K., b. Lebanon, June 25, 1818, d. July 5, 1890; m., Dec. 31, 1846, Mary D. Heafield, b. Aug. 22, 1824; d. July 17, 1887. Bought a farm near his father in Illinois. Children: Eugenie, Rosamond, both m. and have children. John G., b. Lebanon, July 17, 1820; d. Missouri, May 19, 1889; m. and had children, the oldest Sylvester. Drifted from Illinois to Missouri. Isaac F., b. Lebanon, Jan. 20, 1823; d. near Vicksburg, Miss., May 8, 1858; m. and had four children in Illinois. Stephen, son of Robert, b. Enfield, Oct. 13, 1789; d. Canaan, Nov. 6, 1853 (e); m., Dec. 1812, Elizabeth Longfellow, b. Byfield, Mass., June 10, 1785; d. March 12, 1843. Lived on South Road on John Moore farm. His father owned it at the time Col. Levi George owned the place opposite George Ginn's. Robert sold it to his sister, Lois Evans, of Allenstown. Erastus Packard bought of her. Children: Lorenzo D., b. Sept. 9, 1813; d. at sea, Jan., 1838. Went to Cuba summer of 1836, after cedar shingles. In 1837 went on a fishing voyage and never returned. William Longfellow, b. Feb. 10, 1815; d. May 19, 1882 (e); m. (1) Mary Ann Hardy of Enfield, d. Dec. 26, 1841, ag. 24y., 11m.; no children; m. (2) Mary Ann Clough of Canaan, b. Sept. 9, 1823; d. Sept. 14, 1885 (e); lived in Grafton and in Northern Vermont; then returned to West Farms and lived on the old Moses Sawyer farm opposite the Cemetery. Children: Adelbert O., b. Grafton, May 22, 1844; d. Providence, May 27, 1893; m., June 22, 1867, Flora A. Wier of Lyndonville, Vt., b. Oct. 9, 1847. Enlisted Company H, Thirtieth Massachusetts Infantry, Dec. 13, 1861; re-enlisted in 1863, Company F, Fifth New Hampshire. Children: Minnie B., Charles H., Austin, Arthur, Arthur, Mabel. Everett O., b. Canaan, Nov. 2, 1846; m., Dec. 5, 1874, Lizzie M. Copp of Hanover; lives in Enfield. Children: Ida M., Edna A., Mary L., Everett D., Georgia A., Lester R. Phineldo O., b. Newark, Vt., Jan. 4, 1847; m. Nellie B. Marsh, at Groton, Vt., Jan. 29, 1868, b. Aug. 26, 1847; d. 1907 (e). Lived on Peters farm on Goose Pond Road. Children: Lena B., b. Dec. 19, 1868; m., March 12, 1890, James F. Eastman, her cousin, b. Nov. 18, 1856; Mamie P., b. Hanover, Nov. 13, 1871; d. Canaan, Aug. 25, 1872; Maitland, b. Canaan, Nov. 10, 1879; Daniel H., b. July 8, 1882; m. Flossie M. Earle of Canaan; two children. Lorenzo D., son of William L., d. Oct. 4, 1850, ag. 3m; Delevan K., b. Jan. 2, 1852; d. Hanover, Nov. 4, 1898 (e); m. Nettie Goss, dau. of Daniel and Loraine. Children: Henry W., m. Eliza Melendy, and Val M. Rebecca, b. Canaan, Aug. 3, 1853; m., April 7, 1876, Frank P. Clark of Andover; three children: Oren A., Ethel A. and Charles H. Susan L., d. Oct. 16, 1854, ag. 1w. Zylpha M., b. Canaan; d. Manchester, Nov. 30, 1886, ag. 29y., 1m., 14d. Adrista E., d. Nov. 24, 1858, ag. 6w. Abraham Longfellow, son of Stephen,

b. Aug. 24, 1818; d. June 11, 1906; m. (1), Feb. 13, 1845, Chastina Burnham, b. March 18, 1821; d. Aug. 13, 1861; m. (2), Feb. 19, 1865, Irene S. (Hadley) Heath, b. March 31, 1827; d. June 22, 1904. Was born on his great-grandfather's farm; soon afterwards the family moved to the William Longfellow farm, also his great-grandfather's. When seven years of age he went to live with his uncle, Abraham Knowlton, on the John Currier farm. In 1844 he bought of his uncle the Jacob Straw farm. Built a new house in 1852, on a part of the Robert Williams farm. In his will he left three hundred dollars to the town, the income of which to be used to keep the family lots in West Farms Cemetery in good condition, also one hundred dollars, the income to be used to cut the bushes along the road. He left five hundred dollars to the Canaan Town Library to be expended in useful books, provided the town would raise a like amount. The balance of his property he left to Dartmouth College. Had four children: Delevan P., b. March 23, 1848; d. April 20, 1852; Lorenzo D., b. April 2, 1854; d. Dec. 16, 1870; Fremont D., b. Aug. 1, 1856; d. in Brattleboro, Vt. Was a carriage builder there. Chastina B., b. June 22, 1859; m. Dwight T. Cowing, lives in Hadley, Mass. Children: Bertha C., Ethel T., Ruby M., Florence B., Josephine W., Marian M. Samuel, son of Stephen, b. May 18, 1820; d. Enfield, Feb. 4, 1878; m., March 16, 1848, Ursula Day, b. Nov. 6, 1823; d. Canaan, Jan. 9, 1904. Attended Canaan Union Academy and taught one winter in Mississippi. Was a selectman of Canaan and Enfield and representative of Enfield. He bought the Longfellow farm and also the Reuben Gile farm. Moved to Enfield. In fall of 1861 enlisted in Company C, Seventh New Hampshire Volunteers; was promoted to first lieutenant in 1862; was in hosiery business in Enfield under the firm name of Dodge, Davis & Williams. Children: Abbie Jeanette, b. Canaan, Dec. 25, 1849; m. Rev. Francis Parker, b. Gloucester, July 19, 1847. Louis Melville, b. Canaan, Sept. 17, 1851; d. April 26, 1900; m., Feb. 27, 1878, Ella E. Brigham. Four children: Robert Longfellow, Elizabeth Langdon, Henry Trumball, Ursula Louise. Miriam Elizabeth, b. Canaan, April 10, 1853; Susan Augusta, b. Canaan, July 6, 1855. Henry Herbert, b. Enfield, Aug. 20, 1858; d. April 9, 1862; Frank Burton, b. Nov. 29, 1864; m., June 23, 1897, Grace E. Parker. Their children are: John P. and Samuel L. He is a merchant in Enfield. Susan Longfellow, dau. of Stephen, b. June 25, 1824; m., Nov. 14, 1849, James Eastman, b. Jan. 1, 1820; d. Aug. 28, 1899. Lived first in the old homestead of his father, James, with his brother, Richard B., then sold to Richard and bought Robert Williams' old farm, which he sold to John Clough, and then bought the Bartlett Bryant farm in Hanover. Children: Stephen, b. Canaan, Oct. 13, 1851; d. June 16, 1898; m., Jan. 1, 1880, Almeda D. Colby, dau. of Moses T., b. May 17, 1856; five children: Arthur H., Susan E., Mary F., Grant C., Grace H. Martha, b. Hanover, Oct. 20, 1855; d. Manchester, Nov. 15, 1891; m., May 24, 1882, Dr. C. A. Manning. Two children: Susan Pearl, and Roy Eastman. James F., b. Nov. 18, 1856; m., March 12,

1890, Lena B. Williams, b. Dec. 19, 1868; lives on old homestead in Hanover; two children: Martha J. and James F., Jr. Mary Goss, dau. of Stephen, b. Jan. 29, 1826; d. Sept. 22, 1886; m. Leonard Hadley (see him). Stephen, Jr., b. March 14, 1827; m. Rebecca G. Hazeltine, d. March 5, 1855, ag. 22y., 8m. (e); one child: Mira. Samuel, son of Robert, b. 1794; d. ———; m., Jan. 1, 1823, Purnel B. Worth, dau. of Dea. John Worth; lived on his father's farm in the neighborhood of West Farms; she was b. Oct., 1802; d. June, 1875; moved to Genoa, Ill., in 1851. Child: Horace B., b. Canaan, Jan., 1824; d. fall of 1866; m., 1853, Hattie Huntley; lived in Genoa, Ill.; two children: Willie and Clarence. John Worth, son of Samuel, b. Canaan, Feb. 25, 1826; drowned, 1848; Purnel Loraine, b. Canaan, July 8, 1828; d. Enfield, Dec. 10, 1896; m. Daniel Goss of Hanover, son of Joshua (see him). George Evans, b. Sept. 7, 1830; d. in the 60's; m. Mary Oakes, after he went to Illinois with the family, then went to Atlantic, Iowa. Frances Elizabeth, b. Canaan, July 8, 1832; d. Jan. 31, 1890; m. (1), Dec. 9, 1852, in Illinois, John Gilkerson; m. (2), July 4, 1867, John Johnson; three children by first: Hiram, John, Jr., and Ida May; one child, Grant, by second. Katherine, dau. of Samuel, b. Canaan, 1834; d. ag. 18m. (e). Franklin, b. 1837; d. ag. 4 (e); Andrew P., b. 1837; d. ag. 6(e); Lorenzo P., b. 1843; d. ag. 18m. (e); Ellen M., b. July 21, 1842; m., April 19, 1866, Joseph Northgraves; five children: Gertrude M., Isabel F., Albert N., Jennie, Charles K. They lived in Illinois, Texas and Iowa. Sarah, dau. of Robert, b. 1798; d. June 30, 1834; m. (1) Stephen Davis; m. (2) Stephen Hadley of Hanover. By her first husband she had two children: Mary, b. June 21, 1818; m. John Dustin, d. Nov. 9, 1900; Arabella A., b. Canaan, Jan. 17, 1823; m. a Trodd; five children: Martha, Isabelle, Henry, Sarah, Mary J. (see Hadley). Calvin, son of Robert, d. single. Nancy, dau. of Robert, b. Canaan, April 23, 1804; d. Manchester, March 21, 1880; m., Hanover, July 21, 1827, Timothy Parker, b. Oct. 31, 1807; d. Manchester, June 15, 1865. Children: John Carlos, Henry Carlton, Dewit C., Nancy A., Amasa H., Sarah S., Horace W.

Wilson, Levi, d. Feb. 28, 1856, ag. 58; m., Dec. 26, 1803, Mrs. Betsey Wood, d. Jan. 24, 1853, ag. 73 (b). Children: Louisa, b. Feb. 9, 1805; William, b. Feb. 9, 1805.

Wilson, Frederick E., b. 1860; d. 1907 (b).

Withington, Samuel, and Hepsibah, had William Dame, b. Feb. 28, 1823.

Wood, William, and Betsey, had Polly, b. May 19, 1780; Betsey, b. March 26, 1782; William, b. Jan. 28, 1784; Polly, b. Jan. 15, 1786; Sally, b. March 27, 1788; m., April 21, 1816, George Johnson; Rosel, b. May 22, 1790; Levi, b. April 8, 1792; m., May 12, 1814, Abigail Whittier; Eli, b. Aug. 6, 1794; Lois, b. Dec. 26, 1801.

Wooster, David H., son of H. F. and C. H., d. Feb. 18, 1883, ag. 2y., 2m., 19d. (b).

Worth, John, d. April 4, 1845, ag. 70; m., Dec. 10, 1801, Betsey Clark, d. Oct. 12, 1862, ag. 82. Children: Catherine E., d. July 29, 1836, ag. 22;

Eliza C., d. July 22, 1835, ag. 26; m., Oct. 12, 1834, Andrew Pettingill. Child: Julia M., d. April 25, 1857, ag. 21; m., Aug. 21, 1851, George S. Shepard; dau., Jenny M., d. Feb. 26, 1857, ag. 5m. (b). John, Jr., son of John, m., Oct. 21, 1840, Flavilla Kelley. Pernal Barber, dau. of John, m. Samuel Williams (see him). Edmund, son of John, by his wife Sarah, had Arabella, d. Aug. 27, 1853, ag. 20; m. Alfred Barney, son of John. Child: Arabella, d. Aug. 22, 1853, ag. 27d.; Hiram S., son of Edmund, m. Elizabeth Durrell (see her). Sarah, m. (2), March 9, 1839, Benjamin T. Hilliard of Enfield; he m. (2), March 24, 1857, Mrs. Martha Buswell of Lawrence, Mass.

Worth, Mrs. Lydia, wife of John, d. May 12, 1835, ag. 30. Abigail, dau. of John and Lucy, d. Oct. 13, 1792, ag. 13.

Worth, Stephen, m. (1), March 16, 1797, Mrs Molly Worth, d. July 15, 1817; m. (2) Susanna (Bagley) Cross. Children: Abigail, b. Feb. 18, 1798; Life C., b. March 28, 1799; Polly, b. Dec. 6, 1800; d. July 15, 1817; Lucy M., b. April 3, 1802; Lydia G., b. Aug. 24, 1803; Caroline B., b. Jan. 7, 1806; Asa, b. March 1, 1808; Sally F., b. Nov. 21, 1811; Elvira, b. Feb. 22, 1813; d. March 11, 1813.

Worth, Nathaniel, d. Sept. 13, 1791; m., Dec. 12, 1789, Mary Bartlett; a son Nathaniel was b. April 18, 1791.

MARRIAGES FROM THE TOWN RECORDS NOT PLACED.

Where the Residence is Not Mentioned it is of This Town.

Abbott, Hazen, of Groton, Vt., to Rachel Cass of Lyme, Sept. 18, 1825.
Aldrich, William, of Grafton, to Abigail Folsom of Grafton, Oct. 12, 1797.
Angier, James H., to Cynthia P. Heath, May 17, 1843.
Adams, Andrew R., Vermont, to Mary S. Wright, Vermont., June 15, 1861.
Avery, Alonzo, Boston, to Mary J. Cilley, Andover, Nov. 8, 1866.
Atwell, Horace, Enfield, to Emily B. Spear, New Ipswich, May 18, 1873.
Barney, Jacob, of Grafton, to Lois Walker, of Grafton, Feb. 25, 1800.
Barney, Jabez, of Grafton, to Abigail Briggs, of Orange, March 2, 1819.
Barnard, Darius, to Mary A. Noyes, of Enfield, March 12, 1857.
Barnard, George, of Lebanon, to Caroline R. Bartlett, of Dorchester, March 22, 1857.
Batchelder, Jonathan, to Sally Tucker, Dec. 31, 1818.
Batchelder, Reuben, of Orange, to Mercy May, Dec. 3, 1854.
Bennett, David, to Polly Cole, both of Orange, Dec. 14, 1817.
Bennett, Ebenezer, Jr., of Andover, to Lucinda Stickney, Dec. 30, 1855.
Biathrow, Horace A., to Sarah A. Wheeler, both of Lyme, March 9, 1853.
Bishop, Joseph, to Philoma Columbia, Feb. 23, 1851.
Blake, Augustus F., to Harriet A. Flagg, Nov. 29, 1854.
Blood, William, of W. Fairlee, Vt., to Rhoda Brown, of Hebron, March 28, 1814.

MARRIAGES.

Bockwell, Oliver B., of Grantham, to Deborah Gage, of Enfield, April 1, 1827.
Bohonon, Moses, of Salisbury, to Lois Waldo, of Orange, Jan. 1, 1801.
Bowers, Lyman, of Lawrence, Mass., to Sabrina C. Wilson, Oct. 8, 1849.
Bullock, Elisha, of Orange, to Jerusha Leeds, May 22, 1800.
Bro, Joel, to Lucinda Columbia, July 2, 1854.
Brown, Don C. of Hanover, to Delia L. Merrill, of Lowell, Mass., Oct. 7, 1857.
Bridgeman, Isaac, to Lucy Chandler, both of Hanover, Jan. 4, 1820.
Bridgeman, Abel, to Abigail Sawyer, both of Dorchester, June 12, 1825.
Briggs, Nathaniel, to Sally Whittier, both of Orange, Oct. 14, 1824.
Bullock, Coomer, to Zelinda Peck, both of Grafton, Dec. 29, 1796.
Blaisdell, Charles E., to Jerusha Blaisdell, both of Dorchester, Jan. 24, 1850.
Beal, Ira, of Manchester, to Harriet Andrews, of Orange, Jan. 28, 1849.
Burnam, Daniel B., of Enfield, to Axa Davis, of Grafton, Feb. 27, 1834.
Batchelder, Bradford C., to Frances A. Rogers, March, 1837.
Buffum, William C., to Sarah Spooner, both of Grafton, Oct. 5, 1837.
Brock, Benjamin, of Newbury, Vt., to Martha Johnson, of Enfield, Nov. 3, 1839.
Bryant, Roswell C., to Lucy E. Huntoon, both of Enfield, April 7, 1839.
Buffum, James, to Sarah Roberts, both of Grafton, Sept. 20, 1840.
Bailey, John, of Springfield, to Eliza A. Nichols, of Enfield, April 15, 1841.
Barnett, Levi, to Mrs. Hannah Gile, both of Enfield, Sept. 22, 1845.
Bean, Nathaniel W., of Enfield, to Hattie A. Hamlett, Nov. 14, 1860.
Blair, Lewis, to Helen Allard, Aug. 22, 1860.
Besse, Edson P., of Newtonville, Mass., to Minnie M. Hoffman, Sept. 18, 1864.
Brooks, Oliver J., to Emily A. Bickford, April 5, 1867.
Brocklebank, Edson B., to Sarah J. Clough, Sept. 13, 1868.
Blaisdell, Henry G., of Dorchester, to Lillie D. Leonard, of Glover, Vt., July 3, 1869.
Broughton, Charles H., of Enfield, to Susan M. Sharp, Sept. 12, 1870.
Bryant, Joseph M., of Hanover, to Louisa M. Goss, of Enfield, Aug. 17, 1871.
Bailey, Henry, of Groton, to Abbie A. Norris, of Dorchester, Aug. 14, 1871.
Bushway, John, to Delia Bushway, Sept. 4, 1875.
Blood, William A., to Almira R. Smith, March 22, 1880.
Burley, Benjamin, to Polly Norris, both of Dorchester, Feb. 27, 1821.
Clifford, Joseph, to Susanna Saunders, both of Grafton, Oct. 4, 1798.
Clifford, Timothy, to Ruth Buffum, both of Grafton, May 27, 1802.
Chase, Jesse S., to Hannah M. Johnson, both of Dorchester, April 14, 1822.
Colburn, S. H., to Elizabeth Mackress, both of Lyme, Feb. 7, 1822.

Conant, Latham, to Polly Beal, both of Lyme, Feb. 17, 1818.
Columbia, William, to Elizabeth Hall, Aug. 3, 1851.
Church, Hilliard, of Enfield, to Mary J. Quimby, of Springfield, Sept. 27, 1851.
Clement, Leonard, of Columbia, to Almira B. Porter, Nov. 3, 1853.
Columbia, Frank, to Sophia Clough, March 11, 1855.
Carter, Jeremiah, of Dorchester, to Cordelia Wells, of Plymouth, Aug. 19, 1855.
Crocker, David, of Salisbury, to Ann Jones, April 3, 1858.
Crocker, Selden L., to Lucy F. Staples, June 19, 1858.
Chaplin, Allerton, to Mary A. Hanscum, both of Lyme, Nov. 17, 1858.
Carr, Jacob, to Olive Pollard, April 24, 1803.
Choate, Moses S., of Enfield, to Hannah C. Martin, March 8, 1849.
Chase, John, to Sarah Hoyt, Jan. 1, 1815.
Clifford, David, of Grafton, to Betsey Noyes, Feb. 27, 1800.
Colby, John, of Grafton, to Mary J. Flanders, Aug. 19, 1832.
Currier, Lorenz, of Enfield, to Eliza R. Smith, of Grafton, Oct. 18, 1849.
Corliss, Cyrus, to Almira Read, both of Bristol, Sept. 30, 1832.
Clifford, Ira, of Wentworth, to Sally Davis, of Grafton, Jan. 24, 1833.
Chase, Simon P., to Ann Houston, of Orange, April 1, 1838.
Chellis, James, to Lucinda Fellows, both of Orange, Oct. 27, 1839.
Chase, Joseph J., of Haverhill, to Harriet H. Fitz, of Chester, July, 1839.
Carr, Lewis C., of Boston, to Betsey Currier, of Manchester, Oct. 22, 1848.
Colby, Samuel A., to Susannah L. Kimball, Aug. 19, 1860.
Church, Hilliard, to Mary E. Gilbert, both of Enfield, Aug. 8, 1863.
County, George B., to Hannah Crowley, Sept. 28, 1863.
Colby, James M., of Hanover, to Arabella E. Martin, Nov. 6, 1864.
Chellis, Sumner, of Orange, to Emma C. Sherwill, of Orange, Dec. 5, 1866.
Cilley, Nathan G., of Orange, to Mary A. Church, of Enfield, Oct. 19, 1867.
Cooms, Albert E., of Orford, to Rosa F. Scruton, of Alexandria, Feb. 12, 1871.
Carroll, Calvin C., to Lizzie Black, of Dorchester, Dec. 27, 1871.
Cross, Franklin M., to Ella E. Stanford, of Royalton, Vt., Sept. 11, 1871.
Copp, G. O. F., to Mary A. Brown, both of Enfield, Dec. 23, 1871.
Cross, George B., to Lydia Martin, both of Hanover, Aug. 24, 1872.
Columbia, John, to Mary Morse, May 17, 1873.
Collins, James D., to Carrie F. Church, Oct. 2, 1876.
Cook, Paul, to Betsey Berry, Jan. 15, 1817.
Corliss Kimball, of Alexandria, to Betsey Heath, Jan. 29, 1818.
Cross, Sylvester, to Olive S. Lovejoy, of Hanover, Sept. 19, 1846.
Currier, James, of Salisbury, to Abigail Hovey, July 4, 1803.

MARRIAGES.

Day, Daniel, to Jane Danforth, of Orange, Dec. 15, 1817.
Dunham, Orison, to Mehitable Putney, April 13, 1841.
Dome, Eslay, to Polly Stevens, Sept. 19, 1797.
Dupuis, Zeb, of Hanover, to Sophia Columbia, June 6, 1863.
Day, Leonard, to Alma Hall, of Northampton, Mass., June 11, 1863.
Decato, Joseph, to Agnes Hill, Jan. 13, 1873.
Deveraux, William H., of Lebanon, to Mary E. Walcott, Jan. 14, 1874.
Decato, John, to Mary A. Hill, Jan. 6, 1877.
Drake, John H., to Sarah L. Abbott, Dec. 20, 1879.
Drake, George W., to Marilla Read, both of Grafton, June 23, 1824.
Drake, John, of Grafton, to Betsey Cogswell, of Enfield, July 22, 1814, or Dec. 18, 1815.
Derber, Walter, to Dilla Eldridge, both of Hanover, Dec. 28, 1817.
Downer, George, of Lebanon, to Susanna Bullock, of Orange, March 9, 1797.
DeMoranville, Charles, Jr., to Abigail Clifford, both of Grafton, July 12, 1808.
Dickerson, Suel, to Hannah Dickerson, both of Newchester, Jan. 6, 1824.
Doloff, Franklin, of Lawrence, Mass., to Sarah M. Derby, June 29, 1853.
Derush, Andrew J., to Mary A. Cilley, of Orange, Dec. 29, 1855.
Dunham, Austin, to Imogene Knight, March 31, 1860.
Dunham, Willard L., to Lucy Fox, Aug. 18, 1860.
Evans, Thomas, to Betsey Pillsbury, Dec. 22, 1814.
Emerson, Charles A., to Hannah B. Ames, of Newport, Feb., 1851.
Eastman, Daniel, to Matilda Burton, May 16, 1868.
Eastman, Henry, to Hattie H. Brock, both of Orange, Jan. 21, 1871.
Eaton, Edward, to Diana Hadley, Feb. 28, 1844.
Fifield, Ezekiel, to Sarah Ann Hardy, Feb. 9, 1847.
Fifield, David, of Bradford, Vt., to Sally Kimball, Jan. 12, 1815.
Flagg, Jacob, of Orange, to Lois Wilson, May 10, 1826.
Flanders, Dr. Thomas, to Susanna Follensbee, of Grafton, Jan. 9, 1815.
French, Henry, to Sally Sawyer, both of Grafton, June 18, 1815.
Flint, Dr. Benjamin, of Rumford, Me., to Sarah Cushing, of Orange, Feb. 1, 1816.
Fellows, Benjamin, to Pensy Bridgeman, both of Hanover, March 11, 1816.
Flanders, Elijah, to Betsey Winslow, both of Lyme, Jan. 1, 1817.
Foss, Topham, of Danbury, to Anne Reed, of Grafton, Aug. 31, 1824.
Frost, Amasa, of Wentworth, to Clarissa P. Clay, Jan. 4, 1851.
Follensbee, James M., of Worcester, to Julia A. Kittredge, March 3, 1854.
Flagg, William, to Mary A. Currier, Nov. 24, 1853.
Follensbee, John B., of Enfield, to Mrs. Persis B. Keenan, June 7, 1854.

Fellows, Moses, of Dorchester, to Elvira Cole, March 25, 1857.
Fellows, Truman, of Dorchester, to Emily D. Cole, March 26, 1857.
Foss, John C., of Lyme, to Pomelia Fifield, March 4, 1835.
French, Amos, of Lebanon, to Susan M. Johnson, of Enfield, Oct. 9, 1837.
Ford, Horace, to Amelia C. Andrews, both of Orange, June 24, 1838.
French, John, of Orange, to Mary J. Flanders, of Danbury, June 12, 1842.
Ferguson, Franklin, to Nancy E. Blodgett, of Warren, Dec. 19, 1860.
Ford, George N., of Danbury, to Amanda M. Davis, of Grafton, April 21, 1861.
French, Nathan, of Unity, to Ellen Bailey, of Enfield, Nov. 27, 1861.
Fox, John F., of Enfield, to Elizabeth Morse, of Sharon, Oct. 14, 1864.
Fellows, Gilbert G., to Maria H. Booth, both of Franklin, Jan. 19, 1867.
Ford, Richard T., to Mary E. Brown, both of Grafton, July 8, 1869.
Fizette, James, to Clara Brown, Sept. 6, 1870.
Follensbee, Ephraim H., to Aphia P. Wheeler, of Groton, Nov. 20, 1870.
Ford, Herman A., to Clara A. Perkins, of Lyme, June 22, 1872.
Flanders, Moses, to Roxanna Russell, of Dorchester, April 3, 1823.
Folsom, John, to Rebecca Colby, June 9, 1791.
Ford, Luther, to Charlotte Evans, Sept. 16, 1838.
Foster, Benjamin F., to Ruth H. Kimball, April 19, 1832.
Foster, Hezekiah, to Sophia Adams, April 16, 1815.
Freeman, Daniel, of Lebanon, to Mrs. Catherine Lawrence, Nov. 12, 1826.
Fulsom, George, of Exeter, to Polly Colby, Nov. 27, 1800.
Gile, Samuel, to Polly Green, both of Enfield, Jan. 25, 1806.
Gody, Joseph, to Harriet Columbia, Sept. 16, 1855.
Gile, Ira S., of Lebanon, to Maria F. ———, Nov. 12, 1857.
Gile, Nelson of Lebanon, to Amelia B. Dresser, of Enfield, Feb. 16, 1870.
Gilbert, John F., of Pembroke, to Irene Thompson, of Orange, March 4, 1850.
Gilman, John B., to Betsey B. Clark, of Danbury, Feb. 21, 1843.
Gage, Daniel B., of Enfield, to Jerusha Ford, of Orange, Nov. 27, 1845.
Green, Edwin, to Emma Pillsbury, of Enfield, June 11, 1865.
Gale, John A., to Jane Knowlton, both of Danbury, July 25, 1869.
Glode, Peter, to Alvina Columbia, Dec. 20, 1869.
Godette, William, to Flora Columbia, July 31, 1875.
Gile, Stephen, to Lydia Straw, Dec. 31, 1818.
Hazen, Samuel, to Betsey Bewel, both of Dorchester, Jan. 26, 1815.
Hazen, N. H., of Walcott, Vt., to A. S. Snow, of Boston, Jan. 19, 1851.
Howard, Henry, to Sally Powers, both of Grantham, Oct. 29, 1826.
Hadley, Amos, to Mehitable Briggs, of Orange, July 3, 1823.
Heath, Samuel W., of Bristol, to Harriet N. Lord, June 11, 1850.
Hill, Moses, to Lucy A. Kimball, Nov. 20, 1848.

MARRIAGES.

Hills, Tiles, to Margaret Burgous, Dec. 17, 1853.
Hazeltine, David, to Pauline Dean, Aug. 20, 1854.
Hamlet, Henry S., to Sarah M. Lary, Nov. 30, 1854.
Haskell, William H., of Maine, to Abby Fales, Oct. 28, 1856.
Hall, Anthony, to Adaline Hall, May 13, 1856.
Haven, George W., of Newport, to Marcia A. Emerson, May 22, 1849.
Hinkson, George, to Pluma Bullock, both of Grafton, Jan. 3, 1837.
Hill, Napoleon J., to Melvina Bennett, March 29, 1880.
Hoyt, Daniel, to Susan Bartlett, Oct. 7, 1837.
Hoyt, Ebenezer, of Orange, to S. Jennie Sargent, of Grafton, Aug. 7, 1870.
How, Joseph, to Hannah F. French, both of Enfield, Oct. 17, 1839.
Hatch, Horace, of Lebanon, to Ann Colcord, of Enfield, Oct. 2, 1839.
Hill, Thomas J., to Mary E. Merrill, Oct. 24, 1841.
How, Nathaniel, to Mary J. Choate, both of Enfield, Feb. 2, 1840.
Hall, John A., of Groton, to Arvilla H. Dimond, 1842.
Holt, John A., of Lyme, to Emeline Whittier, June 18, 1846.
How, Charles B., to Harriet C. Sargent, both of Manchester, April 30, 1859.
Harvey, Timothy M., to Mary A. Martin, both of Grafton, March 27, 1863.
Hoffman, Edwin A., of Lebanon, to Adelaide L. Roberts, of Enfield, March 16, 1865.
Hazeltine, Hollis B., to Emma L. Loverin, Oct. 11, 1865.
Hale, Moses T., of Groton, to Mary A. Buswell, of Orange, Feb. 6, 1866.
Heaton, Arthur, of Orford, to Amanda Childs, Oct. 13, 1867.
Holt, George E., to Sarah J. Braley, both of Grafton, Nov. 17, 1869.
Huntress, John E., of Boscawen, to Eliza J. Littlefield, of Danbury, Dec. 2, 1869.
Hebert, Noah, to Mary Bonney, July 1, 1872.
Hebert, Joseph, Jr., to Ina Downer, of Thetford, Vt., May 24, 1873.
Hoyt, Moses, to Olive G. Hoyt, Dec. 5, 1875.
Hadley, Henry M., of Pembroke, to Nettie M. Phillips, Nov. 27, 1876.
Hadley, William H., of Hanover, to Mary Bradbury, Aug. 19, 1849.
Hadley, Silas, of Hanover, to Sally Kimball, July 4, 1822.
Hadley, Dan W., to Ann K. Dunham, Jan. 12, 1844.
Hadley, Joshua, to Ruth Davis, of Grafton, Jan. 18, 1815.
Haroon, Samuel, to Eunice Colby, Jan. 10, 1804.
Hardy, Thomas, Jr., of Medford, Mass., to Sarah P. Stevens, June 17, 1846.
Heath, Wilbur R., to Ruth I. Nute, of Dover, Jan. 1, 1850.
Hinkson, Samuel, to Abigail Allen, April 21, 1785.
Hoague, Joseph, to Zilpha Day, May 13, 1847.
Hovey, Jacob, to Sally Stevens, Oct. 4, 1791.
Irvin, Simeon T., to Lucy A. Caswell, Nov. 20, 1869.
Johnson, Mathew H., to Hannah E. Sargent, of Springfield, Jan. 6, 1853.

Jones, Thomas, to Adeline Day, May 5, 1847.

Jessamine, George, to Mary Norris, both of Dorchester, 1834.

Jenness, Francis, to June Columbia, April 5, 1871.

Jackman, Joseph, of Landaff, to Esther Sawyer, of Dorchester, March 10, 1810.

Kimball, Archalus, to Lydia Clough, Oct. 4, 1824.

Kimball, Asa, to Hannah Barber, both of Grafton, Jan. 23, 1814.

Kimball, Phineas P., to Lucy Miller, Jan. 1, 1833.

Kimball, Samuel, to Nancy Whittier, of Enfield, Oct. 31, 1835.

Kinne, Elisha P., of Hanover, to Chloe Waterman, Oct. 22, 1817.

Kimball, John, to Almeda Hutchins, Sept. 1, 1875.

Kimball, Moses, to Nancy Kirk, of Alexandria, Feb. 1, 1866.

King, Nathaniel, of Craftsbury, Vt., to Sophia Kimball, April 9, 1818.

Kilton, George, of Grafton, to Mary A. Foss, of Grafton, Sept. 28, 1855.

Knight, George T., of Warren, to Arvilla A. Colby, of Haverhill, Dec. 18, 1864.

Kimball, Sylvester, of Wentworth, to Jennie L. Kimball, of Enfield, Oct. 12, 1870.

Knapp, Mason, of Sharon, Vt., to Helen M. Emory, of Orange, Sept. 6, 1866.

Kemp, Alvah J., of Dorchester, to Mary J. Clough, of Lyme, April 21, 1868.

Lathrop, Jason, of New York, to Susanna Judkins, of Danbury, Feb. 16, 1817.

Leavitt, Moses, to Joanna Reed, both of Grafton, March 5, 1799.

Lathrop, Harris G., to Mrs. Charlotte Hadley, Oct. 17, 1854.

Lovejoy, Isaac, of Hanover, to Mrs. Laura Hadley, Sept. 7, 1856.

Loverin, Moses, of Grafton, to Eliza E. Wright, of Hanover, Sept. 26, 1839.

Lowell, Elijah C., to Sarah Batchelder, both of Orange, Sept. 8, 1844.

Lawrence, Arthur J., of Nashua, to Augusta B. Johnson, Oct. 16, 1864.

Lowell, Allen G., to Vina L. Terrell, Sept. 20, 1879.

Langley, Orra H., to Ellen D. Fowler.

Lowell, Frank H., to Ellen F. Wier, Dec. 7, 1880.

Langworthy, George K. of Middlebury, Vt., to Arvilla K. Hubbard, Aug. 28, 1832.

Lary, Josiah, to Dolly Sanborn, of Dame's Gore, May 9, 1820.

Lock, David, Jr., of Epsom, to Polly Carlton, Nov. 29, 1819.

Marshall, John, of Bradford, to Mary Clark, Nov. 19, 1835.

Merrill, Enoch, of Warren, to Eliza Ann Currier, Feb. 1, 1843.

Morey, Lewis, to Dorothy P. Gould, March 18, 1818.

Murray, Samuel, to Betsey Flanders, Feb. 2, 1819.

Martin, Simeon, to Mehitable Sanborn, both of Dorchester, Dec. 31, 1816.

Martin, Levi, to Chloe Bullock, Oct. 8, 1817.

Mason, Philip, to Betsey Read, both of Grafton, March 16, 1797.

Martin, Perry, to Hannah Quimby, both of Grafton, Jan. 7, 1799.

MARRIAGES.

Morse, Moses, to Sally Eaton, March 8, 1823.
Mather, Ezekiel, to Sally Piper, both of Dorchester, May 17, 1826.
Merrill, Nathaniel, of Vermont, to Hannah Martin, March 8, 1820.
May, Joshua, to Emily Wheat, April 5, 1853.
May, Albert, to Susanna E. Morse, of Hanover, Nov. 24, 1853.
Martin, John, to Esther V. Williams, July 13, 1851.
Martin, Jonathan H., to Mary A. Richardson, both of Grafton, July 5, 1838.
Martin, James, Jr., to Martha Richardson, both of Grafton, Dec. 5, 1839.
Morse, John, to Hepsibah A. Philbrick, both of Enfield, Aug. 31, 1840.
Miner, Leonard N., to Helen N. Choate, of Enfield, Sept. 2, 1846.
Merrill, Levi, to Louisa Hall, Jan. 24, 1862.
Mitchell, Alonzo, to Rosette Abbott, March 21, 1864.
Morey, Jonathan, of Wilmot, to Mary E. Palmer, of Andover, Oct. 29, 1864.
Maigeux, Adolph, to Julia A. Colombe, April 30, 1864.
May, Obadiah, to Rozett Barnot, Jan. 2, 1867.
Mathews, Charles B., to Ella C. Fellows, of Groton, Sept. 7, 1868.
Morse, John W., of Vermont, to Julia A. Washburn, Oct. 26, 1869.
McGrath, John, to Augusta Westcott, both of Dorchester, Dec. 24, 1871.
Noyes, E. P., to Hannah Flagg, of Grafton, Dec. 31, 1857.
Nye, Willis C., of New London, to Mary E. Adams, June 30, 1875.
Nichols, Benjamin F., of Enfield, to Lydia Welch, June 19, 1834.
Norris, Joseph, of Dorchester, to Rachel Lawrence, Nov. 2, 1820.
Norris, Jacob, to Mary Richardson, of Dorchester, Oct. 3, 1802.
Paddleford, Asa, to Susan Decatur, both of Enfield, Sept., 1843.
Parks, Abel, of Hanover, to Sally May, Jan., 1844.
Pillsbury, John, of Danbury, to Sarah Gould, March 24, 1839.
Pollard, Benjamin N., to Sarah A. Temple, Dec. 18, 1864.
Pollard, John, to Mehitable Freeman, Sept. 14, 1821.
Pressey, Charles H., to Huldah G. Bartlett, Oct. 22, 1835.
Puffer, Daniel, to Chloe Barber, July 15, 1805.
Parker, Ebenezer, of Canterbury, to Emily M. Huntoon, of Orange, Jan. 13, 1842.
Pool, Samuel, of Haverhill, to Susan Heath, of Orange, Nov., 1843.
Phelps, Charles M., of Sutton, to Elida M. Cilley, of Orange, April 27, 1863.
Piper, Isaiah, of Gilmanton, to Sarah E. Kilburn, of Orange, March 8, 1866.
Philbrick, Cyrus H., to Harriet C. Cook, of Concord, Jan. 14, 1871.
Paul, Frank, to Mary D. Mahony, Aug. 10, 1872.
Parsons, Sherburne, of Grafton, to Nancy J. Whittier, of Orange, Jan. 17, 1874.
Purmort, Miner T., to Hannah C. Day, both of Enfield, Dec. 24, 1873.
Pattee, W. Fred, of Alexandria, to Hattie I. Gove, Sept. 4, 1875.
Piper, Samuel, to Clarissa Clark, both of Dorchester, Dec. 24, 1817.

Pierce, Earl, to Betsey DeMoranville, both of Grafton, March 12, 1801.
Pratt, Henry, to Eliza A. Hadley, June 8, 1851.
Palmer, Joseph D., of Bradford, to Clarissa G. Tyler, Nov. 20, 1851.
Plummer, Benjamin F., of Hanover, to Helen M. Daniels, Nov., 1851.
Parkhurst, Lucian C., of Vermont, to Harriet J. Butterfield, June 15, 1856.
Philbrick, David, of Hampton, to Betsey A. Edwards, of Enfield, Aug., 1837.
Philbrick, Porter K., of Wilmot, to Nancy M. Hoyt, of Enfield, Dec., 1837.
Pearley, Joseph G., to Abigail C. Clough, both of Enfield, May 27, 1838.
Putney, Joseph, of Wentworth, to Ann Davis, of Grafton, Jan. 11, 1838.
Pray, Oliver, of Orange, to Ruth G. Stevens, of Grafton, March 31, 1841.
Pettingill, Ephraim H., to Susan Dinsmore, Oct. 22, 1840.
Ray, John F., to Huldah A. Page, July 16, 1873.
Richardson, ———, to Susan Norris, Oct. 26, 1817.
Read, James P., to Elizabeth Wright, both of Grafton, Oct. 22, 1823.
Robinson, Amos, of Lebanon, to Lovinia Bullock, of Orange, Jan. 26, 1797.
Richardson, George A., of Vermont, to Orris J. Brooks, of Hanover, Nov. 1, 1854.
Robinson, Joseph C., to Mary Bradbury, both of Massachusetts, Oct. 19, 1856.
Rogers, Harrison, of Mansfield, Mass., to Nancy Hoyt, June 12, 1837.
Rush, Elijah H., of Vermont, to Mary A. Smith, of Rochester, Sept. 18, 1848.
Rowell, John B., of Plainfield, to Mary A. Currier, April 11, 1864.
Rogers, Charles H., of Enfield, to Sarah J. Riddle, of Grafton, Oct. 6, 1866.
Ranzer, Joseph W., of Vermont, to Julia Abbott, Aug. 6, 1870.
Roberts, Jonathan, of Rumney, to Nellie S. Doloff, of Dorchester, Dec. 26, 1871.
Rogers, Simeon R., to Mary A. Hardy, of Danbury, Aug. 14, 1875.
Randlett, Jacob, to Betsey Bradbury, Nov. 5.
Sargent, Aaron, of Grafton, to Mary I. Stevens, Oct. 21, 1846.
Sawyer, Joseph, to Elizabeth Richardson, March 18, 1798.
Shepard, Reuben F., to Amelia Kimball, Nov. 30, 1843.
Sherlock, William, to Sirene Martin, Jan., 1840.
Sherwell, Walter, to Betsey Danforth, both of Orange, Dec. 7, 1815.
Smith, Daniel L., to Sophronia Richardson, June 2, 1843.
Smith, Joseph D., to Mary Huse of Enfield, Nov., 1837.
Springer, Henry, to Patience Saunders, both of Grafton, Sept. 4, 1823.
Squire, Reuben, of Vermont, to Sally Slocum, Dec. 31, 1806.
Straw, Jacob, Jr., to Deliverance Bowen, of Lebanon, Oct. 23, 1825.
Sweat, John, to Hannah Lawrence, March 1, 1827.

MARRIAGES.

Sanders, William H., of Sanbornton, to Sally Reed, of Grafton, Sept. 30, 1832.

Sanborn, William C., to Susan Paddleford, of Enfield, Sept. 18, 1849.

Skinner, B. F., of Hillsborough, to Malvina E. Morse, of Enfield, Jan. 1, 1857.

Seavy, Andrew, to Angeline L. Pierce, both of Andover, May 9, 1855.

Sanborn, George W., to Laura A. Butman, June 6, 1855.

Sawyer, Peter, to Eliza A. Bridgeman, Dec. 14, 1854.

Stephens, Joshua, Jr., of Enfield, to Sally March, of Springfield, March 23, 1815.

Soomer, William, of Lebanon, to Polly Swett, of Hanover, July 28, 1816.

Smith, Enos, to Martha Silloway, both of Grafton, Feb. 12, 1824.

Stevens, Roland, to Hannah Clifford, both of Grafton, Aug. 15, 1802.

Shattuck, Nathan, to Sarah Briggs, both of Orange, March 14, 1822.

Sanborn, John, to Lydia Piper, both of Dorchester, July 7, 1822.

Sanborn, Edward, to Sally Martin, both of Dorchester, May 9, 1822.

Story, George, of Enfield, to Sarah W. Johnson, of Dorchester, Feb. 6, 1823.

Sanborn, Joseph S., to Ruth W. Johnson, both of Dorchester, Feb. 6, 1823.

Sanborn, Joshua, to Mary Sawyer, both of Dorchester, Aug. 24, 1826.

Sanborn, Ira, of Sandwich, to Betsey Sanborn, of Dame's Gore, Dec. 25, 1820.

Stevens, Joseph P., to Laura Sales, both of Grafton, Aug. 2, 1818.

Smith, Sylvanus, of Northampton, N. Y., to M. A. E. Columbe, Aug. 8, 1850.

Smith, E. W., to Nancy M. Hadley, of Manchester, Feb. 21, 1852.

Sweet, George L., to Mary Clough, of Groton, Nov. 16, 1852.

Smith, Rodney V., to Deborah Claflin, April 5, 1853.

Skinner, John, to Eliza Chesley, both of Enfield, May 8, 1854.

Sweat, Thomas, to Delia Woodward, both of Dorchester, Sept. 19, 1833.

Swasey, Benjamin K., to Mrs. Mary D. Sanborn, Dec., 1837.

Sanborn, Jasper S., of Springfield, to Patience Spooner, of Grafton, Nov. 5, 1837.

Smith, Warren, of Bradford, to Mary Stone, of Hanover, April 29, 1839.

Sleeper, Alfred, of Grafton, to Mary How, of Danbury, Oct. 17, 1839.

Stewart, Urie W., of Cambridge, Mass., to Elizabeth R. Page, of Manchester, Sept. 1, 1845.

Sanders, Oliver H., to Alice Allen, May 23, 1866.

Smith, George H., of Woodstock, Vt., to Angeline C. Varnum, Jan. 23, 1869.

Smith, David F., of Lyme, to Persis W. Chase, of Rhode Island, June 26, 1869.

Shaw, Livingston C., of Stoneham, Mass., to Rosa C. White, of Dorchester, Feb. 14, 1872.

Sleeper, Benjamin C., of Alexandria, to Mary Aldrich, Nov. 11, 1874.

Taber, Luther A., to Lydia W. Bullock, of Grafton, Oct. 22, 1844.

Thurston, Stephen, to Nancy Davis, March 15, 1818.

Tucker, Nathaniel, of Norwich, Vt., to Betsey Straw, Sept. 15, 1822.

Tucker, James, to Mehitable Keniston, Feb. 7, 1805.

Tucker, John, to Hannah Beedle, March 12, 1797.

Tyler, Job, to Mrs. Lydia Dustin, May 18, 1820.

Taylor, Samuel, to Lydia Pillsbury, both of Danbury, Feb. 28, 1814.

Thurston, Jesse, to Eliza Clark, Aug. 1, 1824.

Tucker, Daniel B., of Thornton, to Elizabeth Elliott, April 11, 1850.

Thompson, Caleb, of Lyme, to Elizabeth A. Wilmot, March 22, 1852.

Townsend, George B., to Frances M. Allard, Sept. 28, 1856.

Tenney, Gustavus, of Alexandria, to Pluma Pettingill, of Grafton, June 16, 1860.

Tibbetts, Charles H., to Sarah H. Thurston, of Gilmanton, Oct. 31, 1859.

True, Joseph G., to Dolly C. Chellis, both of Orange, Oct. 26, 1865.

Talbert, Frank, of Enfield, to Elnora Baker, of Royalton, Vt., June 4, 1867.

Towne, William H., to Mary M. Hiscock, Oct. 9, 1879.

Vimieux, Benjamin, of Massachusetts, to Olive Columbe, Jan. 1, 1865.

Waldo, Walter, to Rody Gove, July 17, 1809.

Whipple, Joseph, Jr., of Hebron, to Lydia Blaisdell, of Dorchester, Jan. 29, 1817.

Williams, Samuel, Jr., to Jane Bullock, both of Grafton, Jan. 26, 1797.

Williams, Oliver, to Jemima Barney, both of Grafton, Oct. 24, 1799.

Williams, William, to Hannah Merrill, both of Enfield, March 26, 1811.

Woodworth, George, of Dorchester, to Louisa Hovey, of Lyme, Aug. 14, 1825.

Wood, Amos, to Silva Sargent, both of Lebanon, Feb. 23, 1819.

Willis, Roswell O., to Lydia Stark, both of Hanover, June 24, 1819.

Whitmore, Daniel, to Marie Wells, Nov. 9, 1851.

Winslow, John, of Lyme, to Lydia E. Woodworth, of Dorchester, Aug. 17, 1853.

Wear, Joseph, of Andover, to Ann A. Calif, March 26, 1854.

Withington, Horace H., of Hanover, to Lydia A. Fellows, Oct. 29, 1857.

Washburn, Harvey, to Laurett Aldrich, Nov. 13, 1839.

Woods, Levi C., to Belinda D. Colby, Aug. 19, 1860.

Wood, George H., of Vermont, to Clara P. Follensbee, of Vermont, Oct. 12, 1864.

Webber, John D., to Mrs. Harriet A. Washburn, Nov. 4, 1865.

White, James T., of Vermont, to Lizzie H. Chandler, of Lyme, Nov. 20, 1865.

Washburn, Nahum, to Nancy Chandler, of Hanover, Oct. 5, 1841.

MARRIAGES.

Wentworth, Jacob, of Berwick, Me., to Zilpha L. Morrill, Jan. 12, 1846.
Wheat, Benjamin, of Dunstable, to Sarah Bullock, of Grafton, Jan. 18, 1816.
Whittlesey, John R., to Ann Whittier, March 28, 1836.
Wilson, Joseph, to Sarah Saunders, of Lebanon, Sept. 7, 1802.
Woodward, George B., of Manchester, to Mary J. Clark, Sept. 10, 1843.
York, Daniel, to Hannah Davis, Feb. 2, 1819.

APPENDIX.

APPENDIX.

Votes for Governor.

From 1784 to the formation of the Constitution in 1792 the chief executive of the state was called president. This town does not seem to have left a record of any votes before 1787. The absence of all records during that period may be accounted for, because Canaan probably did not know whether it was going to belong to Vermont or not.

The * shows which candidate was elected.

1787*John Langdon,		23.	1802*John T. Gilman,	87.
John Sullivan,		9.	John Langdon,	17.
1788*John Langdon,		21.	1803*John T. Gilman,	104.
John Sullivan,		1.	John Langdon,	30.
Josiah Bartlett,		7.	1804*John T. Gilman,	110.
1789*John Sullivan,		4.	John Langdon,	42.
John Pickering,		24.	William Tatton,	1.
1790 John Pickering,		14.	1805*John Langdon,	54.
*Josiah Bartlett,		3.	John T. Gilman,	104.
John Sullivan,		2.	1806*John Langdon,	46.
1791*Josiah Bartlett,		37.	Jeremiah Smith,	73.
1792*Josiah Bartlett,		53.	Joshua Richardson,	1.
1793*Josiah Bartlett,		35.	1807*John Langdon,	39.
John Langdon,		7.	Jeremiah Smith,	34.
1794*John T. Gilman,		53.	R. B. Clark,	11.
Beza Woodward,		3.	J. T. Gilman,	3.
1795			Daniel Blaisdell,	3.
1796*John T. Gilman,		42.	1808*John Langdon,	51.
Timothy Walker,		10.	Jeremiah Smith,	49.
1797*John T. Gilman,		47.	John Currier,	5.
1798*John T. Gilman,		18.	R. B. Clark,	5.
Oliver Peabody,		34.	Oliver Peabody,	4.
1799			1809*Jeremiah Smith,	145.
1800*John T. Gilman,		57.	John Langdon,	47.
Timothy Walker,		12.	1810*John Langdon,	42.
Oliver Peabody,		1.	Jeremiah Smith,	140.

1811*John Langdon,	53.	Isaac Hill,	5.
Jeremiah Smith,	123.	Scattering,	11.
Caleb Ellis,	1.	1828*John Bell,	180.
1812*William Plumer,	46.	Benjamin Pierce,	45.
John T. Gilman,	145.	1829*Benjamin Pierce,	77.
1813*John T. Gilman,	134.	John Bell,	156.
William Plumer,	37.	1830*Mathew Harvey,	77.
1814*John T. Gilman,	157.	Timothy Upham,	162.
William Plumer,	49.	Joseph Dustin,	1.
1815*John T. Gilman,	147.	1831*Samuel Dinsmore,	87.
William Plumer,	43.	Ichabod Bartlett,	144.
Daniel L. Morris,	1.	1832*Samuel Dinsmore,	112.
1816*William Plumer,	42.	Ichabod Bartlett,	114.
James Sheaf,	143.	Arthur Livermore,	25.
1817*William Plumer,	34.	1833*Samuel Dinsmore,	134.
James Sheaf,	128.	Arthur Livermore,	54.
Josiah Bartlett,	4.	1834*William Badger,	120.
1818*William Plumer,	42.	Scattering,	2.
Jeremiah Mason,	124.	1835*William Badger,	146.
1819*Samuel Bell,	41.	Joseph Healey,	99.
William Hale,	93.	1836*Isaac Hill,	173.
1820*Samuel Bell,	104.	Scattering,	5.
William Hale,	11.	1837*Isaac Hill,	213.
Scattering,	7.	Thomas Flanders,	1.
1821*Samuel Bell,	75.	1838*Isaac Hill,	158.
Scattering,	16.	James Wilson,	148.
1822*No vote.		1839*John Page,	196.
1823*Levi Woodbury,	105.	James Wilson,	115.
Samuel Dinsmore,	43.	1840*John Page,	189.
1824*David L. Morrill,	59.	Enos Stevens,	115.
Jeremiah Smith,	87.	1841*John Page,	187.
Scattering,	7.	Enos Stevens,	141.
1825*David L. Morrill,	173.	1842*Henry Hubbard,	154.
Jacob Blaisdell,	1.	Enos Stevens,	52.
1826*David L. Morrill,	127.	John H. White,	16.
Benjamin Pierce,	31.	Daniel Hoit,	19.
Scattering,	15.	Amos Miner,	2.
1827*Benjamin Pierce,	115.	1843*Henry Hubbard,	133.

APPENDIX. 671

Anthony Colby,	56.	James Bell,	22.
John H. White,	47.	Asa Fowler,	4.
Daniel Hoit,	35.	Nathaniel M. Baker,	139.
1844*John H. Steele,	89.	1856*Ralph Metcalf,	206.
Daniel Hoit,	124.	John S. Wells,	196.
John H. White,	61.	Ichabod Goodwin,	11.
Anthony Colby,	36.	1857*William Hale,	232.
Henry Hubbard,	1.	John S. Wells,	181.
1845*John H. Steele,	90.	1858*William Hale,	235.
Daniel Hoit,	106.	Asa P. Cate,	168.
Anthony Colby,	96.	1859*Ichabod Goodwin,	229.
1846*Anthony Colby,	85.	Asa P. Cate,	211.
Nathaniel S. Berry,	83.	1860*Ichabod Goodwin,	273.
Jared W. Williams,	132.	Asa P. Cate,	167.
1847*Jared W. Williams,	143.	1861*Nathaniel S. Berry,	226.
Anthony Colby,	120.	George Stark,	153.
Nathaniel S. Berry,	86.	Levi Bartlett,	2.
1848*Jared W. Williams,	168.	1862*Nathaniel S. Berry,	193.
Nathaniel S. Berry,	205.	George Stark,	159.
1849*Samuel Dinsmore,	156.	Paul S. Wheeler,	16.
Levi Chamberlin,	102.	1863*Joseph A. Gilmore,	117.
Nathaniel S. Berry,	62.	Ira Eastman,	191.
1850*Samuel Dinsmore,	164.	Walter Harriman,	75.
Levi Chamberlin,	102.	1864*Joseph A. Gilmore,	209.
Nathaniel S. Berry,	64.	Edward W. Harring-	
1851*Samuel Dinsmore,	137.	ton,	186.
Thomas E. Sawyer,	112.	Onslow Stearns,	1.
John Atwood,	74.	1865*Frederick Smith,	203.
1852*Noah Martin,	189.	Edward W. Harring-	
Thomas E. Sawyer,	84.	ton,	154.
John Atwood,	72.	1866*Frederick Smyth,	208.
1853*Noah Martin,	193.	John G. Sinclair,	143.
James Bell,	67.	1867*Walter Harriman,	197.
John H. White,	44.	John G. Sinclair,	202.
1854*Nathaniel M. Baker,	195.	1868*Walter Harriman,	253.
James Bell,	72.	John G. Sinclair,	228.
Jared Perkins,	54.	1869*Onslow Stearns,	194.
1855*Ralph Metcalf,	202.	John Bedell,	229.

1870*Onslow Stearns,	207.	John M. Hill,	164.
John Bedell,	228.	1887*Charles H. Sawyer,	157.
Scattering,	16.	Thomas Cogswell,	146.
1871*James A. Weston,	235.	1889*David A. Goodell,	186.
James Pike,	202.	Charles H. Amsden,	202.
1872 James A. Weston,	240.	1891*Hiram A. Tuttle,	156.
*Ezekiel A. Straw,	207.	Joseph M. Fletcher,	5.
1873*Ezekiel A. Straw,	167.	Charles H. Amsden,	206.
James A. Weston,	219.	1893*John B. Smith,	148.
1874*James A. Weston,	215.	Luther McKinney,	156.
Luther McCutchins,	155.	1895*Charles A. Busiel,	173.
1875*Person C. Cheney,	204.	Henry O. Kent,	120.
Hiram A. Roberts,	204.	1897*George A. Ramsdell,	171.
Scattering,	3.	Henry O. Kent,	89.
1876*Person C. Cheney.	272.	1899*Frank A. Rollins,	223.
Daniel Marcy,	202.	Charles F. Stone,	123.
1877*Benjamin F. Prescott,	238.	1901*Chester B. Jordan,	225.
Daniel Marcy,	175.	Frank E. Potter,	130.
1878*Benjamin F. Prescott,	242.	Scattering,	4.
		1903*N. J. Bachelder,	203.
Frank A. McKean,	188.	H. F. Hollis,	101.
1879*Natt Head,	235.	1905*John McLane,	204.
Frank A. McKean,	165.	H. F. Hollis,	94.
1881*Charles H. Bell,	222.	1907*Charles M. Floyd,	194.
Frank Jones,	240.	N. C. Jameson,	73.
1883*Samuel W. Hale,	225.	Scattering,	8.
M. V. B. Edgerly,	200.	1909*Henry B. Quinby,	240.
1885*Moody Currier,	196	C. E. Carr,	153.
		Scattering,	5.

REPRESENTATIVES.

1774–76 None, embraced Lebanon, Hanover, Relhan, Canaan, Grafton, Cardigan.
1777 None, embraced Hanover, Canaan, Cardigan.
1783 ———, embraced Relhan, Canaan, Cardigan, Dorchester, Grafton.
1784 William Ayer, embraced Enfield, Canaan, Cardigan, Dorchester, Grafton.

APPENDIX.   673

1785	Ebeneazer Hoyt, embraced Enfield, Canaan, Cardigan, Dorchester, Grafton.		
1786	Jesse Johnson, embraced Enfield, Canaan, Cardigan, Dorchester, Grafton.		
1787	Jesse Johnson, embraced Enfield, Canaan, Cardigan, Dorchester, Grafton.		
1788	None.		
1789	Jesse Johnson, embraced Enfield, Canaan, Cardigan, Dorchester, Grafton.		
1790	Ebeneazer Hoyt, embraced Enfield, Canaan, Cardigan, Dorchester Grafton.		
1791	Ebeneazer Hoyt, embraced Enfield, Canaan, Cardigan, Dorchester, Grafton.		
1792	William Richardson, embraced Enfield, Canaan, Cardigan, Dorchester, Grafton.		
1793	Daniel Blaisdell, embraced Canaan, Grafton, Orange.		
1794	John Burdick, embraced Canaan, Grafton, Orange.		
1795–99	Daniel Blaisdell, embraced Canaan, Grafton, Orange.		
1800–07	Ebeneazer Clark, embraced Canaan.		
1808–09	Moses Dole.	Eleazer Martin,	1.
1810–11	John Currier.	1838 James Arvin,	148.
1812–13	Daniel Blaisdell.	March Barber,	133.
1814–16	Thomas H. Pettingill.	W. P. Weeks,	9.
1817	John Currier.	J. L. Richardson,	1.
1818–20	Moses Dole.	1839 W. P. Weeks,	193.
1821	John H. Harris.	R. B. Clark,	98.
1822	None.	Dunham,	1.
1823	John H. Harris.	1840 W. P. Weeks,	182.
1824–25	Daniel Blaisdell.	March Barber,	98.
1826	Elijah Blaisdell.	Josiah Haynes,	1.
1827–28	James Wallace.	R. B. Clark,	1.
1829–30	Nathaniel Currier.	1841 Caleb Blodgett,	182.
1831–32	Josiah Clark, Jr.	March Barber,	134.
1833–34	George Walworth.	Chamb'n Packard,	2.
1835–36	J. L. Richardson.	1842 Caleb Blodgett,	155.
1837	James Arvin, 140.	John Sweat,	51.
	William P. Weeks, 110.	John B. Towle,	9.
	John Shepard, 8.	1843 James Arvin,	141.

43

	W. E. Eastman,	86.		No Representative.	
	H. C. George,	15.	1850	Allen Hayes,	106.
	Jonathan Kittredge,	13.		W. P. Weeks,	144.
	James Eastman,	3.		Caleb Dustin,	60.
	John H. Harris,	3.		Scattering,	6.
	Jonathan Swan,	1.		No choice.	
	Caleb Blodgett,	1.		No Representative sent.	
1844	Liba Conant,	169.	1851	Jonathan Kittredge,	170.
	William Martin,	105.	(1)	Peter S. Wells,	132.
	Jonathan Kittredge,	1.		Ara Wheat,	5.
1845	No. of ballots.				
	No Rep. sent.			Ara Wheat,	146.
1846	Jonathan Kittredge,	126.	(2)	Peter S. Wells,	95.
	Chamb'n Packard,	97.		Scattering,	3.
	W. W. George,	57.	1852	W. P. Weeks,	197.
	J. E. Sargent,	5.	(1)	Jonathan Kittredge,	129.
	Scattering,	6.		Elzina Wheat,	2.
	Next morning.			Scattering,	3.
	Jonathan Kittredge,	128.			
	Chamb'n Packard,	62.		J. B. Wallace,	172.
	W. W. George,	8.	(2)	Ara Wheat,	84.
	Scattering,	7.		Scattering,	15.
1847	Jonathan Kittredge,	201.	1853	W. P. Weeks,	184.
(1)	Eleazer Martin,	122.	(1)	Allen Hayes,	94.
	Nathaniel Currier,	1.		Scattering,	8.
(2)	W. W. George,	158.			
	J. E. Sargent,	116.		Peter S. Wells,	149.
	Scattering,	34.	(2)	Charles Barney,	55.
1848	Jonathan Kittredge,	182.		Scattering,	5.
	Eleazer Martin,	145.	1854	W. P. Weeks,	180.
	W. W. George,	5.	(1)	Jonathan Kittredge,	75.
	Scattering,	3.		Caleb Dustin,	45.
1849	Eleazer Martin,	141.			
	J. B. Wallace,	100.		Peter S. Wells,	152.
	Job C. Tyler,	53.	(2)	Eleazer Barney,	56.
	Jonathan Kittredge,	6.		Nathan Jones,	53.
	Scattering,	9.	1855	Jonathan Kittredge,	224.
	Seven ballots.		(1)	Jesse Martin,	138.
	No choice.				

APPENDIX.

	Wyman Pattee,	206.
(2)	S. B. Morgan,	125.
1856	Wyman Pattee,	215.
(1)	W. P. Weeks,	191.
	Eleazer Barney,	210.
(2)	Jesse Martin,	181.
	Nathan Jones,	4.
1857	Eleazer Barney,	213.
(1)	W. P. Weeks,	170.
	Scattering,	4.
	Nathan Jones,	208.
(2)	L. C. Pattee,	158.
	Scattering,	1.
1859	James H. Kelley,	226.
(1)	Franklin P. Swett,	206.
	William Doten,	220.
(2)	Hazen K. Farnum,	218.
	Scattering,	5.
	Next day.	
(2)	Hazen K. Farnum,	228.
	William Doten,	225.
	Scattering,	1.
1860	Horace S. Currier,	271.
(1)	Franklin P. Swett,	166.
(2)	William L. Harris,	270.
	William Doten,	163.
	Scattering,	2.
1861	George W. Murray,	222.
(1)	William Doten,	141.
	Scattering,	4.
(2)	Charles Day,	223.
	Arnold Morgan,	144.
	Scattering,	3.
1862	George W. Murray,	175.

(1)	Lewis C. Pattee,	119.
	Harry Follensbee,	77.
	George Harris,	1.
(2)	George Harris,	184.
	Arnold Morgan,	127.
	C. S. Putnam,	66.
	Joseph Dustin,	1.
	Second vote.	
(1)	Harry Follensbee,	199.
	George W. Murray,	192.
	Scattering,	7.
(2)	George Harris,	199.
	Arnold Morgan,	194.
	Scattering,	7.
	No Representative.	
1863	Lewis C. Pattee,	199.
(1)	Harry Follensbee,	184.
	Arnold Morgan,	194.
(2)	Caleb S. Bartlett,	184.
	Scattering,	2.
1864	Harry Follensbee,	210.
(1)	Lewis C. Pattee,	190.
	Scattering,	1.
(2)	Caleb S. Bartlett,	210.
	Arnold Morgan,	190.
1865	Frank Currier,	198.
(1)	Frank P. Swett,	141.
	Scattering,	3.
(2)	William G. Somers,	203.
	Augustus Shepard,	138.
	Scattering,	3.
1866	William W. George,	205.
(1)	Stephen Peaslee,	141.
(2)	George W. Murray,	212.

	George Hinkson,	101.	1873	Otis J. Story,	152.
	Scattering.	6.		Benjamin Norris,	221.
1867	Jonathan Barnard,	180.		W. L. Harris,	151.
(1)	William W. George,	142.		G. W. Davis,	210.
	N. P. Taplin,	27.	1874	Frank Currier,	163.
	S. R. Swett,	20.		G. W. Davis,	214.
	James C. Felch,	18.		William Hall,	160.
				Thomas Sanborn,	221.
(2)	Stephen Peaslee,	205.	1875	Thomas Sanborn,	188.
	George W. Murray,	129.		W. B. Richardson,	212.
	Scattering.	26.		Henry McGrath,	196.
	Second ballot for first.			H. S. Dow,	205.
	Jonathan Barnard,	174.	1876	W. B. Richardson,	273.
	N. P. Taplin,	59.		Albert H. Wilson,	198.
	W. W. George,	33.		Stephen Peaslee,	194.
	Scattering.	59.		H. S. Dow,	267.
1868	Caleb Dustin.	250.	1877	O. L. Rand,	166.
(1)	Stephen Peaslee,	231.		A. E. Barney,	235.
				Levi F. Webster,	164.
(2)	John Q. Perley,	247.		Allen H. George,	229.
	James C. Felch,	231.	1878	C. H. Tower,	161.
1869	James C. Felch,	224.		A. E. Barney,	256.
(1)	Horatio Gates,	205.		O. L. Rand.	166.
				L. S. Welch.	252.
(2)	Joseph D. Weeks,	220.			
	John W. Richardson,	204.	Bien.	J. D. Weeks,	174.
				L. S. Welch,	220.
1870	Hiram Barber,	196.		Charles Davis,	158.
	L. C. Follensbee,	194.		F. D. Currier,	238.
	J. D. Weeks,	241.	1880	F. D. Currier,	220.
	Elijah Smith,	238.		Warren F. Wilson,	239.
1871	Elijah Smith,	242.		Charles Day,	201.
	Nathan Willis,	187.		J. D. Weeks,	252.
	Stephen Peaslee,	243.	1882	J. D. Weeks,	203.
	M. H. Milton.	179.	No.	S. D. Smith,	210.
1872	Stephen Peaslee,	241.	1884	Guilford Doten,	144.
	Otis J. Story,	209.		S. R. Swett,	187.
	Benjamin Norris,	238.	1886	George W. Story,	130.
	W. L. Harris,	210.		L. S. Davis,	154.

APPENDIX.   677

1888	Warren E. Wilson,	169.		F. D. Currier,	232.
	George W. Story,	207.	1900	C. O. Barney,	228.
1890	A. M. Shackford,	137.		O. L. Rand,	131.
	H. J. Goss,	205.	1902	Daniel Goss,	89.
1892	G. H. Lathrop,	132.		H. B. Gates,	210.
	G. H. Gordon,	177.	1904	F. A. Bogardus,	108.
1894	H. A. Gilman,	126.		S. R. Smith,	184.
	G. H. Gordon,	187.	1906	C. M. Murray,	278.
1896	F. A. Doten,	105.		H. P. Burleigh,	71.
	R. R. Smith,	210.	1908	J. B. Wallace,	222.
1898	A. W. Hutchinson,	117.		E. M. Allen,	177.

SELECTMEN.

1770 John Scofield, Joseph Craw, Samuel Benedict (Assessors).
1771 John Scofield, Joseph Craw, Samuel Benedict (Assessors).
1772 Ebenezer Eames, Joseph Craw, Samuel Benedict.
1773 Asa Kilburn, Ebenezer Eames, Joseph Craw.
1774 Asa Kilburn, Joseph Craw, Charles Walworth.
1775 Asa Kilburn, Ebenezer Eames, ———.
1776 Asa Kilburn, Ebenezer Eames, Samuel Jones.
1777 Ebenezer Eames, Richard Clark, 3d, Samuel Jones.
1778 ———
1779 ———
1780 ———
1781 George Harris, Thomas Baldwin.
1782 ———
1783 William Ayer, William Richardson.
1784 ———
1785 William Richardson, George Harris.
1786 William Richardson, Caleb Welch, Eleazer Scofield.
1787 William Richardson, William Ayer, Ezekiel Wells.
1788 Samuel Jones, William Richardson, Samuel Noyes.
1789 John Worth, William Richardson, Samuel Jones.
1790 John Worth, Samuel Jones, William Richardson.
1791 John Worth, William Richardson, Dudley Gilman.
1792 Dudley Gilman, Thomas Miner, John Harris.
1793 Richard Whittier, Thomas Miner, John Harris.
1794 John Harris, William Richardson, Joshua Harris.

1795 Samuel Jones, John Worth, Richard Whittier.
1796 Ezekiel Wells, Daniel Farnum, Richard Whittier.
1797 Ezekiel Wells, William Richardson, Daniel Farnum.
1798 William Richardson, Ezekiel Wells, Daniel Farnum.
1799 Richard Whittier, Gideon Morse, John Currier.
1800 Gideon Morse, John Currier, Ebenezer Clark.
1801 Gideon Morse, John Currier, Ebenezer Clark.
1802 Gideon Morse, John Currier, Ebenezer Clark.
1803 John Currier, Ebenezer Clark, William Richardson.
1804 Ebenezer Clark, James Morse, Moses Dole.
1805 Ebenezer Clark, James Morse, John Currier.
1806 James Morse, Levi Bailey, John M. Barber.
1807 John Currier, Hubbard Harris, Amos Gould.
1808 John Currier, Hubbard Harris, Amos Gould.
1809 John Currier, Hubbard Harris, Amos Gould.
1810 John Currier, Hubbard Harris, Joseph Bartlett.
1811 John Currier, Hubbard Harris, Caleb Seabury.
1812 John Currier, Hubbard Harris, Caleb Seabury.
1813 Daniel Blaisdell, Daniel Pattee, Clark Currier.
1814 Daniel Blaisdell, Daniel Pattee, Nathaniel Bartlett.
1815 Daniel Blaisdell, Daniel Pattee, Nathaniel Bartlett.
1816 Daniel Pattee, John Currier, Elias Porter.
1817 Daniel Pattee, John Currier, Elias Porter.
1818 Daniel Blaisdell, Elias Porter, John H. Harris.
1819 Daniel Pattee, John Currier, John H. Harris.
1820 John H. Harris, George Walworth, Jacob Richardson.
1821 John H. Harris, George Walworth, Jacob Richardson.
1822 Elijah Blaisdell, Nathaniel Currier, James Wallace.
1823 John H. Harris, John Currier, Richard Clark, 3d.
1824 Elijah Blaisdell, James Wallace, Nathaniel Currier.
1825 Elijah Blaisdell, James Wallace, Nathaniel Currier.
1826 James Wallace, Nathaniel Currier, William Martin.
1827 William Martin, Ebenezer Clark, Benjamin Haynes.
1828 Elijah Blaisdell, John H. Harris, Joshua Wells.
1829 James Wallace, Daniel Pattee, March Barber.
1830 James Wallace, Daniel Pattee, March Barber.
1831 Elijah Blaisdell, John Shepard, William Martin.
1832 Elijah Blaisdell, John Shepard, Joseph L. Richardson.

APPENDIX. 679

1833 Joseph L. Richardson, George Walworth, William Campbell.
1834 Joseph L. Richardson, George Walworth, William Campbell.
1835 James Arvin, William Martin, Sylvanus B. Morgan.
1836 James Arvin, William Martin, Sylvanus B. Morgan.
1837 Joseph L. Richardson, March Barber, Daniel Campbell.
1838 Joseph L. Richardson, Daniel Campbell, Caleb Blodgett.
1839 Joseph L. Richardson, Daniel Campbell, Caleb Blodgett.
1840 Caleb Blodgett, James Eastman, Chamberlain Packard, Jr.
1841 Caleb Blodgett, Chamberlain Packard, Jr., Daniel Pattee, Jr.
1842 Daniel Pattee, Jr., James Arvin, Peter Wells.
1843 Daniel Pattee, Jr., Peter Wells, William W. George.
1844 William W. George, Peter Wells, Joseph Dustin.
1845 William W. George, Joseph Dustin, James Arvin.
1846 William W. George, Joseph Dustin, Samuel Williams.
1847 Joseph Dustin, Nathaniel Currier, Nathaniel Shepard.
1848 Nathaniel Currier, Nathaniel Shepard, Caleb Dustin.
1849 Caleb Blodgett, Daniel Pattee, Jr., John H. Swett.
1850 Eleazer Martin, Peter S. Wells, William Doten.
1851 Jonathan Kittredge, Moses G. Kelley, Samuel Williams.
1852 Peter S. Wells, March Barber, Chamberlain Packard, Jr.
1853 March Barber, James Pattee, Benjamin Y. Hilliard.
1854 March Barber, James Pattee, Benjamin Y. Hilliard.
1855 William W. George, Hazen K. Farnum, John S. Shepard.
1856 William W. George, John S. Shepard, Roswell Elliott.
1857 Roswell Elliott, Augustus C. Lovejoy, Horatio Gates.
1858 William W. George, Roswell Elliott, Horatio Gates.
1859 Eleazer Barney, Charles Day, William G. Somers.
1860 Eleazer Barney, Charles Day, William G. Somers.
1861 William G. Somers, Henry C. George, Stephen Morse.
1862 Franklin P. Swett, Henry H. Wilson, Job S. Davis.
1863 Franklin P. Swett, Henry H. Wilson, Job S. Davis.
1864 John S. Shepard, John M. Barber, Job S. Davis.
1865 Eleazer Barney, Franklin P. Swett, William W. George.
1866 Eleazer Barney, William W. George, Isaac Davis.
1867 Peter S. Wells, Benjamin Norris, John W. Currier.

1868 Isaac Davis, Elijah C. Flanders, Moses E. Currier.
1869 Henry H. Wilson, Charles Davis, Levi F. Webster.
1870 Henry H. Wilson, Charles Davis, Levi F. Webster.
1871 Henry H. Wilson, Charles Davis, Levi F. Webster.
1872 Henry H. Wilson, Charles Davis, Levi F. Webster.
1873 Henry H. Wilson, Ephraim F. Wilson, Daniel H. Campbell.
1874 Henry H. Wilson, Ephraim F. Wilson, Daniel H. Campbell.
1875 Eleazer Barney, Otis J. Story, Moses T. Colby.
1876 Eleazer Barney, Otis J. Story, Moses T. Colby.
1877 Isaac Davis, Moses T. Colby, John Currier.
1878 Isaac Davis, Moses T. Colby, John Currier.
1879 Isaac Davis, Nathan C. Morgan, John Currier.
1880 Isaac Davis, Albert H. Wilson, James H. Kelley.
1881 Isaac Davis, Albert H. Wilson, Lewis C. Follensbee.
1882 Isaac Davis, Hollis B. Whitney, Lewis C. Follensbee.
1883 Isaac Davis, Hollis B. Whitney, George W. Hazeltine.
1884 Henry H. Wilson, Isaac Davis, Harris J. Goss.
1885 Henry H. Wilson, Isaac Davis, George W. Hazeltine.
1886 Henry H. Wilson, John Currier, George W. Hazeltine.
1887 John D. Loverin, Milan E. Davis, Guilford Doten.
1888 Leroy S. Davis, John D. Loverin, Alvin Davis.
1889 Leroy S. Davis, Oscar L. Rand, Daniel Goss, Jr.
1890 Leroy S. Davis, Oscar L. Rand, Daniel Goss, Jr.
1891 Leroy S. Davis, Harris J. Goss, Charles W. Dwinels.
1892 Henry H. Wilson, John Currier, Warren E. Wilson.
1893 Warren E. Wilson, Daniel W. Campbell, Eugene Shepard.
1894 John Currier, Eugene Shepard, Arthur A. Austin.
1895 John Currier, Eugene Shepard, Arthur A. Austin.
1896 John Currier, Eugene Shepard, Arthur A. Austin.
1897 John Currier, Claude M. Murray, Horatio B. Gates.
1898 John Currier, Claude M. Murray, Horatio B. Gates.
1899 John Currier, Claude M. Murray, Horatio B. Gates.
1900 John Currier, Albert L. Hadley, Will A. Hoit.
1901 John Currier, Will A. Hoit, William Hall.
1902 John Currier, Will A. Hoit, Frank B. Smart.
1903 John Currier, Will A. Hoit, Frank B. Smart.

APPENDIX.

1904 John Currier, Horace G. Robie, Frank B. Smart.
1905 John Currier, Frank B. Smart, Erwin M. Adams.
1906 John Currier, Frank B. Smart, Erwin M. Adams.
1907 John Currier, Frank B. Smart, Erwin M. Adams.
1908 John Currier, Erwin M. Adams, Arthur E. Mooney.
1909 Frank B. Smart, Eugene A. Shepard, Horace G. Robie.
1910 Frank B. Smart, Eugene A. Shepard, Horace S. Robie.

MODERATORS.

1770–72	John Scofield.	1802	William Richardson.
1773–76	Asa Kilburn.	1803–05	Ezekiel Wells.
1777	John Scofield.	1806	Joshua Richardson.
1778–85	No records.	1807	Simeon Arvin.
1786	Samuel Jones, Caleb Welch, George Harris.	1808–09	Daniel Blaisdell.
		1810–11	William Richardson.
		1812	Daniel Blaisdell.
1787	Richard Clark.	1813–20	Thomas H. Pettingill.
1788–90	Samuel Jones.	1821	Elijah Blaisdell.
1791	William Ayer.	1822	Daniel Blaisdell.
1792	William Richardson, Thomas Miner, John Burdick, Samuel Jones, Dudley Gilman.	1823	Abraham Pushee.
		1824	Daniel Blaisdell.
		1825	William Atherton.
		1826	Daniel Blaisdell.
		1827–28	Elijah Blaisdell.
1793	Samuel Jones, John Burdick, Thomas Miner.	1829	Jacob Trussell.
		1830	Daniel Blaisdell.
		1831	Jonas W. Smith.
1794	William Richardson, Samuel Jones.	1832–34	Elijah Blaisdell.
		1835–36	Caleb Blodgett.
1795	Samuel Jones, Ezekiel Wells.	1837	Joseph L. Richardson.
		1838–42	William P. Weeks.
1796–97	Ezekiel Wells, William Richardson.	1843	Caleb Blodgett.
		1844–45	Jonathan Kittredge.
1798	Ezekiel Wells.	1846	William P. Weeks.
1799	Thomas Miner, Joshua Harris, Ezekiel Wells.	1847–48	Jonathan Kittredge.
		1849–50	William P. Weeks.
		1851	Jonathan Kittredge.
1800–01	Ezekiel Wells.	1852–54	William P. Weeks.

1855-56 Jonathan Kittredge.
1857 Wyman Pattee.
1858 Jonathan Kittredge.
1859-60 James P. Barber.
1861 George W. Murray.
1862-63 Isaac N. Blodgett.
1864-66 George W. Murray.
1867 Isaac N. Blodgett.
1868 James P. Barber.
1869 William P. Weeks.
1870-75 Henry H. Wilson.
1876-79 Albert E. Barney.
1880 S. R. Swett, Bien. Henry H. Wilson.
1881-82 Henry H. Wilson.
1883 Joseph D. Weeks.
1884-86 Henry H. Wilson, Bien. F. D. Currier.
1887 Henry H. Wilson.
1888-96 Frank D. Currier.
1897 S. R. Swett.
1898-1910 Frank D. Currier.

Town Clerks.

1770-72 Samuel Benedict.
1773-76 Caleb Welch.
1777-85 Thomas Baldwin.
1786-88 David Fogg.
1789-90 John Worth.
1791 David Dustin.
1792-96 Oliver Smith.
1797 Caleb Pierce.
1798-1800 Oliver Smith.
1801-06 Moses Dole.
1807 Jacob Trussell.
1808-17 Moses Dole.
1818-24 Daniel Hovey.
1825-33 Timothy Tilton.
1834-36 James Arvin.
1837-38 Eleazer Martin.
1839-45 James Arvin.
1846-51 James B. Wallace.
1852-54 Jesse Martin.
1855 James H. Davis.
1856-57 Mathew H. Milton.
1858-59 C. S. Putnam.
1860-62 John M. Barber.
1863 David Barnard.
1864-66 William A. Wallace.
1867 Charles Barney.
1868 Albert E. Barney.
1869-74 Charles Barney.
1875-83 Alfred M. Shackford.
1884-85 Warren E. Hoit.
1886-87 Willie A. Tucker.
1888-94 George H. Gordon.
1895 Charles H. Tower.
1896-1910 George H. Gordon.

CENSUS OF 1790.

	Free white males of 16 yrs. upward including heads of families.	Free white males under 16 yrs.	Free white females including heads of families.
Ayer, William	2	3	3
Barber, Joseph	1		
Barber, Robert	4	2	4
Bartlett, Josiah H.	1	2	2
Bartlett, Nathaniel	1	1	4
Bean, John	1	1	1
Blasdall, Daniel	1	4	1
Blasdall, Parot	2	1	4
Blood, Enock	1		
Baldwin, Thomas	1	1	5
Booth, Isaiah	1	2	2
Bradbury, William	1		2
Brdshaw, Joshua	1	4	4
Clark, Caleb	1		2
Clark, Currier	2	1	1
Clark, Josha	1		1
Clark, Richard	2	1	4
Clark, Richard, Jr.	1		1
Colby, Daniel	1	3	3
Colkins, John P.	1	4	4
Currier, John	1	1	4
Cushing, Joshua	1	1	2
Duglas, William	1	5	2
Dustin, Daniel	1	1	1
Dustin, Jonathan	4		3
Dustin, Jonathan, Jr.	1	1	1
Eastman, Stephen	1	1	2
Finch, Henry	2	1	3
Flint, Joseph	4	4	6
Falsom, Joseph	1		
Fulsom, Josiah	4		1

	Free white males of 16 yrs. upward including heads of families.	Free white males under 16 yrs.	Free white females including heads of families.
Fulsom, Samuel	1	3	3
Gates, Rowland	1	2	1
Gardner, Ezekiel	1	1	3
Gilman, Dudley	1	2	4
Hadley, Abel	1	2	2
Hadley, Simon	1		1
Harris, Benjamin	1		
Harris, George	4	1	3
Harris, George, Jr.	1		
Harris, John	1	2	3
Heath, Samuel	1		4
Hovey, Jacob	1		
Jones, David	2	1	6
Jones, Jehue	1	4	5
Jones, Samuel	2	1	2
Kimball, Asa	1	2	3
Kenester, Francis	1	1	1
Lathrop, Elias	1		
Lathrop, Thaddeus	1	3	2
Michanm, Samuel	4	4	5
Miller, Jonathan	2		4
Minor, Thomas	3	2	5
Morse, Daniel	1	1	1
Nichols, Ezra	1		1
Norris, Eliphlet	1	3	3
Noys, Samuel	1		1
Otis, Richard	3	2	3
Paddleford, Asa	1		3
Richardson, Enock	2	3	2
Richardson, William	2	2	3
Roynalds, Hezekiah	1	3	1
Samburn, Moses	1		8
Sawyer, Benjamin	3	2	4

APPENDIX. 685

	Free white males of 16 yrs. upward including heads of families.	Free white males under 16 yrs.	Free white females including heads of families.
Scofield, Eleazer	2	2	3
Scofield, John	2	3	5
Sergeant, Samuel	1	3	3
Smith, Jabez	1		
Smith, Oliver	1		3
Smith, William	1		2
Springer, Henry	1	2	4
Stevans, Amos	2	1	3
Sticknor, Jonathan	1		1
Stoddard, Clemont	1		2
Webster, William	1	1	3
Welch, Caleb	4	4	4
Wells, Ezekel	2	2	4
Welch, Samuel	2	2	3
Wells, Ashel	2	2	2
Wells, Ezekiel	2	2	4
Wells, Joshua	2	2	4
Weeker, Nathaniel	2	1	2
Wheeker, Richard	2		
Wilson, Warren	1	1	2
Woodbury, James	1	1	2
Worth, John	3	3	3
Worth, Nathaniel	1		3
Total, 476.	134	126	216

First Inventory on Records, 1782-86.

1782

John Scofield.
Ebenezer Eames.
George Harris.
Joseph Flint.
Caleb Welch.
William Ayer.
Samuel Jones.
Richard Clark.
Robert Barber.
Elijah Lathrop.
Thadeus Lathrop.

Jonathan Stickney.
Richard Otis.
Thomas Baldwin.
Jehu Jones.
John Scofield, Jr.
Eleazer Scofield.
Samuel Meacham.
Ezekiel Gardner.
Mathew Mann.
Josiah H. Bartlett.
William Douglass.
John Bartlett.
Nathaniel Bartlett.
Charles Walworth.
William Smith.
Samuel Hinkson.
David Fogg.
Joshua Harris.

Benjamin Sawyer.
Ezekiel Wells.
John P. Calkins.
Samuel Gates.
William Manning.
James Woodbury.
Henry Springer.
Frances Smith.
Leonard Hoar.
Benjamin R. Burts.
Elias Lathrop.
Gideon Brockway.
Josiah Barber.
Daniel Blaisdell.
James Treadway, n. r.
Ephraim Wells, n. r.
Jonathan Paddleford, n. r.

All the above appear in the inventory of 1786 with the exception of John Scofield, Jonathan Stickney, Matthew Mann, Samuel Gates, William Manning, Frances Smith, Leonard Hoar, Gideon Brockway, Josiah Barber, Ephraim Wells and Jonathan Paddleford with the following additional names. These inventories are copies and do not contain the names of all the men in town.

1786

Caleb Clark.
William Richardson.
Joshua Richardson.
Warren Wilson.
Joseph Stickney.
Caleb Clark, Jr.
Joshua Wells.
Joshua Smith.
Josiah Folsom.
Joseph Kinney.
Benjamin Harris.

Lucy Walworth.
John Currier.
Richard Clark, Jr.
Richard Clark, 3d.
Clement Stoddard.
Isaiah Booth.
Parrot Blaisdell.
Nathan Follensbee.
Nathaniel Whitcher.
Reynold Gates.
Abel Hadley.
Humphrey Nichols.

APPENDIX.   687

Elijah Paddleford, n. r.
Asa Paddleford, n. r.
Asahel Wells.
Samuel Noyes.
Oliver Smith.

George Harris, Jr.
Sargent Blaisdell.
Sarah Scofield.

LIST OF VOTERS IN THE TOWN OF CANAAN QUALIFIED TO VOTE FOR STATE AND COUNTY OFFICERS ON THE SECOND TUESDAY OF MARCH, 1825.

Arvin, James.
Aldrich, Milton.
Aldrich, Abel.
Aldrich, Jedidiah.
Atherton, William.
Annis, Benjamin.
Arvin, Jesse.
Blaisdell, Daniel.
Blaisdell, Elijah.
Blaisdell, James.
Blaisdell, Daniel, Jr.
Blaisdell Parrot.
Blaisdell, Jacob.
Blaisdell, John.
Bartlett, Nathaniel.
Bartlett, Caleb C.
Barber, John M.
Barber, Nathaniel.
Barber, Josiah P.
Bailey, Levi.
Bailey, Levi, Jr.
Bartlett, Joseph.
Barber, Josiah.
Barber, Josiah, Jr.
Barber, March.
Bradbury, William.
Currier, David, Jr.
Currier, John.
Currier, James.

Chase, Moody.
Clark, Josiah.
Carlton, Jona.
Colby, Daniel.
Clark, Joseph.
Cass, Nathan.
Currier, Theophilus.
Currier, Theophilus, Jr.
Currier, Joshua.
Cilley, Thomas.
Colby, Adonijah.
Clark, Eliphalet.
Campbell, William.
Campbell, Daniel.
Clark, Amasa.
Currier, David.
Cilley, Abner H.
Clough, Samuel.
Cross, Nathan.
Clark, Robert B.
Chase, Ezra.
Clark, Richard, Jr.
Currier, Nathaniel.
Colby, Ensign.
Carlton, John.
Clark, Ebenezer.
Clark, Theodore.
Clark, Josiah, Jr.
Cobb, Solomon.

Cobb, Guilford.
Collins, John.
Caswell, Otis.
Cilley, Mark.
Dustin, David.
Dustin, John R.
Doten, James.
Doten, James, Jr.
Davis, Ebenezer.
Dole, Moses.
Dow, Jacob.
Dustin, Joseph.
Derby, Nathaniel.
Davis, Moses.
Dole, Wales.
Davis, Nathan.
Dustin, Caleb.
Dustin, Francis.
Dustin, Dudley.
Drake, Samuel.
Drake, Thomas.
Eastman, James.
Eastman, Phineas.
Eaton, Ebenezer.
Flanders, Moses.
Folsom, Joseph.
Fales, John.
Flint, George.
Flanders, John.
Flanders, John, 2d.
Flanders, Thomas.
Fales, Oren.
Folensbee, Moses.
Foster, Amos.
Gale, Ezra.
Gile, Richard.
Gilman, Ezra.
Gould, Nathan.
Gilman, Caleb.

Gates, Raynold.
Gile, Reuben.
Gilman, Nathaniel.
Gleason, Sewell.
Greeley, Mathew.
Gould, Amos.
Gould, David.
Gove, Elijah.
Goss, Joshua.
Gilman, Samuel.
Gile, Stephen.
Goodrich, Joshua.
George, Levi.
Hadley, Simeon.
Hadley, Moses.
Hadley, Moses, Jr.
Hadley, Amos.
Hinkson, Daniel.
Harris, Joshua.
Harris, Hubbard.
Harris, John H.
Haynes, Benjamin.
Haynes, Josiah P.
Hoyt, John.
Harris, William.
Hovey, Daniel, Dr.
Hovey, Dudley.
Harvey, David.
Hoyt, Robert.
Hoyt, Rufus.
Hoyt, Bartlet.
Heath, Bartholomew.
Jameson, Jeremiah.
Jones, Amasa.
Jones, Asahel.
Jennes, Job.
Jennes, Stephen.
Kimball, Daniel.
Kimball, Abraham.

APPENDIX. 689

Kimball, Daniel, Jr.
Kelly, Moses.
Kimball, Asa.
Kinne, Luther.
Kimball, William.
Kimball, Aaron.
Longfellow, William.
Longfellow, Abraham.
Lawrence, Moses.
Leeds, Harre.
Low, Moses.
Morse, James.
Martin, Robert.
Martin, William.
May, John.
Milton, Joseph.
Miner, Thomas.
Miner, Amos.
Miner, Elisha.
Miller, Jacob.
May, Edwin.
Martin, John.
Noyes, Samuel.
Noyes, Stephen.
Nichols, Ezra.
Nichols, Aaron.
Otis, Richard.
Pattee, Daniel.
Pressey, Calvin.
Pressey, Moses.
Pattee, Daniel, Jr.
Page, Lazarus.
Pilsbury, Joshua.
Pilsbury, Joshua, Jr.
Paddleford, Samuel.
Paddleford, Charles.
Paddleford, James.
Porter, Elias.
Pollard, Adam.

Packard, Chamberlain.
Porter, Daniel.
Pattee, James.
Pattee, James, 2d.
Pattee, Moses.
Quimby, Jonathan.
Richardson, Joshua W.
Richardson, William.
Richardson, Joshua.
Richardson, Nathaniel.
Richardson, Jacob.
Richardson, Moses.
Richardson, Joshua, 2d.
Richardson, David.
Richardson, Amos.
Richardson, Charles.
Rogers, William.
Richardson, Ephraim.
Richardson, Solomon.
Stevens, George.
Smith, Francis H.
Straw, Jacob.
Shepard, Nathaniel.
Shepard, John.
Sawyer, Moses.
Sanborn, Timothy.
Sherburn, Daniel.
Sweet, ——.
Smith, Joseph.
Sanborn, Theophilus.
Smart, William.
Trussell, Jacob.
Tyler, Job.
Tyler, Job C.
Tyler, James.
Tilton, Timothy.
Wilson, Levi.
Wells, Joshua.
Whittier, Samuel.

Whittier, Moses.
Whittier, Daniel B.
Whittier, Rufus.
Welch, Caleb.
Welch, William.
Walworth, Charles.
Walworth, George.
Wilson, Warren.
Wilson, Robert.
Wells, Ezekiel.
Wells, Caleb P.
Wood, William.
Welch, Bailey.
Welch, Uriah.

Wheat, Joseph.
Wallace, James.
Wilson, Washington.
Wilson, Joel.
Williams, Stephen.
Williams, Samuel.
Worth, John.
Wilson, Ephraim.
Wilson, Nathaniel.
Welch, Dan.
Welch, Simeon.
Whitney, Isaac.
Wiggins, Broadstreet.

We hereby certify the foregoing to be a true list of the voters in the town of Canaan according to the best of our knowledge.
Selectmen's office, February 19, 1825.

ELIJAH BLAISDELL
JAMES WALLACE } *Selectmen*
NATHL CURRIER

ENROLLMENT LIST, 1864.

The enrollment list for August 22, 1864, contained these names of men between the ages of 18 and 45, not aliens, capable of bearing arms:

Aldrich, Edgar D.
Avery, Thomas D.
Brooks, Frank.
Butman, Thomas W.
Bradbury, Lewis N.
Blake, Augustus.
Barber, Frank W.
Bartlett, Caleb S.
Barber, James P.
Blodgett, Isaac N.
Bucklin, Alamando.
Chase, George W.

Clark, George P.
Currier, Moses E.
Columbia, William.
Currier, John.
Currier, Henry.
Currier, Frank.
Clark, Byron.
Crockett, John F.
Clark, Benjamin O.
Cobb, Hiram M.
Clark, Henry W.
Currier, John W.

Appendix.

Davis, Daniel G. S.
Davis, Alfred.
Duphonot, John.
Day, Joseph F.
Davis, Alvin.
Dwinnells, Charles.
Derby, Joseph C.
Decato, Albert.
Dunham, Willard L.
Davis, James H.
Davis, John R.
Davis, Walter S.
Doten, Ambrose.
Doten, Guilford.
Eaton, Nathaniel.
Fifield, Edson.
Felch, James C.
Felch, Benjamin F.
Follensbee, Joseph.
Follensbee, Lewis C.
Flint, Edwin.
Gates, Newton B.
Garven, Solomon.
Hall, William.
Hadley, Eben.
Heath, Leonard.
Hall, Frank.
Hazelton, George W.
Hadley, George W.
Hoit, Benjamin W.
Hobart, William E.
Kinne, Freeman F.
Kendall, Charles W.
Kimball, Horace W.
Kimball, John W.
Lary, Alonzo L.
Lary, Benjamin P.
Lary, Walter F.
Lary, Joseph C.

Langley, Charles T.
Muzzey, George E.
Morse, Edwin.
Morey, Horace.
Morse, Orrin H.
Miner, Allen E.
Muzzey, John S.
Pollard, Benjamin N.
Pollard, Frederick R.
Pollard, Joseph D.
Plummer, James B.
Pattee, Lewis C.
Perley, John Q.
Pattee, Burns W.
Pressey, George.
Parker, Freeman S.
Richardson, Dexter.
Richardson, James B.
Randlet, George W.
Shepard, Calvin W.
Shepard, George S.
Smith, Richard R.
Sanborn, Morrison I.
Smith, Leonard W.
Sanborn, Jonathan A.
Smith, Elijah.
Smith, Daniel.
Towle, Stephen H.
Tucker, Moses C.
Tucker, Jonathan A.
Tilton, Smiley.
Weeks, William B.
Webster, Levi F.
Whittemore, Daniel.
Wilson, Warren F.
Whittier, George L.
Wadleigh, Gustavus B.
Wilson, James.
Worth, Hiram S.

Webber, John D.
Welch, Lyman.
Abbott, Hazen.
Aldrich, Aaron.
Butman, Frank.
Baker, James.
Barnard, Darius.
Barber, Hiram.
Barney, Alfred.
Campbell, Daniel H.
Clough, John F.
Clark, John B.
Cilley, Stephen F.
Columbia, Lewis.
Davis, Isaac.
Decato, Charles.
Day, Charles.
Dodge, Simon.
Eastman, Richard B.
Edwards, Elijah W.
Elliott, Henry W.
Ford, Adonirum.
Flanders, Elijah C.
Farnum, Hazen K.
Fales, George.
Goss, Daniel.
George, Levi.
Hazelton, Richman.
Hadley, Gilbert S.
Heath, John R.
Howard, Waterman.
Hadley, Azro B.
Jackson, Heber.
Jepson, Francis.
Kinne, Horace.
Kimball, Abram F.
Kelley, James H.
Lincoln, Josiah B.
Morgan, Nathan C.

Milton, Mathew H.
Miller, Horace W.
Nichols, Benjamin P.
Peaslee, Stephen.
Pressey, Albert.
Shepard, John S.
Stickney, Daniel.
Somers, William G.
Swett, Frank P.
Thompson, Valentine.
Taplin, Nathaniel P.
Tilton, Elbridge.
Whitney, Bela B.
Whitney, Albert.
Whitney, Hollis B.
Wilson, Henry H.
Whittier, Elisha R.
Welch, William.
Whittier, Elijah.
Welch, Frank.
Worcester, Benjamin.
Wells, Charles H.
Smith, William P.
Cobb, George E.
Leeds, Charles H.
Jessamin, Henry L.
Barney, Albert.
Leeds, Hubbard C.
Swett, Harlan P.
Whittier, Jeremiah M.
Plummer, George F.
Wilson, Albert H.
Aldrich, Ezra A.
Prescott, Philip G.
Gordon, William.
Bradbury, Albert.
Dow, Everett.
Gross, Rufus S.
Legro, David.

Martin, Levi.
Washburn, Charles D.
Sharp, Bial.
Cilley, George E.
Miner, George B.
Burbank, John L.
Dunning, Charles L.
Fifield, William H.

Harris, Tilton F.
Jones, Charles S.
Pattee, Henry H.
Shattuck, Edwin E.
Weeks, Marshall.
Webster, Daniel.
Davis, Leroy.

Of these men the following should not have been enrolled: Thomas D. Avery had but one finger on one hand, had tried to enlist but they would not have him. Walter S. Davis, trouble with his eyes. William E. Hobart had but one hand. Stephen M. Towle was an epileptic. Philip Prescott was wounded and dismissed. James H. Davis and Charles Langley were incapacitated. Frank Barber and Isaac Davis were over forty-five years old. Frank Swett was in Idaho. Charles and Albert Decato and John Duphonot were aliens. Charles W. Kendal resided in Wilmot.

Town Appropriations.

For Charges.

1770–1776	No appropriations.	1800	$100.
1777	£3, L. M.	1801	$130.
1778–1785	No records.	1802	$130.
1786	£16, L. M.	1803	$80.
1787	£20, L. M.	1804	$50.
1788	£30, L. M.	1805	$150.
1789	£20, L. M.	1806	$30.
1790	£10, L. M.	1807	$200.
1791	None voted.	1808	$150.
1792	£9, L. M.	1809	$75.
1793	None voted.	1810	$200.
1794	£9, L. M.	1811	$200.
1795	£30.	1812	$300.
1796	£12.	1813	$250.
1797	2s. 6d. on pound, for charges highways and bridges.	1814	$200.
		1815	$260.
		1816	$150.
1798	None voted.	1817	$300.
1799	£60.	1818	$400.

1819	$400.	1864	$6,000.	
1820	$350.	1865	$6,000.	
1821	$750.	1866	$2,000.	$3,000 for old debts.
1822	$200.	1867	$5,000.	
1823	$450.	1868	$4,000.	
1824	$400.	1869	$4,000.	
1825	$400.	1870	$6,000.	
1826	$500.	1871	$4,000.	
1827	$600.	1872	$5,000.	
1828	$800.	1873	$6,000.	
1829	$500.	1874	$6,000.	
1830	$600.	1875	$6,000.	
1831	$1,200.	1876	$6,000.	
1832	$400.	1877	$6,000.	
1833	$600.	1878	$6,000.	
1834	$1,100.	1879	$6,000.	
1835	$800.	1880	$6,000.	
1836	$800.	1881	$6,000.	
1837	$1,200.	1882	$10,000.	
1838	$1,000.	1883	$6,000.	
1839	$1,200.	1884	$3,000.	
1840	$1,000.	1885	$3,000.	
1841	$800.	1886	$3,000.	
1842	$1,000.	1887	$3,000.	
1843	$800.	1888	$3,000.	
1844	$1,000.	1889	Passed article.	
1845	$1,000.	1890	$100.	
1846	$1,000.	1891	$1,000.	
1847	$1,000.	1892	Passed article.	
1848	$1,500.	1893	Passed article	
1849	$3,200.	1894	$1,000.	
1850	$2,500.	1895	$1,000.	
1851	$2,000.	1896	$500.	
1852	$1,000.	1897	$1,000.	
1853	$2,000.	1898	$1,500.	
1854	$2,000.	1899	$1,000.	
1855	$3,000.	1900	$500.	
1856	$3,000.	1901	$300.	
1857	$2,000. $500 extra to apply on town debt.	1902	$300.	
		1903	$500.	
1858	$2,500.	1904	$500.	
1859	$2,500.	1905	$500.	
1860	$3,000.	1906	$500.	
1861	$3,000.	1907	$500.	
1862	$3,000.	1908	$1,000.	
1863	$4,000.	1909	$500.	

INDEX

INDEX

ABBOTT, Charles........................421
 Hazen......................654, 692
 Jane............................583
 Joseph C........................632
 Julia...........................662
 Rosette.........................661
 Royal...........................608
 Sarah L.........................657
ABDY, Mr..............................263
ADAMS, Addie E........................583
 Andrew R........................654
 Angietta........................583
 Benj. W....................370, 619
 Cyrus...........................486
 Erwin M....................488, 681
 Ephraim...................366, 373
 J. W......................245, 247
 John S..........................583
 Matta J.........................583
 Mary E..........................661
 Mary J..........................642
 Placid...........365, 368, 373, 408
 Sophia..........................658
 William....................367, 379
AKERMAN, Ernest S.....................583
 R. Clara........................591
ALDRICH, Aaron............369, 584, 692
 Abel.....................398, 583, 687
 Adelaide........................584
 Almon...........................584
 Anna D..........................584
 Asahel B........................583
 Clark...........................486
 Edgar D..................367, 380, 600
 Edwin C....................420, 583
 Edwin D..................367, 379, 583
 Elbyne.....................583, 642
 Emergene........................584
 Emily...........................584
 Etta C..........................583
 Etta S..........................583
 Eva M...........................583
 Ezra A..........................692
 Gifford.........................583
 Harry...........................584
 Harvey..........................584
 Hubbard W..................489, 583
 Jedidiah........................687
 Julia...........................584
 Laurett.........................664
 Lenora S........................583
 Leonard.........................583
 Lucretia........................649
 Lydia...........................598
 Lyman...........................584
 Marcia A........................584
 Mary............................664
 Mary C..........................604
 Mary E..........................583
 Melvin A........................631
 Milton.....................584, 687
 Mina M..........................584
 Ora L...........................583
 Orpha...........................583
 Persis P........................583
 Richard...................445, 583
 Sidney..........................583
 Serena..........................606
 Smith...........................247

ALDRICH, Welcome......................583
 William...............489, 583, 654
ALFORD, Alden E.......................455
ALLARD, Frances M.....................664
 Helen...........................655
 William E..........365, 375, 617, 647
ALLBE, Sarah I........................638
ALLEN, Abigail........................659
 Alice...........................663
 Edwin M..............490, 584, 598, 677
 Emma A.....................584, 598
 Ethan............................61
 Lena F..........................584
 R. E............................491
 Roxie L.........................492
 Susan...........................515
 T. Wilfred......................584
ALLERTON, Charles H..............378, 382
ALLIS, Abigail........................645
AMBROSE, Rev. Samuel.............168, 182
AMES, Hannah B........................657
 Persis..........................516
 Susie E.........................648
AMHERST GEN..........................VII
AMSDEN, CHARLES H.....................672
ANDRE, Major..........................253
ANDREWS, Alice........................643
 Amelia C........................658
 Benjamin F......................636
 Dexter O........................636
 Harriet.........................655
 Irving B........................598
 James...........................364
 Nancy J.........................649
 T. J............................247
ANGELL, Harvey........................440
ANGIER, James H.......................654
ANNIS, Benjamin.......................687
ARVIN, Albert G...........390, 420, 584
 Elizabeth.......................584
 Emily...........................584
 George..........................584
 Hannah..............93, 435, 499, 584
 James....93, 286, 289, 290, 297,
    298, 299, 303, 401, 411, 584
    673, 679, 682, 687
 Jesse D....................486, 687
 Simeon....75, 76, 88, 128, 130, 133
    137, 145, 176, 186, 232
    404, 409, 415, 435, 440
    452, 584, 681
 Susanna....................584, 594
 William B..................428, 582
ASBURY, Bishop...................293, 294
ASHLEY, Colonel.......................350
ATHATON, Mathew.......................177
ATHERTON, Caroline E..................300
 Edwin W....................300, 584
 George W........................584
 Harriet A.......................584
 James W.................369, 381, 584
 Martha M........................300
 Mary E..........................584
 William......209, 248, 439, 446, 486
    533, 555, 584, 681, 687
ATKINSON, Theodore.............VIII, 4, 5
ATWELL, Cynthia.......................578
 George P........................635
 Guy E...........................635

INDEX.

ATWELL, Horace............654
  Rufus..............418, 635
  Sarah M..............635
ATWOOD, Caleb B............590
  John................671
  Augustus Francis......374, 382
AUSTIN, Arthur A...........680
  Dudley..............486
  George W............584
  Gertrude A........584, 594
  Lettie M............648
  Persis F............209
  Roswell.............224
AVERILL, Sophronia.........578
AVERY, Alonzo..............654
  Elizabeth F.........584
  F. F.............447, 587
  Samuel...........94, 584
  Thomas D......94, 366, 690, 693
AYER, William....6, 41, 56, 57, 58, 60, 64
    65, 76, 141, 144, 312, 313
    344, 346, 352, 437, 444, 447
    672, 677, 681, 683, 685
AYERS, Thomas..........368, 373
BABBITT, Olive.............612
BABCOCK, Joseph............346
BACHELDER, Nahum J.........672
  Nancy...............584
BACON, Owen F..........374, 382
BADGER, Gen. William.......69, 670
BAGLEY, David..............628
  Charlotte...........584
  Henry...............628
  Moses...............584
  Sarah...............628
  Sarah M.............616
  Susanna.............596
BAILEY, Adelaide...........584
  Alfred..............627
  Anna................584
  Betsey...........520, 523
  Ellen...............658
  George..............627
  Henry...............655
  John................655
  Levi....177, 189, 209, 251, 584, 678
  Lucy S..............631
  Lydia...............584
  Polly C.............206
  Rial................584
  Sally...............584
BAKER, Alpheus.............484
  Bishop...........243, 245
  Climena L...........585
  Ellen E.............585
  Elnora..............664
  George P............585
  James..........585, 604, 692
  James M.............585
  Nathaniel M.........671
  Salmon..............498
BALCH, Daniel..........283, 454
  Julia...............325
BALCOM, Willard W..........523
BALDWIN, Erastus.......168, 169
  Mary................603
  Ruth.............169, 170
  Sarah...............170
  Thomas, Rev......21, 26, 27, 33
    44, 50, 52, 54, 55, 63, 68, 71
    126, 142, 143, 166, 168, 170, 171
    175, 181, 188, 343, 345, 346, 350
    389, 445, 495, 508, 518, 677, 682
    683, 686
BALL, Charles O............578
  Elizabeth D.........622
  Ruth F..............503

BALLARD, Sampson...........147
BANE, Fred.................523
BANNISTER, Warren......232, 234, 246
BARBER, Alice..............586
  Anna................586
  Betsey..............586
  Byron J.............586
  Catherine.......441, 585, 600
  Chloe...............661
  Clarissa A..........587
  Daniel..............587
  Deborah.............502
  Deliverance......441, 585
  Frank............585, 603
  Franklin W...300, 480, 585, 690, 693
  George E............586
  Hannah..............660
  Henry H.............586
  Hiram.........300, 442, 585, 585
    586, 588, 676, 697
  Horace H.........300, 585
  Irena............441, 585
  James P.........300, 369, 585
    586, 682, 690
  Jasper..............60
  Jennie M............586
  Jesse...........441, 585
  John M....45, 63, 121, 122, 123, 131
    145, 147, 149, 176, 189
    251, 314, 318, 390, 392
    395, 396, 397, 408, 411
    431, 441, 466, 585, 586
    588, 678, 679, 682, 687
  John M., Jr......95, 300, 359, 434
  Joseph..............683
  Josiah 45, 47, 100, 137, 174, 186, 222
    393, 404, 405, 406, 431
    442, 446, 586, 686, 687
  Josiah, Jr......208, 209, 221
  Josiah P......359, 442, 586, 687
  Louisa..............587
  Mr..................283
  March....91, 193, 260, 268, 272, 277
    280, 297, 299, 303, 397, 400, 410
    417, 441, 585, 673, 678, 679, 687
  Martha J........300, 585, 636
  Mary............441, 485
  Miriam..........441, 585
  Moses...............587
  Nancy C..........363, 586
  Nathaniel ..43, 82, 88, 100, 128, 130
    132, 144, 145, 176, 223
    287, 298, 303, 363, 392
    412, 436, 445, 450, 453
    519, 585, 622, 687
  Nellie J............586
  Nelly...............585
  Pernal.........518, 585, 654
  Polly...............586
  Robert, Capt....35, 41, 42, 44, 56, 57
    60, 61, 62, 63, 69, 70
    77, 81, 101, 122, 123
    124, 130, 139, 145, 146
    147, 149, 172, 176, 232
    251, 314, 315, 343, 344
    345, 355, 357, 390, 422
    435, 437, 439, 440, 446
    486, 519, 585, 683, 685
  Robert, Jr.......498, 499
  Sally.........441, 585, 613
  Sally P.............586
  Salome..............587
  Sarah...........578, 585
  William M...........586
  William P. C........586
  Winthrop G..........585
  Zebulon..........253, 602

INDEX.

BARBOUR, Priscilla B.............643
BARKER, George...................592
  John.............................416
  Joseph...........................246
BARNARD, Burns M.................595
  Clara............................587
  Cora B...........................587
  Darius..............366, 654, 692
  David......365, 366, 486, 587, 682
  Ellen L..........................587
  Emma J...........................587
  Eugene A.........................587
  Francis H........................587
  George...........................654
  Georgianna.......................587
  Hattie F.........................587
  Jonathan......93, 418, 419, 587, 676
  Mary A...........................587
BARNES, Fred O...................587
  Jeanette F..................334, 626
  John O...........................377
BARNET, Levi.....................655
BARNEY, Aaron...............587, 592
  Addie............................587
  Alathea..........................587
  Albert E..............369, 587, 614
                  676, 682, 692
  Alden H..........................491
  Alfred......................654, 692
  Allen W..........................588
  Arabella.........................654
  Arthur J....................491, 587
  Bertha E....................587, 609
  Charles.....................588, 674
  Charles O.......28, 491, 587, 677
  Clarence E.......................587
  Ebenezer.........................601
  Edward A....................587, 614
  Eleazer..........93, 366, 587, 601
            674, 675, 679, 680
  Elsina H.........................587
  Ernest A.........................535
  F. W.............................490
  Harry A..........................587
  Helen............................654
  Jabez............................587
  Jacob.......................486, 654
  Jemima...........................664
  John F...........................587
  Lester O.........................587
  Lillian A........................492
  Lizzie I....................588, 638
  Marjory..........................587
  Maurice H........................587
  Otis........................358, 587
  Pauline..........................587
  Polly M..........................587
  Ralph T..........................587
  S. Addie.........................587
BARNOT, Rozett...................661
BARRY, Jane......................588
BARTLETT, Belinda L..............585
  Betsey......................589, 604
  Caleb C...........397, 416, 588, 687
  Caleb S...............588, 675, 690
  Caroline R.......................654
  Chloe............................527
  Cordelia H.......................588
  Eliza H.....................588, 618
  Frank T..........................589
  Hannah...........................516
  Huldah G.........................661
  Ichabod................272, 273, 283
  John H..............60, 64, 344, 345
                437, 589, 686
  Joseph....47, 100, 131, 158, 159, 209
       431, 443, 445, 446, 588, 678, 687

BARTLETT, Joseph, Mrs............222
  Josiah, Hon.........69, 71, 75, 350
                522, 669, 670
  Josiah Hall..........60, 683, 686
  Levi.............................611
  Lois.............................588
  Mary.............................654
  Matty............................588
  Molly............................589
  Myra H...........................589
  Nancy H..........................589
  Nathaniel......42, 57, 60, 82, 87, 88
          124, 134, 145, 343, 345
          351, 356, 384, 397, 404
         410, 436, 447, 522, 585
            678, 683, 686, 687
  Nathaniel E......................589
  Polly...............588, 603, 618
  Polly H..........................588
  Ruth.............................588
  Sally............................589
  Sister...........................201
  Susan.......................613, 659
  Susanna..........................436
BARTON & BACON...................340
BASFORD, Charlotte...............605
  Joseph...........................499
  Mary........................499, 521
  Olive............................498
  Sarah.............231, 499, 521, 622
  Wealthy..........................498
  Bailey...........................608
BATCHELDER, Bradford C...........655
  Daniel, Capt.....................364
  Jonathan.........................654
  Nancy M..........................628
  Reuben......................489, 654
  Sarah............................660
BATES, Dexter....................246
  Mrs. Ruth........................631
BAXTER, A. F.....................247
  Thomas.................52, 344, 351
BEAL, Ira........................655
  Polly............................655
  Susan............................609
BEALE, Oliver....................246
BEAN, Andrew E...................578
  Benjamin.........................364
  Folsom...........................589
  J. Mowry.........................247
  John.........131, 145, 447, 589, 683
  Lucia P..........................589
  Moses............................589
  Nathaniel W.............366, 377, 655
  Sarah E..........................605
  Susanna..........................589
BEARO, Francis..............370, 382
BEATTIE, Jane....................527
BEDELL, John................671, 672
BEEBE, Jonathan, 3d............4, 46
  Nathan...........................176
BEEDLE, Hannah...................664
  John................344, 345, 352
  Mehitable...................506, 649
  Thomas..............177, 406, 446
BELDING, Samuel..................645
  Stephen..........................645
BELL, Charles H..................672
  Emeline B........................648
  Emma A............................96
  James............................671
  John.............................670
  Joseph...........................473
  Samuel...........................670
  William H........................589
BELLOWS, Col. Benjamin...........350
  General..................69, 72, 76

700 INDEX.

BENEDICT, Samuel...19, 23, 27, 31, 49, 55, 57, 101, 113, 173, 231, 386, 677, 682
BENNETT, David..................654
  Ebenezer, Jr..................654
  Leonard 246
  Malvina 659
  Mary 532, 607
BENSON, Grace E..................589
BERRY, Anna......................577
  Betsey 656
  Charles D.....................589
  N. S..........................671
  N. T.....................109, 111
  Sarah 589
BERT, Dorcas.....................589
BESSE, Edson P...................655
BEWEL, Betsey....................658
BIATHROW, Horace A...............654
  Myra 610
BICKFORD, Amelia A...............589
  Carrie 589
  Emily A......................655
  Ida M........................589
  Jane 589
  Jonathan 589
  Joseph S.....................589
  Lucy J.......................646
  Mary E.......................589
  Sabrina C....................589
  Sarah M......................589
BIGELOW, Ann.....................647
BILL, Mary E.....................641
BILLINGS, Esther.................619
BINGHAM, A. L....................644
  Elisha 53, 344, 351
  Jonathan 54
BIRTS, Ben Rob........52, 60, 61, 344, 345, 351, 686
  Widow 70
BISHOP, Joseph...................654
BLACK, Lizzie....................656
BLAIR, Andrew...............381, 383
  Lewis 655
  Walter 111
BLAISDELLS 502-517
BLAISDELL, Abigail......503, 504, 515
  Abner 503
  Alfred O.....................504
  Alvah 515
  Alzoa 516
  Azubah 504
  Carrie 610
  Charles E....................655
  Charlotte 514
  Clara 515
  Clarissa 504
  Clark 515
  Daniel 40, 41, 42, 43, 44, 45, 46, 47, 57, 64, 69, 74, 79, 80, 87, 88, 89, 101, 108, 121, 122, 123, 124, 127, 128, 129, 130, 135, 137, 138, 143, 145, 146, 148, 149, 151, 185, 187, 188, 189, 192, 193, 219, 233, 314, 318, 343, 344, 345, 352, 389, 399, 412, 445, 466, 467, 501, 502, 505, 506, 514, 518, 519, 669, 673, 678, 681, 683, 686, 687
  Daniel, Jr.........88, 358, 514, 515, 522, 687
  Daniel, 3d...............426, 514
  Edward 517
  Edwin 504

BLAISDELL, Elijah 45, 47, 48, 122, 159, 164, 209, 215, 228, 250, 253, 254, 256, 257, 258, 260, 264, 317, 318, 320, 323, 328, 453, 468, 486, 502, 504, 512, 513, 514, 515, 673, 678, 681, 687, 690
  Elizabeth 514
  Emily 516
  Enoch 503
  Fannie E.....................589
  Frank 517
  George 515
  George H.....................504
  Guilford 516
  Hannah 514
  Harriet 517
  Harriet N....................515
  Harrison 516
  Henry 504
  Henry G......................655
  Horace 516
  Jacob 277, 486, 514, 515, 516, 612, 641, 670, 687
  James 80, 209, 363, 513
  James J.................426, 515
  Jerusha 655
  John 486, 514, 687
  Jonathan 503, 514, 516
  Jonathan H...................515
  Joseph 515
  Joshua 209, 359, 502, 516
  Josiah 515
  Judge 515
  Justin 515
  Justus 515
  Linnie N.....................589
  Lora A.......................589
  Lydia 664
  Malvina 515
  Martha E.....................589
  Mary 505, 515, 649
  Mary A.............299, 514, 515
  Mehitable 589
  Nancy 515
  Nancy A......................600
  Parrott ...70, 89, 344, 345, 352, 445, 503, 504, 506, 514, 516, 683, 686, 687
  Peter 505
  Polly 504, 516
  Ralph 502, 503, 504
  Rhoda ..196, 300, 514, 515, 516, 524
  Ruth 504
  Sally ...196, 501, 504, 514, 515, 516
  Sanborn 589
  Sarah 515, 517
  Sargent 65, 503, 505, 515, 687
  Suel S.......................515
  Timothy 486, 514, 516
  Timothy K...............517, 594
  W. O.........................504
  William 503, 514, 515
  William A....................515
BLAKE, Achsah....................618
  Augustus F.........362, 654, 690
  Benjamin 93, 445, 637
  Ebenezer 234, 246
  Elisha 409
  J. H.........................489
  John F.......................637
  Joseph 363, 445, 603
  Keziah 605
  Marion F.....................629
  Meschack 102, 345, 397, 407
  Polly F......................589

INDEX. 701

BLANCHARD, Harvey A............649
   Israel 589
   Leafy 618
   Simon 123, 174, 445, 461
BLEEKER & SEDGWICK............325
BLISS, Joseph D.............378, 383
BLODGETT, Caleb...142, 162, 273, 274, 276
        281, 282, 284, 285, 288, 297
        298, 299, 300, 303, 309, 337
        417, 541, 589, 621, 673, 674
                679, 681
   Mrs. 216
   Caleb, Jr........293, 337, 346, 427
   Charles H.................589
   Emily R..............300, 589
   Isaac N............331, 337, 486
           487, 589, 682, 690
   Lois 599
   Nancy E..................658
   Roxanna 636
   Sarah A..............226, 337
BLOOD, Bert..................586
   Enoch 683
   Luvia I..................619
   William 654
   William A................655
BLUE, Mary...................505
BOCKWELL, Oliver B............655
BODFISH, Captain.............364
BOGARDUS, Blanche A..........425
   Blanche E................492
   Charles B............425, 600
   Frank A.......425, 590, 600, 677
   Stanley 425, 600
   Wilmer S............425, 590
BOHONON, Moses................655
BOND, Ellen S.................328
   James 380, 382
BONNEY, Mary.................659
BOOTH, Anne..................590
   Edmund C.................643
   Isaiah 120, 590, 685, 686
   Joseph C.................590
   Maria H..................658
BOSTON, Hannah S.............590
BOSWELL, Elder...............198
BOUTWELL, Abbie B............598
BOWEN, Deliverance 662
   Eliza 498
   Lucinda 593
BOWERS, Lyman................655
BOYCE, Lizzie M..............596
BOYINGTON, Huldah M..........590
BOYNTON, Adeline R...........635
   Elvira A.................644
BRACKETT, Edward............277
   Maria C..................277
BRADBURY, Aaron...........590, 633
   Addie R..................590
   Albert A.....367, 379, 590, 624, 692
   Amanda E.................590
   Amos P...................590
   Benjamin 193, 201, 231, 297, 590, 630
   Betsey 590, 662
   David 590
   Dexter F...........367, 380, 590
   Enos W....................590
   Fannie W..................590
   George C......130, 369, 590, 639, 647
   Hannah 590
   Harriet A.................590
   Joshua 590
   Judith 590
   Lewis N..............590, 690
   Mary 198, 590, 659, 662
   Melvin A..................633
   Rebecca 590

BRADBURY, Rosie E............633
   Roswell 590
   Samuel 590
   Sarah 590
   William 65, 231, 389, 447
          590, 622, 683, 687
   William C.................633
   William J.................590
BRADFORD, Mary...............536
BRADISH, Ellen................593
BRADLEY, Charles..........381, 382
BRADSHAW, Joshua.............683
BRALEY, Etta.................646
   Harriet 523
   Sarah J..................659
BRANCH, Thomas................246
   Brewster B...............247
BRIDGMAN, Abel...............655
   Eliza A..................663
   Helen 624
   Henrietta 337
   Isaac 655
   Pensy 657
   Sarah E..................631
BRIGGS, Abigail..............654
   Bathsheba 594
   Howard C.................590
   Joseph 649
   Mehitable 609, 658
   Nathaniel 655
   Sarah 663
BROADHEAD, John..........232, 233
   Joseph 246
BRIGHAM, Ella E..............652
BRO, Joel....................655
BROCK, Benjamin..............655
   Hattie H.................657
BROCKLEBANK, Edson B.........655
   James 419
   Laura R..................591
   Moses A.............489, 591
   Nellie A............591, 612
   Sarah J..................598
BROCKWAY, Gideon.............686
BROOKS, Emma E...............595
   Frank 690
   George F............378, 382
   Oliver J.................655
   Orris J..................662
BROUGHTON, Charles H.........655
BROWN, Abel..............396, 591
   Adeline C................591
   Clara 658
   David 108, 445
   Don C....................655
   Elmer E..................592
   Emily F..................630
   John G...................591
   Josiah, Capt.............350
   Mary A...................656
   Mary E...................658
   Rhoda 654
   Sarah 525
   Susan F..................591
BRUSH, Abner R...............625
   Caroline 625
BRYANT, Bartlett.............196
   Fannie 638
   George N.................247
   George W.................590
   Harrison C...............600
   John 252
   Joseph M.................655
   Mathew 417
   Roswell C................655
BUCK, Sarah..................528
BUCKLIN, Alamando............690

702 INDEX.

BUCKLIN, Allie S..............591
   Alonzo 608
   Arthur M..................591
   David 404, 409, 583
   Mary E....................591
   Matilda A.................607
   Milo 608
BUCKNER, Mary................523
BUELL, Hepzibah..............645
BUFFUM, James................655
   Ruth 655
   William C.................655
BULLOCK, Chloe...............660
   Coomer 655
   Elijah 637
   Elisha 655
   Jane 664
   Lovinia 662
   Lydia 647
   Lydia W...................664
   Martha J..................598
   Pluma 659
   Rosie E...................638
   Sarah 665
   Sarah A...................608
   Seth 481, 482, 483
   Susanna 657
BUNKER, V. E.................198
BUNTIN, Widow................87
BURBANK, John L..............693
BURCH, Delila................650
BURDICK, John....23, 27, 75, 76, 140
          144, 145, 673, 681
   John, Jr..................145
   Shubel 174, 392, 445
BURGE, Dyer..................246
BURGESS, R. A................488
BURGOUS, Margaret............659
BURGOYNE SURRENDER.347, 348, 350, 354
BURNHAM, Rev. Abraham........217
   Adelia A..................591
   Amanda 650
   Asel 364
   Benjamin 246
   Carrie L..................641
   Chastina 652
   Daniel B..................655
   Elizabeth 591
   Elzina ....
   Grover 486, 597, 599
   Hannah C..................583
   Israel 536
   James 591
   John 584
   Joseph 591
   Liona E...................591
   Lucy 591
   Mason 591
   Nellie W..................591
   Ruth L....................591
   Silas 591
   William 604
BURKE, Honora................591
   John W....................591
   Michael 591
BURLEY, Annie M..............558
(Burleigh), Benjamin.........655
   Betsey 577
   Brackett W................642
   Charles R.................642
   Charles W.................642
   Elizabeth 522
   Fannie 588
   George M..................588
   Gordon 83, 281, 283, 289, 423
          444, 535, 540, 642

BURLEY, Harry P........337, 441, 677
   Henry G...................642
   John 588
   Joseph 588
   Joseph B..................588
   Joshua 277
   Judith G..................628
   Louisa 588
   Louisa M..................588
   Lucretia M................642
   Lucy J....................535
   Mary E....................642
   Mary J....................629
   Sarah 599
   Sarah H...................648
   Thomas 599
BURNS, John..................536
   John J....................366
   Letitia 536
   Mary 536
BURPEE, Wesley P.....91, 159, 267, 268
          272, 278, 280, 512
BURRILL, John................626
BURROUGHS, Rev. Eden.........207
BURROWS, D. W................198
BURTON, Matilda..............657
BUSHWAY, Delia...............655
   John 655
BUSIEL, Charles A............672
BUSWELL, Martha..............654
   Mary A....................659
BUTLER, Sally................648
BUTMAN, Blanche..............591
   Charles H.................591
   David H..............367, 368
   Ellen M...................648
   Eva G.....................591
   Frank 591, 595
   Frank H...................591
   Fred E...............101, 591
   George E..................591
   Grace 591
   Laura 591
   Laura A...................663
   Mary 591
   Oscar 591
   Paul 591
   Thomas W..................690
BUTTERFIELD, George..........591
   Harriet J.................662
   William 454
BYINGTON, Orra C.............609
BYRON, Julia F...............528
CADY, Aaron...............3, 48, 113
   Aaron, Jr...............3, 48
   Nathaniel 3, 48, 113, 406
CAHOON, Rev. C. D........240, 241
CALDWELL, Alexander..........159
   William 113
CALEF, Ann...................630
   Ann A.....................664
   John 630
   Mary 606
CALFE, Captain............69, 354
CALKINS, Rev. Charles.208, 209, 210, 248
   John P..........209, 248, 387, 390
          496, 683, 686
   Temperance 496
CALL, Enoch...............96, 591
   Mary A....................617
   Ruth 591
   Sarah J...................591
   William R............566, 591
CALLEMORE, Sarah E...........633
CAMPBELL, Alba A.............592
   Archibald K...............543

INDEX. 703

CAMPBELL, Betsey............592, 637
 Charles A..................592
 Daniel 91, 163, 272, 282, 288
   297, 303, 512, 562
   591, 646, 679, 687
 Daniel H..............369, 591, 680
 Daniel W.................591, 680
 Dorothy 543
 Ella 592
 Giles 234, 246
 Hannah 592
 Katherine A................608
 Mary 592
 Sarah F....................591
 William ...84, 91, 134, 189, 258, 260
   269, 271, 278, 280, 297
   394, 396, 431, 447, 470
   591, 679, 687
 William, Mrs...............244
 William W..................542
CANFIELD, Captain..............354
CAPLES, C. V...............241, 242
CARLTON, Albert................592
 Betsey 478, 579
 Charles H..................588
 Cyrus 30, 407, 446
 Daniel 131, 592
 Edward 222
 Eliza 222
 Frances C..................592
 John 687
 Jonathan ..56, 75, 116, 131, 132, 145
   150, 252, 253, 392, 393
   405, 406, 435, 446, 455
   592, 687
 Jonathan, Jr...............446
 Mary J.....................588
 Miles 592
 Molly 592
 Moses 592
 Nancy 592
 Polly 660
 Sally 602
 Samuel 488, 588
 Thomas J...................375
 Thomas L...................592
CARPENTER, Carrie L............624
 David F....................498
 Louise L...................624
CARR, C. E.....................672
 Daniel 60, 246
 Jacob 656
 Lewis C....................656
CARRIGAN, Darby............374, 382
CARROLL, Calvin C..............656
 Frank W................368, 381
 James 633
CARTER, Abigail................592
 Amaziah 283
 Frank P................116, 453
 George 592
 Jeremiah 656
 John 375, 378, 382
 William 247, 592
CASS, Nathan...............532, 687
 Rachel 654
CASTLE, Mrs....................277
CASWELL, Fauntleroy............359
 Lucy A.....................659
 Otis 688
CATE, Asa P....................671
CAVERLY, Harriet D.............592
CHAMBERLAIN, Abner.........3, 45, 47
 Benjamin 3, 45
 David 3, 48
 John 3, 47

CHAMBERLAIN, Levi..............671
 William 3, 44, 46, 104, 113
 William A..................592
 William, Jr............4, 48, 113
CHAMBERS, William..............522
CHAMPAGNE, August..........378, 382
CHANDLER, Lizzie H.............664
 Lucy 655
 Nancy 664
 Sally 627
 Susan O....................538
CHAPLIN, Allerton..............656
CHAPMAN, Clarissa J............300
 Jane 222
 Lucinda 649
 Lydia 645
 Mary J.....................423
 Pamela 622
 Roswell S..................300
 Samuel 26, 27, 28, 49, 50
   60, 177, 387, 447
 Sarah S....................586
CHASE, Abigail M...............592
 Ambrose 393, 405, 447, 592
 Arthur H...................429
 Baruch 324
 Betsey M...................592
 C. H.......................247
 Charles C..................592
 Charles T..................640
 Clarence J.................592
 Daniel W...................193
 Dorothy S..................602
 Ebenezer 483, 485, 486
 Eliza J....................592
 Elsie 639
 Ezra 222, 445, 592, 687
 Frances M..................592
 Frank W....................589
 George W...........488, 639, 690
 Hannah 592
 Hannah H...................592
 Henry M....................592
 Horace W....297, 309, 419, 535, 592
 Jesse S....................655
 John 656
 John R.....................592
 Col. Jonathan.........34, 345, 346
   350, 351, 353
 Joseph 592
 Moody 687
 Moses 393, 406, 447
 Nathaniel L................247
 Permelia 647
 Persis W...................663
 Philander 73
 Robert 429
 Samuel B...................592
 Sarah 592, 619
 Sarah A................587, 592
 Sarah C....................619
 Simon P....................656
 Viola J....................592
 William 193, 395, 592
 William M..............428, 592
CHELLIS, Dolly C...............664
 James 656
 Mary A.....................635
 Sumner 656
CHENEY, Albert.................622
 Anna 643
 Caleb 622
 Elder 195
 Helen G....................616
 John B.....................607
 Mabel 622

704 INDEX.

CHENEY, Person C............672
   Susanna 644
CHESLEY, Ann................592
   Eleazer 592
   Eliza 663
CHILD, David L...........263, 266
   Mary M....................640
CHILDS, Almira T............592
   Amanda 659
   Ella F.....................578
   Mary E. F.................592
   Oliver B...........366, 377, 592
CHITTENDEN, Abbie B.........644
   Governor 59
CHOATE, Asa.................411
   Benjamin 358, 411, 476
   Helen 623, 661
   Henry 591
   Jonathan 643
   Mahala 300
   Mary J....................659
   Moses 656
CHRISTENSEN, Jacob......376, 382
CHRISTIE, Daniel M...........335
CHURCH, Carrie F............656
   Charles 128
   Colonel 351
   Hilliard 656
   Mary A....................656
   Samuel 396
CHURCHILL, Caroline P........611
   D. C..............109, 111, 299
CILLEY, Abner H...159, 189, 366, 590, 687
   Diancy 590
   Elida M...................661
   George E..................373
   George J..............590, 693
   Hannah 198, 199
   Horatio G.................590
   J. E.......................402
   Levi 393, 395, 408, 447
   Mark 137, 688
   Mary A....................657
   Mary E....................593
   Mary J....................654
   Nathan G.............489, 656
   Stephen F.................692
   Thomas 687
CLAFLIN, Alice E.............611
   Deborah 663
   Dorothy 611
   P. Leon 611
CLAPP, Sarah................222
CLARK, Abigail....228, 411, 414, 521, 613
   Abner 246
   Alice B....................523
   Alma C....................593
   Almeda E..................620
   Amasa 131, 384, 396, 398
            447, 592, 687
   Amos B...............297, 521
   Andrew J..................524
   Angeline L............521, 604
   Anna 522, 524
   Anne 522
   Arthur B..................521
   Austin E...................523
   Benjamin O. T.......593, 643, 690
   Betsey 519, 522, 593, 595
          604, 615, 630, 653
   Betsey A...................590
   Betsey B...................658
   Betsey C...................523
   Burlingame 648
   Byron 690

CLARK, Caleb........32, 42, 52, 61, 120
         123, 124, 126, 158, 386
         401, 443, 520, 683, 686
   Caleb, Jr........228, 518, 521, 620
   Carlton C.............191, 593
   Carrie C...................648
   Charles H..................651
   Charles R..................521
   Chase 521
   Chestina 300, 521
   Clarissa 661
   Daniel 593, 610
   Daniel W..................637
   David 499, 521, 522
   Dorcas 593
   Dorinda 593
   Dorothy 520, 523
   Dorothy B.............300, 602
   Earl L.....................341
   Ebenezer..42, 82, 176, 192, 252, 486
        514, 517, 522, 524, 673
                678, 687
   Eleanor W.................523
   Eliphalet 177, 439, 446, 522, 605, 687
   Eliza 523, 599, 613, 664
   Eliza P....................593
   Elizabeth 425, 522
   Emeline 593, 630
   Emily M...................619
   Emily S....................523
   Emma 648
   Esther 183, 521
   Ethel A....................651
   Frank B...............341, 523
   Frank K...................341
   Frank P..............521, 651
   Fred 521
   Fred B....................489
   George L..................648
   George P.........369, 381, 593, 690
   Rev. George W......240, 241, 247
   Gilman 524
   Gilman W.............362, 520
   Hannah 521
   Hannah S..................594
   Helen A...................593
   Henry H...................522
   Henry W...........593, 648, 690
   Horace 520, 524
   Horace A..................594
   Horatio N.................522
   Hugh T....................341
   Irena 586, 593
   Jacob 522
   Jacob S....................594
   James 19, 57
   Jehiel 362, 524
   Jemima L..................523
   Jennie D...................593
   Jennie S...................521
   Jerusha 594
   Jesse 298, 520, 524
   John 522
   John B...............522, 692
   John H....................521
   John S....................594
   Joseph 88, 145, 174, 228, 397, 447
        520, 521, 524, 643, 687
   Joseph D..................300
   Joshua 522, 683
   Josiah 43, 83, 100, 109, 128, 131
        132, 156, 158, 176, 178
        181, 183, 187, 189, 193
        251, 343, 344, 350, 351
        352, 355, 356, 362, 363
        395, 396, 404, 411, 414

INDEX. 705

CLARK, Josiah....436, 438, 445, 446, 517,
    518, 519, 522, 523, 597,
    607, 687
 Josiah, Jr....298, 519, 584, 673, 687
 Josie 593, 594, 608
 Judith 519, 520, 522, 524
 Laura 593
 Leah 522
 Leonard A................593, 648
 Lizzie M......................594
 Lucina G......................524
 Lucy 524
 Lydia 436, 496, 522, 605
 Mahala D.....................593
 Mary 522, 593, 660
 Mary A.......................524
 Mary G.......................648
 Mary E.......................594
 Mary J..................523, 665
 Miriam J.....................593
 Mrs. 522
 Nancy A......................524
 Oren A.......................651
 Pernell 183, 436
 Pernell E....................523
 Polly 521, 522
 Prescott 74, 80, 81, 89, 233
    402, 499, 521, 522
 Rachel G................593, 602
 Rachel S.....................608
 Reuben 593, 610, 640
 Rhoda 514, 605
 Richard 47, 52, 62, 63, 145, 174
    176, 178, 182, 183, 187,
    250, 344, 351, 353, 355,
    390, 405, 465, 517, 518,
    522, 570, 681, 683, 685
 Richard, Jr....43, 131, 137, 145, 176,
    186, 362, 395, 409, 522,
    524, 686, 687
 Richard, 3d...54, 78, 79, 82, 144, 177,
    192, 196, 393, 447,
    677, 678, 686
 Richard C....................523
 Richard O....................523
 Robert B.....272, 361, 398, 519, 522,
    523, 536, 669, 673, 687
 Ruth 524
 Sally ...515, 519, 520, 521, 523, 609
 Samuel 521
 Samuel S................593, 631
 Sarah 525, 593
 Sarah E......................521
 Sophronia 523
 Susanna 522, 588
 Theoda H................523, 636
 Theodore 593, 687
 Tilton 521
 Timothy 446, 593
 Truman J................584, 594
 Warren W....................594
 Warren T....................594
 Wyman P.....................589
 Wyman R....................523
 Zilpha 522, 593
CLARKSON, Lucy R................492
CLAY, Benjamin 593
 Clarissa P....................657
CLEMENT, Anne B.................594
 Clara F......................621
 Harriet 639
 Joshua, Rev......30, 176, 198, 202
 Leonard 650
 Levi 522
 Oliver F.....................594

CLEVELAND, Rev. Aaron 127, 181, 188, 207
 Clara A......................594
 Deidamia 594
 William A....................594
CLIFFORD, Abigail................657
 David 656
 Hannah 663
 Ira 656
 Jacob 345, 355, 406
 Jerusha 601
 Joseph 655
 Mr. 71
 Temperance 623
 Timothy 655
CLOUGH, Abigail 597
 Abigail C....................662
 Allen J.................594, 649
 Alma A.......................591
 Bert 594, 649
 Clark 594
 Emma A..................594, 627
 Jeremiah 630
 John 93
 John F..................594, 627
 Lydia 660
 Mary 663
 Mary A...........594, 608, 651
 Mary J..................591, 660
 Miriam 594
 Samuel 447, 594, 687
 Sarah J.................594, 655
 Sophia 656
 Timothy 408
 William H....................591
COBB, Abbie P................300, 594
 Abigail 594
 Adelia F............300, 594, 598
 Caroline 594
 Edwin 595
 Elizabeth F.............300, 594
 Fannie L.....................595
 Fanny 594
 George E...9, 333, 369, 491, 595, 692
 Guilford 93, 283, 297, 298, 299,
    440, 486, 584, 594, 692
 Hiram 594, 595
 Hiram M........97, 300, 595, 690
 Lucretia B...............300, 594
 Phœbe 517, 594
 Phœbe P.....................300
 Polly 594
 S. Frances.............300, 595
 Salmon 343, 345, 486, 594
 Salmon P........148, 266, 268, 272,
    278, 280, 284, 297,
    303, 308, 309, 320,
    423, 438, 594, 687
COBURN, Abigail 610
 Blanche M..........425, 492, 600
 Elizabeth 600
 Harry R......................600
 Ida M........................599
 Jesse 192
 John B.......................600
COCHRAN, Abby....................626
 Albert 626
 Clarendon A..................626
 Lizzie 626
COE, Rev. Curtis.................207
COGSWELL, Betsey.................657
 Charles E....................586
 Charles N....................328
 Emma F.......................636
 Frank 489
 John 252
 Susannah 601

45

706 INDEX.

COGSWELL, Thomas............72, 672
COLBURN, Addie...................618
   Capitola B...................638
   Carrie J.....................650
   Elizabeth 395
   J. W.........................446
   Leonard 595
   Mandana B...................595
   Mary J......................625
   Pauline R...................586
   S. H........................655
   Willard 593, 595
COLBY, Aaron C....................362
   Aaron H.....................595
   Abigail 643
   Abner C.............362, 403, 595
   Abner H.....................362
   Adonijah 595, 634, 687
   Almeda D....................652
   Alvin 595
   Anthony 671
   Arvilla A...................660
   Belinda D...................664
   Betsey 89
   Charles A...................618
   Charles M...................596
   Daniel ..176, 181, 189, 221, 343, 344
      353, 356, 396, 436, 446, 595, 683
   Edna R......................596
   Elijah R.......91, 271, 298, 595, 620
   Ella J......................596
   Elizabeth 595, 616
   Enoch 595
   Ensign 7, 143, 193, 297, 298, 397
      446, 479, 595, 602, 687
   Eunice 659
   George M....................618
   James M.....................656
   John 595, 656
   John H......................595
   John S......................595
   Joseph 362, 595
   Joshua 72
   Lizzie M....................596
   Lucy 595, 646
   Martha A....................596
   Mary 610
   Mary C......................595
   Moses 595
   Moses T.....................680
   Nancy R.....................595
   Polly 646, 658
   Rebecca 658
   Reuben 362
   Rhoda 633
   Rowel 486
   Ruth P......................591
   Samuel A................367, 656
   Sarah 595, 620
   Sidney L............366, 381, 595
   Susan T.................591, 595
   Willaba 595
   Willaby 595
COLCORD, Ann......................659
   John 117, 446, 449
   J. M........................177
COLE, Abigail...............83, 196, 505
   Alvin B.....................596
   Amon H......................596
   Caroline D..................642
   Daniel B....................419
   Daniel W....................596
   Elvira 658
   Emily D.....................658
   Etta M......................596
   Joseph H....................596

COLE, Norman W....................596
   Polly 654
   Solomon 204
   Thomas 177, 447, 505, 649
   Viola M.....................596
COLLINS, Chellis E................617
   Err 447
   James D.....................656
   John 688
   Nellie M....................596
COLUMBIA, Alvina..................658
   Anthony 596
   Charles 596
   Dora 617
   Flora 658
   Frank 656
   Harriet 658
   Henry W.....................631
   John 656
   Julia A.....................661
   June 660
   Lasett 596
   Lewis 692
   Lucinda 655
   M. A. E.....................663
   Olive 664
   Perley J....................587
   Philoma 654
   Sophia 657
   William 656
COLT, John G......................482
CONANT, Elizabeth J...............300
   Henry I.....................596
   Latham 656
   Rev. Liba.........198, 224, 299, 674
   Sarah A.....................300
CONGER, Mattie....................586
CONVERSE, Samuel..................118
CONWAY, Daniel................376, 382
COOK, Harriet C...................661
   John A......................622
   Paul 363, 656
COOKE, Thomas.....................486
COOLEY, Abigail................... 64
COOMBS, Rev. S................102, 193
COOMS, Albert E...................656
COPP, Darious W...................595
   Ellsworth W.................596
   G. O. F.....................656
   Henrietta 596
   Lizzie M....................651
CORLISS, Cyrus...................656
   Cyrus L.....................247
   Joseph F....................596
   Kimball 656
CORNING, Amos G...................610
   Minnie L....................610
   Sherburne L.................610
CORSER, Hannah....................627
COTTON, Thomas....................234
COUCH, Carroll M..................642
   William 656
COULT, A. C..................247, 398
COUNTY, Dennis............367, 370, 381
   George B............365, 369, 656
COX, Samuel H................263, 323
COWING, Bertha C..................652
   C...........................247
   Dwight T....................652
   Ethel T.....................652
   Florence B..................652
   Josephine W.................652
   Marian M....................652
   Ruby M......................652
CRADDOCK, Eleanor.................650

CRAM, Bessie..................517
    Charles H..................517
    Charles H., Jr..............517
    Clara......................517
    Harriet B..................517
    Mildred....................517
    Nathan D...................517
    Timothy....................517
    Walter.....................517
CRAW, Joseph........19, 20, 23, 24, 27, 28
        31, 49, 55, 57, 386, 677
CREED, Cornelius............380, 383
CROCKER, Bernice..................615
    David......................656
    Sally......................615
    Sarah......................494
    Selden L...................656
CROCKETT, E................198, 299
CROFOOT, James...................599
CROSBY, Benjamin J..............596
CROSS, Amey......................596
    Bailey..........177, 446, 449, 596
    David......................203
    Dixi C.....................631
    Elizabeth.............596, 642
    Emma P.....................649
    Fannie E...................638
    Fanny.................451, 596
    Franklin M.................656
    Fred.......................399
    George B...................656
    Jonathan B.....343, 345, 352, 596
    Lemira H...................596
    Leonard....................596
    Luther.....................596
    M. E..............384, 437, 499
    Nathan......83, 137, 410, 411, 413
        445, 446, 449, 596, 687
    Olive..........248, 251, 535, 596
    Rebecca...............499, 596
    Susanna....................654
    Sylvester..................656
CROSSMAN, Daniel............19, 24, 27
CROWELL, Joshua............182, 246
CROWLEY, Hannah..................656
CRUMMELL, Rev. Alexander....291, 292
        294, 295
CUMMINGS, Clara A...............542
    Daniel G...................542
    Eunice C...................631
    Martha.....................596
CUNNINGHAM, Grace F.............621
    John B................419, 597
CURRIER, A. H...............368, 372
    Aaron......................597
    Abner......................525
    Abigail H..................598
    Adelaide H.................492
    Albert.....................629
    Alonzo.....................597
    Amos..................525, 597
    Amos H................525, 597
    Ann..............488, 525, 597
    Anna...........525, 526, 527, 533
    Benjamin...................525
    Bernard B..................586
    Betsey.............522, 597, 656
    Charles W..................597
    Clarissa..........526, 532, 607
    Clark..........76, 88, 131, 137, 145
        252, 384, 393, 396, 405, 447
        525, 532, 645, 678, 683
    Daniel........91, 283, 482, 486, 525
    David........193, 412, 447, 597, 687
    Dexter................485, 486
    Dorothy E..................597

CURRIER, Dorothy J..............597
    Eben F................193, 597
    Ebenezer...................525
    Edward................418, 597
    Eliza A...............300, 660
    Eliza H....................522
    Elizabeth.............356, 597
    Elizabeth P................597
    Ephraim....................525
    Eva...................598, 610
    Fanny......................597
    Farrington..........26, 313, 597
    Frank..........300, 366, 597, 622,
        675, 676, 690
    Frank D........338, 452, 488, 597
        676, 677, 682
    Fred B.....................586
    Fred R.....................600
    George K..............300, 597
    Hammond..............598, 610
    Hannah.........489, 524, 525, 526
        529, 533, 597
    Helen R....................597
    Henry.................269, 597
    Henry K...............597, 690
    Henry K. W.................597
    Henry and William......419, 482
    Horace S.......338, 359, 366, 452
        454, 541, 597, 675
    James......218, 526, 529, 656, 687
    Jennie W...................597
    John..........43, 44, 45, 69, 76, 81
        82, 83, 84, 87, 88, 89, 99, 103
        105, 107, 110, 116, 122, 124
        127, 130, 156, 160, 176, 177
        178, 179, 189, 252, 254, 314
        316, 387, 393, 394, 395, 397
        403, 406, 410, 414, 434, 439
        446, 509, 517, 524, 525, 526
        532, 533, 652, 669, 673, 678
        680, 681, 683, 686, 687, 690
    John C.....................488
    John P................597, 608
    John W.........597, 600, 679, 690
    Joseph.....................525
    Joshua..........26, 189, 193, 196
        197, 200, 447, 530, 597, 687
    Joshua E., Jr..............196
    L. K..................367, 368
    Lizzie.....................597
    Lois..............526, 531, 644
    Lorenz.....................656
    Lucy A................243, 602
    Mary.......................525
    Mary A................657, 662
    Mary D................529, 542
    Maud M.....................597
    Miriam.....................525
    Moody......................678
    Moses E........369, 609, 680, 690
    Nancy......................624
    Nancy M....................616
    Nathan............485, 486, 525
    Nathan M...................297
    Nathaniel.........88, 93, 165, 200
        209, 255, 263, 266, 279, 290
        298, 303, 322, 324, 361, 436
        446, 452, 454, 483, 486, 540
        562, 596, 597, 673, 674, 678
        679, 687, 690
    Nathaniel S...........428, 597
    Nellie B...................600
    Oliver C...................597
    Oliver P...................597
    Orpha......................237
    Permilia..............526, 532

INDEX

CURRIER, Persilla 525
  Rebecca 222, 629
  Reuben 177, 597
  Rhoda F. 516
  Rhoda M. 597
  Richard 524
  Richard, 3d 481, 482, 485, 486
  Ruth 598, 620
  Sally 532
  Samuel 404, 524
  Samuel W. 404, 598, 610
  Sarah 525, 526, 528
  Sarepta 195, 532
  Seth 525
  Simeon 598
  Sophronia 597
  Stephen 525
  Theophilus 88, 345, 356, 417, 444, 597, 687
  Theophilus, Jr. 597, 641, 687
  Theophilus S. 597
  Thomas 524
  Webster 488
  William 273, 524
  William A. 597
  William D. 97, 597
  William P. 597
  Willie D. 600
CURRIER'S HALL 302
CURRIER'S STORE 267
CURRIER & WALLACE 93, 541
CURTIS, Charles C. 159
CUSHEN, Deborah 71
  Joshua 71, 683
  Solomon 71
CUSHING Caleb 486
  Sarah 657
CUSHING'S GORE 107
CUTLER, Ezra 373
CUTTING BROS. 201
DALE, Mr. 440
DAINES, Byron 594, 598
  John P. 594
  Louisa 598
  Marcia 598
  Peabody M. 598
  Sadie R. 598
DALPHA, Lida 598
DALY, Charles H. 543
  Gertrude E. 543
  Mabel H. 543
DAME, Theophilus 153, 520
DANA, Hattie 614
DANFORTH, Betsey 662
  Jane 657
DANIELS, Asa 3, 45
  Clement 3, 44, 45, 48, 116
  George W. 101, 632
  Georgia B. 629
  Grace 632, 636
  Helen M. 662
  Ida L. 632
  Lucy M. 633
  Martha A. 633
  Ozias 632
  Seth 93, 397, 409, 447, 533
DARLING, Melinda 648
DARUSH, Andrew J. 365, 374, 380, 382, 657
DAVENPORT, Marion M. 300
DAVIS, Abigail 622
  Abram 604
  Albert F. 367, 368
  Alfred 598, 691
  Alvin 407, 489, 490, 598, 633, 680, 691
  Amanda M. 658

DAVIS, Ann 662
  Arabella A. 653
  Arvilla F. M. 523, 599
  Arthur L. 598, 620
  Axa 655
  Benjamin 237
  Benjamin F. 491
  Betsey 606
  Charles 369, 598, 623, 676, 680
  Charles H. 598
  Daniel G. S. 369, 523, 599, 691
  David 444
  Ebenezer 406, 410, 445, 688
  Ella A. 623
  Ella M. 634
  Eliza 523
  Emma 579
  Enoch 245
DAVIS, George 206, 418, 590
  George W. 128, 138, 169, 367, 409, 489, 490, 506, 598, 676
  Everett T. 598
  Fanny E. 598
  Frank A. 598
  Hannah 665
  Harry A. 598
  Herbert C. 598
  Horace L. 371
  Isaac 366, 598, 625, 641, 679, 680, 692, 693
  J. S. 366
  James H. 594, 598, 682, 691, 693
  Job S. 679
  John R. 691
  Julia A. 598
  Katherine R. 492
  Kitty 590
  Laura E. 598, 608
  Leon A. 598
  Leonard 245, 523, 599
  Leroy S. 590, 676, 680, 693
  Lilla L. 598
  Lillea M. 523
  Lizzie J. 598
  Louisa M. 583
  Lucy D. 609
  Martin 598
  Mary 523, 599, 653
  Mary E. 638
  Milan E. 598, 680
  Moses 688
  Nancy 664
  Nathan 688
  Nettie E. 598
  Orel K. 523, 599
  Peter L. 599
  Phebe 590
  Rollin E. 637
  Roxie L. 584, 598
  Ruth 609, 659
  Sally 656
  Samuel 598, 609
  Sarah 616
  Sarah E. 644
  Stephen 653
  Verne L. 598, 626
  Walter S. 691, 693
  Watts 138, 418, 464, 599
  Wesley 598
  Wesley P. 599
  Willie M. 598
DAY, Adeline 660
  Betsey 578
  Charles 366, 418, 434, 440, 442, 606, 675, 679, 692

INDEX.

Day, Daniel..................657
 David 533
 Flora B..................606
 Hannah C.................661
 John 446
 Joseph F.................691
 Leonard 657
 Lilla 622
 Mamie B..................606
 Samuel 533
 Ursula 652
 Zilpha 659
Dean, Ellen...................596
 Pauline 659
 Velous 599
Dearborn, Rev. Reuben.....242, 247
 Captain 355
Deaver, Henry J...............596
Decato, Albert............691, 693
 Almond K.................378
 Charles 692, 693
 Etta 599
 John 657
 Joseph 657
 Luella 599
 Susan 661
Defosses, Lewis...............447
Del Valle, Nina...............517
 Ysabel 517
De Morainville, Betsey........662
 Charles 657
Dennett, Captain..............354
Dennison, Elizabeth.......426, 634
Derber, Walter................657
Derby, Elihu..............195, 599
 Foster M.................599
 Joseph C.................691
 Lucy C...................599
 Mrs......................440
 Nathaniel 159, 209, 363
     414, 586, 688
 Sarah M..................657
Desmond, Thomas H........378, 383
Devereaux, William H..........657
Dexter, Kitty.................612
Dewey, Andrew............400, 415
Dickerson, Hannah.............657
 Mary E...................647
 Reverend 207
 Suel 657
Dickey, John B................603
Dickson, Macauley.............599
Digby, William......366, 377, 419, 596
 Florence H...............596
 Joseph W.................596
 Rosella E................596
Dimond, Arvilla H.............659
 Mr. and Mrs.........461, 489
Dinsmore, Susan...............662
Dodge, Alvah 132
 Arthur 630
 Clarence 630
 Ella S..............599, 630
 Elmore J.................599
 Harry 599
 Hattie R.................599
 Lena 630
 Samuel 3, 6, 20, 23, 48, 117
 Samuel, 3d........4, 47, 122, 139
 Simon 444, 630, 692
Doe, Mary E...............329, 642
Doherty, Daniel...........367, 374
Dole, Charles A...............341
 Elizabeth S..............599
 Crime of Isaac...........469
 Joseph 533

Dole, Lucy....................222
 Mary 533
 Moses 45, 82, 87
  88, 124, 128, 129, 133, 137
  185, 186, 208, 215, 219, 252
  257, 314, 431, 446, 448, 482
  486, 533, 673, 678, 682, 688
 Tavern 130, 481, 533
 Wales 131, 189, 446, 599, 688
Doloff, Franklin..............657
 Nellie S.................662
Dome, Eslay...................657
Dorsey, William...........370, 382
Doten, Ambrose C......600, 620, 691
 Betsey 222, 593
 Catherine B.........597, 600
 Eleanor 600
 Ellen F..................600
 Frank A.........492, 599, 677
 George W.................600
 Guilford 300, 599, 676, 680, 691
 Hattie F.................600
 Hattie M.................599
 Helen M..................600
 James 82, 285, 298, 392, 394
   440, 445, 486, 599, 688
 James, Jr................486
 L. Linwood...............599
 Lizzie M.................600
 Loiza 600
 Mabel P..................600
 Maria 599
 Martha 599
 Martha T.................599
 Mary 599
 Mary T...................599
 Matilda J................600
 Nellie M.................599
 William 297, 298, 417
    585, 675, 679
Douglass, Caleb...............120
 William 61, 64, 120, 139
  140, 141, 146, 147, 253, 390
  422, 437, 446, 499, 683, 686
Dow, Archie...................587
 Armena 600
 Austin V.................616
 Benjamin 277
 Caleb 300, 600
 Charles S................600
 Daniel 409, 445
 Edith M..................587
 Edwin B..................600
 Elvira 600
 Emma S...................600
 Everett 367, 369, 379, 381, 692
 Hannah 158
 Hervey S............589, 676
 Isaac 600
 Isaac W..................300
 Isophena 600
 Jacob 82, 88, 130, 209
  237, 248, 422, 441, 446
  451, 500, 600, 646, 688
 Jacob T..................600
 Joseph 300, 600
 Mary 300, 600
 Mary J...................624
 Moses, Gen............72, 79
 Pearl E..................587
 Robert W.................600
 Rozetta 600
 Samuel 643
 Sarah 600
 Sylvanus J..........382, 600
 William W................600
Dowling, Fannie 648

Downe, Captain..............352, 353
Downer, George....................657
    Ina...........................659
Downing, Mr.......................293
Downs, D. W.......................247
Drake, George................162, 288
    George W.....................657
    James C......................482
    John.........................657
    John H.......................657
    Samuel..............215, 222, 223
                  287, 432, 688
    Thomas.......................688
Dresser, Amelia B.................658
    Belle M......................598
Drew, Almary......................600
    Calvin S.....................600
    Jacob........................461
    Joseph H.....................615
    Roseanna.....................600
    Sally........................600
Drown, Hattie.....................639
Drugg, Thomas.....................600
Dubia, Ethel E....................599
    James...................491, 492
Dudley, Mr.........................94
    Timothy B....................260
Dunbar, Margaret..................515
Duncan, Margaret..................172
    William H...............299, 416
Dunham, Almon.....................601
    Ann..........................440
    Ann K........................659
    Austin.................367, 380, 657
    Eugene.......................601
    Frances R....................601
    Hiram U......................601
    Louisa.......................601
    Orison.......................657
    Phineas C.....................91
    Phineas O....................691
    Timothy A..............368, 373
    Willard L..............657, 691
Dunklee, Helen....................597
    John C.......................597
Dunning, Charles L................603
    C. U..................245, 247, 486
Duphonot, John................691, 693
Duplesse, Ira I...................601
Dupuis, Zeb.......................657
Durgin, William S.................608
Durkee, Bartholomew...............113
    Nathan.................345, 355
Durocher, Odil....................613
Durrell, Augusta E................601
    Daniel.................601, 616
    Daniel I...............601, 620
    Elizabeth J............601, 654
    Emeline A..............587, 601
    Eunice.......................601
    Eunice S.....................601
Dustins......................499, 502
Dustin, Alfred B.............222, 601
    Betsey.......................500
    Blanche......................601
    Caleb...............94, 234, 236, 246
          247, 417, 486, 500, 617
          622, 674, 676, 679, 688
    Caroline E...................500
    Cassius M....................619
    Charles W...............94, 601
    Daniel..................502, 683
    David..............70, 71, 143, 145, 147
          232, 343, 345, 363, 395, 398
          411, 441, 499, 596, 682, 688
    Dudley B...............500, 688
    Eben R.......................488

Dustin, Emeline..........300, 501, 610
    Emily........................500
    Emily J......................488
    Francis.................500, 688
    Franklin.....................500
    Franklin T..........365, 376, 601
    Gertrude.....................601
    Hannah.............499, 584, 601
    Harriet B...............300, 502
    James..............362, 500, 501
    John.........................653
    John B............359, 457, 501, 653
    John R.......234, 237, 412, 601, 688
    John W.......................601
    Jonathan.............35, 57, 63, 118
          123, 177, 343, 344, 390
          405, 437, 446, 499, 683
    Jonathan, Jr.........446, 499, 683
    Joseph...............47, 48, 91, 122
          162, 212, 275, 281, 283
          297, 298, 308, 344, 359
          362, 363, 366, 440, 499
          500, 501, 514, 670, 679
    Loraine H....................500
    Lydia........................664
    Melvina J....................601
    Minnie.......................601
    Nathan.......................502
    Paul.........................246
    Rebecca A...............300, 502
    Ruth................63, 441, 499
    Samuel..........437, 499, 502, 514
    Silas........................412
    Sophronia....................502
    Susanna......................502
    Sylvester....................601
    William W...........367, 379, 601
Dutton, Silas.....................609
Dwinels, Catherine................601
    Charles W........488, 601, 686, 691
    Daisy........................601
    George.......................601
    James........................601
    Julianna G...................601
    Louisa.......................601
    Moses........................601
    Sarah........................610
    Sarah C......................601
Dyke, Lyman.......................601
Eames, Ebenezer...3, 5, 13, 26, 27, 28, 34
          46, 50, 52, 53, 57, 143
          168, 391, 422, 446, 677, 685
    Joseph......................3, 45
Earle, Flossie M..................651
Eastman, Abigail.............231, 622
    Albert.......................300
    Allie S......................602
    Alphonso.....................606
    Arthur H.....................652
    Bartlett.....................602
    Caroline.....................601
    Caroline M...................606
    Caroline P...................301
    Cogswell.....................601
    Daniel.......................657
    Elwell.......................601
    Enoch........................489
    George S.....................300
    Gertrude A...................618
    Grace H......................652
    Grant C......................652
    Henry........................657
    Ira..........................671
    James........47, 209, 243, 244, 260, 304
          416, 602, 652, 674, 679, 688
    James F..............602, 651, 652
    John.........................601

INDEX.

EASTMAN, Josephine 601
  Larned 202, 243, 602
  Lizzie F. 607
  Margaret 602
  Martha 652
  Martha J. 653
  Mary 602
  Mary A. 601, 641
  Mary F. 652
  Miranda 613
  Miriam 301, 602, 612
  Moses 601
  Moses F. 602
  Obidiah 159
  Peggy 601
  Persis T. 601
  Phineas 93, 131, 193, 239, 268
        276, 280, 281, 454, 601, 688
  Rhoda 602
  Rachel 601
  Richard B. 692
  Ruth B. 649
  Simeon 601
  Sophronia 602, 635
  Stephen 243, 300, 602, 652, 683
  Susan E. 652
  William E. ... 159, 304, 305, 306, 674
EATON, C. E. 247
  Ebeneazer 602, 688
  Edward 657
  George M. 602
  James M. 367, 368, 602, 633
  Lois 610
  Lucinda M. 602
  Mary F. 602
  Mr. 241
  Nathaniel 91, 416, 418, 602, 691
  Sally 661
  Susannah 602
EDGERLY, M. V. B. 672
EDWARDS, Angie 620
  Benton 602
  Betsey A. 662
  Burns W. 367, 368, 602
  Byron 367, 368, 602
  Elijah W. 593, 602, 610, 692
  Perry 602
  Wilks 649
ELDRIDGE, Dilla 657
  Elsa 633
ELKINS, Sarah 622
ELLIOTT, Andrew 356
  Betsey 602
  Carrie E. 524, 608
  Elizabeth 524, 664
  Emeline 602, 642
  Freeman E. 602
  Hattie 602, 634
  Henry E. 602
  Henry W. 602
  Joel 602, 638
  Roswell 524, 602, 679
  Sarah M. 524
ELLIS, Caleb 670
ELMER, Adelia 590
EMERSON, Caleb D. 602
  Captain 354
  Charles A. 657
  Charles E. 602
  Charles H. 616
  Isaiah 240
  Isaiah E. 641
  Jesse E. 287
  Marcia A. 659
  Maria 630
EMERY, Dan G. 644
  Gwendolin 644

EMERY, Mary C. 644
EMMONS, Abigail 609
EMORY, Hannah L. 617
  Helen M. 660
  Richard 246
ENGLISH, John 247
EVANS, Alexander 593
  Asaph 539
  Charlotte 658
  Chloe 197
  Edward 486
  George 193, 194, 196, 197
  Henry 373
  Lois 445, 651
  Lucretia D. 584
  Samuel 378, 382
  Thomas 630, 657
EVERETT, Captain 354
  C. F. 488
EVON, Irene S. 602
FAIRBANKS, Joseph 246
FAIRFIELD, Adelia M. 611
  Anna C. 611
  Arthur P. 611
  Calvin P. 611, 616
  Ella H. 611
  Helen F. 611
  Marion 611
  Marion H. 611
  Payson E. 611
  Sarah L. 611
FALES, Abby 659
  Abigail 301, 603
  Arnold 603, 609
  Augusta A. 603
  Caleb 244, 603
  Caroline E. 603
  Charles H. 588
  Clara J. 588
  David 603, 609
  Dorothy 620
  Dorothy H. 602
  Eliza 602, 622
  Emily D. 603
  Eunice C. 585, 603
  George 159, 443, 588, 692
  Hannah E. 588
  Henry 603
  Horace 603
  Inda 603
  Jabez H. 603, 622
  John 11, 83, 89, 91, 131
        133, 151, 193, 221, 224, 297
        397, 410, 447, 453, 602, 688
  John, Jr. 91, 193, 195, 272, 284
  John D. 603
  Joseph B. 588
  Joseph H. 603
  Julia H. 603
  Laura 603
  Loraine H. 603
  Lucy A. 586, 588
  Maria 588
  Martha J. 603
  Mary 595
  Mary C. 602, 637
  Mary M. 586, 588
  Orrin 159, 443, 588, 603, 688
  Orrin G. 588
  Polly 602
  Sarah 195, 301, 603
  Silvia 595, 602
  Susan C. 603
  Willard A. 602
FARMER, John 210
FARNUM, Daniel .. 60, 79, 80, 313, 314, 392
        405, 407, 444, 603, 678

INDEX.

FARNUM, George W..............603
  Hannah C.....................603
  Hazen R...........675, 679, 692
  Jonathan.....................603
  Lucy S.......................603
  Luther C.....................603
  Phebe........................603
  Ransom.......................300
  Sally S......................603
  S. C....................246, 247
FARRER, Nathaniel.........314, 315
FARRINGTON, Mary................597
FELCH, Benjamin F..............691
  Cora.........................632
  Ella.........................632
  Hannah.......................222
  James C..........632, 676, 691
FELLOWS, Antoinette............622
  Benjamin.....................657
  Eliza C......................661
  Gilbert G....................658
  Lucinda......................656
  Lydia A......................664
  Mercy........................603
  Moses........................658
  Stephen......................487
  Truman.......................658
  Wilfred D....................607
FERGUSON, Franklin.............658
  Persis.......................583
FERNALD, J. H..................489
FESSENDEN, Thomas G.............73
FIELD, Joseph..................645
  Otis....................221, 222
FIFIELD, Adin G................616
  Alice........................603
  Davidson.....................616
  David........................657
  Edson J........369, 381, 616, 630, 691
  Elmer........................616
  Enoch........................434
  Ezekiel......................657
  Frank S.................590, 616
  Georgianna M.................603
  Ira..........................453
  Joseph.......................630
  Libius.......................641
  Mehitable....................585
  Pomelia......................658
  Sarah A......................601
  William......................616
  William H...............630, 693
FINCH, Abigail..................65
  Henry...............422, 603, 683
FISH, Theoda...................603
FISHER, Betsey.................594
  Eva A........................632
  Mahala D.....................610
FISK, Mr........................84
FISKE, Daniel..................641
FITTS, Richard.................647
FITZ, Harriet H................656
FITZGERALD, E..................491
FIZETTE, James.................658
FLAGG, Albion W............595, 599
  Hannah.......................661
  Hannah W.....................603
  Harriet A....................654
  Jacob........................657
  Joseph.......................205
  Lois.........................603
  William......................657
FLANDERS, Abraham H.......300, 428
  Alice M......................604
  Anna.........................222
  Augustus B...................604
  Bertha M.....................604

FLANDERS, Betsey...............660
  Betsey A................604, 618
  Elijah..................362, 637
  Elijah C......434, 604, 630, 680, 692
  Frederick....................604
  George M.....................604
  Georgia......................604
  Gracia..................604, 614
  Hannah.......................533
  Hattie E.....................615
  Irad.........................604
  John...........193, 414, 589, 604
              614, 647, 688
  John B.......................159
  John C.......................604
  Joshua..................362, 604
  Julia A......................604
  Julia Y......................604
  Lydia B......................604
  Margaret.....................603
  Martha.......................607
  Mary.........................533
  Mary J.........585, 604, 656, 658
  Minnie.......................614
  Moses............399, 533, 658, 688
  Sally........................533
  Sarah A. L...................300
  Sarah E......................604
  Sarah J......................604
  Sarah M......................604
  Susan........................604
  Susanna.................270, 299
  Sylvester..........340, 604, 625
  Theodate......................64
  Thomas..........90, 162, 256, 269
          281, 282, 285, 288
          297, 298, 428, 441
          456, 462, 657, 670
  Timothy......................533
FLEETHAM, Constance............595
  Ernest D.....................595
FLETCHER, Daniel...............246
  Joseph M.....................672
  Sarah...................222, 630
FLINT, Abigail..................89
  Benjamin.....................657
  Edward.......................604
  Edwin..............424, 528, 691
  George.........412, 446, 528, 628
  Horace C.....................528
  John...............109, 111, 543
  John C.......................528
  Joseph...60, 61, 64, 108, 145, 174, 253
    390, 447, 506, 533, 604, 683, 685
  Lavinia......................584
  Louisa.......................529
  Lucy....................604, 648
  Lydia........................198
  Mary.........................536
  Oscar W......................529
  Polly...................604, 626
  Sally..............499, 604, 623
FLOYD, Mrs.....................494
  Charles M....................672
FLURY, Frederick...............374
FOGG, David.......60, 63, 65, 143, 300
        389, 441, 499, 682, 686
  George W.....................604
  Harrison..........26, 300, 604, 632
  Lucy.........................604
  Mary....................318, 514
  Samuel.......................604
  Wallace G....................604
FOLLANSBEE, Abi................604
  (Follensbee) Addie M.........492
  Arabella.....................604
  Arthur P.....................491

INDEX. 713

FOLLANSBEE, Betsey..............313
   Clara D....................604
   Clara P................620, 664
   Daniel..................362, 461
   Elizabeth..................597
   Ephraim H..................657
   Frances G..................604
   Hannah.....................515
   Harry..................420, 675
   Henry H....................604
   Herbert E..................604
   Ida........................604
   James..................414, 620
   James M....................657
   John 344, 345, 394, 409, 447, 632
   John B.....................657
   Joseph.................46, 102
   Joseph J..............650, 691
   Lewis C............676, 680, 691
   Lucian A...................604
   Martha.................313, 612
   Mary A.....................604
   Moses......................688
   Nathan ..312, 344, 345, 353, 356, 686
   Nettie M...................604
   Offranda A.................301
   Orrin M....................604
   Perley R...................604
   Rhoda......................620
   Sarah..................313, 612
   Sarah B....................584
   Seth P.................419, 604
   Susanna....................657
   William B..................362
FOLSOM, Abigail................654
  (Fulsom) Angeline S...........603
   Betsey.....................605
   Cyrus......................604
   Elizabeth S................605
   George.................605, 658
   Harry H....................605
   Hiram......................605
   Horace.....................603
   Jeames.....................605
   John.......................658
   John C.....................604
   Joseph...............604, 683, 688
   Josiah...............605, 683, 686
   Lucia A....................595
   Mary.......................595
   Mary J.....................604
   Minnie M...................492
   Navessa....................605
   Rufus H....................604
   Sally..................591, 605
   Samuel..................71, 684
   Samuel, Jr.................605
   Sheleb.....................605
   Stephen................483, 486
   Steven.....................605
   Widow.......................80
FORD, Adoniram.................692
   Charles H..................489
   David T....................591
   Herman A...................658
   Horace.....................658
   George N...................658
   J. Alonzo..................644
   Jerusha....................658
   John.......................593
   John N.....................371
   Luther.....................658
   Richard T..................658
FORTIES, Zephraim............372, 383
FOSS, John C...................658
   Mary A.....................660
   Topham.....................657

FOSTER, Rev. Amos 195, 210–222, 229, 235
          236, 296, 322, 325, 423
          432, 444, 470, 484, 486
          570, 605, 688
   Benjamin F.................658
   Broughton W................605
   Ellen M....................605
   Frances J..................605
   Harriet E..................605
   Herschel...................246
   Hezekiah...................658
   John...................246, 588
   Jonathan....................88
   Mercy......................622
FOWLE, Daniel...........3, 27, 102, 117
FOWLER, Asa....................671
   Ellen D....................660
   Susan A....................599
FOX, Elizabeth.................605
   Fanny O....................605
   Harvey.....................605
   John F.....................658
   Lucy.......................657
   Mary I.....................633
   Sarah.......................71
   William, Jr........3, 46, 113, 449
FRASER, Henry W................542
FREEMAN, Daniel................658
   Jonathan................72, 76
   Mehitable..................661
FRENCH, Amos...................658
   Darwin G...................529
   Deacon......................46
   Emma L.....................529
   George H...................529
   Guy C......................529
   Hannah F...................659
   Hattie W...................529
   Helen......................624
   Helen M....................529
   Henry..................30, 657
   James H...............380, 382
   John.......................658
   Levi.......................529
   Lois M.....................529
   Mary A.....................626
   Moses..................163, 597
   Nancy......................623
   Nathan.....................658
   Polly..............243, 244, 602
   Rhoda......................622
   Samuel.....................222
FROST, Amasa...................657
   Mehitable S................516
FULLER, Rev. E. C.....223, 266, 279, 286
          287, 295, 296
   E. M.......................293
FURBER, George C...............611
   Ida........................611
   James A...............480, 611
   Loraine....................611
   M. T.......................491
   Sarah......................611
FURLONG, James.............367, 379
GAGE, Daniel B.................658
   Deborah....................655
   Lura.......................622
GALE, Ezra................398, 688
   John A.....................658
   Sarah......................630
GARDNER, Ezekiel....50, 61, 70, 145, 176
    344, 345, 355, 445, 450, 684, 686
   George Warner..............426
   Reverend...................202
   Sanford....................364
   William....................356
GARFIELD, Marie................585

GARLAND, Herman T..............605
   Herbert 636
   Lou C.........................628
   Louise J......................605
GARNET, Henry Highland...291, 292, 294
GARVIN, Solomon..................691
GATES, Amanda M..................605
   Americus 91, 271
   Bella 605
   Charlotte 522, 605
   Ennice 605
   Eunice F......................605
   General 351, 355
   Grace L.......................605
   Hannah B......................631
   Horatio 605, 676, 679
   Horatio B......436, 605, 677, 680
   Joshua C......................605
   Josiah, Jr........4, 6, 13, 20, 23, 27
                  46, 57, 117
   Leora A.......................605
   Marvin 605
   Maud S...................605, 637
   Mrs. 202
   Newton B............369, 605, 691
   Pertie J..................605, 637
   Reynold 130, 145, 177, 181
              186, 343, 345, 405
              431, 436, 447, 522
              605, 684, 686, 688
   Samuel J........130, 158, 159, 344
             345, 396, 447, 605, 686
   Samuel T.....................131
   Thomas 4, 5, 46, 113, 344, 350
   William 499
   William H.....................605
   Zebulon 61
GAY, Jerome..................376, 382
GEORGE, Agnes L..................606
   Allen H.................366, 377, 486
              488, 606, 647, 678
   Artemisia 606
   Benjamin P.....93, 94, 142, 159, 605
   Bertha 606
   Betsey 605
   Carlos C......................606
   Carrie M......................606
   Celinda A.....................606
   Charlotte T..............606, 649
   Charles 606
   Clarissa 606
   Eleanor H.....................606
   Elijah 606
   Eudora E......................606
   Estelle A................605, 621
   Ennice W......................606
   Flora M.......................583
   Frances K.....................606
   Frank A.......................606
   Grace I.......................606
   Hannah 605
   Harriet S............301, 606, 614
   Henry C..............91, 339, 416
              606, 641, 674, 679
   Irving T.................339, 606
   Isabelle M........300, 424, 606, 647
   Isaac K.......................606
   Levi 46, 82, 134, 149
           235, 237, 366, 688, 692
   Louisa 606
   Lucinda 606
   Mary 605
   Mary A........................606
   Mary J........................606
   Mary L........................597
   Mercyline 606
   Moses E.......................606

GEORGE, Thomas M.................606
   Wallace B.....................606
   William W....162, 298, 303, 366, 368
            369, 401, 449, 454, 462
            606, 674, 675, 676, 679
GEROULD, Rev. Moses...........224, 337
   Samuel L......................427
   Sarah 589
GERRISH, Col. Henry...........104, 156
GIBBS, Sarah.....................647
GILBERT, John F..................658
   Mary E........................656
GILE, Amos.......................606
   Daniel 417
   Dorothy C. F..................607
   Ezekiel 352
   Hannah 608, 655
   Henry J..................376, 606
   Ira S.........................658
   John 606
   Julia A.......................301
   Lovicy 607
   Lucy 301
   Lydia H.......................301
   Mary A..............206, 606, 616
   Mehitable 606
   Nelson 658
   Reuben 46, 154, 398, 446, 688
   Richard 688
   Samuel 234
   Stephen 658, 688
   Warren N......................607
GILES, Benjamin...................49
GILKERSON, Hiram.................653
   Ida M.........................653
   John 653
GILL, Lydia......................643
GILLETT, Frank...................542
   Evelyn F......................542
GILLIS, Albert S.................607
   Lizzie 607
GILMAN, Alvah.............367, 379, 607
   Arvilla 607
   Betsey 607
   Caleb 222, 287, 607, 623, 688
   Charles H.....................607
   Daniel H.................532, 607
   Dudley 30, 75, 88
            129, 144, 173, 174, 422
            448, 607, 677, 681, 684
   Edward H......................607
   Eliphalet C...........196, 298, 359
              415, 607, 617
   Elmer A..................532, 607
   Ezra 532, 607, 688
   Fred B........................607
   Hannah W......................607
   Horatio A..............491, 607, 679
   James C.......................607
   Jesse 607
   John 382, 383
   John B........................658
   John S........................300
   John T...........76, 79, 607, 669, 670
   Josie 607
   Laura P.......................607
   Lucia 607
   Lydia 191
   Mary 88, 607
   Mary G........................500
   Minerva W.....................607
   Nathaniel 71, 143, 145
           177, 182, 193, 393, 403
           406, 412, 446, 607, 688
   Nicholas, Hon.................86
   Phoebe 601
   Sally 520, 523, 607

INDEX. 715

GILMAN, Samuel......193, 607, 647, 688
   Sarah 183
   Sidney A..................607
   Sidney B..................607
   Steven 607
   Steven S..................300
   Uriah S...................607
GILMORE, Joseph A..............671
   Winthrop 607
GILPATRICK, Josephine...........644
GINN, George...................498
   Harold R..................607
   Mildred P.................607
GLEASON, Elmira................607
   Emily S...............607, 619
   Sewall 189, 398, 410
                   411, 447, 688
   Winsor 607
GLODE, Peter...................658
GLOGGETT, Enos.............367, 379
GOBAR, Charles O...............607
   Lola A....................607
GODDARD, Rev. Samuel...........217
GODETTE, William...............658
GODY, Joseph...................658
GOODELL, David A...............672
   Welthea W.................619
GOODHUE, David.............529, 601
   Elsie 612
   George H......226, 435, 612, 623
   J. Merrill 612
   Merrill 612
   Stephen 397
GOODRICH, B. E.................369
   Joshua 688
   Lydia 614
GOODWIN, Ichabod..............671
GORDON, Charles S..............607
   Clemmie A.................607
   Earl C................429, 608
   Ella A....................607
   Emma F...................492
   Ethelyn A.................608
   Frank L...................607
   George H......488, 490, 491, 533
                   608, 677, 682
   Harold G..................608
   Judith 609
   L. H......................246
   Lawrence O................598
   Leila M...................608
   Lucian N..................375
   Mamie G..................608
   Mary E....................607
   Ralph W..............598, 608
   Ruth C....................608
   Vaughan L.................608
   Willie 607
   Capt. William......379, 440, 454
                   590, 607, 692
   William 297, 418
   William A.................367
GORHAM, Eva S.............594, 624
GOSS, Abbie....................608
   Abby F....................608
   Albert 593, 594, 608
   Anna D....................608
   Beatrice 594, 608
   Ben A................598, 608
   Bernice E............490, 608
   Calista S..................608
   Charley 608
   Daniel 408, 594, 608
                   653, 677, 680, 692
   Dell J.....................492
   Dora 608, 640
   Elmira C..................608

GOSS, Elizabeth................608
   Emma 608
   Hannah A.................592
   Harris J...........434, 489, 491
               608, 626, 677, 680
   Isabelle M.................638
   Jethro 608
   Jonathan 608
   Joshua 608, 688
   Lena 608
   Levi 608
   Levi M....................608
   Lizzie L...................608
   Louisa M..................655
   Nellie S...................608
   Nettie 651
   Orvill 366, 371, 608
   Reuben 418, 608, 620, 637
   Richard 608
   Roxanna 608
   Ruby I....................608
   Rufus S...............367, 380
   Russell 608
   Sarah 608
   Susannah 608
   Susie S...................608
   Wallace R.............524, 608
   Walter 608
GOULD, Abigail.................609
   Alanson 609
   Amos 132, 187, 189, 208, 209
              222, 223, 287, 410, 416
              418, 447, 586, 678, 688
   David 88, 209, 609, 688
   Diadema 609
   Dorothy P.................660
   Hannah 608
   Hannah S.............608, 627
   Huldah 363
   John T....................609
   Joseph T..................609
   Martha H.................614
   Nathan 290, 608, 688
   Rebecca 590
   Sarah 661
   Sarah C...................608
   Sylvester P............609, 614
GOVE, Elijah............356, 412, 688
   Hattie I...................661
   Rody 664
GRAHAM, George................609
   George W.................609
GRANGER, Elihu................486
GRAVES, Nancy.................646
GRAY, Nellie P..................521
GRAVILLE, Joseph............368, 375
GREELEY, Abigail............609, 648
   Achsah 609
   David 458, 609, 628
   Ellen A...................625
   Ephraim 609
   Hannah 609, 640
   Ira 609
   John D...................609
   Lydia 609
   Mathew 81, 129, 131, 209, 344
              353, 356, 447, 609, 688
   Nancy 609
   Sally 609
   Sarah 603
   Shubael 361, 609
   Susan P..................609
GREENE, A. S...........30, 267, 446
   (Green) Edwin...........658
   Emily A..................621
   J. A.................100, 488
   James 370, 376, 382, 383

Index

GREENE, Nelson................247
GREENFIELD, Charles........406, 446
GREENOUGH, Robert................609
GRIFFITH, Amelia B................611
GRIMES, Alice A................587
GROSS, Rufus S................692
GROVES, Anthony................596
    Horace S................619, 624
GUNSCH, Edwin................372
GUSTIN, Thomas........3, 6, 43, 45, 46
    48, 49, 102
    Thomas, Jr................3, 48
HACKETT, Corcellus H.........97, 633
    James................633
HADLEY, Aaron................610
    Abel......61, 64, 131, 144, 145, 174
    176, 252, 366, 371, 396
    431, 609, 610, 684, 686
    Albert L................609, 680
    Amos................609, 658, 688
    Andrew J................488, 610
    Angie E................609
    Arabel................597, 609
    Azro B................692
    Bertha D................492
    Calvin................610
    Charlotte................660
    Charles................610
    Dennis................610
    Diana................657
    Dorcas................593, 610
    E. L................488
    E. S................488
    Eben................610, 691
    Edwin A................609
    Eliza A................661
    Emeline D................595
    Emma................501
    Etta M................597, 610
    Eva M................610
    Florence................610
    George W................111, 609, 691
    Gilbert S................692
    Gilman................610
    Hamlin E................610
    Hannah................641
    Henry M................659
    Howard................610
    Ida A................610
    Isabel R................610
    Jacob................609
    John M................610
    Joshua................609, 659
    Joshua M................637
    Kimball................247
    Laura................660
    Leonard................420, 610, 653
    Linnie C................610
    Lizzie................501
    Lydia................609
    Lyman................610
    Malvina................609
    Marcia................609, 610
    Marcia A................639
    Mariann................609
    Mary E................583
    Miriah................598, 609
    Molly................184
    Moses................160, 174, 184, 195
    198, 447, 610, 688
    Nancy M................602, 610, 663
    Norman................198, 607
    Obadiah................610, 617
    Orra................610
    Relief................609
    Sarah................610
    Silas................659

HADLEY, Simeon..297, 300, 404, 448, 501
    609, 610, 684, 688
    Sophia................603, 609
    Stephen................371, 610, 633
    Stephen, Jr................610, 640
    Stephen, 3d................601
    Susan M................610, 640
    Warren B................610
    William H................659
    William K................590
HADLOCK, G. O................488
HAFFENREFFER, R. H...159, 437, 440, 453
HAGGETT, Albert A................440 594
    Minnie L................594
HALE, Elizabeth................593
    Enoch................350
    Moses T................659
    Samuel W................672
    William................670, 671
HALL, Adaline................659
    Alma................657
    Anthony................659
    Asa A................380, 382
    Bertha................633
    Elder................192
    Eugenia E................632
    Frank................691
    George O................633
    George W................691
    Hendrick................586
    Henry................612
    John A................659
    Joshua................612
    Louisa................661
    Martha S. W................644
    Polly................612
    Sally................612
    William........369, 434, 489, 604
    676, 680, 691
HAM, Asa A................159
    Betsey................454
HAMILTON, Cyrus B................189, 423
    Harriet................222
    Rev. Jonathan................285
HAMLETT, Hattie A................655
    Henry S................300, 372, 659
    Levi................94, 402, 518
    Warren W................372, 383
HANCHETT, Diantha................650
    Elam................650
    Nathaniel................650
    Samantha................650
HANDERSON, Anna M................610
HANNAFORD, Sidney R................639
HANSCUM, Mary A................656
HANSON, Ben................610
    Ebenezer................251, 610
    Hannah................610
    Jeremy S................610
    John................610
    Lucy................610
    Mariame................610
    William G................610
HAPGOOD, Joseph................159
HARDY, A. C................247
    Alden................648
    Almira................610
    Biley................87
    Elder................235, 236
    Gilman................610
    Hannah................591
    John W................246
    Mary A................651, 662
    Mary E................610
    Mercy................65, 244
    Orra H................372, 383
    Rachel C................610

INDEX. 717

HARDY, Sarah A............657
　Thomas J........595, 610, 659
HAROON, Samuel............659
HARPER, Nellie J............630
HARRIGAN, John............590
HARRIMAN, Molly............604
　Capt. Steven..............80
　Walter..................671
HARRIS, Abbie F............591
　Anna............611, 612, 621
　Arabella........301, 612, 621
　Benjamin......61, 612, 684, 686
　Betsey..................612
　Daniel......3, 5, 13, 19, 46, 394
　Dexter........305, 366, 612
　Ebenezer..................3, 46
　Eliza....................612
　Eliza A..................611
　Eliza B..............612, 626
　Elizabeth............516, 612
　Emma J..................612
　Frederick M..............611
　George 3, 5, 13, 19, 23
　　　　24, 26, 28, 30, 34, 40
　　　　41, 48, 57, 61, 104, 123
　　　　165, 231, 312, 445, 496, 611
　　　　612, 677, 681, 684, 685, 687
　George D............367, 612
　George H......222, 223, 224, 287, 292
　　　　305, 313, 344, 416, 435
　George L............612, 675
　George M..................611
　Georgianna..............612
　Gibson 3, 13, 48, 113
　Hannah H......611, 612, 614
　Harriet..................611
　Hubbard ...82, 88, 90, 132, 145, 174
　　　　176, 222, 486, 612, 678, 688
　Hubbard, Jr.......279, 283, 287
　　　　313, 323, 324, 540
　Isaac B..................612
　Israel 102, 128, 176, 445, 612
　James 367, 375
　James S..................612
　Jason E..................612
　Jesse....................612
　John, Hon............316, 324
　John, Dr......40, 69, 75, 123, 143
　　　　148, 252, 422, 446, 677, 684
　John A..................611
　John H......30, 88, 89, 165, 215, 219
　　　　254, 255, 263, 358, 396, 416
　　　　611, 622, 673, 674, 678, 688
　Joshua ..40, 41, 43, 44, 45, 54, 62, 68
　　　　69, 78, 82, 83, 88, 123
　　　　124, 172, 177, 209, 219, 344
　　　　345, 353, 361, 392, 394, 398
　　　　404, 408, 440, 445, 448, 452
　　　　611, 623, 677, 681, 686, 688
　Kittie..................611
　Lemira L................611
　Lenora W................612
　Lois................612, 625
　Lucy............578, 612, 641
　Lucy M..................611
　Lydia....................612
　Marcia M................611
　Martha........209, 270, 470
　Mary................612, 637
　Mary F......222, 265, 266, 611
　Mehitable................612
　Miriam........174, 180, 470
　Octavia..................612
　Oscar W............591, 612
　Polly....................611
　R. L....................637
　Sally................611, 612

HARRIS, Sarah......222, 277, 313
　Sarah F..................301
　Sarah J..................612
　Sarah S............611, 616
　Tilton..................693
　William......102, 176, 398, 411
　　　　412, 445, 612, 688
　William L......366, 612, 675, 676
HARTWELL, H. H............247
HARTY, Capt. John D........363
HARVEY, David..............688
　Mathew..................670
　Timothy M................659
HASKELL, William H........659
HASTINGS, Lydia............324
HATCH, Horace..............659
HAVEN, George W............659
HAWKINS, Captain............355
HAWKS, Mary................639
HAYES, Allen......94, 455, 611, 674
　Idella M................611
　John H..................611
　Joseph..................247
　William A................328
HAYNES, Benjamin......236, 237, 252
　　　　612, 678, 688
　Francis A................612
　George..................612
　John....................612
　Josiah P......159, 297, 413
　Martha J................612
　Ruthy..................612
　Sally..................595
　Sumner..................612
HAYWARD, Augustus R......605, 620
　Captain..................554
　Orinda..................620
　Ruel....................620
　Wilmer H................613
HAZELTINE, Alberto C......613
　Daniel..................369
　David..................659
　Ellen S..................527
　George..................527
　George H................527
　George W......100, 613, 680, 691
　Grace E............613, 618
　Julia....................527
　Hollis B................659
　Jonathan................500
　Minnie E................613
　P. Jennie................527
　Rebecca G................653
　Richman..................692
　Sally............520, 523, 613
　William..................613
HAZEN, Celinda............301
　Edmund..................444
　N. H....................658
　Samuel..................658
HEAD, Nat................672
HEAFIELD, Mary D..........651
HEALEY, Joseph............670
HEATH, A............247, 299
　Bartholomew......222, 287, 412
　　　　432, 688
　Betsey..................656
　Cynthia P................654
　David..................440
　Irene S..................652
　John R............613, 692
　Leonard..................691
　Lora....................648
　Lyman E................613
　Olivia W................301
　Sally..................613
　Samuel............145, 684

HEATH, Samuel W............658
  Susan 613, 661
  Tyler 368, 371
  Wilbur R..................659
HEATON, Arthur...............659
  Charles 648
HEBERT, Esther...............613
  Joseph 226, 613, 659
  Leedus 366, 377
  Noah 659
HEDDING, Elijah............243, 246
HENDEE, Capt. Joshua....350, 351, 352
HENDERSON, Isabelle E.........613
HEYDOCK, W. T................473
HEWS, Eliza..................532
  Sybel 605
HIBBARD, Jedediah....26, 27, 30, 32, 34
                   344, 350, 351, 353, 355
  Laura E..................631
HILL, Agnes..................657
  Cas 113
  Charles 613
  Frank 613
  Freddie A.................613
  Frederick 486
  Harry O...................613
  Isaac 539, 679
  John M...................672
  Mary A...................657
  Moses 613, 658
  Napoleon J..............420, 659
  Col. Thomas...............278
  Thomas J..................659
  Villa A...................613
  Willie G..................613
HILLIARD, Benjamin T..........654
  Benjamin Y..............415, 679
  Samuel 619
HILLMAN, J. H................247
HILLS, James.................355
  Tiles 659
HIMES, Adelphi W.............198
  Rev. Palmer C...........198, 299
HINDS, Justice J.............474
HINKSON, Betsey M............613
  Chamberlain P.............613
  Daniel 410, 411, 434, 444
                    613, 627, 688
  Daniel F................376, 613
  Delia L.................613, 636
  Eleanor L.................606
  George 366, 461, 659, 676
  Leander 613
  Louisa W..................627
  Mrs. 202
  Rodosca K.................636
  Samuel 60, 61, 344, 345, 659, 686
HINMAN, W. S.................528
HISCOCK, Laura E.............664
HOAGUE, Joseph...............659
  Sarah 615
HOBART, Colonel..............351
  I. N....................302, 332
  Nathan 486
  William E...............694, 693
HOBBS, Catherine.............593
  John 593
HOFFMAN, Beletson............372
  Edward A..................616
  Henry 365
  Minnie M..................616
  Sophia E..................616
HOISINGTON, H. G.............247
HOIT, Abigail..............613, 655
(Hoyt) Albert................601
  Albert A..................586
  Anna 609

HOIT, B. F...................234
  Bartlett 91, 95, 209, 272
                    297, 579, 688
  Benjamin H................614
  Daniel 529, 613, 659, 670, 671
  David 613, 645
  Ebeneazer 42, 157, 158
                    514, 659, 673
  Eliza J...................614
  Frank A...................613
  George 613
  George F..................529
  Hannah 455
  Hannah P..................613
  Joel 613
  John 82, 131, 209, 222, 344, 354
                  355, 440, 447, 613, 688
  John, Jr................586, 613
  John G....................613
  John W..........94, 137, 159, 368
                    370, 379, 381, 613
  Josephine A...............614
  Judith 613
  Levi 579
  Levi W....................300
  Lois 633
  Lois M....................529
  Moses 659
  Nancy 613, 662
  Nancy M..................6, 662
  Nathan W..................662
  Ned L.....................614
  Olive G...................659
  Persis 613
  Robert 209, 344, 345, 613, 688
  Rufus 414
  Rufus A.................614, 688
  Rufus S...................614
  Samuel 486, 489
  Sarah 656
  Stephen B.................613
  T. M......................488
  Warren E................614, 682
  Will A............578, 614, 680
HOLCOMB, Eliza J.............625
  James M...................625
  Lucy E....................625
  Mary C....................625
HOLDEN, Zenas D..............644
HOLLENBACK, John C...........642
HOLLIS, H. F.................672
HOLMAN, Joshua.............242, 247
HOLT, Ann R..................614
  George E..................659
  George F..................614
  James S.................376, 382
  John 369
  John A....................659
  Nathan S..................488
  Sadie A...................614
  William 614
HOMAN, Caleb N...............616
  Mabel R...................625
  Samuel N..................625
  Susan 629
HOMER, Jonathan Rev..........156
HONEY, Ichabod................70
HOOPER, Rev. Mr..............173
HOPEY, Fath R................614
HOPKINS, John................610
HORNBROOKE, Mary A...........587
HORR, Leonard......35, 60, 120, 686
HOSLEY, Josette..............587
HOSMER, John.................489
HOUGH, Hannah................611
HOUSE, Captain...............351
HOUSTON, Ann.................656

Index. 719

Hovey, Abigail............................656
   Daniel 88, 89, 208, 209
            345, 350, 354, 423, 484
            486, 612, 614, 684, 688
   Dudley 688
   Edward O..........................614
   George H..........................614
   Jacob 75, 120, 659, 684
   Louisa 664
Howard, Amasa..........131, 422, 446
   Edward 614
   Elvira H...........................614
   Henry 658
   Rice 461
   Sally K............................614
   Waterman 692
Howe, A. B..............................116
(How), Betsey...........................628
   Charles B..........................659
   Elizabeth 614
   F. E..............................491
   Joseph 659
   Mary 663
   Mary E............................492
   Nathaniel 614, 659
   Nathan 209, 222, 246
Hubbard, A. W..........................226
   Arvilla K.........................660
   C. S..............................298
   Henry 670, 671
   Jennie M..........................619
   Porter 650
Huggett, Edna E........................614
   Elmer E...........................614
   William 434, 614
Huggins, William H....................618
Hukins, William..........................71
Hunt, Phylendy R......................614
Hunter, Charles H......................633
Huntington, Ruth......................169
Huntley, Hattie........................653
Huntoon, Caroline......................636
   Emily M...........................661
   George 624
   George A..........................639
   Lucy E............................655
   William 632
Huntress, John E......................659
Hurlbutt, John T......................647
Huse, Daniel......................411, 609
   Harry 488
   James 300, 313
   John F............................634
   Mary 662
   Sarah 588
   Conant & Co.......................416
Hutchins, Almeda......................660
   Hezekiah 352
Hutchinson, Abby A............587, 614
   Alice 342, 530, 542
   Arthur W.....93, 130, 392, 404, 411
        436, 519, 586, 614, 618, 677
   Bessie 587, 614
   Charlotte I.......................614
   Charlotte P.......................614
   Charles 93, 419, 614, 646
   Charles B.........................614
   Fred R............................614
   L. B....................122, 193, 342
   Levi 614
   Lucy J............................614
   Mariam 614
   Mary 614
   Mary E............................614
   Richard W...418, 420, 461, 614, 635
   Rosina 587, 614

Ingalls, C. O..........................491
   John 498
Ingram, John..........................300
   Nathaniel 283
Irvin, Simeon T.......................659
Isham, Charles H......................642
   Ferdinand 642
Jackman, Joseph......................660
Jackson, Carroll......................615
   Frank 377, 382
   George 589
   Heber 630, 692
   Lilla A............................614
   Mary M............................633
   Miles 589, 623
   Solon P...........................615
Jameson, Ada..........................615
   Edith 615
   Fred 615
   Hannah 504
   Jeremiah 688
   Jerome 615
   Leander 419, 615
   N. C..............................672
   Wilbur 615
Jefferson, Alexander..................590
Jenner, Doctor..........................73
Jepson, Francis..................615, 692
   Mary A................588, 615, 639
Jenness, Allen........................615
   Dorothy 615
   Frances 660
   George B..........................615
   Job 688
   Job B..........365, 373, 398, 615
   Lucy J............................615
   Malvina 615
   Mary 615
   Oscar P...........................615
   Roseanna 615
   Sally 615
   Sarah C...........................615
   Stephen 170, 409, 447, 649, 688
Jennings, Sarah F.....................644
Jerrole, Alonzo E.....................625
   Frank H...........................625
   Franklin M........................625
   Hattie 625
   Joseph J..........................625
   Lucy E............................625
   Mary A............................625
Jessamine, George....................660
   Henry I...........................692
Jewell, Clara.........................535
   Clara J............................590
   Jacob 87
   John 298
   John A............................643
Jewett, Sarah.........................630
Johnson, Alta.........................611
   Augusta B.........................660
   Bela 486
   Daniel 177, 624
   Elijah W......365, 368, 373, 378, 615
   Ellen R...........................615
   F. W.............................247
   George 624, 653
   Grant 653
   Haines 247
   Henry 615
   Horace A..........................378
   Ichabod S.........................486
   James 615
   James, Jr..........................82
   Jesse 41, 70, 148, 482, 483, 673
   John 653
   Lura C............................615

INDEX.

JOHNSON, Martha
  Mathew H..................655
  Miriam....................659
  Ruth W....................611
  Sarah M...................663
  Sarah W...................655
  Susan M...................663
  Timothy...................658
  Timothy, Jr........80, 177, 444
JONES, Albert A..................176
  Alfred G..................615
  Almeda................367, 374
  Alvin S.............616, 625
  Amasa....................616
        89, 189, 237, 252
        317, 445, 615, 688
  Ann.......................
  Arden.....................656
  Asahel...............616, 636
  Betsey....395, 412, 418, 615, 688
  Caleb.....................615
  Charles............366, 447, 615
  Charles S.................446
  Charles T..........616, 631, 693
  David.....................616
  Doctor............158, 177, 684
  Ednah.....................423
  Emelie C..............616, 630
  Emily E...................616
  Esther....................301
  Florence M............495, 524
  Frank.....................616
  Frank B...................672
  Harriet S.................616
  Harvey B..................615
  Hezekiah..................488
  Hiram..................30, 177
  Horace M.............367, 379
  Ida M.....................488
  Irena.....................616
  J. S.................616, 624
  Jabez................367, 368
  James.............4, 48, 616
        4, 6, 13, 46, 113
        344, 350, 353, 386, 616
  Jehu......................
        13, 42, 52, 54, 61
        65, 70, 71, 72, 75
        76, 123, 143, 145, 175
        176, 177, 181, 250, 344
        345, 356, 394, 395, 407
        444, 522, 615, 684, 686
  Jesse.....................415
  John......................
  John A........247, 299, 361, 482, 584
  John F....................615
  John S....................525
  Jonathan..................616
  Julia.....................482
  Julia C. A................488
  Julianna..................615
  Lena......................615
  Lizzie A..................616
  Louisa M..............616, 629
  Lucina A..................615
  Lydia A...................615
  Malinda...................
  Maria C...................300
  Mary......................301
  Mary B...............615, 635
  Mary C....................615
  Mary F...............333, 484
  Mary S...............521, 642
  Marilda...................
  Melissa A.................610
  Miriam...............616, 624
  Moses W...............11, 495
  Nancy C...................298
  Nathan....................
        182, 205, 454
        606, 616, 674

JONES, Paul
  Philura...................353
  Polly................616, 641
  Polly C...................616
  Rebecca...................616
  Reuben....................599
  Romie E...................246
  Rosamond..................492
  Ruth K....................629
  Sarah.....................488
  Satira....................616
  Samuel....11, 13, 19, 21, 24, 27, 31, 49
        42, 44, 49, 52, 53, 54, 55, 57
        62, 65, 68, 69, 77, 78, 104
        123, 124, 126, 144, 344, 345
        346, 353, 356, 357, 386, 387
        389, 390, 436, 445, 478, 494
        496, 677, 678, 681, 684, 685
  Sylvester.................
  Thomas...........394, 616, 623
  Thomas E..................660
  Thomas N.........366, 377, 616
  Thomas W..................229
  William F.................615
  William P.................642
JORDAN, Chester B................615
JOSLIN, Samuel...................672
JOSLYN, Henry E..................647
  Lewis.....................555
  Richard................16, 231
  Samuel.....................52
        52, 57, 60, 75, 113
        182, 389, 445, 504
  Sarah.....................
JOYCE, Sarah L...................650
JUDKINS, Susanna.................644
  Widow.....................660
KEAZER, Timothy...............80, 81
KEENEN, Christopher..............503
  Persis B..................616
KEHOE, Mary......................657
  William...................505
KELLEY, Ann P...............377, 382
  Charles H.................617
  Ezra......................590
  Flavilla..................486
  George H.............617, 654
  George W..................616
  Hattie L..................616
  Henry.....................616
  James H...................382
        300, 480, 606, 616
  Jennie E.........675, 680, 692
  John......................616
  Joseph T.........371, 382, 650
  Lydia W...................616
  Marion I..................616
  Mary G....................616
  Moses...........509, 607, 617
        89, 184, 447, 486
  Moses G..........616, 641, 689
  Nancy........298, 453, 616, 679
  William B.................184
        221, 222, 229, 453
  Williamine L....486, 611, 616
  Hall......................611
KELLEY & GEORGE..................204
KELLOGG, Ezra...............401, 452
  Israel....................246
  Stephen..........3, 48, 116, 518
  S. G..................3, 46, 47
KELTON, Almer F..................247
  Edwin A...................617
  Lorenzo F.................617
KEMP, Alva J.....................617
  Lovina....................660
KENDALL, A. S....................613
  Charles W.................247
        691, 693

INDEX. 721

KENT, Daniel..................617
   Elizabeth 617
   George 263, 320
   Henry O..................672
   Moody 320
   William A................158
KENYON, Charles E............605
KERBY, Thomas............370, 382
KERNAGEN, Andrew............246
KESLEY, John.................145
KETCHEM, Sukey..............617
KIDDER, Amos.................440
   Benjamin 297, 585
   Charles W................300
   Emily C..................585
   Jason 46
KILBURN, Asa........26, 27, 28, 34, 53
            119, 344, 350, 677, 684
   Sarah E..................661
KILLIAM, Joseph..........234, 246
KILLIAM, Heman...............599
KILTON, Emeline L............598
   George 660
KENESTON, Abigail............618
   Frances 65, 70, 392, 405, 684
   Mehitable 65, 664
   Nancy 505, 649
   Samuel 618
   William 618
KIMBALL, Aaron...............689
   Abigail A................617
   Abram F.............617, 692
   Abraham 299, 617, 688
   Achsah G...........619, 617
   Adeline 617, 624
   Alfred H.................618
   Amelia 662
   Anner 617
   Archalus 660
   Arvilla 617, 646
   Asa 174, 231, 410, 617, 618
           622, 660, 684, 689
   B. A.....................488
   Betsey H.................536
   Burus C..................618
   Burus J..................617
   Caleb P..................617
   Carrie E.................617
   Charles T................617
   Cromwell 486
   Daniel 45, 174, 183, 193
         344, 350, 354, 356, 410
        412, 414, 617, 618, 688
   David 447, 519, 523
   Diana 615
   Elizabeth A.........617, 618
   Ella A...............523, 599
   Enoch 617
   Eugene E.................617
   Frances B................492
   Fred B...................617
   George 221, 227, 255, 257, 263
       264, 266, 267, 269, 270
       278, 279, 293, 294, 316
       320, 328, 426, 432, 471
   George W................373
   Hannah 618
   Horace W...........617, 691
   James 365, 375
   Jennie L.................660
   John 404, 481, 660
   John W............588, 617, 691
   Joseph 414, 617
   Lonisa 617
   Lucy A..............633, 658
   Mary 617
   Mary A..................425
46

KIMBALL, Moses...........617, 660
   Nancy L..................301
   Nancy L. R...............617
   Nathaniel 618
   Oscar M..................618
   Pamelia S................617
   Parkhurst K..............617
   Phineas P................660
   Relief 618
   Reuben 81, 174
   Richard 447
   Ruth H..............222, 658
   Sally 637, 659
   Samuel 660
   Sophia 660
   Susanna 656
   Sylvester 660
   William 172, 297, 417, 441
          455, 618, 632, 689
   William H................618
KING, Charles P......93, 405, 425, 452
         488, 491, 618, 622
   Edwin R..................618
   Georgie T................618
   George and William...4, 47, 48, 102
           103, 117, 122
   James 622
   James F............613, 618
   James M..................618
   Lizzie M............614, 618
   Lora M...................492
   Marion 618, 622
   Nathaniel 660
   Ronald 585
   Sarah 647
   Vinia E............618, 630
   William A................585
KINGSBURY, Mary..........319, 514
KINNE, Ada I................618
   Amos 159, 196, 618, 647
   Baron S..................618
   Celina A.................618
   Clarence L...............618
   Climena 618
   Elisha P.................660
   Esther 618, 624
   Eunice 618
   Freeman F................691
   G. H.....................490
   Horace 604, 618, 692
   John 686
   John M...................618
   John N...................618
   Joseph 686
   Louisa 618
   Luther 75, 164, 196, 269
       271, 280, 395, 400
       408, 411, 447, 588
          618, 689
   Martin V. B..............618
   Mary A...................618
   Nellie 618
   Rosina J.................618
   Sewell G............196, 618
KIRK, Nancy..................660
KIRKPATRICK, Lydia J........557
KITTREDGE, Alfred H.........300
   Edward C. D........300, 328, 427
   Ellen M..................328
   Jonathan 47, 93, 159, 162, 223
      224, 298, 304, 305, 306
      307, 308, 322, 325, 359
     454, 456, 457, 674, 681
               682
   Temperance Address......325
   Reformation 218, 325, 431
   Jonathan P...............328

722   INDEX.

KITTREDGE, Julia A............301, 657
KNAPP, Mary S....................644
    Mason 660
KNIGHT, George T..................660
    Imogene 657
KNIGHTS, Moses...................401
KNOWLES, Abbie E................583
KNOWLTON, Abraham.......97, 344, 346
                      446, 619, 652
    Jane 658
LADD, David N...................488
    Melissa 649
    Sally 592
LAHEY, James.................381, 382
LAMB, Eleanor.................12, 623
LAMBKIN, Lewis......89, 134, 447, 619
LAMONTAINE, John.............367, 372
LAMOTTE, Adolphus................619
    Irving A......................619
    James 619
    Mary A...................619, 624
    William 619
LAMPHERE, George...............4, 48
LANDON, Mr.......................440
LANGDON, George.............381, 383
    John 68, 69, 75, 669, 670
LANGLEY, Charles T........366, 691, 692
    Iona 619
    Orra H........................660
    Sarah J.......................619
LANGTON, Adolph.................615
LANGWORTHY, George K.............660
LARY, Alonzo L..............619, 691
    Asa 619
    Austin L......................619
    Benjamin P...............619, 691
    Daniel ...157, 158, 356, 445, 519, 619
    Daniel W......................619
    David 363
    Dena 619
    Elizabeth 619
    Esther 619
    Freddie L.....................619
    Harley 619
    Joseph C.................619, 691
    Josiah 660
    Sarah M.......................659
    Uriah F..............418, 592, 619
    Walter P.................619, 691
LASHUA, Charles..................442
    Frank 421, 444
LATHAM, Arthur...................299
LATHROP, Anna....................619
    Annie 620
    Belle 619
    Benjamin G....................620
    Betsey 619
    Caroline 619
    Charles L................620, 637
    Clara 619
    Daisy 620
    Daniel S......................619
    Della C.......................620
    Don 619
    Earl C........................620
    Elias 41, 57, 61, 315, 684
    Elijah 35, 120, 685
    Elisha 62, 619, 620
    Ellen E.......................620
    Emma L...................620, 637
    Frank R.......................620
    George E......................620
    George H.................619, 677
    Harris 619
    Harris G.............48, 411, 619
    Hattie A......................620
    Henry S.......................619

LATHROP, Horace W................620
    James B.......................620
    Jason 660
    Jedediah 3, 13, 48, 113
    John H..................300, 620
    Joshua S.............297, 400, 415
                        418, 602, 620
    Lucinda A............595, 620, 635
    Lulu M........................619
    Malvina C.....................620
    Margaret 620
    Mary 619, 620
    Mrs. 222
    Nancy G.......................619
    Pamela 619
    Polly 209
    Samuel 52, 344, 350, 355
    Susan 608
    Susan B.......................301
    Thaddeus ..61, 69, 130, 131, 143, 145
         177, 389, 393, 446, 619, 684, 685
    Thaddeus, Jr.........82, 131, 397
    Thaddeus S..............415, 619
    Thomas 486, 620
LAUD, William....................631
LAWN, Margaret...................620
    Mary 620
    Rebecca 620
    Robert 620
LAWRENCE, Artemus................585
    Arthur J......................660
    Catherine 658
    David 395
    Hannah 662
    John 443
    Moses 47, 121, 122, 123, 131
           137, 234, 236, 237, 406
             410, 443, 445, 689
    Rachel 661
    Richard 443
    William 585
LAXSON, Flora....................620
LEARNED, Frances M...............619
LEAVITT, George W................603
    Mary A........................609
    Moses 660
LEDLOW, Patrick..............370, 383
LEE, John M.................380, 382
LEEDS, Augusta...............600, 620
    Charles H............369, 620, 692
    Carey 298, 597, 620
    Elmina 620
    Harry 189, 405, 408, 410
              445, 595, 620, 689
    Helen A.................601, 620
    Horace 620
    Hubbard C................620, 692
    Jerusha 620, 645, 655
    Lizzie 620
    Mary 620
    Orinda 620
    Rhoda 620
    Richard C.....................620
    Sarah A..................620, 646
    Tryphoena 620, 629
LEET, Dr. George E...............424
LEGRO, David.............367, 380, 692
LEONARD, Lillie D................655
LESLIE, Maria P..................628
LESTER, George...............376, 383
LEWIS, John..................246, 325
    Sarah C.......................643
    Roswell W.....................325
LIBBEY, William A................590
LILLIS, Mrs. Ross................608
LINCOLN, Josiah S........454, 455, 613
                        616, 692

LITTLE, Colonel............346, 352
   Eliza 642
   James H..................612
LITTLEFIELD, Eliza J..........659
LIVERMORE, Judge...........69, 670
LIVINGSTON, William............358
LLADO, John...................408
LOCK, David, Jr................660
   Jonathan 71
LONG, P., Colonel..............69
LONGFELLOW, Abraham....526, 621, 689
   Elizabeth 621, 654
   Hepzibah 621
   Sarah 356, 621
   Susan 621
   William ..97, 134, 344, 352, 353, 356
        405, 446, 621, 652, 689
   William, Jr...............134
LORD, Harriet N................658
   President 219
LOUGEE, John..................159
LOVEJOY, Angustus 324, 355, 402
        419, 621, 679
   Frederick W...........611, 646
   Helen 646
   Isaac 660
   Lillian M................609
   Marion 646
   Olive S...................656
   Wendell 646
LOVERIDGE, Lewis.............4, 44, 47
LOVEREN, Emma L..............659
(LOVRING), Ernest D............621
   Hannah 621
   John B................366, 377
   John D..........132, 577, 621, 680
   Joseph H.................621
   Laura L..................243
   Lydia 621
   Mary A...................635
   Moses 660
   Nora E...................621
   Susan 621
   Wilbur F.................621
LOW, Mary A...................621
   Moses 26, 689
LOWELL, Ada E.................590
   Allen G..................660
   Belle 592
   Elijah C.................660
   Elizabeth 621
   Frank B..................592
   Frank H..............650, 660
   Gideon 592
   Melissa J................596
   Paulina 632
LULL, Joseph..............234, 246
LUNDY, Benjamin...............323
   Captain 345
LUNT, Ezekiel.................495
McBEAN, Kate..................619
McCAULEY, John............378, 383
McCONNELL, Charles............621
   Jane 621
   Robert 370, 383
McCORMICK, George P...........621
McCOY, William........235, 236, 246
McCULLOM, John............370, 382
McCURDY, Rev..................240
McCUTCHINS, Luther............672
McEWEN, Doctor................424
McGEE, James..............375, 382
McGRATH, Henry................676
   John 661
McGREGGOES, Captain...........355
McINTIRE, Blanch L............523

McKEAN, Frank A...............672
McKEWEN, Margaret.............619
McKINNEY, Daniel..............417
McLANE, John..................672
McLAUGHTON, John..............621
McNABB, Thomas............365, 374
MACKEY, Emily.................647
MACKESS, Elizabeth............655
MAGER, Loftus R...........367, 374
MAHAN, Elizabeth C............625
MAHONY, Mary D................661
MAHR, John....................382
MAHURIN, Ephraim H............462
MAKEPEACE, Orson..............366
MANN, John, Inn................26
   Mathew 60, 686
MANNING, C. A.................652
   Roy E....................652
   Susan P..................652
   William 686
MANSUR, James.................601
MARCH, David..........441, 458, 600
   Frances D................521
   Sally 663
   Sarah 585
MARCY, Daniel.................672
   Mary A...................616
MARGEUX, Adolph...............661
MARKEY, A. M..................247
MARLAND, Alfred...........367, 372
MARRS, Elza A.................621
MARS, John....................240
MARSH, Nellie B...............651
MARSHALL, Dorothy A...........621
   Frank 621
   George 621
   Jane M...................621
   John 374, 660
   Moses H...............366, 377
   Sally 610
   Thomas 366, 378, 621
MARSTON, Captain..............352
   Jacob 234
   Persis 585
   Sarah 634
MARTIN, Abigail........585, 586, 592
   Albert ...300, 452, 543, 560, 612, 621
   Amanda L.................625
   Arabella E...............656
   Arthur 621
   Benjamin 625
   Benjamin F...............625
   Celina 301
   Charles 625
   Chestina 621
   Eleazer 152, 297, 298, 299
        303, 308, 333, 621
        673, 674, 679, 682
   Eleazer and Jesse......93, 159, 283
        288, 444
   Eliza 498
   Eunice 502
   George H.................535
   Hannah 621, 661
   Hannah C. S..........301, 656
   Henry 297, 313, 534, 535
   Helen A..................535
   J. E.....................491
   James 661
   Jesse 97, 297, 298, 303
        309, 316, 340, 452
        621, 674, 675, 682
   John 661, 689
   Jonathan H...............661
   Joshua 599, 414
   Levi 367, 379, 621, 660, 692
   Lillie W.................543

MARTIN, Lucy..................609, 622
    Lydia 656
    Mary 523, 599, 609
    Mary A. 585, 587, 659
    Mary J. 598
    Nelson 247
    Noah 671
    Perry 660
    Polly 621
    Richard K. 373
    Robert ..237, 343, 344, 354, 534, 689
    Roxalina B.......301, 340, 589, 621
    Roseanna 625
    Sally 663
    Simeon 660
    Sirene 662
    Sophia 423
    Susan A. 621
    Walter B. 488, 587
    William 280, 281, 297, 486, 534
                     674, 678, 679, 689
    Willie 374
MARCIZE, Lindor..................375
MASON, David H. 302, 303
    John 58
    Philip 660
MASSEURE, Charles H..............621
    Frances H. 621
MATHER, Ezekiel..................661
MATHEWS, Charles B...............661
MATTISON, H. A. 247
MAXWELL, Doctor..................134
MAY, Albert 622, 661
    C. Augusta 622
    Charles 622
    Eddie F. 622
    Edwin 159, 447, 622, 689
    Edwin H. 622
    Emily 622
    Foster 622
    George 622
    Harriet 605, 622
    Helen M. 622
    John 64, 102, 177, 343, 344
                     398, 407, 445, 612, 622
    Joshua 661
    Lucy 611, 622
    Marcia A. 622
    Mercy 654
    Obadiah 661
    Sally 622, 661
    Sarah A. 622
    Thomas 622
    William 622
MAYNARD, Emeline C. 624
    Louise R. 624
MAYO, William A. 247
MEACHAM, Andrew 231, 622
    Andrew M. 622
    Bettish 622
    Darius 650
    David 650
    Frances 650
    Elam 177, 398, 445, 622
    James 650
    Jeremiah 231, 344, 350, 622
    John 650
    Joseph 622
    Joshua ..134, 177, 231, 398, 447, 622
    Marinda 650
    Miriam 617, 622
    Nancy 650
    Phoebe 231, 622, 645, 646
    Polly 231, 590, 622, 650
    Roseanna 650

MEACHAM, Samuel 3, 5, 13, 26, 46, 53, 60
                     83, 185, 231, 343, 344, 345
                     384, 390, 447, 518, 622
                                         684, 686
    Sarah 231, 622, 650
    Sylvester 650
    Thomas 232, 622
    William 650
MEAD, Emma L. 529
MEEWENS, Lydia A. 622
MELENDY, Eliza 651
    Henry C. 648
MELOON, Abigail 622
MERRIAM, Nettie 598
MERRILL, Betsey 622
    Delia L. 655
    Elvira 622
    Emma M. 590
    Enoch 660
    Hannah 664
    Harriet 517
    Helen M. 492
    Jonathan 370
    Joseph 481, 482
    Julia A. 604, 633
    Levi 661
    Mary E. 659
    Mary S. 644
    Mehitable E. 650
    Nathaniel 661
    Sally 649
    Thomas 274
MESSER, Nathan 11
METCALF, Gov. Ralph 334, 671
MEYER, Ferdinand 376
MILLER, Elijah 260, 286
    Elsie 594, 633
    Elizabeth B. 585, 622
    Horace W. 603, 622, 626, 692
    Jacob 176, 447, 450, 622, 689
    John 382
    Jonathan 684
    Lucy 660
    Lucy K. 617
    Nancy 590, 619, 622
    Pasha 618
    Russell A. 521
    Ruth 603, 622
    Nancy 590, 619, 622
    Silas 120
    T. W. 517
    William 199
MILLETT, Ozias 589
MILTON, Adda 622
    Bella A. 623
    Ella 622
    Ella R. 597
    Frank E. 494, 623
    Jacob 623
    John T. 419, 420, 622
    Joseph 622, 689
    Lora M. 618, 622
    Loraine H. 622
    Lura G. 97, 491
    Mathew H. 226, 543, 622
                                     676, 682, 692
MINER, Allen 12, 77, 499, 604, 623
    Allen E. 624, 691
    Amos 91, 298, 623, 641, 670, 689
    Avery A. 623
    Burton E. 623
    Caroline T. 598, 623
    Charles W. 624
    Clinton 623
    Cynthia 623
    Edwin B. 420, 624, 646
    Elijah 143, 444, 486, 623

Index.   725

MINER, Elisha............88, 623, 689
 Ellen....................623
 Elsie T................590, 623
 George...................623
 George B.............623, 693
 Henry H..................623
 James M..................623
 Leonard.........623, 640, 661
 Lewis....................623
 Lovica..............623, 626
 Lucy.....................623
 Lucy A...................301
 Lucy J...................624
 Lyman....................623
 Marvin...................623
 Michael C................370
 Sophia...................623
 Thomas......4, 5, 12, 13, 20, 27, 32
  33, 34, 42, 44, 45, 46, 50
  52, 54, 56, 60, 70, 71
  75, 77, 78, 82, 99, 101
  113, 119, 120, 123, 135, 137
  172, 173, 174, 176, 178, 237
  252, 312, 344, 345, 346, 355
  386, 387, 390, 404, 518, 623
  677, 684, 688, 689
 Thomas T.................623
 & Fairfield..............416
MITCHEL, Alonzo.......368, 373, 661
 Elder....................192
 Mary J...................647
 William A................628
MONROE, Agnes................626
MONTGOMERY, Hannah...........643
MOODY, Stephen...............320
MOONEY, Arthur E........646, 684
 Kate S...................624
 Maud A...................624
MOORE, Hugh..................369
 John.....................491
 Micaiah.....82, 83, 88, 130, 132, 135
  137, 186, 395, 436, 438
 Nelly....................618
MOORES, John............380, 382
MOREY, Ann M.................640
 Benjamin.................617
 Frank...............266, 371
 Horace...................694
 Israel....................26
 Jonathan.................661
 Lewis...............428, 660
 Mary A...................624
 Nellie L.................624
 Persis L.................624
 Robert C.................624
 Robert R............453, 624
 Sophronia C.........521, 624
 Stephen..................624
MORGAN, Ada C...........624, 639
 Alice....................624
 Alva.....................624
 Arnold...95, 309, 313, 420, 423, 675
 Ben......................424
 Carrie L.................488
 Clarence.................624
 Converse G...............624
 Edna.....................624
 Erasmus B........241, 242, 247
 Frances A................424
 Lizzie B............424, 628
 Nancy....................224
 Nathan C..........36, 300, 488
  624, 680, 692
 Olive B..................624
 Samuel..............483, 486
 Sylvanus B...260, 280, 298, 299, 303
  367, 401, 446, 624, 675, 679

MORGAN, Thomas B.............624
MORIARTY, John........335, 367, 374
MORRILL, Captain.............353
 E. J.....................352
 H. J.....................606
 James...............489, 598
 Joe......................458
 Samuel A.................624
 Sarah E..................592
 Zilpha L.................665
MORRIS, David L..............670
MORRISON, Nettie M...........605
MORSE, Adeline E.............590
 Addie E..................624
 Amos.....................486
 Anna B..............620, 637
 Aphia....................318
 Betsey...................625
 Byron....................625
 Carl E...................625
 Caroline.................625
 Charles N.........367, 616, 625
 Clarence H...............637
 Daniel........391, 405, 447, 624, 684
 Edwin A...........616, 624, 691
 Elizabeth................658
 Ellen....................625
 Elsie T..................625
 Emeline..................625
 Emeline W................625
 Emily C..................624
 Flora....................625
 Frank C..................603
 Frank W..................640
 Franklin P...............624
 Freddie A................637
 George...................625
 George H.................626
 Georgianna...............625
 Gideon..............439, 678
 Hannah S.................301
 Helen....................623
 Henry...............441, 600
 Irene....................624
 James.........174, 177, 305, 445
  612, 625, 641, 678, 689
 James B..................625
 Jesse...............617, 624
 John.....................625
 John W...................661
 Joseph...................222
 Julia...............625, 641
 Julia T..................626
 Lois............526, 625, 631
 Lucinda..................624
 Lucy.....................625
 Malvina E................663
 Martha E............626, 640
 Martin V. B..............600
 Mary............624, 626, 656
 Mary F...................626
 Mary R..............625, 632
 Minnie...................625
 Moses....................661
 Nancy....................625
 Nathan D.................640
 Nathan W............623, 640
 Orrin H.........624, 637, 691
 Persis P.................625
 Peter....................222
 Prudence.................632
 Rachel...................624
 Ruth A...................625
 Sally....................625
 Sarah...............600, 626
 Sarah S..................604
 Silas M..................624

MORSE, Sophia L..................595
　Stephen .366, 408, 418, 618, 624, 679
　Susanna 622
　Susanna E....................661
　Thomas 177
　William C....................626
MOSHER, Alice....................628
MULHOLLAND, John.................372
MUNROE, William C................263
MURPHY, James....................376
MURRAY, Carl B...................626
　Charles A....................644
　Charles E....................626
　Claude M..............626, 677, 680
　Elizabeth E..................644
　Ellen F.....................626
　George W......334, 338, 339, 340
　　　　　　　369, 626, 675, 676, 682
　Grace E......................606
　John 626
　Julia W.....................626
　Katherine C..................644
　Katherine R.............598, 626
　Samuel 660
　Sarah W....................626
MUZZEY, Charley M................632
　Doctor 219
　Edwin A.....................610
　George E..............488, 632, 691
　John S......................691
　Nehemiah 619
　Nella 632
　Nancy 227, 320
NASON, Elizabeth.................641
NEAL, Charles W..................620
NEIDIG, Cora.....................517
NEILEY, Edith....................636
NELSON, George...........222, 423, 541
NESMITH, Alfred J...........225, 626
　Erastus 626
　Lucy R......................626
NEVINS, James..........3, 45, 48, 102
　John 222, 234
NEWHALL, M.......................247
NEWMARCH, John.........4, 46, 47, 102
NICHOLS, Aaron..........412, 626, 689
　Almanda P...................626
　Almeda 301
　Benjamin F..............643, 661
　Benjamin P......369, 612, 626, 692
　Betsey 626
　Charles R...................199
　Colonel 354
　Dexter H..............586, 626
　Eleanor 301
　Eliza A....................655
　Enoch 626
　Ezra 91, 122, 343, 344, 392, 410
　　　411, 604, 623, 626, 684, 689
　H. A........................367
　Humphrey 61, 686
　Josephine S.................626
　Julia A............301, 622, 626
　Kate 626
　Lovica F...................626
　Lydia 626
　Mandana L..................626
　Mary A......................626
　Mrs. 266
　Nancy 626
　Noah 193
　Ralph 626
　Sarah M....................626
　Tilton 297, 367, 626
NILES, Julianna..................617
NORRIS, Abbie A.................655
　Benjamin 234, 626, 676, 679

NORRIS, Bishop...................243
　Clark C.....................532
　David 532
　Eliphalet 70, 177, 252, 445, 684
　Fardey 443
　George 626
　Herbert 309
　Horace R...............367, 626
　J. 283
　Joseph 443
　Lizzie B..............608, 626
　Lydia 70
　Margaret 532
　Mary 660
　Nathaniel 239
　Polly 655
　Samuel 234
　Susan 634, 662
NORTHGRAVES, Albert N............653
　Charles K...................653
　Gertrude M..................653
　Isabel F....................653
　Jennie 653
　Joseph 653
NOURSE, Alton....................489
NOYES, Abigail...................627
　Amos 627
　Amos L......................627
　Ben A.......................619
　Betsey 627, 656
　Charles E...................627
　David 489
　Dudley 177, 362, 444
　E. P........................661
　Emma F.....................608
　Ephraim 209
　Frederic 362
　Jacob 661
　James 627
　Joseph 627, 661
　Lydia 627
　Mary A......................654
　Mattie H....................627
　Moody ...177, 392, 404, 445, 627
　Parker 73
　Relief 627
　Samuel 69, 77, 127, 131, 177
　　　　208, 255, 444, 486, 505
　　　　　627, 684, 687, 689
　Sophia 597
　Sophia A....................627
　Stephen 689
　Theodore 627
NUTE, Ruth J....................659
NYE, Willis C....................661
OAKS, Mary......................653
O'BRIEN, James H................226
O'CONNELL, Robert M.............368
OLCOTT, Edward..................250
　Eunice 647
OLIPHANT, Marion H..............643
OLIVER, Andrew............611, 616
OSBORN, Joel....................593
OSGOOD, Captain.................352
　Charlotte 514
　Marie 524
OTIS, Amos......................627
　Elisha 627
　Erastus 627
　Esther 627
　Ethelinda 627, 647
　Ezra 627
　Israel S....................627
　Lucy 627
　Richard 64, 68, 71, 82, 132, 177
　　　　181, 182, 186, 209, 222
　　　　343, 344, 354, 356, 445

INDEX. 727

OTIS, Richard........627, 684, 687, 689
 Roxanna 627
 Sally 627
 Sarah 627
OWEN, Merrill..............628, 640
PACKARD, Albert.............594, 627
 Betsey 628
 Burton C................594, 628
 Chamberlain 627, 689
 Chamberlain, Jr....91, 162, 271, 298
     401, 673, 674, 679
 Erastus 628, 651
 Ethel 594, 628
 Hannah E...............594, 627
 John 608, 627
 Louisa 628
 Maud E......................628
 Octavia 627, 646
 Rachel 627
 Rachel C....................613
 Samuel 628
PADDLEFORD, Asa..46, 173, 174, 251, 389
    391, 395, 407, 445, 661
       684, 687
 Charles 689
 Elijah 407, 446, 687
 James 627, 689
 Jonathan 686
 Martha 628, 630
 Samuel 260, 689
 Susan 663
 William G....................528
PAGE, Abraham..............209, 627
 Abraham, Jr.................297
 Almira 627
 Captain 351
 Charles 627
 Eliphalet R.............453, 627
 Elizabeth R.................663
 Hannah 92, 627
 Hulda A.....................662
 Jeremiah 104
 John 621, 670
 Lazarus 451, 689
 Leonard 627
 Mary E.......................301
 Rachel R.....................301
 Samuel 627
 Sarah 614
 Sarah A......................627
 Sarah F......................627
 Thomas 486
PAINE, Benjamin.............246
 Col. Elisha........62, 69, 72, 499
 John 234, 246
 Sylvanus 411
 William 614
PALMER, Doctor..............219
 Joseph D....................662
 Mary E.......................661
 Nellia A................339, 606
PARKER, Amasa H.............653
 Cora B.......................589
 Daniel 315, 356
 Dewitt C....................653
 Ebenezer 661
 Francis 652
 Freeman S..............589, 691
 George W....................589
 Grace E......................652
 Henry C......................653
 Horace W....................653
 John C.......................653
 Mary J.......................601
 Master 253
 Nancy A......................653
 Thomas 4, 48, 101

PARKER, Timothy............653
PARKHURST, Catherine........585
 Lucian C....................662
 Sarah 141, 148
 William 88, 141, 146, 148, 177
    358, 438, 440, 446, 585
PARKS, Abel................661
PARMENTER, Ethel M..........642
PARMLEE, H. S...............247
PARSONS, Sherburn...........661
PATTEE, Allen W.............628
 Angeline C...................629
 Ann M.......................628
 Ann R.......................629
 Asa 628
 Betsey 629
 Burns W...........620, 629, 691
 Calvin M....................628
 Daniel 11, 46, 87, 88, 91, 134
  162, 189, 258, 260, 266, 268
   278, 358, 394, 431, 445, 458
  494, 512, 611, 628, 678, 689
 Daniel, Jr....91, 260, 268, 271, 280
   282, 298, 628, 679, 689
 Mrs. Daniel.................222
 Daniel F....................629
 Dorcas 628
 Dorothy 630
 Eliza D.....................628
 Elizabeth D.................628
 Ella 629
 Fred D......................629
 Fred L......................628
 George W....................629
 Gordon B....................628
 Hannah D....................629
 Hattie 628
 Henry H................628, 693
 Hiram 628
 J. Munroe...................300
 James 90, 91, 162, 168, 222, 258
   272, 278, 280, 283, 284
   288, 298, 299, 303, 416
   478, 486, 494, 629, 689
 James C.................93, 628
 James F.....................629
 James H.....................628
 James W.....................629
 Jennie L....................629
 Jesse 629
 John 629
 John B......................628
 Judith 609, 628
 Lewis C...........366, 628, 675, 691
 Louisa M...............628, 629
 Moses D...........162, 229, 689
 Peter 251, 405, 445
 Phœbe 579
 Rhoda J.....................629
 Sadie 628
 Selding 252, 462
 Sylvanus B..................628
 W. Fred.....................661
 Widow 84, 87, 89
 Wyman 300, 629, 675, 682
 & Perley...............93, 419
PATTEN, Daniel G..........297, 648
PAUL, Frank.................661
 Sally 585
 Thomas 267, 291, 292, 293, 294
PAULSON, J. V...............517
PAYSON, Moses P.............324
PEABODY, Col. Stephen.......352
 General 69, 76, 669
 George W....................615
PEACOCK, Elder John.....192, 193, 194
     196, 200, 201

Index.

PEARSON, David..........177, 446, 643
  Lydia 183
PEASLEE, Allie................629
  Charles H...................629
  Daniel 391, 450
  Frankie 629
  Fred W.......................629
  George E.....................629
  Harry O......................629
  Jonathan 629
  Miriam 629
  Sanford 629
  Stephen 418, 454, 629
              675, 676, 692
PECK, Ebenezer................3, 46
  Zelinda 655
PENHALLOW, John..............163
PERKINS, Charles 617
  Clara A......................658
  Cyrus 603, 617
  Cyrus E......................617
  Elizabeth D..................617
  Henry I......................617
  Isaac N......................617
  Isaac W......................529
  Jared 671
PERLEY, John....80, 81, 88, 177, 465, 461
  (Pearley)
  John Q..............628, 676, 691
  Joseph G.....................662
  Lydia 629
  Moses 672
  Nat 629
  Rebecca 628
  Stephen 629
PERRY, Rev. Baxter..............217
  O. H..............122, 422, 437, 452
PETERS, Anna T.................630
  Charles F....................630
  Druzilar 629
  Eliza L......................630
  Fanny 629
  Hannah 598, 629
  Jacob 362, 630
  John 629
  Joseph 584
  Joseph B.....................630
  Mary 630
  William 629
  Willie F.....................630
PETERSON, Turner................61
PETTEE, C. H....................105
PETTINGILL, Andrew.............654
  Benjamin and Polly..........316
  Ephraim H....................662
  Julia M......................654
  Pluma 664
  Polly 605
  Thomas H.......84, 87, 88, 89, 131
      159, 189, 253, 254, 316
      320, 444, 483, 486, 673, 681
PHELPS, Charles M..............661
  Eleazer 234, 246
PHILBRICK, Ann..................625
  Carrie E.....................593
  Charles A................630, 643
  Cyrus H......................661
  Daniel H.....................630
  David 662
  Dorothy A....................608
  Hannah 608
  Hepzibah A...................661
  Hiram 418, 593, 630, 643
  Jane 610
  John W..............366, 372, 593, 630
  Mary 630
  Porter K.....................662

PHILLIPS, Elkanah...............195
  Nettie M.....................659
  Samuel 482
PICKERING, John.................669
  Sarah 642
PIERCE, Angeline L..............663
  Gen. Benjamin................670
  Betsey 500, 630
  Caleb, Dr................82, 130
      150, 176, 251, 422, 435
      438, 440, 628, 630, 682
  Earl 662
  Hannah A....................643
  Louise M.................628, 630
  Nathaniel C........189, 317, 459
              486, 628, 630
PIERO, John..................378, 382
PIERSON, Peter...........365, 368, 373
PIKE and Blodgett.......337, 338, 339
  J. 246
  James 672
PILLSBURY, Addie A.............631
  Betsey 630, 657
  Deborah 630
  Elizabeth 630
  Emma 658
  Harrison 400, 415, 417, 533
  Ithamar P..........228, 428, 628
  J. D. W......................630
  John 661
  Joseph D.....................630
  Joshua 45, 82, 177, 181
      182, 187, 207, 208, 219, 222
      224, 287, 445, 577, 630, 689
  Joshua, Jr..........208, 209, 222
  Lydia 664
  Marcus M....................427
  Mary B.......................630
  Miriam 630, 644
  Sarah 630
  Sarah A. C...................301
PINKHAM, Deborah...............650
  Sarah 650
PIPER, Benjamin................647
  Charlotte 589
  Isaiah 661
  Lydia 663
  Sally 661
  Samuel 661
PITCHER, Henry P...............600
PLANT, Nancy A.................619
PLASTRIDGE, Dr. Charles P....299, 533
  Emma C......................507
  Mary D..................218, 222
PLUMMER, Benjamin F...........662
  Elmore H.................618, 630
  George F.....................692
  Mabel A......................626
  Reuben S.....................630
  William 630, 670
  William A....................626
POLAND, Sarah..................356
POLLARD, Adam.......158, 159, 189, 260
            410, 447, 630, 689
  Benjamin 630
  Benjamin N..............661, 691
  Caroline 630, 633
  Charles W....................630
  David 159, 630
  Elnora 631
  Eva 631
  Fred R...................631, 691
  Hannah 630, 631
  Horace 630
  Isaac 630, 631
  John 661
  Joseph J...........159, 631, 691

INDEX.   729

POLLARD, Louisa..................630
 Louisa H...................604
 Lydia..................590, 630
 Margaret...................603
 Martha.....................630
 Mary.......................630
 Nancy......................634
 Olive......................656
 Perley.....................630
 Rodney.....................630
 Royal S....................631
 Sarah......................630
 Solon K....................630
 Sybil......................630
 Sylvenia...................630
 Walker.....................630
 William....................630
POLLOCK, Ann....................647
POMPEY, Negro...................553
POOL, Samuel....................661
POOR, Lucy......................523
POPE, Isabelle N................639
PORTER, Alfred..................209
 Almina B...................656
 Benjamin....................91
 Benjamin W........272, 274, 280
     292, 607, 631
 Betsey.....................631
 Burrill, Jr................309
 Clarissa..............593, 631
 Daniel......93, 447, 451, 631, 689
 Daniel R...................631
 David......................631
 Elias.......82, 88, 89, 208, 209, 215
   219, 222, 486, 631, 678, 689
 Eliza......................631
 Eliza R....................631
 Fred B. L...116, 122, 441, 444, 631
 Hannah.....................631
 Israel.....................585
 John..............134, 407, 631
 Micah......82, 181, 182, 408, 445, 631
 Noah.......................631
 Osman......................631
 Phebe......................590
 Reuben.....................631
 Ruth M.....................631
 Sarah......................631
 Thomas J...................631
 William....................631
 William H..................631
POTTER, Jeremiah................522
 Frank E....................672
POWELL, Adna J..................631
 Andrew J...................649
 Charlotte..................626
 Hannah D...................631
 Ida A......................649
POWERS, David J.................611
 Frank......................611
 George.....................440
 Loraine....................611
 Sally......................658
 William....................611
PRATT, Abigail..................594
 Betsey.............217, 218, 541
 Charles A..................369
 David......................540
 Henry......................662
 Joseph.....................480
 Louise.....................597
 M. P.......................597
 Rebecca V..................597
PRAY, John F....................662
PRENTISS, Edward................614
 Laura......................614
 Alice F....................633

PRESCOTT, Allie S...............633
 Benjamin...................672
 Benjamin F.................672
 Mamie B....................633
 Philip G..........366, 378, 434
    633, 692, 693
 R. R.......................601
PRESLEY, Thomas.................370
PRESSEY, Addie L................631
 Albert.......193, 319, 324, 631, 692
 Albert L...................692
 Calvin............93, 625, 631, 689
 Celia C....................631
 Charles H..................661
 E. H.................367, 368
 Elvira.....................631
 Elwin H....................632
 Eva........................631
 Friend................602, 631
 George............631, 625, 691
 George P...................631
 Henry A....................632
 Hiram......................647
 Horace.....................631
 James......................631
 John..............356, 489, 631
 John L................159, 631
 Julia M....................631
 Lucia V....................631
 Maria L....................616
 Mary.......................631
 Miranda R..................632
 Moses.................631, 689
 Samuel.....................631
 Sarah......................631
 Sarah B....................631
 William O..................631
PRESTON, Almira A...............643
 Alpheus...............419, 632
 Elizabeth..................632
 Elmer W....................632
 Florence J.................632
 Frank......................632
 George W...................632
 Henry.................371, 382
 Jenette E.............604, 632
 John E.....................632
 Lydia......................632
 Marcellus..................632
 Martin.....................632
 Mary E.....................632
 Munroe.....................632
 Nelson.....................632
 Willie.....................632
PREW, Charles............368, 372, 382
PROCTOR, Almira.................609
 John.................336, 337
PROCKTER, Lucia A...............632
PUFFER, Daniel..................661
 Mary.......................530
 Minnie B...................632
 Reuben.....................447
PURMORT, Luther.................309
 Mark.......................502
 Minor T....................661
PUSHEE, Abraham 172, 189, 209, 363, 410
   465, 483, 486, 540, 681
PUTNAM, Caleb S............632, 682
 Elvira W..............632, 646
 Florina W..................632
 Hattie S...................632
 Hiram E...............578, 632
 Louisa.....................641
 Martha.....................632
 Persis.....................632
 Russell....................504
 Sidney.....................632

INDEX.

PUTNEY, Clara L............624
   Joseph 662
   Mehitable 657
QUEEN, Mary................517
QUIMBY, Aaron..............452
   Hannah 660
   Herbert F................247
   Jonathan 689
   Mary J...................656
   Silas 247
QUINBY, Henry B............672
QUINCY, Josiah........272, 306
RAINEY, Albert J...........632
   Albert R.................632
   Loney E..................632
   Mary A...................632
RALSTON, James.............411
RAND, Herman S.............632
   Oscar L........488, 676, 677, 689
   Oscar S..................632
RANDALL, Rufus......4, 45, 46, 102
   Sargent 663
   Sylvester 4, 46
RANDLETT, George W....369, 604
   Jacob 285, 518, 662
   John W...................632
   Joseph 83, 156, 393, 406, 445
RANSOM, Elder Elisha...168, 172
RANZER, Joseph W..........662
RATHBURN, Isaiah.....3, 46, 122, 441
   Joshua 4, 46
RAY, John F................662
READ, Almira...............656
   Betsey 660
   James P..................662
   Marilla 657
RECORD, William........35, 120
REED, Anne.................657
   C. A.....................247
   Joanna 660
   John K...................644
   Minnie B.................644
   Sally 663
REID, James R..............528
RENNE, Ferdinand...........650
RICARD, Ada M..............632
   Edgar 405, 447, 532
   Maggie 604
RICE, Alice M..............643
   Charles 632
   Clara E..................542
   George E.................542
   Lillian A................542
   Mabel A..................542
   Mary P...................620
RICHARDS, George S........528
   James 378, 383
   Jane 642
   Lester S.................528
   Oliver S.................528
   William J................528
RICHARDSON, Abi...........634
   Abi P...............526, 634
   Abby R...................634
   Adeline R............634, 635
   Albert 590
   Albina L.................601
   Alfred 633, 643
   Alvah 297, 630, 633
   Amos 363, 398, 411, 635, 689
   Anna 209
   Annette 590, 633
   Benjamin 634
   Betsey 634
   Caleb 633
   Caleb H..................634
   Captain 352

RICHARDSON, Carrie M......634
   Charlotte 634
   Charles W......222, 229, 344, 346
              351, 634, 689
   David 26, 47, 159, 209
              410, 577, 634, 689
   Deborah 642
   Dexter 633, 691
   Edna 579, 633
   Eliphalet ...343, 344, 354, 356, 395
         397, 410, 446, 526, 632, 634
   Elizabeth 632, 634, 662
   Ella M..............492, 633
   Emily B..................634
   Enoch 177, 252, 343, 344, 346
         347, 349, 351, 356, 447
           518, 632, 634, 684
   Ephraim 689
   Esther 633
   Eunice 634
   Fred G...................633
   George 209, 229, 426, 634
   George A.................662
   George H............377, 633
   George M.................366
   George W.................376
   Hannah 627
   Hannah G.................635
   Hannah H.................633
   Harriet N............634, 642
   Henry 634
   Herod 91, 271, 633
   Hiram 96, 633
   Hudson M.................634
   Ira 634
   Isaac G..................633
   Jacob 177, 209, 344, 399
            447, 632, 678, 689
   Jacob F..................607
   Jacob M..................222
   James 289, 392
   James B.............633, 691
   John ...173, 174, 177, 343, 344, 349
         351, 447, 632, 633, 634
   John W.............634, 676
   Joseph 634
   Joseph L.....196, 250, 256, 258, 260
         269, 270, 278, 280, 290
         297, 299, 303, 414, 635
          673, 678, 679, 681
   Joshua 82, 134, 174, 177, 229
         305, 343, 344, 347, 354
         356, 390, 446, 681, 686
   Joshua, Jr........209, 633, 689
   Joshua W........297, 356, 634, 689
   Josiah 297, 627
   Julia A..................634
   Loanna 661
   Louisa P.................634
   Lucy A...................301
   Lydia 634
   Maria 633
   Martha 661
   Mary 634, 661
   Mary A.............633, 661
   Mary E.............662, 633
   Mary R...................301
   Moses 177, 344, 345, 392, 405
         441, 453, 632, 634, 689
   Nabby 634
   Nancy 634
   Nancy A. B...............632
   Nancy M..................620
   Nathaniel 447, 663
   Persis A.................633
   Phoebe 634
   Plummer 634

RICHARDSON, Rufus K... 26, 283, 363, 634
   Ruhannah 633
   Samuel D..................... 635
   Sarah 618, 632, 634
   Sarah C.................. 598, 633
   Sarah M..................... 633
   Solomon 689
   Sophia 635
   Sophronia 662
   Susan 632
   Susanna 595, 617, 634
   Theodore 634
   Warren B........... 97, 634, 676
   Willard 633, 640
   William 40, 41, 42, 43, 57, 58, 61
              65, 75, 79, 80, 81, 84
          123, 124, 131, 140, 143, 144
          145, 149, 155, 173, 175, 177
          178, 189, 318, 343, 344, 350
          355, 356, 384, 399, 405, 436
          447, 632, 633, 645, 673, 677
            678, 681, 684, 686, 689
   William G............ 87, 131, 634
   William M................... 633
RIDER, Henry............... 377, 382
RIDDLE, Sarah J................. 662
RINDGE, Daniel 72
   Isaac 6
RING, Harry F.................. 635
   Lucy P...................... 635
ROBERTS, Adelaide L............ 659
   Amelia B.................... 643
   George S.................... 635
   Hiram A..................... 672
   Jonathan 662
   Mary A...................... 635
   Melinda 649
   Orrin 246
   Sarah 655
   Smith 635
ROBIE, Gilbert J........ 367, 380, 635
   Horace G................ 635, 681
ROBBINS, Francis................ 298
   Mr..................... 247, 263
ROBINSON, Amos................. 662
   Asa 439, 527
   Captain 355
   Jennie 648
   Joseph C.................... 662
   Laurenza 635
   Mary E...................... 636
   S. J........................ 247
   Sarah 632
ROBY, Ralph.................... 486
ROCKWELL, John............ 159, 524
ROGERS, Abigail S............... 635
   Charles H............... 635, 662
   Daniel 4, 47, 48, 122
   Eliza M..................... 639
   Ella M...................... 607
   Frances A................... 655
   George W.................... 647
   Hannah 613
   Hannah W.................... 647
   Harrison 613, 662
   Jane 647
   John L...................... 635
   Lafayette W............. 488, 647
   Louise M.................... 647
   Mary A...................... 584
   Mary D...................... 647
   N. P......257, 263, 323, 325, 474
   Letters 227, 294, 321, 322
   Nancy G..................... 647
   Sally 647
   Sally A..................... 618

ROGERS, Wallis L................ 647
   William 635, 646, 689
   William M................... 647
ROLFE, Mr...................... 298
ROLLINS, Arrosina............... 635
   Frank A..................... 672
ROOD, Heman.................... 224
ROSS, Artemus.................. 523
   David 605
   Hubbard P................... 523
   Isaac 109
   Martha 635
   Urvilla M................... 620
   Willie 523
   Willie J.................... 635
   Zaphira 620
ROWE, Smith.................... 647
ROWELL, John B................. 662
   Louisa C.................... 649
ROYNALDS, Hezekiah............. 684
RUDD, Gideon...11, 52, 344, 351, 354, 496
RUNDLETT, Luana P.............. 651
RUNNELLS, Mr................... 450
RUSH, Elijah H................. 662
RUSSELL, Captain........... 346, 352
   Roxanna 658
RUTER, Martin.................. 246
SABINE, Phineas.... 4, 48, 122, 139
SALTER, Captain C............... 352
SAFFORD, Colonel............... 521
   Grace A..................... 587
SALES, Laura................... 662
SANBORN, Abigail........... 635, 636
   Achsah 635
   Addie A..................... 636
   Alma L.................. 635, 636
   Ann J....................... 635
   Belinda 610
   Betsey 595, 635, 663
   Burns W..................... 608
   Charles H................... 635
   Comfort 635
   Dolly 660
   Eben D...................... 634
   Edward 663
   Edwin D..................... 299
   Elizabeth A............. 634, 635
   Emeline F................... 636
   Emmer 635
   Eva M....................... 598
   Garlophelia 636
   George W.................... 663
   Georgie A................... 492
   Georgie M................... 635
   Herbert A................... 635
   Hezekiah H.................. 636
   Ira 663
   Isaac 635
   J. Clark.................... 635
   Jacob 234, 246
   Jasper 663
   John 663
   Jonathan 418, 635
   Jonathan A......... 579, 635, 691
   Joseph S.................... 663
   Joshua 635, 663
   Lewis T................. 634, 642
   Lizzie J.................... 635
   Lula A...................... 636
   Lydia 591
   Maria 635
   Mary 159, 614, 635
   Mary D...................... 663
   Mehitable 660
   Morrison J.............. 636, 691
   Moses 621, 684
   Sally 585

732 INDEX.

SANBORN, Samuel..................408
 Sarah......................635
 Senia......................609
 Sue E......................655
 Susan......................521
 Theophilus..........451, 596, 689
 Thomas........595, 620, 635, 676
 Timothy.............363, 592, 689
 Tristram.............117, 158, 445
       519, 616, 635
 William C..................663
SANDERS, Oliver H.................663
 Samuel.................209, 486
SANFORD, Daniel F.................300
SARGENT, Aaron..........366, 378, 662
 Addie H....................597
 Betsey.....................636
 Edward E...................303
 Frances M..................636
 Hannah E...................659
 Harriet C..................659
 Ida B......................533
 J. Everett......299, 308, 331, 332
       359, 584, 674
 John.......................584
 Mary..................504, 593
 O. B.......................488
 Rebecca S..................643
 S. Jennie..................659
 Samuel.....................685
 Sarah C....................604
 Silva......................664
SATTERLEE, Mary...................504
SAUNDERS, Abbie A.................647
 James......................486
 Joseph................370, 382
 Patience...................662
 Sarah......................665
 Susanna....................655
 William H..................663
SAWYER, Abigail...................655
 Anne.................313, 532
 Augusta....................532
 Azubah.....................636
 Benjamin............57, 60, 61, 64
      65, 92, 684, 686
 Benjamin C.................131
 Betsey.....................642
 Burns......................532
 Charles H..................672
 Esther................632, 660
 Frances W..................606
 John..................222, 532
 John R.....................636
 Jonathan..............411, 636
 Joseph.........533, 634, 662
 Mary.......................663
 Mary C.....................636
 Mary P.....................635
 Matilda....................636
 Moses...............344, 354, 689
 Noah.......................593
 Olivia.....................532
 Peter......................663
 Sally......................657
 Samuel.....................363
 Samuel S...................532
 Sarah H....................636
 Seraph.....................593
 Stephen....................593
 Thomas E...................671
SAYLES, Willard...................486
SCALES, Abigail...................636
 Isaac H....................636
 Ruth.......................636
 Stephen....................636
 William........265, 267, 269, 277

SCAMMEL, Colonel..................353
SCIPIO, Job........................52
SCOFIELD, Benjamin................496
 Betsey.....................498
 Delight.............11, 351, 496
 Eleazer.............11, 52, 53, 63
     102, 123, 174, 250
     395, 403, 445, 495
     496, 677, 685, 686
 James......................498
 Jesse......................498
 John........9, 20, 23, 24, 26, 27, 28
    30, 33, 40, 49, 50, 52, 57
   81, 104, 123, 126, 143, 144
   145, 386, 387, 389, 445, 493
       677, 681
 John, Jr........11, 52, 77, 78, 102
     123, 344, 345, 350, 351
     354, 355, 445, 495, 498
      522, 685, 686
 John B.....................497
 Lewis......................498
 Lucinda....................498
 Lydia.................495, 498
 Miriam.........495, 496, 498, 585
 Nathan......................28
 Sarah...........10, 494, 498, 687
 Temperance...........495, 496
SCOTCHBURN, Helen.................644
SCRUTON, Rosa F...................656
SEABURY, Caleb.....84, 88, 131, 177, 178
    185, 187, 231, 358, 396
    482, 483, 507, 678
SEABLES, Alice....................622
 Blanch.....................622
 William H..................622
SEAVEY, Charles..............444, 634
 Eugene.....................634
 Henry......................634
SEAVY, Andrew.....................663
SEWALL, Samuel E.............263, 323
SHACKFORD, Addie M................636
 Alfred M......116, 488, 586, 636, 677
 Ann A......................636
 Byron W....................636
 Edrick.....................636
 Susan A....................636
 Warren O...................636
SHARON, Israel...............367, 442
SHARP, Abial...........367, 379, 693
 Earl C.....................619
 Susan M....................655
 William....................309
 William H..................619
SHATTUCK, Anna B..................586
 Benjamin...................486
 Edwin E...........375, 648, 693
 Edwin H....................648
 Eliza......................592
 Frank E....................648
 Hattie J..............593, 648
 Isaac W....................648
 Lodena A...................648
 Malvena..............593, 648
 Nathan.....................663
SHAW, A. M........................368
 Elias P....................636
 Livingston C...............664
 Mary E.....................636
SHEA, Patrick.....................374
SHEAF, James......................670
SHEPARD, Abigail.............636, 637
 Alice M....................637
 Ann B......................636
 Anne.......................533
 Arthur D...................636
 Augustus........369, 609, 637, 675

INDEX. 733

SHEPARD, Calvin W..........691
   Edwin 367, 447, 613, 636
   Eliphalet 637
   Eliza T....................636
   Eugene A....132, 605, 637, 680, 681
   George S..............654, 691
   Henry 637
   Herman A.................636
   Jenny M..................654
   John 91, 260, 297, 322, 412, 418
       486, 636, 673, 678, 689
   John S.........523, 636, 679, 692
   Malana 554
   Mary 222
   Moses 131, 189, 636
   Nathaniel 91, 271, 297, 303, 447
       592, 637, 679, 689
   Polly 637
   Reuben F..................662
   Roxie B...................636
   Sarah 637
   Seth B....................636
   Stephen 365, 374
SHERBURNE, Abigail.............637
   Alice 637
   Annabelle 624, 637
   Annah 637
   Caroline 637
   Caroline E............608, 637
   Daniel 159, 305, 411, 637, 689
   Edith 637
   Ella 637
   Emma L...................492
   Henry H..............374, 637
   Ivory L...................637
   Joseph 159, 602, 637
   Lyman J..............620, 637
   Mary 637
   Mary E...................637
   Olivia A..................637
SHERLOCK, William..............662
SHERRY, Joseph.................378
SHERWILL, Emma C..............656
   Walter 662
SHOEMAKER, Theodore............373
SIAS, Solomon..................234
   Colonel 363
SIDNEY, Thomas......291, 292, 294, 295
SILLOWAY, Andrew...............637
   Elizabeth A...............637
SILSBURY, Elmira...............637
SILVER, Mehitable..............525
SIMONDS, Charles F.............620
   Frederick S...........455, 620
   Mary E...................621
SIMPSON, James.............367, 371
SINCLAIR, Captain..............355
   John G...................671
SKEEL, Thomas.................246
SKINNER, B. F.................663
   Captain 346
   Doctor 205
SLACK, John H...........346, 324, 328
SLADE, Susan..................589
SLEEPER, Alfred................663
   Augusta J.................607
   Benjamin C................664
   Caleb A...................362
   Emma 501
   Ethel 501
   Grace 501
   Polly 506, 649
   Samuel 372, 383, 400
   Dea. Stephen..............414
   Walter 246
SLOANE, George................620

SLOANE, James.................482
SLOCOMB, Sally................662
SLOSS, Robert.................226
SMALLEY, Roger D..........611, 616
SMART, Abial..................615
   Frank B...........615, 680, 681
   Leroy E...................615
   Wilfred H.............420, 615
   William 689
   Winnifred S...............615
SMILEY, Nancy.............592, 607
SMITH, Addie B................592
   Alden E...............492, 638
   Almira R..................655
   Alvira 625
   Anna 637
   Anna B...................637
   Arvilla 625
   Asahel 217
   Betsey 638
   Carey 128, 411, 488, 491, 588, 638
   Caroline M................615
   Charles 583
   Charles M.................586
   Cora B....................638
   Daniel 533, 691
   Daniel C..................374
   Daniel L..............635, 662
   David 177
   David F...................663
   E. W. 663
   Edna J....................618
   Elijah 369, 608, 638, 676, 691
   Eliza 637
   Eliza R...................656
   Elizabeth 638
   Eliphalet 637
   Elsa A................301, 586
   Enos 663
   Francis 344, 345, 550, 637, 686
   Francis H.............638, 689
   Frank W...................638
   Franklin S................648
   George H..................663
   Hannah 637
   Harriet A.........301, 586, 638
   Harriet N.................637
   Harry R...................638
   Helen 340, 639
   Herman S..................638
   Ida M.....................638
   Inez C....................586
   Jabez 177, 685
   James 368, 375
   Jennie M..................626
   Jeremiah 669, 670
   John 94, 527, 638
   John B................625, 672
   John E....................648
   Jonas W...............151, 684
   Joseph 461
   Joseph B..............638, 689
   Joseph D..............297, 662
   Joshua 637, 686
   Leonard 638
   Leonard W.................691
   Lillian A..................587
   Lizzie I..................492
   Lucilla A.................618
   Lucy E....................630
   M. Irene..................586
   Maria L...................644
   Mariam E..................586
   Marilla C.................638
   Martin 376
   Mary 637
   Mary A....................662

INDEX.

SMITH, Mary E. 640
  Mary F. 533
  Mehitable 638
  Micajah M. 486, 638, 649
  Minerva 642
  Moses 637, 638
  Nathaniel B. 247
  Ned 638
  Ola 578
  Oliver 68, 88, 145, 146, 170
        176, 178, 189, 251, 252
        390, 440, 447, 519, 612
        637, 682, 685, 687
  Perley B. 618
  Perley E. 648
  Phœbe A. 637
  Plummer 590
  Polly 637
  Rachel G. 615
  Ray 638
  Richard R. 677, 691
  Robert 368, 375
  Rodney V. 663
  Ruth E. 638
  Sally 222, 607, 637
  Samuel 623
  Sarah 637
  Sarah W. 638
  Sidney R. 638, 677
  Simeon 88
  Sophia 586
  Stephen D. 618, 676
  Stephen S. 274, 283, 452
        468, 585, 637
  Steven 637
  Sylvanus 663
  Uriah 173, 187, 637
  Ursula 637
  Warren 663
  William 60, 61, 637, 685, 686
  William C. 419
  William J. 638
  William P. 586, 692
SMITZ, Carlos 370
SMYTH, Frederick 671
SNELL, Malvina 595
SNOW, A. S. 658
  Jonathan 234
SOMERS, William G. 500, 675, 679, 692
  Willie B. 500
SOOMER, William 663
SOUTHARD, George H. 638
SOUTHWORTH, Calvin P. 611
  John P. 611
  Sarah L. 614
SPAFFORD, Mattie E. 523
SPARROW, Richard 3, 46
SPAULDING, Russell H. 247
SPEAR, Emily B. 654
  Velina S. 590
SPENCER, Benjamin 462
  Gideon 171
  Jared 3, 48, 113
SPOONER, Patience 663
  Sarah 655
SPRAGUE, Jonathan 345
SPRINGER, Betsey 638
  Dorothy 638
  Hannah 638
  Henry 60, 107, 145, 174, 205
        252, 343, 344, 354, 446
        638, 662, 685, 686
  John 638
  Joshua 344, 345, 347
  Levi 638
  Lois 638
  Mary E. 638

SPRINGER, Nathan 345
  Relief N. 205, 638
  Sally 80, 514
  Susannah 638
SQUIRE, Reuben 662
ST. CLAIR, General 350
STANFORD, Ella E. 656
STANLEY, Alfred 528
  Carrie L. 527
  Charles A. 528
  Catherine J. 527
  Ellen F. 527
  Frederick J. 528
  Hannah G. 527
  Harriet E. 527
  Henry 527
  Herbert A. 528
  James 527, 528
  John 527
  John C. 527
  John E. 638
  Julia 527
  Julia E. 528
  L. Edgar 528
  Lavinia 527
  Lois 527
  Lyman 527
  Margaret A. 527
  Martha M. 527
  Nancy 527
  P. Jennie 528
  Robert J. 528
  Stella J. 528
  Susie C. 528
  William 527
STANNELL, Mary 525
STAPLES, Lucy F. 656
STARK, Arvilla 617
  Daniel 423
  General 351
  George 671
  Lydia 664
  Mary E. 594
STEARNS, Onslow 462, 671
STEELE, Eleazer 246
  J. A. 247
  John H. 671
STEPHENS, Caroline 610
  Joshua, Jr. 663
  Samuel 617
  Samuel S. 609
STERMON, Cora B. 626
  Elizabeth M. 626
  Joseph 626
STETSON, Sarah 222
STEVENS, Abel 354
  Alfred A. 599
  Alice 638
  Alpha B. 300
  Amos 444, 685
  Belinda W. 638
  Benjamin H. 638
  Betsey 584
  Capitola 492
  Charles C. 638
  Charles R. 615
  Ellen E. 587, 595
  Elvira G. 523
  Enos 670
  Flossie J. 626
  Frank H. 638
  Franklin H. 638
  George 689
  Georgia A. 638
  Hannah 65
  Hannah L. 301
  Hazel 501

Index.

STEVENS, Henrietta A........618
  Henry P........595
  Hilsey R........486
  Hiram H........615
  Ira B........638
  Jemima........639
  John H........247
  Joseph........162
  Joseph P........663
  Joshua........391
  Julia C........615
  Leon........638
  Mabel E........301
  Maria M........607
  Mary........617
  Mary I........662
  Moses........300
  Nancy........599
  Neldora A........638
  Peter........91, 271, 639
  Polly........657
  Rhoda J........639
  Roland........663
  Ruth........597
  Ruth G........662
  Sally........659
  Samuel H........638
  Samuel S........486
  Sarah P........659
  Sophronia........591
  Susanna........619
  Widow........391
  Wyman........587, 595
STEVENSON, Reginald C........587
STEWART, Urie W........663
STICKNEY, Carl........606
  Caroline........639
  Clinton G........606
  Clinton M........606
  Daniel........369, 381, 450, 639, 692
  Frank W........606
  Jonathan........60, 61, 685, 686
  Joseph........60, 61, 685, 686
  Lucinda........624
STILES, E. C........624
  John........611
  Nathaniel........639
STOCKBRIDGE, Joseph F........614
STOCKER, Lilla M........618
  Parker H........618
STODDARD, Clement........177, 446, 627, 685, 686
  Lucy........627
  Polly........627
  Ruth........627
STONE, Captain........354
  Charles F........672
  Edwin P........633, 636
  Elbridge G........590
  Lucy A........590
  Mary........592, 663
  William P........636
STONNING, Evelyn J........614
STORRS, Emma........528
STORY, Abbie........639
  Bertha M........639
  Carl W........639
  Carroll M........639
  Charles O. B........615, 639
  Clara A........639
  David........639
  Ethel C........639
  Frank H........639
  George........663
  George W........639, 676
  Harriet P........639
  J. Clement........369, 339, 639

STORY, Leslie........639
  Mary A........639
  Mehitable P........590, 639
  Otis J........339, 639, 676, 680
  Robin........639
  Walter C........491, 624, 639
STRATE, Kate E........578
STRAW, Aaron........25
  Betsey........664
  Daniel L........669
  Ezekiel A........672
  Hannah........638
  Jacob........134, 446, 652, 662, 689
  Levi........145, 174
  Lydia........446, 658
  Molly........639
  William........446
STRONG, Rev. Harrison W........197
  Serena........197
STURGEON, Rose A........639
  Willie D........639
SULLIVAN, John........68, 69, 460, 669
  Julia A........586
SUMNER, Nathaniel........162
SWAN, Catherine R........639
  Charlotte........639
  Jonathan........195, 298, 478, 674
SWASEY, Benjamin K........663
SWEAT, Enoch........177, 251
  John........177, 205, 246, 445, 662, 673
  Thomas........663
SWETT, Charles........598
  Charles F........639
  Experience........639
  Franklin P........11, 29, 452, 480, 675, 679, 692, 693
  Harlan P........692
  John........639
  John A........300
  John H........679
  Lore........639
  Lui........639
  Mary A........611
  Polly........663
  Stephen R........420, 486, 488, 649, 676, 682
  Walter A........610
SYKES, Emily S........639
SYLVESTER, Joseph........246, 365, 374
TABOR, Luther A........664
TAGGART, Irad........247
  John........247
TALBERT, Emily D........639
  Frank........664
  William H........639
  William P........639
TALLMAN, David........498
TANNER, Thomas........639
TAPLIN, Charles C........639
  Eddie F........639
  George F........368, 379, 639
  John........639
  N. P........639, 676, 692
TAPPAN, Arthur........323
TATTON, William........669
TAYLOR, Augustus W........300
  C. W........247
  Fred D........598
  John........378, 383
  Lydia........648
  Samuel........664
  Susan........595
TEMPLE, Charles........639
  Mary A........640
  Miria A........639
  Roxanna........639
  Sarah A........661

INDEX.

TENNEY, Grace L............633
　Gustavus 664
　Horace B...............586
　Irene A............586, 614
　Jacob P................633
　John 440
　Mary M................633
　Will C.................604
TERRILL, Vina L............660
TEWKSBURY, Edwin...........611
　Melbourne B............611
　Thomas George......368, 373
　Henry 380
THOMPSON, Alice S..........640
　Caleb 664
　Ebenezer 76
　Ernest H...............640
　Irene 658
　Valentine 640, 692
　William 370, 382
THRASHER, James H..........587
THURSTON, Jesse............664
　Sarah H...............664
　Stephen 664
TIBBETTS, Charles H........664
　Jesse 640
　Joseph 640
TIFFANY, Doctor............74
TILTON, William Brackett...217, 423
　Colonel 69
　Elbridge 692
　George 367
　Harriet B.........423, 612
　James A...............423
　Joseph C..........423, 453
　Joseph H..............454
　Smiley 691
　Timothy 89, 189, 208, 209, 218
　　　219, 222, 223, 263, 266
　　　268, 274, 275, 279, 287
　　　317, 423, 432, 458, 482
　　　483, 484, 485, 486, 682, 689
TONKIN, Henry..............198
TOLBERT, William...........365
TOPPIN, Colonel............69
TORREY, Martha.............599
TOWER, Charles H.......676, 682
TOWLE, Allie J.............640
　Almira 633, 640
　Angeline L............640
　Charles 640
　Cynthia 640
　David 668, 610
　Elsina A..............648
　Ephraim 640
　George 640
　Hannah 222
　Harriet N.........610, 640
　Isaac 266, 278, 285, 286
　　　287, 362, 640
　John 640
　John B................673
　John R................640
　John W............375, 640
　Lucinda E.............640
　Martha E..............640
　Martha J..............640
　Mary A................640
　Mary A. C.............640
　Mary E................640
　Mary S................640
　Sarah W...........640, 648
　Shubael 209, 609, 640
　Stephen H......640, 691, 693
TOWNE, Josiah K........216, 217
　William H.............664
TOWNSEND, David........356, 617

TOWNSEND, George B.........664
　Nancy 640
　Ziba 640
TREADWAY, James....34, 52, 64, 75, 108
　　　118, 123, 167, 499, 686
TRIBBLE, John...........3, 46
　The Trapper.........7, 479
TRIPP, Rev. Shubel.........193
TRESCOTT, Bernice E........341
TRODD, Henry...............653
　Isabelle 653
　Martha 653
　Mary J................653
　Sarah 653
TROW, J. H.................247
TROWBRIDGE, Cynthia C......640
TRUE, Joseph G.............664
TRUELL, Sumner B...........632
TRUMBALL, Frank A......491, 600
TRUSSELL, Albert...........640
　Benjamin 184, 185, 209, 217, 640
　Cyrus 640
　Elizabeth 640
　Farnum 640
　Horatio 640
　Ira M.................640
　Jacob ...81, 82, 84, 88, 131, 150, 208
　　　209, 210, 211, 215, 221, 223
　　　258, 260, 264, 266, 268, 271
　　　274, 276, 277, 278, 279, 280
　　　281, 282, 285, 286, 287, 289
　　　290, 323, 344, 423, 439, 454
　　　461, 484, 486, 560, 640, 681
　　　682, 689
　John L................640
　Lorenzo 640
　Mary A................640
　Persis E..............640
　Priscilla 622
　Rozelta 640
　Rozina 640
　Sally 640
　William 640
TUCKER, Albert W...........648
　Alfred B..............636
　Alvin 631
　Almira 632
　Arthur 648
　Benoni 344, 354, 446
　Carrie 648
　Daniel B..............664
　Edrick S..............636
　Edward M.........188, 424, 488
　Eunice 640
　Hannah 633
　Harvey 579
　Howard H.............636
　Jacob 129, 174, 446
　James 664
　John 664
　Jonathan A...........691
　Jonathan K...........640
　Joseph 648
　Joseph M.............636
　Lawrence C...........636
　Leon 648
　Luie A................425
　Luzefor 641
　Marilla D.............640
　Mary 631
　Mary K................492
　Mehitable 578
　Moses 640
　Moses C...............691
　Nathan 643
　Nathaniel 82, 316, 664
　Ross F................644

INDEX.

TUCKER, Sally..................654
    Samuel M..................644
    Sarah.....................640
    Sarah E...................640
    Will A....................636
    Will H....................682
TURNER, Justice of Lyme.......457
    Otis G.....................63
TUTTLE, Hiram A...............672
    Sophia....................536
TYLER, Abigail................515
    Benedict..................498
    Clara.................515, 641
    Clarissa G................662
    Eliza A...............598, 641
    Elizabeth.................623
    Elsie A...................625
    Fannie S..................641
    Fanny.................623, 641
    James......92, 285, 297, 641, 689
    Job............175, 183, 189, 395
            409, 447, 641, 664, 689
    Job C................205, 399, 625
            641, 674, 689
    Joseph....................515
    Lucy..................625, 641
    Nabby.....................641
    Nancy.................616, 641
    Polly.....................641
    Rev. President........217, 218
    Rhoda.................597, 641
    Sarah P...............597, 641
    Theodore.........486, 632, 641
UNDERHILL, Addie B............641
    Anna......................641
    Edgar S...................641
    Ellen S...................607
    Frank T...................641
    John......................641
    Robert....................641
    Susan A...................641
UPHAM, Thomas.................670
VALE, Caty....................637
VARNUM, Abigail W.............640
    Angeline C................663
VAUGHAN, O. A. J..............359
VERMONT, Thomas...............641
VIMIEUX, Benjamin.............664
WADE, Orrin...............374, 382
WADLEIGH, Gustavus B..........691
    Joseph...............175, 176
WADLEY, Washington............641
WALBRIDGE, John J.............488
WAKEFIELD, Thomas L...........303
WALDO, Caroline...............222
    Lois......................655
    Nathan.................30, 86
    Walter....................664
WALDRON, Thomas Westbrook..3, 47, 102
WALKER, Captain...............354
    Elder.....................201
    Isaac......................62
    James H..............377, 382
    Lois......................654
    Timothy...................669
WALLACE, Family...............535
    Amelia M.............542, 555
    Harriet O....301, 543, 565, 612, 621
    Henry................367, 374
    James......93, 208, 209, 211, 218
           397, 452, 462, 469, 484
           486, 536, 673, 678, 690
    James B......93, 94, 97, 297
           299, 428, 452, 530, 538
           542, 544, 674, 677, 682
    John......................536
    John F....................537

WALLACE, Joseph...............536
    Mary..........222, 270, 275, 364
           469, 523, 536
    Mary E....................649
    Margaret..................536
    Oscar F...........267, 293, 542
    Rodney H..................543
    Sophia J.............301, 543
    William...................536
    William A......309, 366, 486, 529
           542, 543, 577, 682
    William J.................341
    House.....................435
WALTERS, Joseph.........52, 68, 344
    Sarah......................71
WALWORTH, Alice...............641
    Amos....3, 5, 13, 19, 20, 27, 46, 641
    Arthur C..................641
    Betsey...............634, 641
    Caroline A................641
    Charles....33, 50, 52, 57, 120, 123
           124, 208, 209, 219, 222
           386, 387, 444, 506, 612
           630, 641, 677, 686, 690
    Charles J.................641
    Clark C..............601, 641
    Dennison..................641
    Ella......................641
    Emily J...................641
    Emma......................641
    Eunice....................641
    Eunice P..................606
    George..88, 255, 260, 394, 444, 616
           641, 673, 678, 679, 690
    James J...................641
    Lucy.................641, 686
    Lula......................641
    Mary A....................641
    Sally.....................641
    Simeon....................641
    Susannah..................641
    William H. H..............641
WARD, Stephen.................260
WARNER, Capt. Daniel...........72
WARREN, Leonard B.............488
WASHBURN, Charles.....366, 378, 583
           634, 642, 693
    Delia S...................634
    Don C................367, 379, 642
    Ella M....................639
    Georgia A............634, 642
    Hannah....................628
    Harriet A.................664
    Harvey....................664
    Horace....................634
    Julia A...................661
    Laurella..................642
    Luther B..................642
    Nahum................642, 664
    Oscar F..............372, 383
    Polly.....................642
WATERMAN, Chloe...............660
    Elisha....................642
    Lucy......................642
WATKINS, Captain..............409
WATSON, Allie V...............642
    Eunice....................617
    J. S......................642
    Miriam....................640
WAUGH, Bishop.................243
WAY, Allen....................528
    Anna......................528
    Frank A...................528
    Laura A...................528
    Spofford A................528
    William J.................528
WEAR, Joseph..................664

47

INDEX.

WEARE, Augusta A............624
  Meschech 59
WEAVER, Elizabeth............586
WEBBER, John D..........664, 692
WEBSTER, Alpheus S...........642
  Angeline F..................591
  Ann C......................488
  C. W.......................601
  Captain 351, 353, 355
  Charles C...........95, 308, 309
  Daniel 86, 693
  Emily F....................642
  Emma 488
  Frank H....................598
  Harry 642
  Herbert L..............407, 533
  Hiram L....................642
  Ira G......................488
  John S................380, 642
  Levi F......488, 533, 676, 680, 691
  Rev. Mr....................182
  Rufus 488
  William 685
WEEKS, Brackett..............642
  Charles M..................644
  Elizabeth P.................642
  Frank C....................644
  Joseph D........309, 335, 367, 428
               642, 676, 682
  Marshall 642, 693
  Mary D................437, 642
  Susan H....................642
  William B...........428, 642, 691
  William P. 94, 160 161, 276, 282, 285
        288, 297, 298, 299, 303
        305, 306, 308, 309, 328
        332, 334 366, 560, 642
        673, 674, 675, 681, 682
WELCH, Abigail...........521, 643
  Alvin C....................644
  Anna C....................643
  Anthony 365, 375, 593
  Arnold 643
  Arnold S...................644
  Austin H...................644
  Bailey 195, 221, 419, 643, 690
  Betsey 643
  Caleb 25, 27, 32, 50, 52
        54, 55, 57, 61, 65
        71, 78, 82, 140, 143
        145, 162, 168, 169, 173
        175, 176, 344, 345, 346
        431, 444, 448, 450, 596
        642, 677, 681, 685, 690
  Caleb, Jr......26, 82, 176, 253, 344
        345, 363, 409, 442, 642
  Carrie E...................643
  Caroline B.................643
  Charles 643
  Charles A..............300, 644
  Charles E..................644
  Dan 642, 690
  Daniel 71, 363, 642, 643
  Edward A..................644
  Eliza 643
  Eliza B....................633
  Elizabeth 643
  Emily D....................642
  Emma R...................644
  Ethel 643
  Eunice J...................643
  Francis 298, 583, 642, 643, 692
  Frank C...................644
  George A..................643
  George O..................643
  George P..............531, 643
  Hannah 198

WELCH, Henry C..............643
  Henry J...................643
  Horace B...........300, 453, 644
  Jane M....................644
  James 644
  James F...................644
  Jennie E..................643
  John C....................531
  John N....................643
  Jonson 195
  Joseph 630, 643
  Lewis C...................643
  Lincoln R.................644
  Louisa M..................644
  Lovena A..................644
  Luther 643
  Lydia 643, 661
  Lydia A...................643
  Lydia J...................643
  Lyman S.....453, 455, 644, 676, 692
  Martin 26
  Mary 643
  Mary A................643, 644
  May B....................644
  Polly 643
  Relief 643
  Reuben 444, 643
  Richard 643
  Russell 26
  Samuel 80, 177, 184, 193
        395, 446, 643, 685
  Simeon 415, 690
  Sophia 643
  Sophronia 642
  Uriah 47, 531, 644, 690
  Willard C..................644
  William ...26, 81, 602, 642, 690, 692
  William H..............421, 642
  William H. H...............644
  Zephy 643
WELLS, Ada E................646
  Alanson 646
  Allen C....................646
  Alvin J....................646
  Amos 113
  Asahel 685, 687
  Benjamin 400
  Benjamin P................418
  Betsey 646
  Betsey P..................647
  Caleb 646
  Caleb P.......119, 413, 647, 690
  Charles H..........300, 434, 589
        632, 646, 692
  Cordelia 656
  Delia F...................647
  Elizabeth J.................588
  Enos 646
  Ephraim 4, 45, 118, 645, 646, 686
  Ephraim, Jr.............3, 6, 48
  Ezekiel 13, 21, 26, 30, 40, 41
       43, 44, 45, 49, 52, 57, 60
       62, 71, 77, 78, 79, 81, 82
       83, 88, 99, 101, 111, 117
       123, 124, 126, 127, 128
       129, 130, 131, 143, 144
       145, 149, 176, 180, 231
       252, 318, 343, 345, 350
       351, 355, 384, 387, 389
       390, 391, 398, 435, 438
       446, 447, 466, 537, 622
       645, 678, 685, 686, 689
               685, 686
  Ezekiel, Jr...396, 407, 627, 646, 690
  Ezekiel, 3d..........396, 409, 646
  F. H......................402
  F. M......................420

Index.

WELLS, Frank C..............646
   Fred B..............367, 379
   Freddie..............646
   George F..............646
   George T..............367
   Hannah..............646, 647
   Harriet..............588
   Hugh..............644
   John..............645
   John S..............671
   Jonathan..............645
   Joshua..............18, 26, 41, 49, 52
       55, 57, 60, 100, 101
       123, 124, 145, 168, 176
       181, 250, 251, 343, 344
       345, 351, 355, 393, 431
       440, 446, 449, 463, 518
       645, 678, 685, 686, 689
   Joshua, Jr..............595
   Judah..177, 397, 407, 445, 627, 647
   Julia..............646
   Lucy..............624, 646
   Lydia..............646
   Mahala..............647
   Marie..............664
   Mary..............614, 645, 646
   Mary A..............646
   Nancy..............646
   Octavia M..............646
   Otis..............647
   Peter S......97, 200, 297, 303, 416
       617, 646, 674, 679
   Phœbe..............600, 646
   Polly..............591, 646, 647
   Rheuanah..............626
   Sally..............646
   Sarah..............645
   Stephen..............400
   Thomas..............3, 48, 113, 644, 645
WENDELSTADT, Mary H..............451
WENTWORTH, Gov. Benning....VII, 3, 19
       99, 153
   Dennison..............227, 257
   J. F..............490
   Jacob..............665
   Gov. John......25, 31, 153, 355, 384
   Capt. John..............3, 46, 102, 103
   Martha..............102
   Capt. William....4, 47, 48, 102, 122
WESTCOTT, Augusta..............661
   Caroline A..............589
   James A..............647
   Melissa L..............646
   Phebe S..............648
WESTON, James A..............672
WHALEY, Clisty..............610
   Minnie..............610
WHEAT, Allen A..............425, 647
   Alvah..............647
   Ara..............278, 424, 428, 674
   Benjamin..............647, 665
   Bridget..............356, 647
   Elizabeth A..............647
   Elvira H..............647
   Elzina..............590, 647, 674
   Emily..............661
   Harold..............647
   Isabelle..............647
   Jane E..............606, 647
   Joseph...90, 131, 187, 188, 189-192
       193, 210, 211, 212, 217
       219, 220, 228, 235, 236
       318, 343, 345, 354, 356
       416, 432, 478, 501, 516
       570, 647, 690
   Joseph, Jr..........93, 131, 304, 400
       460, 606, 647

WHEAT, Lafayette..............647
   Lois..............647
   Lydia..............607, 647
   Nathaniel..............647
   Sally..............647
   Solomon..............647
   William G..............424, 647
WHEATON, Benjamin..............113, 312
WHEELER, Aphia P..............658
   John..............591
   Moses B..............589
   Paul S..............671
   Sarah A..............654
WHEELOCK, Eleazer H..............246
   Elvira W..............632
WHIPPLE, General..............352
   Joseph..............664
WHITE, Rev. Broughton....207, 210, 216
   Rev. Charles..............217, 219
   Harriet A..............605
   James T..............664
   John H..............670
   Rose C..............664
WHITING, Caleb..............3, 46
WHITMAN, Allen.....3, 48, 122, 139, 437
WHITMER, William..............371, 382
WHITMORE, Daniel..............664
   Norman..............648
WHITNEY, Abigail..............649
   Albert W..............640, 648, 692
   Alice M..............648
   Bela B..............452, 648, 692
   Charles A. O..............648
   Clara A..............648
   Emma..............648
   Elsina A..............649
   Esther..............648
   Flora M..............648
   Fred..............648
   Harriet..............648
   Henry O..............648
   Hollis B..............368, 648, 680, 692
   Isaac..............356, 609, 648, 690
   James H..............648
   James M..............648
   Louisa A..............648
   Louisa J..............648
   Lucy J..............648
   Lydia..............356, 609
   Melissa A..............613
   Mina W..............648
   Moses S..............648
   Philip..............648
   Silas..............648
WHITTEMORE, Daniel..............621, 691
   Fannie E..............621
   Lillie E..............621
WHITTIER, Dorothy..............648
   Abi D. P..............649
   Abiah..............450, 648
   Abigail..............505, 653
   Abijah A..............649
   Albion..............648
   Almira..............648
   Ann..............665
   Asa..............486, 648
   Augusta..............648
   Augustus L..............648
   Belinda..............649
   Carrie J..............650
   Charles..............404, 421, 649
   Clinton..............649
   Daniel B......88, 117, 209, 397, 412
       423, 453, 484, 486, 604
       648, 690
   David H..............649
   Dexter..............649

WHITTIER, Dorothy................648
    E. M..........................650
    Eldora V......................627
    Elijah 130, 177, 369, 390
                        445, 505, 649, 692
    Elisha R..................649, 692
    Emeline 648, 659
    Enoch 649
    Francis 119
    George L..........369, 434, 649, 691
    Harriet J.....................649
    Hattie L......................649
    Henry C.......................650
    Hermon D......................649
    Horatio N.....................648
    Ida A.........................636
    Ira A.........................649
    Isabelle 649, 650
    Jane 650
    Jeremiah 369, 400, 414, 649, 692
    Leonard 451, 649
    Louisa 649
    Lucinda G.....................649
    Martha J......................649
    Mary A....................649, 650
    Mary E. J.....................638
    Maud M........................649
    Mehitable 649
    Mellie E......................650
    Miriam B......................649
    Moses 413, 415, 450
                          648, 649, 690
    Nancy 660
    Nancy A.......................649
    Nancy J.......................661
    Nathaniel 41, 145, 176, 405, 406
                   446, 489, 502, 505, 506
                          649, 685, 686
    Nathaniel, Jr.................406
    Nathaniel, 3d.................649
    Polly 649
    Richard 75, 81, 123, 127, 145, 175
                    176, 177, 179, 186, 251, 252
                    343, 345, 355, 446, 448, 525
                          648, 677, 678, 685
    Rufus 451, 486, 649, 690
    Ruth C........................648
    Sally 649, 655
    Samuel 138, 331, 396, 413
                         445, 505, 649, 689
    Samuel W......................649
    Sarah A...................594, 649
    Simeon 648
    Webster 649
    William 606, 649
    Zenas 650
    & Balch...................453, 541
WHITTLESEY, Aaron.................414
    John R........................665
    Polly 650
WIBARD, Richard. .3, 47, 48, 102, 117, 122
WIER, Ellen F.................650, 660
    Emma L........................650
    Flora A.......................651
    Louisa 529
    Mahala E......................650
    Martha 650
    Mary S........................586
    Sarah 650
    Thomas 650
WIGGIN, M. M......................491
WIGGINS, Broadstreet..............690
WIGHT, Freeman 523
    Freeman C.....................523
    Robert F......................523
WILCOX, Leonard...................299
    Melissa 625

WILDER, Caleb.....................174
WILLIAMS, Abbie J.................652
    Abraham L..................97, 651
    Adelbert O..........367, 382, 651
    Adrista E.....................651
    Albert J......................651
    Andrew P......................653
    Arthur 651
    Asa 19, 24, 27, 49, 54
                          57, 344, 350, 355
    Austin 651
    Calvin 653
    Captain 346
    Charles H.....................651
    Chastina B....................652
    Clarence 653
    Dan H.........................651
    Delevan K.................608, 651
    Delevan P.....................652
    Edna A........................651
    Elizabeth L...................652
    Ellen M.......................653
    Esther V......................661
    Etta 651
    Eugenie 651
    Eva 651
    Everett D.....................651
    Everett O.....................651
    Flora 651
    Frances E.....................653
    Frank B.......................652
    Franklin 653
    Fremont D.....................652
    George E......................653
    Georgia A.....................651
    Gratie 650
    Henry H.......................652
    Henry T.......................652
    Henry W.......................651
    Horace B..................300, 653
    Horace P......................651
    Ida M.........................651
    Isaac F.......................651
    J. Frank......................651
    Jared 671
    John G........................651
    John P........................652
    John W........................653
    Katherine 653
    Lena B....................651, 653
    Lester R......................651
    Loraine P.....................608
    Lorenzo D.................651, 652
    Lorenzo P.....................653
    Luis M........................652
    Mabel 651
    Maitland 651
    Mamie P.......................651
    Mary 650
    Mary G...........610, 622, 650, 653
    Mary L........................651
    Minnie B......................651
    Mira 653
    Miriam E......................652
    Nancy 653
    Oliver 664
    Orion H.......................650
    Owen 651
    Phineldo O....................651
    Polly 231
    Purnel L......................653
    Rebecca 651
    Robert 134, 173, 174, 234
                     235, 445, 446, 447, 650, 652
    Robert, Jr................84, 244
    Robert L......................652
    Robert M......................651

Index. 741

WILLIAMS, Rosamond 651
  Samuel 363, 652, 653, 654
                664, 679, 690
  Samuel, Jr. 390
  Samuel L. 652
  Sarah 610, 653
  Sias K. 651
  Stephen 134, 356, 651, 690
  Stephen, Jr. 653
  Susan A. 652
  Susan L. 602, 651, 652
  Sylvester 650
  Sylvester D. 651
  Thomas 650
  Ursula L. 652
  Val M. 651
  Valorous C. 650
  Valorous T. 651
  William 664
  William L. 651
  Willie 653
  Zylpha M. 651
WILLIS, Ara 579
  Ardelia 579
  Clarabelle 579
  George H. 579
  Hannah S. 391
  Holmes 579
  John 396, 447
  John C. 579
  Leona 579
  Lizzie 579
  Nathan 579, 676
  Otis 443
  Otis F. 579
  Perry 579
  Roswell O. 664
  Samuel 189
  William H. 579
  Hall 457
WILMARTH, Rev. Ezra .. 177, 184, 188, 207
  Mary E. 587
WILMOT, Elizabeth A. 664
WILSON, Family 577
  Albert H. 578, 676, 680, 692
  Angie M. 578, 632
  Betsey 577, 634
  Betsey I. 488
  Charles S. 588
  Charlotte 578
  Edna 579
  Effie A. 578
  Elizabeth 578
  Ephraim 189, 267, 297, 299
                577, 578, 690
  Ephraim F. 680
  Frank P. 578
  Fred B. 578, 592
  Fred E. 653
  George 577
  George H. 578
  Gordon 577
  Harriet F. 578
  Hattie S. 578
  Helen 577
  Henry H. 105, 132, 300, 369
        417, 434, 446, 488, 577
        578, 679, 680, 682, 692
  Ida B. 578, 614
  Jabez 445
  Jacob 578
  James 369, 381, 578, 679, 691
  Jane 579
  Jeremiah 445, 579
  Job 445
  Joel 579, 690

WILSON, John 88, 145, 174, 177
               405, 447, 578
  John B. 578
  Joseph 665
  Lemuel 478, 579
  Leon W. 578
  Levi 418, 445, 512, 577
                579, 653, 689
  Levinia 578
  Lois 657
  Loraine 578
  Louisa 653
  Luella 588
  Matilda 579
  Nathaniel 189, 397, 577, 690
  Orissa C. 578, 685
  Presele 578
  Prudence 579
  Robert 82, 87, 92, 174, 447
           577, 579, 633, 690
  Rufus 363, 577, 578
  Sabrina C. 655
  Samuel 478, 579
  Ursula 579
  Warren 89, 129, 145, 177, 343, 344
     356, 384, 445, 447, 577, 685, 686
  Warren E. 578, 677, 680, 691
  Warren F. 369, 402, 415
               417, 577, 676
  Washington 362, 578, 690
  William 653
WING, Persons W. 425
WINSLOW, Betsey 657
  John 664
WISE, Aaron 486
WISWELL, Elsie T. 623
  Grace I. 612, 623
WITHINGTON, Ephraim F. 588, 640
  Herbert F. 615
  Horace H. 664
  Julianna G. 488
  Moses E. 488, 601
  Samuel 486
  Sidney B. 588, 615
  Sylvester 608
  William D. 653
  William H. 615
WOLCOTT, Elias 455
WOLFSON, Carl 593
  Clara C. 593
  Mabel M. 593
  Maurice S. 593
  Sigismond 447, 593
WOOD, Amos 664
  Betsey 653
  Eli 653
  George H. 620, 664
  Rev. Henry 224
  Levi 649, 653
  Lois 653
  Polly 653
  Rosel 653
  Thomas 209, 222
  William 445, 458, 512, 653, 690
WOODBURY, Aaron 650
  Rev. Robert 284
  James 60, 61, 80, 87, 88, 89, 318
          344, 345, 356, 685, 686
  Levi 670
  Mary A. 594
  Ruth 80, 83, 84, 87, 88, 89
WOODWARD, Bezaliel 69, 76, 312, 669
(Woodard)
  Delia 663
  Elvira H. 492
  George B. 665
  H. H. 491

742   INDEX.

WOODWARD, Palmer............635
WOODS, Doctor................265
    Levi C..................664
    Lyndon B................370
WOODWORTH, Lydia E...........664
WOOLEY, Henry J.........238, 246
WOOLFE, Kate M...............597
WOOSTER, David H.............653
    H. B....................448
WORCESTER, Benjamin..........692
WORTH, Abigail...............654
    Arabella................654
    Catherine E.............653
    Edmund..................654
    Elvira..................654
    Eliza C.................653
    Hiram S.........601, 654, 691
    John.........76, 88, 93, 127, 144
                145, 168, 174, 175, 176
                177, 178, 179, 180, 182
                183, 184, 189, 230, 343
                344, 355, 410, 415, 446
                465, 510, 519, 522, 653
                677, 678, 682, 685, 690
    John, Jr..........131, 176, 300
                        396, 445, 617
    Life C..................654
    Lucy M..................654
    Lydia...................654
    Lydia G.................654
    Molly...................654
    Nathaniel......450, 654, 685
    Purnel B............363, 653
    Polly...................654
    Sally F.................654

WORTH, Sarah.................654
    Stephen......109, 138, 176, 186
                187, 318, 397, 408, 410
                418, 445, 464, 596, 654
    Widow....................71
    Tavern..............130, 168
WORTHEN, Amos............231, 622
    Hattie E................598
    James...................411
    Jennie P................598
    John....................607
    Joseph..................160
    Moses...............231, 622
    Sally...................622
WRIGHT, Ahimez...............46
    Eliza E.................660
    Elizabeth...............662
    Hattie P................529
    Lydia R.................598
    Martha M. J.............633
    Mary S..................654
    Oren P..............247, 626
YARDEN, Oliver...........377, 382
YEATON, Lois.............377, 382
    Lois M..................633
YORK, Albert.............368, 372
    Daniel..................665
    Louisa..................588
YOUNG, A. L..................490
    Daniel..................246
    George..............371, 382
    Jacob...................605
    Rev. Mr.................186
YOUNGMAN, Susan L............587

INDEX OF SUBJECTS.

Abolition......90, 258, 273, 277, 279, 284
            285, 288, 289, 290, 319
            323, 326, 329
Academy......................253
Albany, N. Y.............304, 351
Alexandria...................198
Alta, California.....557, 563, 567
Alton, Ill...................324
Amesbury, Mass....7, 56, 57, 312, 435, 436
Andover Theological Seminary......265
Anti-Masonry.............279, 322
Anti-Slavery.........244, 280, 295
Anti-Slavery Almanac.........283
Appropriations...............693
Army, Northern.......352, 353, 354
Artillery Company............361
Arvin Field..................520
Ashes........................452
Aspasia and Demophile.........63
Assembly of Vermont...........67
Assessors....................677
Association Test..............51
Awl Shop.....................455
Baptists.....151, 176, 183, 199, 220, 241
    Church.....63, 126, 142, 166, 183
    First Society...........192
    Parsonage.....193, 281, 298, 324
    First Society Constitution....175
    State Convention........201
Barber Sawmill....87, 387, 389, 403, 435
                                447, 450
Barnard Hall.............491, 492

Bear Pond.................45, 48
Bell, The.................91, 152
Bennington...........351, 352, 355
Birch Corner.............406, 413
Blackwater Bridge............401
Bond Issue................95, 96
Boscawen......................9
Bounties.................368, 369
Bozrah, Conn.................168
Brewster B...................247
Brick Yard...............395, 396
Bridges.....387, 389, 390, 393, 394, 395
                    396, 397, 398, 399
Bridgewater Circuit......233, 234
Broad Street....41, 116, 139, 396, 404
Bunker Hill..........346, 352, 545
Camp-meeting.................240
Campbell Sawmill.............407
Canaan Circuit.......234, 242, 246
    and Bridgewater Circuit....246
    Grenadiers............95, 362
    Lyceum Hall Association....151
    Musical Society..........89
    Social Library...........82
    Street Improvement Society....142
    Tract Society...........209
    Union Academy......163, 297-311
                329, 336, 337, 340, 341
                        427, 428
    Union Academy Catalogue....300
    Union Academy Notes.....297, 304
Cannon.......................361

INDEX. 743

Cardigan 54, 65, 155
   Mountain 72, 140
Casimere Mill......................453
Catholics 226
Cattle at large.....................93
Cavalry Troop......................361
   New Hampshire Battalion......380
Cemetery, Fencing........11, 75, 81
   Near Jones........................95
   Sawyer Hill.................96, 344
   Street 11, 81, 89, 97, 169, 343
   Scofield 10
   Wells 81, 343, 403, 421
   West Canaan..........11, 81, 97, 343
   West Farms.............81, 97, 652
Census 50, 53, 63, 71, 81, 83, 89, 91
   94, 95, 96, 97
Center Deestrick..........250, 253, 519
Charlestown, "No. 4"..............vi.
Charter, First..................1, 192
   Second 3
   Dame's Gore.....................153
Checklist, 1825...................687
Chelmsford Meeting House.........149
Christian Register................272
Church Right............4, 126, 137
Cider 431, 434
Clark Pond....................110, 408
   Hill Road...................164, 414
Clay Bed............................36
Clifford Farm.....................205
Cobble Graveyard........26, 54, 81
   344, 395, 407
Cochran Place.................392, 417
Codfish Hill......................408
Cogswell Hill.....................105
Colchester, Conn.....13, 57, 113, 181, 436
Colored Scholars..................277
Committee Meadow Brook Road 401, 419
   of Safety........51, 52, 54, 61, 350
   of Correspondence................51
   of Vigilence......................91
Common 139
Concord Register..................320
Congregational Church.....184, 207, 230
   257, 292, 296, 399, 533
   Discipline 285
   Meeting House........221, 255, 263
   Society 208, 221
Congregationalists 174, 177, 186
   192, 193, 209, 241
Congress 339, 388
Constitution of Church............175
Constitutional Convention.........70
Continental Money.................66
Cornish 58
Copps Hill........................348
Corner 29, 158, 363, 397
   410, 452, 480
Coroner 68
Court of Common Pleas............391
Crow Bounty.......................83
Crystal Lake House...............438
Culloden, Ship of War............346
Dalton 59
Dame's Gore......41, 47, 48, 83, 87, 103
   107, 108, 109, 110, 111, 137
   153, 163, 410, 411, 412, 413
   Annexation 157
Danbury 319
Danforth Farm....................117
Dartmouth College......31, 217, 289, 299
   302, 316, 324, 325, 327
   332, 335, 336, 339, 340
   341, 403
   Gazette 131
   Graduates 549–551

Devil Music of Deacon Worth......184
Discontinuance of Roads..........393
   Across R. R. at Grist Mill......96
   Arvin to Barber................401
   From Brick Yard Easterly Crossing Intervale................396
   Daniel Blaisdell to Job C. Tyler.399
   To Burying Ground to Daniel Colby 396
   Burying Ground to David Dustin 395
   Campbell Hill to Lebanon Road.400
   Clark to Samuel Gates..........395
   Ensign Colby to D. B. Whittier 397
   Codfish Hill to River...........394
   G. W. Davis to Lebanon.........402
   John Fales......................397
   Near French Shanties...........401
   Nathaniel Gilman to Joseph Randlett 393
   Gilman Hill to Moses Flanders..398
   Goose Pond.....................401
   John Harris to Town Hill Bridge 394
   From Kelley & George Store....401
   Knights to Hanover.............401
   From Thad. Lathrop, Jr., to Two Sawmills 397
   Joshua Martin..................399
   Meacham to Old Road...........393
   J. L. Perley....................401
   Pillsbury to Jenniss............400
   Town Hill......................401
   Tray Factory...................402
   Turnpike beyond F. F. Avery...400
   Through George Walesworth's..394
   Wells Bridge to South Road....398
   Through Wells Cemetery........402
   Wells Hill to S. B. Morgan....401
   F. H. Wells Mill to Enfield....401
   Stephen Wells to Dorchester...400
   To Northeast Corner of Ezekiel Wells 3rd's Orchard...........396
Division of Lands.......23, 42–48, 113
   118, 119, 120, 121
Doctors and College Graduates..422–434
Dorchester ....VII, 65, 70, 110, 111
   118, 129, 155, 156, 198, 403
Drafted Men.......................362
Eames' Mill 28, 56, 124, 384
   403, 437, 521
Eaton Mills......................416
Eighteenth Regiment..............380
El Clamor Publico................556
Eleventh Regiment................377
Enfield ..VIII, 59, 62, 65, 70, 79, 105, 155
   Line 40, 103
Enrollment 383, 690
Factory Village....81, 192, 408, 416, 454
Fairs 2
Farewell Address............281, 283
Felloes 453
Fence-viewers 55
Fifteenth Regiment...........367, 379
Fifth Regiment...................373
Fire Precinct.....................95
First Death.......................20
   N. H. Light Battery........370, 381
   Heavy Artillery................381
Fort Dummer......................VI
Fort Edward......................349
Fort Washington.............352, 353
Fourteenth Regiment..............379
Fourth Regiment..................372
Franconia 59

Index.

Free-will Baptist Church..........203
  Baptists 241
Freemasonry 323, 481
French and Indian War..........VII
Gates Gore...............157, 447
General Sessions Court.....386, 387, 388
                 390, 394, 400
                 408, 411, 415
                 416, 417, 419
General Court Petition..........157
Gilman Dudley Tavern.......252, 519
Girdling Trees...................119
Glebe Right............4, 36, 48, 100
Gore Road.................160, 420
Goose Pond........19, 47, 81, 92, 132
Goose Pond Brook..........46, 393
  Bank 461
  Road 415
Goulding's Mills................419
Governor's Right.........4, 113, 117
  Road 386
Grafton 42, 54, 65, 70, 71, 75
       105, 108, 129, 198, 319
  and Canaan Line.....106, 107, 110
  Turnpike Co......116, 129, 221, 399
    Assessments and dividends
                      134, 136
    Certificate of Sale..........133
    Incorporation 129
    Survey 406, 409, 413, 414
    Toll Rate...................129
Grand Bashaw...................459
  View Hotel..........140, 438, 440
Granite Phalanx..................359
Grantees 3
Grantham ....VIII, 61, 104
Great Island................350, 353
Greeley's Mill................397, 453
Groton ....VIII, 110, 111
Gulf 26, 388
Hammer Shops...............205, 454
Hampstead 57, 352
Hanover ....VIII, 43, 54, 58, 61, 62
            70, 76, 102, 103, 110
            118, 135, 155, 198
  Circuit 233, 246
Harness Shop....................453
Hart's Pond......100, 116, 122, 139, 195
      283, 384, 437, 449, 478, 518
  Orthography 479
Hat Factory......................453
Haverhill 7, 57, 181, 499
Hearse 92
Heath's Inn...................47, 241
Hinsdale VI
Hogreefs 79
Hogs 55, 79
How Some of Our Houses Were
  Built 435-447
Howard Farm.................128, 169
Howe Hill.......................105
Hubbardton, Vt..................351
Incorporation of Towns.........VIII
Incidents 456-480
Indian River........11, 123, 127, 390
  River Grange..................489
Indians 8, 348
  From Canada...................56
Inventory 57, 77, 78, 685
  Blanks 96
Investigating Committee Academy
                      162, 305
Jacobins 288
Juror Meeting, First.............71
Justice of Peace........76, 79, 313
Kimball Union Academy......217, 339
Kittery Point....................352

Knights of Pythias..............490
Ladies' Benevolent Society of Ac-
  worth 217
Lary Cider Mill.................434
  Pond Road....................402
Layout of Roads.................403
Lawrence Mill...................396
Lawyers 312-342
Lebanon ....VIII, 54, 58, 61, 62, 103
  Road 143, 408
License for Selling Liquor...88, 92, 358
Liquor Agent....................434
Lisbon 59
Literary Fund...............161, 298
Littleton 58
Lock Lot 71
Los Angeles Star............553, 556
Lot-Laying Committee 22, 42, 99, 124, 527
Lumber 81
Lyme ....VIII, 58, 103, 110, 111, 129
  Road 103, 391, 392
Maps 4, 106, 108, 123, 155
Markets 2
Marriages 654
Martha's Vineyard...............521
Martin's Hall...............268, 332
  " & Currier's Store....416, 452
Mascoma River........48, 56, 105, 110
                  123, 140, 394
  Valley Assembly...............492
Massachusetts Daily Spy.........545
Masting Pine.....................2
Mausoleum 97
Meredith Association............193
Meeting House......69, 139, 143, 396
  Building Agreement............146
  Dispute over Place............143
  Report on Building............149
  Selling Pews..................144
Methodists 174, 186, 193, 199, 229
  Church 231, 245, 293
  First Church..................238
  First Class...................231
  Preachers' Street.............246
  Preachers' E. C...............247
Methuen, Mass...................352
Mexican War.....................364
Mill Prison.....................353
  Right 29, 116, 122, 422
Military Agent..................369
Militia after Revolution........357
Militia Law.....................357
Mills 20, 23, 26, 28, 51, 56
          81, 100, 168, 394, 435
Milton Hall.................491, 492
Ministers' Right........4, 32, 46, 100
                  126, 131, 207
  Laying 126
  Deed from Baldwin.............127
Minute Men Pay..................76
Mob Midnight........288, 289, 295, 323
Moderators 681
Moose Mountain.........105, 140, 155
  Brook 53, 56, 388
Mount Cardigan Lodge...........491
  Defiance 350
  Independence 354
  Moriah Lodge 317, 319, 459
                481, 533, 535
Mud Pond Brook........123, 390, 409
Music in Methodist Church......238
Musters 93, 358
Nashua Telegraph...............544
Natchitichez 282
Negro Pen.......................257
New Hampshire Conference.......233
  Gazetteer 210

INDEX. 745

Missionary Society.....207, 216, 225
Patriot 258, 260, 270, 272,
                    277, 331, 480
Post 544
Newburyport 65
Newcastle 349, 352, 354
New Hampton Academy.........426
Newmarket 56, 181, 188
Nigger Town Guide Boards.......290
Nine Months Men.........367, 379
Ninth Regiment...............376
Northern Railroad......92, 93, 96, 461
Northern Bear................509
Norwich, Conn.............13, 57
  Military Academy..........423
Noyes Academy....196, 197, 223, 255-296
                    332, 423, 454, 456
  Burning 288, 297
  Diary Relating to..256, 258, 260, 266
                    267, 268, 269, 273
                    276, 280, 288
  Destruction 162, 268, 288, 273
  Moving Bill...............283
  Prospectus 261
  Trustees 257, 261, 263
Oberlin College................265
Old Families..................493
Orchards 461
Orford 129
Orange 46, 59, 70, 75, 79, 86
                    103, 106, 107, 108, 109, 127
                    129, 135, 155, 156, 198
  Association 210
  Dispute Over Line.....106, 108, 110
  Proprietors' Suit with Josiah
    Clark 43, 109
Paper Mill..............138, 435, 453
  Money 65
Peggy's Tavern.............191, 451
Penhallow Pasture..............117
Perambulations 105, 111
Pest House 72
Petition to Annex Land.........76
  for Civil Magistrate.........61
  for Field Officer............62
  to Establish Enfield Line.....104
  of George Harris............25
  for New Town................62
  of Orange.................109
  of Proprietors to Governor Wentworth 24
  to Reimburse Soldiers.......346
Phillips Andover Academy......339
Pierce Tavern..........140, 150, 438
Pinnacle 122, 140, 440
  House 130, 170, 422, 435
Pitch Book and Proprietors Surveys 35, 99, 118
Plainfield ....VIII, 61
Plaisted 7
Plaistow 57, 352, 353
Police Court..................97
Poor Farm........91, 94, 162, 164, 442
  Town 64, 68, 70, 80, 81, 84
                    87, 88, 89, 91, 95, 504
Post Road..........384, 385, 386, 387
  Riders 388, 404, 406
Porter's Intervale.........44, 119
Portsmouth 351, 353
  Plains 363
Potato Road..............417, 444
Pots and Pearl Ashes..........452
Pound 50, 64, 81, 83, 459
Preachers 246, 247
President of Senate............68

Proprietors' Book of Records....22, 34
                    114, 124
  Meetings 22-48
  of Proposed Meeting House....141
  Rights 81, 113
  Surveys 124
  Warnings of Meetings........24
Propagation of Gospel Right....4, 48
                    100, 137
Prospect Hill.........92, 405, 408
Prosperity Assembly...........492
Public Rights.................126
Pythian Sisterhood............492
Rams 75
Rand Hotel....................450
Ranges 117
Recruits 366
  Second Regiment...........370
  Third Regiment............371
  Fifth Regiment............374
  Sixth Regiment............375
  Ninth Regiment............376
  Eleventh Regiment.........378
  Artillery 381
  Battery 381
  Cavalry 380
Re-enlisted Veterans, Second Reg...371
  Third Regiment............372
  Fourth Regiment...........373
Relhan 54, 155
Reporter, The.................566
Representatives 54, 71, 76, 79
                    508, 520, 672
Resolutions on War of 1812......84
Revolutionary Soldiers......343-356
Rhode Island Campaign......349, 352
                    354, 355
Roads 384-421
  Charles Abbott............421
  Adams to Dorchester........400
  Abel Aldrich to Enfield Line..398
  Arvins to Barbers..........401
  Arvins to Deweys Road......415
  Arvins to Dorchester........400
  Thomas Baldwins to Enfield...389
  Barbers to Flints...........390
  Barbers to Meeting House....391
  Barbers to Nichols.........392
  Barnards by Flints to Watering
    Trough 420
  Barney Brothers' Store, North..419
  Birch Corner to Tormeys....412
  To Daniel Blaisdell Land....389
  Blake's Road...............394
  Blakes to Hanover Line....397, 409
  Boscawen to Dartmouth College 403
  Broad Street to Asel Jones....396
  Broad Street by Brick Yard to
    Enfield 395
  Broad Street to Corner......404
  Brick Yard to John Harris...389
  Broad Street to Lebanon City
                    395, 398
  Broad Street to Schoolhouse...403
  Broad Street to Thad. Lathrops 393
  Brocklebanks to Enfield.....419
  Bucklin to Moreau...........395
  David Bucklins to Charles Whittiers 404
  Fred Butmans to Factory Village 394, 408
  Alter from Calkins' and Jones'
    Sawmill 389
  Calkins to Town Hill........387
  Old Cardigan 384
  Cyrus Carlton's to Dorchester..407

746 INDEX.

North Line Jonathan Carlton..393
Carltons by Whittiers..........392
Amasa Clarks to Hanover......398
Deacon Clarks to Orange Line..398
Clark's Bridge to Gales........398
Deacon Clark's Bridge to John
  Worth, Jr..................396
Deacon Clark's Bridge to Deacon
  Sleepers 400
Clark Hill....................399
Clark Pond..............401, 418
Josiah Clarks to Turnpike.....397
Cloughs to Joshua Meachams...408
Cobble Graveyard....394, 395, 407
D. B. Cole's.............401, 419
Committee Brook........401, 419
Corner to Curriers............410
Corner to Turnpike............410
Nathan Cross..................413
Nathan Cross to Haynes on Gore
  Line 399
Cunninghams to John Miltons...419
David Currier to Nathaniel
  Barber 412
Across Clark Curriers.........396
To John Currier's Land........390
John Currier to Woods Mills...397
Clark Curriers to Josiah Barbers 393
Clark Curriers to Richard Clarks 393
John Curriers to Putneys......404
Sam Curriers to A. W. Hutchinsons 390, 392, 404
Across Dames Gore........160, 411
Seth Daniels to Welchs Mills..397
G. W. Davis to Grist Mill..397, 409
Watts Davis..............401, 481
William Digby's Across Horace
  Chase's 419
From Dorchester Road by Whittiers to Carltons........392, 405
Dorchester by John Curriers...403
Dorchester by T. W. Youngs...415
Exchange Dustins to Street....395
To David Dustins..........398, 411
To Eames Mill...124, 384, 386, 395
Eames to Dames Gore...........391
Steven Eastmans to Daniel
  Morse 391
Enfield Road..................396
Enfield by Paddlefords by N.
  Branch Bridge...............391
Farnum Road..............393, 405
Flints to Burdicks............391
Flints to Meeting House.......392
George Flint..................392
David Foggs to Quaker Hill....389
James Follensbees to Road from
  Canaan to Dorchester........44
Gates 418
To Gates Cilleys Ambrose Chases 393
Reuben Giles to John Mays.....398
Giles to Paddleford...........412
Gilman Hill to Birch Corner...393
                        406, 412
Gore Road 420
Gould Road....................399
Elijah Gove...................412
Grafton to Barbers Mill...389, 403
Grafton Turnpike..............413
Explore Greeleys Mills to West
  Farms 397
Grist Mill to Wells Cemetery..403
Grist Mill to Fair Grounds.409, 421
Hanover to Enfield............398
Harris 411

Exchange Harris to James Dotens
 392
Harris to Thad. Lathrop.......393
N. J. Hills...................420
Richard Hutchinson to Sanborn
  Wheel Shop..................418
From Job Jenness..............398
Jerusalem to Shingle Schoolhouse 405, 410
Jehu Jones to Welchs Mill..394, 395
Alter from Joslen to Enfield..389
Otis Jones....................401
Samuel Jones to Barbers Mill..387
John Kimballs down Eastman
  Hill 404
Kimball to Silas Dustin.......412
Kimball to Amos Gould.........410
D. Kimballs to J. Kimball, Sawyer Hill...................414
Luther Kinney.................400
Lary 411
From Thad. Lathrops...........389
David Lawrence, Eliphalet Richardson, at Corner..........395
Straighten from Lawrence Mill
  to Turnpike 396
Moses Lawrence to Nathan Cross 410
Lebanon Road by Kendricks.396, 408
Lockehaven 394, 408
Lower Meadow............386, 387
A. C. Lovejoy............401, 419
Lime to Grafton...............386
Lyme Road near Records...393, 405
Joshua Martins to Aaron Whittleseys 400, 414
Meeting House to J. M. Barbers 396
Hill South of J. M. Barbers...396
Meeting House to Corner.......399
Meeting House to Widow Stevens
 391
Mills to Town Line, South.....386
Thomas Miners Intervale.......386
Lieutenant Miners.............399
Morgan to Sharons.............420
Stephen Morse to Turnpike.....409
Ezra Nichols to Meeting House.392
Moody Noyes to Flints.........392
Across Pattee & Perley........419
Philbrick to Peaslee's Mill..403, 418
From New Road Plymouth....413
From Adam Pollards............397
Post 385, 387, 388
Potato 401, 418
Prospect Hill to Lyme.........391
Reuben Puffers to Campbell Hill
                        393, 406
Across Railroad at Grist Mill.. 96
Ricards to Lashua........393, 405
Amos Richardson....452, 398, 411
Richardson to Kinneson...392, 405
River Road to Dorchester......400
River Road from Fair Grounds 414
Sawyer Hill..............384, 390
Moses Sawyers to Hanover Line
                        411, 413
Scofields to Wells Interval...386
Caleb Seaburys to Road from
  Clark Curriers to Amasa Clarks
                            396
Sharons to Common.............411
Lydia Shattuck to C. L. Kinne 409
Sherburne to Clarks...........411
Lewis Simmons Straightened...398
Cary Smiths to Orange Line...411
South Road to Enfield Line...394
                        407, 415

Widow Stevens to Joshua Stevens 391
Stephen Swett to Road from Depot to Street............420
Switch to March Barbers......400
Town Hill Road................396
Old Tray Factory........394, 407
Tug Mountain.................408
Turnpike to Road from Turnpike to Dorchester................414
Turnpike Near John Flanders..414
To Turnpike by Eliphalet Gilmans....................415
Job Tylers....................395
At Village....................420
Captain Walesworths..........386
H. L. Websters to Enfield Line 394, 407
Wells Cemetery Road..........421
Joshua Wells to Dames Gore.... 41
Wells to Nathaniel Gilmans Round Pond..................403
Captain Wells to Moses Chases..393
Exchange from Wells Barn to Abel Hadleys.................396
Straighten Judah Wells to Meeting House....................397
Ezekiel Wells, 3d, to Bridge over Mud Pond Brook..............409
Joshua Wells to Orange Line..393, 406, 407
Exchange Wells to Post Guide on County Road..................396
Wells Bridge to South Road 399, 413
F. M. Wells over West Farms..420
West Farms to Prospect Hill 393, 405
Joseph Wheat.................400
Whittier to Carlton......393, 406
Sam Whittiers to Deacon Clark's Bridge.......................396
John Worth to Moses Whittier Bars........................415
Stephen Worths...............397
Wolfeboro Road to Mr. Bradburys.....................65, 389
Wolfeboro or Governors.31, 384, 386
First Tax by Proprietors...... 23
First Committee by Proprietors 384, 387, 390
One Who Calls Out Committee to Pay......................391
Districts 387, 389, 390, 391
Indictment 396, 398
Labor 23, 83, 385, 387, 389
Surveyors 390, 391, 393, 394
Surveys 387, 390, 406, 407
Petition Daniel Blaisdell......399
Petition J. S. Lathrop........400
Petition to Hanover......390, 392
Petition through Relhan......384
Royalton, Vt..............55, 345
Ruddsboro Road...............351
Rumney ....VIII, 198
Rutland 345
Sale of Right at Auction.......113
Salisbury 353
Saratoga 346, 349, 351, 352, 353, 354, 355
Sawyer Hill........57, 92, 143, 384, 414
Scofield Bridge.........396, 398, 401
Scholars 251
School and Books.............253
Districts 63
First Report.............. 95
and Literary Fund......164, 282

Interest 162
Punishments 259
Right 4, 46, 126, 128, 131
Laying 32, 126, 128
Subscription Paper...........250
Surplus Revenue.............161
Vote for Money........63, 70, 250
Votes 250, 251
Schools 248-255
Search of Title..............114
Secession of Sixteen Towns....40, 58
Second Regiment..............369
Secret Organizations.....481-492
Selectmen, Pay...............89, 92
Settlers, Award............11, 24
First and Second............. 9
Other Early............18, 57, 444
Seventh Regiment.............326
Shakers 283, 419, 420, 446
Shepard Lot..............108, 109
Sidewalks and Sewers......... 96
Sixth Regiment...............375
Small Pox.................... 72
Smart's Mountain.............140
Social Lodge.................485
Soldiers 343-383
South Road.....19, 27, 57, 114, 117, 123, 143, 241, 387, 394
Squatters 35, 120
St. Armands.................498
St. Lukes' Church............293
State Temperance Society.....326
State's Gore........42, 103, 153
Stillwater 352
Stone House..................444
Stony Point..................353
Substitutes 367, 368, 369, 382
Sugar Hill...................158
Suit for Slauder.............467
Summit Lodge.................488
Surplus Revenue..161, 287, 298, 307, 329
Surveys, Proprietors'........115
of Town........103, 105, 106, 111
Switch 397, 416
Tanneries 29, 448
Taverns 438, 440
Tax on Non-Resident Land.....80, 83
to Build Mills............. 27
Exemption 54
State 56
by Town and Proprietors.... 23
on Proprietors' Rights....28, 42, 44
for Roads, First........... 23
for Preaching.............192
Payers, First List 6
Temperance in Canaan.....430-434
Organization 219
Third Regiment..........355, 371
Thirty-Seventh Regiment...358, 520
Officers, 1808............358
Officers, 1820............358
Officers, 1830............359
Ticonderoga ..348, 350, 352, 353, 354, 355
Timber Lands................. 30
Tithingmen 49, 459
Toll Gates 130
Tontine 453
Town Appropriations..........693
Clerks 682
Hill 118, 143, 386
Road 394
Library 96, 494, 652
Lines 102
Meetings 49-98
Plot 2, 101, 139
Poor 64, 70, 71

Records 77, 88
Tray Factory 402, 408
Trees Set Out on Street..........479
Trenton, N. J...................352
Trespass Committee.............43, 45
Trust Funds....................96, 97
Twelfth Regiment................379
Twenty-Fourth Regiment........62, 229, 357, 527
Twenty-Third Regiment..........357
Union Society................185, 187
Unitarian School................226
United States Pension Bureau......356
Universalists 174, 177
Valley Forge....................351
Vigara 364
Vigilance Committee.............244
Volunteers of '61.....366, 367, 368, 369
  Aid to.......................95
  by Brokers..................382
Vote for Governor..........75, 79, 669
  President, 1787 74
  President, 1788..............74

First Senator.................69
President of United States 69, 72, 76
Representative United States... 69
Walpole VI
War of 1812................84, 87, 362
  Rebellion 95, 364
Warning, First Town Meeting.......24
Weare, Quarterly Conference.......205
Weights and Measures...........71, 75
Welch Crossing...................96
  Mill 56, 394, 397, 398, 421
West Canaan 81, 123
  Farms 252, 405
  Point 354, 355, 428
Westgate G., Tavern..............419
Westmoreland VI
Wheat, Legal Tender............. 71
Wheel Carriages, Tanneries, Pots and
  Pearl Ashes................448-455
Windsor Ministerial Association ...217
Woodstock Association............183
Yale College 228, 428
Yankee Traveler 317

Milton Keynes UK
Ingram Content Group UK Ltd.
UKHW051106250324
439991UK00007B/796